Ernest A. Farrington, M. D.
Born January 1, 1847   Died December 17, 1885.

CLINICAL
MATERIA MEDICA

By

E.A. FARRINGTON, M.D.

Fourth Edition, Revised and Enlarged by
HARVEY FARRINGTON, M.D.

B. JAIN PUBLISHERS PVT. LTD.
NEW DELHI - 110 055

STUDENT'S ECONOMY EDITION

Price **£11·99**

INDIAWISE
78 Milton High St, SITTINGBOURNE
Kent ME10 2AN Tel: 01795 435854

Reprint Edition : 1996
© Copyright with the Publisher
Published by :
B. Jain Publishers Pvt. Ltd.
1921, Street No. 10, Chuna Mandi
Paharganj, New Delhi - 110 055 (INDIA)
Printed at :
J. J. Offset Printers

ISBN 81—7021—029—1
BOOK CODE B-2235

PREFACE TO THE FIRST EDITION.

DURING the year following the death of Dr. Farrington, the editor of this volume published several of the lectures here presented, in the *Hahnemannian Monthly*, *North American Journal of Homœopathy*, and *Monthly Homœopathic Review*. These were well received by the profession. Some of them were, moreover, translated and published in German, French, and Spanish journals. A number of physicians expressed the desire to have the lectures appear in book form. The consent of Mrs. Farrington to such publication was therefore obtained, the Doctor's manuscript was placed at our disposal, and Dr. S. Lilienthal kindly consented to revise the lectures after their completion in manuscript.

In order that the work should be thoroughly representative of Dr. Farrington, those concerned in its preparation for the press decided that the author's style should be closely followed. These lectures are therefore presented exactly as delivered, excepting where a change was suggested by his manuscript or by his published writings.

There have also been incorporated in the volume numerous abstracts from the comparisons in the "Studies in Materia Medica," published in the *Hahnemannian Monthly* in the years 1880, 1881, and 1882. These will be found in the lectures on Lachesis, Apis, Cantharis, and Sepia. The lecture on Moschus is essentially a reprint of the study of that remedy in the *Hahnemannian* for January, 1882. The editor feels no necessity for apologizing for this addition of the above-mentioned matter to the lectures proper, for, as Dr. Korndœrfer truly says in his memorial sketch of his deceased friend, they "belong to the classics of our school." The regret is that they cannot be incorporated in their entirety.

The reader must remember that in a course consisting of seventy-two lectures, it would be utterly impossible to include a complete presentation of the homœopathic materia medica. This fact was always kept in mind by Dr. Farrington. It was his aim, therefore, to present to his students, only such matter as would enable them to establish their knowledge of materia medica on such a firm foundation that their post-graduate study of that *science* would be a comparatively easy task. How well he succeeded in his object can be attested by the many physicians whose fortune it was to receive instruction from his lips.

It should be said of Dr. Farrington's manuscript, that it gave marked evidence of constant study. Interlineations and notes of reference were frequently added. Erasures were few, for what he therein recorded was only placed there after having been thoroughly confirmed by the clinical experience of himself, or of some other competent observer. Fully did he realize the importance to homœopathy of a materia medica which should be, in all respects, perfect.

CLARENCE BARTLETT, M. D.

PHILADELPHIA, October 1st, 1887.

PREFACE TO THE SECOND EDITION.

WHEN the first edition of this work was published, in the autumn of 1887, a large number of copies were printed, sufficient, it was thought, to satisfy the demand for some time to come. So flattering was the reception accorded it, this large edition has been exhausted, and a new one has been called for. In the preparation of this the editor has had, as before, the assistance of the author's manuscript lectures, together with notes of students whose privilege it was to receive instruction from Dr. Farrington in more recent years than was accorded the editor. The result of this revision has been the addition of a number of symptomatic indications for drugs. These additions have been pretty evenly divided over the whole work.

In presenting the second edition of Farrington's Clinical Materia Medica to the profession, the editor cannot refrain from expressing his admiration of the thoroughness of the work of its distinguished author. A review of the index shows that more than four hundred drugs were considered by him; many of these received but minor mention, while others he treated of *in extenso*, as their importance warranted. The therapeutic index shows, moreover, that hardly a class of ailments to which humanity is liable but what has received more or less attention. The therapeutics of diseases like scarlatina, diphtheria, and typhoid fever, as to be expected from their importance, were thoroughly considered. Others, but seldom met with in actual practice, were given but a passing notice. In all his teachings Dr. Farrington showed himself to be a practical physician, fully alive to the demands to be made upon the needs of the student on entering practice.

OCTOBER 1, 1890.   C. B.

PREFACE TO THE THIRD EDITION.

OWING to the continued favor of the profession, the second edition of my father's work is now exhausted, and it becomes necessary to issue a third, which is herewith presented in substantially the same form with the one preceding. I have gone over the whole work, carefully comparing the text with the original material and correcting one or two palpable errors, also pressing into service a large volume of notes on Materia Medica, chiefly comparisons, which was not made use of before.

HARVEY FARRINGTON, M. D.

PHILADELPHIA, PA., August 19, 1896.

PREFACE TO THE FOURTH EDITION.

Farrington's Clinical Materia Medica has made for itself a place among the classics of homœopathic literature. It has become a standard text book in the colleges, and is consulted by practicians generally in this country and, in fact, wherever Homœopathy has made its way. It has been translated and published in the German language, in Spanish (Mexican), and an edition in Bengalee (Indian) has been contemplated, if not already issued.

Though lacking in the perfection that the author himself would have given it had he written it with his own hand, it nevertheless bears the charm and freedom of expression of the fluent lecturer who is well-versed in the materia medica and a past-master in its practical application. In editing this, the fourth edition of the work, these essential characteristics have been faithfully preserved. The revision has consisted chiefly in the elimination of a few inelegant expressions, due to a too literal transcription from the notes of the stenographer. Over forty pages of new matter have been added, including a full lecture on Natrum arsenicatum. But, with only a few minor exceptions, these additions have been made from original manuscript notes and articles from current literature by the author himself.

Much time has been expended in compiling the indexes, which will now be found to contain the names of some of the lesser remedies mentioned in comparisons, the alkaloids and other references previously omitted.

To master the homœopathic materia medica requires years of study and close application. Those who are conscientiously toiling to this end will find much in the following pages to lighten their labor.

In conclusion, I wish to acknowledge my indebtedness to my brother, Dr. Ernest A. Farrington, for valuable assistance in preparing the work for the press.

HARVEY FARRINGTON, M. D.

CHICAGO, ILL., January, 1908.

CONTENTS.

	PAGE
IN MEMORIAM,	9
LECTURE I. Introductory,	17
II. Animal Kingdom,	25
III. The Ophidia—Lachesis,	33
IV. The Ophidia—Lachesis (*continued*),	49
V. The Ophidia—Lachesis (*continued*),	62
VI. Archnida—Mygale, Lycosa tarentula, Tarentula Cubensis, Aranea diadema and Theridion curassavicum,	73
VII. Cantharis,	84
VIII. Hymenoptera—Apis mellifica,	98
IX. Moschus,	115
X. Sepia,	122
XI. Sepia (*continued*),	133
XII. Nosodes—Psorinum and Ambra grisea,	147
XIII. Secale cornutum,	153
XIV. The Vegetable Kingdom—Apocynaceæ; Apocynum cannabinum, Oleander, Vinca minor and Alstonia scholaris,	161
XV. Gelsemium sempervirens,	169
XVI. Nux vomica,	177
XVII. Ignatia,	197
XVIII. Spigelia anthelmintica, Curare and the Juglandaceæ,	205
XIX. Araceæ—Arum triphyllum, Caladium, Dracontium and Pothos fœtida,	208
XX. Anacardiaceæ—Anacardium orientale,	217
XXI. Rhus toxicodendron,	223
XXII. Compositæ—Arnica montana, Artemisia vulgaris, Absinthium, Millefolium, Taraxacum, Eupatorium perfoliatum, Artemisia abrotanum,	237
XXIII. Cina and Chamomilla,	246
XXIV. Melanthaceæ—Colchicum, Veratrum album, Veratrum viride and Sabadilla,	251
XXV. Menispermaceæ—Cocculus Indicus,	259
XXVI. Papaveraceæ—Opium,	264
XXVII. Sanguinaria and Chelidonium,	274
XXVIII. Cucurbitaceæ—Colocynth,	284
XXIX. Bryonia alba,	289
XXX. Coniferæ—Abies nigra, Sabina juniperis, Terebinthina, Pix liquida and Thuja occidentalis; Euphorbiaceæ—Croton tiglium, etc.,	304
XXXI. Ranunculaceæ—Aconitum napellus,	314
XXXII. Actea racemosa, Ranunculus bulbosus and Ranunculus sceleratus,	326
XXXIII. Helleborus and Staphisagria,	334

CONTENTS.

	PAGE
LECTURE XXXIV. Pulsatilla,	343
XXXV. Rubiaceæ—Cinchona rubra,	363
XXXVI. Ipecacuanha and Coffea,	376
XXXVII. Scrophulariaceæ—Digitalis purpurea, Linaria vulgaris, Verbascum, Gratiola, Leptandra Virginica and Euphrasia,	387
XXXVIII. Baptisia tinctoria,	399
XXXIX. Solanaceæ—Belladonna,	404
XL. Stramonium and Hyoscyamus,	423
XLI. Tabacum, Dulcamara, Capsicum and Glonoin,	432
XLII. Lycopodium clavatum,	439
XLIII. The Umbelliferæ—Conium maculatum, Ammoniacum gummi, Asafœtida, Æthusa cynapium; the Berberidaceæ—Berberis and Podophyllum,	447
XLIV. Mineral Kingdom—Selenium,	454
XLV. Sulphur,	463
XLVI. The Carbon Group—Carbo vegetabilis,	479
XLVII. Carbo animalis, Graphites and Petroleum,	488
XLVIII. Halogens, Bromine and Iodine; and Spongia,	501
XLIX. The Acids—Fluoric and Muriatic acids,	515
L. Phosphoric and Sulphuric acids,	526
LI. Nitric, Hydrocyanic and Picric acids,	533
LII. Silicea,	542
LIII. Arsenicum album,	549
LIV. Phosphorus,	562
LV. The Preparations of Antimony—Antimonium crudum and Antimonium tartaricum,	576
LVI. The Preparations of Mercury	584
LVII. The Noble Metals—Aurum,	600
LVIII. The Preparations of Silver—Argentum nitricum and Argentum metallicum,	605
LIX. Platina, Palladium and Alumina,	612
LX. Plumbum and Stannum,	621
LXI. Cuprum and Zincum,	628
LXII. Ferrum and the Magnesia Salts—Magnesia carb. and Magnesia mur.,	639
LXIII. Baryta carb., Strontiana carb. and Lithium carb.,	649
LXIV. The Ammonium Preparations—Ammonium carb., Ammonium mur. and Ammonium phos.,	657
LXV. Salts of Lime—Calcarea ostrearum,	666
LXVI. Calcarea phosphorica and Hepar,	678
LXVII. Preparations of Soda—Natrum carb. and Natrum sulph.,	689
LXVIII. Natrum muriaticum and Natrum arsenicatum,	696
LXIX. Borax veneta,	706
LXX. Salts of Potash—Kali bromatum and Kali hydriodicum,	712
LXXI. Kali bichromicum,	720
LXXII. Causticum,	729
LXXIII. Kali carb.,	736
INDEX OF REMEDIES,	743
THERAPEUTIC INDEX,	777

In Memoriam.*

PROFESSOR E. A. FARRINGTON, M. D.

BY AUG. KORNDŒRFER, M. D., PHILADELPHIA, PA.

The subject of this sketch, Dr. Ernest A. Farrington, was born January 1, 1847, at Williamsburg, Long Island, N. Y., and died at Philadelphia, December 17, 1885. During his early years his family removed to Philadelphia, at which place he received his education, and rapidly rose to eminence in his profession.

Having already, during his early childhood, given evidence of exceptional intellectual ability, he passed through his school-life with the highest commendation of his teachers.

After his entrance to the High School he seemed to develop an intellectual capacity rarely witnessed in one so young. He grasped and utilized facts with such vigor that his teachers looked upon him as quite a phenomenal boy. Often have I heard his teachers, professors of the High School, remark upon his aptness, clearness of thought, and remarkable proficiency in the various studies embraced in the curriculum of the school.

It may here be worthy of passing note, that, during his entire school and student life, he endeared himself to his teachers, not less by his genial manners, than by his remarkable intellectual qualities.

Having completed the prescribed course at the High School, he made a most brilliant examination and was graduated, not only at the head of his class, but with the highest average to that time attained by any graduate of the institution.

During the following summer he visited his birthplace, spending the summer there and in New York city. Early in the fall he returned to Philadelphia, there to resume his favorite occupation, study.

---
*From the *Hahnemannian Monthly*, January, 1886.

Under the preceptorship of his brother, H. W. Farrington, M. D., he in the fall of 1866, matriculated in the Homœopathic Medical College of Pennsylvania.

Here, again, the characteristics of his early life became the remark of his fellow-students, and it was not long before he was looked upon as one of the brightest students of his class. His quickness of perception, his ready memory, his devotion to study, and conscientious estimate of the responsibilities of his calling, marked him as one of the most promising students of our school. Coupled with all this, was an unusually strong religious bent of mind. His religious views were, however, of that happy type which but illuminate life's way, never casting shadows of doubt or gloom. His highest aim was to do right because it was right; that he accomplished this, all who knew him will attest.

When the Hahnemann Medical College of Philadelphia was chartered, in 1867, it became a question of serious import to him as to whether he should continue in the College with which he was connected or join the new institution. After lengthened consideration, he decided to sever his relationship with the old College. He became the second matriculant of the Hahnemann Medical College of Philadelphia. Here, again, he won unstinted praise, and graduated March, 1868, having enforced the full conviction upon the minds of all, both Faculty and class, that he had no superior in the class of "68." To the honor of all, let it be said that envy never tainted the commendation of one; every graduate delighted to accord to him his full meed of praise.

He entered practice immediately after his graduation, establishing himself at the residence of his father, 1616 Mount Vernon Street. His arduous labors in the pursuit of knowledge, during the years of college life, followed by even greater efforts during his early practice, made preceptible inroads upon his otherwise strong constitution; this led him, during the summer of 1869, to take a short European trip, from which he returned much improved in health. He reëntered practice with renewed vigor, and speedily succeeded in securing a large and appreciative *clientele*.

On the 13th of September, 1871, he consummated in marriage an engagement which had for some time existed with Miss Elizabeth Aitkin, of Philadelphia, an event which brought more than usual joy, as in his wife he found a most congenial and helpful spirit, both as to his professional and religious life. Four children, three boys and one girl, have blessed this union.

Dr. Farrington was essentially a teacher among men. Already we find him, in the spring of 1869, filling a lecturer's appointment as teacher of Forensic Medicine in the spring course of the Hahnemann Medical College. These lectures proved to be so satisfactory that the Faculty, on the resignation of the Professor of Forensic Medicine, after the session of 1869-70, elected him to fill the vacancy. Within two years, the chair of Pathology and Diagnosis becoming vacant, he was appointed to fill the same, and in 1874, upon the resignation of Dr. Guernsey, then Professor of Materia Medica, he was called to fill that most important chair.

His ambition was now about to realize the attainment of its highest aim. This had really been his true field of labor—here his deepest studies were made; here was, indeed, his life work.

Possessed of superior analytical powers, he never felt satisfied to accept a view or theory save it were demonstrably true; he, therefore, made deep and thorough research and study upon every question involved in the subject of homœopathy; the law, dosage and potency questions all were subjects of much interest, but above all, his delight lay in the study of the Materia Medica.

His daily association with Hering quickened this his natural desire, and he was soon recognized by that master spirit of our school as one well fitted to a place in the highest rank among the expounders of that most intricate science, Materia Medica. Hering delighted to say, "When I am gone. Farrington must finish my Materia Medica."

His labors in this direction were not restricted to simply reviewing old provings, but were rounded out unto fulness by personally supervising provings of both old and new drugs. While he certainly possessed a wonderful memory for symptoms, the most prominent feature of his teaching may nevertheless be said to have been his ability to thoroughly analyze the specific drug action, showing not only the superficial but also the deeper relationship of symptoms.

Family and class relationship of drugs he studied with deepest interest. In fact, his "Studies in Materia Medica," a few of which have been published in the *Hahnemannian Monthly*, belong to the classics of our school.

On his election to the chair of Materia Medica, he devoted much of his time to the development of a method which, while full and comprehensive, would at the same time present a simplicity which would enable every student to intelligently study this most difficult subject.

He infused such new life into this usually prosy subject, that it soon became the favorite hour with many, and to all an hour of interest and profit. To the earnest student it became rather a recreation than a task. His analytical mind carried the students through labyrinths of symptoms and mazes of modalities, with such clear and concise directions as to the way, that the thoughtful student might ever after feel able to traverse the same alone.

His writings all bear the impress of a master mind. Already in 1871, scarcely three years subsequent to his graduation, we find him dealing with the philosophical elucidation of drug prescribing, in language indicating depth of knowledge rarely found even among our oldest practitioners. In illustration, permit a short quotation from his report of a case published in the *Hahnemannian Monthly*, April, 1871.

"It is a singular fact that all of the tribe of *Senecionideæ*, Ord. *Compositæ* which we have proved (Cina, Artem. vulg., Cham., Tanacet., Arnic., Senecio grac.) have relief from some form of motion.

"The *Artemisia vulgaris* resembles the Cina in nervous troubles, but, as it is in conjunctive relationship, it can not be used immediately before or after Cina. As a disjunctive relative and hence one that follows well, *Silicea* corresponds to the somnambulistic state, and *Silicea*, *Nux vom.* and *Caust.*, to the irritation of the solar plexus giving rise to spasm.

"The *Absinthium* (wormwood), another member of the Artemisiæ, when drunk in brandy (a famous drink used to stimulate the brain by actors, etc.), I have seen produce the delirium embriosorum, which was only relieved by *pacing the floor*, showing again the general relief from motion."

Thus we find him, as a beginner in years, treating the Materia Medica as by the hand of a master. The literature of our school has been greatly enriched by his pen; for though he did not strive to gratify ambition in giving to the profession massive volumes, he performed that which he felt duty to demand, *i. e.*, gave of his time in work not only upon his lectures, but also to societies, and in our journal literature.

The *American Journal of Homœopathic Materia Medica*, the *Hahnemannian Monthly*, the *North American Journal of Homœopathy*, and other journals, have each received valuable articles from his pen. His Studies in Materia Medica alone, published in the *Hahnemannian Monthly*, aggregate about two hundred pages, and his comparisons, published as an appendix to the *American Journal of Homœopathic Materia Medica*, from 1873 to 1875, embrace over 150 pages more. His other articles were numerous and instructive.

Dr. Farrington was a homœopathist by conviction. With him it was not a light thing to be a physician, and he could only practice that which he could see to be true. Expediencies, for the sake of gaining the *éclat* of those who, through want of knowledge, grant unstinting praise to pleasant error, had no attraction for him. He preferred to sacrifice and to sustain his own sense of doing right rather than gain financial success by pandering to the ignorance of wealth, where it demanded departure from the law of cure in an experimental treatment of disease.

The influence which such a mind must exert upon a profession cannot be overestimated. Essentially scientific in its bent, progressive in its character, earnest in its labors, logical in its reasonings, and philosophical in its judgments, the results reached even most presistent opponents were compelled to receive with respect. While thus a true and most consistent homœopath, he necessarily became identified with every movement which might tend toward the advancement of learning. Especially did he desire to see medical education brought to a far higher level than has ever been attained in this country.

Dr. Farrington was also an active participant in our County Society work. On the floor during debate, he was listened to with that attention which ability only can command. In the Chair, which for three successive years he occupied, he presided with dignity and justive.

He was also a member of the State Society and of the American Institute of Homœopathy, which latter he joined in 1872. For many years he was a member of its "Committee on Drug Provings," during which time he was also identified with its Bureau of Materia Medica. At the time of his decease he was chairman of that bureau. In 1884 the Institute appointed him a member of its Editorial Consulting Committee on the new "Cyclopædia of Drug Pathogenesy," etc.

In December, 1879, when the *Hahnemannian Monthly* was purchased by the Hahnemann Club of Philadelphia, he was selected by his colleagues of the Club as the sole editor of the journal, but on account of impairment of health and multiplicity of duties he felt impelled to decline the charge; though later, at the earnest solicitation of the Club, supplemented by that of the General Editor, he accepted the position of Contributing Editor, which position he filled until the time of his death; in fact, his last article, a book review, was written but a few weeks prior to his decease.

Thus we find him throughout his life striving to accomplish the work which he valued so highly. No labor seemed too great, no effort too severe, so long as it tended to promote the advance toward that standard to which he felt the profession should aspire. An earnest advocate of higher education in general, he especially longed for the time when the professional standard should be placed at its highest.

Dr. Farrington was not less esteemed for his generous friendship than for his professional ability. He was noticeably a man of strong convictions nevertheless, with such characteristic breadth of thought and liberality of mind that he never allowed the strongest antagonism in scientific views to chill a friendship once formed.

His genial manners rendered him a most delightful companion, as all who ever had the opportunity to enjoy social intercourse with him will heartily attest.

His last illness began about the 14th of December, 1884, prior to which time he had contracted a cold to which he gave slight heed. Subsequently, owing to necessary exposure in the performance of his professional duties, laryngitis set in; he, nevertheless, delivered several lectures after the throat symptoms had assumed decided severity. During a lecture prior to the Christmas holidays, aphonia took the place of the existing hoarseness, rendering further lecturing impossible.

It became necessary for him to secure a substitute during the month of January, 1885, but feeling much improved, he insisted upon resuming lectures during the month of February He continued his duties in the College until after the Spring examination. During this time the disease invaded the bronchia, developing into a severe bronchitis; this, however, yielded partially during the latter part of March and April. At this time the most careful physical examination did not reveal the slightest sign of lung involvement. He now felt convinced that a trip to Europe would materially advance his recovery. He therefore sailed for Europe, accompanied by his wife, on the 9th day of May. On the 31st of May he wrote from Paris: "I am about the same, as yet, but live in hope." Under the advice of Dr. Herrmann, of Paris, he concluded to "go to Baden-Weiler, a beautiful little town in the Black Forest, noted for its mild climate, mountainous scenery, and restful surroundings." Here again disappointment came to him in that a wet season set in, which continued until his departure, although he remained for several weeks hoping for a favorable change. A stay of several weeks at Brighton, England, highly recommended by several English physicians, afforded no relief. Much discouraged he finally sailed for home. Disappointment and injury alone had resulted from his journey.

He now began to feel that his race was nearly run; that the great work in which he had engaged must be laid aside, and hopes long entertained must be abandoned. The first realization brought a feeling of bitter disappointment, which, however, speedily gave place to a calm conviction that the Lord's way was best. His mind seemed at perfect ease, and though he made fruitless efforts to obtain relief, he maintained an unwavering confidence in the law of cure. Some of his lay friends, seeing that homœopathy must fail, strongly urged him to seek the advice of a prominent allopathist. This he positively refused, afterwards remarking to the writer: "If I must die, I want to die a Christian." His faith in the law was unbounded; he believed it divine in origin, and therefore wholly true.

In religious faith he was a Swedenborgian, holding devoutly to the views of that great expounder of God's law. In his church life, as in his professional, he showed that zeal and learning which soon made him a light among his brethren. He was loved and esteemed by his church as but few laymen at his age are loved. Conscientious, zealous and learned, he seemed destined to be a leader among men. He was early called to his work on earth—that work he faithfully performed. Early the call came to his work on high—confidently he entered thereon. Seeking higher planes of usefulness here, he looked forward to his higher field of labor there in pleasurable anticipation. A good man has been called away. May his living example inspire many to emulation.

A CLINICAL MATERIA MEDICA.

LECTURE I.

INTRODUCTORY.

TODAY we are to begin our study of Materia Medica. At the outset, it will be necessary to give a rambling review of the subject. Before you begin the study of the details of a science, you must understand the construction of that science or art. Were it not for these underlying laws which string together the Materia Medica into one consistent whole you would have no need for lectures on the subject. The ten volumes of the *Encyclopædia of Materia Medica*, issued by Dr. Allen, of New York, contain over nine thousand pages. These do not include clinical symptoms, which would make several thousand more. Then recollect, each physician discovers something new each year, and so a great mass of knowledge is accumulated by a sort of compound multiplication. You can, therefore, well understand why the student might be startled at the idea of attempting to master such a conglomeration. Nor could he master it, were he to attempt to do so by memory alone. Man's mind is composed of more than memory. Memory is the impression made on the mind by a fact. Recollection is another qualification of the mind, which enables one to call up the facts which have been memorized. It is understood that nothing which we take into the memory is ever effaced. It remains there forever. It may be covered with figurative cobwebs and never brought to light, unless the mind is so drilled or so orderly arranged that it may be recalled when occasion requires. The mind should be so drilled and its various faculties so trained that when an external thing occurs similar to an internal fact, *i. e.*, a fact memorized, at once that external thing awakens into recollection the fact or facts bearing on that subject. This is very apt to be so with our feelings, perhaps more naturally than with our intellects, because the latter require more cultivation. Many of us are so strong emotionally that we may call up an emotion without any evident effort of the will or any direction of the understanding. Let me give you an example. A man, on one occasion, was driving along a country road, and ran over a dog and horribly mangled the poor animal. This made him feel very sick. The event was apparently forgotten. Several years later he was driving along the same road, never thinking of the incident, until he came to the spot where the accident happened, when immediately the same sensation of sickness occurred. Then the impression which was made on his mind was recalled, and at once awakened the emotions. Thus must be the intellectual mind of the man who would master the science of medicine. He must see his patient, and when he sees his patient it awakens in his mind the picture of the remedy. This has been termed instinct, but it is not. To do this he must study persistently. You see a physician old in years come into a sick-room. At once he says, this patient needs Sulphur. How did he know that? It was not second sight on his part; but through thirty or forty years' experience he had been studying Sulphur, had been forming in his mind images of Sulphur, and living ideas of Sulphur. The moment he sees these in his patient, that moment he recollects Sulphur. If he had not the idea of that remedy in his mind, he could not see it in his patient. Now, I ask of you not to try to jump over these years that must pass between the beginning and the ending of the art of medicine, and do not make yourselves prophets before your time.

In order to bring some system out of this chaos of Materia Medica, it will be necessary to adopt some plan of study. What is that plan, is asked by every student; one teacher answers in one way, another in another. The method may not be correct, and yet its results may be good. It does well enough for a scaffolding by which you erect your building, after which the scaffolding is removed and the building remains. Some method must be adopted, and that retained to the end. In analyzing the method which I have chosen to adopt it may be well to begin at the beginning and to carry you on until you may see what plan I propose for your adoption. It may not be clear at once. An abstract thing is not at once grasped by the mind. It requires to come up time after time. What seems difficult at first, is plain enough after a while.

In the first place, I will begin by suggesting an analysis of the drug.

We presume now that you have heard of some one substance which has been a popular remedy in your part of the country for years. You think that it ought to be proved. You proceed to get the necessary material. First, you procure your drug. You prepare its tincture and then you potentize it. Now, it is a principle of Homœopathy, to which there is no exception, that you shall learn the action of a drug on the healthy organism before you use it in practice. That is a rule which you cannot neglect. You cannot be too careful, otherwise you throw yourself into confusion, doubt and empiricism, and help to fill the Materia Medica with "bosh," of which there is enough already there.

What you want to know, is exactly what this medicine will do. What would you think of a machinist who undertook to build a machine when he did not know how the parts fitted together? What would you think of a physician who does not know the use of the tools he is about to employ? You now intend to try the effects of this drug on some healthy person or persons. Will it produce alterations in the function or the nutrition of the body or of its organs? If so, a symptom or symptoms will be the result. Symptoms, then, are indications of alterations in the functions or the nutrition of a part or of parts of the body. I have been accused of stepping down from the lofty heights of pure Homœopathy and dressing myself in physiological livery. The statement made against me is that we cannot know what changes are taking place except through symptoms; therefore, if one begins to talk about altered tissue, he at once pollutes Homœopathy. This is true, and it is false. It is true if you take this altered tissue alone. It is not true if you regard this altered tissue as a manifestation of the change in the vital force. I cannot see how there can be a symptom which is not at least the result of a change of function. I do not mean that you must give *Bryonia* because it acts on serous membranes. I do not mean that you must give *Aconite* because it produces dry skin, heat, etc. I do not say that you shall give *Belladonna* because it produces hyperæmia of the brain and dilatation of the pupil; but I do say that these drugs produce these effects, and if these effects are not alterations in function, what are they? We can know changes in the vital force only by results, and these results are symptoms.

Now you get symptoms in your provings. These symptoms you will find to be embraced under two grand classes, subjective and objective. The subjective symptoms are those which the prover himself experiences, and which he has to express to you in certain language. The objective are those which apply directly to your senses. They are such as you may see, hear, touch, taste or smell. For instance, if you give the drug we are speaking of, and the prover says he feels a pain over the right eye, that is a subjective symptom. You cannot see it, touch it, taste it or feel it. It does not apply to your senses. You know what pain is; you have experienced it; you can appreciate it in your own mind. But if a boil is produced by this medicine; if there is a cloudy deposit in the urine, or if there are mucous râles or harsh sounds in the lungs; if the heart itself is altered in its action; if a wart appears on the skin, or if sweat breaks out, you have an objective symptom. Now, what will be the alteration in function which these objective and subjective symptoms express? They are decrease of function, increase of function and alteration of function. If this drug produces photophobia, there is increase of function; if, on the other hand, it causes blindness so great that the patient can gaze at the sun, there is decrease of function; whereas, if it produces cloudiness of the cornea or visions of bright stars, there is an alteration of function. The prover may have increased urination, decreased urination or brick-dust sediment in the urine, this last being an alteration of function. So, when we come to speak of a drug, and to tell you what its effect on the system is, we will have these three classes with which to deal, increase, alteration and decrease. You go on collecting these symptoms, both subjective and objective. If you are skilled in the analysis of the excreta of the body, you should make use of your knowledge to determine the elimination of urates, phosphates, etc. These are facts, and, in their place, are invaluable. I would have you mind this expression, *in their place, valuable; out of place, valueless and even harmful*. An increase in the elimination of urea would weigh nothing in the balance against the mental state. All symptoms of the Materia Medica are not of the same value. They are relative in value.

We include all the symptoms that we can observe. Then what have we? A mass of symptoms seeming to have no connection at all. They come from a human organism that is all order and perfection, and all the parts of which work in perfect harmony. When even one of these parts is out of order, there must be a certain clue to string these effects together and picture a form of disease, and when you get this form of disease, what have you? A pathological state. I hope that no diploma will be granted to any man in this class who does not study pathology.

When you have the changes *in toto* that this substance has made on the system, you have the pathology of the case. You have the totality of the effects on the system. This grand effect of the drug must be in the mind always, qualifying the individual symptoms of the drug. You may express this as you choose. Some call it the genius of the drug; others speak of it as the general action of the drug. This you must have in your mind or the other symptoms are worthless. Did you not do this you would be a mere symptomist, certainly a term of reproach. You must know what the whole drug does or you are not able to appreciate any one part of the drug. You can find twenty drugs with precisely the same symptoms. How will you decide between them? Apparently they are all identical, but not in their general action. How is this general action found? By the study of the drug as a whole. But here is a place where physicians may go too precipitately and fall into pathology. They say that as Belladonna produces a picture of scarlatina and as Arsenicum produces a picture of cholera Asiatica, even unto the growths found in the excrement, therefore these substances must be *the* remedies for their respective diseases. Baptisia produces a perfect picture of typhoid fever, therefore they say Baptisia must be *the* remedy in typhoid.

As we carry out the view I expressed a few minutes ago, when we examine a patient for disease we proceed in exactly the same way as we do in the case of the proving. We note the changes we see and the sensations the patient feels; we look at his tongue, we examine his urine, we put all these together and we make a pathological picture of that man. Suppose you decide the case to be one of typhoid fever. That must not be valued except by comparison, showing how the present case differs from the general disease. If the genius of the case under treatment suits the genius of Baptisia, and, if you give that remedy, the patient will recover whether you call his disease typhoid fever or mumps. If the genius of Baptisia does not suit the genius of the case, then that remedy will do no good. If the patient has the Baptisia symptom, "thinks he is double, or all broken to pieces," that drug will not cure unless the genius of Baptisia is there, too. I may be permitted to recall a remark of Carroll Dunham. At a certain consultation there was chosen for a patient a drug which seemed to have many of his symptoms, but when Dr. Dunham was asked for his opinion as to whether that drug was the similimum, he replied, "No, I think not, for the general character of Ignatia does not correspond with the general character of the patient, which corresponds to Baryta.

You will find his most prominent symptoms under Baryta." One physician decided for one drug, the other for another. Each went by his study of the drug; one understood Ignatia in part, the other by its totality.

It is my duty to show you this winter the genius of each drug, and the relations which drugs bear to one another. I cannot hope to give you all that is characteristic of each, but I think that I can give you an idea of its genius, and show you how drugs are related so that you may fill up the interstices at leisure. You must acknowledge that Materia Medica is the most important of all branches, but you cannot understand it unless you have a thorough knowledge of the others. You must learn symptoms and not mere words, and you cannot put any idea into them until you know their meaning; and unless you can interpret symptoms you can never learn the genius of a drug.

Analysis of a medicine.
- Blood and bloodvessels.
- Lymph and its vessels.
- Nerves, brain, cord and sympathetic; muscles, tendons, ligaments
- Connective tissue.
- Bones, cartilages and joints.
- Serous and synovial membranes.
- Mucous membranes.
- Skin.
- Organs.

We now understand a drug as analyzed according to the schema on the board. We must see how it affects the blood and bloodvessels, the lymph and lymph vessels, the nervous system, including, of course, the brain, cord, and sympathetic nervous system.

The first of these divisions tells us something of the nutrition of the body. The second, the lymph, likewise tells us of nutrition and how well repair is going on. The muscles, ligaments, etc., tell us how the human machine may move; and so we may go through the entire schema.

You will note the deviations from the normal under each of these headings. Under the conditions of the blood you will note increase, as in plethora or hyperæmia; decrease, as in anæmia or ischæmia, and alteration, as in chlorosis or pyæmia. The same is true of the lymph, which may exhibit plus, minus and change, and so on down the list.

When you study the drug by this analysis you quickly arrive at an idea of it as a whole, that is, you get the genius of the drug. But when you have done that you are not through with your difficulties. You must learn to tell one drug from another.

You go into a field and you see two or three hundred cattle. They all look alike to you, yet the man in charge of them knows each one. How does he know them? He knows them by certain distinctions which he has learned by familiarity with them. So can you know one drug from another by studying their points of difference. Drugs impinge in their resemblances, and separate in their differences. Thus we have another form of study, comparison of drugs. That is just as necessary to successful practice as is the first step, the analysis of the drug.

Then again there are drugs which antidote each other. You may have made a mistake. Your patient may be too susceptible to the action of the remedy, and you require to modify its effects. It was only yesterday that I prescribed Nux vomica for a cold. It relieved the patient of his cold, but he became almost crazy with headache. He had had an excess of Nux vomica, so I gave him Coffea, and in ten minutes his head was better. This was done by simply modifying the effects of Nux vomica, not by suppressing the symptom.

Again, there are some remedies which, although they bear a strong resemblance to each other, seem as though they ought to be concordant remedies, yet they are inimical.

So you study the Materia Medica, analyzing one drug after the other until you have analyzed all. Then you must arrange your remedies according to some system in your mind, and so be enabled to recall facts as you need them If you study only one remedy, every case you see fits that remedy. If you have studied Aconite, every case will suggest Aconite. Thus you must have Aconite and its confreres side by side in your mind, before you can use them successfully in the sick room. This is done by systematizing your study.

Now, then, you will find that drugs hold certain relations to each other. You will find five relations. The first I have called the family relation, derived from their similarity in origin. When drugs belong to the same family they must of necessity have a similar action. For instance, the halogens, Chlorine, Iodine, Bromine and Fluorine, have many similitudes, because they belong to one family. So, too, with remedies derived from the vegetable kingdom. Take, for instance, the family to which Arum triphyllum belongs. There you find drugs which resemble each other from their family origin. Take the Ophidians, and you will be perplexed to tell the differences between Lachesis, Elaps and Crotalus. This resemblance through relationship is sometimes so nearly identity that these drugs do not follow each other well. Take, for example, Ignatia and Nux vomica. Both come from the same order of plants; they do not follow each other well, and they do not antidote each other. Then we may have drugs which present marked similarities in action though dissimilar in origin. These are said to be "concordant." Drugs which hold a concordant relation may follow each other well.

There is another relation, that of complement, that is, one drug completes a cure which the other begins, but is unable to effect. Such a relation exists between Belladonna and Calcarea.

Next we have the relation of antidote, of which I spoke a few moments ago.

Lastly, we have the relation of enmity, one that I am unable to explain to you. It is a fact that certain drugs, although resembling each other apparently, will not follow one another with any satisfaction. They seem to mix up the case. Such drugs are China and Psorinum, Apis and Rhus, Phosphorus and Causticum, and Silicea and Mercury.

In carrying out these various ideas we must study Materia Medica as a natural science, for such it must be intrinsically, although it is as yet undeveloped and unworthy of that dignified name in our present understanding of it. Nature's laws in no way dispute the known relations and actions of drugs. They rather harmonize with them.

Each order or class is to receive a separate examination, its resemblances and differences noted and the individual members compared with related remedies. Thus is preserved a uniform progression from *generals* to *particulars*.

We are now ready to begin our study of the various drugs composing the Homœopathic Materia Medica. For this purpose I have arranged the remedies in three grand divisions, according to the kingdom of nature from which they are derived, viz.:

1. Remedies derived from the animal kingdom.
2. Remedies derived from the vegetable kingdom.
3. Remedies derived from the mineral kingdom.

There is also a fourth class of remedies, the nosodes or disease products.

In our next lecture we will begin our study of drugs derived from the animal kingdom.

LECTURE II.

ANIMAL KINGDOM.

TODAY we begin our study of the medicines obtained from the animal kingdom. I desire to preface my lecture on these remedies with a few remarks relating to their properties in general Many of the animal poisons are distinguished by the violence and intensity of their action, and by the decided alterations which they produce in both structure and function. The blood is often changed in its composition and quality. The nervous system suffers and even the lower tissues are affected. The whole tendency of these remedies is to produce diseases, *which are never of asthenic character and always of a destructive form*, tending thus to local as well as to general death of the body. We therefore look upon these poisons as medicines which suit deep-seated diseases, such, for example, as are accompanied by changes in the quality of the blood; such as profoundly affect the nervous centres. Consequently they are indicated in typhoid fevers, erysipelatous inflammations, tuberculosis of different organs and tissues of the body, and many of those dyscrasiæ which underlie and qualify acute diseases. You will find, if you devote time to the study of this portion of the Materia Medica, more time than we can spare or than these lectures will permit, that they are often necessary to arouse vitality and direct the vital forces into a proper channel.

You will find, too, that these animal poisons are apt to affect the mind, especially the emotions. They arouse the lowest qualities in human nature, and produce a condition which is truly shocking. Some of them arouse the filthiest lust, the most intense anger, and passions of a kindred nature. So we may find many of these drugs suitable for persons affected with insanity, whether it be the result of functional or organic cerebral changes; whether or not it be reflex from irregularities in bodily functions.

You will see by the table which I have placed on the board that we have a number of remedies derived from the animal kingdom.

Vertebrata	Mammalia	Moschus, *Castoreum*, *Mephitis*, Oleum animale, Hippomanes, Castor equi, Lac vaccinum, Lac defloratum, Lac caninum, Koumyss, Fel tauri, Fel vulpi, Pulmo vulpis.
	Ophidia	Lachesis, Crotalus, Bothrops, Agkistrodon, Elaps, *Naja*, Vipera.
	Pisces	*Oleum jecoris aselli.*
	Batrachia	Bufo rana.
Mollusca		Sepiæ succus, *Murex.*
Radiata		*Corallium rubrum*, Spongia, Medusa, Badiaga.
Articulata	Hemiptera	*Coccus cacti*, Cimex.
	Hymenoptera	Apis mellifica, Vespa, *Formica.*
	Coleoptera	Cantharis, Doryphora.
	Orthoptera	Blatta.
	Arachnida	*Tarentula, Mygale, Theridion, Aranea.*

I have, for convenience of study, divided these animal substances according to their natural relations. We have first the *Vertebrata*. Within this grand division of the animal kingdom we note the first class, the *Mammalia*, below this the *Ophidia* or great variety of serpents, then the *Pisces* or fishes, and, finally, the *Batrachia*. In the higher order of Mammalia we have a large list of remedies; but these members of the animal kingdom compose only a small portion of it. There are many animal drugs of which we know nothing but their names; they have been used by one individual without any special proving. This is a field which has not been thoroughly investigated, and one, too, the investigation of which has encountered great opposition. Especially has the *Cimex lectularius*, the common bed-bug, been condemned; but this opposition has extended to other remedies of the class. Prejudice goes far. I do not wish to sanction these medicines any more than they deserve. Our notions, our prejudices, and our appetites affect us all. Reviewing the *Mammalia*, we note first the *Moschus*, and here another and similar animal substance, the *Castoreum*. I mention these together that you may remember them as two substances which act on the nervous system somewhat similarly. The origin of *Moschus* you all know; *Castoreum* is a similar product taken from the beaver, and is a very useful medicine for patients, especially women, who are nervous and do not react after typhoid fever. If, after the fever has spent its force, the patient remains irritable, with weak and exhausting sweat, *Castoreum* helps her at once.

Next we have here the product from the animal which you all know as the skunk, *Mephitis putorius*. This *Mephitis* also acts powerfully on the nervous system. If taken in a low potency when one is exhausted, it tones up the nervous system and relieves the exhaustion. The main use of *Mephitis*, however, is in whooping-cough. It produces a well described hard cough, with well-marked laryngeal spasm and a distinct whoop. I have found in using this medicine that it often apparently makes the patient worse, while it really tends to shorten the course of the disease. When the catarrhal symptoms are slight and the spasmodic whoop is marked *Mephitis* is to be selected. The cough is worse at night and after lying down. There is a suffocative feeling; the child cannot exhale; convulsions at times ensue. It vomits its food, sometimes hours after eating. Drinks get into the larynx. In whooping-cough you should compare with *Mephitis*, *Corallium rubrum*, which has, however, smothering *before* the cough, and great exhaustion afterwards. The gasping progresses into repeated crowing inspirations until the child becomes black in the face.

Drosera should also be thought of in this connection. This remedy has spells of barking cough, which come so frequently as not to give the patient an opportunity to recover the breath. They are especially worse after 12 P. M. The child holds each hypochondrium during the cough, and if sputum is not raised, vomiting and retching ensue. The patient may have a diarrhœa with stools containing bloody mucus.

Mephitis has also been recommended in the asthma of drunkards. It may also be used in the asthma of consumptives when *Drosera* fails. In the last-named condition you may think also of *Rumex* and *Sticta*. The former of these is to be given when there is aggravation at 2 A. M. The latter remedy has been recommended by Dr. E. T. Blake when the trouble is associated with splitting headache. The *Mephitis* patient seems to have the power of withstanding extreme cold. He feels less chilly than usual in cold weather. Washing in ice-cold water causes a pleasant sensation. Other symptoms of the drug which are worthy of notice are the following: Wandering pains, with pressure to urinate; fine nervous vibrations reaching to the bones, causing anxiety; awakes at night with congestions to the legs (see *Aurum*); legs uneasy, as if they would become insensible; vivid fancies, unfitting him for mental labor; talkative, as if intoxicated; violent pain in the head after a fulness which was pressing upwards; head dull and numb; head feels enlarged; heaviness and pressure in the back of the head, as from a finger pressing; redness and injection of the conjunctiva; dimness of vision; letters blur and run together.

Below we have the *Oleum animale*. This is similar in its origin to *Castoreum* and *Moschus*. It is the secretion of the mare, which tends to excite the passion of the opposite sex.

Next we have the *Castor equi*, which is the red substance growing on the inside of the legs of the horse. The principal use that has been made of this in medicine has been in sore nipples, when they are cracked and ragged, almost hanging in fact.

Now we come to the milk preparations. I am not going to uphold these. You are to be the judges. No editor of a journal, or college professor, however brilliant he may be, should decide for you. I have been making experiments with them and I believe that some at least will become very valuable remedies. Try them, that you may know them by your own experience. The first is *Lac vaccinum*, or cow's milk; the next is *Lac defloratum*, or skimmed milk. The latter has gained such a foot-hold that less objection has been made to it than to any of the others. It has been used largely in the treatment of diabetes. Patients are directed to drink a pint of milk morning, noon and night, while all food containing starch and sugar is prohibited. The quantity of milk just mentioned is gradually increased until the patient consumes four or five quarts daily. Provings of *Lac defloratum* have been made. It has cured intense headache, located principally in the fore-part of the head. The pains are of a throbbing character, and are associated with nausea, vomiting and the most obstinate constipation and great chilliness. It is especially suitable in anæmic women. Remember these symptoms — anæmic women, throbbing frontal headache, nausea, vomiting and obstinate constipation.

Next we come to the dog's milk, *Lac caninum*. It has been used chiefly in diphtheria by a New York physician. *Koumyss*, another of the milk preparations, is *certainly* no humbug. It is prepared by fermentation from asses' milk, and used largely on the plains of Asia. Many claim that it is an excellent food for the weak and anæmic and especially for the consumptive. It is readily digested and is well tolerated by weak stomachs.

Next we have two substances, *Fel tauri* and *Fel vulpi*, which have been used in constipation and in accumulation of flatus in the intestines.

Pulmo vulpis was introduced by Grauvogl, who, acting according to the law of "*Signatura rerum,*" recommended *Pulmo vulpis* in asthma because foxes were long-winded. I give you this without indorsing it.

We next come to the *Ophidia*. Here we have the large class of serpents, the consideration of which I will omit now, because we will take them up for study at our next meeting.

Among the *Pisces* or fishes, I will mention only the cod-liver oil, or *Oleum jecoris aselli*. This is known as a great remedy in scrofulosis, tuberculosis and debility. It is used, as you know, by physicians of both schools of practice. Many physicians claim that it acts physiologically. This is a mistake. It is a medicine. It does not act by the oil contained as Dr. Hughes claims. If it does, why is it that other oils do not produce as good effects? It is a compound drug and contains Iodine, Phosphorus, and other substances. Dr. Neidhard of this city has made provings of it. He gave the drug in the lower potencies to provers, until he obtained a list of symptoms which he found to be characteristic. I will here give you an outline of the symptoms. You may use it when there are chills running down the back, hoarseness, and soreness through the chest. How many times you will see these symptoms as the beginning of tuberculosis! There may be sharp stitching pains here and there through the chest; the patient complains of burning pain in spots or in some one portion of the chest. Fever is particularly marked toward evening with burning of the palms of the hands. The cough is dry, with an expectoration of a somewhat slimy mucus such as we notice in the initial stages of tuberculosis. These are symptoms which have been noticed in the provings conducted by a conscientious observer, Dr. Neidhard; they are symptoms which, when occurring in the sick, have been cured by the drug. When they are present, you may give *Oleum jecoris aselli* either in potency or in the crude form, and give it, too, on a scientific basis.

Next we come to *Bufo rana*, a variety of toad indigenous to South

America. The surface of its body secretes an oily substance which has the reputation of being poisonous. The native women, when tired of the importunities of their husbands, mix this oily secretion into their husbands' drink for the purpose of producing impotency. Provings have been made of *Bufo*, and it has been found to produce a very disgusting set of symptoms. It causes a sort of imbecility, in which the person loses all decency. He becomes a confirmed masturbator and seeks privacy to indulge his vicious habit Masturbation and even sexual intercourse seem to cause convulsions which simulate those of epilepsy. The aura that begins the epileptic paroxysm starts from the genital organs. The patient may even be thrown into violent convulsions during coitus. That form of epilepsy for which *Bufo* has done the most is that which occurs from sexual over-excitement or else seems to start from the solar plexus. These symptoms are preceded by a singular irritability of the mind during which the patient talks incoherently, and is then vexed because his gibberish is not understood. The convulsions themselves are usually followed by profound sleep. Some years ago, Dr. Wm. Payne cured a case of peritonitis with this remedy in which there were repeated convulsions, finally followed by stupor, unconsciousness, cold limbs, copious sweat, etc. I have recently successfully treated a woman with this drug, the indications being spasms, with suppurating blisters on the skin, in the throat, and in the vagina. The abdomen was exceedingly sensitive, feeling to her as if the same sort of sores were also in the bowels. *Bufo* also cures blisters on the skin, which rupture, leaving a raw surface from which there oozes an excoriating ichorous fluid.

We may here institute comparisons between *Bufo* and its concordant remedies. *Indigo* is indicated in epileptiform spasms which seem to be reflex from the irritation of worms. It is often useful in children when they are aroused at night with this horrible itching at the anus. But it never does any good unless the patient is low-spirited or sad or timid. If he is vehement or excitable, recourse must be had to a vehement remedy like *Nux vomica* or *Bufo*.

Artemisia vulgaris is an excellent remedy in epilepsy, especially when it has been caused by fright or some exciting mental emotion. The attacks are repeated one after the other, and are followed by profound sleep.

From the *Mollusca* we obtain two remedies, *Sepiæ succus* and *Murex*. These I will leave for the present, as I shall have more to say of them by and by.

From the *Radiata* we obtain four medicines, the first of which to be mentioned is the *Corallium rubrum* or red coral. It has several uses, but I shall mention only two. *Corallium rubrum* is useful in a combination of *syphilis* and *psora*. There are smooth spots on the surface of the body, mostly on the palms of the hands. At first they are of a coral-red hue, but they finally become darker, and assume the well-known copper-color characteristic of syphilis. *Corallium* is also useful for chancres when they have this coral-red hue.

The whooping-cough of *Corallium rubrum* has been styled the minute-gun cough, the paroxysms, as already described, coming very close together. During the day the cough is short, quick and ringing in character; when night comes, decided paroxysms of whooping appear, worse towards morning. These seem to take the child's breath completely away, so that when they have ceased, he falls back completely exhausted. In this whooping-cough it is similar to *Mephitis*, which I have already described to you.

Spongia we shall speak of along with the *Halogens*, Bromine, Iodine, etc.

Medusa, or the jelly-fish, has effects which are nearly identical with those of *Urtica urens*. It produces a nettle-rash, and also has some slight action on the kidneys.

Badiaga, the fresh-water sponge of Russia, has two principal points of attack, the first of which is on the lymphatic glands, causing enlargement with induration. It has been successfully used in indurated buboes, especially when they have been maltreated. Here it is similar to *Carbo animalis*. It also has an action on the heart. It is of service in palpitation of that organ caused by any unpleasant excitement; thus it is similar to *Coffea* and *Phosphorus*. It is not indicated in organic heart diseases.

Nitrite of amyl is likewise indicated in functional cardiac affections. It paralyses the vaso-motor nerves and is therefore useful in congestions to various parts of the body, especially to the head or to the chest. The face becomes flushed, and even puffed and red. Respiration is greatly oppressed. The heart beats more frequently, but loses in force. A constrictive sensation about the heart is experienced and the patient must sit up. The urine ordinarily contains a small quantity of albumen. So susceptible is the person, that the opening of a door causes flushing. *Nitrite of amyl* is indicated in flashes of heat at change of life.

Next we come to the *Articulata*, insects whose bodies are in segments, the wasps, bees, etc. We have in this group a great many remedies, some of which have been placed on the board. To the *Hemiptera* belong the *Coccus cacti* and the *Cimex*.

Coccus cacti is a little insect infesting the cacti of South America. The principal use of the drug is in whooping-cough with morning aggravation. The child awakens in the morning and is immediately seized with a paroxysm of whooping-cough, ending in vomiting of clear ropy mucus, hanging in great long strings from the mouth. That is a symptom which you all should remember. I can assure you that it is a positive one, for with this condition present *Coccus cacti*, when administered in the beginning, has cut short the whole disease. Still further, *Coccus cacti* affects the chest. The apices of the lungs are sore, and the patient coughs up this ropy mucus.

Kali bichromicum and *Senega* are concordant remedies of *Coccus cacti* in these conditions. *Kali bichromicum* has a dry, barking cough, worse in the morning. The expectoration is stringy, but it is yellow in color —not clear, as under *Coccus cacti*.

Senega is useful in chubby children. It has tough expectoration, which is transparent like the white of an egg and difficult to raise, but the cough is worse towards evening. If the child is old enough, it will complain of a crushing weight on the chest.

Cimex is a remedy that I have never used. It has been recommended in intermittent fever.

From the *Hymenoptera* we obtain such important remedies as *Apis mellifica*, *Vespa* and *Formica*. This order we must leave for the present.

The order *Coleoptera* gives us *Cantharis*, which will be considered in a future lecture. From this order we also obtain the *Doryphora decemlineata*, or potato-bug. This is highly poisonous, and has been used successfully in inflammations of a low grade; for instance, in gonorrhœal inflammation when the parts are purple or dark red.

Under the order *Orthoptera* we have one remedy mentioned, the *Blatta*, or cockroach. Journals have contained many accounts of cases of dropsy cured with it. Lastly, we have the *Arachnida*, or spiders, the consideration of which we shall leave for a future lecture.

LECTURE III.

THE OPHIDIA.

In considering the remedies derived from the animal kingdom, first I shall speak, *in extenso*, of the large family, formally called Ophidians, or snakes proper. Of those we use in medicine, we have first the *Lachesis trigonocephalus*. This was proved by Dr. Hering, sixty years ago. Next we have the *Crotalus horridus*. There is also a South American species, proved by Dr. Muir, the *Crotalus cascavella*. This has a few symptoms which will not yield to the administration of the other species. Then there are the *Naja tripudians*, one variety of the cobra, and the *Elaps corallinus*, so called from the shape of the scales on the back, which have something the appearance of coral. Lastly, there is the *Bothrops lanceolatus*, a remedy which, for a year or more, I have vainly tried to procure. It causes symptoms similar to that peculiar condition known as aphasia. Of these poisons, the first four are commonly used in medicine.

The poison of the snake is generally held in a little sac behind the fangs. On the under surface of the fangs is a small groove, into which empties a little tube that conveys the poison from the gland. When they are not in use they lie back on the roof of the mouth. If the animal is excited, it opens its mouth, the fangs are pushed forward, and at the same time, by muscular action, a drop of the poison runs down the canal and into the punctured wound. Now, what follows? That depends on various causes. The poison is more potent at some times than at others. The more angry the serpent is, the more active is its venom. If, in inflicting the wound, the fang passes through the clothing, some of the poison may thus be absorbed. Again, the power of resistance of the individual has some effect.

Thus, you may divide the effects of the snake-poison into three sorts: First, that which may be compared to the action of a stroke of lightning or a dose of Prussic acid. Immediately after the bite the patient starts up with a look of anguish on his face and then drops dead. This represents the full, unmodified, lightning rapidity of the poison. In the second form, commonly, the part bitten swells and turns, not a bright red, but rapidly to a dark purplish color the blood becomes fluid, and the patient exhibits symptoms like those characteristic of septicæmia. The heart-beat increases in rapidity, but lessens in tone and strength. The patient becomes prostrated and covered with a cold clammy sweat. Dark spots appear on the body where the blood settles into ecchymoses; the patient becomes depressed from weakness of the nervous system, and then sinks into a typhoid state and dies. Or there follow nervous phenomena. Vertigo; dark spots before the eyes; blindness; a peculiar tremor all over the body; face besotted; dyspnœa, or even stertor. Or the process may assume a slower form. After the vertigo or trembling the patient remains weak, and the wound turns dark or gangrenous. All the discharges, the sweat, the urine and the fæces become offensive. Dysenteric symptoms of a typhoid character show themselves. The patient goes into a low state, and finally dies. These are all phases of the action of these powerful poisons on the blood and the nerves.

The Ophidia, as a group, are characterized by their paralyzing action upon the nerves. They directly weaken the brain and heart action. Then follow decomposition of the blood, changes in the muscular tissue and local death from gangrene. At first there is developed a condition of anxiety mental excitability and oversensitiveness of the brain, with hallucinations, anxious fear, etc. Afterward arises nervous depression, varying from such a debility as is observed in severe or protracted disease and advancing old age to mental confusion, stupor, low delirium and paralysis. Constrictions are noticed, as in the throat, larynx and sphincters in general. Hæmorrhages, which are usually dark, decomposed, oozing from every orifice of the body; thus also, ecchymoses. They are most marked under *Lachesis* and *Crotalus*, less in *Elaps*, least in *Naja*. Face sickly, pale, anxious; bloated, dark red or bluish. Special senses altered; dim vision, excitability of brain and spinal cord, accounting for the mental restlessness and bodily sensitiveness. Predominant, even with the pains, are torpidity, numbness, twitchings, formication.

You already see in what class of diseases you will find these poisons curative Inflammations and fevers of low, destructive type such as gangrene malignant ulcerations, diphtheria, typhoid, pyæmia, carbuncles. etc. With all there are tendency to faint, muscular prostration, trembling as in drunkards, irregularities in circulation, flushes of heat, apoplectic congestions, paralysis.

Nerves especially affected by the snake-poisons seem to be the pneumogastric and spinal accessory; consequently, you expect to find, as eminently characteristic, symptoms of the larynx, of the respiration and of the heart. All of the Ophidia cause choking, constrictive sensation coming from irritation of the pneumogastric. All of them have dyspnœa and heart symptoms.

Moreover, the Ophidia produce a yellow staining of the skin. This is not jaundice, and must not be confused with that affection. It comes from the blood, and is due to the decomposition of that fluid, just as we find in yellow fever, typhus or pyæmia, and not to the staining of the skin with bile. This is most marked in the *Crotalus*. Again, you may find that the skin is dry and harsh, as if there was no vitality in it, or it may be clammy, more characteristic of *Lachesis*. The discharges are fœtid, even the formed fæcal stools of *Lachesis* are horribly offensive. As the heart is weakened by all, we find as characteristic, running through them all, weak heart, cold feet and trembling—not the trembling of mere nervousness, but the trembling of weakness from blood-poisoning. The cold feet are not indicative of congestion, as you find under *Belladonna;* they are attendant upon a weakened heart.

The heart symptoms of *Naja* resemble greatly those of *Lachesis*, but its cardiac symptoms point more markedly to the remote effects of cardiac valvular lesions; those of *Lachesis* more to the incipiency of rheumatic disease of the heart. In *Naja* there is a well-marked frontal and temporal headache with the cardiac symptoms; the heart beats tumultuously. The patient awakes gasping for breath. *Naja* causes more nervous phenomena than any of the snake-poisons.

Under *Belladonna* the head is hot and the feet are cold, because the blood surges toward the head. Under the snake-poisons the feet are cold, because the heart is too weak to force the blood to the periphery.

All of the snake-poisons cause inflammation of the cellular tissue. Accordingly, we find them valuable when cellulitis arises in the course of typhoid fever, diphtheria, etc. The color of the affected part is dark red, purple or black, like gangrene.

In diphtheria *Crotalus* has had more clinical confirmation in the persistent epistaxis.

Elaps claims attention in cases of hæmoptysis, when the blood discharged is dark in color, especially when the right lung is affected.

Antidotes for these poisons are numerous. There is no doubt that alcohol is a powerful antagonist to the snake-venom. It is remarkable how much alcohol can be swallowed by persons bitten by serpents, without the manifestation of the usual physiological effects. Dr. Hering recommends radiating heat as an antidote. The part bitten should be held close to a hot fire. Ammonia and permanganate of potash have been recommended as antidotes, and cures have been claimed for each.

LACHESIS.

Now let us consider *Lachesis*. First of all, in order that you may comprehend the subject, I wish to refer to those symptoms which are universal. We notice that *Lachesis* is especially suitable to persons who have a peculiar sensitiveness of the surface of the body. Even if the patient is lying in a stupor and you touch him, as when you try to feel his pulse, he will show that he is disturbed thereby. Hard rubbing or pressure may cause no trouble at all. Dr. Hering, who first proved *Lachesis*, could never tolerate tight clothing about his neck. He always wore his collars loose. He noticed that, during the proving, this symptom annoyed him more than usual, so he faithfully made note of the occurrence, but did not place much value on it. Since then the symptom has been confirmed many times in practice, and has been found true, not only as a local symptom of the neck, but as a symptom of the body universally. The explanation seems to be that there is an irritation of the peripheral nerves; and because of this the patient cannot bear touch or slight pressure. It is no evidence of inflammation, and must not be confounded with the inflammatory soreness of *Aconite, Arnica* or *Belladonna*. The sensitiveness also differs from that of *Apis*, which has a bruised, sore feeling more acute than that of *Arnica*. It also differs from the sensitiveness of *Nux vomica* and *Lycopodium* which have it about the waist only after a meal.

Next we find that the drug is prone to affect the left side of the body. Homœopaths have been criticised for attributing to drugs the power of acting upon one side of the body in preference to the other. The simple fact that disease chooses sides ought to be enough to lead one to believe that drugs may do the same. The left side of the body is more apt to be affected by drugs having a depressing action, because that side of the body is weaker.

Another peculiarity of *Lachesis*, arising, probably, from its action on the pneumogastric nerves, is its influence on sleep. This is a universal symptom, that the patient is worse from sleep; *he sleeps into an aggravation.* If it is true that *Lachesis* has an influence on the centres of respiration, and is a weakening drug, we can understand why sleep should aggravate. During our waking hours we have some control over respiration. During sleep this voluntary control is lost. It is when this change takes place that the weakening effect of *Lachesis* is asserted.

Lachesis is a very valuable remedy at the climaxis, especially in the woman who has exhausted herself by frequent pregnancies and hard work. In this worn-out condition there occurs a sudden cessation of the menses. Suppression or non-appearance of discharges always makes the *Lachesis* patient worse. Perhaps previous to the climaxis she was worse before the flow than during it. The pulse is weak and tremulous. There are the peculiar headache, and the annoying symptoms of the mind, hot flashes and nervous symptoms characteristic of the drug.

Now, let us consider some of the symptoms of *Lachesis* in detail. First, as to the mental symptoms. The patient is nervous, anxious, loquacious, jumping from subject to subject; sometimes with fear of being poisoned, which causes him to refuse the medicines you offer. Interesting stories excite immoderately and even intensify the bodily symptoms. Sometimes the anxiety assumes a peculiar type, and he imagines that he is dead, and preparations are being made for the funeral. The loquacity may be accompanied with sleepiness, and yet inability to sleep. Ideas chase each other so rapidly through the mind he cannot write them down. He sits up late at night, mental activity then being unusually increased. But this stage of excitement is commingled with another, which soon entirely supercedes it. The mind is weakened. The patient is able to think only with difficulty. He has to stop to think how words are spelled, like *Sulphur, Lycopodium* and *Medorrhinum.* There is vertigo, worse on closing the eyes, or on sitting or lying down. Vertigo with deathly paleness; syncope. In this vertigo, fainting, etc., you may compare *Theridion,* which has dizziness worse with the eyes closed; but, as a distinctive feature, you will find that under the latter remedy, vertigo, pains and nausea are intensely aggravated by noise. Both remedies are useful in sunstroke. *Arsenic, Hydrocyanic acid, Digitalis, Veratrum album* and *Camphor,* you should compare in vertigo and fainting from cardiac weakness.

Laurocerasus or *Hydrocyanic acid* may be needed in long-lasting faints;

there seems to be no reactive power; the face is pale and blue, the surface cold. If fluids are forced down the throat, they roll audibly into the stomach. If the syncope is attendant upon some poison in the system, as scarlatina, the symptoms are similar, the eruption being livid, and, when pressed, regaining its color very slowly (cf. *Ailanthus*).

Digitalis also rivals the Ophidians in syncope, with the antecedent dim vision; the pulse is generally very slow, and the patient complains of nausea and deathly weakness in the epigastrium.

Camphor and *Veratrum album* display coldness and cold sweaty skin; in the latter remedy, the forehead is cold and sweaty. The face may be red while lying, but if raised, it turns pale and the patient faints; the pulse is thready.

Camphor has icy surface, sudden sinking, as in *Laurocerasus*, and although so cold, he throws off the clothing as soon as he is strong enough to move, even though he be still unconscious.

Heaviness of the head on waking, with nausea and dizziness, as in sunstroke. In ill-effects of the heat of the sun, compare *Glonoine*, *Belladonna*, *Natrum carb.* and *Theridion* (see above). The first two, with bloated red face, paralytic weakness (*Glon.*), unconsciousness, etc., resemble *Lachesis*, but the latter displays the effects of heat upon one already exhausted. All the Ophidians are intolerant of warm, relaxing weather, and so we find many ailments returning in spring and summer. In the *Lachesis* case, the patient may be an inebriate or one prostrated by mental fatigue. The sun's heat makes him languid, dizzy, faint, or, if congestions ensue, the face is dark red, and looks at the same time sunken and cadaverous; the extremities are cold. Here *Camphor* may be demanded if vitality is ebbing away, the fainting spells growing worse, and the body icy cold and bathed in cold sweat. Both *Lachesis* and *Natrum carb.* are useful when hot weather fatigues, in which case you should compare, also, *Selenium* and *Natrum mur.*

Returning now, after this digression, to the mental symptoms of *Lachesis*, we find that the delirium is of a low, muttering type. At other times the patient seems to be going deeper and deeper into a torpid state, with coolness of the extremities and trembling of the hands and body. When asked to protrude the tongue, it comes out tremblingly, or catches in the teeth, and is usually coated dark brown, sometimes with little blisters on the tip. The lips crack and ooze dark blood. Loquacity is commonly followed by depression, and by weakness which amounts to a typhoid state; then comes delirium, but not of the violent *Belladonna* type.

These symptoms show *Lachesis* to be an invaluable remedy in typhoid fever, and in fact in all diseases of a typhoid type. The loquacity just referred to is particularly characteristic. Another mental state which these typhoid patients may have is the delusion that they are under some superhuman power. Diarrhœa is usually present, and the stools are horribly offensive, a strong characteristic of *Lachesis*, which will also aid you in diphtheria, scarlatina and other diseases of this type. Even when the stools are formed, and in every way natural, they give forth this horrible odor. *Lachesis* may also be indicated late in the course of typhoid fever, when the patient lies in a stupor with dropping of the lower jaw, and other symptoms indicative of impending paralysis of the brain.

Let me now speak of some of the concordant remedies of *Lachesis* in these conditions. In the loquacity just mentioned *Lachesis* should be compared with *Stramonium, Agaricus, Mephitis, Actea racemosa* and *Paris quadrifolia*.

Stramonium you will distinguish from *Lachesis* by the red face and the other evidences of great sensorial excitement.

Agaricus exhibits great loquacity associated with convulsive movements of facial and cervical muscles; merry, incoherent talk.

In *Mephitis* it is as if one were drunk.

Under *Actea racemosa* the loquacity is usually associated with menstrual suppression, with puerperal mania or as a part of delirium tremens, for which *Lachesis* also is a useful remedy. *Actea* cures wild imaginings of rats, etc., sleeplessness, wild crazed feeling about the head, incessant talking with continual change of subject; the patient must move about. *Lachesis* has more marked trembling of the hands, diarrhœa and greater exhaustion with the loquacity and hallucinations.

Paris quadrifolia causes a garrulity which is much like that produced by tea, a sort of vivacity with love of prattling.

In these typhoid types of fever you may compare *Lachesis* with *Opium, Hyoscyamus, Arnica, Lycopodium, Apis. Muriatic acid, Baptisia* and *Rhus toxicodendron*. *Opium* is indicated in typhoid fever with this threatening paralysis of the brain, but the symptoms under it refer to a very different condition from that of *Lachesis*. The symptoms which indicate *Opium*, in addition to this dropping of the lower jaw, are unconsciousness, stertorous breathing, and a dark or brownish-red hue of the face. The darker red the face the more is *Opium* indicated. With *Lachesis* the cerebral condition is due to the effect of the typhoid poison on the brain. With *Opium* it is a secondary effect of the intense congestion of that organ.

Hyoscyamus is perhaps more like *Lachesis* than is *Opium*. Here we find the lower jaw dropped; the patient is weak and trembling, and there is twitching of the muscles. This last is a necessary symptom of *Hyoscyamus*. Here, too, there is snoring breathing, as in *Opium*, with involuntary stool and great prostration.

Arnica is also indicated when there is great congestion of the brain. The patient lies in a stupor, with lower jaw dropped and eyes fixed, but, even in stupor, as if the bed was too hot and hard. The face is dark red, and stool and urine are passed involuntarily. In addition to these symptoms, we find under *Arnica* a symptom which differentiates it from the drugs just mentioned, namely, dark spots here and there on the body, irregular in outline and having a black and blue appearance—ecchymoses, as they are called.

Lycopodium is the complement of *Lachesis*, and is, therefore, more apt to be indicated after it than any remedy I have mentioned. The symptoms which indicate *Lycopodium* are these: The patient lies in a stupor, with lower jaw dropped and rattling breathing. There is a rattling of phlegm in the throat during both inspiration and expiration, and the eyes are fixed and set, and are filled with mucus. *Lycopodium* is the most important remedy we have in impending paralysis of the brain; by that I mean to say that it is the most frequently indicated.

Apis has not so markedly the dropping of the lower jaw, but resembles *Lachesis* in muttering delirium, trembling tongue, etc. The bee-poison, however, causes a nervous fidgetiness with sleepiness and inability to sleep; later, muttering delirium; happy, strange expression; abdomen swollen and extremely sensitive, hands and forearms cold, involuntary stools. This sensitiveness is a bruised feeling, differing from the hyperæsthesia of *Lachesis*.

Muriatic acid displays a sunken face, tongue smooth as if deprived of papillæ, or brown, shrunken and hard; sliding down in bed from muscular weakness.

Baptisia has dark, besotted face, drowsiness and stupor, goes to sleep while answering questions; discharges from the bowels dark, fluid and very offensive.

Rhus tox. may simulate *Lachesis* in one phase of its action, namely, when drowsiness appears and there are muttering; dry, cracked tongue, sordes and involuntary stool. In degree the snake poison is undoubtedly lower than *Rhus*, and, therefore, other things being equal, comes in later. *Rhus* has a well-marked restlessness with relief from motion; loquacity is not prominent; the tongue has a red, triangular tip, and the discharges are never so offensive as those of the former remedy. You must bear in mind that *Rhus* is an erethistic remedy, and must be very similar to existing symptoms if it is to be continued after torpidity sets in without erethism.

Leaving the mental symptoms of *Lachesis* and the indications of it and its analogues in typhoid fever, we will next consider its head symptoms. We find that it produces a pulsating headache usually in the left temple and over the eyes, with mental confusion before the development of a coryza, relieved as soon as the coryza appears. This is a universal characteristic—as soon as a discharge is established the patient feels better. I have relieved dysmenorrhœa with *Lachesis* when there was a headache preceding the dysmenorrhœa, but relieved as soon as the flow was established. At the menopause there is burning in the vertex.

In catarrhal and rheumatic headaches you may compare *Mercurius, Cinchona, Pulsatilla, Bryonia* and *Gelsemium*.

Mercurius relieves headache from suppressed coryza when there is pulsating headache with pressure towards the nose, worse when warm in bed and from damp, windy weather. *Cinchona* when the pain is worse from the least draught of air. *Bryonia* and *Pulsatilla* come into use when the checked catarrhal secretion is thick, and yellow and green, respectively. *Gelsemium*, when motility is lessened and the patient is drowsy, with neuralgic pains from occiput to forehead and face.

The headache may also arise from disordered stomach or bowels, or may be an accompaniment of fevers and of diseases of zymotic origin. The patient has an upward tendency of the blood, with throbbing in the head, dark redness of the face, puffed face, confusion of the mind, all the way from simple confusion to absolute stupor, often accompanied, too, by partial blindness, palpitation of the heart, and fainting. The pains about the head are briefly as follows: Sharp sticking, which seems to concentrate at the root of the nose; at other times the pains go from the zygoma to the ear. This direction of the pains is characteristic. As a parallel of this shooting pain from the zygoma to the ear we have pains from the head going down through and into the eyes.

These are all characteristic pains of *Lachesis*. There is an additional one that I will now mention, which is probably of rheumatic origin; pains in the head, going down into the shoulders and neck of the affected side, and often accompanied by slight stiffness of the neck, either catarrhal or rheumatic.

You may have *Lachesis* indicated in severer forms of the head trouble; for instance, in inflammation of the membranes of the brain; sharp pains in the head, making the patient scream out; tongue showing papillæ; strawberry tongue; patient rolls the head from side to side, and bores it into the pillow. Particularly useful is *Lachesis* when an exanthem, like scarlatina or erysipelas, has not developed or has been repercussed. The patient is at first very drowsy, but unable to sleep; there is trembling or palpitation of the heart. Soon stupor ensues, and he becomes heavy and sleepy, and you can rouse him only with difficulty.

In intense head pains, as in meningitis, you should remember the relation between *Belladonna* and *Lachesis*, the difference between these drugs being rather one of degree. Both are suited to meningitis from erysipelas, to scarlatina, to apoplexy, etc.; but the former represents the initial stage of these diseases, or the state in which, even though there be stupor, there are still evidences of irritation and not wholly of depression. Thus, under *Belladonna*, the patient often starts from his heavy sleep, cries out, grinds the teeth, awakens frightened, etc. His pulse is usually strong and the surface congestions are bright red, or if more intense, deep red and livid. If there is an eruption, as in scarlatina, it is red, even if sparse, but vitality is not so low that the extremities are cold or the rash bluish, and the cellular tissue infiltrated and threatening an unhealthy suppuration, as in the snake-poison. Often, however, after the use of *Belladonna* we find evidence of cerebral exhaustion, or blood-poisoning, or impending paralysis, in which case *Lachesis* may be required. The patient still cries out in sleep or awakens frightened, the tongue still shows elevated papillæ, the head is hot, and the face is red; but the pulse is quicker and more feeble, the feet are cold, the surface heat is irregularly distributed; the mind is more befogged and drowsiness is stealthily creeping on, the inflamed part or the pseudo-membrane or the eruption, as the case may be, is becoming more purplish—these indicate the change.

Considering the action of *Lachesis* on the special senses, we find the eyes to be affected by the drug. Dim vision, worse on awaking; dark spots appear before the eyes; sight suddenly seems to fade away; feeling of faintness and palpitation of the heart; with these, nervous trembling. *Lachesis* is one of the leading remedies for dim sight as an evidence of heart disease and vertigo. We may also use it with good effect for what we may term retinal apoplexy. There it acts very well in causing an absorption of the blood.

The nearest remedies to *Lachesis* in this condition of the retina are *Crotalus, Phosphorus, Arnica, Belladonna* and *Hamamelis*.

Scrofulous ophthalmia calls for *Lachesis* when the symptoms are decidedly worse after sleep. There are great photophobia and pains of a burning, stitching, shooting character, extending to the temples, top of the head and occiput. There are also itching and stinging in the eyes and lids, worse from touch. Vision is misty, with black flickering before the eyes.

Crotalus may also be called for in keratitis when there are cutting pains around the eyes, lids swollen in the morning, ciliary neuralgia with these cuttings, worse during menses.

In the diseases of the ear, *Lachesis* may be remedial for roaring and singing in the ears, and other sorts of tinnitus aurium, which are relieved by putting the finger in the ear and working it. This shows that the tinnitus is not congestive, but of catarrhal origin especially from occlusion of the Eustachian tube. The wax is altered in quality and becomes pasty and offensive. There is swelling between the ear and the mastoid process, with throbbing pain and stiffness. You can here compare *Nitric acid, Capsicum, Aurum, Hepar,* and *Silicea*.

Elaps and *Crotalus* also have an action on the ears. *Elaps*, like *Lachesis*, produces a catarrh with black cerumen, buzzing in the ears, and otorrhœa. In *Elaps*, the discharge is yellowish-green, liquid and bloody. Only *Lachesis* seems to have the Eustachian stoppage, better from shaking the finger in the external meatus. *Crotalus* causes a stuffed feeling in the ears, worse on the right side, associated with a feeling as if hot ear-wax was trickling out.

The face in the *Lachesis* patient varies, of course, with the condition that obtains in the system at the time. In many of the diseases in which the remedy is indicated the face has an earthy pallor. In exanthematic diseases it is apt to be bloated or puffed, and bluish-red; if the eruption comes out, it appears sparsely and is of a dark color

Anxious and painful expression with the stupor; face disfigured, puffy, hot, red and swollen, as after a debauch; blue circles around the eyes. With abdominal troubles, as in ague, the face is earthy gray.

Lachesis also has convulsions of the face; lockjaw; distortion of the face; stretching the body backward; screaming; feet cold and itching. Sudden swelling of the face.

For swollen face, you may compare: *Apis, Belladonna, Arsenic, Lycopodium, Hyoscyamus, Rhus tox., Pulsatilla, Stramonium, Kali carb.,* and *Phosphorus.*

For sickly, pale, or earthy complexion: *Arsenic, Bufo, Lycopodium, Carbo veg., Rhus tox., Cinchona, Phosphorus,* and *Phosphoric acid.*

Blue around the eyes: *Arsenic, Cuprum, Phosphorus, Secale cornutum,* and *Veratrum album.*

Debauched look: *Baptisia, Hyoscyamus, Carbo veg., Nux vomica, Sulphur, Opium, Nux moschata.*

In facial convulsions compare: *Nux vomica, Hyoscyamus, Belladonna, Hydrocyanic acid, Lycopodium, Cicuta, Camphor, Phytolacca, Arsenic.*

Apis, Arsenic, and *Kali carb.* agree in puffing of the face even without any redness. In the first, there are also smarting of the eyelids, and a sensation of stiffness. In the second, the swelling is noticed about the eyes, glabella and forehead (also *Natrum ars.*). *Kali carb.* has the well-known sacs of the upper lids, and also sudden swelling of the cheeks.

The expression, complexion. etc., of *Arsenic* are very similar to those of the snake-poisons. The anxiety and pain are marked by more restlessness, irritability, fear of death, etc., and the sunken face is more completely Hippocratic, with pointed features, sunken eyes and cold sweat. When yellow or earthy, it is cachectic. If trismic symptoms are present, the patient will be found lying pale, and as if dead yet warm. Suddenly he arouses, and goes into severe convulsions, only again to relapse into this sort of cataleptic rigidity. The eyes are partly open, with gum on the conjunctiva.

Lycopodium has pale or yellow face, deeply furrowed, looking elongated. The convulsive movements are unique. All through the provings of this remedy you will note an alternation of contraction and expansion. And in the face you note the tongue pushed out and withdrawn, spasmodic trembling of the facial muscles, angles of the mouth alternately drawn up and relaxed, alæ nasi alternately expanded and contracted. The eyes may be partly open and covered with mucus—a bad symptom, generally being indicative of brain exhaustion.

Phosphorus has a pale face, but it is distinguished by its ashy, anæmic appearance. This should be remembered, since this remedy, like the Ophidia, has puffy face, sunken features, blueness around the eyes, and blue lips.

Hyoscyamus is very similar to *Lachesis* in facial expression and in the convulsive phenomena. It has a marked stupid, drunken look; the face is distorted and blue, or swollen and brownish red; starting; twitchings of single groups of muscles are noted. Hunger appears before the attacks.

Stramonium is readily distinguished by its swollen, turgid face, fright on awakening, renewal of spasms from light, and contracted gloomy expression, with wrinkles of the forehead.

Hydrocyanic acid closely agrees in convulsive symptoms and in the color of the face. As in *Elaps*, fluids roll audibly into the stomach; but in the latter it is more as a spasmodic contraction of the sphincters, followed by sudden relaxation. In convulsions, the surface, in the acid, is pale blue, and the muscles of the face, jaw, and back are affected. Suddenly a shock is felt, which passes like lightning from head to foot, and then comes the spasm. Here, the remedy is more like *Cicuta* and *Helleborus* than *Lachesis*. But *Cicuta* has, like the snake-poisons, great difficulty in breathing from spasm, and, more than any remedy, it produces staring; the spasm is followed by disproportionately severe weakness.

Camphor is readily distinguished from *Lachesis* by the coldness and by the withdrawing of the lip, showing the teeth.

Lachesis is indicated in erysipelas of the face. Characteristically, the disease will be most marked on the left side. The face at first may be bright red, but it soon takes on a dark bluish hue. There is considerable infiltration into the cellular tissue, so that we have puffiness of the eye of the affected side. Now the characteristic bluish face is due to the accompanying weakness. Even in the beginning, while the skin is still red, the pulse, though accelerated, is weak, the feet are apt to be cool, and the head is affected sympathetically, so that the patient readily becomes drowsy, with muttering delirium; or the opposite condition of pseudo-excitement—the loquacity which I have already mentioned—obtains.

You must now distinguish this erysipelas of *Lachesis* from that of the remedies which are akin to it; among these is *Belladonna*. In its early symptoms, *Belladonna* bears no resemblance to *Lachesis*. But ir the course of the disease, when the inflammation is so intense that the bloated face grows bluish red, threatening gangrene, or when the brain becomes affected, differentiation is necessary. Here, both have hot head and cold feet, delirium, dry tongue, etc. But *Lachesis* suits when the cerebral symptoms fail to yield to *Belladonna*, and the excitement gives way to muttering stupor. The pulse is weak and rapid, and the cool surface of the limbs is plainly due to failing vitality rather than to the upward tendency of the blood. *Crotalus* holds the same relation to *Belladonna*.

Apis mellifica is indicated in erysipelas when the affected parts exhibit a tendency to become œdematous. If the face is involved, the eye-lids protrude like sacs of water. The face is usually of a pinkish hue, or it may be dark purplish, but it never has the deep bluish-black hue of *Lachesis*.

Although there may be a similar destructive tendency, the condition of nervous irritation produced by the bee-poison is very different from that of any of its congeners. It is a fidgety, nervous state, a fretted feeling, which deprives the patient of sleep, although he feels sleepy.

Rhus toxicodendron is suited to the vesicular form of erysipelas. The patient is drowsy, as under *Lachesis*, little blisters form on and about the face, and the face is dingy red, not the bluish-black of *Lachesis* nor the purple of the intensified *Apis* case.

If vesicles form in the *Lachesis* case, they quickly fill with pus. Speaking relatively, *Rhus* produces more vesiculation and burning, stinging and itching, with more aching of the limbs and restlessness; *Lachesis*, more bluish-red inflammation, with gangrenous tendency.

Euphorbium, since it causes gangrene with erysipelas, anxiety as from poison, apprehensiveness, dim vision, etc., deserves your notice. The right cheek is of a livid or dark red hue, vesicles form as large as peas, and are filled with a yellow liquid. The pains are boring, gnawing and digging in character, and extend from the gum into the ear, with itching and crawling when the pains are relieved.

Lachesis may be indicated in prosopalgia when the pain is worse on the left side, and when there are tearing pains above the orbit and digging and screwing pains around the malar bone. Delirium appears as soon as the eyes are closed.

The teeth decay and crumble. The gums are swollen and bluish, with throbbing pains. *Lachesis* may be successfully used in periodontitis and abscess at the root of a filled tooth (compare *Mercurius, Hepar, Silicea, Fluoric acid* and *Petroleum*.

Of the allied remedies in toothache none is so similar as *Mercurius*, which, like *Lachesis*, relieves when the gum is inflamed and the tooth decayed, with abscess at the root. It is said to have a direct action on the dentine. The pains are tearing and pulsating, and shoot into the face and ears. In *Lachesis* the gum is swollen, and at the same time dark red and livid, or it is tense and hot and looks as if it would crack. *Mercurius* is markedly worse from the warmth of the bed. *Lachesis* often follows the latter, or is needed at once if the patient has been previously salivated. Only *Mercurius* has dirty gums, with white edges.

In sore mouth, aphthæ, etc., *Lachesis* should be compared with *Baptisia*, *Nitric acid*, *Muriatic acid*, *Arsenic* and *Apis;* while *Mercurius* compares more with *Carbo veg.*, *Staphisagria*, *Kali chlor.*, *Iodine*, *Sulphuric acid*, *Nitric acid*.

Baptisia has blood oozing from the gums, which look dark red or purple, salivation, *fœtororis*, offensive stools, and thus far is precisely like *Lachesis*. Both, too, are indicated in the stomacace attending the last stages of phthisis. Decide by general differences and also by the tongue, which, in the former, is yellow or brown down the centre, with red, shining edges. In the latter, it is red, dry and glistening, especially at the tip, and has its sides and tip covered with blisters.

Nitric acid causes an acrid saliva; the pains in the mouth are pricking in character, as from a splinter; the aphthæ and gums are usually whitish; there are raw places, with shooting pains.

Muriatic acid presents deep, bluish ulcers, with dark edges; the mucous membrane is denuded in places, the raw spots being dotted with aphthæ.

Arsenic looks very much like *Lachesis*, with livid, bleeding gums, edges of tongue blistered, or ulcerating diarrhœa. The burning is more intense, and is associated with restlessness, compelling motion in spite of the weakness. In *gangrena oris* it causes more acute pain, and heat in the mouth; both have bluish or black sloughing ulcers. *Arsenic* has more mental irritability.

Apis has blisters marking the border of the tongue, or in clusters. The mouth is usually rosy-red, swollen, and there are marked stinging pains; the margin of the tongue feels scalded, as does the mouth generally.

Carbo veg., *Staphisagria* and *Sulphuric acid* agree more with *Mercurius;* the gums are white, spongy, ulcerated, rather than livid. *Staphisagria* may cause sores, which look bluish-red or yellow; especially is it needed after abuse of *Mercury*, or in syphilitic cases when the general debility is marked with sunken face, blue around the eyes, etc. *Sulphuric acid* produces great debility, yellowish-white gums, yellow skin; the patient is nervous and hasty, and constantly complains of trembling, which, however, is not observed by others.

Salicylic acid causes the common canker sores, with burning soreness and fœtid breath.

Lycopodium produces similar sores near the frænum of the tongue, *Lachesis* at the tip, and *Nitric acid*, *Phytolacca*, *Natrum hydrochlor.* on the inner sides of the cheeks.

Phytolacca has some systematic resemblance to *Lachesis* here as well as in the throat (see next lecture). Both cause great weakness, dim vision, sunken face, blueness around the eyes, sore mouth, tongue blistered along the edges, tip of tongue red, roof of mouth sore, profuse saliva. The poke-root may be distinguished by the great pain at the root of the tongue when swallowing. These pains are a part of the tired aching and soreness which are general over the body.

Helleborus produces canker in the mouth, but the sores are yellowish, with raised edges.

Returning to the subject of decayed teeth, it may be noted that *Kreosote* cures pains extending from teeth to left side of face; teeth decay rapidly, gums bleed, the blood being dark; but the accompanying facial pains are burning, and the patient is excitable, nervous, even, as in children, thrown into convulsions.

Thuja causes a decay just at the border of the gums, leaving the crown apparently sound. Gums dark-red in streaks. Teeth turn yellow and crumble.

LECTURE IV.

THE OPHIDIA

Lachesis (*continued*).

NEXT we take up the action of *Lachesis* on the nose, throat, and chest, so far as catarrhs are concerned. *Lachesis* produces watery discharge from the nose, which is often preceded by throbbing headache, worse in the left temple and forehead, and relieved as the coryza establishes itself. Accompanying this coryza sometimes are vesicles about the nose, redness, puffiness of the face and lids, creeping chills over the body, palpitation of the heart, and great relaxation of the whole system; hence it is suitable for a cold which occurs in relaxing weather, consequently in the spring of the year. *Lachesis* may also be used in ozæna of mercurial or syphilitic origin. Here you may compare *Kali bichromicum*, which follows *Lachesis* well; and also *Aurum*, *Nitric acid*, *Mercurius*, and *Lac caninum*. The last-named drug cures syphilitic ozæna and angina when the corners of the mouth and alæ nasi are cracked.

The cold may extend to the throat, and then we will find that the tonsils are enlarged, particularly the left one, or the inflammation may tend to spread from the left to the right tonsil. The throat, when examined, exhibits a red hue, not bright or rosy-red, but bluish. The patient complains of a sense of constriction, as though the throat were suddenly closing up, or a sensation as though there were a lump in the throat which he must constantly swallow, but which as often returns. Pains in the left side of the throat extending to the tongue, jaw, ear. Rawness and burning. The throat externally is exceedingly sensitive to touch. Unless the tonsils are going on to suppuration, there is relief from swallowing solids, while swallowing of liquids and empty swallowing increase the pains. I except suppurating tonsils because, when they are large and stop up the fauces, nothing can be swallowed; then the attempt to take anything is followed by a violent ejection of the food, through either the mouth or the nose. But with the ordinary catarrhal sore throat, when the tonsils are not parenchymatously swollen, the swallowing of food often relieves the irritation for a time.

The cold may travel farther down and involve the bronchial tubes, when a different class of symptoms develops. The patient may suffer from tickling, irritating cough, which is especially apt to come on as he drops off to sleep, arousing him as if he were choking. He can bear nothing to touch the larynx or throat, so that he loosens his neckband. These, briefly, are the catarrhal symptoms of *Lachesis*.

But suppose, while we are considering this locality, we look to more serious affections which may manifest themselves in these parts, diphtheria, for example. *Lachesis* may be indicated in diphtheria of one or all of these parts. Symptoms for which you will be called upon to prescribe it are mostly those that I have already given you, with these points in addition: The discharge from the nose is thin, sanious, and excoriating; a really dangerous objective symptom. The throat is, if anything, a darker red than in the catarrhal state. The membrane is more marked on the left tonsil, or has an inclination to go from the left to the right. It early develops that gangrenous state which obtains in diphtheria, with the attendant fœtid breath, and the increased danger of systemic infection. The tissues surrounding the throat are often infiltrated so that you have swelling of the glands about the neck, and also of the cellular tissue. The swelling may be so great that the neck becomes even with the chin and sternum. The lymphatic glands are swollen, too, and have a dark purplish hue, and threaten suppuration. When pus does form, it is not a laudable pus. The child is drowsy, even though feverish; the heart, though beating more rapidly than normal, is evidently greatly weakened, as is shown by the feebleness of the pulse and coolness of the extremities. This is the kind of diphtheria in which you can hope much from the use of *Lachesis*. The diphtheritic deposit may extend down into the larynx, and the remedy still be indicated. You must not infer from this that *Lachesis* is *the* remedy for laryngeal diphtheria; but when it has the characteristic symptoms which I mention, it may be needed; the patient arouses from sleep smothering, and has a diphtheritic, croupy cough.

Crotalus and *Naja*, like *Lachesis*, have relieved in diphtheria. The former has been selected when the epistaxis is persistent; blood oozes from the mouth, not merely coming from the posterior nares but escaping from the mucous membranes of the buccal cavity.

Naja has helped in cases just like *Lachesis*, when the larynx is invaded; the patient grasps at the throat, with a sensation of choking, the fauces are dark-red; there is fœtid breath, and short, hoarse cough, with raw feeling in larynx and upper part of the trachea.

Lac caninum is very similar to *Lachesis* in diphtheria, but is readily distinguished by its peculiar habit of alternating sides. Starting on one side, frequently the left, the soreness and swelling, and even the membrane, suddenly shift to the opposite side, only to return, in a few hours, to the starting point. The membrane is grayish-yellow and curdy, and if ulcers form, they shine like silver-gloss.

Lycopodium, which also resembles *Lachesis*, has aggravation of the symptoms from 4 to 8 P. M. The right side is mostly affected; the child awakes from sleep frightened or cross and angry.

Apis is to be distinguished by the œdema of the throat, the stinging pains, the blisters on the border of the tongue, etc.

Again, you may find *Lachesis* of great service in affections of the lungs. We may use it in asthma when there are present one or more of these few symptoms. The patient arouses from sleep with the asthmatic paroxysm, and cannot bear the least pressure about the neck or chest; finally, he coughs up a quantity of watery phlegm *with great relief*. This last is a neglected characteristic of *Lachesis* in asthma. I have succeeded with it in relieving an incurable asthmatic for months.

In pneumonia *Lachesis* may be useful, but not in the early stages of the disease. There is nothing in the provings of *Lachesis* to suggest that it will be useful in pneumonia. It does not cause the engorgement of the lungs, the fever or the fibrinous deposit. But it may be indicated in the later stages of the affection, when it assumes a typhoid form, especially when an abscess forms in the lungs. Brain symptoms, such as low muttering delirium and hallucinations, appear. The sputum is frothy, mixed with blood, and purulent, and the patient is bathed in a profuse sweat.

Sulphur is, perhaps, the better remedy to prevent suppuration when there are no typhoid symptoms, but be careful how you give *Sulphur* if tuberculosis has been developed by pneumonia. To do so is almost like giving a person running down hill another push. It will only hasten the end.

In chest affections *Elaps* is sometimes of great service. It affects the right more than the left lung, but both may be diseased. In the morning there is pain in the right side severe enough to prevent the patient's getting up. There is a feeling of coldness in the chest after drinking. The cough is accompanied by intense pains in the chest, worse in the right apex, as if it were torn out, and the sputum consists of black blood.

You may use *Lachesis* in phthisis, not necessarily to cure, but to relieve. Remember it when, in the course of typhoid fever or pneumonia, tubercles have been deposited in one or the other lung. You may use it in the advanced stages of tuberculosis of the lungs when the patient has a retching cough, which arouses him from sleep, and which ends in expectoration of tough, greenish muco-purulent matter, which causes gagging, and is vomited rather than clearly expectorated; when the patient sweats during every nap, the sweat being most copious about the neck, shoulders and chest, and when the strength is greatly reduced and the pulse indicates extreme prostration.

Next we turn our attention to the alimentary canal from the mouth down. I referred to the tongue in speaking of the typhoid condition. *Lachesis* is useful for weakness of digestion in patients who, from some vicious habits, from abuse of Mercury, or of Quinine, or of alcohol, have so exhausted their stomachs that even the plainest food causes indigestion. Acids especially disagree, aggravating the stomach symptoms and causing diarrhœa. Sometimes a gnawing pain is relieved by eating or improves immediately after a meal, but soon a heavy pressure, as from a weight in the stomach, and other symptoms of indigestion show themselves. There may be a craving for coffee and oysters, which may not disagree.

The liver is affected by *Lachesis*. Like all the snake-poisons, it causes jaundice. Even when abscesses form it may be useful by reason of the tenderness on pressure, intolerance of clothing, and deep throbbing in the right hypochondrium.

The bowel symptoms are not numerous, though they are important. We find diarrhœa caused by the drug, with watery, horribly offensive stools; diarrhœa during the climaxis; diarrhœa of drunkards. Especially may *Lachesis* be used in chronic diarrhœa with great debility and aggravation in spring weather. The tongue is smooth, red and shining (*Kali bi.*). The abdomen is bloated; very sensitive to touch about the waist. Constant tormenting urging in the rectum, but not for stool. It is merely a spasmodic condition of the bowels with an unduly irritable sphincter. The rectum protrudes and is held by the constricted sphincter; after stool there is often a sensation in the rectum as from the beating of little hammers. These symptoms are common enough in dyspeptics, particularly in those who have abused alcohol. They are not infrequently associated with large, protruding hæmorrhoids, which are worse at the menopause, or with scanty menses, with stitches upward at each cough or sneeze. They occur also in connection with constipation. The patient attempts to strain at stool, but must desist on account of pain in the sphincter. Unsuccessful urging; the anus feels closed. Stool hard, like sheep's dung, and excessively offensive.

In dyspepsia *Lachesis* is very similar to *Hepar*. The latter remedy, however, has relief of the symptoms from the use of condiments.

Under *Hepar* the plainest food disagrees. The cravings are unique. As if knowing instinctively what will "tone up" the stomach, the patient longs for condiments or wine. Eating relieves the relaxed feeling, but food annoys as soon as the digestive process begins its slow and imperfect work. The bowels move very sluggishly, even when the stools are soft.

Cinchona, too, enfeebles digestion and induces great weakness and languor after meals. It also has a craving for coffee-beans. Fruits induce diarrhœa with intestinal fermentation. Both cause fulness after eating, but only in *Cinchona* is the fulness so severe as to cause pain, with little or no relief from belching. Bitter eructations and bitter taste belong to each; the latter has the altered taste after swallowing, food retaining its normal taste while being masticated. The discharges from the bowels and the flatus are offensive; yellow watery stools, undigested. But the marked aggravation at night, after a meal, and the resulting prostration, are not at all like *Lachesis*. In dysentery, etc , when putrid or gangrenous changes occur, the choice is more difficult. Both have cadaverous smelling discharges of a chocolate color, with coldness and great debility. And, although *Cinchona* is far preferable if the disease is of malarial origin, such a complication does not contra-indicate the snake-poison. The apparently close similarity is also enhanced by the nervous excitability in both. Light touch is distressing, the epigastrium is sensitive, and clothing annoys in each remedy. But this in *Cinchona* is an increased general sensibility, while in *Lachesis* there is general torpor, with hyperæsthesia of the cutaneous nerves. The former is suitable when the offensive discharges follow a severe, rapidly exhausting inflammation, or when the frequency and quantity of the evacuations have greatly reduced the vitality, thus favoring retrogressive changes. If hectic symptoms are present, the choice is rendered more certain. In addition, we may also refer to the well-known anæmic symptoms of *Cinchona*, paleness, ringing in the ears, easy fainting, etc., which show at once how it affects the blood.

Mercurius presents many points of similarity with *Lachesis*. The latter frequently follows the former, and also antidotes its abuse. There are loss of appetite, coated tongue, nausea with oppression, and epigastric tenderness. Pressure in the pit of the stomach produces a deadly faintness. The stomach hangs heavily, even after a light meal of food of ordinary digestibility. The sensitiveness of the stomach to the clothing is a part of a symptom which is completed by a similar tenderness over both hypochondria, with fulness and upward pressure from the abdomen. The patient cannot lie on the right side. If hypochondriacal, he is suspicious, anxious and restless at night, with vascular erethism and sweat. In fact, this erethism is directly contrary to the torpid *Lachesis*.

In abdominal inflammations with suppuration, as in typhlitis, both remedies are useful and follow each other well. *Mercurius* has its ever-present perspiration without relief; stools slimy, or much straining, with or without stool. *Lachesis* follows when the symptoms threaten a typhoid condition. The patient can lie only on the back with the knees drawn up; if he turns to the left side, a ball seems to roll over in the abdomen.

In the rectum and anus, *Mercurius* has more persistent tenesmus; protrusion of the rectum, which looks inflamed and blackish; *Lachesis*, more spasmodic tenesmus, with constriction of the anus, which tightly constricts the prolapsed rectum. Both have chronic constipation. The former induces much straining, with tenacious or crumbling stools; chilliness during defæcation.

Arsenicum intensifies the gastric and systemic weakness to which we referred in the remedies just considered. While it is true that the patient does not fully realize his want of strength, and hence does not care so much to lie quietly, nevertheless the actual amount of his vitality is seriously reduced. In a word, he is excessively weak without feeling so fatigued. Any exertion produces fainting. Taste is lost, or is bitter, sour, and putrid. The stomach feels swollen as if full of water. Craving for acids and for coffee; the latter, as in *Lachesis*, agrees with the patient. There are burning feelings, red rough tongue, and anxiety and distress after eating, as in subacute gastritis, which no remedy pictures better. Nausea is frequent, and often periodical (12 P. M.) and is accompanied by great prostration. The vomiting is of many kinds, but is distinguished from the bilious, slimy, or bloody emesis of *Lachesis* by its irregular convulsive character, indicative of gastric irritability. *Lachesis* is adapted to the nervous weakness and trembling of drunkards; spasm of the stomach, spasmodic constrictions, relieved temporarily by eating; vomiting of bile or mucus; *Arsenic* is adapted to burning periodical pains, with sour acrid vomiting; violent thirst, but vomits the water.

Cadmium sulph. has nausea, yellowish or black vomit, saltish rancid belching, cold sweat of the face, burning, cutting in the stomach; cramps after beer, griping in the lower part of the bowels. Both this remedy and *Lachesis* induce marked sensitiveness to touch upon stomach or abdomen, spots of burning soreness here and there over the swollen abdomen (peritonitis); offensive, bloody, chocolate-colored discharges, as in dysentery, with constriction in the bowels; cutting pains in bowels. But in *Arsenic* there is more lamenting with agonized expression; restless moving despite the pains. The constriction of the intestines is torturing; the patient declares he cannot stand it, and rolls about in agony, despairing of his life. The extreme tenderness of the pit of the stomach denotes a more positive state of acute inflammation than *Lachesis* causes.

In the vomiting of yellow fever *Lachesis* has, in addition, brown coating on the teeth and abdominal tenderness.

Arsenic has also spasmodic protrusion of the rectum; very painful tenesmus with burning; hæmorrhoids, especially in drunkards; they protrude at stool with burning. Alvine discharges are offensive, dark, sometimes involuntary, with great weakness and coldness. But *Lachesis* has less tenesmus recti, the distress there being attributable to a constriction of the anus not found in the other drug. *Arsenic*, moreover, causes more acridity of the stools, with rawness and excoriation of the anus.

All that I have here stated regarding the difference between these two drugs might be tersely stated thus: One causes intense irritability and acute inflammation of tissue, mental anguish, and extreme prostration; the other, torpidity, with loss of vitality, but associated with nervous excitability, constrictions, and cutaneous hyperæsthesia. Still, some minds require more attention to detail; and every one retains general mental impressions more accurately if they are formed with due attention to particulars.

When there is ulceration of the bowels, tendency to sloughing, with offensive, purulent, or bloody discharges, the two remedies are very nearly allied. Vitality is at a very low ebb; blood oozes from the cracked lips and tongue, and the extremities are cold. But even here the best distinctions are the mental irritability of *Arsenic*, and the intolerance of pressure of *Lachesis*.

Carbo vegetabilis resembles *Lachesis* in weak digestion, complaints of drunkards, flatulent asthma, constriction of the œsophagus, annoyance from clothing about the waist, offensive, bloody, decomposed, purulent stools, collapse, etc.

There is craving for coffee, but it does not relieve. Milk disagrees in both remedies, but only the snake-poison has craving for it. *Carbo veg.* has aggravation from fats, tainted meats, fish, oysters, foods causing flatulency, ices, vinegar, and sour cabbage—the latter principally on account of the flatulency it causes. Eructations are sour, rancid. Both drugs have relief of flatulent distension from belching, but *Lachesis* has an ill feeling in addition, which is relieved. Both drugs experience freer breathing after belching. In *Carbo veg.* this is expressed as the lessening of a tension and upward drawing which marks the costal attachments of the diaphragm; in *Lachesis* there is a relief after eructations which seem to suffocate him. They come rapidly, and induce the ever-present *Lachesis* constriction of the throat. The latter remedy also has empty eructations, which intensify the pains.

Carbo veg. has heaviness, fulness, sleepiness after eating, with fulness of the abdomen, almost to bursting. Burning in the stomach is also increased. This heaviness is very characteristic, and is noted likewise in the abdomen, which seems to hang heavily; also in the head, which feels as heavy as lead. The burning is attended with a creeping feeling up to the throat. In *Lachesis*, the fulness and pressure is as from a load, and the sense of repletion induces lowness of spirits. There is, also, a feeling as if a lump were forming in the stomach and also in the bowels; burning, with hard abdominal distension, and a feeling as if a stone was descending; he must stand still or step cautiously. This lump is presumably a part of the *Lachesis* constriction, which we have so often designated as highly characteristic. In *Carbo veg.* the flatus is more rancid, putrid, or, when passed per anum, burning, moist, offensive. Its incarceration with burning is a cause of many of the symptoms, and it is more in quantity than in the snake-poison. It also causes a bearing down upon the bladder and sacral region. *Lachesis* relieves a gnawing gastralgia, when eating lessens the pain; *Carbo veg.* cures when there is burning, with a constrictive cramp, bending him double; the pains are paroxysmal and take his breath. The burning spreads up to the chest and down into the abdomen, seemingly following the sympathetic.

Tenesmus recti is most prominent in *Carbo veg.*, anal constriction in *Lachesis*. It is this latter symptom which explains, as we have before observed, the ineffectual urging to stool; while in *Carbo veg.* the urging is fruitless on account of the pressure of flatus. Both have bluish, protruding piles, as after debauchery. This constriction distinguishes them, as do also the headache and diarrhœa. In each there is throbbing headache, but *Carbo veg.* has more of the heaviness, and the diarrhœa is thin.

In typhoid conditions, whether the specific fever, or as a sequel to peritonitis, dysentery, etc., *Carbo veg.* causes the more perfect picture of collapse, while in *Lachesis* the cardiac debility, drowsiness, cool extremities, etc., indicate failing vitality, but the patient is not so near death as in the former drug. In the collapse of *Carbo veg.* there are tympany; cold legs, especially to the knees; filiform pulse; cool breath; absence of discharges from the bowels; or involuntary, putrid, bloody, purulent diarrhœa.

In hernia, *Carbo veg.* has anxiety, as in *Arsenic*, but with uneasiness rather than restless change of place; and it resembles *Lachesis* in the annoyance of the clothing, foulness of the parts, if strangulated, etc. There is, however, more meteorism and fœtid flatus.

Graphites has anxiety, melancholy; tip of the tongue blistered; feeling of a lump in the left side of the throat, over which the food seems to pass with difficulty; on empty deglutition, a constrictive retching from the œsophagus up to the larynx; must loosen the clothing after eating; gastralgia, relieved by eating; chronic gastritis, especially after abuse of alcoholic drinks. Sensation of a lump in the stomach; flatulent distension of the abdomen, with congestion to the head; fœtid flatus. Suffocative spells arousing from sleep, must jump out of bed; compelled to eat something to relieve the pain. Offensive stools.

But this remedy causes more flatulence than *Lachesis*. The gastralgic pains are burning and griping, and the feeling of a lump in the stomach is accompanied by a constant beating; the heartburn is rancid. The suffocative spells are usually worse after 12 P. M. instead of during or after a sleep at any time; and the constriction noticed on falling asleep is of the chest instead of the larynx. The offensive movements from the bowels are half-digested, dark and pappy indicating the imperfect digestion which is so characteristic of this remedy.

There is some resemblance in the constitutional symptoms of *Graphites* and *Lachesis*, since both are needed at times in phlegmatic patients: but the former is related to a distinguishing type; fat. cold and costive; skin herpetic, rough and disposed to crack and ooze a glutinous fluid.

Aside, then, from a few resemblances to the snake-poison, *Graphites* belongs more with *Arsenic*, *Nux vomica* and *Lycopodium*. It resembles the first two in gastritis and gastralgia; the latter in flatulency.

Sulphuric acid resembles the snake-poisons somewhat, especially in the ailments of drunkards. Its corrosive effects, however, are distinctively prominent, as shown in the violent inflammation of the alimentary canal. But the nervous system is so involved that several symptoms look like those of *Lachesis*, as, for instance, epigastrium sensitive, constrictive feeling in the bowels, griping, cutting, twisting, with faint-like nausea; trembling, pale face, apprehensiveness; fluttering pulse; cramps in the pharynx; he cannot swallow; œsophageal stricture; great weakness, etc. Both, moreover, crave brandy.

The acid acts well when the patient is weak, emaciated and complains of trembling, which, however, is more subjective than objective. He is anxious and restless; must do everything hurriedly. The face is pale, and sometimes presents dry, shrivelled spots, especially when the hæmorrhoids are worse. Eructations are sour. The stomach feels relaxed and cold. Wine may palliate and distilled liquors aggravate, as in *Lachesis;* but the peculiarity of the acid is that the stomach rejects cold water unless it is mixed with brandy. The abdominal muscles are spasmodically retracted. Stools are yellow, like *Lachesis*, but present a chopped appearance, and are stringy; they are watery, diarrhœic and very offensive. Piles are moist, burn and may prevent defæcation.

As the acid causes croupous formations, it should be remembered with *Lachesis* when the stools indicate such a condition in the intestine.

The acid also resembles *Elaps;* drinks feel like ice in the stomach; but only the former has the relief from the admixture of spirit. The *Elaps* diarrhœa resembles that of the rest of the order, but this remedy is particularly called for when the stools consist of black, frothy blood with twisting pains in the bowels.

Colchicum deserves mention here, especially since, like *Lachesis*, it causes coldness or cold feeling in the stomach (*Elaps*), intolerance of pressure of the clothing, burning in the stomach, vomiting and purging, *spasms of the sphincter ani*, urging to stool, offensive flatus, offensive diarrhœa, sensitiveness to the least touch, very much exhausted, slow breathing, feeble pulse. But there is generally present nausea, worse from the smell of food; if the patient sits or lies very quietly, the vomiting is suppressed (like *Veratrum*). Senses too acute; a bright light, touch or *strong odors* irritate him (like *Nux vom.*). Vomiting and purging as in cholera morbus; the sphincter ani contracts after each stool, with fruitless urging. The similarity, then, exists chiefly in the sensitiveness to touch and the constrictions of sphincters with weakness, other symptoms being so different as to render a choice easy. (See also below.)

In cholera *Lachesis* has been employed when the vomiting was renewed by the least motion and the nausea was attended with a great flow of saliva. As *Colchicum* has precisely the same symptoms other indications must decide.

In reflex irritation, as convulsions with variegated, slimy stools in teething children, and rolling of the head, *Colchicum* resembles *Podophyllum*.

Belladonna, Lachesis, Rhus tox. and *Baptisia* constitute a group serviceable in peritonitis, enteritis, etc.

Belladonna differs from all in the character of the inflammation. It is only when the affection becomes asthenic that the others are needed. *Lachesis* follows *Belladonna* when, especially in children with inflammatory diarrhœa, constipation suddenly sets in with abdominal swelling and tenderness, particularly at one spot, or if suppuration ensues and *Mercurius* fails, or, again, if gangrene threatens.

In peritonitis *Lachesis* is indicated late in the disease, when the fever still continues and is worse after 1 P. M. and at night. The slightest touch on the surface of the body is intolerable. Typhoid symptoms complicate the case. It may even be indicated when there is typhlitis after the formation of pus. It follows, particularly *Belladonna, Bryonia* or *Mercurius corrosivus*. It is also similar to *Rhus tox.*, but, having more typhoid symptoms, comes in later in the case.

Rhus tox. requires drowsiness, the fever remaining high or increasing; restlessness; tongue dry, parched, brown, with red, triangular tip; diarrhœa slimy, watery or putrid, yellowish-brown and bloody, involuntary during sleep; generally it is accompanied by tearing down the thighs, while *Lachesis* has painful stiffness from the loins into the thighs. In typhlitis, in which affection either may follow *Belladonna*, *Rhus tox*. has relief from pressing the swelling gently from below upward; *Lachesis*, intolerance of touch.

In periproctitis *Rhus tox*. may be needed if the inflammation is of traumatic origin; *Lachesis*, if an abscess forms and fails to point, the surrounding tissues presenting a purplish hue.

Colchicum compares with *Lachesis* when the prostration is extreme, with coma, hot abdomen, cold extremities, and thready pulse; if raised, the head falls back and the jaw drops; the face is hippocratic, the tongue is protruded with difficulty, and the bowels move involuntarily. But the tympany is more marked in the former; and the stools contain white flakes or shreds; the tongue is either thickly coated brown or it is bright red, except at the root, where it is coated. According to provings and cases of poisoning, *Colchicum* does not cause sensitive abdomen below the epigastrium.

Arnica develops a profound stupor, with blowing respiration, dry tongue, brown down the middle, distended abdomen, and involuntary fæces and urine. It may be distinguished by the ecchymoses and the bruised aching, inducing restlessness, which latter is relieved if the patient's clothing is smoothed down and his position changed.

Among the remedies causing constriction of the anus, the following are worthy of notice: *Bellad.*, *Caustic.*, *Nitric ac.*, *Nat. mur.*, *Ignat.*, *Kali bi.*, *Opium*, *Plumbum*, *Mezereum*, *Coccul*.

The first has pressing and urging toward the anus and genitals, alternating with contractions of the anus; spasmodic constriction of the anus, as in dysentery.

The second, *Causticum*, causes fruitless urging to stool, with anxiety and red face.

Nitric acid causes sticking in the rectum, as from a splinter; the constriction occurs during stool and lasts for hours afterward; the rectum feels as if torn.

Natrum mur. has a sensation of contraction in the rectum during stool; the fæces tear the anus; frequent ineffectual urging; spasmodic constriction of the anus.

Ignatia induces a proctalgia; contraction, with cutting, shooting pains; contraction of the anus worse after stool. Symptoms are inconsistent, irregular, fitful, as in hysteria.

Kali bi. has a sensation of a plug, similar to *Lachesis;* diarrhœa of a brown, frothy water, spurting out in the early morning and followed by tenesmus ani.

In *Opium* the anus is spasmodically closed during the colic, with obstinate constipation. *Plumbum* is very similar.

But all these are readily distinguished from *Lachesis* by the characteristic symptoms of the latter: Tormenting urging in the rectum, but on account of constriction of the anus it becomes so painful he must desist; protruding piles, with constricted anus.

Much nearer, and indeed almost identical here, is *Mezereum;* after the stool, the anus is constricted around the protruded rectum. In other respects, however, the two remedies are widely different.

Kali bichromicum must also be remembered as a relative of *Lachesis* in dysentery. Both have red, cracked, smooth tongue; blackish stools; hence both are useful in severe or typhoidal cases, and here they follow each other well. The offensive odor of the discharges distinguishes the latter; the jelly-like, sometimes stringy mucus, the former.

A peculiar feature of *Cocculus* is tenesmus recti after stool, with faintness, and yet peristalsis is lessened. (Compare *Ignatia*.)

LECTURE V

THE OPHIDIA.

LACHESIS (*continued*).

Lachesis causes in the male an increased lasciviousness with diminution of the physical powers. The mind is a prey to all sorts of allurements, but erections and emissions are imperfect.

Upon the female organs, *Lachesis* acts very powerfully. It seems to have special affinity for the ovaries, particularly the left ovary; ovaritis, ovaralgia, and tumor, may be relieved when there are tenderness to pressure of the clothing and other characteristic symptoms of the drug Menses scanty, feeble, blood lumpy, black, and very offensive; pains in the hips, bearing down in the region of the left ovary—all better when the flow is established. The uterus is also intolerant of the least pressure.

Lachesis may be used in puerperal metritis, especially when the lochial discharge is foetid. The face is purple and the patient unconscious.

It is indicated in ovarian tumors when the disease shows a tendency to extend from left to right, even when suppuration has taken place. It is especially called for after *Hepar* or *Mercurius* when there is great adynamia.

In syphilis, *Lachesis* is called for as an antidote to mercury or when the chancre becomes gangrenous. Its characteristics are found in its peculiar sore throat, the blue surroundings of the ulcers, nightly bone-pains, violent headache, and the phagedenic chancre.

The syphilitic ulcers on the legs are flat and have blue surroundings; caries of the tibia; the parts are sensitive and livid; ulcers in the throat; bone-pains at night; all after abuse of mercury.

The bluish ulcers ally it with *Hepar, Asafœtida, Lycopodium, Silicea, Arsenic;* the pimples, blisters, or pustules surrounding the ulcers ally it with: *Arsenic, Phosphorus, Lycopodium, Mercurius, Hepar, Silicea*, etc.; the burning in the areola with: *Arsenic, Lycopodium, Mercurius, Silicea;* the offensive pus with: *Arsenic, Asafœtida, Lyco-*

podium, Silicea, Sulphur, Hepar; the ulcers, being flat, with: *Arsenic, Asafœtida Lycopodium, Mercurius, Silicea, Phosphoric acid,* etc.; if they become black or gangrenous, with: *Arsenic, Secale Silicea, Plumbum, Carbo veg., Euphorbium, Muriatic acid.* But *Lachesis* has the burning most marked when the ulcer is touched. The surrounding skin is mottled. Ulcers on the legs tend to spread superficially (rather than deeply, as, for example, in *Kali bi.*), the discharge is scanty and the strength is failing. Dark blisters encircle the ulcers and the surrounding skin is dead. Sometimes the discharge ceases, the patient is stupid, cold, the leg becomes œdematous, and a bluish-red swelling along the course of the veins shows that phlebitis exists. All this looks like *Arsenic, Carbo veg., Bufo, Secale, Cinchona,* etc. But *Arsenic* presents more vascular excitement and nervous irritability with the prostration. *Carbo veg.* induces still greater prostration than *Lachesis,* cold sweat, cool breath, collapse. The ulcer has a cadaverous odor. In mild cases there is no resemblance at all between the two, for *Carbo veg.* causes much burning, rawness in the folds of the skin; borders of the ulcer hard, but not oversensitive, as in *Lachesis.*

Hepar should be remembered as a concordant of *Lachesis,* especially because it is so useful after abuse of mercurials. The areola of the ulcer is very sensitive, but there is a sore, bruised feeling, together with hyperæsthesia. And, although the suppurating part may turn bluish and the patient experience weakness, yet there are no evidences of loss of vitality and gangrene, such as suggest the later-indicated drug, *Lachesis.*

Lycopodium is here again a complement of the snake-poison. If syphilitic ulcers appear in the throat, they are dark grayish-yellow, worse on the right side. The forehead exhibits a coppery eruption and the face is sallow, often furrowed, but lacks the small red bloodvessels which shine through the yellow skin in *Lachesis.* Chancres are indolent. Condylomata are pediculated. Ulcers on the legs refuse to heal, with tearing burning, worse at night; they are made worse by poultices or by any attempt to dress them. The pus is often golden-yellow. There is flatulent dyspepsia.

Nitric acid, should it seem similar in phagedenic chancre, ulcers on the tibia, etc., may easily be distinguished by the irregular edges of the ulcer, which also presents exuberant, easily-bleeding granulations; and its mouth and throat symptoms may be differentiated by the cracks of the commissures of the lips, sensations of a splinter in the throat, etc.

Kali iodatum exhibits a very different train of symptoms from *Lachesis*. Gnawing, boring bone-pains; throbbing and burning in nasal and frontal bones; greenish-yellow, excoriating ozæna; papules ulcerating and leaving scars; rupia; chancres with hard edges and curdy pus; ulcers deep-eating; violent headache, much more severe than in the snake-poison, and causing hard lumps on the head. Tendency to interstitial infiltration of soft tissues and also of bones, thus more extended than with *Lachesis*, which infiltrates only the soft tissues.

In the uterine and ovarian symptoms of *Lachesis* your attention is directed to the following comparisons.

Platina has profuse, dark menses instead of scanty flow, and the hauteur is much more pronounced. The nymphomania is accompanied by titillation and tingling of the genitals or with vaginismus. In ovarian affections this drug has relieved after *Lachesis* failed, as in suppuration of the ovary, the pus having been evacuated under the action of the latter. The pains are burning, with violent bearing down.

Palladium has relieved induration and swelling of the right ovary, as has *Lachesis*. Mentally the two are widely different. The former develops an egotism which manifests itself in the patient's concern for the good opinion of others, consequently her pride is often injured. Mental emotions aggravate the ovarian pains, as in the snake-poison, but in a different way. The *Lachesis* patient is ecstatic or at least excitable; the relating of stories moves her to tears. The *Palladium* patient is easily agitated in society; a lively conversation or some evening entertainment increases her pains and tries her mentally and bodily.

In ovarian affections *Apis* stands closely allied to *Lachesis*, but it acts more on the right ovary than on the left. There is a bruised, sore feeling, or a stinging, burning. At other times the pains are described as lancinating.

In prolapsus uteri or during the menses the bearing down seems to be in the right ovary; pains followed by a scanty dark mucus.

Both have pains from the left to the right ovary, but in *Apis* these are experienced while stretching. There is also a strained feeling in the ovarian region, very characteristic. The pains may ascend in either, but in *Apis* they are in the right ovary, with pain also in the left pectoral region, and cough.

Mentally there is considerable similarity (see Mind). Both have jealousy, with talkativeness and increased sexual desire; restlessness, with bustling manners.

Arsenic affects the ovaries and uterus, and has metrorrhagia of dark blood, and increased sexual desire. But this powerful agent affects more the right ovary, with marked burning, tensive pains and restlessness, which is somewhat relieved by constantly moving the feet; menstrual colic, better from warm applications.

Lycopodium reverses the *Lachesis* direction of pains, shooting from right to left. Its gastro-enteric symptoms are also always present.

Although *Graphites* more often affects the left ovary it will also relieve when pains in the right ovarian region are followed by a discharge from the vagina, but constitutionally this drug and *Lachesis* differ.

A marked symptom of *Lachesis* is the relief of pain when the blood flows. Compare *Moschus*, drawing, pulling at beginning of menses, ceasing with the menstrual flow; *Zincum*, relief of boring in the left ovary (just like *Lachesis*).

Platina and *Ammonium carb.* have pains which continue with the flow, the former even with a profuse discharge, the latter with flow between pains. In *Actea racemosa* the more profuse the flow is the greater is the pain.

Now, the heart, circulation and fevers. *Lachesis*, as I have already intimated, affects the circulation markedly; it causes flushing of heat, as at the climaxis; rush of blood headward, with coldness of the feet; palpitation of the heart, with a feeling of constriction about the heart as if tightly held by cords. These latter symptoms, with the oppression of the chest, the dyspnœa on awaking, and the inability to lie down, have led to the use of *Lachesis* in hydrothorax and hydropericardium when dependent on organic disease of the heart.

Lachesis is indicated in general dropsy when the urine is dark, almost blackish, and contains albumen, and the skin over the œdematous parts is dark bluish-black. I remember a man, sixty years of age, who had just this sort of dropsy, and continued to live for six months under the action of *Lachesis*, and whose death, when it came, was painless. It is especially useful in the ascites following scarlatina and the ascites of drunkards, when the above symptoms are present.

In renal and vesical affections *Lachesis* is to be selected more by the general than by the local symptoms. For instance, in albuminuria or morbus Brightii, the respiratory symptoms, aggravation after sleep, and blue surface are more characteristic than the urinary symptoms

In cystitis the drug is indicated when the offensive mucus introduces the universal characteristic of tendency to putrescence. And the more this offensiveness of the urine is disproportionately intense, when compared with the time of the vesical retention of the mucus, the more likely is *Lachesis* to be the remedy.

In hæmaturia the drug, like its powerful rival *Crotalus*, is called for when the symptoms occur as an evidence of blood degeneration, as in low fevers; hence there is the characteristic deposit of disintegrated blood-cells, of fibrin, etc., presenting the appearance of charred straw. In albuminuria after scarlatina there is dropsy from delayed desquamation, and the urine is black or contains black spots. This spotted appearance is precisely like *Helleborus*. Other remedies causing black urine are *Colchicum*, *Natrum mur.*, *Carbolic acid* and *Digitalis*. *Apis*, *Ammonium benz.*, *Arsenicum*, *Benzoic acid*, *Arnica*, *Opium*, *Carbo veg.*, *Kali carb.* and *Terebinthina* produce dark turbid urine. *Lachesis* alone, however, has the foaming urine and the general characteristics already discussed.

Helleborus is to be distinguished by the sensorial apathy, muscular weakness, pale puffed face and jelly-like, mucous diarrhœa which accompany its dropsy. The patient may breathe better when lying down, which is the converse of *Lachesis* and *Arsenicum*.

Digitalis, with blackish, scanty, turbid urine, faintness from weak heart, with bluish face, looks very much like *Lachesis* here. In the latter there is more laryngeal constriction, as well as oppression and constriction of the chest; in the former the suffocative constriction is as if the internal parts of the chest had grown together. *Digitalis* has also sinking or faintness at the stomach, as if life was becoming extinct.

Terebinthina has smoky and turbid urine, depositing a sediment like coffee-grounds. It is often indicated in dropsy after scarlatina. The sediment contains disintegrated blood-corpuscles; hæmaturia. Dyspnœa; the patient must be propped up in bed There is great drowsiness. The tongue is dry and glossy. Clinically, *Terebinthina* has proved useful in the early stages of renal disease, when congestion predominates, that is, before renal casts appear in any great quantity. It causes more intense burning and pain in the back than *Lachesis*, and the urine may have a violet odor. In typhoid fever both renal and alvine discharges resemble those of *Lachesis*. Fœtid stools, hæmorrhages from the bowels, caused by ulceration; the blood is dark, sooty and looks like coffee-grounds. Fœtid urine; disintegrated blood in the urine. In addition, *Terebinthina* causes stupor, dry, smooth, glossy tongue and great weakness. But it is distinguished by a preponderance of tympanites, with burning, which is accompanied by a smooth tongue, as if it had lost its papillæ.

Apis simulates *Lachesis* in post-scarlatinal dropsy, for both remedies have albuminuria, scanty urine, which is dark from decomposed blood, and dyspnœa. But *Apis* usually requires thirstlessness, pale waxen skin and an eruption here or there resembling nettle-rash, red pimples or an erysipelatous rosy appearance of the anasarcous limbs.

Arsenicum is needed in cases of renal disease when the urine is scanty and albuminous without blood, the remedy being required on account of its well-defined heart symptoms or its mental restlessness, etc. Thus far it needs no differentiation here. But if the urine is dark, turbid, blood-mixed, depositing a coffee-like sediment, if there is orthopnœa with cold legs, bronchial catarrh, great difficulty in breathing until phlegm is raised, spasmodic constriction of the larynx, the choice may demand further comparison. *Arsenicum* cures when the urine looks like dark dung-water, and renal casts are abundant. The dyspnœa is noticed more when the patient attempts to lie down in the evening, and again it arouses him after 12 P. M.; it is relieved by the expectoration of mucus. In *Lachesis* the dyspnœa is worse when, after lying down, he drops off to sleep; relief follows the hawking loose or coughing up of a small amount of thick adherent mucus, and there is far more annoyance from the contact of the clothing than there is with *Arsenicum*. In the latter the clothing is torn loose lest its pressure smother the patient; in the former there is added a cutaneous hyperæsthesia.

Colchicum causes an intense congestion of the mucous membrane of the stomach and bowels, and also of the kidneys. The urine is dark, turbid, albuminous, bloody and as black as ink. There is dropsy. But *Colchicum* is readily distinguished from *Lachesis* by the prominence of irritation of the sphincter vesicæ with tenesmus of the bladder after urination. It is especially indicated in gouty patients, who at the same time suffer from a nervous weakness, which is combined with hypersensitiveness. If this latter symptom seems to resemble *Lachesis*, we may readily distinguish by the general effects of *Colchicum*, namely, oversensitiveness to touch (except perhaps the tympanitic abdomen); senses too acute, especially over-affected by strong odors; gastric symptoms are prominent; mental labor fatigues, causing inability to fix the thoughts or to think connectedly; headache, the skin of the scalp feels tense; coated tongue; nausea; great weakness, yet easily irritated by external impressions. A peculiarity of *Colchicum* is that if there are copious salivation and urinary secretion, the stools are scanty and attended with tenesmus, and *vice versa*.

I need not dwell upon the fevers of *Lachesis*, because I mentioned them in speaking of the mental symptoms of the drug. I may, however, speak of the intermittent fever which recurs in the spring-time in spite of the use of quinine in the fall. The chill comes on at one or two o'clock in the afternoon. During the chill—and here is a symptom which is characteristic—the patient feels that he must have clothing piled on him, not so much to keep him warm as to keep him still. He wants to be held down firmly to relieve the shaking and the pains in the chest and head. The fever is characterized by burning pungency, by the oppression of the chest and the heart, and by the associated drowsiness and loquacity. Desire to be held down during chill is also characteristic of *Gelsemium*.

Carbo veg., like *Lachesis*, has annual return of the paroxysms, loquacity during the hot stage, thirstlessness during the fever, oppressed breathing. The patient is very weak from protracted disease and abuse of quinine. But the thirst is greatest during the chill, not before it, and the chill is often accompanied by cold breath, coldness of the knees, even when wrapped up in bed. Flushes of burning heat in the evening attacks, without thirst. Flatulency. One-sided chills, left side generally. Collapse more marked.

Capsicum agrees in thirst before chill, desire for warmth, chill beginning in the back; irregular, intermittent pulse. But with the red pepper the chill commences in the back and spreads thence; the thirst continues into the chill, and drinking aggravates (see *Elaps*). The patient is relieved by hot applications, as by a hot water-bottle applied to the back.

Menyanthes is preferable when the disease manifests itself as a coldness of the tip of the nose, the ear-lobes, and the tips of the fingers and toes. Feet to knees icy cold. Hands and feet icy cold, rest of the body warm. When *Lachesis* is called for in such irregular cases, with cold nose, etc., the livid skin and great weakness, as shown by the filiform pulse, are sufficiently distinctive.

Agreeing more accurately are the following remedies, all of which produce weak or thready pulse, coldness or blueness of the skin, and, of course, great prostration: *Carbo veg*. (see above).

Veratrum album, but in this drug the chill is associated with thirst, and (if internal) runs downward, not upward. Skin blue, cold, inelastic; hands blue; face, mouth and tongue cold; breathing oppressed and labored; heart weak; cold, clammy sweat, worse on the forehead. Heat has no palliative effect.

Arsenic, external heat relieves; mouth and tongue cold; face blue; single parts of the surface blue. Anxious restlessness despite the great debility; cold, clammy sweat. Suffocative attacks of breathing.

Camphor, icy-cold surface, but hot internally, so he throws off the clothing; face deathly pale; limbs blue; breath generally hot. Spasms, or, if conscious, voice altered. Sopor follows.

Hydrocyanic acid, marble-like coldness of the whole body. Pulse feeble or imperceptible. Long-lasting faints. Drinks roll audibly down the œsophagus. Clutches at the heart as if in distress. Spasms; especially muscles of back and jaw are stiff.

Helleborus, muscles relaxed; suddenly he falls, with coldness, cold sweat on the forehead; slow pulse. Horrible convulsions, with extreme coldness. Rheumatic pains in the knees.

Digitalis, like the snake-poison, weakens the heart. The skin is very cold. Copious sweat, but the heart symptoms are not relieved. Pulse intermits every third, fifth or seventh beat; very slow pulse. It will be remembered that *Lachesis* has oppression of the chest, with cold feet. As the latter become warmer the oppression lessens.

Secale, cold surface; sunken, pale face and blue lips. Will not be covered. Tingling in the limbs; holds the hands with the fingers widely spread apart. Cold, clammy sweat. Speech feeble, stuttering.

Hyoscyamus resembles *Lachesis* in the chill up the back, objective coldness of the body, convulsions, delirium. But the chill is worse at night, and spreads from the feet to the spine, and thence to the neck. The lowering of the temperature is accompanied by slow arterial action, drowsiness, or by delirious and excited talk; picks at the bed-clothing, fears being poisoned, hallucinations, fibrillary twitchings, etc.

Lachnanthes, like *Lachesis*, causes glistening eyes during the chill, icy coldness of the body, relieved by warmth. But only the former has brilliant eyes and circumscribed red cheeks with the fever and delirium.

Lycopodium follows *Lachesis*. It is needed in fevers when the patient becomes drowsy or stupid; coldness, as if lying on ice. One foot warm, the other cold—an important symptom. Feels as if the blood ceased to circulate.

In intermittent fever the chill begins in the back, as in *Lachesis*. It is worse from 4 to 8 P. M., or at 7 P. M.; hands and feet numb and icy cold. Sour eructations or vomit are almost invariably present, especially between chill and heat. Thirst mostly after the sweat. Desires hot drinks only.

Apis here, as in many other instances, favors the snake-poison. Both are suited to old or maltreated cases; afternoon chill, oppression of the chest, nose cold, pulse fluttering, skin of hands and arms blue, and general appearance of collapse. But the bee-poison has aggravation from heat, *Lachesis* has not; the former has much more marked oppression of the chest, with consequent smothering. The tongue is red, raw, and covered on tip and borders with vesicles. Thirst during and not before the chill. Urticaria.

Cuprum combines coldness with convulsive phenomena. Icy coldness of the whole body. Severe cramps in the extremities, with cold sweat, blue surface; also collapse. Urine suppressed. Employed successfully in the cold stage of cholera, after *Camphor*, but also useful in other forms of collapse. For instance, it has antidoted snake-bite, with cramps, delirium, and finally torpor.

Lachesis may also be indicated in scarlet fever, but not in the Sydenham variety of the disease, but in those forms which have a malignant tendency. The child is drowsy and falls readily into a heavy sleep. The rash comes out very imperfectly or very slowly, and has a dark purple hue. It may be interspersed with a miliary rash. It is apt to be complicated with a membranous deposit in the throat having the character I have already described to you when speaking of the remedy in diphtheria. The cellular tissue of the throat is inflamed and threatens suppuration. The cervical glands are swollen. On looking into the throat you find it to be dark red with a dirty white deposit on the tonsils, especially the left. The tongue is coated dirty yellow at the base, and the red papillæ show prominently through this coating. The pulse is weak and the surface of the body cool. There is apt to be dark blood oozing from the mouth and nose.

The majority of physicians make a mistake in beginning their treatment of scarlatina. A mistake in the beginning means one of two things, either a long, tedious illness, or a short one, ending with death. The mistake made is to give *Belladonna* in every case. Let us look for a moment at the differences between *Belladonna* and *Lachesis*. Both remedies have the strawberry tongue, the throbbing headache, the red face and the high fever. *Belladonna* is indicated *only* in the sthenic type when there is an active delirium, the throat is bright red in color, the pulse is full and bounding, the rash is bright red and smooth. *Lachesis* on the other hand, is suitable where asthenia predominates, with purplish, tardily-appearing rash, drowsiness, marked swelling of the cervical glands, and other symptoms of malignancy above enumerated.

In carbuncle and cancer we think of *Lachesis* when the surrounding area is swollen and purple or blackish, and pus forms very slowly. *Lachesis* given under these circumstances increases the quantity and improves the quality of the pus, and the patient's strength improves also.

When giving *Lachesis* for malignant pustule you should accompany the remedy with brandy. That is an experience of Dr. Dunham.

I will next say a few words respecting the modalities of *Lachesis*. Modalities, as you know, express the mode or manner by which symptoms are qualified. They are therefore important in the study of drugs and especially in differentiating allied remedies. Two medicines, for instance, may induce supraorbital pains of a shooting character. But if one has the pains modified by pressure, the other by sleep, we are thus enabled to distinguish them in practice. Modalities, then, qualify symptoms and are as essential as adjectives to nouns. Care must be exercised, however, that they be not substituted for the symptoms they modify. Too often we see cases reported, the only homœopathic resemblance between which and the remedy selected is a mere modality, as, for instance, worse after sleep.

The modalities of *Lachesis*, then, are as follows:

Worse.—During sleep, especially the throat symptoms, choking, which arouses him; worse after sleep, especially in the morning

Time of Day.—Generally worse from noon until 12 P. M.; still there are some prominent symptoms aggravated in the morning and forenoon. This is partly owing to the bad effects of awaking, but, as some symptoms appear later in the morning, we may ascribe them to causes then at work. For instance, the patient has vertigo on awaking, yet this returns, on closing the eyes, at 11 A. M. Headache in the left frontal eminence in the morning. Weakness in the morning on rising. Finger tips numb. On sitting up quickly in the morning, breathing becomes slow, difficult and whistling.

In the evening and before 12 P. M., we find the following especial exacerbations: Throat sensitive; diarrhœa; dry, hacking cough. Chill beginning some time between noon and 2 P. M., but fever is marked in the evening and night; worse before 12 P. M.

Temperature, Weather, etc.—Worse in the cold air, from change of temperature and from the warmth of the bed (see below under Motion, etc.); worse from getting wet, wet weather, windy weather; worse before a thunderstorm; worse from the sun; worse in the spring. Better often from warmth, wrapping up, near the stove, etc. Excessively cold or excessively warm weather causes debility.

Motion, Rest, Position, etc.—Worse on and after rising from bed; worse while sitting and better after rising from a seat; better lying in bed on the painless side, but worse from the warmth of the bed (see above under Temperature) and from lying on the painful side. Some symptoms are better from moving but not if continued long.

Touch, Pressure, Injuries, etc.—Almost invariably worse from touch, however slight. Useful for the bad effects of injuries, as penetrating wounds, with much hæmorrhage or gangrene.

LECTURE VI.

ARACHNIDA.

Of the Arachnida or spider-poisons used in medicine I shall call your attention to the following:
1. Mygale lasiodora.
2. Lycosa tarentula.
3. Tarentula Cubensis.
4. Aranea diadema.
5. Aranea scinencia.
6. Theridion curassavicum.

The action of the drugs in this group is a two-fold one; they all poison the blood, and they all act prominently on the nervous system, producing spasmodic diseases, as chorea and hysteria. Among other nervous symptoms produced by them are anxiety, trembling, great restlessness, oversensitiveness and nervous prostration; periodicity.

The system is profoundly affected by spider-poisons; hence, they may be used in serious and chronic ailments.

Taking up the study of these drugs *seriatim*, we come first to the *Mygale lasiodora*.

MYGALE LASIODORA.

The *Mygale lasiodora* is a large black spider, native to the island of Cuba. It was first proved by Dr. J. C. Houard, of this city. It is one of our best remedies for uncomplicated cases of *chorea*. The patient is apt to be low-spirited and depressed. She complains of dull pain in the forehead. She has constant twitchings of the muscles of the face. The head is often jerked to one side, usually to the right. There are also twitchings and jerkings of the muscles of one arm and leg, usually the right. Control over the muscles is lost. On attempting to put the hand up to the head it is violently jerked backward. When an effort to talk is made the words are jerked out.

I can recall one case of chorea in which, under the use of this remedy, the convulsive symptoms were speedily removed, and the patient, a little girl, remained well for years. Dr. Houard, to whom I just referred as having proved this drug, has given me the following symptoms indicating its use. The muscles of the face twitch, the mouth and eyes open and close in rapid succession; cannot put the hand to the face, it is arrested midway and jerked down. Gait unsteady; legs in motion while sitting and dragged while attempting to talk; constant motion of the whole body.

The most similar remedy to *Mygale* in chorea is *Agaricus*,* which also has these angular choreic movements. But as a distinctive symptom we have itching of the eyelids or of different parts of the body, as if they had been frost-bitten. The eyelids are in constant motion. The spine is sensitive to touch.

Actea racemosa is to be employed in chorea when the movements affect chiefly the left side, and when the disease is associated with myalgia or rheumatic ailments, or occurs reflexly as a result of uterine displacements.

Tarentula is indicated in chorea affecting the right arm and right leg. The movements persist even at night.

Ignatia is called for in chorea of emotional origin.

Zizia may be used in cases in which the choreic movements continue during sleep.

The *Stramonium* chorea is characterized by the following symptoms. Features continually changing; now he laughs and now appears astonished; tongue protruded rapidly; head thrown alternately backward and forward; spasmodic twitching of the spine and whole body; the extremities are in constant motion, though not always jerked, for sometimes their motion is rotary, gyratory, even graceful. The muscles of the whole body are in constant motion. There may be stammering. If the mind is affected, the patient is easily frightened; he awakes from sleep terrified; or he often assumes an attitude of prayer, with fervent expression and clasped hands. He frequently lifts his head from the pillow.

*By a very ingenious selection of *Agaricus* by Dr. Korndœrfer, in the case of a two-year old child, who had evident meningitis, and who was not relieved by *Apis*, *Sulphur*, etc., the rolling of the head ceased, alarming forewarning of imbecility happily vanished, and the patient fully recovered. I used the drug in a case of typhoid, in which the child rolled her head and bit her nightgown. Some improvement followed. *Tarentula* was then given, with slight aggravation, followed by lasting improvement. The two should be remembered in impending imbecility. E. A. F.

Returning now to *Mygale*, I give you the following symptoms in addition to those already described: Delirious talk about business; restlessness all night; fear of death; despondency, with anxious expression; nausea, with strong palpitation of the heart, dimness of sight, general weakness; tremulousness of the whole body in the evening; severe chill, thirty minutes, then fever, with trembling; pain in the head in the morning, worse in the eyes and from temple to temple.

Mygale, after having been given to a boy for some time, produced, during the spasmodic symptoms, violent erections of the penis. The penis, when erect, was curved, not straight, and consequently the patient suffered great pain. Dr. Williamson, by whom this observation was made, was then led to a successful use of the remedy in chordee. He used it in a low potency, but it has since been used high with equal success.

LYCOSA TARENTULA.

In poisoning by the bite of the Tarentula, the symptoms are strikingly similar to those of the Ophidia. The bitten part becomes swollen and discolored, and the lymphatic glands are enlarged. By conveyance of the poison to the neck the cellular tissue there is affected, giving rise to swelling of a dark red or purplish hue. Choking seems imminent, when epistaxis, with discharge of dark clots, appears and relieves the symptoms. Evidence of cerebral congestion is given by the violently throbbing carotid arteries. But with all these symptoms there is a pale, earthy hue to the face. The fauces appear swollen and purplish, and there is a difficulty of swallowing which is of paralytic origin. The patient has burning thirst for large draughts of water. The stools are dark and fœtid, and the urine scanty and voided with difficulty. Thus far, there is but little to aid us in distinguishing this condition from a *Lachesis* case. But there are other symptoms—nervous phenomena—which typify the drug. Nervous symptoms are present in all the spider-poisons, but *Tarentula* applies, more than other members of the group, to hysteria. There is marked spinal irritation, and what I have found to be very characteristic is great excitability of the terminations of the nerves. The patient keeps the hands in constant motion, trying to work off this overexcitability. The playing of a lively piece of music excites her and starts her to acting like one crazy. When there are no observers she has no hysterical attacks. As soon as attention is directed to her she begins to twitch, etc. When she has headache it is better from rubbing the head against the pillow. Rubbing seems to relieve.

Tarentula acts on the uterus and ovaries. It is palliative in enlargement of these organs. There is pain in the uterine region associated with constrictive headache. There is also burning pain in the hypogastrium and hips, with sensation as of a great weight in the pelvis. The menses are profuse and are followed by pruritus vulvæ. The patient feels sore and bruised all over, particularly when moving about. She longs for sleep, but is so nervous that she cannot sleep.

Now let us study for a moment the concordant remedies of *Tarentula*, taking up first *Kali bromatum*. We have no remedy in the Materia Medica which has so many reflex symptoms as *Kali bromatum*. Any little irritation, such as dentition or indigestion in children, may bring on convulsions. The symptom, however, which I wish particularly to emphasize is peripheral irritation, with relief from motion or using the part affected.

Crocus deserves mention because of the hysterical state it is capable of exciting, together with choreic symptoms. It causes jumping, dancing, laughing, desire to kiss everybody, contractions of single groups of muscles. She is angry, and then suddenly repents; or angry and talkative, laughing alternately. As in *Tarentula*, music affects her. Hearing one sing, she begins involuntarily to join in; but there is not the subsequent relief from music which is noticed in the spider-poison.

Actea racemosa resembles the spiders in producing sleeplessness, restlessness, trembling and fear of death; and, too, these evidences of nervousness are often, in *Actea* as in *Tarentula*, reflex from uterine affections. The former has, after going to bed, jerking, commencing on the side on which she is lying, compelling change of position, nervous shuddering and nervous chills. Mentally the two drugs differ. *Actea* causes nervousness; she feels as if the top of the head would fly off; delirium with jumping from subject to subject; sees strange objects; great apprehensiveness, as a concomitant of uterine irritation; pains darting into the eye-ball, through to the occiput. Feels grieved, troubled, with sighing; next day, tremulous joy, mirth and playfulness.

This head symptom of *Actea* is not quite the same as that of *Theridion*, under which remedy the patient's head feels as if she could lift it off.

Hyoscyamus is useful in well-marked local jerkings and twitchings of groups of muscles. The patient is sleepless and nervous, or sobs and cries in sleep. The head falls from side to side. She laughs at everything in a silly manner. Stuttering. Mental excitement; talkativeness; she is nervous, suspicious, troublesome, but not maniacal.

Causticum bears some resemblance in causing restless moving at night; she can find no quiet position. Intolerable uneasiness in the limbs in the evening. Anxiety and timidity in the evening. Trembling. Uneasy at night; she awakes from a short sleep with anxiety, which scarcely allows her to remain in one place ten minutes; she is obliged to turn her head involuntarily from one side to the other, until, exhausted, she falls asleep. During sleep frequent motions with her arms and legs. She jerks, mostly the right side of the body. Convulsive motions of mouth and eyes, with sleeplessness and restlessness, after repercussed eruptions. It is especially suited to rheumatic patients, or to those who suffer from paretic affections, especially of one side of the face or of the tongue; the mouth, in consequence, is distorted.

Belladonna produces a bodily inquietude, as in chorea. The patient is obliged to move to and fro, especially to move the hands and feet; he cannot stay long in any position. The predominant jerking is backwards, although this may alternate with a forward bending. There is a boring of the head into the pillow, not mere rubbing against the pillow as in *Tarentula*. *Belladonna* also has constrictions, hyperæsthesia, mania, with laughing, dancing, wild crying, etc. But it is distinguished by the intensity of its symptoms; there are violent congestions throbbing of the carotids, wild look, dilated pupils and injected eyes.

In hysterical states *Ignatia*, though agreeing in many respects with *Tarentula*, has a well-defined individuality of its own. The nervous system is over-impressionable, incoördinate in function and contradictory in action. The patient is extremely susceptible to emotional influences. Fear and grief affect her seriously; the least contradiction offends; she is readily chagrined, and is thus often reduced to grief and tears by the slightest causes. Her mental states, however, are not usually exhibited in violence and rage. On the contrary, she nurses her troubles in seclusion and silence, and broods over them until they prey upon her whole system. She thus grows more and more nervous, and, at the same time, more and more weakened. The heart beats nervously, with variable pulse; she frequently sighs heavily and deeply; suffers from goneness at the stomach, with qualmishness and flat taste in the mouth; feeling of a lump in the throat, swelling sympathetically with the intensity of her mental disturbances. Sleeplessness or violent startings of the limbs. Grief, fright, disappointed love or some other similar cause may develop hysterical or choreic paroxysms. The moods change with wonderful rapidity; now she laughs and jokes, then, quickly, she bursts into tears. Her manner becomes hurried, so that everything is performed hastily, and hence imperfectly and awkwardly. She is afflicted with intense headaches. These are characterized by the predominance of a sensation of pressure; the pain goes to the eye, which feels as if pressed out, or to the root of the nose, or, again, it is confined to one small spot, like a nail pressing; hence the name, clavus hystericus. At the height of the paroxysm she becomes restless and chilly, and often describes a peculiar perversion of vision; she sees fiery zigzags when looking out of the line of vision (see *Theridion*). Finally, a profuse flow of colorless urine terminates the attack.

While, then, both remedies induce sadness, indifference, profound melancholy and hysterical states, only *Ignatia* has the introverted state of mind; only *Tarentula*, the cunning attempts to feign paroxysms and wild dancing.

Platina should not be confounded with the spider-poisons here, because it develops a different form of hysteria. True, there are present deranged coördination of functions, anxiety, trembling, fear of death, which seems to the patient to be imminent; also alternation of depression with gayety and laughter; sexual excitement and convulsions. But the patient assumes a *hauteur*, a self-exaltation, which is foreign to the other drugs considered. Her mental disturbances develop into a condition of self-esteem, during which she looks disdainfully down on all around her. Her paroxysms of laughter are not only loud and boisterous, but ill-timed, occurring even under circumstances of a sad nature. The headaches are of constrictive character, as in *Tarentula*, but there is, in addition, a squeezing, cramplike pain, with numbness, and the pains gradually increase and as gradually decrease.

Indurated uterus belongs to the symptoms of both remedies.

Palladium is readily distinguished by its unique mental phenomena. The patient is not haughty, but she is irritable, and is, unfortunately, given to strong and violent language. Music, society or animated conversation excites her and produces pains in the right ovary; the following day she feels correspondingly exhausted. Her egotism is displayed in a fondness for the good opinion of others, hence she is continually being "slighted." The uterine symptoms are characterized by a weakness, as if the womb were sinking; an empty feeling in the groins, as if eviscerated.

Moschus repeats the scolding of *Palladium*, but the patient keeps it up until her lips turn blue, her eyes stare and she falls to the floor in a swoon. She suffers from sudden suffocation from closure of the glottis or cramp of the chest. She also has faint spells; palpitation; tremulousness of the whole body; coldness of the body; hysterical headache, with fainting spells; copious pale urine; fear of death, like *Platina* and *Tarentula*, but with pale face and fainting; she talks only of approaching death. Vertigo, nausea, dim vision. Vertigo, objects turn in a circle. (Musk relieves when *Theridion* produces vertigo; worse when the eyes are closed.) Headache, as from a weight pressing here or there on the head. An oft-observed symptom with the nervous is fidgetiness of the legs, at times preventing sleep. In addition to *Tarentula* the following remedies may be studied in this relation:

Zincum induces moving of the feet for hours after retiring, even continuing in sleep.

Asafœtida has several times relieved restlessness, as has also *Ammonium carb.*; *Actea racemosa* has already been mentioned.

Arsenicum, so useful in stubborn cases of chorea, has the following: Uneasiness in the legs, must change the position of his feet all the time or walk about for relief.

Mephitis has relieved uneasiness in the legs, as if they would become insensible.

Sticta pulmonaria has produced a sensation as though the legs were floating in the air. One prover became so lively that she lay down on a lounge and began to kick, exclaiming that she felt as if she wanted to fly away. This excitability reminds us of the desire to jump which *Tarentula* causes. (Compare *Stramonium*, *Agaricus*, *Cicuta*, *Hyoscyamus*, *Crocus* and *Natrum mur.*, which latter has jumping high up, regardless of near objects.)

Asarum induces a feeling as if the body were hovering in the air; it also causes shivering and coldness from any emotion. But it offers no essential similarities to *Tarentula*, though it has some slight resemblance to *Theridion*, in that noises become intolerable. The distinction is evident. *Asarum* is so sensitive that a thrill runs through the patient on merely thinking of the scratching of silk, which she is continually impelled to do.

Although I have tabulated several drugs as bearing symptomatic resemblance to the Spiders, only the following hold any intimate relationship:

Ignatia, Moschus, Actea racemosa, Agaricus, Stramonium, Belladonna, Magnesia mur. (the latter in uterine cramps).

TARENTULA CUBENSIS.

Tarentula Cubensis, the hairy spider, causes a perfect picture of carbuncle, even to the sloughing, and claims place as a rival to *Arsenicum* and *Carbo veg.* It may be used effectually when there are great prostration and diarrhœa, with intermitting fever of evening exacerbation. In relieving the atrocious pains accompanying this condition it acts almost like magic. It should, therefore, be compared with *Arsenicum*, and no less with *Lachesis, Anthracinum* and *Silicea.*

ARANEA DIADEMA.

Aranea was suggested by Grauvogl as one of the remedies for what he called the hydrogenoid constitution, this being a constitution which could not tolerate moisture. Under *Aranea* all the symptoms are worse during damp weather or from dwelling in damp localities. Especially is this true with what we may call chronic intermittent fever, for which *Aranea* is the remedy when the symptoms are aggravated during every spell of damp weather. The patient may feel very comfortable on a sunny day, but as soon as it becomes damp he gets sick. During this aggravation he complains of chilliness, as if the bones were made of ice, bone-pains, followed by little or no fever. The chill is apt to be typical, occurring at the same hour every other day, every week, or at some regular period. You find also that the spleen is enlarged and the patient is subject to hæmorrhages. He may or may not have been previously treated with quinine.

Cinchona and *Chininum sulphuricum* are both very similar to *Aranea diadema* in the periodical return of symptoms, and both are indicated in cases of swollen spleen, and of ague from living in damp places.

Cedron, of which it has been asserted that it will relieve the bite of the rattlesnake and modify hydrophobia, may also be regarded as an analogue of *Aranea diadema* and of the spider-poisons generally. It is said to act best in nervous, excitable and even voluptuous patients, especially females. The febrile and neuralgic symptoms return with clock-like regularity. It is used in ague contracted in warm countries or in low, marshy lands, in which latter respect it offers some similarity to *Aranea*. But the former remedy has won favor mainly in hot climates, while the latter works well in chills contracted in cold and wet localities. The chill predominates, heat being slight or wanting. In *Cedron*, on the contrary, there is congestion of the head, flying heat in the face alternating with chill, and dry heat with full, quick pulse.

So far as proved, *Aranea* does not develop the extreme excitation of the other three spiders mentioned above. Still there is evidence that it affects the nervous system. Confusion of the head and headaches after eating, relieved by smoking; headache ceases in the open air; sudden, violent pains in the upper and lower jaws at night immediately after lying down; restless sleep with frequent waking, always with sensation as if the hands and forearms were greatly swollen, as if they were twice as strong and large as natural, a symptom common to remedies that affect the cerebro-spinal nervous system.

Aranea also cures diarrhœa, and these patients are often troubled with this disorder. The stools are watery, and are associated with great rumbling in the bowels, as if considerable fermentation were going on within.

The toothache is especially worse in damp weather, and also as soon as the patient gets into bed. Here it reminds you of *Mercurius*.

There is a symptom of *Aranea* which I have not had the opportunity of observing in practice, and that is numbness of the parts supplied by the ulnar nerve.

Aranea also attacks the bones. It is especially indicated in disease of the os calcis when the patient complains of violent, dull, boring pain in that bone. This may be due to a simple periostitis, or it may be associated with caries. Sometimes there is a sensation as if the bones felt like ice. This is purely subjective.

Theridion Curassavicum.

Theridion compares with *Tarentula* in headache, nervousness and hysteria. According to the provings, there is a similar restless, busy state; he desires to occupy himself, though he finds pleasure in nothing. But there is a strong distinctive characteristic in the sensitiveness to noise. This qualifies the vertigo, headache, and even the gastric ailments. Vertigo and nausea, worse when the eyes are closed, from motion and from noise.* Every sound penetrates the teeth. Every penetrating sound and reverberation extends through the whole body. Headache worse if others walk over the floor. I have relieved most intense headache with *Theridion* when this hypersensitiveness was present, as well as nausea and aggravation from motion. The general accompaniments are true spider-effects: Weakness, trembling, coldness and anxiety. Hysteria, too, has yielded to *Theridion*. Time passes too quickly; hilarity; talkativeness; feels as if her head did not belong to her, as if she could lift it off. Luminous vibrations before the eyes. Sensitive to light; if she looks into the light, dark vibrations are produced; double vision. Faints after every exertion. Anxiety about the heart, with sharp pains through the left chest, or to the left shoulder. Bites the point of the tongue during sleep—all with weakness, chilliness, or easily excited cold sweat. Nausea and vanishing of thoughts, greatly intensified by closing the eyes.

Theridion is very similar to *Spigelia*, which has sharp neuralgic pains over the left eye. Under *Spigelia*, however, the pain comes up from the nape of the neck and over the head, settling above the left eye. The *Spigelia* sick headache is very apt to follow the sun, beginning in the morning, reaching its acme at noon, and gradually subsiding at sunset. The antidote to *Theridion* when it causes this headache is *Moschus*.

Bryonia is at times very similar in headache. I once treated a lady suffering from intense headache and nausea that were worse from the least motion. *Bryonia* was given, but failed. However, when the patient added the fact that noises made both headache and nausea worse, I found the similimum in *Theridion*.

In headaches worse from jarring the floor compare *Belladonna* and *Sanguinaria*.

Another use you may make of *Theridion* is in the sea-sickness of nervous women. They shut their eyes to get rid of the motion of the vessel, and they grow deathly sick.

The spine is very irritable. We have what is known as spinal irritation. Examination reveals great sensitiveness between the vertebræ.

---

*In vertigo worse closing the eyes compare *Lachesis*, *Apis*, *Arnica*, *Piper methysticum*, *Arsenicum*, *Thuja*, *Petroleum*, *Chelidonium*, *Sepia*.

So great is this hyperæsthesia that the patient sits sideways in a chair in order to avoid pressure of the back of the chair against the spine.

A rather peculiar employment of *Theridion*, but one which I have had occasion to confirm, is its use in *phthisis florida*. It is claimed that the drug tends to stay, and in some cases stop, the rapid progress of this fatal affection. One symptom I know is good, violent stitches high up in the left chest through to the back. Dr. Baruch succeeded in removing this symptom with *Theridion* after other physicians had utterly failed.

Myrtus communis and *Pix liquida* vie with *Theridion* in pains in the upper left chest. The first has pain through to the shoulder-blade, a symptom which it often relieves, even in consumptives. *Pix* selects a spot at the third left costal cartilage, where it joins with the rib. (If it fails, consult *Anisum stellatum*, which affects *either* side at the third rib.) Râles through the lungs and muco-purulent sputum are further symptoms of the tar.

Dr. Baruch has also made use of *Theridion* in scrofulous diseases of bones, particularly after *Sulphur, Calcarea, Lycopodium* and the ordinary remedies have failed. I think that it may even cure ozæna with caries, since it attacks the bones and so often removes the yellowish or yellowish-green, thick and offensive discharge from the nose.

LECTURE VII.

CANTHARIS.

The remedy which I propose to bring before you for study today is *Cantharis*, the so-called Spanish fly. It is my purpose to speak of the more important symptoms produced by the drug, comparing it superficially with a number of others having effects similar to it. First of all, for the sake of completeness, let me give you notes on two other drugs, the *Lytta vittata* and the *Cantharis strygosa*. The first of these is the potato-fly, not the potato-bug, the pharmacopœial name of which is *Doryphora*. The potato-fly acts much like *Cantharis* when applied to the skin. It produces first a dermatitis, which is soon followed by the formation of vesicles. The affected parts become red, almost erysipelatous in appearance. The vesicles finally rupture, leaving an ulcerated surface. Finally, death of the part may ensue.

The *Cantharis strygosa* is a species of *Cantharis*, which infests the cotton plant. This, too, has vesication for its characteristic.

There are other varieties of this *Cantharis* among which are the *C. cinerea*, *C. marginata*, *C. atrata*, *C. nutalli* and *Mycabis cichorii et Phalateria*, these last two being imported from China.

Cantharis, or Spanish fly, has long been used by allopaths as a counter-irritant; when applied to any part of the surface of the body it excites a violent inflammation. This inflammation begins, of course, with erythema, rapidly advancing to vesication. The blisters thus formed are filled with a yellowish-white serum. As the inflammation progresses they enlarge, and their contents assume a purulent character. Finally, death of the part ensues, presuming, of course, that the application is continued long enough. At other times large blisters, termed bullæ, may form. These are sometimes as large as a silver half-dollar. They are raised above the surface, and are filled with a fluid which is excoriating. *This irritating property of Cantharis is the foundation-stone of the whole proving.* The pains incident to this kind of inflammation are, of course, very severe. They are of a burning character. At times, when the nerves seem to be implicated in the inflammatory process, there will be sharp lancinating pains along their course.

But *Cantharis* is not the only drug that has these highly irritating effects when applied to the skin or taken internally.

Thus, from external use the following will, sooner or later, cause vesicles to develop on the skin: Varieties of *Cantharis, Formica;* varieties of *Rhus, Anacardium orientale et occidentale;* Ranunculous plants. as *Clematis, Ranunculus bulb., Ranunculus sceleratus, Pulsatilla, Aconite, Caltha, Helleborus, Actea spic.;* Araceæ, especially *Arum mac., Arum tri., Palladium, Pix, Terebinthina, Thuja, Nux juglans, Chininum sulph.;* several species of *Plumbago, Allium sat.;* Euphorbious plants, particularly *Croton tig., Hura, Euphorbia corol., Euphorbium offic., Mancinella, Sinapis, Piper nigrum, Capsicum, Mezereum, Thapsia garganica, Chloral, Cotura matura, Drosera, Podophyllum, Chimaphila, Oleander, Chelidonium, Cochlearia arm., Veratrum album, Camphor, Picric acid, Ammonium causticum, Calcarea caustica, Sulphur, Sulphuric acid, Kali hydrosulphuricum, Nitric acid;* Arsenic preparations, *Carbolic acid, Mercury, Cuprum arsenicosum, Antimonium tart.,* etc.

Rhus tox. and *Anacardium* cause vesication, with much redness of the skin and infiltration. The latter adds loss of appetite and other gastric symptoms as essential concomitants. The former causes red skin and numerous vesicles, surrounded with a red rim from infiltration. A well-defined advance-line of inflammation marks the progress of the disease. The predominant sensations are itching or tingling, while in *Cantharis* burning and smarting, as from salt, are leading sensations. The latter, in some cases, when topically employed, induces an eczematous eruption around the plaster, and in others the vesicated surface assumes a soft, pultaceous, almost gangrenous appearance; but the skin is not the reddish-brown of *Rhus*.

Croton tiglium gives rise to myriads of small, terribly-itching vesicles on a red base. When the genitals are attacked there is pain on urinating, and some of the blisters become large, others break, leaving a red, moist surface. The vesicles may develop into pustules, which finally break and form grayish crusts.

Hura Brasiliensis, a near relative of the former, also produces red vesicles. Both of these remedies cause a tension of the skin, a hidebound feeling, which is best confirmed in *Croton;* but *Hura* carries this feature into its vesication, for the blisters become so tense that, on opening, their serous contents fairly burst forth. A characteristic of this remedy is a sensation as of a splinter under the thumb-nails. The eruption prefers projecting portions of bone, as the skin over the malar bones.

Formica, locally applied, sets up inflammatory redness, with itching and burning, slight exudation and desquamation. The urine is albuminous and bloody, and there is much urging to urinate.

Clematis crispa is food for the Spanish fly. The *Clematis erecta* we know irritates the skin to the production of burning vesicles, which pustulate and discharge a yellowish corrosive ichor. The urine is discharged in drops, or intermittingly, from a narrowed urethra.

Ranunculus bulbosus and *Ranunculus sceleratus* act similarly. In the former the vesicles may become blue-black, or they may discharge a secretion which becomes horny. The latter raises blisters, which leave a raw surface with acrid discharge, and resembles *Cantharis* in pemphigus. In blueness *Ranunculus bulbosus* rather resembles *Lachesis*; the latter causes deep-seated bluish blisters (which appear after scratching). In horny crusts it resembles *Antimonium crudum*.

The several species of Spurge have caused vesication, and the variety called *Euphorbium officinarum* has been employed in vesicular erysipelas; red cheeks, covered with yellow vesicles as large as peas (from an application of the juice); violent fever. Like *Hura*, this plant and the *Euphorbium cyparissias* have an affinity for the malar region. *Cantharis* attacks the surface of the nose (like *Graphites*). *Euphorbia peplus* also attacks the nose, as well as the cheeks.

Mancinella is so irritating that even the water dropping on the skin from the leaves may raise blisters, but the accompanying erythema far exceeds that of *Cantharis*. It resembles the blush of scarlatina, and has been used in that disease.

Thapsia garganica, an umbelliferous plant, closely resembles *Croton*. It causes more pustules, however, and these fill rapidly with pus.

Mezereum develops numerous small vesicles, with intolerable itching; but the secretion quickly forms into thick, high scabs, from beneath which an acrid pus oozes.

Capsicum, *Camphor*, *Terebinthina*, *Pix* and *Piper nigrum* vesicate very slowly. Several of them are used rather as rubefacients. The first may be distinguished by the fact that the blisters appear on surfaces which have been wet with sweat, and the sensation is a pungent burning, while in the fly it is a smarting burning, as from salt.

Camphor, topically, causes an erysipelatous dermatitis, with bright redness, and, eventually, blisters (from concentrated solution). We generally think of it when there has been a retrocession of skin disease, with its well-known symptoms of collapse and convulsions.

Pix and *Terebinthina* cause violent itching, especially the former. The skin becomes cracked under *Pix*, with sleeplessness and bleeding when scratched.

Potash preparations favor more a papular than a vesicular eruption, the latter form being intermediate between the papule and the pustule. *Kali hydrosulphuricum* and *Kali nitricum* develop papular vesicles when locally applied. *Kali bromatum* causes vesicles about the hair follicles (from internal use). *Kali bichromicum* induces an eruption, which presents vesicles with a depressed centre; they suppurate, and on healing leave a cicatrix. *Kali hydriodicum* causes papular vesicles (from internal use), the resulting vesico-pustules contain minute quantities of Iodine. None of these, therefore, resemble the superficial blister of the fly.

Chloral is capable of producing several forms of eruption. Its vesicles are surrounded with a marked capillary hyperæmia.

Chininum sulphuricum has caused an erythematous appearance strongly resembling scarlet fever, but it also forms confluent vesicles, which ulcerate or dry into crusts. Pemphigus, also, may appear.

In pemphigus *Cantharis* compares with *Causticum, Rhus tox., Ranunculus sceleratus*, etc. The following have induced this form of eruption, and deserve a trial: *Caltha, Nitric acid, Copaiva, Sulphuric acid, Chininum sulphuricum, Carboneum oxygenisatum.*

In *Caltha* the bullæ are surrounded by a ring and itch a great deal. On the third day they are transformed into crusts.

Copaiva affects mucous membranes, then the stomach and bowels, and later the skin. A red, miliary rash forms on a red base; urticaria, pemphigus, with excessive offensive discharge.

Carboneum oxygen. is prone to excite vesication along the course of nerves (sciatic, trigeminus, etc.), and hence resembles herpes zoster, a disease which *Cantharis* has occasionally cured. It also causes "large and small vesicles of pemphigus."

Cantharis has a most remarkable affinity for the urinary organs; in fact, experience has demonstrated that nearly always when it is indicated cystic or renal symptoms are present. Marked symptoms of the kidneys and bladder may result even from the use of the drug externally. The same is true when the drug is taken internally. Let us now look at some of its symptoms. We find dull pressive pains in the region of the kidneys. At other times violent cutting, burning pains extend from the kidneys down either ureter to the bladder. The parts externally over the region of the kidneys are very sensitive to touch. There is persistent and violent urging to urinate. Often, too, these cutting pains extend along the spermatic cords to the testicles and down the penis, attended by drawing up of the testicles. At other times there is pain in the glans penis, exhibited in children by frequent pulling at the organ. This pain in the glans penis may not be of an acute nature, but may be simply an uneasy, uncomfortable sensation. When in children you notice this symptom *Cantharis* is generally indicated; at other times you may think also of *Mercurius solubilis;* of course, the symptom may be a habit which the child has been allowed to practice. That, of course, does not call for these remedies.

Coming to the bladder itself, we find here, too, extreme superficial sensitiveness over the hypogastrium (especially when the bladder is distended with urine), and almost unbearable tenesmus vesicæ. Sometimes the patient will have the desire to urinate every two or three minutes. The urine does not pass freely or copiously, but dribbles away in hot, scalding, sometimes bloody, drops, with burning, cutting pains which could not be worse if the urine were molten lead. This burning and urging continue after urination, so that the poor sufferer is really in constant torture. Exacerbations come on every few minutes as calls to urinate become too urgent to resist. The urine itself shows changes in its composition. Blood is more or less thoroughly mixed with it, according to the part of the urinary tract from which the hæmorrhage proceeds. The urine, however, is of a deep red color, independently of its containing blood, and deposits a sediment of mucus. Fibrinous casts, epithelial cells, small rolled-up membranous pieces of the lining of the parts through which it passes—the tubules of the kidney, the ureters and the bladder—are observed under the microscope.

This is the picture of the effects of *Cantharis* as they attain their maximum. From these extreme symptoms you have all grades of severity down to the slightest irritation at the neck of the bladder, with aggravation after micturition.

Now these symptoms characterize *Cantharis*, and indicate it in a variety of affections. You would expect it to be of use in inflammation of the kidneys, particularly in acute inflammation of one or the other of these organs rather than in chronic Bright's disease.

We find, too, that *Cantharis* is a valuable remedy in the passage of renal calculi, especially when the pains are very violent. It has been stated in controversy that it was nonsense to talk about relieving the pains from the passage of renal calculi by homœopathic medication. The ureter is a narrow tube and the stone is frequently large, and it is said that this cannot be passed without pain. This is a mistake. The indicated remedy may so lessen local irritability that the pain attendant on the passage of the renal calculi may be greatly modified.

Often you find *Cantharis* indicated in gravel in children when they have this irritation extending down the penis, with almost constant pulling at that organ.

Cantharis you will find indicated in acute cystitis more frequently than all other remedies put together.

It is also indicated in hæmaturia of inflammatory origin.

It also has a secondary action in producing retention of urine, an effect due to the severity of the preëxisting symptoms.

In gonorrhœa *Cantharis* is indicated *when there is most intense irritation;* not a simple discharge with the necessary burning and smarting, but with violent and painful chordee, marked sexual erethism and discharge that is purulent or bloody. It is also indicated in cases in which the disorder has been suppressed by the use of injections and the disease involves the neck of the bladder.

Now, a word as to related remedies.

Cannabis sativa is very similar to *Cantharis* in its urethral phenomena. It has the same yellow, purulent discharge from the urethra, but is more important when the discharge is thin, and there is smarting and burning on urination. There seems to be more burning and smarting under *Cannabis*, while there is more tenesmus and cutting under *Cantharis*. The glans penis is dark red and swollen. Chordee may be present. *Cannabis sativa* may be indicated in simple acute nephritis, but it is not likely to be of much use in Bright's disease of the kidneys. It has, however, drawing pain in the region of the kidneys, extending into the inguinal glands, with anxious nauseous sensation in the epigastrium.

Cannabis Indica is much used in Asiatic countries. It produces the most wonderful mental phenomena, far exceeding *Opium* in its effects. The two central points of the mental phenomena of this *Cannabis Indica* are delusions as to distance and as to time. Time and space seem to be greatly extended. For example, the patient tells you that he is hungry, that he has eaten nothing for six months, when the dishes from which he has just partaken are yet by his bedside; or, on looking out of the window he tells you that objects but a few feet off are many yards distant. But it is the urinary symptoms of *Cannabis Indica* that concern us more particularly just now. It is very similar to *Cantharis*, and is said to be even superior to that drug for gonorrhœa when the chordee is well marked. In renal disease *Cannabis* is indicated by burning, stitches, aching in the kidneys, pains when laughing; also when uræmia sets in attended by severe headache, with a sensation as if the vertex were opening and shutting. If delirium appears, it is associated with the delusions respecting time and space just mentioned.

Equisetum hyemale is a plant growing in water. It contains a large quantity of silicic acid. It acts very similarly to *Cantharis* on the kidneys and bladder. There are, however, less escape of blood and less tenesmus vesicæ than may be found under *Cantharis*. The urine is less scalding and does not contain so many fibrinous flakes. *Cantharis* is not called for so often as *Equisetum* when there is an excess of mucus in the urine. The bladder is tender and sore, with severe dull pain, which is worse after urination. There is constant desire to urinate, sometimes with a feeling of distension in the bladder and with profuse urination. During urination a burning pain is felt in the urethra. *Equisetum* has won most favor in enuresis. It has proved curative in these cases even when vesical irritation is marked, especially in women, and the urine contains blood and albumen.

Linaria is another drug which has produced and cured enuresis with frequent painful urging to urinate, causing the patient to rise at night.

Eupatorium purpureum is similar to *Equisetum* in vesical irritability of women, for which condition it was used by Dr. Richard Hughes, of England. It causes frequent and painful urging with either excessive or scanty flow of high-colored urine containing mucus.

Petroselinum, one variety of the parsley, is indicated by frequent sudden and irresistible urging to urinate. In the case of a child, he will be suddenly seized with the desire to urinate; if he cannot be gratified immediately, he will jump up and down with pain. You will find *Petroselinum* useful in gonorrhœa with this sudden urging and strangury. *Cannabis, Cantharis* and *Mercurius* all have the sudden urging to urinate, but it is strongest under *Petroselinum*.

Clematis erecta is to be selected when there is mucus in the urine, but not pus; when the urine flows by fits and starts, or the patient has to wait a long time for the urine to come, and then passes only a few drops, with intense biting and burning along the urethra, followed by a full, painless stream. *Clematis* is to be thought of in "first cases" of gonorrhœa when the inflammation develops stricture.

Conium is useful in urethral and bladder diseases when there is pus in the urine; otherwise it is like *Clematis*. It has "passage of the urine by fits and starts," cutting in the urethra after micturition, urine flows more readily while standing (*Sarsaparilla*).

Doryphora is indicated in urethritis in children under ten years of age when the trouble has been provoked by local irritation. In these cases think also of *Hyoscyamus*.

Capsicum is sometimes useful in gonorrhœa, especially in fat persons of lax fibre and of rather indolent disposition. The discharge is of a thick yellow character. The patient complains of fine stinging pains in the meatus urinarius and of stitches in the urethra between the acts of micturition.

Copaiva and *Cubeba* have been so abused by allopaths that I think we are too apt to neglect them. *Copaiva* causes a urethritis with burning at the neck of the bladder and in the urethra. The discharge is of a milky color and of corrosive character. The meatus urinarius is tumid and inflamed and sore as if wounded.

Cubeba causes cutting and constriction after micturition. The discharge is of a mucous nature. Both *Copaiva* and *Cubeba* are useful in the irritation attending thickening of the lining membrane of the bladder. Neither remedy has so violent an action as has *Cantharis*.

Thuja gives us symptoms of continued or oft-repeated gonorrhœa. The patient has continued desire to urinate. The urging is violent, yet he passes only a few drops of bloody urine at a time; or, if these do not pass, there is intense itching. The urethral discharge is thin and green. Warty excrescences appear on the genitals and about the anus. At night there are painful erections which drive away sleep. In *Cantharis* the erections prevent urination; this is not the case in *Thuja*.

Argentum nitricum follows *Cannabis* in gonorrhœa when the discharge becomes purulent and the urethra feels sore and swollen.

Mercurius solubilis and *corrosivus* follow when the discharge becomes worse at night and is green and purulent. The corrosive mercury causes the more violent tenesmus, burning and swelling, hence it is very similar to *Cantharis*. The meatus urinarius is very red. *Mercurius solubilis* has more burning between micturition than has *Cantharis*.

Chimaphila has been found useful in catarrh of the bladder caused by stones. It produces frequent urination at night with increased debility and smarting pain extending from the neck of the bladder to the end of the urethra.

In irritation of the neck of the bladder you may use a number of remedies, some of which I shall mention:

Erigeron, with or without bloody urine.

Pulsatilla is indicated when micturition is followed by cutting pains and there are pressure and soreness over the pubes.

Under *Ferrum phos.* the symptoms are worse the longer the patient stands, and better after urination.

Epigea, *Apis* and *Copaiva* should also be studied in this connection, the latter especially in old women.

Capsicum has spasmodic contracting and cutting in the neck of the bladder; *Mercurius aceticus*, cutting just at the close of urination, like *Natrum mur*.

The *Digitalis* patient finds relief on lying down, as that position relieves much of the pressure upon the neck of the bladder.

Sulphur comes in to remove the remnants of a gonorrhœa.

Ipomea nil, which is one variety of the morning-glory, was a remedy used by the late Dr. Jacob Jeanes for the passage of stone from the kidney to the bladder when he had the following symptoms present: Severe cutting pain in either renal region, extending down the ureter on the corresponding side. The distinctive feature which separates it from other remedies is that these pains excite nausea.

Hydrangea has also been used for the intense pain attending gravel and calculus.

Sarsaparilla is useful for gravel in children when they scream or cry with pain after passing urine; then there is found a grayish sand in the diaper.

Ocimum may be employed in renal colic when there is considerable hæmorrhage; when the urine not only has a brick-red sediment, as under *Pareira brava*, but contains considerable blood. It favors the right side.

Terebinthina, like *Cantharis*, has marked action on the kidneys, but it differs from the latter remedy in that the urine is always dark, cloudy and smoky, from admixture of blood. This is due to congestion of the kidneys.

Cochlearia armoracea, or the horse-radish, is a valuable drug. It produces burning and cutting in the glans penis during and after urination, with a great deal of strangury. The urine becomes thick like jelly on standing.

Then we have the *Uva ursi*. This remedy finds no equal when cystic and urethral symptoms are referable to stone in the bladder. You have, as symptomatic of the drug, burning, scalding urination; the flow of urine stops suddenly as if a stone had rolled in front of the internal orifice of the urethra. When the urine passes it is ropy from the admixture of mucus and blood. The drug seems to diminish inflammatory thickening of the cystic walls, and relieves suffering until the stone can be removed by operation.

Similar to this is *Pareira brava*, which is an excellent drug in gravel and in cystic calculus, when the patient has to get down on all fours to urinate. The tenesmus is great; the urine passes in drops; pains shoot from the kidneys down the thighs, and even into the feet; the urine deposits a copious uric acid sediment and also blood.

This brings to mind *Berberis vulgaris*. This remedy suits when there is kidney affection, with sharp stitching pains radiating from the renal region in all directions, particularly downward and forward, filling the whole pelvis with pain. There are pains in the loins and in the hips. The urine when passed is more slimy than is the *Pareira brava* urine, and deposits copiously a loamy sediment having a yellowish turbid appearance. *Berberis* is an excellent remedy in case of stone in the pelvis of the kidney or in the ureter. Now, you see the difference between the two remedies. *Pareira* has pain going down the thighs, *Berberis* only in the hips and loins.

You may expect to be called upon to use *Camphor* when strangury, retention of urine, etc., have resulted from the abuse of *Cantharis*.

In some cases *Kali nitricum* may be substituted for *Camphor* when renal symptoms have been produced by *Cantharis*.

Apis, too, is said to have relieved the cystitis caused by the Spanish fly.

Aconite frequently suits the incipiency of renal and cystic affections, which, unmodified, progress into a *Cantharis* condition. The urging to urinate, the dysuria and hæmaturia are accompanied by an anxious restlessness and high fever altogether different from the expression of *Cantharis*.

Just as *Cantharis* acts on the tissues, producing inflammation, so does it excite the brain Thus we find the patient violent at times, with paroxysms of rage, tearing his clothing and biting at anyone who approaches him. He barks like a dog. The slightest touch aggravates the symptoms, as does also any dazzling object, as a looking-glass or glass of water. These symptoms greatly resemble those of hydrophobia.

They also point to *Cantharis* as a remedy useful in puerperal convulsions and in inflammation of the brain. The eyes are bright, the pupils widely dilated, and the face is pale or yellowish, and bears an expression of deep-seated suffering.

These symptoms, indicative of inflammatory action in and about the brain and meninges, find their nearest concordant in *Belladonna*, which has the majority of the symptoms above mentioned, if not all of them. Even the intolerance of water is present under *Belladonna*. The difference between the two remedies is found in the expression of the face, *Belladonna* having a bright-red face with throbbing carotids; *Cantharis* usually exhibiting a face that is pale, yellow and wrinkled, with a constant frown and an expression of extreme suffering. When *Cantharis* is the remedy dysuria is almost always present.

Camphor and *Arsenicum* are also nearly related to *Cantharis*. In all three of these drugs the anxiety, the restlessness and the expression of suffering on the face indicate the severity of the disease and betoken a sinking of the vital forces.

Arsenicum closely resembles *Cantharis* in violent inflammations, with intense burning, agony, thirst and subsequent collapse. The two drugs may also meet in uræmia. *Arsenicum*, however, lacks the sexual erethism, and its delirium is associated with a tendency to self-mutilation or to suicide. The patient exhibits fear of death, and restlessness often alternates with the stupor.

Camphor, like *Cantharis*, causes delirium, convulsions, sexual mania, priapism, strangury, internal burning with external coldness, hyperæmia or inflammation of internal parts, as brain, stomach, bladder, etc. The coldness and the sinking of the vital forces in *Camphor* are usually regarded as its most characteristic effects, the symptoms of excitement being reactionary. In *Cantharis*, on the contrary, the principal effects are those of excitement, coldness expressing the result of its prolonged or continued action. Practically, you may decide upon *Camphor* when delirium, mania or convulsions exist with coldness and extreme prostration, especially if caused by a suppressed eruption.

On the mucous surfaces we find that *Cantharis* causes just as violent an inflammation as it does on the skin. It is indicated in inflammation of the throat of a diphtheritic character, accompanied by severe burning and raw feeling in the throat, great constriction of the throat and larynx, amounting almost to suffocation, on any attempt to swallow water. Even the bladder symptoms are aggravated by water. It seems as if the sight or sound of water brings about a constriction of the sphincter muscles. *Cantharis* has been used very successfully in diphtheria when these throat symptoms and the dysuria were present, and when the debility was very marked.

While *Belladonna* has constriction of the throat, worse from swallowing liquids, and intense inflammation of the throat, it lacks the burning, vesication, etc., so characteristic of the Spanish fly.

Much more nearly related to *Cantharis* in its throat symptoms are *Mercurius corrosivus*, *Arsenicum*, *Arum triphyllum*, *Diffenbachia* and *Capsicum*.

The first is all but identical in symptoms; the distinctive mercurial features must decide, although *Mercurius cor.* causes more swelling, especially of the tongue. Deep ulcers form, rather than the extensive vesication of *Cantharis*.

Arum triphyllum is distinguished by the sore, cracked corners of the mouth and tongue, the acrid coryza and the excoriating saliva.

Diffenbachia has caused an intense stomatitis with blisters and burning.

Capsicum relieves burning vesicles; mouth and throat swollen and dark, constriction of the throat, flat ulcers; worse *between* the acts of swallowing.

Cinnabar is also used in scarlatina, but the mucus from the posterior nares is dirty yellow, ropy, and there is dryness of the throat, waking the patient at night.

Apis bears some resemblance to *Cantharis* in erysipelatous states of the mouth and throat, and in diphtheria; but the debility in the latter condition is early in *Apis*, while it is the sequel only in *Cantharis*.

In the alimentary tract we find *Cantharis* producing inflammation of the stomach, of the same character as the symptoms already mentioned, rawness, great thirst with aversion to drinks, and vomiting.

It is of use in dysentery. The discharges are bloody and slimy, and are mixed with flakes that look like scrapings of the intestines. These, I believe, are not really portions of the bowel or pieces of the mucous lining, but are fibrinous formations, resulting from the inflammation. Tenesmus is marked and is almost always associated with dysuria. The pains in the abdomen are colic-like, doubling the patient up; they are of a cutting, burning, griping, wandering character.

In dysentery *Cantharis* has several concordant remedies. One of these is *Colocynth*, which has colicky pains, doubling the patient up. The stools are bloody and slimy, and are made worse by any attempt to eat or drink. They also contain the so-called scrapings of the intestines. *Colocynth* differs from *Cantharis* in that the colicky pains cease after stool, and the patient is relieved by bending double and by pressing firmly against the abdomen. Looking at the two remedies from a pathological standpoint, *Cantharis* has more inflammation and *Colocynth* more nervous symptoms.

Another remedy very similar to *Cantharis* is *Colchicum*. This remedy has tympanitic distension of the abdomen. The discharges from the bowels are composed of white jelly-like lumps, and are followed by violent tenesmus and constriction of the anus, tormenting the patient more than the urging during stool.

Another concordant remedy is *Capsicum*, which is good for dysentery occurring in moist weather. It is best indicated in stout flabby persons. The pains and other symptoms are increased by the slightest draft of either warm or cold air. The drinking of water causes shuddering and increases the pains.

Sulphur you will find best adapted to chronic or persistent cases, especially when the tenesmus continues from one evacuation to another, like *Nux vom.*, or when the bleeding and tenesmus have abated but the stools are still slimy with frequent sudden urging.

Zincum sulphuricum has several times cured subacute cases of dysentery. The pains are referred to the sides of the abdomen, probably in the colon.

Kali bichromicum follows *Cantharis* when, though the "scrapings" continue, the discharges become more jelly-like.

We have yet to speak of the action of *Cantharis* on the sexual organs. *Cantharis* inflames the sexual appetite, producing a violent, almost insatiable, desire for coitus, with erections so violent and so persistent as to amount to priapism; even sexual intercourse does not always reduce the erections. These symptoms call for the drug in chordee during the course of gonorrhœa. They also point to its use for uncontrollable passion, whether the result of mental disease or not.

This priapism of *Cantharis* should not be confounded with that of

Picric acid. Under this remedy the priapism is associated with some spinal disease, such as myelitis, meningitis or locomotor ataxia. Erections are violent and the penis is distended almost to bursting.

Cantharis also acts on the female genital organs, producing nymphomania, for which condition it may be a useful remedy.

We may also make use of *Cantharis* in labor. The drug has the property of expelling moles and other foreign materials from the uterus. We may make use of this effect in cases of retained placenta, either after labor at full term or after a miscarriage.

Cantharis is a useful remedy in erysipelas, especially of the vesicular form. The erysipelatous inflammation begins on the nose, either with or without vesicles. It then spreads to one or the other cheek, with the formation of vesicles which break and discharge an excoriating fluid.

Graphites also has erysipelas commencing on the nose, but it is better adapted to chronic cases.

Cantharis should be remembered as of use in burns. It is remarkable what this remedy will do in allaying the painful symptoms and accelerating the repair of affected surfaces. It may be given internally in potency and applied locally at the same time. If administered early enough in slight burns, the formation of blisters may sometimes be prevented.

In burns you may compare *Cantharis* lotion with *Sapo soda*, *Soda bicarb.*, *Arsenicum* and *Carbolic acid*—the last named when the affected parts ulcerate.

LECTURE VIII.

HYMENOPTERA.

From the order Hymenoptera we derive *Apis mellifica*, *Vespa crabro*, *Formica rufa* and *Bombus*. The local effects of the poisons from these insects are well known. The skin becomes red and swollen, with burning pain; finally, even sloughing may ensue. In susceptible persons, or after the injection of considerable quantities of the poison, general symptoms may develop, such as fainting, prostration, chills and coldness; great restlessness, or insensibility, and even death may result.

The stings of certain ants (*Formica*, not *Termites*, which are neuropterous) contain a poison, the chief ingredient of which is called *Formic acid*. This highly irritating acid is also found in the glands attached to the hairs of stinging nettles, in some caterpillars and in old oil of turpentine.

Apis Mellifica.

For this remedy we have two names, according to the manner in which the preparation is made. It is either *Apis mellifica*, the honey-bearing bee, or *Apium virus*, the poison of bees. The original preparations of the remedy were made in the following manner: A large white dish was placed under a bell jar, in which there was a perforation through which a stick was inserted. Several hundred bees were then placed beneath the jar. The stick was then moved about, and, irritating the bees, caused them to sting the jar and the dish. After a while the bees were allowed to escape, and on the bell jar and plate were seen numerous specks. Alcohol was poured over these, and thus was obtained a powerful extract of the poison of the bee. This is *Apium virus*. Subsequently the whole bee was used. Triturations were made of the entire insect. Thus we obtain *Apis mellifica*. The symptoms of the two preparations have not been separated.

Apis mellifica is an invaluable acquisition to our Materia Medica. In order to understand its symptomatology let us look at its toxicology. Take, if you choose, a sting on the hand or finger as an illustration. Just after the sting, which causes a sharp sticking or burning pain, there commences, very promptly, swelling of the part, with extreme soreness. The part feels as if it had been bruised or pounded. The swelling is at first of a rosy pinkish hue. It spreads very rapidly; the pains become intense. They are of a burning, stinging or shooting character, seldom throbbing. Heat of the part increases with the burning and stinging pains. This may end very speedily in resolution or it may go on. If it pursues the latter course, you will notice that this rosy appearance becomes more intense, in fact, assumes an erysipelatous appearance. Still later, it changes its color and takes on a pale but bluish hue, and the swelling pits on pressure, showing that the parts are œdematous. After a while, if the condition of the system is such as to permit it, gangrene of the part takes place.

Experience teaches us that some such dermal or cellular symptoms are usually present in every case for which *Apis* is the remedy. They, therefore, deserve to be emphasized. The soreness is as important as the more frequently described burning, stinging pains, and varies from a bruised, sore feeling to an exquisite sensitiveness to contact. The swelling is the result of a rapid serous effusion into the cellular tissues. It is a universal symptom.

The inflammation produced by *Apis* is, therefore, not of a sthenic type. It is not, for instance, such as would be cured by *Aconite*, with sudden swelling of the part coming on rapidly and ending in resolution; nor is it such as would be cured by *Belladonna*, with bright red swelling accompanied by throbbing pains and ending either in resolution or suppuration. The *Apis* inflammation is distinctly asthenic, with whitish discoloration and a tendency to gangrene and destruction of tissue. In one case, where the sting was on the hand, the patient suffered also from a carbuncle on the back of the neck.

The vitality is speedily and sometimes alarmingly reduced by the action of *Apis*. This is shown in the severe prostration, desire to lie down, deathly faint feeling premonition of approaching death, nervous trembling, coldness and loss of consciousness, especially in eruptive diseases. The heart is weak, beats slowly or almost imperceptibly, with pulselessness at the wrists.

In the majority of cases calling for *Apis* the nervous system is irritated notwithstanding the accompanying prostration. The patient is excitable and dances with excessive joyousness; she laughs at the greatest misfortune as she would at a comedy; she is always changing her occupation, and will not keep steadily at anything.

As will be inferred from the symptoms mentioned, *Apis* may be employed in states of mind resembling hysteria. The fidgetiness, restlessness, excitability and ill-timed laughter, together with fickleness at work, have led to its successful use for nervous girls. In addition, it has been observed that they are awkward, dropping things and then laughing in a silly way at their clumsiness. The sexual passion is too active, and they are prone to jealousy.

The confusion of mind and unconsciousness just noted indicate the remedy in severe adynamic forms of disease, such as malignant scarlatina, diphtheria, typhoid fever, etc. A complete stupor after apoplexy is said to have yielded to *Apis* when *Opium* failed.

In scarlatina the fever runs high, and the attending restlessness is one of nervous agitation. The mouth and throat are very red, with blisters on the borders of the tongue, and swollen puffy fauces; there are burning, stinging pains and a scalded, raw feeling in the mouth and throat. The skin pricks as from needles, the rash being interspersed with a miliary eruption. There is always puffiness of some part of the surface. Prostration comes on early, with scanty or suppressed urine, high fever and drowsiness.

In meningitis or in meningeal irritation *Apis* holds a prominent position as a curative agent. It is often the remedy, no matter what the ailment, when shrill outcries in sleep lead to the suspicion of cerebral irritation. Such cases frequently begin with the nervous fidgetiness so characteristic of the bee poison, and advance to more serious conditions. In tubercular meningitis, or in acute cerebral effusions, a suppressed or undeveloped eruption is a good guide to the choice of *Apis*.

We may profitably compare *Apis* here with *Belladonna*, *Helleborus*, *Arsenicum*, *Bryonia*, *Zincum*, *Sulphur*, *Cuprum*, *Glonoine*, *Lachesis*, *Rhus tox.*, *Hyoscyamus*, *Natrum mur.*, *Bovista*, etc.

Belladonna is doubtless frequently employed when *Apis* would suit better. A little care, however, will enable the practitioner to distinguish the fidgety nervousness of the latter from the more intense cerebral irritation of the former. The congestions of *Belladonna* are more violent, with throbbing of the carotids, injected red eyes, and drowsiness broken by starts and frightened outcries. The adynamia is much less than in *Apis*. If the disease is scarlatina, the rash is smooth and bright red, but not miliary. The skin is hot and the face red, or, in some cases, pale; but not pale and œdematous as in *Apis*. The cervical glands may be swollen, but there is not the cellular infiltration with an erysipelatous blush, as in the bee-poison.

If there is meningeal irritation, *Belladonna* is needed when the congestive symptoms are intense; *Apis*, when the nervous agitation predominates, with the shrill cry, which betokens stabbing, piercing pains or excitement. In meningitis *Belladonna* is decreasingly indicated as the symptoms of effusion increase, while *Apis* is increasingly indicated as long as symptoms of irritation obtain and the cephalic cry is marked.

Helleborus claims precedence when the irritation of *Apis* gives place to mental torpor, with want of reaction. The forehead is wrinkled, the pupils dilated, and the lower jaw tends to drop; the sopor is complete. There are automatic motions of one arm and one leg; the forehead is bathed in cold sweat. In such cases *Helleborus* may bring about reaction so that another remedy will cure. In typhoid fever they differ widely. *Apis*, although it has great weakness, apathy and stupor, has a dry, blistered tongue and exquisite soreness of the abdomen. *Helleborus* has complete sensorial apathy, dark, sooty nostrils, slow pulse, and no response to touch or pressure.

Bryonia bears some slight resemblance to *Apis*, especially as it may be needed, like the latter, for cerebral effusions following suppressed exanthemata. The sensorium is benumbed, but the senses are not so perverted as in either *Apis* or *Helleborus*. There is a constant chewing motion; the face is dark red, the lips parched; when offered a drink it is taken hastily and impatiently. If the child is moved, it screams with pain. Later, when the sensorial depression amounts to sopor, *Helleborus* follows well, even if the chewing motion and hasty drinking continue. *Apis* follows if the sopor is accompanied by a more shrill cephalic cry than in either of the other remedies.

Cuprum compares with *Apis* when meningitis results from a suppressed exanthem, but the symptoms are very diverse. *Cuprum* causes loud screaming, followed by violent convulsions; the thumbs are clenched, and the face is pale with blue lips; the eyeballs are constantly rotating. If convulsions occur in the *Apis* case, they are less violent, consisting of restlessness and twitching of one-half of the body; the other half is lame and trembles.

Much more closely related in suppressed eruptions is *Sulphur*. The two follow each other well.

Glonoine, like *Apis*, has the cephalic cry; there is a sensation as if the head were enormously expanded. Spasmodic vomiting of cerebral origin is most prominent in the former, as is also intense congestion and throbbing.

Zincum produces cerebral irritation; the child awakes with fear, rolls the head; cries out and starts in sleep. There is constant fidgety motion of the feet. The drug is indicated in anæmic children who are too enervated to develop an exanthem. In typhoid states the prostration is very great, with impending cerebral paralysis. Unconsciousness develops, with blue hands and feet, coldness, weak pulse: lower jaw dropped. Here the *Oxide* has been successfully employed.

Rhus tox., though incompatible with *Apis*, has many similar symptoms. In scarlatina, for instance, both suit in adynamia, swollen throat, erysipelatous inflammation of the skin of the neck, miliary rash, drowsiness and œdema. In *Rhus*, however, the eruption is darker, the erysipelas dusky red, and there is great bodily restlessness —not the fidgetiness of *Apis*.

Arsenicum is similar to *Apis* in many respects. Both have anxious change of place, fear of death, restlessness, great weakness. (See also in several instances below.) Irritability of mind occurs in both, but it is more an anxiety and fear in *Arsenicum;* more a nervous restlessness in *Apis*.

If they meet in cerebral affections, as possibly they may, especially in hydrocephaloid, *Arsenicum* is to be selected by hot skin, pale and hot face. The child lies in a stupor; suddenly it twists its mouth and a jerk goes through the body; or the child lies as if dead, with half-open eyes, dried mucus on the conjunctivæ, and no response to touch upon the eyelids.

Hyoscyamus and *Lachesis* are similar in jealousy.

Natrum mur., *Bovista*, *Lachesis*, *Æthusa*, *Ignatia*, *Nux vom.* have awkwardness; the first is most similar to *Apis*.

I have already hinted that *Apis* may be of use in dropsies. The symptoms calling for it are briefly these. In general dropsies we find it indicated by the peculiar appearance of the surface of the body. The skin has a transparent, waxen look, with a whitish or perhaps slightly yellowish tinge. The urine is scanty, and there is almost always absence of thirst. The characteristic symptoms are the transparency of the skin and the thirstlessness. Now as to cause. *Apis* is especially useful in dropsies of renal origin, whether the result of scarlatina or not. The urine is scanty and highly albuminous, and contains casts of the uriniferous tubules. There is a swelling about the eyelids. The surface of the body feels sore and bruised; in some cases the pain is of a burning character. If the dropsy is of cardiac origin, the feet are œdematous, especially after walking. This is attended with almost intolerable soreness and burning.

Even when the dropsy has invaded the chest and we have hydrothorax *Apis* may be the remedy, especially when the trouble is of cardiac origin. The patient is unable to lie down. He has the same constrictive feeling about the chest that we find under *Lachesis*. He has a dry cough, which seems to start from some place in the trachea or larynx, usually the trachea, the cough not ceasing until a small quantity of phlegm is loosened. Thus far the remedy is exactly like *Lachesis*. But *Apis* has, in addition to these symptoms, a mental symptom which comes from the chest, namely, a constant feeling as though he could not live. It is not a feeling of dyspnœa, but appears to be a sort of anguish of mind; the patient cannot understand how it would be possible for him to get another breath, so great is this suffocative feeling. Associated with these chest symptoms, the patient often has a strange feeling as though he were going to die, but there is not the intense fear and sthenic fever of *Aconite*, nor the great restlessness of *Arsenicum*, but more of a fidgety anxiety.

In pleuritis with exudation *Apis* is one of the best remedies we have to bring about absorption of the fluid. *Apis* and *Sulphur* will cure the majority of these cases.

Apis also acts on the synovial membranes, giving a perfect picture of synovitis, particularly when it affects the knee. It is indicated when there are sharp, lancinating, stinging pains shooting through the joint, with aggravation from the slightest motion.

Bryonia affects the joints and their synovial membranes, but the pains are stitching in character, with tension, and they are better from the warmth of the bed, while the *Apis* pains are better from cold applications.

Iodine is useful in dropsy of the knee, and has followed *Apis* well, especially in scrofulous children (compare also *Kali iod.*).

We have still another form of dropsy in which *Apis* is a remedy, namely, dropsy of the brain, a condition which used to be called hydrocephalus. It is not so often indicated in true hydrocephalus, that is, when from some mechanical cause there is inflammation set up in the membranes of the brain, followed by accumulation of serum; but it is in tubercular meningitis that this remedy is useful. *Apis* is here indicated in the first stage. The symptoms which call for it are these. The child bores its head backward into the pillow, and rolls it from side to side; every little while the child arouses from sleep with a shrill, piercing cry. This peculiar shriek is due to pain. One side of the body twitches and the other lies as if paralyzed. Strabismus is usually present. The pulse is rapid and weak, and the urine scanty. There is no remedy which can do any good in this stage if *Apis* does not. *Apis* has a peculiarity which I should mention, and that is slowness of action. Sometimes you will have to wait three or four days before you notice any effects from its administration. The favorable action of the remedy is first shown by increased flow of urine.

In dropsies, *Apis* may be compared first of all with *Arsenicum*, which has the same transparency of the skin, and is also of use in dropsies of renal, cardiac or hepatic origin. The differences between the two remedies are these. *Arsenicum* has intolerable thirst, but the patient usually drinks only a small quantity at a time, because water annoys the stomach. Eating and drinking both cause vomiting. I have seen cases in which even a single teaspoonful of medicine provoked vomiting. The patient exhibits marked restlessness.

Another remedy for comparison is *Apocynum canabinum*. This is much used in the West for general dropsies, swelling of any part of the body, ascites, hydrothorax, etc., usually without any organic disease as a cause. The patient cannot tolerate any food. Food or water is immediately ejected. There is a sunken, gone, exhausted feeling at the pit of the stomach.

The next remedy similar to *Apis* is *Acetic acid*. This is useful in dropsies when the face and also the limbs have this waxen or alabaster appearance. It is especially indicated when the lower parts of the body, that is, the abdomen and limbs, are swollen, hence it is useful in ascites. Thus far it is similar to *Apis*. But it has thirst, which *Apis* has not, and gastric disturbance is almost always present; sour belching, water-brash and diarrhœa. *Acetic acid* is an undeservedly neglected remedy in dropsy. You see how it stands between *Apis* and *Arsenicum*. It differs from both of these remedies in the preponderance of gastric symptoms.

In hydrocephalus, the most similar remedy to *Apis* in the stage of exudation is *Sulphur*. *Sulphur* is indicated more on general principles than for its particular affinity for the meninges. Tubercular meningitis cannot occur in an otherwise healthy child. There must be a diathesis at the bottom of the trouble. *Sulphur* helps in the same stage as *Apis* when *Apis* fails to bring about a reaction, particularly when the child is scrofulous and has other *Sulphur* symptoms The child lies in a stupor, with cold sweat on the forehead, with jerking of the limbs, particularly of the legs, with spasms of the big toes and sometimes of the thumbs also. The urine is suppressed. *Sulphur* is all the more indicated if there has been a retrocession of some eruption before the disease displayed itself.

Helleborus is also similar to *Apis* in hydrocephalus. *Apis* is useful while there is still some irritation of the brain, as indicated by the cephalic cry. *Helleborus* comes in when torpor predominates and the child lies wholly unconscious. The eyes do not react to light. The urine is suppressed. There is automatic motion of one side of the body. You will notice, too, a peculiar corrugation of the muscles of the forehead, particularly the occipito-frontalis. In milder cases, before the stupor is profound, you will find *Helleborus* indicated by these symptoms. This corrugation of the muscles of the forehead is present, together with a constant chewing motion of the mouth. The child seems to have no wants. It asks for nothing; yet, when given water, it drinks with avidity.

Now, a word respecting the difference between *Belladonna* and *Apis*. *Belladonna* is not usually indicated in tubercular meningitis. It is the remedy above all others for simple meningitis, but not for the tubercular form of the disease. *Belladonna* has the very essence of acuteness in its symptomatology. Every symptom appears suddenly and with great intensity. But tubercular meningitis is a slowly developed disease. If the premonitory symptoms are violent, however, you may use *Belladonna* in tubercular meningitis in the stage of hyperæmia with acute pains, restless tossing about, crying out in sleep, and boring the head into the pillow; but it ceases to be a remedy when the exudation is established. The range of action of *Belladonna* is at an end when that of *Apis* begins.

There is another remedy which sometimes comes in between *Belladonna* and *Apis*, and that is *Bryonia*, which acts on serous membranes, causing copious exudation. It is indicated after *Belladonna*. The child becomes more stupid from increased pressure on the brain. The face suddenly flushes and then pales, usually a bad symptom. The child cries out, particularly when moved, even the least bit; this is a characteristic symptom. The abdomen is distended and the tongue is usually coated white down the middle. So much for *Apis* and its concordant remedies in dropsies.

The next use we may make of *Apis* is in erysipelas. It is useful particularly in erysipelas of the face, when the eruption commences under or about the right eye, and spreads thence across the face to the left side, the parts quickly becoming œdematous, and at first assuming a pinkish rosy hue. The soreness soon becomes severe, and burning stinging pains follow. There is high fever, with dry skin and usually no thirst. Now, if the disease is not checked, and the face assumes a purplish livid hue, as in phlegmonous cases, in which the inflammation involves the deeper structures, causing destruction of tissue, *Apis* may still be the remedy.

There are several concordant remedies in erysipelas. First of all, *Belladonna*. The difference lies in this: *Belladonna* is required when the swelling of the face is smooth, bright red, streaked red, or, from intensity, deep dark red. There is not much tendency to œdema or to the formation of vesicles. The pains are always acute, with throbbing in the affected parts. The brain almost always sympathizes markedly, causing throbbing in the head and visions as soon as the patient closes his eyes. The patient jerks in his sleep. The pulse is full and hard.

Another remedy, more similar to *Apis* even than *Belladonna*, is *Rhus tox*. You should be particular in differentiating these two remedies, because they are inimical, and one cannot be given after the other. Under *Rhus tox.* the color of the face is dusky red and not the bright red of *Belladonna*, nor the rosy or purplish livid hue of *Apis*. There is almost always a formation of blisters, which burn and sting. They are distinguished from those of *Apis* by the preponderance of itching. Under *Rhus tox.* the disease usually travels from left to right when attacking the face. *Apis* stands between *Rhus* and *Belladonna* in nervousness, partaking somewhat of the former's restlessness, with the latter's cerebral excitement. Neither produces exactly the livid or blue-red hue noticed in some *Apis* cases. Here *Lachesis* is nearest. The other symptoms will enable you to decide.

When the nose is mainly attacked *Apis* compares with *Cantharis*, but the latter has larger blisters and more burning.

When the face, after a spell of erysipelas, is sensitive to cold, compare *Rhus tox., Belladonna, Hepar, Silicea, Sulphur*, etc.

Apis may be of use in urticaria when there suddenly appear on the surface of the body long pinkish-white blotches raised above the skin. The itching, burning and stinging are almost intolerable. The eruption may come as a result of cold or during the course of intermittent fever.

Here *Apis* is similar to *Arsenicum*, which also produces hives, and to *Urtica urens*. This latter remedy is indicated in hives when the welts are smaller than in *Apis*. The itching and burning are intolerable. It is especially indicated when the disease has been produced by eating shellfish.

Terebinthina and *Copaiva* are also useful in urticaria after eating shellfish.

Kali bromatum is indicated when the hives occur with nervous diseases.

Rhus tox. is to be thought of when they are an accompaniment of ague or rheumatism.

Bovista is required when they are attended with diarrhœa, the stools being followed by tenesmus and burning.

Pulsatilla comes in when the hives are of gastric or uterine origin.

Calcarea ostrearum is especially suited to chronic cases, and *Sepia* and *Rumex* are indicated when the trouble is worse in the open air, the latter especially if worse while undressing.

Apis may also be given in variola when there are intense itching and swelling.

Apis may be used in rheumatism, whether of articular or muscular origin, but it is more frequently indicated in the articular type, commonly called acute inflammatory rheumatism. The affected parts feel very stiff and exceedingly sensitive to pressure. There is often a sensation of numbness. The joint or joints affected are swollen and give the patient a kind of "stretched-tight feeling." The swelling is rather pale red in color, and some fluctuation may be detected about the joint. There are burning, stinging pains, worse on any motion.

Apis has often been successfully employed in paralysis following devitalizing affections, such as diphtheria or typhoid fever, and also when meningeal effusions remain after inflammations. In all such cases suppressed or preëxisting exanthemata constitute a leading indication for the 'bee-poison, and the re-appearance of skin symptoms calls for its discontinuance as long as the improvement thus instituted lasts. *Sulphur* is a great aid here.

In these cases of prostration the patient is either nervous, restless and oversensitive, or hot and drowsy, whether thirsty or not.

Apis produces an intermitting type of fever, and is therefore of service when this type is found in the sick. The chill occurs characteristically at 3 P. M., and is accompanied by thirst and an oppression of the chest as if it were too full, which may be actually the case on account of congestion of the thoracic viscera. The chill is worse in the warmth. It is followed by burning heat of the whole body, with an increase of the oppressive feeling of the chest, drowsiness, but usually no thirst, and the warmth of the room becomes intolerable. Then comes the sweat, which may, however, be imperfect. There is never any thirst during the sweat. This is characteristic.

During the apyrexia many characteristic symptoms are present. The patient often complains of pains under the ribs on either side. The feet are swollen and œdematous, the skin is sallow or waxen, the urine is scanty, and urticaria breaks out. Such symptoms are found in rather severe forms of this affection when excessive use of quinine has spoiled the case, and in chronic forms which have undermined the general health and produced disease of the liver, spleen, etc.

The most similar concordant of *Apis* here is *Natrum mur.* This is indicated in exactly the same type of intermittent fever as *Apis;* the chief difference between the two remedies lies in the time of appearance of the chill; at ten o'clock in the morning in the case of *Natrum mur.*, and at three o'clock in the afternoon in the case of *Apis.*

In typhoid types of fever *Apis* is to be selected primarily by the mental state. The delirium is not of an active type; the patient lies in a stupor with muttering; the face is either flushed red, or, more frequently, pale and waxen, wearing a look of anxiety as from visceral disease or a happy expression. The skin in this type of fever is burning hot in some places, while in others it is unnaturally cool; it is almost always dry; should there be sweat it is usually of a transient character; the prostration is so great that the patient slides down in bed; he cannot exercise sufficient muscular force to retain his position on the pillow. The tongue is dry, cracked and red, and, like that of *Lachesis*, it catches on the teeth when the attempt is made to protrude it, and it trembles; there is often a whitish or darker coating on the dorsum of the tongue, while the edges, especially about the tip, are red and covered with little blisters and vesicles. Very important is the bruised soreness of the swollen abdomen.

In these cases *Apis* resembles *Muriatic acid*, which has this prostration, but with the characteristic acid diathesis.

In scarlatina most of the indications for *Apis* have already been given. Here, too, we find the same defective effort on the part of nature to produce a fever. The body is very hot in some places and cool in others. The rash is deep-red in color, very much like that of *Belladonna*, but differing from that remedy, you remember, in the presence of this miliary eruption which *Belladonna* does not have. The child is drowsy, sleeping most of the time, or he is drowsy but cannot sleep. This symptom you must remember because it is identical thus far with one of *Belladonna*. Associated with this sleepy or wakeful state the patient is fidgety and restless. You notice, too, that he is peevish, and manifests every symptom of being very irritable.

This restless state of *Apis* must be distinguished from those of *Rhus tox.* and *Belladonna*. In *Rhus tox* it is a general restless state of the whole body, and of the mind as well. The patient lies first on one side and then moves to the other, but is not affected with anxiety as in *Arsenicum*. In *Apis* the restlessness or desire to move comes from a general nervous feeling.

The inability to go to sleep in *Belladonna* comes from inflammation or congestion of the brain The hyperæmia produces this drowsy state, and the brain is so exhausted that the patient cannot go to sleep.

In addition to the symptoms already mentioned for scarlatina, we have *Apis* further indicated when the condition advances to effusion of serum about the brain. The throat symptoms are unimportant. You often find patches on the tonsils. The throat inside is swollen and rosy-red, while externally it is engorged, with an erysipelatous blush to it. *Apis* may also be used late in the disease for the sequelæ—that is, when the kidneys become affected and dropsy appears with albuminuria.

Again, we find *Apis* of service in diphtheria. The disease advances so insidiously that its presence is not suspected, or, from the very beginning the child is thoroughly prostrated, with high fever and drowsiness. The pulse is rapid, but not strong. At first the throat has a varnished appearance, as though the tonsils and fauces were coated with a glossy red varnish. The membrane forms on either tonsil, oftener on the right than on the left, and it is thick, looking like wash-leather. The tongue is often swollen, so that the child can scarcely swallow. If the child is old enough, he will complain of a feeling of fulness in the throat which necessitates swallowing, but makes it very difficult. The explanation of this is found in the next symptom, that is, the uvula hangs down like a sac of water, and consequently there is a feeling of fulness. If you examine the throat thoroughly, you will find the rim of the glottis swollen, red and œdematous, and breathing is labored owing to the narrowing of the entrance of the larynx. In some of these cases the breath is very fœtid, while in others there is little or no fœtor. In still other cases you will find as characteristic of *Apis* a red rash over the surface of the body, making the case appear like one of scarlatina. The external throat is swollen and erysipelatous. The above symptoms may indicate *Apis* in non-diphtheritic œdema of the glottis also.

Now, there are several remedies similar to *Apis* in diphtheria. One of them is *Arsenicum*. *Arsenicum* is indicated, as you might expect, in rather severe cases of diphtheria when the throat is very much swollen inside and outside, the membrane has a dark hue, and there is great fœtor. There is a thin, excoriating discharge from the nose. The throat is œdematous, just as it is in *Apis;* the patient is restless, especially after midnight; the urine is scanty, and the bowels are either constipated or else there is an offensive, watery diarrhœa.

In still other cases, when, despite the dark purplish hue of the throat, and the marked swelling and great prostration, there is not much pain, *Natrum arsenicosum* is the remedy. Here, also, the uvula is infiltrated with fluid.

Still another remedy is *Kali permanganatum*. This remedy, which is seldom used in the high potencies, is indicated when the throat inside and outside is swollen and œdematous, the breath is horribly offensive, and a thin discharge issues from the nose. The great characteristic is the extreme fœtor.

Apis causes an irritation of the mucous lining of the larynx and trachea, and also soreness in the chest-walls.

It has been found most useful when laryngeal symptoms accompany erysipelas, œdema of the throat, glottis, or larynx, or suppression of eruptions; less often in simple laryngitis or laryngeal catarrh.

Difficult breathing, and especially the unique symptom, "he does not see how he can get another breath," has led to the successful employment of the drug in hydrothorax, hydropericardium, œdema pulmonum and asthma.

The lancinating, darting pains, palpitation, orthopnœa, etc., render *Apis* valuable in cardiac inflammations and dropsy. The essential symptoms seem to be œdema or sudden mucous swelling, dyspnœa, sudden, lancinating or stinging pains, restlessness and anxiety.

Compare: *Lachesis, Arsenicum, Sulphur, Belladonna, Kali carb., Spigelia, Digitalis, Asparagus, Apocynum cannabinum.*

Arsenicum and *Apis* have many resemblances. So apparently alike are the restlessness, changing of place, and dyspnœa, that one remedy is often given when the other should be. The best distinction lies in the fidgety restlessness peculiar to *Apis*. If dropsy obtains, both may be needed in pale, tensely swollen limbs, but *Apis* often has redness, itching or an erysipelatous condition present, as well as thirstlessness.

Belladonna is too often mistaken for *Apis* in laryngeal affections. The latter has more œdematous swelling, with consequent dyspnœa; the former more spasmodic constriction.

In cardiac affections *Arsenicum, Apocynum cannabinum, Digitalis*, and *Asparagus* bear some similarity to *Apis*, especially in great debility and dropsy. *Apocynum cannabinum* is needed when the pulse is small and weak, the heart-beat irregular, now weak, now stronger; and there is sinking at the epigastrium. *Asparagus* suits in the aged, with weak pulse and pain about the left acromion. *Digitalis* causes a doughy appearance of the skin; the pulse is slow or weak, quickening with every bodily movement; a gone, deathly sick feeling develops in the epigastrium soon after eating.

The cough of *Apis* is frequently encountered in cases where this remedy is needed. It resembles, more or less, *Lachesis, Carbo veg., Rumex, Belladonna, Chamomilla, Crotalus horridus, Nux vomica, Bryonia, Ignatia, Arsenicum, Hyoscyamus.*

Lachesis, Nux vom., Bryonia and *Hyoscyamus* agree in adherent mucus.

But *Lachesis* has intolerance of touch, even clothing, about the neck, a symptom not marked in *Apis*, except with the sense of suffocation.

Rumex has a teasing, persistent cough, aggravated by cool air, or by anything which increases the volume or rapidity of the inspired air.

Chamomilla differs mentally.

Nux vomica cures cough from adherent mucus high up in the trachea; but there is a rough, scraped feeling in the throat.

Bryonia adds epigastric irritation to the suprasternal, and the pains in the trachea and chest-walls are sharp, stitching, as well as bruised, aching.

Ignatia induces a nervous cough, and the more the patient coughs, the more annoying is the irritation.

Arsenicum causes more of a burning tickling, referred to the suprasternal fossa; but since it so often concurs with *Apis*, it should be compared with the latter, especially when the cough accompanies dropsy, heart disease, etc.

Belladonna may be misapplied for *Apis*, but can be distinguished by its greater constriction of the throat, and deeper inflammatory redness.

Carbo veg. agrees in hoarseness, rawness, and tickling cough, but the irritation is as from vapor of sulphur.

Now, the action of *Apis* on the genital organs. *Apis* is often indicated in diseases of the female organs. Nearly all the provers experienced symptoms referable to the uterus and ovaries. There is increased sexual desire with stinging in the ovaries. This is sometimes a symptom in widows, and *Apis* will often relieve it. Tendency to abort at or before the third month. *Apis* produces and will check abortion when the symptoms agree. Therefore it must be given cautiously during pregnancy, because if given in low potency and frequent dosage it may bring about a miscarriage, especially before or at the third month. We may use it in amenorrhoea when we have congestion of the head as a result of the suppression of the flow, bearing down in the uterine region, thirstlessness, and intolerance of heat. Particularly is it indicated in girls with this amenorrhoea at the age of puberty. They are nervous, hysterical, awkward and silly. It is not a natural awkwardness, but one that comes from incoordination of the muscles. With these symptoms there is flushing of the face.

We may also use *Apis* in affections of the ovaries, especially of the right side. It holds the same relation to the right ovary that *Lachesis* does to the left. It is indicated in ovaritis with extreme soreness in the right ovarian region, together with burning or stinging sensations, and some tumefaction, detectable either over the pelvis or, more characteristically, through the rectum or vagina.

In ovarian cysts, *Apis* is an excellent remedy to control the growth, especially in the incipient stages. We have here, in addition to the burning and stinging pains, numbness down the thigh and over the right side of the body, and a feeling of tightness across the chest, with cough. This is not a symptom of lung disease, but is reflex from the uterus.

Now there is a combination of honey with salt, known as *Mel cum sale*. This was for years a popular remedy in Germany for bladder troubles and for diseases peculiar to women. I have used this remedy in prolapsus uteri and even in chronic metritis, especially when associated with subinvolution and inflammation of the cervix. The special symptom which leads to the selection of the remedy is a feeling of soreness across the hypogastrium from ilium to ilium.

Apis may be of use in diseases of the eyes. I have seen several cases of asthenopia cured by this remedy, when reading caused smarting in the eyes, with lachrymation and itching of the eye-lids and some burning and stinging. *Apis* is also a remedy for staphyloma, whether of the cornea or sclerotic coat. In external diseases of the eye, it is not without value. The eyes are over-sensitive to light. The conjunctiva is reddened or puffy and chemotic. But this swelling of the palpebral conjunctiva under *Apis* is more from congestion than from a true chemosis, as under *Rhus tox.*, which is very similar, especially in œdematous swelling of the lids, chemosis, hot, gushing lachrymation; erysipelas. But *Apis* has less tendency to the formation of pus—a symptom highly characteristic of *Rhus tox.* In the former the pains are stinging, the time of exacerbation is the evening, and cold water relieves the inflamed lids. If erysipelatous, the lids are a bluish red, looking watery, as if semi-transparent. In the latter, the pains are worse at night, particularly after midnight; warmth relieves; the erysipelatous lids are of a dusky red, and, together with the cheeks, are studded with small watery vesicles. The pains in *Rhus tox.* are usually of a drawing, tearing character, although in erysipelas they may be burning or stinging, but with more itching than in the bee-poison. The eyelids often feel heavy and stiff.

Arsenicum compares with *Apis* in hot tears, violent pains and œdematous lids. But the lachrymation is more acrid. The œdematous lids are pale, not bluish-red. The palpebral conjunctiva and the edges of the lids are very red. The restlessness is more pronounced. Relief is usually obtained from warm applications, though the scrofulous patient can open his eyes in the cool open air, but not in the room, even if dark. The symptoms are worse at and after 12 P. M.

To return to the eye symptoms of *Apis*, the lids are swollen, red and œdematous. There is burning of the tarsi, with agglutination of the lids. Sudden and very severe pains shoot through the eyes, and these are relieved by the application of cold water. The eyes are generally worse in the first part of the night. *Apis* is often indicated in scrofulous ophthalmia, in which affection it is often followed by *Kali bichromicum.*

It now only remains for me to speak of the intestinal symptoms of *Apis*. It may be of value in diarrhœa, such, for instance, as comes on during the course of typhoid fever or scarlatina, or as the result of the debilitating influence of continued heat.

You will find it useful in the diarrhœa of children who are very much debilitated. Irritability of the brain is generally present with the condition known as hydrocephaloid. The symptoms are much like those indicating *Apis* in hydrocephalus. The child wakens with a scream. The stools are thin, watery, yellow in color, and usually worse in the morning. At every motion of the body the bowels move, as though the sphincter ani had no power. The stools may or may not be offensive.

Apis differs from *Bryonia*, which has morning diarrhœa, worse from motion; in the diarrhœa of *Apis* the motion aggravates, not because of its general effects, but because the sphincter ani is so uncertain.

In bad cases you will find the urine scanty.

Apis may also be thought of in panaritium. The finger swells rapidly, with tense, glossy-red surface and violent burning, stinging pains.

In this respect it is very similar to *Sulphur*, and may be followed by *Sulphur* when its action is imperfect.

Modalities: *Apis* has general relief from cold applications. Many complaints are worse evenings and night, though diarrhœa increases in the morning. Motion generally aggravates, as does a warm room.

Apis is antidoted by *Plantago* and *Lachesis*, and is complementary to *Natrum mur.*

Ledum was proposed by Teste as an antidote for the stings of insects. Dr. Drysdale has cured nightly itching of the feet with it.

In closing, let me ask you to remember the relation of *Apis* to *Arsenicum*, *Acetic acid*, *Belladonna* and *Sulphur*. Remember, also, its inimical relation to *Rhus tox.*

LECTURE IX.

MOSCHUS.

The order of *Ruminantia* furnishes us with an article called *Musk*, which is obtained from the *Moschus moschiferus*, or musk-deer. It is found in a sac just behind the umbilicus, and probably consists of a secretion from the preputial follicles.

The second word, "moschiferus," is a necessary qualification, since several species of the musk-deer, as the Tragulus Javanicus and the Meminna Indica, are unprovided with the musk-bearing pouch.

So penetrating is the odor of this substance, that it is with great difficulty removed from a room, even after extensive cleansing and alterations.

Moschus is of some value in nervous affections, and also in several grave forms of disease. Injected into the veins of animals, it has produced narcotism with muscular spasms, bloody stools and finally death. Wood regards its action on man as feeble and uncertain, though he admits its clinical worth when the nervous system is exhausted, with accompanying restlessness, etc. Ringer regards it as ill-adapted to medicine on account of its sickening odor. Bartholow, Flint, Hammond and Rosenthal do not use it in hysteria. German writers, Jolly, for instance, admit a temporary benefit from its use in hysteria. Like some American authorities, they employ it more confidently in pneumonia and in spasmus glottidis. Trousseau, with characteristic conservatism, rejects the overdrawn laudations of older writers, and proceeds, in his own unique fashion, to define its accurate application to diseases.

In our own school, precise prescribing has had its influence in more clearly defining the power of *Musk*, and in thus limiting its action within reasonable bounds. The experiments of Joerg and Sunderlin, which Allen has seen fit to incorporate in the *Encyclopædia*, are considered by some to be contradictory. Still, they are not opposed to other provings obtained with potencies or by inhalation, and so are of value and deserve to be retained.

Homœopathically employed, *Moschus* is of use in various affections when the nervous symptoms predominate. The disease, in consequence, does not follow its normal course, but remains uncured or develops serious symptoms, indicating nervous exhaustion. It is also sometimes called for in hysteria and hypochondriasis.

Moschus, then, produces numerous symptoms referable to the nervous system. The following are especially worthy of note:

Excited as from alcohol; pulse full and frequent; temperature slightly elevated; congestion of the brain; raves, speaks rapidly and confusedly; scolds until her lips are blue, her face pale, and she falls unconscious; anxiety; starts at any noise; anxious about death. Anxiety, with fainting; faints, with coldness, pale face, complete unconsciousness; hysteria; cries one moment and bursts into uncontrollable laughter the next; delirium; sleeplessness; muscular twitching; ataxia; the face wears an expression of surprise; convulsions, more tonic than clonic.

Accompaniments: palpitation of the heart, as from anxious expectation; nervous, busy, but weak; soon drops things; tremulous nervousness; fainting spells, with pale face and coldness; sleepy during the day; rush of blood to the head, with staring eyes; dizzy unsteadiness, as of something rapidly moving up and down; vertigo; headaches and pains in the back and limbs, which are described as a sensation of tension, stiffness, pressure or drawing; the muscles and skin are tightly drawn (tonic spasm). She frequently complains of nausea, and there is cramping about the navel, or a jerk-like clawing. Uneasiness in the legs, worse while she is sitting; great tympanitis, with fainting; copious watery urine; spasmus glottidis. The menses are too early and too profuse, preceded by the tense, drawing sensations, and also a drawing and dragging towards the genitals. Sexual desire is increased, with local titillation.

Sudden sensation in the upper part of the larynx, as if it closed upon the breath. A kind of "cramp" in the lung, beginning with an inclination to cough, gradually increasing and making him perfectly desperate. Suffocative constriction in the chest.

The most important hysterical symptoms of *Musk* are: attacks even to fainting or unconsciousness; coldness of the surface; pale face; suffocative paroxysms; scolding until she falls unconscious.

Compare *Castoreum, Nux moschata, Asafœtida, Gum ammoniac, Valeriana, Ignatia, Magnesia muriatica.*

Camphor antidotes many of the symptoms of *Musk*, especially if unconsciousness and coldness are present.

Castoreum is derived from the preputial sacs of the beaver. Like *Musk* it causes nervousness, twitching, and deranged menses. But it is more adapted to the nervous symptoms which precede fully developed hysteria. It suits women who suffer from irritable weakness, abdominal symptoms predominating.

Chargé, for example, employs it for women who, during convalescence from a prostrating disease, as typhoid fever, suffer from spasmodic affections, twitchings of muscles, with extreme exhaustion. The want of nervous reaction, therefore, tends to prolong convalescence unduly, and *Castoreum*, by strengthening the nerves, hastens recovery.

Trousseau employs this remedy for nervous colic with pallor, cold sweat, and sudden loss of strength, caused by emotions, chilling the feet, etc. Also for amenorrhœa, with painful tympany; the menstrual blood, owing to uterine tenesmus, escapes only in drops. Teste agrees with him in the main.

The provings develop a train of symptoms quite consistent with these clinical effects. The woman is nervous, apprehensive and sad, growing fitful during the menses. Tearing pains, better from pressure or rubbing. Tearing pressure in different parts during menses.

Abdomen distended with flatus; dragging in the groins, inclination to stool during menses. Cutting about the navel.

Stools of bloody mucus, or of whitish water, with burning in the anus. Green mucous stools, which burn. Cutting colic before stool, better from pressure or bending double.

A Spanish physician has confirmed the modality of *Castoreum*, relief of pains from pressure, and we may profit by French and Spanish authorities in their treatment of nervous affections, since from national peculiarities they have ample opportunities to treat such cases.

The similarities between *Musk* and *Castoreum* are rather in the kind of affections in which they are indicated than in special symptoms. Still Trousseau places them together in nervous attacks, when the aura starts from the abdominal viscera. But only the *Musk* has clearly developed hysterical attacks, with pulmonary and laryngeal spasms and unconsciousness.

And we may say, in passing, only *Castoreum* has cured watery or green mucous stools in delicate, nervous children, who weaken under summer heat or during dentition, and who will not rally under the usual remedies.

Nux moschata exerts a very novel influence upon the mind. The state varies from a bewilderment, in which the surroundings are strange, dreamy, or fanciful, to a condition of absentmindedness, sleepiness, and finally deep stupor, with loss of motion and sensation. Mental states may alternate. At one time she laughs, as if everything partook of the ludicrous. She jests even about serious subjects. Suddenly her mood changes to sadness, with weeping and loud crying; or her expression grows stupid, all ideas vanish, and she appears as if overwhelmed with sleep. There are, likewise, errors of perception; a momentary unconsciousness she regards as having been of long duration. Her hands look too large. Objects gradually diminish in size as she looks at them steadily. The bodily functions come under the same influence; great weakness and bruised feeling of the small of the back and the legs; the knees feel weak, as after a long journey; prostration; tendency to faint; oppressed breathing, rush of blood to the heart, skin cold and dry. So relaxed that pulse and breath are scarcely discernible. Head drops forward, the chin resting on the breast. Head rolls about as if bulky. Bowels enormously distended with wind, as from weak digestion. Even soft stools are evacuated with difficulty. It is this mental and bodily atony which has led to the excellent cures made with *Nux moschata*, not only in hysterical weakness, but in typhoid fever and cholera infantum. The hystero-spasmodic symptoms of the drug are intimately commingled with the above symptoms; head jerked forward; jaws clenched; heart as if grasped; sudden oppression of the heart, with choking sensation; tonic, followed by clonic spasms; unconsciousness or fainting.

Accompaniments are: great dryness of the mouth and throat, which, on account of her tendency to magnify, she complains of extremely. The least emotional excitement renews the symptoms, increases the distension of the abdomen, etc. Skin dry and cool, no disposition to sweat. Palpitation of the heart; heart-beat and pulse changeable.

Valeriana is so much abused as an antispasmodic that Homœopathicians are too apt to neglect it. But it occupies its definite place in the treatment of hysteria, differing from *Musk*, *Asafœtida*, and all other "nervines." It is not so much adapted to hysterical spasms, with unconsciousness, like the drugs already considered, as it is to a general state of nervous and vascular excitement. Both mind and body are in a condition of irritation. The patient is lively, joyous, talking rapidly, with rapid sequence of thoughts. Sometimes she imagines she is beset with dangers, or surrounding objects seem strange. She suffers from headache, giddiness and restlessness. Her muscular organism is so irritated that she cannot keep quiet; she *must* move. The same state influences her pains. The provings show twinging, drawing, cramp-like, stinging, or darting-tearing pains, all worse when she sits and better when she walks. The circulation, too, is excited; her head feels full to bursting; constant heat and uneasiness; dry heat in the evening while sitting, flushes of heat. She is wide awake and restless all night, falling into a dreamy sleep toward morning. Digestion is disturbed. Before dinner she has a taste as of fœtid tallow, while early in the morning, on awaking, the taste is flat or slimy. Nausea, as if a thread were hanging in the throat; nausea beginning in the region of the umbilicus, and gradually rising to the fauces. Bloated abdomen.

From the order of *Umbelliferæ* we derive two gums which have often been used in nervous affections. I refer to *Gum ammoniac*, and, especially, to *Asafœtida*.

The latter acts most prominently upon the abdominal ganglia, and thence upon the whole nervous system. Its most characteristic effects are as follows: reversal of the peristaltic action of the bowels, stomach, and particularly of the throat; rancid eructations, with profuse saliva, greasy taste; the head feels dull and compressed; burning in the stomach and œsophagus; enormous meteorism of the stomach; stools papescent, brown, offensive; spasmodic tightness of the chest, as if the lungs could not be fully expanded; oppression to an agonizing degree; heart congested and distended, with small pulse. Drawing and tightness, here and there; pulse small, contracted, with shivering in the lumbar region. Pressure in various places, usually from within outward. Cutting, labor-like distress in the region of the uterus. Urine brown, of pungent odor. Later, as the patient weakens, there are malaise, yawning, shuddering from time to time, vertigo, vanishing of sight and cold sweat.

Clinically, it has been determined that *Asafœtida* is suited to nervous patients, when their condition is the direct sequel of the checking of habitual discharges, such as the external healing of running ulcers, the sudden suppression of a diarrhœa, etc. Also after abuse of mercury, when, besides the nervousness, affections of the bones and periosteum, such as caries, are likewise present. There are extreme sensitiveness in the region of the carious ulcer, and severe pains at night. Women are sometimes helped by *Asafœtida* when a habitual expectoration is checked and hysterical symptoms, together with oppression of the chest, follow. Here the drug displays a family resemblance to *Gum ammoniac*, which has frequently been given for such a condition of the lungs.

Musk and *Asafœtida* agree in producing globus hystericus, spasm of the chest, and palpitation. The former is best adapted to a full-fledged hysterical spasm, with fainting or unconsciousness. The latter has more offensive discharges, and the globus is part of an extensive reverse peristalsis. Fainting has not been noted (except in one case, when the intensity of the pain caused it). Tympany is also well marked.

Magnesia muriatica resembles the last remedy and also *Musk*. Like other *Magnesia* preparations it affects the stomach and bowels and the nervous system. Thus the *Carbonate* and *Phosphate* are indicated in neuralgia, especially in cases subject to repeated attacks by reason of nervous debility. The *Muriate*, however, has been proved to be eminently useful in hysteria. We observe prominent abdominal symptoms; nausea, with accumulation of water in the mouth; liver enlarged; tongue large, flabby and yellow; she must hurry to stool, which is crumbly as if burnt; and, as if to show a combination of abdominal and nervous symptoms, there are rumbling in the abdomen, with dragging, griping, cutting, tension, and then pain as if the bowels were cut to pieces; feeling of something rising into the throat like a ball, almost taking her breath; relieved by eructations. Flatus collects in the stomach and abdomen, causing reflex spasmodic symptoms through irritated nerves.

This is still further confirmed by the following: attack of faintness during dinner; anxiety with nausea and pale face; trembling of the body; relieved by eructations. Or, again, sudden heaviness on the chest during dinner, nausea, water in the mouth; heat mounting to the face; it seems as if eructations or vomiting would relieve her.

Illusions of fancy have been observed. Very important is the headache; griping and raging in both temples, sensation as though she would become dizzy and lose consciousness, disappearing on pressing the head with both hands. Headache relieved by wrapping up the head.

The menstrual flow is black, clotted, with pains in the back while walking and in the thighs when sitting. Uterine spasms, with tension in the groins (Hale thinks in the broad ligaments); cutting in the lower abdomen during menses. Cramps in the abdomen, with pressure upon the rectum and genitals.

Palpitation of the heart, not, like *Musk,* "as from anxious expectation," but, nonetheless, non-organic, for it comes on while sitting and on rising from a seat, and disappears on moving about. This has been several times confirmed.

Briefly, by way of summary: *Moschus,* excited, scolding, fainting; coldness; spasm of the glottis and lungs.

Castoreum, exhausted, pains better from pressure; menstrual colic with pallor and cold sweat.

Nux moschata, errors of perception, drowsy; faints; enormous tympany; oppression of the heart and throat; skin dry, cool.

Valeriana, nerves irritated, cannot keep still; tearings, cramps, better when moving; taste of tallow or slime.

Asafœtida, reverse peristalsis, rancid eructations, offensive flatus; tightness of the chest; checked discharges.

Magnesia muriatica, faints at dinner; relief from eructations; head better from pressure and wrapping up; palpitation better on moving about; stools crumble.

Moschus, has been employed by allopathic physicians when, in the course of pneumonia, a purely nervous delirium obtains. The brain is violently excited and the patient talks nonsense with furious vivacity (Trousseau).

We need remedies for just such cases, remedies which will calm the irritable weak nerves, and permit the disease to proceed in its normal course.

The following may prove beneficial in diseases embarrassed by a condition of non-reaction from irritable weakness: *Musk, Ambra grisea, Asafœtida, Valeriana, Castoreum, Coffea, Scutellaria, Cypripedium, Coca, Zincum ox., China, Camphora, Agaricus, Tarentula.*

LECTURE X.

SEPIA.

BELONGING to the Mollusca is an animal called the *Sepia*, or cuttle-fish. A hard calcareous substance belonging to the cuttle-fish is, you all know, used for the feeding of birds. The animal itself possesses a little sac or pouch which contains a dark brown, almost black, fluid. When pursued by larger fish it ejects this fluid, thus clouding the water and protecting itself from its foe. This was for a long time supposed to be the only use for this fluid. It was supposed to be entirely inert when taken into the human system. Since Hahnemann's experiments have shown the fallacy of this belief, it is safe to suppose that the cuttle-fish uses it also to kill the smaller fry upon which it preys.* The name *Sepia* is the common term used to designate this remedy in our Materia Medica, the juice just referred to being the part employed. This juice is used by artists. The history of the introduction of this substance into our Materia Medica is as follows:

It is stated on the authority of Dr. Hering that an intimate friend and patient of Hahnemann, an artist, was in the habit of wetting his brush, containing India ink, with his saliva. Failing to cure him of his chronic ailments, Hahnemann suggested the ink as the probable cause of his persistent symptoms. The artist doubted this, but nevertheless modified his custom by covering the lips with a thin layer of sponge moistened with water, the mouth being protected by an impervious though pliable shield, and his obscure illness shortly passed away. Hahnemann then instituted provings with the *Sepiæ succus*. All the symptoms observed by him have since been confirmed. In 1874 the American Institute of Homœopathy, acting under the notion that our old remedies should be reproved, performed this task for *Sepia*. There were made some twenty-five provings of the drug in the third to the two-hundredth potencies. These were reported at the meeting of the Association in 1875. They testify to the fact that the provings left us by Hahnemann cannot be improved upon.

Sepia is a remedy of inestimable value. It acts especially on the female organism, although it also has an action on the male. It is particularly adapted to delicate females with rather fine skin, sensitive

---

*See also Teste. *Materia Medica*, page 299.

to all impressions, usually with dark hair, although not necessarily so; the face is apt to be sallow and the eyes surrounded by dark rings.

It acts upon the vital forces as well as upon the organic substances of the body. It very soon impresses the circulation, which becomes more and more disturbed as the proving progresses. Even as early as the fourth hour there are developed flushes of heat and ebullitions. These flushes end in sweat, with a weak, faint feeling. Any motion or exertion is followed by hot spells and free sweats.

Hand in hand with this orgasm is an erethism of the nervous system, causing restlessness, anxiety, etc.

These two sets of symptoms indicate the disturbing influence of the drug upon the nervous system of animal life, and also upon the vasomotor nerves. Thence arise headaches, various local congestions, etc.

Quickly following these symptoms are those marked by relaxation of tissues and nervous weakness. The prover becomes languid, prostrated, faint. The joints feel weak, as if they would easily become dislocated. The viscera drag downward, and thus originate the well-known goneness, etc. Venous congestions still continue, and, indeed, on account of vaso-motor weakness increase. The prolapsed uterus becomes more and more engorged, the portal stasis is augmented and the liver is heavy and sluggish. The bloodvessels are full, and hence the limbs feel sore, bruised and tired. The general depressing influence upon the vital powers is further displayed in great weakness, faintness and trembling. The limbs feel heavy, as if paralyzed; stiffness and unwieldiness of the legs, especially after sleep.

The sphincters, as well as all structures depending for power upon non-striated muscles, are weak. Hence the rectum becomes prolapsed, evacuations of bowels and bladder are tardy and sluggish, and yet there is no complete paralysis.

Organic changes are produced as exhibited in the complexion, which is yellow, earthy; in the secretions, which are offensive, sour, excoriating, etc.; in the condition of the skin, which has offensive exhalations, and is disposed to eruptions, discoloration, desquamation, ulcers, etc.

Among the conditions which modify the *Sepia* case, none is so important as the effect of motion. Two or three provers experienced decided relief of the symptoms (one prover excepting horseback riding) from violent exercise. But many symptoms are made worse from exertion. How, then, are we to discriminate? Since many of the symptoms arise from lax tissues, with torpidity, and, above all, with surcharged veins, exercise, by favoring the return of blood to the heart, relieves. The aggravation from horseback riding or from the motion of a ship, since it jars the sensitive parts and even tends to increase venous fulness, necessarily augments the troubles. But the headache, faint, exhausted condition, the sacro-lumbar pains, and often, too, the prolapsus uteri, are naturally intensified by walking.

Briefly, it has been found that *Sepia* acts well in men, or, more often, in women who are puffed and flabby, less frequently emaciated; who have a yellow, or dirty yellow-brown blotched skin; who are inclined to sweat, especially about the genitals, armpits and back, suffer with hot flashes, headaches in the morning, awaken stiff and tired, and are the subjects of diseases of the sexual organs. The man has sexual erethism, but without energy, and coitus induces great exhaustion (neurasthenia). The woman is erethistic, with hysteria, or with prolapsed uterus, palpitation, orgasm of blood, faintness, etc. In both cases, there may be portal stasis, with imperfectly acting liver, with atonic dyspepsia, sluggish bowels, uric acid deposit in the urine, and attending evidences of impaired digestion and assimilation. The general attitude is never one of strength and healthful ease, but rather of lax connective tissue, languor, and easily produced paresis.

It is to be further remembered that the *Sepia* symptoms are notably worse in the forenoon and evening, the afternoon bringing a time of general mitigation. Of this fact there are numerous confirmations.

We are now prepared to review the symptoms in detail, and to determine whether they sustain the assertions thus far made.

To understand the symptomatology of so prominent a drug as *Sepia*, which has in its pathogenesis some two thousand symptoms of more or less importance, we must consider the action of the substance upon the various tissues. First of all the blood. *Sepia* causes great disturbance in the circulation; many of its symptoms seem to depend upon venous congestion, and this is especially noticeable in the portal circulation. Reviewing some of the symptoms based on this pathological condition, we find flashes of heat which seem to begin about the trunk and go upward to the head, with anxiety, and, of course, an oppressed feeling, ending in perspiration; throbbing all over the body, particularly in the epigastrium, in the hepatic region, in the uterine region, and in the small of the back. This symptom is very common in hysteria and chlorosis. Nose-bleed, either from mechanical causes, as a blow or a fall, from being in a hot room, or from suppressed menses. Throbbing pain in the uterus; the uterus when examined is found to be swollen, engorged with blood, sensitive to the touch, and as we shall see when speaking of the local symptoms, displaced. The hands are hot and the feet are cold; or, as soon as the feet become hot the hands become cold. This is an excellent indication for *Sepia*.

If we look at the symptoms of the skin, again we find the action of *Sepia* due to defective venous circulation. We know that when the vaso-motor nerves are inactive the skin is more sensitive to the effects of irritation, and is particularly apt to develop herpetic eruptions, especially about the elbow and knee-joints. Ulcers may form about the joints, particularly about the joints of the fingers. Under *Sepia* these are generally painless. There are only two other remedies that I know of with this symptom, namely, *Borax* and *Mezereum*. *Sepia* has been many times confirmed as a remedy in herpes circinatus.

Sepia also causes yellowish-brown spots, itching, redness, vesicles, humidity and rawness, scaling pustules. The warm room makes the urticaria patient feel comfortable; but the warmth of the bed aggravates the pricking of the skin. Dunham, guided by the tendency to scaling, recommends the drug as an antidote to *Rhus* poisoning.

Sepia stands well in the treatment of psoriasis, though inferior to *Arsenicum* and *Arsenicum iodatum*.

These yellowish-brown spots have also been removed by *Lycopodium*, *Nux vomica* and *Sulphur*. *Curare* is used by Dr. Baruch, of New York.

Besides *Sepia*, *Calcarea ostrearum*, *Baryta carb.* and *Tellurium* have been recommended for ringworm. *Baryta carb.* has never been successful in my hands. *Tellurium* is useful for ringworm over a great portion of the body in intersecting rings.

In scabies *Sepia* is indicated after *Sulphur*, when pustules intersperse the itch-vesicles.

Sepia has a marked action on connective tissue, weakening it, and thus producing a great variety of symptoms. Thus, there is weakness of the joints, which give out readily when walking; weakness about the pit of the stomach, not relieved by eating and evidently the result of a sagging down of the viscera. This effect of *Sepia* may be utilized in cases in which the joints are readily dislocated.

Now, taking up the organs *seriatim*, we find *Sepia* to have a marked action on the mind. It produces a mental state which is quite characteristic, and which ought to be present when *Sepia* is the remedy. The patient, usually a woman, is low-spirited, sad, and cries readily. This sadness is usually associated with irritability. It will not do to find fault with the *Sepia* woman. At other times she manifests a condition of perfect indifference. She does not care for her household affairs or even for her own family.

This mental state of *Sepia* is to be distinguished from that of *Pulsatilla*, *Natrum mur.* and *Causticum*.

Pulsatilla is without doubt the nearest analogue. Like *Sepia*, it develops a state of weeping, anxiety with ebullitions, peevish ill-humor, solicitude about health, etc. But only the former has the mild yielding disposition, clinging and seeking consolation There may be moroseness and peevishness, or irresolution, but there is the angry irritability and the cool indifference of the latter.

Natrum muriaticum is complementary to *Sepia;* they agree in causing weeping mood, depression of spirits, persistent recalling of past unpleasantnesses, irritability, indifference, loss of memory, and alternation of mental states. The former has prominently, "worse from consolation." Clinically, we may say the same of *Sepia*. Both remedies, too, have ailments aggravated by vexation or anger. The two are evidently similar in causing weak and irritable nerves, but their complemental relation consists in the fact that *Sepia* causes more vascular erethism; hence it is that under *Sepia*, disturbed feelings induce congestion of the chest and head, animated conversation causes hot face, and sweats follow excitement. In *Natrum mur.*, the symptoms point more to nervous excitement or weakness alone, hence emotions induce headache, and drawing up the spine; and unpleasant thoughts cause sadness, paralytic weakness, or irritability without ebullitions. If hypochondriacal, it is a state of melancholy from mental depression, caused by inert bowels; while in *Sepia* the same state depends also upon portal stasis, and therefore is more persistent and associated with more irritable temper. *Natrum mur.* may be called for when the mental state depends upon uterine disease or menstrual irregularity, but this will be only a prolapsus, never the uterine engorgement of *Sepia*. The indifference of *Natrum mur.* is born of hopelessness and mental languor; while that of *Sepia* includes an undisguised aversion to those nearest and naturally dearest.

Causticum induces sadness, especially before the menses. The face is yellow; but the anxiety is more a timid, fearful state. She is full of forebodings. She dreads the possibility of accidents to herself and others.

Lilium tigrinum stands very near to *Sepia*. It affects the circulation, particularly of venous blood, and, as reflex symptoms from uterine and ovarian irritation, there are nervous irritability; desire to be busy, yet cannot do much; hurried manner. Depressed, full of apprehension of incurable disease, of accidents, etc. Feels that she will go crazy; weeping mood.

Both remedies suit the weakened system, especially that of the female; fearful about one's health; hurried, nervous, fidgety; so nervous that the least excitement causes cold, clammy hands, palpitation, etc. In both, the cause of debility seems to be a relaxation of the ligamentous structures, serous sacs and veins. The first two account for the empty, gone feelings; weak knees (even cracking in *Lilium*, from deficient synovial fluid); prolapsi, etc. The last explains the readiness to portal stagnation (*Sepia*), fulness of the chest, heart, and the veins of the extremities.

There is, however, an essential difference in this, that the *Lilium* patient finds relief in diverting her mind by busying herself; while the *Sepia* patient has many nervous symptoms relieved by violent exercise. It is, in the former case, a sexual erethism which is thus relieved; in the latter, relief is general, by favoring venous circulation, nervous erethism being but slight, and being associated with lessened venereal passion, and aversion to coitus. Moreover, *Lilium* has a marked remission of its symptoms in the forenoon, while *Sepia* is more apt to find relief during the afternoon.

Hepar develops a mood which it may not be inappropriate to consider. Sadness; unpleasant events return to mind; sad in the evening, even with thoughts of suicide; peevish; the slightest thing makes him break out into violence; he does not wish to see the members of his own family.

But this latter condition is not quite the indifference of *Sepia*. It arises more from a contrary mood. And, further, only *Hepar* has such violent outbursts of passion.

Platina is similar in its depressed moods. "Indifference; he does not seem to care whether his absent wife dies or not." But the digression is into haughtiness; or into anxiety, with fear of imminent death; or into that contracted mental state akin to the feeling of personal superiority, in which "everything seems too narrow; with weeping mood." And, besides, as we shall see anon, the uterine symptoms differ materially.

Let us now consider the head symptoms of *Sepia*. There is a disease of the head called hemicrania, for which *Sepia* is one of our main remedies. The symptoms which indicate it here are the following: pains over one eye (usually the left), of a throbbing character; deep, stitching pains which seem to be in the membranes of the brain; the pains almost always shoot upward or from within outward; they are so severe as to extort cries, and frequently culminate in vomiting. The paroxysms are renewed or aggravated by motion, light noise or by a thunderstorm and are relieved by sleep or rest in a dark room. Usually, with women, there are soreness of the face, uterine malposition, or disturbance of menstruation. We find, too, that the patient may have a jerking of the head backward and forward, worse while sitting and in the forenoon. This has been utilized in nervous women (with hysteria for instance), and also in children with open fontanelles. In these cases you should not give *Sulphur*, *Calcarea*, or remedies of that type. Study the symptoms and you will find that *Sepia* is indicated. *Sepia* is also useful in arthritic headaches, especially when, like those of *Nux vomica*, they are worse in the morning, with nausea and vomiting. The liver, of course, is affected, and the urine is loaded with uric acid.

In headache from brain-fag *Sepia* is to be selected by its general cachectic condition. It is said to be particularly efficacious when a one-sided occupation has led to brain exhaustion. Compare *Natrum mur.*, *Nux vom.*, *Sulphur*, *Picric acid*.

In hemicrania you may compare *Sepia* with *Belladonna*, *Sanguinaria*, *Iris*, *Pulsatilla*, *Nux vomica*, *Arsenicum*, *Theridion*, *Silicea* and *Thuja*.

Belladonna is to be selected in hemicrania when there are violent hyperæmia, with throbbing carotids, red face, intolerance of the least jar, light or noise. It is indicated, you will see, in plethoric patients, and not in the cachectic, as with *Sepia*.

Sanguinaria produces a right-sided headache, the pains coming over from the occiput. They increase and decrease with the course of the sun, reaching their acme at mid-day. The paroxysms end with profuse urination (as in *Silicea*, *Gelsemium* and *Veratrum album*). They recur every seven days. *Sanguinaria* also has a menstrual headache which attends a profuse flow. In *Sepia* the menses are scanty. In *Sanguinaria* the pains are on the right side; in *Sepia* they may occur on either side.

You will use *Iris versicolor* in hemicrania when the attack begins with blurring of sight and the paroxysms are attended with sour, watery vomiting. The pains involve the infra-orbital and dental nerves, with stupid or stunning headache.

Pulsatilla is very similar to *Sepia*. Both are indicated by scanty menses; bursting, throbbing, boring or stitching pains on one side of the head; obscuration of sight, white tongue, nausea and vomiting. *Pulsatilla* has more vomiting, and a thickly-furred tongue with clammy mouth, and relief from cold air. The pains are shifting in character, and are associated with chilliness. They are worse in the evening. In *Sepia* the pains recur in shocks or flashes, with proportionate increase of heat in the head; the blurring of sight is associated with heavy eyelids; and the face, though red with headache in either remedy, is ordinarily yellow with *Sepia* and pale with *Pulsatilla*.

Nux vomica is more suited to men than is *Sepia*. It cures a drawing, aching feeling as of a nail driven into the head, or as if the brain were dashed to pieces. The face is pale sallow, or sallow on a red ground. The attacks commence early in the morning, and generally increase to a frantic degree. As under *Sepia*, the exciting causes may be hæmorrhoids, abdominal plethora or brain fatigue. In general, however, the two drugs are very different.

Arsenicum will cause a throbbing, stupefying headache over the left eye. In this particular it resembles *Sepia*, but the prostration and restlessness of the two drugs are very different, as is also the intensity of the angry irritability, even to swearing, which *Arsenicum* induces. The *Arsenicum* headache exceptionally derives a temporary relief from the application of cold water to the head.

Theridion has, more accurately speaking, flickering before the eyes, then blurring. The nausea of this remedy is made worse by closing the eyes, and also by noise. The effect of noise is more intense than in *Sepia*. It seems to intensify the pains, and, as it were, penetrates to the teeth, so sensitive are the nerves to this sort of vibration.

Silicea may be needed after any unwonted exertion, if moderate. The pains excite nausea and fainting, and are followed by obscuration of vision.

Sepia is very useful in diseases of the eyes. You will find it indicated in asthenopia attending uterine diseases. You may differentiate *Sepia* from other remedies by the time of its aggravation, the patient generally being worse in the evening; in the morning and afternoon she is quite free from symptoms.

In conjunctivitis you will find *Sepia* indicated when the inflammation is of a sluggish type, occurring generally in scrofulous children. The symptoms are subacute. There is muco-purulent discharge in the morning. The eyes feel comparatively comfortable during the day, while in the evening there is an annoying dryness of the conjunctivæ.

The remaining eye-symptoms of *Sepia* we may summarize as follows: cataract; trachoma, with or without pannus; scaly lids; pustular lids with eruptions on the face; eyes irritable to light, lids close in spite of him; eyelids droop; aching, sticking pains, worse from rubbing. Causes: uterine or liver diseases, scrofula, tea drinking. Worse morning and evening, in hot weather; better from cold washing, and in the afternoon.

I have for years employed *Sepia* in blurring of sight, etc., with prolapsus uteri. I have likewise found it efficient in asthenopia, associated with exhaustion dependent upon loss of semen, whether of voluntary or involuntary occurrence. In these respects the drug is similar to *Natrum mur.*, *Lilium tig.*, *Jaborandi*, *Kali carb*. The first of these superadds muscular weakness (internal recti), stiff sensation in the muscles of the eyes on moving them, etc. There is running together of letters or stitches, but not the sudden vanishing of sight so marked in *Sepia*.

Lilium tigrinum causes smarting of the eyes; blurring with heat in the eyelids and eyes; sharp pains over the left eye; thus symptomatically resembling *Sepia*. It has also burning, smarting in the eyes after reading, better in the open air, like *Pulsatilla*. Spasm of accommodation (study *Jaborandi*).

Cyclamen and *Pulsatilla* may also be considered with *Sepia* in sudden vanishing of sight; the first with profuse and dark menses, the second with scanty dark flow. But the *Cyclamen* blindness accompanies a semi-lateral headache of the left temple, with pale face, nausea referred to the throat, and weak digestion.

Under *Pulsatilla*, which you may also use in conjunctivitis, there is a discharge of muco-pus, but it is bland and is worse at night, with agglutination of the lids in the morning. There are fine granulations on the lids. The patient is subject to repeated highly-inflamed styes.

Graphites you may employ when the canthi crack and bleed, and the edges of the lids are pale and swollen as well as scaly.

Thuja is indicated in eye affections of tea drinkers. Brown, bran-like scales accumulate about the cilia, and there are little tarsal tumors like warts.

Nux vomica will be called for in eye affections associated with liver diseases. The symptoms are worse in the morning, and some of them are relieved by cold bathing.

Natrum mur., like *Sepia*, is indicated in eye affections reflex from uterine disease; the lids droop. But under *Natrum mur.* there is more spasmodic closure of the lids in conjunctivitis; the discharges are thin and acrid; there are cracks in the canthi and also in the corners of the mouth; pains over the eyes are present, worse when looking down.

Alumina likewise has falling of the lids, dryness, burning, dim sight; but *Alumina* has aggravation in the evening and at night. The inner canthi are affected.

Next we shall consider the action of *Sepia* on the abdominal organs. It is indicated in the form of dyspepsia mentioned above, and also in the dyspepsia incident to uterine diseases, when it is associated with a gone, empty feeling in the epigastrium or the abdomen, with sour or bitter taste in the mouth, and with a longing for acids or pickles, which seem to relieve these symptoms. The tongue is coated white, the bowels are usually constipated, the stools are hard, dry and insufficient, or, even if not indurated, they are expelled with difficulty. The abdomen is swollen and distended with flatus, and there is almost always soreness in the hepatic region. On making a physical exploration you find the liver enlarged, not from fatty or amyloid degeneration, but from congestion.

Hæmorrhoids are also an indication for *Sepia* when there is bleeding at stool, with a feeling of fulness in the rectum as though it were distended with some foreign material, which seems to excite an urging to stool. The urine has a peculiar fœtid odor, and is very turbid. When standing it deposits a uric acid sediment, which adheres tenaciously to the side of the vessel.

Lycopodium is a worthy rival of *Sepia* in the condition just described. The distinction between the two remedies may be given in a very few words.

A sensation of emptiness in the epigastrium is more characteristic of *Sepia*; repletion after eating, of *Lycopodium*. Indeed, with the last-named drug, the repletion overshadows the other symptoms, often existing without any alterations in the appearance of the tongue. Sour taste and sour or burning eructations are, however, very common. The abdomen is in a state of ferment. After eating, the circulation is disturbed, with irresistible drowsiness. The urine contains a sediment of free red sand. The bowels are constipated, with urging and constriction of the anus. The urine, however, is not so offensive as under *Sepia*.

Sulphur resembles *Sepia* in many respects. Both are suitable in torpid cases with defective reaction. There are abdominal plethora, congested liver, piles, constipation, hunger about 11 A. M.; bitter or sour taste; eructations, sour or tasting like bad eggs; fulness from little food, etc. In *Sulphur* the face is more blotched, red, and at times spotted. Saliva nauseates him. He vomits food. He craves brandy or beer and sweets; but they disagree. He experiences hunger at 11 A. M.; while in *Sepia* it is more of a gone, faint feeling. The constipation is attended with ineffectual urging like *Nux vomica*.

For gone, empty feeling in the epigastrium, compare *Sepia* with *Calcarea ostrearum*, *Cocculus*, *Kali carb.*, *Stannum*, *Ignatia*, *Carbo an.*, *Sarsaparilla*, *Niccolum*, *Oleander*, *Ipecac.*, *Thea*, *Staphisagria*, *Actea rac.* and *Hydrastis*.

Cocculus has the weakness extending all over the abdomen and chest. It tires her to talk. The feeling is renewed by over-exertion and especially by loss of sleep.

Kali carb. has empty feeling before eating, out of proportion to the feeling of vacuity caused by hunger, with undue bloating after eating, especially after soup in small quantity.

Under *Stannum*, the sensation continues after eating, and extends all over the chest.

With *Ignatia*, it is attended by sighing.

Under *Carbo animalis*, it arises from loss of vital fluids.

Sarsaparilla has it associated with rumbling in the abdomen.

Niccolum, without desire for food.

Oleander, with sensation of distended abdomen; the chest feels empty and cold.

Actea racemosa is excellent when, with the faint, empty feeling in the epigastrium, there is a trembling, wavy sensation spreading from the stomach over the body.

Hydrastis relieves when there is sinking sensation, palpitation of the heart, and mucus-coated stools.

Thea produces a gone, faint feeling; sick headache radiating from one point, and pains in the left ovary.

LECTURE XI.

SEPIA—(*continued*).

Let us resume our study of *Sepia*. Going still lower in the abdomen, we find it exhibiting a very marked action on the uterine organs, causing, as I mentioned the other day, engorgement of the uterus with displacement. In a well-advanced *Sepia* case the uterus is enlarged and the cervix is indurated. The organ is either prolapsed or retroverted. Leucorrhœa is a very prominent symptom, the discharge being of a yellowish-green color and somewhat offensive. With these objective symptoms we find bearing-down pains in the abdomen and in the small of the back. This is so extensive at times that it seems to interfere with breathing. Sometimes the patient feels as if everything would be forced out through the vulva. This feeling is relieved by sitting with the limbs crossed. With the bearing down there is associated a backache, referable to the lumbar or sacral region. It is decidedly worse when the patient is standing or walking. There are burning pains in the uterus, and sometimes pains of a sharp character shooting upward; or there may be a sensation as if the uterus were clutched by a hand, a symptom to be found also under *Cactus* and *Lilium tigrinum*. The menses are usually late and scanty, although exceptionally they may be early and profuse.

The most similar remedy to *Sepia* is *Lilium tigrinum*, for the provings of which we are indebted to Dr. William Payne, of Bath, Maine. He was led to make the provings after learning that the flowers of this plant had caused convulsions in a child. He thought that it might prove to be a valuable remedy in the convulsions of children. In his provings he was assisted by Dr. Dunham and a number of ladies. He observed convulsions in the course of the provings, but in almost every instance some alteration in the functions of the uterus and ovaries was noticed. The uterine symptoms of *Lilium tigrinum* are those which often accompany or follow pregnancy and labor. It is indicated in cases of subinvolution. The uterus does not regain its normal size after confinement and the lochia lasts too long. When the patient rises to walk, the uterus falls by its own weight.

The patient complains of a heavy, dragging sensation, principally in the hypogastric region. She feels the need of some support to hold up the abdominal organs. This is very similar to *Sepia*. In *Sepia*, as stated, the woman sits with her legs crossed, thus giving an artificial support to the uterus. The leucorrhœa, too, is very similar. Under *Sepia* it is yellowish-green or milky, somewhat fœtid, and often excoriating Under *Lilium* I think the most characteristic leucorrhœa is watery, yellowish, or yellowish-brown, and excoriating. This excoriating property of *Lilium* is characteristic. The provers of *Lilium* had in two cases prolapsus, and in one, retroversion of the uterus. There is urging to urinate under *Lilium;* when the urine passes it causes burning and smarting, the same kind of feeling at the meatus urinarius as the leucorrhœa causes at the vulva. Then, too, you will find urging to stool; morning diarrhœa, hurrying the patient out of bed, the stool being yellow, papescent, and causing an excoriating feeling at the anus. Here *Lilium* rubs against *Sulphur*, which has characteristically early morning diarrhœa. The *Lilium* symptoms are usually worse in the afternoon, while those of *Sepia* are worse in the forenoon.

Lilium has some chest symptoms which are worthy of note. Patients experience a full, crowded feeling in the chest, as though there were too much blood there; they want the windows open, as fresh air gives them relief. This oppression of the chest is caused by venous stasis. With it there is a taste as of blood in the mouth, reminding one of *Pulsatilla* and *Hamamelis*, both of which have that symptom. There is a feeling as of a rivet or a bullet in the mammary region; also a feeling of coldness about the heart. *Natrum mur.* cures this last symptom when it appears during mental exertion; *Lilium*, when it occurs as a result of uterine disease. *Kali bichromicum*, *Kali chloratum*, and *Carbo animalis* also have it and Dr. Richard Hughes reports a case in which he cured it with *Petroleum*.

"*Helonias*," according to Dunham, "produces profound melancholy; deep, undefined depression, with a sensation of soreness and weight in the womb; 'a consciousness of a womb.' *Lilium* dulls the intellect, produces a sensation of hurry, with debility, and distress based on an apprehension of having some fatal or serious malady." And, further, *Helonias* is an excellent remedy when there is a tired, aching feeling, and some burning in the back and legs. This is common enough with women, and no remedy, unless it is *Picric acid*, relieves more promptly. The debility of *Helonias* is the result of impaired nutrition. Experiments have clearly demonstrated the fact that a diminution of red corpuscles and a general impoverishment of the blood results from its use.

Sulphur is often needed to aid *Sepia* in a chronic case. The complementary relation lies in the common power of the two drugs to correct abdominal congestion and other vascular irregularities. Sometimes, when the latter is in use, a forenoon "goneness" becomes marked as an eleven o'clock faint, hungry feeling; or, flushes of heat persist. Again, a one-sided headache persistently returns and weakens the patient. Piles grow worse. The bearing down becomes continuous, with a weak feeling in the genitals. Then *Sulphur* is substituted, and improvement is at once noticed. After awhile, however, the symptoms shift pointedly *Sepia*-ward; and so the two alternate. Several such cases have been observed. One patient from the West was entirely cured with these two drugs, and remains well. She had been an invalid for years.

Murex, also a mollusc, bears a family resemblance to *Sepia*. The provings are, as yet, meagre, but clinical experience has confirmed some of the symptoms. Dr. Dunham, and after him, Dr. B. F. Betts, have made comparisons between *Murex* and *Sepia* which are sufficient guides in their differentiation.

Murex, like its relative, causes uterine congestion, epigastric "goneness," cystic irritation, muscular debility, and mental depression.

It differs, however, in that it causes sexual excitement; desire so violent as to fatigue the reason; venereal desire renewed by the slightest touch.

The secretions are more copious than is usual with *Sepia*. Thus the menses are profuse instead of scanty. There is copious urination at midnight with pale urine; the patient wakes with a start, and a violent desire to urinate. This is not so marked in *Sepia*. Both, however, have intermittent menses.

Both remedies are useful in affections of the uterine cervix. *Murex* when there is a sensation of soreness, or "a feeling as though something was pressing on a sore spot in the pelvis"—(Betts). Lancinating pains extending upward to the abdomen or thorax; thick, green or bloody leucorrhœa. *Murex* agrees rather with *Lilium* and *Platina* in sexual erethism; and with *Kreosote* in the urinary symptoms.

Clinically it has been used for polyuria, with frequent urging at night. *Kreosote* has sudden urging; he cannot get out of bed quickly enough; he urinates with great haste, and passes a large amount of offensive urine.

Kreosote, moreover, bears some relation to *Sepia*. Both have intermittent menstrual flow, dragging downward in the back, and pressure outward in the genitals; painful coitus; vomiting of pregnancy; the urine deposits a red sediment, and is turbid and offensive.

But the menses are usually copious. They are accompanied by somewhat different reflex symptoms from those belonging to *Sepia*, notably, difficult hearing, with humming and roaring in the head. The dragging in the back is relieved by motion, not aggravated as in *Sepia*, and the leucorrhœa is more acrid and irritating; it excoriates the parts over which it flows. Sometimes it is yellow, and has the odor of fresh green corn.

This acridity of the leucorrhœa marks clearly the divergence of *Kreosote* from *Sepia*, as well as from *Murex*. This led to the employment of the drug in cancerous and other ulcerations of the cervix uteri. And we now choose it when there are burning, sensitiveness and tumefaction of the cervix, with bloody ichorous discharges; sensitiveness to touch or to coitus; and a putridity, which is foreign to the other remedies mentioned.

Stannum resembles *Sepia* in simple prolapsus uteri et vaginæ, with "goneness," bearing down and melancholy. But its characteristic is falling of the uterus and vagina during hard stool. Dr Hughes writes approvingly of its use in relieving the sensation of bearing down so common with womankind, and adds: "I have been astonished at its power over prolapsus. It seems to strengthen the uterine ligaments." (*Pharmacodynamics*, 4th edition).

Nux vomica agrees with *Sepia* in causing portal stasis; uterine congestion; hæmorrhoids; urging to stool; backache, worse from motion; awakening at 3 A. M. But *Nux* produces a peculiar irritability of the tissues, rendering the patient over-sensitive, while the functions are performed fitfully, spasmodically, and inharmoniously. Gastric symptoms predominate and they are just those which result, in a nervous person, from abuse of stimulants, highly seasoned food, etc. Thus, after a meal the clothing feels uncomfortable; retching predominates over actual vomiting. There are nausea, weakness, and a faint feeling after eating, as if produced by a strong purgative, but never the "goneness" of *Sepia* or *Murex*. There is frequent but ineffectual urging to stool, not inertia of the rectum. The menses come too early, but are not very profuse, and are accompanied by more spasmodic pains and spasmodic movements in the abdomen than in *Sepia*, and by less steady bearing down and dragging. *Nux* has one symptom, common after lacerated perineum, namely, internal swelling and burning of the vagina like a prolapsus.

Aloe acts on the liver, increases the bile, causes griping in the bowels, and diarrhœa. Its action on the bowels and uterus reminds one of *Sepia*, for it causes a determination of blood to the parts, with repletion of the veins and consequent irritation. But the relaxation, which is expressed in *Sepia* by dragging and "goneness," with weakness of the sphincters, is described by the *Aloe* patient as a more complete atony—a paresis. It is expressed as heaviness, weight, with dragging down. This heaviness belongs to the pelvis, uterus, perineum, rectum, sacral region and the lower bowels. In fact, it is universal, characterizing even the headache; dull headache across the forehead, with heaviness in the eyes and nausea—she must make the eyes small with the pain—weight on the vertex. That the headaches belong to bowel and uterine affections is proved by the fact that they alternate with symptoms of the latter (like *Podophyllum*).

Coupled with heaviness and congestion, there is a weakness of the sphincters. The patient feels a lack of confidence in them; she fears lest some stool will escape with flatus—the fæces and urine will pass together—every time she passes urine, there is a feeling as if some thin stool would escape—sudden urging in the morning.

Aloe, then, is needed when, with uterine congestion and prolapsus, there are heaviness in the abdomen and back, and uncertain control of the rectum. The woman frequently suffers from loose bowels. Without any warning, she feels faint, with a sensation as if she were about to have diarrhœa. If the bowels move, there is more wind than substance, and she becomes prostrated and covered with a clammy sweat. If she has hæmorrhoids, they protrude, and are relieved by cold applications.

Podophyllum suggests itself here. It, too, acts on the liver, causes diarrhœa and prolapsus of the uterus and rectum; hollow feeling in the epigastrium; pains in the ovaries (right) and down the anterior crural nerve; burning in the hypogastrium and sacral region, with retarded menses.

The prolapsus uteri of this remedy, however, is nearest akin to that of *Stannum*, with bearing down as if the genitals would come out during stool. But in *Stannum* it is recorded as occurring during hard stool; hence *Podophyllum* causes the more relaxation in the pelvic region.

Podophyllum, it would seem, affects first the stomach and liver, and then the uterus and rectum. We find it, therefore, most effective when its gastric symptoms concur with those of the uterine region. While it resembles *Sepia* in causing bearing down in the hypogastric and sacral regions, relieved by lying down; aching in the ovaries, etc., it differs in gastro-hepatic symptoms; fulness, weight, and dragging about the liver, soreness, better from rubbing. Diarrhœa only early in the morning or during the day; sometimes the passages are wholly fæcal, but they are too frequent. Watery, gushing diarrhœa, continuing from 3 A. M. into the forenoon. Prolapsus ani before stool. After stool a weak, faint feeling in the abdomen, weak rectum and prolapsus ani. This weakness resembles *Aloe*. It is the paresis of a violent purgative, not the general relaxation of *Sepia*.

Pulsatilla nigricans is very nearly related to *Sepia*. It cures scanty, late menses; bearing down; uterine cramps; backache; fainting; hemicrania; clavus. It is especially suitable for women who are irresolute, yielding and lachrymose, or silent, peevish and difficult to please. There is anxiety, which seems to come from the epigastrium or from the heart, with qualmishness. Anxiety as if in a hot atmosphere; also at night, as from heat. The patient is faint, she must have air. She is chilly, yet is generally better in the open air; chilly with the pains; anæmia; chlorosis.

The uterine pains of *Pulsatilla* are cutting and pressing, with a feeling of heaviness, converging toward the pudenda. The weighty sensation is compared to that of a stone, and is observed in the hypogastric and sacral regions. Constrictive, colicky, cramping pains predominate; actual bearing down is not so marked. Hence we employ it frequently in delayed menses and in labor. It acts fitfully; hence the uterine pains come by fits and starts, as does the menstrual flow; labor-pains are spasmodic, irregular, and finally end in complete inertia. Thus there is want of power from the very beginning, shown in the fitful character of the contractions, and in their final utter failure. *Sepia* causes more bearing down with the cramp. If indicated in labor, it is when an indurated and unyielding cervix retards progress.

There may be spasmodic contractions of the os and upward-shooting pains. Here it favors *Gelsemium* and *Calcarea carb.;* while *Pulsatilla* favors *Caulophyllum* and *Secale.*

In temperament, *Pulsatilla* is tearful, mild, or peevish, whimsical, cross; *Sepia* is tearful, depressed, but easily irritated and excited, or indifferent.

As already intimated, *Sepia* is of use in a congested or indurated state of the cervix uteri, with soreness and burning. *Aurum met., Aurum mur.* and *Aurum mur. natronat.* are similar. *Gold* causes hyperæmia, but it acts very differently from *Sepia.* On studying its effects one is impressed with the prominence of two sets of associated symptoms, namely, nervous excitation and vascular irritation; and yet the first no more represents innervation than the second does true plethora. They indicate irritable weakness. Hepatic, renal and uterine congestion appear to arise secondarily to a cardiac irritation with hyperæmia.

The prolonged action of *Gold* develops a fever not unlike that of *Mercurius,* with profuse sweat, salivation and copious urine. There is also a tendency to an overgrowth of fibrous tissue, whence result cirrhoses. The glands, at first stimulated, eventually become enlarged and indurated. The periosteum is diseased, and finally the bones become carious.

In keeping with these changes are its characteristic symptoms. Under its influence the emotions become greatly affected; the patient is easily enraged by trifling contradiction; there may be cheerfulness, but the most persistent state is one of melancholy and disgust for life, with a tendency to suicide She imagines she has lost the affections of her friends; the fates are against her; she is no longer fit for this world, and she longs to die. She is seized with præcordial anxiety and tremulous fearfulness. Rush of blood to the chest develops when walking fast or for a long time, with bursting fulness. There is bruised pain in the uterine region. She is oversensitive to pain, nervous, tremulous, and agitated. The uterus is congested and prolapsed by its very weight. Sexual desire is increased.

While, then, there are congestions, prolapsus and melancholy in *Aurum,* as in *Sepia* and *Murex,* the course of the symptoms is different, and the mental symptoms differ especially. In *Aurum* there is melancholy with depression, because of supposed loss of friendship; in *Sepia* there is indifference to friends. Anxiety in the former is præcordial; she must move from place to place (as in *Arsenicum*); a mere noise makes her anxious. Anxiety in the latter comes, it is true, with disturbed circulation, but it is not especially cardiac, and is accompanied by flushes of heat. Both produce weariness of life, with desire to die, even amounting to suicidal tendency; *Aurum*, because she has lost the affections of her friends (Talcott); *Sepia*, from sheer loathing of life.

Platina favors on the one hand *Aurum*, and on the other *Sepia*. All three have weariness of life. *Platina*, however, has with the weariness, a great dread of death, which the patient believes to be near at hand. As in *Aurum*, the *Platina* patient feels as if she were alone, but she has a peculiar state of mind, which finds a physical parallel in her power of vision. She is out of sorts with the world, for everything seems too narrow. Things in her own home look strange on her return after a short absence. Persons are looked down upon as pitiful, insignificant and very inferior to her. And similarly, *objects about her appear smaller than natural.*

Neither *Aurum* nor *Sepia* compares with *Platina* in the pronounced nymphomania and voluptuous irritation of the genitals. The menstrual flow in the latter is profuse and clotted instead of scanty.

Platina and *Sepia* have uterine cramp, but in the latter it is clutching, as if suddenly seized and then released; in the former it is a decided cramping followed by numbness—a symptom which is universal in this remedy.

The carbons should be compared with *Sepia*. They come into use when induration or ulceration is present, with "venosity," offensive excoriating discharges, and with gastric disturbances characterized by accumulation and passage of offensive flatus.

Carbo animalis has proved itself equal, if not superior, to *Sepia* in indurations of the cervix, with burning, tearing pain across the pubes. There are labor-like pains in the pelvis and sacrum; the leucorrhœa stains yellow; the menses are followed by great weakness, she is so weak that she can hardly speak; there is "goneness," not better from eating. She desires to be alone; she avoids all conversation; she is oppressed with anxiety and orgasms. The carbons act on the veins, favor offensive flatus, offensive discharges and excoriations, the latter being superficial and irregular in outline. Inflammations are sluggish, and tend to suppuration or death of the parts, with burning pains, great weakness and collapse.

Carbo animalis causes violent pressing in the back, groins, and thighs during the menses, with unsuccessful urging to eructate. It is distinguished from *Sepia* by a throbbing headache, which follows the menses. It has also copper-colored acne on the face.

Carbo veg. has caused bearing down in the rectum and vagina; the os is usually open; there is a feeling of weight in the uterus and right ovary; *the menses have a strong odor;* the leucorrhœa excoriates; the genitals are sore in places, and they smart, itch, burn, and are aphthous. Anxiety, with distended veins; a wretched, nervous feeling in the uterus, which culminates in the thighs; nervous, fidgety. Mental depression before the menses.

Carbo veg. may cure varicose veins of the genitals, with blueness and burning—bluish tumors (*Carbo animalis* being preferable if they are indurated), ulcers or fistulæ. The vaginal discharges are excoriating, thin, and ichorous, while in *Sepia* they are less excoriating and are thicker. There is burning across the sacrum, dragging from the abdomen to the small of the back. Burning pain deep in the pelvis, increasing and decreasing (Leadam).

Graphites is an impure carbon which contains traces of iron. It combines the offensive secretions, flatulency, and skin symptoms of the carbons, with anæmia.

According to Dunham the onset of the menses is accompanied by a variety of accessory symptoms, as with *Sepia.*

The remedy is not often required for prolapsus uteri, but it is clearly indicated when there is a feeling as if the womb would press out the vagina; the patient complains of a heavy load in the abdomen, and of lancinating-like electric shocks down the thighs (Leadam).

The leucorrhœa is profuse, coming in gushes, and is excoriating. The remedy affects the ovaries more decidedly than does *Sepia;* the left ovary is indurated and swollen, and pains are felt when the parts are touched.

Like *Sepia* it causes the nipples to inflame and crack. It is very useful to soften or remove cicatricial tissue in the mammæ (like *Phytolacca*).

But *Graphites* is best adapted to women who are anæmic, though obese, who are constantly cold, constipated, and subject to a rough, herpetic condition of the skin. The eruptions are moist, and the sweat is offensive, as in *Sepia*, but glueyness of the secretions is well-marked only in *Graphites*. The skin grows hard, cracks and bleeds. There is less desquamation than in *Sepia.*

Graphites, by virtue of its effect upon cicatricial tissue and indurations, ought to prove useful for softening the cervix, when, as is often the case, a laceration has remained unhealed, acting as a source of irritation.

Natrum carbonicum and other soda salts are complementary to *Sepia*.

The carbonate is needed when there is bearing down as if all would come out. The patient is melancholy, apprehensive and over-sensitive to music. There is backache very much like that of *Sepia*; heaviness, worse sitting, better moving; bruised pain over the back at night, tension, boring from the tip of the left scapula forward through the chest. The skin is dry and rough.

Clinically, it has served when the cervix is enlarged, with ill-shaped os. Dr. Betts has had good results with it in congenital defective growth of the anterior vaginal wall, and this ill-shaped os.

Natrum muriaticum is suited to anæmic women, with thin worn face and general emaciation. They are melancholy; easily angered; suffer from nervous weakness, with palpitation, trembling, anxiety, and predominant chilliness; inclined to sweat; sweat in the axillæ with chilliness over the back; prolapsus uteri; cramps, scanty menses, urine with red sediment; painful coitus. It therefore resembles both *Pulsatilla* and *Sepia*. But consolation aggravates (*Pulsatilla* is easily pacified, and rather seeks consolation); the headaches are congestive, pseudo-plethoric, with bursting pains, worse from the least motion, even of the eyeballs; the mucous membranes smart as under *Sepia*, but there is an abnormal dryness; thus, the tongue feels dry, the eyelids are dry, the rectum feels dry and smarts, etc. With this dryness there is a tendency to erosions, with smarting burning; thus the tongue is sore and ulcerated; the gums are sore and bleed. The skin is unnaturally dry. The prolapsus uteri is worse in the morning; she must sit down to prevent it, with backache, which is relieved by lying on the back. She complains of tension in the hypogastric and inguinal regions as if the skin were tight (*Apis*). There is greenish leucorrhœa with smarting and a feeling of dryness. Cutting in the urethra, which is most marked after urination. Menses scanty, or scanty a day or two and then copious.

Natrum hypochlorosum differs somewhat from its congeners. According to the prover, Dr. R. T. Cooper, it is useful in debilitated persons, of lax fibre and rather sluggish mentally and physically.

The debility is accompanied by emaciation, nervous exhaustion and other evidences of deep-seated changes in the organism. There are vertigo with falling, associated with aching across the forehead and uterine bearing down; swimming feeling as if the top of the cranium were about to float off. Pains across the forehead and eyes or on the vertex, with uterine symptoms. The brain feels paralyzed, also the limbs; the fingers feel numb; fainting spells. The tongue is large, and takes the imprint of the teeth; flatulency, constipation, bloating after meals, flatulent asthma—all indicating abdominal plethora.

These symptoms are met with in connection with uterine diseases. Black clotted menses; sleepiness; dark circles around the eyes. Bearing down in the uterus, which may be congested, enlarged and sensitive; constant oozing of blood, worse from any exertion. The womb feels as if it opened and shut, thus not precisely the clutching and relaxing of *Sepia*. She feels as if the womb were pushed up when she sits down (a symptom of *Ferrum iod.* also). Swelling low down in the abdomen, going up to the chest, and causing dyspnœa, worse after eating. A weight seems to fall from the chest to the abdomen, with aching on the top of the head. Swelling in the left ovarian region at the menstrual period. The drug appears to cause the prolapsed uterus to rise into its place, reminding one of the experiments of Dr. Jackson with *Sepia*. Pruritus; weak feeling about the chest; easily overcome with heat. The latter is also a symptom of *Sepia* as well as of *Natrum mur.* and *Natrum carb.*

Actea racemosa is invaluable in the treatment of women. It is especially adapted to those who are predisposed to muscular rheumatism and myalgia. It causes hyperæmia of the brain and cord, and even inflammation in the cervical and dorsal spine. Hence come its occipital pains, lightning-like pains, delirium, etc. (see below). Here it resembles *Absinthe*, *Abrotanum*, and *Gelsemium;* the last named remedy, however, has more drowsiness and muscular paresis with less excitement. *Sepia* also causes fulness of the spinal vessels, but it is less marked than in *Actea*, more passive, more torpid. The sensory nerves are excited in *Actea*, while, at the same time, they are weak, like the motor nerves and the muscles. The heart acts feebly and nervously, the pulse is either very quick and feeble or slow and intermittent. With this there is scanty urine, depositing a red or yellow sediment. There is a general feeling of uneasiness, restlessness and fidgets; or tremors, nervous chills. The muscles feel sore, bruised and stiff; there are severe myalgic pains, with numb feeling. The pains are violent and dart like lightning. Phillips recommends it even for anasarca, with the above condition of heart and urinary secretion, "even when *Digitalis* failed."

Actea, then, is preeminently a remedy for "irritable weakness." As with *Sepia*, there are nervousness, restlessness, melancholy, scanty menses with bearing down, etc. But *Actea* produces a more decided nervous excitement, amounting to delirium, with hallucinations of rats, etc.; it develops an overwhelming apprehensiveness—without apparent cause—which the patient cannot overcome, and which reduces her to despair. In her excited state she feels as if the top of her head would fly off, and she would go crazy. She becomes suspicious, irritable and is dizzy, as if intoxicated. All these symptoms form a part of the general nervous state, which depends upon an irritated condition of the uterus and ovaries; or is, at least, perpetuated thereby. The disturbed state of the uterus seems to be based upon a rheumatic diathesis. She suffers more from neuralgia than the *Sepia* patient; dull aching from the occiput to the vertex; aching soreness in the eyeballs, sharp pains thence to the vertex, with red, congested eyes—all associated with flexed or irritable uterus. Very important, too, are neuralgic pains in and about the latter organ; the uterus is sensitive to touch, pains shoot across from side to side; there is bearing down, with tightness around the hips; scanty menses, with pain continuing after the flow begins. The epigastric faintness is not quite the "goneness" of *Sepia*. It is accompanied by nervousness; tremors; waves spreading from the epigastrium all over; a feeling as if frightened. *Sepia* may be needed in asthenopia, reflex from the uterus; *Actea* rather in hyperæsthesia of the retina or in ciliary neuralgia, reflex from the uterus. Both are very useful at the climacteric; *Sepia* for the flushes of heat; *Actea*, according to Hughes, for irritability, pain at the vertex, and sinking at the stomach.

Kali ferrocyanidum has relieved bearing down; pus-like leucorrhœa, profuse but not irritating; sadness even to tears; sinking sensation at the epigastrium; passive uterine hæmorrhages with consequent debility (Bell, McClatchey).

But these effects ought not to be confounded with those of *Sepia*. For the drug is an intense poison, acting on the muscles and heart, etc. The epigastric sinking is connected with weakened heart, the heart-beats becoming diminished in number and force, with consequent coldness, sinking, vertigo, numbness and tremors. The remedy, then, suits debilitated cases in which the heart is failing. It is closely allied to *Kali carb.* in weak heart.

Calcarea ostrearum causes a pressure in the lower abdomen, on physical exertion. Bearing down, worse standing; aching in the thighs. Sore pain, tension when standing erect or bending backward. Stinging in the cervix; stitches. But the menses are profuse and too early, and the general symptoms are, as is well known, very different from those of *Sepia.*

Calcarea phosphorica (like *Phosphorus*) produces a weak, sinking feeling in the hypogastrium; empty sinking sensation at the epigastrium. The uterine prolapsus is worse during stool or micturition, with a sense of weakness and distress. Aching in the uterus. Cutting through to the sacrum. Cream-like leucorrhœa. Burning in the vagina, with pain on both sides of the bladder and uterus. Burning like fire up into the chest. Flushes of heat, anxiety, faintness, debility; she sweats easily.

But the menses are profuse and there is sexual excitement. She is weak and emaciated, perhaps tuberculous; she suffers from partial profuse sweats, but they are not offensive as in *Sepia.* Every exposure increases her rheumatic pains, and, with these, her distress in the uterus.

Among the remaining remedies I may briefly refer to the following:

Mitchella repens has engorged, dark red, swollen cervix. This is associated with an irritation at the neck of the bladder, with urging to urinate. There are, however, no general resemblances to *Sepia.* The remedy is rather to be classed with *Eupatorium purpureum* in vesical irritability in women (Hughes); with *Hydrocotyle* in irritation of the neck of the bladder, with heat and itching of the vagina and red cervix uteri (confirmed by Dr. Mitchell); with *Vespa* in ulcers around the os; and with *Apis* in dysuria.

Sepia ought not to be confounded with *Secale cornutum* or *Ustilago;* for although the three cause bearing down, congestion, aching distress, and prolapsus uteri, the conditions are quite different. The last two act on the muscular coat of the bloodvessels and on involuntary muscular fibres in general. Secondarily, from undue relaxation, they favor tumefaction and passive hæmorrhages. Their "bearing down" is prolonged, and marked (like *Caulophyllum*). *Ustilago* has relieved uterine hæmorrhage; also vomiting of blood in a lady with uterine disease; passive flow of blood; the examining finger detects a soft, patulous cervix, and is stained with blood (Woodbury).

Viburnum opulus has caused and cured pains, occurring as in *Sepia*, around the pelvis and uterine region; also "goneness;" empty feeling at the stomach; bearing down; nervousness. But the bearing down is much more violent, and culminates in the uterus in intense cramp; thus favoring *Caulophyllum*, *Actea rac.*, *Secale*, etc., rather than *Sepia*.

Inula and *Hedeoma* have been proved, but clinical experience is wanting. Like *Sepia*, they cause uterine pains and bearing down; the first, dragging in the genitals and spine; urging to stool and to micturition; the second, bearing down with great weakness in the legs.

Sepia, in a few instances, has relieved choreic symptoms; sudden jerking of the head backward and forward; twisting pain in the stomach rising to the throat.

Among similar remedies we should not forget to include *Zizia*. It causes an increase of blood in the uterus, with backache, smarting, burning in the back, spasmodic movements of the face and limbs. The mind is at first exhilarated, then depressed, and finally a state of indifference obtains. The most marked characteristic, however, is restless, choreic movements, worse during sleep.

When prolapsus uteri is a symptom of general defective nutrition, with little or no local congestion, *Sepia* yields to *Aletris*, *Caulophyllum*, *Abies Canadensis*, *Lac defloratum*, *Calcarea phos.*, *Natrum mur.*, *Helonias*, *Natrum hypochlor.*

In threatened abortion, *Sepia* is indicated not so much by the pains as by the evidence of disturbed circulation. This, together with irritable nerves and laxness of tissue, makes up the cause of the impending catastrophe. It will be noticed that there are, or there have been, fulness and pressure of blood to the head and chest, feeling of heaviness in the abdomen, flushes of heat, with faintness and momentary attacks of blindness—observed especially when the patient is in a warm or close room, kneeling in church, when using the eyes steadily, etc. A common attendant, clearly expressive of the nature of the *Sepia* case, is the excellent keynote of Dr. H. N. Guernsey: sense of weight in the anus like a heavy ball.

This last symptom is unique, differing materially from the urging of *Nux* and *Sulphur*, the pressure of *Lilium*, and the fulness and weight of *Aloe*. The latter has also a sensation of a plug wedged in between the symphysis pubis and os coccygis.

LECTURE XII.

NOSODES.

This class of remedies, as I have already intimated in my introductory lecture, consists of disease products. Many of them have been demonstrated to possess medicinal properties, and hence they are useful in the treatment of diseases of the human frame. The field here is certainly an immense one. As yet, we hardly know the commencement of our labors in this direction. I think that the time will come, when the medicines composing the group, will prove themselves to be of immense service in the treatment of chronic diseases. Some of the nosodes have been derived from the diseases of animals, others from those of plants.

Great objections have been made to the nosodes as remedies in homœopathic practice. It is well that you should understand the prejudices which you will meet, both among the laity and in the profession. Objections have been made to *Psorinum*, which you know is obtained from the itch eruption and also to *Syphilinum*, the syphilitic poison, on the ground that they are nasty and filthy. This objection is certainly absurd, because nobody would for one minute entertain the idea of administering these substances in a low potency; and this being the case, no one will maintain that there is anything nasty or disagreeable to one's feelings in administering to a patient *Psorinum*, for instance, in the two hundredth attenuation.

Another objection that has been raised against the nosodes, and one which apparently carries some weight with it, is, that the use of these substances interferes with the progress of Homœopathy by confusing it with Isopathy. We may reason as much as we will, but we must always keep in view the facts of the case. We must fall back on the tribunal before which all our prescriptions must go, and that is experience. Now, I do not know how far I should care to go into these nosodes. Correctly applied, they are not isopathic remedies. What I call pure Isopathy is the practice proposed by Dr. S. Swan, of New York. For example, if a patient is so constituted that he cannot eat strawberries without being made ill thereby, Dr. Swan potentizes the strawberry and administers it to the patient and claims that thus the idiosyncrasy is destroyed. Isopathy rests on the bold assertion that what causes disease will cure it when administered in a high potency. The use of the nosodes in homœopathic practice differs from this because in Homœopathy we start with an experimental fact. We have taken these substances, proved them on the healthy, and have administered them at the bedside. We have found them efficacious, therefore we have the same right to claim them as medicines as we have any molecular substance. We will now proceed with their symptomatology, beginning first with

PSORINUM.

Psorinum has been sufficiently proved to enable us to use it successfully in the treatment of disease. We find it especially indicated in constitutions which are psoric (to use Hahnemann's word), in patients who are subject to glandular and cutaneous affections, and who do not react to the apparently well-chosen remedy. Suppose, for example, that the remedy suited to the case is *Pulsatilla*. The symptoms seem to call for it. The prescription is in accord with every rule of Institutes, and yet relief is but transient. In such a case, there is some dyscrasia underlying the disease, and this must be removed or modified before it will be possible to cope successfully with the disease. Again, in certain cases of scarlatina your prescriptions avail nothing, and the little ones die. Many of these cases could be saved if we investigated this branch of our materia medica more thoroughly. The various constitutions or dyscrasiæ underlying chronic and acute affections are. indeed, very numerous. As yet, we do not know them all. We do know that one of them is due to gonorrhœa. This disease is so frightfully common, that patients with a dyscrasia arising from it are very rapidly increasing. Now I want to tell you why this is so. It is because allopathic physicians, and many homœopaths as well, do not properly cure it. Gonorrhœa is not a local disease, and, if it is not properly cured, a constitutional dyscrasia is developed, which may be transmitted to the offspring. I know, from years of experience and observation, that gonorrhœa is a serious difficulty, and one, too, that complicates many of the cases that we have to treat. The same is true, in a modified degree, of syphilis. Gonorrhœa seems to attack the nobler tissues, the lungs, the heart and the nervous system, all of which are reached by syphilis only after the lapse of years.

To return from this digression. *Psorinum*, like *Sulphur*, is to be thought of in cases where there is a decided psoric taint, and the well-chosen remedy refuses to act. Let us look at some of the symptoms, and note the way that *Psorinum* affects the tissues. It causes an eruption on the skin, usually herpetic in character, and accompanied by great itching. This itching is intolerably worse as soon as the patient gets warm in bed. By and by you will observe that the skin has a dirty, dingy look, as though the patient had never washed himself (which may indeed be the case). In some places the skin has a coarse look, as though bathed in oil. The sebaceous secretion is excessive. In children the eruption is especially noticeable about the head. It may involve the whole scalp, but it spreads characteristically from the scalp down either side of the face, involving the cheeks and ears, like tinia capitis, which in fact it is. This eruption is, at times, moist, and oozes a matter which is very offensive. At other times it is dry, furfuraceous, as it is then called, and may disappear in the summer, only to reappear when cold weather sets in. There is usually associated with these skin symptoms an otorrhœa, which is thin, ichorous and horribly offensive, having an odor like that of rotten meat. Ulcers appear on the legs, usually about the tibia or around the ankles or other joints. These ulcers have but this to characterize them, *they are slow to heal;* they are indolent. I may also observe here, that the herpetic and itching eruptions just referred to are apt to appear in the bends of joints, in the bends of the elbows, and in the popliteal spaces. The child is pale, sickly and greatly emaciated. The entire surface of the body emits an offensive odor, which persists despite the most careful washing. This comes from defective action of the cutaneous glands. They do not properly eliminate, and consequently the discharges remain and undergo decomposition and give off this odor, which can never be cured until the child's skin is cured.

In summer time these children are very apt to have cholera infantum. There is no remedy that replaces *Psorinum* in its range of symptoms in this disease. The children are apt to be nervous and restless at night as a precursory symptom to the cholera infantum. They awake at night as if frightened, or they cry out during sleep; then, two or three nights afterward, they begin with diarrhœa; the stools are profuse and watery, dark brown or even black in color, very offensive, almost putrid in odor, worse at night, or driving the patient out of bed early in the morning

Psorinum cures a form of chronic cephalalgia with bursting, throbbing pains in the head, preceded by flickering, dimness of vision or spots before the eyes, and accompanied by hunger. Sometimes the patient is inordinately hungry the day before the attack. This hungry feeling is a frequent concomitant of *Psorinum* complaints. Canine hunger preceding an attack of diarrhœa. Hunger at night, must get up and eat something, like *Phosphorus* and *China*, a condition sometimes met with in pregnancy.

We also find *Psorinum* indicated in the bad effects of suppressed itch. This disease is produced, you know, by the itch insect. You are justified in using as a local application anything that will kill the insect but not suppress the disease. Such an application you have in *Oil of lavender*, which kills both the insects and their ova. When itch has been suppressed, *Psorinum* is an excellent remedy to develop it; usually, too, it will cure the disease after its redevelopment.

Psorinum is also useful when pustules or boils remain after itch has been cured by some other remedy.

There is another use that may be made of *Psorinum*, which I have not mentioned, but which is as important as any other. Sometimes, after acute or violent diseases, we find the patient greatly prostrated. For instance, after typhoid fever he is depressed in mind, weak in body, low-spirited, hopeless of recovery, and yet you know that there is no absolute certainty that the patient cannot get well; that there are no organic lesions remaining. He has weakening night-sweats. Perhaps *Sulphur* has been given without result. In such cases *Psorinum* is the remedy.

Here you may also consider *China* or *Cinchona*, which is an excellent remedy for rapid exhaustion following acute diseases, especially when there has been loss of blood, protracted or profuse diarrhœa, or profuse sweat. It is similar to *Psorinum* in the night-sweat; but the latter is the remedy when there is the mental state just described—the despair of recovery.

Laurocerasus is to be thought of when there is lack of reaction, especially in chest troubles.

Capsicum is indicated in lack of reaction occurring in persons of lax fibre.

Opium is a very superior remedy in these cases when the patient is stupid and drowsy.

Valerian, *Moschus* and *Ambra grisea* are to be used in nervous affections when the apparently well-chosen remedy fails.

Carbo veg. is indicated in cases of abdominal disease when there is great coldness of the body. The breath is cold, and the pulse rapid.

Psorinum is very similar, as you see, to *Sulphur*. It complements that remedy. It is inimical to *Lachesis*, and is antidoted by *Coffea*.

AMBRA GRISEA.

Ambra grisea is supposed to be a disease-product derived from the whale. It has a decided medicinal action, and, like all substances having a strong odor, it acts prominently upon the nervous system. Unless there are some nervous symptoms present in the case, you can hardly expect it to do good service. *Ambra* affects the cerebro-spinal nervous system, causing spasmodic symptoms here and there over the body. The muscles of the face twitch. It may also be used in sleeplessness arising from worriment of mind, as from business troubles. The patient may, in these cases, retire to bed feeling tolerably tired, yet as soon as his head touches the pillow he becomes wakeful. Such a case as that frequently yields to *Ambra*. This remedy is particularly indicated in thin, spare men, who have a decidedly nervous temperament, in whom nervousness predominates at the expense of nutrition. It is particularly indicated for the nervous complaints of old people, especially when they are forgetful and cannot remember the simplest facts. Vertigo comes on when the patient moves about, and the legs are unsteady; he totters when he walks. He has numbness of the feet and tingling in the limbs. The limbs go to sleep readily. These symptoms show you that there is either functional or organic weakness of the cerebro-spinal nervous system. We may use the drug in cases of softening of the brain and spinal cord, whether of senile origin or not.

There is another use we may make of *Ambra grisea*. It is a very quick-acting remedy. We may, therefore, give it in nervous diseases when there is defective reaction. We have already learned of a similar use of *Psorinum;* under the latter remedy, the defective reaction arises from constitutional taint. But under *Ambra grisea* it arises from nervous weakness. We find many such cases, particularly among men.

We may use *Ambra* for cough which is worse when strangers are in the room, or under any other circumstances which would tend to excite the nervous system. It is then a cough that is reflex from mental influences. In these cases, it is exactly similar to *Phosphorus*.

Ambra is also indicated for cough, whether whooping-cough or not, when the cough is followed by eructations of wind from the stomach. There are not many remedies that will cure this symptom. *Ambra grisea* is one of the best; others are *Sulphuric acid*, *Arnica*, *Sanguinaria* and *Veratrum album*. Sometimes the eructations come during the cough, which is usually a very annoying and painful symptom. Here *Ambra* coincides with *Arsenicum*, *Cimex*, *Lachesis* and *Angustura*. We may use *Ambra* in asthma when it is accompanied by cardiac symptoms, oppression of breathing, and a feeling as of a load or lump in the left chest and fluttering in the region of the heart. This comes probably from a constrictive feeling there, not as if a hand were grasping the heart, but as if something in the left side of the chest were squeezed up in a lump. It is usually accompanied by palpitation of the heart.

Ambra grisea acts markedly on the female genital organs, its action here being important and quite unique. It causes atony of the uterus. The menses are regular as to time or they come a few days too early, but they are very profuse, and are accompanied by nosebleed and by an increase in the varicose veins on the legs, if such a condition is present. There is a discharge of blood between the periods. Any little excitement or extra effort, such as straining at stool, brings on a vaginal discharge of blood, showing how engorged is the uterus and how relaxed and weak the tissues. The leucorrhœa consists principally of mucus, which has a bluish or bluish-gray tinge to it.

You may also use *Ambra* during the lying-in period, especially when constipation is severe. It is suited to those nervous women who are thin and scrawny-looking, who have frequent ineffectual urging to stool accompanied by great anxiety and restlessness, and inability to pass stool while the nurse or any one else is in the room.

LECTURE XIII.

SECALE CORNUTUM.

Secale cornutum is commonly called "spurred rye." *Ergot*, a term borrowed from the French, is the name of the drug in the old school pharmacopœia. The drug is not obtained from the rye itself, but from a fungous growth which attacks the grain, probably when it is very young.

Secale cornutum, or *Ergot*, has long been used in the dominant school on account of its well-known property of producing contraction of non-striated muscular fibres when given in appreciable doses. It exerts this action particularly on those involuntary muscular fibres which have a circular or transverse direction. I believe that it does this through an influence exerted over the vaso-motor nerves, and that all its symptoms are explainable on this ground. In the first place, the effects of *Secale* may be divided into two sets, those referable to the circulation, and those referable directly to the nervous system. We shall consider the last-named first. We find *Ergot* producing a peculiar type of convulsions, which constitute a prominent symptom of Ergotism, a condition of chronic poisoning produced by *Ergot*. Ergotism is not at all uncommon on the continent of Europe, especially in some of the provinces of Germany, where the farmers grow a great deal of rye. Rye is the principal grain, and thus *Ergot* poisoning is frequent. Of late years, by exercising more care, the number of cases of Ergotism has lessened. Let us now return from this little digression and describe the character of the convulsions.

At times the body is rigid and at others the rigidity alternates with relaxation; particularly is this noticed in the fingers. The hands are clenched, or the fingers are spread wide apart. The facial muscles twitch. Twitching commences in the face and spreads over the whole body. The abdomen is drawn in by the contraction of the musculi recti abdominales. There is suppression of urine, and at the same time retention from spasmodic contraction of the neck of the bladder. By the use of the catheter a small amount of prune-juice-like fluid may be obtained. There is a great deal of spasmodic retching, but not much real vomiting. The stomach is violently contracted.

Coming now to the action of *Secale* on the circulation, we find that the symptoms referred to disordered circulation are traceable to the action of the drug on the involuntary muscular fibres of the blood-vessels. The first effect is one of contraction, while the secondary action produces a dilatation. The fingers look bluish-black, as though the blood had settled there. The skin is wrinkled and dry. After a time sloughing of the whole or part of the limb results. Now, the explanation of this is as follows: there has been a prolonged contraction of the capillaries, interfering with the circulation, and bringing about a stasis of blood. Thus local nutrition is deranged and the part in consequence dies. This action of *Secale* has led to its use in dry gangrene, especially of the toes in old people.

Coming next to the uterus as a muscular organ containing non-striated muscular fibres, we find that *Ergot* produces marked contraction of this viscus, acting more on the pregnant than on the non-pregnant uterus, more upon the uterus of parous than of nulliparous women. The more the uterine muscular fibres are multiplied the more powerful is the action of *Ergot*. What symptoms does the drug produce? You know that it has been used to bring on contraction of the uterus, to cause abortion, to hasten the expulsion of the fœtus when abortion is inevitable, to increase labor-pains, to expel the after-birth, and in fact whenever it is desirable to create uterine contractions. One of its characteristic symptoms is prolonged but ineffectual uterine pains. Another, which you will sometimes notice in cases of retained placenta, is hour-glass contraction of the uterus. This peculiar contraction prevents the expulsion of the placenta. You may remove the after-birth by the aid of the hand, but the safer plan is to give a few doses of *Secale*.

Secale may also be used in thin and scrawny women, with dry, harsh, shrivelled skins, and sallow faces, who are very weak in labor. The labor-pains seem to be entirely wanting. The uterus is as flabby as though it were merely mucous membrane, instead of a muscular organ. At other times the woman will complain of a sort of prolonged bearing down feeling in the abdomen and the sacral region.

Ergot affects the blood itself; it seems to lessen the coagulating function of that fluid. Hence it will cause hæmorrhages, which are dark, thin and persistent; hæmorrhage from the uterus or from any of the cavities of the body. You may give it in uterine hæmorrhage when the flow is passive, dark in color and, it may be, offensive. The woman may be reduced to such an extent that she is almost exsanguinated and lies unconscious and cold. Before losing consciousness she complains of tingling all over the body, and requests the attendants to rub her limbs. Formication is the best word to describe this tingling sensation under *Secale*. She constantly holds her fingers spread asunder. This symptom seems to bother her even more than the hæmorrhage itself. In such cases *Secale* is the remedy.

Again, we may use *Secale* in retained placenta, when it arises, not from hour-glass contraction of the uterus (although this condition may obtain), but after miscarriage, especially that occurring during the early months of pregnancy. The discharge corresponding to the lochia is offensive. The patient is cold and often almost pulseless, from loss of blood; the uterine contractions are very imperfect, or else there is prolonged tonic contraction. In such cases, *Secale* is further indicated by its mental symptoms. The patient has mania, during which she laughs, claps her hands over her head, in fact, seems to be beside herself.

Secale acts very prominently on the gastro-enteric organs. It produces a picture very much like that of cholera, and will be found useful whether it be cholera infantum, cholera morbus, or cholera Asiatica. It is indicated when the patient is cold and almost pulseless, with spasmodic twitching of the muscles in various parts of the body; the spreading asunder of the fingers is especially noticeable. The eyes are sunken, and the features pinched. There is a great deal of spasmodic retching, although not much vomiting. The surface of the body is harsh, shrivelled, and dry, as though there were no moisture left in the system. The urine is suppressed. There is tingling or formication all over the body. The stools are profuse and watery, and are ejected with great violence. The patient, though cold, cannot bear to be covered.

In cholera infantum *Secale* is indicated more particularly by profuse undigested stools, which are watery and very offensive, are discharged by fits and starts, and are followed by intense prostration. Now, *Secale* must be separated from the remedies that are similar to it, or you cannot use it to the best advantage.

It has been observed in the case of a manufactory in which substances containing arsenic were made, that the fumes of the arsenic destroyed all the surrounding vegetation with the exception of the rye, which grew more luxuriantly under the fumes of this factory than it did in other localities. When we come to study the medicinal effects of *Secale* and *Arsenicum* we find that they have many symptoms in common. Both produce shrivelling of the tissues, both produce gangrene, both produce choleraic symptoms, and they follow each other well. The following few distinctions are sufficient: in the first place, the *Arsenicum* gangrene and almost all of its other symptoms are worse from cold and better from warmth. The patient wants to be wrapped up warmly. The *Secale* patient finds relief from cold. The same is true of ulcers. If you have an indolent ulcer, with burning pains and discharge of an ichorous offensive pus, you almost always think of *Arsenicum*. Yet *Secale* is the remedy if there is relief from cold.

In cholera, both remedies have profuse, offensive, watery stools, which are very exhausting. *Arsenicum* lacks the tingling which is almost always present when *Secale* is the remedy. *Arsenicum* has more restlessness, anxiety, anxious tossing about and irritability of fibre. The patient wants to be warmly wrapped, while the *Secale* patient wants to be cool.

During the stage of collapse, *Secale* is indicated by the symptoms I have mentioned. Here, it is very similar to *Carbo veg*. The latter remedy is indicated when the prostration is so great that the patient lies quiet, too weak to move, with passive hæmorrhage from the nose, and, perhaps, from the bowels as well. The body is cold, especially from the feet to the knees. The pulse is rapid, almost threadlike, and the breath is cold. In such alarming cases *Carbo veg*. may sometimes save the patient's life.

Another similar remedy, *Camphor*, is to be used in preference to *Secale*, *Arsenicum*, or *Carbo veg*. in cholera, when the system is overwhelmed by the suddenness or violence of the poison, before there is any vomiting or diarrhœa, and when the prostration is intense and the body is as cold as ice. The voice is squeaky or husky. *Camphor* is here used in the mother tincture, a few drops in water, and a dose given every fifteen minutes until the reaction takes place, when some other remedy may be needed.

Veratrum album resembles *Secale* in the coldness and blueness of the surface, with profuse watery stools; but it differs in one symptom, namely, the cold sweat on the forehead. None of the remedies just mentioned have this symptom except *Arsenicum*, and under this remedy the restlessness is greater than under *Veratrum*, while the cold sweat on the forehead is less marked.

In the uterine symptoms, hæmorrhages, etc., we have to remember some remedies that are closely allied to *Secale*. I may incidentally mention *Carbo veg.* here as a remedy similar to *Secale* in persistent epistaxis. The bleeding continues day after day, apparently not decreasing in the least, the blood being dark and non-coagulable. You must distinguish between the two remedies by their other characteristic symptoms.

Ustilago is to be remembered as a companion of *Secale*. It is a fungus which grows on corn and is similar in action to *Ergot*. Careful chemical analysis shows that it contains Ergotin just as does *Secale*. *Ustilago* may be used in hæmorrhages somewhat different in character from those of *Secale*. The hæmorrhages in which it is most effective are those from the uterus, when the flow is bright red, partly fluid, and partly clotted. With this condition present you may use *Ustilago*, whether the hæmorrhage occur at the climaxis or during labor, abortion, or menstruation. Unlike *Secale*, this remedy causes passive congestion of the uterus. It is especially indicated when the slight manipulation necessary for a digital examination causes oozing of blood. Another condition for which it is the remedy is menorrhagia from retroflexion of the uterus. I have generally used it in the sixth potency. It seems to give tone to the uterus, so that the organ no longer feels soft and spongy to the examining finger. The circulation through the uterus is improved, and bleeding takes place less readily.

We have two or three other remedies useful in these cases of engorged uterus, and as this condition is so difficult to cure I will give them to you here.

One of them is *Bovista*, the puff-ball. When this plant is mature, the envelope of the ball bursts, and there is ejected from the cavity a brownish powder, which consists of the spores of the plant. This, when applied to the skin, produces an eruption resembling herpes, which bleeds readily. *Bovista* affects the circulation in a very peculiar way. It seems to produce a relaxation of the entire capillary system, but whether it acts through the blood or through the nervous system, I am unable to state. This relaxation of the capillaries favors the hæmorrhagic diathesis. On account of this unique action of *Bovista*, we find it useful in epistaxis, associated either with menstrual irregularity, or with traumatism.

Bovista is indicated in uterine hæmorrhage when the uterus is engorged, particularly when there is a flow of blood between the menstrual periods from any little over-exertion. Here it is exactly like *Ambra grisea*, but the menstrual flow of *Bovista* occurs *chiefly or only at night or early in the morning*. It would seem that the exercise during the day, by favoring the circulation, tends to diminish the uterine congestion.

Hæmorrhage when the uterus is engorged is also found under *Ustilago* and *Secale*.

Another peculiarity of *Bovista*, which I might mention here, is a puffy condition of the surface of the body. A lady, for instance, after holding her scissors, notices that a deep crease has been made in the thumb and finger by the instrument, showing that there is a slight œdematous condition produced by the sluggish passage of the blood through the veins.

Bovista also produces some symptoms of suffocation. It is used, in some countries, to stupefy bees in order to facilitate the collection of honey. The symptoms of asphyxia are very much like those produced by the fumes of charcoal, and *Bovista* has proved useful as an antidote to the effects of charcoal fumes.

Other antidotes to charcoal fumes are *Arnica* and *Opium*.

In addition to these symptoms of *Bovista*, you should remember another group, likewise dependent upon the circulation. The heart feels enormously large, with oppression of the chest and palpitation after a meal and during menstruation. Associated with the heart disease, and also with deranged menses, is a headache deep in the brain, with a feeling as though the head were enormously large or swollen.

Mitchella repens may be used in cases of engorged uterus when the flow is more active than in the case of the remedies already mentioned. The blood is brighter in color, and the hæmorrhage is associated with dysuria.

The next remedy that I want to mention as similar to *Secale* in hæmorrhages is *Trillium pendulum*. This remedy is useful in an entirely different type of hæmorrhage from that calling for the former. It is indicated when the flow of blood is bright red and profuse, and is attended by a faint feeling in the epigastrium, pain in the back, coldness of the extremities, prostration, and rapid, feeble pulse. It is more closely allied to *Cinchona* than to any of the remedies thus far mentioned. It is indicated more by the active acute hæmorrhage than by the chronic slow oozing calling for *Secale*. There is gushing of bright red blood at every least motion. She feels as though the sacro-iliac synchondroses were falling apart and wants the pelvis tightly bound.

Hamamelis is likewise indicated in hæmorrhage. It acts as you know principally upon the veins. It is called for when there is hammering headache, especially about the temples. Strange to say the patient exhibits no alarm or anxiety concerning the hæmorrhage. The flow is dark and rather passive and there is a feeling of soreness in the affected part. The patient is greatly exhausted by the flow of blood.

Erigeron Canadensis is indicated in hæmorrhages from the uterus associated with painful urination. How can you distinguish it from *Mitchella?* The *Erigeron* hæmorrhage comes in fits and starts; it comes with a sudden gush and then stops again.

Sometimes the cavity remaining after the extraction of a tooth bleeds persistently. If you can clean out that cavity so as to remove the clot, and apply to it a piece of cotton soaked in tincture of *Trillium*, you will often check the hæmorrhage even when other styptics fail. I have never used *Erigeron* in that way and cannot, therefore, tell what effect it would have. I have used *Trillium* in the same way in nosebleed.

I would like to mention here *Ferrum phosphoricum*. It acts upon the circulation very much as does *Hamamelis*. It is an excellent remedy in that stage of inflammation which we describe as "dilatation of the blood-vessels." If administered then, it prevents further extension of the disease. Thus in engorgement of the lungs, it prevents the subsequent pneumonia. The chest feels sore and bruised, the pulse is full and round, but not rope-like as under *Aconite*. The expectoration is scanty and blood-streaked. Whenever the discharge contains blood and you have not the sthenic fever that belongs to *Aconite*, you may depend upon *Ferrum phos*. Sometimes in the summer diarrhœa of children, the bloodvessels of the intestinal tract become greatly distended. The stools are watery and contain mucus and blood. There may be a little urging to stool but no tenesmus. If tenesmus appears, *Ferrum phos*. ceases to be the remedy. If your case advances to the production of pus or muco-pus, *Ferrum phos*. can do no good.

You may also use *Ferrum phos*. in the beginning of hydrocephaloid, when, during a violent attack of summer complaint, the child becomes drowsy and heavy, its eyes are suffused with blood, and there is a full, soft pulse. It has not the hard, tense pulse of *Aconite* or *Belladonna*.

LECTURE XIV.

THE VEGETABLE KINGDOM.

I HAVE now reviewed the majority of the medicines derived from the animal kingdom, and also the most important of the nosodes. We come next to the second grand division in natural history, the vegetable kingdom. The vegetable kingdom offers us many varieties of medicinal substances, some of great practical utility and others having but a limited sphere of usefulness. Drugs obtained from this kingdom owe their medicinal effects to the juices which they contain, or to certain properties which reside in the roots, flowers, or seeds. The medicinal qualities of a plant may be obtained from various parts of it, and these qualities may vary with the part. It is said of *Belladonna*, for instance, that one part of the plant gives us more of the acrid qualities of the drug, while another gives us more of the narcotic properties. We must be careful then in making a proving of a vegetable drug, that we are certain of the part of the plant we are using; and in publishing our proving, we should state whether the whole plant was used, or only a single part of it. If but a single part was utilized, we should state accurately which part, as the root, the flowers, the seeds, etc.

A study of the vegetable kingdom involves to some extent a study of the mineral kingdom, because many of the medicinal properties of vegetable remedies owe their existence to substances derived from the minerals in the soil in which they grow. The principal effects of some of the grasses are the result of the large quantity of *Silica* they contain. Ninety-nine one-hundredths of the effects of *Laurocerasus* come from its *Hydrocyanic* or *Prussic acid*, which is commonly classed with the inorganic compounds. The same may be said of *Amygdala persica*. Now these substances derived from the mineral kingdom and contained in the vegetable kingdom, become more active in their new environment; that is to say, a given chemical substance, if made synthetically in the laboratory, would possess less marked medicinal virtues than if it were obtained from a plant. The above remarks also apply to the animal and vegetable kingdoms. Substances existing in the animal kingdom and found also in the vegetable, are far more active in the former. Thus the Colorado potato bug, which feeds on potato-plants and derives from thence *Solanine*, presents more powerfully the symptoms of the latter than does the *Solanine* itself.

We shall study the remedies derived from the vegetable kingdom according to the classification of botanists. There are some incongruities in the botany of to-day; for instance, in the leguminous order of plants from which we get peas and beans, which are very nutritious, is also placed the Lathyrus. which has very poisonous properties. Because there is an outward resemblance between the Lathyrus and sweet-pea, it seems not a little incongruous to put them together, when their effects are so different.

The five relations of drugs, which I have already mentioned, apply here as in the animal kingdom. There is this to be remembered, that substances having the same origin generally do not follow each other well. For example, if you have given *Ignatia*, it is not well to follow it with *Nux vomica*, and *vice versa*, because they both contain *Strychnia*. Though they have many symptoms in common, they act too much in the same line. Another example may be noted in *Glonoin* and wine. When *Glonoin* was proved, it was found to have a decided action on the pulse. All the symptoms were aggravated when the provers took wine. Wine produces an excitement very similar to that of *Glonoin*, but its action seems to be in the same direction, consequently it intensifies the effects of the latter.

But the different orders, sub-orders and classes into which botanists divide plants are so extensive and cover such vague resemblances, that we cannot confine ourselves strictly to the above rule regarding the sequence of drugs. Take for instance the Ranunculaceæ, from which we obtain *Pulsatilla, Aconite, Helleborus*, and *Staphisagria*. Now the resemblances between these four drugs are not so close that they cannot follow each other without injury. If we find, then, from our study of symptomatology of the drugs that there are no marked resemblances between them, the rule does not apply. In the Anacardiaceæ the rule does not apply with regard to *Anacardium* and *Rhus tox*. These drugs bear a family resemblance, but their points of divergence are so great that one drug may act as an antidote to the other. The rule, however, does apply to *Ignatia* and *Nux vomica*, and to *Pulsatilla Nuttalliana* and *Pulsatilla pratensis*. I will now take up the consideration of the individual drugs derived from the vegetable kingdom.

APOCYNACEÆ.

In the order of *Apocynaceæ* there are a number of plants which we use as medicines. Among these may be mentioned *Apocynum cannabinum* and *androsæmifolium, Gelsemium sempervirens, Vinca minor, Oleander, Nux vomica, Ignatia, Curare, Alstonia scholaris,* and *Spigelia.* By some authorities *Gelsemium, Nux vomica, Ignatia, Curare,* and *Spigelia* have been included in another order, the *Loganiaceæ.* This order of plants is very poisonous; they depress the nervous system, causing prostration, and even narcosis and paralysis; some of them cause death.

APOCYNUM CANNABINUM.

Apocynum cannabinum was said by Pliny to be fatal to dogs, and from this circumstance its name was derived. It has a tough fibre, like hemp, which has been used for cordage.

Apocynum has a marked effect in increasing the flow of urine. It is not sufficient, however, in the present course, to study the drug simply as a diuretic, because it has such a decided action on the vital forces that it demands a more extended notice. It depresses the vital forces greatly, as evidenced in the relaxed sphincters, loss of muscular power, etc. This loss of power is an important general symptom, since it qualifies, as we shall see presently, the cardiac, renal and intestinal symptoms.

In the last few years *Apocynum* has come into very extensive use in the treatment of many forms of dropsy. When I give you a resume of its symptoms, you will see that its indiscriminate use in dropsical conditions is by no means strictly homœopathic. When not properly indicated symptomatically, it is necessary to exhibit it in large doses in order to produce any effect. *Scoparius* (broom-corn) and also the pods of some of the Leguminosæ, cause increased functional activity of the kidneys and so aid in the elimination of the dropsical effusion. But *we* have to deal with an art that admits of no such prescribing. It aims at definiteness, not generalization. It teaches the selection of a similimum, not of a temporary palliative.

When indicated *Apocynum* demands that the following symptoms be present: bewilderment and heaviness of the head; drowsiness and debility or disturbed, restless sleep. The functions are sluggish. The pulse is slow. The bowels are constipated, although the fæces are not hard. The kidneys are torpid, or else the urine is copious and urination is almost involuntary from relaxed sphincters. The nose and throat are filled with thick yellow mucus on awakening. The patient has a sense of oppression at the epigastrium and chest; he can hardly get breath to speak, even after lighter meals than usual; he must take frequent deep inspirations. There are also fluttering of the heart, and dartings and prostrated feeling in the cardiac region. The pulse is irregular, intermittent and at times feeble, then slow. The heart beats regularly, then flutters and becomes feeble, then slow and labored, now and then losing a beat. This is just the group of symptoms characteristic of cardiac dropsy, and it shows what an affinity the drug has for the cardiac region. It will often palliate even in fatty degeneration of the heart, with dropsy, in old people.

Here you may compare several remedies: first, *Arsenicum*. This remedy has the same thirst and the same sinking at the epigastrium as has *Apocynum*, but it is indicated in more advanced cases, and the patient always presents more irritability of fibre.

I showed you the distinction between *Apis*, *Acetic acid*, and *Apocynum* when I lectured on *Apis*.

Helleborus and *Digitalis* are similar to *Apocynum* in causing torpidity, slow pulse, etc. But I think that *Apocynum*, as a rule, is the preferable remedy, unless the symptoms point very strongly to one of the other two.

Apocynum also has some action on the joints, producing a rheumatic condition. The joints feel stiff, especially on moving in the morning.

You may recall that I mentioned *Apocynum* as a remedy in hydrocephalus. The head is large; there is bulging of the frontal bones; the fontanelles are wide open; there is squinting, and, in extreme cases, the patient is blind; one side is paralyzed. The case closely resembles *Apis*, but lacks the cephalic cry. It is indicated in more advanced cases than *Apis*. One or two cases have been cured by the continued use of the remedy.

There is a diarrhœa which may call for *Apocynum*. The stools are copious, yellow, watery, or brownish, and sometimes contain undigested food. They are discharged with an expulsive force like a cork from a bottle. The sphincter ani is so weak that stools escape unbidden, or while the patient is passing flatus. After stool, he feels weak or has an "all-gone feeling" in the abdomen. The face is pale and covered with a cold sweat.

Aloe has a similar weakening effect on the sphincter ani, and great prostration after stool; but the stools under this remedy contain a *jelly-like mucus*, are apt to be worse in the morning, and there is a colic which is relieved by bending double.

Gamboge has stool preceded by excessive cutting about the navel. The stool is expelled "all at once" after considerable urging, and is followed by a feeling of great relief.

Apocynum also has hæmorrhoids, which are associated with a feeling as if a wedge were being hammered into the anus.

Anacardium is another drug which has a sensation as though a plug were being forced up into the anus.

OLEANDER NERIUM.

The *Oleander nerium* is a native of Palestine, but it is also found wild in Southern Europe and is much cultivated in gardens and hothouses everywhere; it thrives especially in damp places. As a plant it is highly ornamental, its large rose-colored flowers making it particularly attractive. It is, however, very poisonous, causing a decided prostration of the nervous system with symptoms of narcosis. Do not fail to remember this depressing character of the drug. It produces weak memory and forgetfulness. Not only does it have this effect, but it also produces slowness of perception. The patient has great difficulty in catching the meaning of remarks. Accompanying these mental symptoms is a vertigo which is the result of weakness. Everything points to depression of the sensorium. *Oleander* is an important remedy when the symptoms just mentioned are the forerunners of paralysis.

Some years ago I succeeded in curing a case of headache with *Oleander*. The patient was a young lady. The headache was relieved by forcibly looking cross-eyed. While hunting for this symptom in the materia medica, I found that *Oleander* had pain in the head relieved by looking sideways. On that symptom I prescribed the remedy.

Studying the action of *Oleander* on the abdominal organs, we find emptiness and goneness in the pit of the stomach, even after eating, relieved by taking brandy. You will find this symptom indicating

Oleander in very weak women who have infants at the breast. Immediately after nursing, the patient is seized with a tremor, and is so weak that she is scarcely able to walk across the room.

Carbo animalis is also suited to this condition.

Oleander is useful in diarrhœa. The stools are thin and contain undigested food, the characteristic symptom being that the patient passes, undigested, the food he had eaten the day before. This symptom you may notice in children with cholera infantum and marasmus. Another symptom calling for *Oleander* in infants and children is, "every time they pass wind they soil their diapers."

Here you must study *Oleander* in conjunction with *Ferrum*, *Arsenicum*, *Argentum nitricum*, and *Cinchona*. *Ferrum* has diarrhœa with stool containing undigested food. The stool is unattended with pain, and is apt to occur during a meal.

Arsenicum is indicated in diarrhœa caused by chilling the stomach by the ingestion of cold substances. The stools are of a yellow color and are attended with pain of a burning character. The patient is worse after midnight, and there is the peculiar *Arsenicum* thirst.

Argentum nitricum is indicated in diarrhœa in which the bowels move as soon as the patient drinks.

Cinchona is useful in debilitating diarrhœa, with watery evacuations containing undigested food; caused or made worse by eating fruits. The stools may escape involuntarily after a meal.

Apis mellifica is a good remedy in cholera infantum with wide open anus and involuntary escape of fæces.

Phosphorus and *Aloe* also have involuntary escape of fæces; the symptom may best be expressed as a want of confidence in the sphincter ani. With *Phosphorus*, the fæces pass as soon as they enter the rectum, as if the anus remained open.

In paralysis, *Oleander* is indicated when the disease invades one or the other limb; it is painless, and is usually preceded for a long time by vertigo. I think that *Oleander*, like *Gelsemium*, is indicated only in functional paralysis. I do not believe that it will cure paralysis of central origin. It goes further than *Gelsemium*, however, in implicating the sensory as well as the motor nerves.

Oleander also has an action on the skin. It produces marked sensitiveness of the skin, so that very slight friction causes soreness and chafing, especially about the neck or between the scrotum and thighs. There is violent itching of the skin on undressing. It also produces an eruption on the scalp and behind the ears, simulating crusta lactea, and oozing a fluid which hardens into scabs beneath which vermin breed. It is just as important a remedy in this disease as *Sulphur*, *Mezereum*, *Viola tricolor*, etc. The distinction which you may make lies in the other symptoms, *i. e.*, if the characteristic gastro-enteric symptoms are present, *Oleander* will be the remedy.

For symptoms produced by acute poisoning with this remedy, *Camphor* is the best antidote. For the chronic symptoms, particularly if there be any cutaneous disorder, *Sulphur* is probably the best remedy, because it is the most similar, but of the value of this last suggestion I am not positive. I merely offer it to you for what it is worth.

Vinca Minor.

Vinca minor is one variety of the periwinkle. It contains a bitter and astringent principle, making it of service as a "tonic," to use old-school language, and also as a styptic to control hæmorrhage. These properties it retains in the potencies. For instance, it may be used for profuse menstruation or passive menorrhagia when the blood flows in one continuous stream, associated of course with great debility. I find that Dr. Richard Hughes, in his *Manual of Pharmacodynamics*, speaks of three cases of post-climacteric hæmorrhage, all of which were improved by *Vinca minor*. In one a permanent cure resulted; in the other two there was a return of the hæmorrhage, and in one of these the trouble was due to carcinoma.

Vinca minor, like its relative, *Oleander*, produces an offensive smelling eruption on the scalp and face and behind the ears, in which vermin breed. It develops a crust which allows the discharge to remain beneath, and decomposition furnishes pabulum for the vermin; the hair falls out and is replaced by gray hair.

Vinca minor is also useful in plica polonica, a condition in which the hair is matted together.

In these skin symptoms you may compare *Vinca minor* with several remedies; first with *Viola tricolor*. This is useful in crusta lactea, when the exudation is very copious. Like *Vinca*, it mats the hair together, but there is this peculiarity which always enables you to distinguish between the two, namely, *Viola* has urine with a peculiar pungent odor, which has been aptly compared to that of cat's urine. You may think of it when persistent eczema is accompanied by disturbance in the urinary organs, either too copious urination, or sudden cessation of the urinary secretion.

Another remedy is *Arctium lappa*, which is useful for moist offensive eruption, forming grayish-white crusts, especially when the adjacent glands are swollen; the axillary glands may even suppurate. There is polyuria with pain in the bladder after voiding the urine.

Still another remedy for crusta lactea or tinea favosa is *Nux juglans*. It has soreness on and behind the ears, like *Graphites;* the scalp is red and itches violently. Scabs appear on the arms and in the axillæ (also *Arsenicum iod.*).

Staphisagria is a good remedy for an oozing fœtid eruption, worse on the occiput; the hair falls out. Scratching seems to cause the itching to change place. It is particularly indicated in sickly children with pale face and dark rings around the eyes. They are easily angered and reject proffered gifts, just as under *Chamomilla*. It is especially indicated after the abuse of mercury.

Ustilago has caused, but it has not yet been reported to have cured, a filthy eruption of the scalp, in which part of the hair came out, leaving the remainder matted. A watery serum oozed continually from the eruption.

Alstonia Scholaris.

Alstonia, so far as proved, causes debility, low fever, often with diarrhœa, and, when pushed, rigors, sweat, etc., purging, cramps and vertigo. Clinically, it has been used in chills and fever, in diarrhœa of malarial origin, here vieing with *China*, and for chronic intermittent fevers suppressed by quinine.

It contains *Ditaine*, which, like *Curare*, paralyzes peripheral motor-nerve filaments. This is not, as in *Chininum*, preceded by reflex excitement. *Ditaine* evidently paralyzes vaso-motor nerves. It seems to resemble *China* in diarrhœa, chills, etc., but has not the irritability of the latter.

LECTURE XV.

GELSEMIUM SEMPERVIRENS.

GELSEMIUM SEMPERVIRENS is a yellow-flowering plant indigenous to the South. It is an evergreen, and puts forth its fragrant flowers among the earliest in the spring. It is highly poisonous; especially active in this respect is the bark of the roots. During our late civil war this plant was largely used in the South as a substitute for *Opium* as a narcotic.

It is a member of the Loganiaceæ, all of which are more or less poisonous. From this order we obtain also *Nux vomica*, *Ignatia* and *Spigelia*.

Its alkaloid, *Gelsemine*, is a mydriatic like *Atropine* and *Duboisine*. Applied locally or used internally in large doses, it dilates the pupil. Given internally in small doses, however, it contracts the pupil.

To acquire a thorough knowledge of *Gelsemium* will not tax you much. Its sphere of action is well defined. In poisoning cases we find that the prominent and universal symptom is paralysis of the motor nerves. Keep this fact before you and the symptoms of this remedy will be readily understood, especially if you apply the paretic action to both voluntary and involuntary muscles. The mind is at first clear; or there may be a slightly stupefied condition as in the case of alcoholic intoxication, a sluggishness in thought and in emotion. Later in the toxic effects of the drug you will note that the sphincters become relaxed: the anus remains open, permitting the escape of fæces. Urine escapes freely and involuntarily. Still later, respiration becomes labored, as though the muscles had not the power to lift the chest. Finally, the heart-muscle gives out, and the patient dies. Looking, then, at these symptoms as presenting in a nutshell the action of this drug, we find that it is a depressant. It acts upon the cerebro-spinal system, particularly upon the anterior columns of the cord. We also see that, by producing this sluggishness of thought, this stupid state of the mind, it must have an action on the vascular system. It is through the vaso-motor nerves that it produces passive congestion, and this congestion may be either venous or arterial. Passive congestion is generally of venous origin; but under *Gelsemium* the passive hyperæmia refers to both arteries and veins. In addition to this nervous action of the drug, it has something of an affinity for the mucous surfaces, giving rise to catarrhal inflammations. It is not difficult with this outline of the drug to fill in the characteristics.

We find that, in obedience to its paralytic action, it causes diplopia. This double vision, when *Gelsemium* is the remedy, comes from paresis of the muscles of the eye:

Ptosis, or paralysis of the upper lid, calls for *Gelsemium* when it is associated with thick speech and suffused redness of the face. The eyeballs feel sore, the soreness being worse on moving the eyes. In this last symptom it is similar to *Bryonia*.

In ptosis we may compare *Gelsemium* with *Causticum, Rhus toxicodendron, Sepia, Kalmia,* and *Alumina*. *Rhus tox.* is useful in ptosis, or, in fact, in paralysis of any of the ocular muscles, when the disease occurs in rheumatic patients as a result of getting wet.

Sepia is indicated in ptosis when it is associated with menstrual irregularities.

Kalmia is also useful in ptosis of rheumatic origin, when attended with a sensation of stiffness in the lids.

Causticum, in the ptosis of rheumatic subjects.

Alumina is indicated in ptosis associated with rectal inertia and consequent constipation.

Returning now to *Gelsemium*, we find that there is difficulty in swallowing, dysphagia, as it is called. This symptom is due to defect in the muscles of deglutition.

Gelsemium also acts upon the larynx, causing aphonia, or want of voice; the patient may be able to whisper, but he can scarcely utter any sounds on account of the paretic state of the laryngeal muscles. This symptom is frequently observed in hysterical women especially after emotions of a depressing character. Paralysis after emotion is noted under other drugs; for example, under *Natrum mur*, which has, "the arm almost loses its power after a fit of anger;" *Stannum*, paralysis mostly left-sided with perspiration of the affected part; *Staphisagria*, paralysis of one side from anger.

The heart is affected by *Gelsemium*; on going to sleep the patient is suddenly aroused by a feeling that the heart will stop beating. He feels that the heart would cease to beat if he did not move about. Here the heart-muscle is in a weakened state, and there is a sort of instinct on the part of the person to move about to stimulate it to act.

Digitalis has a symptom which is just the reverse of this, namely, the patient fears that the heart will cease beating if he makes any motion.

Grindelia robusta has great weakness of the heart and lungs. When the patient drops off to sleep he wakes up suddenly with a sensation as if respiration had ceased.

In post-diphtheritic paralysis, *Gelsemium* is our most valuable remedy. In one very severe case of this disease under my care, *Gelsemium* effected a perfect cure. The child did not have sufficient strength to hold herself up. The spine in the upper cervical region was bent backward. One side of the body was paralyzed. In attempting to walk, the child would shuffle along as though she had no control over the muscles. If she attempted to turn around she would fall. The speech was thick and heavy, as though the tongue were too large for the mouth. There was marked strabismus. But sensation was nearly perfect. I ordered the patient to be stripped twice a day, laid on the bed, and thoroughly rubbed. I gave her *Gelsemium* internally, and under the use of this remedy she made a perfect recovery.

I doubt whether *Gelsemium* will cure paralysis of organic origin, where there are tissue alterations in the brain, the spinal cord, or the peripheral nerves themselves.

Gelsemium is useful in some cases of headache. I said a few moments ago that it causes a passive congestion, and by that I mean, not a violent, sudden afflux of blood to a part, but a dilated condition of the bloodvessels, such as may be found under *Ferrum phos.* The headache begins in the nape of the neck, passes up over the head, and settles down over the eyes. It is usually worse in the morning, and is accompanied by stiff neck, or it begins at 2 or 3 A. M. and reaches its acme in the afternoon. The patient cannot think effectively or fix his attention. He becomes listless and stupid; he has dizziness with blurred sight and heaviness of the head. These symptoms are alleviated by the discharge of watery-looking urine.

Oleum animale has cured megrim with polyuria, the urine being perfectly clear. Compare also *Ignatia, Sanguinaria, Kalmia, Melilotus, Aconite* and *Silicea.*

The face is a suffused red color. The eyes grow heavy and bloodshot. There is great difficulty in lifting the upper lids; often, too, the speech is thick, as though the tongue were unwieldy. Altogether, the face has the appearance of one under the influence of liquor. Thought is slow, so that the patient answers questions either slowly or imperfectly. This condition is accompanied by a pulse which is full and round, and seems to flow under the fingers like a current of water. It resembles the *Aconite* pulse, but lacks the tone of the latter. It is not hard and unyielding like the pulse of *Aconite*. Not infrequently the headache is preceded by blindness, as under *Psorinum*.

Here, then, you have symptoms which suggest *Gelsemium* in a variety of diseases. How useful it ought to be in the congestive stage of spotted fever! In addition to the symptoms already mentioned, there is another which is characteristic of spotted fever, namely, depression; the system seems to be laboring under the effect of some poison which it cannot overcome. So you have every indication here for the use of *Gelsemium* in that dreaded disease. But when the case advances to active inflammation, or when there is effusion, *Gelsemium* gives place to other remedies.

In addition to the headache above described, there is another form which is associated with a feeling as though there were a band around the head, or across the forehead.

Let us now consider the fever of *Gelsemium*. It causes a fever which is remitting or intermitting in its type. You will find it a valuable remedy in the remitting types of fever in children. During the febrile exacerbation they are very nervous and restless, tossing about continually. (You must not give *Aconite* in these cases, unless the mental symptoms of that remedy are present.) The face has the suffused redness I mentioned above, and there is drowsiness. When aroused from this drowsy state the child is peevish, irritable, nervous, even somewhat excitable, but there is never the violent tossing about of *Aconite*. In extreme cases the drowsiness may give place to convulsive motion. The muscles of the face twitch; the child becomes rigid as though it were about to have a convulsion. There is usually not very much thirst, but there is great prostration, so that the child seems too weak to move. Every part of the body seems to be so sore that he cries out if you move him. These symptoms will remit and, possibly, the next morning, slight perspiration will show itself. The next afternoon the symptoms return as before.

In intermittent types of fever you may select *Gelsemium* in the beginning. The chill runs up the back or starts from the feet and extends upward. It is sometimes associated with copious urination and with bruised aching all over the body. The patient wants to be held so that he will not shake so much. Then comes the fever with the symptoms that I have already mentioned. Sometimes irritability is exhibited. He can neither bear noise nor light. The sweat is slight or partial, but it relieves all the pains. The tongue is coated white or yellow. Speech is thick. The bowels are constipated and the stools are yellow. It is especially indicated in intermittent fever of non-malarial origin.

In adults we find *Gelsemium* the remedy in bilious fever, particularly bilious remittent fever. The reason that it is useful in bilious fever is that it causes a passive congestion of the liver. The blood flows sluggishly through the liver. This is not the portal stasis found under *Nux vomica*, but it is a lazy flow of blood. Thus the liver becomes overcharged with blood, the bile cannot be properly secreted, and there is a bilious type of fever.

In typhoid fever *Gelsemium* is indicated, particularly in the initial stages; when, during the first week, the patient feels sore and bruised all over, as if he had been pounded. He dreads to move. He has headache. More than that, he has loss of muscular power. He is drowsy, and has this same suffused red face. In these cases *Gelsemium* will so modify the course of the fever that the patient will pass through it with comparatively mild symptoms.

We may find *Gelsemium* indicated in catarrhs excited by warm, moist, relaxing weather, with excoriating discharge from the nose, making the nostrils and wings of the nose raw and sore. There are frequent paroxysms of sneezing, especially in the morning, and sore throat, the tonsils being red and somewhat tumefied, with difficulty in swallowing. I would remind you, in passing, that this difficulty in swallowing is not what it is under *Belladonna*. Under the latter remedy the difficulty comes from the extent of the swelling, and also from spasmodic contraction of the fauces, owing to the hyperæsthesia of the nerves. No sooner does water touch the throat than it is expelled through the nose. With *Gelsemium* the dysphagia is the result of the paretic state of the muscles, or the patient was muscularly weak when he caught cold. With this cold you will find dry teasing tickling cough, with very little expectoration. There is a sensation of dryness in the mouth, although it is not dry, which reminds us of *Nux moschata* and *Natrum mur*. The right nostril is red and sore; there is a feeling as if hot water were passing over the mucous membrane of the nostrils; relief comes when near the fire. You find general prostration, and often, too, neuralgia of the face.

Quillaya (or soap bark) cures colds contracted in warm relaxing weather. Like *Gelsemium* there are muscular languor, desire for rest and quiet, general bruised feeling, even of the eye-balls, etc. The former, however, has more of a stuffed sensation in the nose; the latter a fluent, excoriating coryza with neuralgia of the face and head.

Now in prosopalgia *Gelsemium* may be of use when the disease affects one side, and is intermitting in its type. The seventh pair of nerves is involved, and the patient makes all sorts of grimaces.

Gelsemium has some slight action on the skin. It produces redness and an itching which is violent enough to prevent the patient from falling asleep. A fine eruption, consisting of small pimples, and somewhat resembling that of measles, may appear. *Gelsemium* may, therefore, be used in measles in the beginning, when fever is a prominent symptom, and we have the watery discharge from the nose, excoriating the alæ nasi and the upper lip. There is apt to be associated with this a hard, barking, croupy cough and hoarseness.

Aconite, other things being equal, is the best remedy we have for the beginning of measles. If you have a case that you presume is going to be measles, with fever, restlessness, photophobia, coryza, sneezing, and hard, croupy cough, you are justified in giving *Aconite*.

If there be any fever *Pulsatilla* is not the remedy.

When the skin is moist with the fever, *Belladonna* is more likely to be the remedy.

When the characteristic drowsiness and suffused face is present, you may give *Gelsemium* in the beginning of any eruptive disease, even if there be convulsions present.

Next I want to speak of the action of *Gelsemium* on the genital organs. On the male organs it produces a condition very nearly approaching impotence. There are frequent involuntary emissions at night, with relaxation of the organs, no lascivious dreams, and often cold sweat on the scrotum. It is indicated especially in those cases which arise from masturbation.

I would have you note here another remedy, namely, *Dioscorea*. This is excellent for what we may term atonic seminal emissions. The organs are so relaxed that two or three dreams, with emissions of semen, occur in a single night. The day following the emissions the patient feels weak, particularly about the knees In these cases I know of no remedy like *Dioscorea*. I usually give it first in the 12th potency, and afterward in the 30th.

Caladium seguinum is indicated for the bad effects of sexual excesses, when wet-dreams occur without any lasciviousness or any sexual excitement whatsoever.

Agnus castus is the remedy for spermatorrhœa in old sinners. The parts are cold and relaxed; the sexual appetite is gone and the patient is melancholic.

Other remedies which may be compared with *Gelsemium* in its action on the male organs are *Digitalis*, *Phosphorus*, *Nux vomica*, *Calcarea ostr.*, *Lycopodium* and *Camphor*.

Sepia, *Selenium*, and *Conium* produce a similar seminal weakness, with erethism and easy emissions.

In gonorrhœa, *Gelsemium* is indicated in the beginning when there is marked urethral soreness. There are also burnings at the meatus and along the course of the urethra. The discharge as yet is slight, not having become purulent. The disease may have been suppressed, and, as a result, may be complicated with epididymitis. In gonorrhœal rheumatism it may be a useful remedy.

In diseases of the female organs, *Gelsemium* is an invaluable remedy. First of all, we find it useful in rigid os uteri. You must not confound this condition with the more common spasm of the os, which calls for *Belladonna*. Often we find in labor, after it has lasted several hours, that there has been tardy dilatation of the os. The examining finger finds the os unyielding, hard and thick. The patient is hysterical and full of nervous excitement. The pains leave the uterus and fly all over the body or shoot upward and backward. At other times the pains go from before backward and the uterus seems to push upward. Or there is a sensation of a wave rising from the uterus to the throat, ending in choking. This condition calls for *Gelsemium*.

Another condition, exactly opposite to this, also calls for *Gelsemium*, namely, complete atony of the uterus. The neck of the uterus is as soft as putty. It is perfectly flabby. The body of the uterus does not contract at all. The bag of waters bulges freely from the os, but there is no attempt whatever at expulsion. In such cases, give a few doses of *Gelsemium*.

In the premonitory stages of puerperal convulsions *Gelsemium* is an admirable remedy. Albuminuria may be present. The convulsions are preceded by drowsiness, and twitching of different parts of the body. The os is either rigid, as I first mentioned, or else everything is perfectly inactive; the pulse is full and large, but soft. Sharp, distressing, cutting pains in the abdomen go from before backward and then upward, and with every pain the face flushes.

Gelsemium may also be used in the non-pregnant state. The uterus is markedly anteflexed and feels as if squeezed by a band. The uterine symptoms are associated with a frontal headache and dim vision. The head feels enormously enlarged, with a wild confused feeling in it. These symptoms alternate with sharp labor-like pain in the uterus extending to the hips and back, and even down the thighs. *Gelsemium* is often useful in neuralgic and congestive dysmenorrhœa when bearing down coexists.

Caulophyllum is similar to *Gelsemium* in dysmenorrhœa and follows it well.

Actea racemosa and *Sepia* have headaches reflex from uterine irritation.

Gelsemium is useful for the effects of emotions, particularly after fright or fear. A suddenly appearing diarrhœa, coming on from excitement, as for instance "stage-fright" or the anticipation of some trying ordeal, calls for *Gelsemium*. The stools are copious, yellow and papescent. The tongue is coated white or yellowish.

Other remedies coming into play in cases of diarrhœa arising from emotional influences are *Opium, Veratrum album, Argentum nitricum* and *Pulsatilla*.

Opium in cases coming on as a result of fright, especially when the image of the thing which caused the fright constantly appears before the mind.

Veratrum album in diarrhœa after fright, associated with cold sweat on the forehead.

Argentum nitricum when diarrhœa follows great excitement, especially when the imagination has been played upon. Diarrhœa from anticipation.

Pulsatilla in diarrhœa from fright, when the stools are greenish, yellow and slimy, or very changeable and worse at night; trembling; weeping.

Gelsemium may even avert impending abortion from depressing emotions, with the peculiar pains mentioned above in connection with labor. In this condition you should compare *Aconite* and *Opium*.

Conium, Physostigma and *Tabacum* intensify the action of *Gelsemium*.

Gelsemium is antidoted by stimulants, and by *Belladonna, Digitalis, China* and *Coffea*.

LECTURE XVI.

NUX VOMICA.

Nux vomica, another member of the Loganiaceæ, is a drug that was known as early as 1540, A. D., in which year, one Valerius Cordus wrote a remarkably accurate description of it. The fruit of the tree is about the size of an orange and contains a bitter, gelatinous pulp. This pulp, it is said, is eaten by some of the birds of India, although it is well known to contain *Strychnine*. The *Nux* itself is the seed deprived of the pulp and shell. This seed is disk-shaped, and about one inch in diameter and one-quarter of an inch thick. Its surface is satiny by reason of a thick covering of adpressed radiating hairs.

You will recall that I have already mentioned that *Ignatia* and *Nux vomica* both contain as active principles two alkaloids known as *Strychnia* and *Brucia*. The *Brucia* occurs in much smaller quantities than the other, and is present more in the bark of the tree than in the nut itself. Its properties are somewhat similar to those of *Strychnia*. Both alkaloids are combined with an acid known as *Igasuric acid*, which is identical with the malic acid found in apples and pears. *Strychnia*, the principal alkaloid of *Ignatia* and *Nux vomica*, has a well-described symptomatology, being a poison not uncommonly used for suicidal and homicidal purposes, and also for the extermination of the lower animals, cats, rats, etc. *Strychnia* causes restlessness, trembling of the limbs, stiffness of the neck and jaws, constriction of the throat and tetanic convulsions with opisthotonos. These tetanic convulsions differ from those of true tetanus only in the fact that the muscles relax between the paroxysms. The temperature of the body is not so high as in true tetanus, and trismus comes late in *Strychnia* poisoning. These *Strychnia* convulsions are re-excited by impressions made on the senses, particularly by the slightest touch, while rubbing relieves; the patient is conscious throughout the attack. In very large or in oft-repeated doses, *Strychnia* causes paralysis of afferent nerves. Finally, collapse ensues as the result of exhaustion of the motor centres. I give you these symptoms of *Strychnia* for two purposes. One is that you may be familiar with them in order to recognize them in case one of your patients is unfortunate enough to be poisoned with the drug. The other is that you may the better understand the action of *Nux vomica*, for *Strychnia* being its principal ingredient, you will find running all through its symptomatology this over-impressibility; by this I mean that everything impresses the patient excessively. External impressions, such as sounds, odors and noises, excite him, and this symptom, I say, is characteristic of the drug

The smallest fatal dose of *Nux vomica* is said to be three grains; that of *Strychnia*, one-half a grain

Strychnia resembles *Picrotoxine*, *Veratria*, *Cicuta virosa*, *Thebaine*, *Hydrocyanic acid*, *Belladonna*, *Stramonium*, *Aconite*, *Physostigma*, *Passiflora*, *Curare*, *Camphor*, *and Phytolacca;* but especially are its effects like traumatic tetanus.

Picrotoxine, according to Bartholow, is synergistic with *Strychnia;* but respiration is accelerated, not so much from spasm of the respiratory muscles as from spasm of the glottis; and there is less susceptibility to slight touch. Gubler asserts that *Picrotoxine* produces more choreic symptoms.

Veratria causes incoordination by producing relaxation of some fibres with contraction of others; that is, following prolonged contraction of muscles comes a state of partial relaxation with fibrillary contractions. Herein it somewhat resembles *Strychnia;* but it differs widely in purging and vomiting, and in general paralysis occurring, not from exhaustion, but from direct devitalizing of the muscles.

Thebaine causes tetanus, but may be distinguished by its hypnotic symptoms. It is said to be the most poisonous of the active principles of *Opium*.

Physostigma, which contains the alkaloid *Eserine*, can be confused with *Strychnia* only in a limited range of symptoms. It increases the irritability of the sensory nerves and also causes tetanic spasms of involuntary muscles. But in the main, it differs widely from *Strychnia*, causing spinal paralysis and diminished reflex action. Hence, when such symptoms as constriction of the throat, cramps in the stomach and bowels, tenesmus recti, stiff spine and legs, tight feeling in and about the eyeballs, etc., suggest a similarity to *Strychnia*, such consentaneous evidences of spinal paralysis as the following will serve for differentiation: trembling; so feeble he can hardly walk; finds difficulty in making the muscles obey the will (like *Gelsemium* and *Conium*); unsteady when walking with the eyes closed. In *Strychnia*, death results from asphyxia caused by tetanic spasm of the respiratory muscles; in *Physostigma*, from paralysis. The pupils, too, differ; the former causes dilatation during the convulsions, with contraction during the interim; the latter causes contraction with defective accommodation and twitching of the eyelids.

If, now, the remote effects of *Strychnia* are to be considered—such effects as follow severe but not fatal poisoning, or such symptoms as are frequently produced by potencies—we may still discriminate by the characteristic irritability, which is more marked in *Strychnia;* everything makes too strong an impression; odors cause fainting; there are muscular tremors with excitement; desire for coitus, but during the act the penis becomes flaccid.

Curare, although it contains *Strychnia*, acts quite differently from the latter on account of the presence of the alkaloid *Curarine*. This substance destroys the irritability of the end-organs of the motor nerves, leaving the muscles themselves intact. Reflex action is diminished or destroyed, and respiration is paralyzed. Sensation is not materially altered. Owing to paralysis of the vagus, the heart's action is accelerated, but blood-pressure is not increased. In fact, from paralysis of vaso-motor termini, the bloodvessels dilate, lessening resistance to the blood currents. Increased peristalsis is not due to spasm, but to paralysis of the inhibitory splanchnic fibres.

We have no very trustworthy provings of *Curare*. Baruch has used it for so-called "liver-spots;" and Dr. Paul Pitet records several interesting cures of muscular weakness, embarrassed respiration from deficient power, immobility with fixed gaze on awakening, and eczema of infants, worse on the face and behind the ears, especially in scrofulous children (*World's Homœopathic Convention*. vol. i).

It has also been used by Baruch, I think, for catalepsy, with spasms of the lower jaw, and for paralytic weakness in the hands and fingers of pianists.

Phytolacca differs essentially from *Strychnia* in its acrid-narcotic properties, as well as in its tardy gastro-intestinal irritation and collapse. Still the convulsive symptoms are somewhat similar; the limbs are stiff, the hands firmly shut, the feet extended and the toes flexed; the jaws are clenched and the lips everted showing the teeth; opisthotonos is present; the chin is drawn down to the sternum; there is alternate relaxation and spasm of the facial muscles.

Passiflora incarnata has cured cases of tetanus in hot countries, where, unhappily, they are but too common. Dr. Archibald Bayne, of Barbadoes, W. I., reports two cures with the tincture and the ix (*Hahnemannian Monthly*, May, 1881).

Angustura is placed among aromatic bitters and is called a tonic. But it is more than this. It causes drawing, tension, and stiffness of the muscles and joints, with a bruised, sore feeling, as after a blow. This tension is marked enough in the temporal and masseter muscles to suggest trismus. The drug also affects the bones. There are points of resemblance between *Angustura* and another of the Rutaceæ, the *Ruta graveolens*. Injury to periosteum frequently suggests the latter; and it is very probable that injury with incipient muscular contractions may need the former.

Dr. Hering, who was fully aware of the confusion of *Angustura* with *Strychnia*, nevertheless reported a cure of tetanus with the former, and printed the symptoms thereof in his *Guiding Symptoms*. Dr. Hubbard reports a cure made with *Angustura* (*Medical Investigator*, April, 1870).

That *Angustura vera* acts on the bones has been fully confirmed. Ægidi used it when the long bones were affected (see *Raue's Pathology*) Dr. C. G. Raue writes me that the preparation with which he cured podarthrocace was unquestionably the *vera*. It was Jenichen's, and this manufacturer carefully distinguished between *Angustura vera* and *Angustura falsa*, or *Nucis vomicæ cortex seu Brucea antidysenterica*.

Dr. Aug. Korndœrfer, Sr., used Jenichen's 200th for necrosis of the lower jaw. One side of the jaw had been successfully excised; but the disease made its appearance on the other side; the cure was complete.

Among the general characteristics of *Angustura* we may refer to irritation from a slight offence (with caries). Craving for coffee (clinical, but confirmed by Dunham, Bœnninghausen, and Ægidi). Tenesmus recti, with soft stool; urging to urinate, with copious flow (see Dr. Edmundson's case, *Hahnemannian Monthly*, October, 1876). I cannot, then, quite agree with Dr. Hughes, who asserts that *Angustura* has no recognized therapeutic place.

Aconite in one of its manifestations, causes a general tension of nerves and vessels, characterized by the well-known anxiety, heat, etc. (see Hughes's *Pharmacodynamics*). It also induces trismus, stiffness of the limbs, and even opisthotonos. We see now why Reynol could use it successfully in trismus of horses ('Trousseau's *Therapeutics*, vol. ii); and, further, why it is recommended in the beginning of traumatic tetanus.

It does not, however, like *Strychnia*, cause increased reflex excitability. There is present rather a diminution or perversion of sensibility, expressed by tingling numbness.

In impending tetanus we certainly have efficient preventives of the full-fledged disease. *Aconite*, with fever, anxiety, tension of muscles, tingling and numbness; *Veratrum viride*, *Hypericum*, with excruciating pain in the wound; *Belladonna*, *Cicuta*, *Silicea*, and possibly *Angustura*, if the wound is suppurating or has suddenly ceased to discharge pus.

Hydrocyanic acid was first recommended in tetanus by Bégin; and Dr. Hughes, in his paper on that acid, read at the World's Convention in 1876, cited poisoning cases which prove its homœopathicity to epilepsy and to tetanus. The relation of this acid to the latter disease is more fully brought out in Dr. Hughes's *Pharmacodynamics*, where we read: "*Hydrocyanic acid* causes tetanus; there is not, as with *Strychnia*, evidence of increased reflex excitability; but, as with *Aconite* and *Cicuta*, persistent tonic spasm; this it produces by direct action upon the spinal cord."

It seems especially useful when the tetanic symptoms show themselves mostly in the muscles of face, jaws, and back; there are trismus, risus sardonicus and embarrassed respiration, with lividity and frothing at the mouth. Dr. Charles A. Barnard reports two cases of traumatic tetanus relieved with this acid. In each instance only the spasms of face, jaws, and chest were ameliorated, other remedies being needed for the remaining symptoms (see *New England Medical Gazette*, October, 1882). This affinity of *Hydrocyanic acid* for the upper part of the body does not contra-indicate the medicine in opisthotonos and general tetanic rigidity, for under its baneful influence both trunk and extremities are thrown into spasm. In one case, spasms commenced in the toes and spread over the body. But the acid undoubtedly affects the medulla oblongata most powerfully, and consequently lungs, heart, and larynx suffer through the pneumogastric nerve. It bears but little resemblance to *Strychnia*, but is similar to *Cicuta*, *Lachesis*, and *Nicotine*.

Lachesis has relieved when, with trismus and spasm of the larynx, there is blueness from asphyxia and the patient sleeps into the paroxysm.

Cicuta virosa contains a volatile alkaloid termed *Cicutine*, which is chemically identical with *Coniine*. According to Boehm, this plant causes vomiting, diarrhœa, and tetanoid convulsions, and in man also syncope and strabismus. *Cicutoxine* is another alkaloid derived from *Cicuta*. It is the most powerful of the *Cicuta* derivatives, causing in frogs, alternate tonic and clonic spasms. The respiration is hurried, the inspiratory so far exceeding the expiratory act that the animal becomes distended with air. In mammals, the first effect is profuse salivation, quivering of the muscles, and then spasms. The breathing grows very rapid, and then suddenly convulsions develop. Respiration, as with *Strychnia*, is suspended by contraction of the respiratory muscles. If irritated, spasms return; after the paroxysms subside, the animal lies completely exhausted.

Now these views of the action of *Cicuta* embody characteristics which have for years guided the homœopathist in the choice of this powerful remedy; sudden rigidity; then jerking and violent distortion, followed by *utter prostration;* tonic spasm renewed by touch; *great oppression of breathing;* lock-jaw; face dark red; froth at the mouth; opisthotonos; *loss of consciousness.*

The seizure in the *Cicuta* case is more epileptiform than in *Strychnia* and there is generally loss of consciousness. Reflex excitability is less marked in the former. The exhaustion of *Cicuta* is equalled only by *Chininum arsenicosum.*

Tabacum and its alkaloid *Nicotine*, which is also closely related to *Coniine*, cause drawing back of the head, with rigidity of the muscles of the neck and back; contraction of the eyelids and the masseter muscles; hissing respiration from spasm of the laryngeal and bronchial muscles; alternate tonic and clonic spasms, followed by general relaxation and trembling; retraction of the abdominal muscles; contractions of parts supplied with involuntary muscle-fibres, as the intestines, ureters, etc.; these contractions are accompanied by intense pain, nausea, cold sweat and speedy collapse, with asphyxia.

Tobacco, then, acts upon the spine, especially upon the medulla oblongata, and also upon the abdominal ganglia. Its tetanic symptoms with asphyxia resemble those of *Hydrocyanic acid* rather than those of *Strychnia*. A characteristic difference between *Tobacco* and *Nux vomica* is well brought out in their respective applications to renal colic. In *Nux* there is pain down the right ureter into the genitals and leg, nausea and vomiting; in *Tabacum*, pains down the ureter, with *deathly sickness and cold sweat.*

Veratrum album causes trismus with spasm of the glottis and constriction of the chest, amounting almost to suffocation; the hands and feet are drawn inward, and the pupils are contracted. It may be distinguished from *Strychnia* by the fact that under *Veratrum album* the convulsions are secondary to exhausting diseases and are never primary, as under *Strychnia*.

Stramonium, like *Strychnia*, causes tetanic convulsions, which are worse from touch or from light. The chief distinction is that with *Stramonium* mania is almost always present, while under *Strychnia* the mind is clear to the last hours of life.

Camphor is similar to *Strychnia* in tetanic spasms. It has showing of the teeth from drawing up of the corners of the mouth, but when *Camphor* is indicated in tetanic spasms, we find the ever-present deathly coldness.

In studying *Nux vomica*, you should remember these prefatory remarks.

Next let me say that *Nux vomica* is complementary to *Sulphur* By that I mean that after *Nux vomica* has done as much as its symptoms will allow it to do, very frequently the remaining symptoms find in *Sulphur* the remedy that will complete the cure.

Now, let me give you the *Nux vomica* temperament. It does not necessarily follow that you must not use *Nux* if the constitution is not what I am going to describe; but it does follow that it acts better in the constitution about to be mentioned. *Nux vomica* is best adapted to rather thin, spare patients It does not seem to act so well on the fleshy. Especially is it indicated if the patient is rather irascible and is quick and active in his motions. He has a nervous temperament. He is extremely susceptible to external impressions and hence cannot tolerate noise, odors or light. The face is rather sallow or yellowish. There is a sort of false plethora that gives the patient at times red cheeks on the yellow background. Generally, too, you will find that he suffers from any strain on the mind, particularly if this overtaxing of the mental powers is intensified or rendered more injurious by sedentary habits. Thus you will find the drug of great value for those who deprive themselves of sleep and exercise in pursuance of their studies. You will find it frequently indicated in ministers who take very little exercise and who have become dyspeptic. They have headache and are tired in the morning when they awake. The *Nux* patient frequently lies awake at night the mind is so wrought up that he cannot sleep. Thoughts run through the mind in confusion. He does not fall asleep until long after midnight, and then awakes in the early morning, perhaps at four or five o'clock. Falling asleep again, he awakes once more, feeling as if he had been on a spree, and his sleep had done him no good. He has a bitter taste in the mouth; the tongue is coated; he complains of dull headache, and, in fact, of every symptom that points to wearing out of the system from overwork. This, then, is the kind of patient in which you will find *Nux vomica* most effective.

Nux may avert an oncoming cerebral softening especially when sedentary habits and severe mental strain have preceded it, as well as in cases where intemperance antedates the disease. The patient complains of headache when he exerts his mind. His memory is fickle, he is dizzy and his walk grows unsteady. The remedy may be followed by *Phosphorus, Picric acid* or *Sulphur*.

The *Nux* patient, you will find, has a great deal of trouble with the digestive organs. He suffers from headache, situated either in the occiput or over one eye, usually the left. When the pain settles over the eye, it usually begins in the morning, and increases until night, and is accompanied generally by a sour taste in the mouth (less frequently by a bitter taste), by accumulation of flatus, and by annoying retching. This may be associated with vomiting of food and of sour matter, but the prominent feature of the vomiting is the violent retching, often more or less ineffectual, showing the irritated condition of the stomach. He has the characteristic peculiarity of waking in the early morning and then falling asleep, only to awake again feeling worse than at first. The bowels are constipated; and this constipation consists, characteristically, in ineffectual urging to stool. Thus you see that it is not due to atony of the rectum, but to irregular, fitful action. He suffers, also, from gastralgia which is usually made worse by eating. It is sometimes worse, however, when the stomach is empty. The pain starts in the epigastrium, and radiates in various directions, into the back, etc. The paroxysms are very apt to recur periodically every morning, and are often associated with vomiting of sour matter and ineffectual urging to stool. The pains themselves are of a griping, clawing character, as though a hand were scraping the inside of the stomach; they are often relieved by hot drinks. Now, you will notice that the symptoms I have mentioned for *Nux vomica*, if mentioned in pathological language, would have to be put under the term gastric irritability. The nerves are in such a state of hyperæsthesia that the ingestion of food causes spasmodic action of the stomach and ejection of its contents. This, you will notice, is pathologically similar to the condition of the rectum.

In this extreme gastric irritability, we find *Nux vomica* a remedy without which we cannot well get along. You are treating a patient who has been prostrated by disease; as soon as he swallows food, up it comes. *Nux* is here one of the remedies to be thought of, particularly in children who are very excitable, and in men when they have indulged in excessive eating or in debauchery.

In other cases, where there is much burning in the stomach with the violent ejection of food, *Bismuth* is the remedy. The *Subnitrate of Bismuth* is the remedy for pure gastralgia, that which is not associated with any catarrh, or with any of the symptoms of indigestion. The epigastric pains may be burning, griping, or lancinating, extending into the adjacent spine. Pressure, heaviness and burning in the stomach, convulsive gagging. The patient vomits at intervals when the stomach becomes full, and then the amount of vomited matter is enormous. Water is vomited as soon as it reaches the stomach. But unlike *Nux*, the pains are usually relieved by cold drinks, and, though the patient is greatly prostrated, the surface of the body is warm.

In still other cases, we find *Arsenicum* the remedy, when, in addition to the burning pains, we have the intolerable restlessness and anxiety, thirst, etc. It produces a perfect picture of subacute gastritis. A remedy more valuable than any yet mentioned is *Kreosote*. *Kreosote* is excellent for this irritable weakness of the stomach. Food cannot be digested. But its distinctive character lies in the fact that, though the stomach retains the food several hours, it finally ejects it undigested.

Another form of stomach trouble to which *Nux* is applicable is a dyspepsia in which there is marked aggravation an hour or so after eating. About twenty-four hours before the attack comes on, the patient complains of great hunger. He craves meats, gravies, and fat foods, and is averse to coffee. He has violent thirst, but water distresses the stomach and causes distension; after even a light meal, he is obliged to loosen his clothing. He is troubled with sour and bitter eructations, and hiccough.

In gastric symptoms following debauchery, when *Nux* fails, *Carbo veg*. is a good remedy, although *Sulphur* may be required.

Pulsatilla is preferable to *Nux vomica* when the symptoms have resulted from a mixed diet, such as meats, pastry, nuts, ice cream, etc., especially if the temperament agrees.

In constipation, *Nux* is similar to several other remedies. *Lycopodium* has constipation with ineffectual urging to stool, but under this remedy the ineffectual urging is caused by constriction of the rectum and anus.

Carbo veg. has an urging to stool similar to that of *Nux*, but it is relieved by the passage of flatus, showing at once the cause of the urging.

Under *Opium*, *Bryonia*, and *Alumina* the constipation is unattended by urging to stool. *Opium* has constipation from inactivity of the bowels; the stool consists of hard, round, black balls.

The *Bryonia* constipation results from dryness of the alimentary tract. The stools are large, dry, and hard.

Marked inactivity of the rectum characterizes *Alumina*. The evacuation of even a soft stool requires great effort.

Nux vomica has a marked action on the liver. It is particularly indicated in liver affections in those who have indulged to excess in alcoholic liquors and highly-seasoned food, or who have abused themselves with drastic purgatives. *Nux* is one of the best remedies we have to counteract the effects of allopathic dosing. In taking charge of a case that has been under old-school treatment you will frequently find it necessary to administer *Nux* before you can get a clear picture of the symptoms. In these cases you will often find the liver swollen, hard and sensitive to the pressure of the clothing. Colic is frequently present, and may come from an accumulation of flatus, which presses either upward toward the chest, producing inconvenience in breathing, or downward toward the rectum and bladder, developing both urging to stool and desire to urinate. Or it may be a hæmorrhoidal colic. By this I mean abdominal pains which follow the sudden stoppage of hæmorrhoidal flow. The patient has perhaps been subject for years to piles, with bleeding at stool. If from some cause, this flow is suddenly checked and headache or colic results. *Nux* will help him. If the liver is enlarged, you should give *Nux* in repeated doses, and you will often be gratified to find the liver resume its natural proportions. If it does not, then you must fall back on *Sulphur*, *Sepia* or *Magnesia mur*.

Nux may also be indicated in the enlarged liver of drunkards.

Here you may compare it with *Sulphur, Lachesis, Fluoric acid, Arsenicum* and *Ammonium mur.*

Nux vomica is also useful in jaundice provoked by violent anger, by abuse of quinine, or by too high living. The patient has attacks of faintness, after which he feels very weak.

Chamomilla may be employed in jaundice resulting from a fit of anger, as also may *Bryonia, Natrum sulph.* and *Aconite.*

Bryonia is especially useful in jaundice when the case has been spoiled by the abuse of calomel or blue mass.

In jaundice from the effects of quinine you should compare *Hepar, Mercurius, Pulsatilla* and *Arsenicum.*

Carduus marianus is indicated in jaundice with dull headache, bitter taste in the mouth, and white-coated tongue, especially in the middle, with the tips and edges red. There is nausea with vomiting of an acid green fluid. The stools are bilious, and the urine golden-yellow. There is an uncomfortable fulness in the region of the liver.

In hæmorrhoids, *Nux* may be useful when there is itching, keeping the patient awake at night, and frequently so severe as to compel him to sit in a tub of cold water for relief. There is frequent ineffectual urging to stool, and the piles are apt to bleed. But unless *Nux* is thoroughly indicated in such cases, it should not be prescribed, for while it may cure the piles, it is likely to excite some other trouble more unbearable than the one it has relieved.

The analogues of *Nux* in hæmorrhoids are several. *Æsculus hippocastanum* is a wonderful remedy in abdominal plethora. You will find it indicated when there is throbbing deep in the abdomen, particularly in the hypogastric region. The hæmorrhoids, which may or may not bleed, are accompanied by a feeling of dryness in the rectum, as though little sticks or splinters were pricking the folds of the mucous membrane. This is the keynote for *Æsculus*. *Æsculus* also has weak feeling at the sacro-iliac symphysis, as though the back were about to give out at this point.

The next remedy to be mentioned in this connection is *Aloe*. This drug has abdominal plethora and flatulence, like *Nux* and *Sulphur*, and hæmorrhoids like *Nux, Sulphur* and *Æsculus*. But it differs from these remedies in that it acts almost entirely on the rectum, producing catarrh of its mucous lining. The stools are accompanied by an expulsion of copious flatus. The hæmorrhoids protrude like a bunch of grapes and are greatly relieved by cold water. There is also a sort of uncertainty about the rectum, shown in a feeling as if the bowels were about to move. *Aloe* also cures a headache which, like that of *Nux vomica*, is situated over the eyes It is attended by a sensation as though a weight were pressing the eyelids down. Relief comes from partially closing the eyes.

Collinsonia is indicated in hæmorrhoids when there is a sensation of sticks in the rectum. Constipation is usual. 'The bowel symptoms are worse in the evening and at night. *Collinsonia* is also useful in prolapsus uteri complicated with hæmorrhoids. It is just as frequently indicated in this condition as is *Podophyllum* in prolapsus uteri with diarrhœa and prolapsus recti. *Collinsonia* has a symptom found also under *Opium*, namely, dry balls of fæcal matter are passed from the rectum; but they differ from those of *Opium* in that they are of a light color.

Hamamelis is called for in hæmorrhoids when there is considerable hæmorrhage with marked soreness of the affected parts. The back feels as if it would break.

Nux vomica may be used in diarrhœa coming on after a debauch. The patient is usually worse in the morning. The stools are papescent or watery, and are scanty and accompanied by urging, thus keeping up the character of the remedy. The patient retches in the morning, vomiting perhaps a little froth or sour fluid. He craves liquor, of course, but his stomach is so irritable that he vomits the stimulant as soon as it is taken. Such persons seem to be particularly intolerant of milk.

We may give *Nux* in dysentery when there is frequent ineffectual urging to stool, ceasing as soon as the bowels move. The stools are bloody, slimy, watery and scanty. The patient is worse in the morning. *Nux* is indicated by these symptoms whether the disease is the result of cold, or whether it comes from the suppression of an excretion, such as the perspiration.

Mercurius is distinguished from *Nux* in dysentery by the fact that in the former the urging to stool does not cease with the evacuation, no matter how free the latter may be.

Another concordant remedy in dysentery is *Aloe*. This drug is useful in dysentery when there is griping pain in the hypogastrium before stool, resembling *Nux vomica* very closely here. The stool consists of blood and mucus, coming out in jelly-like masses. The griping may or may not cease after stool. In addition, an extraordinary amount of mucus must be expelled.

Nux is a valuable remedy in hernia, whether inguinal or umbilical. It is indicated when, on rising in the morning, the patient complains of a feeling of weakness in the abdomen, particularly in the region of the inguinal canal. It affects especially the left side.

Lycopodium may be used for right-sided inguinal hernia.

Cocculus Indicus comes into play in umbilical hernia after *Nux vomica* has failed.

Let us now study the action of *Nux* on the eyes. We find it indicated in many eye diseases. You may give *Nux* in ordinary conjunctivitis, particularly when it is worse in the morning. This period of aggravation is so well marked that it becomes characteristic of the drug. There is agglutination of the lids and photophobia in the morning. For instance the child buries its head in the pillow in the morning and forenoon, while in the afternoon it uses its eyes freely. These symptoms may also indicate the drug in scrofulous ophthalmia and in blepharospasmus.

In inflamed eyes *Euphrasia* should be compared. It has the morning agglutination but the photophobia is especially noticeable in artificial light. The tears are profuse and acrid, causing the lids to smart, while with *Nux* the lid-edges itch and burn without discharge.

In spasms of the eyelids *Agaricus* is generally the best remedy, but you should consult also *Belladonna*, *Natrum mur.*, *Euphrasia*, *Pulsatilla*, etc.

Nux may also be indicated when the deeper structures of the eye are involved. For instance, it may be given in that dread disease, atrophy of the retina, whether it comes from choroido-retinitis or not.

We find it indicated, too, in another condition of the retina, namely, retinal hyperæsthesia. It is indicated by intolerance of light, worse in the morning; the least attempt to use the eyes is followed by intense pains and spasmodic motion of the ocular muscles; with this there may be excoriating lachrymation and frequent pains in the top of the head.

In amblyopia or impairment of vision due to the effects of tobacco and intoxicating liquors or of debauchery, no remedy will do more toward restoring the power of the weakened optic nerve. Even when atrophy has commenced, *Nux* will palliate if it does not entirely cure.

Another condition in which you find *Nux* indicated is in ecchymoses of the sclerotic coat, when a certain amount of blood is effused beneath the conjunctiva. These often follow debauchery or sitting up late at night to study, in persons subject to dyspepsia.

If these ecchymoses are of traumatic origin, you should study *Ledum*, *Arnica* and *Hamamelis*.

Now for *Nux vomica* in catarrhs. *Nux* is suited to the initial stages of the ordinary coryza, particularly when it has been caused by dry, cold weather, or by sitting in cold places, especially by sitting on cold steps. The trouble is associated with sneezing, and a stuffed-up sensation in the nose at night and in the open air, with fluent coryza in a warm room and during the day. The eyes water, and there is a scraping rawness in the throat. These symptoms are associated with aching all over and chilliness, worse from moving, even when covered up warmly in bed.

The rawness of *Nux* differs from that of *Mercurius*. It is not a sore, raw feeling as if the skin were off, so much as it is a rough, scraping sensation. *Mercurius* is useful in coryza, with rawness and soreness of the nose and throat, with aggravation in damp weather.

Pulsatilla is the remedy for a "ripe" cold, in which the discharge is green and bland. If *Pulsatilla* is prescribed in the beginning, it usually spoils the case.

If, despite the use of *Nux*, the cold travels downward and involves the chest, I have found *Phosphorus* to follow well.

There is an epistaxis curable by *Nux vomica*. It occurs in persons of a hæmorrhoidal disposition, and is preceded by headache or red cheeks. It usually comes on at night during sleep, although it may occur at any time.

Nux may also be used in Eustachian catarrh, when there is itching and tingling along the Eustachian tube, inducing a frequent desire to swallow.

You will sometimes find symptoms of the mouth suggesting *Nux* as a remedy. Ulcers form on the lips, accompanied by burning and sticking pains. Ulcers also appear on the gums. The stomacace of *Nux vomica* is of gastric origin.

Cough is not a prominent symptom of *Nux vomica*. You may employ it in coughs of nervous origin: for instance, in coughs which are provoked by mental work. It may also be used in coughs of gastric origin. The patient suffers from cough after eating and in the morning. There is usually severe headache and soreness in the stomach and bowels.

In diseases of the chest we do not find *Nux* indicated very frequently. It is sometimes useful in asthma, not often in the purely nervous type, but commonly in that arising from gastric disturbance. It is associated with a feeling of fulness and oppression in the stomach, particularly manifested after a hearty meal, during which the patient must loosen all the clothing about the hypochondria in order to obtain relief. The abdomen is distended with flatus. The asthmatic symptoms are worse after a meal, after 12 o'clock at night, in the morning, and are always increased by cold air or any exertion, particularly ascending a height. Belching relieves.

There is a drug analogous to *Nux vomica* which is often overlooked by members of our school, and that is *Zingiber*. *Zingiber* or ginger, unless given too frequently, has a tonic effect on the stomach. It is not a safe article of food for children, or for those who have any kidney affection, as it rather favors the development of morbus Brightii. As a medicine, *Zingiber* may be used in asthma of gastric origin. The attacks come on in the night toward morning. The patient has to sit up to breathe, but despite the severity of the paroxysms, there seems to be no anxiety.

Carbo veg. and *Lycopodium* are similar to *Nux* in asthma from abdominal irritation with marked flatulence.

In hæmoptysis or blood-spitting, *Nux vomica* is indicated when the trouble results from debauchery. The attack usually appears after a drunken spree or after some violent emotion, such as anger, but it may also result from suppressed hæmorrhoidal flow.

Nux vomica is a useful remedy in diseases of the genito-urinary organs. It is indicated in renal colic, when one kidney, usually the right, is the seat of the disease. The pains extend into the genital organs and down the leg, and they are usually associated with intense backache. We must here differentiate *Nux* from *Lycopodium*, *Cantharis*, *Belladonna* and *Berberis*.

Lycopodium, like *Nux*, usually chooses the right side, but the pains extend along the course of the ureter and end in the bladder; they do not descend the leg. The backache is relieved by urination. It may be given after *Nux*.

One of the best remedies during the paroxysms of renal colic is *Cantharis*, which relieves the patient by lessening the amount of local irritation and thus permitting nature to get rid of the stone with less suffering to the patient.

Belladonna is another remedy for renal calculi. The pains are of a sharp, shooting character and differ from those of *Nux* in the fact that they come suddenly and radiate in various directions from the central point of irritation. The patient grows feverish and excitable. *Belladonna* relaxes the spasmodic constriction caused by the stone and allows it to pass more readily.

Berberis is an excellent remedy for renal calculi. The pains are of a shooting character. The patient cannot make the slightest motion, and must sit bent over toward the painful side to obtain relief. If, in addition, he complains of sharp, darting pains following the direction of the ureter and extending into the legs, there is no remedy like *Berberis*. You find in the urine a reddish deposit, consisting of mucus, epithelium, and amorphous urates.

Berberis sometimes has biliary calculi associated with the renal disease. *Belladonna* is also useful in cholelithiasis, but the remedy to cure the condition permanently is *Cinchona*. This has been highly recommended by Dr. Thayer, of Boston. Unless some symptom or symptoms call specifically for another drug, put your patient on a course of *Cinchona* and have him continue it for a number of months.

In the passage of gall-stones, when remedies fail to relieve, I find that ether, externally and internally, is very good, acting better here than chloroform.

We find *Nux* indicated in hæmaturia, when it is traceable to the same cause as the hæmoptysis described above, namely, to debauchery.

Nux vomica is indicated also in affections of the bladder, particularly in strangury accompanied by painful urging to urinate, with the passage of only a few drops at a time, causing burning and scalding and other uncomfortable sensations. With this urging to urinate there is also urging to stool.

In gonorrhœa *Nux* is useful after the abuse of cubebs or copaiva, when the discharge is thin. Sometimes I have noticed that after gonorrhœa has been cured so far as the discharge is concerned, the patient still complains of irritation far back in the urethra, probably in the prostate, causing an uncomfortable feeling which the patient refers to the root of the penis. *Nux* often relieves this condition.

Nux is useful in sexual excesses, especially for the bad effects of early masturbation. It is one of a group of remedies used in these cases ever since the days of Hahnemann. This group consists of *Nux vomica*, *Sulphur*, *Calcarea carb.* and *Lycopodium*. *Nux* is to be given when the patient has headache, frequent involuntary emissions at night, especially towards morning; he complains of backache and difficulty in walking. Do not repeat your medicine too often, and when improvement ceases under *Nux*, *Sulphur* will almost always be the next remedy indicated.

Calcarea carb. usually follows *Nux* and *Sulphur*, particularly when night sweats follow every emission; or, after marriage, every coitus is followed by weakness of mind and body.

Lycopodium is indicated still later, when the case has gone on to complete impotency. The erections are either absent or imperfect. The genitals are cold and somewhat shrivelled.

Staphisagria is called for in the bad effects of masturbation, particularly if there is great emaciation, with dark rings about the eyes, sallow face, and well-marked peevishness and shyness.

There is still another remedy which I would mention in this connection, and this is *Cobalt*. This is an excellent remedy for backache in the lumbar region, following seminal emissions, whether voluntary or involuntary; the backache is particularly worse while sitting.

Nux is indicated in a variety of diseases of the female sexual organs. We find that it has caused and therefore can cure prolapsus uteri. It is to be used when the disease is of recent origin, and has resulted from a sudden wrenching of the body. These symptoms are often associated with constipation accompanied by ineffectual urging to stool. If *Nux* does not entirely cure, the best remedy to follow it is *Sepia*.

The menses, under *Nux vomica*, are almost always profuse, are generally dark in color and are accompanied by retching and cramps in the abdomen. The patient has frequent fainting spells about the time of the menses, especially when in a warm room.

During pregnancy, *Nux* is a useful remedy for the morning sickness. The patient rises in the morning feeling haggard and sick at the stomach. The more retching predominates over vomiting, the more can we expect of *Nux vomica*. Jaundice, even, may be present. The skin is sallow, the bowels are constipated, and the appetite is lost. Still later, the patient complains of great pressure upward, as though she could not breathe.

During labor, *Nux* is the remedy when the constipation calls for it. The labor pains may be very spasmodic and severe; the woman has a constant inclination to stool and urine. This symptom, when *Nux* is the remedy, is not due to mechanical causes, such as the pressure of the child's head, but it is purely of reflex origin. Frequently, you will find fainting during the pains, or the pains begin in the back and descend thence to the buttocks and thighs. We may also give *Nux* when the labor pains nearly or entirely cease, exactly as in *Pulsatilla*. The temperament of the patient will enable you to decide between the two.

Nux is often useful to prevent the return of metrorrhagia, preceding the climaxis or during labor. There are the urging to stool, faintness, etc., already mentioned.

Now let us take up the action of *Nux vomica* on the spine. It produces, as we have seen when speaking of *Strychnia*, irritation of the motor centres and efferent nerves. The backache cured by *Nux* is that located in the lumbar region. It is usually worse at night when lying in bed, and the patient cannot turn over without sitting up. It is thus useful in lumbago. The longer he lies in bed in the morning the more does his back ache.

Picric acid should be mentioned here. This substance is known chemically as trinitrophenol, and is a violent poison. It is to be thought of when, after every severe mental effort, the patient suffers from intense headache of a throbbing character, felt more particularly at the base of the brain. There is often an accompanying congestion of the spine, with an increase of sexual excitement, so that erections become violent enough to be termed priapism.

Nux vomica is indicated in torticollis, arising from cold or due to spinal disease.

Belladonna is the best remedy for stiff neck of rheumatic origin or from cold. The stiffness is apt to be on the left side.

Causticum has stiffness of the sterno-cleido-mastoid muscle of the right side, with drawing. The torticollis may be due to paralytic weakness, as in affections involving the spinal accessory nerve. Here *Agaricus* and *Lachnanthes* are also to be compared.

In spinal irritation you must use *Nux* when the backache just described is present in association with the following symptoms. Sudden loss of power in the legs in the morning; the hands and feet go to sleep easily; stiffness and tension in the hollow of the knees; the clothing about the waist feels too tight; sensation as of a band about the waist; desire to lie down; numbness and formication along the spine and in the extremities. These symptoms also indicate *Nux* in myelitis, and in the early stages of locomotor ataxia, especially when the trouble has occurred from exposure to cold or from sexual excesses.

Phosphorus is in many respects very similar to *Nux*. Both cause an increase in impressionability; both cause spinal anæmia. But *Phosphorus* tends toward complete paralysis, *Nux* generally toward partial paralysis dependent upon exhaustion. Both have proved useful in spinal softening.

Physostigma has a symptomatology almost typical of spinal irritation. Under this drug every nerve of spinal origin is irritated. Pressure of the finger between the vertebræ causes the patient to wince. *Physostigma* causes rigidity of the muscles from meningeal irritation. It finally develops trismus and tetanus.

Ambra grisea, like *Nux vomica*, is suited to thin, "dried up," nervous subjects. It has marked numbness of the skin. Various parts of the body go to sleep readily. There are also stiffness in the small of the back after sitting and tension in the lumbar muscles, worse on awaking. Even the scrotum and penis feel numb. Patients who complain of these symptoms are apt to be excessively nervous and weak. In company they are easily embarrassed and speak and act hastily. They are driven by nervousness to an impetuous desire to talk, but quickly give out (like *Cocculus*, *Veratrum album*, *Calcarea ostrearum*, *Alumina*, *Sulphur*, and *Kali carb.*). Conversation and exercise quickly cause fatigue.

Asarum Europœum is suited to still another style of nervousness. It is especially adapted to irritable females, who are so exceedingly sensitive that even the *thought* of any one scratching silk or making some similar noise causes an aggravation of their symptoms.

Castoreum is indicated when females are nervous and do not react after sickness. Hence, it may be used after typhoid, especially when the patients are subject to headaches which leave the head very sensitive to touch. These are attended by tingling, creeping sensations which are relieved by sleep.

Nux is useful in rheumatism when it involves the larger joints and muscles. It is especially indicated in rheumatism of the trunk. The swelling in the joints is usually rather pale. The symptoms are almost always worse towards morning.

Nux has been recommended for the acne of drunkards and also for acne from eating too much cheese. Constipation from eating cheese requires *Colocynth*.

Sulphur should be preferred when, with other symptoms, the face is red in blotches, and *Ledum* when there are red blotches and pimples in which sticking is induced by every least touch. *Kreosote* and *Lachesis* are also to be compared with *Nux* in this condition.

Next we shall look at *Nux vomica* in typhoid fevers. In the selection of *Nux* in such cases, you are guided by the gastric and bilious symptoms, bitter taste in the mouth, especially in the morning, nausea, vomiting of bile, and characteristic constipation of the drug. The weakness which necessarily belongs to the typhoid state is expressed under *Nux* by a strong inclination to lie down. The nights are passed in nervous, excited sleep; slight noises cause him to start. He moans and whimpers in his slumber and his dreams are full of bustle and hurry. He may even be delirious.

Nux vomica is useful in intermittent types of fever, when the chill is preceded or accompanied by blueness of the finger-nails; gaping and yawning are well marked. There is always aching in the limbs and in the back; this is followed by fever, and that by sweat. During the apyrexia we have prominent gastric and bilious symptoms.

A peculiarity of *Nux* well worthy of mention is that it seems to intensify the action of *Sepia*. The same relation exists between *Sepia* and *Lilium tigrinum*, and between *Sulphur* and *Mercury*. *Nux vomica* is inimical to *Zincum*.

The *Nux* patient is always better after an uninterrupted sleep. Led by this symptom, Dr. P. P. Wells cured his friend, Dr. Dunham, of diphtheria with *Nux*, a characteristic symptom of the case being marked relief from a nap. When the sleep is disturbed, the *Nux* patient is always worse. Early in the evening he is irresistibly drowsy.

Nux acts best when given in the evening. According to Hahnemann, sensitive persons should not take it fasting in the morning or on first awaking, because its most powerful symptoms are then called out. Neither should it be taken just before or after a meal, or when the mind is on a strain.

LECTURE XVII.

IGNATIA AMARA.

IGNATIA AMARA, or, more properly speaking, *Strychnos ignatia*, is a large climbing shrub growing in the Phillipine Islands and in Cochin-China. The fruit is spherical or ovoid, and about four inches in diameter. Its shell is smooth and brittle, and encloses some twenty or thirty seeds. Its name is attributed to the Jesuits, who called it St. Ignatius's bean, in honor of its virtues. Though chemically and botanically similar to *Nux vomica*, *Ignatia* differs materially from that remedy in symptomatology, and this, too, despite strong family resemblances.

Ignatia is preëminently a spinal remedy, as is also *Nux vomica*. Like the latter, it seems to intensify the impressionability of all the senses, perhaps even more than *Nux* does. Under *Nux*, however, this over-excitability is exhibited by anger, vehemence and irascibility; in *Ignatia*, by melancholy with tendency to weeping. Now, while there is this melancholy tearful mood, yet the patient smothers her grief. The *Ignatia* patient nurses her sorrows, keeping them from others, while the *Nux vomica* patient is vehement and angry; he strikes any one who may oppose him; he is so overbearing that one can scarcely live with him. You must separate this melancholy mood of *Ignatia* from that of *Pulsatilla*.

The *Pulsatilla* woman is tearful, sad, and melancholy like *Ignatia*, but there is not that introspective mood which develops in the *Ignatia* patient. She makes her grief known to every one who comes near her. She seeks sympathy. She is timid and yielding in her disposition.

We find *Ignatia* indicated in nervous women who are burdened with grief, particularly when they dwell upon their troubles in secret. Such cases find relief in *Ignatia*, especially when of recent origin.

For the chronic or long-lasting effects of grief, we have *Phosphoric acid* and *Natrum muriaticum*. Often when the former remedy is indicated, the patient complains of night sweats, not from organic disease, but from sheer exhaustion. She has little or no appetite, and complains of a sensation as of heavy pressure on the top of the head, as though a great load lay there. Emaciation, ennui, and night sweats are characteristic symptoms. In some cases the symptoms are such as to make *Phosphorus* preferable to *Phosphoric acid*.

Natrum mur. is very similar to *Ignatia* in its mental state but shows more of irascibility with its melancholy. Consolation aggravates and elicits an angry rebuff. There is headache in the vertex, emaciation and tremulous palpitation from every strange noise. When *Ignatia* fails to remove the symptoms entirely *Natrum muriaticum* frequently comes in to complete the cure.

Ignatia we find, then, to be useful for the ill-effects of grief, and also, by reason of this great sensitiveness to external impressions which it produces, greater even than that of *Nux vomica*, we find it indicated in hysteria, especially when the patient alternately laughs and cries, or, in other words, exhibits a changeable mood. The face flushes at every emotion. Sometimes the laughing becomes spasmodic and ends in screams and even spasms of the chest with blueness of the face. We have also globus hystericus or feeling as if a ball were rising in the throat. This is often relieved by belching, while drinking water causes an aggravation of the convulsive action in the throat. The patient may fall into a half unconscious state, with clenched thumbs and blue face, as we find under *Cuprum*. Finally a sigh and a long-drawn breath announces the return to consciousness. Now let us consider some of the concordant remedies of *Ignatia* in these hysterical states.

Platina is indicated in hysterical women with violent mania or lofty, supercilious mood.

Hyoscyamus is called for when the mental condition of the patient exhibits marked jealousy. She is full of suspicions. She fears that she will be poisoned, and may on that account refuse all food and medicine.

Asafœtida, like *Ignatia*, has the globus hystericus; flatus accumulates in the abdomen and, pressing up against the lungs, produces oppression of breathing. It is especially useful in hysterical convulsions after suppression of discharges.

Moschus is particularly suited when the patient faints readily. She sits down to her meals and faints dead away from taking even a small amount of food into the stomach. She also has violent spasms of the chest, in which it would almost seem that she must die. She turns blue in the face and foams at the mouth. She may be of a scolding disposition, and even this causes fainting.

Valerian is useful in these hysterical women, when the slightest exertion causes violent headache. They often complain of a sensation as if a string were hanging down into the throat. In the latter part of the evening, they exhibit a tendency to flushes of heat. The slightest pain causes fainting. They complain of a warm sensation rising from the stomach into the throat with the globus hystericus. You will often have to use *Valerian* for pains in the limbs, which simulate those of rheumatism. They are worse while the patient sits and better when she walks about.

Cocculus has a mood somewhat like that of *Ignatia*. Sensitive, anxious, with frightened look; loss of memory, mental confusion, vertigo; spasms of the uterus; great weakness and nausea even to fainting. A sort of semi-paralytic condition pervades the whole body: choking constriction in the upper part of the fauces with difficult breathing; hysterical palsy. These symptoms in *Cocculus* are usually the result of night watching or loss of sleep.

Nux moschata is indicated in hysteria, associated with frequent emotional changes and enormous bloating of the abdomen after a light meal. The patient complains of an overpowering drowsiness and of excessive dryness of the mouth, even when that cavity exhibits the normal degree of moisture. There is also a marked tendency to faint.

Belladonna is indicated in hysterical states, when the patient is boisterous and wild, with red face, etc.

The *Valerianate of Zinc* I have used for a common symptom of hysterical persons and of nervous patients generally, and that is, what has been termed the fidgets. They cannot sit still, or they must keep the legs in constant motion. I have used it, and I do not remember to have failed to cure in a single instance. This uneasiness of the feet is not an uncommon symptom in old cases of uterine disease; I usually give the remedy in the second or third potency.

The headache of *Ignatia* is usually situated in one spot in the head, just as though a nail were being driven into the skull at that point. Any little mental work, or in fact any work that is irksome or more severe than usual, any strong odor, whether pleasant or otherwise, any emotion which would be borne without trouble by one whose nervous system was in a natural state, may bring on this headache. The attack often ends with vomiting. These headaches are often periodical, returning every two days. They often terminate with a copious flow of pale, limpid urine. Several other remedies have headache, relieved by copious urination. They are: *Aconite*, *Gelsemium*, *Kalmia*, *Melilotus*, *Sanguinaria*, *Silicea* and *Veratrum album*. Sometimes the *Ignatia* headache is of a throbbing character, worse in the eyes, and about the eyebrows and the root of the nose; it is relieved for a time by a change of position. Again, *Ignatia* may be indicated in headache, when the head feels heavy, as if from congestion, and yet the pain is better from leaning forward; sometimes aggravation occurs from stooping, thus giving us what Hahnemann calls an alternate effect. The *Ignatia* headaches are aggravated by talking or listening intently, and by coffee.

The power of *Ignatia* to produce increased excitability renders it useful in spasms, not only of hysterical origin, but also in those occurring in delicate women who are not hysterical, and in children. The spasms are excited by emotions, such as fright or fear. For example, the child has a convulsion after being punished. Afterward, when the child goes to sleep, there is whimpering in the sleep. Under ordinary circumstances the child will get over the trouble without any treatment; but if it happens to be extremely delicate, or if the trouble occurs during the period of dentition, or there is some reason for fearing convulsions or hydrocephalus, *Ignatia* may prevent a great deal of trouble. During the convulsions in which *Ignatia* is the remedy, you will usually find the face deathly pale, although at times it is flushed. There is twitching of individual muscles, particularly those about the eyelids or the mouth, and the child stiffens out. As was said before, *Ignatia* is especially indicated when the convulsions have appeared after grief, fright, or some violent emotion.

Nervous women in labor may require *Ignatia* for spasms. These spasms, however, are to be distinguished from those calling for *Belladonna*, *Stramonium*, etc., by the absence of fever or severe congestion, and from *Hyoscyamus* by the absence of unconsciousness or mania.

In these convulsions produced by emotions, unless you have clearly in your mind the distinctions between several remedies, you may not make so prompt a cure as you should. *Opium*, like *Ignatia*, is a remedy for the immediate effects of emotions. It does little or no good for the protracted effects. It, too, is worse after punishment, fright or fear. The body stiffens out, and the mouth and the muscles of the face twitch. Thus far it is exactly like *Ignatia*. The distinction lies in this particular: under *Opium* the face is dark red and bloated, and the spasms are more frequently associated with loud screams than under *Ignatia*.

Glonoin produces sudden violent congestions of the head, as does *Opium*. Like *Opium* and *Ignatia*, it may be used for the sudden effects of violent emotions. In the convulsions the fingers are spread asunder and extended, a symptom which you also find under *Secale*.

Veratrum album also is suitable for convulsions after sudden violent emotions, but the face is cold and blue, with cold sweat on the forehead.

Hyoscyamus has sudden starting and twitching of the muscles, more so than *Ignatia;* one arm will twitch and then the other. The motions are all angular. There is a great deal of frothing at the mouth. The patient seems to be wild.

Belladonna is probably more frequently indicated than any other remedy for convulsions following violent emotions, anger, etc., with bright red face, wild straining eyes, hot head, and spasms of the glottis.

Opium is probably the best remedy when, from fright of the wet-nurse, the child has retention of urine.

Cuprum is indicated in convulsions where the fingers are clenched. There is marked blueness of the face and mouth. Any attempt to swallow fluids causes gurgling in the throat.

Chamomilla is useful in convulsions of children after any emotion. It is easily distinguished from *Ignatia* by the petulant angry disposition of the child. One cheek is red and the other pale, and there is hot sweat about the face and head.

There is a sore throat curable by *Ignatia*. The patient complains of a sensation as though there were a plug in the throat, worse when not swallowing. Examining the tonsils, you find them studded with small superficial ulcers having a yellowish-white color. There is a constricted feeling about the throat, with a great deal of nervousness and insomnia.

The cough of *Ignatia* arises from constriction of the larynx, or from a sensation as of a feather there. The more the patient coughs, the worse does the tickling become.

Ignatia may be used in chills and fever when there is thirst during the chill, and when the warmth of the stove or other artificial heat relieves the chill. This is not a common symptom. It is very different from *Nux vomica*, which usually finds no relief from covering up or from the heat of the stove. *Capsicum* has relief from applying the hot water bottle. *Lachesis* has longing for the heat of the fire, yet the chill is not shortened thereby. *Arsenicum* has chill relieved by warmth. Other remedies are *Rhus tox.*, *Menyanthes*, *Nux moschata* and *Sabadilla*.

The action of *Ignatia* on the genital organs must also be mentioned, as we find it indicated in dysmenorrhœa, associated with what is termed menstrual colic; that is, when there is a great deal of bearing down in the hypogastric region. The patient exhibits hysterical symptoms. The pains are labor-like in character, and are seemingly relieved by pressure, by lying down, and by change of position. The menses are dark, frequent and copious.

The nearest remedy here is *Cocculus Indicus*. This has uterine spasms and dark menstrual flow, but the backache always enables you to differentiate this drug from others. It has a weak, lame feeling in the small of the back, as though the patient were about to be paralyzed. The limbs tremble when she begins to walk. In addition to this, she often complains of a feeling of emptiness or hollowness in various cavities of the body, especially in the chest and abdomen.

Pulsatilla is at times indicated for this menstrual colic, particularly when the menses are dark in color and delayed. The flow is usually fitful. The patient is apt to be chilly, and the more severe the pains are, the more chilly does the patient become.

Chamomilla is a third drug similar to *Ignatia* in uterine spasms. It is indicated by the mental symptoms. The patient is so cross that she can scarcely answer any one civilly.

I would like you to remember also *Magnesia mur.*, which is indicated in uterine spasms accompanying induration of the uterus, whether of a scirrhous nature or not.

Actea racemosa is called for in uterine spasms when the pains fly across the hypogastrium from side to side.

In disorders of digestion *Ignatia* is useful when the patient complains of bitter or sour-tasting mucus in the mouth and copious salivation. There is fanciful aversion to certain foods. He asks for a certain food, but after tasting, refuses it. Food may be regurgitated. Gastralgia is present. He has hiccough, aggravated by eating and smoking, and, especially in children, by emotions. There is an empty, gone feeling at the epigastrium, with qualmishness. In some cases there is empty retching, relieved by eating. The patient vomits at night the food taken in the evening. The bowels are disordered.

Hyoscyamus is one of our best remedies for hiccough occurring after operations on the abdomen.

Stramonium and *Veratrum album* for hiccough after hot drinks, and *Arsenicum* and *Pulsatilla* after cold drinks.

Teucrium marum verum is useful in jerking hiccough after nursing.

Cajuputum suits hiccough coming on the slightest provocation (*Sulphuric acid*). There is spasmodic stricture of the œsophagus, the tongue feels swollen. Flatulence is present.

Ammonium muriaticum is characterized by hiccough with stitches in the chest, and empty, gnawing sensation in the stomach after a full meal.

Ignatia is useful in prolapsus ani, which may or may not be accompanied by hæmorrhoids. You have as a characteristic symptom sharp stabbing pains shooting up into the rectum. This prolapsus ani may annoy the patient, even if there is soft stool. There is distressing constriction at the anus, aggravated after stool, and better while sitting. Itching and creeping at the anus as from ascarides, in which condition *Ignatia* is sometimes an excellent remedy.

Indigo is said to be a good remedy for ascarides, especially in melancholy children. Honey given night and morning will act as a palliative. *Teucrium* should also be thought of in this connection.

Ignatia produces a variety of symptoms referable to the eye, making it a useful remedy in several diseases of that organ. Like *Agaricus*, it has nictitation of the eye-lids, with spasmodic action of the facial muscles. There are neuralgic pains about the eyes. These are exceedingly severe, and are often associated with the globus hystericus. *Ignatia* may also be useful in phlyctenular ophthalmia, when there is intense photophobia and a feeling of sand in the eyes.

The toothache of *Ignatia* is worse between than during acts of eating. Now this is in perfect harmony with the throat symptoms of the drug; that is, there is a feeling as of a lump in the throat which is not felt *during* but *between* the acts of deglutition. The "lump" may feel sore while swallowing, but it is felt more markedly between acts of deglutition. This symptom has led to the selection of *Ignatia* in aphthous sore-throat (the tonsils being swollen and studded with white flat patches), and even in diphtheria.

14

Zincum holds a very peculiar relation to *Ignatia* and to *Nux vomica*. It follows *Ignatia* well, while it is inimical to *Nux vomica*.

Natrum muriaticum follows *Ignatia* well, especially in mental ailments.

LECTURE XVIII.

SPIGELIA ANTHELMINTICA, CURARE AND THE JUGLANDACEÆ.

SPIGELIA.

Spigelia is another member of the order *Loganiaceæ*. To understand it as a remedy is not a difficult thing to do, if we start with the idea that it acts on the nerves, having as a grand characteristic, neuralgia. Associated with these neuralgic symptoms we almost always find symptoms sympathetic from the head, whether these be neuralgic or not. Mentally, we find the patient exhibiting fear, anxiety, forebodings, as though something were about to happen. This is a very common symptom with nervous, neuralgic subjects, especially those whose nerves are very much weakened. Another symptom which sometimes appears is fear of pointed things; for instance, the patient is afraid of pins. There is often, also, præcordial anguish.

The neuralgia itself, if it involves the head, begins in the occiput, coming forward and settling over the left eye. It may also involve the cheeks, especially the left. There are burning, jerking, tearing pains, worse from any noise or from any jarring of the body. They are usually aggravated by change of weather, and are especially worse in stormy weather. At the acme of the pain there is often bilious vomiting. The period of exacerbation is marked. The pain begins in the morning with the sun, increases during the day, and diminishes toward evening.

We often find *Spigelia* indicated in sick-headache when the patient can bear neither noise nor jarring of the body.

This remedy is our mainstay in ciliary neuralgia. The pain may be in either eye; more frequently, however, it is in the left. There may be photophobia from slight retinitis; sharp stabbing pains in the eye, or radiating from the eye. The supraorbital region is tender to touch. The eye-ball feels swollen, or as if it were too large for the orbit. Associated with these symptoms are lachrymation and coryza.

Three remedies are here to be compared with *Spigelia*. The first of them is *Mezereum*. This is useful in ciliary neuralgia. The pains radiate and shoot downward. There is a cold feeling as though a stream of cold air were blowing on the eye. *Mezereum* is especially indicated when the bones are involved, a frequent sequence of mercury.

Another remedy useful in ciliary neuralgia is *Thuja*. Like *Mezereum*, it has a cold feeling in the eye, but the pains take the opposite direction; they go upward and backward instead of downward.

Still another remedy to be thought of is *Cedron*, which has neuralgia recurring at the same hour with clock-like regularity.

Spigelia is a valuable heart remedy. It is to be thought of when there are sharp stitching pains referred to the left chest, shooting into the arm and neck; on placing the hand over the heart, there is a peculiar "purring" feeling. The patient is worse from the slightest motion of the hands or arms. He cannot lie down. The pulse is not synchronous with the heart-beat.

Spigelia may be used for worms. It should be given when there are strabismus from abdominal irritation, jerking over the eyes, paleness of the face, with blue rings around the eyes. The patient feels faint and nauseated on awaking in the morning, when there is also hunger, which is relieved by eating breakfast; there is colic, worse about the navel; stool consisting of mucus, fæces and worms.

CURARE.

Curare or *Woorari*, the famous arrow poison of South America, is derived from the bark of the *Strychnos toxifera*. The commercial preparation is a brownish-black paste of variable composition, the most active ingredient being the alkaloid *Curarine*.

Curare acts on the periphery of the motor nerves, producing paralysis of motion without any disturbance of sensation. When taken internally it causes violent symptoms, sudden vertigo associated with great weakness of the legs. Sooner or later this is followed by vomiting of bile. Some time ago I treated a man with cirrhotic liver. Every morning, at ten or eleven o'clock, he had an attack of bilious vomiting, followed by a chill. The vomiting continued for three or four weeks, and nothing seemed to stop it. But as he had the dizzy feeling just mentioned, I finally gave him *Curare* 500th, and it stopped the vomiting very promptly. The man lived two or three months after that.

Dr. Pitet, of Paris, recommends *Curare* for the dyspnœa of emphysema when the patient seems to be pretty far gone. He administers the drug in the 3d or 6th potency.

Closely allied to *Nux vomica* are certain remedies derived from the order—

JUGLANDACEÆ.

All the Juglandaceæ seem to produce a condition of the blood in which that fluid becomes dark and pitch-like in color. They all cause hæmorrhages.

Juglans regia, or the walnut, is useful for menses which come on too soon, and are composed of nothing but black coagula.

All the members of the order cause cutaneous eruptions. The most important here is *Juglans cinerea*, sometimes called *Juglans cathartica*.

uglans cinerea is one of our best remedies in occipital headache. The pains are of a sharp, shooting character; when this symptom is present you may use the remedy in diseases of the brain or spinal cord.

Juglans cinerea also causes jaundice, just like *Nux vomica*, with stitching pains about the liver, and pain under the right scapula (*Chelidonium* and *Bryonia*); the patient wakes at three o'clock in the morning and cannot go to sleep; these symptoms are often associated with the occipital headache just described. The stools are bilious, or yellowish-green, burning the anus, and associated with tenesmus.

In dropsy of the chest *Juglans cinerea* is useful when there are red spots on the skin, looking very much like flea-bites.

LECTURE XIX.

ARACEÆ.

THE order of plants which we shall study to-day is the *Araceæ*, or, more correctly speaking, the *Aroideæ*. The plants in this group all contain in their juices an acrid principle in more or less quantity. The *Diffenbachia*, when taken into the mouth, produces a frightful stomacace; the mouth is covered with a yellowish-white membrane; ulcers form upon the lips, tongue and fauces. This drug was proved by one of the students of this College. Since then it has been used in the treatment of violent forms of stomacace.

The members of this order which we shall consider are *Arum triphyllum*, *Arum dracontium*, *Caladium seguinum*, *Pothos fœtida*, *Acorus* (of which we know little or nothing), and *Diffenbachia*.

Araceæ
- Arum triphyllum
  - Ailanthus, Ammonium causticum, Nitric acid.
  - Muriatic acid, Lycopodium.
  - Selenium.
- Caladium
  - Graphites.
- Dracontium
  - Balsam of Peru.
  - Pix liquida.
  - Guaiacum.
  - Eryodiction Californicum.
- Pothos fœtida
- Acorus
- Diffenbachia

ARUM TRIPHYLLUM.

The so-called "Jack in the pulpit" is the first drug in the order for our consideration. This remedy has an interesting history. Some twenty-five years ago there appeared an epidemic of scarlet fever, in the course of which nearly every case that was not promptly cured in the beginning died. The percentage of losses under homœopathic as well as under other systems of treatment was truly frightful. The reason for this was that we had no remedy which covered the symptoms of the epidemic. In a poor family, living in a small street, there were five children sick with this epidemic form of scarlatina. The physician who was called to attend them had lost so many cases under the usual remedies that he thought it useless to have recourse to these. He thought it better to try something new. *Arum triphyllum* had only been experimented with to a certain degree, but still it had been known to produce certain symptoms which led him to the selection of the drug, which he administered in a low potency. All the cases recovered. It was afterward prescribed in other cases during the same epidemic, with marked success. From that time to this, *Arum triphyllum* has been looked upon as a valuable drug in the treatment of diphtheria, malignant forms of scarlet fever, and also other fevers having a typhoid form.

In scarlatina, we may use *Arum triphyllum* when there is an excoriating discharge from the nose and mouth, making the nose and upper lip raw and sore. The tongue swells; its papillæ are large and red, giving it a rough feeling comparable to a cat's tongue. The throat is very sore, and the tonsils are much swollen. There is often a dry cough which hurts the child so much that he cringes under it and involuntarily puts the hands to the throat as if to modify the pain. The discharge from the mouth, also, makes the lips and surrounding parts of the face sore, cracked and bleeding, even the saliva itself being very acrid; scabs form; the child will not open his mouth. He is excitable and irritable in mind as well as in body. Thus, you see that *Arum triphyllum* is an exceedingly irritating drug. The child is restless, tosses about, is cross and sleepless at night. The eruption may come out very well and there may be double desquamation. At other times the rash is dark and imperfectly developed; the child picks and bores its fingers into its nose, or nervously picks at one spot till it bleeds. In mild cases, the urine may be very profuse; in severe cases the urine is greatly diminished and the appearance of profuse urination is a sign that the remedy is acting well. In very bad cases, however, those in which the malignancy shows itself in both the internal and external symptoms, you will find a perfect picture of uræmia. The child tosses about the bed unconscious and has this involuntary picking at one spot or boring the finger into the nose; the urine is completely suppressed. The brain is very much irritated, as shown by the restless tossing about and the boring of the head into the pillow. In such a case, *Arum triphyllum* may save the patient, although, at the best, the case is an **exceedingly doubtful one.**

I have never seen inflammation of the brain yield to *Arum triphyllum*, unless some of these symptoms were present; either irritation about the throat, mouth, or nose, or else this peculiar picking or boring at the nose or at one spot till it bleeds. I think that as a rule it is indicated when the cerebral inflammation comes from the suppression of some violently acting poison, such as we find present in scarlatina or diphtheria. Nor would I think of giving *Arum* in uræmia if it arose in the course of ordinary Bright's disease. I do not think it can be the remedy unless the symptoms already referred to are present.

Arum triphyllum has a marked effect upon the larynx. It produces a hoarseness which is characterized by a lack of control over the vocal cords. If the speaker attempts to raise his voice it suddenly goes up with a squeak. With this symptom you may use *Arum* in clergyman's sore throat, whether this affection be the result of overstraining the voice or of cold.

Possibly the remedy most similar to it in this hoarseness and uncertainty of voice is *Graphites*, which is excellent for singers who cannot control their vocal cords, and who develop hoarseness and cracked voice as soon as they begin to sing.

In *Carbo veg.* the voice is deep, failing when the endeavor is made to raise it.

Another remedy for this condition is *Selenium*. The patient gets hoarse as soon as he begins to sing.

Other remedies for the effects of increase of the voice are *Arnica*, *Rhus tox.*, *Causticum*, *Phosphorus* and *Natrum muriaticum*.

Now let us study for a few moments the analogues of *Arum triphyllum*. First of all we shall consider *Nitric acid*.

This was formerly the only remedy we had for scarlatina maligna. It has the excoriating discharge from the nose. No remedy has it more marked, not even *Arum*. The discharge from the nose makes the nostrils and lips sore. This is attended by great prostration. The throat is extremely sore and is covered with membrane of a diphtheritic character, either dark and offensive, or else yellowish-white. The mouth (whether the disease be diphtheria or scarlatina) is studded with ulcers, which appear principally on the inside of the cheeks, on the lips and on the borders of the tongue. This ulceration is accompanied by salivation, the saliva usually being watery and very acrid. The pulse frequently intermits every third or fifth beat a very bad symptom. *Nitric acid* is also preferable to any of the other remedies in diphtheria with these excoriating discharges when the disease advances and affects the stomach (whether or not the membrane in these cases spreads to the stomach, I cannot say); when, with great prostration and membrane in the throat and nose, there is distress and uneasiness referred to the stomach, with total rejection of all food.

Muriatic acid is another remedy in these malignant cases of scarlatina and diphtheria. Under this remedy there is the most intense prostration. The patient seems to have scarcely life enough to move. He is worse at about ten or eleven o'clock in the morning. The mouth is studded with deep ulcers having a dark or black base. They tend to perforate the parts on which they are situated. *Muriatic acid* frequently has the intermittent pulse of *Nitric acid*, but accompanying this symptom there are involuntary stool and urine.

In addition to *Nitric acid* and *Muriatic acid* in cases having this dangerous group of symptoms you should think of *Alcohol*. Grauvogl, you may remember, found that diphtheritic membrane was dissolved and its growths destroyed by several substances, one of them being *Alcohol*. So this agent has become a remedy for diphtheria. *Alcohol* in the form of brandy and water tends not only to destroy the growth, but also aids in counteracting the terrible prostration.

Lycopodium is similar to *Arum triphyllum* in scarlatina and in diphtheria. It has a similar nasal discharge, usually associated, however, with dull, throbbing headache at the root of the nose or over the eyes. The nose is so stuffed up that the child cannot breathe at night. The patient bores and picks at the nose just as under *Arum triphyllum*. But in the *Lycopodium* case the diphtheritic deposit travels from the right to the left side. The patient is always worse from sleep even after a short nap. He suddenly awakens from sleep, crying out as if frightened; nothing can be done to pacify him. He is irritable and peevish. In more advanced cases calling for *Lycopodium*, you will find the child unconscious and in a deep sleep. The lower jaw drops, the urine is scanty or even suppressed, and what does pass stains the bedding or clothing red and deposits a red sand. The breathing is rapid, rattling, with waving of the alæ nasi and snoring. The mucous membrane of the throat is ulcerated and œdematous. Every symptom points to impending paralysis of the brain.

Ammonium causticum was first suggested by Dr. J. P. Dake as a remedy in diphtheria appearing in the nasal cavities, with a burning, excoriating discharge from the nose, and great prostration. The symptoms above mentioned led Dr. Dake to use the remedy in an epidemic which appeared in Nashville, Tennessee.

Lastly, let me mention *Ailanthus*. This drug is a member of the order of *Simarubaceæ*. It is analogous to *Quassia, Cedron, Brucia*, etc., all of which are of bitter taste and have anti-malarial properties. Its history is as follows: Dr. P. P. Wells, of Brooklyn, had two cases of poisoning in children. From his statement of the symptoms, it would certainly seem that he had to treat malignant cases of scarlatina; but there being no such epidemic about at that time, he looked for other causes, and found that the little patients had been chewing the blossoms of the *Ailanthus*. This told him at once that the *Ailanthus* would probably become a remedy in scarlatina. He made provings of the drug, and found that they fully confirmed what he had already learned from these poisoning cases. Since then this remedy has been successfully used many times. A year ago I attended a boy with scarlatina. The child lay in a stupor with his mouth wide open. The throat was swollen, the nose stuffed up, and the slight rash that had appeared on the body was dark and mixed with bluish spots. I gave *Lycopodium*, without any benefit whatever. The child grew worse instead of better. I then thought of *Ailanthus*, and gave it in the sixth potency, with the result that the child was completely cured. I believe the patient would have died had it not been for the *Ailanthus*.

Ailanthus resembles *Arum triphyllum* in the acridity of the discharges. There are excoriating discharges from the mouth and nose, making the lips sore. We find a similar swelling of the throat, both inside and outside. So far as these superficial symptoms are concerned, the remedies are identical. But there is a great difference to be recognized in the other symptoms. The *Ailanthus* patient becomes drowsy and lies in a stupor, hence this drug is indicated when there is torpidity rather than the restless tossing about of *Arum triphyllum*.

The *Ailanthus* rash comes out imperfectly; it is dark red or bluish, and is mixed with petechiæ.

Some little time ago, several members of the class asked me to speak of the remedies useful in diphtheria, and while I am on the subject of *Arum* and its analogues in this affection, I shall take the opportunity to comply with that request.

Baptisia tinctoria has long enjoyed a great reputation in typhoid fever. It has lately been used in diphtheria, and in scarlatina also when the child is very much prostrated and lies in a half-stupid state, almost like one intoxicated. The face is dark-red, and has a besotted look, and the discharges from the mouth and nose are horribly offensive, so much so, indeed, that one might suppose that gangrene of the affected parts had taken place.

Rhus tox. we find indicated in rather severe cases, when the membrane is dark in color and bloody saliva runs out of the mouth during sleep. These symptoms are associated with inflammation of the glands about the neck, of a dark erysipelatous hue.

Phytolacca decandra we find useful when, in the beginning of the disease, there are creepy chills and backache. The patient is weak, and feels faint when he sits up in bed. On looking into the throat you find it dark-red, almost purple. There is great burning in the throat, with aggravation from hot drinks.

Amygdala amara is indicated when there are sharp, lancinating pains in the swollen tonsils. The palate and fauces have a dark-red hue, and the patient is very much prostrated.

Naja tripudians is to be administered when there is impending paralysis of the heart. The patient is blue. He awakens from sleep gasping. The pulse is intermittent and thready. Dr. Preston, of Norristown, has been very successful with *Naja* when the symptoms I have mentioned were present.

Apis mellifica is indicated in diphtheria, when, from the very beginning, the child is greatly prostrated. He is feverish and drowsy at 3 P. M. The pulse ranges from 130 to 140, and is very weak. At first the throat has a varnished appearance as though the tonsils and fauces were coated with a glossy red varnish. The membrane forms on either tonsil, oftener on the right than on the left, and it is thick like wash-leather. The tongue is often swollen. If the child is old enough to talk to you, he will complain of a sensation of fulness in the throat, necessitating swallowing but making the act very difficult. The uvula, in fact the whole throat, is œdematous and swollen. The rima glottidis is swollen, red, and œdematous, making breathing difficult. In some of these cases the breath is very fœtid, while in others it is not so in the least. In some cases a red rash appears over the body, greatly resembling that of scarlatina. The child is often thirstless in spite of the presence of fever.

Arsenicum album is called for in rather severe cases of diphtheria, when the throat is very much swollen both internally and externally, and the membrane has a dark hue and is very fœtid. There is a thin, excoriating discharge from the nose. The throat is œdematous, just as it is under *Apis*. The patient is restless, especially after midnight, and is greatly prostrated. The urine is scanty; the bowels are constipated, or else there is an offensive, watery diarrhœa.

Natrum arsenicosum is the remedy when the throat is of a dark purplish hue, with great swelling and prostration, but without much pain.

Kali permanganatum is useful when the membrane is horribly offensive. The throat is œdematous, and there is a thin discharge from the nose; the chief characteristic of the drug is this extreme fœtor.

Lachesis is called for when the membrane forms first on the left tonsil and spreads thence to the right. It is to be distinguished from other drugs which act in a similar manner by the fact that the symptoms are worse from empty swallowing, and are often relieved by eating or swallowing solid food. There is a constant feeling as of a lump on the left side; this descends with each act of deglutition, but returns again. Sometimes, on waking from sleep, there is a feeling as if there were needles in the throat, which create suffocation. When the tonsils are very much swollen, fluids are apt to return through the nose. The fauces are of a dark purplish color, and there is great prostration. The heart is weak in its action. There is aggravation after sleep, and the throat is sensitive to the slightest touch.

Belladonna is not a prominent remedy in diphtheria. When you do give it in this disease, make sure that it is the remedy or you will lose valuable time. It may, however, be the remedy in the early stages when the violence of the attack calls for it, if there is congestion of the head before the membrane has formed.

Other frequently indicated remedies are *Kali bichromicum*, *Iodine*, *Bromine*, *Mercurius biniodatus*, *Mercurius cyanatus*, etc. Some of these I have already given you, and the others you will get in future lectures.

CALADIUM SEGUINUM.

Caladium is indicated in stout persons of flabby fibre who are subject to catarrhal asthma; that is, asthma with the production of mucus which is not readily raised, but which, when raised, gives relief to the patient.

It is a remedy to be remembered in spermatorrhœa or in seminal weakness, particularly in nocturnal emissions, when there is complete relaxation of the organs so that emissions occur without any dreams, or if there be a dream, it is entirely foreign to sexual subjects. So you see it is indicated in far advanced cases without erections.

DRACONTIUM.

I bring this drug before you in order to say a few words concerning the remedies similar to it. *Dracontium* has never been proved in the high potencies. It produces symptoms similar in nature to those of *Arum triphyllum*, but its action is on the lower portion of the respiratory apparatus. *Arum* produces a laryngeal cough. *Dracontium* acts on the trachea and bronchial tubes, giving rise to a violent attack of bronchial catarrh, with rapid formation first of a watery, burning discharge, and later, of pus or muco-pus; hence its symptoms are: yellowish purulent discharge, with great burning, rawness, and other symptoms of violent inflammation.

Beside *Dracontium* I have placed on the board a list of remedies, some of which may be unknown to you. The *Balsam of Peru* should be remembered as an admirable remedy in bronchial catarrh when there is formation of muco-pus. When you place your ear to the chest you detect loud rales, and the expectoration is thick, creamy, and yellowish-white. The *Balsam of Peru* is an excellent remedy, even though night sweats and hectic fever show the disease to be progressing alarmingly. This drug I use in a low potency.

Next below I have placed *Pix liquida*, which is not only an excellent remedy in bronchial catarrh but also in phthisis pulmonalis. It is indicated by the expectoration of purulent matter, offensive in odor and taste, and accompanied by pain referred to the left third costal cartilage (really in the left bronchus). This pain may or may not apparently go through to the back. In such cases *Pix liquida* is the remedy. It is especially indicated in the third stage of phthisis.

Next to this I have placed *Guaiacum*, which is also to be thought of in the late stage of tuberculosis, when there are pleuritic pains referred to the left apex, and in addition offensive muco-purulent sputum.

Eryodiction Californicum (also called *Yerba santa*) has as yet a very limited symptomatology, but it has been used successfully in what we may call bronchial phthisis. The patient has night-sweats, and the body wastes away. There is great intolerance of food. It is called for in phthisis, the result of frequent bronchial catarrhs, and also in asthma relieved by expectoration.

POTHOS FŒTIDA.

Pothos fœtida is a remedy you should remember in asthma. It is useful for asthma that is worse from any inhalation of dust, as, for example, the inhalation of the dust in a hay-loft, and that is relieved by stool.

It also includes within its therapeutic range marked hysteria. Absent minded, irritable; hysterical paroxysms resembling tetanus, with enormous bloating of the abdomen.

LECTURE XX.

ANACARDIACEÆ.

To-day I introduce to you for study a group of plants known as the *Anacardiaceæ*. This is a valuable order, from which we obtain several very useful medicines. 1. The *Anacardium orientale*, which comes from the East. 2. The *Anacardium occidentale*, the western *Anacardium* or cashew nut. 3. The *Comocladia dentata*, which is the *Rhus* common to the southern parts of the United States and Cuba. Upon the blossoms of this plant bees feed in certain seasons of the year. Those who partake of the honey at such times are liable to become affected with an eruption very much resembling that of erysipelas. The *Comocladia* is very similar to *Rhus tox*. Both remedies have pain with relief from motion; both may be called for in erysipelas; both cause scarlet redness of the body, with burning and itching; both produce weakness, numbness, restlessness, etc. They differ in their eye-symptoms. *Comocladia* has pains in the right eye with a sensation as if it were larger or were being pushed out of the head. These eye-symptoms are worse near a warm stove; while those of *Rhus* are relieved by this influence. *Apis* has eye-symptoms aggravated from being near a warm stove. The ophthalmia of *Mercurius*, *Argentum nitricum* and *Antimonium crudum* is also worse from radiated heat. *Comocladia* resembles *Euphorbium officinarum* in its skin-symptoms, even in the red stripes on the skin. 4. *Rhus toxicodendron* or the poison ivy, which I will consider at length in my next lecture. 5. *Rhus glabra*, or the common sumach; it is not so poisonous a variety of the *Rhus* as those already mentioned. It has cured occipital headache, and also epistaxis proceeding from the left side. 6. *Rhus radicans*, which is regarded by many as identical with *Rhus tox*. 7. The *Rhus venenata*, an exceedingly poisonous variety. It has a large blossom of a dark reddish-brown color. It is a small tree, growing sometimes to the height of ten feet, and very much resembling the *Ailanthus*.

All the plants of this order are poisonous; they affect the blood, and develop an eruption on the skin which is, at first, vesicular and finally pustular and eczematous. They may also produce an erythema ending in erysipelas. Despite the similarities thus far mentioned, there are great differences in their physiological action; in fact, these differences may be so great that, in some points, they may bring some of the members of the group into an opposite relation to each other.

ANACARDIUM ORIENTALE.

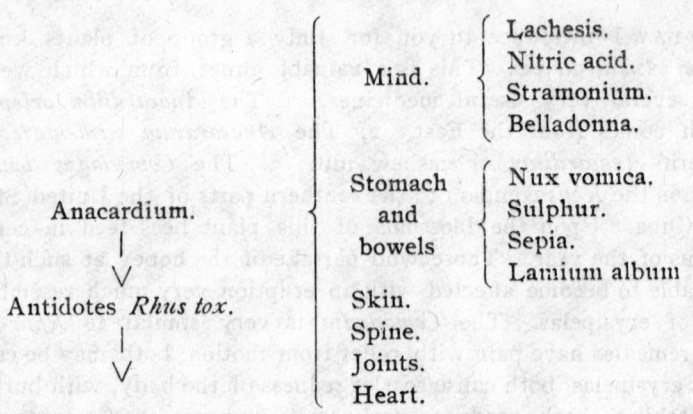

Anacardium.
|
V
Antidotes *Rhus tox*.
|
V

Mind. { Lachesis. Nitric acid. Stramonium. Belladonna.

Stomach and bowels { Nux vomica. Sulphur. Sepia. Lamium album

Skin.
Spine.
Joints.
Heart.

Is antidoted by Juglans.

Anacardium exerts a depressing influence on the system, not only as to the mind, but as to the body as well. It produces a weakness of memory; this symptom we often meet with as the result of acute diseases; for example, the acute exanthemata, such as small-pox. The eruption of *Anacardium* is analogous to that of variola. Taking these two symptoms, loss of memory and eruptions simulating that of variola, we find an excellent reason for prescribing this remedy when loss of memory appears as one of the sequelæ of that disease. *Anacardium* may also be useful when this disturbance of memory occurs in old people, or as the result of softening of the brain.

In addition to this effect on the intellect, we find the emotional mind very much disturbed; the *Anacardium* patient imagines that he hears voices afar off talking to him. Here it is something like *Stramonium*. He has a sensation as though he had two wills—one commanding him to do what the other forbids. This is not an uncommon symptom in typhoid fever, in which disease plants which poison the blood, as do those under consideration, may be exceedingly useful. This feeling, as if the patient had two wills, is also found under other remedies. You will find it, for example, under *Lachesis*, which, you will remember, has: "The patient thinks that he is under the control of some superhuman power." A similar symptom is also found under *Belladonna.*

Another mental condition characterizing *Anacardium* is a propensity to swear. Now, do not suppose that I recommend *Anacardium* for the cure of profanity when it exists as the result of low morals; far from it. When, however, the propensity to swear comes as a result of mental disease, *Anacardium* may do noble work. I once treated a minister who exhibited a remarkable *penchant* for profanity; try as hard as he would, he could not help it. This trouble did not affect him until he suffered from a peculiar headache, characterized by a sensation as if a plug were in the head. *Anacardium* made a complete cure in his case.

Another remedy producing disposition to swear is *Nitric acid;* but I have never seen it do any good in these cases excepting after the abuse of mercury. I also wish to call your attention to a symptom of the drug, on the authority of Dr. Talcott, of Middletown, N. Y., namely, inclination to commit suicide by shooting, a symptom which you will also find under *Antimonium crudum.*

We also find *Anacardium* a remedy for the bad effects of over-use of the mind; for mental fatigue, in other words. Mental exertion brings on a tearing headache, the pains being situated mostly in the forehead and back part of the forehead. In other cases, the headache may assume a different phase, in which the patient complains of the plug-sensation spoken of above, or of a constrictive sensation as though a band were tied about the head. These headaches of *Anacardium* are associated with great mental irritability, which is not, however, always so great as to lead the patient to indulge in profanity.

Hypochondriasis is one of the marked features of *Anacardium.* The patient is apt to be clumsy and silly in his behavior, and very much depressed. There is again this idea of duality, that his mind is separated from his body, that a stranger accompanies him. These symptoms of the mind frequently owe their origin to gastric disturbance. In the woman they may develop after child-birth. She imagines that her child is not her own, that her husband is someone else.

The gastric symptoms of *Anacardium* are these, and they are very characteristic. You will note that the patient is hungry much of the time; he feels better while eating, but worse after eating. He is apt to have constipation; there is frequent desire for stool, but when an attempt to move the bowels is made, the urging passes away. The rectum seems powerless; he complains of a sensation as of a plug or of some foreign substance in the rectum; this symptom is not the mechanical result of the retained fæces. Here again you notice the sensation as of a plug or some foreign substance interfering with the normal function of the organ. Now these symptoms that I have mentioned are more common than we think. When they do occur, we are more apt to think of *Nux vomica*, *Ignatia*, and *Sulphur*, and forget *Anacardium*.

Especially does *Anacardium* resemble *Nux vomica* in the morning nausea. Like *Nux*, the former may be useful for the morning sickness of pregnancy; the patient is relieved while eating, but the symptoms return soon after. There is also a resemblance in the mental symptoms of the two drugs. Wherein do they differ? There is an essential difference in the pathology of the cases calling for these remedies. While you will note that *Anacardium* has urging to stool, it also has in addition a powerlessness or inefficiency of the rectum, thus exhibiting a paretic state which does not belong to *Nux vomica*, the last-named drug being suited to irregular peristaltic action of the bowels. Then, too, that sensation as of a plug in the rectum, is not found under *Nux vomica*.

Do not forget the distinction I have given you between *Anacardium* and *Nux*, I admonish you again, because I know we often give *Nux* when we should have given *Anacardium*.

Sepia is similar to *Anacardium*. This remedy has urging as if some foreign substance were in the rectum; a constant full feeling in the rectum, even after stool. In addition to this, it has inactivity of the rectum, so that even a soft stool is expelled with difficulty. It is true that these symptoms of *Sepia* almost always require the presence of some uterine disease to make it the remedy.

A French physician has recommended *Anacardium* as an invaluable remedy in internal hæmorrhoids. He administers the drug in the thirtieth potency, several times daily, for several weeks. He claims to have made many cures; I have not been able to confirm his experience.

The same physician uses *Lamium album* for external piles. This remedy has a headache accompanied by a peculiar backward and forward motion of the head.

Let us now study the action of *Anacardium* on the skin. We find it useful when the face is swollen, particularly on the left side, and covered with small blisters which have a pock-like appearance. These blisters are umbilicated; they may also occur on other parts of the body. They discharge a yellowish serum which hardens into crusts in the open air. The itching is extreme, so great, indeed, as almost to compel the patient to dig the nails into the skin. These cutaneous symptoms are often accompanied by some of the gastric symptoms just mentioned.

The *Anacardium occidentale*, or cashew nut, although the kernel is edible, causes a vesicular eruption, usually on the face, but on other parts of the body also, with almost intolerable itching, and as you might expect, it also causes umbilicated pustules, as in small-pox. It produces an erysipelatous eruption on the face, and this spreads from the left to the right. Now, this is in the proving. You remember that I said in my lectures on Institutes, when in a proving the symptoms move in one direction, that the remedy producing the symptoms ought to cure a disease going in the opposite direction. For instance, in the proving of *Rhus tox.* the erysipelatous inflammation goes from right to left, hence it cures erysipelas going from left to right. As this variety of *Anacardium* has symptoms like *Rhus*, but moving in an opposite direction, it may act as an antidote to *Rhus tox*.

We shall now speak of the action of *Anacardium orientale* on the heart. *Anacardium* is indicated in palpitation of the heart, especially in the aged, when it complicates such slight difficulties as an ordinary coryza. This palpitation is often associated with defective memory.

We also find it indicated in rheumatic pericarditis characterized by sharp stitches through the cardiac region, these stitches being double, that is to say, one stitch is quickly followed by a second, and then there is a long interval.

Next we shall say a few words about the action of *Anacardium* on the spine, back, and limbs. *Anacardium* may be selected in diseases of the spinal cord. The symptoms which indicate it here are, sensation as though a band were tied around the body; a feeling as though a plug were stuck in the spine so that any motion of the body gives rise to a pain as if the plug were sticking still further into the body. The knees, particularly, seem to feel weak in these spinal affections. They feel as if paralyzed. The patient is scarcely able to walk, and in addition has a feeling as though the knees were bandaged tightly.

Looking into Bœnninghausen's works, you will find that *Anacardium* has an action on the knee-joint. The swelling of *Anacardium* is of a chronic character, and is attended by a sensation as of subcutaneous ulceration.

Anacardium, you should remember, is not antidoted by *Rhus tox.*, although, under some circumstances, it is an antidote to this remedy. But it is antidoted by the *Juglans*—also by strong coffee without sugar or milk.

Next we come to the different varieties of *Rhus*. *Rhus toxicodendron*, as I have already intimated, will be considered in full in my next lecture. I will now say a few words concerning *Rhus radicans*, and the antidotal treatment of *Rhus* poisoning. *Rhus radicans* is highly recommended for occipital headache associated with rheumatic stiffness at the nape of the neck.

Many antidotes to *Rhus* poisoning have been suggested. One of the best is *Croton tiglium*. This, when applied locally, and also when taken internally, produces an eruption almost identical with that of *Rhus tox.* First, an erythema appears, with decided inflammation and pitting on pressure. Small vesicles form, very close together, attended by almost unbearable itching, burning, and stinging. These vesicles fill with a yellowish serum, and finally break and form more or less thick crusts.

Ammonium carb. has also been suggested. It may be used both internally and locally. It produces a fine red eruption, with great burning and itching, worse at night.

Western physicians have of late been using *Grindelia robusta*. It is not much used here.

Arsenicum is to be thought of when the eruption is attended by fiery, burning pains in the skin and great restlessness.

Chronic *Rhus* poisoning finds its best remedy in *Graphites*, but *Sulphur* and especially *Sepia* are also of great use in curing obstinate cases.

This *Grindelia robusta*, to which I have referred so briefly, has a remarkable action on the pneumogastric nerves. It seems to produce a paresis of those nerves, so that when the patient drops off to sleep he stops breathing and, of course, is aroused by the desire for oxygen. You see that it is allied here to *Lachesis* and *Gelsemium*.

LECTURE XXI.

RHUS TOXICODENDRON.

The drug of which I wish to speak this morning is the chief member of the Anacardiaceæ, namely, the poison-ivy or *Rhus toxicodendron*. You must remember it as complementary to *Bryonia*, a fact discovered by Hahnemann in his experience with an epidemic of war-typhus, during which he treated many cases, losing but two; the success he then gained was acknowledged on all sides. Many lives have since been saved by the exhibition of these two remedies in alternation; *i. e.*, an alternation which consists in giving *Bryonia* when *Bryonia* symptoms are present, and *Rhus tox.* when the patient manifests symptoms calling for that remedy. This is a legitimate alternation. We must also remember a fact of which I have spoken before, but which is so important that I here reiterate it, namely, that *Rhus tox. bears an inimical relation to Apis mellifica*. Although the symptoms of the two are superficially similar, for some reason which I cannot explain, these drugs do not follow each other well.

We find *Rhus tox.* forming the centre of a very large group of medicines. If we were to study them all comparatively, it would take several hours. For example, holding as it does important typhoid relations, it has radiating from it many drugs employed in typhoid states of disease. *Bryonia*, as I have already said, stands close to it. Then we have diverging in another radius *Arsenicum*, in still another *Muriatic acid*, *Phosphorus*, *Carbo veg.*, etc., with *Baptisia* and a number of others.

First, we shall study the action of *Rhus tox.* on the circulatory system. We find that it causes an erethism, an increase in the circulation; in other words, ebullitions of the blood. It acts on the central organ of the circulation, the heart. Thus we find it indicated in uncomplicated hypertrophy of that viscus, *i. e.*, hypertrophy not associated with valvular lesions. From what cause? From the effects of over-exertion, as may frequently happen in athletes and in machinists who wield heavy tools.

Rhus tox.
↓
Bryonia.

1. Blood. { Heart, pulse. / Typhoid symptoms.
2. Fevers.—Intermittent, etc.
3. Fibrous tissues. { Aponeuroses, tendons. / Joints. / Cellulitis. / Over-exertion.
4. Skin. { Eruptions. / Erysipelas.
5. Mucous membranes. { Influenza. / Diarrhœa.
6. Organs.

Compare Rhus with

Arnica, Bromium, Aconite, Kalmia, Pulsatilla, Actea r., Phytolacca dec.	In cardiac affections.
Phosphorus, Arsenicum, Muriatic acid, Carbo veg., Baptisia, Arnica, Phosphoric acid, Taraxacum, Bryonia.	In typhoid fever.
Arnica, Arsenicum, Sulphur, Petroleum, Ruta, Staphisagria, Kali carb., Ledum, Valerian, Anacardium, Conium, Lycopodium, Pulsatilla, Ferrum, Rhus rad., Kalmia, Colchicum, Rhododendron.	In rheumatic affections.
Lachesis, Ailanthus, Arum triphyllum, Belladonna, Calcarea ostrearum.	In scarlatina.
Mezereum, Nux juglans.	In eczema.
Cinchona, Sulphuric acid, Belladonna, Spigelia, Carbo animalis.	In head symptoms.
Calcarea ostrearum, Sepia, Gelsemium, Kalmia.	In eye symptoms.

Other remedies useful in this condition are *Arnica* and *Bromium*. These remedies, when indicated, must be given persistently for days and even weeks, until you have succeeded in bringing about a proper absorption of the surplus cardiac muscular fibres. We also find *Rhus* indicated in palpitation of the heart, following over-exertion. When *Rhus tox.* is the remedy in heart disease, you usually find accompanying the disorder a sensation of numbness of the left arm and shoulder. The patient experiences a weak feeling in the chest, as if the heart muscle were tired, and this is worse after any exertion. The palpitation at times seems worse when he is sitting still.

Aconite has tingling in the fingers in association with heart disease. The fingers feel as if they were going to sleep. Anxiety is always present with this drug.

So, too, with *Kalmia*, which has the same symptom in the left arm, with cardiac affections.

Cactus has this symptom associated with constrictive sensation as of an iron band about the heart; and *Sumbul* with heaviness and sharp, wiry shooting pains in the fingers.

Pulsatilla has numbness, particularly about the elbow, very frequently with hypertrophy or dilatation of the right ventricle.

Actea racemosa has the sensation as though the arm was bandaged tightly to the body.

Phytolacca, however, affects the right side of the body. It has the same sensation in the right arm that *Aconite*, *Kalmia* and *Rhus* have in the left.

Now the pulse of *Rhus tox.* *Rhus* produces a depression of the system, hence its pulse is not apt to be so full and strong as we find under *Aconite*. It is accelerated, but with this acceleration there is apt to be weakness of its beat. At other times, it is irregular or even intermittent; all these are characteristic of *Rhus tox.* With these different kinds of pulse, we often find the numbness of the left arm which I have just mentioned.

Let us next take the typhoid symptoms of *Rhus;* by this I mean typhoid-like symptoms, symptoms which indicate sinking of the vital forces such as appears in diseases assuming a low type. Other things being equal, you may rely on *Rhus* whenever acute diseases take on a typhoid form. Dysentery assuming this form may call for it. The same is true of peritonitis, pneumonia, scarlatina and diphtheria under similar conditions and when no other remedy is positively indicated. *Rhus* must, therefore, act on the blood, poisoning that fluid.

The symptoms which indicate it in typhoid fever proper are these: in the first place, the temperament helps you a great deal. The patient is of a rather mild temperament. The delirium is of a mild character, and not violent. At times, it is true, the patient may exhibit a disposition to jump out of bed, or to try to escape, but when he is more or less conscious, he manifests little petulance or irritability. It is not, then, a violent anger that characterizes *Rhus tox*. You will notice that this delirium is associated with restlessness, not only mental but physical as well. The patient constantly tosses about the bed. He is first lying on one side of the body, then on the other. At one moment he is sitting up, during the next he is lying down. You observe then a constant desire to move, and it is even possible that the patient is relieved by the change of position. Sometimes we find exceptionally, in the beginning of the disease, that the patient wants to lie perfectly quiet. This is on account of the great weakness. He feels perfectly prostrated. In fact, the sense of debility is an early symptom, far outstripping the rest of the symptoms in their course, and out of proportion to them. He is indifferent to everything. Sometimes the patient has hallucinations. He fears that he will be poisoned. He will not take the medicines you leave him, or the food and drink that is offered him, as he fears that his attendants desire to poison him. As the stupor progresses, he answers very slowly, as if reluctantly or else in a petulant way; but he is not violent. He has severe headache, the pain of which he compares to a sensation as of a board strapped to the forehead. This is often associated with a rush of blood to the head, as shown by sudden flushing of the face He has epistaxis, and this relieves the headache. The blood that escapes is dark in color. His sleep is restless and he dreams of roaming over fields or of great exertion, as climbing, swimming. The typhoid fever may affect the lungs and produce pneumonia, with the usual cough, difficult breathing, and rust-colored sputum attending that affection; with all these symptoms you find the tongue dark brown, dry and cracked. The cracks gape considerably and at times bleed. Sometimes the tongue and mouth are covered with a brownish, tenacious mucus; at others, you find the tongue taking the imprint of the teeth. Now, let me beg of you not to give *Mercurius* simply because the latter symptom is present. *Mercurius* has very little application to typhoid fever; it will spoil your case unless decided icteroid symptoms are present. The tongue of *Rhus tox*. very often has a triangular red tip, which is quite different from the more evenly coated flabby tongue of *Mercury*. There is disturbance of the stomach and bowels. The patient has diarrhœa with yellowish-brown or greenish stools of a cadaverous odor. Stools may come involuntarily, during sleep. The urine escapes involuntarily, and sometimes leaves a reddish stain. The patient complains of tearing pains in the limbs with almost intolerable backache. Sometimes (like *Bryonia*) he dreams of the business of the day. (*Aurum, Causticum,* and *Aurum mur.*, also have this restlessness of the limbs, worse at night.) The surface of the body is dry and hot, and often redder than normal. Sometimes red spots will be found on the skin. If he has sweat, it is copious and sour-smelling, and is accompanied by a miliary rash. The abdomen is tympanitic; and it is especially sensitive over two important points, the right iliac region and the region of the spleen, which organ, by the way, is swollen. Finally, the stools become scanty and greenish and are unattended by tenesmus. In women a uterine hæmorrhage may complicate the case, but this gives no relief to the symptoms. Symptoms of pulmonary congestion appear. Râles are heard all through the chest, especially in the lower lobes of the lungs. The cough is at first dry, and then becomes more frequent and loose, with expectoration of blood-streaked sputum. These, then, are the main symptoms which lead you to prefer *Rhus* in the treatment of typhoid fevers. Very briefly let me show you how it may be distinguished from its concordant remedies; and first, I shall speak of some of the remedies that may follow *Rhus tox*.

Phosphorus follows *Rhus* well when the pneumonic symptoms have failed to yield to that remedy, and when the diarrhœa continues. The stools are yellow and blood-streaked, sometimes looking like "flesh-water."

Arsenicum follows *Rhus* in the erethistic form of typhoid fever. Notwithstanding the terrible prostration, the patient is still irritable and anxious, even to the last hours of life. The profound weakness continues, the mouth grows blacker and the diarrhœa persists, notwithstanding *Rhus*. Here let me give you a word of caution. Beginners are apt to give *Arsenicum* too soon. If this is done, they only hasten the troubles that they are endeavoring to prevent. *Arsenic* is an excellent remedy when indicated, a dangerous one when misused. I therefore say, "do not give it early in the course of typhoid affections, unless the symptoms clearly call for it." Like *Rhus, Arsenicum* has restlessness, prostration and prominent abdominal symptoms. Thirst is intense. Pains are of a burning character. The stools are dark-brown, offensive and bloody, and more frequent after midnight.

Muriatic acid is also useful in the erethistic form. It has many symptoms in common with *Rhus*. It is to be preferred when the decomposition is still more evident; the prostration is great, the patient being so weak that he slides down toward the foot of the bed. The stool and urine escape involuntarily.

Hyoscyamus has the symptom, fear of being poisoned, in a more marked degree even than *Rhus*, but otherwise has no great resemblance.

But we also find *Rhus* similar to remedies which suit the torpid form of the disease. Foremost in this list is *Carbo veg*. The *Rhus* patient often runs into a *Carbo veg.* state, in which case he lies perfectly torpid, without any sign of reaction. The limbs are cold, especially the legs from the feet to the knees, and are covered with a cold sweat. The pulse is rapid and with little volume, the discharges from the bowels are horribly offensive.

Still another remedy is *Baptisia*. This is indicated when we have, as under *Rhus tox.*, brown or blackish coated tongue, and well-marked fever. The face presents a dark red, besotted appearance, like that of one intoxicated. The discharges from the bowels are dark, fluid and very offensive. The patient is drowsy and stupid; he goes to sleep while answering questions; or he is restless, tossing about the bed with the illusion that he is double, or is scattered about, and must try to get himself together again. He complains of the bed feeling too hard. The tongue is often studded with aphthous ulcers.

Arnica and *Baptisia* both have a drowsy, stupid state; the patient complains of the bed feeling too hard, and goes to sleep while answering questions. But, under *Arnica*, there is complete apathy ecchymoses and bed-sores appear on the body, there is also involuntary stool and urine; and, if the lungs are affected, the sputum is bloody.

Phosphoric acid follows well after *Rhus* when there is increased debility or prostration with perfect apathy. The stools are bloody and slimy. Nose-bleed, when it occurs, brings no relief.

Taraxacum should also be borne in mind. Bœnninghausen's son was taken with typhoid fever and was attended by his father. Among his symptoms was the restlessness I mentioned as characteristic of *Rhus tox.*, yet that remedy gave no relief. Looking up the materia medica,

Bœnninghausen found that *Taraxacum* had this same restlessness of the limbs with tearing pains, and in addition it also had a symptom which was present in his son's case, mapped tongue. He gave *Taraxacum* with prompt result.

The indications for *Bryonia* in typhoid states I will defer until next month, when I lecture on that drug in detail.

Next we see the disturbances in the circulation produced by *Rhus* exhibited in another form of fever, namely, intermittent fever. *Rhus* is suitable for intermittent types of fever when the chill begins in one leg, usually in the thigh, or between the shoulders or over one scapula. It is very important always to note the point it which the chill starts in this disease. For instance, under *Eupatorium* and sometimes *Natrum mur.*, it begins in the small of the back; under *Gelsemium*, it runs up the spine. In the *Rhus* case, during the chill there is a dry, teasing cough, a symptom which you will also find under *Cinchona*, *Sulphur*, *Bryonia* and *Sabadilla*. Along with the external chill there is internal heat. Thirst is absent. Often, too, we find skin symptoms, as urticaria and fever blisters, the latter being situated about the mouth. The sweat is very general, excepting about the face.

We now come to the study of the action of *Rhus* on the fibrous tissues. Allow me to include under this tissue the aponeuroses and tendons of muscles, the ligaments about joints and the connective tissue. No remedy has a more profound action on the fibrous tissues than has *Rhus tox*. First of all, I will speak of its action on the tendons of muscles. We find *Rhus* useful whenever these tendons are inflamed, whether it be from over-exertion or from a sudden wrenching, as in the case of a sprain. We find, also, that we may give *Rhus* in other affections arising from over-exertion. For example, if a musician from prolonged performing on wind instruments suffers from pulmonary hæmorrhages, *Rhus* will be his remedy. If from violent exertion a patient is seized with paralysis, his trouble may yield to *Rhus tox*. In sprains, *Calcarea ostrearum* follows when *Rhus* has relieved, but failed to cure.

Let me here speak of a few other remedies applicable to the bad effects of over-exertion, in order that you may differentiate them from the drug which is the subject of this lecture.

Arnica acts more on the muscular tissue than on the ligaments. Hence, we would find it indicated when, as a result of long exertion, there is a great soreness of the muscles. The patient feels as if he had been pounded. It has not that strained feeling of *Rhus*. When a joint is clearly sprained, *Arnica* is not the best remedy, unless there is considerable inflammation of the soft parts other than the ligaments.

Arsenicum is to be thought of for the effects of over-exertion, particularly if that exertion consists in climbing steep hills and mountains. Here you have the effects of breathing rarefied air as well as those of the exertion. It is also useful for inflammation and soreness in enarthrodial joints from concussion, as, for instance, when the head of the femur is jammed violently into its socket.

The general characteristic, however, which helps you to decide for *Rhus* in all these cases is this: *the patient has relief of his symptoms by continued motion, while he experiences aggravation on beginning to move.* The reason for this symptom is that the fibrous tissues become limbered up as the patient continues to move.

I may say that there is somewhat of an exception to this characteristic, and that is in that painful disease known as lumbago. I find that in the beginning of this affection *Rhus* is the remedy, whether the patient is better from motion or not. The symptoms calling for *Rhus* are great pains on attempting to rise, stiff neck of rheumatic origin from sitting in a draught, rheumatic pains in the interscapular region, better from warmth and worse from cold. There may also be constrictive pains in the dorsal muscles, relieved from bending backward.

Sulphur also has rheumatic pains, with stiffness in the lumbar region, and with sudden loss of power on attempting to move.

Petroleum and *Ruta* are useful when these rheumatic pains in the back are worse in the morning before rising.

Under *Staphisagria*, the lumbar pains compel the patient to get up early.

Kali carb. has sharp pains in the lumbar region, worse at 3 A. M., compelling the patient to get up and walk about. The pains shoot down the buttocks.

Ledum has pain in the back, which may be compared to a feeling of stiffness after sitting still for a long time. There is a crampy pain over the hips in the evenings. In the morning the feet are stiff and rigid.

Valerian causes, and therefore will cure, violent drawing, darting, jerking pains in the limbs, which appear suddenly. They are worse from sitting and better from motion. The patient also has a strained feeling in the lumbar region, subject to the same modality as the pains in the limbs.

In rheumatism *Rhus* is indicated, not so much in the inflammatory form as in the rheumatic diathesis, when the characteristic modality just mentioned is present, and when there is aggravation during damp weather, or from dwelling in damp places. Another peculiarity of *Rhus* is that prominent projections of bones are sore to the touch, as, for example, the cheek-bones. This shows you that *Rhus* affects the periosteum. Still another characteristic is that the patient cannot bear the least exposure to cool air.

Rhus may also be used for either horse or man when the patient has become warm from exercise, and the resulting free perspiration has been checked by rain or dampness.

In these various rheumatic affections, I wish you to compare, first, *Anacardium*, which has a stiff neck, worse from beginning to move.

Conium has worse from beginning to move, but relief from continued motion.

Lycopodium and *Pulsatilla*, which are worse on beginning to move but better from slow motion.

Ferrum, which has neuralgic and rheumatic pains worse at night, relieved by slowly moving about at night.

Capsicum, which has many symptoms relieved by moving about.

Rhus radicans has drawing, tearing pains in the legs. It has also rheumatic pains in the back of the head. It is useful in pleurodynia or false pleurisy, when the pains go into the shoulders. In the provings made by Dr. Joslin it caused pains following the course of the ulnar nerve.

Kalmia latifolia has tearing pains down the legs, without any swelling, without fever, but with great weakness. You see that it here resembles *Colchicum*.

Rhododendron has great susceptibility to changes in the weather, particularly from warm to cold, and to electric changes in the atmosphere. Associated with this susceptibility to changes in the weather are numbness, formication, etc.; pain in the limbs, especially in the bones of forearms, hands and feet. As under *Rhus*, these pains are worse during rest. Sometimes the patient complains of a weak, paralytic feeling. Symptoms may remit for hours or days. *Rhododendron* is particularly useful in chronic rheumatism affecting the smaller joints. It is one of the best remedies for what has been termed rheumatic gout, and for a hard, rheumatic swelling of the big-toe joint, often mistaken for bunion.

Ledum is an invaluable remedy in gout, and in rheumatism affecting the smaller joints. The pains characteristically travel upward. There are nodes about the joints. In gout, *Ledum* is useful when the pains are worse from the warmth of the bed and ameliorated by cold applications; when there is an œdematous condition of the feet; when *Colchicum* has been abused, and the patient has become greatly reduced in strength by this asthenic remedy. You will find that both *Ledum* and *Colchicum* cause acute tearing pains in the joints, with paralytic weakness of the limbs, and numbness and coldness of the surface. As in *Rhus tox.*, the brain feels sore at every false step. *Ledum* also has drawing pains in the joints, aggravated by wines; the muscles feel sore as if out of place.

You note from the schema that *Rhus* has an action on the cellular tissue. It is useful in cellulitis accompanying diphtheria, and in orbital cellulitis, with the formation of pus. Herein lies a positive distinction between *Rhus* and *Apis*, which *never* produces cellulitis with abscess.

In carbuncle, another form of connective tissue inflammation, *Rhus* is indicated in the beginning, when the pains are intense and the affected parts are dark red. If given early, *Rhus* may abort the whole trouble. If not, you may have to resort later to *Arsenicum, Carbo veg.*, or even *Anthracinum.*

Rhus has a most remarkable action on the skin. It produces an erythema, rapidly progressing to vesication, often accompanied by œdema and with the final formation of pus and scabs. The cutaneous surface about the eruption is red and angry-looking.

Rhus is indicated in eczema. If the face is attacked, there is œdema of the loose cellular tissue about the eyelids, with pains which we may denominate burning, itching, and tingling, to make a nice distinction between this remedy and *Apis*, which has burning and stinging pains. The eruption is moist, offensive and suppurating, at times impetiginous. A red line marks the spread of the disease.

Rhus gives us also a perfect picture of vesicular erysipelas. The structures for which this drug has a special affinity are the scalp and the skin of the face and the genital organs. The affected parts are dark red, and the inflammation (in the sick) travels from left to right.

The erysipelas of *Apis* travels from right to left; the affected parts are rosy-red, pinkish or dark purple; thirst is absent; but *Apis* requires the presence of œdema.

In scarlatina *Rhus* is indicated, especially in the adynamic forms, and should very quickly supplant *Belladonna* when these symptoms appear. The child grows drowsy and restless. The tongue is red and sometimes smooth, a very unusual symptom is scarlatina. The fauces are dark red and have a peculiar œdematous appearance. The cervical glands are enlarged and there may be an enlargement of the left parotid. There may even be impending suppuration of these parts. The cellular tissue about the neck is inflamed, so that the cutaneous surface here has a dark red or bluish erysipelatous hue. If the child is delirious, the delirium is always mild. The eruption does not come out fully, but when it does appear it is of a dark color, and is apt to be miliary. *Rhus*, you see, thus acts on the vital forces. It depresses the sensorium, as shown by the drowsiness and mild delirium. The secretions are altered, becoming acrid. Not only the cervical glands, but the glands in all parts of the body may become enlarged, and especially those of the axilla. The body is emaciated and the patient grows weaker.

Lachesis and *Ailanthus* follow *Rhus* well in this condition, but they present an even more adynamic picture. *Ailanthus* is especially indicated when the skin is covered with a scanty dark bluish rash. The throat inside is swollen. The cellular tissue of the neck is infiltrated. There is excoriating nasal discharge and the child is drowsy and stupid.

Arum triphyllum is similar to *Ailanthus* in that it has the excoriating coryza. The corners of the mouth are sore, cracked and bleeding. The saliva even is acrid. The child is irritable and restless. (See lecture on *Araceæ*.)

Belladonna also has this enlargement and induration of the axillary glands, but it is often neglected in this condition. It is especially useful for the symptom occurring in females at the climaxis.

In scarlatina compare *Calcarea ostrearum*. The parotid glands become affected. The rash recedes, leaving the face puffed and pale.

In variola you will find *Rhus* indicated when the pustules turn black from effusion of blood within, and when there is diarrhœa with dark bloody stools.

In eczema you should compare *Mezereum* with *Rhus*, especially in scrofulous cases when hard, thick chalky crusts form, which crack and ooze copiously of pus. Itching is more intense at night when the patient is warmly wrapped up. Sometimes pimples surround the main seat of the disease.

Nux juglans is one of our very best remedies in tinea favosa, especially when it occurs on the scalp and behind the ears. Itching is intense at night, so that the patient has difficulty in sleeping. Scabs appear on the arms and in the axilla.

Psorinum produces a scaly dirty-looking eruption with itching worse from the warmth of the bed.

Graphites has more rough skin and oozing of glutinous fluid.

We next study the action of *Rhus* on the mucous membranes. It produces a copious coryza with redness and œdema of the throat. It is indicated in influenza with severe aching of all the bones, sneezing and coughing. The cough is dry in character, and is worse in the evening until midnight and from uncovering the body; cough from tickling behind the upper half of the sternum. Especially is *Rhus* indicated when the trouble arises from exposure to dampness.

Mezereum has cough worse from sunset to 12 P. M. *Sanguinaria* and *Pulsatilla*, evening cough better sitting up in bed, the former with relief from belching.

Hepar resembles *Rhus* in the exaggerated sensitiveness to cold air so that even the exposure of a hand excites the cough, which, however, is usually moist.

In diarrhœa calling for *Rhus*, the stools consist of blood and slime mixed with reddish-yellow mucus. Thus you see that it is of dysenteric character. With this character to the stool, *Rhus* is indicated in dysentery, when there are tearing pains down the thighs during defæcation. I once cured with *Rhus* a case of small-pox which had degenerated into a hæmorrhagic type, pustules containing bloody pus; the indications for the remedy were: stools of dark blood, with pains tearing down the thighs during stool.

In other abdominal inflammations assuming a typhoid type, *Rhus* may be indicated, as I have already said, whether the affection be peritonitis, enteritis, typhlitis, perityphlitis, or metritis. In diseases of the puerperal state, *Rhus* is a capital remedy when the symptoms are of a typhoid type.

There is a colic curable by *Rhus*. It may or may not be of rheumatic origin. The pain is relieved by bending double *and moving about*. It thus differs from *Colocynth*, which has relief from bending double, but not from motion, although the severity of the pain may drive the patient into moving about.

Now, the head symptoms of *Rhus*. There is a form of vertigo, common with old people, which comes on as soon as the patient rises from a sitting posture. It is associated with heavy feelings in the limbs, and is doubtless indicative of some senile changes in the brain. *Rhus tox.* is one of the remedies which can palliate this condition. Sometimes they have a swashing feeling in the brain when moving about. In this swashing feeling in the brain, compare with *Rhus* the following: *Cinchona, Sulphuric acid, Belladonna, Spigelia,* and *Carbo animalis.*

Rhus is of value in many affections of the eye. We find it useful in scrofulous ophthalmia when phlyctenules form on and about the cornea. Most intense photophobia is present. The eyelids, which are also involved in the inflammatory process, are spasmodically closed. If you force the lids apart there will gush forth a yellow pus. The pains in the eyes are worse at night.

You may use it in conjunctivitis caused by getting wet (also *Calc. ost.*).

Rhus may also be used in iritis either of rheumatic or traumatic origin. The inflammation may extend to and involve the choroid, and still *Rhus* will be the remedy. Pains shoot through the eyes to the back of the head, and are worse at night. On opening the eyes there is a profuse flow of hot tears. In some cases the inflammation may go on to suppuration.

In glaucoma, *Rhus* has sometimes proved useful.

In orbital cellulitis, it is almost a specific. It should always be given in cases in which the symptoms indicate no other remedy.

It is also one of the best remedies we have for ptosis in rheumatic patients after exposure to dampness.

Causticum is here the nearest concordant remedy of *Rhus*, but you must also think of *Gelsemium, Sepia,* and *Kalmia* in this symptom. The last-named remedy has a sensation of stiffness in the eyelids and in the muscles about the eyes.

The otalgia of *Rhus* is accompanied by pulsations in the ear at night; sensation as if some one was blowing in the ear; whistling, etc., becoming loud, as if the membrana tympani had burst, when lying down.

A local symptom of the face calling for *Rhus* in rheumatic patients is pain in the maxillary joints as if the jaw would break. Every time the patient makes a chewing motion with the mouth the jaw cracks. Easy dislocation of the inferior maxilla calls for *Rhus*. *Ignatia* and *Petroleum* are here similar.

In toothache, *Rhus* may be indicated when the pains are made worse by cold and relieved by warm applications. There is an exception to this however, *i. e.*, in jumping toothache, when the pain is momentarily relieved by the application of the cold hand. The teeth feel loose, or as if they were too long and as if asleep. The gums are sore and feel as if ulcerated.

In various forms of paralysis, *Rhus* may be indicated, especially in rheumatic patients when the trouble has come on from over-exertion or exposure to wet, as from lying on the damp ground. In the latter case, the trouble probably finds its origin in a rheumatic inflammation of the meninges of the cord.

If, however, the exposure to wet excites a myelitis, *Dulcamara* is the remedy.

Rhus may also be used in the acute spinal paralysis of infants.

In these different forms of paralysis, *Sulphur* holds a complementary relation to *Rhus*.

LECTURE XXII.

COMPOSITÆ.

The next order of plants to be considered is the *Compositæ*, a very large order, from which we obtain a number of drugs; namely, *Arnica, Chamomilla, Cina, Eupatorium perfoliatum* and *purpureum, Artemisia vulgaris, Artemisia abrotanum, Artemisia tridentata, Absinthium, Millefolium, Taraxacum,* and *Calendula.*

Compositæ.
- Arnica.
  - Capillaries.
  - Typhoid.
  - Injuries.
  - Organs.
- Chamomilla.
- Cina.
  - Abdomen.
  - Brain and spine.
  - Fever.
  - Organs.
- Artemisia vulgaris.
- Absinthium. } Brain and medulla.
- Millefolium.
- Eupatorium perf.
- Eupatorium purp. } Fever.
- Taraxacum. Liver.

We shall now proceed to study the first one of these.

ARNICA MONTANA.

Arnica montana is commonly called leopard's bane. The tincture of the drug should be prepared from the roots of the plant rather than from the flowers, because the latter are infested by little insects, the bodies of which, together with the eggs, considerably modify the action of the pure drug, and, of course, add symptoms which are foreign to the genuine effects of *Arnica*. We also find an essential oil in the flowers differing somewhat from that found in the roots. I do not know why the plant has been called the leopard's bane, for it is hardly poisonous. While there have been a few cases of death resulting from its extravagant use, most of them have been traced to preparations in which the flowers were used, so that it is not unlikely that the fatal result was due to the insects. The species which is officinal in our materia medica, the *Arnica montana*, does not grow in this country, but is indigenous to Europe. Its essential oil contains an imperfectly known alkaloid called *Arnicin*, and a starchy substance known as Inulin.

To understand *Arnica* properly as a whole you must know that it affects the blood vessels. Exactly how it does this, I can hardly tell you, for it is not clearly defined in my own mind; but the results I *can* tell you. It so affects the walls of the blood-vessels, particularly of the capillaries, that dilatation of the small vessels and extravasation of blood becomes possible. This weakening of the capillary wall, which admits of extravasation of blood, explains the applicability of *Arnica* to trauma. It also explains the relation of the drug to typhoid conditions. Now if you will keep before your minds this fact, that *Arnica* so alters the capillaries that blood may ooze through their walls, you will understand its symptoms. There seems to be a venous stasis producing an extravasation of blood. This form of oozing cannot occur from a healthy vessel.

Arnica is applicable to both the acute and the chronic effects of injuries. The acute injuries for which it is useful are the following: simple bruises in which there are well-marked ecchymoses; concussions of the brain or spine or of both. We have no remedy which equals *Arnica* in these last-named cases. Even compression of the brain comes within the range of *Arnica*, whether this compression be the result of a displaced fragment of bone in cranial fracture, or the result of effusion of blood within the cranial cavity. *Arnica* cannot, of course, cure in the former of these cases; an operation is demanded in order to obtain permanent relief.

You may use *Arnica* in injuries of the muscles from a strain or from a sudden wrench, as in case of heavy lifting, and in hæmorrhages of mechanical origin. Fractures of the bones may call for the use of *Arnica*, both externally and internally, to relieve the swelling and tumefaction of the limb, and also to relieve the twitching of muscles, a reflex symptom of the fracture.

In the chronic effects of injury we may use *Arnica* when diseases (which may even be entirely foreign in their appearance to the ordinary symptomatology of the drug) may be traced to a traumatic origin. No matter what that disease may be. whether of the brain, eyes, lungs or nerves, if the injury is the exciting cause, the administration of *Arnica* is proper.

Again, as *Arnica* undoubtedly acts on the muscular tissue itself, we may use it for the consequences of diseases in the muscle ; for instance, when one has been working very laboriously, and in consequence the whole body feels sore and bruised, as if pounded ; or again, when heavy work may have caused hypertrophy of the heart. This lastnamed is not strictly a disease, but it ends in disease. The heart is a muscle that grows under the stimulus of exercise as much as does the biceps of the arm. As a result of the cardiac hypertrophy, the patient complains of swelling of the hands on any exertion. They become redder than usual, and swell when the arm is permitted to hang down. The pulse you will find to be full and strong. When the heart has reached this stage of hypertrophy, there are local symptoms in addition to those mentioned. The heart feels as though tightly grasped by the hand. The whole chest feels sore and bruised, and he cannot bear his clothing to touch it.

This will at once suggest to you *Cactus*, which has that constriction about the heart. *Cactus*, however, does not have a traumatic origin for its symptoms.

The sensitiveness of the chest suggests *Lachesis*, but is a different symptom under *Arnica*, which lacks the sensitiveness of the peripheries of the nerves that *Lachesis* has ; but has a genuine soreness from fulness of the bloodvessels.

Other remedies to be compared with *Arnica* in this hypertrophy of the heart are .

Rhus tox., especially if there is rheumatic diathesis.

Arsenicum, if it has resulted from climbing high places.

Bromine has also been successfully used in this condition.

Now let me give you the typhoid symptoms of *Arnica*, which, although very different from those just mentioned, depend upon a similar condition of the bloodvessels.

The changes in the bloodvessels due to the typhoid poison favor the formation of ecchymoses here and there over the body. There is also a passive congestion of the brain. This is shown by drowsiness and indifference to those about him and to his condition. The patient falls asleep while answering questions, just as we find in *Baptisia*. With these symptoms you almost always find the head hot and the body not hot. The symptom in the materia medica reads, "the head is hot and the body cool, or at least not hot," implying that there is a difference in temperature between the head and the rest of the body, and this has been so often confirmed that it is well for you to remember it. The patient complains of a bruised feeling all over the body, so that the bed feels too hard to him. He is restless and tosses about the bed to find a soft spot on which to rest; and yet the fault is not with the bed, but with himself. Sugillations from hypostasis appear on the back. The lungs become affected—and here, too, the same character of *Arnica* shows itself. There is a cough, with expectoration of mucus and blood. If the patient is still sufficiently conscious he will complain of sore bruised feeling in the walls of the chest. There is a brown streak down the centre of the tongue. As the case progresses still further, *Arnica* may yet be called for, when the pressure of the blood in the brain is sufficient to cause apoplectic symptoms. The breathing becomes heavy, and even stertorous. The lower jaw drops. Petechiæ appear on the skin, and both stool and urine are passed involuntarily, the patient, of course, being in a stupor. These are the typhoid symptoms of *Arnica*.

Now for the muscular symptoms. *Arnica* develops a true myalgia. The pains occur in the muscles of any part of the body. They are of traumatic origin, or they come from over-exertion, and are accompanied by this sore, bruised feeling, which is so necessary to the choice of the drug.

In rheumatism, you may employ *Arnica*, not for true inflammatory rheumatism, but for the local rheumatism which occurs in winter weather, and which seems often to be the combined effect of exposure to dampness and of cold and strain on the muscles from over-exertion. The affected parts feel sore and bruised. Any motion, of course, aggravates this sensation. There are sharp, shooting pains, which run down from the elbow to the forearm, or which shoot through the legs and feet. The feet often swell and feel sore and bruised.

In cases of injury, the drugs to be thought of in connection with *Arnica* are these: first, *Rhus tox.*, which, as I have already told you more than once, is preferable to *Arnica* when the ligaments of a joint, rather than the soft parts, are involved in an injury. It acts on the fibrous structures. *Arnica* is suited more to tumefaction of the other tissues.

Calendula is to be thought of when the injury causes a torn or ragged wound, possibly with loss of substance. *Calendula* removes the inflammatory condition of the part, and so permits of healthy granulation.

Hypericum is to be substituted for *Arnica* when the nerves have been injured along with the other soft parts. Nothing equals *Hypericum* in cases of mashed finger. It relieves the pain and promotes healing. It often follows *Arnica* in concussion of the spine. Dr. Ludlam, of Chicago, was very partial to *Hypericum* in this trouble of the spinal cord, and with good reason, for not only has he relieved some severe cases with it, but the provings show a perfect picture of the results of spinal injury.

Another drug is *Staphisagria*. This is the remedy for smooth clean cuts, such as are made by the surgeon's knife, and hence it is called for in symptoms which are traceable to surgical operations. Even if the symptoms which follow are not apparently connected with the symptomatology of *Staphisagria*, you may expect, when they arise from this cause, to obtain relief by its administration.

Ledum is useful after *Arnica* when the latter remedy fails to relieve the soreness. It is also suited to injuries inflicted by pointed instruments, therefore in punctured wounds.

Symphytum officinale is the proper remedy for bone injuries. For example, when a blow on the eyes injures the orbital plates of the frontal bone. It may also be administered in case of irritable stump after amputation; and also for irritability of bone at the point of fracture.

If the latter condition is the result of impaired nutrition, *Calcarea phos* should be prescribed.

For violent burning, stinging pains in a stump after operation, *Allium cepa* is the remedy.

Arnica may be used as a preventive of pyæmia. It is thought by some physicians that this remedy promotes the evacuation of pus, that it promotes the appearance of pus on the surface of a sore. With the object of preventing pyæmia, some surgeons use *Arnica* after operations, applying it locally and giving it internally at the same time.

This property of *Arnica*, to prevent pyæmia, lies at the foundation of the routine practice among physicians of giving this drug to women after delivery. It tends to relieve the soreness following parturition and promotes proper contraction of the uterus and expulsion of coagula and of any portions of the membranes that may have been retained.

Arnica has an action on the skin, producing crops of boils all over the body. They begin with soreness and go on to suppuration, and are followed by another crop. It may also be used in boils and abscesses which have partially matured but which, instead of discharging, shrivel up by reason of absorption of the contained pus. *Arnica* given internally and applied externally redevelops the abscess.

Further, in connection with the action of *Arnica*, I would call your attention to the effects of the drug on the gastro-intestinal tract. We find it indicated in dyspepsia, when, after a meal, there is impending apoplectic congestion of the brain with throbbing headache and drowsiness ; and also, when there is some difficulty in the digestion of food ; there are foul breath, slimy yellow coating of the tongue, eructation of gas tasting like rotten eggs, tympanitic distension of the abdomen and foul-smelling stools.

Arnica may be called for in cholera infantum, diarrhœa or dysentery ; the stools have a foul odor and are slimy, bloody, and even purulent, and are accompanied by great urging and straining to stool. The dyspeptic symptoms just mentioned will be present, and there are sharp, stitching pains through the abdominal walls. The patient is thirsty, and yet he does not know what he wants to drink.

I should like, in closing my remarks on *Arnica*, to mention its use in whooping-cough. It is indicated in children who have a violent tickling cough, which seems to be excited whenever the child becomes angry. The child loses its breath when it cries. Before a paroxysm it begins to cry. Why? The lungs and trachea are sore. The little sufferer knows what is coming and dreads it ; that is the interpretation of the symptom. The expectoration is frothy, slimy and always mixed with blood.

In compression of the brain from apoplectic extravasation of blood, *Arnica* may be used when associated with the hemiplegia ; there is an aching soreness all over the body. Bed-sores form very readily.

Artemisia Vulgaris.

Artemisia vulgaris, another member of the order Compositæ, is a very serviceable remedy in epilepsy, brought on by violent emotions, and especially by fright. The attacks come in rapidly repeated seizures, that is to say, several convulsions come close together and then there is a long interval of rest. The paroxysms are usually followed by sleep. Again, *Artemisia vulgaris* seems to be of some use in that form of epilepsy known as "*petit mal.*" The patient is walking in the street, when, suddenly, he stops, stares into vacancy, possibly mumbles a few words, regains a normal condition, and then goes his way totally unconscious of anything unusual having happened.

Artemisia, like other members of the order (*Cina* more prominently than any of the others), has an effect on the eye. We find under the drug the symptom: "colored light produces dizziness;" for example, when seated near a stained-glass window the patient becomes dizzy. In addition to this it causes a well-developed asthenopia. On attempting to use the eyes the patient experiences pain in them, together with blurring of the vision, the latter symptom being momentarily relieved by rubbing the eyes. This is easily explained; the asthenopia is due to muscular defect and error of accommodation. By rubbing the eyes, the accommodation is temporarily restored.

ABSINTHIUM.

Absinthium, another form of wormwood, is of interest to you not only as a medicine, but also because you will meet with cases of its abuse in those who indulge in it as a drink. The first effect of *Absinthe* is an exhilaration of the mind, soon followed by damaging results, among which is horrible delirium and eventually epileptiform spasms. In this delirium the patient is obliged to walk about. You will note this symptom running through all the remedies of the order. *Chamomilla* and *Cina* have relief from moving about; *Artemisia* has desire to move about; and here under *Absinthium* the patient walks about in distress, seeing all sorts of visions. The use we may make of *Absinthium* is in the sleeplessness of typhoid fever when there is congestion at the base of the brain.

MILLEFOLIUM

is of interest to you as being a remedy in hæmorrhages from the lungs, uterus, bowels, etc. The flow of blood is bright red, and usually profuse.

It is distinguished from *Aconite* by the absence of anxiety.

Taraxacum,

or the ordinary dandelion, is a decided liver remedy. If given long enough, it will produce a free flow of bile. The symptoms to guide you in its selection are these: the tongue is mapped, and there are bitter taste in the mouth, chilliness after eating or drinking, pain and soreness in the region of the liver, and bilious diarrhœa. The use of this drug in typhoid fever was mentioned in a recent lecture on *Rhus tox*. *Artemisia tridentata* also suits bilious patients who suffer from headache, vertigo, nausea, bitter taste, backache, etc.

Eupatorium Perfoliatum,

or the bone-set, is a popular remedy in malarial districts for chills and fever. In this disease it is indicated by the following symptoms: the chill begins from seven to nine A. M., preceded by headache and insatiable thirst, which rarely continues into the fever. It first appears in the back and is accompanied by aching in the limbs, as though every bone in the body were being broken. This is followed by high fever with increase of the aching, and this by sweat, which is scanty or profuse. In some cases there is a double periodicity; the chill comes in the morning of one day and in the evening of the next.

You may also think of *Eupatorium perfoliatum* in influenza with hoarseness worse in the morning, and cough with extreme soreness along the trachea and even to the finest ramifications of the bronchial tubes. With this there will be the aching all through the body as if in the bones, which impels the sufferer to move, but no relief is obtained thereby.

Eupatorium purpureum has been used for chill beginning in the back. I do not know of any symptom distinguishing it from *Eupatorium perfoliatum*.

(Artemisia) Abrotanum.

Artemisia abrotanum, or Southernwood, has an intensely bitter taste, is suited to cases of suddenly appearing spinal inflammation and to chronic myelitis. There are sudden aching pains in the back which are relieved by motion; numbness and paralysis. It is especially called for in rheumatic patients with lameness and stiffness of the joints. It is useful in patients of the class who are suffering from the effects of suppressed conditions. There is a strong tendency to metastasis. Thus rheumatism, either spontaneously or from meddlesome local treatment, leaves the extremities and goes to the heart. After the extirpation of hæmorrhoids or the checking of diarrhœa, gastric symptoms supervene.

Abrotanum is one of the remedies which is applicable in the metastasis of mumps to the testicle or mammary gland, and should be studied along with *Pulsatilla, Carbo vegetabilis* and perhaps *Arsenicum.*

We also find it indicated in marasmus occurring in weak children who are emaciated, wrinkled, pale, with blue rings around the eyes, gnawing hunger and bloated abdomen. You may distinguish it from other drugs that have like symptoms, especially by the fact that the emaciation is first noticed in the lower extremities.

LECTURE XXIII.

CINA AND CHAMOMILLA.

Cina.

The medicinal virtues of *Cina* are largely, although not entirely, due to a poisonous active principle which it contains; that active principle is *Santonine*, the central point of action of which is the abdominal ganglia, whence are reflected nervous impressions to all other parts of the body, but principally to the brain and spine. As a result of this primary action on the abdominal ganglia, we have as reflex symptoms, convulsive twitchings and jerkings of the limbs and even violent spasms, these latter usually being of a tonic character. Strabismus also is present. Under the influence of *Cina*, the face is pale, and it continues so, even if there be fever. *Ipecacuanha* and *Bryonia* also have this symptom. With the pale face of *Cina*, there are usually associated dark rings about the eyes. The pupils are dilated. The child grinds its teeth during sleep. It also picks or bores at the nose with its finger. The sleep is restless and attended by crying out. This is the general action of *Cina*. You now know what you may expect of the drug. Taking these symptoms into account, we are led to the use of *Cina* for the presence of worms in the alimentary tract. The most careful analysis of clinical experience has demonstrated that *Cina* is most powerful for the elimination of round worms. The sickly appearance of the face, the blue rings about the eyes, and the grinding of the teeth, associated with canine hunger, give a perfect picture for the drug. *Cina* so far corrects the abdominal organs and so far tones up the abdominal ganglia, that the mucous membrane of the alimentary tract pours forth a normal secretion, and the worms, no longer having a proper pabulum on which to subsist, die and are expelled. This, then, is the use of *Cina*.

With the oxyures, those little worms which appear about the anus and get into the rectum, *Cina* is of no avail, because the symptoms caused by them are not symptoms of *Cina*. For these, we have another group of remedies.

Aconite, when the child is feverish and cannot sleep.

When the child is simply much excited, you may give *Ignatia*.

Indigo is the best remedy when convulsions result from the worms. If all these fail, think of *Quassia*.

Caladium seguinum is the best remedy in little girls when the worms travel over the perinæum and get into the vagina. The irritation they produce may thus excite masturbation.

We may also make use of *Cina* in affections of the eyes, especially in asthenopia from defective accommodation. When the patient attempts to read, the eyes begin to ache, the letters become blurred and a cloud comes over the field of vision. Relief is obtained by rubbing the eyes. The same condition I have already told you is found under *Artemisia vulgaris*. It is also a symptom of *Euphrasia*, being due to the mucus which gathers in a film over the cornea.

A very peculiar effect on the eye produced by *Santonine* is, that objects look yellow.

Cina being a spasmodic remedy, we may expect it to be useful in whooping-cough, in which disease it is indicated when the paroxysms come regularly through night or day and are accompanied by tonic convulsions. Just after a paroxysm, a gurgling sound is heard. *Cina* may also be used in cough reflex from the irritation of worms.

As a concomitant of all these conditions, we find the temperament of *Cina*. It is indicated in children who are irritable, nervous and peevish; who resent being touched or even looked at. They are obstinate and permit no one to approach them.

Cina seems to have some effect on the bladder, producing wetting of the bed at night, usually during the first sleep. The urine is pale and turbid and sometimes has a very strong odor. This latter symptom would remind you of *Phosphoric acid*, which also has enuresis in the fore-part of the night.

Probably the remedy most frequently called for in enuresis during the first sleep is *Sepia*, although it will also be found under *Benzoic acid* and *Kreosote*.

Cina is not often used in intermittent fever, but it is sometimes indicated by thirst during the chill and occasionally during the fever also. Pale face is present even during the hot stage. There are also vomiting, canine hunger, and clean tongue.

Like many of the other members of the order Compositæ, the *Cina* patient finds relief from moving about.

Chamomilla Matricaria.

The *Chamomilla* of the homœopathic materia medica is the German variety, the *Chamomilla matricaria*. The drug apparently acts best upon patients with a morbidly sensitive nervous system. It is like *Coffea*, *Ignatia* and *Belladonna* then, in so far as it lessens nervous excitability.

Slight impressions produce distress and anguish of mind; pains often result in fainting. Here it is similar to *Valerian*, *Hepar*, *Veratrum album* and *Nux moschata*. It is especially applicable to these symptoms when they appear after long-continued use of narcotics.

In every disease in which *Chamomilla* is indicated, we notice this peculiar excitability. The patient, whether it be child or adult, a woman in labor or with toothache, is cross and excitable. Unless this mental state is present, *Chamomilla* will most likely fail you.

When violent emotions, like anger, affect the viscera, as, for example, the liver with jaundice, you may think of the drug under consideration. In this condition it stands related to a few drugs.

Staphisagria is indicated in children or adults when colic follows a fit of anger.

Bryonia has gastro-enteric symptoms after anger. Under this remedy, however, the symptoms are associated with chilliness, under *Chamomilla* with heat; under *Bryonia* the face is dark red, under *Chamomilla*, pale with one red cheek. The *Bryonia* tongue is coated white, that of *Chamomilla* yellow.

Colocynth has vomiting, diarrhœa and violent colicky pains from a fit of anger, but may easily be distinguished by the fact that the pains are relieved by bending double and from firm pressure.

Continuing the nervous symptoms of *Chamomilla*, we find the drug useful for insomnia in children, when they start during sleep and the muscles of the face and hands twitch. With these symptoms there is apt to be colic; the face is red, especially one cheek, and the head and scalp are bathed in a hot sweat. A word of explanation is here necessary. Sometimes, during an attack of fever in a child, the cheek on which it lies becomes red; now that is not a *Chamomilla* symptom. These nervous symptoms of *Chamomilla* are generally reflex from the abdomen. There is very little evidence of delirium in these cases. When brain complications are present *Chamomilla* ceases to be the remedy, and *Belladonna* comes in.

When, during dentition, *Chamomilla* fails, *Belladonna* is the remedy, because it is suited to a more advanced state.

This same nervous state of *Chamomilla* may be applied to the use of the drug in rheumatism. Rheumatic pains drive the patient out of bed and compel him to walk about. He is thirsty, hot, with red cheeks and almost beside himself with anguish. Stitching pains jump from place to place, but unlike *Pulsatilla*, they leave a sense of weakness and numbness. Sweat does not relieve him, but his pains are better *after* sweat.

The analogous remedies here are *Rhus tox.*, which lacks the excitement of *Chamomilla*; *Ferrum metallicum*, which has rheumatism better from moving about slowly; *Veratrum album*, which has maddening pains, compelling the patient to walk about. With the latter remedy there is not the feverishness and excitement which characterize *Chamomilla*.

Chamomilla also acts on mucous membranes, causing symptoms of catarrh. It is indicated in the catarrhs of children, when the nose is "stopped up," and yet there is a dropping of hot, watery mucus from the nostrils; there are sneezing and inability to sleep; and with these a dry, teasing cough, which keeps the child awake, or may even occur during sleep; or there is rattling cough, as though the bronchi were full of mucus. Especially is *Chamomilla* useful in colds brought on by cold windy days.

Nux vomica is also indicated in catarrhs, when there is a "stopped-up" feeling in the nose, but there is no secretion whatever.

Sambucus is indicated in catarrh, when the child starts up suddenly as if suffocating.

Sticta suits a hard, dry, barking cough; the nose is "stuffed up" and dry; the real condition is this, the nasal secretion dries so rapidly that it cannot be discharged.

Chamomilla has a number of gastric symptoms. It is useful in biliousness produced by anger. We find it also indicated in gastralgia, especially when the food eaten seems to lie like a load in the stomach. There is distension of the hypochondria, the tongue is coated yellowish-white, and there is a bitter taste in the mouth; there are colicky pains in the abdomen, which are relieved by drinking a cup of coffee.

Chamomilla produces a diarrhœa with hot, yellowish-green stool, looking like chopped eggs, and often mixed with bile, causing soreness at the anus, and having an odor of sulphuretted hydrogen; it is especially worse toward evening; it is apt to occur during dentition.

Chamomilla is here frequently followed by *Sulphur*, because both remedies produce the same stools with soreness of the stomach. If there is much tenesmus with these symptoms *Mercurius* is the remedy.

If the stool is worse in the morning, and comes with a gush, we should think of *Podophyllum* and *Sulphur*.

Chamomilla is an invaluable remedy in the lying-in room; it is indicated when labor pains begin in the back and pass off down the inner side of the thighs. There is great nervous excitement; the labor seems exceedingly painful. After the labor is over, the lochial flow is dark and too profuse, and the after-pains are violent and intolerable.

Chamomilla may be used in threatening abortion caused by anger, when the pains are of the character just described, and there is a flow of dark blood.

Viburnum is useful in threatening miscarriage when these pains come down the lower part of the abdomen and go into the thighs. It will stop the pains even if it cannot prevent the miscarriage.

LECTURE XXIV.

MELANTHACEÆ.

Melanthaceæ.
- Veratrum album. — Mind. Abdomen.
- Veratrum viride. — Circulation.
- Sabadilla.
- Colchicum.
  1. Nerves.
  2. Abdomen.
  3. Fibrous tissues.
  4. Organs.

FROM the *Melanthaceæ* we obtain the following medicines: *Veratrum album*, *Veratrum viride*, *Sabadilla*, and *Colchicum*. Of these drugs, I may say that I am pretty well persuaded that the *Veratrum album* and *Veratrum viride* are well understood, and are, therefore, not easily misapplied. I am also well persuaded that *Colchicum* has not the place in practice it deserves. True, it comes to us from the allopathic school as a remedy highly recommended for gout. We ought not, however, from the exorbitant use of the drug by that school, to go to the opposite extreme, and neglect it altogether as a remedy.

COLCHICUM.

The symptoms of *Colchicum* I have arranged under four headings. The first, the nerves, includes typhoid conditions and debility. You must know that the drug tends to produce great prostration, and from this arises the great danger in administering it in large doses as a routine remedy in gout and rheumatism. While the paroxysms of pain may be relieved thereby, there is apt to be induced a condition of debility which runs the patient into other and new dangers.

Let us see how we can use this effect of the drug under our law of cure. We find it indicated in debility, particularly in debility following loss of sleep; for instance, when one does not retire as early as usual in the evening, so that he is deprived of a portion of his accustomed sleep, he awakens next morning feeling tired and languid;

he can hardly drag one leg after the other ; the appetite is gone ; bad taste in the mouth and nausea are present. The debility, then, starts from or involves digestion as a result of loss of sleep. You can see how close this comes to the *Nux vomica* condition. The debility, however, is greater even than that of *Nux vomica*. There is, at times, an aversion to all food ; the odor of food cooking makes the patient feel sick ; he becomes irritable ; every little external impression annoys him ; here it is precisely like *Nux vomica*.

As another form of debility or debilitating fever, we find *Colchicum* indicated at times in typhoid fever. Now, the position of *Colchicum* in typhoid fever is between *Arsenicum* and *Cinchona*. First, we find that the patient's intellect is beclouded. But although his mind is befogged, he still answers your questions correctly, showing you that he is not in a complete stupor. Unless questioned concerning it, he says nothing about his condition, which does not seem dangerous to him. There is not that fearfulness, that dread of death, which characterizes some other drugs indicated in typhoid fevers. The pupils are widely dilated, and very imperfectly sensitive to light. There is a cold sweat on the forehead ; here you will at once note a resemblance to *Veratrum album*. When the patient attempts to raise the head from the pillow, it falls back again and the mouth opens wide. You thus see how weak are the muscles in the *Colchicum* case. The face has a cadaverous appearance. The features are sharp and pointed, the nose looks as though it had been pinched or tightly squeezed, and the nostrils are dry and even black. The tongue is heavy and stiff, and is protruded with difficulty. In extreme cases it is bluish, particularly at the base. There is almost complete loss of speech, and the breath is cold. There are often nausea and vomiting, the latter being attended with considerable retching. These symptoms are associated with restlessness and cramps in the legs. The body is hot while the extremities are cold. Coming to the abdominal region, we find tympanites is exceedingly well marked. Stools are watery and frequent, and escape involuntarily. These are the symptoms which lead you to *Colchicum* in typhoid states. They greatly resemble those calling for *Arsenicum* and *Cinchona*. They resemble *Arsenicum* in the intensity of the debility and *Cinchona* in the tympanitic condition. *Colchicum* seems to stand between the two, combining the restlessness and debility of *Arsenic* with the tympany of *Cinchona*. You will notice that the *Colchicum* symptoms are principally abdominal. Some of them suggest *Veratrum album*. You must, therefore, place this remedy in your mind by the side of *Colchicum*, that you may make the necessary distinction between the two.

Carbo vegetabilis is allied to *Colchicum* in the coldness of the breath, in the tympany, and in the great prostration. But *Carbo veg.* seems to suit when there is giving out of the vital forces. The patient lies cold and almost pulseless. The pulse feels much like a slight ripple beneath the examining finger; there is no decided pulsation. The feet and the legs below the knees are cold, or there may be coldness of the knees and feet, the parts between them not being cold. A watery stool is not so characteristic of *Carbo veg.*, the discharges being either absent or, if present, dark brown and horribly offensive.

Next we come to the abdominal symptoms. The tympany and the diarrhœa have already been mentioned. In addition to these symptoms we have others which strongly point to the drug as a possible remedy in cholera. There are nausea and vomiting, the nausea seeming to be provoked by the smell of food. Whenever the patient sits up, the nausea and vomiting become worse. The matters vomited are watery and bilious. When dysenteric symptoms are present, the stools are frequent, watery and bloody, and contain shreds which were formerly supposed to be portions of the lining membrane of the bowels, but which are now known to be a plastic formation from exudation. Tenesmus is violent, and is followed by spasm of the sphincter ani. If you have a case of dysentery with these symptoms, *Colchicum* will help you out. If there is tympany also, all the more is it indicated, being then far preferable to *Cantharis*, *Mercurius* or any other remedy in our materia medica.

The third heading on the board is "Fibrous tissues." This brings us to the consideration of *Colchicum* in rheumatism and gout. Now, *Colchicum* has a special affinity for the fibrous tissues. I include under this term the tendons and aponeuroses of muscles, ligaments of joints and even the periosteum. The swelling produced by it is either dark red or pale in color, with no particular tendency to suppuration, extremely sensitive to touch, and with a strong tendency to shift from joint to joint. In rheumatism proper, *Colchicum* is indicated when it begins in one joint and travels thence to another, or in one side of the body and then flies to the other. The pains are worse in the evening. The joint is extremely sensitive to the slightest motion. The urine is dark red and scanty, just such as you would expect to find in gout or rheumatism. You will find such patients exceedingly irritable. Every little external impression, as light, noise or strong odors, annoys them, and pain seems to be unbearable. The only difference between these symptoms and those of gout is that in the latter the great-toe is involved, and the paroxysms occur in the night.

Sometimes we have metastasis of rheumatism or gout to the chest. Even then *Colchicum* may be the remedy. In valvular heart disease or pericarditis following rheumatism, it is indicated by violent cutting and stinging pains in the chest, particularly about the heart, with great oppression and dyspnœa. There is also the sensation as if the chest were being squeezed by a tight bandage. *Colchicum* stands almost alone in gout and rheumatism. There are no remedies similar to it in action here.

Colchicum is sometimes indicated in dropsy with suppression of urine. The dropsy is particularly liable to appear as hydrothorax. What urine does pass contains blood, and is almost as black as ink, and is loaded with albumen. Hence you see that it is indicated in dropsy depending upon Bright's disease. Here it resembles, quite closely, *Lachesis*, which also has this black urine.

It also resembles *Terebinthina*, which causes congestion of the kidneys with rupture of the fine capillaries, and consequent pouring out of blood into the pelvis of the kidneys. The urine contains tube-casts. It is smoky in appearance, and has a dirty pinkish deposit.

Thus you have seen when *Colchicum* may be used in rheumatism, when in typhoid fever, and when in simple debility. The fact that the protracted use of *Colchicum* is followed by great prostration will lead you to study the drug, when after frequent acute attacks of gout the patient becomes greatly weakened.

In affections of the heart *Colchicum* is closely allied to *Spigelia*.

When *Colchicum* has been abused, *Spigelia* is the remedy to be used as an antidote.

Veratrum Album.

Veratrum album is not a difficult remedy to understand. It has been used since the days of Hahnemann for cholera Asiatica, cholera morbus and other abdominal affections. Its symptoms in this relation are well known, but unless you are careful you will neglect an equally important use of the drug, and that is in mental symptoms. In poisoning with *Veratrum*, there are very few symptoms referable to the brain.

It seems to act prominently on the abdominal organs, probably through the splanchnic nerves. When these nerves are paralyzed, the blood-vessels become over-charged with blood and pour forth their serum. In this respect it is similar to *Elaterium*. The prostration, the coldness and the terrible sinking sensation that belong to *Veratrum* all start from these nerves. But *Veratrum* may affect the brain as well. Even then the symptoms are not unlikely to be associated with coldness, weakness, etc.

We may have *Veratrum album* indicated in delirium. That you should notice particularly, as, in this respect, it becomes closely allied, apparently, to *Belladonna*. The delirium is associated with restlessness, with desire to cut and tear the clothing, with loquacity and rapid, earnest, loud talking; he strikes those about him; anxiety; frightened at imaginary things; lasciviousness; lewdness in talk; he springs out of bed and rushes about the room as if thereby to obtain relief. Thus far the symptoms are such that you can only with difficulty distinguish them from those of *Belladonna* and *Stramonium*. The distinction lies here: *Veratrum album has coldness of the surface of the body with cold sweat on the forehead.* Sometimes the face is red and the lips are blue, and there is tingling through the limbs.

Veratrum album is also suitable for women when they suffer from abnormal mental impressions arising from disturbance in the sexual sphere; in nymphomania, for instance. The patient is lewd to an extreme. She rushes about the room endeavoring to kiss every one. These attacks are especially prone to appear before each menstrual period. She is constantly framing lies of the most outrageous character.

Veratrum is also to be thought of when after fright, there is great coldness of the body with diarrhœa. *Gelsemium*, *Argentum nitricum*, *Aconite* and *Opium* also have diarrhœa after fright. Under *Veratrum*, it is associated with coldness and prostration.

Now for some of the abdominal symptoms. *Veratrum album* is indicated in affections of the bowels, in cholera morbus, cholera infantum and cholera Asiatica and in intussusception of the bowels. The stools in the diarrhœa calling for *Veratrum* are profuse, watery and greenish, containing sometimes little flakes that look like spinach. At times, too, they are bloody, and are always associated with sharp cutting pains in the abdomen, and often, too, with cramps in the limbs. There is great weakness, almost to fainting, with every effort at stool, and copious, frothy vomiting. Cold sweat on the forehead is present.

In the various choleraic affections more particularly, *Veratrum* is indicated by the following symptoms : vomiting and purging at the same time, colicky pains through the abdomen with cramps, especially in the calves of the legs, profuse watery stools, rice-water stools, as they are called. They are attended with great prostration and cold sweat, especially on the forehead. It is useless to give *Veratrum* in choleraic affections unless there is pain. The patient is worse at night. Emaciation is rapid.

The first remedy to consider here in its relation to *Veratrum album* is *Camphor*. Like the former, it produces coldness and symptoms of collapse. *Camphor* is better suited to cholera when the discharges are scanty and the nausea marked. Sometimes the upper lip will be drawn upward, showing the teeth, making the nauseous expression of the face more hideous. The entire body is cold. The voice is squeaky or high-pitched.

Jatropha curcas also produces a perfect picture of cholera. It causes vomiting of ropy albuminous matters with purging like water from a hydrant, coldness, nausea and gurgling in the abdomen.

Podophyllum resembles *Veratrum album*, in that it produces a perfect picture of cholera morbus. It is especially indicated when the case is characterized by the absence of pain. Herein, it is very different from *Veratrum*. The attacks generally come on during the summer. The stools are watery and come out with a gush and a splutter like water from a hydrant. There is marked loathing of food. The bowels are more apt to move after midnight and toward morning. The stools are very liable to vary in color, now yellow, now green, etc.

There is a remedy which is, I think, better suited to the summer complaint of children than is *Veratrum*. I refer to *Iris versicolor*. It produces marked inflammatory symptoms, with excoriated raw feeling at the anus. The patient is worse at two or three o'clock in the morning. There are nausea and sour and sometimes bilious vomiting. The stools are either watery, or are yellowish-green and mixed with bile or oily particles.

Pulsatilla is called for in after-midnight diarrhœa caused by a diet of pastry, etc.; or by eating ice-cream immediately after a meal.

Croton tiglium comes in when the movements are yellowish or yellowish-green, pouring out with a rush or splutter, like water from a hydrant. They are provoked by every attempt to eat or drink.

Elaterium is the remedy for profuse watery stools when they are of an olive-green color.

I have often found *Veratrum album* useful for cardiac debility following acute diseases, when the heart-muscle becomes so weak that the pulse is thread-like. The patient faints on moving. On lying down the face is red; on sitting up, it turns deathly pale. Often you will find the hands cold and clammy.

Veratrum Viride.

Although the name of this drug is similar to that just considered, you must not reason thereby that it produces the same symptoms. *Veratrum viride* produces congestion of the base of the brain and of the upper portion of the spinal cord. It thus interferes with the function of the pneumogastric nerves. At first it seems to produce engorgement of the lungs, just such as we witness in the beginning of pneumonia. This is associated with a high degree of arterial excitement. If these symptoms go on unchecked, we have dizziness and faintness on attempting to sit up, nausea, cold sweat and orthopnœa, and in fact every symptom of paralysis of the heart from over-exertion of that organ. Thus you will see that *Veratrum viride* comes in as an invaluable remedy in those violent congestions which precede pneumonia. It may even abort the whole disease.

Veratrum viride also produces œsophagitis, in which disease it may be indicated even when the disorder has arisen from traumatic causes. It is called for by the difficulty of swallowing and the fiery burning pains in the œsophagus.

In chorea it is also indicated, when in addition to the choreic twitching, there is violent congestion of the nerve-centres. Given in a low potency it relieves the congestion, and therefore the nervous disturbances.

We may depend on *Veratrum viride* even in puerperal convulsions. The cerebral congestion is profound. The patient lies in a condition like that of apoplexy. Between the convulsions she is not conscious, but lies in a deep sleep. The face is red, the eyes are injected and there is violent convulsive twitching. The pulse is full and bounding.

In some cases *Gelsemium* helps when there is a dull, drowsy state of mind, but here the pulse, though full, is soft and flowing.

SABADILLA.

Like *Veratrum album*, *Sabadilla* is a useful remedy on account of its mental symptoms. It may be used with success in cases of imaginary disease. For example, the patient imagines that she is pregnant when she is merely swollen from flatus; or that she has some horrible throat disease which will surely end fatally.

Thuja has the symptom, imagines herself double or treble, or that she is made of glass, and is in constant fear of being touched lest she be broken.

Sabadilla is useful in influenza and that troublesome affection, hayfever. There are violent spasmodic sneezing and lachrymation on going into the open air; the throat also is affected, giving you a perfect picture of tonsillitis. The difficulty begins on the left side, and extends to the right; the pain is worse on empty swallowing and is relieved by warm drinks. Sometimes there is a sensation as of a thread or string in the throat, or else a sense of constriction in the throat, as if it was tied by a string. *Lachesis* as you know has sore throat going from left to right. It is readily distinguished by the marked aggravation from hot drinks and after sleep.

We may also make use of *Sabadilla* in worms, when there are nausea and vomiting associated with a peculiar colic, as though the bowels were being whirled around like a wheel.

LECTURE XXV.

MENISPERMACEÆ.

The *Menispermaceæ* is not a very large order of plants, there being derived from it but one remedy that we shall consider in this course of lectures. That remedy is *Cocculus Indicus*. The name given to the order has been derived from the shape of the seeds.

Cocculus Indicus.

Cocculus Indicus owes its properties to an active principle called *Picrotoxine*, this term being derived from two Latin words meaning, when combined, "bitter poison." You will notice by the schedule on the board that I have arranged the symptomatology of the remedy under two heads, first, the nerves, and secondly, the organs in general.

Cocculus Indicus.
1. Nerves.
   - Cerebro-Spinal.
   - Debility.
   - Typhoid.
   - Spasms.
2. Organs.

Now, whatever individual characteristics you may have for a drug in an individual case, these characteristics should agree with the general effects of the drug; otherwise, you are making a partial selection. To illustrate: under *Belladonna*, you know of the symptom, "sleepy, but cannot get to sleep;" that is characteristic of the remedy. But we find the same symptom under *Cinchona*, *Ferrum*, and *Apis*. How are you to distinguish between them? By taking the general effect of *Belladonna* as a groundwork, into which the particulars must fit.

Now, we shall find under *Cocculus* symptoms that are under many other drugs, but in no other drug do they hold the same relation as they do here. What, then, is the general effect of *Cocculus Indicus?* This effect is the well-known action of the drug on the cerebro-spinal system, it having very little influence on the nerves and the ganglionic system. How can you find this out? Not very easily, I confess, but yet this has been done, by studying the drug as a whole, by endeavoring to discover, by means of physiology, pathology, or any other science that bears on the subject, on what portions of the body it acts, what functions it alters, and what tissues it changes. Then you have a strong basis on which to build your symptomatology.

Cocculus acts on the cerebro-spinal system, producing great debility of these organs; the action of the drug on the brain itself I will explain to you when I come to speak of its use in typhoid fever. We will now consider the remedy as it affects the spinal cord. It causes a paralytic weakness of the spine, and especially of its motor nerves; thus we find it a certain and frequent remedy in paralysis originating in disease of the spinal cord. Especially is it indicated in the beginning of the trouble, whether it results from functional or from severe organic disease of the cord; whether the disease be spinal irritation from loss of seminal fluid, softening of the spinal cord, or locomotor ataxia. It is especially indicated in these cases when the lumbar region of the spine is affected; there is weakness in the small of the back, as if paralyzed; the small of the back gives out when walking. There is weakness of the legs; and by legs I mean the entire lower extremities; the knees give out when walking; the soles of the feet feel as if they were asleep; the thighs ache as if they had been pounded; first one hand then the other goes to sleep; sometimes the whole arm falls asleep, and the hand feels as if swollen. These symptoms lie at the foundation of the symptomatology of the whole drug; they all seem to depend upon spinal weakness. We find these symptoms common enough in women with menstrual difficulties, when the back gives out in the morning, after venereal excesses, and also from loss of sleep.

There is a concomitant symptom which you almost always find associated with those just mentioned, and that is a feeling of hollowness in some one of the cavities of the body, either in the head, chest, or abdomen. It is more than a weakness; it is an absolute feeling as though the parts were hollow. Talking tires these patients very much.

The debility of *Cocculus* is of spinal origin. Especially is it apt to follow loss of sleep; the patient cannot sit up even one or two hours later than usual in the evening without feeling languid and exhausted throughout the entire day following.

Let me next enumerate the typhoid symptoms of *Cocculus*; under this heading I shall speak of those of the brain. You would not expect

Cocculus to be indicated in a case of typhoid fever when the changes in or ulceration of Peyer's patches are marked, or where there are profuse diarrhœa, pneumonia, and similar complications. But in the nervous type of the fever, when the cerebro-spinal system is bearing the brunt of the disease, *Cocculus* becomes one of the remedies that will help us through the case. The symptoms indicating it are the following: the patient complains of great vertigo, and this is made worse when sitting, or when attempting to change from a reclining to a sitting posture. It is often associated with nausea, inclination to vomit, and even fainting. *Bryonia* also has this symptom. So far as the symptom itself is concerned there is no difference between *Bryonia* and *Cocculus*, yet, if you examine the case thoroughly, you will find that in *Cocculus* it is weakness of the cerebro-spinal nerves that gives origin to it. There is great confusion of the mind; a sort of bewildered, heavy state might better explain what I mean. It requires a great effort to speak plainly. In some cases they cannot find the words they wish to convey their meaning. Generally, such patients lie quietly wrapped in thought; the eyelids are heavy, as though they could hardly be lifted. Here is a symptom reminding you of *Gelsemium*. If the patient is still conscious enough to describe to you his condition, he will complain of a feeling of tightness of the brain, as though every nerve in the head were being drawn up tightly. At other times, he has this empty hollow, vacant feeling in the head. Any attempt to move the patient produces faintness or even fainting away. The tongue is usually coated white or yellow; there is bitter taste in the mouth. The abdomen is greatly distended and tympanitic; this tympanites under *Cocculus* is not the same as under *Cinchona*, *Carbo veg.*, *Colchicum*, *Sulphur*, or even *Lycopodium*.

There are several origins of tympanites. It may come from the blood-vessels, from the air swallowed with the food, from changes in the food itself, and also from retention of flatus. The latter condition is the cause of the tympany under *Cocculus Indicus*. It is not to be thought of as a remedy when flatus results from decomposition of food. That calls for *Carbo veg*. *Cocculus* has considerable oppression of the lungs, this being of nervous origin. It is usually referred by the patient to the walls of the chest. The patients are sleepless, or at least business thoughts crowd on the mind and keep them in a half-waking state, here again resembling *Bryonia*. These are the symptoms which lead you to *Cocculus Indicus* in typhoid states.

The next division for consideration is "Spasms." *Cocculus Indicus* is useful in spasmodic affections when the patient is greatly debilitated as to the cerebro-spinal nervous system. Irritable weakness is the condition which gives rise to the spasms for which *Cocculus* is the remedy. It is especially useful when spasmodic symptoms ensue as a result of prolonged loss of sleep. This condition we meet with more frequently in women than we do in men. The former are also more subject to spinal weakness. You may also use *Cocculus* for spasms after suppressed menses. The eyes are usually closed during these convulsions, and there is rapid oscillation of the eyeballs beneath the closed lids. But the woman must be of a weak, nervous temperament, or *Cocculus* is decreasingly indicated.

Under the heading "Organs" we still have a word to say about *Cocculus*. First, as to the headache. Some years ago there was an epidemic of spotted fever in this city. During that epidemic many children died, especially in its earlier days. After a while there was discovered a symptom characteristic of the epidemic, and that was intense headache in the occipital region, in the lower part of the back of the head, and in the nape of the neck. The intense headache was manifested in various ways. Children in a stupor would manifest it by turning the head back, so as to relieve the tension on the membranes of the brain; others, who were conscious, would put their hands to the back of the head, while still others complained of pain in the back of the head, as if the part were alternately opening and closing. That symptom was under *Cocculus*. There were very few fatal cases after *Cocculus* was used. Occipital headaches are hard to cure. *Cocculus* is a good remedy. *Gelsemium* is another. In the latter there is passive arterial congestion, by which I mean that the arterial blood flows freely to a part, the pulse being full and round, and not hard and tense, as under *Belladonna* or *Aconite*. There is often thick speech, too, with *Gelsemium*.

Still another remedy for occipital headache is the *Juglans cathartica*, sometimes called *Juglans cinerea*, or the butternut. This I consider to be the best remedy for sharp pains in the occipital region. They are often accompanied by nausea, dull pain in the right hypochondrium, jaundice and other symptoms of liver involvement.

We have already anticipated some of the symptoms of *Cocculus* pertaining to the female genital organs. The menses are either profuse, coming too often or with a gush, and very debilitating, or they are tardy in their appearance, and the patient suffers each month from what has been termed menstrual colic. We have a little group of remedies for this condition, consisting of *Cocculus*, *Pulsatilla* and *Chamomilla*. First let me describe the symptoms of *Cocculus*. This remedy is indicated by a colic in which the pain is as if there were sharp stones rubbing against each other in the abdomen. There is very often with this colic excessive distension of the abdomen from accumulation of flatus. The colic is especially liable to awaken the patient at midnight. It is relieved by belching, but returns again from the re-accumulation of flatus. The patient is, of course, irritable.

Under *Chamomilla* the menstrual flow is very dark. The mental symptoms described to you in my lecture on that drug are necessarily present.

Pulsatilla has scanty menstrual flow, coming by fits and starts, griping pains doubling the patient up; but the disposition is mild and tearful.

Cyclamen is similar to *Pulsatilla*. It has chilliness with the pains; crying, tearful mood; dyspepsia, made worse by eating fat food and pastry; scanty menses; menstrual colic. But we make the distinction here: *Cyclamen* does not have relief in the cool air or in the cool room, and in many cases *Cyclamen* has thirst. The resemblance between *Cocculus* and *Cyclamen* lies in the fact that both remedies suit a depressed condition of the cerebro-spinal nervous system. More particularly the indications for *Cyclamen* are these: the patient feels dizzy; is weak from any motion; is highly anæmic; and usually worse when sitting up. These symptoms are commonly associated with dimness of vision. We also find under *Cyclamen* this flatulent colic, arising from wind in the bowels, coming on at night, and relieved only by getting up and walking about. Compare also, in menstrual colic, *Ignatia* and *Nux vomica*.

LECTURE XXVI.

PAPAVERACEÆ.

We now proceed to study the *Papaveraceæ*, an order of plants from which we obtain *Opium, Sanguinaria Canadensis,* and *Chelidonium majus.* As an order, they act on the circulation of the blood, tending to produce narcosis of a greater or less degree by engorging the blood-vessels of the brain. The effect thus produced on the sensorium ranges all the way from sleepiness to stupor. This, you know, is eminently true of *Opium,* and, to a less degree, of *Sanguinaria* and *Chelidonium. Fumaria officinalis* contains an enormous amount of potash in its ashes; *Argemone Mexicana,* the Mexican poppy or yellow thistle, has been used in the treatment of tinea. It has a yellow juice, which, when exposed to the air, looks like Gamboge. We shall now take up the study of these drugs *seriatim.*

OPIUM.

Opium.
- Brain. Emotions.
- Spasms. Paralysis.
- Marasmus.
- Constipation. Bladder.
- Sleep.
- Chest. Lungs. Heart.
- Defective reaction.

Opium is obtained, as you probably know, from the unripe capsules of the poppy plant, *Papaver somniferum.* The unripe capsules are usually employed in its manufacture, because they are more powerfully soporific. In some respects opium is the most remarkable drug in our materia medica. You know that many drugs owe the majority of their effects to active principles which they contain. Thus *Belladonna* contains *Atropine; Stramonium, Solanine; Nux vomica, Strychnine,* etc.; but *Opium* seems to embrace an endless number of these active principles and each succeeding year adds to the list. Let me enumerate them—they are as follows:

      Morphine,   Protopine,
      Pseudo-morphine,   Methylnornarcotine,

Codeine,	Deuteropine,
Apocodeine,	Laudanine,
Thebain,	Codamine,
Cotamine,	Papaverine,
Hydrocotamine,	Rhœagenine,
Apomorphine,	Rhœadine,
Desoxymorphine,	Dimethylnornarcotine,
Nornarcotine,	Meconidine,
Thebenine,	Cryptopine,
Laudanisine,	Narceine,
Narcotine,	Meconic acid,
Lanthopine,	Lactic acid.

These various substances are derived from *Opium*, by more or less complicated processes. They have more or less narcotic properties akin to those of *Opium* itself. The action of some of these alkaloids is well-known, while of the action of others we are as yet ignorant.

Morphia (used principally in the form of the sulphate) is probably the best understood of these. It is largely used by old-school physicians in hypodermatic medication for the relief of pain. But we may make use of it as a homœopathic remedy. In such violent diseases as cancer *Morphia* has been successfully given for one of its secondary symptoms, extreme susceptibility to pain; pains are so violent as to threaten convulsions, or cause twitching and jerking of the limbs; under these circumstances *Morphia* is a homœopathic remedy. It does not cure, but relieves the pains, not as an opiate by stupefying the patient, but according to the law of Homœopathy.

Morphia has the property of producing tympany. This is a very important fact for you to bear in mind, as you may find it necessary to differentiate incipient peritonitis from *Morphia* effects.

Codeine, another of these alkaloids, is a useful drug in the treatment of phthisis. It is indicated in that dry, teasing cough which annoys the patient night and day.

Furthermore *Codeine* has caused and cured twitching of the muscles, especially of the eyelids. This is a very annoying symptom; it is sometimes relieved by *Crocus*.

Apomorphia causes and cures vomiting. Now this vomiting is not of the kind for which you give *Ipecac.*, *Tartar emetic*, *Lobelia*, etc. It is a reflex vomiting usually from the brain. *Apomorphia* produces vomiting if injected hypodermatically, long before it can have any local action on the stomach. You may utilize this effect of the drug in vomiting of cerebral origin, and also in that annoying disease from which many people suffer, and for which they get little sympathy, seasickness. In these cases of cerebral vomiting you may also think of *Belladonna*, *Glonoin* and *Rhus tox*.

There are several other of these alkaloids of which we have some provings, but nothing that has been definitely described. There are also numerous preparations made from *Opium ;* these are largely used in allopathic practice ; we have nothing, however, to do with them, except to undo the mischief they produce. The various preparations of *Opium* enter into the composition of cough-mixtures and soothing-syrups, used largely in popular practice. Their effects are decidedly pernicious, especially in children. A prominent old-school authority says that the use of soothing-syrup for children is decidedly reprehensible. It stunts their growth, makes them irritable and cross, and interferes sadly with the brain development. *Nux vomica* is one of the antidotes in cases of injury from anodyne preparations. Still better, perhaps, as an antidote, is *Chamomilla*, which is suited when opiates have been given for some time, and have produced their secondary effects ; the little one is wakeful ; slight pains are unbearable. When this condition is present, *Chamomilla* is your remedy, whether the patient be child or adult.

No drug is more freely abused by both allopath and homœopath (!) than is the one we are studying to-day. I would that I had both opportunity and ability to convince the practitioner of the old school of medicine of the absurdity of his indiscriminate use of opiates, and I could hope still more earnestly to dissuade homœopathicians from hiding their ignorance under the anodyne effects of an occasionally interpolated dose of *Morphine* or *Laudanum*. The one class, ignorant of any other means of assuaging pains, and the other class, too lazy to study their cases, seek relief for their patients in anodynes. Call them to task for their unscientific practice and they meet you with the remark, "my duty is to relieve the sick." Let me rejoin, "At any cost? Must you do what you know to be wrong?" "No, but how do you make it wrong?" Let me reply by a brief resumé of the *modus operandi* of *Opium*, and then if this question is not answered I make no further objections to anodynes.

In small doses, *Opium* has primarily a transient exhilarating effect. It seems, however, to affect the emotional more than the intellectual sphere. The mind feels as if floating in the air, unincumbered by the laws of space and gravity. The imagination has full play. If now the dose be increased, either in quantity or by frequent repetition, there follows a sleepy state. This sleep varies all the way from a pleasant feeling of easy drowsiness to the most profound stupor. This narcotic and anodyne effect of *Opium* is the result of the increased circulation of blood in the brain, brought about not only by increasing the amount of blood supplied to the brain but also by interfering with its return to the heart. Let me digress for a few moments and speak of the physiological explanation of sleep. Hammond has shown that during this state, the quantity of blood circulating in the cranial cavity is greatly diminished. If you give *Opium* to produce sleep, what do you do? Do you produce anæmia of the brain? No, just the reverse. I ask you, then, is the administration of opiates for their anodyne effects at all rational?

Returning to the effects of *Opium*—the face becomes deep red and swollen from the distension of the blood-vessels. The more profound the stupor, the darker red is the face. It may even become of a brownish hue. The pupils become contracted. The pulse is full and slow. Respiration is deep, and as the stupor grows in intensity it becomes heavier and finally stertorous. What is the meaning of this stertor? It means that as the poisonous effects of *Opium* increase, a paretic and finally a paralytic condition of the muscles of the palate and cheeks appears. These parts, thus being thoroughly relaxed, flap back and forth with each respiration. The pulse is full, round and slow, showing you that the heart is acting with the full volume of blood, but not with the usual speed. As the case goes on hour after hour, you find a picture of complete paralysis developing. The practical application of this I will give you when speaking of typhoid fever. The sphincters lose their control, so that there is involuntary escape of urine and fæces. The pupils now are dilated and the skin is bathed in cold sweat. The lower jaw drops and finally death ensues.

In these fatal cases autopsies show the cerebral convolutions to be flattened, the vessels of the cerebro-spinal axis engorged with blood; and there is effusion of serum beneath the arachnoid and into the ventricles of the brain.

These are the symptoms of acute *Opium* poisoning.

Now these phenomena depend upon the action of *Opium* on the nerves. From irritation comes the first brief excitation. From the subsequent paralyzing action come the drowsiness, muscular relaxation and coma. From the beginning, the cerebral vessels are surcharged with blood, and this gradually increases until sopor ensues. Now, gentlemen, let me ask, is it rational practice to assuage pain with a substance which paralyzes and so relieves by taking away, *not the disease*, BUT THE ABILITY TO FEEL, THE CONSCIOUSNESS OF SUFFERING?

What are the effects produced by the habitual use of the drug? The first effect is one that I have already described to you, one of dreamy imaginative activity of the emotional mind. Later, as the use of the drug is continued, every tissue of the body becomes affected. The skin grows dry and sallow and hangs in folds, the limbs emaciate, and the intellect becomes dulled.

The best antidote to *Opium* is strong black coffee, given repeatedly until there is some sign of reaction. In addition to that you should use electricity. You should also remove any of the poison that may be in the stomach by means of an emetic or the stomach-pump, and you should force the patient to walk about to prevent stupor.

Opium has so far been sufficiently described for you to see readily in what classes of disease it is indicated.

You see the picture of *Opium* in typhoid fever with profound cerebral congestion resulting in paralysis of the brain, dropping of the lower jaw and stertorous breathing. Often when *Opium* is called for in this disease, the body is bathed in a hot sweat. This sweat is not critical. It is a bad omen. It is a symptom of approaching death, in that it is a result of paralysis of the sweat glands. This symptom is also found under *Stramonium*.

In typhoid fever with threatening paralysis of the brain, you should remember *Lachesis*, the symptoms of which I described to you when lecturing on that drug; also *Hyoscyamus*, which has the stertorous breathing; but there are differences, as you will learn in a future lecture.

Opium must be considered in the treatment of apoplexy. It is natural to suppose that a remedy producing such fulness of the cerebral blood-vessels might, in persons predisposed, readily cause their rupture, and the consequent symptoms of extravasation of blood into the cerebral substance. *Opium* is indicated by the color of the face, by the stertorous breathing, and by tetanic rigidity of the body. Especially is it indicated in the apoplexy of drunkards. *Opium* follows *Belladonna* in apoplexy.

In apoplexy occurring in drunkards, you should think also of *Baryta carb*. and *Lachesis*.

Arnica suits in apoplexy, when the pulse is full and strong. The paralysis is on the left side and there is stertorous breathing.

Apis is called for when the coma fails to yield to *Opium*.

For apoplexy with convulsions, think of *Belladonna, Hyoscyamus, Lachesis* and *Opium.*

For apoplexy followed by paralysis, *Arnica, Belladonna, Lachesis, Nux vomica* and *Rhus tox.*

When followed by idiocy, *Helleborus.*

In apoplectic congestion with sleepiness after meals *Opium* should be compared with *Nux vomica* and *Arnica.*

Opium is useful in *mania a potu* or delirium tremens. Especially is it indicated in "old sinners;" in those whose long lives of excess have thoroughly destroyed their constitutions; in those who have had the disease time after time. It takes but a small quantity of liquor to throw them again into the delirium. The face wears a constant expression of fright or terror.. They have visions of animals springing up from various parts of the room. They imagine that they see ghosts, devils, etc., with whom they converse, though they are terrified by the subjects of their visions. If they succeed in obtaining sleep, it is of the stertorous character already referred to.

There are several remedies which, if given soon enough, will enable you to carry your patients with delirium tremens safely through the attack. I have already mentioned *Opium;* another is *Lachesis;* especially is this indicated when the patients have visions of snakes and other hideous objects; sensation in the throat as if choking; and springing out of sleep suddenly as if from a dream.

Another remedy is *Stramonium*, to which you will be guided by the violence of the symptoms. The patient starts from sleep in perfect horror, with visions of animals coming toward him from every corner of the room; he makes efforts to escape; his face is bright red.

Still another remedy is *Cannabis Indica*, or the hashish. This is one of the best. It has thus far been given only in low potency. The symptoms which seem to characterize it are, ideas of grandeur and errors of perception as to space and as to time.

In other cases we have to use *Arsenicum*, when there is fear of death and the patient will not permit himself to be left alone.

A remedy often forgotten, but useful, nevertheless, is *Calcarea ostrearum*. The minute the patient closes his eyes he sees visions which compel him to open them again in affright.

You may use *Opium* in cholera infantum when the face is red or pale, and is associated with fatally advancing stupor; the pupils react to the stimulus of light either not at all or else very sluggishly. The disease seems to begin by involving the brain, or such a mishap threatens during its course; as yet there is neither diarrhœa nor vomiting; the child appears as if it had been drugged. *Opium* administered in a case like this will restore the patient to consciousness. Diarrhœa sets in, and the disease proceeds naturally to recovery. This remedy may also be given when there is a lack of vitality, and the well-selected remedy refuses to act. The patient is either sluggish or drowsy. It is just as useful in these cases as are *Carbo veg.*, *Sulphur*, *Valerian*, *Ambra grisea*, *Psorinum*, or any of the other drugs called for in defective reaction.

There is a remedy which I wish to give you here, but with some caution, because it is what has been termed a "breech-presentation," that is, it was used clinically before provings of it were made. That remedy is *Ferrum phos.* It is called for in cholera infantum when the discharges from the bowels are frequent; within twenty-four hours the child is greatly reduced, and falls into a stupor, with red face, dilated pupils, rolling of the head, and soft, full-flowing pulse. We know that Iron has that kind of a pulse; we know that congestion belongs to all the preparations of Iron. In one of my cases with the above symptoms, *Belladonna* and *Sulphur* were each given in turn, but failed. I then gave *Ferrum phos.*, and in twelve hours the child returned to consciousness, and is alive to-day.

You may also use *Opium* in suppuration of the lungs occurring in those greatly addicted to the use of intoxicating liquors; the breathing is labored, and is attended with rattling and snoring. Cough is very difficult, and is attended with smothering spells; the face becomes blue during the cough.

Another affection of the lungs occurring in drunkards, namely, hæmoptysis, calls for *Opium* when the chest is hot and the limbs are cold; the cough is violent, and is attended with an expectoration of frothy mucus and blood; the patient is drowsy with the cough.

Antimonium tartaricum also has cough with drowsiness and gaping.

We find *Opium* sometimes indicated in spasms, especially when they occur as the immediate result of fright or anger; or when a nursing infant has a convulsion after its wet-nurse has been frightened; the body is in a condition of tetanic rigidity; opisthotonos; the spasm is ushered in with a loud shriek ; there is foaming at the mouth ; the face becomes dark red, or even purple, and the body is often bathed in a hot sweat ; deep, snoring sleep follows the spasm.

Opium causes and cures constipation ; a constipation in which there is inertia of the rectum and the entire intestinal tract ; there is no inclination whatever for the bowels to move ; thus the bowels become impacted with fæces ; flatus accumulates in the upper portion of the intestines and presses upward against the chest. This symptom is very common after diseases that are debilitating or long-lasting. In such cases I have been in the habit of giving *Opium* in repeated doses until colicky pains are produced ; this indicates restoration of peristaltic action of the bowels. I then order an injection of cocoa-nut oil or soap and water to soften the fæcal masses, when an easy evacuation of the bowels follows. The *Opium* stool in its complete picture consists of little hard, dry, black balls. This form of constipation reminds us of that of *Alumina*, *Plumbum* and *Bryonia*.

Bryonia has constipation with inertia of the rectum and lack of intestinal secretion ; the stools are large and dry.

Plumbum closely resembles *Opium*, but there is some spasmodic constriction of the anus ; the stools consist of hard, black balls.

Alumina has inertia of the rectum with hard, dry, knotty stools, but often attended with soft fæces.

In tympanites or accumulation of flatus, especially in advanced stages of peritonitis, compare *Opium* with *Terebinthina*, *Lycopodium*, *Carbo veg.*, *Colchicum*, and *Raphanus*.

The characteristic symptom calling for the last-named remedy in tympanites is, that the patient passes flatus neither upward nor downward for days.

Opium may be used in bladder troubles, especially in retention of urine. It is indicated when this retention has resulted from fright, and when it follows parturition. This last-named symptom I have twice confirmed.

In this retention of urine after labor, compare with *Opium*, *Hyoscyamus*, *Causticum*, and *Arsenicum*.

In suppression of urine you may think of *Stramonium*, *Zingiber*, *Lycopodium*, and *Pulsatilla*.

The power of *Opium* to cause shriveling of every fibre of the body suggests its use in marasmus in children. The patient is wrinkled and like a little dried-up old man ; the characteristic *Opium* stupor is present.

When the above-named condition has been produced by *Opium*, *Sulphur*, *Argentum nitricum*, or *Sarsaparilla* may be used as an antidote. *Muriatic acid* is the remedy for the continued muscular debility following the use of *Opium*.

We may find *Opium* indicated in that very dangerous condition, strangulation of the bowels. There are violent colicky pains and vomiting of matters having a fæcal odor.

In colic it may be given when there is great tympany and pressure downward on the rectum and bladder; there is a great deal of belching without relief.

Compare here *Nux vomica*, *China* and *Lycopodium*.

Veratrum album has colic as if the bowels were twisted; abdomen tense. The longer delayed is the emission of flatus, the more difficult is it to pass. *Opium* has been of service in incarcerated hernia, ileus and typhlitis, with complete constipation, vomiting of fæcal matter or at least of substances of a fæcal odor.

Sometimes we find *Opium* useful in metrorrhagia, whether after labor or not. The patient is restless; the sheets feel hot to her; she is sleepy, but cannot sleep.

In fevers other than typhoid, it may be given when the chill is accompanied by heat of the head and great drowsiness; the body is burning hot, even when covered with a copious sweat; desire to uncover; unconsciousness; feels as if his legs belonged to some one else. (Compare *Baptisia* and *Stramonium*.)

Puerperal fever sometimes calls for *Opium*, especially when caused by fright. There is over-excitement of all the senses; even distant sounds annoy the patient; the discharge from the uterus is very fœtid. The case approaches a condition of stupor.

In hæmorrhage from the uterus, compare *Belladonna*, which has a flow of bright blood feeling hot to both physician and patient.

Hyoscyamus also has this. But under this remedy there is a great deal of spasmodic jerking of the body.

You will see from what I have said that *Opium* is an invaluable remedy for the bad effects of fright, whether that emotion produces convulsions or diarrhœa.

Gelsemium, *Pulsatilla*, and *Veratrum album*, you will recall as being useful in diarrhœa after fright.

For the remote consequences of fright *Opium* does not always suffice you should then remember *Natrum muriaticum*, *Silicea*, and *Phosphorus acid;* the first named especially for chorea or paralytic weakness of this origin.

Opium, like *Bovista* and *Arnica*, is useful for the bad effects of inhalation of charcoal vapors.

In spasms of the lungs, compare *Moschus* and *Ipecac*.

Drosera is likewise indicated in the spasmodic cough of consumption, coming on in the evening, and perhaps again after midnight. Every effort to raise a little phlegm ends in retching and vomiting.

LECTURE XXVII.

SANGUINARIA AND CHELIDONIUM.

BEFORE proceeding with our study of *Sanguinaria*, I will say that there is a variety of the poppy plant which grows in Mexico called the *Argemone Mexicana*. It is used in Mexico in much the same manner as we use *Opium*. It causes cutaneous eruptions and has been used in the expulsion of tape-worm. The juice of the plant when collected and dried has much the appearance of gamboge. I mention this, not because it is a matter of importance, but as a piece of information that may in time prove beneficial.

We shall now take up the study of another member of the Papaveraceæ, the *Sanguinaria Canadensis*, or blood-root. This is a plant which is readily recognized by the character of its root, which, when cut, is red, and exudes a fluid having the appearance of blood, hence the plant has been aptly named "blood-root." The seeds of *Sanguinaria* are somewhat narcotic. You can see a resemblance between it and *Opium*, not in the completeness of its symptomatology, but a family resemblance sufficient to place it by the side of *Opium*, yet having differences so great that there can be no danger of confounding the two drugs. In extreme narcosis from *Sanguinaria* we find languor and torpor, dilated pupils, with disordered vision and irregular pulse. The symptoms are not unlike those which follow poisoning with *Stramonium*. In studying the drug we may save all unnecessary multiplication of symptoms by attention to the following schemæ:

Compare with Sanguinaria Canadensis,
- Belladonna, Iris versicolor, Paullinia, Melilotus, — In headache.
- Veratr. viride, Phosphorus, Antim. tart., Sulphur, — In pneumonia.

SANGUINARIA CANADENSIS irritant to
- *Brain*: Anxiety, irritability.
- *Nose*: Faint from odors.
- *Ears*: Sensitive to sudden sounds.
- *Circulation*:
  - Headaches.
  - Vertigo.
  - Hæmorrhages.
  - Climaxis.
  - Fever.
  - Menstruation.
  - Phthisis florida.
  - Local congestions.
- *Mucous membranes*:
  - Dry feeling or rawness.
  - Cough.
  - Croup.
  - Ulceration.
  - Polypi.
  - Diarrhœa.
  - Pneumonia.
- *Glands*: Salivation.
- *Skin*: Acne, ulcers.
- *Muscles*: Rheumatism, myalgia, languor, nausea, faintness.

Sanguinaria in the first place is an irritant, whether taken into the mouth, applied to the skin, or when carried by the blood to other tissues. For the primary and most important effect of the drug, then, we have irritation of tissue. For instance, the brain is irritated by *Sanguinaria*. This is mentioned first because of the predominant importance of all mental symptoms, be they emotional or be they intellectual. Anxiety is almost always present with the *Sanguinaria* ailments. This anxiety, however, is not an isolated symptom. It appears qualifying the headaches, the gastric difficulties, the heart and chest symptoms, and in fact all the ailments in which *Sanguinaria* is applicable. Like almost all anxiety, it is accompanied by irregularities or disturbances in the circulation. There is also an irritability of temper which makes the patient morose, irritable, peevish or excitable. We note, too, that the ears are irritated by the drug but as a result, primarily, of the irritating action on the circulation. There is increased redness of the external ear, with humming and roaring in the ears from increased circulation of blood through the aural structures. *Sanguinaria* also produces a hyper-excitation of the auditory nerves with the following symptoms as characteristic : painful sensitiveness, especially to sudden sounds ; sensation as if the patient were in a railroad car or in some vehicle which was moving and jarring her, with a feeling as if all about her were talking rapidly and confusedly ; the patient desires to be held in order to remove this nervous vibratory sensation through the body. Thus you see the primary irritating effect on the ear reflected through the entire nervous system, producing these symptoms, which, by the way, are not uncommon in women about the time of the climaxis. *Sanguinaria* is equal to *Glonoin* in these cases.

This desire to be held reminds one of *Gelsemium*, which has heart disease and chills with tremor of the whole body and desire to be held still, and *Lachesis*, which wants to be held down during the chill in intermittent form.

Next we come to the nasal symptoms. The sense of smell is usually increased ; hence we notice a peculiar susceptibility to odors, which causes the patient to feel faint. This is not an uncommon symptom in "rose-cold." It also belongs to hysteria, and places *Sanguinaria* by the side of *Phosphorus*, *Ignatia*, *Valerian*, *Nux vomica* and similar remedies.

The disturbances in the circulation we find first exhibited in the vertigo. There is rush of blood to the head with this dizziness; the patient feels sick and faint, as if she would fall when she attempts to rise from a sitting posture.

Then, too, we have the circulatory disturbances represented in the sick-headache, and *Sanguinaria* has no equal in this affection especially in that form which is so common in this country as to receive the name of "American sick-headache." The patient suffers from rush of blood to the head, which causes faintness and decided nausea, the nausea even continuing until vomiting sets in. The pains, which are of a violent character, begin in the occipital region, spread thence over the head, and settle over the right eye. They are of a sharp, lancinating character, and at times throbbing. At the height of the disease the patient can bear neither sounds nor odors. Mark the effect on the auditory and olfactory nerves. She can not bear any one to walk across the floor, for the slightest jar annoys her. As the headache reaches its acme nausea and vomiting ensue, the vomited matters consisting of food and bile. The patient is forced to remain quiet in a darkened room. Sometimes a profuse flow of urine relieves; otherwise the only respite she has is when sleep comes to relieve her. Sometimes the pain is so violent that the patient goes out of her mind, or she seeks relief by pressing against her head with her hands or by pressing the head against the pillow. This is the *Sanguinaria* sick-headache in its completeness. Not only does the remedy palliate, but it cures.

Studying *Sanguinaria* with its concordant remedies, you will find coming into your mind most prominently *Belladonna* as affecting the right side, as having throbbing pains, cerebral congestion and intolerance of light and noise. You see that the two remedies are very similar. Practically speaking, *Sanguinaria* is the more useful of the two in the gastric form. In *Belladonna*, you almost always find cold feet with the hot head, which may not necessarily be present under *Sanguinaria*. Then again, the *Belladonna* patient is not relieved by lying down, but by sitting propped up, while *Sanguinaria* has relief from lying down. Further, the symptom of pain coming from the occiput over the head, etc., is not so prominent under *Belladonna* as it is under *Sanguinaria*.

Melilotus, one variety of the clover, produces a most violent cerebral congestion with headache, which drives the patient almost frantic. It really seems to the patient that the brain would burst through the forehead. The throbbing pain is almost as violent as it is under *Glonoin*. In one proving of this drug, a lady had this congestive headache with prolapsus uteri and violent palpitation of the heart. The pain is sometimes relieved by profuse flow of urine.

Still another drug closely allied to *Sanguinaria* is *Iris versicolor*. This drug is useful for sick-headaches, particularly when they are periodical in their appearance, recurring, for instance, every Sunday. This is because the strain of the preceding six days has been relieved and now the patient feels its effects and has this sick-headache. It is especially suited to school teachers, college professors, students, etc. The pains are intense and of a throbbing character and supra-orbital. They often affect the eyes and cause temporary blindness. At the height of the headache vomiting often ensues, the vomited matters being bitter or sour, or both.

I wish also to mention *Paullinia sorbilis*. This has some little history. A number of years ago there appeared a specific, in the form of pills, for sick-headache, the principal ingredient of which was this *Paullinia*. It proved itself to be an efficacious remedy. The objection I have to the drug is that it must be given in large doses, consequently I do not think that it has a true symptomatic relation to the ailment for which it was recommended. Its active principle is said to be identical with *Caffeine* and *Theine*.

Continuing our study of the effects of *Sanguinaria* on the circulation, we find it sometimes indicated for hæmorrhages, not very frequently it is true, yet when the symptoms call for it you should bear it in mind. It is especially indicated in metrorrhagia occurring at the climaxis. The blood is bright red, clotted and frequently offensive. Especially is it to be used when the metrorrhagia is accompanied by the form of sick-headache which I have already described, and by flushing of the face and flushes of heat which are incident to change of life in women. The face becomes scarlet. This high color passes off with moisture and faint, weak, sick feeling. Here then you must place *Sanguinaria* with *Glonoin*, *Nitrite of Amyl*, and *Lachesis*. The menstrual flow of *Sanguinaria* is bright red, clotted and offensive, later becoming dark and losing its offensiveness.

Still another fact which illustrates these irregularities of the circulation, is the application of *Sanguinaria* to phthisis florida. In detailing to you the symptoms calling for this remedy in phthisis florida, I will also mention the character of the cough and also the application of the drug in pneumonia, because the symptoms in each case are similar, although belonging to different diseases. You find the patient suffering from hectic fever. The fever usually comes at about two or four o'clock in the afternoon; the cheeks have a bright circumscribed flush. The cough is usually dry at first, and seems to be excited by tickling or crawling in the larynx and upper portion of the chest, probably in the trachea, and perhaps in the beginning of the bronchial tubes. There is a great deal of burning and fulness in the upper part of the chest, as if it were too full of blood, which it really is. The patient complains of sharp stitching pains, especially about the right lung and in the region of the nipple. These pains are in all probability myalgic. The affected muscles of the chest are sore. There is also great dyspnœa. Thus early in the disease, *Sanguinaria*, by calming the circulation, by removing the congestion of the chest, by lessening the hectic fever, will save your patient from what would end fatally in a few months.

When pneumonia calls for *Sanguinaria*, we have, in addition to the symptoms already mentioned, rust-colored sputum with the cough (just as you find in the stage of red hepatization), a very distressing amount of dyspnœa, and the hands and feet burning hot, or else just the reverse, icy cold. Sometimes, even before the amount of hepatization will account for it, you have failure of the heart's action. The pulse becomes weak and irregular. There is a weak, faint feeling about the heart. The patient is faint. He is covered with sweat and he suffers from nausea.

Localized congestions are frequent enough in the symptomatology of *Sanguinaria*. You have seen how it causes cerebral congestion, circumscribed redness of the cheeks, etc. You may also use it for a teasing cough compelling the patient to sit up at night. The cough ceases so soon as the patient passes flatus by the bowels or belches. Connected with this form of cold, there is a feeling as of a warm current running from the chest to the stomach. The disease may be transferred from the chest to the abdomen, the whole difficulty ending in diarrhœa.

Sanguinaria resembles several drugs in pneumonia. It bears a resemblance to *Veratrum viride* in the engorgement of the lungs and in the intensity of the symptoms. *Veratrum viride* has, more marked than *Sanguinaria*, arterial excitement. As yet, hepatization has not taken place. *Veratrum viride* given then lowers the pulse, reduces the congestion and modifies the pneumonia. It also resembles *Sanguinaria* when the engorgement is so profound as to threaten the death of the patient. The pulse becomes rapid and quivering, the face livid, and every symptom of approaching paralysis of the lungs is present. But when hepatization has taken place, *Veratrum viride* is not indicated.

Phosphorus resembles *Sanguinaria* in pneumonia. Its symptoms I will mention when I lecture on that drug.

Antimonium tartaricum resembles *Sanguinaria* when the face becomes livid; the blood is surcharged with carbon; rattling cough, etc.

Sulphur resembles *Sanguinaria* during the stage of resolution when the hepatized lung does not clear up properly, and the sputum becomes purulent. In these cases, either remedy is indicated, *Sanguinaria* being preferable when the expectoration is very offensive, even to the patient himself.

Returning to *Sanguinaria* and reviewing its action on the mucous membranes, we find that it has a highly irritating effect, causing at first extreme dryness, whether it be of the conjunctiva, the mucous membrane of the mouth, nose or any other mucous surface. Alternating with this dryness and indicating the drug in another phase of the case, is rawness with burning, as though the mucous membrane were denuded of its epithelium. This is common enough in catarrhs. You find the nose sore and raw with fluent excoriating coryza. The cough is as I have described, and seems to depend upon this dryness or irritation of the mucous surfaces.

When the laryngeal mucous membrane is affected, we have very distressing symptoms. There is aphonia and, in addition, a feeling of swelling in the throat as though the patient would choke. *Sanguinaria* is indicated in laryngeal catarrh, whether it be from phthisis or from simple cold or exposure.

The croup for which we may use *Sanguinaria* is one in which there may be a formation of pseudo-membrane with dryness, burning and swollen feeling in the throat, and metallic croupy cough which cannot be characterized by any other words than wheezing-whistling. It is too shrill to be only "wheezing," and it is too moist to be "whistling" alone. If it is associated with the dryness and burning, and some of the other catarrhal symptoms, *Sanguinaria* will quickly cure the entire affection.

Sometimes we have ulceration of the mucous surface with the qualifying symptoms already mentioned.

Another effect on the mucous surfaces is the formation of polypi. These may be found in the nose or in any other part of the body. *Sanguinaria* is especially useful for mucous polypi when they bleed profusely. When occurring in the nose, they are associated with the form of coryza already referred to. There is also profuse salivation, showing that the drug irritates the salivary glands.

The skin is also affected under *Sanguinaria*. It produces acne on the face, particularly in women who have scanty menstruation and are subject to irregular distribution of blood.

Lastly we find the drug affecting the muscles, inflaming them, and giving a picture of acute muscular rheumatism. The pains are erratic, sharp and stitching, with great soreness and stiffness of the muscles, especially those of the back and neck. *Sanguinaria* exhibits a special affinity for the right deltoid muscle. The pains are intense. The patient is unable to raise the arm to the head. *Sanguinaria* holds the same relation to the right deltoid that *Ferrum* does to the left.

So much for *Sanguinaria Canadensis*.

CHELIDONIUM MAJUS.

Chelidonium.
- LIVER, LUNGS, *Heart*.
- *Neuralgia, Toothache.*
- Eyes, Kidneys, Fistula.
- Joints, Diaphragm.
- Skin, Chills and Fever.

Compare with Chelidonium majus,
- Antim. tart.
- Mercurius.
- Kali carb.
- Bryonia.
- Lycopodium.

I shall be brief in my remarks on *Chelidonium*, as we have not the time to treat exhaustively of the drug. It is a unique remedy, possessing points of similarity with its congeners, *Sanguinaria* and *Opium*, and also with *Nux vomica*, *Mercurius*, *Phosphorus* and *Kali carb*. The plant yields an acrid, yellow, bitter juice, which, when applied locally, produces inflammation and even vesication. The principal value of *Chelidonium* lies in its action on the liver, lungs and kidneys. The patient is low-spirited, inclined to weep, but knows no reason therefor; restless, must move from place to place, with mental anguish; headache, with coldness extending from the neck into the occiput; the head is so heavy he can scarcely raise it from the pillow; pressure in the occiput toward the left ear.

Chelidonium may be indicated in many affections of the liver, from a simple congestion to a positive inflammation. It produces pains in the right hypochondrium all the way from a simple soreness to the most aggravating variety of sharp stitches, which shoot from the liver down into the stomach, or down into the back from the posterior aspect of the liver. There is marked pain under the angle of the right shoulder-blade. That is the key-note for the drug in hepatic disease.

In addition to this you have the usual hepatic symptoms, swelling of the liver, chills, fever, jaundice, yellow-coated tongue, bitter taste in the mouth, tongue taking the imprint of the teeth, as you find under *Mercury*, and desire or craving for milk, which exceptionally agrees. There is usually also a craving for acids and for sour things, as pickles and vinegar. The stools are characteristically profuse, bright yellow and diarrhœic, or they may be clayey. These are the symptoms of *Chelidonium*, and they are very definite. Let me tell you how to apply them. You may use the drug in simple biliousness; in hepatic congestion or inflammation, and also in pneumonia with bilious symptoms, in what has been termed bilious pneumonia. The symptoms indicating it in the latter affection I will give you presently.

This pain under the angle of the right scapula of *Chelidonium* brings to mind pains of a similar character found in other remedies. *Chenopodium* has dull pain lower than the angle of the right scapula and nearer the spinal column.

Ranunculus bulbosus has pain along the whole inner edge of the left scapula, at times extending below its inferior angle and through the left chest.

Lobelia syphilitica has pain under, not below, the inner border of the left scapula, worse after weeping.

Angustura has sharp cutting pain from just beneath the right scapula to the breast near the nipple.

Bryonia is very similar to *Chelidonium* in hepatic affections. Both remedies have sharp stitching pains, both have pain under the right shoulder blade, both have bitter taste in the mouth and yellow-coated tongue, and both have swelling of the liver. But *Bryonia* differs in its stool, which is either hard, dry and brown or, if loose, it is papescent and profuse and associated with a colic very much like that of *Colocynth*. Sometimes the stools have an odor of old cheese.

Lycopodium, which bears some resemblance to *Chelidonium*, is easily differentiated, especially in the rumbling of flatus in the left hypochondrium, in the sour rather than the bitter taste, in the sour vomiting, in the fulsomeness after partaking of small quantities of food, and in the character of the pains, which are dull and aching under *Lycopodium*, and sharp and lancinating under *Chelidonium*.

You may use *Chelidonium* in neuralgia of the face. The pains go from the right cheek bone into the teeth or into the eye, or the pain may be located in the supra-orbital nerves. This neuralgia will not yield to *Chelidonium*, however, unless you have some of the hepatic symptoms of the drug present. It is a neuralgia dependent on disorder of the liver, and not an idiopathic prosopalgia.

Chelidonium is useful, as I have already intimated, in bilious pneumonia. It is also indicated in the capillary bronchitis of children when these hepatic symptoms are present, especially when it follows measles or whooping cough. The face in these cases is apt to be deep red. There is great oppression of the chest, as shown by the efforts to breathe and a fan-like motion of the alæ nasi (a *Lycopodium* symptom, by the way), one hot and one cold foot (another *Lycopodium* symptom), and stitching pain under the right scapula. The cough is usually loose and rattling. The expectoration is not easily raised.

Mercurius is sometimes indicated in bilious pneumonia. It differs from *Chelidonium* in the character of the stool more than in anything else. The *Mercury* stool is slimy and is attended with great tenesmus before, during and after the stool, while in *Chelidonium* it is quite free. The *Mercurius* expectoration is apt to be blood-streaked, and there are sharp pains shooting through the lower portion of the right lung to the back, a symptom which, however, may also be in *Chelidonium*.

Antimonium tartaricum has yellow skin, urine and vomit, in bilious pneumonia; stinging under right false ribs, frothy yellow tenacious sputum, rattling in chest with suffocation, fan-like motion of alæ nasi, great oppression, strong heart beat.

Kali carb. is a remedy often forgotten in pneumonia. It is not indicated in the beginning, but later, when there is copious exudation into the lungs, with great rattling of mucus during the cough. The symptoms are worse toward two or three o'clock in the morning. The expectoration contains little globules of pus. There may even be cyanotic symptoms with puffiness of the upper eyelids.

LECTURE XXVIII.
CUCURBITACEÆ.

Cucurbitaceæ.
1. Colocynthis cucumis.
2. Bryonia alba.
3. Citrullus (Water-melon). The seeds are diuretic.
4. Cucurbita (Squash).
5. Momordica balsamina.—Flatulency.
6. Elaterium momordica.—Bowels and fever.

TO-DAY we begin our study of the *Cucurbitaceæ.* This order gives us some six or eight drugs, and also some edible fruits. Among the latter are the water-melon, canteloupe, and cucumber. The seeds of some of these have diuretic properties, and those of the water-melon, pumpkin and squash have been used as a cure for worms.

Of the medicinal substances obtained from this order we may say that they all act prominently on the alimentary tract. They seem to have in common a cathartic action. They probably act paralyzingly on the vaso-motor nerves of the abdomen. They produce griping pains, gushing watery diarrhœa. This last symptom is most prominent under *Elaterium.*

Let us now enumerate these medicines. Fifth on the list is the *Momordica balsamina;* of this we have but one characteristic symptom, and that is accumulation of flatus in the splenic flexure of the colon, precisely like *Lycopodium.* It is a very convenient thing to know this. For instance, if, during the course of a more or less chronic disease, this one symptom becomes very annoying, and you do not want to destroy the action of the drug you are giving, you simply interpolate a dose of *Momordica,* which removes the symptom and enables you to go on with the treatment as before.

Elaterium, another member of the order, has been used principally in our school of medicine, in a peculiar form of diarrhœa. Like the *Cucurbitaceæ*, it acts powerfully on the alimentary tract, producing a sudden and enormous effusion of serum into the bowels. Thus it causes a watery diarrhœa, the stools flowing out very profusely. The characteristic symptom of the drug, and the one which will lead you to its selection in cholera infantum, is watery stools of an olive-green color, coming out with a gush, with cutting pains in the abdomen. Thus, you see, it is comparable with *Croton tiglium, Podophyllum, Veratrum album*, and remedies of that type.

It is readily distinguished from *Croton tiglium*, which is adapted to a profuse, yellow, watery stool, which is provoked every time the patient eats and drinks.

Podophyllum has, as you all know, the morning aggravation to distinguish it.

The remaining medicines belonging to the *Cucurbitaceæ* are the *Citrullus*, or water-melon; the *Cucurbita*, or squash, the seeds of which, as well as those of the pumpkin, have been used for tænia; the *Colocynth*, and the *Bryonia alba;* the last two being drugs of great importance, we shall proceed to their consideration *in extenso*.

COLOCYNTHIS CUCUMIS.

Colocynthis.
1. Nerves. { Neuralgia. Cramp.
2. Bowels.
3. Urine.
4. Gout.

The *Colocynthis cucumis* furnishes us with a gourd about the size of an orange with a smooth marbled green surface. When dried it appears of a brownish color. It is not indigenous to this country, but is imported from Syria and Turkey. Often, however, it is found in the market, peeled and dried, looking like a pithy ball, full of seeds and very light in weight. It is inodorous, but it has an intensely bitter taste.

Like the other members of this group, *Colocynth* causes violent intestinal irritation, first of watery evacuations and later of mucus and blood. The pains are atrocious; griping, cutting, etc. But this is not all. The drug also affects the nervous system powerfully, whence comes its beneficial effects in the treatment of various neuralgias. (In its neurotic symptoms, *Colocynth* is closely allied to *Dioscorea villosa*).

Furthermore, this remedy so long restricted to the relief of colic alone, has lately wrought cures in certain deep-seated ovarian diseases, as ovarian tumors. *Colocynth* acts directly on the ovaries, and also upon the epididymis. It is a mistake to assert, as was done formerly, that it can cause no inflammatory action; for in a case of poisoning, the autopsy revealed freshly-glued intestines, thus showing an inflammatory exudate. It is indicated in affections of the ovaries by stitching pains as from a needle deep in the right ovarian region, and crampy pains relieved by bending over or from pressure.

Two cases of ovarian tumor have been reported as cured by *Colocynth* on these symptoms.

I remember having cured a lady of ovarian colic from which she had suffered for three years, with *Colocynth*. The pains in this case were of a griping character and were relieved by bending double. There were no organic changes present.

Now let us examine the action of *Colocynth* on the abdomen and its contents with the concomitant symptoms: persistent bitter taste; violent thirst; empty eructations; nausea; vomiting of a bitter fluid or of food; griping pains which force him to bend double or to press firmly against the abdomen. This griping is the well-known key-note of the drug, and it is indicatory whether it be of local origin or reflex, whether arising from flatus, undigested food, or cold; or whether resulting from violent emotions, as in what has been termed "nervous colic." The stools may be fluid, copious, fæcal, flatulent and papescent; or slimy and bloody and preceded by severe tenesmus; but in every case there is this griping which more often precedes the stool and is relieved afterward, although sometimes it continues after stool. These evacuations are provoked by the slightest food or drink, as is also the pain. In some instances the griping develops into cutting, stabbing pains, which spread all over the abdomen and down into the pelvis. They are relieved by the emission of flatus or by stool. The pressure of flatus may incommode the bladder, relief, however, instantly following borborygmi. The urine is fœtid and deposits a mucous sediment.

We shall now compare *Colocynth* with some of its concordant remedies.

In the bad effects of anger, *Colocynth* is closely allied to *Chamomilla* and *Staphisagria*, and more remotely, to *Causticum*. It resembles *Chamomilla* in the violence of its emotions. Both drugs may be used in children when violent emotions produce cramps and even bilious stools. *Chamomilla* differs from *Colocynth* in the violence of its congestive symptoms, hot sweat on the head, etc. The characteristic *Chamomilla* temperament also helps you to decide.

Staphisagria is sometimes to be substituted for *Colocynth* in the effects of violent emotion in women and children when the violent abdominal cramps fail to yield to the latter remedy.

In its abdominal and gastro-enteric symptoms you should compare it with *Aconite, Veratrum album, Bovista, Croton tiglium, Elaterium*, and *Mercurius*.

Veratrum album has abdominal pains forcing the patient to bend double, but he must walk about for relief. He also has cold sweat on the forehead. It is especially suitable in ileus or intussusception of the bowels.

The colic of *Bovista* finds relief from bending double and after eating. The urine is red.

Croton tiglium has griping pains with profuse watery diarrhœa. The stools are yellowish, brownish or green in color and profuse, coming out with a gush, like water from a hydrant. They are aggravated after nursing or eating.

As shown by the symptoms, *Colocynth* is a remedy sometimes needed in summer complaint and in dysentery. It differs from *Croton tiglium*, which has stools whenever the patient eats or drinks, in that the latter has movements which are profuse and watery, and gushing like water from a hydrant. *Elaterium* again changes the picture by producing olive-green stools, profuse and gushing. *Croton tig.*, it is true, causes green stools, but they are a brownish green.

Colocynth differs from *Mercurius* because in the former the tenesmus, etc., cease after stool. It differs from *Nux vomica* also, for although the pain ceases after stool in *Nux*, the movements are scanty and there is frequent ineffectual urging.

The griping already referred to is not, in *Colocynth*, confined to the intestinal tract. We may confidently employ the remedy when the griping involves the bladder in some forms of strangury or of spasm of that viscus, and also in menstrual colic, whether uterine or ovarian. All that is requisite is that the nervous element should predominate over the inflammatory, with the relief from bending double and from firm external pressure.

Transferring this action of the drug upon the sympathetic to the "voluntary system," or cerebro-spinal system, we find symptoms like the following: left-sided tearing crampy pains after vexation or mortified feelings; boring, tearing pains in the head, boring stitches, sharp cutting pains in the eyeballs and extending thence up into the head; worse at rest and on stooping, and better from firm pressure and from walking; eye, on stooping, feels as if it would fall out; profuse acrid tears. These symptoms suggest *Colocynth* as a remedy in gouty and bilious headaches, and also in the intense pains of iritis, ciliary neuralgia and glaucoma.

He we may compare *Chamomilla*, *Cedron*, *Spigelia* and *Prunus spinosa*.

Chamomilla also has left-sided tearing headache from anger, biliousness, etc., but it has more red face, hot sweat, etc.

Cedron has periodical pains about the eyes; it is usually, however, supra orbital, and it may be of malarial origin.

Spigelia is very similar to *Colocynth*. The eye feels too large; the pains are stabbing, tearing and radiating; they are aggravated by pressure and motion; *Colocynth* finding relief by walking in a warm room, and on pressure.

Prunus spinosa has more crushing pain; a feeling as if the parts were pressed asunder, or violent bursting pain shooting back to the occiput.

Colocynth has proved useful in hip-disease, especially of the right side; dull stitches during walking, must stand still; followed by heaviness and insensibility of the affected parts; crampy pain as though the parts were screwed in a vise; lies on the affected side with the knee drawn up.

In studying these symptoms we also see the application of the drug to sciatica; pains extending down the sciatic nerve to the knee or even to the heel, aggravated by any motion. The attacks of pain are followed by numbness of the whole limb and partial paralysis. If the case is of long continuance, the nutrition of the limb is deficient. Sometimes the cramps in the leg are so severe that the patient feels as if the whole leg were fastened down by iron bands. The pains are usually worse at night.

Gnaphalium is very similar to *Colocynth* in sciatica. It has intense neuralgic pains along the course of the sciatic nerve, alternating with numbness.

In cramps of the muscles you should compare *Colocynth*, *Nux vomica*, *Veratrum album* and *Cholos terrapinæ*. I know of no remedy better adapted to simple cramps in the muscles than the last named in this list.

In rheumatism, *Colocynth* may be useful, especially for the stiffness of the joints following the acute disease.

If, however, there are concretions in the joints, you should think of *Causticum* and *Guaiacum*.

Guided by its constrictive qualities, physicians have used *Colocynth* in paraphimosis.

Colocynth is antidoted by *Coffee*, *Camphor* and *Staphisagria*.

LECTURE XXIX.
BRYONIA ALBA.

Bryonia.
1. Blood.
2. Serous Membranes.
3. Muscles.
4. Skin.
   a. Rash; Measles.
   b. Scarlatina.
   c. Suppressed eruptions.
5. Mucous membranes.
6. Organs.

THERE are three species of *Bryonia*, but so nearly identical are they that Allen has classed them under one heading in his Encyclopædia. *Bryonia alba* is one of the oldest remedies in the homœopathic materia medica, and is one of the best proved. It grows plentifully in England and on the continent in Europe. The tincture is prepared from the roots. It is a polychrest, suitable to many kinds of disease. To give you all its symptoms, even all its characteristic symptoms, would take two or three hours of steady hard work. I will endeavor in the hour before us to explain the action of *Bryonia* so far that you may be able to apply the drug, and, as I have said before, supply the deficiencies at leisure.

We find *Bryonia* indicated first of all in changes in the blood; in changes affecting its quantity, its quality and its circulation. For example, it is indicated in febrile conditions; in fevers of an intermitting type, although not frequently; in those of a remitting type, very often; sometimes, too, in synochal fever; and also in rheumatic, gastric, bilious, traumatic and typhoid fevers, in all of which, gastric symptoms are prominent. The symptoms which characterize its fevers are in general these: there in an increased action of the heart, giving rise to a frequent hard tense pulse, very much as you find under *Aconite*. There is actually an increase in the force and power of the heart's action. This action is augmented by any movement of the body, consequently the patient is anxious to keep perfectly quiet.

Then you find that there is almost always intense headache with these fevers. This is usually of a dull throbbing character or there may be sharp stabbing pains in the head. This is almost always associated with sharp pains in or over the eyes. All of these parts are exquisitely sensitive to the least motion. The patient will avoid moving the eyes, for instance, because it aggravates the pain. The least attempt to raise the head from the pillow causes a feeling of faintness and nausea. The mouth is very dry and the tongue is coated in the milder forms of fever as, for instance, in the synochal fever or in the light gastric type of fever. The coating on the tongue is white, and is especially marked down the middle. The edges of the tongue may be perfectly clean.

As the fever grows in intensity, it approaches more a typhoid type. Bilious symptoms predominate. The white tongue becomes yellowish and is associated with a decidedly bitter taste in the mouth. There are splitting headache, tenderness over the epigastrium, with stitches, soreness, or tenderness in the right hypochondrium. As the typhoid symptoms increase, the tongue becomes more and more dry, but still maintains its coating. If the fever is of an intermittent type, you will always find the chill mixed with heat; that is, during the chill the head is hot, the cheeks are a deep red and there is a decided thirst, which is generally for large quantities of water at long intervals. In some cases it may be a continuous thirst. The pulse is hard, frequent and tense. The sweat is provoked by the least exertion and has either a sour or an oily odor.

In typhoid fever, *Bryonia* is indicated in the early stages and by the following symptoms : there is some confusion of the mind ; the sensorium is depressed but there are no perversions of the senses. During sleep there is delirium, which is usually of a mild character. On closing his eyes for sleep, he thinks he sees persons who are not present. On opening them, he is surprised to find that he is mistaken.

Sometimes this delirium is accompanied or preceded by irritability. The speech is hasty, as you find under *Belladonna*. As the disease increases, some little heaviness almost approaching stupor accompanies sleep. The patient has dreams, which have for their subject the occupation of the day. Frequently with this delirium, the patient suffers from an agonizing headache. This is usually frontal. If the patient is able to describe it to you, he will tell you that his head feels as if it would burst. No better term than "splitting headache" could be used to describe it. It is congestive in its character. The face is usually flushed and of a deep red color. This is intensified like all the other symptoms of the drug, by any motion of the head, and is often accompanied by nose-bleed. The epistaxis is particularly liable to come on at three or four o'clock in the morning, and is frequently preceded by a sense of fulness in the head. In very severe cases, you will notice that the patient puts his hand to his head as if there were some pain there, and his face is expressive of pain. Yet so stupid is he, that he makes no complaint other than that expressed by these automatic movements. Another symptom to be noted in these typhoid fevers, is the dryness of the mucous membranes, especially those of the mouth and stomach. This is the result of deficient secretion. In no case is the condition more apparent than in typhoid states. The mouth is dry, as I have already intimated, and yet there may be no thirst. If there is thirst it seems to have the character I mentioned in speaking of intermittent fever. The patient drinks large quantities but not very frequently. After drinking water or while attempting to sit up, the patient has a deathly nauseated feeling and sometimes even vomits. At other times he complains of a heavy pressure in the stomach, as if a stone were lying there. This symptom is no doubt due to the same pathological condition we found in the mucous membrane of the mouth. The secretion of gastric juice is deficient, consequently food lies undigested in the stomach. When *Bryonia* is called for the bowels are usually constipated. When they do move, the stools are large, hard and dry, and are either brown or black in color. They are expelled with difficulty owing to the atony of the rectum. Sometimes in well-advanced cases of typhoid fever, you will find soft, mushy stools, calling for *Bryonia*. There is a symptom which sometimes accompanies typhoid fever at about the end of the first week of the fully developed fever, and that is a form of delirium in which the patient expresses a continual "desire to go home." He imagines that he is not at home and longs to be taken there in order to be properly cared for. This symptom is a strong indication for *Bryonia*, and frequently disappears after two or three doses of the remedy.

In these febrile conditions, it is necessary to place *Bryonia* in its proper relations with its concordant remedies. First of all *Aconite*. *Aconite* bears an intimate relation to *Bryonia* in all these types of fever except gastric, intermittent and typhoid fevers. *Aconite* has not in its totality any special relation to any of these, however incorrectly it may be given to lessen the temperature. The symptomatology of *Aconite* is opposed in every respect to that of typhoid fever. In gastric fever, it may be given in the beginning when there is the full pulse, hot and dry skin and restlessness, indicating that drug; but as the fever advances, it is then not indicated unless there are bilious complications. Then it is an all-sufficient remedy. The distinctions that you are to make between *Aconite* and *Bryonia* are as follows: in the first place, they hold the relation of *Aconite* and *Bryonia* and not *Bryonia* and *Aconite;* that is to say, *Aconite* is given earlier in the case than is *Bryonia*. *Aconite* suits the hyperæmia, the congestion or even the chill which precedes an inflammatory fever. *Bryonia* is indicated later when *Aconite* fails. The mental symptoms of the two drugs are so distinct that you ought not to confuse them. *Aconite* demands that the mind be excited, that the patient be restless, tossing about the bed, full of fears. He imagines that he is going to die. The *Bryonia* patient may suffer just as much as the one to whom you would give *Aconite*, but he is perfectly quiet. He is quiet because motion aggravates his symptoms. Early in typhoid fever, and sometimes in rheumatic fever, you may have *Bryonia* indicated by this symptom: the patient is restless and tosses about the bed impelled by nervousness, and yet he is made worse by the motion. If there is anxiety in *Bryonia* it assumes more the form of apprehension; he fears that he will not have the wherewithal to live.

Still another remedy to be thought of in connection with *Bryonia* in these fevers is *Belladonna*, and particularly in the beginning of typhoid fever. Now there is really nothing in the symptomatology of *Belladonna* which would call for it in a well-advanced case of typhoid type of fever. Only in the beginning could you confuse it with *Bryonia*. In the first place it has erethism. Here you distinguish it by its delirium, which is of a violent character. The patient jerks his limbs and starts during sleep. He springs up from sleep in affright. As soon as he closes his eyes, he sees all sorts of objects and people, which disappear as soon as the eyes are opened. *Belladonna*, then, has more cerebral erethism, and more violence in its delirium than has *Bryonia*. With the *Belladonna* headache there are throbbing pains, and the patient may be obliged to sit up rather than keep perfectly quiet in order to obtain relief.

Another remedy to be compared with *Bryonia* is *Rhus tox*. This is often indicated in typhoid fever. You all know the historic fact that Hahnemann, during one of the war-epidemics of typhus, cured many cases with these two remedies. Since the days of Hahnemann, this use of these remedies has become universal. Remember, however, that they are not specifics. Each epidemic may so change in character as to require other remedies. *Rhus tox.* is indicated, when there is marked restlessness. The patient, first lying on one side, changes to the other. For a few moments, he feels better in his new position. Then he begins to ache and back he turns again. Like *Bryonia*, it has nose-bleed, when nose-bleed relieves the patient's symptoms, and the headache I described to you last month as "a sensation as though a board were strapped tightly across the forehead." There are rheumatic aching pains through the joints and muscles of the limbs. The tongue differs from that of *Bryonia*. It is brown and dry and even cracked, and has a red tip, also an excellent indication for *Sulphur*. With *Rhus tox.*, there is frequently diarrhœa from the very beginning. *Bryonia* usually has constipation.

I just referred to the symptom under *Belladonna*—"the patient sees persons and objects on closing the eyes; these disappear as soon as the eyes are opened." Both *Calcarea ostrearum* and *Cinchona* have this symptom. Under the latter remedy, however, it does not occur in typhoid fever, but after hæmorrhage.

Next, I wish to talk about the action of *Bryonia* on serous membranes. *Bryonia* acts powerfully on these, producing inflammation. Hence we are called upon to prescribe it when the meninges of the brain and spinal cord, the pleuræ and the peritoneum, and the synovial membranes are inflamed. The indications for *Bryonia* in these serous inflammations are particularly to be looked for after exudation has taken place. There are sharp stitching pains, worse from any motion. The fever may still be high or it may have been partially subdued by the remedy which preceded.

Comparing *Aconite* with *Bryonia* once more, you will see the same rule applicable here as before; *Bryonia* is indicated after and not before *Aconite*. Take for purpose of illustration a typical case of pleurisy. In the beginning of the disease when fever is high you select *Aconite*, but just as soon as the fever commences to decrease, and effusion begins, as indicated by the friction sounds, *Aconite* ceases to be of any benefit and *Bryonia* comes in as an all-sufficient remedy. It is customary with some physicians to give *Aconite* for the fever and *Bryonia* for the pleuritic trouble. But this is useless. *Bryonia* is adapted to the whole case. It has not the same restlessness which demands *Aconite*. The patient is quiet and is full of pain. He lies on the affected side. Why? Because by the pressure thus exerted on the ribs, he moves the affected parts less than he would were he lying on the sound side.

When the meninges of the brain are affected, *Bryonia* is a valuable drug, but here, except in some rare cases, it follows *Belladonna* rather than *Aconite*. *Belladonna* ceases to be the remedy in meningitis, whether tubercular or otherwise, when effusion within the ventricles or beneath the membranes commences. It then gives place to *Sulphur* in some cases, *Apis* in others, and *Bryonia* in still others. *Bryonia* is indicated when meningitis follows the suppression of some eruption, as that of scarlatina or measles. The child's face is pale, or else it is red and pale alternately, the tongue white. The child screams out suddenly as if it were in great pain, which it really is. These pains are of a sharp lancinating character and are especially manifested on moving the patient. There is marked squinting with one or both eyes. The bowels are usually constipated, the abdomen distended and the child has well-marked sensorial depression which seems to border on stupor. If you arouse the child and offer him drink, he takes it impetuously or hastily, just as under *Belladonna*. The latter remedy has more rolling of the head.

For the sake of convenience we shall next study the catarrhs of *Bryonia* and the effects of the drug on the lung structure. We find *Bryonia* indicated in nasal catarrh when there is either great dryness of the mucous membrane of the nose, with hoarseness, sneezing, or more frequently, when the discharge is thick and yellow. It is also indicated when the discharge has been of the character just indicated and has been suddenly suppressed. As a result, there is dull throbbing headache just over the frontal sinuses. *Bryonia*, however, is not often indicated in catarrhs without some stomach and bowel symptoms. The treatment of colds is a severe test of the skill of a physician. If you can successfully treat them, you must understand homœopathy well. They are the most difficult class of cases we have to contend with. There are two reasons for this. One is that the patients are constantly exposed, and the other is that they are not watched sufficiently closely. If you are given the opportunity to watch the cases carefully, so that you may prescribe as the indications change, you will cure promptly. *Lachesis* is also useful for suppressed coryza. But it has not so marked an aggravation from motion; nor has it the yellow discharge. *Aconite* should be given in cases where the suppression is due to dry cold winds, and there is red face, fever, etc. *China* comes in with headache worse from the least draught of air and better from pressure.

We may also use *Bryonia* in pneumonia. The type of the disease in which it is indicated is in the true croupous form. Just as we found *Bryonia* indicated in pleurisy with effusion, so is it of use in pneumonia after the croupous exudation has taken place. Usually when it is called for there is also some pleuritis, hence it is applicable to pleuro-pneumonia. It is not indicated in the beginning of the disease because the exudation does not occur in that stage. It is indicated after *Aconite*, with the following easily understood condition. The fever still continues, but the skin is not so hot, the face so red and the patient so restless as when *Aconite* was indicated. The patient is more pacific, and his face and whole demeanor are expressive of anxiety. I would have you discriminate between this condition and that calling for *Aconite*. It is not so much the mental anxiety that *Aconite* pictures as it is an expression of pulmonary oppression. That you *must* remember. The cough which under *Aconite* was of a dry teasing character, with frothy sputa, perhaps still remains troublesome, but it is looser and more moist. There is very little expectoration yet, but what little there is, is either yellowish or streaked with blood. Owing to the accompanying inflammation of the pleura, sharp pleuritic stitches are felt in the chest. They are worse on the left side. The patient complains of heavy pressure just over the sternum. The pulse is full, hard and tense. The urine is dark-red and scanty.

Still another remedy that ought to be thought of along with *Bryonia* in pneumonia is *Antimonium tartaricum*. It is indicated in pneumonia that begins as a bronchitis and extends downward. It is especially suited to cases that begin on the right side, and that have these sharp stitching pains, high fever, great oppression of the chest, as in *Bryonia*. But it is called for more in catarrhal than in croupous pneumonia. Mucous râles are heard distinctly in the chest. The colds of *Bryonia* if they begin in the nose tend downward.

Several remedies other than *Bryonia* have these pains in the chest-walls. *Gaultheria* has pleurodynia, with pain in the anterior mediastinum.

Ranunculus bulbosus is decidedly the best remedy for intercostal rheumatism; it has sharp, stitching pains, and a sore *spot* in the chest, and these are worse from any motion (even breathing), pressure, or change of temperature. The dyspnœa in these cases is sometimes distressing.

Arnica is sometimes of use when the sore and bruised feeling of the chest predominates.

Rhus radicans is called for in pleurodynia when the pains shoot into the shoulder.

Senega acts best in fat persons of lax fibre. It is useful in cold with stitches, soreness in the thoracic walls, sensation of tightness, and much mucus in the chest. There is hoarseness; the throat is so dry and sensitive that it hurts the patient to talk; the cough often ends with sneezing.

Rumex crispus has sharp, stitching or stinging pains through the left lung; it is indicated more in the early stages of phthisis. When the patient turns the left side feels sore.

Asclepias tuberosa has sharp stitches through the lower part of the left chest, worse from motion. *Kali carb.* has stitches irrespective of motion, worse 2 or 3 A. M.

Trifolium pratense has hoarseness and choking spells at night with the cough. The neck is stiff; there are cramps in the sterno-cleido-mastoid muscles which are relieved by heat and friction.

Actea racemosa has pleurodynia; worse on the right side, especially in nervous women.

In bronchitis, *Bryonia* is indicated with this same pressure over the sternum; the dyspnœa is great; the cough is dry, and seems to start from the stomach. Bursting pain in the head with every cough. Sometimes a little tenacious blood-streaked sputum is raised. The cough is worse after a meal, when it may even end in vomiting. During the cough the patient presses his hand against his side to relieve the stitching pain. The same symptoms will indicate this remedy in whooping cough. The child coughs immediately after a meal, vomits what it has eaten, then returns to the table.

Returning now to the action of *Bryonia* on the serous membranes, we find it producing synovitis. The affected joint is pale-red and tense. There is, of course, effusion into the synovial sac. There are sharp, stitching pains, aggravated by any motion. *Bryonia* is indicated in these cases whether the synovitis be of rheumatic or traumatic origin.

The nearest concordant remedy to *Bryonia* here is *Apis*, which is an excellent remedy for synovitis, particularly of the knee-joint. Sharp, lancinating, and stinging pains, and effusions into the joint, are further indications for the remedy. *Apis* seems to be preferable to

Bryonia when this synovitis is of scrofulous origin, or at least appears in a scrofulous constitution. *Apis* also has another kind of inflammation, which ends in the thickening of the serous sac and of the tissues and cartilages about the joints, giving you the well-known white swelling.

You should also remember *Sulphur* in these cases. This remedy supplements *Bryonia* and *Apis*, and urges them on when they fail to do their work.

We come next to the study of *Bryonia* in its action on the muscular system. It is one of the few drugs which produce a positive inflammation of the muscular substance; consequently you expect to find the drug of use in muscular rheumatism. The muscles are sore to the touch, and at times swollen, and, as you might expect, there is aggravation of the pains from the slightest motion. *Actea racemosa* also acts on the muscular substance itself.

Bryonia may also be indicated in articular rheumatism. We find that the fever is not very violent, and the pains and swelling either shift not at all or else very slowly. The local inflammation is violent; that is characteristic of *Bryonia*. The parts are very hot, and dark- or pale-red. The pulse in these cases is full and strong, and the tongue is either uniformly white or, more characteristically, dry and white down the centre. The bowels are constipated. It is needless for me to say that the pains are worse from motion.

The difference between *Bryonia* and *Rhus tox.* is principally this: *Rhus* is suitable for rheumatism after exposure to wet, especially when one is overheated and perspiring. Then, too, the *Rhus* patient finds relief from moving about. *Rhus* attacks the fibrous tissues, the sheaths of the muscles, *Bryonia* the muscular tissue itself.

The difference between *Ledum* and *Bryonia* may be described in this way: *Ledum* is useful for rheumatic or gouty inflammation of the great toe; instead of tending to copious effusion the effusion is scanty, and tends to harden into nodosities. In hot swelling of the hip and shoulder joints, *Ledum* should be remembered as more successful than *Bryonia*.

Actea spicata has a special affinity for the smaller joints. It has this characteristic: the patient goes out feeling tolerably comfortable, but as he walks the joints ache and even swell.

Viola odorata has a specific action on the right wrist.

Caulophyllum is especially suited to rheumatism of the phalangeal and metacarpal joints, particularly in females.

Sabina also affects the small joints; gouty nodes; pains worse in a warm room.

In *Colchicum* we have marked aggravation in the evening; the affected joints are swollen and dark red. It is especially useful in weak debilitated persons, or in those who, despite local rheumatic inflammation, exhibit general symptoms of torpor. The stomach is generally affected; nausea when smelling food. The urine is scanty and red, and burns in passing along the urethra. The pains are of a tearing or jerking character, and appear as if in the periosteum. The pains are superficial in summer and deep in winter. In metastasis of rheumatism to the heart, both remedies are to be studied.

Bryonia has great oppression under the sternum, worse from motion; sharp stitches in the cardiac region, pericardial effusion, with strong pulse. *Colchicum* has pericardial effusion, fulness and oppression while lying on the left side, compelling him to turn over. The pulse is small, weak, and accelerated. The *Colchicum* pains appear about the neck and shoulders, or in a small part of the body at a time, and then shift quickly.

Guaiacum is useful in chronic forms of rheumatism when the joints have become distorted by the concretions. It is also indicated in pleurisy during the second stage of phthisis with muco-purulent sputum.

Arctium lappa may also be compared with *Bryonia* in rheumatism. It cures soreness of the muscles, dull pains, all worse from motion; high-colored urine. All the provers were so weary and sleepy, they could not work.

Next we shall study the alimentary canal. We have already spoken of *Bryonia* here so frequently that its symptoms require but a passing notice. There are the dryness of the mucous lining throughout, the white coating of the tongue, the characteristic thirst, a feeling as though a stone or heavy weight were lying clogged in the stomach, the hard, dry, brown stool, passed with difficulty owing to the hardness of the fæcal matter, atony of the rectum, and intolerance of vegetable food. The symptoms are worse in summer. It seems that the *Bryonia* patient cannot tolerate the heat of the sun.

The liver also is affected. We find it congested, or even inflamed. The gastric symptoms just mentioned complicate the case. The peritoneum covering the liver is inflamed, consequently there are sharp stitches in the right hypochondrium, worse from any motion and better when lying on the right side. In jaundice from duodenal catarrh, you may give *Bryonia*, especially when the trouble has been brought on by a fit of anger. Although the patient appears hot, he complains of feeling chilly.

Chelidonium is an admirable remedy for symptoms very similar to those just enumerated. Sharp pains in the region of the liver, shooting in every direction, up into the chest, down into the abdomen; well-marked pain under the scapula, even going through the chest like a rivet; and diarrhœa with either clay-colored or yellowish stools. It differs from *Bryonia* particularly in the character of the stool, and the peculiar pain under the scapula.

Bryonia is also similar to *Kali carb.*, which is indicated in bilious affections when there are these sharp pains in the right hypochondrium, shooting up into the chest; often there is sharp pain, coming from the lower lobe of the right lung. The difference between these pains and those of *Bryonia* is that these are not necessarily made worse by motion.

Yucca filamentosa is an admirable remedy for biliousness, with pain going through the upper portion of the liver to the back. There is bad taste in the mouth; the stools are diarrhœic and contain an excess of bile. A great deal of flatus passes by the rectum.

Chamomilla, like *Bryonia*, is indicated in biliousness following anger. With *Bryonia* there is apt to be chilliness with the anger; with *Chamomilla* the patient gets hot and sweats.

Berberis vulgaris also has sharp stitching pains in the region of the liver; but the pains shoot downward from the tenth rib to the umbilicus.

The bowels, I have said, are usually constipated under *Bryonia*, but in some cases the reverse condition obtains. *Bryonia* is indicated in diarrhœa when the attacks are provoked by indulgence in vegetable foods or stewed fruits, and also by getting overheated in the summer time. The movements are especially worse in the morning after rising and beginning to move around, thus distinguishing them from those of *Sulphur* and making them similar to the stools of *Natrum sulph*. In other cases, the patient is seized with sudden griping pains, doubling him up, accompanied by copious pasty stools. Sometimes the stools are dark green, from admixture of bile. They have the odor of old cheese.

The mental symptoms of *Bryonia* have been pretty thoroughly described to you in speaking of typhoid fever. I will merely say here that the patients are irritable and easily angered. This condition is present with the bilious symptoms, with the headache, and with the dyspepsia—in fact, it is characteristic of the remedy.

The headache of *Bryonia*, I have also told you, is worse from any motion; even a movement of the eyeballs aggravates the pain. The pain begins in the occiput, or else in the forehead, going back into the occiput. It is worse when awaking in the morning, after violent fits of anger, and from stooping. Its exciting causes are exposure to heat, especially moist, hot, foggy air; taking cold; debauchery and rheumatism. Headache from ironing.

The nearest remedy that we have to *Bryonia* here is *Gelsemium*, which has headache with this soreness of the eyes on moving them.

Natrum mur has a headache which feels like the beating of little hammers, with aggravation on moving the head and eyes.

With the occipital headache of *Bryonia* we should also compare *Petroleum*, which has throbbing occipital headache.

Juglans cathartica has occipital headache with pains of a sharp character.

Carbo veg and *Nux vomica* have occipital pains with bilious attacks.

On the external head, we find *Bryonia* developing an oily perspiration with a sour odor.

A similar symptom referred to the face is found under *Natrum mur*.

Bryonia is a valuable remedy in diseases of the eyes, but not when the external coats of the eyes are affected. It is to be thought of for metastasis of rheumatism to the eyes. The pains are violent and shoot through the eyeball into the back of the head, or up toward the vertex. They are aggravated by any motion of the head or eyes. There is also a sensation of tension as if the eyeballs had been put on a stretch. *Antimonium tartaricum* also has metastasis of rheumatism to the eyes. Now you know, from what I have said, that *Bryonia* is indicated in inflammation of the serous membranes with effusion. *Bryonia* ought, both symptomatically and pathologically, to be a remedy in glaucoma. The tension of the eyeball is greatly increased. Hot tears flow from the eyes. Photophobia and diminution of vision are present.

Bryonia is useful after operations on the eye when burning pains and vomiting follow.

The toothache of *Bryonia* is of a rheumatic origin and comes from cold. You will frequently find it occurring in teeth showing no signs of decay, which would lead to the conclusion that it is the nerve which is affected. More than one tooth may be involved and relief is momentarily obtained by firm pressure of the head against the pillow, or by the application of cold.

Toothache in children from decayed teeth, with relief from the application of cold water, finds its best remedy in *Coffea*.

Kreosote has neuralgia of the face with burning pains increased by motion and by talking, especially in nervous, irritable persons whose teeth decay rapidly.

In aphthous sore mouth, *Bryonia* may be useful. The child seizes the nipple, but at once lets go and cries. When its mouth becomes moistened by the milk, however, it nurses well enough. We note here the characteristic dryness of the remedy.

The urine of *Bryonia* is dark, almost brownish red, without any deposit. This change in its appearance is due chiefly to excess of urochrome.

Bryonia has some action on the female genital organs. It is sometimes indicated in menstrual difficulties when the flow is dark red and profuse, but more especially is it useful when the normal flow has been suppressed and we have what has been termed vicarious menstruation.

Here you should compare *Pulsatilla* and *Phosphorus*, especially if the suppression of the flow produces hæmoptysis or hæmatemesis.

Senecio is to be thought of if the patient has cough with bloody expectoration.

Hamamelis, *Ustilago* and *Millefolium* come in for hæmatemesis.

Bryonia is indicated in the lying-in chamber. For years I have been accustomed to using it for the so-called milk fever. I consider it indicated here more often than any other remedy because the symptoms of this affection are those of *Bryonia*. The fever is not very marked, there is tension of the breast with headache, tearing in the limbs and the patient is weary and wants to keep still.

In threatening mammary abscess, *Bryonia* is indicated when there are sharp stitching pains, tension of the breast, and swelling of a pale red color.

In incipient mammary abscess you should compare first of all *Belladonna*, which is useful when the symptoms are violent; areas of redness spread out in radii from the central point of the inflammation.

Phytolacca is an excellent remedy when from the beginning the breasts show a tendency to cake. Especially is *Phytolacca* the remedy if suppuration threatens. When the child nurses, pain goes from the nipple all over the body, streaking up and down the spine. The flow of milk is apt to be excessive.

Phellandrium aquaticum is an excellent remedy when pains course along the milk-ducts between the acts of nursing.

Croton tiglium is to be selected when there is pain from the nipple through to the back when the child nurses, as though the nipple were being pulled by a string.

Bryonia should be remembered in measles. Here it is indicated principally by the tardy appearance of the rash. There is a hard, dry cough which makes the child cry. The little one doubles up as if to resist the tearing pain which the effort of coughing causes. There may be little or no expectoration. The eyes are inflamed. In other cases the eruption suddenly disappears and cerebral symptoms appear. The child is drowsy. Its face is pale and there is twitching of the muscles of the face, eyes and mouth. Any motion causes the child to scream with pain. In other cases instead of these cerebral symptoms you have inflammatory diseases of the chest, such as bronchitis or even pneumonia.

In scarlatina, *Bryonia* is not often indicated, but when it is, you find some one or all of these symptoms to guide you. The rash has not that smooth character observed under *Belladonna*. It is interspersed with a miliary rash. It comes out imperfectly and the chest symptoms and cerebral symptoms just mentioned are present. Now while all the senses are benumbed in these cases, there are no absolute hallucinations of the senses as under *Belladonna;* the patients do not hear voices talking to them as under *Anacardium;* they do not awaken from sleep clinging to those about them, as with *Stramonium* or *Cuprum*.

When an eruption has been suppressed and the brain is affected in consequence, you may also look to *Cuprum*, which is the remedy when the symptoms are violent. The child starts up during sleep. There are decided perversion of the senses, and the spasms characteristic of *Cuprum*.

Helleborus suits when the entire sensorial life is suspended and the child lies in a profound stupor.

Zincum is to be preferred if the child is too weak to develop an eruption. The rash comes out sparingly. The surface of the body is rather cool. The child lies in a stupor, gritting its teeth; it starts up during sleep. Dilated pupils, squinting and rolling of the eyes are observed, and there is marked fidgetiness of the feet.

Ipecac. is to be thought of when the chest is affected from the recession of the rash of measles, if there is difficulty in breathing, cough, etc.

Tartar emetic ought to be given in preference to *Bryonia* when the disease is variola.

Bryonia is complementary to *Alumina.*

It is antidoted by *Chamomilla, Nux vomica, Pulsatilla, Rhus tox.* and *Senega.*

It antidotes *Rhus tox., Rhus venenata* and *Chlorine.*

LECTURE XXX.

CONIFERÆ AND EUPHORBIACEÆ.

CONIFERÆ.

ABIES NIGRA.—Stomach.

SABINA JUNIPERUS.—Abortion.

PINUS SYLVESTRIS.—Infantile atrophy.

TEREBINTHINA.
- Kidneys, bladder, etc.
- Mucous membranes.
- Uterus.
- Typhoid states.
- Renal dropsy.

Compare *Arsenicum, Cantharis, Copaiva, Camphor, Phosphorus.*

PIX LIQUIDA.—Lung; Eruptions.

Compare *Anisum stellatum.*

THUJA.
- Nervous system.
- Sycosis.
- Syphilis.
- Variola.
- Marasmus.

Compare *Pulsatilla, Kali bichromicum, Spigelia, Mercurius, Nitric acid, Natrum sulph., Euphrasia, Staphisagria.*

The large order of *Coniferæ* or cone-bearing plants is the subject for our study to-day. From this order we obtain the different varieties of pine, hemlock, and spruce from which the various preparations of turpentine have been obtained. The principal remedies of this group you will see in the schedule on the board. They are *Abies nigra*, or black spruce; *Sabina juniperus*, one form of the juniper, from which the oil of savin, a well-known remedy for the production of abortion, has been taken; *Pinus sylvestris*, a variety of the pine; *Terebinthina*, or turpentine, obtained from many of the pines; *Pix liquida*, or pitch; and *Thuja occidentalis*, the arbor vitæ or tree of life.

Abies Nigra.

This remedy is not an important one, but I cannot forbear mentioning one of its symptoms—one, too, that has been frequently confirmed. I refer to the symptom occurring in dyspepsia, which the patient describes as a feeling as though he had swallowed some indigestible substance which had stuck at the cardiac orifice of the stomach. This is the main symptom and the keynote of the drug. There are also present the low-spiritedness, the hypochondriasis, and the constipation incident to dyspepsia.

Sabina Juniperus.

I am obliged also to slight *Sabina juniperus* for want of time. You know of it as a remedy in the treatment of uterine disease, and as a drug to prevent impending abortion, especially at the third month. The symptoms indicating it here you will learn from the Professor of Gynæcology, Dr. Betts. I shall only say in brief that they are: pain which commences in the small of the back and goes around and through the pubes; drawing-aching pains—which are so common in abortion: and pains which run through from the sacrum to the pubes. This last symptom is very characteristic of *Sabina*. In addition to these pains there is a bright-red clotted flow of blood, increasing with every motion. You may also use *Sabina* in post-partum hæmorrhage when the placenta is retained and the symptoms just mentioned are present.

Terebinthina.

Terebinthina, or turpentine, is a drug which has been much abused by old-school physicians, and has therefore been greatly neglected by homœopaths. In the revulsion from the misconceptions of the old-school physicians, we often avoid a drug altogether. All that I have time to say concerning *Terebinthina* is that its main action is on the kidneys and bladder. When you find metritis, peritonitis, pneumonia, hydrocephalus, typhoid fever, scarlatina, or, in fact, any serious disease of low type, with the following renal symptoms, *Terebinthina* comes in as your remedy: dull pains in the region of the kidneys; burning in the kidneys; pains extending from the kidneys down through the ureters; burning during micturition; strangury and albuminous urine. The urine is characteristically dark, cloudy and smoky-looking, as though it contained decomposed blood, which in fact it does. It also has the odor of violets like *Cantharis, Copaiva, Osmium* and *Selenium*. The real pathological condition of the kidneys in these cases is not one of acute Bright's disease, nor one of croupous formation in the kidneys, but one of renal congestion, with oozing of blood into the pelvis of the kidney. The condition is not infrequently the result of living in damp dwellings. When the above urinary symptoms are present, you may give *Terebinthina* with confidence, no matter what the patient's disease may be.

Other symptoms characterizing these low states are feeble heart in pneumonia; intense burning in the uterus in metritis with typhoidal symptoms; burning in peritonitis; and tympany from paresis of the bowels.

Terebinthina often acts powerfully on mucous membranes. It produces burning in the air-passages, with thin expectoration, very difficult of detachment. It also is occasionally of use in humid asthma with the urinary concomitants of the drug.

Worms have been removed by *Terebinthina*. The child starts and screams out in sleep; picks at its nose; has a choking sensation and a dry, hacking cough; there may even be convulsions.

Alcohol favors the action of *Terebinthina*.

Pix Liquida.

Pix liquida has but two symptoms worthy of note. One proceeds from its action on the lungs. You may give it with confidence in suppurative processes affecting the left lung, with pain at the third left costal cartilage.

Anisum stellatum has the same pain, but here it is referred to the right third costal cartilage. The above symptoms of *Pix* and *Anisum* have stood the test of experience over and over again.

Remedies having pains in the left side of the chest, which are here worthy of mention, are: *Myrtus communis* (upper part), *Sumbul* (many pains), *Fluoric acid, Oxalic acid, Actea rac.* (under the nipple), *Lilium tigrinum* (through the heart or through the mamma to the back), *Kali carb., Sulphur* (through to the back), *Sarsaparilla* (from the back through to the left chest), *Pulsatilla nuttaliana* (on the left side, under the arm near the back), *Guaiacum* (stitches at about the upper three ribs; purulent sputum), *Theridion, Phosphorus* and *Silicea*.

Pix liquida also causes an eruption, especially on the dorsum of the hands, which cracks, itches intolerably at night, and bleeds when scratched.

Thuja Occidentalis.

The remainder of the hour will be devoted to *Thuja occidentalis*, the last member of this group, and we shall consider it fully. The history of the introduction of this drug is somewhat novel. Hahnemann received in his office on one occasion a patient who complained of some symptoms about the genital organs, which were, to say the least, suspicious. There was a thick purulent discharge from the urethra, with burning on urinating. There were also small pimples, attended with itching, about the glans penis, and some swelling of the parts. Hahnemann charged his patient with having contracted gonorrhœa. This was stoutly denied by the patient, who, by the way, was a theological student. However, on the principle prevailing in every court to consider a man innocent until he has been proved guilty, Hahnemann determined to give the young man no medicine, and directed him to report in three days. At the end of that time he came back well. Hahnemann was puzzled. He questioned the patient closely, but found no cause. Then the young gentleman remembered that as he sauntered through a garden a few days before he picked some leaves of the arbor vitæ and chewed them. This led Hahnemann to investigate the properties of *Thuja*, when he discovered that the theological student had told the truth.

Do not think, however, that *Thuja* has no other field of usefulness than in sycosis, because it has several interesting actions on the system, especially upon the nervous system. While you must remember that these nervous phenomena may rest on a sycotic basis, you should also know that they may exist without the presence of any such taint. Grauvogl tells us of the "hydrogenoid constitution," in which the poison of gonorrhœa acts most virulently. If one with this constitution contracts the disease, he is more apt to retain the constitutional taint. This constitution, we are told, may exist without any sycotic taint. In those who are afflicted with it, vaccination is most injurious. When you find a patient suffering from vaccination, the virus being pure, you may set that patient down as belonging to the hydrogenoid constitution. We have two antidotes to these bad effects of vaccination: *Silicea*, which suits almost any of the symptoms, even convulsions, and *Thuja*, which is especially suitable if diarrhœa results and the vaccine pustules are very large. It was on account of this last-named symptom that Bœnninghausen recommended *Thuja* in variola. He gave it just as soon as the vesicles began to turn into pustules, and he claimed to have thereby prevented scarring.

But to return to a study of the action of *Thuja* on the nervous system. The patient exhibits a manner which is hurried and impatient. He talks hurriedly. His movements are unnaturally active and hurried. His temper is easily aroused. Even trifles make him angry and excited. Some of the gentler emotions also are awakened. For instance, music causes weeping and trembling of the feet. There is a form of insanity or mania in which you will find *Thuja* the only remedy, and that is one in which there is the fixed idea in the patient's mind, that he is made of some brittle substance, and he will not permit himself to be approached for fear that he will be broken. This is not the *Antimonium crudum* condition. It is not an irritability of mind that drives any one and every one away, and will not permit one's self to be even looked at, but it is a symptom that comes from some fixed delusion as to his bodily composition.

Or he thinks that his body and soul are separated or that a stranger is by his side.

Another singular characteristic of *Thuja* is one that was first met with in an old maid. She experienced a sensation as though a living child were in the abdomen. This symptom has suggested the use of *Thuja* in pseudocyesis.

Accompanying these symptoms of the nervous system indicating the drug in melancholia, and other forms of insanity, we find many disturbances in the circulation, such as ebullitions of blood, pulsations all over the body, and præcordial anxiety. The action of the drug on the nervous system is further shown in various forms of neuralgia. Thus it is indicated in the form of headache known as clavus, in which the patient has a sensation as though a nail were being driven into the vertex, or into one of the frontal eminences. *Thuja* may also be used in neuralgia affecting either the head or the face or both. The pains are of an intense stabbing character, and are well-nigh unbearable. If the patient sits up these pains almost drive him to distraction; they may even produce unconsciousness. He therefore maintains the horizontal posture. The pains seem to begin about the malar bones and eyes, and go back toward the head. They may be due to a suppressed eruption. This neuralgia reminds us of *Mezereum* and *Spigelia*, but we distinguish it from that of the last-named remedy by the direction of the symptoms; in *Spigelia* the pains begin in the back of the head and come forward.

After detailing to you these unique nervous symptoms, I pass to the application of the drug to sycosis. Remember that these nervous phenomena may or may not have a sycotic basis. *Thuja* is a remedy which tends to alter the sycotic constitution, to change the soil in which this poison grows. There are two elements which make up disease; they are the elements of the disease itself, and those of the constitution in which it grows. The sycotic constitution to which I have referred modifies every subsequent disease, and that, too, whether there be any urethral discharge or not.

In gonorrhœa you may use *Thuja* when the discharge is thin and greenish, and there is scalding pain during urination. After urination there is a sensation as if a few drops of urine ran down the urethra. Warts or condylomata appear on the genitals, at the anus, about the perineum and upon mucous surfaces. I have treated one case in which the wart formed on the centre of the tongue. This was speedily cured by *Thuja*. These warts may have a seedy look, or they may be of a cauliflower shape. Cauliflower-like excrescences are especially apt to grow from the cervix uteri. In other cases, these warts are moist and ooze a glutinous, foul-smelling fluid. Sometimes we find ulcers about the genitals, and these have very much the appearance of chancroids; they have a dirty yellow base with hard edges. Very characteristic are such ulcers if they seem to have originated from warts. Sometimes we note fissures, or furrows about the anus, on the perineum, scrotum or glans penis. These are deep and are covered with pus. There is sweetish-smelling sweat about the genital organs. The inner sides of the thighs are red and excoriated. The testicles are often involved, one or the other of these organs being drawn up in consequence of contraction of the cremaster muscle. The testicle is swollen and aches as if bruised. There may be balanorrhœa, that is, a purulent inflammation of the inner surface of the prepuce and of the sulcus behind the corona glandis.

In the female organs we find the cauliflower excrescences which I have already mentioned; fungous growths of venereal origin about the genitals; and condylomata with thick green leucorrhœa, corresponding to the thin greenish-yellow gleet of the male.

Again, if a gonorrhœa be checked by injection, by cold or by any other influence, constitutional symptoms may arise which call for *Thuja*. Especially is this remedy indicated if the complication be articular rheumatism, or prostatitis; the hair dries and splits at the ends; the scalp becomes scaly and covered with dry scurf; iritis appears, accompanied by condylomata on the iris; the eyelids are inflamed and become warty. Ozæna may be an additional complication, with a discharge that is thick and green. The teeth decay at the root, the crowns being apparently normal. Other symptoms worthy of mention are pustules, which have considerable resemblance to those of *Tartar emetic;* chilliness during urination; nervousness and restlessness during both night and day; otorrhœa; foul breath; hoarseness.

Thuja has the singular property of *softening hard tissue, tissue naturally hard, as the nails.* Herein lies the explanation of the ability of the drug to remove warts; it softens them and causes their absorption.

The drug has a specific action in sclerotitis.

The cough of *Thuja* is worse during the day; seldom occurring at night. The sputum is like old cheese.

Thuja is a remedy in scrofula and marasmus. Such cases are not necessarily sycotic, but they have just such constitutions as favor the growth of this taint. The stools are watery, gurgling, forcibly expelled, and are daily worse after breakfast, and accompanied by much loud flatus; tinea ciliaris, with dry bran-like scales; irregular and imperfect eyelashes; children are pot-bellied; they scream on awaking, and are a long time becoming fully awake.

I propose now to devote the remaining moments of the hour to a consideration of the remedies similar to *Thuja* in the above-mentioned conditions. One of the nearest allies to *Thuja* is *Pulsatilla*, in that it has ozæna with thick greenish discharge. In gleet, also, the remedies have the same discharge, it being thicker under *Pulsatilla*. Then, too, gonorrhœal rheumatism, orchitis and prostatitis, are just as characteristic of *Pulsatilla* as of *Thuja.*

Kali bichromicum is useful in ozæna occurring in sycotic constitutions, the discharge being yellowish or more often greenish. The nose feels unnaturally dry. Dark greenish plugs are hawked from the post-nasal space.

Nitric acid resembles *Thuja* in the condylomata or warts. It is also of use in ulcers, when they are ragged in outline, and in enlarged tonsils, whether these affections be of syphilitic or of gonorrhœal origin. *Nitric acid* also has moist fissure of the anus (which is also present, as you know, under *Thuja*), balanorrhœa and thin greenish leucorrhœa. *Nitric acid* has, however, to distinguish it from *Thuja*, more aching pains in the bones, especially in those localities devoid of muscular tissue covering, as along the tibia, and over the sternum and cranium.

Staphisagria suits long filiform condylomata. The system generally is depraved, as shown in the sallowness of the face, the dark rings about the eyes, the spongy gums, the yellowish-white skin, and the great debility. It is especially indicated when there has been previous mercurialization. There is generally induration of one or the other testicle.

I would like to mention here *Jacaranda*. This is a South American plant that was first proved by Muir. It is an excellent remedy for balanorrhœa, and for red chancroid or chancroid-like sores about the penis. It has been proved conclusively to be a good remedy.

Corallium rubrum is an excellent remedy for chancre-like sores that are very red.

Mercurius resembles *Thuja* in the iritis, the balanorrhœa, the green urethral discharge and the rheumatism. The difference lies here: in *Mercurius*, sweating aggravates the symptoms as does also the warmth of the bed. *Thuja* has a symptom which is not often met with, but which saved a life for Bœnninghausen, namely, sweat upon uncovered parts of the body only.

Sabina is useful for condylomata which itch and burn, especially in women.

Euphrasia is called for when the condylomata are large and look like a cock's comb.

Cinnabaris is an excellent remedy when there is a combination of syphilis and sycosis. The figwarts are apt to be fan-shaped. There is a great deal of itching, especially about the joints.

The complement of *Thuja* in these sycotic troubles is *Natrum sulph*.

Sarsaparilla is indicated when there is a sycotic eruption consisting of little spots scarcely raised above the skin, often scaling a little, but looking like the roseola of syphilis, itching intolerably, and developing an aggravation in the spring; also when a moist eruption appears on the scalp, the pus from which causes inflammation of any part which it touches. Sycotic headache is found under *Sarsaparilla*. The pain begins in the back of the head, and comes forward and settles at the root of the nose, with swelling of the nose; moist eruption about the genitals, or between the scrotum and the thighs.

Petroleum also has this last-named symptom; and in addition another, namely, membranous shreds about the anus.

EUPHORBIACEÆ.

The members of the *Euphorbiaceæ* contain an acrid principle which in some cases is oily in character, in others resinous; in the latter case, the juice escapes from the plant as a milky fluid, which dries into a gum. These oils or gums have two properties. If applied to the skin they produce redness and vesication. The vesicles fill with yellowish-white serum, and may even suppurate and form scabs of a honey color. They all act more or less intensely as purgatives, producing a watery diarrhœa, associated with colic, tenesmus, flatulence, burning, nausea and vomiting. The medicines which we derive from this order are *Croton tiglium*, *Jatropha curcas*, *Yucca filamentosa*, *Euphorbium officinarum*, *Euphorbia corollata*, *Mercurialis perennis*, *Hippomane mancinella* and *Ricinus communis*.

CROTON TIGLIUM, ETC.

This remedy produces a diarrhœa with yellowish watery stool pouring out like water from a hydrant, often associated with nausea and vomiting. This nausea is of a very aggravating character, and is attended by faintness and loss of sight. Colic appears and is better from warm drinks. The stool returns with any effort to eat or drink.

The nearest analogue to *Croton tig.* is *Jatropha curcas*, which produces a perfect picture of cholera Asiatica, with great prostration and simultaneous vomiting and purging. The vomited matters look like rice-water or the white of an egg. There are also cramps in the calves and coldness of the body.

The next similar drug is the *Euphorbia corollata*. This produces vomiting and purging, just like the previous remedy, with cold sweat all over the body. It has more markedly than the other members of this group a peculiar mental state—the patient wants to die.

Cascarilla or Sweet-bark has abdominal symptoms relieved by warm drinks, but it seems to be useful in a different class of cases from the foregoing remedies. We use it when there are knotty stools covered with mucus, like *Graphites*, and associated with colic and burning just like the other remedies of the group. *Cascarilla* also has frequent pale red hæmorrhages from the bowels. These hæmorrhages do not consist of a simple oozing of blood, such as often follows a stool when hæmorrhoids are present, nor is it a hæmorrhage from the bowels from hepatic disease, but it comes from disease of the blood-vessels.

Yucca filamentosa has a predominance of the bilious symptoms over the gastric and intestinal. It has frontal or temporal headaches, frequent flushing of the face, yellow or sallow face, tongue coated yellow or yellowish-white and taking the imprint of the teeth. There are also dull aching about the centre of the liver, poor appetite, distended abdomen which is sensitive to the touch, colic or colicky pains, tenesmus with frequent passage of flatus, and frequent watery or yellowish-brown stools.

Now let us study the action of these remedies on the skin. When *Croton tiglium* is applied to the skin it produces an erythema, soon followed by a group of vesicles which are almost confluent, and which burn and itch intolerably. If the action of the drug is allowed to continue, these vesicles form a yellowish scab much resembling that of milk-crust, in which disease it may be indicated, especially when the bowel symptoms suit.

Hippomane mancinella was first proved by Dr. Muir. Its power of producing vesicles has been utilized in scarlet fever. Its symptoms are these: delirium; sore throat, with inability to swallow on account of the constriction in the throat and œsophagus; burning of the eyes, made worse by closing the lids.

Yucca produces an erythematous redness of the skin. In two provers it produced a burning and swelling of the prepuce with redness of the meatus urinarius. An examination of allopathic text-books will show you that *Yucca* has been recommended for gonorrhœa.

Euphorbium officinarum differs somewhat from the others. Like them, it produces an erythematous and vesicular eruption. Its chief value, however, arises from its action on the bones. It is used in diseases of these structures with burning pains, especially after the abuse of mercury.

Ricinus communis, or Castor oil, has the effect of increasing the quantity of milk in nursing women. It is here similar to *Urtica urens*, which is an excellent remedy for absence of milk after confinement. Castor oil, when abused, is antidoted by two remedies, *Bryonia* and *Nux vomica*. *Bryonia* is useful on account of a specific relation to the symptoms of *Ricinus*, and *Nux* on account of its relation to drastic remedies in general.

LECTURE XXXI.

RANUNCULACEÆ.

Ranunculaceæ.
{
Aconitum napellus.
Helleborus niger.
Clematis erecta.
Pæonia.
Pulsatilla.
Hydrastis Canadensis.
Staphisagria.
Actea racemosa (Cimicifuga).
Actea spicata.
Radix coptidis.
Ranunculus bulbosus.
Ranunculus sceleratus.
}

TODAY we have on the board the *Ranunculaceæ*, an order of plants containing many medicines. It receives its name from the different varieties of the buttercup. As a whole, the order seems to be characterized by acridity, and some of its members are slightly narcotic. From this order we obtain *Aconite, Actea racemosa, Actea spicata, Radix coptidis, Ranunculus bulbosus, Ranunculus sceleratus, Hepatica, Pulsatilla, Hydrastis Canadensis, Clematis erecta, Staphisagria, Helleborus* and *Pæonia*. *Staphisagria* contains Delphinine. *Hydrastis Can.* when fresh is said to be narcotic as well as acid. It is used for its tonic action, and it is said to cause, when abused, symptoms like those of Sulphate of Quinine, such as tight feeling, buzzing and ringing in the ears and reduction of the pulse. The *Clematis vitalba* is so caustic that it has been used as a substitute for Cantharides. Similar properties belong to *Clematis crispi*, on which the Spanish flies feed with avidity. The *Clematis viorna* whose tough shoots are made into paper, is also vesicant. We shall have time to study only the principal members of this order, and first of all let us consider *Aconite*.

ACONITUM NAPELLUS.

Aconitum napellus is the monkshood. *Aconite* itself means "without dust." The plant has been so named from the botanical fact that it grows on dry rocks, with scarcely enough earth about to enable it to take root. This shows the hardiness of the plant. It is called the monkshood because of the shape of the flowers, which turn over and give the appearance of a hood thrown over the head.

Aconitum napellus contains a crystalline alkaloid called *Aconitine*. It is found in largest quantity in the root. Several other active principles occur with it. They are of uncertain composition and are difficult to isolate. In fact, commercial *Aconitine* practically always contains some of these substances. *Aconitine* and its related active principles are found in differing proportions in many of the members of the order. *Aconitic acid* is said to occur in some of them combined with calcium. I have heard that some of the inhabitants of Persia dry the tops of the *Aconitum ferox*, and eat them with impunity. I cannot say how true this is, but it is known that this species of *Aconite* contains *Pseudo-aconitine*, which is less toxic than true *Aconitine*. It is also asserted (this, too, I cannot vouch for) that, in some parts of Switzerland, *Aconite* is grown in rows along the streets, and the tops are cut off and used as greens. Perhaps this illustrates the fact that plants alter their properties under domestication.

When taken in poisonous doses, *Aconite* acts as a depressant to the cerebro-spinal nervous system. It produces a sensation of numbness attended with pricking and tingling in the extremities, and even complete anæsthesia. It also affects the circulatory system. After the first sensation of diffused warmth is experienced, there follows an intense internal heat and profuse hot sweat. At other times the skin becomes covered with a miliary rash which itches intensely. The pulse and respirations are greatly accelerated. Secondarily, the surface of the body becomes cool with cold clammy sweat, the pulse grows feeble and death ends the scene.

Aconite does not at first impair the intellect and the emotions. In its action on the nerves it thus differs from *Cocculus Indicus*, which early disturbs consciousness. This drug, moreover, produces a complete motor and not sensory paralysis. It differs also from *Gelsemium*, *Conium* and *Nux vomica*, which early destroy motor rather than sensory activity. As regards its symptoms of collapse, they resemble those of *Camphor* and *Veratrum album*. But only *Veratrum* has the characteristic purging and vomiting, with cold sweat on the forehead. Both *Aconite* and *Nux vomica* cause tetanic convulsions, but they are only partial in *Aconite*, and are accompanied by great muscular weakness.

Aconite produces two different sets of symptoms, entirely distinct in their character, and as separate as though the drug were composed of two substances, each developing its own symptoms. The second set of symptoms, that which is most thoroughly known, is the tendency of *Aconite* to develop fever and inflammation. This it does through its action on the sympathetic nervous system. We find it indicated in genuine inflammatory fever of the type called synochal or sthenic fever. These terms apply to a fever which has about it no quality of weakness or asthenia. The symptoms of the fevers calling for *Aconite* are these: there are usually dry heat of the skin, and full, hard, bounding pulse. This fever is always associated with anxiety. The mental symptoms and those which are local, Hahnemann has told us, are the true guiding symptoms in the selection of *Aconite*. It cannot be the remedy unless there are present anxiety, restlessness and fear of death. The sweat which follows the fever is usually critical, and gives relief to all the symptoms; it is profuse, warm or even hot. It has been proved that *Aconite* does not produce any alteration in the quality of the blood; hence, you cannot expect it to be indicated in any form of fever in which there is a poison in the blood, destroying that fluid or impairing its corpuscles, altering its plasma, or in any way changing its quality. The type of the *Aconite* fever is sthenic and continuous, and not intermittent or remittent. It has no symptom in its pathogenesis which points to intermittency. Beginning with the initial chill or chills, the dry heat follows and continues until sweat brings relief. Then the fever is over so far as *Aconite* is concerned. It has no typical return of these febrile attacks. Hence, you cannot give *Aconite* in intermittent fever. Then, again, it must be borne in mind that sometimes the fever is not the disease itself, but a symptom which is necessary for the proper development of the disease. You should no more attempt to remove this fever by the administration of *Aconite* than you would attempt to remove a single symptom in any other disease. Hence when fever is only a symptom, *Aconite* should not be given to control it. Take scarlatina, for instance. The fever here may run high, the skin may be hot and dry, and the pulse hard. Superficially, *Aconite* appears to be indicated, yet you know, with the other symptoms present, backache, vomiting, sore-throat and the existence of other cases of the disease in the neighborhood, that scarlatina is developing. You know, by removing this fever, you take away a symptom which is necessary for the proper development of the rash belonging to the disease. Therefore, *Aconite* is rarely to be thought of in scarlatina. There may be exceptional cases, when the fever is disproportionately severe and the characteristic mental symptoms are present, in which *Aconite* may be administered, but nine cases out of ten would only be spoiled by its administration.

Again, a mistake is made in giving *Aconite* in typhoid types of fever to diminish the pulse and control the temperature. *Aconite* has no relation whatever to typhoid fever. It is here given from mere symptom practice and not through any knowledge of pathology and symptomatology. Let me beg of you not to commence this practice; it will only lead you to alternation.

In traumatic or inflammatory fevers, *Aconite* must give way to other remedies unless this restlessness or anxiety is present. One of these remedies is *Bryonia*, which has full, hard pulse, increased action of the heart, dry skin and aggravation of all the symptoms by motion. The patient lies perfectly quiet. He is not at all restless.

It is important that you distinguish between *Aconite*, *Gelsemium* and *Apis mellifica* in febrile states. I will therefore give you in detail the symptoms and conditions which make the selection of one or the other of these remedies certain. If I repeat what has already been said, the repetition will only serve to impress the distinction between these remedies more firmly on your minds.

Aconite typifies the synochal fever; *Gelsemium* the remittent or intermittent; *Apis* the intermittent or typhoid. *Aconite* causes decided chill, followed by dry, hot skin and full, hard, bounding pulse, followed later by a warm, profuse, critical sweat, with relief. *Gelsemium* causes partial chill, beginning in the hands or running up and down the spine, followed by general heat, most decided, about the head and face. Sweat is gradual and moderate, but always gives relief. *Apis* causes a chill, which is followed by burning heat all over, or heat in some places and coolness in others. The heat is felt particularly in the abdomen. The skin is hot and dry, or alternately dry and moist. Sweat is absent or breaks out only in spells, soon drying off.

Under *Aconite* the pulse is, as stated, full, hard and bounding. Under *Gelsemium* it is full and flowing, but not hard—the so-called "waterhammer pulse." Under *Apis* it is accelerated, full and strong, or fluttering, wiry and frequent. *Aconite* presupposes that the blood is not qualitatively altered. *Gelsemium* admits of any change which may favor depression. *Apis* tends towards toxæmia, with a typhoid type.

Aconite, therefore, is the remedy only when the fever is sthenic, such as arises from exposure to dry, cold winds; from exposure after overheating; from cooling suddenly when warm and sweating, etc. In bilious fever it is indicated in the early stages when the fever is sthenic, especially because it acts on the liver. It is also the remedy in inflammatory fever, whether traumatic or not, the type agreeing, it is particularly applicable to full-blooded, robust individuals, who readily suffer from sudden active congestions. It bears no relation to the intermitting type of fever, and, when given during such a fever, acts only by subduing the heart's action, and never curatively, hence never homœopathically. Neither does it hold any relation to typhoid fever. *Gelsemium* is the remedy when the fever develops under circumstances which favor a paresis of motor nerves of both voluntary and involuntary muscles. It corresponds to that stage in which the blood-vessels are dilated and full, but lack the firmness and resistance of a fully developed sthenic inflammation. Such a form of fever is accompanied by languor, muscular weakness, desire for absolute rest, and drowsiness. Under such conditions congestions might still be arterial, as under *Aconite*, but they exhibit a passivity which is sufficiently characteristic. The pulse is full, flowing, but not hard. So *Gelsemium* may be indicated in bilious fevers, the liver being passively congested. Again, it applies in typhoid forms, but never after the languor and drowsiness belonging to relaxation, and consequent passive congestion of the brain, pass into great prostration and stupor.

Apis has an apparent resemblance to the sthenic fever of *Aconite* in its hot skin, strong pulse, etc., and this is especially so in the beginning of erysipelatous inflammations, or, still more, in inflammation of serous or synovial membranes. But the tendency of *Apis* is toward typhoid or toward effusions; *Aconite* never develops either. Thus *Aconite* may suit the fever attending the initiation of a meningitis, pleuritis or synovitis; but its power ceases when the cri cephalique, the dyspnœa and dull percussion note, or the puffy, doughy swelling about the joint, announce the appearance of effusion. In its intermittent form of fever, *Apis* bears no resemblance to either *Aconite* or *Gelsemium*. Even in a rheumatic type, in which *Aconite* and *Apis* both appear, the resemblance is only superficial; for *Apis* either develops an erysipelatous inflammation, or causes burning-stinging pain and an exquisite soreness, all referable to the blood-vessels.

In its lower forms *Apis* deserts *Aconite* and completely supersedes

Gelsemium. It is indicated in genuine scarlatina, in diphtheria and in typhoid fever. There is a tendency to defibrination of the blood, and lastly to decomposition of the fluids. In such cases the anxious restlessness of *Aconite* and the irritability or drowsiness of *Gelsemium* are replaced by a fidgety restlessness and stupefaction. The excitement and delirium of *Aconite* and the semi-conscious muttering of *Gelsemium* are changed into low muttering delirium and unconciousness. Arranging the respective symptoms according to the requirements of the Organon, we have each remedy characterized as follows: *Aconite*, anguish; despair; restless tossing about during the fever; fears he will die; throws off the clothes; pulse full, hard, bounding; skin hot, dry; all symptoms end in copious sweat. *Gelsemium*, irritable; sensitive; children sometimes wakeful; nervous; even threatened with convulsions; or drowsy; eyelids heavy; look as if intoxicated; want to remain perfectly quiet. Chill up and down the back, followed by fever with increased drowsiness; pulse full, flowing. Sweat moderate, gradual, but giving relief. *Apis*, fidgety restlessness; wants to sleep, but so nervous, cannot; or low, muttering delirium; sopor. Chill begins in the knees or abdomen at three P. M.; heat, with dry skin or occasional transient spells of sweating; desire to uncover; great oppression of the chest; skin hot in some places and cool in others. Pulse accelerated and strong; or, as debility shows itself, wiry and frequent, intermittent, or imperceptible.

Belladonna comes in as another concordant remedy to *Aconite*. This drug, as we shall see in the future, does not act primarily on the vasomotor nerves or sympathetic ganglia; hence it does not control the calibre of the blood-vessels. It acts primarily on the cerebro-spinal nervous system, and we therefore find it indicated in fevers which begin with symptoms of the brain and spinal cord, or in fevers which have commenced with the *Aconite* type, but have, by extension, involved the brain. Thus we often find *Belladonna* following *Aconite* well. Remember that *Belladonna* requires the presence of brain symptoms, such as starting from sleep, throbbing headache, hot head and cold body and extremities.

Veratrum viride takes the place of *Aconite* in fever marking the onset of pneumonia, when there is great arterial excitement and engorgement, as indicated by full rapid pulse; labored and difficult breathing; or later, nausea on rising, faintness, slow pulse and coldness.

When synochal fever fails to yield to *Aconite*, the best remedy is *Sulphur*. The symptoms that will lead you to the selection of this remedy are these: despite the administration of *Aconite*, the dry heat persists; either no perspiration shows itself, or, if any, it is simply transient. The patient, at first sleepless and restless, becomes drowsy and answers questions slowly or permits an interval to elapse between your question and his reply, as if not fully comprehending The tongue becomes dry and the speech a little thick. The patient gives evidence of falling into a typhoid state owing to the continued exhaustion from this heat.

Ferrum phosphoricum, of which I have already spoken more than once, should be distinguished from *Aconite*. It acts upon the blood-vessels, producing a sort of semi-paretic state, in which they become dilated as in the second stage of inflammation. The pulse is full and rather soft; not hard or tense, as with *Aconite*. It is indicated in congestions of any part of the body when the discharges from that part are blood-streaked. This may be applied to dysentery; to hæmoptysis, or to secondary pneumonia.

Arsenicum album, like *Aconite*, causes intense fever, with anxiety, restlessness, and fear of death; but the fever and inflammation of *Arsenic* are such as belong to intense local disease, to inflammation progressing to the destruction of the part, to fever of a typhoid type with putrid discharges, etc.

Aconite may be used in inflammatory affections of the brain. You must, however, distinguish between an idiopathic cerebral inflammation and one arising from deep-seated disease. *Aconite* can have but little influence over tuberculous meningitis. But in meningitis or cerebral congestion from lying with the head exposed to the direct rays of the sun, especially when asleep, it is the best remedy, being superior here to either *Glonoin* or *Belladonna*. But *Glonoin* and *Belladonna* are preferable in sunstroke from exposure under ordinary conditions. *Aconite* may further be indicated in sunstroke when the great heat has had a paralyzing effect on the circulation. At first the heart works harder. It then begins to lose its force and beat from 120 to 130 beats per minute.

Amyl nitrite causes a similar picture. The face is flushed; the eyes protruding; there are roaring in the ears, vaso-motor paralysis and paralysis of the heart secondary to reduced pressure in the capillaries. *Aconite* may also be used when cerebral congestion results from a fit of anger.

You may use *Aconite* in affections of the eyes. It is of service in conjunctivitis following surgical operations, or resulting from a foreign body in the eye. It is also indicated in inflammatory affections of the eyes, arising from exposure to dry cold winds. There is a great deal of heat, dryness and burning in the eye. The eye feels as if full of sand, and is exceedingly sensitive. The pains are so intense that the patient wishes to die; he declares that he cannot stand them. The eye-ball feels as if forced out of the orbit, and aches; this aching is worse when the affected part is moved or touched. Photophobia is intense. The pupils are contracted, and there is a blue circle around the cornea, and violent aching in the eye-balls as in episcleritis. Even glaucoma may demand *Aconite* when, in addition to the symptoms above enumerated, there are pains extending down the face, as in *tic douloureux*, especially after exposure to intense cold or to cold winds or in rheumatic patients. If, however, *Aconite* does not relieve promptly, you must resort to other measures at once, as this disease may destroy sight in an incredibly short time.

Sulphur is indicated in conjunctivitis from irritation of foreign bodies when *Aconite* fails.

Spigelia has many pains similar to those of *Aconite*, especially in the left eye; but its inflammation is less general than in the case of *Aconite*.

You will recall that I said *Aconite* had two distinct types of action. We have considered the second and better known type; let us now study the other, which is very different from the former. The symptoms of this type belong more to the cerebro-spinal nervous system. First, we shall speak of the symptoms of the mind itself. We find *Aconite* useful for mental disease or hysteria when there is particular aversion to excitement, especially to busy streets. The patient dare not cross these streets because of fear that something will happen to him. This symptom is perfectly normal under some circumstances, but when extreme, denotes over-excitement of the brain, common enough in hysterical patients. They are anxious. They show an intolerance of music. They can bear no sounds, so sensitive are the ears. They imagine that some part of the body is deformed, *e. g.*, a limb displaced, lips too thick, or features distorted. They imagine that they do all their thinking from the stomach. Sometimes such patients, during attacks of illness, have "spells" in which they predict the hour of death. You may note this symptom in puerperal fever. *Argentum nitricum* and *Coffea* also have the symptom, prediction of the hour of death, the latter especially in child-bed.

Furthermore, *Aconite* causes paralysis; a paralysis which may easily be remembered from two or three subjective symptoms; paralysis accompanied by coldness, numbness and tingling. Unless there is tingling in the affected part, we seldom find *Aconite* indicated. Even paralysis of both legs—paraplegia—may yield to *Aconite* with this characteristic coldness of the limbs and tingling. We may also use *Aconite* in various forms of local palsies, as facial paralysis, when associated with the above-mentioned symptoms, and when traceable to exposure to dry cold winds. But this paralysis is never of organic origin.

Sulphur is the main antidote when paralysis results from overdoses of *Aconite*.

Cannabis Indica and *Staphisagria* should be remembered in paralysis, with tingling in the affected parts; *Rhus tox.*, *Sulphur* and *Causticum* are preferable later, especially in paralysis from cold.

The neuralgia for which *Aconite* is the remedy, is caused by exposure to dry cold winds. Especially is it indicated when there is violent congestion of the affected part, which is usually the face. The face will be red and swollen. The pains drive the patient almost to despair. There is usually tingling in the affected part. You may here compare *Spigelia*, which is indispensable in left-sided prosopalgia, with severe burning, sticking pains. The patient exhibits intense excitement and great intolerance of the pains.

Colchicum is likewise indicated in left-sided prosopalgia. The pains are associated with a paralytic weakness of the muscles, but lack the severity of those of *Spigelia*, and the excitement and intolerance of pain which characterizes that remedy is wanting under *Colchicum*.

Amyl nitrite may be needed rather than *Aconite* in prosopalgia with much local congestion.

Aconite is a very important remedy in the treatment of affections of the heart. The symptoms indicating it in these cases are numerous and important—necessarily so, since *Aconite* disturbs the blood-flow so markedly, and in addition exerts a special action on the heart and its nerves. There are congestions to both heart and lungs, palpitation with anxiety, cardiac oppression, and even syncope. The palpitation is worse when walking. Lancinating stitches occur and prevent the patient from assuming an erect posture or taking a deep inspiration.

Attacks of intense pain extend from the heart down the left arm, and are associated with numbness and tingling in the fingers.

In hypertrophy of the heart, *Aconite* is indicated by this numbness and tingling in the fingers. It is in uncomplicated hypertrophy of the heart only that you should give this remedy. In hypertrophy from valvular disease it may do great harm. You should here compare *Aconite* with *Arnica*, *Aurum met.*, *Rhus tox.*, and *Cactus grandiflorus*. *Kalmia* and *Rhus tox.* also have numbness and tingling in the left arm with heart disease.

Aconite may be used in the first stage of pneumonia when the fever is high and has been preceded by a chill. Symptoms of engorgement of the lungs are present. The cough is usually hard and dry and rather painful. The expectoration is serous or watery, and a little blood-streaked, but never thick and blood-streaked. The patient is necessarily full of anxiety.

Veratrum viride, as already indicated, competes with *Aconite* in the incipiency of pneumonia. It acts admirably when the pneumonic engorgement is severe, with violent excitement of the heart, as indicated by rapid full pulse, nausea, faintness on rising, tongue red down the centre.

Bryonia comes in to take the place of *Aconite* especially when hepatization has commenced. The cough is still hard and painful, and is associated with thicker expectoration. The anguish is now traceable to oppression of breathing and not to the fever; the patient prefers to lie still rather than to toss about.

Aconite may also be indicated in pleurisy, in the very beginning, before there is any exudation; there are sharp stitches on either side of the chest, with chills followed by febrile action. *Aconite* is to be thought of here particularly when the trouble has arisen from a checked perspiration or confinement from the fresh air.

In croup you should give *Aconite* when the trouble has arisen from exposure to dry cold northwest winds. The patient is aroused from sleep with long suffocating attacks. The cough is of a hard, dry, barking character, and may be heard all over the house. There are great difficulty of breathing, anxiety, and high fever.

Spongia is to be used when the breathing becomes "sawing." The cough is still barking, harsh, and rasping. It is especially indicated in light-complexioned blue-eyed children, when the trouble is worse before midnight.

Hepar should be given when the cough is worse toward morning, and on uncovering, and is associated with rattling of mucus.

Sambucus is called for when there is spasm of the glottis. The breathing is of a wheezing, crowing character, and is worse after midnight and from lying with the head low.

In hæmoptysis calling for *Aconite* the blood is bright red. The trouble is always associated with anxiety, and fever is invariably present. In hæmoptysis, you may compare with *Aconite* the following remedies:

Millefolium, which has hæmoptysis, with profuse flow of bright red blood, but without fever.

Ledum for hæmoptysis of drunkards or persons of a rheumatic constitution. The blood is bright red and foamy.

Cactus grandiflorus for hæmoptysis with strong throbbing of the heart and a sensation of constriction, as of a band about the chest. It has, however, less anxiety and less fever than has *Aconite.*

Aconite is frequently of use in abdominal diseases, especially if they be inflammatory. You may use it in gastritis or gastric catarrh, when the trouble has been caused by exposure, by the checking of an acute eruption, or by sudden chilling of the stomach from drinking ice water. There is pressure in the stomach as if a cold stone lay there, persisting even after repeated vomiting. Compare also *Colchicum, Arsenicum, Elaps,* etc. You may also give *Aconite* in inflammatory colic when the pains force the patient to bend double, yet are not relieved by this or any other position. This symptom is invaluable in the beginning of inflammatory processes within the abdomen, and also in some cases of ovarian dysmenorrhœa. *Colocynth* may be compared here This drug lacks the inflammation, however, and finds relief in bending double and from pressure.

Aconite may be used in dysentery, especially if the disease occurs in the autumn, when warm days are followed by cold nights; the stools are scanty, bloody and slimy, with much tenesmus. In this disease, *Aconite* is followed very well by *Mercurius.*

The diarrhœa of *Aconite* is of inflammatory origin. It usually appears in summer, as the result of indulgence in cold drinks or from checked perspiration. The stools are watery, slimy and bloody.

Cholera infantum calls for *Aconite* when the stools look like chopped spinach, and the inflammatory symptoms already mentioned are present.

You should also remember *Aconite* in incarcerated hernia, when inlammation has started in the strangulated bowel, with burning pain in the affected part. There are also vomiting of bile, great anxiety and cold sweat.

In incipient nephritis, whether true Bright's disease or not, *Aconite* has relieved when the patient complains of sharp cutting pains going in a circle from the renal region around to the abdomen over each ilium.

Coming now to the genital organs, we find *Aconite* sometimes indicated in dysmenorrhœa supposed to result from thickening of the peritoneum over the ovaries, and in suppression of the menses, due to anger or fright. The characteristic colic which I described a few minutes ago is present.

During pregnancy, *Aconite* may be administered for certain mental symptoms, such as fear of death, excitable temperament, etc. It may also be used for impending abortion caused by fright or anger.

During labor itself it may be given when the pains are unnaturally violent, rapid and frequent. The patient complains that she cannot breathe; that she cannot bear the pains. She is restless and anxious, and the body is covered with a hot sweat.

In the so-called "milk-fever," *Aconite* is to be given when the mammary glands are hot and swollen, and the skin hot and dry. These symptoms are associated with restlessness and anxiety.

Suppression of the lochia is an indication for *Aconite*, when the trouble is caused by exposure or by some violent emotion, provided high fever, thirst and anxiety are present. The mammæ are lax, and the abdomen is distended and sensitive to touch.

Aconite is not often indicated in puerperal fevers because they are generally of septic origin, but for one form of child-bed fever it is the only remedy capable of subduing the whole affair within a few hours. The nurse, perhaps, has carelessly exposed the patient after a hard labor, or she has bathed her with too cold water, or has thoughtlessly changed her clothing without the necessary precautions, and the following symptoms result. High fever; thirst; eyes glaring and wild; sharp, anxious expression; abdomen distended and sensitive to touch; mammæ lax and without milk. When you have this symptom-picture, you may confidently give *Aconite*.

While *Aconite* is not called for in scarlatina, still it may be used during that disease, after the stage of desquamation, when the child catches cold and acute Bright's disease results. The child starts up from sleep in perfect agony, with cold sweat on the forehead and with cold limbs. Dropsy is also present.

In measles *Aconite* is called for early in the case, where there are high fever; redness of the conjunctivæ; dry, barking cough; restlessness; and itching, burning of the skin. It precedes *Pulsatilla*, and may be relied upon so long as the high fever lasts. The rash is rough and miliary.

Gelsemium differs in that it causes more drowsiness and desire to remain quiet.

In acute coryza you will find *Aconite* indicated when the nasal mucous membrane is dry and hot, and when there is most violent throbbing headache, better in the open air. Or, the coryza may be fluent and hot, with frequent sneezing. The muscles all over the body feel sore, so that sneezing forces him to support his chest. There are fever, restlessness and the accompanying symptoms. All these are provoked—not by damp weather, and not, as some teach, by exposure to *any* sort of atmosphere capable of producing cold, but by cold, dry winds, or checked sweat.

You may compare *Nux vomica* in colds caused by cold weather. The nose is stuffed and dry, and the throat feels rough as if scraped.

Belladonna is to be given if the head is intensely hot, the throat red and the tonsils swollen.

China is useful if there is headache from suppressed coryza, with pains worse in the open air, instead of better, as under *Aconite*.

In skin diseases, *Aconite* is sometimes indicated. It is not a remedy for scarlatina, but you will sometimes find it useful in so-called scarlet-rash, with high fever, anxiety and other appropriate symptoms.

Sulphur is the proper remedy when *Aconite* has been abused.

LECTURE XXXII.

ACTEA RACEMOSA, RANUNCULUS BULBOSUS AND RANUNCULUS SCELERATUS.

Actea Racemosa.

We have in the homœopathic materia medica two varieties of the *Actea*, namely *Actea racemosa*, *Cimicifuga* and *Actea spicata*. The last-named of these may be dismissed in a very few words. It acts upon the joints, especially upon the smaller joints, as those of the hands and feet. It is useful in rheumatism affecting these parts, especially if the hands and wrists are involved.

Actea racemosa acts upon the cerebro-spinal nervous system, and especially on the motor nerves It seems to have a decided influence over the nerves distributed to muscles, producing a perfect picture of myalgia.

Actea racemosa is also valuable by reason of its reflex nervous symptoms. It has neuralgia of any part of the body as a reflex symptom from uterine or ovarian disease. One of its most important symptoms arising from this cause is a sensation of heat on the top of the head just behind the centre. Other symptoms which you may note about the head are feeling as if the top of the head would fly off, sharp lancinating and neuralgiform pains in and over the eyes, and supra-orbital pains shooting up to the top of the head. These symptoms indicate *Actea racemosa* in some of the diseases peculiar to women and in diseases of the eye proper. In any disease of the eye, when pains of the above-named character are present, *Actea* is one of the first remedies to be considered.

Spigelia has similar pains. Under this remedy the neuralgia comes and goes with the sun; that is, it reaches its height at noon and subsides in the evening. The *Actea* pain is worse at night rather than during the day. The *Spigelia* pain begins in the back of the head and comes forward, settling over one or the other eye. This remedy also has a sensation as if the eye-ball were enormously large; but when this latter symptom is traceable to uterine displacement, *Actea* is preferable.

Cedron is an invaluable remedy in neuralgiform affections when the pains involve the supra-orbital nerve and the eye, and are worse on the left side. The eye burns as if it were on fire. The pains recur regularly at the same hour each day.

Another remedy to be mentioned in this connection is *Kalmia latifolia*, which has supra-orbital neuralgia, worse on the right side.

Actea may also be used for headache attended with a feeling as if the patient were going crazy. Especially is it of value when uterine symptoms are present.

It is also called for when there is pain in the left infra-mammary region, dependent upon uterine disturbances.

We come now to the action of *Actea* on the female sexual organs. It is indicated in labor or in threatened miscarriage when the pains fly across the abdomen from side to side (*Lycopodium*, from right to left; *Ipecac.*, from left to right and associated with nausea). The pains seem to double the patient up. It may also be used in the early months of pregnancy for those pains in the abdominal walls which so distress the patient.

When there is a great deal of soreness in the abdomen, the local application of a solution of *Hamamelis* is a good remedy.

The labor-pains of *Actea* seem to be associated with fainting spells or with crying out in agony, so severe are they.

In after-pains it is useful only when they are intense, when the patient is exceedingly sensitive and cannot tolerate them, and when they are worse in the groin.

Actea may also be used in puerperal mania. The patient declares that she will go crazy, and her every action apparently indicates that she is keeping her word. She is suspicious. Her talk is nonsensical, and yet she seems to be conscious of what she is doing, and she says she cannot help it. Sometimes she has visions of rats, etc. These symptoms may also indicate the drug in delirium tremens.

Here you may compare *Lachesis*, which has "awakening from sleep and springing from bed, not only with superhuman strength, but in great terror."

Arsenicum often follows *Lachesis* when the patient is afraid to be left alone.

Calcarea ostrearum has visions of rats and mice as soon as the patient closes her eyes.

Another symptom that we find indicating *Actea* in labor is "rigors, or nervous chills" in the first stage of labor. *Gelsemium* also is useful in this condition.

Actea racemosa does not cause phthisis, yet it may be one of the first remedies indicated when the disease is not of hereditary origin, especially if the trouble has been brought on by exposure, or in any case in which the well-defined cough of *Actea* is present. This cough is dry, teasing, worse at night, with little or no sputum, and usually associated with pleurodynia.

In pleurodynia associated with tuberculosis, you will find *Guaiacum* to be a remedy that rarely fails.

You may use *Actea* in angina pectoris when the pains radiate over the chest, and are associated with cerebral congestion and unconsciousness. The face is livid, and the left arm feels as if bound tightly to the body.

Another use that we may make of *Actea* is in that condition known as spinal irritation. Especially is it indicated when the upper and lower cervical vertebræ, particularly the latter, are sensitive to pressure; hence the patient will not lean back in her chair because of the uneasiness which it produces. This symptom of *Actea* is usually reflex from uterine irritation.

We have several remedies similar to *Actea* in spinal irritation. One of these is *Natrum mur.*, which also produces sensitiveness between the vertebræ. The main distinction is that the patient finds relief from lying flat on the back, and that, too, even when there is a uterine displacement. Another indication calling for *Natrum mur.* is a partial paralysis from weakness of the spine. Especially is it indicated when these symptoms arise from grief, anger, etc.

Physostigma, or the Calabar bean, develops a perfect picture of spinal irritation. It produces all sorts of burning and twinging sensations referable to the spinal column, with numbness of the feet and hands and other parts of the body, crampy pains in the hands, and sudden jerking of the limbs on dropping off to sleep. The muscles of the back become rigid, and even a tetanic condition may ensue.

Agaricus muscarius also produces a perfect picture of spinal irritation, with well-marked tingling or formication in the back, itching or burning of the skin as if frost-bitten, twitching of the muscles, especially of the eyelids, and sensations in different parts of the body as if needles of ice were being thrust into the skin.

This spinal irritation may develop a partial paralysis, in which case we have two remedies to fall back upon. The first of these is *Zincum metallicum*. This produces a perfect picture of irritable spine, with aching in the back at about the last dorsal vertebra, worse from sitting than from either walking or lying. Accompanying this symptom there is weakness of the legs, especially at noon, when the patient is hungry. You should also remember that the spinal symptoms of *Zinc* are made worse by wine.

The second remedy is *Cocculus Indicus*. This we use in females with weak spine, when there is paralytic aching in the small of the back. The patient feels as if she could scarcely walk. Along with these symptoms there is also an empty, gone feeling in the abdomen, which feels as if it were a hollow cavity.

Among men we do not find these symptoms present except as a result of sexual excesses, in which case *Nux vomica* is the remedy.

Cobalt is of use for spinal irritation from sexual excesses when there is backache, worse when sitting, with weakness in the legs.

Ranunculus Bulbosus.

Ranunculus bulbosus.
{ Serous membranes.
Muscles.
Effects of alcohol.
Skin. }

Compare with *Aconite, Arnica, Cactus, Bryonia, Rhus tox., Arsenicum, Mezereum.*

We have two varieties of the *Ranunculus* to consider to day. These are the *Ranunculus bulbosus* and the *Ranunculus sceleratus*. Both of these plants possess a juice or sap which is exceedingly irritating to the skin. When applied locally, it produces erythema followed later by an eruption which is at first vesicular in character and attended with burning, smarting and itching. If the symptoms continue, by reason of the intensity of the action of the drug ulceration and even gangrene of the parts may follow, the gangrene being associated with fever and delirium. This is an extreme picture, yet it is one which may follow the prolonged use of some of the species of *Ranunculus*.

We shall now consider *Ranunculus bulbosus*. First as to its action on serous membranes: we may think of *Ranunculus bulbosus* in inflammation of serous membranes, particularly of the pleura or peritoneum, when there are acute stabbing pains, accompanied by an effusion of serum into the serous sac. Accompanying this effusion we find great anxiety, dyspnœa and distress, caused partly by the accumulation of fluid and partly by the anxiety from the pains themselves. Now these are symptoms not commonly known among physicians, yet you will find that here *Ranunculus* will serve you as well as *Apis*, *Bryonia* or *Sulphur* or even better than these, if the pains are of the character just described.

The second heading in our schema is "Muscles." We find *Ranunculus* acting here as a curative agent. It is especially indicated in rheumatism of the muscles, particularly in muscles about the trunk. Intercostal rheumatism yields far more quickly to this drug than to any other. There is usually a great deal of soreness to touch, and the muscles have a bruised feeling, as if they had been pounded. I know that *Aconite*, *Arnica* or *Bryonia* is often given when *Ranunculus* is indicated.

Aconite may be the remedy in pleurodynia when there is high fever (which is not often), especially if you can trace the trouble to exposure to cold after being overheated.

Ranunculus bulbosus may also be used in the case of persons who are subject to stitches about the chest in every change of weather.

Again, it may be used for sore spots remaining in and about the chest after pneumonia. The characteristic sensation attending the *Ranunculus* soreness is a feeling of subcutaneous ulceration, which is purely subjective. This symptom is also characteristic of *Pulsatilla*.

Again, *Ranunculus* may be used for pains about the lungs from adhesions after pleurisy.

The rheumatic pains of *Ranunculus* are worse in damp weather and particularly from a change of weather or change of temperature. Even a rheumatic headache having this aggravation, may call for *Ranunculus*.

We may find it indicated also in diaphragmitis, when there are sharp shooting pains from the hypochondria and epigastrium through to the back.

Another remedy that I have found of service in this latter disease is *Cactus grandiflorus*, which is an excellent remedy for sharp pains in the diaphragm, particularly if there is a feeling as though a band were tied around the waist marking the attachments of the diaphragm to the borders of the ribs.

You should remember *Ranunculus bulbosus* as a remedy for the bad effects of excess in drink, in hiccough and even in epileptiform attacks and delirium tremens.

Ranunculus bulbosus is useful in herpes zoster or zona. Vesicles appear on the skin and are filled with serum. Sometimes these vesicles have a bluish-black appearance. There is marked burning. Especially is *Ranunculus* indicated when the trouble follows the course of the supra-orbital or intercostal nerves and is followed by sharp stitching pains. Here you may compare *Rhus tox.*, *Arsenicum* and *Mezereum*.

Ranunculus may also produce pemphigus. Large blisters form, which burst and leave raw surfaces.

Again, you may use *Ranunculus* in eczema, attended with thickening of the skin and the formation of hard horny scabs.

Here it is similar to *Antimonium crudum*, which has also horny excrescences or callosities on the soles of the feet.

The ulcers which *Ranunculus* causes are flat and are attended with a great deal of stinging pain. The discharge is ichorous.

Lastly, we may mention the action of *Ranunculus* on mucous membranes. It is one of the remedies useful in hay fever. You will find that there is smarting in the eyes; the eyelids burn and feel sore; the nose is stuffed up, especially toward evening, with pressure at the root of the nose and tingling, crawling sensation within its cavity. Sometimes this sensation attacks the posterior nares, causing the patient to hawk and swallow, and endeavor in every way to scratch the affected part. *Arsenicum* and *Silicea* also have this symptom. You will notice, too, that there is with this hay fever, hoarseness, general muscular soreness and very likely sharp stitching pains in and about the chest. The neck of the bladder may be affected, producing some burning on urinating.

Ambrosia artemisiæfolia should be compared in hay fever. The provings by Dr. E. E. Holman contain the following: stuffed sensation in the nose and chest; oppressive pain in the left chest, must sit up to breathe comfortably; worse in the evening until midnight; awakens suddenly with pertussis-like cough; face dark red; eyes congested, smarting, watery; nose red, swollen; watery coryza.

Sulphur does not follow *Ranunculus* well.

Ranunculus Sceleratus.

Ranunculus sceleratus. { Tongue, etc.
{ Skin.

Compare with *Natrum mur.*, *Arsenicum*, *Taraxacum*, *Rhus tox*.

Ranunculus sceleratus is more irritating in its action than is *Ranunculus bulbosus*. In its action on the skin it produces a vesicular eruption with thin, yellow, acrid discharge, something like that of *Ranunculus bulbosus*. It also develops more markedly large isolated blisters. When these burst, an ulcer is formed, the discharge from which is very acrid, making the surrounding parts sore.

In stomacace, and sometimes even in diphtheria or in typhoid fever, you will find *Ranunculus sceleratus* indicated by the presence of denuded patches on the tongue, the remainder of the organ being coated. Thus we have the condition known as mapped tongue. *Natrum mur.* has this symptom and so have *Arsenicum*, *Rhus tox.*, and *Taraxacum*, but none of these remedies have the same amount of burning and rawness that *Ranunculus sceleratus* has. The acridity of the drug differentiates it from all others.

Like *Ranunculus bulbosus*, *Ranunculus sceleratus* may be indicated in ordinary catarrhs with sneezing, fluent coryza, pains in joints, and burning on urination.

LECTURE XXXIII.

HELLEBORUS NIGER AND STAPHISAGRIA.

HELLEBORUS NIGER.

Helleborus niger.
- Sensorial depression.
  - Sweet spirits of nitre, Phosphoric acid, Opium.
- Dropsies.
  - Apis, Digitalis, Zincum (Brain), Terebinthina.

I PROPOSE considering first, to-day, *Helleborus niger.* This is also termed the Christmas rose, because it blossoms in midwinter. It has a dark brown root, which contains two active principles, *Helleborin* and *Helleborein.* The latter is said to be the poisonous constituent of the plant. It is an active cardiac poison, and also causes violent purging, vomiting, abdominal pains, and finally collapse. This purgative action resembles *Veratrum album,* and the collapse, *Camphor, Carbo veg., China,* etc. *Veratrum album* has not the apathy of *Hellebore; Carbo veg.* has cold feet and cold knees, rarely unconsciousness; *Camphor* has most prominently the coldness, sometimes with an internal feeling of heat, impelling the patient to throw off the clothes. The *Helleborin* is either inoperative, or, according to some authors, exerts a narcotic influence, and produces paresis of both sensation and motion.

The action of *Helleborus* has been marked out for you on the board. It blunts the sensorium, producing sopor, typhoid symptoms, paralysis of muscles, collapse, and lastly dropsies. Before going any further I wish to say that by collapse I mean not a simple weakness, but a condition in which there is a positive diminution of temperature, so that the thermometer, instead of registering 98½° registers 96°, or thereabouts, according to the intensity of the collapse.

In its action on the sensorium we find that *Helleborus* blunts or depresses sensorial activity. This condition is exhibited in a variety of symptoms; for instance, we note diminished power of the mind over the body; the patient is slow in answering questions, as though he did not comprehend what was asked him; he sees imperfectly, or does not seem to comprehend what he sees; hearing is imperfect: taste is absent, or nearly so; he has the desire to work or to occupy himself, but lacks the muscular strength to do so. So you see that all the senses are benumbed by the action of *Helleborus*. Even what has been termed the muscular sense is affected by it. Muscles do not obey the will readily unless the mind is strongly exerted. If, for instance, the patient is holding anything in his hand and you speak to him, and so divert his mind, the muscles in action relax and he drops what he is holding. Even the heart muscle does not escape these paretic effects, and we have slow action of that organ. The patient feels a heaviness or weight over the entire body. There is a pressing headache of a stupefying character. Sometimes there is a sensation as though the contents of the head were bulging at the forehead and eyes. *Belladonna* is thus not the only remedy that has the sensation as though the brain were being pushed through the forehead. The face is expressive of the stupidity under which the patient is laboring.

We may find *Hellebore* indicated in typhoid fever, or in other conditions in which this sensorial depression, with the symptoms already enumerated, is present. In these cases you will also note the following symptoms: there is a dark soot about the nostrils; the nostrils are dry; the tongue is yellow and dry, with red edges; the breath is horribly offensive; drinks roll audibly into the stomach. The fever accompanying these symptoms is most marked in the afternoon, from 4 to 8 P. M. The face is at times pale and almost cold, and the pulse faint, weak, and almost imperceptible. There is also meaningless picking at the lips or clothing.

In this sensorial depression *Helleborus* is similar to *Phosphoric acid*, *Sweet spirits of nitre* and *Opium*. Like *Phosphoric acid*, it has sensorial depression, apathy, and perfect indifference. The patient is wholly indifferent as to his fate; he cares not whether he lives or dies. The difference between the two drugs is that under *Phosphoric acid* there is drowsiness from which the patient is easily aroused, and then is perfectly conscious; this is not the case with *Helleborus*, which has a condition more nearly approaching the stupor of *Opium*. *Phosphoric acid* lacks the complete muscular relaxation belonging to *Helleborus*. It also has not so markedly black soot about the nostrils.

Sweet spirits of nitre is a remedy recommended by Hahnemann in these cases of typhoid fever when the key-note to the whole case is sensorial apathy, there being, of course, no other symptoms present to indicate any other remedy. The patient seems to be in a sort of torpor, from which he may, by exertion, be aroused, but he falls back immediately into the same indifference. In these cases Hahnemann dissolved a few drops of the crude drug in half a glassful of water and administered it every two or three hours until reaction was manifested or some other drug indicated. You will find that *Sweet spirits of nitre* and *Phosphoric acid* differ from *Helleborus* in degree only, *Sweet spirits of nitre* having apathy in the lowest degree, *Phosphoric acid* coming next, while *Helleborus* has it most marked.

Opium, the last drug on the list, you will recognize at once as similar to *Helleborus*. The cerebral congestion is more profound under the *Opium*. The breathing is loud and stertorous, a symptom not marked in *Helleborus*. Then, too, the face is dark, brownish-red, or often blue; under *Helleborus* it is pale, and often cold or at least cooler than natural, and at times livid and covered with a cold sweat. The pulse will help you to discriminate between these two remedies, it being full and slow under *Opium*, and small, weak, and almost imperceptible under *Helleborus*.

Arnica is also to be thought of as a remedy producing this drowsy stupid state, from which the patient may be temporarily aroused.

Hydrocyanic acid and *Cina* have the symptom, "drinks roll audibly into the stomach." *Cina* has it in whooping-cough, but when it occurs in approaching paralysis of the lungs and brain, *Hydrocyanic acid* is the best remedy. *Phosphorus* has it in typhoid conditions. *Cuprum* has gurgling in the œsophagus when drinking.

In muscular exhaustion you may compare *Helleborus* with *Muriatic acid*, *Opium*, *Gelsemium*, *Saponin*, *Conium*, *Curare*, and *Kali carb*.

Next, we find *Helleborus* called for in meningitis when exudation has taken place. You have present all or some of the symptoms of sensorial apathy already mentioned, showing you the depressed condition of the system. In addition you have shooting pains in the head. If the patient is a child, it will, of course, be unable to describe this last symptom, but you will notice by the sudden screaming or crying out that it has these sharp shooting pains. The child bores its head into the pillow; the head is hot, and the forehead wrinkled into a frown from contraction of the corrugator supercilii muscles. There is automatic motion of one arm and one foot. This automatic motion may recur at regular intervals. I remember one case in which, every three minutes, the child's head was jerked to one side and the arm thrown up over the head, it would then utter a half-pitiful cry and become quiet again. In the *Helleborus* child, the eyeballs are drawn upward, so that you can scarcely see the cornea; the face becomes flushed, and then gradually turns pale. When offered a drink of water the child seizes the proffered glass with avidity, as though it were thirsty; this it does, not only on account of the thirst, but also because of the nervousness. The bowels are usually constipated or, if there is any stool, it is white, scanty, and jelly-like. The urine is dark, scanty, and loaded with albumen.

We can readily conceive that summer-complaint may demand *Helleborus* if these symptoms are present. In addition we may have sore mouth, salivation, rubbing of the nose, etc.

The nearest remedy to *Helleborus* in tuberculous meningitis is *Apis*. This drug has more of the *cri encephalique* and more excitement and irritability than *Helleborus*, which has, characteristically, sensorial depression. In *Apis* we often find spasms of the flexors, so that the big toes are drawn upward. This symptom has not been noticed under *Helleborus*.

Digitalis is very similar to *Helleborus* in dropsies of the brain. Both remedies cause great depression of the sensorium, both are suited to post-scarlatinal dropsy, and both cause meningitis with effusion. *Digitalis* is to be chosen by the scanty, albuminous urine, and by its characteristically slow pulse, which may be even slower than the beating of the heart. In addition to these symptoms there may be a cold sweat on the surface of the body.

Zincum is useful in cases where one of the exanthemata has been checked, or has not developed properly. The child is so enervated that it has not sufficient strength to develop an eruption. It arouses from sleep as if in fear; it has constant fidgety motion of the feet.

Other forms of dropsy in which *Helleborus* is indicated are general dropsy or anasarca, and especially ascites. Here you may give *Helleborus* when the trouble has arisen from post-scarlatinal nephritis. The urine is dark and scanty, or smoky from the admixture of decomposed blood. On standing it deposits a sediment looking like coffee-grounds. The stool contains jelly-like mucus, and is passed with much straining.

The nearest remedy here is *Terebinthina*, which cures dropsy dependent on congestion of the kidneys, as indicated by dull aching in the renal region and by the smoky-looking urine.

In dropsies compare also *Arsenicum* and *Apocynum*.

As illustrative further of the depression of *Helleborus*, I may mention its successful employment in a case of shock from a blow on the head. *Arnica* had failed, and the patient became drowsy; one pupil was larger than the other; the patient answered questions slowly as if comprehension were imperfect; one leg was dragged in walking. The pulse was scarcely fifty per minute, and the patient in general was worse from 4 to 8 P. M. *Helleborus* cured the case.

STAPHISAGRIA.

Staphisagria.
|
∨
Colocynthis.
Causticum.

1. Blood.
   Sycosis,
   Scurvy.
2. Loss of Fluids.
3. Organs.

Similar to
Nux vomica,

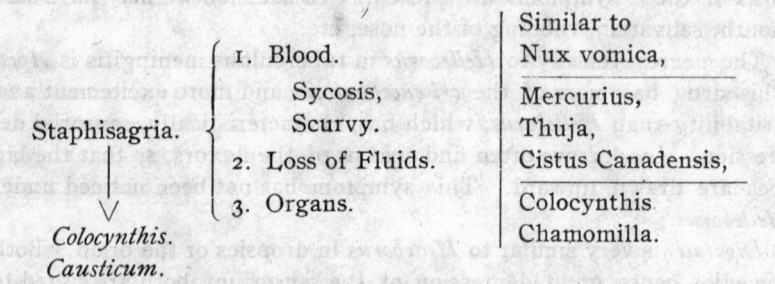

Mercurius,
Thuja,
Cistus Canadensis,

Colocynthis
Chamomilla.

Staphisagria is indicated in patients who appear pale, and are worn out and exhausted, especially as regards their nervous system. Both brain and spinal cord are weakened under its influence. The face is rather sunken, the nose is peaked and pointed, and the eyes are sunken and surrounded by blue rings. Mentally, the *Staphisagria* child is rather impetuous and irritable, reminding one strongly of *Chamomilla;* the adult *Staphisagria* patient is hypochondriacal. There may be one of several causes producing this last-named mental state. First, sexual excesses: it is called for in these hypochondriacal moods after self-abuse, and also when this mental state occurs in young men and young women as a result of permitting the mind to dwell too much on sexual subjects. Owing to his bad habit the boy becomes apathetic and gloomy, and has the complexion and sunken face that I have described. He rather prefers solitude, and is shy of the opposite sex. Locally, there is to be noted an irritability of the prostatic portion of the urethra. This state of affairs usually follows self-abuse; it is seldom the result of excessive sexual intercourse.

Platina was recommended by Grauvogl as a drug capable of curing spasms or convulsions, emaciation, and that train of symptoms which follows prepubic abuse of the sexual organs.

Still another remedy, *Caladium*, is to be thought of when, from masturbation, the glans penis is as flabby as a rag. The prepuce, when it is withdrawn behind the glans, remains there, not having contractility enough to replace itself. Nocturnal emissions occur either without dreams or with dreams that are foreign to sexual subjects.

Other remedies indicated in this condition are *Dioscorea*, *Gelsemium*, and that well known group to which I have already referred in a previous lecture, *Nux vomica*, *Sulphur*, *Calcarea ostrearum* and *Lycopodium*. Among the new remedies, *Bromide of Potassium* or *Kali bromatum* has been suggested. I have seen it do good when there was mental depression and weakness of the legs after self-abuse.

In the female, in whom masturbation is not so common, we find ovarian symptoms resulting from the habit. *Staphisagria* becomes the remedy when these organs are in a state of irritability, especially in nervous excitable women. It may also be used in women of this class when these symptoms occur in the prolonged absence of their husbands. When pruritus vulvæ is also present, *Caladium* often helps.

Staphisagria has another set of mental symptoms of a different type from those just mentioned. The patient is easily excited to anger, sensitive to the least impression, and takes offence at every little meant or unmeant insult.

We find *Staphisagria* indicated in what I have already termed a mental colic; that is crampy pains in the abdomen following a fit of anger, just as we found present under *Chamomilla* and *Colocynth*.

Chamomilla is called for in these cases when hot face, red cheeks and hot perspiration are associated with the colic; and *Colocynth*, when the severe pains cause the patient to double up for relief. *Staphisagria* is here complementary to *Colocynth*, stepping in to complete the cure when *Colocynth* is insufficient.

We find *Staphisagria* indicated also in diseases of the skin and of the bones. This drug has long been used as a local wash to destroy lice or vermin. You may use it internally when an eczematous eruption appears on the skin. This may occur on any other part of the body, but it is especially apt to be found on the head and face. The eruption is usually dry, and formed of very thick scabs, and itches violently, this last being an indication for the local application of

Staphisagria. The peculiarity of this itching is that when scratching stops it in one place, it goes to another. At other times these scabs are moist, and are yellowish in color and very offensive, even breeding lice. Thus you see *Staphisagria* is suited to crusta lactea or eczema capitis.

Again this drug may be indicated in children who are weak and broken down as the result of a syphilitic or sycotic inheritance. In such children you almost always find the teeth decaying rapidly. The milk-teeth are scarcely full grown before they become black in creases or spots and crumble away. In this respect *Staphisagria* rivals *Kreosote*, which is one of the best remedies for premature decay of the milk-teeth, when they first become yellow, then dark and finally decay. In *Thuja*, as you will remember, the teeth decay at the edge of the gums.

Next to these remedies you may think of *Antimonium crudum*, and in other cases still, *Chamomilla* and *Coffea*.

In the *Staphisagria* patient the gums are unhealthy, swollen, spongy and bleed easily when touched by food or by the finger, this condition being associated with painful swelling of the submaxillary glands. It is especially indicated after the abuse of *Mercury*.

Staphisagria is useful in children suffering from inflammation of the eyes, particularly of the lids with hardened styes.

For those little cystic tumors which form in the eyelids midway between the inner and outer surfaces, *Graphites* is the best remedy. *Baryta carb.* also cures tarsal tumors.

The *Staphisagria* children have an eczematous eruption composed of yellow scabs about the ears. The exudation from these is bloody and seems to cause rawness of the skin. Still further, we find *Staphisagria* affecting the bones. It causes swelling of the periosteum with subsequent suppuration.

It also produces fig-warts or condylomata on the skin; these are usually pediculated. This symptom places *Staphisagria* among the sycotic remedies. Thus we find it a suitable companion of *Thuja*, being preferable to that remedy when there are present the form of eruption already mentioned, the crumbling of the teeth and the pediculated condylomata.

In some cases we find it indicated in syphilitic ulceration after the abuse of *Mercury*, the discharge being thin and acrid. An examination with the probe reveals diseased bone beneath.

STAPHISAGRIA.

We have several remedies similar to *Staphisagria* in bone affections, whether of syphilitic or scrofulous origin. One of them is *Stillingia*. This is of great use in syphilitic affections of the long bones, such as the femur, tibia, humerus, etc., and in periosteitis or in osteitis, the pains being worse at night and in damp weather. In addition to this you almost always find an excoriating coryza, the well-known syphilitic ozæna.

Another remedy is *Mercurius*. Still another is *Kali hydriodicum*, especially when there is a combination of syphilis and mercury in the case.

Strontiana carb. is suited more to the scrofulous constitution. It is indicated in osteitis, particularly of the femur, with ulcers which discharge more or less broken-down bone. With the bone trouble there is apt to be a profuse exhausting diarrhœa almost like that accompanying hectic fever.

Another remedy is *Chloride of Gold and Platinum* which is useful for either caries or necrosis.

Gettysburg Salts, which owes its effectiveness to the lithium carbonate it contains, is useful especially in caries of the vertebræ and of the hip-joint.

Another use of *Staphisagria* is found in its application to gout. It is not so useful for the acute paroxysms as it is when gout becomes systemic, and the sodium urate, instead of being eliminated by the kidneys, is deposited in the various joints and organs of the body, producing arthritic nodes.

It is also indicated in arthritic ophthalmia. The eyes burn and feel very dry, notwithstanding which there are smarting and profuse lachrymation. The pains go from the eyes into the teeth.

In these gouty affections of the eyes, *Colocynth* is also a good remedy.

Upon the stomach *Staphisagria* seems to produce a relaxation, so that the organ appears to hang down and is flabby and weak. This same symptom you will find under *Ipecacuanha* and *Abrotanum*. In *Staphisagria* there is a desire for brandy, wine or something stimulating. Such patients are subject to colic, which greatly resembles that of *Colocynth*.

You must also remember *Staphisagria* as a remedy in colic following operations about the abdomen. It is also efficacious when an incised wound, whether inflicted by the surgeon or by accident, is unduly sensitive.

In diarrhœa in children *Staphisagria* is indicated when the disorder is associated with a peculiar form of stomacace; the tongue and gums are white and spongy, while there are cutting pains before and after stool, with a great deal of tenesmus of the rectum during stool, and escape of flatus, which is usually hot and smells like rotten eggs (here being similar to *Chamomilla*), stool being renewed by any attempt to take food or drink.

In its action on the female organs, *Staphisagria* causes prolapsus uteri, and this prolapsus is almost always associated with a flabby condition of the stomach. The whole abdomen—contents and parietes—feels as if it would drop, so relaxed is it. If you investigate thoroughly, you will find that disappointed love or permitting the mind to dwell on sexual subjects has favored this relaxation. The leucorrhœa which accompanies this condition is yellow and excoriating.

LECTURE XXXIV.

PULSATILLA PRATENSIS.

Pulsatilla.
{ Blood-vessels.
Mucous membranes.
Synovial membranes.
Organs. }

Compare with *Bryonia, Nux vomica, Antimonium crudum, Ipecac, Sulphur, Sulphuric acid, Arsenicum, Colchicum, Kali bichromicum, Caulophyllum, Ignatia, Actea racemosa, Helonias, Hamamelis, Sepia.*

To-day we shall study *Pulsatilla*. The species which we shall consider is the *Pulsatilla* of Hahnemann, the *Pulsatilla pratensis*, and not the American plant, the *Pulsatilla Nuttalliana*. There is some little difference in the action of the two drugs. The "*pratensis*" has been better proved. The concordant remedies of this drug are almost without number. The reason for this is that it is a well-proved remedy, and one, too, that is often indicated. Its complementary remedies are *Sulphuric acid* and *Lycopodium*.

Its antidotes are *Chamomilla, Coffea, Ignatia* and *Nux vomica*.

The relation of *Pulsatilla* or *Sulphuric acid* calls for particular notice. The latter remedy follows the former in gastric troubles. *Pulsatilla* is also antidotal to *Sulphuric acid*. When this acid has been used for the cure of the appetite for liquor, *Pulsatilla* has been proposed as the remedy best suited for the diarrhœa which ensues.

Pulsatilla pratensis is a pretty little flower belonging to the anemone. It has been called the wind-flower, and its name is in keeping with its symptoms, as they are as fickle as the wind. Changeableness of the symptoms is characteristic of the drug. This is especially marked in the hæmorrhages, which apparently stop and in a few hours return. It is also true of the diarrhœa, the stools continually changing their appearance—at one time being green, at another mixed with yellow, and at still another slimy.

The mental symptoms are of the same fickle nature, the patient now being irritable, then tearful, and again mild and pleasant. These are illustrations of the changeableness that I have described.

Pulsatilla seems to be especially adapted to the female organism, although it affects men as well as women. It is one of those remedies which we are apt to select by the predominance of the mental symptoms. It is especially indicated in patients of a mild, tearful disposition, having a rather slow, phlegmatic temperament. They are never irascible, although at times peevish. Thus, in the case of a child with some gastric ailment, *Pulsatilla* may be used when it is peevish, pale, chilly, and satisfied with nothing. This is not the *Nux vomica* condition, nor is it like *Chamomilla*, both of which remedies have decidedly more violence with their anger.

The *Pulsatilla* woman is tearful and easily discouraged. Sometimes she is full of anxiety, with forebodings of some impending disaster. This anxiety comes from the epigastrium and is very likely to be associated with indigestion. It is often accompanied by chattering of the teeth, palpitation of the heart and flushes of heat. These are the main mental symptoms of *Pulsatilla*. They are present, more or less, in every disease in which it is the remedy.

In these mental symptoms you should compare *Sepia*, which, you will recall, has a similar mental state; but it differs from *Pulsatilla* in the presence of irritability and anger. There is also indifference to her household affairs, to which she was formerly attentive.

Natrum muriaticum also has tearful disposition similar to that of *Pulsatilla*, but consolation under *Natrum mur.* aggravates, while under *Pulsatilla* the patient seeks consolation.

Stannum metallicum likewise has this tearful disposition. The patient is very much discouraged, or is tearful over his chest symptoms. He fears that he will go into a decline.

The *Ignatia* patient is sad, but she hides her grief from others.

Pulsatilla is especially suitable for chlorotic or anæmic women, when they complain constantly of a feeling of dulness, but in spite of this find relief for many of their symptoms in the open air. They cannot tolerate a close room. The pains from which they suffer seem to be accompanied by chilliness. This chilliness is more marked the more decided the pains are. The mental symptoms already mentioned are present. Especially is *Pulsatilla* the remedy when chlorosis has been complicated by the abuse of iron and quinine. Chlorotic patients, coming to you from allopathic hands after iron and quinine have failed to relieve, thus showing you that these remedies are not suitable to the case, will find their first, if not their only remedy, in *Pulsatilla*.

You will frequently find this hint of service to you in practice, not only in chlorosis, but in other affections as well, when they arise, not so much from local disease, as from a general defective state of nutrition; the whole system is worn out; every tissue is relaxed. The woman suffers from mal-position of the uterus. The menses are late and scanty, dark, clotted or changeable in character. *Pulsatilla* does not always cure after the abuse of iron, but it stands in the same relation to this substance that *Nux vomica* does to the abuse of drastic purgatives, and *Camphor* to cantharides.

To understand how these phenomena of *Pulsatilla* are caused—whether in women, where they are most frequently met with, or more exceptionally in men—you must remember that the drug acts upon the vascular system, especially upon the right heart, and upon the veins and capillaries. Thus we find that whatever weakens the venous portion of the circulation, whatever retards the return of blood to the heart, must of course provoke just the class of symptoms for which *Pulsatilla* may be indicated. We know, for instance, that a warm, close room will provoke these symptoms. If a person sits in a close room or in one where the temperature is too high, the veins will become tortuous and there will be some oppression about the chest and retardation of the heart's action. When these symptoms occur in disease they suggest *Pulsatilla*. It acts on the right heart more than on the left, consequently, despite the chilliness which arises from the anæmia, the open air acts as a stimulus to the venous circulation, and this improves the symptoms depending upon the sluggish flow of blood. You will find many symptoms throughout the entire body calling for *Pulsatilla* when there is this disturbance in the venous circulation.

In the chest there is a feeling of soreness referred to either the right or the left sub-clavicular region, or to the apex of one or the other lung. This soreness is felt when the patient lies on the affected side or presses against the chest. It seems to involve the muscular structures about the shoulder and even down the arm of the affected side. This symptom indicates venous congestion, or, at least, sluggish circulation through the upper part of the lung. It has been a valuable symptom to me and to many physicians in the incipiency of tuberculosis, especially in women of the *Pulsatilla* temperament. Along with this soreness in the lung there may be some cough with expectoration. Although there may be no symptoms indicating the positive existence of tuberculous infiltration we will have other symptoms indicating the onset of the disease. *Pulsatilla* has several times relieved these cases.

Then, too, we have *Pulsatilla* indicated in varicose veins, whether occurring on the limbs or about the testicle (varicocele). The affected parts are bluish and annoy the patient by the soreness and stinging pains in them.

The epistaxis of *Pulsatilla* is of a passive character. The flow comes steadily, but it is not bright red and does not come in gushes as it does in epistaxis dependent upon arterial lesions. It often occurs vicariously, taking the place of the menses. The same is true of the blood-spitting or hæmoptysis, which is either associated with this soreness or passive congestion of the chest or is dependent upon suppressed menstruation.

Pulsatilla has an important analogue, namely, *Hamamelis*, in these venous symptoms. Before *Hamamelis* was proved *Pulsatilla* was the only remedy we could depend upon in the class of symptoms enumerated. *Hamamelis* is the preferable drug in varicose veins unless constitutional symptoms call for *Pulsatilla*, especially in the case of varicocele. Varicocele has been cured by *Hamamelis* applied externally and taken internally. The great characteristic of this drug, and that which makes its choice certain, is soreness of the affected part. It is a soreness which is not exactly the bruised feeling of *Arnica;* it is not the sensitive soreness of *Lachesis;* nor the stinging soreness of *Apis;* but *it is that sore feeling which belongs to venous congestion.* You may apply *Hamamelis* successfully in any condition in which that is present. I have often made use of the drug in pregnancy, when varicose veins appeared over the abdomen, and when the patient could not make any motion without experiencing a bruised sore feeling. *Hamamelis* is not the panacea which druggists would have us believe. It does not cure everything, sprains, etc., but it *does* cure the class of symptoms I have mentioned.

Another concordant remedy of *Pulsatilla* is *Lilium tigrinum*, which, like the former, affects the right heart, producing engorgement of the veins, relief in the open air, scanty menses, and taste of blood in the mouth. But it differs from *Pulsatilla* in the decided tendency to prolapsus uteri, with bearing down, relieved by supporting the abdomen, or by crossing the limbs; and in the mental state, which is one of irritability and restlessness with constant desire to hurry. Furthermore, when *Lilium* is indicated, a sharp pain, extending from the left nipple through the chest to the back, is apt to be present.

Another analogue is *Sepia*, which has many of the *Pulsatilla* symptoms. *Sepia*, also, is indicated in anæmia and chlorosis, and it also has the mild tearful temperament, but there is a difference in the mental symptoms. With *Sepia* there may be irritability or at times vehemence.

The *Sepia* patient has complete aversion to her usual household duties.

Let us now consider the action of *Pulsatilla* on mucous membranes. This is easily remembered. It produces a catarrhal inflammation of the mucous membrane, which ends in the production of bland yellow or yellowish-green mucus. You have here an indication which you may apply to any mucous membrane.

Conjunctivitis calls for *Pulsatilla* when the discharge is thick, yellow or yellowish-green, and bland; hence it is not indicated in the beginning of the disease, but later in its course, when the symptoms have matured. It is an invaluable remedy in ophthalmia after measles, in purulent ophthalmia, and in ophthalmia neonatorum (whether these troubles are of gonorrhœal origin or not), when the discharge is of the character just described. Its analogue here is *Argentum nitricum*, which has precisely the same symptoms in more marked degree, and is to be used after the failure of *Pulsatilla*. The latter in turn sometimes serves as an intercurrent to spur on the action of *Argentum nitricum*.

Mercurius corrosivus is suitable in cases which, despite the use of *Argentum nitricum*, threaten to ulcerate and perforate the cornea.

These are not by any means the only eye symptoms of *Pulsatilla*. Dr. George S. Norton, of New York, published in the *Hahnemannian Monthly*, some years ago, a paper on the use of this remedy in diseases of the eye, which covered some six or eight pages. In addition to the conjunctival inflammation just noticed, *Pulsatilla* causes obscuration of vision, with vertigo and nausea, diplopia, starry apparitions, circles of fire, etc. (these generally being reflex symptoms); pustules on the cornea, with very little dread of light, but with lachrymation, worse in the open air; pressing, stinging pains in the eye; swollen lids; styes, relieved when in the open air; margins of the lids inflamed and swollen, but not excoriated.

In ophthalmia, with very little photophobia, it resembles *Graphites*, but has not the cracks along the lid-edges.

Pulsatilla is also an excellent remedy in small central corneal ulcers, with no vascular supply, especially when occurring in scrofulous subjects. It may still further be used in lachrymation from disease of the lachrymal duct when the symptoms just enumerated are present, and for lachrymation worse in the wind.

Pulsatilla also affects the nasal mucous membrane, developing here symptoms which indicate it in the advanced stages of a cold. It should not be given in the beginning of a cold unless the temperament and other symptoms decide, because sneezing and serous excoriating discharge are not characteristic *Pulsatilla* symptoms. But when you find a nasal catarrh "ripened," that is, when the nasal discharge is thick, muco-purulent, yellowish or yellowish-green, and not in the least excoriating, you have a perfect picture of *Pulsatilla*.

In chronic nasal catarrh you may give *Pulsatilla* if the discharge is of this character. You must give the drug frequently and persistently, in order to cure. In addition to the symptoms already enumerated, there is still another symptom, namely, loss of taste and smell. There is a remedy known as *Cyclamen*, which is very similar to *Pulsatilla* in its symptomatology. It seems to be suited to nasal catarrh when there are loss of taste and smell, and this thick discharge just like that of *Pulsatilla;* but it has, in addition, spasmodic sneezing and aversion to the open air.

Penthorum sedoides is useful in the incipiency of coryza when there is rawness in the nose and throat. The patient complains of a constant wet feeling in the nose, but without coryza. Later, there is a formation of thick purulent discharge, just as in *Pulsatilla*.

Spigelia is one of our best remedies for catarrh of the posterior nares. The symptoms indicating it are profuse discharge of mucus through the posterior nares; nasal mucus passes off only through the posterior nares. This drug has accomplished some good cures in the hands of Dr. Aug. Korndœrfer, who also recommends *Theridion* for this affection.

Hydrastis is also suited to post-nasal catarrh. The discharge is of a thin watery character, and is attended with a great deal of burning and rawness, together with a sensation as of a hair in the nostrils.

Pulsatilla is an invaluable remedy in affections of the ears. In otitis externa you may use it when the external ear is hot, red, and swollen, and there are darting, tearing, pulsating pains, which are worse at night.

In otitis media also it is useful when there is a profuse thick yellow or yellowish-green discharge from the ear.

Pulsatilla is one of our leading remedies in catarrhal otitis. There is deafness, with a feeling as if the ears were stopped up, with rushing noises in the ears, isochronous with the pulse. *Silicea* is the nearest remedy to *Pulsatilla* in catarrhal otorrhœa.

Belladonna and *Mercurius* have a deeper action than *Pulsatilla*, acting on the cellular tissues.

Chamomilla is similar to *Pulsatilla* in the ear symptoms, but the pains are more violent, and are attended with red cheeks; the patient cannot bear pain.

Plantago major is to be thought of when earache is associated with toothache.

Tellurium causes catarrh of the middle ear, which may penetrate into the cells of the mastoid process and establish an abscess there, or may even involve the internal ear or the brain. Pus forms in the middle ear, and finally, perforating the membrana tympani, escapes externally. The resultant discharge is thin and acrid, causing blisters wherever it touches, and smells like fish-brine.

In catarrh of the throat you will find *Pulsatilla* sometimes, though not frequently, the remedy. It would here be indicated by the appearance of the parts. There are a marked redness of the tonsils and a varicose condition of the blood-vessels of the parts, and the fauces have a dark red or purplish hue. There are also stinging pains in the throat (here reminding you of *Apis*), worse usually from swallowing saliva or after eating food.

Leaving the pharynx we next come to the stomach, where we find *Pulsatilla* indicated in catarrhal conditions. The tongue is coated with a thick rough white fur. The mouth feels dry, and yet there is not much thirst, thirstlessness being a characteristic of the remedy. There are also nausea, and sometimes vomiting, the vomited matters consisting either of food or mucus, and also of bile. The food vomited may have been that eaten a long time before, thus showing the weak digestion of the remedy. There is a feeling of fulness and heaviness in the stomach after eating, sometimes associated with a feeling of rawness in the stomach as from ulceration. The latter is merely a subjective symptom and is a common sensation in *Pulsatilla*. Usually there is diarrhœa, with slimy or watery stools, worse after midnight. Attending these gastric symptoms is heartburn and sometimes, though rarely, water-brash. When water-brash calls for *Pulsatilla* there is a putrid taste in the mouth in the morning, better after drinking. The patient craves lemonade. He may complain that his mouth is dry, yet it seems to contain plenty of mucus. Other symptoms experienced are: feeling of weight in the epigastrium an hour after eating, relieved by eating again; feeling in the œsophagus as if food were lying there (also *China, Abies*); throbbing in the epigastrium; much flatulence which moves about, causing pinching pains and rumbling, worse on awaking or just after supper. Now these are the symptoms calling for this remedy in gastric catarrh. What are the exciting causes? First of all and most important, *Pulsatilla* is called for when the trouble has arisen after partaking of fatty food or of pastry. It is also indicated in gastric catarrh arising from a mixed diet, as turkey, vegetables, coffee, etc., especially if eaten at night; also after chilling the stomach with ice-cream or ice-water, especially if the stomach is warm. In still other cases it may be indicated after getting wet, especially after getting the feet wet when suppression of the menses ensues.

Let us now differentiate this remedy from the others commonly used in these dyspeptic symptoms. The most important remedies besides *Pulsatilla*, having aggravation from eating fatty foods, are *Ipecac., Thuja* and *Carbo veg*. *Arsenicum* and *Carbo veg* have aggravation from eating ice-cream, and *Nux vomica* and *Ipecac.* from partaking of a mixed diet, or aggravation from eating at night; in this condition you may think also of *Cinchona*. In desire for lemonade, compare *Cyclamen, Sabina* and *belladonna;* nausea at the thought or smell of food, particularly if rich or fat, *Sepia* and *Colchicum;* in vomiting of food long after eating, *Kreosote*.

Bryonia produces a catarrh of the stomach with white coated tongue, putrid taste in the mouth and a feeling as of a heavy load in the stomach. It may also be indicated in gastric catarrh brought on by chilling the stomach, although it is more suitable when the trouble has been brought on by the heat of summer weather. *Bryonia* usually, however, has constipation as an accompanying symptom, or if it has diarrhœa, it has not this yellowish-green or watery stool. Instead of this, the stools are papescent and have a putrid odor like old cheese.

Nux vomica resembles *Pulsatilla*. Both are serviceable in catarrh of the stomach arising from overeating or from a mixed diet. Especially is *Nux* indicated after indulgence in alcoholic drinks. Dryness of the mouth with little or no thirst and uncomfortable feeling about the stomach, are also found under *Nux vomica*. The bowels are constipated. Comparatively speaking, we may say that heartburn is more characteristic of *Pulsatilla* and water-brash more characteristic of *Nux vomica*. The mental symptoms of the two remedies differ widely, and they should be easy to distinguish on this account.

Antimonium crudum resembles *Pulsatilla*, but the tongue under this remedy is coated white as though it had been whitewashed. Vomiting predominates over the other symptoms. A slight quantity of food excites nausea and vomiting. It is an excellent remedy in children.

Ipecacuanha is a first-class remedy in these gastric catarrhs caused by chilling the stomach with ice-water or by eating pastry, confectionery or other indigestible substances. Usually the tongue is clean. It seldom has the thick coating belonging to *Pulsatilla* or *Antimonium crudum*, and nausea predominates over every other symptom.

Arsenicum is complementary to *Pulsatilla* when gastric catarrh arises from chilling the stomach with ice-cream or ice-water.

Under *Pulsatilla* there is a sensation as of a stone in the epigastrium. You will find a similar symptom under *Abies nigra*, which has been successfully used in gastric troubles when the patient experiences a sensation as of a hard-boiled egg in the stomach after eating.

You may use *Pulsatilla* in constipation occurring in pregnant women or following the abuse of *Cinchona* and its preparations. The stools are large, with much urging and backache, or they are insufficient and finally consist of nothing but yellow mucus. You may also use it for diarrhœa when the stools are of a greenish-yellow color or are very changeable. The trouble is usually caused by partaking of a mixed diet late the night before, and the symptoms are apt to be markedly worse after midnight.

Here you should compare *Iris versicolor*, which is one of the best remedies we have for cholera morbus, coming preferably at two or three o'clock in the morning with vomiting of food and sour, bilious matters, accompanied by purging. It differs from *Veratrum album* in the absence of coldness and symptoms of collapse.

In cystitis or catarrh of the bladder we find *Pulsatilla* indicated when there is frequent urging to urinate from pressure on the bladder as if the bladder were too full. There is pain in the urethra. The urine itself is often turbid from the admixture of mucus. Clinically, we have not found *Pulsatilla* a first-class remedy in cystitis, but we have found it almost always the remedy in cystic symptoms accompanying pregnancy. It yields to *Cantharis*, *Equisetum* and *Dulcamara* in cystitis.

Gonorrhœa calls for *Pulsatilla* when the discharge is thick, bland and yellow or yellowish-green. There are usually pains in the groins when this drug is indicated, and I have noticed, too, pains going across the hypogastrium from side to side, a symptom that has sometimes been produced by overdosing with *Pulsatilla*. After giving it a few times in these cases, the patient returns, complaining of this aching across the stomach. This symptom occurring thus, calls for the lengthening of the intervals between the doses, or else for its stoppage altogether.

In suppression of gonorrhœa, *Pulsatilla* is indicated if orchitis, or rather epididymitis, ensues. The testicle is retracted, enlarged, very sensitive to the touch and the skin of the scrotum is dark red. There are sharp dragging pains following the course of the spermatic cord. Unless some other symptoms contra-indicate it, *Pulsatilla* will restore the discharge and relieve the distressing pain, but the patient must be kept quiet and the scrotum must be supported in a suspensory. In some cases I have used hot water locally as an adjuvant. While it seems to increase the swelling, it relieves the pain.

In some of these cases there appears to be an absence of symptoms of a subjective character. All you can observe is that the testicle is swollen and exquisitely sore to the touch. The gonorrhœal discharge has almost if not entirely ceased. In these cases *Hamamelis* is your remedy.

Clematis is an excellent remedy for gonorrhœal orchitis when the testicle is indurated and is "as hard as a stone."

Rhododendron also is a useful remedy when the orchitis becomes chronic and the testicle is indurated exactly like *Clematis*. Under *Rhododendron*, however, the testicle tends to atrophy. There is also a feeling in the gland as if it were being crushed.

In induration of the testicle you may compare *Conium*, *Arnica*, *Staphisagria*, *Spongia*, *Aurum metallicum*, besides the remedies already mentioned. You may give *Oxalic acid* when there are terrible neuralgic pains in the spermatic cords, worse from the slightest motion, and even on thinking of them.

Ustilago and *Hamamelis* also cause neuralgia of the testicle.

Mercurius is called for when the glands are swollen, and when what little discharge remains is greenish, and when there is phimosis.

Pulsatilla is of use in enlargement of the prostate. It is indicated by the mechanical symptom, fæces, when they escape, are small and flat.

Hydrocele, especially the congenital form, may yield to *Pulsatilla*.

Next let us study *Pulsatilla* in its relations to synovial membranes. *Pulsatilla* has not an affinity for the true serous membranes, as we found under *Aconite* and *Bryonia*, but it acts on the synovial sacs, which are slightly different from the pure serous membranes. The remedy is indicated in rheumatism of the joints, and in gouty, gonorrhœal and traumatic synovitis. The joint is, of course, swollen, and the pains are of a sharp stinging character, and are accompanied by a feeling of soreness or of subcutaneous ulceration about the affected joint. The pains in these joint inflammations are usually erratic, now here and now there. The tearing pains in the joint force the patient to move the affected part. Pressure relieves. These tearing pains often extend down the limb, and are accompanied by jerking, probably through irritation of the muscular nerves, and are relieved by slowly moving about. I dwell upon these pains because they so frequently call for *Pulsatilla*. They are usually worse from warmth, and are relieved by cold. They are worse in the evening.

Pulsatilla rivals *Apis* in synovitis, but the latter drug has more effusion than the former, and is indicated when there is a great deal of œdema about the joint.

Ledum and *Lac caninum* have pains worse from warmth. In the former they travel downward; in the latter they shift from one limb to the other and back again.

In rheumatism with erratic pains, you may compare *Kali bichromicum*, *Sulphur* and *Bryonia*.

Chamomilla has stitching pains, jumping from place to place, worse in the knees and ankles, but they are accompanied by numbness and a sense of weakness. The temperament is totally unlike that of *Pulsatilla*.

Kali bichromicum is called tor in gonorrhœal rheumatism. The pains are better in a warm room.

By reason of its action on the digestive organs, *Pulsatilla* becomes of value in gout or in the gouty diathesis, especially when the trouble has been brought on by indigestion. If the disease persists despite its use, *Colchicum* follows well.

Now let us consider the action of *Pulsatilla* on the various organs. We have already studied the mental symptoms of the drug. We have yet to speak of its headaches. These we may summarize as being mostly frontal and supra-orbital. They are generally of uterine, neuralgic, rheumatic or gastric origin. They are aggravated by mental exertion and by warmth. They are usually worse in the evening, although the gastric symptoms are worse in the morning. When of rheumatic origin, the pains are sharp and seem to go from the head into the face and almost drive the patient mad, so severe are they. In other cases they may be erratic, wandering from one part of the head to the other.

In some cases the headache accompanies menstrual suppression. The head is hot. The pain in the head is better in the open air and is often accompanied by nose-bleed.

In these headaches you should compare *Pulsatilla* with the following remedies:

Ranunculus bulbosus, headache on the vertex as if the head were being pressed asunder, worse in the evening and on going from cold to warm air and *vice versa*.

Ranunculus sceleratus, gnawing in the vertex in a small spot.

Cocculus Indicus, pain in the occiput as if it were opening and shutting.

Spigelia, sensation as if the head were open along the vertex.

Carbo animalis, feeling on the vertex as if pressed asunder; must hold it together.

Veratrum album, pressure on the vertex, with pain in the stomach; head relieved by pressing the vertex, and aggravated by motion.

Menyanthes, compressive headache in the vertex and sensation when ascending steps as if a weight pressed on the brain, better from pressure, and accompanied by cold hands and feet.

Phellandrium, pain as from a weight on the top of the head, with aching and burning in the temples and above the eyes, which are congested; eyes water; can bear neither light nor sound.

The eye symptoms of *Pulsatilla*, and some of those of the ear, have already been considered. We shall now proceed with the remaining ear symptoms. *Pulsatilla* has long been known as a remedy for otitis externa or inflammation of the external auditory meatus. The pains are very severe, as indeed they must be from the confined nature of the canal, surrounded as it is by bone. The external ear is swollen and red. The pains are usually worse at night. The trouble may end with otorrhœa, which has the character already described.

We come next to the action of *Pulsatilla* on the female organism. It is here that *Pulsatilla* has won its laurels. We find it indicated in girls at the age of puberty, when the menstrual flow has not established itself normally, or has not appeared at all. It is especially at this time that you may find soreness of the apices of the lungs, calling for *Pulsatilla*, and you know that unless you remove this symptom and establish the menstrual flow, your patient will have some form of phthisis. When the menses are established they are apt to be too late and too scanty. The flow is fitful in its character, now coming on and now stopping, now appearing as dark clotted blood, and again as an almost colorless watery flow. It is preceded by menstrual colic. The pains are of a crampy, griping character, and so severe that the patient can hardly bear them. She almost smothers if the room is close She has the *Pulsatilla* temperament well-marked. Amenorrhœa may call for *Pulsatilla* when it occurs during the ordinary period of menstruation, or as a result of wet feet, and when nose-bleed acts vicariously for the menses. In some of these cases a single dose will bring on the menstrual flow, while in others you are obliged to give the drug repeatedly.

During pregnancy you may find use for *Pulsatilla*. Soreness of the uterus and of the abdominal walls may call for it as well as for *Hamamelis*.

Then again it may correct malpositions of the fœtus in utero, if the cause is not mechanical. Now I know that in making this statement I am venturing on debatable ground. I do not mean to say that *Pulsatilla* will make the fœtus turn around. But I do mean to say that *Pulsatilla* will act on the muscular walls of the uterus, and stimulate their growth. Sometimes the uterus in its growth during pregnancy develops more on one side than another. Hence there is irregularity in its development, and the fœtus must assume an irregular position. *Pulsatilla*, by altering the growth of the uterus, permits the fœtus to assume its proper position.

During labor *Pulsatilla* is called for when the pains are slow, weak and ineffectual. Then, again, we may find the pains spasmodic and irregular, and they may even excite fainting, as in *Nux vomica*. The patient feels as if smothering, and calls on you to open the windows.

Again *Pulsatilla* may be called for after labor when the placenta remains adherent. In these cases it will not only bring about release of the placenta, but will so tone up the uterus as to avoid post-partum hæmorrhage. *Cantharis* and *Gossypium* are also useful in this condition.

Again *Pulsatilla* is many times the remedy in simple retained placenta, which allies it with *Sepia, Sabina, Secale* and *Caulophyllum.*

Pulsatilla may also be used for after-pains, the temperament agreeing. These pains, however, call more frequently for *Chamomilla, Caulophyllum* and *Xanthoxylum.* The last two remedies are particularly useful.

Cuprum metallicum is a good remedy for severe crampy after-pains in women who have borne many children.

Pulsatilla may also be used for scanty or suppressed lochia.

It may also be indicated as frequently as *Hamamelis* in phlegmasia alba dolens, or "milk-leg."

The mammary glands are affected by *Pulsatilla* before, during, and after pregnancy. It is indicated when mechanical irritation, as, for instance, carrying school-books, excites the flow of milk. After labor you may still give this remedy when the breast is swollen and painful and the flow of milk scanty or absent, the patient being gloomy and tearful.

In this connection I may mention several remedies that are more important than *Pulsatilla.* I think that *Urtica urens* is the best remedy for non-appearance of the milk without any other symptoms, there being no apparent reason for the agalactia.

Still another remedy is *Ricinus communis* or castor oil. This has, when used externally, developed milk. It may also be successful when given internally in low potency.

Agnus castus is useful in agalactia when the mind is greatly depressed.

Causticum is called for in women of a rheumatic diathesis. The face is usually sallow and the patient gloomy and depressed.

In its relation to diseases of women, *Pulsatilla* has a great many allies. First of all we may mention *Actea racemosa* or *Cimicifuga.* This remedy resembles *Pulsatilla* because it acts on the uterus. Both remedies favor normal labor. Here *Actea* is probably the superior of the two. It also resembles *Pulsatilla* in its action during labor, being indicated for labor-pains which are very distressing. The symptoms, however, are not intermittent, but rather continuous, and as to temperament, we find *Actea racemosa* differing from *Pulsatilla.* For instance, it is indicated in a high degree of nervousness, both during labor and out of labor, during which the woman has an intensely apprehensive mood. She has a dread or fear of something about to happen, and this haunts her from day to day. At other times she has a dread of undertaking anything, even ordinary work. *Actea racemosa* is also indicated in any deviation from normal in the position of the uterus when there are sharp cutting pains across the hypogastrium from side to side. It is also to be used for neuralgia reflex from uterine irritation, and that, too, whether it be the nerves of the head, chest or limbs that are involved.

Another remedy to be compared with *Pulsatilla* is *Caulophyllum*. This is a remedy that we have not had many years, and yet it is so useful that we would not now be able to get along without it. Its main characteristic is intermittency of pains. If they are neuralgic and reflex from uterine disorder, they are intermittent in character. They are usually sharp and crampy, and appear in the bladder, groins and lower extremities. During labor *Caulophyllum* is indicated when there is extreme uterine atony. The pains may be as severe as ever, yet there is apparently no expulsive effort. It is often indicated in nervous women in whom pain seems to be intolerable. The pains are spasmodic and fly about from place to place, now in the groins, then in the abdomen, and next in the chest, never going in the direction of the normal pains. The patient seems to be exhausted. There is great exhaustion of the whole system. She can scarcely speak at times, so weak is the voice. These are symptoms which indicate *Caulophyllum*. It has been used here by most physicians in the low potencies, although all potencies may be used. It may also be indicated during the last weeks of pregnancy when the patient suffers from false labor-pains, these consisting of painful bearing-down sensations in the hypogastrium. I have known a single dose to stop them after they had lasted for hours.

I have next to speak of *Helonias dioica*, or the false unicorn, one of the order of Liliaceæ. This is one of the new remedies, and it is one which has proved itself worthy of a place by the side of the well-tried *Pulsatilla*. It is serviceable in females who are run down as to their nervous system; who are easily fatigued by any work and who complain of a tired backache, this tired feeling extending into the limbs. They seem to feel better when they are working than they did when they commenced to work. Now this is not the *Rhus tox*. condition. It is not due to a limbering up of stiff joints as under the latter remedy. The reason for the symptom is, that some of the languor passes off as the patient continues her labors. The backache is usually situated in the lumbar region just over the site of the kidneys, or it may appear lower down and affect the sacral region. Pain in either of these locations may accompany uterine disturbances. You will find also that *Helonias* is useful for suppression of the menses (here it is closely akin to *Pulsatilla*), when the kidneys are congested. It seems as if the monthly congestion, instead of venting itself as it should through the uterine vessels, has extended to the kidneys, giving rise to albuminuria. The urine is scanty and turbid. Then, again, you find *Helonias* called for after confinement, when there is a tendency to prolapsus and other malpositions of the uterus. The patient complains of heaviness and dragging in the pelvic region. There is a sensitiveness which has been expressed as "consciousness of the existence of a womb." You know that we are not conscious of our internal organs. They move and perform their respective functions without any sensation. The minute our sensations tell us that we have a stomach or liver, that minute we begin to have disease there. Accompanying these symptoms of prolapsus and of uterine over-sensitiveness is apt to be too long-lasting lochia, if I may use that term. To be more exact, I should say that there is a sanguineous discharge, which continues for weeks after confinement. I can recall a case which I treated last winter. It was that of a lady who gave birth to a very large child, and suffered afterward from prolapsus uteri. I gave her several remedies without relieving her, so that at the end of three months she was still uncured. About this time she began to complain of tightness across the chest, with cough and some little bloody sputum. Her mother had died of phthisis after giving birth to twins, so I feared serious lung affection. *Phosphorus* did no good; *Nux* did no good. I studied up the case more thoroughly. She told me that she felt as though there were a heavy weight over the chest on the sternum, and a feeling as though the chest had been gripped in a vise with the sore feeling which follows. This annoyed her when she awakened at night. These symptoms were symptoms which had been noticed only in the male provers of *Helonias*. Nevertheless I gave that drug, and it entirely removed both the chest symptoms and the prolapsus. Then, again, under *Helonias* you frequently find a tendency to inflammation of the vulva and vagina with formation of pus. You may also use it in ulceration of the cervix uteri. With this there is a leucorrhœa which has a bad odor, and every little exertion tends to produce a flow of blood. With these symptoms there is almost always persistent itching about the genitals with or without the formation of blisters or sores. We know little or nothing concerning the value of *Helonias* during labor.

A drug to be placed by the side of *Helonias* is *Senecio aureus*. This drug causes inflammation of mucous membranes, hence it is useful when there is a tendency to catarrh of the nose, throat and lungs, particularly in women. It is especially suited to nervous, excitable women who suffer much from sleeplessness, traceable to uterine irritation, as from prolapse or flexion of the uterus. The patient suffers from scanty menstruation, and she is apt to be tearful. There is dry teasing cough, with stitching pains in the chest and blood-streaked sputum. The bladder sympathizes with the uterine disease. There is much pain at the neck of the bladder causing burning and tenesmus. After the onset of the menstrual flow the chest and cystic symptoms become modified or cease, thus showing how intimately they are related to the irregularity in the menstrual effort.

Another drug is *Aletris farinosa*. This is one of the most bitter substances known. It is closely allied to *Senecio* and *Helonias*. In allopathic parlance it is a "tonic." It is especially useful in women who, in addition to uterine trouble and leucorrhœa, have extreme constipation, great effort being required to effect an evacuation from the bowels. There is great accumulation of frothy saliva. *Aletris* is a remedy also for weakness of digestion; food distresses the patient and lies heavily in the stomach.

Cyclamen is very similar to *Pulsatilla*. They are both suited to chlorotic and anæmic women, and they both have some trouble with the digestion, and intolerance of fatty foods. The menstrual colic and irregularities are almost identical in the two drugs. The same kind of melancholy is common to both. *Cyclamen* may be distinguished from *Pulsatilla* by the following symptoms. Generally, but not always, there is more thirst with the *Cyclamen* patient. The *Pulsatilla* patient feels better in the open air, the *Cyclamen* does not. The *Cyclamen* patients suffer from a peculiar kind of torpidity, both of mind and body, with languor. They cannot think. They are better when aroused and forced to exercise, something like *Helonias*. When they get up in the morning they feel so heavy and languid that they feel as though they could scarcely go through the day's duties, but when they once get to work they go on tolerably well until night time. That is *Cyclamen*, and it is very much like *Helonias*. They suffer, too, from dulness of the senses with flickering before the eyes. You often find this in weak anæmic women. They see various colors before the eyes, very much as under *Santonin*, *Conium*, *Kali bichromicum*, etc. Sometimes they have half-sight. The indigestion with which they are troubled has this to characterize it: formation of flatus which causes colic at night, forcing the patient to get up and walk about till the flatus passes and gives relief.

It yet remains for me to speak of *Hydrastis Canadensis*. This is a remedy which acts even more powerfully on mucous membranes than does *Pulsatilla*. It causes catarrh of the mucous membranes of the nose, stomach, bowels, bladder, uterus and vagina, the discharge, however, being more acrid than it is under *Pulsatilla*, and of a thick yellow or bloody appearance; in uterine affections *Hydrastis* is indicated for prolapsus uteri with ulceration of the cervix. The leucorrhœa is watery at times, and at other times thick, yellow and excoriating: this condition being associated with gone, weak feeling at the pit of the stomach and well-marked palpitation of the heart. The tongue is moist, and coated a dirty yellow color, and takes the imprint of the teeth. The face is sallow, and the eyes are sunken and surrounded by dark rings. The bowels are apt to be constipated, the stools being coated or intermixed with mucus.

Lastly may be mentioned *Lilium tigrinum*, which helps in uterine complaints when there are sharp pains across the abdomen from one ilium to the other; in addition there are marked bearing-down pains, making the patient cross her limbs. She places her hand over the vulva to support the viscera.

Pulsatilla cures a fever with these symptoms: the head is hot and the lips are dry; the patient is constantly licking his lips to moisten them, yet he does not wish to drink. It may also be used in intermittent fever after the abuse of quinine when thirst appears at two or three o'clock in the afternoon; then comes chill without thirst, and anxiety and oppression from venous congestion of the chest. The patient is sleepy, yet she cannot sleep. Sometimes one hand is hot and the other cold.

Pulsatilla acts on the larynx, causing hoarseness which comes and goes capriciously. Such a hoarseness frequently marks the termination of a "cold," and this remedy may prevent its becoming chronic. It also cures purely nervous hoarseness appearing with every emotion.

In the chest we again have symptoms of a catarrhal nature.

Bronchitis with thick yellow expectoration; or dry, tickling cough from irritation in the trachea, worse in the evening and on lying down, with dry air passages or a scraped, raw feeling. Occasionally there is dyspnœa or constriction of the chest.

I warn you not to select *Pulsatilla* for a loose cough unless you are sure that all the symptoms of the case call for it. It often tightens such a cough without curing it.

Bloodspitting has already been mentioned. This may be vicarious or it may belong to incipient consumption. In the latter case there may be added soreness in the chest, worse under the clavicles; burning in the chest, especially in the region of the heart; stitches in the sides of the chest.

Pulsatilla Nuttalliana has sharp pains below the left arm-pit near the back.

In dry night-cough compare *Hyoscyamus*, *Conium*, *Actea racemosa*, *Laurocerasus*, *Bryonia*, etc.

Pulsatilla is indicated in measles, but I think that it is often given in the wrong place. It is indicated when the catarrhal symptoms are prominent and we have coryza and profuse lachrymation. The cough is usually dry at night and loose in the day time. The child sits up in bed to cough. It may also be used when there is earache. Do not give *Pulsatilla* in the beginning when the fever is high. You should begin the case with *Aconite* or *Gelsemium*. The eruption may come out to its full extent or it may have a dusky appearance.

Kali bichromicum is to be used when, instead of simple catarrh of the eyes, you have pustules developed on the cornea. The throat is swollen and pains go from the throat into the ears; the salivary glands are swollen, and there is catarrhal deafness.

In neuralgia, *Pulsatilla* is indicated when the pains are jerking, erratic and paroxysmal, and as they continue they become more and more unbearable.

Spinal irritation is also an indication for the drug. The neck, and in fact the whole body, feels as stiff as a board. The small of the back feels as if tightly bandaged. There are pains in the sacral region, worse on sitting and when bending backward. The joints feel weak, as if they would become readily dislocated. Rest relieves these symptoms, hence the patient is better after sleep.

In backache, worse from sitting, you may think of *Zincum*, *Cobalt*, *Sepia*, *Cannabis Indica*, *Agaricus*, *Berberis*, *Rhus tox.*, *Valerian*, etc.

The sleep symptoms of *Pulsatilla* are very characteristic. The sleep is restless with frequent waking and troubled dreams; on waking the patient is dull and listless.

In sleep symptoms *Pulsatilla* and *Nux vomica* differ very much. While the former is wide awake and full of ideas in the evening, *Nux* is sleepy in the evening. The *Nux* patient awakes at three or four o'clock in the morning feeling rested. Then he goes to sleep again and awakes at the usual time feeling a great deal worse.

Cocculus has sleeplessness from pure mental activity. Ailments folow very slight deprivation of sleep.

Sulphur has "slightest noise at night awakens the patient."

LECTURE XXXV.

RUBIACEÆ.

Rubiaceæ.
- Cinchona.
- Ipecacuanha.
- Coffea.
- Rubia tinctoria. (Madder.)
- Galium. (A red dye.)
- Mitchella.
- Gambier.

To-day, gentlemen, we have before us an order of plants from which we derive three very valuable drugs, *Cinchona*, *Ipecacuanha* and *Coffea*. This order also gives us *Gambier* (a drug not used in our materia medica) and *Mitchella*, besides several dyes, as the famous Madder and Galium.

From the fact that these dyes are red, the order derives its name.

The first drug on the board is the *Cinchona*, frequently, although improperly, called *China* in our nomenclature. We shall now proceed with its consideration:

Cinchona Rubra.

Cinchona
- Ipecac., Arsenicum, Ferrum met., Veratrum album, Carbo veg.
- Phosphoric acid, Phosphorus, Rhus tox., Bryonia, Pulsatilla.
- Nux vomica, Podophyllum, Eupatorium perf., Natrum mur.
- Chininum sulph., Aranea diadema.
- Lachesis, Cornus florida, Eucalyptus.
- \> Pulsatilla, Arsenicum, Ipecac, Veratrum album.
- < Selenium, Digitalis.

Cinchona.
- Loss of fluids.
- Anæmia.
- Ill-effects of sudden or acute diseases.
- Hæmorrhage.
- Fevers: malarial, intermittent, hectic.
- Digestive organs.
- Rheumatism.
- Neuralgia.

Cinchona is certainly a wonderful drug, wonderful in the many varieties of its species, wonderful in its composition and wonderful in its effects. It also has a historical value to homœopathists as being the drug which led Hahnemann to the discovery of the law of cure and enabled him to establish Homœopathy as a fixed science. It is not a little singular that the natives of Peru, especially in the early days, would not permit the *Cinchona* tree to be touched, as they believed it to be poisonous and under the charge of special gods. They were, therefore, greatly astonished when Europeans became engaged in the occupation of stripping the bark from the trees and exporting it to Europe. The *Cinchona* industry has now grown to such an enormous extent as to demand certain restrictions in its gathering and exportation lest the species become extinct. New trees are being continually planted, so that there is no danger of extermination of the drug.

There are several varieties of the *Cinchona* bark, of which, however, I can mention but three, namely, the pale bark, the *Calisaya* or yellow bark, and, lastly, the red bark, or *Cinchona rubra*. There are some thirty other species known.

A physician in the West, the value of whose experiments I am inclined to doubt, claims to have discovered in *Cinchona rubra* a certain specific against intemperance, or the thirst for liquor. He gives the bark in appreciable doses, and claims that in a time varying from one to four weeks it will cure the most confirmed inebriate of his pernicious appetite.

In publishing the accounts of his observations in the journals, he says that he was led to his discovery on treating an "old sot" who had never known a sober day until he had chills and fever, which was cured by red bark.

Cinchona contains a number of alkaloids which are closely related chemically; in fact, many of them are isomeric. They are associated with various organic acids peculiar to the group.

The most important of the *Cinchona* alkaloids are given below:

Quinine, $C_{20}H_{24}N_2O_2$.
Quinidine, $C_{20}H_{24}N_2O_2$.
Cinchonine, $C_{20}H_{24}N_2O$.
Cinchonidine, $C_{20}H_{24}N_2O$.
Quinamine, $C_{20}H_{24}N_2O_2$.
Quinic acid, $C_7H_{12}O_6$.
Cincho-tannic acid.
Quinovic acid, $C_{24}H_{38}O_4$.

It now remains for us to study the general effects of *Cinchona* before we proceed with our consideration of its symptomatology.

It has been determined that a solution of *Quinine* of one part to ten thousand acts destructively on bacteria and infusoria. Thus it will destroy the poisons that propagate many of the contagious diseases, as puerperal fever, scarlatina, etc. You may make use of this property when going from one case of puerperal disease to another, for if you bathe your hair and whiskers in a solution of *Quinine* in bay-rum, this will destroy all danger of carrying the contagion and will not prove a source of annoyance to yourselves. On the contrary, it will aid the growth of the hair and beard.

Quinine and its salts when topically applied to a denuded surface or to a mucous membrane, act as decided irritants.

Quinine also has a toxic action upon all protoplasm. It is particularly active in preventing amœboid movement, which, as you know, is possessed by the leucocytes. This is one reason why allopathic physicians have used it to prevent inflammation. *Quinine* also inhibits enzyme action, thus retarding tissue metabolism. That is one explanation of its tonic effect. You will see, however, that this property of retarding waste is still more marked in *Coffea*.

Quinine also acts upon the heart substance, weakening that structure. Thus there is impaired circulation.

Another effect of *Quinine* is that large quantities injected subcutaneously destroy the oxygenating power of the blood. Furthermore it has the ability to reduce hyperpyrexia. This appears to be accomplished mainly by a direct action on the heat-producing foci

It also tends to act on the spleen, producing congestion, inflammation and enlargement of that viscus.

There is still one other property of *Quinine* which it may be well to remember, and that is its power of abolishing reflex action when taken in large quantities.

Now let me give you the symptoms of cinchonism, that is, the symptoms which follow the excessive use of *Cinchona bark* or of *Quinine*. You will find prominent among these symptoms an increase of appetite from stimulation of digestion. Soon nausea and vomiting appear, and even diarrhœa may be added to the gastric disturbances. Then the head becomes affected. There is a peculiar sensitiveness to external impressions, to noises, to bright lights or to anything that is apt to render the patient irritable. There is experienced a peculiar form of headache, which is characterized by dull aching and at other times by throbbing in the head. There are well-marked ringing or roaring sounds in the ears, a very characteristic effect of *Cinchona*. Vertigo still further complicates the case. If the use of the drug is still persisted in, deafness follows.

In other cases there appears a sort of *Cinchona* intoxication which is not unlike that produced by alcohol This is followed by delirium, dilated pupils, then complete stupor with difficult respiration and finally convulsions, these convulsions arising from anæmia of the nerve centres and not from congestion, as is the case with *Belladonna*. In extreme cases collapse and death from paralysis of the heart end the patient's life. These, then, are the general effects of *Cinchona*, when that drug is given persistently in increasing doses and at short intervals. They may vary in severity from a simple ringing in the ears to all the symptoms of complete poisoning.

Hahnemann has taught us that *Cinchona* is useful only when debility or anæmia comes from loss of fluids. In the allopathic school it is used in all forms of debility, given either alone or in combination with iron or sherry wine. But, as I have said before, we have learned from Hahnemann that it is useful only in the anæmia which results from loss of fluids. Hence, you may use it for the results of hæmorrhage, whether it be from the mouth, lungs or uterus. You may use it when long-lasting diarrhœa has exhausted the patient. It may even be used when the condition has proceeded further than a simple debility, and that horrible disease known as hydrocephaloid has developed.

In such cases, when *Cinchona* is the remedy, the child has these symptoms: after violent or long-lasting cholera infantum, it becomes drowsy; the pupils may be dilated, the breathing is very rapid and superficial; the diarrhœa may have ceased, or the movements may be involuntary; the surface of the body is rather cool, especially the prominent features about the face; thus, the ears, nose, and chin are cold. In just such cases as this, *Cinchona* will, if there is any vitality remaining, restore the patient to health.

If it should fail, you may still fall back on *Calcarea phosphorica*, a similar but more deeply-acting drug.

In applying *Cinchona* to the debility resulting from sexual excesses, remember that it is only curative for the debility resulting from the excessive loss of semen. If there are constitutional troubles it is worse than useless.

Now let us pause and study the relation which *Cinchona* bears to other drugs applicable to debilitated and anæmic conditions.

Ferrum is indicated in pure anæmia, with an appearance of plethora.

Arsenicum is the remedy for debility resulting from overtaxing of the muscular tissues, such as follows prolonged exertion, climbing mountains, etc.

Phosphorus is preferably indicated in prostration which is very sudden in its onset, when the nervous system is exhausted. Hence, we may have to use this drug in a variety of diseases, in scarlatina, in measles, in diphtheria, and, in fact, in any disease in which the nervous system seems to have sustained a sudden shock or blow. This is not a *Cinchona* case, remember.

Phosphoric acid is somewhat different from *Phosphorus*. It is to be thought of in debility of nervous origin, when it is not connected with any pain except, perhaps, a simple burning in the spine or in the limbs. The mind is rather apathetic, and the patient is inclined to be drowsy and sleepy. The characteristic of this sleepiness is that he is easily aroused from it and is wide awake.

Zincum is good when the brain becomes affected in the course of nervous diseases, scarlatina or summer complaint of infants. Especially is it useful in scarlatina when the child has not sufficient strength to develop an eruption.

You may use *Cinchona* for hæmorrhages, and here you can scarcely do without the drug. The hæmorrhage may come from any orifice of the body; the blood is apt to be dark and clotted; the flow is so profuse as to have almost produced exsanguination of the body; there is coldness of the face, of the whole body in fact; the features show the presence of collapse; there is gasping for breath; the patient demands to be fanned. Now, this fanning is desired, not for the purpose of cooling the patient, but is called for because of the instinctive demand for more oxygen, which the fanning produces by changing the strata of air about the patient's head. *Cinchona* is frequently called for in ante-partum and post-partum hæmorrhages; in such cases you do not give it in a single dose, but repeatedly, at short intervals, until the consequences of the hæmorrhage have been removed.

There is another condition in which I would recommend *Cinchona*, and that is, when retained placenta is attended with hæmorrhage. *Pulsatilla* does no good. I know that it has been recommended in these cases to take away the after-birth by manual interference, but it has been my practice to administer *Cinchona* until the tonicity of the uterus is restored, and then remove the placenta.

The nearest remedy to *Cinchona* in these symptoms is *Ipecacuanha*, which is useful when there is profuse bright red flow of blood, usually accompanied by nausea, and sometimes by very hard, labored breathing. Sometimes there is coldness of the surface of the skin, which is covered with cold sweat. It is one of our best remedies in the hæmoptysis of incipient phthisis.

Belladonna is useful when the hæmorrhage is of bright blood, coagulating rapidly, and feeling hot to the parts over which it flows.

Trillium controls hæmorrhage when the flow is either bright red or dark, and occurs in women who flood after every labor.

Millefolium is suited for a profuse, bright red flow, unattended with pain; it is much like *Aconite*, but it lacks the restlessness, anxiety and fever of that remedy; it has, also, continuous flow after an injury.

Sabina is to be used when the flow is bright red with clots, and is worse from any motion. The hæmorrhage is attended with pain extending from the pubes through to the sacrum, and with pains in the legs.

Carbo vegetabilis is to be given when there is a continuous dark passive hæmorrhage. The patient wants to be fanned. The skin is cool and bluish, and the pulse rapid and weak.

Secale is said to be best adapted to thin scrawny women. The flow of blood is passive; it is attended with tingling in the limbs. Although the surface of the body is cold, the patient persistently expresses her desire to be uncovered.

Erigeron is said to be useful in profuse hæmorrhage similar to that of *Sabina*, but associated with irritation of the bladder and rectum.

Hamamelis is suited to passive venous hæmorrhages, especially when the part from which the flow of blood proceeds feels sore and bruised.

Acalypha Indica is useful in hæmoptysis after fits of dry coughing.

Cinnamomum, profuse hæmorrhage from a strain or misstep.

Cyclamen, profuse hæmorrhage, with dizziness and obscured vision, as from a fog. This is different from the natural syncope resulting from excessive or sudden bleeding. It may follow slight losses of blood in women of a delicate build, whose weakness is cerebro-spinal.

You may also compare *Ledum*, *Vinca minor* and *Phosphorus* if the hæmorrhage is caused by uterine polypi.

When reaction has been established after hæmorrhage, you may still give *Cinchona* if there is headache with violent throbbing of the carotid arteries. This is not a *Belladonna* symptom. It is here an indication of anæmia, whereas under *Belladonna*, this symptom is indicative of hyperæmia.

It is a general characteristic of *Cinchona* to produce a nervous erethism with its symptoms of debility, a fact which allies it more with *Arsenicum* than with the torpid *Carbo veg*. The mind is over-active, although lacking endurance. Ideas crowd on the mind in unwelcome profusion, preventing sleep. On closing the eyes he sees persons and figures. The surface of the body is sensitive to the touch. This susceptibility is more imaginary than real. If the patient has a slight pain he feels it unbearably, and he dreads the slightest attempt to approach him lest you touch him, yet firm pressure or rubbing relieves. He exhibits a similar sensitiveness to a draught of air, which always makes him worse. These hints are appropriate to neuralgic and other pains. *Arnica* has this fear of being approached in gout; *Spigelia* has an actual sensitiveness of the whole surface, the least touch sends a sudden shock through the entire frame.

You may have to use *Cinchona* to cure asthenopia, but only when it occurs as the result of hæmorrhage or loss of fluids. An examination with the ophthalmoscope shows the disk to be pale and anæmic. The pupils are apt to be dilated; the eyes ache on attempting to use them, as in reading or writing, and objects appear blurred.

We now come to the study of the action of *Cinchona* on the digestive organs. It is very useful for dyspepsia occurring especially after loss of fluids. Digestion is so weak that the stomach cannot tolerate any food at all. Should the patient's supper come to him later than usual, he is sure to suffer in consequence. The stomach is distended with flatus, but belching relieves only momentarily or not at all. The least food or drink taken increases this symptom, so that after taking but a small quantity, he feels full, as though he had eaten an enormous meal. He complains often after eating of a sensation as of a lump in the mid-sternum, as though food were lying there. This is situated higher up than is the "hard-boiled egg" sensation of *Abies nigra*. *Pulsatilla* also has the same sensation in the same locality. This state, when *Cinchona* is the remedy, is often the result of loss of fluids, drinking tea to excess, and beers, fruits, etc. The appetite is often voracious when not capricious; thirst for cold water; drinks little and often; longs for acids, brandy, sweetmeats; buzzing in the ears.

Aconite has anxiety, relieved by very cold water or ice. *Veratrum album* desires ice-cold water. The following also crave cold water: *Pulsatilla*, *Plumbum*, *Scilla*.

Cinchona is an excellent remedy in the gastric troubles of children who are continually asking for dainties, but who reject substantial kinds of food. On awaking in the morning they are cross and irritable. They have a bad taste in the mouth and a white-coated tongue.

Cinchona is useful in some diseases of the bowels, especially when associated with marked tympany. The abdomen is enormously distended; when you percuss it, it gives forth a sound almost like that caused by striking the tense head of a drum. It is particularly when this tympany occurs early in the disease that *Cinchona* does good; then this symptom shows early debility. Later in the course of the disease, when it results from decomposition, *Cinchona* is less valuable, and you must resort to such remedies as *Terebinthina*, *Colchicum*, etc.

The diarrhœa of *Cinchona* is very characteristic. The stool is lienteric in character. It is worse at night and after eating. This is attended with rapid exhaustion and emaciation. In appearance the stools may be yellow, watery or brown, and very offensive. *Cinchona* is one of our best remedies for diarrhœa occurring in hot weather after eating fruits.

The nearest allies to the drug here are *Ferrum metallicum*, *Arsenicum album*, *Phosphoric acid*, *Oleander*, *Iris versicolor* and *Podophyllum*.

Arsenicum and *Ferrum* both have profuse lienteric diarrhœa, coming on during or after eating.

Phosphoric acid differs from *Cinchona* in that, while the stools are frequent and copious, they are not attended with much debility.

Iris versicolor is indicated in summer diarrhœa. The stools are copious and are associated with vomiting. The patient is worse at about two or three o'clock in the morning. It differs from *Veratrum album* in the absence of coldness.

Podophyllum is to be used for profuse gushing diarrhœa, coming on in the morning, or more during the day than at night. The stools may contain undigested food and often, in children, deposit a mealy sediment.

The *Oleander* diarrhœa is also lienteric. The patient passes in his stool the food which he had eaten the day before.

Cinchona, as you all know, is a valuable remedy in the treatment of chills and fever. It is useful either in fevers of the tertian or of the quartan type. The chill is unaccompanied by thirst, but there is thirst either before or after the chill. During the chill the patient sits as near as possible to the fire or wraps himself warmly in blankets; but the *warmth thus obtained does him no good*. The chill is followed by long-lasting heat, during which the patient desires to uncover. He is then usually without thirst. His face is fiery red, and he is often delirious. The sweat which follows is profuse and debilitating, with intense thirst. The apyrexia is by no means free from symptoms. The face is sallow, dingy yellow, from bilious complications, the spleen is enlarged, and there are aching sore feeling in the splenic region and either total loss of appetite, or canine hunger. The feet become œdematous, sometimes from disturbance in the composition of the blood, but mostly from interference with the hepatic and splenic circulations. Sleep is greatly disturbed, and the patient, as soon as he closes his eyes, sees figures, etc., before him.

The *Sulphate of Quinine* has these same symptoms, with this in addition, the chills recur with clock-like regularity, usually at 3 A. M., with blue nails, and pain in the dorsal vertebræ. But both drugs may be indicated in an anteponing type of fever. The heat is accompanied by excessive thirst and red face. The tongue is yellow down the centre, with pale edges. The heat gradually breaks into a sweat which relieves. The patient is very weak between the periods. *Cinchona* and its preparations have been so much abused in the treatment of intermittent fever that it is necessary to differentiate them carefully from their concordant remedies.

First of all may be mentioned *Cornus florida*. This drug has sleepiness long before the chill; the patient feels chilly, but is warm to the touch; the heat is associated with drowsiness, and is followed by profuse sweat.

Menyanthes is excellent when the chill predominates, with icy coldness of the tips of the fingers; in fact, all peripheral parts of the body get cold.

In *Capsicum* the chill begins in the back, with thirst. The patient feels better from heat applied to the back and from wrapping up, just as under *Ignatia*.

Eupatorium perfoliatum is useful when the chill comes in the morning, or in the morning of one day and in the afternoon of the next; the usual time, however, is nine o'clock in the morning. The chill is often preceded by thirst and bitter vomiting. The drinking of water makes the patient chilly. The fever is usually followed by very slight sweat.

Lachesis may be used after the abuse of *Quinine*, when the chills return in the spring.

Canchalagua is indicated in spring ague, with severe chill; the hands are puckered up like a washerwoman's.

Eucalyptus is a remedy which has been highly recommended in malarial fevers, but I must say to you that I know little or nothing about it.

Ipecacuanha is useful in intermittent fever when the type has been spoiled by *Quinine*. You can obtain no clearly defined picture of the case. Everything is confused. *Ipecacuanha* seems to have the property of developing the symptoms and of curing the case, or it provides you with sufficient data to enable you to select the appropriate remedy. The characteristic symptom of *Ipecacuanha* during the paroxysm is short chill, followed by long fever. Usually we find gastric symptoms, with a preponderance of nausea.

Sepia is also to be thought of in cases that have been spoiled by *Quinine* or by bungling administration of Homœopathic remedies.

Another remedy which may be utilized for the removal of the bad effects of *Quinine* is *Arsenicum album*. It is called for when the paroxysms occur more or less periodically. Thirst is great. The spleen is swollen. Dropsical symptoms appear. Paroxysms of neuralgia appear in the face, and recur regularly. *Arsenicum* may be indicated when almost any form of disease assumes the malarial type. In these cases you will find the ordinary remedies of no value whatever.

Still another remedy in severe cases is *Carbo veg*. This is especially of service after the abuse of *Quinine*, when there is thirst during the chill; when the body is icy-cold, and especially is this coldness noticed from the knees down; and when there is lack of reaction. You will be surprised to see how nicely an apparently hopeless case will rally under one or the other of these remedies.

There is a constitution developed by the marsh miasm for which it is necessary to use deep-acting remedies. Foremost among these stands *Aranea diadema*. This drug is suited to persons who may not have any distinct type of fever, but who suffer at every cold or damp change in the weather. The symptoms seem to be ill-defined. At one time they feel dyspeptic, at another they ache all over; but in all cases the constitutional taint is at the bottom of the whole trouble. *Aranea diadema* will so change the type of constitution that the patient will escape any further injury when exposed to dampness. *Malaria officinalis* should be compared in this condition.

In some cases you will have to use *Ferrum metallicum* as an antidote to *Quinine*, especially when we have the masked anæmia peculiar to this drug. The face is easily flushed, and the bloodvessels throb. The spleen is enlarged, and dropsical symptoms are manifested mostly about the feet.

Cinchona—to return to that drug—is also of essential service in the treatment of hectic types of fever, such types of fever as indicate a long-lasting suppurative process. The surgeon is called upon to employ this drug very frequently when, after emptying an abscess, symptoms of hectic fever develop. The cheeks are red. The patient is excessively nervous, the nervous irritability being greatly disproportionate to the patient's strength. He is so greatly prostrated by the fever that he can scarcely raise his head. Diarrhœa adds to his weakness. Copious night-sweats also exhaust him. Along with *Cinchona* in this connection you must place in your mind its analogues, which are chiefly *Arsenicum album* and *Carbo veg*. You will often meet with a severe case in which *Cinchona* runs its course, and no longer produces improvement. You will then have to select *Arsenicum* or *Carbo veg.*, according to the symptoms of the case.

Carbo veg., as well as *Cinchona*, is to be remembered as a remedy to prevent collapse following the opening of a cold abscess, such as occurs in spinal caries. The symptoms of the two remedies are almost identical, and your choice between them may be difficult unless you find other symptoms in the case pointing distinctly to one or the other drug.

Psorinum, like *Cinchona*, is useful in some cases of night-sweats. It is indicated when profuse sweats occur after acute illnesses, as typhoid fever, etc. The patient is very despondent, hopeless of recovery; remains weak, with trembling of the hands and weak back and joints. *Sulphur* is very similar.

Another form of suppurative trouble in which you may use *Cinchona* is in suppuration of the lungs, particularly in drunkards, when the trouble is associated with hectic fever.

You may also be called upon to use *Cinchona* in disorganized states, either of the external tissues or of the lung substance. In the latter case the remedy is indicated by the hectic symptoms and by the fœtid breath. Here *Cinchona* vies with *Arsenicum*, *Secale*, and *Lachesis*.

Do not confound the fœtid breath just mentioned with that arising from certain forms of bronchitis, in which the sputum is retained a long time and undergoes decomposition in the lungs. While the patient is breathing quietly you can notice no extraordinary odor. As soon as he gives a deep cough the breath becomes horribly offensive. This kind of cough calls for *Capsicum*, and, perhaps next in importance, for *Sanguinaria Canadensis*.

You will find *Cinchona* often indicated in inflammatory rheumatism, not in the beginning of the disease, but later when the fever has become intermittent in its character. The joints still remain swollen. The characteristic pains in these cases are jerking and pressing. The patient will not permit you to approach, crying out with pain if you touch the affected parts, so exquisitely sensitive is the surface. *Quinine sulphate* is also useful in a similar condition.

Cinchona is also a neuralgic remedy. It is especially suited to neuralgia of the infraorbital nerve on either side when the symptoms are typical in their return, and when the slightest touch or draught of cold air makes the patient worse. If the neuralgia is of malarial origin *Cinchona* is increasingly indicated.

You may here compare *Cedron*, which is applicable to malarial neuralgia, usually supraorbital, when the attacks return with clock-like regularity.

In jaundice you should use *Cinchona* when the surface of the body and the sclerotica are yellowish. The liver is swollen and sensitive to the touch, and there is a feeling in the right hypochondrium as of subcutaneous ulceration. The stools are whitish, and are accompanied by fœtid flatus, or else there is diarrhœa. It is especially indicated in

RUBIACEÆ.

jaundice arising from sexual excesses, from loss of animal fluids, from abuse of alcohol, and from gastro-duodenal catarrh.

The antidotes to *Cinchona* are *Arsenicum album*, *Ipecac*, *Carbo veg.*, *Lachesis*, *Pulsatilla*, *Ferrum metallicum* and *Veratrum album*. The indications for most of these have already been given you.

Cinchona and *Morphia* are antagonistic in brain symptoms.

Cinchona and *Belladonna* are antagonistic in heart symptoms, temperature, etc.

LECTURE XXXVI.

IPECACUANHA AND COFFEA.

Ipecacuanha.

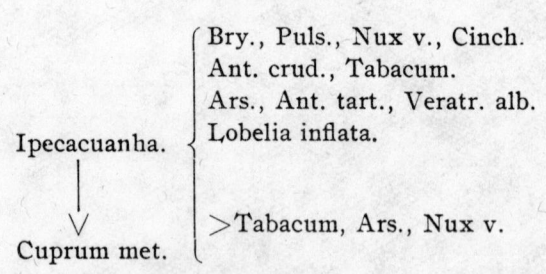

Ipecacuanha. { Bry., Puls., Nux v., Cinch. Ant. crud., Tabacum. Ars., Ant. tart., Veratr. alb. Lobelia inflata.

∨
Cuprum met.

>Tabacum, Ars., Nux v.

IPECACUANHA CEPHAELIS is a small shrub growing in Brazil. It is bitter, acrid and nauseous, and possesses a peculiar odor which, in some persons, excites sneezing and even asthma. In many cases the conjunctivæ are injected, with puffiness under the eyes, profuse coryza and tension over the eyes.

Ipecacuanha contains as its active principle a substance called *Emetin*, which gives to the drug its property of producing vomiting. It also contains an acid called *Ipecacuanhic acid*, and a small quantity of a fœtid volatile oil. The latter constituent probably has something to do with the action of the drug on the pneumogastric nerve and its consequent use in the treatment of asthma. *Ipecacuanha* is easily studied. It acts upon the nerves (especially the pneumogastric) and mucous membranes. It has been employed by allopathic physicians as an anti-spasmodic in asthma and in pulmonary catarrhs. In the latter class of troubles it is used to provoke vomiting, and, of course, gives temporary relief.

Ipecacuanha seems to have a special affinity for the mucous membranes lining the bronchial tubes and alimentary canal. One of the most prominent features of this drug is its property of producing nausea and subsequently vomiting. So prominent is this symptom that you will find it present in almost all the cases in which *Ipecacuanha* is required.

Studied more particularly, *Ipecacuanha* is found suitable for patients who are easily irritated, full of desires, but know not for what. If a child, the patient cries and screams almost continually. As an adult, he is irritable and morose, holding everything in contempt.

Thus you will find *Ipecacuanha* indicated in headaches. These are of rheumatic origin. The characteristic sensation is a pain as if the head or bones of the head were bruised or crushed, this feeling seeming to go down into the root of the tongue. This headache is accompanied by nausea and vomiting. *Ipecacuanha* may also be used in unilateral sick headaches with deathly nausea. In these cases the face is usually pale, blue rings surround the eyes, and the expression about the mouth betrays the intensity of the nausea. Now, these symptoms are not so necessarily present in the adult as they are in the child. You see the corners of the child's mouth drawn, and a line extending from the alæ of the nose to the corners of the mouth, giving to the child an expression of nausea, and at once suggesting to your mind such remedies as *Ipecacuanha*, *Antimonium tartaricum* and especially *Æthusa cynapium*.

In that bursting headache of *Ipecacuanha* compare *Veratrum album*, which has that bruised feeling here and there in the brain. There is still another drug which has this symptom, and that is *Ptelea*.

The gastric symptoms of *Ipecacuanha*, in addition to those already mentioned, are such as would call for the exhibition of this drug after indulgence in rich food, such as pastry, pork, fruits, candy, ice-cream, etc. Nausea is constant with all complaints; vomiting of bile; vomits just after eating (like *Arsenicum*); vomits after eating rich or indigestible food; vomiting of mucus; morning sickness. The tongue is usually clean, a symptom which differentiates *Ipecacuanha* from *Nux vomica*, *Antimonium crudum*, etc. Distress in the stomach; it feels relaxed as if hanging down (like *Staphisagria*, *Theine*, *Lobelia*, *Tabacum*).

These gastric symptoms of *Ipecacuanha* should be compared with those of three other remedies, the most important of which is *Pulsatilla*. You will at once recognize the similarity of the two drugs. They are both useful for gastric disturbances caused by indulgence in mixed diet, pastry, ice-cream, pork, fatty food, etc. *Pulsatilla* may be considered the better remedy of the two early in the attack, when the stomach still contains the food which disagrees, while *Ipecacuanha* is better when the stomach is empty and the effects only of the indulgence remain. The best distinction between the two remedies, however, lies in the condition of the tongue. In *Ipecacuanha*, the tongue, as above stated, is clean or only slightly coated, whereas in *Pulsatilla* the tongue is almost always foul, white or yellow, with a very disagreeable taste in the mouth.

Arsenicum album must follow or supplant *Ipecacuanha* when an actual catarrh of the stomach has been produced by indigestible food, especially after sudden chilling of the stomach with ice-cream or ice-water. There are vomiting, burning pains in the stomach, diarrhœa, restlessness, etc.

Antimonium crudum, like *Ipecacuanha*, is suitable for gastric catarrh, following a mixed diet of pastry, etc. The tongue is thickly coated white, as if it had been whitewashed.

Ipecacuanha may be indicated when, in the case of children, indulgence in rich food has produced convulsions. It may even be useful in the convulsions of teething children, or convulsions following suppressed eruptions, cold, etc. They are of the rigid tetanic form. Sometimes the rigidity alternates with flexing of the arms and jerking of the arms toward each other.

Colic may occur, and this is of a griping character. Either the pain is situated about the umbilicus, as though a hand were tightly clutching the intestines; or the colic consists of cutting pains which shoot across the abdomen from left to right. The stools are either green, as in diarrhœa of infants, or they are yellow and liquid, and covered with mucus and blood. Sometimes they have a fermented appearance and look like molasses. That is as good a comparison as I can give you; the stool looks just like molasses when it is frothy. At other times the stools are black from admixture of bile. Some of these diarrhœas are associated with tenesmus, indicating catarrh of the lining membrane of the bowels.

Ipecacuanha is frequently indicated in the commencement of cholera infantum. You find present pallor of the face, with blue rings around the eyes; the fontanelles are still open, showing defective nutrition; the child may have nose-bleed with the pale face; it is drowsy, with starting and jerking of the muscles during sleep. The child is subject to frequent attacks of nose-bleed. The condition already simulates that of hydrocephaloid. You must not think because *Ipecacuanha* is associated so closely with stomach symptoms, that it cannot be indicated in this reflex cerebral state. You will find nausea and even vomiting usually present. The child eats or drinks and vomits what it has taken almost immediately afterward. Particularly is *Ipecacuanha* indicated in these cases as a remedy preceding the exhibition of *Arsenicum album*. *Arsenicum*, as already indicated, is complementary to *Ipecacuanha* in these abdominal affections.

In some of these cases of gastro-intestinal troubles in children *Ipecacuanha* and the other remedies just mentioned will sometimes fail you. Then it will be well for you to bear in mind the following remedies, which, though infrequently indicated, may prove themselves to be of inestimable value.

Œnothera biennis, the evening primrose, commonly seen in the fields and waste places, is an invaluable remedy in exhausting, watery diarrhœa. It does not act, as has been suggested, as an astringent, by its tannic acid, but is a genuine homœopathic remedy, producing and curing diarrhœa. The evacuations are without effort, and are accompanied by nervous exhaustion, and even by incipient hydrocephaloid.

Gnaphalium causes a watery, offensive morning diarrhœa, which recurs frequently during the day. The provers were children, and well have they portrayed a very common group of cholera infantum symptoms. They had rumbling in the bowels, colicky pains, and were, at the same time, cross and irritable. The urine was scanty, and the appetite and taste were lost. A writer in the *Homœopath* mentions having used this drug very successfully, and Dr. Hale refers to it in his *Therapeutics*.

Geranium maculatum is also a successful baby's remedy. Dr. Hale devotes eight pages to *Geranium* and other astringents, dividing their action according to his rule of primary and secondary symptoms, and deducing thence two propositions for use in practice. The provings, brief though they are, help us in the choice of the drug; constant desire to go to stool, with inability for some time to pass any fæcal matter, then the bowels move without pain or effort; mouth dry; tip of the tongue burning. The Allopaths use *Geranium* as an astringent.

Paullinia sorbilis has been suggested for diarrhœa, which is green and profuse, but odorless.

Opuntia comes to us recommended by so careful an observer—Dr. Burdick—that, although I have not used it, I do not hesitate to present it anew. Nausea in stomach and bowels; feels as if the bowels were settled down into the lower abdomen (confined in adults). In infants we may, perhaps, look to this drug when the lower part of the abdomen is the seat of disease, as this seems to be its characteristic seat of attack.

Nuphar luteum causes a yellow diarrhœa, worse in the morning, either painless or with colic. It has been employed for diarrhœa during typhoid, and indeed seems to cause nervous weakness. Whether it will be of service for infants remains to be seen. We should look to it when *Gamboge*, *Chelidonium*, etc., fail, and when exhaustion is a prominent attendant.

Kali bromatum has been given successfully several times in cholera infantum, when there were great prostration, cool surface and symptoms of hydrocephaloid. Compare *Cinchona* (incipient hydrocephaloid, following prolonged or oft-repeated diarrhœic discharge), *Calcarea phos.*, *Carbo veg.*, *Veratrum album*, *Camphor*, etc.

Returning now to *Ipecacuanha*, we should note another effect of the drug which is just as characteristic as its action on the bowels, namely, its action on the mucous membrane of the respiratory tract. Thus it may be used in coryza. The nose feels as if stuffed up; there is often epistaxis, loss of smell, nausea and some catarrh of the bronchial mucous membrane.

You may compare here *Allium cepa*, which is an excellent remedy for simple nasal catarrh when the nasal secretion is watery and acrid and the lachrymation mild. There are rough raw feeling in the throat and cough provoked by tickling in the larynx. I may say in qualifying these symptoms of *Allium*, that although it quickly stops the nasal catarrh it frequently seems to drive the trouble to the chest. *Phosphorus* appears to stop this action of *Cepa*.

Euphrasia is very similar to *Cepa* in nasal catarrh. Here, however, we have excoriating lachrymation and bland nasal discharge.

Arsenicum album follows *Ipecacuanha*, in the catarrhs of fat, chubby children.

Affecting prominently, as *Ipecacuanha*, does, the pneumogastric nerves, we should expect it to be useful in affections which involve these nerves, such as asthma, in which disease it is indicated when there is a sensation as of constriction of the chest, worse from the least motion. When the patient coughs you hear the rattling of mucus in the chest, yet none is expectorated. Especially will you find this kind of asthma calling for *Ipecacuanha* in stout persons of lax fibre, either adult or child, who are particularly sensitive to a warm moist atmosphere.

Very similar to *Ipecacuanha* in asthma is *Arsenicum album*, which often follows it well either in catarrhal or nervous asthma.

Cuprum metallicum is useful in asthma when the spasmodic element predominates. The face gets blue; there is constriction of the throat; the patient almost goes into convulsions.

Another drug closely allied to *Ipecacuanha* is *Lobelia inflata*. This has, with the asthma, a weak sensation in the epigastrium, spreading up into the chest, nausea, profuse salivation and a feeling as of a lump in the stomach.

Ipecacuanha is one of the best remedies we have for capillary bronchitis in infants, especially if caused by the kind of weather I have described. There is a great accumulation of mucus in the chest. The examining ear hears râles all through the chest, both anteriorly and posteriorly. The cough is spasmodic and usually attended with vomiting of phlegm. There may be fever and *Ipecacuanha* still be indicated. The child may have difficulty in breathing from the marked accumulation of mucus in the chest. In such cases, I have used the remedy in all potencies; that is to say, from the third to the twenty thousandth, and I have been well satisfied with its action. When *Ipecacuanha* is indicated, the stage for giving *Aconite* has passed, because exudation has begun. If you adhere to the principles of homoeopathy, you will not give *Aconite* and *Ipecacuanha* in alternation. After giving *Ipecacuanha*, you will notice that the mucus does not adhere so firmly to the walls of the bronchial tubes, but it becomes less tenacious and is raised more readily.

Let me warn you that there are two or three changes of symptoms which will call for concordant remedies. One of these changes calls for *Antimonium tartaricum*, and that is when the cough grows less and less frequent, the quantity of mucus in the chest not diminishing in amount. The infrequency of the cough is not a good symptom, although the mother will think so. The chest is so filled with mucus that the child cannot cough. He grows more and more drowsy. In giving *Antimonium tartaricum* in these cases, give it in frequent doses until the cough increases.

Another change calls for *Phosphorus*. This should be given when the inflammatory symptoms increase, the substance of the lungs becomes involved and pneumonia supervenes. Then *Ipecacuanha* ceases to be the remedy. Any one who practices in the colder parts of the country will find these catarrhs frequent, and with *Aconite*,

Ipecacuanha, *Antimonium tartaricum* and *Phosphorus*, he can manage the great majority of his cases.

Still other remedies may be needed. In some cases *Antimonium tartaricum*, though apparently well indicated, fails to control the symptoms. Then we may have recourse to *Sulphur*, which produces in the healthy a catarrh of the bronchial mucous membrane with loud râles all through the chest, particularly in the left lung. Especially is it indicated when there is atelectasis. I have used *Sulphur* with great success in just such cases.

Another remedy is *Terebinthina*, which I have used when the child was drowsy and the lungs seemed to be all clogged up. The urine is apt to be scanty and dark from the admixture of blood. *Terebinthina* must be given repeatedly.

Still another remedy is *Lycopodium*, which affects more markedly the right lung. Loud râles are heard all through the affected part. The expectoration is yellowish and thick.

We may be called upon to give *Ipecacuanha* frequently in whooping-cough, by virtue of the spasmodic character of the cough and the action of the drug on the pneumogastric nerve. You will find in addition to the symptoms already mentioned, that spasmodic convulsive symptoms are present. During the cough the child stiffens and becomes rigid from tonic spasm of the extensor muscles; loses its breath and turns pale or blue in the face. Finally it relaxes and vomits phlegm, which of course relieves. While *Ipecacuanha* is of excellent service here, you are reminded of two other drugs which are similar.

One of these is *Cina*, which I must ask you to remember as being something more than a mere worm remedy. This remedy is useful in whooping-cough with the same kind of rigidity that I have described for *Ipecacuanha*, but there is in addition a clucking sound in the œsophagus as the child goes out of the paroxysm. If in addition to this symptom you also have grinding of the teeth, *Cina* is certainly a better remedy than *Ipecacuanha*.

Cuprum metallicum is the complement of *Ipecacuanha* in spasmodic affections and in whooping-cough. It is especially indicated in convulsions from worms and during the course of whooping-cough. Spasms of the flexors predominate.

In fevers we may use *Ipecacuanha*, especially in those of an intermittent type. It is one of the best drugs to give when your case is mixed up. It is particularly indicated when there is a short chill, followed by long fever with nausea and vomiting, especially after the abuse of *Quinine*.

Ipecacuanha is an excellent drug for hæmaturia, for hæmorrhage from the kidneys when the trouble is attended with nausea, oppression of the chest, hard breathing, and cutting pains in the abdomen.

In some cases those who work in *Ipecacuanha* are affected with a violent inflammation of the conjunctiva. Now this fact led Jousset to apply the drug in the treatment of ophthalmia, and he claims many cures with it in the intense conjunctivitis of scrofulous children. There are tearing pains in and about the eyes and copious lachrymation. Tears gush forth every time the lids are separated. When, however, there is marked keratitis, he prefers *Apis*.

In closing let me give you the *Ipecacuanha* temperament. Studied as a homœopathic remedy, you will find it indicated in patients who are full of desires they know not for what. The child cries and screams continually. The adult is irritable and morose, holding everything in contempt.

Bismuth seems to hinder the action of *Ipecacuanha*.

Opium increases its action on the bronchial mucous membrane.

Coffea Arabicum.

Coffea is extensively used as a beverage. Its alkaloid, *Caffeine*, is identical chemically with several others, such as *Theine*, the active principle of tea, and is related chemically to the purin bodies, xanthin, uric acid, etc.

Caffeine lessens the amount of urea excreted in the urine. It is useful when there is an extra drain on the system, particularly after hard work in hot weather, at which time the system is doubly exhausted by the fatigue and the heat combined.

Then a cup of coffee is a very good thing. So, too, it may be used after loss of sleep, when fatigue is more marked than it is after labor. Other things being equal, coffee is not so useful for the young as for the old. A man in active business life or one who works hard all day, or an elderly man in whom waste is out of proportion to repair, finds great benefit from coffee. In fact, it is almost instinctive on the part of workmen to fall back on coffee as a beverage, because it gives them what their food will not, a certain amount of strength and an antidote to the wear and tear of labor.

The effects of *Caffeine* on the system bear a certain resemblance to *Strychnia*. It seems to excite reflex action, and, if persistently given, tetanus as well. It produces sudden starting from the slightest touch of the surface of the body (like *Strychnia*), and increased susceptibility to all external impressions. This increased "excito-motor" action explains many of its symptoms. Violent emotions, whether of pleasure or of pain produce symptoms. Patients experience sudden joy, and they are at once sick from the excitement. They awaken at night without any desire whatever to return to sleep.

Coffea also produces an ecstatic state of mind. Here it finds a concordant remedy in *Cypripedium*. Especially is the latter remedy indicated in children who awaken at night from sleep, and are unnaturally bright and playful, and evince no desire to go to sleep again. Such symptoms are often preliminary to some brain affection, which the timely use of *Cypripedium* may avert.

Apoplectic congestion may be cured by *Coffea*, particularly if an excited state of the mind has been the cause of the excessive fulness of the cerebral blood-vessels. So, too, an animated conversation in which the party interested becomes greatly warmed up and has cerebral congestion will call for *Coffea*. This remedy is of value, however, only in the beginning of these cases; then it is all-sufficient. But if the trouble goes on to effusion (not inflammatory effusion, but effusion of serum by oozing through the distended capillaries), you must have recourse to *Belladonna*, *Bryonia* or some remedy more adapted to effusion than is *Coffea*.

Coffea is also a remedy in eruptive diseases, when the eruption keeps the patient awake on account of the excessive itching and burning of the skin; the patient scratches even until the parts bleed. This symptom is due, in the *Coffea* case, to the hypersensitiveness of the skin.

Moreover, *Coffea* has fear of death, thus allying it with *Aconite;* this fear usuallly being present with the severe pains. All pain in the *Coffea* patient is intolerable. Even a slight pain causes great complaint and crying and whining.

Coffea is often indicated in the toothache of children and of nervous people. Sometimes you will be led to give *Chamomilla* in these cases. You find the mental symptoms indicating that drug, yet it does no good, or it affords but partial relief. You may give *Chamomilla* when the face is red, when the child cannot bear the least pain and is cross and irritable, and when cold water in the mouth relieves for an instant. But if cold water relieves permanently, *Coffea* is the remedy.

The senses are all too acute under *Coffea*, not only the sense of touch but that of sight and of hearing also. Under the stimulating influence of this remedy the patient may see fine print with a degree of distinctness altogether unnatural. Distant noises seem to be magnified.

Coffea has a condition almost the reverse of the hyperæsthetic state. It results from the secondary or depressant action of the drug.

In its effect upon the circulation, at first it seems to increase the frequency of the pulse, showing that there is increased action of the heart. This is followed later by cardiac depression, with palpitation and irregular pulse. It must be remembered that this increased frequency of the pulse is not attended with an increase of force, as under *Aconite*, *Bryonia* and *Baptisia*. So you see that the stimulation is not genuine. On the contrary, it weakens the heart muscle, so that after a while, if this drug be given long enough, or if coffee be indulged in as a beverage to excess, the heart exhibits a tendency to dilate.

We find *Coffea* also indicated in diarrhœa, particularly that occurring among housewives; those who have a great deal of care and trouble in the management of the household.

Remember also the use of *Coffea* for fatigue arising from long journeys, especially during hot weather.

I wish to mention two or three other drugs analogous to *Coffea*, that have recently been proved. *Piper methysticum*, also called *Kava-kava* and *Awa-samoa*, is largely used in Polynesia as a beverage. It has also been proved as a medicine. Its effects seem to be something like those of coffee, for it produces at first a feeling of buoyancy or tension, as though every nerve were " strung-up " to its highest pitch. The prover feels that he can work hard without fatigue. If these effects reach their extremes, there is a feeling of mental tension as though the head were large, almost full to bursting. There is dizziness also; dizziness on closing the eyes or on directing the attention to any object. The vessels of the brain, and particularly those about the base of the brain, fell full, as if ligated (that is the symptom given in the language of the prover). Thus far you see it is somewhat similar to *Coffea*. But the secondary action quickly follows the use of *Piper*, and this reverse effect is characterized by what we may call brain-fag. The brain feels tired on awakening, as one feels after being out late at night and losing considerable sleep, or after a hard night's study. There is heavy, dull aching in the head, which is worse from reading, thinking or any use of the mind. The mental symptoms, be they those of excitement or of depression, are relieved by diversion of the mind. Further than this, *Piper* seems to produce convulsions, and it has cured them. The spasms simulate those of catalepsy. The mind is tired and yields to the least pressure. There is over-sensitiveness to all external impressions.

LECTURE XXXVII.

SCROPHULARIACEÆ.

Scrophulariaceæ.
- Digitalis.
  - Myrica cerifera.
  - Spigelia.
  - Kalmia.
  - Helleborus.
  - < China.
- Gratiola.
- Leptandra.
- Euphrasia.
- Verbascum.
- Linaria.

From this order of plants we obtain *Digitalis, Gratiola, Leptandra Virginica, Euphrasia, Verbascum* and *Linaria*. These drugs are not all thoroughly proved, but those that are well known are sufficiently distinct to be easily remembered. The most important member of the group is the

Digitalis Purpurea.

Digitalis contains among other ingredients two substances, one known as *Digitalin*, the other as *Digitoxin*. The latter is found in larger quantity than the former. *Digitalin* has been proved separately from the *Digitalis*. Its symptomatology, however, is, like most other active principles, very nearly identical with that of the original drug.

Digitalis produces, very early in the proving or in poisoning cases, among other symptoms, the most distressing nausea and vomiting. This emesis is often accompanied by a deathly faint, sinking sensation at the pit of the stomach. The surface of the body is often cold, and sometimes covered more or less with cold sweat. The pulse is irregular. These early symptoms of *Digitalis* remind one of several other drugs, notably, *Antimonium tartaricum, Tabacum* and *Lobelia*. It is probable that these drugs and *Digitalis* all cause this nausea and vomiting by affecting the base of the brain, acting there upon the pneumogastric nerves as they leave their origin. Such symptoms as this deathly nausea and vomiting might suggest the use of *Digitalis* in the vomiting attendant upon cerebral disease; in meningitis, for instance, whether the meninges of the cerebrum alone, or of the cerebrum and cord combined, were involved in the inflammation.

The drug may even be used in the nausea and vomiting of pregnancy, and in the incipiency of abortion. One of the provers, a pregnant woman, took an overdose of *Digitalis*, and in consequence was seized with this same deathly nausea and a flow of blood from the vagina.

We may also study *Digitalis* in its action on the heart. Through irritation of the pneumogastric nerves we have inhibition of the heart's action. As a consequence of this effect of the drug, the pulse becomes slow. Arterial tension is greatly increased, probably owing to the action of the drug on the vaso-motor centre, which is supposed to be at the base of the brain; the pulse is, therefore, primarily slow and strong. In addition to the effect of the drug on nervous structure, we must remember that it also affects muscular tissue, both of the striated and non-striated varieties. Thus it causes weakness of the cardiac tissues. This weakness varies in intensity from simple weakness to complete paralysis of the muscular fibre. Consequently, we may very soon have added to these other symptoms, weakness of the pulse. Every little extra exertion, such as that incurred while rising from a sitting to a standing posture, increases the rapidity of the pulse, but the force of the beat is diminished. This quick pulse may become irregular and even intermittent. With this view, then, of the physiological action of the drug, you may understand the following symptoms of the heart and respiration connected therewith.

But first let me here give you a word of caution respecting the use of *Digitalis* in heart affections. The tendency of this drug, like that of *Lachesis* and *Arsenicum album*, is downward. You must not use it, therefore, indiscriminately or carelessly, but only when you are guided to its selection by the symptoms of the case, or you will certainly make your patient worse. In organic diseases of the heart, *Digitalis* must be used with extreme caution, because it may hasten the period when nature is no longer able to compensate by hypertrophy of the heart-muscle for the interference in the circulation. Nature thus may be compelled to give out. Then the heart yields to the pressure of the blood within its cavities and begins; and we shall have the train of symptoms which I intend to describe to you shortly, as belonging to *Digitalis*. This warning is particularly applicable to the use of the drug in large doses. Given thus it may relieve for a time, but it only hastens the fatal end. With this word of warning I now proceed to give you in detail the heart symptoms of *Digitalis*.

The heart feels as though it stood still, and this sensation is attended with great anxiety. There is a sort of indescribable uneasiness in the cardiac region, which may be expressed as a sense of oppression or tightness about the heart, or as an uneasy feeling with weakness and numbness in the left arm. There is a feeling of goneness or sinking at the epigastrium. This is sometimes relieved by eating, but often comes on worse after eating, particularly after breakfast. There are sharp sticking pains in the region of the heart. Sometimes there is choking when trying to swallow, from reflex spasm of the glottis. The pulse is slow, often slower than the beating of the heart. In these cases the heart beats so imperfectly that some of its pulse waves are not transmitted appreciably to the radial artery at the wrist. Any movement such as rising from a chair, getting out of bed, or increasing the speed in walking, increases the rapidity of the pulse but causes no increase in the force of its beat. The irregular distribution of the blood caused by these alterations in the heart's functions is exhibited in a variety of symptoms. In extreme cases, for instance, we find even cyanosis, which suggests *Digitalis* as a possible remedy for cyanosis neonatorum. The child turns blue and falls into a syncope on the slightest motion, or else it becomes deathly sick, as you see from the expression of the face and from the involuntary gagging. If you can feel the pulse, you will find it irregular both in rhythm and volume; the surface of the body is cool. The borders of the lips are blue or purple. The child is blue around the eyes. The veins wherever they show through the skin are seen to be dark.

Other and more common illustrations of the irregular distribution of the blood may be shown in the sleep. The patient's sleep is uncomfortable and restless. He dreams a great deal; he starts up from sleep dreaming that he is falling from a great height Sometimes he awakens with an anxious or distressed feeling, which he may be unable to locate, but which results from the cardiac affection. Mentally, the *Digitalis* patient, besides being anxious, has those gloomy forebodings incident to heart disease. He has an apprehensive feeling, ill-defined it is true, yet none the less terrible. He is apt to be sad and depressed, as well as anxious. The respiration is of course affected by this action of the heart. We frequently find the breathing deep sighing and slower than normal. This symptom is almost pathognomonic of heart affection. There is often a desire to take a deep breath, but an attempt to do so seems to result in only half-filling the lungs, which do not expand to their full capacity. This is often attended with dry cough, which seems to be excited by deep inspiration. The deeper he attempts to breathe, the more likely is he to cough. This is altogether a bronchial symptom, and comes on from an overfilling of the blood-vessels there. Suffocative spells with painful constriction of the chest, as if internal parts of the chest were grown together, are not uncommon. Sometimes these attacks force the patient to sit up in order that he may breathe. If these cardiac symptoms are present you will find *Digitalis* indicated in several varieties of disease starting remotely from the heart, and yet depending for their existence either directly or indirectly upon the disease of that organ.

In almost all the affections in which *Digitalis* may be used there is present either a slow pulse or a feeble pulse, becoming irregular or quick.

For instance, dropsy may call for *Digitalis*. This dropsy is not of renal origin. You would hardly think of *Digitalis* in dropsy resulting primarily from a liver or kidney disease, but in that form occurring primarily from cardiac debility, it is at times an invaluable remedy.

Digitalis may be used with profit in a number of forms of dropsy. You may give it in anasarca when the surface of the body is bluish, rather than of the alabaster-like appearance characteristic of renal dropsies. Local dropsies, too, are present. Thus you find *Digitalis* indicated in hydropericardium, and even in hydrothorax and ascites, if they are connected with heart disease. In dropsies of the chest there is a remedy that is often forgotten, and that is the *Sulphate of Mercury* or *Mercurius sulphuricus*. Especially is this remedy useful when the chest-dropsy occurs from heart or liver disease. When the drug acts well it produces a profuse watery diarrhœa, with great relief to the patient. A very common form of dropsy calling for *Digitalis*, is infiltration of the tissues of the scrotum and penis. We may even use *Digitalis* in hydrocele when the cardiac symptoms calling for the remedy are present. The urine is often suppressed or very scanty.

This deficiency in the renal secretion depends upon disordered circulation, and not upon primary disease of the kidneys. The urine may be dark red or albuminous.

We find *Digitalis* causing some liver symptoms which are worthy of notice. I think, however, that *Digitalis* has no direct action on the hepatic cells; it does not appear to affect the bile secretion directly. But in jaundice, in which the primary trouble is a cardiac disease of the type already mentioned, with ashy white stools, *Digitalis* certainly acts admirably. The liver is enlarged and feels sore, as if bruised. Objectively examined, it is found to be somewhat indurated. With this symptom we have jaundice. The taste is bitter, or at other times, sweetish. The tongue may be perfectly clean, or it may be whitish-yellow. The pulse is slow, even slower than the beating of the heart. Drowsiness may supervene and even increase to stupor. The stools are of the character above mentioned. The urine is high-colored from admixture of bile pigment. The jaundice calling for *Digitalis* is not that which follows retention of bile or is caused by catarrh of the duodenum or by some obstruction of the biliary ducts, but it is due to an actual functional imperfection of the liver, that organ not taking from the blood the elements which go to form the bile.

A remedy which here compares favorably with *Digitalis* is *Myrica cerifera*, which has the following symptoms. First, despondency, which depends upon the disordered condition of the liver. The symptoms of *Myrica* are similar to those of *Digitalis* because in each case the jaundice is due to the imperfect formation of bile in the liver, and not to obstruction of the flow. But the two remedies are very different in their absolute effects on the system. With *Digitalis*, the jaundice is traceable to the condition of the heart. With *Myrica*, the case seems to be functional rather than organic. For some reason the bile is not properly formed, and therefore its elements remain in the blood. The heart is affected secondarily, slowness of the pulse thus being produced. The symptoms calling for *Myrica* are these: Despondency, dull, heavy headache, worse in the morning; the eyes and sclerotic have a dirty, dingy, yellowish hue, the lids themselves being abnormally red; the tongue is coated a dirty yellow. Weak sinking feeling in the epigastrium after eating. The patient is weak and drowsy and complains of muscular soreness and aching in the limbs. The pulse is slow but intensified. The stools are ash colored. The urine is dark and turbid. You recognize at once the resemblance to *Digitalis;*

but it is more superficial in its action than is that remedy, and would not be suitable for so violent a case as the latter.

In heart affections you may compare *Digitalis* with a number of remedies, notably, with *Kalmia*, *Arsenicum album*, *Helleborus* and *Conium*.

Kalmia latifolia is a drug which belongs to the order *Ericaceæ*, with *Rhododendron*, *Ledum palustre* and other remedies. It is a valuable remedy in rheumatism when it affects the chest. The pains in the *Kalmia* affection of the heart are sharp, taking away the breath; the patient almost suffocates, so severe are they. The pains shoot down into the abdomen or stomach; the pulse is slow, almost as slow as that calling for *Digitalis*. *Kalmia* is especially useful when gout or rheumatism shifts from the joints to the heart, especially after external applications to the joints. I refer here especially to the application to the joints of substances that are not homœopathic to the case. If you were giving *Arnica* internally and applying it locally, and if it were the indicated remedy, there would be no danger of metastasis. But if some one were to apply the tincture of *Aconite* to the affected joint there would be danger of the inflammation travelling to some more vital part. The *Kalmia* rheumatism, unlike that of *Ledum*, usually travels downward, thus following the direction of its pains.

Helleborus is similar to *Digitalis* in the slowness of the pulse. The respiration is also slow and the temperature of the body is greatly diminished, often being as low as 95° or 96° F. There is generally cerebral disease.

Spigelia also must be compared with *Digitalis*. It has the following symptoms. Sharp pain shooting through the heart to the back, or radiating from the heart and down the arm or over the chest and down the spine; great oppression or anxiety about the heart; palpitation of the heart worse from any movement of the arm or body; thrilling or purring sensation felt over the cardiac region (this is just such a thrill as you feel when stroking a cat's back when the animal is purring); blowing sound over the heart. You will find *Spigelia* indicated when these heart symptoms accompany other affections, for instance, neuralgia, particularly if it affects the left side of the face, commencing in the occiput and settling over and in the left eye. That is the *Spigelia* headache. Its aggravation follows the course of the sun. It commences in the morning, reaches its acme at noon, and diminishes toward night. You may also use it in ciliary neuralgia with these accompanying sympathetic symptoms of the heart. Sharp pain shoots through the eyeball and radiates in all directions, almost driving the patient mad. At other times there is a sensation as if the eye were being squeezed in a vise or as if it were enormously enlarged and were being pushed out of the head. It is one of the chief remedies to be thought of in iritis with excessive pain. I wish also to mention a symptom for *Spigelia* that the late Dr. Jacob Jeanes confirmed many times, and that is intermittent pulse. He prescribed this remedy as an intercurrent, in many varieties of disease, when the pulse assumed this character.

Convallaria majalis presents heart symptoms associated with uterine symptoms; soreness in the hypogastrium; pain in the sacro-iliac synchondrosis, extending down the leg. Itching of the meatus urinarius and vulva.

Another remedy is *Magnolia grandiflora*, which has sadness; nervousness; weak heart, with sensation of constriction in the cardiac region; worse on walking fast; and at times the sensation as if the heart stopped beating.

It will not be unprofitable for us next to study the action of *Digitalis* on the brain. It causes symptoms which are very much like those of meningitis, even meningitis with effusion, or of hydrocephalus, and also of cerebro-spinal meningitis. The symptoms from which you will have to decide are these: there is throbbing headache, which is referred to the forepart of the head; delirium, which may be so violent as to simulate mania; decided errors in vision; bright balls of fire appear in the field of vision, or, like *Santonin*, objects appear of various colors, as yellow or green. Still later, as the trouble progresses, mental confusion increases and amaurotic congestion of the retina takes place; the pupils become dilated and fail to respond to light, and finally coma appears. There is great general prostration with coldness of the body, which is covered with a cold sweat. Even in these forms of cerebral disease, when *Digitalis* is to be your remedy, the pulse comes in as your chief guide. If the symptom, buzzing in the ears, should suggest *Cinchona*, I entreat you not to give it after *Digitalis*, for Hahnemann tells us that, although there is a similarity in the cerebral symptoms and in the weakness, yet the drugs are inimical.

Lastly we shall speak of the action of *Digitalis* on the urethra and genital organs. *Digitalis* produces a catarrhal irritation of the bladder, particularly about its neck. There are strangury and frequent urging to urinate, especially when the patient is standing or sitting pressure on bladder not relieved by urinating. The patient may also have frequent urging to urinate at night. The urethra is inflamed so that we have burning in the urethra with purulent discharge, thick in character and bright yellow in color. Now, if you combine these symptoms with another one, namely, that the glans penis becomes inflamed with copious secretion of thick pus over its surface, you have a perfect picture of *Digitalis* in gonorrhœa. This form of the trouble, *Digitalis* will cure, whether the pulse be slow, fast, soft, weak, or what not. Often, too, when *Digitalis* is indicated in this trouble, you will find the prepuce puffed up and infiltrated with serum. Let me say, in passing, that if the prepuce becomes indurated, *Digitalis* will do no good, but *Sulphur* will.

The nearest remedy to *Digitalis* in gonorrhœa is *Mercurius*. This is a good remedy for gonorrhœa associated with inflammation of the prepuce, but with less œdema and more dark purplish swelling of the parts with phimosis or paraphimosis.

Mercurius corrosivus is good in these cases when the glans has a dark red or gangrenous appearance.

In the beginning of these cases of paraphimosis, we may give *Colocynth*, which will sometimes relieve the spasm and enable the prepuce to be drawn forward over the glans.

Petroselinum is to be thought of as an intercurrent remedy in gonorrhœal affections when the neck of the bladder is involved, and there is sudden urgent desire to urinate. It seems as if the patient can hardly retain his urine until he gets to a convenient place.

Digitalis also produces violent erections, even chordee. It is one of our best remedies for involuntary seminal emissions during sleep, even without dreams. The emissions are followed by great weakness.

Linaria Vulgaris.

This drug acts powerfully upon the sympathetic nerves. It may be serviceable in fainting of cardiac origin when the patient faints dead away without apparent cause. *Linaria* has repeatedly produced this symptom. It is true that there is some difficulty in confirming such a symptom as this, because, in most cases, the patient quickly returns to consciousness without recourse to any remedy. But if a patient who is subject to attacks of fainting of this kind is not only relieved but is cured by taking the drug, you know that this is the result of the remedy.

It also has some action upon the bladder, causing and also curing enuresis with painful urging to urinate.

VERBASCUM.

Verbascum is to be thought of as a remedy for catarrhs or colds when they are associated with neuralgia of the left side of the face, which appears periodically, generally twice a day, the same hour in the morning and afternoon of each day. It is described as a dull pressure on the malar bone as from a finger, with tension of the cheek and numb feeling. It is worse from every change of temperature, especially a change from warm to cold. There is considerable coryza and lachrymation present.

Verbascum has a peculiar cough which is characteristically laryngeal and tracheal. It could be produced only in a hard unyielding tube like the larynx or trachea.

The cough is hollow, hoarse, barking or trumpet-like, and is associated with hoarseness, the voice itself being deep and hard, a sort of "*basso profundo.*" It bears some resemblance to *Drosera*, *Spongia* and *Sulphur*.

GRATIOLA.

Gratiola is useful in diarrhœa. It produces and cures a profuse yellowish, gushing, watery diarrhœa, comparable to water rushing from a hydrant. This diarrhœa is very common in summer, and seems to have as its exciting cause excessive drinking of water, whether it be cold or not. It is concordant with *Croton tiglium*, *Elaterium*, *Podophyllum* and several other drugs.

LEPTANDRA VIRGINICA.

Leptandra Virginica is a drug which acts prominently on the liver. Locally, we find dull aching in the right hypochondrium, in the region of the gall-bladder, and also posteriorly in the posterior portion of the liver. This aching is often accompanied by soreness. At other times the congestion is great enough to produce burning distress in and about the liver. This often spreads to the stomach and abdomen. As accompanying symptoms we find drowsiness and despondency, which belong to liver affections of this character, and also diarrhœa, in which the stools are black, almost as black as pitch. These stools are accompanied by burning, distressing, colicky pain at the umbilicus. In other cases we have vomiting of bile with this burning distress, and occasionally clay-colored stools. The tongue is coated yellow or more frequently black, or dark-brown, and black down the middle. With these symptoms present, *Leptandra* may be indicated in bilious and typhoid fevers.

Leptandra resembles *Mercurius*. The main distinction between them is that *Mercurius* almost always has, characteristically, tenesmus continuing after stool. *Leptandra* has not this symptom, although it may have griping colicky pains after stool.

Iris versicolor should also be mentioned here. This drug irritates the whole alimentary tract, hence there are burning, serous diarrhœa, even rice-water discharges; cramps and vomiting. In cholera morbus coming at 2 or 3 A. M. it is superior to *Veratrum*. It also produces inflammation of the pancreas. *Leptandra* acts more on the liver; if the stools are not black, they are watery, muddy, and worse in the morning after beginning to move.

EUPHRASIA OFFICINALIS.

Euphrasia is particularly of use to us as a medicine acting on mucous membranes, especially the conjunctiva and the nasal mucous membrane.

It has long been known as a remedy in affections of the eyes. First it produces an inflammation of the eyelids, a blepharitis. The eyelids become reddened and injected, particularly on their inner surface. They become puffed, red or even dark red; ulceration takes place, giving us a discharge which is thick and excoriating. The tears themselves are profuse and excoriate the cheeks. There is marked photophobia; the patient cannot bear sunlight, but even more objectionable to him is artificial light. It has been urged by some physicians that it is "splitting hairs" in attempting to differentiate between aggravation from sunlight and that from artificial light. I cannot see where this objection has any force, for sunlight and artificial light are very different in their compositions.

Belladonna has aggravation from artificial light, and *Aconite* from sunlight.

In conjunctivitis, *Euphrasia* is sometimes indicated in scrofulous cases. Little blisters or phlyctenulæ form on or near the cornea; the discharges from the eyes are acrid and purulent and a film of mucus seems to collect over the cornea, causing a difficulty in vision. This blurred sight is relieved by wiping the eye or by winking.

We find *Euphrasia* indicated also in conjunctivitis of traumatic origin, when the above symptoms are present. *Arnica*, which is more of a remedy for bruises, has no application to this acrid discharge or to the formation of these little blisters; so when these form after an injury, *Euphrasia* is the preferable drug.

Although *Euphrasia* affects principally the superficial structures of the eye, we find it indicated in rheumatic iritis. If you examine the eye, you find that the iris reacts very tardily to light, and the aqueous humor is cloudy from the admixture of the products of inflammation. The pains are burning, stinging, shooting in character, are worse at night, and are attended with this acrid lachrymation.

Euphrasia is indicated in coryza which is perfectly bland with lachrymation which is excoriating.

If we compare it with its concordant remedies we find, beginning with the eye symptoms, that it is a close ally of *Mercurius solubilis*. Both remedies have this well-marked blepharitis and conjunctivitis coming from cold. But under *Mercurius* the discharge is thinner than under *Euphrasia;* moreover *Mercurius* has marked aggravation from the heat of the fire, and in damp weather.

Next we find *Euphrasia* similar to *Arsenicum album*. Both have the acrid discharge and the formation of phlyctenulæ on the cornea, and both are indicated in scrofulous cases. But *Arsenicum* has more marked burning—burning like fire, especially after midnight. This symptom is frequently though not always relieved by the application of hot water. Nor have we in *Euphrasia* the marked restlessness we have in *Arsenicum*.

Another similar drug is *Rhus toxicodendron*, which has profuse gushing tears, excoriating the check; profuse purulent discharge from the eyes. But the pus is thinner under *Rhus* than it is under *Euphrasia*. *Rhus* more often attacks the right eye; *Euphrasia* attacks either eye. *Rhus* has pains in the rheumatic iritis, darting from the eye through to the occiput, with a great deal of restlessness, agony, tossing about at night, and relief from motion and applied heat.

In studying the coryza we are accustomed to associate *Euphrasia* with *Allium cepa*. We make this differentiation between the two remedies: *Cepa* has excoriating coryza and bland lachrymation; *Euphrasia*, bland coryza and acrid lachrymation.

There is still one other application we may make of *Euphrasia*, and that is in paralysis of the third pair of nerves, causing ptosis, especially when caused by catching cold, in rheumatic patients.

The allies here are *Rhus toxicodendron* and *Causticum*, both of which have exactly the same symptom. This gives you very nearly the precise position of *Euphrasia* in the treatment of catarrh of the eyes and nose.

We may also make use of the drug in the treatment of condylomata. It is useful in broad, flat condylomata of the anus, of course of sycotic origin. Usually there is some oozing of moisture about them.

LECTURE XXXVIII.

BAPTISIA TINCTORIA.

Baptisia tinctoria. { Gelsemium.
Rhus tox., Bryonia.
Arnica, Muriatic acid, Lachesis, Arsenicum album.
Ailanthus.

I HAVE selected for our study to-day a member of the leguminous plants, namely, *Baptisia tinctoria,* or the wild indigo. *Baptisia* is a drug which has a short history, but an exceedingly interesting one. Our journals are replete with glowing accounts of cures of typhoid conditions made with it. *Baptisia* causes, in general, the changes in the blood, both quantitative and qualitative, which are exhibited in typhoid fever. The offensive exhalations, the mental and nervous phenomena which it develops are characteristic of this disease. *Baptisia* is suitable to all stages of typhoid, early or late. Its symptoms I will divide into two classes: first, those which indicate the remedy early in typhoid affections, and, secondly, those which call for it late. The drug may of course be indicated even if all the following symptoms are not present in any one case. But I shall give you the characteristic symptoms of the remedy, and unless several of these are present it would not be proper to give *Baptisia*. These symptoms are as follows: excitement of the brain, just such as precedes delirium; wild, wandering feeling; the patient cannot confine his mind to any one subject; restlessness, constant desire to move from place to place; disturbed sleep. The patient awakens at two or three o'clock in the morning, and then is so restless that he tosses about, unable to sleep any longer. During sleep his dreams are of the most extravagant character. He dreams that he is chained to the bed, or that he is swimming a river, or undergoing some ordeal which makes a great demand on his strength. He may suffer from nightmare, from which he awakens with a sensation as though the room were insufferably hot, making breathing almost impossible. If he still has strength he goes to the open window to get air. Now this is not a true asthma; it is not due to a spasmodic contraction of the bronchioles. There is a fulness of the chest, causing the oppressed feeling. One prover described the symptom, not as a true difficulty of breathing, but as a feeling as though he had not strength to lift his chest.

The patient makes frequent errors as to his own person, supposing at times that he is double or that his body is scattered about, and that he must toss about the bed to collect the pieces. Now these evidences of nervous excitement are accompanied by excessive prostration; the back and limbs ache; the back feels stiff; the patient feels tired and bruised all over; he complains of the bed feeling too hard; this makes him restless, and he tosses about the bed to find a softer spot; weakness develops, progressing so far that he becomes unable to walk; he suffers from an indescribable weak or faint feeling, with or without vertigo.

The face is hot and flushed and has a heavy, besotted look, as in the case of one intoxicated. The eyes, also, are heavy and stupid in appearance. The tongue is at first white or slightly yellowish: frequently, too, the papillæ are raised and project through this whitish or yellow coating. The edges of the tongue are of a deep red color.

There is a dull, heavy headache, with the sensation as if the head would be pressed in; sometimes the pressure in the forehead seems to go down into the root of the nose. Again, the patient complains of a sensation which he describes "as though the skin of the forehead were being pulled back towards the occiput." This is evidently due to tonic contraction of the occipito-frontalis muscle. At other times the patient simply describes the sensation as though the skin of the forehead were tense, or tight, or drawn. These symptoms of the head are often accompanied by a numb, tingling feeling in the forehead or scalp. At other times the head feels enormously large.

The typhoid type of fever is very characteristic of *Baptisia*, it being one of the few remedies which actually produce this type of fever. There is always an increase of temperature. The pulse is usually accelerated in direct proportion to the intensity of the fever. Even in the early stages of typhoid fever, you may find *Baptisia* indicated by the abdominal symptoms, slight sensitiveness in the ilio-cæcal region, and yellow putrescent stools These, then, are the symptoms calling for the early exhibition of *Baptisia* in typhoid fever.

I can say confidently that if you select the drug on its homœopathic indications as just outlined, you will succeed in aborting a large percentage of typhoid states. I say this despite the assertions of many other physicians who have argued to the contrary. The properly-selected drug *will* abort typhoid fever. The disease need not run its course, as prominent old-school authorities claim it must necessarily do.

Later in the course of the disease, during the second or third week, you will find *Baptisia* indicated when the prostration is profound. The patient is in a stupor. He falls asleep while answering questions. His face is now dark-red in color and has, more marked than ever, this heavy, besotted look. The tongue has changed its yellow or white coating to one which has a brown streak down the centre, the edges of the organ still remaining red. All the exhalations and discharges from the patient are exceedingly offensive. The teeth are covered with sordes having an offensive odor. The breath is fœtid. The stools are yellowish or dark, and are horribly putrid. The urine and sweat are both offensive. So you see, *Baptisia* applies to cases in which there is an evident decomposition of vital fluids and rapid disintegration of tissue.

To give *Baptisia* its legitimate position among other typhoid remedies it will be necessary to compare it with those nearest like it in symptomatology. The first of these remedies to which I shall call your attention is *Gelsemium*. This usually precedes *Baptisia* when there are malaise and muscular soreness, and the patient suffers from chills and "crups," which go down the back. This is on the first day, remember. In the afternoon comes the fever with accelerated pulse, this being full and flowing, not tense and resisting as under *Aconite*. The fever is usually associated with drowsiness; the face is red in color, uniformly suffused; and even as early in the case as this there may be prostration. *Gelsemium* causes paralysis of the motor nerves, hence there must be weakness of the muscles. By the next afternoon if the fever rises, despite *Gelsemium*, you may change to *Baptisia*, provided the above-mentioned symptoms develop. The reason I dwell on the relations of these two drugs is because of the great similarity of their symptoms. Both of them have this intense muscular soreness and prostration; both have drowsiness and nervous excitement, with prostration; both have this feeling of expansion, as though the head or some part of the body were enormously enlarged; and both have the afternoon exacerbation of the fever. The relation between the two drugs is one of degree or intensity. *Gelsemium* is the milder acting drug of the two.

Another remedy which is not unlike *Baptisia* is *Rhus tox*. Like *Baptisia*, *Rhus* has restlessness, brown tongue and soreness of the muscles. I must confess that the distinction between the two remedies is not always easy. Formerly, *Rhus* held undisputed sway in almost all diseases which threatened to assume a typhoid type, whether the disease was diphtheria, scarlatina, peritonitis or pneumonia. Now this honor is shared with *Baptisia* The main differences between the drugs, briefly given, are these: *Rhus* has restlessness, caused more by rheumatoid pains than by muscular soreness alone. The tongue, under *Rhus*, has a red, triangular tip, which is not noticed under *Baptisia*. Delirium is of a muttering character under *Rhus*, unaccompanied, so far as I know, by these delusions respecting personal identity. Neither are the putrid discharges of *Rhus tox*. quite so offensive as those of *Baptisia*. If diarrhœa progresses to a severe type under *Rhus*, the stools are watery, sometimes bloody and involuntary. The pneumonic symptoms which often complicate typhoid fever are more prominent under *Rhus*.

Arnica claims a relationship with *Baptisia*. It is similar to the latter remedy in the stupor, in the intolerance of the bed (the patient complaining that it feels too hard), and in the falling asleep while answering questions. *Arnica*, I think, is more suitable when there is a tendency to apoplectic congestion and when the stupor is so profound that both stool and urine are passed involuntarily. The intensity of the involvement of the brain is shown by the loud, snoring respiration. Then, too, in *Arnica* we find suggillations, sometimes called ecchymoses.

Lachesis also comes forward as similar to *Baptisia*. You will recognize the resemblances between the remedies in the offensiveness of the discharges, in the putridity of the exhalations and in the excessive prostration. I believe that I have seen apparently hopeless cases react under the benign influence of this remedy. As an animal poison, I think it penetrates more deeply than *Baptisia*, and in consequence should be called for in worse cases. It may be distinguished by the following symptoms: trembling of the tongue when attempting to protrude it; the tongue catches on the teeth during the act. When he succeeds in getting it out, it hangs there tremblingly, and he may not even have sense enough to draw it in again. Hæmorrhages are frequent in the *Lachesis* patient. Blood may escape from every orifice of the body. The lips crack and ooze a dark or blackish blood. Dark blood escapes from the bowels. This, after standing awhile, deposits a sediment which looks like charred straw. In severe cases there is marked intolerance to light pressure. Even when the sensorium appears to be perfectly benumbed the patient resists the slightest touch about the neck. In still worse cases, you have to distinguish it from *Baptisia* when there are approaching cerebral paralysis, dropping of the lower jaw and involuntary discharges.

Muriatic acid bears some resemblance to *Baptisia* in the great prostration, in the decomposition of fluids, and in the low form of delirium. But the general character of its symptoms is not sufficiently similar to those of the other remedy to make a distinction difficult. The *Muriatic acid* weakness is so great that the patient is unable to make the slight exertion required to maintain the head on the pillow; he therefore slides down to the foot of the bed.

Now, a word about *Baptisia* in diseases other than typhoid fever. In such affections it is indicated by the symptoms already mentioned. In dysentery you will give it when the discharges are offensive, bloody and are attended by tenesmus, but with a significant absence of pain, showing an alarming depression of vitality.

Baptisia comes into play in the treatment of phthisis. It is especially useful during the later stages of the disease in relieving the fever, particularly when it increases in the afternoon with slight drowsiness, thick speech and bewilderment of mind.

Baptisia has proved itself one of our best remedies in diphtheria when it has assumed a typhoid type. Some of the symptoms already mentioned will be present. The mouth is excessively putrid. The membrane is dark and exhibits a gangrenous tendency. Sometimes, early in the disease, you will observe this characteristic: the patient can swallow only liquids. Give him milk and he will drink it. Give him solid food and he rejects it at once.

Ailanthus is to be compared with *Baptisia* in typhoid conditions, in scarlatina and in diphtheria. It produces even more profound stupor than the latter remedy. There is a well-marked, excoriating, watery discharge from the nose, making the upper lip sore. The rash, if any exist, is of a livid purplish hue, thus denoting the poisoned state of the blood.

I wish to impress upon you the need of correlating properly in your mind *Gelsemium*, *Baptisia*, *Rhus tox.* and *Lachesis*. These remedies present so many distinct clinical pictures, which, when recalled in time of necessity and used according to their symptomatic indications, form a quartette invaluable in the treatment of disease.

LECTURE XXXIX.

SOLANACEÆ.

Solanaceæ.
{ Belladonna.
Hyoscyamus. } Mydriatic—Acro-narcotic.
Stramonium.
Solanum nigrum.
Tabacum.
Dulcamara.
Capsicum—Acrid.

The drugs composing this group of remedies present great symptomatic similarity. The first three remedies on the list are continually in use, even in an average practice. There is scarcely a symptom of one of them which cannot be found under one of the others. The resemblances are, in fact, perplexingly similar.

I have arranged the remedies on the board, not botanically, but rather according to their medicinal relations. For instance, the first four on the list attack prominently the brain and have narcotic properties; they are, therefore, placed in one group. Then we have *Tabacum*, which also has narcotic properties, but which acts also on other parts of the body besides the brain. Next comes *Dulcamara*, which contains a small quantity of *Solanine*, and is only slightly narcotic. A large quantity of this drug would be required to develop the soporific effects which can be obtained from *Stramonium* or *Hyoscyamus*. Lastly, we have *Capsicum*, which is decidedly irritant or acrid. Placed on the skin, it acts as a blister or counter-irritant. It has possibly some narcotic effects, but it differs almost entirely from the other members of the group.

The resemblances between the first three members of the group are so great, in fact the drugs are so nearly " *idem*," that it is not well to follow one with the other. There are some symptoms of *Belladonna* and *Hyoscyamus* which are opposite, not so much in the phraseology in which they are expressed, for they may read almost exactly alike, but in the fact that they are results acting in opposite directions; consequently, they sometimes serve to antidote each other. Especially is this true of the skin symptoms.

BELLADONNA.

Belladonna.
- Sphincters contract.
- Nerves.
  - Irritates the centres.
  - Irritates, then paralyzes the peripheries.
  - Disturbs the circulation; worse in the brain.
  - Disturbs the circulation; fever.
- Ailments.
  - Violent, sudden.
  - Usually with brain symptoms.
- Inflammation.
- Hyperæmia with tendency upward.
- Brain cells.

Belladonna, or the deadly nightshade, was known to the medical world as early as 1500 A. D. The Venetians named the plant "*herba bella donna*," from the circumstance that the ladies used it distilled in water as a cosmetic to brighten the eyes and flush the cheeks. The plant, especially the leaves, yields the well-known alkaloid *Atropine*. The root, too, contains *Atropine*, although in variable proportions. *Belladonna* is intensely poisonous to man, though herbivorous animals may eat it with impunity.

Studied as a poison, *Belladonna* causes the following symptoms: eyes dry and injected; face red, turgid, and hot; skin scarlet or studded with papillæ, all but identical with those in scarlatina; violent congestions especially of the head; mouth and throat distressingly dry; this last sensation extends downward, compelling frequent swallowing, and suffocative spasms of the fauces and glottis. Thirst is violent, yet water aggravates; there are vertigo, confusion, hallucination, and finally stupor. The pupils are so markedly dilated that the iris is hardly visible.* There are jactitation of the muscles; convulsions. Such poisoning cases are not uncommon in Europe, where the plant is

---

**Belladonna dilates the pupil by stimulating the sympathetic; *Physostigma* contracts it by stimulating the third cranial nerve; *Gelsemium* dilates it by paralyzing the third cranial nerve.

native, and where its berries have been mistaken for cherries. In this country, too, it has been taken accidentally, and also employed in attempts at suicide. To antidote it, use the stomach pump, emetics of hot mustard water, and strong coffee without milk or sugar.

Belladonna as a homœopathic remedy is almost as old as the art itself. Our symptomatology from provings and poisoning cases enables us to employ the drug with mathematical certainty so far as its selection is concerned. But like all polychrests, it is abused by hurried and careless practitioners, and so is often given when its resemblance to the cases under treatment is only superficial and partial. Of all drugs, it has the power of producing opposite effects most markedly.

Belladonna has been so often mentioned in the preceding lectures of this course in comparing it with other drugs that you are already somewhat familiar with it. For this reason many of the symptoms of the drug may be passed over in brief review. But first of all let me tell you something of the general character of *Belladonna*. It seems to be best suited to rather fleshy and phlegmatic persons of a plethoric habit who are subject to congestions, especially of the head. This is something like the constitution of *Calcarea ostrearum*, but *Belladonna* has not the pallor of that remedy. The *Belladonna* patients are pleasant and jolly enough when well, but they become exceedingly irritable and overbearing when ill. This pleasant sociability which makes them so companionable, seems to be converted into the opposite condition when they are afflicted with disease. It is also suited to precocious children, with big head and small body, who may be scrofulous, with a tendency to swelling of the lips and enlargement of glands. They learn things rapidly; sleep is unnatural; the head is hot and the cheeks red; they scream out during sleep. *Belladonna*, when it is to be used for children, demands the presence of some cerebral symptoms. There must be some irritation of the brain, as shown by jerking of the limbs, irritability and fretfulness, or even some absolute meningeal inflammation.

A peculiarity of *Belladonna* is its faculty of exciting constriction of the circular fibres of blood-vessels, contraction of sphincters, etc. This universal quality of *Belladonna* is exemplified in the constriction of the throat, worse from liquids; constriction of the anus, which, with tenesmic urging and pressing in the rectum, suggests the drug in dysentery; spasmodic constriction of the os uteri, retarding labor; and ineffectual or frequent urging to urinate, with scanty discharge.

The disease in which *Belladonna* is indicated is acute, sudden and violent. The very rapidity of the onset of the trouble should at once suggest *Belladonna*. For example, a child is perfectly well on going to bed. A few hours afterward it begins to scream out during sleep, and is soon aroused with violent symptoms, such as jerking of the limbs, irritation of the brain, restlessness, can't lie still; ceaseless motion, especially of the arms. All these symptoms suggest *Belladonna*.

Again if inflammations come suddenly, and are violent or almost overwhelming in their intensity, *Belladonna* is suggested. We may think of it in abscess, when pus develops with lightning-like rapidity, whether it be an abscess of the tonsil, a boil, or any other kind of abscess. Hence we find it indicated in phlegmonous erysipelas, which quickly goes on to suppuration. The affected parts become greatly swollen. Pus works its way through the tissues between the various muscles. The very suddenness of the attack suggests *Belladonna*. The pains are quite consistent with this character of the drug. They come suddenly and last a greater or less length of time, and then cease as suddenly as they began. So much for the general character of *Belladonna*.

Belladonna acts on muscular tissue and on the joints. It is one of our best remedies in acute and chronic rheumatism. The pains are cutting and tearing, running along the limbs like lightning. The joints are swollen, red and shining; streaks of red radiate from the inflamed joint; rheumatic fever, with pains attacking the nape of the neck, shoulders and upper arms. It is one of the best remedies in rheumatic stiff neck, caused by cutting the hair, getting the head wet, or sitting with the head and neck exposed to a draft.

The action of *Belladonna* on the brain must be understood before we can proceed further. In reviewing the symptoms of the drug, it seems to me that it does not develop positive inflammation of the meninges, but rather the collateral symptoms of the inflammation only. Thus *Aconite* causes an absolute inflammation of the meninges with an increase of exudation; *Bryonia* causes inflammation, with an exudation of leucocytes and blood plasma, constituting complete inflammation. But *Belladonna* seems rather to provoke congestion only. The surcharged blood-vessels seem to have ruptured, producing little reddish spots or ecchymoses in the tissues, thus exciting a congestive irritation of the brain beneath the membrane. If exudation follows this congestive irritation the exudate is serous, and is just the kind that results from venous congestion. It is not the inflammatory exudation, rich in plasma, which is pictured under *Bryonia*, *Apis* and *Sulphur*.

Nevertheless, *Belladonna* produces so many collateral symptoms of cerebral irritation, that we find its use indispensable in this condition. In the first place, it causes congestion of the head. In its milder form, this may be simply a feeling of heat about the head, the feet being cold. At other times and in more violent forms we find the face red and the whites of the eyes somewhat injected. The patient complains of a severe throbbing headache. He may be either drowsy or very wakeful. Frequently these latter symptoms alternate, that is, at times the patient is drowsy and falls into a heavy slumber, awaking later with a start, and crying out, or giving some other evidence of cerebral irritation, such as jerking of the limbs and twitching of individual muscles. As this form of irritation advances, we find the eyes very red, the whites of the eyes looking almost like raw beef. The carotid arteries throb so violently that their pulsations are plainly visible. This congestion proceeds to an inflammatory irritation. We find intense throbbing in the head, with sharp shooting pains, making the patient scream or cringe, so violent are they. These pains come almost like a flash, and disappear as suddenly as they came. At first the patient cannot sleep. He is in the unfortunate predicament of being sleepy, yet unable to sleep. As the symptoms advance, especially in children, there is boring of the head into the pillow; the head is thrown backward and there is rolling of the head from side to side. Some squint is noticed. The pupils are dilated. There is grinding of the teeth. The face is now bright red or else the congestion is so violent as to make it almost purple. If the patient is a child whose anterior fontanelle has not yet closed, you can feel it, tense and bulging, above the convexity of the skull, throbbing and thumping with each pulsation of the heart. Convulsions often ensue, particularly in children, and these convulsions are very violent, distorting the body in every conceivable manner, opisthotonos predominating. The urine is either scanty or suppressed. Now the various symptoms, subjective and objective, which belong to this condition are, first, jerking in sleep, or even when awake; on closing his eyes the patient is very apt to see abnormal visions. These usually disappear on opening the eyes. At other times he has a sensation as though he were falling; the patient, if a child, suddenly arouses from sleep, clutches at the air, and trembles as if from fear. Sometimes this symptom is due to dreams; at other times it comes from severe pain in the head, which, by its intensity, wakens the child in great alarm. At still other times it results from the sensation as if the child were falling.

Sometimes we find the patients with this cerebral irritation lying in a stupor. They can scarcely be aroused, and when aroused they are always violent, tossing about, striking those near them and tearing their clothes. All these are evidences of excitement, which, if not due to actual inflammation, at least approach that condition.

In inflammation of the brain or its membranes, *Belladonna* must give place to other drugs when exudation takes places, whether the meningitis be simple or tuberculous. There is very little relation between *Belladonna* and tuberculous meningitis. Tuberculous meningitis is slow in its course. Thus we have suggested at once *Sulphur, Calcarea ostrearum, Apis,* and other remedies deeper and slower-acting than *Belladonna.* Then again, when exudation has taken place, as indicated by the persistence of the rolling of the head and sudden shrieking, we know that we must resort to other remedies, principally to *Apis. Bryonia,* too, often comes in after *Belladonna,* when the face is flushed red or is alternately red and pale. The slightest attempt to move the child makes it shriek with pain. The pupils do not react readily to light. The child moves the mouth as though it were chewing or sucking. The resemblances between the two remedies are so great as to make a selection often perplexing. Both remedies have haste in drinking water, both have crying out with pain, both have aggravation from motion, and both have constipation. At times you will find it very difficult to distinguish between the two.

To separate *Belladonna* from *Aconite* is easier. The fevers caused by the two drugs are distinguished in the following manner: *Belladonna* does not produce fever primarily from its action on the sympathetic nervous system; *Aconite* does do this. *Belladonna* acts secondarily on the sympathetic and primarily on the cerebro-spinal nervous system, hence is of use only when that system is involved, which in children occurs very early in the case. In adults it is apt to commence as a fever, cerebral symptoms ensuing; thus *Belladonna* becomes the remedy. In the beginning of fever, *Aconite* is preferable when there is violent anguish of mind, with restlessness, tossing about, fear of death, dry, hot skin, full, bounding pulse, some hallucinations, some crying out in sleep, and some muttering or foolish talk which belongs to the fever. These cerebral symptoms result from the high temperature and not from direct inflammation of the brain. But suppose this case goes on until the brain becomes involved. The skin becomes so hot that it almost burns the examining hand, or, if you raise the bed-clothes, a hot steam seems to come forth from the patient. That is the kind of heat that belongs to *Belladonna*. At other times, hot sweat, particularly about the head and face, accompanies this heat. You see the sweat standing out in beads on the forehead, and if you feel it you will find that it is hot. This is not at all characteristic of *Aconite*. The two remedies may be, however, distinguished by the fact that *Belladonna* has jerking in sleep, hallucinations, visions, and courting of death rather than fear of it. This is often the case in rheumatic fever. The whole system seems to be involved, producing general fever with pain in the joints flying about from place to place. This fever is almost always associated with profuse sour sweat, which gives no relief whatever. The patient seems to soak everything about him with the sweat, and the more he sweats the less sign is there of improvement. *Aconite* does no good here, but *Belladonna* does.

When the fever has subsided somewhat, and the sweat still continues, *Mercurius* is the proper remedy to follow.

In typhoid types of fever, *Belladonna* is indicated sometimes in the beginning of the disease. It is indicated in the stage of excitement when the congestion of the brain predominates. We find furious delirium, with screaming out and violent efforts to escape from the bed or the house. The face is red. either a bright or deep red, bordering on purple; the pupils are dilated and the eyes injected. The patient is full of fear, imagining that all sorts of accidents are about to happen to him. The urine is scanty, and when passed it is usually a bright deep yellow, with or without sediment. The feet are apt to be cold. The patient now falls into a heavy snoring sleep; this is not a quiet sleep, for there is apt to be some evidence of cerebral irritation, such as jerking of muscles, twitching of limbs, and crying out. No matter how profound the sleep may be, it is *never* a perfectly quiet stupor; if it is, *Belladonna* is not the remedy. You will see from this that *Belladonna* is indicated, not from any changes in the brain caused by the poisoned blood, but from changes resulting from congestion or inflammation. When the disease has gone so far as to cause alterations in the fluids of the body, *Belladonna* is decreasingly indicated as these changes advance. Then you should have recourse to such remedies as *Hyoscyamus*, *Rhus tox.*, *Lachesis*, and others.

Sometimes we have a condition differing from the one already described, in which *Belladonna* may be the remedy. The face is pale instead of red. Now this indication is just as characteristic of *Belladonna* as is the red face. It is usually associated with irritation of the brain and starting in sleep. It occurs usually in summer complaint, during dentition, and in colic and in similar diseases.

The pulse is either full and hard, as under *Aconite*, or it is slow. It is slow when the cerebral congestion is great enough to cause some pressure on the brain. Here, again, you find an illustration of the alternating effects of *Belladonna*. The pulse may be rapid for a while, and then it becomes slow, and so alternates.

The headaches of *Belladonna* are nervous and congestive. The vertigo also is congestive; the patient feels as if he would pitch forward; or he suddenly falls backward unconscious. The nervous headaches are semi-lateral, right sided, worse from 4 P. M. to 3 A. M., worse from lying down; the brain feels as if it were swashing about. The headache is worse from light, noise or *any* jarring. Vomiting; can't keep quiet; fidgety. The congestive headaches are of a throbbing character, with aggravation from inclining the head toward the part of the brain most markedly congested. The pains are often of a stabbing, shooting character, driving patient almost wild. When the whole head is affected, the patient sits up with the head supported so as to keep it from bending; accompanying the headache there is generally a red face, and violent throbbing of the carotid arteries. The mind is often affected; the patient becomes delirious, wild and excited, and has all sorts of hallucinations.

We have already seen how *Belladonna* may be indicated in inflammation of the brain. It is also a valuable remedy in inflammation of other parts of the body. For instance, we find it to be the best, though by no means the only, remedy in otitis media, or inflammation of the middle ear. This disease will perplex you at times. The symptoms are very severe. The child puts its hands to its head, and you may erroneously presume the trouble to be there. The pains are digging, boring and tearing in character; they are necessarily so on account of the anatomical relations of the parts affected. They come suddenly, and are very violent. They seem to shoot into the other ear, or into the head, with buzzing and roaring in the ears. Now if you examine the ear you will find the membrana tympani bulging outward, its blood-vessels very much injected; in fact, it presents a highly inflamed appearance. There is rapid formation of pus, which seeks to escape either by bursting the membrane, by the Eustachian tube, or through some internal part. In case it takes the latter course, it produces alarming if not fatal symptoms. It is your duty to recognize this disease early, while there is still a chance of saving the ear. *Belladonna* is believed to be our best remedy for the disease in its early stages; later, we have other remedies indicated such as *Hepar* and *Tellurium*.

Tellurium causes inflammation of the middle ear, with rupture of the membrana tympani and pouring out of pus, which may, at first, be bland, but soon becomes very offensive, having an odor like that of herring-brine.

In inflammations of the eyes, as in conjunctivitis or sclerotitis, we find *Belladonna* indicated by the suddenness of the attack, by the severity of the pains, and by the violence of the symptoms. There is great intolerance of light. The eye feels as if enormously swollen. The conjunctiva is bright red These symptoms give you a perfect picture of *Belladonna*. It seems to attack the right eye more than the left. It is the intense congestion which guides us to the selection of *Belladonna* in eye-affections; the same remark applies equally to neuralgias in and about the eye.

Spigelia has many eye-pains like those of *Belladonna*, but they are left-sided, and lack the intense congestion.

Amyl nitrite is similar to *Belladonna*, being indicated when the eyes and face are red.

Paris quadrifolia is excellent when there are pains as if the eyes were drawn back by strings; the eyeballs feel too large (like *Spigelia*).

Prunus has a crushing pain, or sensation as if the eyes were pressed asunder, or sharp piercing pains through and around the eye.

The parotid gland is inflamed by *Belladonna*, especially on the right side; there are stitches, extending into the ear; the gland is swollen, hot and red; the orifice of Steno's duct is painful, as if abraded; the saliva is thick, gluey, yellowish and tenacious; mucus coats the mouth and throat with a thick tenacious layer; the tongue is white and fissured.

Belladonna produces inflammation of the throat. The *Belladonna* tongue is usually bright red, the papillæ are enlarged or elevated, giving it a resemblance to the strawberry (and hence it has been called the strawberry tongue). At times you find the dorsum of the tongue coated with a thin white layer, through which the enlarged red papillæ show. But, as the case advances, this coating peels off, leaving a bright red, highly-inflamed tongue.

The throat is a prominent point of attack in the *Belladonna* proving. The inflammation which it develops there is of a very common kind. Looking into the throat, you find the fauces inflamed and bright red, the tonsils, particularly the right one, enlarged, with a tendency of the disease to extend toward the left. All these symptoms have the same rapidity of progress that we noticed with the *Belladonna* symptoms elsewhere. There is great contraction of the fauces and glottis, so that any attempt to swallow is followed by sudden constriction of the throat and ejection of the food through the nose and mouth. The patient makes an attempt to drink, and the moment the water touches the fauces it is ejected, and escapes in any way it can. The patient seems to be worse from swallowing fluids, more so, in fact, than from either saliva or solids. The tonsils rapidly suppurate; the glands in the neck, externally, are commonly involved, and are to be felt as hard but very sensitive kernels in the neck.

Sometimes you find a pearly-white exudate on the fauces, which is seen to be mucus and not fibrin. There is, therefore, strictly speaking, no resemblance between the *Belladonna* inflammation and that characteristic of diphtheria or membranous croup, so that when *Belladonna* is administered in diphtheria it must be indicated on other symptoms than those belonging to the membrane. The general character of diphtheria is that of blood-poisoning, while *Belladonna* does not poison the blood. When you give *Belladonna* in diphtheria, therefore, be certain that it is the remedy or you will lose valuable time. It may, occasionally, be the remedy in the early stages when the violence of the attack calls for it.

Let me here remind you that *Lycopodium* affects the right tonsil, that it produces high temperature, crying out during sleep, and awaking from sleep cross and irritable. These symptoms we found under *Belladonna* also; so be sure when you give the latter remedy that *Lycopodium* is not the one that is indicated.

Then, again, you should think of *Apis*. *Apis* is a magnificent remedy in diphtheria. The exudate is more on the right tonsil; the throat is bright red and rosy; the tongue is red and the fever very high; the skin is dry and hot, the pulse accelerated, and the patient very restless.

But, in tonsillitis or quinsy, *Belladonna* stands at the head of the list of remedies. Here it far exceeds *Apis* in therapeutic value, because it attacks the parenchyma of the organ. The inflammation caused by *Apis* is superficial, only involving the mucous surface.

In throat diseases *Belladonna* forms an interesting little group with *Hepar*, *Mercurius*, *Silicea* and *Sulphur*. When, in spite of the exhibition of *Belladonna*, pus forms in the tonsil, as indicated by rigors and chills and by sharp, lancinating pains with throbbing, you should change from that remedy to *Hepar*. Even then you may be able to prevent abscess-formation.

You should change to *Mercurius* if pus has already formed; the tonsil is enlarged and encroaches on neighboring parts and the breathing is labored. When pus has thus shown itself, *Mercurius*, given low and repeatedly, will cause a quick breaking of the abscess, relieving all the symptoms. If you give *Mercurius* at first you will greatly lengthen the course of your case.

Sometimes you must have recourse to *Silicea* when the abscess has discharged and refuses to heal. Pus keeps on forming and grows dark and fœtid and disagreeable to the taste.

In some of these cases *Silicea* fails; then you should interpolate a few doses of *Sulphur*, which generally has the desired effect. It may be necessary to have recourse to *Fluoric acid*.

There is another remedy that has been used to some extent, namely, *Amygdala amara*. The drug causes a dark red injection of the fauces, uvula and tonsils, with sharp pains, causing considerable difficulty in swallowing; sometimes they are so severe as to make the patient cry out. If these symptoms are present the drug may be used in diphtheria. I have myself cured cases of this disease with *Amygdala amara* alone when there were present this dark red color of the throat, the sudden sharp pains, and marked general prostration. *Amygdala* develops the prostrated, tired feeling which is incident to the first days of diphtheria.

Belladonna is of use in œsophagitis with sense of *constriction;* there are painful swallowing and breathing. *Veratrum viride*, *Rhus tox.* and *Arsenicum* are also remedies sometimes indicated in œsophagitis.

In gastric symptoms, *Belladonna* is called for when there are cramp-like pains in the stomach, worse during a meal; stitching pains; must bend backward and hold the breath; burning. These gastralgic pains always go through to the spine. Pressure is a prominent gastric symptom; it is worse after eating and comes also at times when walking.

Calcarea ostrearum has pressure as of a stone, relieved from motion. *Chininum arsenicosum* has caused pressure in the "solar plexus" with tender spine just behind it.

Bismuth has gastralgia going from throat to the spine, relieved by bending backward. It thus closely simulates the *Belladonna* case, but lacks the extreme nervous and febrile excitement; *Bismuth* is inclined to be cold, with pale face, although the pain may be accompanied by anxiety and restlessness.

In inflammation about the abdomen we sometimes find *Belladonna* the remedy; for instance, in peritonitis, whether accompanied by metritis or not, and whether or not it is of puerperal origin. The symptoms which call for it are: commencing tympanites the abdomen is swollen like a drum, and very sensitive to touch, so much so, in fact, that the patient wants all the bed-clothing removed. The least jarring in the room makes her worse. For instance, if you should unexpectedly kick your foot against the bed in walking near her, you cause her to wince and complain bitterly of pain. You will also notice the pungent heat of which I have already spoken. The abdomen feels extremely hot to your hand. On raising the bed-clothes there appears to issue forth the hot steam to which reference has already been made. There is marked cerebral irritation. The lochial discharge is apt to be scanty or suppressed.

Tilia Europea is a drug that I feel certain has not received due credit from the profession. It is useful in puerperal metritis when there is intense sore feeling about the uterus; there is also marked bearing-down with hot sweat which gives no relief.

A remedy very commonly used by allopaths is *Terebinthina*. Now, the symptoms which this drug has actually produced are: bearing down in the uterine region; burning like fire about the hypogastrium; burning on urinating; dark, cloudy, muddy urine. In these cases the tongue is apt to be dry and red.

For this feeling of soreness in the uterus Dr. Jeanes used a preparation of honey with salt, *Mel cum sale*. He used it in the third or sixth attenuation. His key-note for the selection of the drug was a feeling of soreness in the hypogastric region extending from ilium to ilium. This is an important indication in uterine displacements and in the commencement of metritis.

Under *Belladonna*, the urine is yellow and clear; turbid with red sediment, or profuse. There may be involuntary urination in sleep This latter suggests the use of the drug in children. It will not often disappoint you when the other symptoms concur. There is not a true atony present, but a relaxation of sphincters and an over action from the loss of balance of the longitudinal muscular fibres. There is a feeling in the bladder as of a ball rolling there (also *Lachesis* and perhaps *Lycopodium*), tenesmus of the bladder; strangury; dark, turbid and fiery red urine; frequent desire to urinate with scanty discharge of urine. In enuresis with actual relaxation look to *Plantago major*, *Causticum*, etc. *Belladonna* may have to be followed in these cases by *Calcarea ostrearum*, *Sulphur* or *Silicea*. *Kreosote* is indicated in enuresis especially when the patient urinates when dreaming of the act. *Hyoscyamus* should also be considered.

We have next to speak of the action of *Belladonna* on the skin. It causes at first an erythema, a bright scarlet redness of the skin; the skin becomes exceedingly sensitive to the touch. Sometimes, this erythema consists in a uniform blush over the entire surface of the body such as we have in the Sydenham variety of scarlatina. At other times it has an erysipelatous appearance, coming, as it does, in streaks which start from some central point and radiate in all directions, the color usually being very bright, the swelling rapid with early involvement of the cellular tissue beneath the skin, and in some cases rapid formation of pus, which burrows deeply into the cellular tissue. Thus you have a true picture of phlegmonous erysipelas. With these symptoms you do not often find development of vesicles or pustules. Instead of this you find the surface smooth, shining and tense. Pains are violent and sharp. They are of a lancinating and stinging character and are usually associated with a great deal of throbbing, particularly if the deeper parts are involved in the inflammation.

If the erysipelas should attack the face, it almost always begins on the right side, with a tendency to extend toward the left. There is almost always a tendency manifested. Do not confound this cerebral irritation with metastasis of erysipelas to the brain. It is a simple irritation caused either by the amount of fever, by the severity of the pain, or by the poisoning of the blood, or possibly all three; but it is not a true metastasis. If metastasis should take place, *Belladonna* may still be called for. If, however, *Belladonna* fail in these cases, we have other remedies: for instance, *Lachesis*, when cerebral metastasis fails to yield to *Belladonna*, the face is of a purplish or bluish hue rather than of the bright or deep red of *Belladonna*. The patient is weaker, the pulse more rapid and lacking in force, and there is more drowsiness than we find under *Belladonna*.

Still another concordant remedy is *Crotalus*, which is very similar to *Lachesis*—so similar, indeed, that I cannot give you any points of distinction between the two.

Cuprum is to be thought of for this metastasis, if the patient is threatened with convulsions. There are vigorous contractions of the flexor muscles.

Ailanthus suits when there is profound stupor and the face is livid and mottled. *Apis* and *Sulphur* also come within this sphere.

Returning now to the erythema of *Belladonna*, we learn that when the condition becomes general, it suggests the employment of the remedy in scarlet fever. In this disease, it is indicated, first of all, by this bright rosy hue of the whole body; secondly, by the irritation of the brain and this of an active kind, the symptoms ranging from a simple starting from sleep or twitchings of individual groups of muscles to the most violent delirium with shrieking and jumping out of bed. The rash itself must be of the smooth kind. *Belladonna* does *not* cause a miliary rash. Vomiting is violent. *Belladonna* produces vomiting just as severe as that of *Ipecacuanha;* particularly is it indicated in cerebral vomiting. Throat symptoms are prominent. There is bright red swelling of the throat, the tonsils are glistening, the tongue has the strawberry appearance, or if it is coated, the coating is thin and the elevated papillæ show through. The pulse is full, strong and accelerated, and there is great restlessness, as you might expect. You may have swelling of the glands, particularly of those about the neck. You may have suppression of urine or copious urination. Either of these conditions is incident to the *Belladonna* case. The drowsiness or sleep is not that of clearly marked coma. There is not the sleepiness or stupor that is developed by poisoned blood, in which condition the brain is so imperfectly supplied with oxygen that it loses its activity. That is not the *Belladonna* condition. The *Belladonna* sleep may be profound; the patient may snore; he may sleep "as heavy as a log," but the sleep is not quiet and passive. He cries out in his sleep, the muscles twitch, the mouth is in constant motion as if chewing; there is grinding of the teeth. In fact there are almost always present symptoms showing that there is irritation of the brain of an active character. When the patient is aroused from sleep he is violent, looking around the room wildly, and striking at those about him. When, however, the disease from its very onset is of a malignant type, or when it becomes so despite *Belladonna*, you cannot change too soon to some other remedy. You must at once select another, such for example as *Lachesis, Rhus tox.*, or *Hyoscyamus*. *Lachesis* has, in these cases, many symptoms similar to those calling for *Belladonna*. We find in both remedies, crying out during sleep, restlessness, irritability on awaking, strawberry tongue, redness of the whole surface of the body, suppressed urine, sore throat and vomiting. But wherein do they differ? They differ in the very essence of the disease. In the case of *Lachesis*, the disease is adynamic and the blood poisoning is profound. The cerebral symptoms do not develop to a *Belladonna* *furore*, but there is more stupor. The skin-eruption has not the bright erythematous hue of *Belladonna*, but it is either pale, purplish or bluish. It is apt to be irregular, coming out imperfectly. The throat shows you not only enlarged glands externally, but swelling of the connective tissue all around, in the tissue about the fauces as well as in them. The affected parts are rather of a purplish color. If there is a tendency to the formation of pus which is offensive *Lachesis* is even better indicated.

Rhus tox. often precedes *Lachesis*, particularly when cellulitis is a complication and before it has assumed that purplish hue. The inflammation is of a low type. The rash is of the miliary variety (also *Hyoscyamus, Stramonium, Bryonia* and *Lachesis*).

Returning again to *Belladonna*, we find that it sometimes fails in cases of the Sydenham variety of scarlatina, although the symptoms seem to call for it. The remedies to be thought of in this case are these: *Sulphur*, which, just as strongly as *Belladonna*, produces a smooth erythema of the entire surface of the body, and may, in fact, sometimes be indicated in the beginning of the case.

Calcarea ostrearum, which is complementary to *Belladonna*, often completes what that remedy only partially cures. So in scarlatina, we find it indicated when the rash comes out under *Belladonna* but begins to pale off. The face becomes pale and bloated. The cervical glands are swollen. The urine is scanty or even suppressed, and the brain symptoms suggestive of *Belladonna* may yet be present.

And *Lycopodium* which comes in when the child grows stupid and yet still awakes screaming in affright, is cross and strikes its attendants.

Another action of *Belladonna* on the skin is the production of boils or abscesses. You may give it in mastitis or inflammation of the mammæ. It is here indicated by the violence of the symptoms, by the radiating redness, by the throbbing and tendency towards suppuration. The same symptoms call for it in abscess of any kind and in any situation. Even a bubo which is specific in its character may call for *Belladonna* if the symptoms are of the violent character already mentioned, and it will here do good service for the time being. We also find it the remedy for boils that recur in the spring.

Belladonna may be used successfully in the summer complaint of very young infants. We find it to be the remedy when there is crying or screaming hour after hour without any assignable cause. We find it also indicated in indigestion of infants, associated with sharp pains, suddenly screaming out and bending backward, not forward as under *Colocynth*. Sometimes the transverse colon is so distended that it protrudes like a pad in the umbilical region. This symptom sometimes occurs in lead colic. Then, too, we find *Belladonna* indicated in diarrhœa. It is particularly suited to a dysenteric diarrhœa, that is, a diarrhœa from cold with enteritis, the discharges being associated with considerable tenesmus (for you must remember that *Belladonna* has great affinity for sphincter muscles), the discharges being slimy and bloody. In summer complaint the stools are yellowish or green, and contain lumps looking like chalk, consisting no doubt of fat and casein.

You must remember *Belladonna* as complementary to *Chamomilla* in this colic and diarrhœa of infants.

In neuralgia, *Belladonna* is indicated when the pains come on suddenly, last a longer or shorter time, and then as suddenly disappear; the pains are lancinating, burning, tearing and shifting. They are worse from motion, light, noise, or the slightest jar, and from lying down; and are better when sitting up. In prosopalgia the right side is mostly attacked, especially the infraorbital nerves, and the face is hot and red. In sciatica the pain is worse in the hip-joint at night, compelling change of position. All these pains, as well as the fevers, are apt to show exacerbation at 2 or 3 P. M., and again at 11 P. M. The power of this drug to excite neuralgic pains in any of the spinal nerves has led to its recommendation in the atrocious pains which mark the beginning of locomotor ataxia.

In neuralgia compare *Aconite, Amyl nitrite, Cactus grand., Verbascum,*

Platina and *Ferrum carbonicum*. The last named has vascular excitement, red face, etc., which are very similar to *Belladonna*.

Belladonna is very often called for in the treatment of convulsions. Epilepsy is readily modified by it, and at times cured. So is that dread disease, puerperal eclampsia. And spasms of children during dentition, from repelled eruptions, etc., keep the remedy in almost daily demand. In all these cases the cerebral symptoms are prominent. Hot head, flushed face, throbbing carotids, starting from sleep in terror, etc., foam at the mouth having an odor of rotten eggs. The convulsive movements may be a combination of emprosthotonos and opisthotonos; or the patient, usually a child, becomes suddenly rigid, stiffens out, with fixed, staring eyes. In puerperal cases the woman is unconscious, and each pain re-excites the spasm. Between them she tosses about, moaning and crying, or lies in a deep sleep. In teething children the gums are swollen and the mouth is hot and dry.

In epilepsy we should remember *Absinthium*, which causes congestion of the cerebral meninges and the medulla and even produces a fibrinous exudate under dura mater. Hallucinations are terrible; brilliant eyes; epilepsy, followed by obtuse state of the mind, a dazed condition. Epileptic vertigo or momentary unconsciousness. *Artemisia vulgaris* is botanically similar to *Absinthium*, and helps in epilepsy occurring after fright, and when numerous attacks follow one another rapidly. Great restlessness is characteristic of *Absinthium*, *Artemesia*, *Cina*, *Chamomilla* and other members of the order compositæ.

In ailments during dentition compare: *Kreosote*, child worries all night; must be patted and tossed all night; teeth decay rapidly. *Colchicum*, stools changeable; convulsions during teething, reflex from abdominal irritation. *Cina*, convulsions, face pale, child stiffens out; restless. *Dolichos*, gums intensely sensitive; seem to itch. *Æthusa*, swollen red gums; vomiting of curdled milk, followed by stupor, etc.

Glonoin to *Belladonna* is similar in child-bed; *Chamomilla* in children, cross, face red, hot sweat. *Opium*, dark red face, sopor, especially after fright.

We come now to speak of the action of *Belladonna* on the female genital organs, upon which the drug has a decided action. It causes constant and violent bearing down, worse on lying down, and relieved by standing. *Sebia* is opposite to this, and *Aconite* has bearing down, worse from rest and relieved by motion.

Under *Belladonna* the menses are early and copious, bright red, and attended with cramp-like tearing pain in the back, arms, etc.; throbbing headache; most intensely painful congestive dysmenorrhœa; bearing down; cutting pain from behind forward or *vice versa;* menstrual flow, which, without any apparent cause, is offensive; lochia offensive without apparent cause. Uterine hæmorrhages; blood pours out and feels hot; uterine hæmorrhage with bearing down in the back; leucorrhœa with this bearing down; spasmodic contraction of the os uteri, which feels hot and very tender; pain in the back as if it would break. Labor-pains come and go suddenly; pains violent but ineffective.

Belladonna may be used during labor when the os does not dilate on account of a spasmodic condition of the cervix. The labor-pains are violent and cause great distress, and yet the child does not advance. The examining finger finds that the os remains rigid and spasmodic. A few doses of *Belladonna* will usually be sufficient to correct the trouble. *Gelsemium* should also be remembered in rigidity of the os uteri.

On the respiratory tract *Belladonna* has some action. It causes cough from tickling in the larynx, as from dust; face red, eyes sparkling; cough dry, hacking, coming in very violent attacks; cough with dryness and tightness in the upper part of the chest, worse just after lying down in the evenings and at night. The mechanical concussion of this cough is more severe than the existing cause warrants, which is in keeping with the violence of the drug's action. The sputum is composed of blood-tinged mucus. Larynx sore and hot internally, worse from pressure. Burning in the chest; sticking pains from coughing and motion, but not affected by breathing. The pains are worse under the right clavicle. Pressing in the chest and between the scapulæ, with dyspnœa, walking and sitting.

Calcarea ostrearum also has cough just after lying down.

Phosphorus differs from *Belladonna* in having the irritation lower down in the respiratory tract. It has more rawness, and the larynx is sore, worse from talking or pressure thereon. In *Belladonna* it is only sore from pressure.

Under *Causticum* the cough is tickling; the voice is almost gone; there are soreness and rawness of the trachea, but not of the chest.

Rumex has dry cough from tickling in the supra-sternal fossa, aggravated by the least cool air or by deep inspiration.

With *Cepa* the cough causes a feeling as if the larynx would split; it makes the patient cringe; coryza.

Lachesis has cough from tickling lower down than in the *Belladonna* case, and is aggravated by the slightest pressure of the clothing.

Belladonna acts in muscular tissue and also in the joints. It is one of our best remedies both in acute and chronic rheumatism. The affected joints are swollen, red, shining and often have red streaks radiating from them along the limbs. It is one of our best remedies for stiff neck caused by cutting the hair, getting the head wet or sitting with the head and neck exposed to a draft. *Bryonia*, *Nux vomica* and *Guaiacum* are nearly related in this affection.

Belladonna is complementary to *Calcarea ostrearum*. It is antidoted by *Coffea*, *Nux vomica* and *Opium*. *Hyoscyamus* antidotes its abuse in skin affections and cough.

LECTURE XL.

STRAMONIUM AND HYOSCYAMUS.

Datura Stramonium.

Stramonium stands between *Hyoscyamus* and *Belladonna*. It excites the sensorium and perverts its functions. The special senses are affected. Thus there is double vision. Objects appear double or oblique. The mental symptoms are as follows: the mania or delirium is of a wild character, the face being of a bright red; the eyes have a wild and suffused look, although they are not so thoroughly congested as under *Belladonna*. The hallucinations terrify the patient; he sees objects springing up from every corner; animals of every kind and grotesque creatures arise and terrify him. The patient, if a child, cries for its mother even when she is near. The eyes are open and the pupils widely dilated. If an adult, he is decidedly loquacious in his delirium. At times he manifests a merry mood in his loquacity, and at others he has the "horrors." At one moment he will be laughing, singing and making faces, and at another praying, crying for help, etc. He often has photomania or desire for light. He seems to have great fear of the dark. Sometimes he insists upon it that he is conversing with spirits. Again the mania assumes a silly character. He talks in a foolish and nonsensical manner and laughs at his own attempts at wit. The loquacity differs from that of *Lachesis*. In *Stramonium* the loquacity consists of a simple garrulity, whereas in *Lachesis* it is a jumping from subject to subject. During the delirium of *Stramonium*, as under many narcotics, the patient frequently attempts to escape.

Agaricus seems to stand between *Stramonium* and *Lachesis*, having some resemblance to both.

A condition simulating that of hydrophobia sometimes calls for *Stramonium*. In this state any bright object causes furious delirium, spasm of the throat and horrible convulsions. The dilirium, especially in typhoid conditions, is excessive and seems to exhaust the patient completely.

The spasmodic motions of *Stramonium* are characterized by gracefulness rather than angularity; they are more gyratory than jerking. Especially is this condition noted in young children when there is a non-appearance of the eruption during one of the exanthemata. *Stramonium* acts better on children and young infants than does *Belladonna*. Take, for instance, a case of measles. The rash does not come out properly; the child is hot; its face is bright red; it tosses about, crying out in a frightened manner as soon as it falls asleep; it knows no one; its movements, though convulsive, are not jerking and angular. This is a case for *Stramonium*.

Similar to *Stramonium* in these cases is *Cuprum metallicum*, which has, like the former remedy, aggravation on arousing from sleep, and also this same terror. It is characterized by the violence of its symptoms. The abnormal movements are decidedly angular. The face is apt to be of a bluish color. It is especially indicated when the rash has been repercussed and these violent cerebral symptoms appear.

Another similar remedy to *Stramonium* is *Zincum metallicum*. This, too, has crying out in sleep and awaking from sleep terrified. There is considerable evidence of debility, the child being so weak that it has not sufficient strength to develop an eruption.

Another nervous affection which yields to *Stramonium*, or is at least modified by it, is nervous asthma; the patient can scarcely draw in the breath on account of the spasm; there is aggravation from talking. *Stramonium* is also indicated in locomotor ataxia. The patient cannot walk in the dark or with his eyes closed. If he attempts to do so he reels and staggers.

Mental abnormalities as to shape seem to be characteristic of the *Stramonium* patient. For instance, he imagines that he is very large, or that one arm is very large. Sometimes he feels as if he were double, or that he had three legs instead of two. These errors as to shape and size in the *Stramonium* patient bring to mind several other remedies, particularly *Baptisia*, which, however, does not in the least resemble *Stramonium* in other symptoms. It is to be remembered that both of these remedies have these illusions as to shape. The *Baptisia* patient feels that he is double, or, what is more characteristic, that his body is scattered about, and he must try to get the pieces together. Other remedies have this symptom; we find it under *Petroleum* and *Thuja*. Under the latter remedy the patient imagines that he is made of glass, and he walks very carefully for fear that he will be broken. These symptoms may indicate the drug in typhoid fever.

In erysipelas, with involvement of the brain, you may find *Stramonium* indicated when the disease assumes an adynamic type. The symptoms are very much like those of *Rhus tox.*, but you distinguish it from the latter by the violent cerebral symptoms, the delirium, the restlessness, and the screaming out as if terrified. And yet with all these symptoms there is little or no fever.

Stramonium may also be called for in the incipiency of scarlatina when the rash fails to appear and the brain suffers, but it has less fever and throat symptoms than has *Belladonna*. There may be suppression of urine, which is especially characteristic of this drug if it is free from pain or other discomfort.

As in all remedies that irritate the brain, we find grinding of the teeth. We may also find stuttering, which, by the way, has been compared to the spasmodic urination of children, when the least excitement will cause them to pass urine in little jets; in a similar way are the words jerked out. Particularly does the patient find it difficult to combine vowels with consonants.

Another remedy for stuttering or stammering is *Bovista*.

The tongue of the *Stramonium* patient is red or whitish, and covered with fine red dots, and is dry and parched. In some cases it is swollen and hangs out of the mouth.

Stramonium may excite a decided nymphomania, during which the woman, though very chaste when in her normal condition, becomes exceedingly lewd in her songs and speech. She may become very violent in her manner. Often these symptoms occur in women before menstruation, in which case *Stramonium* acts most admirably. The menstrual flow is apt to be very profuse, showing that it is the high degree of congestion that produces the nymphomania. There is a strong odor about these women, reminding one of the odor of animals in the rutting season.

I would also like to call your attention to the diarrhœa which *Stramonium* cures. The stools are very offensive, smelling almost like carrion. They are apt to be yellowish. They may or may not be dark, but the offensiveness is the most important symptom.

Absence of pain is characteristic of *Stramonium* excepting in abscess, particularly when it affects the left hip-joint, in which case it may be so intense as to throw the patient into convulsions.

The antidote for *Stramonium* poisoning is lemon juice.

Hyoscyamus Niger.

Botanically and, in a measure, therapeutically, *Hyoscyamus* is similar to *Belladonna*. This interesting drug, though innocuous to some animals, is poisonous to fowls, and has received the name of henbane.

Hyoscyamus seems to be especially adapted to acute mania, to mania without any evidence of absolute inflammation, to mania which has for its key-note extreme excitation of the sensorium. The patient, under such circumstances, has many strange notions, all arising from these abnormal impulses. He imagines, for instance, that he is about to be poisoned. Possibly he will refuse your medicine, declaring in angry tones that it will poison him. Or he imagines that he is pursued by some demon, or that somebody is trying to take his life. This makes him exceedingly restless. He springs out of bed to get away from his imaginary foe. The senses, too, are disturbed. Objects look too large or else are of a blood-red color. Sometimes objects appear as if they were too distinct; that is, they have an unnatural sharpness of outline. The patient talks of subjects connected with everyday life, jumping from one subject to another pretty much as in *Lachesis;* all this time the face is not remarkably red, possibly it is only slightly flushed. The pupils are usually dilated, sleep is greatly disturbed, the patient lies awake for hours. As the mania advances he seems to lie in a sort of stupor, and yet it is not a real stupor, because the slightest noise rouses him into all these forms of violent mania. Every little impression causes excitement of the sensorium. Accompanying these symptoms we find characteristic debility, this debility showing itself in the great prostration on every attempt to move or walk about, and in paralysis of one or more muscles following the maniacal attacks. As the sensorium becomes more and more depressed he answers questions slowly or else gives irrelevant answers. Sometimes he will be in a stupor from which he can be readily aroused and will answer your questions quite correctly, but he will relapse into the stupid state immediately. With this there is a sort of adynamic condition of the brain resulting from this prolonged over-excitement, and in this condition we still find delirium, but the patient is greatly prostrated, stool and urine pass involuntarily, the pulse is no longer full and accelerated, but it is quick, rapid and without volume, and irregular. Stupor is now complete, sordes appear on the tongue and around the teeth, the lungs are engorged, not from a pneumonic process, but because of hypostatic congestion. Associated with this we have snoring-rattling during breathing. The mouth is opened, the lower jaw dropped, and the patient lies quietly with occasional twitching of groups of muscles. This condition will soon be followed by death unless relief can be obtained. At other times we find the delirium returning anew and the symptoms take another form. The patients are silly and laugh in a flippant manner. Sometimes, for hours at a time, they will have a silly, idiotic expression of the face. Again they become exceedingly lascivious, throw the covers off and attempt to uncover the genital region. The abnormal movements accompanying these symptoms are rather angular; they are not all of the gyratory character significant of *Stramonium*.

Still another form in which the cerebral symptoms of *Hyoscyamus* may appear, particularly in women, is jealousy, and also the effects of powerful emotions, as disappointed love, fright and other emotions that are more or less exciting and at the same time depressing.

Coming now to inflammation of the brain or meninges, we find *Hyoscyamus* sometimes indicated when we have present some of the symptoms already enumerated and in addition to these symptoms relief from shaking the head or sitting with the head bent forward. Here it is exactly opposite to *Belladonna*. The patient complains of pulsating waves through the head.

We have a cough quite characteristic of *Hyoscyamus*. This cough comes from elongation of the uvula, the result of relaxation or inflammation. The uvula hangs down and rests on the root of the tongue, causing irritation and the consequent cough. This cough is worse when lying down, the patient having almost complete relief when sitting up. It is usually worse at night and also after eating and drinking and from talking.

There are two or three remedies to be compared with *Hyoscyamus* here. One of them is *Rumex crispus*. This is a splendid remedy for tickling cough from an annoying tickling in the supra-sternal fossa. The patient wants to breathe warm air. Anything which disturbs the temperature of the respired air excites the tickling, and hence the cough. The tickling may extend down into the chest and still *Rumex* be indicated.

Natrum muriaticum also has a dry cough from elongated uvula.

There is another remedy which has the same symptom, and one

which has been confirmed, too. It is *Mentha piperita*. It is inferior to *Rumex*, however. I have heard it said that eating apples will relieve this kind of cough.

Hyoscyamus is also to be considered as a remedy for sleeplessness. It is useful in the sleeplessness of children when they twitch in sleep, cry out and tremble, and awaken frightened.

It is also a valuable drug in convulsions. It is one of the most reliable remedies we have for epileptic convulsions, that is, if there is no other remedy indicated. In the *Hyoscyamus* convulsion we find the patient twitching and jerking. These angular motions that I have described seem to be provoked by eating. Especially is this to be noted in children; the child will wake up from sleep hungry; the face is apt to be of a deep red color, almost on the purple during the paroxysm. There are also frothing at the mouth and biting of the tongue. These symptoms are almost always followed by profound sleep. Convulsions that are puerperal in origin also call for *Hyoscyamus*, which may readily be separated from *Belladonna* and *Stramonium* by the prominence of nervous agitation, reflex excitability, etc.

In epilepsy compare *Cicuta virosa*, which has shocks from the head down, staring eyes, screaming, red face, limbs greatly distorted, respiration greatly impeded. Trembling before and after the spasm and great weakness afterwards. See also *Œnanthe crocata*.

We have *Hyoscyamus* indicated also in chorea. The patients are very weak with tottering gait. They seem to have abnormal impressions of distances. They reach for something that seems to be just within their grasp, when, in reality, it is on the other side of the room.

Stramonium is also a remedy to be thought of in chorea, particularly if the brain is affected. The child awakens from sleep with a scream. It sings and laughs without reason.

Still another remedy is *Veratrum viride*, which is particularly indicated when there is great congestion in the nervous centres, and the pulse is much over-excited.

Now let me speak of the fevers of *Hyoscyamus*. I have already given you the symptoms which would indicate the drug in typhoid fever. We have to see how we may apply it in the treatment of fevers with skin symptoms, as scarlatina. *Hyoscyamus* is indicated in scarlatina, although not very frequently; yet it may be called for in cases that have been spoiled by *Belladonna*. The rash is of a miliary type and is dark or dark red in color. It is rather scanty, too, from partial repercussion. There are also picking at the bed-clothes, crying out in sleep and stupor, all denoting the alarming progress made by the disease.

Stramonium is indicated in scarlatina when the symptoms are violent, something like those we have seen in *Belladonna*. The face is very red, the rash seems to be scattered over the surface, the prostration is excessive, the skin is apt to be very dry and hot without as much of the hot sweat as we have found under *Belladonna*. If sweat does come it does not relieve.

Now let us compare the three remedies, *Belladonna*, *Stramonium* and *Hyoscyamus*, one with the other. In general, we find that *Belladonna* causes more congestion or inflammation of the brain, *Stramonium* congestion with more sensorial excitement, and *Hyoscyamus* more nervous irritation and less of congestion and inflammation than either of the others.

The type of the delirium in *Belladonna* is wild; there is a desire to escape; the patient bites and strikes; the face is red and the eyes suffused with violent throbbing of the carotids. He either complains of these hallucinations on closing the eyes or he stares at one point with eyes *wide* open. Then, too, there is sleepiness with inability to sleep. If there is stupor it is rather the result of the congestion and inflammation of the brain, and is attended with some symptoms of irritation so that the patient, when aroused, is violent or he alternates between delirium and stupor, there being no evidence of serious blood changes.

Hyoscyamus has a similar desire to escape; the patient attempts to bite and strike those about him; he has the same desire to uncover, but he lacks the violent throbbing of the carotids and intensity of the redness of the face and suffusion of the eyes. The *Hyoscyamus* patient has a particular aversion to light and has especially marked the fear of being poisoned or of being betrayed. Lying quietly in the bed, he suddenly sits up and stares around as if looking for some one whom he expected to see in the room. At a word from the nurse he lies down again and goes off into a sleep. He may expose his sexual organs. His wakefulness is very different from that calling for *Belladonna*. He is nervous, whining, crying and twitching.

Phosphorus stands nearest to *Hyoscyamus* in this desire to uncover the person. But *Veratrum album* is also closely allied in nymphomania.

Hyoscyamus is used very extensively in insane asylums for acute non-inflammatory mania. You will always find these patients weak; the pulse often lacks volume; they either have no appetite whatever or else an enormous appetite. Eating is at once followed by an aggravation of the symptoms. Allopathic physicians use very largely the alkaloid *Hyoscyamia*. This is very similar to *Kali bromatum*, having the power of exciting the sensorium without inflaming the brain. Thus we find *Kali bromatum* indicated in the acute mania of children when they arouse from sleep with screams and imagine that some one is going to hurt them. The patient may also have the insane impression that he is to be murdered or that his honor is at stake, or that those in his house dislike him and intend to do him harm.

Hyoscyamus is indicated in these cases particularly if they are puerperal in their origin. We also find these symptoms of *Hyoscyamus* in typhoid fevers. The tendency, you will see, is to run into a low type of disease; it is more of an adynamic remedy than *Belladonna*. In typhoid fever you should compare *Phosphoric acid, Rhus, Lycopodium* and *Lachesis*. But all of these, excepting perhaps *Phosphoric acid*, act more powerfully than *Hyoscyamus* and hence follow *Hyoscyamus* well, the latter being insufficient.

Belladonna may be indicated in the beginning of the disease when there is the wild and furious delirium. *Hyoscyamus* comes in later when the stupor becomes more marked; when the patient picks at the bed-clothes or at his fingers in a somnolent sort of way and occasionally reaches out as if grasping for something in the air. You will find the tongue, in such cases, dry and red; speech, of course, is difficult; and, as the case progresses, we have the sordes on the teeth with involuntary stool and urine and dropping of the lower jaw. I would like to say here, by way of caution, that in some instances, although a case for *Hyoscyamus* is clearly made out by these symptoms, yet it does not always act. I cannot tell you why. I can see no cause except that the drug does not act deeply enough. In such cases, I usually look up *Lachesis, Lycopodium, Muriatic acid* and *Arsenicum*.

In fevers of this type *Stramonium* differs from *Belladonna* and *Hyoscyamus*. The patient sees objects which seem to rise in every corner of the room and move towards him. He has a mania for light and company, which is just the opposite of *Belladonna*, is excessively loquacious and laughs, sings, swears and prays almost in the same breath. The desire to escape is present; there is sudden spasmodic lifting of the head from the pillow and then dropping it back again; he awakens from sleep in fright and terror, not knowing those around him; the motions that he makes are quite graceful and easy, although they may be violent. At times, the body is bathed in a hot sweat which does not give any relief to the patient. The desire to uncover is similar to that of *Hyoscyamus*, but it is more an uncovering of the whole body rather than of the sexual organs. The tongue is often soft, taking the imprint of the teeth; screaming in sleep, often with hiccough; the face is usually bright red, but not as deeply congested as in *Belladonna*.

LECTURE XLI.

TABACUM, DULCAMARA, CAPSICUM AND GLONOIN.

TABACUM.

TABACUM contains several active ingredients, the most important of which is Nicotine. Ever since smoking was an "art," attempts have been made to get rid of this Nicotine. Every one acknowledges that it has a serious effect on the body. There are three groups of symptoms which may follow the use of tobacco. The primary symptoms are the well-known gastric symptoms deathly nausea and vomiting. The patient is deathly pale, does not care whether he lives or dies. Sometimes cold sweat breaks out on the body. The secondary effects are more remote, coming months or even years after using the weed, and these are dyspepsia, amblyopia and also some symptoms of the heart.

These symptoms of the heart I would have you remember. If they are not caused by tobacco, *Tabacum* will be a very valuable remedy in their cure. I refer especially to dilated heart when these symptoms are present: there are frequent pallor, with lividity of the face: diarrhœa, alternating with constipation; palpitation when lying on the left side; muscæ volitantes, tinnitus aurium and dry cough, which is cardiac in its origin; paroxysms of suffocation, with tightness across the upper part of the chest; feeble and irregular pulse; pains like those of angina pectoris shoot from the heart down the left arm or up into the neck, and involve different plexuses of nerves; the extremities are cold and covered with a clammy sweat. Another symptom that may come as a secondary symptom of tobacco is neuralgia of the face. This symptom, when thus caused, is curable by *Sepia*, as is also the dyspepsia.

Impotence also follows tobacco and often yields to *Lycopodium*.

The tertiary effects of tobacco include apoplexy.

Tobacco, in its effect on the gastric organs, very much resembles *Hydrocyanic acid*, *Veratrum* and *Camphor*. For instance, we find it indicated in cholera, when the nausea and cold sweat persist after *Veratrum*, *Secale* or *Camphor* has stopped the diarrhœa. This nausea is accompanied by burning heat about the abdomen, the rest of the body being cold. The patient persists in uncovering the abdomen.

I would remark here that this kind of sickness suggests *Tabacum* in renal colic or in strangulated hernia. There are this deathly nausea and sickness, with slimy stool, from irritation of the bowels.

The resemblance to *Hydrocyanic acid* is found in asphyxia. The latter drug acts upon the medulla, and, hence upon the heart through the pneumogastric nerves. Consequently, the symptoms you would expect it to produce are those of the heart and lungs. We find it producing convulsions, with drawing at the nape of the neck from irritation at the base of the brain. Along with this, respiration is irregular or gasping, and there is great distress about the heart, with repeated weak "spells" and coldness and blueness of the surface of the body. It is well to remember this fact in uræmic convulsions when the medula is affected. *Hydrocyanic acid* is then our only hope.

Tabacum is used as an antidote to the bad effects of *Cicuta virosa*.

The primary effects of tobacco are generally relieved by *Ipecac*.

Nux vomica is indicated for the bad taste in the mouth and the headache worse in the morning from excessive smoking.

It is said that *Plantago major* produces a distaste for tobacco. I have seen one or two patients who, after taking it, supposed they had contracted a dislike to tobacco.

DULCAMARA.

Dulcamara, or the "bitter-sweet," contains a small quantity of *Solanine*, a much smaller quantity, in fact, than any other member of the group. The tender leaves and twigs have been used for the preparation of the tincture. Several accounts of poisoning from the berries of the *Dulcamara* have been recorded. The symptoms thus produced are hard griping pains in the bowels, followed by unconsciousness and spasms which are tetanic, and are accompanied by hot, dry skin, trismus, loud rattling breathing, and, in one case, death.

The ordinary symptoms produced by the drug are not so severe. We find as the very central point around which all the other symptoms of the drug group, this one: aggravation from cold, damp weather or from changes from hot to cold weather, especially if these changes are sudden. Thus we find *Dulcamara* useful in rheumatism made worse by sudden changes in the weather; twitching of the muscles of the eyelids or mouth whenever the weather becomes damp; dry coryza, sore throat, with stiffness of the neck; colic from cold, especially with diarrhœa at night; earache, when it returns with every such change in weather.

Dulcamara has a marked influence on the nervous system; but here again its use in practice is often based on the above aggravation. We have the tongue paralyzed in damp weather, with impaired speech; hyperæmia of the spinal cord with the paretic state belonging to that disease when caused by lying on damp, cold ground, and intensified by every return of damp weather. It is also indicated in paralysis of the bladder aggravated by damp weather.

It is also of use in incipient paralysis of the lungs in old people, especially if the symptoms are aggravated by change in the weather.

Dulcamara has a specific influence on the lining membrane of the bladder, causing catarrh of that organ. The urine is very offensive, and is loaded with mucus.

It also exerts a marked action on the skin. Thus, it develops a bright red eruption on the surface of the body. Here and there will be large wheals, which may be white or red, and along with these there is usually burning and itching.

It is indicated in urticaria traceable to gastric disorder when there is relief from cold air.

The complement of *Dulcamara* is *Baryta carb.*, which also has aggravation in cold weather, especially in scrofulous children.

Capsicum Annuum.

Capsicum possesses few, if any, of the narcotic properties of the Solanaceæ, but it has, highly marked, the irritating properties of the group in high degree; but little of the drug is required to produce this irritation. It is eliminated from the body through the kidneys, producing strangury with burning when passing water. This drug acts best in persons of lax fibre, rather stout in build, who do not respond readily to medicine because they are of lax fibre, and also because of impaired digestion.

The *Capsicum* patient has weak digestion or weak stomach, hence the whole man is weak. Such patients are irritable and easily angered. This is true of either adults or children. They are worse from the least draft of air, even though this air be warm. They are clumsy in their motions.

They are subject to chills and fever. The chill commences in the back. Although the patient is thirsty, yet drinking causes shivering.

The *Capsicum* patient is subject to catarrhal asthma with red face and well-marked sibilant râles. He coughs, and a successful cough raises phlegm, which relieves the asthma.

Capsicum has a symptom of the chest not often met with in practice, and that is very offensive breath during the cough.

It also has a well-marked action on the ear, especially on the middle ear. It is of use in rupture of the membrana tympani from disease when there is soreness or inflammation of the mastoid process of the temporal bone.

For abscess of the mastoid process the preferable remedies are *Aurum* and *Nitric acid*.

For chronic suppuration of the middle ear you may think of *Silicea*.

Capsicum is of importance in diseases of the throat. It is indicated in diphtheria or in gangrene of the throat when there are burning blisters in the roof of the mouth and when there is an odor from the mouth like that of carrion. The throat feels constricted as if spasmodically closed. The patient is worse when not swallowing and in extreme cases greatly prostrated.

The most similar remedy here is *Cantharis*.

Capsicum is also indicated in elongation of the uvula.

In dysentery it is indicated when the stools are frequent but small and attended with violent tenesmus and burning in both rectum and bladder. The stools are bloody and slimy and contain shaggy pieces. There is thirst, and yet drinking causes shuddering.

GLONOIN.

Glonoin. { Blood. Trauma. Convulsions. }

Glonoin or nitro-glycerine is considered in this part of the course of lectures on account of its symptomatic resemblance to *Belladonna*. It is a very easy drug to study. Though its main point of attack is the blood, it does not affect the quality of that fluid so much as it does its circulation. It acts very quickly and very violently. The key-note to the whole symptomatology of the drug is expressed in this one sentence: "*A tendency to sudden and violent irregularities of the circulation.*"

With that for our foundation we can easily work out the other symptoms. The symptoms which are traceable to the irregularities in the circulation are these : very characteristic, indeed, is a throbbing headache. The pain may be in the whole head, or it may be in the forehead, vertex, occiput or any one part of the head. This throbbing is not a mere sensation; it is an actual fact. It really seems as though the blood-vessels would burst, so violent is the congestive action of the drug. The throbbing is synchronous with every impulse of the heart. The blood seems to surge in one great current up the spine and into the head. The bloodvessels externally become distended. The external jugulars look like two tortuous cords, the carotids throb violently and are hard, tense and unyielding to pressure. The face is deep red. This throbbing is either associated with dull, distressing aching or with sharp, violent pains.

We find *Glonoin* applicable to sunstroke, indicated either by the symptoms already mentioned, or by symptoms which show that the prolonged congestion has produced depressing effects upon the brain. The face becomes rather pale, the pulse, which was at first full, grows soft and feeble, and the respiration labored. There is not as much pressure about the chest as about the medulla oblongata, thus interfering with the nerves of respiration. The eyes are often fixed. The patient may even be unconscious. *Glonoin*, then, we find to be our best remedy for the effects of heat, whether the trouble arises from the direct rays of the sun, from hot weather or from working in the intense heat of a furnace, as in the case of foundrymen and machinists. These effects of the sun or heat are not confined to the head alone, but may involve the whole body. Thus we note oppression of breathing, with palpitation of the heart and nausea and vomiting, with white coated tongue. This nausea is not gastric in origin, but cerebral, as under *Rhus tox.*, *Belladonna* and *Apomorphine*. The appetite is gone; there is no desire for food; there is a horrible sunken feeling in the epigastrium, and often, too, diarrhœa. All these symptoms call for *Glonoin*.

Still other effects of this congestion are found in the eye. The eyes feel as if too large and protrude as though bursting out of the head. *Glonoin* is indicated in eye diseases arising from exposure to very bright light, as in the case of one obliged to work at a desk beneath a hot, bright light, as a bright Argand burner. If you should examine such an eye with the ophthalmoscope, you will find the bloodvessels of the retina distended or, in extreme cases, apoplexy of the retina.

Again the effects of the increased blood pressure under *Glonoin* may be noticed in the symptoms of the mouth. For instance, there is difficulty in conversation from diminished power of the tongue, this due to pressure on the cerebral centres. Wine aggravates all these symptoms. Sometimes the congestion is so great as to make the patient frantic; he tries to escape, to jump out of the window.

Another effect of the cerebral congestion is convulsions. *Glonoin* is an admirable remedy for the convulsions coming on during labor, puerperal convulsions. The face is bright red and puffed the pulse full and hard and the urine albuminous. The patient froths at the mouth; she is unconscious. The hands are clenched, the thumbs being in the palms of the hands. At other times the hands are stretched out as under *Secale*, and the patient is unconscious. I think that *Glonoin* is one of the best remedies we have for the congestive form of puerperal convulsions, that form which is announced by rush of blood to the head, especially if there is albuminuria. It is also invaluable in congestion to the head from suppressed menses.

The mental symptoms traceable to this congestion are syncope or sudden fainting, the face being pale or often livid, black spots before the eyes, sudden onset of unconsciousness, well-known streets seem strange to the patient. This last symptom is one decidedly dangerous. It may be the forerunner of an actual attack. A person who is subject to apoplectic congestion is suddenly seized in the streets with one of these attacks and does not know where he is. *Glonoin* is the remedy for him.

Another remedy for this loss of location is *Petroleum*.

Glonoin is also useful for the bad effects of fear. I mentioned that briefly when speaking of *Opium*. There is horrible apprehension and also sometimes the fear of being poisoned. This last symptom places it alongside of *Hyoscyamus, Lachesis, Rhus tox., Bromide of Potassium* and *Baptisia*.

Another use of *Glonoin* is its application to trauma. It has been found an excellent remedy for pains and other abnormal sensations, following some time after local injuries. Long after the reception of an injury, the part pains or feels sore, or an old scar breaks out again; then *Glonoin* seems to relieve.

Natrum sulphuricum should be compared, especially after head injuries.

It is necessary for you to remember the distinctions between *Belladonna* and *Glonoin*, because they meet in the congestions and inflammations of the brain in children and old persons. They divide the honors in these diseases, because each has a number of confirmed cures. We have the *cri encephalique* in *Glonoin* which is not so marked under *Belladonna*, so it would seem that the *Glonoin* case is more severe than that of *Belladonna*. The symptoms which would help you to differentiate the two drugs are these: First, *Glonoin;* the head symptoms are worse by bending the head backward; worse in damp weather; worse from the application of cold water, which may even cause spasms; better from uncovering; better in the open air; sometimes the patient is obliged to get up and walk about despite the soreness that jarring causes. A very marked symptom which anticipates puerperal convulsions, and which is an early symptom in congestion of the brain from suppressed menses, and a prominent symptom in the bad effects of the heat of the sun, is a feeling as if the head were enormously large. The head seems as if it were expanding. Although that symptom is found under *Belladonna*, it is not so characteristic of that drug as of *Glonoin*.

Now *Belladonna* has relief from bending backward, from sitting up with the head quiet *Belladonna* usually has relief from covering the head, while *Glonoin* has relief from uncovering, although the latter symptom is of less importance than the others.

The best antidote to *Glonoin*, that I know of, is *Aconite*.

LECTURE XLII.

LYCOPODIUM CLAVATUM.

Lycopodium clavatum.
1. Constitution.
2. Blood.
   a. Fevers.
   b. Ebullitions; pulse.
   c. Varices.
   d. Typhoid.
   e. Scarlatina.
   f. Diphtheria.
3. Liver.
4. Dropsy.
5. Catarrhs.
6. Kidneys.

LYCOPODIUM or club moss is a member of the Lycopodiaceæ, so called from their resemblance to a wolf's foot. It has long been used in pyrotechnic displays, for the production of artificial lightning and in legerdemain.

In legerdemain it is used as a coating to the hand, after which that member may be dipped into water and removed from thence perfectly dry. As a medicine, it was considered wholly inert by members of the allopathic school of practice, and was used only as a drying powder by nurses. Nevertheless in the experience of some it was found quite severe symptoms followed the use of this powder. Others, on the contrary, used it for months, and years, and declared it to be positively inert. Now why was this? The Cryptogamia, unlike other plants, instead of seeds, have spores, which are sometimes arranged under the leaves, as in the case of *Lycopodium*. Now these spores have a hard, shell-like covering, within which we find a small quantity of oily substance, which is the active part of the spore. As long as the *Lycopodium* used consisted of unbroken spores it was inert; when, however, these were ruptured, it became active and symptoms followed its local application.

In the preparation of *Lycopodium*, great care should be taken to see that all the spores are broken. When thus prepared, we have in it a truly valuable medicine which Hahnemann proved for us, and one, too, which we need in practice almost every day. I love to extol the virtues of this remarkable drug, for Hahnemann, with his infallable *Law*, rescued it from its ignominious use as an infant powder, and elevated it to the highest rank among the antipsorics.

In order that you may understand the symptomatology of the drug, I have arranged the schema which you see before you on the board.

First of all, we will study the general character of the drug. *Lycopodium* affects profoundly the vital forces, causing a series of symptoms that indicate it as invaluable in brain fag, typhus, scarlatina, etc., when the brain symptoms point to an alarming paralytic state.

We find it indicated most frequently in emaciated persons who are muscularly weak; the mind, however, is well developed. Particularly is this noticeable in children. They are precocious and unusually obstinate. The emaciation is noticed particularly about the upper part of the body and neck. There is a predisposition to liver troubles, and also to affections of the lungs; the face is often pale and sallow; the eyes being sunken and surrounded with dark bluish circles. Often, too, the face is furrowed with creases and wrinkles, indicating deep-seated disease. The face readily flushes, the cheeks become red. This is often so in the evening and after eating. As to temperament, the *Lycopodium* patient is rather impatient and irritable, and easily made angry. At other times, sadness or tearfulness is marked. When sick, such patients are apt to become domineering and rather imperious in manner; or to consider themselves of great importance and those about them of no importance, so they order others about with an angry vehement manner. As to the intellectual part of the mind, we find the memory always weak. Thus we find the drug often indicated when there are frequent mistakes in speech. The patient forgets words or syllables. He cannot read, for the meaning of certain words is confused; he cannot find the right word while speaking, but if the subject is very important, so as to call forth his utmost energy, words flow with ease. Compare *Sulphur*, *Lachesis*, *Fluoric acid*, *Silicea*.

All the symptoms are aggravated from 4 to 8 P. M. *Lycopodium* is not the only remedy that has this. It is also found under *Sabadilla*, *Nux moschata* and *Helleborus*. *Helleborus* bears some relation to *Lycopodium*, not only because of its aggravation from 4 to 8 P. M., but also because of the arousing effect of directing the will to the work.

The changes made in the blood by *Lycopodium* are not numerous. In febrile states we sometimes find it indicated by chill coming at three or four o'clock every or every other afternoon; this chill being followed by sweat without intervening heat; or the case may be characterized by chill coming at this hour and sour vomiting with or without heat.

The pulse in *Lycopodium* is not very characteristic. In the provings the pulse is changed very little, except that it is slightly increased in frequency towards evening. The arms feel numb, heavy and weak, relieved by using them.

Next, I have to notice varicose veins. *Lycopodium*, by reason of its action on the liver, tends to produce swelling or enlargement of the veins, particularly those which are more or less imperfectly supplied with valves; so we have varices characteristic of *Lycopodium*; varices in the legs, particularly the right; varices of the genital organs; the labia are swollen by varicose veins; this latter condition occurring during pregnancy, being a symptom which calls for *Lycopodium*; also *Carbo vegetabilis*.

So, too, we often find nævi modified by *Lycopodium*. Now, do not suppose that every nævus is curable by medicine, for such is not the case. It is, however, your duty to cure them by medicine when you can. For this purpose, *Lycopodium* is one of the remedies. Still another remedy, and one, too, which is better than any other, and has also produced nævi, is *Fluoric acid*.

So, too, carrying out a similar line of symptoms, you will find *Lycopodium* indicated in bleeding piles, piles which contain a far greater quantity of blood than the size of the vein involved would warrant; also in piles which do not mature, but which, from partial absorption of their contents, remain as hard bluish lumps.

Then, again, in erectile tumors which have now an increase and then a decrease of the amount of blood in them, *Lycopodium* may be useful.

Lycopodium must have some effect on the blood and on the nervous system because of its general use in typhoid states. It is not the remedy in the beginning of typhoid fever, but when the disease has gone on, despite your treatment, to a state which is very alarming. The patient becomes stupid, lies with dropped jaw, half open eyes, the conjunctivæ being coated with a glazing of mucus and directed into vacancy. Passes urine involuntarily. Again, about the fourteenth day of the fully-developed fever, when the rash belonging to the disease does not appear and the patient sinks into an unconscious state, with muttering delirium, picking at the bed-clothes or grasping at flocks, distended abdomen, great rumbling of flatus, constipation, sudden jerking of the limbs here and there, breathing, snoring and rattling, pulse rapid, intermitting; involuntary urination or retention of urine; if the urine is passed in bed it leaves a reddish sandy deposit in the clothing. Here is a condition of non-reaction which must end fatally unless quickly remedied; *Lycopodium* often does it.

These indications are very similar to those calling for *Calcarea ostrearum*. *Calcarea ostrearum* has been found to be the remedy in this stage of typhoid fever when the rash does not appear. But *Calcarea* may have either constipation or diarrhœa. *Lycopodium* always requires constipation. *Calcarea* has more hallucinations. The patient sees visions when he closes his eyes; he cannot sleep; although he may be fully conscious, yet he is continually frightened by some imaginary object. In such cases *Calcarea* develops the rash and brings the patient out of this precarious state.

In *Hyoscyamus* the urine leaves streaks of red sand on the sheet. The distinction between this remedy and *Lycopodium* in impending cerebral paralysis is chiefly one of degree—the *Lycopodium* being the deeper acting of the two. Further it has this more pronounced afternoon aggravation and less nervous irritability, etc.

In these typhoid conditions we have an indication for *Lycopodium* in the tongue. The tongue seems swollen and the patient cannot protrude it, or when the patient does put it out it rolls from side to side like a pendulum. Almost always, too, the tongue is dry and has blisters on it. These are symptoms enough to warrant you in the choice of *Lycopodium*.

In scarlatina, *Lycopodium* is not indicated by its power to produce an eruption and fever similar to those of scarlatina; it is called for, rather, in those cases which do not take a normal course, but which go on to a fatal issue by reason of the constitution. You are guided here by the typhoid symptoms just mentioned, and also by another symptom which anticipates these and leads you to *Lycopodium* long before such serious symptoms appear. I refer to the condition of the child after sleep. The child wakens cross and irritable, kicking the clothes off and striking every one about it, or it raises up terrified and clings to its mother as if for protection against some object of alarm.

LYCOPODIUM CLAVATUM.

Although this symptom may seem insignificant, it is not so by a means. It is the beginning of mischief, and if not checked, stupor and impending cerebral paralysis will follow. Here it resembles *Cuprum*, *Belladonna*, *Stramonium* and *Zincum*, all of which remedies have arousing from sleep as if frightened. The element of irritability and the absence of symptoms characteristic of the other drugs lead you to *Lycopodium*.

Related remedies having more of the element of irritability are *Chamomilla*, *Arsenicum*, *Kali carbonicum*.

Lycopodium is often needed when the child becomes suddenly obstinate; breathes rapidly in sleep; worries, cries; muscles become flabby it is unable to walk any more.

We may make another use of this symptom. Sometimes children have a disease called "gravel," in which lithic acid is passed in sufficiently large quantity in the urine as to cause pain on passing water. They awake from sleep screaming out with pain and kicking at all around them. Here *Lycopodium* is indicated by both the subjective and the objective symptoms; it is related to *Sarsaparilla*. *Zingiber*, *Pulsatilla*, *Arnica*, *Prunus spinosa*, etc., should be compared in ischuria.

Often, too, when *Lycopodium* is indicated in scarlatina, you will find that one or the other parotid gland is inflamed and discharging purulent matter.

Probably the very best remedy in the materia medica for parotitis accompanying scarlatina is *Rhus tox*. The next best is *Calcarea ostrearum*, and next to that *Lycopodium*. *Lachesis* is only indicated when the swelling is purplish and the pus is not laudable but thin, excoriating and ichorous.

Lycopodium is often overlooked in diseases of the eye, when, nevertheless, it is here a very useful remedy, although indicated principally in cases that have become chronic. You may use it in granular lids, which are dry and smarting, in retinitis pigmentosa and even in cataract. It will also cure styes, especially occurring near the inner canthus.

In diphtheria, *Lycopodium* is to be thought of when the diphtheritic deposit is most copious on the right side of the throat, with a tendency to spread toward the left. There is a constant desire to swallow, amounting almost to spasm of the throat, with violent stinging pains. The patient is worse from swallowing drinks, especially cold drinks. You often find the symptoms aggravated from four to eight P. M.

The cervical glands are swollen. Generally, when *Lycopodium* is the remedy in either scarlatina or diphtheria, the nose is invaded by the disease. The patient cannot breathe through his nose. The tonsils are very much swollen, as is also the tongue, so that he is obliged to open the mouth and protrude the tongue in order to get breath. Sometimes, after you have given *Lachesis*, the membrane goes to the right side. Then *Lycopodium* comes in as a substitute.

Arum triphyllum and *Nitric acid* are very similar in diphtheria of the nose. *Phytolacca*, dark red throat, worse on the right side, but there is inability to swallow hot drinks.

Next we come to the action of *Lycopodium* on the liver. *Lycopodium* acts very strongly on this organ, producing quite a number of symptoms. First, beginning with the mouth, we find the tongue coated, sour or, exceptionally, putrid taste in the mouth on arising; violent hunger, almost amounting to canine hunger; yet a few mouthfuls of food seem to produce fulsomeness, as though the patient were "full up to the throat," quickly followed by hunger again; distress in the stomach *immediately* after eating, *not some little time after*, like *Nux vomica;* cannot bear the pressure of the clothing about the waist, here being somewhat like *Lachesis;* but it is distinguished from *Lachesis* in that the latter has the sensitiveness all the time, but *Lycopodium* only after a meal. The region of the liver is very sensitive to touch. Sometimes there is a feeling of tension there, and this feeling of tension is a subjective symptom which leads you to the choice of *Lycopodium* in chronic hepatitis when abscesses have formed. The diaphragm is very apt to be affected in this state. There is a feeling as though a cord were tied around the waist. There is marked collection of flatus. Possibly that is the reason why a small quantity of food fills the patient up. This flatulence tends upwards rather than downwards; rumbling of wind in the splenic flexure of the colon, with distention of that portion of the intestinal tract. There is great fermentation in the intestines, this being followed by discharge of flatus, and even by diarrhœa. The bowels are usually constipated, however, with ineffectual urging to stool. After stool there is a feeling as of a great quantity remaining unpassed.

Now these symptoms, especially if associated with ascites, will lead you to the choice of *Lycopodium* in that disease known as cirrhosis of the liver.

Lycopodium, in these gastric and hepatic symptoms, has many analogues, one of which is *Nux vomica*. *Nux* may be distinguished from it by the following: Although *Nux vomica* has sour taste in the mouth, aggravation in the morning and fulness after eating, yet the immediate distress is more prominent under *Lycopodium*. In the accumulation of flatus, of the two remedies *Nux* has more pressure downwards, giving frequent urging to stool and pressure on the bladder. Both remedies have prominently constipation, with ineffectual urging to stool. The difference between the two remedies is this: *Nux vomica* has this ineffectual urging from its fitful action; under *Lycopodium* it arises from contraction of the sphincter ani.

Sulphur is also similar in the accumulation of flatus and in the sour and bitter taste; but the characteristic place for the accumulation of flatus in *Sulphur* is in the sigmoid flexure, and is referred by the patient to the left groin.

Momordica balsamica is another remedy that has incarcerated flatus in the splenic flexure. *Cepa* has pain in the region probably due to the same cause.

Raphanus is also to be thought of in cases with accumulation and retention of flatus. Dr. James B. Bell, of Mass., one of our most eminent surgeons, performed an operation on the abdomen. The patient was decidedly tympanitic, and yet he passed no flatus whatever, although the bowels moved. That symptom is under *Raphanus*. Dr. Bell gave that remedy, and the patient recovered.

Next we come to the dropsies curable by *Lycopodium*. We find the remedy indicated in dropsies, particularly in the lower half of the body. The upper part of the body is emaciated, the muscles of the arms and chest are shrunken, the abdomen is distended, and the legs swollen and covered with ulcers, from which serum continually oozes. Now, there are three remedies which may be given when ulcers form on the legs in dropsy. They are *Rhus tox.*, *Lycopodium* and *Arsenic*. The cause of the dropsy indicating *Lycopodium* is liver disease. It has also been used successfully for hydropericardium in heart disease after the failure of *Arsenic*.

We next come to the catarrhs of *Lycopodium*. *Lycopodium* may be thought of in catarrh affecting the nasal mucous surface, particularly when the nose is "stuffed up" and the child cannot breathe. The child starts up from sleep rubbing its nose.

You may also think of it in bronchial catarrh, whether the larger or smaller tubes are involved, when there is accumulation of mucus, as indicated by rales, rattling breathing, cough and dyspnœa and waving of the alæ nasi.

It may also be given in hectic fever with suppuration of the lungs, particularly when the right lung is worse than the left.

It is also useful in pneumonia when the hepatization is so extensive that the patient has great difficulty in breathing, and there is alternate contraction and dilatation of the alæ nasi. It may also be employed in typhoid pneumonia, the symptoms agreeing, and also for the bad effects of maltreated pneumonia, particularly if suppuration of the lungs impends.

I come now to the action of *Lycopodium* in the muscular and fibrous tissues. It weakens the muscles and so becomes of use in delicate persons whose muscles are poorly developed. The arms feel weak and heavy, but that this weakness is mainly functional is shown by the fact that the patient when he tries to use them, finds that he can work quite well with them. The limbs easily go to sleep, with numbness and formications. These sensations accompany rheumatism, neuralgia, etc. *Lycopodium* is found effective in chronic rheumatism and gout when the pains are worse from damp weather and relieved by slow motion and warmth, and the characteristic gastric and urinary symptoms are present. The right side is principally the seat of trouble.

In diseases of the kidneys we find *Lycopodium* indicated for a trouble to which I have already referred, the presence of lithic acid in the urine, and also in renal colic affecting the right side.

There is one symptom for *Lycopodium* that I would yet like to add, a symptom not uncommon in typhoid fever, pneumonia, and scarlatina, and that is coldness of one foot while the other is warm or even hot. This symptom may appear insignificant on paper, but I can assure you that it is of inestimable value in practice.

Sulphur has coldness of one foot, but it is usually the left foot that is affected.

Lycopodium is complementary to *Lachesis*.

LECTURE XLIII.

THE UMBELLIFERÆ, THE BERBERIDACEÆ AND SPIGELIA.

The Umbelliferæ.

The Umbelliferæ are an order of plants which have a marked action on the nervous system, developing in some cases symptoms akin to hysteria. They also affect the glandular system, producing either engorgement or atrophy of glands. They all act on the mucous membranes, producing catarrh, and some of them act upon the skin, developing pustular eruptions. The remedies obtained from this order are as follows:

>Conium maculatum,
>Cicuta virosa,
>Œnanthe crocata,
>Phellandrium aquaticum,
>Petroselinum,
>Asafœtida,
>Ammoniacum gummi.

We will now proceed to consider the one first mentioned on this list.

Conium Maculatum.

Conium maculatum acts as a depressor of the cerebro-spinal system. It develops a paretic state which spreads from below upwards, the lower part of the body giving out before the upper. When the drug is taken in poisonous doses we find at first a difficulty in walking, as though the legs could not be moved. As the action of the poison increases, other and more vital organs are involved. The lungs are attacked; there is dyspnœa; the pulse is irregular, showing the fitful action of the heart muscle. Up to this time the mind is perfectly clear. Finally unconsciousness ensues, and the patient dies from paralysis of respiration.

We may utilize *Conium* in those exhausted states of the system resulting from old age. It may also be used after severe diseases, as diphtheria and typhoid fever, and for the sequelæ of that vice of vices, masturbation. In the paralyses of *Conium*, sensation is but little involved. Its analogues here are *Gelsemium* and *Cocculus*, which produce functional motor paralysis and are prominent remedies in post-diphtheritic paralysis.

In the treatment of the effects of sexual excess, we find *Conium* of great utility by reason of its mental symptoms. It produces a perfect picture of hypochondriasis. The patient is melancholy, averse to society, yet fears to be alone. *Conium* may also be given when this mental condition arises from celibacy.

Zinc oxide is here very similar to *Conium*. The latter is a depressing remedy, while the former is irritating as well as weakening.

You may use *Conium* in vertigo, when it is the result of cerebral anæmia and when it is characterized by exacerbations on turning over in bed. It is often associated with a numb feeling in the brain, as if that organ were stupefied.

Acting as *Conium* does upon the glandular system, we would expect it to be a scrofulous remedy. It is indicated in scrofulous ophthalmia; a characteristic symptom calling for it in this trouble being intense photophobia disproportionately severe to the degree of inflammation present. In addition to this there are ciliary neuralgia and prosopalgia, usually on one side, and worse from cold, under the influence of which the cheek becomes of a dark red color and swells.

Conium affects the wax in the ears, increasing it in quantity and making it a dark color, something like chewed-up paper.

The proper treatment in these cases is to remove the accumulation of wax by careful syringing, and then give *Conium* to prevent its formation anew.

Conium does not act very prominently on the chest. However, we find it useful in consumptives when they find it impossible to expectorate the sputum; they must swallow it again. It is especially useful for tormenting night cough, from tickling as from a dry spot in the larynx, which is relieved as soon as the patient sits up in bed. There is scarcely any cough during the day.

Conium weakens the heart, causing the pulse to be one moment full and regular and the next soft, weak, and irregular. This symptom is not an uncommon indication for *Conium* in aged people.

The use of *Conium* in glandular diseases and in malignant forms of tumors comes from its power of producing enlargement of the glands, adenomata. The glands affected are of a stony hardness. These indurations are quite common in the mammæ, in the testicles, and in the uterus. Usually, there is little or no pain; although, sometimes, there may be darting pains. *Conium* is indicated in the beginning of scirrhus. It is also indicated after contusions or bruises when induration is the result.

There is an inflammation of *Conium* which closely simulates that of malignant disease. In the mouth it gives us a picture of noma; the tongue and mucous surfaces are swollen, with offensive discharge; the parts have an ashy, grayish hue, and may even be gangrenous. There is great difficulty in swallowing, with spasm of the throat.

In cancer of the stomach, there is vomiting of blood, and of a grayish-black substance which is made up of decomposed blood and broken-down gangrenous tissue.

Conium is complementary to *Nux vomica* in constipation, especially when there is faint feeling after stool.

Ammoniacum Gummi.

Ammoniacum gummi is a gum obtained from a very large tree growing in Arabia. It has gained quite a reputation as a cure for diseases of the eye. I have used it successfully in asthenopia, when the eyes smart and burn, especially if used at night by artificial light. The eyes become injected, and often throb, especially in the inner canthus of each eye. It thus stands between *Belladonna*, which is used for affections of the eyes from overwork when there is great congestion, and *Ruta*, which is indicated for irritability of every tissue of the eye from overwork or from using the eyes on fine work.

Asafœtida.

Asafœtida is a gum having a decided alliaceous odor. It is especially useful in two classes of disease: First, in nervous diseases developing a perfect type of hysteria; it acts upon the muscular fibres, producing a reverse peristaltic action in the œsophagus and intestines. Thus, it causes a sensation as though a ball started in the stomach and rose into the throat; this being provoked by over-eating, by motion, or by anything that can excite the nerves. It produces a bursting feeling, upwards, as though everything in the abdomen were coming out at the mouth. This is common in colic from hysteria, after belching of wind of a strong rancid taste, and is associated with an empty gone feeling in the stomach at 11 A. M. like *Sulphur.*

The second action of *Asafœtida* is upon the bones. It produces periosteal inflammations, resulting in ulcers, especially upon the shin bones. A characteristic of these ulcers is an intolerance of all dressings. The parts around are exceedingly sensitive to the application of even charpie.

We find *Asafœtida* curing hysteria arising from the sudden suppression of discharges.

Asafœtida produces inflammations of the eye. Thus it may be indicated in iritis after the abuse of mercury, especially when it is of syphilitic origin, with burning, throbbing pains, and soreness of the bones around the eyes. The nearest remedy here is *Aurum*, which has relief by warmth. *Asafœtida* has relief from pressure on the eyeball itself, which *Aurum* has not.

Phellandrium aquaticum we find to be indicated in headache which involves the nerves going to the eye. There is a crushing feeling on the top of the head, with burning of the eyes and lachrymation.

Phellandrium also causes sharp pains in the course of the lactiferous tubes when the child nurses.

Petroselinum comes into use in urethral disease, especially in gonorrhœa, when the inflammation has travelled back, and the patient complains of pain at the root of the penis. There is a sudden irresistible desire to urinate, and itching deep in the perineum.

Conium causes chronic cystitis, with intermittent urination. The urine flows and stops. That symptom of the drug I have utilized in the treatment of enlargement of the prostate in old people.

ÆTHUSA CYNAPIUM.

Æthusa cynapium is a frightful poison, having narcotic properties as well as paralyzing effects. The principal use we make of the drug arises from its action on the stomach. It produces a deathly nausea and sickness, with vomiting. In the case of a child the vomit consists of curdled milk, which is often green. After vomiting, the child falls back exhausted and goes to sleep. It awakens hungry, eats and vomits again. The face is pale, and there are dark rings about the eyes. The analogue here is *Antimonium crudum*, which differs from *Æthusa* in having a white-coated tongue. *Calcarea ostrearum* or *Calcarea acetica*, has vomiting of curdled milk, and the child is apt to have diarrhœa with sour-smelling stools.

Cicuta virosa, another member of the order, when taken in any quantity produces congestion at the base of the brain and in the medulla oblongata. At first, the patient is rigid, with fixed staring eyes, bluish face and frothing at the mouth and unconsciousness. Next, there passes a shock, or series of shocks, from the head through the body. The jaws are locked, the patient bites the tongue. These spasmodic symptoms are followed by profound exhaustion. These symptoms indicate *Cicuta* in epilepsy, spasms from worms, and also in some forms of puerperal spasms.

We notice, too, that *Cicuta*, in addition to these symptoms, develops phenomena which resemble the remote effects of concussion of the brain. The pupils are dilated; there are vertigo and headache, and sometimes epileptiform convulsions.

Cicuta also attacks the skin, producing a pustular eruption, with yellowish honey-colored scabs, particularly about the mouth, and matting the whiskers It has even cured two cases of epithelioma when the cancerous growth was covered by these honey-colored scabs.

Next, we will study the

BERBERIDACEÆ.

Of this order we have time to study but two drugs, namely, *Berberis vulgaris* and *Podophyllum peltatum*.

BERBERIS VULGARIS.

Berberis vulgaris belongs to this order along with *Caulophyllum* and *Podophyllum*. It contains an alkaloid called *Berberina*, which is also found in *Hydrastis Canadensis*, *Zanthorriza*, *Menispermum Canadense*, *Coptis root*, etc. Some chemists have even asserted that what is sold as *Muriate of Hydrastine* is not *Hydrastine* at all, but *Muriate of Berberine*. This *Berberine*, when given in large doses to animals, produces restlessness, convulsive trembling, thirst, diarrhœa and, finally, paralysis of the posterior extremities. Man is far less readily poisoned by it than are the lower animals. In the old school it is used as an antiperiodic and also as a bitter tonic.

Berberis vulgaris acts more on the kidneys and bladder than on any other parts of the body; next to these the liver, and, lastly, the mucous membranes. It also affects the vital powers and damages nutrition, as shown by the sunken face and excessive prostration.

First of all we will consider the kidney symptoms as the most important. Just as I would recommend *Digitalis* for several diseases when the heart symptoms decide for it, so would I recommend *Berberis* in certain affections, as peritonitis, metritis, etc., when marked by the *Berberis* kidney symptoms. We find in the renal regions sticking, digging, tearing pains, worse from deep pressure, for they are evidently in the kidneys themselves. These tearing pains extend down the back and into the pelvis along the course of the ureters. There is a sort of tensive, pressive pain across the small of the back, which feels stiff and numb; pains of a sticking or tearing character radiate from the kidneys down into the small of the back. Another symptom which seems to be peculiar to *Berberis* is a bubbling feeling as if water were coming up through the skin. It is a peculiar symptom, and one that may point very strongly to *Berberis* as the remedy.

Coming next to the bladder, we find here very marked cutting which extends down the urethra, and burning pain even after urinating. The urine itself presents marked characteristics. We find it yellow, turbid and flocculent. Sometimes there is whitish sediment, later becoming red and mealy. With these urinary symptoms are the tearing pains just mentioned. Now, whenever you have these renal and vesical symptoms, you must think of *Berberis*, whether the trouble be inflammation of the uterus, of the bowels, of the peritoneum, or of any other part of the body. The face is usually expressive of deep-seated disease, being sunken and worn looking. General prostration is great.

Sometimes the same condition obtains in liver affections. You find very characteristically sticking pain under the border of the false ribs on the right side. These pains seem to shoot from the hepatic region down through the abdomen. These symptoms may well be indicative of gall stone colic.

The stools of *Berberis* are accompanied by violent burning in the anus, as if the surrounding parts were sore; frequent or constant desire for stool. These symptoms have suggested the use of *Berberis* in fistula of the anus.

In fistula compare *Silica*, *Sulphur*, *Ignatia* and *Calcarea phos.*, the latter when lung symptoms are present as the result of an operation for removal.

You may also use *Berberis* in complaints of females, when the leucorrhœa or menstrual difficulty is associated with the peculiar urinary symptoms of the drug.

Berberis is to be studied alongside of *Pareira brava*. The difference between the two drugs is this: in the latter drug the pains go tearing down the thighs, while in the former they seldom go further than the hips, and the patient is unable to urinate unless he gets down on his hands and knees. Urine ammoniacal.

We may also use *Berberis* in disease of the joints, when accompanied by the tearing and burning pains and the bubbling sensation just mentioned. It is also a very useful drug in rheumatism or gout, when characteristic urinary symptoms are present. This places it by the side of *Lithium carb.*, *Benzoic acid*, *Calcarea ostrearum* and *Lycopodium*.

Benzoic acid is useful in gout and in rheumatism with urinary symptoms, when the urine smells strong, like that of the horse.

Calcarea ostrearum has very offensive urine, with a white instead of a turbid deposit.

Lycopodium is useful in rheumatism or gout when the urine contains a lithic acid deposit.

Podophyllum Peltatum.

Podophyllum peltatum is the mandrake or May-apple, a plant that grows to the height of some two or three feet, with leaves spread out like an open hand. It is found mostly on the borders of woods. The parts used in medicine are the roots and fruit of the plant. When applied externally, *Podophyllum* produces a rawness of the skin, resembling intertrigo. If the powdered plant gets into the eyes it produces a severe inflammation and even a perforating ulcer of the cornea.

The central point of attack of the drug, however, is in the abdomen. Shortly after it is taken there follow diarrhœa, colicky pains, the well-known morning stool pouring out like water from a hydrant, preceded by retching and vomiting and spasmodic contraction of the stomach, making the child scream out; a diarrhœa such as would make us think of *Sulphur*, *Dioscorea*, *Bryonia*, *Natrum sulph.*, and a few other remedies. The stools are renewed immediately by eating, like *Croton tiglium*, etc.

In addition to its intestinal action we find it acting on the liver, and here is the main use that is made of the remedy. It is indicated in the torpid or chronically congested liver. The liver is swollen and sensitive, and friction over the right hypochondrium relieves this sensation. The face and sclerotica become tinged yellow. There is bad taste in the mouth, evidently arising from the degeneration of food in the intestinal tract. The tongue is coated yellow or white, and takes the imprint of the teeth. The bile may become inspissated in the gall bladder, forming gall-stone; thus we find *Podophyllum* indicated in that tormenting disease, bilious colic. The stools are of the nature already mentioned; or they are constipated and clay-colored, showing the absense of bile. These symptoms of *Podophyllum* much resemble those of *Mercurius*. They have won for the drug the name of vegetable mercury. It is much less injurious, however, than is *Mercury*.

In constipation of bottle-fed babies *Podophyllum* will sometimes relieve. The stools are dry and crumbling.

Of the remedies having the symptom, the tongue takes the imprint of the teeth, *Mercurius* stands at the head of the list. Next to that we have *Podophyllum*, and then *Yucca filamentosa*, and, finally, *Rhus*, *Stramonium* and *Arsenicum metallicum*.

Podophyllum also produces prolapsus recti with the diarrhœa. The rectum protrudes before stool (*Nux vom.* after), especially in the morning. *Podophyllum* also seems to have the power of producing and curing prolapsus of the uterus with attendant symptoms of bearing down in the hypogastric and sacral regions worse from motion, and neuralgia in the right ovary, extending down the anterior crural nerve, backache, retarded menses, thick transparent leucorrhœa and often coexisting with these, prolapsus recti.

As concordant remedies to *Podophyllum* in this prolapsus we have *Nux vomica* and *Sepia*, the indications for which I have already given you in a former lecture.

Very few would think of *Podophyllum* as a remedy for tonsillitis and yet it has some very clear cut indications in this affection. The trouble is apt to start in the right side and extend to the left, like *Lycopodium*. There is great dryness of the throat, aggravation from swallowing liquids and in the morning and pain going into the ear.

Podophyllum is a valuable remedy during dentition. It does not seem to act on the brain, yet it causes reflex cerebral irritation, whether this be from the abdominal symptoms alone or from the teeth. The symptoms which indicate it in addition to those already given are moaning and whining during sleep, not crying out with a sharp, sudden noise, as under *Belladonna*, but a sick cry; the child grates its teeth; the head is thrown back and rolled from side to side.

Next we find *Podophyllum* indicated in fevers, usually of a remittent type, particularly in bilious remittent fever. The drug does not produce many characteristic symptoms during the chill, but during the fever the patient is sleepy and sometimes delirious.

LECTURE XLIV.

MINERAL KINGDOM.

I propose now to begin the study of the drugs obtained from the mineral kingdom. I have placed on the board (*see next page*) for your study the elements, arranged in order according to some of their relations, just as we find them in chemistry. I wish to explain here the general idea of the relation of drugs, and especially of those belonging to the mineral kingdom. If you consult chemistry you will find that the elements hold to each other an electrical relation. They hold to each other a relation of polarity as positive electric and negative electric. Certain of these elements are emphatically negative, and others are just as positively positive. Some of the elements, as gold, silver, etc., hold a middle relation, being rather neutral. These I have placed at the neutral point of the magnet. The advantage of this method of study will be seen as we proceed. The negative electrics are known to be conductors of light, the positive conductors of heat. The extreme effects in this respect are noticed at either pole, diminishing as we approach the curve of the magnet. Another fact which is well worth knowing is this general statement: the electro-negatives act on the bowels in the morning, and the chest in the afternoon; that is, they act upward on the body during the day. Exactly the opposite holds true with the electro-positive. These act on the chest in the morning, and on the bowels in the latter part of the day. Most of you are acquainted with the morning diarrhœa of *Sulphur*, which hurries the patient out of bed. You know how the asthma of that remedy increases in the afternoon. Taking the remedies at the other extreme, we have the *Kali* salts as examples; you know that they have aggravation of their chest symptoms in the forenoon, and of their bowel symptoms in the afternoon. This is, of course, a very general statement, but it may be of great use to you in enabling you to differentiate between drugs. Let me illustrate. You have a case of scrofula and you are obliged to decide between *Sulphur* and some salt of lime. You will be astonished to see how similar are many of the symptoms of these two drugs. The very fact of the diarrhœa

Electro—.   Electro+.

Electro—.	Electro+.
Oxygen. Ozone. Nitric ac. Amyl nitr.	Antozone.
Sulphur. Selenium. Sulph. ac. Carboneum sulph.	Hydrogen.
Fluoric ac. Iodine. Spongia. Bromine. Chlorine. Muriatic ac. Cyanogen.	Ammonium. Kalium. Natrum. Lithium.
Carbo veg. Carbo an. Graphites. Petroleum. Cosmoline. Silicea.	Calcarea. Baryta carb. Strontia carb.
Phosphorus. Phosphoric ac. Arsenicum alb. Arsenicum iod. Tellurium. Antimon. crud. Antimon. tart.	Zincum. Magnesium. Cadmium. Alumina. Plumbum. Stannum.
Aurum. Argentum. Mercury. Thallium. Cuprum.	Ferrum. Manganum. Niccolum. Kobaltum.

Platina.   Iridium.
                                           Indium.
        Palladium.   Rhodium.
                 Osmium.

coming in the morning or afternoon, insignificant as it may appear under other circumstances, serves as a differentiation between these two drugs. Now in making this statement I do not mean that because *Sulphur* produces a morning diarrhœa, that it must *always* be the remedy when that symptom is presented; but I do mean that when you are compelled to decide between two remedies having opposite directions in action, this relation becomes of great importance. As you approach the remedies or chemicals at the neutral point of the magnet, you find these effects less marked, until, finally, they are unnoticeable.

There is another fact which we may learn from this arrangement of drugs. You notice that here we have oxygen and sulphur. They are chemical elements, which are placed near together in chemistry, and are similar not only as chemicals but also as medicines. Next on the list we have nitrogen, which is used in medicine in the form of *Nitric acid*. Below this we have a list of remedies which constitute a group in chemistry known as the halogens; they consist of *Fluorine*, *Fluoric acid*, *Iodine*, *Bromine*, and *Spongia*. The latter drug is placed here not as a chemical substance, but as a drug which owes its medicinal properties to the iodine and bromine which it contains. It is of practical value to remember these drugs in this connection, because they are not only chemically similar, but they are also similar as medicines. Moreover, this grouping of remedies enables you to keep in mind a group of remedies from which you may choose one to suit your case. I have introduced cyanogen here because it holds important chemical and medicinal relations to the halogens. Below we have the carbon group, *Carbo veg. Carbo animalis*, *Anthrakokali*, the diamond, and *Graphites*. I have also placed in this group *Petroleum* and *Cosmoline* or petroleum jelly, two oily substances, rich in carbon, and having many resemblances to the pure carbons.

In a future lecture I shall give you the characteristics which belong to all the carbons, so that you can say here is a patient who needs some preparation of carbon, which shall it be? This you determine in the same way as you selected one of the halogens. Next we have a group composed of *Phosphorus* and its acid and *Arsenicum*. Below, we have *Tellurium*, *Antimonium crudum* and *Antimonium tartaricum*, which is similar enough to the sulphide to be placed along side of it. This group of drugs possesses many similarities. *Phosphorus* and *Arsenic* are continually placed in contrast in the physician's mind, and it is often difficult for him to decide which he shall give.

The *Antimony* preparations are similar in form and isomorphous with *Sulphur* and *Selenium*. There is another fact which we may borrow from chemistry, and that is that substances of similar crystalline structure have similar medicinal effects. These substances often replace each other in chemistry. I give you these facts so that you may have a rational conception of drugs, not as mere individuals, but as consistent with nature and with themselves. Here below we have the noble metals, gold and silver. Then we may go up on this side tracing the drugs through the same relation we did on the other. Every one knows how closely related, chemically and medicinally, are *Barium* and *Strontium*. This relation is very much like that of similarity in origin. They are not apt to follow one another well. Here are *Sulphur* and *Sulphuric acid;* suppose you are going to decide between them and suppose it to be a perplexing case. You say "I will give *Sulphur*, and if he is not better to-morrow I will give *Sulphuric acid*." That is bad practice. It would be much better to say that I will give *Sulphur* to-day and *Calcarea* to-morrow. Why? They are similar drugs, but entirely foreign in their family relations and origin. Why do I dwell on these two relations? Because I want you to distinguish between that which is the same and that which is similar. *Ignatia* and *Nux vomica* are too much as though they were the same thing. *Ignatia* and *Zinc* are concordant remedies which are similar but which are not identical. You note that I have placed hydrogen above all the potash salts. You notice that here is placed antozone. *Ozone* is negative oxygen, and antozone is positive oxygen. *Ozone* exists in the sea-air and how many times do you send your patients to the sea-shore for relief. We may derive a hygienic fact from this statement; if I have a patient who is something of a *Sulphur* patient, I would think that sea-air would do him good because sea-air is rich in ozone, and ozone in a general way suits his condition. On the other hand, if he belongs more to the "salt" class of drugs I would not send him to the sea-shore. I would send him where antozone exists, as in fogs We will now proceed to study the drugs derived from the mineral kingdom. The remainder of the hour I will devote to the consideration of *Selenium*. To-morrow we will study the king of remedies, *Sulphur*.

Selenium.

| Selenium. | Arum tri.
Caust., Carbo v., Phos., Spong.
Sulphur. | <Cinch.
<Wine.
>Ign.
<Puls. |

Selenium is isomorphous with *Sulphur* and resembles it both chemically and medicinally. We find it producing very little effect on the blood and lymphatic vessels, but it acts on the nervous system. We often find it the remedy in nervous diseases. It seems to produce a weakness or general debility involving all parts of the body. This debility is expressed by easy fatigue from any exertion or labor. If the patient sits up a little too late at night, or exerts his mind a little too much, he is exhausted the whole of the next day and is thereby unfitted for either mental or physical work. Particularly is he weakened from hot weather. It is evident that the hot weather weakens him. This is further shown by the fact that he becomes stronger as the sun sinks and the temperature with it. He is sluggish on account of this debility. He wants to sleep from sheer exhaustion, and yet he is always worse after sleep. He cannot bear any nervous exhaustion, consequently he is made worse by seminal emissions, whether voluntary or involuntary. As a result of the seminal loss, the next day he is irritable, suffers from mental confusion, headache, almost paralytic weakness of the spine, involuntary escape of prostatic fluid, dribbling of semen during sleep, and after stool and urination. Now you will notice at once the resemblance of the drug to *Sulphur*. Both have bad effects of mental exhaustion and loss of sleep, and both have involuntary emissions and prostatorrhœa. The distinction lies in the fact that *Selenium* has more of the relaxation. Here you find two substances suitable in similar conditions, and yet the shade of difference is sufficient to enable you to know which one is the more useful for your case. Both have impotence. With *Sulphur* there is more coldness and shrivelling of the genital organs. With *Selenium* there is more of this total giving up or relaxation, so that semen dribbles away involuntarily.

We may be called upon to use *Selenium* for the sequelæ of typhoid fever. When the patient begins to walk about, there is such great debility of the spine that he fears that he will be paralyzed. Again you see the great similarity between *Sulphur* and *Selenium*. *Sulphur* is invaluable in the exhaustion consequent upon protracted diseases. This again we have in *Selenium*. In *Selenium*, such characteristic *Sulphur* symptoms as flushes of heat on the least motion are lacking. *Sulphur* has more of that gone weak feeling in the forenoon, which is not marked under *Selenium*.

We find *Selenium* also indicated in headache of nervous origin. The pain is of a stinging character, and is usually situated over the left eye, and it is worse from the heat of the sun. Notice again how hot weather influences the *Selenium* patient. The headaches return quite periodically every afternoon, and are increased by any strong odor, as the odor of tube-roses, musk, etc. This headache is evidently nervous because it is associated with profound melancholy and profuse flow of clear limpid urine. You often find this last symptom in hysterical patients. Other remedies, however, have it in more marked degree, as, for instance, *Gelsemium*, *Ignatia*, *Lac defloratum*, *Moschus*, etc.

Again, another indication of the nervous origin of this headache is seen in the fact that the patient is worse from drinking tea and from certain acids, notably lemonade. Even tamarind-water aggravates. Here again we have resemblances to the *Sulphur*, in the periodical return of the headache. With *Sulphur*, however, it does not return every afternoon, but every week; nor has this remedy the aggravation from tea, although it has from coffee.

You will find both remedies indicated in the headache of drunkards and of those who have been guilty of debauchery. The *Sulphur* headache is worse from all forms of alcoholic drinks. The *Selenium* headache is sometimes improved by brandy, as are also the gastric symptoms. You will find that the patient has a longing for brandy. Now this is not the drunkard's craving. It is the result of a peculiar weakness in the stomach, a feeling as if the patient wanted something to stimulate him, and brandy is desired, as it has a temporary palliating effect. The same symptom you find under *Staphisagria* and *Hepar sulphur*, both of which have that great relaxation and dragging or want of tone in the walls of the stomach and consequent insufficiency in the secretion of gastric juice.

Selenium comes to us well-recommended, in a peculiar form of constipation, though it failed me in the one case in which I used it. The constipation for which it is indicated is one purely due to atony of the intestinal tract. Peristaltic action is almost nil, so that fæces become impacted. The fæces are hard and dry from absorption of their moisture, and require removal by artificial means, yet *Selenium* is said to tone up the rectum and prevent the recurrence of this symptom. The same symptom is found under *Alumina*, *Opium*, *Plumbum* and *Bryonia*, but these are probably not indicated so often during convalescence.

Another peculiarity of *Selenium* which qualifies its symptoms is the character of the sleep. The patient sleeps in cat-naps. He awakens often in the night, or is easily aroused by any slight disturbance. He awakens at precisely the same hour every morning before his usual rising time, when all his prevailing complaints are worse. Here again it resembles *Sulphur*. These "cat-naps" are characteristic of *Sulphur*. The true *Sulphur* sleeplessness is this: The patient is aroused from sleep and is then wide awake. He has not this periodical hour of awakening each morning, which calls for *Selenium*.

Another resemblance between the two drugs you will find in affections of the skin. *Selenium* is useful in skin diseases, particularly when there is itching in the folds of the skin as between the fingers, and about the joints, particularly the ankle joint. The itching may also occur in small spots and is associated with tingling, here again showing involvement of the nervous system. The hair falls off, not that of the head, the eyebrows and whiskers, but of other parts of the body. You will find on the scalp an eczematous eruption which oozes a serous fluid after scratching. Here, again, it bears a striking resemblance to *Sulphur*, but is distinguished from that remedy if the patient is old enough to describe his case, by this tingling in spots.

We sometimes find, although not often, that *Selenium*, like *Sulphur*, is indicated in chronic affections of the liver. Especially is it called for in enlargement of the liver with loss of appetite, particularly in the morning; there is white coating on the tongue, thus separating it at once from *Sulphur*. Then, too, with loss of appetite, *Sulphur* has increase of thirst, which is lacking in *Selenium*. There are sharp stitching pains in the hepatic region, worse on any motion and worse on pressure and sensitiveness of the liver. Now if there is a peculiar fine rash over the hepatic region, *Selenium* is the only remedy you can think of to suit your case.

Selenium has a very marked action on the larynx and lungs. Several animals were poisoned with *Selenium*. It produced inflammation of the lining membrane of the larynx and congestion of the lungs with exudation into the pulmonary substance. Post-mortem examination showed the mucous membrane to be congested, with dark purplish spots here and there through it. Oozing of blood and frothy serum followed the incision of the knife. I have used *Selenium* successfully in the hoarseness of singers, particularly when the hoarseness appears as soon as they begin to sing. It may also be used when hoarseness appears after long use of the voice. There is frequent necessity to clear the throat by reason of the accumulation of clear starchy mucus. These symptoms point suspiciously towards incipient tubercular laryngitis. Here *Selenium* is grouped with *Arum triphyllum*, *Spongia*, *Causticum*, *Carbo veg*. and *Phosphorus*.

Arum triphyllum has entirely different effects, but it bears a strong symptomatic resemblance to the throat symptoms of *Selenium*. It is also useful for the hoarseness of singers and orators, but especially indicated when the voice suddenly gives out during use. For example, the patient is talking in a sort of monotone when the voice suddenly breaks and goes up to a higher key.

The antidotes to *Selenium* are *Pulsatilla* and *Ignatia*. *China* and wine are inimical to it. The debility caused by *Selenium*, so says Hahnemann, is very much increased by the use of *Cinchona*. Now the emaciation caused by *Selenium* is very similar to that of *Cinchona*. We have debility and emaciation from loss of animal fluids, a condition also found under *Cinchona;* yet the two drugs are inimical.

LECTURE XLV.

SULPHUR.

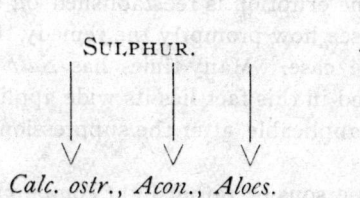

SULPHUR.
  ∨   ∨   ∨
Calc. ostr., Acon., Aloes.

{ Psorinum.
Merc., Nitric ac., Lach.
Nux, Puls., Bry.
Bapt., Arsenicum.
Calc. ostr., Lyc., Silic., Sepia.
Aconite, Bell., Bry.
Phos., Ant. t., Ars.

> Nux, Puls., Merc.

Sulphur is an element with which you are all familiar. You must be careful, if you prepare the medicine yourself, that you obtain it perfectly pure. The sublimed *Sulphur* that you buy in the shops is very impure. It contains some of the oxygen acids of *Sulphur*, some *Selenium*, and often, too, *Arsenic*. When chemical substances are associated in this way in nature, it is a fact that they must be related medicinally. There is also a relation between the plant and the soil in which it grows. Thus, *Belladonna*, which grows in lime earths, is related medicinally to *Calcarea*. The *Agaricus* will never grow where there is coal. You will find no relation between *Agaricus* and the carbons. *Cistus Canadensis* grows where there is mica, consequently you may expect some relation between that drug and *Magnesium*.

Sulphur may be said to be the central remedy of our materia medica. It has well-defined relations with nearly every drug we use. The great utility of *Sulphur* arises from this peculiarity, it is our mainstay in defective reaction. When the system refuses to respond to the well selected remedy, it matters not what the disease may be, whether it is a disease which corresponds characteristically with the symptomatology of *Sulphur* or not, it will often be the remedy to clear up the case and bring about reaction, and either itself cure the case or pave the way for another drug which will cure. This quality of *Sulphur* arises from its relation to what Hahnemann called psora. Hahnemann taught what is practically true, that when a disease is suppressed (and a disease is suppressed when it is driven from the surface to the interior of the body), there is formed a constitution or dyscrasia which will afterwards modify every abnormality from which the patient may suffer. For instance, an eruption on the skin is dried up or is driven in by some external application. Afterwards (it may be some time), another disease appears, not necessarily as a skin affection, however. Pathologically, it may be entirely different from it. For instance, as the result of exposure to cold, the patient contracts pneumonia. This condition due to the suppression of the eruption so modifies the disease that it is not curable until that same eruption is reestablished on the skin. Then you will be amazed to see how promptly the remedy that before refused to act now cures the case. Many times has *Sulphur* restored such suppressed diseases, and in this fact lies its wide application in practice. Particularly is it applicable after the suppression of itch.

Sulphur is especially adapted to persons of rather light complexion who are easily angered, although dark-complexioned persons may also yield to its influence if they exhibit *Sulphur* symptoms. It is one of our mainstays in the treatment of the negro. Whether this is owing to the rapid growth of scrofula in that race or not, I cannot say. It is also suited to persons who are subject to skin affections, particularly to those who have harsh, rough skin, which very readily breaks out with eruptions of various descriptions, varying from a simple erythema to a positive eczema. There is apt to be also an offensive odor from the body. This odor may arise partly from uncleanness, for the typical *Sulphur* patient is not very fond of water. Bathing aggravates his complaints. There is, moreover, a positive distaste or dislike for water. This peculiar disagreeable odor or exhalation from the skin is not removed by washing; hence, you must consider it to be for the most part an abnormality arising from impure excretions from the skin. The patient is rather of coarse fibre. His hair is harsh and coarse. There is craving for alcoholic drinks, especially those of the coarser type, as beer, ale, whiskey, etc.

The patient walks rather stooped from weakness of the spine. Then, too, as I have already said, he fails to react to the apparently indicated remedy.

In defective reaction, *Sulphur* does not stand alone. I have already spoken of the value of *Psorinum* in this connection. *Cuprum* should also be thought of. We also have *Laurocerasus* in chest affections, particularly in diseases of the lungs which do not respond to treatment; *Valerian* and *Ambra grisea* in nervous diseases; and *Carbo veg.*, particularly in abdominal affections and in the collapse which is marked by cold breath, cold knees, etc.

Now, let me speak of the action of *Sulphur* on the circulation. In almost every instance in which it is the remedy you will find deranged circulation. It seems to act more prominently on the venous circulation, producing a sort of plethora. But this is not a true plethora. It is the result of irregularities in the distribution of the blood, by which certain parts of the body become congested. These congestions, generally speaking, are such as occur particularly from abdominal troubles, especially fulness of the portal system, a very common trouble nowadays. Especially is *Sulphur* indicated in plethora that has arisen from sudden cessation of an accustomed discharge, particularly a hæmorrhoidal flow. For example, piles have suddenly stopped bleeding, and fulness of the head, with distended blood-vessels, fulness of the liver, etc., show that congestion of these parts has resulted. *Sulphur* will, in these instances, ease the congestion and restore the accustomed discharge. Then you may proceed with *Sulphur* or with some other remedy, according to the indications of the case, to cure this abnormal discharge in the proper way.

The congestion of the head, for which *Sulphur* is indicated, is accompanied by roaring in the ears indicating that there is congestion about the auditory nerves—redness of the face, worse in the open air and better in the warm room, and heaviness and fullness almost to bursting. The patient feels worse when he stoops.

Sulphur is frequently indicated in congestion of the chest with or without hæmoptysis. There is great difficulty in breathing. The patient feels oppressed and wants all the doors and windows opened. These symptoms are accompanied with violent palpitation of the heart, resulting from the endeavor of that organ to compensate for the increased supply of blood to the thoracic cavity.

If I may be allowed to use the expression, there is too much blood in the heart. The blood rushes into that organ and is not removed by its contraction rapidly enough. This is a very common symptom indicating *Sulphur*, and especially calls for it when the patient is disturbed at night with sudden rush of blood to the heart. with violent palpitation, gasping for breath feeling as if the patient would suffocate if fresh air is not obtained. These symptoms may also be experienced during the day from ascending a height or from exercise where the heart is called upon to do extra work. Often the patient feels as if the heart were too large for the thoracic cavity, a symptom also belonging to *Glonoin, Eupatorium perfoliatum* and *Grindelia robusta.*

As further evidence of the irregular distribution of the blood in *Sulphur*, we have redness of the various orifices of the body, a very strong characteristic of the remedy. The lips are of a rich red color. This symptom often indicates *Sulphur* in pneumonia, scarlatina, dysentery and anæmia. Redness of the ears may be noticed even when the rest of the body is not abnormal in color. With this last indication, *Sulphur* has ofter prevented earache in children. With this indication it has often prevented erysipelas. We also find this redness along the borders of the eyelids, giving them an appearance as if they had been painted. We find redness at the anus, with soreness of the part, a symptom which is particularly useful in the diarrhœa of children. The child screams with pain when the bowels are moved. That symptom alone may frequently lead you to decide that *Sulphur* is the remedy. The same is also true of the vulva, which is found to be red.

Another and very common expression of the irregularity in the circulation is flushes of heat, not only the flushes of heat that occur at the climacteric for which *Sulphur* is so frequently indicated, but the flushes of heat which may occur in any disease and do occur during convalescence. The "flush" is followed by more or less moisture, which gives relief. To be purely characteristic of *Sulphur*, this must be associated with other symptoms, such, for instance, as sensation of heat on the top of the head. The feet, in such cases, are apt to be cold and the patient complains of weak feeling in the epigastrium, especially in the forenoon from ten to twelve. While you often cure flushes of heat with *Sulphur* when this symptom is absent, you never fail if you have the heat on the top of the head, cold feet and sinking feeling in the epigastrium. In the flushes of heat at climaxis you may also think of *Lachesis, Sulphuric acid, Nitrite of Amyl* and *Kali bichromicum;* in the weak faint feeling at 11 A. M., *Phosphorus, Hydrastis, Asafœtida,* and *Zinc.*

Another illustration of the action of *Sulphur* on the circulation is shown in the fever of the remedy. *Sulphur* is not particularly indicated in typhoid or septic conditions. There is no indication that *Sulphur* makes changes in the structure of the blood such as belong to scarlatina, typhoid fevers and the septic conditions generally, so that from this fact we could not give *Sulphur*. There are other reasons than the septic changes that enable us to prescribe *Sulphur* with success. It is indicated when the fever is of a remittent or continued type. It may be used after *Aconite* for the pure synochal fever when, despite the use of that remedy, the dry, hot skin remains and there is no reaction or no critical sweat, which will give the necessary relief. Hour after hour, day after day, this fever continues; hence its name, continuous. Or it may be what has been termed a "continuous remittent;" that is, there is an exacerbation each evening and a slight fall towards morning, the fever never going away entirely. You may give *Sulphur* when this fever approaches the typhoid condition, led by these indications: the patient begins to be drowsy with his fever. His tongue is dry and red at the edges and tip, and he responds to your questions very sluggishly and slowly. He is literally burning up with fever. The consumption of oxygen of the system is producing these symptoms. *Sulphur* acts marvellously in these cases.

Sulphur may also be indicated in intermittent types of fever. It is not a specific for intermittent or malarial fever, and yet it has periodicity in its symptoms. Here you must select it from the well-known symptoms, torpor with slowness in answering questions, chills that will not stop despite your well-selected remedy, particularly if the intermittent assumes the remittent type, or, more frequently, if the remittent type commences and runs into the intermittent. It may also be called for in malarial neuralgia occurring mostly in the face and recurring quite periodically and resisting other remedies. Here, too, you must remember *Cinchona*, *Arsenicum* and *Chininum sulph*.

In these fevers I would have you place *Sulphur* alongside of two other remedies, which usually follow that remedy because in their symptomatology they suit a more advanced case. These two remedies are *Baptisia* and *Arsenicum*. *Baptisia* typifies a fever which is decidedly typhoid in its tendency. The torpor does not stop with this sluggishness in responding to questions, but it goes on to stupor, so that the patient even falls asleep while answering you. The tongue becomes of a brown or blackish hue down its centre and sordes form on the teeth. The discharges from the mouth and from the bowels have an offensive odor; the face has a besotted look; the blood is actually decomposed from septic poisoning or from the prolonged high temperature.

Arsenicum suits inflammatory fever further advanced than that calling for either *Sulphur* or *Aconite*. It has some symptoms which remind you of the latter remedy, notably, restlessness; full, bounding pulse; hot, dry skin; anxiety and fear of death; yet beneath all these symptoms, there is evidence of prolonged tissue-changes. The inflammation is going on to destruction of the parts involved, whether the disease be typhoid fever or a simple inflammatory affection from cold as in gastric catarrh. The symptoms are aggravated after midnight; there is burning thirst with tendency to drink little and often, or burning thirst with refusal to drink water because it aggravates these symptoms, especially the burning like coals of fire in the part affected. With all these symptoms the brain may remain perfectly clear.

Next, we come to the consideration of the action of *Sulphur* on the lymphatic system, including under this head the glands and the vessels themselves. *Sulphur* is our mainstay in scrofula, which is, as you know, an affection involving this lymphatic system. It is the prince of remedies here. It is especially useful in the very commencement of the disease, when its first evidences are presented, particularly in patients having the temperament which I have already described to you as characteristic of the *Sulphur* patient. The patient sweats about the head, particularly during sleep. There is a marked tendency to eruptions such as crusta-lactea, boils, and, in older children, acne. In the case of children, the head is large in comparison with the rest of the body. The fontanelles, particularly the anterior, remain open too long from defective osseous growth. There is tendency to bone affections, to caries, and, particularly in early childhood, to rickets and to curvatures of the spine. The child has a voracious appetite. This it expresses by greedily clutching at all that is offered it, whether edible or not, as if it were starved to death. There is defective assimilation. Glands are so diseased that, while sufficient food is taken into the system, it is not appropriated to the nourishment of the body, so that the child is always hungry and yet emaciated. The child looks shrivelled and dried up, like a little old man; the skin hangs in folds and is rather yellowish, wrinkled and flabby. All these are precious symptoms for the exhibition of *Sulphur*. You may occasionally have to use *Sulphur* in the beginning in a sort of negative condition. You are certain from a majority of symptoms that you have a case of scrofula, and yet no particular remedy appears to be indicated. Then you should give *Sulphur*, which develops the symptoms and shows you what you have to contend with

In marasmus of children you may give *Sulphur* when many of the symptoms already mentioned are present. The child is ravenously hungry, especially at 11 A. M. Now, in regard to this eleven-o'clock hunger, I would say that if you want to use *Sulphur* successfully in these cases, you must also have these symptoms present: hunger at 11 A. M., heat on top of the head and cold feet. If you have these three symptoms present, *Sulphur* never fails you. If there is heat on the top of the head alone, you must think of *Calcarea* or *Phosphorus*.

Another affection of which I wish to speak under the head of the lymphatic system is tuberculosis, not that I wish to say that scrofula and tuberculosis are identical, but that the lymphatic vessels have considerable to do with the spread of tubercle. *Sulphur* is a valuable drug in tuberculosis, no matter what part of the body it may invade. It is especially useful in tubercular hydrocephalus. Here it has done good work, not in the third stage, when the case is nearly hopeless, but in the commencement of the pathological process, when there are violent convulsions, sudden flushing of the face; the child cannot hold its head up from weakness of the cervical muscles. The child wants to lie with its head low. That symptom expresses a great deal, because, when the head is low, there is less effort of the neck required to hold the head up. The child cries out in its sleep. Often, on falling off to sleep, there is sudden jerking of one or both legs. It cries out in sleep as if frightened. The face is red and the pupils are dilated. *This is not a case of Belladonna. Belladonna cannot, never did, and never will cure tubercular meningitis.* The symptoms tend to appear more or less periodically. Associated with these few cerebral symptoms you will have very many general symptoms, some of which I have already mentioned, and some of which will be spoken of before the end of the lecture. When I give you these symptoms in different groups, I do not wish to convey the idea that these symptoms indicate the drug only when they occur in their respective groups.

In tuberculosis affecting the lungs, *Sulphur* is indicated only in the beginning. I would here caution you as to how you use the drug. If carelessly or wrongly given, it may precipitate the disease which it was your desire to cure. You must not repeat your doses too frequently, and you must never give it unless you are certain that it is *the* remedy, for the tendency of *Sulphur* is to arouse whatever lies dormant in the system. The particular indications for *Sulphur* are these: the body feels too hot. The patient wants the windows open, no matter how cold the weather may be. There are frequent flushes of heat, empty feeling in the stomach, heat on top of head, cold feet, etc., palpitation of the heart on ascending, pain through the left chest from the nipple to the back. Now you may, in this condition, give *Sulphur* as high as you choose, one, two, or three doses and await results. Watch your patient carefully, and in many instances a cure will result, but not in all.

In tuberculosis affecting the mesenteric glands *Sulphur* is indicated by the symptoms that I have already mentioned under emaciation and scrofula.

You may also find *Sulphur* indicated in hip-joint disease, and in white swelling, both of which are probably of tubercular origin. You will be aided in your selection of the drug by the general symptoms.

In these tubercular troubles you may compare with *Sulphur*, *Calcarea ostrearum* and *Phosphorus*. Both of these remedies are suited to scrofulous children, generally after *Sulphur*. They are indicated more by the general character of the patient than by the brain symptoms alone. All three remedies, as you know, have the same imperfect growth of tissue. The *Sulphur* patient is apt to be thinner than the one of *Calcarea ostrearum*, but *Calcarea* especially suits a fat, flabby, apparently well-nourished child; the paleness and the softness of flesh show you that the growth of fat has been obtained at the expense of other tissues. The sweat of the *Sulphur* patient has an offensive odor; with *Calcarea* the sweat is on the scalp, and is cool.

Calcarea phosphorica gives you these symptoms: There is a tendency to emaciation rather than obesity; the abdomen may be large, but is more apt to be flabby; the fontanelles, especially the posterior, remain open too long.

Still another remedy is *Apis*. You know that *Apis* is one of the best remedies in tubercular meningitis. It is very similar to *Sulphur*. Both remedies are indicated in cerebral symptoms arising from the repercussion of some eruption—*Sulphur*, if it is a chronic eruption, and *Apis*, if it is an acute one. Even here they collide. The best distinction to make is this: *Apis* is indicated when there is well-marked effusion on the brain; the patient cries with a piercing shriek. Then, again, the restlessness of the two remedies ought to be compared. With *Sulphur*, the patient does not sleep at all, or starts up from sleep suddenly, or sleeps in cat-naps. In *Apis*, we have this picture: the child is sleepy; it suddenly awakes from sleep with a shrill cry; it may be wholly or partly conscious; it is sleepy, but cannot sleep.

Sulphur acts as powerfully on the nervous system as it does on the circulation. It affects the brain, producing first some alterations in the functions of that organ. For instance, it may be useful in hysterical states, when the general symptoms of *Sulphur* are present; when the patient has the insane idea that she is very wealthy; she tears up her clothes regardless of the consequences; she plays with and examines old soiled rags with pleasure, evidently regarding them as objects of beauty. At other times there is profound melancholy, with disposition to do nothing at all; she is perfectly listless. This is not the indifference of *Phosphoric acid*, but listlessness or torpidity that is very common in hypochondriasis. At other times the patient is affected with a religious mania; even this mania is remarkably egotistic, the patient fears that she will not be saved; she is anxious about her own soul, but perfectly indifferent concerning the salvation of others. At other times the patient is intolerably irritable and peevish; this is particularly true with children.

Again, *Sulphur* may be indicated in hydrocephaloid. I have tested it fully in this condition, and know it to be invaluable. For instance, hydrocephaloid comes on during the course of cholera infantum. The little patient lies almost in a stupor. The face is pale, and bathed in a cold sweat, particularly the forehead. Do not mix the case up with *Veratrum;* that drug is not indicated. The eyes are half open, and you find the pupil reacting very sluggishly to light, the urine is suppressed (a very alarming symptom); the child occasionally twitches or jerks one or the other limb, and may now and then start up from sleep with a cry. This is a condition in which you will find *Sulphur* to act like a charm, and that, whether the diarrhœa continues or not. There is no remedy which can take its place. The violent rolling of the head, the suffused face, or the crying out of *Belladonna* are not present, nor is there the *cri encephalique* belonging to *Apis*, but there is a group of symptoms peculiar to *Sulphur*.

Sulphur acts on the spine, producing several conditions there; first of all, it is useful in spinal irritation. On pressing between the vertebræ you notice that the patient winces. *Sulphur* may also be used in spinal congestion, when the trouble results from suppression of the menses, or, still more characteristically, from the suppression of a hæmorrhoidal flow. The back is so sensitive that any sudden jarring of the body causes sharp pains along the spine; there is dry heat, particularly in the small of the back, and this is often associated with cold feet.

We also find it indicated in paraplegia, or paralysis of both legs. *Sulphur* has produced this, and it can cure it. I do not think that *Sulphur* is well indicated in far advanced cases resulting from either sclerosis or softening of the cord, or from chronic inflammation of its meninges; but it has done good work in paralysis of both legs, with total retention of urine, and numbness extending up to the umbilicus. When the urine is drawn by the catheter it is found to be turbid and highly offensive. Now *Sulphur* must be given persistently in these cases. I must say that it will not always cure, for many cases are incurable, but it will cure some cases in which the central cause of the trouble is not so chronic, and in which the alterations in the structure of the cord are not so profound but that they can be removed.

General weakness of the spine, not classed under any particular name, has been sometimes cured by *Sulphur*. The patient has the characteristic stoop-shouldered appearance. The chest feels empty and weak; it tires him to talk; there is weakness in the epigastrium during the forenoon. We may also use *Sulphur* when these symptoms occur during convalescence from various acute diseases.

We next have to speak of the action of *Sulphur* on the muscles, ligaments, tendons and joints. *Sulphur* is indicated in acute and chronic rheumatism, particularly the latter, when the inflammatory swellings seem to ascend; that is, they begin in the feet and extend up the body. The pains are worse in bed, and at night. The patient uncovers on account of burning heat of the feet. Especially do we find *Sulphur* useful during the course of acute inflammatory rheumatism for that annoying symptom, jerking of the limbs on falling asleep,

We may also use it in synovitis, particularly after exudation has taken place. *Sulphur* here produces absorption, and very rapidly, too, particularly in the knee.

We come next to study the action of *Sulphur* on the serous membranes. I have already spoken of its use in tubercular meningitis, so I now speak of its action on the pleura. We find *Sulphur* indicated in pleurisy, particularly when you have that sharp stitching pain through the left lung to the back, worse lying on the back, and worse from the least motion. It is also useful in cases that refuse to respond to the well-chosen remedy, particularly when there is well-marked pleuritic effusion. *Apis* is also to be thought of in this condition.

In peritonitis *Sulphur* is indicated more by the general symptoms than by those directly referable to the affected part itself.

We next come to the action of *Sulphur* on the mucous membranes. Here we will consider its use in catarrhs and pneumonia. We find *Sulphur* indicated first of all in conjunctivitis. It is especially useful when the trouble has resulted from a foreign body in the eye, particularly after *Aconite* fails. It is also useful in scrofulous inflammations of the eye, especially with the characteristic tendency of this remedy to congestion. The eyes are red and injected, and there is a feeling as of a splinter of glass in the eye. The inflammation is worse in hot weather. During the winter the child is comparatively free from trouble. This symptom then is due to the relaxing influence of heat. The child is worse when near a hot stove. With the above symptoms to guide us, we may also use *Sulphur* in keratitis. Also when the condition results from the injury or irritation of some foreign body as a grain of sand or a cinder, and *Aconite* has failed to cure.

In nasal catarrh or coryza we find *Sulphur* indicated in those who are subject to catarrhs, especially chronic catarrh, when scabs form in the nasal cavity, the nose bleeds readily, and is swollen, the alæ especially are red and scabby, this redness at the outlet of the nose being quite consistent with the *Sulphur* condition. The nose is "stuffed up" while in doors, but when the patient is out in the open air, breathing is unobstructed.

Coming next to the throat and lungs, we find *Sulphur* indicated in laryngitis and also in bronchial catarrh. Hoarseness is present, and this makes the voice very deep, a sort of basso profundo. In other cases there is aphonia, which is worse in the morning. The more chronic the case is the more is *Sulphur* indicated.

In bronchitis, especially chronic bronchitis, *Sulphur* is indicated when there seems to be an enormous and persistent accumulation of thick muco-pus. The patient suffers from spells of suffocation, with palpitation of the heart. He must have the windows open. The cough is worse when he is lying in a horizontal position, and may then be so violent as to cause nausea and vomiting. *Sulphur* may sometimes prevent pneumonia by relieving the lungs of that hyperæmia which necessarily precedes the deposit of plastic matter. If in the very beginning you give *Sulphur* you will prevent the disease, providing, of course, that remedy is indicated. If you are too late to prevent it you may still use *Sulphur* when exudation has commenced—that is, in the beginning of the stage of solidification. Even then it will modify the course of the disease. Again you may give it in torpid cases to bring about a reaction when resolution will not take place rapidly enough, and you fear the formation of tubercles. You may also use it in pneumonia with typhoid tendency, with slowness of speech, dry tongue, etc., and also at the later stage of pneumonia when the lungs refuse to return to their normal condition and you fear the breaking down of lung tissue. All sorts of râles may be heard in the chest. Expectoration is muco-purulent, the patient has hectic type of fever, loses flesh, etc. *Sulphur* will save the patient. But you should not give it after tubercies have formed. The proper remedy then is *Lachesis*. *Sulphur* is indicated only in the early stages of phthisis. It is seldom indicated in the advanced stages. But in the very incipiency, when you have an increase of blood in the chest, beginning dulness on percussion in the apex of either lung, diminished respiratory movement in the upper portion of the chest, *Sulphur* will, by equalizing the circulation, cure the case.

In affections of the bowels we find *Sulphur* a very useful remedy. You may give it in diarrhœa when these characteristic symptoms are present: the stool changes frequently in color, at one time it is yellow, at another slimy, and at another watery. It may contain undigested food, especially in the case of scrofulous children. It is particularly worse in the morning, driving the patient out of bed.

You may also use it in dysentery, particularly after the tenesmus has ceased, and mucus and blood are still being discharged. It is necessary that you distinguish several other remedies from *Sulphur* in moving diarrhœa.

In the first place, *Bryonia*, which is useful for early morning diarrhœa, which comes on as soon as the patient begins to move about.

Natrum sulphuricum is similar to *Sulphur*, and is oftener required in scrofulous cases. It also has diarrhœa in the morning after getting up and moving about, but the stool is associated with a great deal of flatus.

Another remedy is *Rumex crispus*, which has exactly the same symptom as *Sulphur*—early morning diarrhœa, hurrying the patient out of bed. But it is indicated after catarrhs, with the characteristic cough of *Rumex*.

Still another remedy that is not infrequently confused with *Sulphur* is *Podophyllum*. This has early morning diarrhœa, hurrying the patient out of bed. Like *Sulphur*, the stools are of a changeable color. It differs from *Sulphur* in that the diarrhœa continues through the whole day, although worse at noon. Then, too, with *Sulphur* you will almost always find the tendency to soreness and rawness of the anus.

Phosphorus has morning diarrhœa, with green, painless stool.

Dioscorea also has morning diarrhœa, but it is associated with griping, colicky pains, pretty much of the same character as those calling for *Colocynth*, but they are apt to fly off to other parts of the body, and contrary to *Colocynth* the patient must bend backwards.

I wish now to say a few words about the skin symptoms of *Sulphur*. I have referred to them already in brief, so that I am only supplementing what has already been given to you. You will remember that the skin is apt to be harsh, rough, coarse, and measly in the genuine *Sulphur* patient. There is very little tendency to perspiration, or if there is perspiration, it is only partial, and offensive, sour, or musty. There is tendency to the formation of acne, principally on the face. Pustules form here and there over the body, which heal very slowly, indeed. Freckles are spread plentifully over the face, hands, and arms. There is also a tendency to intertrigo; soreness and rawness appear wherever there is a fold of skin, in the groin, mammæ, or axillæ, or in the folds of the neck.

We find *Sulphur* indicated in that affection known as itch. Now, Hahnemann was the author of the theory that the suppression of itch by external salves, as by sulphur ointment, is responsible for the appearance of many other diseases. He cited hundreds of cases to prove his assertions. Some years after this announcement a Corsican found the little *sarcoptis homines* burrowing beneath the skin and laying its eggs in these burrows. He showed this to be the cause of the itch, and then thought he had effected the complete destruction of the psora theory. But there is another side of the story. A man who is a victim of the "itch" goes along the street and meets two friends, A. and B., with both of whom he shakes hands, and A. contracts the disease while B. escapes. Now, there must be a difference in the constitutions of these individuals, or they would both have taken the itch or both escaped it, for they were both exposed to the same extraneous influences. A.'s system must have been unsound or he could not have taken it, for the itch insect cannot find a suitable dwelling-place in a healthy organization. So, after all, the Corsican's discovery did not overthrow Hahnemann's psoric theory. The term psora is an unfortunate one, but it serves to indicate the constitution which favors the growth of the sarcoptis.

Sulphur is a valuable remedy in this affection, because it conforms so closely to the symptoms of the disease. It has itching in the bends of the joints and between the fingers as soon as the patient gets warm in bed. The skin becomes rough and scaly, and little vesicles form. As the disease progresses, you find occasional pustules appearing here and there over the eruption. Now, in order to rid your patient of this sarcoptis, wash the parts thoroughly in warm water with soap, and then have him rub the skin thoroughly with a common crash towel. Then apply the oil of lavender, which will kill both the eggs and the fully-developed insect without suppressing the disease. Then you may give *Sulphur* or some other indicated remedy internally. If *Sulphur* has been used externally and the itch suppressed, you may have other remedies to choose from.

Give *Mercurius* when pustulous and eczematous eruptions complicate the case.

Give *Sepia* particularly when constitutional symptoms appear. There are occasional large and well-formed pustules, which develop into an impetigo.

Causticum is especially useful when itch has been suppressed by ointments of either mercury or sulphur.

I next wish to say a few words about the action of *Sulphur* on the digestive apparatus. *Sulphur* is useful in disorders of the stomach, liver and intestinal canal. It may be indicated in dyspepsias of many varieties. The particular indications of the drug may be set down as these: first, in a general way, you find it indicated in patients who suffer from abdominal plethora or passive congestion of the portal system, as indicated by a sensation of tightness or fulness in the abdomen, with feeling of repletion after partaking of but a small quantity of food. The liver is congested, enlarged and sore on pressure. The bowels are constipated, with frequent ineffectual urging to stool, and with hæmorrhoids which are the direct results of this abdominal plethora. Constipation frequently alternates with the diarrhœa. In these cases the diarrhœa is not apt to be the early morning diarrhœa of *Sulphur*. This remedy may also be the remedy for gastric ailments arising from the suppression of an eruption, whether that be erysipelas, eczema, itch or the like.

Dyspepsia of drunkards, after excessive use of brandy and beer rather than wines, sometimes calls for *Sulphur*. Here, too, you often find the enlarged or congested liver.

Sulphur is also indicated in dyspepsia from farinaceous food. It seems as if in every case of disease of the liver in which *Sulphur* is indicated, the patient cannot digest farinaceous food, which calls upon the pancreatic juice and bile as well as upon the gastric juice itself. The patient vomits a great deal. He cannot take any milk. If he attempts to do so he vomits it at once. That, as you know, is a common symptom in drunkards. The vomited matters are apt to be sour and mixed with undigested food. In addition to these symptoms you find all sorts of abnormalities of appetite. The patient is hungry at ten or eleven o'clock in the forenoon, even after eating a moderate breakfast. He has goneness, faintness or gnawing feeling in the epigastrium, as if he must have food or sink. When he gets the food and relieves his hunger, he begins to feel puffed up. He feels heavy and sluggish, and so low-spirited that he scarcely cares to live. It will be well to remember that *Sulphur* is indicated not so much in the beginning of these affections as after *Nux vomica*. You find almost exactly the same symptoms under *Nux*. When that remedy only partially relieves, *Sulphur* comes in to complete the cure.

Lachesis should be used in the enlarged liver of drunkards when the case has gone on to a low grade of symptoms, especially if inflammation ensues and abscess forms in the liver.

If the liver wastes away, secondarily to the congestion, we must depend upon the other remedies, the most important of which are *Phosphorus* and *Laurocerasus*, the former especially if there is fatty degeneration of the liver substance.

Next, a word or two in regard to *Sulphur* in diseases of the sexual organs. There is a trio of medicines, *Nux vomica*, *Sulphur* and *Calcarea*, which are useful in cases of masturbation and excessive venery. Beginning with *Nux* you note some improvement in the patient; by and by you will find symptoms of *Sulphur* presenting themselves. If *Sulphur* fails after producing partial relief, *Calcarea* completes the cure. The symptoms calling for *Sulphur* are these: you will find the patient weak and debilitated, having many of the gastric ailments that I have mentioned, particularly faintness, flushes of heat, cold feet and heat on the top of the head. There is frequent involuntary emission of semen at night, exhausting him the next morning. The seminal flow is thin and watery, and almost inodorous, and has lost all its characteristic properties, being nothing more than a shadow of the normal seminal secretion. The genital organs are relaxed; the scrotum and testicles hang flabbily; the penis is cold, and erections are few and far between. If coitus is attempted, semen escapes too soon, almost at the first contact. The patient suffers from backache and weakness of the limbs, so that he can scarcely walk. He is, of course, low-spirited and hypochondriacal.

You may find *Sulphur* indicated in gonorrhœa, whether the discharge be thick and purulent, or thin and watery, when there are burning and smarting during urination, and when there is this bright redness of the lips of the meatus urinarius. *Sulphur* may also be used when phimosis occurs, especially when there is inflammation and induration of the prepuce.

Sulphur also acts on the female genital organs. The main symptoms it produces are those which come from congestion of these organs. They are associated with flushes of heat and abdominal plethora; there are bearing down and weight in the uterine region, a feeling of fulness and heaviness there, standing is a very annoying position to her, and there is burning in the vagina, often in association with pruritus and appearance of papules on the mons veneris.

The nearest remedy to *Sulphur* here is *Aloes*, which produces precisely the same symptoms, the same bearing down, the same fulness of the abdomen from abdominal plethora. *Sulphur* has, in addition to the above symptoms, aversion to washing. *Aloes* acts more on the rectum than on any other portion of the alimentary tract. There is a constant desire for stool. When stool is expelled it is accompanied by a great deal of flatus. The hæmorrhoids of *Aloes* protrude like bunches of grapes, and are always relieved by cold water.

In closing my remarks on *Sulphur,* I want to mention two or three uses you can make of the crude article. *Sulphur* has in its totality of symptoms a perfect picture of cholera Asiatica. It suits the incipient symptoms. It bears a resemblance to the course of the disease, and also to the subsequent symptoms. We have, then, in *Sulphur* a true prophylactic of that dreaded epidemic. It may be used by placing a little flowers of sulphur inside of the stockings, as recommended by Dr. Hering several years ago. This sulphur is absorbed, as shown by the exhalation of sulphuretted hydrogen with the sweat.

Flowers of sulphur burnt in a closed room may be used as a disinfectant.

LECTURE XLVI.

THE CARBON GROUP.

Carbo animalis (contains phosphate of lime)
Carbo vegetabilis (contains carbonate of potash)
Graphites (contains iron).
Aniline sulphate.
Carboneum (Lampblack).
Coal gas.
Bisulphide of Carbon.

I invite your attention this morning to the medicines obtained from the carbon group. Carbon in its purity is found only in the diamond. We have it comparatively pure, however, in lampblack, or *Carboneum*. Carbon will necessarily be somewhat different in its action, according to the source from which we obtained it. Hahnemann used principally three carbons, *Carbo animalis*, *Carbo vegetabilis* and *Graphites*. The first he derived from the animal kingdom, the second from the vegetable, while the last was an artificial product found principally lining the interior of large iron retorts. *Carbo animalis* is obtained principally from bones. It contains some phosphate of lime. *Carbo veg*. contains some carbonate of potash. It is obtained principally from a variety of the beech-tree. *Graphites* is always contaminated with more or less iron. Hence you see that these are not pure carbons. I have also placed on the board the *Sulphate of Aniline*, which behaves like a carbon and is a carbonaceous compound. Then, too, we have *Carboneum* and *Carbonic oxide*. *Carbonic acid* gas does not seem to possess active medicinal properties. It is not very poisonous. Its main deleterious effects are due to deprivation of oxygen. *Carbonic oxide* is much more poisonous, producing death, not only by suffocation, by displacing the needed oxygen, but by another remarkable peculiarity. It has the property or peculiarity of displacing oxygen from the blood and taking its place there. You know that oxygen is carried along in the blood by the red corpuscles. *Carbonic oxide* has the power of supplanting the oxygen in these structures. For a time, it seems to act like oyxgen, but soon its poisonous properties are manifested with all the inevitable results of asphyxia. Coal gas, which we obtain by slow combustion of coal, and the illuminating gas used in our large cities, are of this character. They produce serious effects when taken in large quantities, especially when the subject is deprived of the ordinary atmosphere. It is said that this coal gas is beneficial in the treatment of whooping-cough. I have known of but one case thus treated, and that one died. *Bisulphide of Carbon*, which has also been proved has some valuable symptoms.

Now, all of the carbonaceous substances have some properties in common. For instance, they all have a tendency to relieve putrescence or putrid discharges or putrid exhalations from the body and offensive sores. You all know the mechanical properties of charcoal, what an absorbent it is, and how it can purify the atmosphere or substances that are undergoing decomposition. The animal charcoal, which is more porous, is here more effectual than the vegetable. If you bury a dead rat or mouse in charcoal for several months, you will not find any odor from decomposed tissue at the end of that time, but only a clean white skeleton. But this property, I would have you know, is not entirely mechanical. In the potencies, it may be exemplified in the human system. Now I do not mean that potentized charcoal will remove the odor from a decomposing animal, but I do say, that in a potentized state it exerts similar effects on the human system.

All the carbons act also on the skin, producing excoriations and intertrigo. They affect the glands also, causing enlargement and induration of the axillary and other lymphatic glands, even as in the case of *Carbo veg.* and *Carbo animalis*, simulating cancerous enlargement and infiltration. They all affect the mucous membranes, producing catarrhs of the nose, throat and lungs, and also of the bowels. They all tend to produce asphyxia. We find this prominently in *Carbo veg.*, less so in the *Carbo animalis*, and very marked in *Aniline* and *Carboneum*. *Carboneum* may produce asphyxia with convulsions simulating those of epilepsy. Coal gas and *Carbonic oxide*, too, are calculated to produce dyspnœa from deprivation of oxygen. We find, also, that all the carbons act on the veins, producing varicose veins. We find, too, that all the carbons tend to produce flatulence This is one of the reasons why I object to toast as an article of diet for the sick. Toast, when the bread is nicely dried through by gentle and continuous heat, is very beneficial, but when it is charred, it tends to produce flatulence. The flatus is offensive and has an odor like that of rotten eggs.

CARBO VEGETABILIS.

Carbo veg.
- Ars., China, Phos., Phos. ac.
- In collapse, Camph., Veratr. alb.
- Caust., Kali c., Sulph.
- Paralysis of lungs: Ant. tart., Ammon. c., Baryt. c., Mosch., Nitr. ac., Lauroc., Lach., Opium.
- Kali c., Phos.
- Bry., Nux v., Puls., etc.

As I have already intimated to you, *Carbo veg.* contains some carbonate of potash. It is also a fact worthy of note that *Kali carb.* is complementary to *Carbo veg.*, especially in lung and throat affections and also in dyspepsia. *Carbo veg.* is also complementary to *Phosphorus*, here, too, in chest affections, in the throat more than anywhere else and, in excessive debility, particularly in the threatened paralysis of the whole system as a sequel to severe disease. The drug is antidoted by *Arsenicum* and *Camphor*, and holds an inimical relation with *Causticum*. The inimical relation between *Carbo veg.* and *Causticum* is not so marked as that between the latter remedy and *Phosphorus*.

Carbo veg. is especially indicated in patients who are advanced in life, and consequently debilitated. It is called for in weak, delicate persons who are old dyspeptics, especially if they have abused their digestive organs by debauchery.

In analyzing the drug we will speak first of its effects on the blood. We find *Carbo veg.* indicated in affections in which the composition of the blood is decidedly changed. There is decided sepsis or blood poisoning in many of the diseases in which *Carbo veg.* is the remedy. We find the drug indicated in hæmorrhages, hæmorrhages, too, of a very low type. Thus we give it in epistaxis or nose-bleed when the face is pale and sunken and almost hippocratic. The blood flows persistently for hours, perhaps for days. It is dark and rather fluid. It is apt to occur in old and rather debilitated persons and during the course of diphtheria. You find nearly the same symptoms under *Camphor* and *Mercurius cyanatus*.

We also find *Carbo veg.* indicated in hæmorrhages from the lungs, not only in hæmoptysis but also in bronchorrhagia. In these cases the patient suffers from great anxiety and yet without any particular restlessness. The anxiety is very evident in the face and in the efforts at breathing, but there is no particular restless tossing about. The patient complains of burning pain in the chest. *Carbo veg.* is to be used especially in well advanced cases of lung degeneration. The pulse in these cases is apt to be intermittent and thready, the face is pale and often covered with cold sweat. The patient wants to be fanned, because fanning brings more air to the lungs.

These same symptoms indicate *Carbo veg.* in hæmorrhages from the uterus, whether metrorrhagia or menorrhagia. Here, again, you find marked burning pains across the sacrum and lower portion of the spine. If the hæmorrhage continues any length of time you will notice the same trouble in the chest, with the difficulty in breathing above mentioned.

Carbo veg. will here work hand in hand with *Cinchona* and *Arsenicum*. *Arsenicum* is useful in these persistent hæmorrhages of a low type, depending upon some degeneration in the organ affected. Both it and *Carbo veg.* have these violent burning pains. With the *Arsenicum*, however, you have, as a distinction which applies in all conditions, irritability of fibre and mind, which is not the case with *Carbo veg.* *Carbo veg.* is a torpid, sluggish remedy, while *Arsenicum* has irritability, with restless tossing about, anxiety, etc.

Ipecacuanha should also be remembered in hæmorrhages, especially in hæmorrhages from the lungs and uterus, when the patient takes long breaths, as if panting. Unless there is present coldness, amounting almost to collapse, you may prefer to begin with this drug rather than with *Carbo veg.* or *Cinchona.*

Next we find *Carbo veg.* useful in varicose veins which occur on either the arms or legs, or even on the female genital organs. These varicose veins tend to ulcerate. They are bluish or livid, looking as though the blood had long remained in them. In the resultant varicose ulcers you will find very similar symptoms to those in other ulcers in which *Carbo veg.* is the remedy; burning pains, and mottled appearance of the surrounding skin as though the smaller veins had become enlarged. Ecchymoses are seen beneath the skin. The ulcers have a decidedly indolent appearance.

Carbo veg. is also useful in ulcers other than varicose when they are of a very low type. They are flat, tending rather to spread on the surface than to dip deeply into the parenchyma. They discharge not a laudable pus, but instead that which is ichorous, corrosive, thin, burning and offensive in character. The burning is worse at night, depriving the patient of sleep and keeping him in torture the whole night. Even in cancerous ulcers, as in ulcerating scirrhus, you will find *Carbo veg.* useful.

It may also be administered in carbuncle, particularly when the affected parts are bluish or livid, and when the discharges are offensive and associated with burning pains. In these cases it is not only your duty to give it internally, but also to apply it externally as a plaster. It tends to prevent decomposition of fluids, sweetens the sore and so prevents poisoning of the system. The same is true for gangrene. When carbuncles or boils become gangrenous, *Carbo veg.* may be indicated. In these cases it is distinguished from *Arsenicum* by the absence of this extreme restlessness.

In febrile conditions, *Carbo veg.* is useful for the typhoid and intermittent types of fever, for collapse during fever, and for yellow fever. It is a preventive of yellow fever just as *Sulphur* is of cholera. If all the ejecta of the patient are buried in charcoal, the spread of the disease will surely be prevented. When the disease is fully established, *Carbo veg.* is of no more use than *Sulphur* is during the course of cholera.

The intermittent type of fever in which you may employ *Carbo veg.* is of a low grade. The case is one of long standing, and has been abused by quinine. There is thirst during the chill. The feet are icy-cold up to the knee a very characteristic symptom of *Carbo veg.* When the heat comes, it is in burning flashes. The sweat is either sour or else exceedingly offensive from alterations in the discharges of the skin. During the apyrexia the patient is pale and weak. Memory is weak; the mind seems to be befogged. The patient is decidedly low-spirited and melancholy.

In the hectic type of fever, *Carbo veg.* is indicated by pretty much the same symptoms as those which I have already mentioned. It is particularly useful for hectic fever dependent upon long-lasting suppuration, whether due to abscess in the lungs, or in the hip-joint, or about the vertebræ. *Menyanthes* is the remedy in quartan fever when the legs below the knees are icy-cold

You know that abscesses accompanying diseases of the spine may have to be opened. Sometimes surgeons are afraid to do this before they have prepared the system for it, because reaction is so slow that the patient may not survive. The danger from opening these abscesses may be greatly lessened by the use of *Carbo veg*. or *Cinchona*, according to the particular indications.

In collapse from various causes you may use *Carbo veg*. There is decided lack of animal heat. The nose, cheeks and extremities are cold. It is indicated in the late stages of typhoid fever; after protracted loss of vital fluids, as after long-lasting hæmorrhages; during cholera Asiatica; during pneumonia; and, in fact, in any form of disease in which these symptoms appear. The body may be icy-cold, especially about the extremities; the breath is cool; the pulse is thread-like, scarcely perceptible and intermittent. The lips may be bluish from cyanosis. Breathing is very weak and superficial; the patient may be either conscious or unconscious. Now, *Carbo veg*. in just such cases comes in as a savior, and rescues many a case that would otherwise die.

There are other remedies similar to *Carbo veg*. in collapse. *Camphor*, especially, is similar to it in cholera Asiatica, but it is indicated rather in the beginning of cholera without any vomiting or diarrhœa; when the poison seems to have depressed or shocked the nervous system, so that the patient is icy-cold, dry or in a cold sweat; the tongue is cold. If he can speak it is in a squeaky or in a high-pitched voice, or else it is a husky, toneless voice. *Camphor*, in such cases, brings about reaction very quickly. *Carbo veg*. would be indicated in the later stage, when the prostration is the result of the drain on the system by the alvine discharges.

Veratrum album is also similar to *Carbo veg*. in collapse. It has cramps in the calves of the legs, the thighs and the chest, and characteristically cold sweat on the forehead.

I wish next to say a word about the action of *Carbo veg*. on glands. The glands, especially the mammæ, become indurated. There are burning pains in the swollen glands, with tendency to suppuration. When they do suppurate, the discharged pus is not of a laudable character.

We find *Carbo veg*. indicated in catarrhal troubles which are provoked by warm moist atmosphere, such as we have in this latitude with southwest or southerly winds. The patient is worse in the evening or less characteristically in the morning. He has aphonia recurring regularly each evening, painless or associated with raw feeling down the larynx and trachea. There is dry tickling cough, at times quite spasmodic in character.

It is here analogous to *Phosphorus*, and is often preceded or followed by that remedy. The *Phosphorus* aphonia is associated with rawness of the larynx, and is worse in the evening.

In the morning aphonia, *Carbo veg.* is more closely allied to *Sulphur*, which has loss of voice, particularly in the morning.

Still another concordant remedy is *Causticum*, which is suited to laryngeal catarrh in singers with rough hoarse voice, associated with tracheo-bronchial catarrh, and rawness and burning under the sternum. This group is found under both remedies. The main difference is that *Causticum* has hoarseness worse in the morning, and *Carbo veg.* in the evening. *Causticum* has aggravation in dry, cold weather, and *Carbo veg.* in a damp warm atmosphere.

Another remedy is *Eupatorium perfoliatum*, which I use for hoarseness with soreness in the larynx, trachea and bronchial tubes. The hoarseness is worse in the morning, and is apt to be associated with aching all over the body.

Carbo veg. may also be used in asthma, particularly in the asthma of old people and of people who are very much debilitated. They look, during the asthmatic attack, as if they would die, so oppressed are they for breath. They are greatly relieved by belching wind. It is especially indicated in asthma which is reflex from accumulation of flatus in the abdomen.

It may also be used in threatening paralysis of the lungs in typhoid fever, after pneumonia, and in old people. The "paralytic catarrh" of old people calls for *Carbo veg.* There are loose rattling râles when the patient coughs or breathes, a marked symptom of emphysema. The bronchial tubes are greatly dilated. In addition to this you will find coldness, symptoms of collapse, etc.

The nearest approach to *Carbo veg.* in emphysema is *Ammonium carb.*, which, like *Carbo veg.*, has blood poisoned by carbonic acid, giving you the coldness, blueness, etc., incident to that condition.

In threatened paralysis of the lungs, we have a great many remedies to consider, most of which I will reserve until we come to speak of *Phosphorus*, which stands very close to *Carbo veg.* Then, too, you should also remember *Moschus* and *Antimonium tartaricum*.

Antimonium tartaricum applies when there are loud râles heard in the chest. It seems as if there was an immense amount of mucus there, and yet the patient can scarcely raise any of it. The extremities are cold and blue from the cyanosis developed by the blood poisoning.

The patient soon becomes drowsy and passes into a stupor from which he can be aroused, but into which he readily relapses. You should also remember *Antimonium tartaricum* when, in the course of lung affections, whether there be bronchiectasia or catarrh on the chest in children (and here it is especially called for), the cough ceases or becomes more rare and yet there is no diminution in the mucus-production itself. Your practiced ear placed on the chest detects just as copious an exudation, and just as much rattling of phlegm in the lungs, and yet the child does not cough so frequently. The mother thinks the child is better, but in reality it is worse, for the lungs are losing their power.

Carbo veg. is an excellent remedy for the terrible dyspnœa of chronic aortitis, especially when the patient has become very anæmic, dropsical, etc. Here you should compare *Arsenicum*, *Cuprum* and *Lachesis*.

Still further, I want to speak of the action of *Carbo veg.* on the stomach and bowels. We find it here, rivalling other well-known remedies in dyspepsia or indigestion, and those of a rather low type, too. We find it indicated, too, for the bad effects of debauchery, for excessive indulgence in table luxuries, and for bad effects from wines and liquors and all kinds of dissipation. As a result of dissipation, we may have just such symptoms as call for *Carbo veg.* headache, particularly in the morning when the patient awakens from sleep, having spent the best part of the night carousing; dull headache referred to the back part of the head, with a great deal of confusion of mind. There is humming or buzzing in the head as though a hornet's nest had taken its place there. The patient feels worse in the warm room. The pain also seems to go from the occiput through the head and into and over the eyes, with dull heavy aching in that region. There are nausea and usually a sort of burning distress and weakness referred to the epigastrium. He is unable to take any fat food, whether meat, gravy or fried food. He cannot drink milk because it produces flatulence. After eating the stomach feels heavy, as if it were dragged down. The abdomen is distended with flatus and both belchings and borborygmi are offensive. The wind belched has a rancid or putrid taste, and a decidedly offensive odor when passed from the bowels. He suffers from constipation with piles. The piles get worse every time he is on a spree; oozing of moisture from anus; perineum, sore, itching.* Sometimes they protrude and are bluish, they are so distended with blood. At other times, he has morning diarrhœa with stool which is very watery and thin and accompanied by a great deal of straining. We find *Carbo veg.* particularly indicated here after the failure of *Nux vomica.* The patient is peevish, easily angered. Vertigo reflex from the gastric disturbance is present. It is especially worse after a debauch and excessive indulgence in high living. It is often associated with syncope, especially at meals or after eating.

The nearest concordant remedy here is *Arsenicum.* Both remedies have bluish protruding piles, both have burning in the epigastrium, both have anxiety, and both are suitable for the bad effects of ice-cream, and ice-water in hot weather. The difference may be expressed in these few words: *Carbo veg.* is torpid, *Arsenicum* is always irritable; of the two remedies, *Carbo veg.* has the burning most marked especially in internal parts, as in the stomach.

Nux vomica impinges on *Carbo veg.* in the bad effects of over-eating and high living. As I have already said, *Carbo veg.* comes in when *Nux* has ceased to act. The *Nux* toper is a thin, spare, yellow, wiry fellow. That of *Carbo veg.* is sluggish, stout and lazy.

Next we are to distinguish *Carbo veg.* from *Cinchona.* This is easily done, because the two drugs meet only in the flatulent dyspepsia and in debility. *Cinchona* is suited to a peculiar functional debility, when the system is devitalized by loss of animal fluids. *Carbo veg.* is the better remedy when the debility arises from organic causes, and we have a picture of collapse with hippocratic face and coldness of the body, particularly of the knees. Both remedies produce great flatulence. *Cinchona*, however, does not have the rancid belching with burning. Belching temporarily relieves the symptoms in *Carbo veg.* In *Cinchona* they sometimes seem to be worse therefrom.

Lycopodium also typifies perfectly this state of tympanites. The abdomen is enormously distended. The distinction to be made is this: *Carbo veg.* produces more flatulence of the bowels, *Lycopodium* more of the stomach. Again, *Carbo veg.* produces rancid belching, or else passage of offensive flatus, with bitter taste in the mouth. *Lycopodium* has more of a sour taste with its belching.

---

* *Perineum, moist, raw, oozing,* etc.; Ammon. c., Alum, Natr. m., CARBO V., CARBO A., NITR. AC., GRAPH (and cracked), SULPH., *Rhus tox.*, *Arsenic.*, ANT. CR. (mucous piles), THUJA (offensive oozing), SILICEA (moist), *Sulphuric acid*, *Capsic.*, Petroleum (see also Fissures), *Borax* (slimy, purulent oozing), *Sepia* (oozing).

Carbo veg. may be indicated in dysentery. Here it is called for in very severe cases. There are burning pains situated deep in the abdomen, usually in one or the other of the bends of the colon. The abdomen is greatly distended and tympanitic. The pulse is weak and intermittent. The discharges from the bowels are horribly offensive and brown, watery and slimy in appearance. You see what a desperate case we have here, one that calls for great skill in prescribing. Here you must distinguish between two other remedies and *Carbo veg.*, namely, *Arsenicum* and *Cinchona*.

Arsenicum helps when there is, as I have said, that irritability of fibre. The patient is just as sick and just as near death's door as is the *Carbo veg.* patient, but he is restless, and complains of burning thirst and yet exhibits an intolerance of water. The discharges from the bowels are about the same in character under the two remedies. *Arsenic*, however, has less tympanitic distension of the abdomen.

Cinchona and *Carbo veg.* are also similar in these cases. Both have these dark offensive fluid discharges, both have the distension of the abdomen, both have great weakness and hippocratic face. With *Cinchona*, however, the movements from the bowels are provoked by every attempt to eat or drink. Belching gives but temporary relief. Again, the flatus is not so offensive as with *Carbo veg.*, nor are the burning pains so marked as under *Carbo veg.* or *Arsenicum*.

LECTURE XLVII.

CARBO ANIMALIS, GRAPHITES AND PETROLEUM.

Carbo Animalis.

Carbo animalis. $\begin{cases} \text{Bromine.} \\ \text{Sepia, Natr. m.} \\ \text{Silic., Phos.} \\ \text{Badiaga.} \\ \text{Merc. iod., Nitr. ac.} \end{cases}$

↓

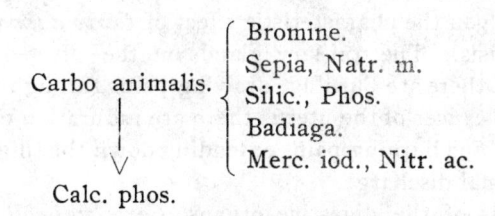

Calc. phos.

CARBO ANIMALIS and *Carbo veg.* do not follow each other well. They are so far inimical that one may not be given with benefit after the other. They are too nearly alike. *Carbo animalis* contains some phosphate of lime. *Carbo animalis* is complementary to *Calcarea phosphorica*, especially in affections of the glands.

Carbo animalis is suited to old persons and to those who are greatly debilitated by disease, especially when there is a predominance of what is known as venous plethora. You find such patients particularly inclined to blueness of the skin. The hands and feet readily become blue, with distended veins showing through the skin. They become ill from very slight causes. The cheeks often get bluish. Both remedies are indicated in decomposition of tissue of the body, as in gangrene and ulcerations of the surface or of internal parts, with putrid discharges. Both, too, are indicated in weakness of the digestive organs, both are indicated for the bad effects of loss of animal fluids, particularly during lactation.

Now, as a general distinction between the two drugs, you may remember this: although both drugs act on the glands, the predominance is in favor of the *Carbo animalis* for glandular affections. For instance, we find it indicated in induration of glands, of the axillary glands and of the glands in the groin, particularly in syphilitic or gonorrhœal patients. These buboes are hard like stone: *Carbo animalis* is especially useful when these have been opened too soon, and when there is a gaping wound which has partly healed, leaving the surrounding tissues of an almost stony hardness.

Badiaga rivals *Carbo animalis* in just these cases, particularly in indurated buboes that have been maltreated.

Again, we find *Carbo animalis* indicated in cancer more frequently than *Carbo veg.;* particularly is it useful in cancer of the breast or of the uterus. In mammary cancer you have the glands indurated in little nodes; or small circumscribed portions which are as hard as stone. Later the skin around the induration becomes bluish and mottled, thus showing you the characteristic effect of *Carbo animalis* in producing venous stasis. The axillary glands on the affected side become indurated and there are burning, drawing pains through the mammæ. In the case of cancer of the uterus there are induration of the cervix, metrorrhagia, and burning pains extending down the thighs, and thin, offensive vaginal discharge.

In affections of the digestive organs, *Carbo animalis* differs from *Carbo veg.* in this: we find that under *Carbo animalis* there is goneness and empty feeling in the pit of the stomach, not relieved by eating, and in this respect it is very similar to *Sepia*.

We find these symptoms indicating *Carbo animalis* in preference to *Carbo veg.* in the weakness of nursing women; we notice that every particle of food taken distresses the stomach, just as we found under *Carbo veg.*, but with *Carbo animalis* there is coldness about the stomach, which is relieved by pressing firmly with the hand or by friction over the abdomen, thus showing you the weak debilitated condition in which the patient is, who requires this remedy. *Carbo veg.* has dragging heaviness about the stomach to distinguish it. Both remedies have piles with this weak digestion, but there is oozing of a thin, inodorous fluid from the rectum in *Carbo animalis* which does not exist as markedly under *Carbo veg.*

Both drugs meet again in affections of the chest. We find them both indicated in the late stages of pneumonia, bronchitis, or of phthisis pulmonalis, when there is destruction of the lung tissue and decomposition of the fluid which is expectorated. It is just here that you are most liable to make a mistake in selecting one drug for the other. *Carbo animalis* has this symptom to distinguish it, suffocating hoarse cough producing shaking of the brain as though the brain were loose in the head. And a cold feeling in the chest. Expectoration is green, purulent and horribly offensive, and comes generally from the right lung, in which you probably will find by examination, a cavity. As soon as the patient closes his eyes he feels as if he were smothering.

Other remedies having cold sensation in the chest are: *Bromine*, *Paris quad.* and *Camphor.*

The *Carbo veg.* cough is spasmodic, with deep, rough voice or else with aphonia. There is decided burning in the chest and expectoration is profuse, particularly in the bronchitis of old people. It is yellow and very fœtid, more so than in *Carbo animalis.* The patient has dyspnœa, worse on turning over in bed and on dropping off to sleep. There is a great deal of rattling in the chest.

Carbo animalis is more useful than *Carbo veg.* in constitutional syphilis, and for this reason: while both may be indicated in constitutional or tertiary syphilis, after the abuse of mercury, particularly when the glands are affected, and there is great emaciation. *Carbo animalis* is indicated more by these symptoms: it has coppery-red blotches on the skin, particularly on the face. That you know to be the characteristic hue of syphilitic eruptions. In this respect it resembles *Mercurius bin.*, *Nitric acid* and *Badiaga* more than it does *Carbo veg.*

In debility we find *Carbo veg.* always superior to *Carbo animalis.* There are very few characteristic symptoms indicating the latter as a remedy in the last stages of typhoid fever, pneumonia and scarlatina. The only difficulty you will have in deciding between the two drugs will be in the debility attendant upon lactation.

In affections of the ears we find *Carbo veg.* and *Carbo animalis* again meeting. Thus, we find both drugs causing otorrhœa. The discharge is thin, ichorous, bloody and excoriating in both remedies. With *Carbo animalis* there is also associated a swelling of the periosteum behind the ears over the mastoid process. Here it is similar to *Nitric acid*, *Aurum* and *Capsicum*. With *Carbo veg.* we find this otorrhœa particularly as a sequel to exanthematous diseases, as measles and scarlatina. There is no swelling of the periosteum back of the ear. Both remedies are indicated in deafness. *Carbo animalis* has this peculiar symptom: they cannot tell whence sound comes. *Carbo veg.* is indicated in deafness when the ears are too dry from the absence of the cerumen or wax, or when there is discharge of offensive cerumen.

In eye affections we find *Carbo animalis* indicated when the patient is far-sighted; while walking along the street objects seem to him to be far off. The eyes seem as if they were loose in their sockets. This feeling is due to relaxation in the connective tissue similar to that found in the brain. Old people have dimness of sight on attempting to read, but this is relieved by rubbing the eyes.

Carbo veg. is indicated when the patient is near-sighted; objects have to be placed near to the eye to be seen. This symptom is worse after exerting the eyes or after using them steadily for any length of time.

GRAPHITES.

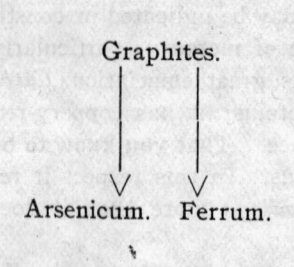

Graphites.
∨ ∨
Arsenicum. Ferrum.

{ Sepia, Pulsatilla.
Kali carb., Phosphorus, Calcarea ostr.
Sulphur, Lycopodium, Silicea, Hepar.
Phytolacca.
Mezereum, Petroleum, Iris, Rhus.
Mercurius, Antimon. crudum.
Staphisagria.
Ratanhia, Pæonia, Nitric acid. }

Graphites.
{ Slight erethism; then weak, relaxed, anæmic; chlorotic.
Fat, chilly, costive; lymphatic glands swollen.
Skin: cracked, rhagades, fissures, herpes, eczema, oozing of scanty gluey humor.
Cicatrices are softened.
Mucous membranes: scanty secretion, cracks, fissures, etc. }

Graphites is not a pure carbon. Even the purest specimens of it contain some iron. You will note that I have placed beneath it two complements, namely, *Arsenicum* and *Ferrum*. It has many symptoms in common with *Ferrum*, acting complementary to that drug, and many more allying it to *Arsenicum*.

It is a relative of *Ferrum*, principally in that class of symptoms belonging to anæmia or chlorosis of females, such as irregularities in the distribution of the blood, and pallor of both skin and mucous membranes.

It is complementary to *Arsenic* in many of the skin symptoms, in affections of the glands, burning in internal parts, etc. Besides these complementary remedies, *Graphites* has quite a number of concordant remedies. It is antidoted by *Arsenicum*, and in some of its gastric symptoms by *Nux vomica*. *Arsenicum*, you thus see, holds two relations to *Graphites;* one of antidote and one of complement. It is complementary in one series of effects, and antidotal in another. It antidotes especially the mental symptoms of *Graphites*.

The *Graphites* patient is sad and full of grief, particularly if a female. She has an anxious, apprehensive state of mind. She has forebodings of some imaginary accident or mishap which is about to take place; and this makes her anxious and restless; impelling her to move about from place to place; she cannot be kept quiet. It is this group of symptoms which *Arsenicum* antidotes. We find this anxious, apprehensive state of mind in *Graphites* to be a very important symptom. You all know how important in making a homœopathic prescription the mental symptoms are. We find this apprehensiveness, this low spiritedness, qualifying many of the *Graphites* conditions. We see it in the chlorosis, in the skin symptoms, in the inflammations of the eye, etc., as you will discover later on.

We find *Graphites* acting best in constitutions in which there is a tendency to obesity. This obesity, I would have you remember, is not the healthy, solid flesh, that belongs to a full-blooded, strong, hearty individual, but it is of the kind which you find under *Calcarea ostrearum*, showing improper nutrition. The two remedies run close to each other in these fat but unhealthy individuals. The *Graphites* constitution is also one in which there is deficient animal heat, owing to the defective oxygenation of the blood. These patients are always cold, whether they are in or out of doors. The circulation is at first excited, followed by loss of energy and consequent venous hyperæmia. Syncope readily occurs, with great anxiety. Motion is impaired and tissues are relaxed, but paralysis is not complete. In the case of chlorosis, the *Graphites* patient has these symptoms: there is a tendency to rush of blood to the head, with flushing of the face, exactly like that which belongs to *Ferrum*. The patient feels a sudden shock about the heart, and this is followed by rush of blood to the head. She thinks she has heart disease. On lying down at night, she experiences throbbing all through the body. That is not due to true plethora. The blood is decidedly "watery," and, if you were to examine it microscopically, you would find an excessive number of white blood corpuscles. The menstrual flow in these cases is too late, too pale and too scanty. The mucous membranes are apt to be pale, just as you find under *Ferrum*. The lips are pale. There is leucorrhœa, which is watery and quite profuse, sometimes excoriating the parts over which it flows.

Now, you may say, how are we going to distinguish this from *Pulsatilla?* Like *Graphites*, *Pulsatilla* has late and scanty menses, with pale or dark flow in chlorotic or anæmic patients; also in patients who are apt to be chilly, and who are low-spirited, crying at every imaginary trouble. How will you distinguish between these remedies? The main distinction lies in this: the *Graphites* patient always has some skin symptoms to aid us, *Pulsatilla* scarcely any. The *Graphites* patient has a rough, harsh, dry skin, with very little tendency to sweat. Little pimples, whether containing pus or not, appear on the body, and are apt to be worse at the menstrual periods. While in *Pulsatilla* there is strong tendency to diarrhœa, in *Graphites* there is strong tendency to constipation. These symptoms are sufficient to always enable you to distinguish between these two closely allied remedies.

Next, as most important in our study of *Graphites*, I wish to call your attention to the action of the remedy on the lymphatic glands, and also upon the skin. It produces enlargement of the lymphatic glands, of the neck and of the axillæ and also of the inguinal and of the mesenteric glands. This, together with marked skin symptoms, calls frequently for its use in scrofula. Now, we find it running parallel with *Calcarea ostrearum*, *Sulphur* and *Silicea* in scrofulosis, particularly of children. We find the abdomen large and hard. The children thus affected suffer from diarrhœa, with stools which are thin, offensive and contain partially digested food.

In inflammation of the eyes, of a scrofulous character, we have no remedy, not even *Calcarea*, *Sulphur* or *Arsenic*, that excels *Graphites*. The cornea is apt to be covered with superficial ulcers, or again, it may be inflamed. There is thickening of the eyelids, particularly along the edges, which are covered with scurf or scales. The lids may be agglutinated or not, but the grand characteristic which makes the choice of *Graphites* certain is this: the blepharitis is worse in the angles of the eye, in the canthi. If there is tendency for the edges of the lids to crack and bleed, you need not hesitate to use *Graphites*. The thickening of the cartilages of the lids may be so great as to produce ectropion or entropion. Then, too, the eyelashes become wild, turn in towards the ball of the eye and irritate the conjunctiva. Hardened styes may appear along the edges of the lids. *Graphites* also affects the vision. Letters appear double and run together. An eczematous eruption appears about the eyes, on the cheeks, on and behind the ears, on the top of the head and down the occiput. It may also be scattered here and there over the surface of the body, particularly in the bends of the joints. Behind the ears it assumes the form of intertrigo, being moist and sticky. If the child lies on its ear, the ear will be glued fast to the head. Sometimes you find *Graphites* indicated in phlyctenular ophthalmia. Little vesicles form on the cornea and on other parts of the eye, producing profuse, burning lachrymation. These tears are mixed with pus, which is thin, and excoriates the cheek over which it flows. The discharge from the nose, which is partly from the eye by the way of the puncta lachrymali, is also thin and excoriating, and you find cracks and crusts around the nostrils quite in harmony with the condition of the borders of the eyelids.

I would now like to mention briefly a few of the distinctions between *Graphites* and its allied remedies. *Petroleum* or coal-oil is similar to *Graphites* in many of its symptoms. It has an eruption very much like that of *Graphites* and is particularly indicated when the most marked symptom is an intertrigo behind the ears. If the child is old enough, he will also complain of aching and other painful symptoms in the back of the head. The main distinction between the two remedies is that *Graphites* pictures more of a herpes and *Petroleum* a pure eczema.

In prescribing *Calcarea ostrearum* the local symptoms, particularly those of the eyes, do not help you much. They are too general. They are just the symptoms of scrofulous ophthalmia. But you would be aided in your selection of the drug by its general symptoms, sweat of the head and cold, damp feet which are not prominent under *Graphites*. You may also remember that *Calcarea ostrearum* is the best remedy for the results of scrofulous ophthalmia, rather than the acute symptoms themselves. It is best suited to the opacities of the cornea and the thickening of the lids.

Arsenicum has the same burning, excoriating discharge from the eyes, but is distinguished by this: the lids are spasmodically closed. Otherwise the symptoms are provokingly similar.

Sulphur will help you when the edges of the lids are redder than natural, while under *Graphites* the edges of the lids are paler than they ought to be.

Euphrasia is useful in phlyctenular ophthalmia with excoriating discharge, etc. But although the discharge is excoriating under *Euphrasia* it is also thick and purulent, while under *Graphites* it is thin.

Mercurius is also useful in scrofulous cases, especially when the patient is worse at night and from the heat and glare of the fire. *Mercurius* is decidedly preferable if syphilis complicates scrofulosis.

Hepar is very similar indeed to *Graphites*. It is preferable when there is throbbing in and about the eye. Now even if the child is not old enough to describe its symptoms you will notice from its actions that there is pain and you will see evidence of the formation of pus; for instance, suppurating styes form on the lids. *Hepar* suits the suppurative process better than does *Graphites*. You will also notice that the *Hepar* child will not allow anything to press on the eye, because the parts are so sensitive.

Graphites is said to prevent the return of erysipelas when that disease becomes constitutional. The affected parts feel hard and tough, and if it be the face that is involved, are very much distorted. There are burning, stinging pains, as we found under *Apis*. It usually commences on the right side and goes to the left. It is particularly useful when *Iodine* has been abused.

Still further, you must remember the use of *Graphites* in the removal of cicatrices. This remedy seems to have the property of causing the absorption of cicatricial tissue. It was long ago noticed in workers in graphite, that wounds on the hands healed and the cicatrices disappeared very rapidly. Dr. Guernsey has made use of this property of the drug for the removal of cicatrices that form after mammary abscess. Professor Korndœrfer greatly relieved a child's eye by the remedy. The child had been operated on, and cicatrices formed which contracted more than the surgeon expected they would. *Graphites* so far relieved the case that the parts assumed their normal position.

We next have to speak of the action of *Graphites* on the digestive organs, and here it is allied particularly to the other carbons, *Carbo veg.* and *Carbo animalis*. We find the patient complaining of disagreeable taste in the mouth in the morning, as though he had been eating eggs. This symptom is more marked here than in any other carbon. The patient is worse from all meats. This symptom you find under *Pulsatilla*, *Ferrum*, and, in fact, under all chlorotic remedies.

Sweet things nauseate and disgust the patient. After eating, the stomach becomes distended with wind. There is burning pain in the stomach; also a crampy, colicky pain—a real gastralgia, in fact. The patient wakes up at night gasping for breath; sudden dyspnœa, which is temporarily relieved by eating. The gastralgia is also relieved by eating. In this respect it again resembles *Petroleum*, *Chelidonium* and *Anacardium*, all of which have a similar modality. The abdomen is greatly distended from flatulence, and with this distended abdomen we have rush of blood to the head. The liver is apt to be hard and enlarged, with extreme tenderness to the pressure of the clothing after eating. The bowels are usually constipated. The characteristic stool is covered with mucus or contains shreds of mucus. That is a very characteristic symptom of *Graphites*, and of *Cascarilla* also. The patient suffers from hæmorrhoids, which burn and sting; the anus is so extremely sore that the patient is very much annoyed when sitting. Fissures form in the anus. *Graphites* is here one of our best remedies.

Now we have several similar remedies here. First, *Lycopodium*. This has distension after eating, with great accumulation of flatus, but the flatus is not rancid or putrid, as it is under *Graphites*. That is a sufficient distinction between the two remedies.

Again, we have this list of remedies: *Ratanhia*, *Pæonia*, *Nitric acid* and *Silicea*. *Ratanhia* is an excellent remedy for fissure of the anus, and is to be recommended when there is great constriction of that orifice. Stools are forced out with great effort and the anus aches and burns for hours afterward.

Pæonia is also useful for fissures of the anus with a great deal of oozing, thus keeping the anus damp and disagreeable all the time. This is associated with great soreness and smarting, and enormous hæmorrhoids.

Nitric acid is also a remedy for fissure of the anus, particularly when there is a feeling as if there were splinters or sticks pricking the anus.

Now *Graphites* is distinguished from all these by the fact that they have more or less tenesmus or constriction of the anus, while *Graphites* has little or none.

Silicea is also a remedy for fissure of the anus. The patient tries to force a stool, but it partly decends and then slips back again.

Now the mucous membranes: *Graphites* is useful in nasal catarrh when there is an extreme dryness of the nose. You often find this in scrofulous cases. This alternates with the discharge of lumps, or clinkers, as they are sometimes called. At other times, the discharge is very offensive and bloody. You notice how the offensive character of the discharge shows itself in these carbons. The borders of the nostrils are sore and scabby, and crack readily. Here you have a resemblance to *Antimonium crudum*, to *Calcarea* and to *Arum triphyllum*. The sense of smell is too acute. The patient cannot bear the odor of flowers. There is a cracking or roaring in the ears when swallowing or chewing. This tells you that there is catarrh of the Eustachian tubes. On examining the ear with the speculum, you will find the membrana tympani not perforated, but quite white. The ears are apt to be dry, and there is a lack of natural secretion (just as you found under *Carbo veg.*), with hardness of hearing, better from riding in a carriage. It is not the riding that improves the hearing but the noise made by the carriage.

Graphites may also be used in chronic sore throat with sensation as of a lump in the throat. This is worse after empty swallowing. Here it is similar to *Sulphur* and *Calcarea ostrearum*.

The cough of *Graphites* is not very characteristic. It is a dry cough with a great deal of strangling, making the face red and the eyes water. It is worse during deep inspiration.

On the male genital organs, *Graphites* acts quite prominently. We find it producing uncontrollable sexual excitement and violent erections. The most important symptom of *Graphites* is impotence. There is a want of sensation during coition with no discharge of semen.

It also acts on the female organs. We find affections of the left ovary with enlargement of that gland, and with scanty delayed menses, chilliness, constipation and coexistent eruptions. The uterus is displaced under *Graphites*. The os is far back and presses against the posterior wall of the vagina, hence the remedy is indicated in anteflexion and in anteversion. With this, there is bearing down extending into the hypogastrium. The leucorrhœa is watery and profuse, sometimes coming in gushes. Often, with these symptoms, there exists an eczematous eruption about the vulva.

Petroleum.

This is a highly carbonaceous oil, but it is not pure carbon. Medicinally, it stands somewhat between *Sulphur* and *Phosphorus* on one hand, and *Graphites* and *Carbo veg.* on the other. We find that those who work in coal-oil are subject to eruptions on the skin. Thus a wheal appears across the face or body looking like a hive, and this itches and burns. Then, again, a vesicular eruption appears there which develops into a perfect picture of eczema, forming thick scabs and oozing pus. The skin soon grows more harsh and dry, and there form deep cracks and fissures which bleed and suppurate. These symptoms make *Petroleum* an excellent remedy for eczema wherever it may appear. We find it useful in rhagades, particularly when they occur in winter, when the hands chap, crack and burn and itch intolerably. Sometimes ulcers develop.

Again, *Petroleum* has been used in sprains of joints, especially in old rheumatic patients. It is particularly indicated in rheumatism, when the knees are stiff, this stiffness being associated with sharp sticking pains in them and with stiffness of the neck and cracking sounds when moving the head, owing to roughness of the muscular fibres.

Next we find *Petroleum* to be remembered in diseases of the mucous membranes. It may be used successfully in ozæna. Here the discharge is quite in agreement with the character of the eruption. Scabs and purulent mucus are discharged from the nasal cavities. The nose is sore and the nostrils are cracked as in *Graphites*. The post-nasal space is filled with purulent mucus, causing much hawking.

Then, too, we find the eyes affected under *Petroleum*. It is especially useful in blepharitis marginalis. It is also indicated in inflammation of the lachrymal canal, when suppuration has commenced and a fistula has formed. This tendency to the formation of fistula is also seen in the gums, anus, etc. It is a general characteristic.

The cough of *Petroleum* is also to be remembered. It is a dry teasing cough which comes on when lying down at night. We often find that cough in children with a diarrhœa which, however, appears only during the day.

Next we find *Petroleum* affecting the sweat itself, producing profuse offensive sweat in the axilla and on the soles of the feet.

The only important chest symptom of *Petroleum* is cold feeling about the heart. This symptom is strong under *Natrum mur.*, which has it very well marked, especially when exerting the mind. It is also found under *Kali chloricum, Graphites, Kali nitricum, Carbo animalis* and *Kali bichromicum.*

Next we study *Petroleum* in its action on the stomach and bowels. It produces nausea and vertigo with vomiting of bile, worse in the morning, worse from riding in a carriage and worse during pregnancy. Then, too, *Petroleum* is useful in sea-sickness.

Petroleum produces a diarrhœa which is somewhat akin to that of *Sulphur*. The stools are offensive and watery, and often contain undigested food. They come early in the morning and are associated with emaciation of the body. They differ from *Sulphur* in coming on also during the day. We have another diarrhœa curable by *Petroleum*, and that is a diarrhœa with disordered stomach made worse by the use of cabbage, sauer-kraut and cole-slaw. There is offensive stool with great flatulence, and belching of gas, tasting of cabbage.

Petroleum also acts as a nervous remedy. We sometimes find it indicated in typhoid fever, when there is a slight delirium. It also produces forgetfulness. The patient loses her way in well-known streets. If this symptom has been produced by exposure to great heat, then you should give *Glonoin*.

Another mental symptom curable by *Petroleum* is she imagines that she is double, or that somebody is lying beside her. This symptom has been utilized in this way: a lady in childbed imagined that she had had two babies, and she was very much concerned as to how she could take care of them both. *Petroleum* cured her.

Petroleum has also been used as an antidote to lead poisoning.

LECTURE XLVIII.

HALOGENS.

Halogens.
- Highly irritant to the mucous membranes.
- Spasm of the glottis.
- Pseudo-membranes.
- Glands, etc.

Halogens.
- Bromine.
  - Phos., Ant. tart.
  - Carbo an.
  - Acon., Spong., Hep., Kaol.
  - Kali brom.   >Amon. c
- Fluorine.
- Iodine.
  - Merc., Phos., Sulph., Calc. ostr.   >Sulph.
  - Ars., Calc., Arg. n.   >Starch.
  - Spong., Hep., Kaolin.   >Hepar.
  - Ant. tart.   >Arsen.
- Chlorine.

To-day we begin the study of the chemical elements termed halogens; *Iodine*, *Bromine*, *Fluorine* and *Chlorine* are the elements in this group. As a group the halogens may be remembered by this great characteristic symptom, they all act upon the larynx and bronchial tubes, and in fact upon mucous membranes generally. They are decidedly irritating to the mucous membranes, producing violent inflammation, rawness and excoriation, as anybody can testify who has once inhaled the fumes of *Chlorine*, *Iodine* or *Bromine*. They all produce spasms of the glottis and this is most marked in *Chlorine*, although they all have it. They all tend to produce pseudo-membranous formations on the mucous membranes. All excepting *Chlorine* tend to produce croupous membranes; *Chlorine* tends more to diphtheritic than pure croupous membrane. All of the halogens act upon the glandular system, producing enlargement, induration and even abscess in glands. Thus we find them all useful in scrofulosis, especially *Iodine*, which leads the list. *Cyanogen* also belongs to this group chemically, although it is properly considered as belonging to organic chemistry. It has many similarities to these drugs, and, like *Chlorine*, is useful in diphtheritic deposits. Thus we use *Hydrocyanic acid* and *Amygdala Persica* (which contains *Hydrocyanic acid*) for diphtheritic sore-throat, and we may use the *Cyanide of Mercury* for some of the worst forms of diphtheria. The same is true to a less degree of *Cyanide of Potassium*. These general characteristics of the halogens lead you at times to say: "This patient needs one of the halogens, which shall it be?" To answer that question we must study these four elements separately and by comparison.

BROMINE.

I will first call your attention to *Bromine*. *Bromine* produces a rather peculiar effect on the sensorium, causing a sort of vertigo, which is worse from running water. Anything moving rapidly produces this vertigo. It is associated with a peculiar anxious state of mind. Now this anxiety belongs to all of the halogens. It hardly originates in the mind, probably coming from some defect in the body itself. It is a common symptom in heart and lung affections, and it is probably thence that the symptom springs. This anxiety is expressed in this way: the patient expects to see objects jumping about or he feels as if on turning his head he must see something or some one. This is an effect of *Bromine*, and those of you who are familiar with *Bromide of Potassium* will recognize whence it gets its anxiety. The vertigo is relieved by nose-bleed, showing at once that it is congestive in character. Another symptom indicative of congestion under *Bromine* is this: after dinner there is sensation deep in the brain as though a fit of apoplexy were impending. The patient feels as if he would lose his senses.

The *Iodine* mental condition is more marked than that of *Bromine*. It is a decided erethism, during which the patient is very excitable and restless, moving about from place to place, now sitting here, now sitting there; he fears that every little occurrence will end seriously. In his anxiety he shuns every one, even his doctor. He has a great dread of people. At times he becomes quite excited and delirious, with vertigo, red face and anxiety. In children with tabes mesenterica here is a characteristic irritability, screaming when looked at.

Next, the lymphatic system. Like all the other members of this group, *Bromine* attacks the glands and causes enlargement and induration of the glands. Hence it is called for in scrofulosis. It is particularly suited to scrofulous patients, children usually, when the parotid gland or glands are indurated, when there is a tendency to suppuration, with excoriating discharge, persistent hardness of the gland around the opening, and undue amount of warmth or heat in the gland. I have merely mentioned the parotid gland for purpose of illustration. *Bromine* also affects the mammary gland, for cancer of which it has been a very useful remedy. You may perhaps remember that I told you the other day that it was similar to *Carbo animalis*. Like *Carbo animalis*, it has induration of the glands in the axilla with burning pains. But *Bromine* also has cutting pains. The breast is hard and on palpation, a dull subdued sort of throbbing may be felt in it. Sometimes the drawing or cutting is so marked that it feels as if a string were pulling from the gland into the axilla, a symptom more often calling for *Croton tiglium* or *Paris quad*.

The testicles are acted upon by *Bromine*. We find them swollen, hard and perfectly smooth and unduly hot. The pain is worse from jarring. You will find that glandular affections yield to *Bromine*, especially in persons of light complexion, with fair skin and light blue eyes. I mention this symptom here to make use of it in a few moments as a symptom of comparative value. I do not mean to say that every scrofulous child with blue eyes must have *Bromine*, but I do mean that this symptom is of use to enable us to distinguish *Bromine* from the other halogens.

The tonsils, too, are affected in *Bromine*. Thus we find them deep red and swollen and covered with a network of dilated bloodvessels. They are worse when swallowing, and are accompanied usually with swelling of the glands externally. There is a feeling of rawness in the throat with this tonsillitis. This, too, as you know, is common enough in scrofulous children. Many have a strong temptation to excise the tonsils, but this is not good practice, for you can often cure this trouble by internal medication. In some cases, this enlargement of the tonsils may be looked upon as a forerunner of tuberculosis.

We find *Bromine* indicated in enlargement of another gland, namely the thyroid gland, and curing what has been termed bronchocele or goitre.

We next have to speak of *Bromine* in its action on mucous

membranes. Beginning with the nose, we find that it is useful in coryza or in nasal catarrh, when the discharge is profuse, watery and excoriating. The nostrils, alternately, seem to be stopped up. There is peculiar headache associated with this coryza, a heavy pressure in the forehead which seems to be pushing the brain down and out at the root of the nose. The nose is very sore inside and also around the alæ. This is a smarting soreness, just such as you would expect the fumes of *Bromine* to cause. Later, ulcers form in the nose, with the escape of crusts or scabs, which are blown out and which are always bloody. Every attempt to blow the nose is followed by a discharge of crusts and blood. This you know is common enough with scrofulous children.

Coming now to the throat and lungs, we find *Bromine* indicated in spasm of the glottis, sometimes called laryngismus stridulus. This is a very difficult disease to cure. It is often central in its origin. It commences by sudden closure of the glottis. The child turns blue in the face, and its body becomes convulsed. One spell ceases only to be followed by another. In the second stage, general convulsions appear, followed by emaciation. The trouble may be reflex from dentition, or from indigestion, or from enlargement of the thymus gland. If it can be found to be the result of enlargement of the thymus gland, then *Iodine* is clearly indicated. When it has been caused by retarded dentition, I think that *Calcarea phosphorica* promises better than anything else. Dr. Dunham records a case that had been given up by an allopathic physician, but, knowing the symptoms of *Chlorine*, which, above all other remedies, will produce this spasm of the glottis, he generated some *Chlorine*, and allowed the child to inhale the fumes, with almost instantaneous relief and final cure. All the halogens are useful in this condition, but *Chlorine* is here the best of them all. Their symptoms differ but little so far as the local symptoms are concerned. We may also think of *Sambucus, Antimonium tartaricum, Belladonna, Lachesis, Arsenicum* and, in some cases, *Phosphorus.*

Lachesis is particularly indicated when the patient awakens from sleep with it.

Ignatia, whenever a cross word or correcting the child brings on the spasm.

Another remedy is *Cuprum*, especially when the spasms are general and the child clenches its thumbs.

Ipecacuanha may be of some use in some cases, but I have no confidence in it.

Nor have I in *Sambucus*, because, under *Sambucus*, I think the trouble is more in the chest, whereas, with *Cuprum*, the halogens, *Calcarea phos.*, *Lachesis* and *Belladonna*, the trouble is in the larynx itself.

This spasm of the glottis often comes in the course of croup, in which disease *Bromine* may be the remedy when inspiration seems to be exceedingly difficult; the child is suddenly aroused from sleep as if choking. These symptoms are relieved by a drink of water, which seems to quiet the spasmodic condition. In membranous croup *Bromine* is indicated by the following symptoms in addition to the spasm already referred to: the child has at first a deep, rough voice, which, in the evening, amounts almost to aphonia. It cries with a hoarse, husky voice. The membrane seems to come up from the larynx into the throat. Every inspiration provokes cough, especially every deep inspiration. Breathing is hoarse, rasping and whistling, as though the child were breathing through a sponge or through some loose metallic substance which is vibrating. This is caused by the vibration of membrane as it is deposited more or less uniformly over the interior of the larynx. Later, there is rattling in the larynx. When the child coughs it seems as if the larynx were full of the loose mucus.

Antimonium tartaricum is very similar to *Bromine* in croup. It has rattling and wheezing, extending down the trachea as well as in the larynx.

Now, I wish to say a few words about other remedies in connection with croup, especially concerning *Aconite*, *Hepar*, *Spongia* and *Kaolin*. *Kaolin* is a kind of porcelain-clay, a combination of lime and silica, and has proved very useful in membranous croup. The relation which these remedies hold is this: *Aconite* is useful in the beginning of croup, whether spasmodic, catarrhal or membranous. It is indicated by the child suddenly arousing from sleep as if it were smothering. There is great restlessness. The skin is hot. There must be some anxiety present. Breathing is dry. There is no sound of mucus. Soon the child seems better and falls asleep, only to be aroused again. *Arnica* is especially indicated in these cases if the symptoms have followed exposure to dry, cold winds. Do not stop your remedy too soon. If you do, while the child will be better in the morning, the symptoms may return with renewed violence the next night, and, before you know it, the mucous membrane of the larynx and trachea will take on fibrinous exudation and you lose your patient.

You will need to change to *Spongia* when you have these symptoms present: breathing during inspiration is hard and harsh, as though the child was breathing through a sponge. The cough has a decidedly hard, barking, ringing sound. As yet the sputum is scanty. *Spongia* follows *Aconite*, especially after exposure to dry, cold winds, and in light-complexioned children with blue eyes. The symptoms are usually worse before midnight. Suppose this fails you, then you may have recourse to *Hepar sulphuris calcarea*.

Hepar usually is worse after midnight and towards morning. The cough has the same harsh, croupy sound, but there is a great deal of moisture with it. This is the indication for *Hepar*. It, too, is worse from exposure to dry, cold winds. Sometimes all these drugs fail, and we have to resort to the halogens, especially to *Bromine* and *Iodine*.

I have already given you the symptoms of *Bromine;* let me tell you how to distinguish it from *Iodine*. *Iodine* is particularly indicated after the failure of *Hepar*, when the membrane has formed; inspiration is exceedingly difficult, both from spasms of the throat and occlusion of the lumen of the larynx by the membranous formation. Inspiration is wave-like or in jerks. The cough is moist but harsh, just as you found under *Hepar*. The voice is almost extinct from the hoarseness. The child grasps its throat to relieve the pressure, throws its head far back so as to straighten the route from the mouth to the lungs and favor the passage of air. It is particularly worse in the morning. *Iodine* is especially adapted to dark-complexioned children with dark hair and eyes. This in itself is a great distinction between *Iodine* and *Bromine*. That is why I spoke of the use of *Bromine* in light-complexioned children, because this fact has been proven to be a good distinction between these two drugs, and hence, as a comparative symptom, is one of great value to you. *Iodine* is particularly adapted to cases that come from damp weather. Long-continued damp cold weather will produce just such a cough as *Iodine* will cure. Do not change the remedy in these cases too often. Do not change your remedy on account of alarming symptoms that spring up, *unless you are certain that they indicate a change.*

Kaolin has been used successfully for membranous croup even when the membrane dips down deep into the trachea. There is extreme soreness of the chest. The patient does not want anything to touch him. He will not permit you to use steam or hot cloths, because the chest is so sore.

Returning to the study of *Bromine*, we find it useful in affections of the lungs. It is indicated in asthma, when the patient feels as if he could not get air enough into his lungs, consequently he breathes very deeply. The explanation of this lies not only in the lungs, but also in the constriction of the glottis. Although the patient expands his chest well, air does not go in on account of the narrowness of the opening in the larynx. It is especially indicated in asthma coming on, at or near the seashore.

We also find *Bromine* useful in pneumonia, particularly when it affects the lower lobe of the right lung, hence lobar pneumonia. We often find nose-bleed as a concomitant symptom when *Bromine* is indicated in these cases. The patient also has the symptom just mentioned under asthma, "seems as if he could not get enough air into the chest;" while there seems to be plenty of mucus, the patient does not appear to be able to expectorate it.

We also find *Bromine* indicated in tuberculosis of the lungs, particularly when the tubercular deposit is more manifest in the right lung. The patient suffers frequently from congestion of the head and chest, which is relieved by nose-bleed. Notice how often that symptom occurs under *Bromine*. There is also pain in the mammary region going up into the axilla. The eyes seem to be affected along with the chest symptoms giving rise to a chronic conjunctivitis.

Bromine produces a very characteristic picture of uncomplicated hypertrophy of the heart, by which I mean, muscular enlargement without valvular lesion. The patient finds it difficult to exert himself on account of the oppression about the heart. He has palpitation when he begins to move and when he gets up from a sitting to a standing posture. The pulse is full, hard and rather slow, which is just the character that belongs to an over-active enlarged heart. It has cured many cases of this hypertrophy of the heart. I think it was Dr. Thayer, of Boston, who cured many cases of this trouble with *Bromine*. It may also be used in cardiac asthma, especially when the asthmatic paroxysms are better at sea than on land.*

You here find *Bromine* similar to *Aconite*, but it lacks the anxiety of that remedy. Both remedies are suited to uncomplicated cardiac

---

* Professor Farrington refers above to the asthma of *Bromine* as coming on at or near the seashore, and here he speaks of cardiac asthma better on sea than on land. Both may be right, for being *at sea* differs from being *at the seashore,* where you may have land breezes.—S. L.

hypertrophy, but *Aconite* has fear and anxiety. The patient fears that he will drop dead in the street.

It is also similar to *Aconite* and *Rhus tox.*, both of which remedies have uncomplicated hypertrophy of the heart from over-exertion.

IODINE.

So much for *Bromine;* now for *Iodine;* and first let me speak of the symptoms arising from its abuse. *Iodine* is an absorbent; it has the property of causing absorption, particularly of glandular structures. Its absorbent properties extend to other tissues, involving, finally, even nervous structures. We find, for instance, in persons who are poisoned with *Iodine*, great emaciation. With the female, the mammary glands become atrophied and the ovaries, too, no doubt. With the males, the testicles suffer in the same manner and there is the inevitable progressive loss of sexual power. The skin becomes dark yellow and tawny, dry from deficient action, the sclerotica become yellow, yellow spots appear on the face and also on the body. There is excessive appetite, he is anxious and faint if he does not get his food. He is relieved while eating and yet he emaciates despite the amount of food he eats. Sooner or later the nervous system becomes involved and he is afflicted with tremor. He becomes nervous and excitable; every little annoyance, which would be unnoticed in his normal condition, causes trembling. He has a longing for the open air, as if the cold fresh air gave him more health. This gives a fair idea of the condition to which the patient is reduced by the over use of *Iodine*. One of the best antidotes to this state is *Hepar*. Some cases require *Sulphur*. The individual symptoms decide.

Now compare *Iodine* with *Bromine* in chest affections. *Iodine* is indicated in pneumonia, more so, perhaps, than *Bromine*. It is especially useful when the disease localizes itself, that is, when the plastic exudation* commences. There is a decided cough with great dyspnœa, difficulty in breathing, as though the chest would not expand (and here the trouble is situated in the chest itself), and blood-streaked sputum. You will find some portions of the lungs beginning to solidify. You may also give it later in the disease, after the stage of hepatization, in the stage of resolution, when instead of absorption

---

*Under *Mercurius* and *Iodine*, exudates are plastic; *Bryonia*, serous and plastic; *Hepar*, purulent.

and expectoration of the exudate, slow suppuration appears with hectic fever and emaciation; the patient feels better in the cool open air than he does in the warm room.

Phthisis pulmonalis sometimes calls for *Iodine*. You here find it indicated in young persons who grow too rapidly, who are subject to frequent congestion of the chest, who are rather emaciated, and who suffer from dry cough, which seems to be excited by tickling all over the chest. The patient cannot bear the warm room. Expectoration is tough and blood-streaked. There is a well-marked feeling of weakness in the chest, particularly on going up stairs, The patient has a very good appetite, and is relieved by eating.

The nearest remedy to *Iodine* here is *Phosphorus*, which is also well adapted to phthisis in the rapidly-growing young.

Iodine is also indicated in enlargement of the heart, whether or not accompanied by disease of the valvular structures. There is palpitation of the heart, particularly after any manual labor. It is suited especially to dark-complexioned persons, with dark hair, etc. The heart feels as if it were being squeezed by a firm hand. At other times there is excessive weakness in the chest, with "goneness" or exhausted feeling. The patient can scarcely talk or breathe, so weak does he feel. This shows that *Iodine* acts on the connective tissue. In valvular affections there is a feeling of vibration over the heart, just such a sensation as you get when stroking a purring cat.

Spigelia has that same purring, vibrating feeling over the region of the heart.

Now let me give you the difference between *Iodine* and *Bromine* in scrofulous affections. *Iodine* causes induration of the glands more marked than does *Bromine*. They are hard, large and usually painless. There is a characteristic of *Iodine* which is universal, and that characteristic is torpidity and sluggishness. The very indolence of the disease is suggestive of *Iodine*. It also produces atrophy of the glands. The mammæ waste away and the testicles dwindle. We find it indicated in scrofulosis of children, when they emaciate rapidly, despite a ravenous appetite. They are hungry all the time. They cry for their dinner, they feel better while eating, and yet they do not gain any flesh. They are always better in the open air and worse from any confinement in the warm room. The mesenteric glands are enlarged, and you have what is known as tabes mesenterica. This indicates *Iodine*, particularly when you have these other symptoms present together with excessive mental irritability.

We find *Iodine* causing a rather singular diarrhœa. In such cases the spleen is enlarged, quite hard, and very sensitive to the touch. The liver, too, must be affected, because the stools are whitish; sometimes they are wheylike. This last symptom you will often find connected with obscure disease of the pancreas. *Iodine* has such an affinity for glandular structures, that it, no doubt, attacks the pancreas as well as other glands.

We also find *Iodine* affecting the ovaries. It is indicated in ovarian dropsy. In such cases as this, the single fact that *Iodine* has helped in ovarian dropsy must not lead you to give *Iodine* in every case of that trouble. Other remedies have proved themselves useful. *Apis*, *Colocynth*, and other drugs, have cured cases, and they have sometimes failed. If the whole picture of the patient calls for *Iodine*, it is your duty to give that drug, but not unless such is the case. It must be given for weeks or months before it will bring about absorption of the tumor.

We also find *Iodine* indicated in cancer of the uterus, particularly with profuse hæmorrhages. The leucorrhœa is characteristic, being yellowish and very corrosive. This, in conjunction with the other *Iodine* symptoms, sallow, tawny skin, ravenous appetite, etc., makes *Iodine* the remedy which will relieve many cases and cure some.

In this connection we have other remedies to remember, and notably among these, *Hydrastis*, which has cured epithelioma, and may be a remedy for uterine cancer. I have, however, had no personal success with it. It has been used both externally and internally, when indicated by symptoms which have already been given you in another lecture; especially has it marked goneness at the epigastrium, and palpitation after every motion.

There is a substance, or remedy, known as *Lapis albus*. It is one of Grauvogl's remedies. He, at one time, went to a certain spring, the waters of which, it was claimed, would cure tuberculosis, scrofulosis, and even cancer. On examining the spring, he noticed that the water had gradually worn a crevice in the rocks. He took away a piece of this rock over which the water was falling, and made triturations of it. With this he cured several cases of goitre, and also several cases of scirrhus. This rock has been analyzed, but the analyses differ so that I hardly know which one to recommend.

Iodine is sometimes indicated in rheumatic joint affections, with effusion and emaciation. Hydrarthrosis yields, according to Jahr, Jousset and others, to *Iodine*. In acute cases, compare *Apis*; in the chronic, *Sulphur*.

Both *Iodine* and *Bromine* are of some use in ulcers. *Iodine*, for instance, is useful in ulcers rather of a scrofulous form, with spongy edges, and discharges of a bloody, ichorous, or even purulent character.

Now, *Bromine* is somewhat similar. It is useful in ulcers which have a carrion-like odor, with threatening gangrene. The surrounding skin has a greenish-yellow hue. That is the form of ulcer to which *Bromine* is especially adapted.

Now, a few words about *Chlorine*. I do not know much about it as a medicine. It may be given in a crude form by allowing the gas to be absorbed by ice-cold water, and thus it may be prepared for the cases to be enumerated. *Chlorine*, and in fact all its combinations, seem to have a special affinity for mucous membranes. Hence we find it indicated in catarrhs. *Chlorine* produces a watery discharge from the nose, with a thin, excoriating coryza, making the nose sore, both inside and about the alæ. On examining the mouth, you find it, too, affected with a low grade of inflammation. *Chlorine* here produces small, putrid-smelling ulcers, yellowish-white, which are aphthous in character.

Chlorine is indicated in scorbutic states of the blood, as are all the chlorides. We find under *Natrum mur.* and *Kali chloricum* the same kind of stomacace, with excessive fœtor of the breath.

We find *Chlorine* also acting on the nervous system, probably through the blood. It is indicated in typhoid conditions; the patient has a fear of becoming crazy, or that he will lose his senses. He is very forgetful; he cannot remember names, etc. There is a constant fear of some impending disease. There is also, under *Chlorine*, a peculiar painful sensation in the vertex, passing down the left side of the body. This is a precursor of typhoid fever. It is worse after eating. In such cases *Chlorine* will often modify the fever.

Chlorine is also indicated in impotence, but when this impotence has been produced by inhalations of the fumes of *Chlorine*, *Lycopodium* is the proper antidote.

Chlorine is a very good antidote to *Sulphuretted hydrogen*.

SPONGIA.

Spongia.
{ Acon., Bell., Hep., Iod., Brom.
Anacardium.
Caust., Selen., Phos.
Badiaga.

Spongia is not a chemical substance. It is derived from the animal kingdom, but, because its symptoms are closely allied to those of the halogens, it is convenient to study the drug here. *Spongia* contains *Iodine*, also some *Bromine* and some calcareous matter, and probably other ingredients of minor importance. It differs from *Iodine*. In the first place, it is adapted to light-complexioned persons, and it has not the same property of producing plastic or fibrous exudates that *Iodine* has. It acts, however, on structures very similar to those influenced by the halogens, especially the glandular system and mucous surfaces. We find it of service in tuberculosis, and we shall find it invaluable in the treatment of heart disease.

First, let us study its action on the glands. It is indicated just as are the halogens in indurations and enlargement of the glands. Thus we find it indicated in goitre. The swelling is hard and large, one or both sides are swollen, sometimes even with the chin, and particularly is this associated with suffocating spells at night. This suffocation does not come alone from the size of the goitre, because some very small goitres give rise to this symptom in a very great degree. I would also call your attention to the fact that goitres will vary in size at different times. They will be larger at one time than another. It is said that they increase and decrease with the moon. It has, therefore, been suggested that you give *Spongia*, or whatever drug you select, with the waning moon. In this way you hurry its decline.

Spongia acts on the testicles just as powerfully as the halogens, producing hardness and swelling of these glands. It is particularly useful in cases of maltreated orchitis or inflammation of the testicle after checked gonorrhœa. There is a peculiar sort of squeezing pain in the testicle and cord, worse on any motion of the body or clothing.

In cases of orchitis, our first remedy is not *Spongia*. *Pulsatilla* stands at the head of the list, and next to it we may rank *Hamamelis*, or witch-hazel. The latter drug should be used both locally and internally. It relieves the intense soreness and enables the patient to attend to his duties. Still another remedy is *Mercurius solubilis*, particularly when what little gonorrhœal discharge is present is yellowish-green.

Another remedy in the very beginning is *Gelsemium*.

When, however, you have this peculiar screwing-like, squeezing pain in the cord and testicles, with hardness there, *Spongia* comes in as one of our best drugs.

We find *Spongia* indicated in acute laryngitis. This is an alarming disease. It is indicated after *Aconite*, when there are harsh, barking cough and suffocative spells during sleep, arousing the patient. The larynx is extremely sensitive to the touch. Do not give *Lachesis* in these cases, for the sensitiveness is not due to hyperæsthesia of the cutaneous nerves, but it is the result of the inflamed condition of the laryngeal cartilages. Simply turning the head will bring on a suffocative spell.

Now there is another remedy that I would have you remember in this connection, and that is *Sambucus*. This is useful when these spasms of the larynx occur frequently during the course of acute laryngitis.

The same symptoms that suggest *Spongia* in laryngitis also indicate it in laryngeal phthisis.

I will not speak of the application of *Spongia* to croup, because I gave that to you in the early part of this lecture when speaking of *Bromine* and *Iodine*.

We come next to the lungs. We find *Spongia* indicated in true tuberculosis of the lungs. It is especially called for in the beginning of the stage of solidification of the lung tissue. You find the apices of one or both lungs dull on percussion. The cough is of a hard, ringing, metallic character. It is excited by deep breathing or by talking, by any little excitement, or by dry, cold winds, seldom by damp weather. It is relieved for awhile by eating or drinking. *Anacardium* also has this same symptom, eating relieves the cough. There is a great deal of congestion of the chest, especially when the patient is moving about, walking in the street for instance. This is accompanied by sudden weakness as if the patient would fall. In such cases *Spongia* has cured when given early.

Spongia is followed well by *Hepar* when the same kind of cough continues, but with rather more rattling from the production of mucus, whether blood-streaked or not. The symptoms are worse towards morning, while with *Spongia* they are worse before midnight. You find, too, that the *Spongia* patient is subject to frequent flashes of heat in these phthisical cases, and these return whenever he thinks about them. He also experiences a chill which usually commences across the back. He shakes even when near a warm stove. The heat which follows is all over the body except the thighs, which remain numb and chilly.

Spongia is useful in organic affections of the heart. The patient cannot lie flat on the back with the head low without bringing on a spell of suffocation. He is frequently aroused from sleep as if smothering. He sits up in bed with an anxious look, flushed face, and rapid, hard breathing.

You will find a loud blowing sound over one or the other valve. *Spongia* is particularly indicated after *Aconite*. Here there is the same arousing from sleep with great distress, the face is red and there is probably great congestion of the chest. *Aconite* suits only the hyperæmia that precedes endocarditis. *Spongia* comes in when exudation has commenced and the mischief has been already done. While it does not remove the deposit, it prevents the disease from advancing. In treating heart cases do not begin too soon with *Lachesis, Hydrocyanic acid* or *Arsenicum*. Begin rather with *Aconite*, *Spongia*, *Spigelia*, *Bryonia* or *Phosphorus*. *Arsenic* and such remedies come in later. If you give them too soon you weaken the patient. Unless you have a complete picture for the remedy, do not give in the first stages one usually indicated in the last stages of a disease.

LECTURE XLIX.

THE ACIDS.

Fluoric acid.	Phosphoric acid.
Muriatic "	Hydrocyanic "
Nitric "	Picric "
Sulphuric "	Lactic "
Oxalic "	Malic "
Citric "	Silicic "

Arsenious acid.

THERE are many of the acids, many more in fact than have been placed on the board. There are not many of them, however, with which we are thoroughly acquainted, and there are but few facts that need be stated with reference to others. The very idea of acid, you will at once understand, implies more or less of an electro-negative character. They all combine very readily with the electro-positive substances, as potassium and sodium. You must rid yourself of the impression that the term "acid" necessarily implies that these substances are sour, for all acids are not sour nor do all acids redden litmus paper. It was formerly supposed that all acids contained oxygen, and that oxygen was one of their necessary ingredients. This has been disproved, for certain acids—as hydrofluoric and muriatic acids—contain no oxygen. These acids are derived from the mineral and vegetable kingdoms. Of those derived from the former, we use in medicine *Fluoric* and *Muriatic acids*, which are obtained from the halogens; *Nitric acid*, a combination of nitrogen and oxygen; *Sulphuric acid*, *Phosphoric acid*, *Silicea* or *Silicic acid*, which exists as sand in nature and is by no means sour. So, too, the substance which we term *Arsenicum* is an acid—*Arsenious acid*.

From organic chemistry *Hydrocyanic acid*, sometimes called *Prussic acid*. That, we shall find, exists in a great variety of plants. Then here is *Oxalic acid*, with which you are already somewhat familiar. Many of you who have tasted the "sorrel grass" know how sour the leaves are. It is *Oxalic acid* which gives them their acidity. It exists also in the rhubarb. Rhubarb, either the medicinal or the edible variety, may or may not be poisonous. When raised on new ground it is very apt to contain an undue amount of *Oxalic acid*, and thus may make some persons very sick. *Malic* and *Citric acid* are derived from the vegetable kingdom. *Malic acid* is found more particularly in apples and pears and also in raspberries. *Citric acid* is found chiefly in oranges and lemons. *Acetic acid* is an organic acid, and is the principal ingredient of vinegar. *Lactic acid* is derived from sour milk.

In the first place we may say a few words about the acids in general and tell what characterizes them as a class. It has been determined by careful experimentation with the acids as a class that they decrease the acid secretions of the body and increase the alkaline. If, for instance, a quantity of acid, such as *Citric acid*, is taken into the stomach, it will diminish the secretion of the gastric juice. On the other hand, it will increase the secretion of the saliva. The practical value of this hint is hygienic rather than therapeutic, and yet in that degree it is of great use. For instance, we know how intolerable, at times, thirst is in fevers. Now this thirst may be due, at least in part, to lack of secretion from the salivary glands. The mouth is parched and dry; the tongue cleaves to the roof of the mouth. In such cases as this, acidulated drinks, by acting reflexly, increase the flow of saliva, and will give your patient great relief. For instance, you may give lemonade, providing, of course, it is not antagonistic to your indicated remedy. There are some medicines which *Citric acid* will antidote and some which will disagree with it. Again, if you are giving *Belladonna*, you would not think of using vinegar, as vinegar retards the action of that drug. But when giving *Belladonna* you may use lemonade, as that aids the action of the remedy. *Antimonium crudum* will not tolerate acids, but you may use tamarind water. Now if you find the mouth or throat sore in fever, the "edge" must be taken off the acid by the admixture of some mucilaginous substance to the drink. You might use gum Arabic, but that interferes with digestion somewhat. Irish moss, Iceland moss and slippery-elm are too medicinal. They all act powerfully on the lungs, and you might induce medicinal symptoms if you employ them. Flaxseed has some medicinal effect, but not sufficient to make its use inappropriate. Another substance which may be used is gelatin, that is, if you know that it is pure. Some of it is made from the refuse of the tanner; some from fish-bones, and this is quite palatable; but best of all is that made from calves' feet. This last may be used in water to relieve the sharpness of the acid.

We find that vegetable acids may be useful in dyspepsia, simply for their hygienic value. You may give them, for instance, in sour stomach. You then administer the acid before eating. Allow the patient to drink lemonade before meals and you will often find that the usual heartburn and sour risings after eating are thus diminished. Pepsin, which is often used as an adjuvant in the treatment of dyspepsia, is perfectly allowable, as it does not interfere with the action of any medicine and is not itself a medicine. It is often aided in its action by some kind of acid, particularly in the digestion of nitrogenous articles of food.

Vinegar has been used as an antidote for intoxication.

There is a property of *Lactic acid* which is well worth noticing. This is a very corrosive acid. It will eat into every tissue of the body. In fact, it will dissolve the enamel of the teeth, so that great care must be used in its administration. When prescribed in material doses, it is usually administered through a tube, which prevents it from touching the teeth. Dr. Hering was in the habit of recommending that the teeth be washed occasionally with cream that had become sour by keeping twenty-four hours.

Muriatic and *Lactic acids* favor digestion. Some persons are greatly relieved by drinking sour milk.

Sulphuric acid must be avoided in any form whatever, because it tends to make the food insoluble by combining with its albuminous constituents. *Sulphuric acid* is not used in dietetics, except by children in the cheap candy called "sour-balls," which are acidulated almost exclusively with this acid.

Hydrocyanic acid certainly aids digestion. There are some persons who have been cured of dyspepsia by eating peach-kernels, which contain this acid.

There is a distinction between the mineral acids on one side and the organic acids on the other. The mineral acids, as a class, all produce an irritability of fibre together with weakness and prostration. I am now speaking of their medicinal effects. You will find them to produce an irritable weakness—with the weak and irritable pulse— whereas the vegetable acids produce weakness without irritability. The acids, too, as a class, check hæmorrhages. This is a quality that belongs to nearly all of them. We all know that *Acetic acid* is useful in this sphere. When I have a patient who is subject to hæmorrhage, I am in the habit of instructing the nurse, in case hæmorrhage sets in before I can be called, to dip a cloth in vinegar and place it over the pubes. In many cases, this will be successful. We all know, too, that *Citric acid* will produce and cure hæmorrhage. A child, after eating too freely of lemons, had hæmorrhages from every orifice of the body, even from the conjunctiva. We shall see that *Phosphoric, Sulphuric* and *Arsenious acids* all produce and all check hæmorrhages. It is said that they all do this by reason of their astringency. But how can this be so when they act favorably even in the two-hundredth potency?

Another quality of the acids is their tendency to produce pseudo-membranes. Thus we find some of them indicated in diphtheria; *Muriatic, Phosphoric, Sulphuric* and *Nitric acids,* for instance. Here, again, caution is necessary. As these acids, particularly the vegetable acids, may cause croupous deposits, do not permit a child convalescing from croup to partake of acid fruits. When the child is susceptible, any one of these acids may tend to produce this disease again.

We find that all the acids cause a peculiar debility. This is not a simple functional weakness, such as might result from a rather exhausting diarrhœa, such as you find under *Cinchona*, or such a functional weakness of the nerves as will be curable by *Zinc*, but it is a debility which arises from defective nutrition, particularly from blood disease. Thus we find them called for in very low types of disease, disease in which blood poisoning is a prominent feature, in typhoid states and in scarlatina, particularly when of a low type, in conditions of exhaustion from abuse of various organs of the body. Thus drunkards, who have long been indulging in liquors to excess, may be relieved by *Sulphuric, Phosphoric* and *Arsenious acids*.

We find them indicated, too, in diabetes mellitus. The principal acids for this condition are *Phosphoric* and *Lactic acids*.

We find, too, that many of the acids are useful in scurvy, particularly when it has arisen from a diet of salty food with deprivation of vegetables. So much for our general review of the acids. We will now begin to speak of the acids in order, and, first of all, of *Fluoric acid*.

Fluoric Acid.

Fluoric acid.
- Silicea, Calcarea ostr., Calcarea fluor.
- Kali carb.
- Arsenicum, Phosphoric acid.
- Mercurius.
- Rhus tox.

This is a highly excoriating acid, eating, as you know, even into glass. It is to be particularly remembered by its action on the bones and on the skin. It acts especially upon the lower tissues of the body. We find it indicated in caries, particularly when the long bones, as the femur, humerus and radius are affected. The discharges from the affected parts are thin and excoriating. The symptoms are frequently relieved by cold applications. *Fluoric acid* is frequently useful for caries of the temporal bones, and especially of the mastoid process, and that, too, whether it be the result of syphilis, or of scrofulous catarrh of the middle ear.

We also find it indicated in dental fistulæ. The discharge is bloody, and has a saltish, disagreeable taste, rendering the mouth foul, and gradually undermining the whole constitution. *Fluoric acid* will here relieve. There is another remedy which has not been thoroughly proven, but which seems to act better here than the *Fluoric acid* and that is the *Fluoride of Calcium* or *Calcarea fluorica*.

Calcarea fluorica is especially useful for osseous tumors and for enlargement of bones with or without caries. Last summer a lady came to my office with what the dentist had pronounced to be necrosis of the lower jaw on the left side. The teeth had been removed by him, but the patient, instead of getting better, grew worse, and there was a continual discharge from the cavity. The molar just back of the one taken out had been filled with gold, and that I found on examination to be rough at its root; and when she pressed her jaws together tightly, there would ooze, apparently from its socket, a fluid which was offensive, dark and bloody, and mixed with fine pieces of decayed bone. The gum around the bone was purple and offensive in itself. The dentist had said that a surgical operation was necessary. The first remedy given was *Silicea*, which seemed to have some effect. This was followed by *Fluoric acid*. These two remedies are complementary, and you will frequently find in the bone disease that you will have to give one after the other. *Fluoric acid* is especially indicated when *Silicea* has been abused. It is also indicated when *Silicea* apparently does some good, but fails to complete the cure. Now, in the case I have just related, *Fluoric acid* also helped for awhile, but improvement again came to a stand-still, and now I noticed a swelling of the bone on the outer surface. This led me to think that *Calcarea fluorica* would act better, and I gave it in the sixth trituration. That she had been taking since the first of August. A week ago* the discharge had entirely ceased. The tooth, which had been filled with gold, was no longer painful. Pink granulations were springing up all over the gums. The probe can no longer detect bone which is diseased.

You will remember, as a distinction between *Fluoric acid* and *Silicea* in bone affections and ulcers, that *Fluoric acid* has relief from cold, whereas *Silicea* cannot bear anything cold. The slightest draught is intolerable.

We next have to speak of the action of *Fluoric acid* on the skin. It seems to produce a decided roughness and harshness of the skin, developing cutaneous eruptions of various kinds. There is itching. I do not know of any remedy that causes such general and persistent itching as does *Fluoric acid*. There is itching in small spots here and there over the body. This is worse from warmth and better from a cool place. You will find, under *Fluoric acid*, that old cicatrices will become redder than normal and itch. By and by, little vesicles will form on or near the cicatrix, thus showing you the affinity of *Fluoric acid* for this kind of tissue. Little red blotches appear on the body, and you have well-marked tendency to desquamation. No remedy has this more marked than *Fluoric acid*. You will find that *Fluoric acid* also attacks the nails, causing them to grow rapidly. *Thuja* has the effect of making the nails grow soft.

We may use *Fluoric acid* in felons, particularly in bone felons. Here, as in case of other diseases of the bones, the discharge is offensive. Here, also, we may make the same point of distinction between it and other remedies, namely, by relief from cold applications.

Fluoric acid also acts upon the muscles. Here its effects are rather novel. It causes an increase in muscular endurance. Under its influence a person is able to withstand unusual muscular exertion. More than this, he seems to be better able to withstand the heat of summer

*The lecturer was speaking on October 17th.

and the cold of winter. Thus the drug has a general invigorating or tonic effect.

This same effect we find under other drugs. We know how *Rhus tox.* will enable persons to withstand muscular fatigue. The same is also true of *Arsenicum*. But the remedy that has this property, more than any other I know of, is *Coca*. This interesting plant is used by the people of South America, particularly by those who climb the Andes. It prevents all the symptoms arising from the fatigue of the journey and from the disproportion between the external and the internal atmospheric pressures. We may make use of this in persons who are weak, particularly for old people who get out of breath easily and particularly if they cannot stand a rarefied atmosphere. In that condition *Coca* relieves.

Under the influence of *Fluoric acid*, a short sleep seems to refresh. This effect may also be produced by low potencies of *Mephitis putorius*.

We find that *Fluoric acid* has produced, and therefore ought to cure, varicose veins. Little blue collections of veins in small spots were caused in two or three provers by the drug. It may also be of use in nævus.

Other remedies here are *Hamamelis*, especially in acute cases. It is often used externally and internally in the treatment of enlarged veins.

Muriatic Acid.

Muriatic acid.
{ Debility, typhoid fever.
  Diphtheria.
  Scarlatina.
  Muscular weakness from Opium.

Muriatic acid.
{ Rhus tox., Bry., Phos., Phos. ac.
  Apis, Rhus tox., Arsenicum.
  Opium.
  Nitr. ac.
} > { Camphor.
      Bryonia.
      Alkalies.

Now that we have obtained an idea of the acids in general, we will find *Muriatic acid* a very easy drug to study. The continued use of *Muriatic acid* must give us pathological effects. Now this acid, when abused, produces pathogenetic effects, which present two series of symptoms for study. We find its mental and nervous disturbances under two stages or classes. Under the first effects of the drug there is considerable excitement. The patient is irritable and peevish, and the senses are all too acute. Thus light hurts his eyes, distant noises cause buzzing or roaring in the ears, or aggravating headache. Both smell and taste are abnormally acute. The patient is restless and changes his position frequently. His mind is actively engaged in visions in reference to the past and present and even to the future. The cheeks are quite bright red, the tongue and mouth are apt to be dry, and the heart-beat is quick and irritable but lacking in energy and force. If he is at all delirious, it is only slightly so. He is sleepy but unable to sleep, or he tosses about, dreamy and restless, all through the night. Now these are the transient symptoms of excitement or erethism which may occur under the influence of *Muriatic acid*. You are able to trace beneath these symptoms, from beginning to end, a certain amount of weakness. There is an appearance of over-strength, but it is in a weakened constitution. You know that it is not a true "hyperaction," but only an irritability, that comes under the head of irritable weakness.

The next stage, or that of exhaustion, has several grades, of course. Beginning with the mental symptoms, we find that the patient is apt to be sad, and is absorbed in self, taciturn, introspective, sad and brooding. If you question him you will learn that he is anxious about something real or imaginary. Headache may now appear, he feels as if the brain were being torn or bruised, or there is heaviness as if the occiput were made of lead. The patient becomes unconscious, with muttering delirium, sighs and groans during sleep, the tongue grows more dry and seems to have actually shrunken and become narrow and pointed; so dry is it that when he attempts to talk, it rattles like a piece of wash leather in his mouth. Still later, the tongue becomes paralyzed, so that he can scarcely move it at all. The heart-beats are regular and feeble. The pulse intermits characteristically at every third beat. He now becomes so weak that the muscles refuse their office. He has diarrhœa, which is watery and is accompanied by prolapsus of the rectum. Stool is involuntary when straining to urinate. He slides down in bed. He actually has not sufficient strength to keep his head upon the pillow. Paralysis of the brain is now threatening. This is indicated by vacant, staring eyes, dropping of the lower jaw, coldness of the extremities, and this, if not checked, is followed by death. Now these are the symptoms that call for *Muriatic acid*, particularly in typhoid fever.

The concordant remedies of *Muriatic acid* here are *Rhus, Bryonia, Apis, Phosphoric acid, Nitric acid* and *Arsenicum.*

Bryonia resembles it in the early stages of typhoid fever. Both have that nausea when sitting up in bed, both have dry tongue and soreness through the body, but there are quite a number of other symptoms which will enable you to distinguish, and which have been mentioned in the lecture on *Bryonia.*

Rhus tox., like *Muriatic acid*, has this restlessness in the beginning. The patient is continually moving and tossing about the bed. He cannot sleep at night. There is slight delirium, with muttering. All these symptoms are under both *Rhus* and *Muriatic acid*. *Rhus* has not so much debility as the latter, hence it is followed rather than preceded by the *Muriatic acid.*

Phosphoric acid resembles *Muriatic acid*, but resembles it in this respect: *Phosphoric acid* has apathy and indifference; a complete "don't care condition;" indifferent to what may happen to himself, or to others. That is not the condition calling for *Muriatic acid*, for taciturnity is not indifference. Then again, *Phosphoric acid* does not cause the same prostration that we find under *Muriatic acid*. The characteristic stupor of *Phosphoric acid* is this: the patient is easily aroused from stupor, and is perfectly rational when aroused, no matter how soon he may drop off again to sleep.

Apis resembles *Muriatic acid.* Both remedies have this dry and shrunken tongue, both have sliding down to the foot of the bed, impending paralysis of the brain, etc. The *Apis* tongue is very characteristic, and differs from that of *Muriatic acid.* It is covered with little blisters, especially along the border. The patient cannot put the tongue out; it seems to catch on the teeth, or, if he does get it out, it trembles.

Arsenicum you can readily distinguish by the symptoms, which I will give you next week when I lecture on that drug.

You should also remember in this connection *Baptisia*, which has, in common with *Muriatic acid*, this great weakness. *Baptisia*, however, has a besotted look to the face; the teeth are covered with black sordes, and the tongue is red on the edges and yellowish-brown down the centre.

Now, a word of caution. Do not mistake the symptoms of *Muriatic acid* for those of *Belladonna.* The novice is apt to do it. For instance, you notice the flushed face, the over-excitement of the senses, desire to sleep but cannot; these are all symptoms of *Belladonna*. But try to find the meaning of the *Belladonna* symptoms and then of those of *Muriatic acid*, and you will find that they are by no means the same. The *Belladonna* symptoms apply to hyperæmia, and to the beginning of the disease, and not to overwhelming of the system by disease, as in *Muriatic acid*.

Next I wish to refer to *Muriatic acid* in scarlatina. The body is intensely red. There is rush of blood to the head, with bright red face and great drowsiness. Now the rash comes out very sparingly, and is scattered irregularly over the surface of the body, and interspersed with petechiæ, with bluish or purplish spots. The child is very restless, throws off the clothes, and will not be covered, As the symptoms progress, the skin becomes purplish and the feet decidedly blue. Catarrhal or even diphtheritic symptoms, the diphtheritic symptoms already referred to, may complicate the case. A thin, excoriating discharge escapes from the nose, making the upper lip sore. And so irritating are the discharges from the mouth that the mucous membrane becomes intensely red, and even denuded of its epithelium. By and by, yellowish-gray deposit forms in the mouth, and particularly in the fauces, and on the tonsils, uvula, and posterior wall of the pharynx. One of the provers had symptoms that made it difficult to decide between those of diphtheria and those produced by *Muriatic acid*. The breath becomes very fœtid, and the uvula, œdematous. Sometimes the latter hangs down as thick as your thumb, and lies on the tongue, causing the child to gag and choke. These are the diphtheritic and catarrhal symptoms, and they may occur with or without scarlatina.

Belladonna is apparently, not truly, a concordant remedy here. These symptoms may cause you to give *Belladonna*, and incorrectly, too. The drowsiness and disturbed sleep, etc., of this remedy are caused by congestion of the brain, which is not the case under *Muriatic acid*.

More closely allied are *Apis* and *Sulphur*, which both produce redness of the skin to a marked degree.

Kali permanganicum resembles *Muriatic acid* in the throat symptoms, especially in the œdematous uvula, but is marked by excessive fœtor. Other remedies having this symptom are *Apis*, *Natrum arsenicosum*, *Mercurius cyanatus*, *Capsicum*, *Kali bichr.*, *Arsenicum* and *Hydrocyanic acid*. This last remedy resembles *Muriatic acid* in its throat symptoms, and in the blueness of the surface, and in the presence of petechiæ in the rash.

Sulphuric acid resembles *Muriatic acid* in scarlatina in that both remedies have these bluish spots, great weakness and diphtheritic membrane. *Sulphuric acid* does not have relief from uncovering. Then again, there are appearances on the skin like suggillations. Spots appear that look as though the parts had been bruised.

I have also found *Muriatic acid* useful in the last stages of dropsy from cirrhosed liver. Of course it may be used in any other serious disease of the liver in which the symptoms indicate it. The dropsy progresses as it does ordinarily in cirrhosed liver. The patient finally develops a typhoid condition, and becomes drowsy. Now these are the symptoms for which I have selected *Muriatic acid*. It does not cure; it will only relieve. The patient is drowsy, and becomes very much emaciated. The mouth is dry or it is aphthous. The stools are often watery and involuntary. The stomach is so weak and irritable that no food can be retained.

Nitro-muriatic acid is also to be remembered in these cases of weak digestion. Its symptoms you will find recorded in Allen, and are very similar to those of *Muriatic acid*.

The antidotes to *Muriatic acid* are *Camphor* and *Bryonia* for the dynamic effects of the drug, and alkalies for its acute poisonous effects.

Muriatic acid may also be used for the muscular debility following the prolonged use of *Opium*.

LECTURE L.

PHOSPHORIC AND SULPHURIC ACIDS.

Phosphoric and Sulphuric acids. { Debility — Aphthæ — Typhoid.
Hæmorrhages.
Diarrhœa. }

Phosphoric Acid.

Phosphoric acid. { Rhus tox.
China, Arsenicum, Veratrum.
Nux vomica.
Ferrum >Camphor.
Baptisia. }

To-day we have to study *Phosphoric acid*. This is a combination of oxygen with phosphorus. *Phosphoric acid* produces weakness or debility. Sometimes it causes a transient excitement, but the main characteristic of the drug is this debility, which is characterized by indifference or apathy, by torpidity of both mind and body, by complete sensorial depression. The patient is disinclined to answer your questions. His answers are short, consisting generally of "Yes" or "No," and are made in a way that show that it is annoying to him to speak. The delirium is quiet, not violent, but accompanied with this characteristic depression of the sensorium and muttering, unintelligible speech. He lies in a stupor, or in a stupid sleep, unconscious of all that is going on about him; but when aroused he is fully conscious. That is characteristic of *Phosphoric acid*. You see it is depressing to the sensorium and to the body in general, and yet these changes are in a certain sense superficial. It does not seem to dip deep down into the tissues, so to speak, and affect those serious changes in them that call for some such drug as *Lachesis*. You will find the quality above-mentioned pervading every *Phosphoric acid* symptom I shall mention.

So, you would not expect to give the drug in advanced stages when the stupor is complete.

Now the symptoms which indicate *Phosphoric acid* in typhoid fever are these: pointed nose; dark blue rings around the eyes. The patient may suffer from nose-bleed, but which, however, gives no relief to the symptoms in the early stages of typhoid fever. This is the very opposite of *Rhus tox.*, which is otherwise similar to *Phosphoric acid*. *Rhus* has epistaxis in the beginning of typhoid fever, but the symptoms are relieved by the hæmorrhage. The *Phosphoric acid* patient bores his finger into the nose. Now do not suppose because the patient is picking at the nose that he has worms and that you must give *Cina*. He may have itching of the nose. The symptom may also come from abdominal irritation not due to worms. With *Cina*, it occurs from worms; with *Phosphoric acid*, from the irritation of Peyer's patches, consequently you will find the abdominal symptoms plentiful. For instance, the abdomen is apt to be distended and bloated. There is a great deal of gurgling and rumbling in the abdomen. There is often diarrhœa with stools that are watery, sometimes involuntary, and contain undigested food. For instance, the milk which you have given your patient passes more or less undigested, and there is copious escape of flatus with the stool. The tongue is dry, and may have a dark-red streak down its centre; but it is apt to be pale and clammy, and sometimes covered over with slimy mucus. Sometimes the patient bites the tongue involuntarily while asleep; this is a spasmodic motion; while the jaws come together the tongue protrudes. The urine you will find to be highly albuminous; it has a milky appearance, decomposes very rapidly and you will find it also loaded with earthy phosphates. These are the main symptoms which would suggest the selection of *Phosphoric acid* in typhoid fever.

The nearest remedies here are *Rhus* and *Phosphorus*. *Phosphoric acid* often follows *Rhus* after the latter has relieved the restlessness but not the diarrhœa, and the patient goes into this quiet sort of stupor.

Phosphorus has more dryness of the tongue, more sensorial excitement; all the senses are irritated; the patient cannot bear any noises or odors. If diarrhœa is present, the stools are blood-streaked and look like "fresh-water."

In this sensorial apathy you should also remember the *Sweet spirits of nitre*. The patient lies in bed, perfectly indifferent to every one. He answers questions readily enough, but is apathetic. That is the condition in which Hahnemann gave *Sweet spirits of nitre*. I have found it to succeed when *Phosphoric acid* failed.

Arnica is also to be placed by the side of *Phosphoric acid*. Like the acid, it has apathy or indifference. The patient does not seem to realize that he is as sick as he is. But the *Arnica* condition is more advanced state. The depression and stupor are more profound. He goes to sleep when answering your questions, showing you how overpowering is the stupor. Then, too, you have the petechiæ or ecchymoses common to this remedy, and, still later, involuntary stool and urine.

Opium is more than *Phosphoric acid*, a remedy for stupor when that stupor is progressive. It is only in the beginning of the *Opium* state that the patient can be aroused from sleep. The stupor goes on until no amount of shaking can bring the patient to consciousness. Breathing grows more and more labored and stertorous; the face, instead of being pale, sunken and hippocratic, as in the acid, is deeper red, almost a brownish-red. The browner the red, the more is *Opium* indicated.

Another important series constitutes the emotional symptoms of *Phosphoric acid*. It is one of the best remedies we have for the bad effects of grief and depressing emotions, particularly for the chronic effects of disappointed love. It is here particularly indicated after *Ignatia*. *Ignatia* suits the acute symptoms and *Phosphoric acid* the chronic.

Phosphoric acid is also indicated for homesickness. The patient is sad; he often has hectic fever and flushing of the face, especially in the afternoon, evening or toward night. He has sweat towards evening, and complains of crushing weight on the vertex. That last symptom is very characteristic of *Phosphoric acid*. Now, we may carry these indications further than this. We all know how the emotions affect the body, how bad news affects the digestion, how mother's milk is made poisonous by some powerful emotion. We may find in *Phosphoric acid* a remedy for uterine and ovarian diseases which arise remotely from emotional causes. Thus you may use it in prolapsus uteri which seems to have been precipitated by depressing emotions. If you have other symptoms to aid you in its selection, then all the more promptly will you find both local and constitutional symptoms removed by its administration.

In homesickness you should also think of *Capsicum*.

Natrum mur. may be placed alongside of *Phosphoric acid* for the chronic effects of grief with the "vertex headache," sadness, weeping, emaciation, etc.

Next, I would like to say a few words about the diarrhœa caused by *Phosphoric acid*. It is particularly indicated in diarrhœa which is preceded by rumbling in the bowels. The stools are frequent and persistent. Particularly is it indicated in young persons who grow rapidly. But the diarrhœa, despite its frequency does not proportionately weaken the patient. The mother will tell you that her child has had diarrhœa for six weeks, with a great deal of rumbling of flatus, and yet it does not seem to be much weakened thereby. The stool may contain undigested food, and it may follow a meal.

The distinction between *Phosphoric acid* and *Cinchona* lies in the fact that the *Cinchona* diarrhœa exhausts the patient excessively.

Then another symptom of *Phosphoric acid* is, that the patient, though quite weak, is rested by a very short sleep. I presume that this action of the acid is owing to the stimulating effect of the *Phosphorus* it contains.

Phosphoric acid is suited more to the remote effects of the loss of animal fluids rather than to the acute symptoms. Thus we find it indicated for the long-lasting effects of seminal emissions, whether occurring during sleep or when awake, with every effort at stool or urination or from excessive venery, especially onanism. The whole system seems to be weakened. The patient is dizzy, feels as if he would fall. There is another peculiar form of dizziness. On lying down he feels as if the feet were going higher up than the head. The scrotum and testicles hang down flabby and relaxed. The penis has no power of erection, or erections are deficient. Semen escapes too soon during coitus. The patient complains of formication over the scrotum. The back and legs are weak, so that he totters when he walks. He has little or no absolute pain, except perhaps a burning in the spine, which is worse at night.

Phosphoric acid is very similar to *Cinchona*, in fact it is superior to it in the chronic effects of loss of seminal fluid. *Cinchona* is useful for the acute effects. For instance, a man has emissions for three or four consecutive nights, and is thus much weakened; then *Cinchona* will relieve him promptly.

When you give *Phosphoric acid* for this relaxed condition of the genitals, give it low.

In headache, *Phosphoric acid* occasionally comes into play, especially when the trouble occurs in school-girls; the headache comes on when they study and continues as long as the mental effort is maintained.

Phosphoric acid, furthermore, is to be thought of as a remedy for the debility arising from excessive study.

Phosphoric acid also affects the mucous surfaces. We have to remember it particularly in chest affections. The cough arises from tickling in the chest, in the region of the ensiform cartilage. It is worse in the evening after the patient lies down. In the morning we find expectoration, which is yellowish or muco-purulent, and usually tasting salty. We may think of it, although less frequently than of *Phosphorus* in cases of tuberculosis, when there is great weakness of the chest, so that the patient can hardly talk. This weakness seems to be a cause of dyspnœa. Every draught of air gives him fresh cold. He wraps his chest up warmly; he cannot bear a draught of air to touch his chest. When these symptoms are present, the acid is superior to *Phosphorus*.

Next, the action of *Phosphoric acid* on the bones. You may give it in scrofulous affections of children; for example, in hip diseases and in curvature of the spine from caries of the vertebra. when this symptom is present: if the child is old enough he will complain of a feeling as if the bones were being scraped with a knife. This is from inflammation of the periosteum. This symptom is worse at night and may occur after the abuse of mecury.

Phosphoric acid, like all the mineral acids, affects the kidneys. It produces first what we may call polyuria or copious urination. The symptom, as it was produced in the prover, was this: the urine flowed so rapidly and so frequently that it came out as though the urethra were twice its natural size. You may see in *Phosphoric acid* a possible remedy for diabetes mellitus. The symptoms which led you to it are, first of all, this frequent and profuse urination, requiring the patient to rise often at night. The urine is often milky in appearance. Sometimes it deposits jelly-like masses, particularly in catarrh of the bladder.

I would also like to call your attention to *Lactic acid*. As a remedy in diabetes I have used it with great benefit. There are pronounced anæmia, nausea after eating, canker sores in the mouth, salivation and polysuria.

Phosphoric acid has been recommended for growing pains. *Guaiacum* is also said to be useful for these.

Sulphuric Acid.

Sulphuric acid. { Arnica, Conium, Ruta.
Pulsatilla, Nux vomica.
Lachesis.

∨ Pulsatilla.   >Pulsatilla.

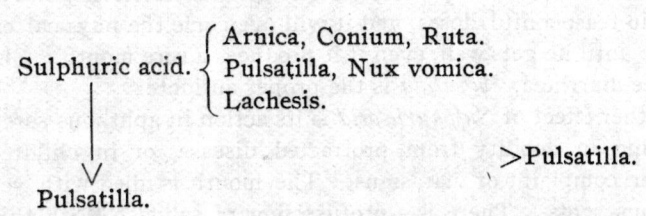

Sulphuric acid is indicated when the patient is hasty, quick and restless in his actions, sometimes, too, when there is the opposite condition, one of great depression, as in typhoid states. He answers questions slowly and with great difficulty, just as does the *Phosphoric acid* patient. You find that there is a general sensation of trembling in the *Sulphuric acid* patient. He feels as if he were trembling from head to foot, although there is no sign of it on the surface. The face in these conditions is rather peaked and is apt to be pale with blue rings around the eyes. Sometimes there is a feeling as though white of egg were dried on the skin. The patient is particularly weak about the digestive organs; thus there is a cold, relaxed feeling about the stomach, making the patient long for some strong or stimulating drink, as brandy, and this, too, in persons who are not addicted to drink. So weak is the stomach they vomit all food; the ejected matters are very sour.

You will find *Sulphuric acid* indicated especially for inebriates who are on their "last legs." They have run down completely, and have long since passed the *Nux vomica* condition. You find them pale, shrivelled-looking and cold; their stomachs so relaxed as not to be able to tolerate any food. They cannot even drink water unless it contains whiskey. The liver is enlarged. They have a dry stomach cough, often followed by belching, the act of coughing hurting the liver. The diarrhœa is watery and offensive, and is accompanied by excessive irritability of mind. They have a quick, hasty manner of doing everything. There is always dampness or oozing of moisture from the rectum. They frequently suffer from piles which burn, and are so large that they fill up the rectum. These cases are relieved by *Sulphuric acid*.

There is another use we may make of *Sulphuric acid*, and it is derived from its power of modifying the thirst for spirituous liquors. You should take two or three drops of the pure acid and dissolve them in a glass one-half full of water. Give it to the inebriate every two or three hours in teaspoonful doses, and it will overcome the physical craving. Give it until he gets well, even if it produces a sore mouth. Should it produce diarrhœa, *Pulsatilla* is the proper antidote.

Another effect of *Sulphuric acid* is its action in aphthous sore mouth occurring in debility from protracted disease, or in children with summer complaint or marasmus. The mouth is filled with yellowish aphthous spots. There is a profuse flow of saliva. With this there is apt to be vomiting of sour milk or sour mucus. The child smells sour despite the most careful washing. The stool is yellowish or slimy, having the appearance of chopped eggs. The child is very apt to have a cough, which is very likely a stomach-cough, with belching of wind after the cough.

You may think of *Sulphuric acid* also in diphtheria. The tonsils are bright red and quite swollen, so swollen in fact that liquids escape through the nose. The child is deathly pale, so pale that it looks like a corpse. It is inclined to drowsiness or somnolence. It can hardly breathe or talk, or make any noise on account of the abundance of membrane.

Sulphuric acid is also useful as a traumatic remedy. It may be used for bruises of soft parts after *Arnica;* in bruises of glands after *Conium;* in injuries of bones after *Ruta*. Particularly may it be used when there are long-lasting black and blue spots with soreness and stiffness.

Again, *Sulphuric*, more than any other acid, is useful in hæmorrhages. It causes hæmorrhage from every orifice of the body, the blood being dark and thin.

You may differentiate *Sulphuric acid* from *Carbo veg.* in the dyspepsia of drunkards by the fact that *Sulphuric acid* is more of a "sour remedy" and *Carbo veg.* a "putrid remedy."

LECTURE LI.

NITRIC, HYDROCYANIC AND PICRIC ACIDS.

Nitric Acid.

Nitric acid.
{ Calcarea ostrearum, Kali carb., Lycopodium.
Arsenicum, Carbo veg., Phosphorus, Moschus, Antimonium tart.
Phosphoric acid, Muriatic acid.
Hepar, Mercurius.

∨

Arum triphyllum.

Nitric acid.
{ Erosion of the mucous membranes, worse where they join the skin.
Offensive discharges.
Ulcers, irregular, exhibiting exuberant granulations; worse from touch, from which they will bleed.
Abuse of mercury.
Typhoid.—Debility.
Catarrh.
Fibrous and osseous tissues.

NITRIC ACID as a chemical substance need scarcely be explained to you, as you know its properties so well. I therefore pass on to consider its use as a medicine. You know its effects on the tissues, staining the skin a dark and yellowish-brown. It is a highly corrosive acid, eating into the flesh. Hence it has been used for the removal of warts, tumors, ulcers and exuberant granulations.

It acts very powerfully on the mucous membranes, and has a particular affinity for the outlets of mucous surfaces where skin and mucous membrane join. Hence you will find its symptoms chiefly about the mouth, lips, nostrils, meatus urinarius and anus; in fact, wherever skin and mucous membrane come together, there has *Nitric acid* a prominent action.

As an illustration, we find it useful in stomacace or ulceration of the mouth. True to the character of the drug, this stomacace will present its most violent symptoms about the lips. There will be blisters and vesicles on and around the lips in connection with the sore mouth. Ptyalism will be present, particularly in cases that have been abused by mercury. So, too, you will find that the diarrhœa is associated with soreness and rawness of the anus.* Even fissures may be present, as I have already said.

The characteristic discharges produced by *Nitric acid* are offensive, thin and excoriating, and, if purulent, are of a dirty yellowish-green color and not at all laudable.

The ulcers calling for *Nitric acid* are offensive and characteristically irregular in outline, tending to spread at the periphery, but more deeply than those arising from the action of *Mercurius*, which produces a superficial flat ulcer. These ulcers of *Nitric acid* are very apt to be filled with profuse exuberant granulations, which bleed readily from the slightest touch. Even the dressing that you apply makes the ulcer bleed. The pains are of a sticking character, as if splinters were sticking into the affected parts. They are often associated with burning pains. The ulcers are worse from the application of cold water. *Nitric acid* is particularly indicated in syphilitic ulcers after abuse of mercury, and also in those of a scrofulous character after *Calcarea* has failed.

Another evidence of the offensiveness of the exhalations and secretions in *Nitric acid* is found in the urine, which has a strong odor, very much like that of the horse. It probably contains an excess of hippuric acid. This symptom is most highly developed in *Benzoic acid*. So characteristic is it in that drug that you will seldom if ever find it absent in the great variety of diseases curable by *Benzoic acid*.

The leucorrhœa is acrid, fœtid, thin, brown, watery or stringy.

The stools, too, show the putridity of *Nitric acid*. They are very offensive, and are green in color, and in children contain lumps of casein. They are also slimy from excess of mucus and are associated with much straining; the tenesmus here closely allies it to *Mercurius*. At other times, particularly in scrofulous children, the stools are pale from deficiency of bile, and pasty and sour as well as offensive.

Nitric acid affects the mucous membranes, producing catarrhs. We find it indicated in coryza, particularly when it is associated with some malignant disease, as scarlatina or diphtheria. Yellow fœtid eczema

---

*Sore excoriated anus: MERC., SULPH., CHAM., *Arsenic*, Puls., Graph., China.

with ulcers; the Eustachian tubes obstructed. In nasal diphtheria, *Nitric acid* is one of the chief remedies. The discharge from the nose is watery and very offensive, excoriating every part which it touches; frequent epistaxis. If you examine the nose, you will find that there is a well-developed white deposit therein. Another symptom, which is a very characteristic symptom, accompanying these conditions, is intermittent pulse. If the membrane has descended into the throat, you will have fœtid odor from the throat, too. The child will complain of a feeling as though there was a splinter there. This is a general characteristic of *Nitric acid*, a sensation as of a fish-bone, splinter or piece of glass sticking into the affected part. It runs all through the symptomatology of the remedy. You find it in the ulcers, and you find it in the rectum associated with the fistulæ and piles, and you find it here in the throat.

Nitric acid is here very similar to its complement, *Arum triphyllum*, which, like the former, causes excoriating discharge from the nose, making the lips sore; the corners of the mouth crack so that the child cannot open its mouth on account of the soreness.

Another remedy is *Muriatic acid*, which has thin excoriating discharge from the nose, intermittent pulse and loss of appetite.

Another effect of *Nitric acid*, and one, too, in which it has no superior, is its use to remove the bad effects of mercury. The particular symptoms which call for it in this condition are these: irritability, restlessness and mental anxiety. This irritability amounts to cursing and swearing. There are also periosteal pains; ophthalmia; inflammation or ulceration of the cornea, with tendency of the ulcers to perforate; hardness of hearing from catarrh of the middle ear and Eustachian tube; ptyalism; ulcers in the throat; caries of bones, particularly of the mastoid process of the temporal bone; dysentery, etc.

It is adapted to secondary more than to primary syphilis, and more especially adapted to secondary syphilis after the abuse of mercury. Chancres have even returned and are phagedenic. There is great soreness in the bones at night, particularly in the bones of the head and along the shins, and this is worse from every change in the weather. On a damp day he will have a boring pain in the bones. Ulcers appear in the throat or on the surface of the body, and these are characteristically irregular in outline. Warts develop, and these are almost always more or less pediculated. There are yellowish-brown spots or copper-colored spots all over the body. There is great debility, with sweat and exhaustion.

When mercury has been abused, *Hepar* is probably the best antidote we have. When mercurialization is conjoined with syphilis, *Nitric acid* is the preferable remedy.

Nitric acid may be needed in the treatment of phthisis. There are sudden rush of blood to the chest, and decided hectic fever, which indicates ulceration of the lungs from breaking down of tubercles. The chest is extremely sore to the touch. The patient suffers from frequent hæmorrhages from the lungs, the blood being bright red and profuse. There is great dyspnœa, so that the patient cannot talk without getting out of breath. There are also morning hoarseness, exhausting phthisical diarrhœa, worse in the morning, and sharp stitches through the right chest to the scapula. The pulse is intermittent. The least attempt at exertion causes palpitation of the heart and dyspnœa. The sweat comes particularly at night and towards morning, and exhausts the patient very much. The skin is apt to be cold towards morning. He is chilly on getting into bed. Heat comes in flashes, or it is only in the hands and feet. The cough is of a tickling character, and seems to annoy him all night. You hear on examination, loud râles all through the chest, and the expectoration is offensive, bloody and decidedly purulent, and of a dirty green color, not being yellowish-green and laudable, as you find under *Lycopodium* and *Pulsatilla*. Sometimes the cough is loose and rattling in character. The patient is usually of thin build, with dark hair and eyes.

Nitric acid is very often indicated in phthisis after *Calcarea ostrearum* or *Kali carb*. *Calcarea* is especially suited to leucophlegmatic patients. The face is pale and sallow. There is soreness of the chest, which is very much aggravated by touch or pressure. The cough is loose and rattling. Diarrhœa, if present, is worse in the evening. Hoarseness, through persistent, is painless. When, however, the *Calcarea* condition has run into the acid debility, *Nitric acid* is one of the very best remedies to follow. It does not often cure, but it relieves and prolongs life for years.

Still another application that we may make of *Nitric acid* is in typhoid fever, particularly in the ulcerative stage, when Peyer's patches have begun to break down. You will find the patient greatly exhausted. The characteristic indications for *Nitric acid* are these: stools are green, slimy and offensive, and sometimes purulent from the pus coming from these ulcers, and there is profuse bright red hæmorrhage from the bowels, with fainting on the slightest motion. The tongue is either white and studded with vesicles or little sore spots, or it is brownish and dry. We may have well-marked pneumonic complications. There seems to be threatening paralysis of the lungs, which you know is by no means an uncommon thing in typhoid fever. This incipient paralysis of the lungs is expressed by loud rattling of mucus in the chest. The pulse, in such cases, you will find to intermit at every third beat.

Now, do not forget *Moschus*, *Phosphorus*, *Antimonium tart.*, *Arsenicum* and *Cuprum* and other remedies that I have mentioned in this connection.

In hæmorrhage from the bowels during typhoid, you may also remember *Alumen*, which is useful when there are large clots passed.

Arsenicum is called for in this hæmorrhage when the flow consists of dark watery blood, and is associated with anxiety and restlessness.

We find *Hamamelis* indicated when there is a dark venous flow, without anxiety. Sometimes the blood is dark and pitch-like.

Still another remedy is *Leptandra*, which is useful in typhoid fever with symptoms of a bilious character, when the stools consist of black blood, looking like pitch.

Hydrocyanic Acid.

Hydrocyanic acid. { Spasms; epilepsy; tetanus. Cholera. Scarlatina. Heart; cough.

Hydrocyanic acid acts upon the cerebro-spinal nervous system, and particularly upon the medulla and upper portion of the spinal cord. It produces convulsions which are very much like those of the fully-developed epileptic attack. Dr. Hughes, of Brighton, England, recommends it as a specific for epilepsy. This, of course, it is not. To cure any disease, you will have to take into consideration the symptoms of each case, and prescribe accordingly.

Hydrocyanic acid also produces a tetanus which resembles very much that produced by *Nux vomica*. The body is stiffened and thrown back, there is cramp in the nape of the neck like *Cicuta;* breathing comes in paroxysms, the jaws are set, there is foaming at the mouth, but the face is flushed.

It is also useful in convulsions during severe attacks of illness, when the face is blue, and the prostration is very great. There are gasping breathing, clutching at the heart, and livid color of the surface of the body.

You may also give *Hydrocyanic acid* for very severe cases of prostration, with approaching paralysis of the brain and lungs, and when there is gurgling from the throat to the stomach when swallowing.

In cholera, *Hydrocyanic acid* is to be placed by the side of *Camphor*, being indicated in marked collapse with sudden cessation of all discharges, as vomiting and purging.

In scarlatina it is indicated in almost hopeless cases of a malignant type, in which the rash is livid from the very beginning. The feet are almost always cold.

Hydrocyanic acid may be given for the cough of heart disease when it is reflex from organic changes in the heart. It may also be used for the dry tickling cough of consumptives.

You may prefer *Laurocerasus* for the dry, teasing cough of consumptives, worse at night, and indeed for heart cough. You may also give it for cough with expectoration which contains little specks of blood scattered through it.

Picric Acid.

Picric acid at first causes congestions. These are soon followed by weariness and mental inactivity, showing how intensely the remedy attacks the vital forces. This weariness progresses from a slight feeling of fatigue on motion to complete paralysis. It is accompanied by indifference, want of will-power, and desire to lie down and rest. Animals, poisoned with this acid, were affected with paralysis of the hind legs, with slow breathing and great muscular weakness. At the autopsies made on them, the cortex cerebri, the cerebellum, medulla oblongata and spinal cord were found reduced to a soft, pulpy mass. The blood was dark brown in color, and loaded with little shining, greasy particles. The urine was rich in phosphates and uric acid and poor in sulphates and urates. Albumen and sugar were also found in the urine. The liver was full of fat granules and its borders dark with stagnant blood.

These symptoms and pathological observations bespeak the use of *Picric acid* in diseases of the brain and spinal rd. To give it, we need not wait until paralysis has set in. We may find it useful in typhoid conditions and also in conditions of brain fag when the mind has been over-worked. In the latter affection, *Picric acid* is one of our best remedies.

It is also useful in neurasthenia. You will find dull headache with aggravation from the slightest attempt at using the mind. This may be in the forehead or in a still worse place, in the occiput, and may then extend down the spine. The patient complains of feeling constantly tired and heavy. Any attempt to study brings on anew these symptoms of the brain, and also develops burning along the spine and very great weakness of the legs and back, with soreness of the muscles and joints. Sometimes sleep is restless and disturbed by priapismic erections. With these, of course, there will be frequent seminal emissions. Sometimes you will find severe pains in the neck and occiput going up to the supraorbital notch or foramen, then extending down into the eyes. There are hot feeling in the lower dorsal region, and aching and dragging in the lumbar region, which is worse from motion. On awaking from a sleep the patient has a tired aching in the lumbar region. The legs are heavy and, at the same time, weak. With this heaviness of the feet he sometimes complains of dull frontal headache. Sometimes he complains of numbness and crawling in the legs, with trembling and with pricking, as if from needles. He has tingling of the lips, formication about the head, and crawling as of ants over the surface. The least exertion causes prostration. He also has vertigo, worse when he stoops, walks or goes up-stairs. He has headaches, with dull, throbbing, heavy, sharp pains, worse from study or movement of the eyes, and better from rest, the open air, or binding the head tightly. The pupils are dilated. Sparks appear before the eyes, which may even smart and burn. Thick matter forms in the canthi. The eye symptoms are worse from artificial light. Accompanying the congestion of the head is nose-bleed. The nose is full of mucus. The patient can breathe only when the mouth is open. The saliva is either frothy or stringy. The taste in the mouth is like that of the acid itself, sour and bitter. The throat feels rough and scraped; better from eating and worse from empty swallowing, and worse after sleep. There is thick, white mucus on the tonsils. On swallowing, the throat feels so sore that it almost seems as if it would split. Sour eructations may accompany the frontal headache. Now, these gastric symptoms may accompany the brain fag. Nausea, which is worse about five o'clock in the morning and worse when attempting to rise. He also complains of pressure and weight about the stomach. He wants to belch, but does not seem to have the power to do it. The irritating effect of the drug is further shown by diarrhœa with stools which are thin, yellow and sometimes oily, with a great deal of burning and smarting at the anus, with prostration and unsuccessful urging to stool. The kidneys are congested. The urine has an abnormally high specific gravity, and contains sugar. It is also albuminous. The conjunctivæ are yellow, just as you find in jaundice. Papules appear on the face and turn into small boils. The feet are apt to be cold. These, then, are the main symptoms of *Picric acid*. Now, let us study those of a few of its related remedies.

Phosphorus, like *Picric acid*, causes fatty changes in the blood, kidneys, brain and spinal cord. Both remedies meet in sexual excesses and priapism, and both may be indicated in brain fag; both have congestive vertigo and crawling and tingling sensations here and there over the body. The distinction lies principally here: *Phosphorus* causes more irritability with the weakness, as displayed by over-sensitiveness to all external impressions. Hence, the senses are too acute, or, if failing, there are present photopsies; loud noises in the ears; sensitiveness to odors, to electric changes in the atmosphere; head weak; cannot think, with aggravation from loud noises. *Phosphorus* also has backache, with feeling as if the back would break on any motion, and with burning spots in the back, better on rubbing. Sexual excitement is very strong, but the erections are not so intense as under *Picric acid*, although the lasciviousness is more marked. Even when, in extreme cases, all irritability has ceased, the history shows that it once characterized the case.

Nux vomica resembles *Picric acid*, somewhat, in the brain fag and in the gastric symptoms, in the sour eructations, in the aggravation towards morning, and in the inability to study. *Nux* is distinguished by the prominence of its gastric symptoms.

Oxalic acid, more than *Phosphorus*, resembles *Picric acid* in the extreme picture of spinal softening. There are weakness about the loins and hips, extending down the legs, and numbness in the back. *Picric acid* has more heaviness and *Oxalic acid* more numbness. The legs are apt to be bluish and cold. The patient complains of paroxysms of dyspnœa. Another symptom, and one indicative of spinal meningitis, is intense inflammatory pain all through the back. A general symptom of *Oxalic acid* is pains coming in small spots, and greatly aggravated on thinking of them.

Another remedy closely related to *Picric acid* is *Sulphur*. This causes congestion of the lumbar spine, so intense congestion that paraplegia, with numbness and tingling, results. Heat in the spine. Retention of urine.

Phosphoric acid suits cerebro-spinal exhaustion from over-work. The least attempt to study causes heaviness, not only in the head but in the limbs; numbness; vertigo; confusion of thought; tingling, formication, especially in small of back; back and legs weak, yet no pain, except a subjective sense of burning; emissions even during stool; genitals relaxed.

Argentum nitricum has backache, worse when first rising from a seat and better from moving about, with trembling weakness of the limbs; vertigo, with fear of projecting corners, etc.; bones at sacrum give out; limbs tremble; impotency; organs shrivelled.

Alumina is indicated in cases somewhat like those calling for *Picric acid*, but is distinguished by the pains in the spine as though a hot iron had been thrust into the part. The patient staggers when walking in the dark. He also has painful feeling about the soles of the feet.

Silicea is quite similar to *Picric acid*. It is useful in nervous exhaustion, where the patient dreads any exertion either of body or mind. When he is warmed up to his work, he can get along pretty well. He also has numbness in the toes, fingers and back, and the constipation peculiar to *Silicea*.

Zinc causes nervous exhaustion. Its backache is worse at the last dorsal vertebra, and is worse while sitting; burning along the spine; formication in the calves; weak limbs; weak back and limbs, with goneness when hungry, especially at 11 A. M. All the nervous symptoms are worse from wine.

Of the remedies which cause violent erections you may compare the following: *Cantharis, Phosphorus, Capsicum, Agaricus, Pulsatilla, Platinum, Opium, Ambra grisea, Zincum, Physostigma, Petroselinum* and *Mygale*.

LECTURE LII.

SILICEA.

Silicea { Asaf., Phosphorus, Conium, Graphites.
Sulphur, Calcarea ostr., Lycopodium.
Gettysburg water.   <Mercurius.

SILICEA in its crude state is inert. It is insoluble, and hence has very little effect on the system. When potentized according to the formula of Hahnemann it becomes one of the most valuable drugs in our materia medica. It is a grand illustration of the efficacy of potentization.

The great and important effect of *Silicea* lies in the nutritive changes which are made by it. As nutritive changes are more evident in the growing child than in the adult, you will find *Silicea* symptoms appearing mostly in children from infancy up, not that it is contraindicated in the adult, but its use is shown more evidently in the young. The child, then, is imperfectly nourished, not from defective quality of the food it takes, but from defective assimilation. The head is disproportionately large; the fontanelles, especially the anterior, are open; the body is small and emaciated, with the exception of the abdomen, which is round and plump, as is often the case in scrofulous children. The head, including the scalp, neck and face, is covered with an offensive sweat. The face is pale, waxen, earthy or yellowish. The bones are poorly developed, as are also the muscles, consequently the child is slow in learning to walk. *Silicea* is especially adapted to rachitic children. The fibrous parts of the joints are inflamed, swollen or ulcerated. This gives the joints, especially the knees, a knob-like appearance.

Silicea is complementary to *Thuja*, especially in nervous affections and for the bad effects of vaccination. Whatever we may say in favor of the necessity of vaccination, we do know but that this operation may be followed by unhappy symptoms, and that, too, when the purest of virus has been used. Hence, at times, you have to counteract the bad effects that may follow the operation. We know that in Paris some 30,000 or 40,000 children were vaccinated after each was given a dose of *Sulphur*, and this is supposed to prevent the outbreak of any other disease than the vaccinia itself. If such bad effects as erysipelas, convulsions or diarrhœa should follow, then you will give *Silicea*, which will cure the case. *Thuja*, itself, is complementary here, and comes in very well for diarrhœa following vaccination, and also when the vaccination fever is high. Pustules, like those of small-pox, together with a rash, appear all over the body. *Melandrinum* is also useful for ill-effects of vaccine, but as yet it has been only imperfectly proven.

You notice that to the right on the board I have placed *Mercurius*, prefixed by a "crescendo" mark. That means that *Mercurius* does not follow well after *Silicea*. Their symptomatologies are apparently similar, and yet they do not seem to agree, although *Silicea* will antidote some of the effects of crude mercury, but, as potentized medicines, they do not follow each other well, hence you must be careful in deciding between the two drugs.

Fluoric acid antidotes the over-use of *Silicea* in bone affections.

Hepar also antidotes some of the effects of *Silicea*.

We are now ready to take up the effects of the drug. First, on cellular tissue. *Silicea* has long been known as a valuable drug, because of its affinity for cellular tissue. It produces inflammation of this extensive tissue of the body, going on to suppuration, and suppuration, too, which is rather indolent or sluggish in type, not necessarily malignant, but tending to perpetuate itself and become chronic. The termination of the *Silicea* cellulitis, then, is in suppuration, which is persistent, in ulceration which is persistent, or in induration. I have already illustrated this in the application of *Silicea* to the tonsils when these glands suppurate and refuse to heal, *Silicea* is more than ever the remedy when this occurs in rachitic children. You will see it also in the treatment of boils or furuncles, furuncles which occur in crops and which do not heal readily, but continue to discharge a rather thin, watery and even ichorous pus, usually having a foul odor, or less commonly a thick pus. *Silicea* may frequently be suggested as a remedy to prevent boils, on account of its tendency to produce inflammation of the connective tissue.

So, too, it would be suggested in that dread disease, carbuncle, particularly when it is situated between the shoulder and nape of the neck, a common site for carbuncle.

Silicea may also be used for induration. For instance, following the treatment of boils and abscesses, or other inflammations of this kind involving the parenchyma of an organ, you may have plastic exudation, which results in induration. This induration *Silicea* will cause to be absorbed, thus placing *Silicea* alongside of *Graphites*, a drug which you will remember tends to absorb indurated surfaces, even going so far as to effect the obliteration of cicatrices.

The same has been said of *Phytolacca*, but I think that this lacks confirmation. It certainly lacks the confirmation that *Graphites* has had.

Sometimes you will find that *Silicea* is unsuccessful in these indurations. Then a dose of *Sulphur*, interpolated, makes *Silicea* act better.

Silicea may be given with good result in all forms of ulcers, both benign and malignant. Its distinctive features are ulcers from bone diseases, as caries or necrosis, scrofulous ulcers which appear about joints ulcers which appear in the back from vertebral caries, and ulcers which appear about the hip in hip-disease, particularly if connecting with fistulæ. The pus is thin and offensive, and often mixed with blood and sometimes with little particles looking like cheese. There is very little tendency to heal spontaneously. These ulcers are relieved by warm and aggravated by cold applications.

Silicea acts upon the bones. We find it indicated in scrofulous children where the bones are curved, as for instance in spinal curvature. Not only is it indicated in lateral curvature, but where there is caries of the vertebral column itself.

It may also be indicated in diseases of the hip, or knee-joint, when the discharges are thin and offensive, and when there are fistulous tracks opening into the joint. The patient is of a scrofulous diathesis, and presents the constitutional characteristics that I have already mentioned as belonging to the *Silicea* patient. In addition to the symptoms there enumerated, the *Silicea* patient may have an offensive foot sweat, and this tends to make the toes sore and even raw. Sometimes there is an offensive axillary sweat. (I believe that the best remedy for axillary sweat is *Petroleum*.) The child also has tendency to swelling of the glands, which suppurate. Now with these symptoms there is a peculiar susceptibility to touch. I would here compare it with *Lachesis*, which as you will remember has extreme hyperæsthesia of inflamed parts. I dwell on this symptom for two reasons; first because it will help you to differentiate from the closely allied lime salts, and secondly because it illustrates a property of *Silicea* which you will see when we come to speak of its action on the nerves.

Let us now stop to compare *Silicea* with its related remedies. *Asafoetida* has offensive discharges from the bones. It is distinguished, however, by the intolerable soreness around the ulcer. For instance, in caries of the tibia, with an external outlet and discharging pus, the parts around the ulcer are so sore and tender to the touch that the patient cannot bear the softest dressing.

Phosphorus is very similar to *Silicea* in bone disease. It resembles it in abscess, particularly in mammary abscess, with fistulous openings. It is similar, too, in the caries of bone, particularly in necrosis. *Phosphorus*, like *Silicea*, has over-excitability of the nervous system.

Platinum mur. is also a valuable drug in caries of the bones.

Another is *Angustura*, which is particularly useful in caries of the long bones, as the humerus, tibia, femur, etc.

Strontiana carbonica is especially useful in caries of the femur with coexisting watery diarrhœa.

Gettysburg salt is rich in carbonate of lithium, and is very useful for symptoms precisely like those of *Silicea*, namely, carious ulcers, or ulcers about joints, such as occur in hip-disease or in caries of the vertebræ. The discharge is acrid and excoriating.

Sulphur, *Calcarea*, and *Lycopodium* are similar to *Silicea* in the scrofulous diseases of children. The distinction between *Calcarea* and *Silicea* is as follows: the *Calcarea* head sweat is confined to the scalp, and is sour rather than offensive. The feet also are damp from sweat, but the sweat does not, as in *Silicea*, make the feet sore or raw. *Calcarea* lacks the sensitiveness to touch of *Silicea*.

In this sweating of the head, the body being dry, *Silicea* is exactly opposite to *Rhus tox.*, which has sweating of the body, the head being dry.

The mucous membranes do not escape the action of *Silicea*. We have otorrhœa, the discharge from the ear being offensive, watery, and curdy. Often you find the membrana tympana perforated, the purulent discharge thence containing little pieces of bone, the result of involvement of the mastoid process or the ossicles of the middle ear by the disease.

There is keratitis, especially with tendency to the formation of sloughing ulcers, which tend to perforate the cornea like those of *Nitric acid*. In the *Silicea* child they are not vascular, so there is not much infiltration of the surrounding tissues. Hypopyon is present. The lids are swollen and covered with suppurating styes.

The nose is also affected. *Silicea* is especially useful in nasal catarrh when ulcers exist on the mucous membranes, and these discharge a thin, bloody excoriating matter; or they may be dry, and then there is annoying dryness of the nose. It is also useful when the catarrhal process extends backwards and involves the outlets of the Eustachian tubes, producing an intolerable itching and tingling in this locality.

We also find *Silicea* indicated in some forms of hay-asthma, especially that which begins with itching and tingling in the nose and violent sneezing and excoriating discharge from the nose.

Silicea has also an action on the lungs. It produces hoarseness and roughness and dryness, with a tickling cough which seems to come from the supra-sternal fossa very much like *Rumex crispus*. There is also a feeling as if a hair were lying in the throat, larynx or trachea. The cough is excited by cold drinks, as under *Rhus tox*. and *Scilla*, by the very act of speaking, as in *Phosphorus*, *Rumex*, *Ambra grisea*, etc., and worse at night when lying down, just like *Rumex*, *Phosphorus* and *Lycopodium*. Sometimes it ends in the vomiting of mucus.

Silicea is useful in the suppurative stage of tuberculosis, when the cough, at first dry, becomes loose, with the expectoration of offensive muco-pus. You will find it of great service in the phthisis mucosa of old people. After great exertion the patient expectorates nasty pus, which is horribly offensive. But *Silicea* will seldom cure these cases. It can only palliate.

Phellandrium aquaticum is an excellent remedy in the last stages of phthisis when the expectoration is terribly offensive.

I would advise you to remember *Capsicum* for bronchial catarrh when the breath is not offensive except during the cough. You know that the *Capsicum* patient is of lax fibre and cannot get up the expectoration; so some of it lies there and undergoes decomposition. The air of ordinary expiration is not offensive, but as soon as the patient brings that from the very depths of the lungs, the offensive odor becomes quite marked.

In the *Silicea* diarrhœa the stools are offensive and usually painless and lienteric. The child vomits its food. These symptoms are associated with the characteristic skin lesions and constitutional peculiarities which go to make up the *Silicea* child.

The constipation of *Silicea* is quite characteristic. The stool partially escapes from the rectum and then seems to slip back again. I think that this symptom is easily explained. There is defective expulsive power on the part of the rectum. With a great deal of straining the stool is partly pushed down. When the bearing ceases then it slips back.

Next you have to remember the action of *Silicea* on the nervous system. It has here a very peculiar effect, which was pointed out first by Dr. Dunham. It causes a tendency to paralysis and paralytic weakness. Here, too, the trouble seems to be due to defective nutrition of the nerves themselves, both in the brain and spinal cord. Then you will have to remember it as a remedy in paralytic weakness accompanying disease of the spinal column. Often, with this condition, there is the peculiar constipation I have just described. With all these paralytic troubles there is an over-susceptibility to nervous stimuli. The senses are morbidly keen. The brain and spine cannot bear even an ordinary concussion or vibration. The surface of the body is tender and sensitive to the touch. Cold aggravates the symptoms and heat relieves.

Silicea may be given in convulsions of an epileptic character, with well-marked aura, when it starts from the solar plexus, as in *Bufo* and *Nux vomica*. The attacks are also said to come in certain phases of the moon. The patients are worse from any over-strain of the mind or emotions.

The headache of *Silicea* is of a nervous character, and provoked by any excessive mental exertion. It is generally worse over the right eye. It is aggravated by any noise, motion or concussion, and better from wrapping the head up warmly. It is not the pressure, but the warmth, that relieves. Sharp, tearing pains rise from the spine into the head. At the height of the paroxysm there is apt to be nausea and vomiting from sympathetic involvement of the stomach.

You should here compare *Menyanthes*, *Paris quadrifolia* and *Strontiana carb*. *Menyanthes* was first confirmed by Dr. Dunham. It has a peculiar headache coming from the nape of the neck, over the head. There is a bursting pain, as if the membranes of the brain were tense, and were pushing the skull open. This is relived by pressure rather than by warmth.

Paris quadrifolia has headache of spinal origin, which arises from the nape of the neck and produces a feeling as though the head were immensely large.

Strontiana carb. produces headache coming up from the nape of the neck and spreading thence over the head. It is just exactly like the headache of *Silicea*. You will have to distinguish by the collateral symptoms.

There are other nervous symptoms produced by *Silicea*. The patient has vertigo, which, like the pains, seems to rise from the spine into the head. It also causes difficulty in balancing. He has a fear that he will fall, and always to the left. Speech is somewhat confused. He finds it difficult to grasp the exact expression he wishes, and this even in ordinary conversation, and yet, when warmed up to his subject, he sometimes speaks quite fluently. Sluggishness is a contraindication of *Silicea* in nervous conditions. You cannot use it in torpid, flabby, nerveless persons. Remember that exactly the opposite is the case with disease of the lower tissues.

Silicea acts just as powerfully on the spine as it does on the brain, causing general motor weakness. Here, too, it is attended with the same irritability. The neck is stiff, causing headache. This stiffness of the neck is not from cold, not from rheumatism of the various muscles, but from spinal irritation. The small of the back aches as if beaten or pounded. The patient complains of pains about the coccyx, and cramps such as one experiences after sitting a long time or after riding a long time over a rough road. The legs tremble. They easily grow weary, particularly in the morning. Loss of animal fluids causes marked aggravation of the symptoms. For instance, seminal emission or coitus causes, or is followed by, bruised aching all over the body. There may also be symptoms of the spine which indicate locomotor ataxia. The fingers feel stiff, with loss of power in them. The part of the body on which he lies goes to sleep.

Silicea is useful in chronic rheumatism. It is one of the remedies on which to depend in treating hereditary rheumatism. The pains are predominantly in the shoulders and in the joints, and are worse at night and worse when uncovering.

A related remedy here is *Ledum*, which has exactly the opposite aggravation to that of *Silicea*. The patient is worse from covering up. The symptoms usually extend from the feet upwards.

LECTURE LIII.

ARSENICUM ALBUM.

Arsenicum.
- Aconite, Sulphur.
- Phosphorus, Rhus, Lachesis.
- Ipecac., China, Veratr. alb., Colchicum, Ferrum.
- Baptisia, Muriatic acid, Phosphoric acid, Nitric acid.
- Antimonium crud., Antimonium tart., Nux v., Pulsatilla.
- Secale, Camphor, Carbo v.
- Apis.
- Ailanthus.
- Anthracinum.

Arsenicum.
↓
Phosphorus.

- >Sesquioxide of iron.
- >China.
- >Ipecac.
- >Ferrum.
- >Graphites.
- >Camphor.
- >Veratr. alb.

Arsenicum.
- Irritability.
- Inflammations: stomach, uterus, etc.
- Fevers: continued, typhoid, intermittent.
- Skin: exanthemata, indurations, gangrene, carbuncle, cancer, ulcer.
- Nerves: neuralgia, convulsions, stupor, exhaustion, fainting.
- Catarrhs: eyes, nose. throat, lungs. etc.
- Dropsy: anasarca, hydrothorax.

TO-DAY we take up for study the last of the acid remedies. I refer to *Arsenious acid* or *Arsenicum album*. It has quite a number of concordant remedies, and quite a list of antidotes. Its complementary remedies are *Phosphorus* and *Allium sativa*.

Arsenicum has long been known as a speedy means of destroying life, hence it has been frequently used for suicidal and homicidal purposes. It has the property of uniting with animal tissues, probably with the albuminous portions, hardening them and causing them to resist the usual process of decay. This fact is taken advantage of by taxidermists in stuffing birds and animals. Cases of accidental poisoning with *Arsenic* are quite common, and this is all the more so because of the use of *Arsenic* in the arts. In the form of Scheele's green, or arsenite of copper, it enters into the composition of certain paints. It is used frequently in the manufacture of certain green wall-papers, and also in artificial flowers. It is also introduced into pastes to be used in sealing packages, which are to protect goods from insects. All these uses of *Arsenic* render poisoning, especially chronic poisoning, by it not at all uncommon.

In certain districts *Arsenicum* is indulged in as an article of diet. The women take it for the purpose of beautifying the complexion, and the men indulge in it because it enables them to work hard with little or no fatigue. The drug acts on muscular tissue so as to increase its power of endurance. We may make use of this fact when some disease has resulted, from climbing mountains or a long journey, as a provoking or modifying cause. The "*Arsenic*" vice is very objectionable, and certainly very injurious. After awhile these persons will suffer from *Arsenic* poisoning; especially if they move away from the region where they are living. The symptoms of slow arsenical poisoning are these: the eyelids are œdematous and the patient suffers from slight conjunctivitis; the eyes are always red and injected, and smart and burn. Associated with these symptoms is dim sight. Whether this comes from the inflammation externally, or from any internal ocular trouble, I am unable to say. The mucous membrane of the mouth, nose and throat is unnaturally red and dry. The sufferer complains of almost constant thirst. Digestion is most certainly deranged. The patient will tell you that he is dyspeptic. The skin assumes rather a dry, dirty look; it is only exceptionally clear and transparent. The patient suffers frequently from nettle-rash. Long wheals appear, and these itch and burn intolerably. Still later, eczema makes its appearance. The patient also suffers from stubborn neuralgia in different parts of the body. These are the most common; and the most certain symptoms indicating arsenical poisoning. In addition to these there will be some acute symptoms. For instance, there will be times when he has attacks of vomiting, with deathly nausea. He will vomit everything he drinks. At other times he has symptoms indicating cholera morbus, *e. g.*, vomiting and purging, and coldness of the surface of the body.

You may frequently be called upon to antidote arsenical poisoning. If it is an acute case you should excite vomiting and administer the sesquioxide of iron as an antidote. Dialyzed iron has also been recommended. It has the advantage of being more stable than the sesquioxide. For the nausea occuring during chronic poisoning, *Ipecac* acts very nicely. In the acute attacks simulating those of cholera morbus, *Veratrum album* relieves.

Cinchona also suits many of the symptoms; particularly the debility, dropsy and neuralgia.

Graphites is one of the best remedies to cure the skin symptoms of chronic arsenical poisoning.

Now we will consider the symptoms of *Arsenicum* in their totality. Quite a universal symptom of the drug, and that, too, whether the result of poisoning or of proving, is what I have already mentioned as an irritability of fibre. This is prominent in the worst cases in which *Arsenicum* may be used. Death may be almost certain, and yet there is this irritability of fibre showing the universal characteristic of the drug. Even when the patient lies unconscious, his stupor is broken by anxious moans and restlessness. Consistently with this quality of the drug, we find *Arsenic* indicated in patients who are anxious and restless, frequently changing their position, full of fear of death; hence they do not wish to be left alone for fear they will die. Delirium is violent, more violent than in any other of the acids except *Nitric acid*. It is worse at night, particularly after midnight. The patient has visions of ghosts and other fanciful figures, with trembling of the whole body. You cannot here fail to recognize the similarity to delirium tremens or mania-a-potu. *Arsenicum* here is of great use, particularly in old offenders who are seriously diseased by the use of alcohol, and who, from some cause or other, cannot get their usual drink.

The pains which the *Arsenicum* patient experiences, whether neuralgic or otherwise, make him desperate and angry, and at times almost furious. When falling asleep, he jerks and starts. During sleep his dreams are frightful and fantastic. Before going any further, I want to introduce a caution in regard to *Arsenic*. *Arsenic* is not a remedy usually called for in the beginning of diseases. The tendency of the symptoms is deathward. If you give the drug too soon, in a disease which in itself tends deathward, you may precipitate the result which you are anxious to avoid. I have myself several times made the mistake despite great caution. Do not give *Arsenicum* early in typhoid fever unless the symptoms call for it unmistakably. Here it is especially dangerous to give it too soon. Often *Rhus tox.* precedes its use. I will say the same thing in regard to tuberculosis. In the last stages of this disease this restless tossing about is not an *Arsenic* symptom, and *Arsenicum* will not relieve it. That is only a precursor of death. You must be certain that the mental state is undisputably that of *Arsenic*, or you will do harm instead of good to your patient. There is one exception to this word of caution, and that is in inflammations of the gastro-enteric system. I may say that *Arsenicum* may here be given quite early in the case without doing any harm, on the contrary with much benefit.

Now for the inflammations and fevers of *Arsenicum*. *Arsenicum* alters the blood. It is useful, as we shall learn, in low types of disease, when the blood-changes are serious. The inflammations of this remedy are characterized by their intensity, and by their tendency to the destruction of the tissue which is inflamed. In these local inflammations of *Arsenic* you will find burning lancinating pains the characteristic sensations. This is described by the patient as though hot coals were burning the part. It is often accompanied by throbbing. Now this burning when *Arsenicum* is the remedy indicates destruction of tissue, hence it calls for this remedy in gangrene, in sloughing, in carbuncles, and in that dreadful disease cancer. And it does not call for *Arsenic* when this burning is a mere sensation. Patients occasionally complain of burning pains, here and there, which arise from nervous causes only. *Arsenicum* does no good then. I have often seen physicians give *Arsenic* when women complained of burning pain in the ovaries. There was no evidence whatever of active inflammation; the burning was purely an ovaralgia. *Arsenicum* could do no good here. If, however, there is ovaritis with the pain, *Arsenic* becomes an invaluable remedy. All these cases in which *Arsenic* is called for are relieved by hot applications, and greatly aggravated by cold.

The most important sites for the *Arsenicum* inflammations are the stomach and bowels primarily, and next to these the heart. The inflammation in the stomach and bowels may vary from slight irritation to the most destructive gastritis and enteritis. The mouth is dry, the tongue white as if whitewashed, or, in some cases with irritable stomach, the tongue is red with raised papillæ. Thirst is intense, but the patient drinks but little at a time because water molests the stomach. An ordinary amount of food causes a feeling of fulness or repletion. In this symptom it is similar to *Lycopodium*. The least food or drink is vomited as soon as taken. But we may have another group of symptoms : weak, sinking sensation at the pit of the stomach, relieved by eating, but so soon as he begins to eat, he has urging to stool with diarrhœa. Here the drug is similar to *Cinchona* and *Ferrum*.

There is very distressing heartburn. Sometimes burning in the stomach like coals of fire is associated with the diarrhœa. The stools are undigested, slimy and bloody, and are attended with violent tenesmus and burning in the rectum. If this goes on, the stools become brownish or blackish, and horribly offensive, showing that it is indicated in most serious cases of enteritis and dysentery. The exciting causes for these various sets of symptoms are sudden chilling of the stomach with ice-water or ice-cream, alcoholic drinks in excess, certain poisons, as the ptomaine of sausage meat that has spoiled, rancid fat, spoiled butter or fat that has undergone decomposition, and lobster salads at certain seasons of the year.

Arsenicum also excites intestinal disease which is almost identical with cholera Asiatica. Even the organic growths of cholera are found in the discharges from the *Arsenic* proving. Do not conclude from this that *Arsenic* must be *the* remedy for cholera Asiatica. It is only the remedy when we have the following symptoms : intense vomiting and purging, the stools being not so much like rice-water as they are brownish-yellow, profuse, and offensive. The vomited matters are green, yellow and bilious. There is burning thirst, with the intense agony which belongs to *Arsenicum*. The surface of the body is as cold as ice, but internally, the patient feels as if on fire.

Arsenicum is also useful in cholera infantum, and in atrophy of infants. It is indicated by many of the symptoms that have already been enumerated. The symptoms of the bowels are, undigested stool, diarrhœa which is provoked just as soon as the child begins to eat or drink, aggravation after midnight (particularly the restlessness and the diarrhœa), and rapid emaciation. The child's skin is apt to be harsh and dry, and often yellowish and tawny. The little patient is restless, evidently being in constant distress. Here, too, we often have to give *Arsenic* quite early in the case, because here the symptoms have been going on before your arrival. It stands in close relation with *Nux vomica* and *Sulphur* in atrophy of infants. For instance, early in the case of marasmus, you may give *Arsenicum*, providing diarrhœa is present, in a case which would call for *Nux vomica* or *Sulphur* were constipation present. The same dried-up mummy which you find in the *Sulphur* case, with the peculiar gastric symptoms of *Arsenic*, would call for *Arsenic*. In far-advanced cases, the resemblance is not to these remedies, but to *Cinchona*, or *China*, and to *Argentum nitricum*.

Now let us study some of the related remedies of *Arsenicum* in gastro-intestinal troubles.

Argentum nitricum has slimy, greenish stools, with excessive flatulence, worse at night. Although both remedies have restlessness, it is not the same in each case. *Arsenicum* has a restless desire to change place, now sitting, now standing. The restlessness of *Nitrate of Silver* is purely nervous. The patient has difficulty in breathing, with long sighs.

Much more frequently will you be called upon to differentiate between *Arsenicum* and *Carbo veg*. *Carbo veg*. is somewhat similar to *Arsenicum* in abdominal affections arising from chilling the stomach, as with ice-water. It has, perhaps, less of the distinctive restless tossing about, but at the same time it may have a nervous, irritable, anxious state, without tossing about. *Carbo veg*. is also a similar remedy to *Arsenicum* when rancid fat has excited gastro-enteric symptoms.

Secale cornutum is very similar to *Arsenicum* in many of its symptoms. The two drugs are complementary. They agree well one with the other. In the abdominal symptoms both drugs meet in cholera Asiatica. *Arsenicum* may be distinguished from *Secale* by these few symptoms: the movements in *Secale* are copious and come in spurts; *Secale* has not the same restlessness that belongs to *Arsenicum*. Now, when there are any spasmodic symptoms present, as is often the case, you will find, under *Secale*, fingers spread asunder, with tingling in the hands and feet, intolerance of heat.

Veratrum album is somewhat similar to *Arsenicum*, in cholera morbus. The latter has not so copious a stool as the former, and cold sweat on the forhead is more marked in *Veratrum*.

Do not forget that *Cadmium sulphuricum* is similar to *Arsenicum* in black vomit, whether that symptom occur in yellow fever or in any other disease.

We find *Arsenicum* often indicated in intermitting types of fever. We all know how often *Arsenic* succeeds *Cinchona* in the treatment of chills and fever. It has cured many cases, especially after the failure of *Quinine*, or after the abuse of that drug; or when the fever has been contracted in salt marshes along the seashore. The chill is not well defined; in fact, it is rather irregular, but the heat is unmistakable. It is intense, with burning thirst, especially for hot drinks; cold drinks make the patient feel chilly. Sweat does not always relieve. Sometimes it appears very tardily. The apyrexia is marked by severe symptoms, dropsy showing itself as the result of enlarged spleen or liver. The patient is scarcely able to sit up. He is often annoyed by neuralgia, which is typical in its recurrence. The pain usually affects one side of the face and seems to be almost maddening, driving the patient from place to place. At the height of the attack there are nausea and vomiting and buzzing in the ears. *Arsenicum* may be also used in intermittent, semilateral headache of malarial origin, especially after the abuse of quinine.

There are several drugs similar to *Arsenicum* in these malarial neuralgias. *Cedron* has neuralgia, returning at precisely the same hour each day.

Chininum sulphuricum is also suited to periodical attacks of neuralgia, relieved by hard pressure.

Valerian is to be thought of in hysterical patients.

Cactus grandiflorus has neuralgic and other forms of pain, which are sure to appear when the patient misses an accustomed meal.

Kalmia and *Kreosote* are useful in neuralgia, especially when there are burning pains.

Magnesia phos. is called for in neuralgia which occurs regularly each night, and is relieved by heat and pressure.

Mezereum has neuralgia in the cheek-bone or over the left eye. The pains leave numbness. They are worse from warmth. It is especially useful when there have been herpetic eruptions after the abuse of mercury. It is one of the remedies we use for the neuralgia of zona.

Robinia has: jaw-bone feels as if disarticulated. With this there is intensely sour taste and waterbrash or sour vomiting.

Other remedies to be borne in mind are *Cinchona, Spigelia, Platinum, Stannum* and *Chelidonium.*

In typhoid fever *Arsenicum* is indicated late in the disease, when the blood changes have so far progressed that you have a picture of complete exhaustion. The patient thinks himself still able to move about until he finds out how weak he is. He has fainting attacks, which are very alarming; he faints dead away, with cold sweat on the body. The delirium is worse after twelve P. M., and is attended with great restlessness. He is sleepless at three A. M. on account of the great heat. The mouth and tongue are covered with sordes, and with a dark brownish coating. Sometimes the tongue is very red. Around the dorsum and tip of the tongue you will find the papillæ red and raised, as under *Belladonna*, but the concomitant symptoms enable you to differentiate it from that remedy at once. The mouth is full of blisters and aphthous ulcers which bleed readily. In other cases, the tongue is bluish with ulcerated edges. Sometimes, in severe cases, water cannot be swallowed because of partial paralysis of the œsophagus. You do not often find much tympany in the *Arsenic* case. The bowels are very much disturbed. Diarrhœa is almost always present, and seems to be provoked by every attempt to eat or drink. Sometimes, stool and urine are involuntary. The stool is yellowish and watery in character, horribly offensive and worse after midnight. At other times the stools contain blood, slime and pus. In some cases the urine is retained from atony of the muscular fibers of the bladder. The fever is intense, being almost sufficient to consume the patient. Sometimes, you have the hæmorrhagic diathesis to deal with, and there is oozing of blood from various parts of the body, from the eyes, nose, etc. This is a dangerous symptom.

Colchicum is a remedy which we are very apt to neglect in typhoid fever. It seems to stand in typhoid conditions between *Arsenic* and *Cinchona*, having the excessive weakness of the former remedy and the marked tympany of the latter. The chief symptoms of *Colchicum* are abdominal. They are, this great tympany, involuntary, forcible, watery stools, accompanied with nausea and frequent vomiting of bile. The body is hot and the limbs are cold, just as in *Phosphorus*. The nose is dry and blackish. The teeth and tongue are both brown. The mind is somewhat cloudy. He answers questions correctly, but otherwise says nothing. He seems not to know the danger he is in.

The relations of *Arsenic* to other remedies in typhoid fever have been described to you elsewhere. I need not, therefore, repeat them here.

Arsenicum may also be useful in continuous fever, which, in its early stages, so closely resembles that of *Aconite* that you may not be able to distinguish between the two drugs. There are hot skin, full bounding pulse, restlessness and anxiety. Thus far, it is exactly like *Aconite*. But it does not end here. It goes on to a continuous type of fever without any intermissions, and with only slight remissions. The heat increases, the patient grows more restless and weaker, the tongue becomes brown and typhoid symptoms develop.

Now, the distinction between *Arsenic* and *Sulphur* is easily made. *Sulphur* is also useful in continuous fever. *Arsenic* is indicated when the great restlessness and burning show you that the case has gone beyond simple continuous fever.

Now, the action of *Arsenicum* on the mucous membranes. We find it an excellent remedy in winter colds. The nose discharges a thin, watery fluid, which excoriates the upper lip, and yet the nasal passages feel stuffed-up all the time. This is accompanied by dull throbbing frontal headache. Repeated attacks of this kind of catarrh or coryza result in the discharge of thick, yellowish, muco-purulent matter. Ulcers and scabs form in the nose. Sneezing is a prominent symptom. Now this sneezing in the *Arsenic* case is no joke. It does not give the relief which one usually gets from a good sneeze. It is a sneeze which starts from irritation in one spot in the nose as from tickling with a feather. After the sneeze, this irritation is just as annoying as it was before. As the cold creeps downwards, you find the case complicated with catarrhal asthma. Dyspnœa appears. The patient cannot lie down, particularly after midnight. He is greatly relieved by cough with expectoration of mucus.

Arsenicum jodatum closely resembles the "*album*" in coryza, hay-fever and influenza. It has the same thin, acrid discharge, and chilliness, but owing to the *Iodine* it contains there is a marked affinity for lymphatic glands.

You will at once recognize the similarity between the symptoms of *Arsenic* and those of hay-fever. Other remedies which you may remember for this condition are: *Ailanthus*, *Silicea* (which has itching or irritation in the posterior nares or at the orifices of the Eustachian tubes), *Lobelia inflata*, and a remedy introduced by the late Dr. Jeanes, *Rosa Damascena*.

This *Rosa Damascena* is useful in the beginning of rose-cold when the Eustachian tube is involved and there is some little hardness of hearing and tinnitus aurium.

Sinapis nigra is indicated when the mucous membrane of the nose is dry and hot. There is no discharge. The symptoms are worse in the afternoon and evening. Either nostril may be affected alone or alternately with the other.

Wyethia is pecific when with the usual symptoms of hay-fever there is itching of the soft palate.

Arsenic is one of our prime remedies in asthma, whether acute or chronic, with aggravation after midnight and from lying down. The patient is beside himself with anguish. The case may be complicated with emphysema, expiration being very much prolonged as in that disease. It follows *Ipecac* well.

In emphysema you should compare *Lachesis*, *Sulphur*, *Ipecac*, *Antimonium tartaricum*, *Naphthalin*, *Carbo veg*, and above all the *Arsenite* of *Antimony*.

In diphtheria, *Arsenicum* comes into use as a most valuable drug. Arsenic crude kills the microscopic growths which produce the disease. In its potentized state it cures when there is fœtid breath, adynamic fever and a great deal of somnolence, which is broken by starts, crying out and by jerking of the limbs. The membrane looks dark and is gangrenous. The pulse is rapid and weak. I would advise you to substitute *Arsenicum iodatum*, if, in addition to the usual *Arsenicum* symptoms, there is marked enlargement of the lymphatic glands.

I have stated that *Arsenic* acts on the heart. It gives us a list of cardiac symptoms which are, in brief, these: the heart-beat is too strong, it is visible to the person standing by and is audible to the patient himself. It is worse at night and is particularly aggravated when the patient is lying on his back. There may be palpitation with great irregularity of the heart's action. Or the pulse may be accelerated and weak. In cardiac inflammations, endocarditis or pericarditis, we find *Arsenic* indicated after the suppression of measles or scarlatina. You then find present the characteristic restlessness and agony of the drug, tingling in the fingers, especially those of the left hand. Œdema is more or less general, beginning with puffiness of the eyes and swelling of the feet and ending with general anasarca. There is great dyspnœa. Now there are two varieties of dyspnœa which belong to heart disease, one which depends upon the defective carrying of the blood through the lungs and the system generally, and the other which is due to accumulation of water in the chest, hydrothorax and hydropericardium. There are spells of suffocation, worse at night, particularly after midnight and on lying down. The skin is cool and clammy, while internally, the patient is burning hot. Now if this condition calling for *Arsenic* goes on uncured, Bright's disease of the kidneys develops. The urine is highly albuminous and contains waxy and fatty casts. Dropsy appears. Little blisters form in the œdematous limbs on the legs, and these burst, and serum oozes forth. The skin itself is rather tense and has a pale waxen hue. Exhausting diarrhœa usually accompanies these symptoms. There is very apt to be also a burning thirst with intolerance of water.

I wish you now to recall the comparison that I have already given you between *Arsenicum* and *Apocynum*, and *Acetic acid*, which stands midway between *Arsenicum* and *Apis*. I would also have you recall the similarity between *Arsenicum* and *Mercurius sulphuricus* in hydrothorax.

In kidney affections you may compare *Arsenicum* with *Apis, Helleborus, Phosphorus, Aurum, Terebinthina* and *Digitalis*.

Now the *Digitalis* symptoms are these: there is venous hyperæmia of the kidneys. You are to study it, therefore, in renal affections when there are present dropsy, feeble or slow pulse, scanty dark turbid urine, which will, of course, be albuminous. It is exactly like *Arsenic*, without the restlessness and irritability of that remedy.

Again, we find *Arsenicum* indicated in that dreadful disease, angina pectoris. The patient is obliged to sit upright; he cannot move a muscle of his body without great suffering. He holds his breath, so painful is it for him to breathe. The pain seems to radiate from the heart all over the chest and down the left arm. In extreme cases there is cold sweat on the forehead, the pulse becomes scarcely perceptible, and, with all this, there is apt to be burning around the heart.

I would now like to refer to the action of *Arsenic* on the skin. You have already seen that it tends to produce induration or hardening of the skin. This renders it a valuable remedy in eczema, in fact, in every variety of skin disease in which there is thickening of that structure, with copious scaling. *Arsenicum* is also useful in eczema proper, when vesicles appear which turn into pustules and form scabs.

Arsenicum is specifically indicated for bran-colored scales on the head, coming down over the forehead. It may also be called for when there is a thick scabby eruption on the scalp, oozing pus, and very offensive.

Arsenicum compares with *Sepia*, *Rhus tox.*, and *Graphites*. Like *Sepia* there is a dry scaly desquamation, but in *Sepia* this "peeling" follows vesicles which were not surrounded by very red skin, or it follows a fine rash, worse about the joints, or a circular eruption like herpes circinatus.

Rhus tox has vesicles on a red erysipelatous surface, chiefly about the genitals and on hairy parts.

Graphites looks very much like *Arsenicum*, but has oozing of a glutinous fluid.

Clematis is similar to *Arsenicum*, but has more rawness, aggravation from washing and moist, alternating with dry scabs.

Hydrocotyle has eczema with skin thick and scaly, but less burning than in *Arsenic*.

Under *Kreosote* the scales pile up into large masses; eruptions on the extensor surfaces of the limbs. Restlessness. *Natrum muriaticum* on the other hand produces scaly eruptions on flexor surfaces and the bends of joints; dandruff alternating with catarrh and loss of smell.

In the exanthematous diseases we find *Arsenicum* indicated first of all in urticaria. Here it is a valuable drug when the wheals are attended with burning, itching, and restlessness. Particularly may it be indicated for the bad effects of repercussion of hives. Even croup may be cured by *Arsenic* if it follows the retrocession of nettle-rash.

In scarlatina *Arsenic* is to be used in some of the worst cases when the rash does not come out properly. The child is thrown into convulsions, and lies pale and in a sort of stupor, with restlessness and moaning. Suddenly it seems to arouse, and immediately goes into convulsions, and then relapses into stupor again. *Arsenicum* is also useful when, during the course of scarlatina, the parotid glands swell and suppurate, after the failure of *Rhus*.

Arsenicum is useful in gangrene, particularly in the dry gangrene of old people, with great soreness and burning in the affected part, with relief from warm or hot applications. This modality furnishes you with a sufficient distinction between *Arsenic* and another great gangrene remedy, *Secale*, which is useful in dry gangrene, with relief from cold applications. *Lachesis* is one of the best remedies for gangrene after injuries, as when the edges of a lacerated wound turn black.

Cinchona suits in gangrene with hæmorrhage or after great loss of blood.

We may use *Arsenicum* in carbuncles or in boils with pepper-box openings and dipping deeply into the cellular tissues. It is indicated by the character of the pains, which you know run all through the *Arsenicum* symptoms, cutting, lancinating, burning pains, with aggravation after midnight, and irritability of mind and body.

Arsenicum sometimes fails in carbuncles. Then we have to resort to *Anthracinum*, chiefly in the thirtieth potency. It has precisely the same symptoms as *Arsenicum*, but to a more intense degree.

Phytolacca is a remedy to be thought of in this affection when there are lancinating, jerking pains. It is said to promote suppuration.

Carbo veg. and *Lachesis* are remedies that we neglect in this disease. If we use *Carbo veg.* it is well also to use a charcoal poultice over the carbuncle.

Arsenicum may be used in cancer. I am not going to propose that this drug will cure cancer. Epithelioma has been cured by *Conium*, *Hydrastis*, *Arsenic*, *Clematis* and a few other remedies. But in cases of genuine open cancer I have not seen any cases cured; but even if these cases cannot be cured, it is still possible to give them some relief. The pains of cancer you know to be torture. They are of a sharp lancinating character; a red hot knife thrust into the part could not be worse. *Arsenic* sometimes relieves these cases when indicated.

In some cases *Arsenicum iod.* relieves when *Arsenicum album* fails. In others *Belladonna* brings relief.

The ulcers for which *Arsenicum* may be given are not usually very deep. They are rather superficial. The pains are of the character already described, burning and lancinating. The discharge is apt to be excoriating, dark and sanious and they are apt to bleed very readily

Lastly, we will consider *Arsenicum* as a remedy in nervous affections. It is indicated in hemicrania when the pains are worse over one eye, and are of a severe lancinating character. They often alternate with colic or affections of the liver. They are worse from any motion, and are temporarily relieved by cold applications.

It may also be used in epilepsy. The patient falls down unconscious, and then writhes in convulsions. Before the attack he has spells of vertigo and intense aching in the occiput. The convulsions are followed by stupor, which, however, is not complete, but is broken by the ever present restlessness.

LECTURE LIV.

PHOSPHORUS.

Phosphorus.
- Nux vom., Coffea, Ambra.
- Rhus tox., Muriatic acid, Lachesis.
- Carbo veg., Arsenicum, Nitric ac., Kali carb.
- China, Veratr. alb.
- Sulphur. Calcarea ostr., Silicea, Lycopod., Calcarea phos.
- Cepa, Bryonia.
- Zinc
- Terebinthina.
- Osmium.

— >Nux vomica, Terebinthina.
— <Causticum.

THIS hour I wish to say a few words about *Phosphorus*. It has two complements, *Arsenicum* and *Allium cepa*. I have placed *Nux vomica* and *Terebinthina* as the antidotes. The use of *Terebinthina* comes to us from the old school. It seems to antidote *Phosphorus* by chemical action in rendering it inert. It also has antidotal effects when used in potency. *Nux vomica* is good when *Phosphorus*, as a remedy, has produced over-effects, or when it has been incorrectly given.

In the study of *Phosphorus* we have to remember, first of all, as most important and as a quality that permeates every part of the *Phosphorus* proving, its action on the nervous system. Its symptoms in no instance point to increase of power or vitality, or to any genuine stimulation of function, but rather to that condition which we found under *Arsenic*, irritable weakness. The patient is exceedingly susceptible to external impressions. He can bear neither light, sounds nor odors; he is very sensitive to touch. Electric changes such as occur in sudden changes of the weather, but particularly in a thunderstorm, make him anxious and fearful, and aggravate all existing symptoms. His mind, too, is excitable and impressionable. He is easily angered and becomes vehement. This is not a simple peevishness. He actually gets beside himself with anger, and, just like the

Nux and the *Chamomilla* patient, he suffers physically in consequence. At other times he is anxious and restless, especially in the dark or about twilight. He has all sorts of fanciful or imaginary notions. He sees faces grinning at him from every corner of the room. His thoughts may be so stimulated that they fairly rush through his mind; but this effect is only transient, and followed either by inability to think and remember, or by aggravation of all his symptoms on mental exertion. He cannot stand mental tax. Here again it impinges on *Nux vomica*. As further evidence of the irritable weakness of *Phosphorus*, we have the delirium of that remedy. Now this delirium may be associated with typhoid fever, with jaundice, or with sexual erethism. It may be quite violent. It is characterized by a condition of ecstacy. The patient has a notion that his body is all in fragments, and he wonders how he is going to get the pieces together. He imagines that he is a great person surrounded by grand accoutrements, the mania of grandeur it is sometimes termed. At other times the mania takes the form of sexual excitement. He uncovers his person without any shame and seeks to gratify his sexual appetite, no matter who may be the victim. These delirious attacks pass into a state of coma, or into stupid condition of mind or state of apathy, during which he answers questions not at all or very reluctantly. *Phosphorus* is here very similar to *Hyoscyamus*, and often follows that remedy to erotic mania. It also bears points of resemblance to *Stramonium*, *Baptisia*, *Rhus tox*. and *Muriatic acid*.

The same quality of the drug is shown in the symptoms throughout the body. Headache, for instance, is attended with increased sensitiveness to odors; the sense of smell is very acute, so that the patient faints away from the smell of flowers. There may be pulsating, throbbing headache, worse from music. The hearing for the sound of the human voice is imparied; associated with this is roaring in the ears, as from rush of blood. Sounds reverberate unpleasantly in the ears. There is also sexual excitement with frequent erections, lascivious thoughts entirely beyond the control of the patient, and frequent seminal emissions during sleep.

Symptoms of the spinal irritation are very characteristic of *Phosphorus*. These are associated with palpitation of the heart, worse from any emotion, whether it be grief, anger or pleasure. The spine, as in all these cases of spinal irritation, is exceedingly sensitive to touch. With all this there is a weakness of the spine. The back feels weak, as if it would soon give out. There is weakness of the limbs, with trembling, on beginning to walk. The patient stumbles a great deal, catching his toes in every little projection of the floor or pavement. He totters, and there seems to be imperfect coördination. He is sleepless from excessive heat. When asleep, his dreams are of a horribly exciting character. These are illustrations of the erethism of *Phosphorus* and also of diminished resistence to external stimulants. Such persons may degenerate into various diseased conditions. The loss of animal fluids, as blood, semen, or milk, or too frequent child-bearing, or too rapid growth in the young, is sufficient to precipitate nervous diseases such as paralysis, chorea and spinal disease, or tuberculosis.

You will find *Phosphorus* indicated in locomotor ataxia, when there is a great deal of burning along the spine. There is also great tingling and formication along the spine and in the affected extremities. In the beginning the patients have extreme sexual excitement. That is a sort of *sine qua non*, either that they are excessively excitable, or else have been so.

You seldom find *Phosphorus* indicated in impotence, unless it has resulted or has been preceded by over-excitation of the sexual organs. This is a valuable hint. I find it especially indicated in young men who are trying to restrain their natural passion, and yet there is locally this erethism. This *Phosphorus* helps most wonderfully to control. If, by reason of celibacy or of over-indulgence in sexual pleasures, the sexual organs lose their power and the patient becomes impotent, *Phosphorus* is the remedy when this has been preceded by over-excitation. It is different from *Conium*, in which the patient may have been naturally excitable, but has gone on to this weakness.

Phosphorus is indicated in locomotor ataxia also, when it can be traced to excessive loss of animal fluids, as semen.

Softening of the brain is another form of atrophy of the nervous tissue in which *Phosphorus* has won many laurels. The patient has a dull pain in the head, a wearied, tired feeling all the time, and slight difficulty in walking. It is particularly indicated after the use of *Nux vomica*. The question is sometimes asked, and quite properly, too, how can you put *Nux vomica* down as the antidote of *Phosphorus*, and then speak of it as a remedy that can precede or follow it? First, the antidote may follow the drug and may be needed, not to antidote it, but because symptoms which come up have an opposite polarity, and, consequently, require an opposite remedy; and, secondly, a remedy may be antidotal in some of its symptoms and concordant in others.

Phosphorus may be used very successfully in chorea when it occurs in children who are growing too fast. The patient is very weak and walks as if paralyzed.

Continuing the nervous symptoms of *Phosphorus* still further, we find it indicated in low types of nervous fever and in typhoid types of fever. I am induced to use this expression, typhoid types of fever, in order to show that you can consider *Phosphorus*, not only in typhoid or typhus fever, but in any form of fever which assumes a typhoid form when these symptoms appear. It is indicated when there is great cerebro-spinal exhaustion. It is particularly the brain and spine which seem to have suffered from typhoid poison. The face is apt to be of an ashy or waxen hue or appearance. The tongue is covered with a viscid, thready sort of slime, which is expectorated with great difficulty. It seems to collect on the teeth and around the gums and on the tongue. It is tenacious and the patient is weak; and these two incompatibles make it difficult for him to cleanse the mouth. The body is hot,—and by the body I mean the trunk,—the head being rather cool and the limbs decidedly cold. There is congestion of both chest and abdomen. The breath is hot, and there is almost always either bronchial catarrh or pneumonia. I refer now more particularly to the pneumonic infiltration which belongs to typhoid fever, in which case *Phosphorus* is often indicated. The patient has burning thirst, which is relieved by drinking cold water. The thirst is worse from three to six o'clock in the afternoon. The patient is better from cold water until the water becomes warm in the stomach, when it is violently ejected. *Phosphorus* does not often do any good in vomiting, except in the chronic vomiting of dyspeptics, unless this condition is present.

This is quite different from *Arsenic*. It is also very different from *Bismuth*, this last-named remedy has vomiting immediately after taking food, with burning, cardialgic pains.

It is different from *Kreosote*, which has vomiting of undigested food hours after eating.

Let us return to *Phosphorus* in typhoid types of fever. The bowels are always affected. You will find that the liver is sore to the touch and usually enlarged. This is also true of the spleen. The patient has diarrhœa as soon as he eats. Here it is identical with *Arsenic*. Now, the stools in the *Phosphorus* case are flaky, dark, and often bloody, and there is extreme weakness after stool, that being a decided cerebro-spinal symptom. You find it in the cerebro-spinal remedies, in *Conium*, in *Nux vomica*, and especially in *Phosphorus*. When there is constipation you may have what has been called characteristically "dog stool," *i. e.*, long, slender stool, which is evacuated with considerable effort. During this fever, which I say is mostly congestive and affects the chest and abdomen, the patient continually throws off the bed-clothes. He puts the arms out of bed to cool off. There is profuse sweat which does not relieve. Now I would like to caution you here that *Mercury* is not indicated in typhoid fever unless there be clearly defined icteroid symptoms, consequently you will not often have occasion to give it in this fever, and never should you give it for this symptom, "profuse sweat without relief," unless it is so well defined by the icteroid and bowel symptoms that you are certain that you have the properly indicated remedy. Other remedies than *Mercury* have this symptom, notably *Phosphorus*, and also *Rhus tox.* and *Chamomilla*, the latter particularly in children. *Phosphorus* is indicated even in extreme cases of typhoid fever when there is threatening paralysis of the lungs. The patient lies in a sort of coma, with hot breath and rattling breathing. It seems as if there was a large quantity of phlegm rattling in the lungs. The limbs are cold and are covered with a cold sweat. The pulse is scarcely perceptible.

I would here remind you of *Carbo veg.* as also being suitable in collapse. It follows *Phosphorus* very well. It is distinguished, theoretically at least, from the latter remedy by this: *Phosphorus* acts more upon the cerebro-spinal nervous system and *Carbo veg.* more upon the sympathetic nerves, particularly on the solar plexus.

Next I wish to speak to you of a property of *Phosphorus* which does not depend upon the action of the drug on the nervous system, and that is the power of the drug to produce fatty degeneration. *Phosphorus* seems to affect the blood, how is not exactly known. It decomposes the blood, rendering it more fluid, rendering it difficult to coagulate. At the same time it produces hyperæmia of one part or another. Thus you will find tendency to congestion of the head or of any of the viscera of the body. This hyperæmia is not an active arterial congestion, but rather a stasis of blood. The affected part becomes engorged with blood, and as this is of an impoverished quality, it does not nourish properly and we have setting-in fatty degeneration of the part. This may be in the brain or spine (of this I have already spoken), it may be in the heart or lungs, but it is especially apt to occur in the liver and kidneys. The muscles even may undergo fatty degeneration.

On the liver, *Phosphorus* acts very prominently. The symptoms here are directly connected with fatty degeneration. When *Phosphorus* is taken for a long time you will find at first this hyperæmia of the liver. That organ is consequently enlarged with the attendant symptoms, well-marked soreness and jaundice. The stools are apt to be grayish-white, showing the absence of the secretion of bile. The abdomen becomes decidedly tympanitic. By and by, the jaundice increases to an alarming extent, the pulse becomes weak and thread-like. These symptoms are traceable to two causes: first, the inevitable alterations in the blood which *Phosphorus* produces; and secondly, the poisoning of the blood by the retention within it of the elements which go to make bile. These have a depressing effect on the heart, making the pulse slow or else weak and thread-like. If you examine the liver at this stage, you find that it is beginning to atrophy, this atrophy depending upon destruction of the hepatic cells proper and increase of the stroma of the liver. The connective-tissue framework of the liver has undergone inflammatory increase. The pressure which this exerts on the hepatic cells causes their destruction. Thus we have what has been termed cirrhosis of the liver. Then comes ascites, and you find varicose veins coursing all over the abdomen. The blood becomes so poisoned that the patient goes into the delirium which I have already described. The urine may be highly albuminous in these cases. The icteroid symptoms increase and finally, death ensues.

Phosphorus is useful in acute yellow atrophy of the liver, a condition which it also produces.

Again, it may be useful in fatty degeneration of the liver as a sequel of heart disease. It may also be indicated in waxy liver dependent upon long-lasting bone disease, as caries of the vertebra or of the hip-joint.

Phosphorus is also indicated in hepatitis when suppuration ensues with hectic fever, night sweats, enlargement in the right hypochondrium, and marked soreness over the liver.

The jaundice of *Phosphorus* is not functional in origin, but is indicative of organic disease; it is associated with anæmia, with brain disease, with pregnancy or with malignant diseases of the liver.

Phosphorus has a marked action on the alimentary tract. The tongue is coated white, and this, as under *Bryonia*, is more along the middle of the organ. With bilious affections, the tongue is coated yellow; in typhoid affections, it is brownish or blackish and very dry. Here it is very much like *Rhus*. The throat and adjacent parts may be inflamed, particularly the uvula. White, transparent mucus collects in the throat. The patient is very hungry, particularly at night. This symptom may almost amount to bulimy, which is also an indication for *Phosphorus* in chills and fever. He wakes up hungry and lies awake until he gets something to eat. There is longing for cold things, ice-cream, ice-water, etc. Cold food seems to relieve until it gets warm in the stomach, when there appears the characteristic vomiting of the remedy. *Phosphorus* may cure vomiting in chronic dyspepsia when there seems to be simple exhaustion of the stomach. Perhaps the inner surface of the viscus is coated with mucus, thus preventing the action of the gastric juice on the food.

We also find *Phosphorus* useful in spasmodic stricture of the œsophagus, especially at its cardiac end. Food seems to go down a certain distance and then it is violently ejected.

Coming to the stomach itself, we find *Phosphorus* indicated in that very dangerous disease, perforating ulcer of the stomach. We find it there indicated by the pain by the vomiting of food as soon as swallowed, and by the vomited matters containing a dark, grumous, semi-solid substance looking like coffee-grounds.

We also find *Phosphorus* indicated by these same symptoms in cancer of the stomach, particularly when it is about to pass into the stage of ulceration.

Phosphorus is one of the few remedies that act on the pancreas. It is especially useful if there be fatty degeneration of that organ. The symptoms indicating it here are the gastric symptoms just enumerated, and oily stool. Sometimes the stool looks like frog spawn, or, to speak more accurately, like cooked sago. *Phosphorus* may also be remembered in diabetes mellitus and Bright's disease when these have been preceded or are accompanied by disease of the pancreas.

The intestinal tract is attacked by *Phosphorus* almost as violently as it is by *Arsenicum*. It produces constipation, the character of which I have already explained to you. It also produces diarrhœa. The stools may be profuse and watery, and worse in the morning. Here it runs against *Sulphur* and *Podophyllum*. It also produces green mucous stools, worse in the morning. The stools are apt to contain undigested food and are very debilitating to the patient. We find *Phosphorus* indicated in cholerine, or diarrhœa occurring in time of cholera epidemics. Paralysis of the bowels is also produced and cured by *Phosphorus*, particularly when the lower portions of the bowels, the colon and rectum, are affected. The anus seems to stand wide open and exudes moisture.

In diseases of the urinary organs *Phosphorus* is a first-class remedy. It is to be thought of in the diseases classed under the general term, Bright's disease. It is useful in fatty or in amyloid degeneration of the kidneys, especially if associated with a similar pathological condition of the liver and of the right or venous heart, with the consequent symptoms of venous stagnation and venous hyperæmia in different organs, with œdema of the lungs and all the symptoms of pulmonary engorgement which indicate pneumonia. The urine contains epithelial, fatty or waxy casts.

Phosphorus may cure hæmorrhages from any part of the body, particularly from the lungs and stomach when associated with Bright's disease.

Phosphorus is a decided irritant to the sexual organs in either sex, producing nymphomania in the female and satyriasis or uncontrollable sexual desire in the male.

It does not affect the female organs very prominently. The menstrual discharges seem to be altered. They are often too profuse and long-lasting, the menstrual blood being too pale. There is always a weeping, sad mood at that time. However, we find *Phosphorus* indicated more when the menses are checked; amenorrhœa when vicarious blood-spitting, epistaxis or hæmaturia ensues.

In diseases of the mammary gland, *Phosphorus* is especially useful when abscesses have formed. The inflamed gland has an erysipelatous appearance. Red streaks radiate from the opening in the abscess. The pus discharged is not laudable, but is of a thin, watery, ichorous character. Here it is complementary to *Silicea*, and very similar to *Belladonna*.

Next we take up the action of *Phosphorus* on the respiratory passages. In nasal catarrh we do not find it often indicated except it be chronic catarrh or ozæna. Then it is indicated by the color of the discharge, which is green mucus and blood-streaked. Green mucus *not* blood-streaked does not often require *Phosphorus*.

Nasal polypus, when it bleeds much, calls for *Phosphorus*. It may also be used in polypi of the ears or uterus. Other remedies to be thought of here are *Teucrium, Calcarea, Calcarea phos., Thuja* and *Sanguinaria*.

On the larynx it acts more prominently than any other remedy we have. The symptoms indicating it here are hoarseness, which is usually worse in the evening, at which time it may amount to aphonia, and extreme sensitiveness of the larynx. The patient is worse from talking or coughing. It hurts the larynx for him to cough or talk, so sensitive is it to the vibrations thus produced.

It also causes catarrhal and membranous croup, but it is not usually indicated here in the beginning. But it acts as a sort of prophylactic to prevent the return of the disease. It is useful also in advanced cases of croup when the cerebro-spinal system is giving out, just as we found in typhoid states. Thus there are aphonia, rapid sinking of strength, cold, clammy sweat, rattling breathing, sunken, pale face and dropping of the lower jaw. The pulse in such cases is weak, thready and intermittent. In this group of symptoms *Phosphorus* is very similar to *Lycopodium*.

You find *Phosphorus* indicated in tracheitis and bronchitis, especially in tall, slender persons of rather tuberculous habit or tendency, rather inclined to stoop and to be hollow-chested. The cough is particularly worse on going from the warm room into the cold air, or in changes from warm to cold. It has dry, tickling cough caused by irritation in the larynx and beneath the sternum. In extreme cases it is associated with tremor of the whole body, so nervously weak is the patient. It is frequently accompanied by almost intolerable pain in the larynx from laryngeal catarrh, by splitting pain in the head just as you found under *Bryonia*, and by burning rawness down the larynx and trachea. There is tightness across the upper third of the lungs. Now, a word of caution respecting this tightness. It is not a feeling as from a band around the chest, but as though the lungs themselves were constricted.

The relation between the fauces, larynx and trachea, as a starting point for cough, has been aptly mapped out by Dr. Dunham and carefully distributed among three remedies. For instance, *Belladonna* acts upon the fauces. It causes dry, tickling, teasing cough. The throat is bright red and the tonsils enlarged.

Going further down, you find tickling in the suprasternal fossa. Every change in the breathing causes cough. This condition calls for *Rumex*.

When the irritation extends down still further, into the bronchi, then *Phosphorus* becomes the remedy.

We find *Phosphorus* indicated in a great variety of coughs. Thus it is useful in stomach or hepatic cough coming on after the patient eats, and starting from tickling at the pit of the stomach. It is also indicated in cough made worse by the entrance of a stranger into the room ; this being purely a reflex nervous symptom. It is also called for in cough provoked by strong odors. In fact, perfumes or anything that will disturb the balance of the nervous system will bring on cough under *Phosphorus*.

Phosphorus is indicated in bronchitis or bronchial catarrh, whether the disease involves the bronchial tubes high up or whether it extends down into the bronchioles. The symptoms are as follows: cough, with tearing pain under the sternum, as if something were being torn loose; suffocative pressure in the upper part of the chest, with constriction of the larynx. You will also find the lungs to be engorged with blood, mucous râles through the chest, panting and labored respiration and even emphysema. The sputa are of various kind. Thus we may have bloody and mucous sputum. Very characteristic is sputum, consisting of yellowish mucus, with streaks of blood running through it. It may be rust-colored, as in pneumonia, or it may be purulent and have a sweetish or salty taste.

In pneumonia, *Phosphorus* is indicated when the bronchial symptoms are prominent. Then it is almost certain to be the remedy. It does not cause hepatization of the lungs, so that it would not be indicated when the lung or lungs are in a complete state of hepatization. But it may be indicated for typhoid symptoms in the course of pneumonia (these symptoms I have already given to you), especially in the latter part of the period of deposit and in the early part of absorption, that is, just when hepatization is coming on and just when it is going off. There is great dryness of the air-passages, with burning, excoriating, raw feeling in the upper part of the chest.

In tuberculosis you find *Phosphorus* indicated particularly in youths, and by this expression I mean both young men and women who have grown too rapidly, who have delicate skin, long silky eyelashes, and who are of easy, graceful manners. The mental development is excellent, yet they have not the physique to support this keenness of mind. Particularly is it indicated if they have a hereditary tendency to consumption, or have had bone diseases in early childhood. The early symptoms, you will notice, are these: the patient catches cold easily; he suffers from rush of blood to the chest; he has the above-mentioned constriction across the chest with every little cold; pains through the apex of the left lung; cannot lie on the left side; aphonia; dry cough; hectic flush of the cheeks, particularly towards evening; oppression of the chest at night, forcing him to sit up; empty feeling at the pit of the stomach, particularly in the forenoon at ten or eleven o'clock; he awakens hungry at night, feeling that he must eat, and that he would faint if he did not. Finally, the hectic fever grows more prominent. There is rapid formation of vomicæ or cavities in the lungs. These are the indications for *Phosphorus* in pneumonia, and I must supplement them with a warning. Unless you give the drug cautiously, you precipitate what you would prevent. Be certain that it is the remedy, and do not give it too often, or you will hasten the process you are anxious to avoid. I would not advise you to give *Phosphorus* in well-marked tuberculous patients. If tubercles have been deposited in the lungs, you should hesitate before giving it, unless the "picture" calling for it is so strong that you cannot possibly make a mistake.

I may say that the same is true also of *Sulphur*. *Sulphur* is adapted to the onset of the disease. Then, a dose or two allowed to act will frequently head these symptoms off. But after tubercles have been deposited, you must be careful how you use the drug.

I would next say a few words about the action of *Phosphorus* on the heart. It is particularly indicated in affections of this organ when the right side of the heart is involved more than the left. Its symptoms point more to the bad results that follow disease of the right heart than disease of the left; in a word, venous stagnation. It is suited to all forms of palpitation; palpitation from emotion, as from the sudden entrance into the room of an unexpected visitor, welcome or unwelcome; from motion; and also from rush of blood to the chest. Particularly does this latter occur in the rapidly-growing young

Phosphorus must also be remembered in endocarditis, in which disease it is often forgotten. Particularly is it indicated when endocarditis or myocarditis occurs during the course of acute inflammatory rheumatism or during pneumonia.

Phosphorus is also useful for fatty degeneration of the heart. You distinguish it from *Arsenicum* by the involvement of the right heart, by venous stagnation and puffiness of the face, particularly under the eyelids. *Arsenicum* has more symptoms of the left heart, more oppression of the chest in breathing, more orthopnœa, and more anasarca or general dropsy.

Phosphorus acts upon the bones. We find this illustrated in the necrosis of the lower jaw, formerly so common among matchmakers. The fumes of the *Phosphorus* cause necrosis of the lower and sometimes of the upper jaw. You may ask, is this not a local effect produced by inhalation of the fumes? If it is a local effect, why does it affect by preference the lower jaw? Why not the upper? But, when persons have been poisoned by eating *Phosphorus*, if necrosis results, it is the lower jaw that is affected, thus showing you that the drug has a special affinity for this bone. It is to be remembered in caries or necrosis of the lower jaw. This you sometimes meet with from teething or from an inflamed or suppurating gland. *Phosphorus* affects other bones as well as the lower jaw, however. We find it not infrequently indicated in caries of the vertebra in scrofulous children. The concomitant symptoms have to decide the remedy for you. For instance, the child is of the characteristic *Phosphorus* build. There is diarrhœa, worse in the morning, much like that of *Sulphur*, the stool containing undigested food. There is tendency to involvement of the lungs. For instance, the patient catches cold easily, with marked tendency to bronchitis. Still further, we may be called upon to use *Phosphorus* in caries of the vertebra when the inflammation has extended inwards and involved the spinal cord itself. This you notice to be expressed first by burning in certain portions of the spine. The patient cannot tolerate any heat near the back. A hot sponge on the back causes him to wince. There will be a feeling as of a band around the body. The difficulty in walking increases until finally the child cannot walk at all. There is often partial loss of control over the sphincters.

Phosphorus also affects the joints, the hip and knee-joints in particular. Hence, it may be indicated in morbus coxarius or in white swelling, both common, as you know, in scrofulous children. Here, too, you have to separate it from the other antipsorics by the general symptoms. I would say, for your guidance, that *Phosphorus* belongs with *Silicea* and seems to complement it. It is useful when *Silicea* has been partially successful in these joint-diseases.

Fistulæ in the glands and about the joints are apt to form with *Phosphorus*. These fistulous ulcers have high edges from exuberant granulations, the purulent discharge being rather thin and ichorous.

Around the ulcer *Phosphorus* has, probably more than *Silicea*, an erysipelatous blush, often radiating as in *Belladonna*. There will frequently be burning, stinging pains, well-marked hectic fever with night sweat, diarrhœa, and anxiety towards evening.

These same symptoms apply to inflammation of the mammary glands when there are fistulous ulcers, as in *Silicea*, but distinguished from that remedy by the erysipelatous blush.

Burning and stinging pains also suggest *Apis*, but *Apis* does not cause deep seated suppuration, such as that in the parenchyma of an organ.

Next, I wish to say a word about the action of *Phosphorus* on the eyes. While it may not be the best remedy for affections of the external parts of the eye, it certainly does lead the list for diseases involving the deeper structures of that organ, as the retina, choroid and vitreous humor. It is particularly in nervous affections of the eye that we find *Phosphorus* indicated, and by "nervous" I mean belonging to the nerves of the eye. Thus it is suited to hyperæmia of the choroid and retina, which may even result in retinitis or choroiditis, and when it does so result, it is apt to be a serious trouble. Vision is greatly lessened. The patient sees all sorts of abnormal colors, black spots in the air and gray veils over things; it seems as if he were constantly looking through a mist or fog. Objects look red. Letters appear red when reading. That symptom, I believe, is under no other remedy but *Phosphorus*. Other remedies have red vision, but under *Phosphorus* alone is it that in reading the letters look red.

This remedy is also indicated in retinitis accompanying kidney affections, retinitis albuminuria.

It may also be indicated in retinitis with suppression of menses or some other uterine or ovarian disorder. When you have an eye affection to deal with do not forget that the eyes are not the whole body. Remember that lesion in the eye may have as a starting point, disease in some other part of the body. Therefore, in making your prescription, do not forget to look for the constitutional symptoms that may be present.

We also find *Phosphorus* indicated in either amblyopia or asthenopia, particularly when associated with Bright's disease or resulting from loss of fluids. When the patient attempts to read the letters blur and run together, and the eyes smart and burn. It is useful in amblyopia occurring after typhoid fever, sexual excesses or loss of fluids. It is also suited to blindness after lightning-stroke. In these cases the patient almost always sees a green halo around the candle-light.

I would like to say that *Phosphorus* will retard the growth of cataract. Other remedies that may suggest themselves in this condition are *Silicea, Baryta carb., Conium, Secale, Natrum mur., Calcarea ostr.* and *Magnesium carb.*

In addition to producing oversensitiveness to sound, as already mentioned, *Phosphorus* has the opposite effect, deafness or hardness of hearing, particularly for the sound of the human voice. We have exactly the opposite symptom under *Ignatia*. This deafness may be purely nervous, as after typhoid fever. It may also indicate the drug in congested states when the hardness of hearing is associated with buzzing and roaring in the ears.

Phosphorus acts on the blood, destroying its coagulability. Thus it is that small wounds bleed much. I think that these are the words of the symptom as Hahnemann gave it to us. The way that he found that to be characteristic of *Phosphorus* was this: one prover noticed that when he pricked his finger it was difficult to stop the bleeding. Hahnemann put this down as a possible symptom of *Phosphorus*. Later, a patient came to him, and described the totality of her symptoms. She had this bleeding. He gave her *Phosphorus* which cured her. Since then this drug has been used many times for this hæmorrhagic diathesis. *Lachesis* has a similar symptom, but has not been so thoroughly confirmed as has *Phosphorus*.

Phosphorus is also indicated in hæmatemesis. This may be vicarious as from a suppressed menstrual flow, or it may result from simple congestion of the stomach, or even from organic disease of the stomach, particularly open cancer or round ulcer of the stomach. The vomited matters contain dark grumous substances, looking like coffee-grounds.

Phosphorus may also be used in hæmoptysis, when indicated by the symptoms already given.

LECTURE LV.

THE PREPARATIONS OF ANTIMONY

Antimony.
- Depresses the heart and circulation.
- Increases sweat.
- Mucous membranes:—catarrhs.
- Nausea, vomiting, purging, fainting, collapse.
- Skin:—rash; pustules.

WE take up for study to-day two of the preparations of antimony, *Antimonium crudum* and *Antimonium tartaricum*. The term *Antimonium crudum* does not imply that it is the metallic antimony but that it is the ore, the form in which it is most frequently found in nature. *Antimonium tartaricum* is a compound salt the tartrate of antimony and potash. There are other Antimony preparations used in medicine, but we shall only consider the above-named as they are the most important.

Antimony exerts a depressing influence on the heart and circulation. Respiration too is disturbed by it, and in the majority of cases, perspiration is increased. The next important seat of action of antimony is the mucous membranes, particularly that of the alimentary canal. It causes nausea, vomiting and purging, with faintness and relaxation. The vomited matters you will find at first to consist of mucus and food. Later they contain bile, and finally blood. It is not because antimony has a special effect on the liver that we have this bilious vomiting, but because it causes a regurgitation of bile. Cramps occur in the limbs. These are accompanied by purging and thus you have a perfect picture of collapse such as you find in cholera or cholera morbus. Now, the emetic properties of antimony are not local. Experiments have been made by which the stomach has been extirpated, a bladder placed in its stead, and antimony injected into the blood. Retching will ensue, and yet there is no stomach. It therefore acts through the pneumogastric nerves.

Antimony will cause convulsions. This convulsive action is traceable to disturbance in the circulation at the base of the brain.

The lungs become engorged with blood by any preparation of antimony. It is said that hepatization of a portion of the organ may follow poisoning by it, especially by its tartrate. This has been doubted of late. It has been claimed that this so-called hepatization was in reality atalectasis.

You also find antimony causing emphysema, particularly of the borders of the lungs.

Animals fed on antimonic acid will have fatty degeneration of the liver, heart, etc.

The skin is attacked by the antimonies. The irritation they here produce is rather slow and tardy, but the result is very characteristic. There will be, at first, slight redness; this is followed by development of papules, and these papules become pustules. Pustular eruptions are very characteristic of antimony, particularly of the tartrate. These pustules resemble the eruption of small-pox, so much so that *Antimonium tartaricum* has been used as a remedy in that disease, and with success.

Antimony is particularly useful when pustules appear about the genital organs, whether they be syphilitic or not.

While the preponderance is in favor of *Antimonium tartaricum* for pustulation, *Antimonium crudum* carries off the palm for horny excrescences and callosities on the feet and hands.

We will now consider

Antimonium Crudum.

Antimonium crudum.
{ Bryonia, Ipecac., Nux vomica, Pulsatilla.
Chamomilla.
Sulphur, Arsenicum, Hepar.
Ranunculus bulbosus.
Æthusa cynapium. }

In the above schema I have placed no complementary remedy to *Antimonium crudum*. *Scilla* has been said to be complementary to it, but I have not satisfied myself that such is the case.

When *Antimonium crudum* is indicated, we find mental symptoms that are quite prominent. It is frequently used in children when they are cross and peevish. They will not even permit themselves to be looked at. If an adult, the patient is sulky or sad, almost like the

Pulsatilla patient. In some cases, there is a slightly erotic condition of mind, connected with sexual erethism. The patient becomes ecstatic and fancies that some beautiful female is the object of his sentimental love.

In children, this peevish mental state is associated with nausea, hot and red face and irregular pulse. The child is particularly cross when washed in cold water, but not so much in warm water. Now, the symptoms often occur in children in association with those of the stomach.

The gastric symptoms of *Antimony* are very well marked. It is suited to gastric catarrh, whether it be developed from cold or from improper food. In the first place, the tongue is coated white, and this coating is apt to be spread uniformly over the whole dorsum of the tongue. It has well been compared to a coat of whitewash. The tongue may be dry, and often is so, as in *Bryonia*. Sometimes, we find this white coating assuming a slightly yellowish tinge, especially on the back part of the tongue. At other times, you will find the borders of the tongue sore and red; often, there is an accumulation of yellowish mucus in the pharynx. There are nausea and vomiting; the latter is very prominent, and occurs as soon as the child eats or drinks. *Antimonium crudum* is especially useful in vomiting from overloaded stomach; from eating indigestible substances; after the abuse of fat food, acids, sour wines, vinegar, etc., or from the excessive heat of summer. The vomited matters contain food; or, in the case of very young children, they consist of curdled milk. The appetite is impaired. There may be colic, in which case there is almost always a deposit of lithic acid in the urine. The bowels are affected also; there is often diarrhœa; the stool is watery and contains little lumps of fæcal matter. This diarrhœa is made worse by vinegar and other acids, by cold bathing and by being overheated. If there is constipation, as is often the case when vomiting predominates, the stools will consist of white, hard and dry lumps that look like undigested curd. In older persons, particularly in the aged, for *Antimonium crudum* suits both extremes of life, we have an alternation of constipation and diarrhœa: the stool, in constipation consisting of hard, dry lumps; that in diarrhœa, of water mixed with fæcal lumps.

Now let us make some distinctions between *Antimonium crudum* and its concordant remedies. *Æthusa cynapium* is our mainstay for vomiting of curdled milk in infants during dentition, or at other times.

The vomited matter comes with a "rush," and the vomiting exhausts the little patient. It then falls into a sleep from which it awakens hungry, eats and again vomits. In *Antimonium crudum*, the child is hungry as soon as it rids itself of the milk. *Æthusa* is suited to severe cases that have been prostrated by a long course of bad diet, by summer complaint or by the irritation of teething. I have known *Æthusa* to relieve the pain and soreness in the gums of teething children when vomiting is a prominent symptom.

Like *Antimonium crudum*, *Ipecacuanha* has vomiting after a meal, after coughing and after acids; and hence it is suited to similar cases. But *Ipecacuanha* usually has more nausea than has the other. Vomiting and retching predominate in *Antimonium crudum*, and nausea in *Ipecacuanha*. Then, too, the latter remedy usually has clean or slightly coated tongue; whereas the former requires a thick white coating of that organ.

Bryonia is similar to *Antimonium crudum*. It has white tongue, dry mouth and constipation. It is suited to gastric catarrh from over-eating in persons of irritable temperament. The *Bryonia* tongue is a little different from that of *Antimonium crudum*, in that it is white down the middle, the edges not being coated. Then, too, the *Bryonia* stool is large, hard, dry and brown. If there is diarrhœa, the stool is offensive and watery, and smells like old cheese.

Still another remedy is *Pulsatilla*. Here we find resemblances in the state of mind. We have both remedies called for in gastric ailments from the use of pork. But *Pulsatilla* has not the characteristic vomiting of *Antimony*, and the stool of *Pulsatilla* is usually greenish, or yellowish-green, and slimy. It is especially suited to cases after indulgence in mixed diet—ice-cream, cakes, pastry, etc.

Antimonium crudum acts upon the skin, producing thick, horny callosities in this tissue. It is often indicated in eczematous eruptions, when the skin is of this character.

It also has a marked action on the nails, causing deficient growth. If, after an accident which has split the nail, the latter does not heal readily, but grows cracked and thick, *Antimonium crudum* will make it grow as it should. I have also used the drug successfully in treating a split hoof, in the case of my own horse.

Children who need *Antimonium crudum* often have an eruption, consisting of crusts which are of a honey-yellow color. They are thick, just as we have seen with the callosities. The affected portions of the skin crack readily. This is particularly well-marked about the nostrils and corners of the mouth.

Now, I know of one case of diphtheria cured by *Antimonium crudum* when the symptoms were these: the child was very cross; whining and crying simply because it was looked at; this was especially so on awaking from sleep; and there were these crusts around the nostrils and in the corners of the mouth. *Antimonium crudum* not only removed these but cured the diphtheria.

The eyes are inflamed. They are worse from any bright glare, as the sunshine, or the glare of a bright fire, here reminding you of *Mercurius*. *Antimonium crudum* is distinguished from *Graphites* by the fact that the rawness is confined to the canthi, whereas under *Graphites* the inflammation involves the whole border of the lids.

On the female genital organs *Antimonium crudum* has some action. It is useful in prolapsus uteri when there is constant bearing-down feeling, as if something were pushing out of the vagina, and tenderness over the ovarian region, particularly when the menses have been suppressed by cold bathing. The leucorrhœa is watery and contains little lumps.

There is one more use of *Antimonium crudum* to mention and we are done with it, and that is in adults who are tormented with gout. It is especially useful when gout has become constitutional. There will be gouty nodes in many of the joints. It here helps, provided the gastric symptoms characteristic of the remedy are present, but not otherwise.

Antimonium Tartaricum.

Antimonium tartaricum.
1. Throat and Lungs.
   - Baryta c., Lachesis.
   - Ipecac., Kali hyd.
   - Phosphorus, Sulphur, Carbo v.
   - Laurocerasus, Ammonium carb.
   - Bromine, Iodine, Spongia.
2. Skin.—Conium, Mercurius, Kali bi., Kali hyd.
3. Bowels.—Veratr. alb., Merc.

Antimonium tartaricum or *Tartar emetic*, as it is also called, is a compound salt of antimony and potash, both of which substances depress the circulation. Hence you will expect to see symptoms due to this cause intensified under *Antimonium tartaricum*. It causes more weakness of the heart and lungs than does antimony itself.

Under *Antimonium tartaricum* we find the head confused, with warmth of the forehead and confused feeling, as if the patient ought to sleep. This drowsiness is worse in the forenoon. Often there is a headache, with sensation as if a band were tied around the forehead. This is a common symptom of headache due to passive congestion of the brain. You find it under *Gelsemium*, *Mercurius*, *Carbolic acid*, *Sulphur*, and several other remedies. Cool air and moving about seem to brighten the patient up. Bathing the head relieves; this is contrary to the general modality of *Antimonium crudum*. There is sometimes throbbing, particularly in the right side of the head. Still another form of headache is drawing in the right temple, extending down and into the jaw-bone. This is a sort of rheumatic tearing pain in the periosteum. If the patient is a child we note an unwillingness to be looked at or touched, and if you persist in your unwelcome attention it may have convulsions. On awaking from sleep the child seems stupid, and is so excessively irritable that he howls if one simply looks at him. Vertigo is often an accompaniment of the *Antimonium tartaricum* ailment; this vertigo seems to alternate with drowsiness.

We often find *Antimonium tartaricum* indicated in cases of suppressed eruptions when there result these symptoms of the head. Particularly is it called for when the eruption of scarlatina, measles or variola does not come out properly, or has been repelled; then we have, in addition to the symptoms I have already mentioned, great difficulty in breathing. The face is bluish or purple, the child becomes more and more drowsy and twitches. There is rattling breathing. All of these symptoms indicate a desperate case. *Antimonium tartaricum* will frequently restore the eruption and save the child. Now, these symptoms that I have mentioned accompany two grand sets of phenomena for which *Antimonium tartaricum* may be useful, namely, pulmonary and gastro-enteric affections.

For children it is an invaluable drug in disease of the chest. For instance you find it indicated in whooping-cough, and, in fact, in any cough, whether from dentition or other causes, when the cough is provoked every time the child gets angry, which is very often. Eating brings on the cough, which culminates in the vomiting of mucus and food.

Again, there is another form of chest trouble in which *Antimonium tartaricum* is indicated. A nursing infant suddenly lets go of the nipple, and cries as if out of breath, and seems to be better when held upright and carried about. Now, this may be the beginning of capillary bronchitis. On examination you will probably detect fine subcrepitant râles all through the chest. *Antimonium tartaricum* here nips the whole disease in the bud and saves the child much suffering. Again, there is another form of cough in which it may be used. There is marked wheezing when the child breathes. The cough sounds loose, and yet the child raises no phlegm. This symptom increases until the child grows drowsy. Its head is hot and bathed in sweat. The cough then grows less and less frequent, the pulse weak, and symptoms of cyanosis appear. In these cases, the quicker you give *Antimonium tartaricum*, the better for your patient.

Antimonium tartaricum is also indicated in affections of old people, and particularly in orthopnœa, or threatening paralysis of the lungs in the aged. You hear loud rattling of phlegm in the chest, and yet the patient cannot get up the phlegm. Here *Baryta carb.* is complementary to *Antimonium tart.*, and often succeeds when the latter remedy only partially relieves.

Now for a few of the concordant remedies in these cases.

Ipecacuanha often precedes *Antimonium tartaricum* in catarrh of the chest in children. Loud râles are heard through the chest. When they cough they gag, but raise but little phlegm.

In this threatening paralysis of the lungs you must compare *Antimonium tartaricum* with several other drugs; with *Lachesis*, which has aggravation when arousing from sleep; with *Kali hydriodicum*, especially when there is œdema pulmonum and a great deal of rattling of mucus in the chest, and what little sputum can be raised is greenish, and frothy like soap-suds.

Carbo veg. also suits these cases, but here the rattling is accompanied by cold breath and by coldness of the lower extremities from the feet to the knees.

Moschus comes in when there is loud rattling of mucus and the patient is restless. It is especially indicated after typhoid fever. The pulse grows less and less strong, and finally the patient goes into a syncope.

Also, do not forget *Ammonium carbonicum* in this condition.

Antimonium tart. is indicated in the asphyxia at the beginning of life, asphyxia neonatorum, when there is rattling of mucus in the throat.

Laurocerasus is useful in the asphyxia of new-born children when there is great blueness of the face, with twitching of the muscles of the face, and gasping without really breathing.

Antimonium tartaricum produces a perfect picture of pleuro-pneumonia. Certain portions of the lungs are paralyzed. Fine rales are heard, even over the hepatized areas. There is great oppression of breathing, particularly towards morning. The patient must sit up in order to breathe. It may also be indicated in bilious pneumonia, that is, pneumonia with hepatic congestion and with well-marked icterus. The pit of the stomach is very sensitive to touch or pressure. There are meteorism, nausea and vomiting. It may be used in the pneumonia of drunkards with these complications.

Antimonium tartaricum produces pustules very nearly identical with those of small-pox; hence, it may be a very useful remedy in that disease. It is very useful in the beginning before the eruption appears, and the patient has a dry teasing cough, which, under other circumstances, might suggest *Bryonia*. Here, however, you should give *Antimonium tart.*, because it covers all the symptoms. It suits the cough and also the reason for the cough. It also suits the eye symptoms which occur during eruptive diseases, as small-pox, scarlatina, measles, etc.

In diseases of the intestinal tract we find it indicated by the following symptoms: nausea with great anxiety, eructations tasting like rotten eggs, yawning and drowsiness. The vomited matters are green and watery, and sometimes frothy, and contain food. The vomiting itself is associated with trembling of the hands, and is followed by drowsiness. Vomiting and purging may take place, with every symptom of collapse, coldness of the surface, the hands and feet are like ice, and the stools are profuse and watery. Thirstless or drinking little and often. Desire for acids, fruits, &c., cutting colic. Here you have an almost perfect picture of *Veratrum*. The distinction between the two remedies is that *Veratrum* has more cold sweat on the forehead, and *Antimonium tart.*, more drowsiness.

When *Antimonium tart.* has produced pustules, the antidote is *Conium*.

LECTURE LVI.

THE PREPARATIONS OF MERCURY.

Mercurius vivus and solubilis.
" dulcis.
" corrosivus.
" aceticus.
" protoiodatus.
" biniodatus.
" cyanatus.
Cinnabaris.
Mercurius sulph.
" præcip. rub.

Hepar.
Cinch.
Nitr. ac.
Dulc.
Kali hyd.
Aurum.
Asafœt.
Staph.
Lach.
Iodine.
Mezer.
Stilling.

WE begin this morning with the study of *Mercury* and its combinations. *Mercury* has long been known and used as a medicine in the old school of practice. Its abuse, when given in excess or inappropriately, has rendered it a very unpopular remedy among the laity. There are many physicians in the so-called old-school practice who have endeavored to obtain for *Mercury* a substitute which would answer the same purpose without deleterious results. They have been more or less successful, but they have never really obtained anything equivalent to that remedy in its genuine usefulness. Of late days, there are not so many allopathic physicians who give the great doses of *Mercury* that used to be so common. This caution in its administration is no evidence of improvement of the medical world, scientifically speaking, but only that they have been driven to this course by their unfortunate results and by popular clamor. There are many physicians who are afraid to let their patients know that they are taking mercurials. The eclectics have substituted such plants as *Podophyllum* and *Leptandra* for *Mercury*, especially in liver affections.

We, of the homœopathic school, are not afraid to use mercurials, because we do so according to a fixed law, guided by their effects on the human system; therefore, we are not in any danger of the bad results which follow overdosing or misapplication of the drug. You notice that I have placed on the board a number of mercurial preparations. All of these have some medicinal properties, but we have not the time, nor will it be proper, to dwell on them all. Our main object is to treat of the principal actions of *Mercury* in general, and then to teach you the principal characteristics which will enable you to prefer one of these preparations rather than others. From the general character of the patient, you know that he needs some mercurial preparation, and you want to know which one. We have here two preparations, *Mercurius vivus* and *solubilis*, that I have placed on the same line. I do not know enough to separate them symptomatically. The provings have been separately placed in Allen's *Encylopædia*, but I have not been able to see any essential differences between them. These preparations are the quicksilver, or metallic *Mercury*, and the *Soluble Mercury* of Hahnemann. *Mercurius solubilis* is not a pure mercurial preparation. It contains some *Ammonia* and some *Nitric acid*. There are only traces of *Nitric acid*, however, and yet these traces must modify its symptomatology somewhat, but to what degree I do not know. The provings of the "*solubilis*" are excellent. They are complete, much more so than those of the "*vivus*." These latter are collected more from poisoning cases and from clinical cases than from actual provings. If, then, the symptoms are clearly placed in the *Encyclopædia* under *Soluble Mercury*, I would advise you to use that preparation. Below the *Mercurius vivus* and *solubilis* on the board we have two preparations of *Mercury* with *Chlorine*. Next comes *Mercurius aceticus*, of which we have but few symptoms. Next we have the two *Iodides of Mercury*, which are very important. The *Biniodide* is red, the *Protoiodide*, yellow. Then we have the *Cyanide of Mercury*. Next we have *Cinnabaris*, which is the *Sulphide of Mercury*. Beneath this we have the *Sulphate of Mercury*, and then the *Mercurius præcipitatus ruber*. Of the latter three we have but few symptoms. *Cinnabaris*, the two iodides, the corrosivus, the solubilis and the vivus are the most frequently used.

You see here on your right a list of antidotes to *Mercury*. That is in itself evidence of the numerous ill-effects which may result from its abuse. They are not all of equal importance. As I mentioned the other day, *Hepar* is the most important antidote for *Mercury*, and also for many of the other metals. It is useful for the mental symptoms that may follow a course of *Mercury*, the anxiety, distress, and even the suicidal mood; also for the bone pains, sore mouth, ulcers and the gastric symptoms.

Nitric acid is particularly to be remembered when the lower tissues are attacked, as the periosteum, the bones and the fibrous tissues. The patient has bone-pains worse at night, aching in the shins in damp weather, ulcers in the throat; particularly if secondary syphilis is complicated by mercurial poisoning.

Cinchona is said to antidote the chronic ptyalism produced by *Mercury*.

Dulcamara has been successfully used for the salivation of *Mercury*, particularly when it is aggravated with every damp change in the weather.

Kali hydriodicum, or the *Iodide of Potassium*, is a well-known antidote for *Mercury*, and has come into practice of late years, and is given by both schools of medicine very extensively, whether the case be syphilitic or not. Like *Nitric acid*, it is particularly indicated when syphilis and *Mercury* combine to make the patient sick, especially when the lower order of tissues are involved, as the bones, the periosteum and the glands; when there is the well-known syphilitic ozæna, a thin watery discharge from the nose, making the upper lip sore and raw. You will find it the best drug we have for the repeated catarrhs which may follow the abuse of *Mercury*. Every little exposure to a damp atmosphere, or even to cool air, causes coryza. This, remember, is a case of mercurial poisoning which the *Iodide of Potassium* is to antidote. The eyes are hot, and watery, and swollen. There are neuralgic pains in one or both cheeks, the nose feels stuffed up and is swollen, and discharges at the same time a profuse watery scalding coryza, and there is more or less sore throat. These symptoms recur at every fresh exposure. There is scarcely any drug which will cure these quicker than will *Iodide of Potassium*.

There is another salt of potash that has an antidotal relation to *Mercury*, and that is *Kali chloricum*. This is an efficient antidote when the poison has developed a sort of scorbutus, and the gums are spongy, soft, and bleed easily; there are ulcers of an aphthous character in the mouth and throat, and fœtor of the breath.

Aurum has next mention. This we find particularly called for in the mental depression and suicidal mania which may develop after a course of *Mercury*, and also for the caries of the bones, particularly of the bones of the palate, nose, etc.

Asafœtida also comes in as a drug to be thought of in the bone affections developed by *Mercury*. Here you have, as a characteristic distinguishing it from the others, extreme sensitiveness around the diseased portion of bone. For instance, in the case of an ulcer communicating with a carious tibia, the parts are so sensitive that the patient can scarcely bear the dressing that you apply. You will find that the tissues are firmly adherent to the bone for some little distance around the inflamed portion. Then, too, you find *Asafœtida* sometimes indicated for iritis following mercurialization. Here, to distinguish it from other remedies, you have the same characteristic, extreme soreness of the bones around the eye.

Staphisagria is an antidote for *Mercury*, and in rather bad cases, too, when the system is very much depreciated by the mercurial poison. We find the patient wasting away and sallow, dark rings around the eyes, well-marked mercurial mouth and throat, with spongy gums, tongue flabby, ulcers on the tongue and in the throat and well-marked bone pains.

Lachesis is an occasional antidote for some of the symptoms, when the mercurial poison has been engrafted upon the constitution and the special characteristics of that remedy are present.

Iodine comes in as an antidote, especially when the glands are affected.

Mezereum is excellent when the mercurial poisoning has invaded the nervous system and neuralgia has developed. This neuralgia may appear in the face, in the eyes or in any part of the body.

Lastly, we have *Stillingia*, which is called for in broken down constitution with periosteal inflammation and nodes on the bones.

Mercury, it is well known, enters into loose combination with the tissues of the body. It has been found in every tissue and may be excreted by almost every channel. It has been found in the perspiration, urine, bile, fæces and saliva. It has even been found in the child in utero and, again, in the nursing infant, when the drug has been taken by the mother. I said that the combination of *Mercury* with the tissues is a loose one, by which I mean it is early disrupted. If a person is poisoned with *Mercury*, it will be readily displaced by one of the above remedies. It is only the chronic cases that need give you concern, and the cure of which you may despair of. When mercurialization is combined with other poisons, as with syphilis and scrofula, then you will have greater difficulty.

The symptoms of poisoning by *Mercury* are these: after exposure to the poison, the breath takes on a sickening sort of odor hard to describe but easy to remember. There is also a metallic taste in the mouth. These are very early symptoms and assert themselves long before the well-known characteristics of the drug appear. The patient feels languid and is frequently sick at his stomach. He vomits his food without any apparent cause. His face becomes rather pale, with dark rings around the eyes; the lips are rather livid and purplish. He complains of heat, particularly in the forehead and down the root of the nose. He cannot bear the warmth of the bed. As soon as he gets warm in bed, his aches and pains begin. Then his mouth begins to feel sore. The mucous membrane becomes puffed, swollen and redder than natural. The salivary glands begin to secrete more rapidly and the mouth is filled with saliva, which is, however, normal in its composition. In a more advanced case, the saliva becomes vitiated. It is no longer the pure secretion, for the glands are overworked. The breath becomes more and more offensive, the gums swell and are tender to touch and the teeth become loose. A dark red line sometimes appears on the gums below the teeth. Later, the gums grow spongy and yellowish-white and ulcerate and discharge an offensive matter. The tongue swells and readily takes the imprint of the teeth. The glands then become involved and you find more or less tumefaction of the parotid and cervical glands. If you were to look into the mouth at this stage, you would find the opening of Steno's duct red and inflamed and, in some cases, even ulcerated. Other glands, too, are affected. We find the pancreas attacked by *Mercury*. The liver also comes in for a share of the poison. You are probably aware that the liver is markedly affected by *Mercury*, and that allopathic physicians have been accustomed to give blue mass or calomel in almost every attack of "liver-complaint." Quite recently, several eminent physicians in the old school have declared that *Mercury* does not increase the flow of bile and hence is not useful for torpid liver; but, however that may be, it is certain that *Mercury* does affect the liver in one way or another. It has caused catarrh of the duodenum, and this catarrh has extended along the bile-duct into the liver. This is a form of trouble which frequently causes jaundice, and a form, too, for which *Mercury* is useful. It has also produced and cured hepatitis, particularly when one or more abscesses have formed in the liver. Individual susceptibility and age vary these symptoms considerably. You will find that it is more difficult to salivate children than adults. Some persons are salivated by very small quantities, while it is difficult to affect others. The scrofulous are very seriously affected by *Mercury*, as you all know.

The more remote symptoms of mercurial poisoning are these: you will find that the blood becomes impoverished. The albumin and fibrin forming of that fluid are affected. They are diminished, and you find in their place a certain fatty substance; the composition of which I do not exactly know. Consequently, as a prominent symptom, the body wastes and emaciates. The patient suffers from fever which is rather hectic in its character. The periosteum becomes affected and you then have a characteristic group of mercurial pains, bone pains worse in changes of the weather, worse in the warmth of the bed, and chilliness with or after stool. The skin becomes of a brownish hue; ulcers form, particularly on the legs; they are stubborn and will not heal. The patient is troubled with sleeplessness and ebullitions of blood at night; he is hot and cannot sleep; he is thrown quickly into a perspiration, which perspiration gives him no relief. The entire nervous system suffers also, and you have here two series of symptoms. At first, the patient becomes anxious and restless and cannot remain quiet; he changes his position; he moves about from place to place; he seems to have a great deal of anxiety about the heart, præcordial anguish, as it is termed, particularly at night. Then, in another series of symptoms, there are jerkings of the limbs, making the patient appear as though he were attacked by St. Vitus's dance. Or, you may notice what is still more common, trembling of the hands, this tremor being altogether beyond the control of the patient and gradually spreading over the entire body, giving you a semblance of paralysis agitans or shaking palsy. Finally, the patient becomes paralyzed, cannot move his limbs, his mind becomes lost, and he presents a perfect picture of imbecility. He does all sorts of queer things. He sits in the corner with an idiotic smile on his face, playing with straws; he is forgetful, he cannot remember even the most ordinary events. He becomes disgustingly filthy and eats his own excrement. In fact, he is a perfect idiot. Be careful how you give *Mercury;* it is a treacherous medicine. It seems often indicated. You give it and relieve; but your patient is worse again in a few weeks and then you give it again with relief. By and by, it fails you. Now, if I want to make a permanent cure, for instance, in a scrofulous child, I will very seldom give him *Mercury;* should I do so, it will be at least only as an intercurrent remedy.

I have placed on the board in tabular form, a list of the mercurial salts together with the parts of the body on which they act. Wherever you notice the cross, you know that the preparation acts on the part of the body placed on that line under the heading of *Mercurius vivus.* This table is only a convenient form. There is nothing practical or scientific in it.

Mercurius Vivus.	Bin.	Prot.	Cyan.	Dulc.	Corros.	Cinn.	Sulph.	Rub.	Acet.
Eyes	—	+	—	+	+	+	—	—	—
Nose	+	+	+	—	+	+	—	—	—
Mouth and Throat,	+	+	+	+	+	+	—	—	—
Kidneys and Bladder,	...	—	+	—	+	—	—	—	+
Heart	—	+	+	—	+	—	+	+	—
Lungs	+	+	—	—	+	+	+	—	—
Genitals	+	+	+	—	+	+	—	+	—
Glands and Bones,	+	+	+	+	+	+	+	+	+
Skin	+	+	+	—	+	+	—	+	—
Stomach and Liver,	+	+	—	—	+	+	+	—	—

Taking *Mercurius vivus* as a type of the whole, we find that it is indicated in persons who are of a scrofulous habit, whether of syphilitic constitution or not, in whom the glandular system is active. This glandular activity shows itself in two ways. In the first place, we may have a condition simulating plethora. In more advanced stages, we may find *Mercurius* indicated in enlarged glands with emaciation and deficiency of blood. We find *Mercurius* indicated also in scrofulous children who have unusually large heads with open fontanelles, particularly anterior fontanelles. They are slow in learning to walk, the teeth form imperfectly or slowly, the limbs are apt to be cold and damp, and there is a damp, clammy feeling to the limbs. You may distinguish it from *Calcarea, Silicea* and *Sulphur* by these characteristics:

the head is inclined to perspire in the *Mercurius* case, but the perspiration is offensive and oily. It is not as often indicated as *Calcarea*, *Silicea* or *Sulphur*, nor is it as certain or as permanent in its effects. But it may come in as a remedy to partially relieve, and it may be indicated as an intercurrent remedy in a course of treatment with *Sulphur* when the latter remedy seems to fail. You will find the *Mercurius* patient illustrating plethora with anxiety and restlessness, tossing about, moving from place to place. It is one of the remedies useful for nostalgia or home-sickness. The patient becomes anxious and irritable. This anxiety seems as if it were in the blood, that is, it is always attended with ebullitions of blood. This distinguishes it from other remedies.

The congestions of *Mercurius* indicate it after *Belladonna*. There are resemblances between the two remedies, which have been well confirmed clinically. It often follows *Belladonna* in inflammations, even in inflammation of the meninges of the brain, when, as under *Belladonna*, there are the same hasty speech and quick, nervous manner. The child talks so rapidly that one word runs into another. You will find the face flushed very much as in *Belladonna*, but you have, in addition, to distinguish it from that remedy, glandular swellings, and tendency to sore mouth.

Mercurius is often indicated in catarrhal or gastric fevers when the face is puffed, when the throat is swollen, both internally and externally, from involvement of both glands and cellular tissue; when there are aching pains in the joints, which are made worse by the warmth of the bed, and are not relieved by sweat. In addition to this you almost always find that there is a tendency to catarrh of the bowels, characterized by slimy, bloody stool, accompanied by great tenesmus, this tenesmus not ceasing after stool. Here, too, you will find that *Mercurius* follows *Belladonna* well.

We find *Mercurius* indicated in hæmorrhages. It is often called for in nose-bleed or epistaxis, particularly when the blood coagulates and hangs from the nostrils like icicles. This is a useful hint. Suppose that nose-bleed appears in a scrofulous child or in a full-blooded patient, a boy at the age of fifteen or sixteen, when congestions are so frequently noticed. You have given *Belladonna*, *Hamamelis*, and *Erigeron*, and have failed to check it. The blood is quite bright, and runs in streams. Medicines do not stop it. Then comes this *Mercurius* condition. You give that remedy and cure, not only that attack, but you prevent the return of others. The same indications apply to uterine hæmorrhage or menorrhagia when the flow is profuse, dark and clotted. Then, if the glandular swelling, sore mouth, and other symptoms are present, *Mercurius* is certain to be the remedy.

We find *Mercurius* indicated in pneumonia. Here it requires that the right lung be affected, and that there are also icteroid symptoms. The skin is yellow. There is sharp stitching pain through the lower portion of the right lung. There will be other pathognomonic symptoms of pneumonia present, but these need not be specified separately.

We find it indicated in peritonitis, and here again it follows *Belladonna* when suppuration has commenced and you have tympanitic abdomen, evidence of effusion, which will be partly serous and partly purulent, sweat, rigors, etc. Here *Mercurius* prevents the further spread of the suppurative process.

Another condition in which we may use *Mercurius* is one of inflammation which has gone on to suppuration, whether the disease be a boil, a tonsillitis, or any other form of inflammation. *Mercurius* belongs to an interesting little group of medicines which you will use very often; they are *Belladonna*, *Hepar*, *Mercurius* and *Lachesis*. To these we may also add *Silicea* and *Sulphur*. You should prefer *Belladonna* in the beginning of inflammation as in tonsillitis. The throat is bright red and swollen, and there is difficulty in swallowing fluids, and sharp pains through the tonsils.

You should change to *Hepar* when the sharp sticking pains and chills indicate the beginning of suppuration. It may prevent suppuration when given in the incipiency of that process.

Mercurius is suited to a still more advanced state when pus has formed and you wish it evacuated. *Mercurius* does not prevent the formation of pus, but rather favors it. If you give it too soon you will spoil the case. In felons, if it is given low, it will generally favor the rapid formation of pus.

When pus continues to discharge and the wound refuses to heal, *Silicea* follows *Hepar*. In some of these cases, the benefit under *Silicea* will cease. Then a dose or two of *Sulphur* will excite reaction and *Silicea* can effect a cure.

Lachesis is indicated when the pus degenerates and becomes of a dark, thin, offensive character, with the sensitiveness to touch of that drug.

Mercurius vivus is indicated in ophthalmia, usually of scrofulous or syphilitic origin. The patient suffers from the glare and heat of the fire, consequently he avoids the fire and warm rooms. You sometimes find it indicated in blepharitis of men who work in and about fires, as foundrymen. The pains are usually worse at night. The lids are thickened, especially at their tarsal edges, and the eyes discharge a thin acrid muco-pus, and you find little pimples scattered over the cheeks. Ulcers may form on the cornea. These ulcers are usually superficial, and have an opaque look as though pus were between the corneal layers. In syphilitic iritis *Mercurius* will be sometimes indicated when there is hypopyon. Now let us distinguish between this and other preparations of *Mercury*.

The *Biniodide of Mercury* is indicated in inflammations of the eye. The symptoms are very similar to those of "*vivus*," but there is more glandular swelling.

The *Protoiodide* is more frequently indicated in eye diseases than is the *Biniodide*. It is called for in corneal ulcers which look as if they had been chipped out with the finger nail. There is, usually, a thick yellow coating on the base of the tongue, the anterior portion being clean and red.

Mercurius dulcis, or calomel, is selected more by its general symptoms, which are these: it suits in scrofulous children who are pale, and who have swelling of the cervical and other glands. The skin is rather flabby and ill nourished. The flabby bloatedness and pallor are the indications for calomel.

Next to this we have *Bichloride of Mercury* or *Mercurius corrosivus*. This is indicated in inflammatory symptoms of the most violent character. There is no mercurial that produces such intense symptoms as does the *Bichloride*. It produces burning, agonizing pains, with most excessive photophobia and profuse excoriating lachrymation, making the cheeks sore, almost taking the skin off, so excoriating is it. There are tearing pains in the bones around the eye. There is ulceration of the cornea, with tendency to perforation. In such cases you will, as a matter of course, have hypopyon. *Mercurius corrosivus* is almost a specific for syphilitic iritis. If the symptoms of the case do not point to some other drug as the remedy, you should give it in this disease. If you choose to use atropia locally, do so in order to prevent the adhesions which will otherwise almost inevitably take place in these cases. You will also find *Mercurius corrosivus* indicated in retinitis albuminurica.

Cinnabaris is next. As a remedy for quite a variety of inflammations of the eye. I will only give you one symptom for it, and that is pain which shoots across the eye from canthus to canthus, or seems to go around the eye.

Next, the action of *Mercury* on the nose. We find *Mercurius vivus* indicated in catarrhs of the nose and throat, which are provoked by damp, chilly weather, and by the damp, cool evening air. The nose itches and burns and feels stuffed-up; with this there is thin coryza. The throat feels raw and sore. There is aching in the various joints. These are the symptoms which will indicate *Mercurius* both as to the exciting cause and as to the symptoms present. You may have with these a hot feeling. The face flushes up and gets red, perspiration breaks out but it gives no relief. There is another form of coryza in which you may give *Mercurius*, and that is when the cold is "ripe," and the discharge from the nose is yellowish-green, thick and muco-purulent.

Here it rivals *Pulsatilla* and *Kali sulphuricum*, both of which are useful for these thick, yellowish-green nasal discharges, when the patient is better in the open air and worse in the evening. *Pulsatilla*, independently of its other symptoms, is distinguished by the fact that the discharge is never irritating, but is perfectly bland. The discharge in *Kali sulph.* is more apt to be yellow.

You are also to distinguish *Mercurius* from *Nux vomica*, which is suited to coryza caused by exposure to dry cold, and when there are soreness, roughness and a harsh, scraped feeling in the throat. *Mercurius* always has a smarting, raw or sore feeling.

Now, the throat symptoms of *Mercurius vivus* may lead you at times to think of it in diphtheria. Think of it as much as you choose, but think of it only to reject it. It is not indicated in diphtheria. I do not believe it indicated even in diphtheritis. But there are other preparations of *Mercury* which may be used here. Both the *Biniodide* and the *Protoiodide of Mercury* are indicated in diphtheritic sore throat, or even in true diphtheria. The *Biniodide* is of use when the left tonsil is inflamed and there is a yellowish-gray membrane forming there. The glands of the neck are swollen. There is also some involvement of the cellular tissue around the throat. The patient may have an accumulation of slimy or sticky mucus in the mouth and throat. The symptoms are worse from empty swallowing, so that the simple attempt to swallow saliva excites more pain than does the swallowing of food.

The *Protoiodide of Mercury* is to be thought of more when the deposit forms on the right side of the throat, with swelling of the glands in the neck and with the accumulation of this tenacious mucus in the throat. Here there is almost always present that thick, yellow, dirty coating on the base and posterior part of the tongue, the tip and sides being red. These two remedies are often indicated in diphtheritic sore throat.

Next you will notice the *Cyanide of Mercury*, which is a combination of hydrocyanic acid and mercury. We have in this drug one of the very best remedies in diphtheria, especially when it is of a true adynamic or malignant type. By reason of the presence of the prussic acid you will find it indicated in cases in which the patient is very much prostrated from the beginning. The pulse is quick. It may be as high as 130 or 140, and it has no volume to it at all. The membrane at first is white, covering the velum palati and tonsils. The glands soon begin to swell, however, and then the membrane becomes dark, threatening even to grow gangrenous. Weakness is extreme. The breath is fœtid. There is loss of appetite. The tongue is coated brown, or, in severe cases, even black. Nose-bleed sets in, and this you know is a dangerous symptom. The remedy may also be used in diphtheria of the larynx. The expectoration is thick and ropy and there is harsh, barking, croupy cough, with dyspnœa. Here, the *Cyanide of Mercury* has saved life, but it will not always do so.

You will notice its resemblance to *Kali bichromicum* in diphtheritic croup. The fact lies in the larynx and in the thick, tough, tenacious expectoration. The distinction lies in this: the *Cyanide of Mercury* has great weakness. Now this weakness is not a simple prostration caused by the efforts of the child at breathing. It is due to poisoning of the blood, which is represented by the blueness of the surface, coldness of the extremities, and quick, weak pulse. If you have not these, *Kali bichromicum* is to be preferred.

Cinnabaris is a remedy not often thought of in catarrhal troubles. It is indicated in nasal catarrh when there is great pressure at the root of the nose, a feeling as though something heavy was pressing on the nose, a heavy pair of spectacles for instance. We also frequently find throat symptoms with this form of catarrh. The throat is swollen and the tonsils are enlarged and redder than normal. There is great dryness in the throat, and this is more annoying at night, waking the patient from sleep. Remember this sensation across the bridge of the nose and the character of the throat symptoms in connection with it. These symptoms may occur in the syphilitic, in the scrofulous, or in persons in whom there is tendency to catarrh. We have found *Cinnabaris* of use in the sore throat of scarlatina, which is often diphtheritic in its character, when there is quite an accumulation of stringy mucus in the posterior nares. That symptom being prominent, *Cinnabaris* will be the remedy for the emergency.

I have used *Mercurius corrosivus* successfully when the accumulation of mucus in the nose is quite thick; in fact, almost like glue. In some cases of syphilitic disease of the nose, you find *Mercurius corrosivus* indicated from the fact that the ulcers perforate the nasal septum, there are burning pains, and discharges are acrid, corroding the tissues over which they flow.

The throat symptoms of *Mercurius corrosivus* are very violent. I can conceive of cases where it would be required in diphtheria, though I have never given it in that disease. The uvula is swollen, elongated and very dark red. There is intense burning in the throat, just as intense in fact as that of *Arsenicum album*, *Arsenicum iodatum* or *Capsicum*. This burning pain is rendered intolerable by any external pressure. It is accompanied by violent constriction of the throat. Any attempt to swallow, be the matters swallowed solid or liquid, causes violent spasms of the throat, with the immediate ejection of the solid or liquid.

You here recognize a resemblance to *Belladonna* in the spasmodic character of the symptoms. *Mercurius corrosivus* is at once distinguished from *Belladonna* by the inflammatory tendency of the symptoms as indicated by these extreme burning pains. Thus it has the constrictive quality of the *Belladonna plus* the most intense, destructive inflammation of the throat. You may further distinguish between the two remedies by the pulse. In *Mercurius corrosivus* the pulse is quick, weak, and irregular, and not full and strong as under *Belladonna*.

Next, a word or two about the *Mercuries* in their action on the genitals and the glands. The *Mercuries* have long been used in the treatment of syphilis. *Mercurius solubilis* or *vivus* is indicated in primary syphilis for the so-called soft chancre or chancroid. The ulceration is superficial rather than deep, and the base of the sore has a dirty, lardaceous appearance. *Mercurius sol.* has produced such an ulcer as this, and, therefore, it will cure it. The sore throat which often ushers in the syphilitic fever six or seven weeks after the appearance of the primary lesion, is also found under *Mercurius solubilis*.

The *Iodides of Mercury* are the preferable remedies for the Hunterian or hard chancre. That is a form of ulcer which the *Protoiodide* and *Biniodide* have both produced, therefore they will cure it. There is no necessity whatever for such external applications as caustics, for the proper internal remedy if it does not entirely prevent the onset of secondary symptoms will at least lessen their intensity.

Mercurius corrosivus is to be preferred to any of the drugs mentioned for syphilitic symptoms when the ulceration is very destructive. The ulcer is serpiginous; it has a ragged edge, eating out and destroying in a few days nearly half the penis.

Secondary syphilis may be treated with one or the other of these preparations, if the drug has not been abused in the primary stages. *Mercurius solubilis* very quickly helps the syphiloderms on the palms of the hands, which are red, itch slightly, and scale off.

There is another use of *Mercurius* which should be mentioned here: if a child continually pulls at the penis, it may be on account of irritation. *Mercurius* is the remedy—or perhaps *Cantharis*.

Returning to *Mercurius vivus*, I want to say a few words concerning its use in diseases of the liver. The tongue is coated a dirty yellowish-white and takes the imprint of the teeth. Scorbutic symptoms are usually present. The gums ulcerate and become spongy. There is a fœtid or disagreeable odor from the mouth. The skin and conjunctiva have a well-marked jaundiced or icteroid hue. There is tendency to rush of blood to the head. The region of the liver is sore to the touch; the abdomen rather tympanitic and swollen, particularly across the epigastrium and in either hypochondrium. The patient cannot lie on the right side. You will find the liver enlarged and often indurated. The stools are either clay colored, from absence of bile, or they are yellowish-green, bilious, passed with a great deal of tenesmus and followed by a "never-get-done" feeling.

Mercury is indicated in dysentery, especially when it occurs in a season when warm days are followed by cold nights.

Nux vomica has many resemblances to *Mercurius*, but it differs in that the pains and tenesmus usually cease after stool; whereas, with *Mercurius*, they continue after stool.

Aconite often precedes the exhibition of *Mercury* in the weather I have spoken of, hot days followed by cold nights. In the incipient stages, such troubles may be checked by *Aconite*. If *Aconite* fails, then *Mercurius* will be indicated. Often, after the tenesmus and blood have ceased, and the mucus still persists, *Sulphur* will be the remedy.

There is another remedy to be remembered in connection with *Mercury* in bilious troubles, and that is *Leptandra*. Both of them have these yellowish-green stools, or stools black like pitch, and horribly offensive stools. The distinction lies here: *Leptandra* has urging to stool, griping continuing after stool, but not the tenesmus. *Leptandra* frequently has dull, aching, burning pains in the posterior portion of the liver.

LECTURE LVII.

THE NOBLE METALS—AURUM.

IN this group we have *Aurum metallicum, Aurum muriaticum, Argentum metallicum, Argentum nitricum, Platinum* and *Palladium*. There are also two or three others of which we know but little.

Aurum and *Argentum* have many symptoms in common, and yet their distinctive characteristics are sufficient to enable you to separate them readily in practice. I will give you the general distinctions between the two drugs before I consider them individually. Gold affects more the circulation of the blood. It also acts on the mind, producing emotional symptoms. Now, by this I mean that if you find symptoms of the nervous system in *Aurum*, they will be followed by symptoms of the circulation as the primary or most important features of the case.

Argentum has more symptoms of the respiratory organs and intellectual part of the mind. With *Aurum*, we have tendency to hyperæmia; in *Argentum*, more nervous phenomena; only, *Aurum* seems to attack the bones. We find very few symptoms of *Argentum* indicating it in bone affections. The latter, however causes an arthralgia or neuralgic pains in the joints. It also attacks the cartilages of joints. For instance, you find *Argentum metallicum* useful in the arthralgic pains of women who suffer from prolapsus uteri. They can scarcely move their joints, and yet a most careful investigation shows no rheumatic inflammation.

Aurum suits in scrofula with redness of the face, thus keeping up the tendency to hyperæmia or fulness of the bloodvessels. In these scrofulous cases, you will find that the opacities and ulcers on the cornea are surrounded by well-filled bloodvessels; here, again typifying the hyperæmic quality of the drug.

Argentum suits in chlorosis. It affects the oxidizing power of the blood; it shrivels the body. Thus *Aurum* affects the distribution of the blood, giving us fulness or hyperæmia, whereas *Argentum* affects its quality, rendering it incapable of fully carrying oxygen. Hence, all parts of the body dwindle from malnutrition.

Silver, and especially its nitrate, coagulates albumen, and this is the reason why the latter has been used locally for so many years as a caustic. When applied with moisture to animal tissues, it immediately coagulates the albuminous portions, and so tends to destroy whatever process is going on. Its action does not extend deeply, however, on account of the formation of this layer of coagulated albumen.

Argentum nitricum more than the mental itself, causes gastro-enteric inflammation, very much like *Arsenic*. In poisoning cases it also seems to affect the epithelial layers. For instance, when animals that have been fed on it for quite a while die, the epithelial layers in all parts of the body seem to be more or less destroyed. That is the reason why you find it of use in cancer and in hæmorrhages, in both of which conditions the epithelial structures are diseased.

AURUM METALLICUM.

Aurum met.
$\begin{cases} 1.\ \text{Mind.} \\ 2.\ \text{Hyperæmia.} \\ 3.\ \text{Induration.} \\ 4.\ \text{Bones.} \\ 5.\ \text{Fatty degeneration.} \end{cases}$

Aurum met.
$\begin{cases} \text{Belladonna.} \\ \text{Mercurius, Nitric acid.} \\ \text{Arsenic, Asafœtida.} \\ \text{Ammonium carb} \quad >\text{Hepar.} \\ \text{Natrum mur.} \quad >\text{Bell.} \\ \qquad\qquad\qquad\quad >\text{Merc.} \end{cases}$

Aurum is a remedy of not very extensive application, but still it is well marked in its limited sphere. Its antidotes are principally *Hepar*, *Belladonna* and *Mercurius*. I am not positive that there is a complement to *Aurum*. Now, in studying the action of this remedy, we are to keep in mind, first, its marked power of producing hyperæmia; and, secondly, its action on the emotional mind more than on the intellectual.

First, let us study the hyperæmia of *Aurum*. We find this in every part of the body upon which the drug acts. It affects the heart, causing increased activity of that viscus, as shown by increased force of the heart-stroke, just as you find in pure cardiac hypertrophy without dilatation. As a result of this increased action, there is enlargement and secondarily, actual hypertrophy of the heart. Consecutive to this trouble, you have a list of symptoms that are very characteristic. The lungs are too full of blood, so that the patient on attempting to walk up hill, or use any little exertion, feels as though there were a crushing weight under the sternum. He feels that if he did not stop walking the blood would burst through the chest. *Aurum* relieves this kind of a case very nicely. According to Kafka, *Aurum muriaticum* is here preferable to the *metallicum*.

This is very similar to *Ammonium carb.*, which has a similar sensation of crushing weight on the sternum, but more tendency to somnolence and venous fulness than has *Aurum*.

Owing to this condition of the heart there is necessarily hyperæmia in other organs. We find, for instance, this tendency to rush of blood to the head aggravated by mental labor, because study always increases the amount of blood in the brain, if there is any tendency to cerebral congestion. There is a feeling of fulness in the head, accompanied by roaring in the ears. The head feels sore and bruised, and the mind is confused. The face, in extreme cases of congestion, is rather bloated, and has a glassy look. Sparks or flashes of light before the eyes show pressure on the retinal vessels. Still further evidence of the hyperæmia in the eye is revealed by the ophthalmoscope. You find a sensation in the eye as though it were being pushed out, with a certain amount of tension there. Two errors of vision may be associated with these symptoms; either he sees double, or he suffers from what is known as half-sight. Now, these symptoms are suggestive of hyperæmia of the brain, which may occur from various causes, among the most prominent being overuse of the eyes, or working in hot places.

Glaucoma may suggest *Aurum*.

In scrofulous ophthalmia we frequently find *Aurum* indicated, if there are present those symptoms of congestion. The bloodvessels are very much injected; pannus is present; great vascularity is a characteristic in these cases calling for *Aurum*. In addition, you will find profuse scalding lachrymation. The eyes are very sensitive to the touch.

Aurum may be used in cases of syphilitic iritis when the eye is decidedly worse from touch. There is a very characteristic soreness around the eye, as if in the bones. Especially is it indicated in syphilitic cases after the abuse of mercury.

In retinal congestion, you should compare with *Aurum*, *Belladonna*, *Glonoin* and *Sulphur*.

In syphilitic iritis, with that sore, bruised sensation around the eyes, compare *Asafœtida*. This remedy, however, has it in less degree. You may also compare here, *Mercurius corrosivus* and *Nitric acid*.

The nose, too, is congested and has a red, knobby tip, greatly disfiguring the face. This may exist as a sequel to the long indulgence in alcohol, or it may be found in children as a symptom of scrofula. If the latter is the case, it is often accompanied by the characteristic catarrh for which *Aurum* is the remedy.

In nasal catarrh or ozæna the nostrils are sore and cracked. There is fœtid nasal discharge, often accompanied by caries of the nasal bones. There is ulceration of the soft parts with perforation of the nasal septum. It is especially indicated in cases of scrofulous or mercurio-syphilitic origin.

The *Aurum* ear symptoms are not very numerous but are suggestive. The ears are congested, and you find roaring in the ears, as I suggested a few moments ago. Further than this, you find great sensitiveness to noises. Now, it is sometimes indicated in catarrh of the middle ear. In these cases you note a fœtid otorrhœa. In addition to this you will very likely find the membrana tympani seriously damaged. The external auditory meatus and the mastoid process of the temporal bone become affected by direct spread of the disease. There are boring pains in the mastoid process. The trouble may progress to caries. I have already shown you illustrations of the effect of *Aurum* on the bones. You noticed that it was indicated in iritis with pains in the bones around the orbits; and you know also that it affects the nasal bones, producing caries there.

In caries of the mastoid process *Nitric acid* is the nearest ally to the *Aurum metallicum*.

For simple soreness or inflammation, beginning in the mastoid cells, *Capsicum* has won some laurels, but for caries of this process, *Aurum*, *Silicea* and *Nitric acid* are the best remedies.

Aurum has some throat symptoms. The tonsils are apt to be red and swollen, and the parotid gland on the affected side feels sore, as if contused. The hard palate may be carious. With all this, there is a mercurial or syphilitic history. I have dwelt on these symptoms because they are those which *Aurum* has most frequently removed.

Returning to the circulatory disturbances of *Aurum*, we find a hyperæmia of the kidneys. This is shown in the beginning by simple increase in the amount of urine passed. By and by the kidneys begin to undergo fatty degeneration. The urine then grows scanty and albuminous, or there may be granular or cirrhosed kidney. *Aurum* will not do any good in these cases. unless the renal trouble is secondary to some heart affection.

The nearest remedy, pathologically, to *Aurum* in granular kidney is *Plumbum*.

We find, too, that the genital organs are affected by this hyperæmia and there is strong tendency to erections. The testicles become inflamed, particularly the right. *Aurum* is especially suited to chronic orchitis, particularly when the right testicle is affected.

As another sequel to this effect of *Aurum*, we find hepatic congestion. The liver is swollen consecutive to cardiac disease. This hyperæmia is associated with burning and cutting in the right hypochondrium. As the hyperæmia continues, the liver becomes cirrhosed or else undergoes fatty degeneration. Ascites appears. The stools are of a grayish or ashy-white color from defective secretion of bile, and we have here, as in almost all ailments in which *Aurum* is the remedy, a peculiar state of the emotional mind, a melancholy or a low-spiritedness, which I shall describe to you presently.

The lungs are also hyperæmic. There is great oppression of the chest, which is worse at night, particularly in the first part of the night; it is worse from prolonged exercise, from prolonged walking. The face may be purple. In extreme cases, syncope may take place.

On the female organs we find *Aurum* acting powerfully, causing congestion of the uterus. The uterus becomes prolapsed from its great weight. It is enlarged from chronic congestion. This is the form of prolapsus which *Aurum* will cure, and no other. The ordinary remedies for prolapsus, such as *Lilium* or *Nux vomica*, cannot relieve this case, because the prolapsus is not the main characteristic. The cause of the prolapsus is the weight of the organ and not the relaxation of the ligaments or weakness of the general system.

There is another salt of gold which has been successfully substituted for *Aurum metallicum* in these cases, and that is *Aurum muriaticum natronatum*. This has been used in the second and third potencies for prolapsed and indurated uterus.

Aurum has some very characteristic mental symptoms. In almost all cases in which it is the similimum, there is present a melancholy, with disposition to weep, or with a feeling of self-condemnation. as if he was not fit to live. This feeling of self-condemnation or worthlessness may amount to despair, sometimes even taking the form of religious mania. He prays all the time. He is sure that he is going to be condemned to the lower regions. He has suicidal thoughts, if he does not make actual attempts at suicide. With all this there is a great deal of mental anguish, associated with præcordial distress, by which I mean distressed feeling referred to the cardiac region. In addition to the melancholy, *Aurum* also produces weakness of the memory. Decided anger may also be characteristic of the remedy. Any contradiction or dispute excites the patient furiously. He becomes red in the face and his pugnacity is aroused. Mental labor becomes irksome to the patient. He is very apt to suffer from headaches which are of a congestive character, as has already been described.

Aurum on the bones I can dismiss in a very few words, as much of it I have already given you. It is useful in caries of the cranial bones, and of the bones about the nose and palate, particularly after the abuse of mercury, whether the case be syphilitic or not.

LECTURE LVIII.

THE PREPARATIONS OF SILVER.

Argentum Nitricum.

Argentum nitr. $\begin{cases} \text{Arsenicum, Nitric acid.} \\ \text{Plumbum, Cuprum.} \\ \text{Zinc.} \end{cases}$ >Natrum mur.

ARGENTUM NITRICUM, or the *Nitrate of Silver*, in its action on the brain and spine furnishes us with a list of symptoms that lead to the use of the remedy in many forms of nervous diseases, from simple nervous debility to full-fledged locomotor ataxia, or paralysis. Among the anomalous sensations which it causes are the following, which are characteristic of the drug: a very common general symptom which may be present in the headache, ovarian affections and in many other diseases, is this, a feeling as if the body or some part of the body were expanding. In the case of headache, the patient has a sensation as if the head were enormously large. Sometimes, with the ovarian pains, the patient says that she feels as if there were an immense swelling in the side affected; and yet an examination shows no enlargement of the painful organ. We find this symptom under several other drugs, but very prominently under *Argentum nitricum*, however. Again, vertigo is almost always present when it is the remedy. This vertigo is associated with general debility and trembling from nervous weakness. The patient staggers and reels as if he were intoxicated. The vertigo is so severe at times that he becomes momentarily blind in association with mental confusion, buzzing in the ears, nausea and trembling. The patient suffers from mental anxiety. He is very impulsive. He must be always busy and yet he accomplishes nothing. He is subject to frequent errors of perception. He hurries restlessly about to fulfill an engagement, thinking that he will be too late, when, in reality, he has an hour or so more than is necessary. In some cases, there is profound melancholy. He imagines if left alone he will die; full of apprehension that he has some incurable disease of the brain. He constantly makes mistakes as to his estimation of distances. For instance, when walking the street, he dreads to pass a street corner, because the corner of the house seems to project and he is afraid that he will run against it. All these errors are traceable to imperfect coördination of muscles. This last is no imaginary symptom; it has been met with a number of times and it has been cured by *Argentum nitricum*.

This defective coordination of muscles is a prominent symptom in the disease known as locomotor ataxia, for the treatment of which allopaths have long employed *Argentum nitricum* as a most valuable remedy. We also may use it when the following symptoms are present: the patient staggers in the dark or when his eyes are closed. The legs are weak and the calves feel bruised as after a long journey. There is a feeling of soreness in the lumbo-sacral region; also pain in the small of the back, very severe when rising from a sitting posture, but rather relieved by walking. *Zincum* is also better from walking and worse from sitting. The difference between the two remedies is that *Argentum nitricum* has pain when rising. Sometimes there is pain in the sacro-iliac symphyses, a feeling as if the bones were loose there. Here it is similar to *Æsculus hippocastanum*. Another symptom which I would like to specialize is trembling of the hands, which causes the patient to drop things. He is very nervous at night. When he does sleep, he has all sorts of horrible dreams. These nervous symptoms are especially worse at eleven A. M. So you see that *Sulphur* is not the only remedy that has this eleven A. M. aggravation.

You will at once see the resemblance between *Argentum nitricum* and *Kali bromatum* and *Natrum mur*. That trembling weakness, with palpitation, is the exact counterpart of the *Natrum mur.* condition. This fearful and apprehensive mood, this imagining that he cannot pass a certain point, reminds you of *Kali bromatum*.

But there are less severe symptoms that will call for *Argentum nitricum*, and one of them is what we may call functional paralysis, such as follows exhausting diseases, post-diphtheritic paralysis, for example. *Gelsemium* is here a concordant remedy of *Argentum nitricum*.

Other nervous affections, for which we may use *Argentum nitricum*, are the following: it is one of the best remedies we have for hemicrania. This is not a simple neuralgia. It is a deep-seated neurotic disease, and by some is supposed to be of epileptic nature. It comes periodically; for its relief the remedy under consideration is one of the best. There is frequently boring pain in the head, which is worse in the left frontal eminence. This boring is relieved by tight bandaging of the head, hence the wearing of a tight-fitting silk hat relieves. It is excited by any mental emotion of an unpleasant kind, or by anything that depreciates the nervous system, as loss of fluids, loss of sleep or mental strain. Sometimes the pains become so severe that the patient loses his consciousness. The paroxysms frequently culminate in vomiting of bile or solid fluid.

There is another form of headache which is mostly neuralgic, and for which *Argentum nitricum* is the remedy. The bones of the head feel as if they were separating, or the head feels as if it were enormously large. The pains about the head increase to such a degree that the patient almost loses her senses. These attacks end in vomiting, probably to recur once more within a few minutes or an hour.

We also find *Argentum nitricum* indicated in prosopalgia, particularly when the infraorbital branches of the fifth pair and the nerves going to the teeth are affected. The pain is very intense and at its height is accompanied by unpleasant sour taste in the mouth. The pains are of the same character as those already described for the hemicrania. I do not believe that this sour taste in the mouth is of gastric origin, but I think that it is due to some abnormality or disturbance in the gustatory nerves. The face, in almost all these cases, is pale and sunken, rather sallow than pure pale, and in extreme cases, when the blood is very much affected, the surface of the body is of a dark, muddy, leaden hue.

We also find *Argentum nitricum* indicated in that troublesome disease, gastralgia, a neurosis of the stomach. It is especially indicated in delicate nervous women. The gastralgia is excited by any emotion, by loss of sleep, and frequently at the catamenial period. There is a feeling in the stomach as though there was a lump there. This is sometimes accompanied by gnawing ulcerative pain referred to the pit of the stomach. From this spot, pains radiate in every direction. These pains seem to increase and decrease gradually, just as under *Stannum*. With this there is apt to be intense spasm of the muscles of the chest. The patient cannot bear to have a handkerchief approach the mouth, as it would cause dyspnœa. The patient cannot bear the least food because it makes this pain worse. Sometimes the pain is relieved by bending double and pressing the hand firmly into the stomach. The paroxysms end with vomiting of glairy mucus which can be drawn into strings, or what is more common, they are accompanied with enormous accumulation of wind. The patient for a long time cannot belch, but when he does succeed in so doing, the flatus comes in an enormous volume. This is often accompanied with general tremor, and a nervous feeling, or by a sensation as if the head was being squeezed in a vise.

The nearest ally to *Argentum nitricum* here, is *Bismuth*, which is indicated in pure nervous gastralgia. The main distinction between it and *Argentum nitricum* is in the vomiting. Just as soon as food touches the stomach it is ejected.

Another nervous disease in which *Argentum nitricum* is indicated is epilepsy. The strong indicating symptom for *Silver nitrate* is this: for days or hours before an attack the pupils are dilated. After the attack, the patient is very restless and has trembling of the hands. It is especially indicated in epilepsy caused by fright or in that which comes on during menstruation.

It may also be used for puerperal convulsions, when between the attacks, the patient is very restless, and tossing about, now on one side and now on the other.

Nitrate of Silver is also indicated in angina pectoris. The patient complains of intense pain in the chest and about the heart. He can hardly breathe.

We also find it indicated in pure nervous asthma. There are present spasms of the respiratory muscles. Marked with dyspnœa, worse in a crowded room.

Leaving now the action of *Argentum nitricum* on the nervous system, we come to its use in inflammations and ulcerations. First of all, under this head, we will consider it in diseases of the eye. *Nitrate of Silver* cures purulent ophthalmia, and by this term I mean any inflammation of the lids or eyes which develops ulceration or pus. This pus is thick, yellowish and bland. It is useful in ophthalmia neonatorum when the pus is of the character just mentioned and is profuse. Especially is it called for after the failure of *Pulsatilla* or one of the mercuries.

You may also use it for the purulent ophthalmia of adults with pus of this character. Like *Pulsatilla*, the symptoms are relieved in the open air and become intolerable in the warm room.

In purulent ophthalmia, *Pulsatilla* stands very closely allied to *Argentum nitricum*. You will notice that both have profuse, thick, bland, purulent discharge, and both have relief from the cool open air. It has been determined clinically that when *Argentum nitricum* ceases to act, a dose of *Pulsatilla* interpolated, helps.

You may also use *Argentum nitricum* in blepharitis when there are thick crusts on the lids, suppuration and induration of tissues. Even the cornea has become affected by the continued inflammation. The heat of the fire makes the patient a great deal worse. This symptom you also find under *Mercurius*.

Granular conjunctivitis also calls for *Argentum nitricum*. The conjunctiva is almost scarlet, and there is profuse muco-purulent discharge.

Rhus tox. is very similar to *Argentum nitricum*, but it has more spasmodic symptoms. There is spasmodic closure of the eyelids, and when you force them open, hot, scalding tears gush forth, and these cause pimples around the inflamed eyes.

Euphrasia is similar in granular lids; it differs from *Argentum nitricum* in this: the purulent discharge is excoriating, and there is, in addition, excoriating lachrymation.

Kreosote may be used in inflammation of the eyelids, whether in the infant or the adult. There is a discharge of hot, scalding tears from the eyes, occurring early in the morning.

Argentum nitricum may be useful in asthenopia from want of accommodation. Even the coarsest kind of work strains the eyes.

Coming now to the mucous membrane of the mouth and throat, we find *Argentum nitricum* producing a dark red appearance of the fauces. Thick mucus collects in the throat and the patient complains of a sensation as of a splinter there. With all this, there may be ulceration. The cause may be mercury, syphilis or scrofula. The papillæ of the tongue are elevated. The gums are tender and bleed readily, but are very seldom swollen, thus giving you a distinction between it and *Mercurius*. There is often the sensation as of a splinter in the throat like *Nitric acid*, *Alumina*, etc.

The larynx suffers from the action of *Argentum nitricum*. There is muco-purulent sputum, seeming to come from the posterior wall of the larynx. There is also marked hoarseness and sometimes even loss of voice. Singers frequently complain of a feeling as if there were something clogging the vocal organs.

Manganum is similar to *Nitrate of Silver*, causing laryngeal symptoms, particularly in anæmic or tubercular patients. The hoarseness is usually worse in the morning and grows better as they succeed in hawking up lumps of mucus. The *Manganum* patient has cough from loud reading, with painful dryness and roughness of the larynx. The cough is usually relieved by lying down.

Selenium is also similar to *Argentum nitricum*.

Paris quadrifolia is a neglected drug in laryngeal affections. We find it indicated when expectoration is noticed mostly in the morning and when it is green and tenacious.

Nitrate of Silver may be used in ulceration of the cervix of the uterus when it is enlarged and indurated, with copious yellow, corroding leucorrhœa and frequent bleeding from the points of ulceration.

Next, I would refer you to the action of *Argentum nitricum* on the kidneys, because little attention is paid to this action of the drug. I think that it was Dr. Preston, of Norristown, who used the drug mostly in such cases. He gave it very frequently in nephralgia from congestion of the kidneys or from passage of calculi. The face is of a rather dark hue and has a dried-up look; there is dull aching across the small of the back and also over the region of the bladder. The urine burns while passing and the urethra feels as if swollen. There is sudden urging to urinate. The urine is dark and contains blood, or else a deposit of renal epithelium and uric acid. It is especially useful when *Cantharis*, which it resembles, fails.

Nitric acid is to be thought of for urinary calculi when the urine contains oxalic acid and when that substance is the principal ingredient of the stone.

Lastly, I have to speak of the action of *Argentum nitricum* on the bowels. Here it is very similar to *Arsenic*. The stools are green and shreddy and consist of blood, slime and epithelium. This is often associated with the discharge of a great deal of flatus and is often provoked by the use of sugar. Especially is it indicated when diarrhœa follows any excitement, such as fright, the anticipation of some ordeal, or when the imagination has been played upon. The bowels are apt to move as soon as the least food or drink is taken.

In cholera infantum it is indicated in children who are thin, dried-up looking, almost like mummies. The legs are apparently nothing but skin and bones. The stools are green and slimy, with noisy flatus, and are worse at night.

Natrum mur. is the proper remedy to antidote the abuse of *Argentum nitricum*, or the after effects of cauterizing by the crude drug.

Argentum Metallicum.

Argentum metallicum produces spasms which simulate those of epilepsy. The attacks are followed by delirious rage. The patient jumps about and tries to strike those near him.

It produces spasmodic pain in various parts of the body; thus it gives rise to pain in the head, which gradually increases and, after reaching its acme, suddenly ceases. This pain is usually on the left side and is often associated with vertigo. The patient is extremely forgetful. The heart muscle sympathizes in these neuralgic pains. Thus, there will be spasmodic twitching of the heart muscle, particularly when the patient is lying on his back.

Now, the debility which naturally follows is very easily understood if you remember one quality of the *Argentum metallicum*, and that is its action upon joints. It has a particular affinity for the cartilages of joints. Thus, we find general debility, with bruised feeling in the small of the back from the weakness of the spine, general weariness forcing the patient to lie down to obtain rest. The knees are particularly weak. There will be, not a true articular rheumatism, but an arthralgia, with pains of the same character as those of the head. All these symptoms are common enough. We find them in nervous, hysterical women and in men after loss of fluids, particularly semen.

Argentum metallicum acts upon the mucous membrane of the throat and larynx. It produces in the larynx a copious exudation of pure mucus, not purulent or not serous, but looking exactly like boiled starch. It is associated with burning and rawness in the larynx, which rawness and burning are excited by talking and protracted use of the voice. The mucus is easily expectorated.

Argentum metallicum acts upon the left ovary, causing bruised pain in that organ and, sometimes, a feeling as though the ovary was growing large. (*Argentum nitricum*, the right ovary.) This is a purely subjective sensation. Associated with this bruised pain there is often a prolapsed uterus.

LECTURE LIX.

PLATINA, PALLADIUM, AND ALUMINA.

PLATINA.

Platina.
- Mental symptoms.—Bell., Pallad., Phos., Lyc.
- Nervous system.—Bell., Helon., Stan., Plumb.
- Sexual organs { Pallad., Arg. met., Helonias, Puls., Phos., Aurum.

THE action of *Platina* is to be studied under three headings, namely: the mental symptoms, its action on the nervous system in general, and its effects on the sexual organs of both the male and the female. The *Platina* patient is rather haughty and proud, egotistical. She seems to look down upon everybody and everything as beneath her. There is often accompanying this mental condition a peculiarity of vision; objects look smaller to her than natural. *Platina* also produces an excitation of the mind and of the whole nervous system. Things seem horrible to her. In her imagination she sees ghosts, demons, etc. Here it resembles *Kali bromatum* and *Hyoscyamus*, both of which have this symptom. Everything seems strange to the patient. When she enters her own home objects appear strange to her; she does not know where she is. At other times the patient is decidedly melancholy. She thinks that death is near at hand and she fears it, very much as we found under *Arsenic* and *Aconite*. *Aconite* predicts the hour or time of death, but otherwise the two drugs differ immeasurably. She may have a decidedly hysterical mood, with alternation of attacks of laughing and crying, especially when these are respectively inappropriate. Now these mental symptoms seem to depend upon excitement in the sexual sphere. The genitals, particularly those of the female, are acutely sensitive. There is constant titillation or tingling in the sexual organs, internally and externally. This excites the unfortunate victim to such a degree as to produce that horrible disease known as nymphomania. The patient seems to have the strength of a giant. She wishes to embrace everybody.

These nymphomaniac symptoms are accompanied by prolapsus with induration of the uterus, just like *Aurum*. The ovaries are very sensitive, and are the seat of burning pains. *Platina* has even succeeded in curing ovaritis when pus has formed, and *Hepar* and *Lachesis* have been insufficient to effect its evacuation. The menses are too early and too profuse, and consist of dark, stringy, clotted blood. They are accompanied by spasms, or by painful bearing-down in the uterine region. Now these spasms of *Platina* are quite frequently met with in hysterical subjects. They consist of a sort of tetanic rigidity with trismus, and this alternates with dyspnœa.

When, as will sometimes happen, nymphomania occurs as the result of worms escaping into the vagina and there exciting irritation, *Caladium* is the remedy.

This menstrual flow of *Platina* brings to mind two or three other remedies, which are here deserving of mention. *Crocus* has a dark or black clotted flow, with or without miscarriage, and associated with a sensation as if there were something moving around in the abdomen.

Chamomilla has profuse, dark, clotted menstrual flow, but its mental symptoms are different from those of *Platinum*.

Millefolium and *Sabina* have bright-red, partly-clotted blood.

Belladonna, like *Platina*, has a sensation in the forehead as if all would come out; face burning red; bearing down in uterus, etc.; but in *Belladonna* the pains come and go suddenly, and the flow is bright; or, if dark, it is offensive in odor.

Lycopodium is the nearest analogue in the egotistic state of mind.

The *Platina* patient often suffers from neuralgia in various parts of the body. These neuralgias are very easily studied on account of their well-marked characteristic symptoms. The pains are of a cramping character, and cause numbness and tingling in the parts affected. You find them frequently in the head. There will be pain at the root of the nose, as though the part were squeezed in a vise, and this is followed by tingling and numbness, which will indicate to you that it is in the course of the nerves that this symptom lies. The pains increase gradually, and decrease just as gradually as they came, as you will find under *Stannum*.

Now, in these neuralgic symptoms, the nearest remedy we have to *Platina* is *Belladonna*. In both remedies there is decided congestion of the head, with bright red face and delirium, but the gradually increasing, and just as gradually decreasing, pains distinguish *Platina* from *Belladonna*.

Capsicum is suited to patients of lax fibre who suffer from burning pungent pain in the face, worse from the slightest draught of air, whether warm or cold.

Verbascum is indicated in prosopalgia when there is a numbing, crushing as with tongs in the painful parts, worse from talking, sneezing, change of temperature, at times associated with numbness, and daily from 9 A. M. to 4 P. M.

Gnaphalium has neuralgia alternating with numbness, especially in the lower limbs.

Arsenicum has prosopalgia, with darting, needle-like, burning pains.

I have yet a few words to say about the action of *Platina* on the male system generally. We find it indicated for the ill-effects of pre-pubic masturbation. It is called for by the melancholy and the sheepish look that the children have. Also when, as a result of this unnatural vice, spasms of an epileptiform character appear. The youth has hollow eyes and yellow skin. During the attack the face is pale and sunken; in fact, it may be so at all times. Consciousness is not often lost. The limbs are usually drawn up and thus spread apart.

It may also be used for spasms during labor. Teething children may require *Platina* when they are anæmic and pale; the jaws are locked, and after the spell the child lies on its back with flexed legs and knees widely separated. The spasms, both in adults and children, alternate between convulsive actions and opisthotonos.

Platina may also be used in hysterical spasms or spasms caused by nervous excitement, when they are preceded or followed by constriction of the œsophagus and respiratory embarrassment, a sort of asthma in other words; sudden arrest of breathing when walking against the wind. In this last symptom it is similar to *Calcarea ostrearum* and *Arsenicum*. *Moschus* is similar to it in hysteria.

In its abdominal symptoms, *Platina* very much resembles *Plumbum*, and it has been used very successfully for the cure of the well-known colic produced by the latter remedy. Like *Plumbum*, *Platina* produces a constipation from inertia of the bowels. It is attended with frequent unsuccessful urging to stool. The stools when passed seem to be like putty or glue, and adhere tenaciously to the anus. It has been highly recommended for the constipation of emigrants.

The *Chloride of Platinum* has only one symptom that I care to mention, and that is caries of the tarsus. You may use it in syphilitic cases, or after the abuse of mercury.

Platina has some further action on the female genital organs, as I have already intimated. It is useful in cases of indurated and prolapsed uterus, associated with continual pressure in the groins and back; parts are painfully sensitive to touch. The patient exhibits sensitiveness, even vaginismus, during coitus.

In indurated uterus compare *Sepia*, *Aurum* (which has more suicidal mania), *Argentum nitricum* and *Helonias*.

For sensitiveness to coitus compare *Sepia*, *Belladonna* (from dry vagina), *Kreosote* (when followed by bloody flow), *Ferrum*, *Natrum mur.*, *Apis* (when associated with stinging in ovaries), *Thuja*, etc.

PALLADIUM.

Palladium is chemically and symptomatically near to *Platina*. It is of use principally for its action on the female genital organs. Its characteristic mental symptoms seem to find origin in the sexual symptoms, and form, with the latter, a useful and precise group for practical use. The patient is inclined to weep. She suffers from mental excitement, particularly in company. She always has an aggravation of her symptoms the day following an evening's entertainment. She is easily put out of humor, and is then inclined to use pretty strong language. She imagines herself very much neglected, and as she attaches great importance to the good opinion of others, this annoys her very much. The *Platina* woman is very different. She is egotistical in another form. Under *Palladium*, pride is easily wounded. In *Platina* the patient is haughty and egotistical; she looks down on others as not being good enough for her.

Palladium has a very characteristic headache, which makes the patient very irritable. It extends across the top of the head from ear to ear. The face is sallow, with blue rings around the eyes. There are also nausea, usually worse in the evening, and very acid eructations The bowels are constipated, the stools often being whitish in color.

We come now to the special uterine symptoms of *Palladium*, and these we find quite numerous. They are as follows: soreness in the abdomen with downward pressure, a very common symptom in uterine diseases; pain in the uterus and bladder after any exertion during the day; knife-like cutting pains in the uterus, which are relieved after stool; constant tired feeling in the small of the back; she is so tired that she actually reels; she feels drowsy; she complains that she feels sore and bruised all over; heaviness as from lead, deeply seated in the pelvis, worse from any exertion, and worse standing; walking is much less irksome to her than is standing; lying on the left side relieves; swelling in the region of the right ovary, with shooting pains from navel into the pelvis, and with this there is bearing down, relieved by rubbing. Jelly-like leucorrhœa. These local symptoms, together with those of the mind, make up the complete *Palladium* picture.

Argentum metallicum, like *Palladium*, has affections of the ovaries and uterus. It is useful in prolapsus uteri when accompanied by symptoms of the left ovary. The special characteristic sensation in *Argentum metallicum* is a feeling as though the left ovary were growing enormously large.

Still another drug is *Lilium tigrinum*. This resembles *Palladium* and *Platinum* both, and you will have to keep these three remedies together in your minds. They all have irritability, "easily angered," and "things don't go right," but only *Palladium* has this over-sensitiveness to offence, and only *Platinum* the *hauteur*.

Helonias is also similar to *Palladium*, in its irritability, soreness and, above all, a feeling of "tiredness."

ALUMINA.

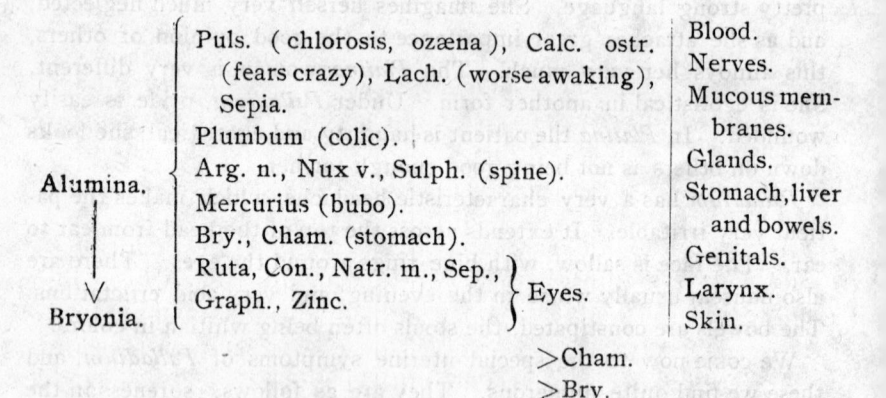

Alumina.
↓
∨
Bryonia.

{ Puls. (chlorosis, ozæna), Calc. ostr. (fears crazy), Lach. (worse awaking), Sepia.
Plumbum (colic).
Arg. n., Nux v., Sulph. (spine).
Mercurius (bubo).
Bry., Cham. (stomach).
Ruta, Con., Natr. m., Sep., }
Graph., Zinc. } Eyes.

Blood.
Nerves.
Mucous membranes.
Glands.
Stomach, liver and bowels.
Genitals.
Larynx.
Skin.

>Cham.
>Bry.

Alumina or the oxide of *Aluminium*, is a form of pure clay and is known as *argilla*. According to Hering, the symptoms which Hartlaub obtained are not pure, because he simply washed his preparation of clay, while Hahnemann subjected his to a red heat.

You notice by the table on the board that I have placed *Bryonia* as the complement of *Alumina*. This is particularly true of the gastric symptoms These drugs follow each other well in gastro-enteric affections. *Bryonia*, also, acts as an antidote to *Alumina*, as does also *Chamomilla*. I have placed several of the concordant remedies with a few words in parenthesis to indicate the points of resemblance. Thus *Pulsatilla* is marked by chlorosis and ozæna, showing that in these two affections particularly, *Pulsatilla* is concordant with *Alumina*. Then you notice that *Plumbum* is similar to it in colic, and *Nux* and *Sulphur* in spinal affections, etc.

Alumina acts best in aged persons of spare habits, who are rather wrinkled and dried-up looking, or in girls at puberty, especially if they are chlorotic, and also in delicate or scrofulous children, particularly children who have been artificially fed—that is, nourished by the many varieties of baby foods with which the market is glutted. Such children are weak and wrinkled; nutrition is decidedly defective. The bowels are inactive. This constipation is characteristic. There is a great deal of difficulty in voiding the stool even though the fæces be soft, showing you at once that the inactivity of the bowels is the main influence at work in its causation. Here, it is like *Bryonia*. Excepting that the latter has more hardness and dryness of the fæcal matter. The child suffers from ozæna or chronic nasal catarrh, with a great deal of dryness of the nose. This you know by the dry sniffling sound which the child makes in breathing through its nose. The child, too, when teething, may suffer from strabismus. This comes from weakness of the internal rectus muscle of the affected eye. This symptom is sometimes curable by medicine, and when it is so, this method is preferable to any surgical procedure. Sometimes, it follows worms. Then *Cina* is the remedy; when it comes from brain irritation, *Belladonna*; and *Cyclamen* when from menstrual or gastric irregularities.

The *Alumina* patient is very low-spirited and inclined to weep, like *Pulsatilla*, and this low-spiritedness is worse on awakening, here resembling *Lachesis*, *Pulsatilla*, *Sepia*, etc. At other times, you find the patient troubled with an apprehensive state of mind, a fear that he will go crazy, and this is an exact counter part of *Calcarea ostrearum*, *Iodine*, etc. This shows you the irritable state of brain fibre. Another peculiarity that may be present, particularly in hysteria, is suicidal tendency when the patient sees blood, or a knife, or something of that kind.

Men in whom *Alumina* is useful are hypochondriacal. There is a great deal of lassitude and indifference to labor or work. An hour seems to them half a day. They are exceedingly peevish and fretful; and here you find *Alumina* rivalling *Nux vomica* and also *Bryonia*.

Now, on the right side of the board, you will notice several headings under which I propose to consider *Alumina*. First, what changes are made in the blood by *Alumina?* I cannot tell you how it alters the blood, but there are diseases of the blood to which it is applicable, and it is convenient here to bring these to your notice. We find it indicated in anæmia, and also in chlorosis especially in young girls at puberty, when the menses are pale and scanty, and there is an abnormal craving for certain indigestible articles, such as slate pencils, chalk, whitewash, etc. The leucorrhœa to which they are subject is usually transparent, and quite ropy and tenacious, or else is composed of yellowish mucus, which is profuse, sometimes running down the limbs to the feet. This exhausts them very much, because it is rich in albumen. With these symptoms, you will almost always find the mental states that I have given you.

Now in nervous affections. *Alumina* has been used in nervous affections of a very grave character. Bœnninghausen used the metal *Aluminium* for the following symptoms in that dreaded disease, locomotor ataxia: frequent dizziness; objects turn in a circle; ptosis, diplopia or strabismus; inability to walk in the dark or with the eyes closed without staggering; feels as if walking on cushions. There is formication, or sensation as from creeping of ants in the back and legs. The nates go to sleep when sitting. The heels become numb when walking. A feeling in the face as though it was covered with cobwebs, or as though the white of an egg had dried on it. Pain in the back, as though a hot iron were thrust into the spine. These are the symptoms indicating *Alumina*, and these are the symptoms which led Bœnninghausen to *Aluminium*, and enabled him to cure four cases of the disease.

Next, the mucous membranes. *Alumina* is a unique drug here. It acts in a limited but very well-described class of cases. It causes unmistakable dryness of the mucous surfaces. If you keep that fact in mind you can explain all the symptoms which it causes. You have at once the key to its dyspepsia, nasal catarrh, sore throat and constipation. There is dryness of the mucous membranes. After a while, there is formation of mucus, which is thick, yellow, and very difficult of detachment. Let me show you a few illustrations of this. In the eyes, for instance, it will be indicated in blepharitis particularly, with great dryness of the conjunctiva. The lids feels stiff and they crack, so dry are they. The nearest analogue here is *Graphites*, which has the same symptoms, only it has more bleeding than has *Alumina*.

Alumina is useful in asthenopia from irritated conjunctiva; also in granular lids and chronic blepharitis.

For dry eyes, Allen recommends, also, *Berberis, Natrum carb.*, and *Natrum sulph.*

Eyes dry on reading, *Crocus, Argentum nitricum, Cina, Natrum mur.*

Drooping eyelids, *Nux moschata, Sepia, Rhus, Gelsemium.*

Alumina also has loss of power over the internal rectus. Here it is like *Agaricus, Jaborandi, Conium, Ruta,* and *Natrum mur.* The latter, according to Woodyat, is the best.

In nasal catarrh you will find *Alumina* indicated in children with great dryness of the nose, formation of scabs and remotely, thick, tenacious yellow phlegm or mucus, which is difficult of removal.

The cough indicating *Alumina* is dry and spasmodic. It is worse in the morning when the patient coughs until he detaches a small amount of tightly adherent mucus, which relieves for a while.

You find it indicated in disease of the throat, in a relaxed condition of the mucous membrane, just that condition you meet with in clergymen's sore-throat. The throat is very dry on waking with husky, weak voice. It is dark red, the uvula elongated. The patient is better from hot drinks. Hoarseness appears worse in the morning, with a feeling as of a splinter in the throat when swallowing. This last symptom you find also under *Hepar, Argentum nitricum, Nitric acid,* etc.

The mucous membrane of the stomach is dry, and, therefore, there is defective secretion of gastric juice. Here you have the same dyspepsia as is curable with *Bryonia*. The distinctive symptoms for *Alumina* are these: there is a feeling of constriction along the œsophagus when swallowing food. The patient is always worse from eating potatoes; that is a good indication for *Alumina*. There is aversion to meat and a craving for indigestible substances. The liver is sensitive to touch, and there are stitching pains in that organ, as under *Bryonia*. You find the constipation with urging to stool already described, even though the stool be not dry and hard. Piles itch and burn, and are moist.

Next, we consider the action of *Alumina* on glands. Here I have only one symptom for you, and that is the use of the drug in treating buboes. You may give it in gonorrhœal bubo when there exists with it a yellowish gonorrhœal discharge, with burning and itching along the urethra, particularly at the meatus.

Lastly, the skin. *Alumina* acts here just as it does on the mucous membranes, producing dryness and harshness of the skin; as a consequence, we find it indicated in rough, dry eruptions, which crack and may bleed, although not often, and which itch and burn intolerably, and are worse in the warmth of the bed.

You will recall here that *Argentum nitricum*, *Nux vomica*, and *Sulphur* are similar to *Alumina* in spinal affections.

Mercurius is the most similar remedy.

Alumina has been used as an antidote to the colic caused by *Plumbum*.

LECTURE LX.

PLUMBUM AND STANNUM.

Plumbum Metallicum.

Plumbum. { Belladonna, Platina, Nux vomica, Cuprum, Opium.
China. } > { Opium.
Alumina.

The symptoms of *Plumbum*, or lead, may be studied from its main property, that is, its tendency to cause contraction of muscular fibre, both voluntary and involuntary. It will cause this contraction of muscles, and it will also cause contraction of the bloodvessels, because it affects the involuntary or non-striated muscular fibres. The first symptom that usually follows poisoning by lead, whether taken by the stomach in small doses, as in case of drinking water impregnated with it, or whether by inhalation, as in the case of painters, is lead colic, and this consists of horrible griping cramp-pains, with retraction of the abdominal walls, making the abdomen concave rather than convex. There is understood to be spasm of the recti muscles; as these are contracted, of course they draw the abdominal walls in. Pain radiates in all directions, generally following the course of the nerves, sometimes causing delirium when extending to the brain, dyspnœa when involving the chest, retraction of the testicles when extending in that direction, and violent cramps in the legs when reaching the nerves there. With this colic there is obstinate constipation, and in some cases, even stercoraceous vomiting.

The colic is antidoted by *Alumina, Alumen, Platina, Opium, Nux vomica, Arsenicum, Colocynth, Sulphuric acid, Zincum,* or *Belladonna,* and is prevented by alcohol.

Next the symptoms of *Plumbum* that are of a paralytic character. The first characteristic symptom here is wrist-drop from paralysis of the extensor muscles of the wrist. This *Plumbum* has cured when it has arisen from other causes than lead-poisoning. This paralysis extends to other parts of the body, always involving extensor muscles in preference to flexors. There appears on the border of the gums a blue line, known as the gingival line of lead poisoning. It is caused by the sulphur that exists in the tartar on the teeth combining with the lead in the bloodvessels, and forming a deposit of insoluble sulphide of lead. As I have said, the paralysis extends and involves other parts of the body, and then it is characterized by atrophy of the affected parts, which is therefore due to true organic changes. Thus you find *Plumbum* indicated in paralysis from disease of the spinal cord when that nervous structure has undergone fatty degeneration or sclerosis.

Plumbum suits very nicely that disease known as multiple cerebro-spinal sclerosis. It is indicated by this symptom: tremor, followed by paralysis.

We often find *Plumbum* indicated in paralysis with contracture.

Progressive muscular atrophy may also call for *Plumbum*.

Plumbum tends to produce non-development of the uterus. We may, therefore, find it indicated in cases of tendency to abortion. The fœtus in utero increases in size, but the muscular fibres of the uterus do not develop in proportion, hence the uterus is no longer able to accommodate the growing fœtus and abortion ensues.

Sometimes we find *Plumbum* indicated in delirium, very much like that of *Belladonna;* the patient bites and strikes at those near him; but it differs from that of *Belladonna* in this: there is tremor of the head and hands, and yellow mucus collects about the mouth and teeth. The delirium, moreover, alternates with colic, which is not the case in *Belladonna*.

Other cerebral disturbances from lead-poisoning are not common, but still the following may be met with: insomnia, severe headache, either occipital or frontal, with or without vertigo; noises in ear; disordered vision; diplopia; amaurosis; contraction of pharynx, though liquids are swallowed in gulps and greedily; mind weak, morose, and sad; preceded by albuminous urine.

Plumbum has frequently caused epilepsy. The characteristic symptoms which indicate it are paralytic heaviness of the legs before the attack, and paralysis and prolonged snoring sleep afterwards. It is especially indicated in convulsions from cerebral sclerosis or tumor.

In constipation you may use *Plumbum* when the retraction of the abdomen already mentioned is present, and when there is marked spasm or contraction of the sphincter ani. There is urging to stool, and the patient complains of a sensation as though a string were drawing the anus up into the rectum.

It may be mentioned in passing that *Baryta carbonica* has a colic with retraction of the umbilicus like *Lead*. *Thallium* has the same symptom as an accompaniment of violent lancinating pains through the stomach and bowels, following each other rapidly like electric shocks. This remedy has relieved the fulgurating pains of locomotor ataxia.

In its action on the kidneys *Plumbum* produces granular degeneration or cirrhosis of those organs. There is very little dropsy or albuminuria, but a marked tendency to uræmia and consequent convulsions.

STANNUM.

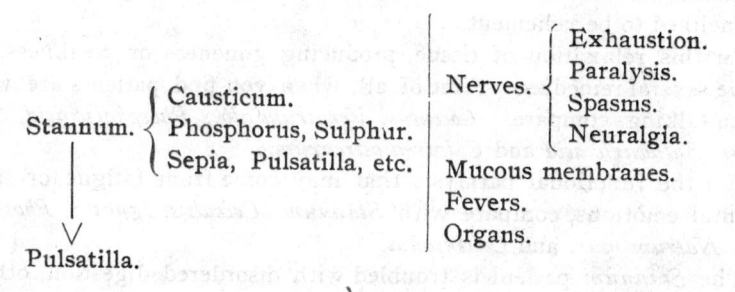

Stannum
{ Causticum.
Phosphorus, Sulphur.
Sepia, Pulsatilla, etc. }

Nerves. { Exhaustion. Paralysis. Spasms. Neuralgia. }

Mucous membranes.
Fevers.
Organs.

∨
Pulsatilla.

Stannum is a drug that has not many symptoms; hence it can be disposed of very quickly. Its complement is *Pulsatilla*.

The *Stannum* patient is usually sad and lachrymose, just like *Pulsatilla*. Crying usually makes the patient worse. This low-spiritedness is found in the lung troubles for which *Stannum* is your remedy. This is rather different from the usual mental state of consumptives, who, you all know, are generally hopeful, almost to the last hour of life. *Stannum* is particularly indicated when they are low-spirited, hence it is rarely indicated in true tuberculosis. The woman for whom *Stannum* is indicated is also nervous and weak; so nervous, irritable, and weak is she, that she becomes anxious and has palpitation of the heart, even from so little exertion as giving directions concerning her household affairs. She complains of a sensation of goneness in the stomach and chest. This nervous exhaustion is exhibited in various ways; it is particularly induced when the patient goes down stairs, more than when ascending. She feels as if she could not walk down stairs, or as if she had not sufficient strength in her limbs.

This exhaustion may be exhibited in another way: the patient does not complain much about walking, but on trying to sit down she fairly drops into the chair. This is not an imaginary symptom. You will meet it in uterine affections.

In the mental symptoms you may compare *Stannum* with *Natrum mur.*, *Pulsatilla*, and *Sepia*. *Natrum mur.* has melancholy, sad, weeping mood, but consolation seems to aggravate. On trying to comfort him, he becomes enraged.

The *Pulsatilla* patient is of a mild, tearful, yielding disposition. She rather likes consolation. She has scanty, delayed menses, while *Stannum* has the opposite.

The *Sepia* patient has sadness concerning her own health, while she exhibits great indifference to her family. She is easily offended and is inclined to be vehement.

In this relaxation of tissue, producing goneness or weakness, we have several remedies. First of all, when you find patients are weak from talking, compare: *Cocculus*, *Veratrum alb.*, *Phosphoric acid*, *Sulphur*, *Sulphuric acid* and *Calcarea ostrearum*.

For the functional paralysis that may come from fatigue or from mental emotions, compare with *Stannum*, *Cocculus*, *Ignatia*, *Phosphorus*, *Natrum mur.* and *Collinsonia*.

The *Stannum* patient is troubled with disordered digestion, otherwise called dyspepsia. There are nausea and vomiting in the morning, or, as in *Colchicum*, the odor of cooking causes vomiting. This last symptom is a particularly strong indication for *Stannum*, especially in women. There is weak, gone feeling in the stomach, as in *Sepia*; also bitter taste in the mouth. The rectum is inactive. Much urging is required to evacuate even a soft stool. The face is apt to be pale and sunken, with dark rings around the eyes. These symptoms indicate debility, with which women suffer, and they may call for the exhibition of *Stannum* when worms are present. Even when convulsions result from the irritation of these parasites, *Stannum* is still the remedy if other symptoms agree, thus placing it alongside of *Cina*, *Artemisia*, etc.

Men may require *Stannum* when they are hypochondriacal. They have gastralgic pains, which compel them to walk about for relief, and they are so weak that this exercise is very fatiguing to them. The tongue is coated yellowish.

The *Stannum* patient suffers from prolapsus uteri. This prolapsus so often calls for *Stannum*, that Dr. Richard Hughes generally finds this remedy useful for simple prolapsus uteri. You will find, too, that under *Stannum* the vagina is prolapsed. These prolapsus symptoms are worse during stool. The menses are always profuse. The leucorrhœa corresponds with the prevailing character of the drug. It is yellowish or else it is clear mucus, and is always associated with unbearable weakness. The patient is so weak that she can scarcely move about. The prostration is so great that, on dressing in the morning, she has to sit down several times to rest. There is trembling of the arms and legs. The limbs feel as heavy as lead. This weakness is always worse when descending, as when going down stairs or assuming a sitting posture. These uterine symptoms may be associated with weak or gone feeling in the chest. The patient feels so weak she can scarcely talk.

As somewhat similar to *Stannum* in prolapsus uteri, with aggravation of symptoms during stool, you may remember *Podophyllum*, which has prolapsus uteri with diarrhœa. The stool is usually green, and comes with a rush.

Calcarea phosphorica, *Nux vomica*, *Pulsatilla* should also be studied in this connection.

As you might expect, a patient, so thoroughly weakened as to the nervous system as is the *Stannum* patient, must suffer from neuralgia. The general characteristic guiding you to its use is, *the pains increase and decrease slowly*. They are especially liable to occur in the course of the supra-orbital nerve. With this character to the pain, we find *Stannum* useful in prosopalgia following intermittent fever and abuse of quinine.

In these pains that increase and decrease slowly, the nearest remedies are *Platina* and *Strontiana carb*. *Spigelia*, *Kalmia* and *Natrum mur.* also have the symptom, though perhaps less markedly.

Epilepsy has been treated with *Stannum*, particularly when reflex from abdominal irritation, as from the presence of worms in the intestinal canal. The patient has a pale face and dark rings around the eyes, and colic, which is relieved by pressing firmly on the abdomen. If the child is old enough to describe his sensations, he will complain of a sweetish taste in the mouth. It is also useful in epilepsy with sexual complications; opisthotonos; clenching of the thumbs.

Hysterical spasms may also call for *Stannum*, especially when associated with pain in the abdomen and diaphragm.

Next, the action of *Stannum* on mucous membranes. When it is the remedy, you find that there is copious secretion from the mucous membranes. This is bland and unirritating, and is yellowish or yellowish-green; hence it is a muco-purulent secretion. Sometimes, although not so often, this mucus is tenacious, viscid and intermixed with blood. It accumulates in the throat and is detached with great difficulty, even exciting vomiting. The mucus collects very rapidly in the chest and is quite easily expectorated, with great relief to the patient. The oppression, the weakness, and the tightness of the chest are all relieved when this sputum is raised. The voice, which is husky and hoarse, seems to be raised in pitch by this expectoration. Dyspnœa, too, is decidedly better after expectoration. The cough is very annoying and teasing. It is worse at night, and is excited by talking and walking rapidly. The patient, in addition, complains of that weakness of the chest. It seems as if he had no strength there whatever. Dyspnœa comes on, worse towards evening.

Now these are the symptoms which indicate *Stannum* in cases of neglected cold. They also suggest the drug in what has been very properly termed catarrhal phthisis. There is marked hectic fever. The chills come characteristically at ten o'clock in the morning. Towards evening the patient becomes flushed and hot, with aggravation of his symptoms on any exertion. At night he has profuse sweat, which is particularly worse towards four or five o'clock in the morning. Let me say here that in this hectic fever, with chill at ten o'clock in the morning, I have several times tried *Natrum mur.*, but without obtaining any benefit from it.

Stannum is a remedy which you must select with great care, or it will surely disappoint you. This symptom of weakness must be present if you expect results. When you find *Stannum* insufficient in catarrhal phthisis, you may think of the following remedies:

Silicea is indicated in catarrhal as well as in true tubercular phthisis when there is cough, which is increased by rapid motion. There is copious rattling of phlegm in the chest. The expectoration is more purulent than that of *Stannum*. There are usually vomicæ in the lungs. You will find *Silicea* frequently indicated in the catarrhal phthisis of old people.

Phosphorus must often be carefully compared with *Stannum*, as the two remedies are frequently misused for each other. Both have hoarseness, evening aggravation, weak chest, cough, copious sputum, hectic, etc. *Phosphorus* has more blood or blood-streaks, tightness across the chest, aggravation from lying on the left side and thirst for ice-cold water.

Senega is a drug which produces great soreness in the walls of the chest and great accumulation of clear albuminous mucus, which is difficult of expectoration. These symptoms are often accompanied by pressure on the chest as though the lungs were pushed back to the spine. It is especially indicated in fat persons of lax fibre. This *Senega* contains *Senegin* or *Polygalic acid*, which is identical in composition with *Saponin*, the active principle of the *Quillaya saponaria*. This also produces the same kind of relaxed cold as the *Senega* does.

Coccus cacti is useful in whooping cough, with vomiting of great ropes of clear albuminous mucus. It may be useful in catarrhal phthisis when, with this ropy phlegm, there are sharp stitching pains under the clavicles.

Balsam of Peru is indicated in catarrhal phthisis by copious purulent expectoration. We know but little concerning this drug. We must, therefore, adopt the expedient of selecting it by a process of exclusion.

Yerba santa or the *Eriodiction Californicum* is indicated when there is asthmatic breathing from accumulation of mucus. There are considerable emaciation and fever.

Among other remedies with much phlegm on the chest are *Antimonium crudum* and *tartaricum, Chamomilla, Belladonna, Calcarea ostrearum, Calcarea phosphorica* and *Ipecacuanha* (in children), *Lycopodium, Sulphur, Phosphorus, Balsam of Peru* (purulent sputum), *Hepar, Scilla, Yerba santa* (fever, emaciation, asthma from mucus), *Copaiva* (profuse greenish-gray, disgusting-smelling sputa); *Illicium anisatum* (pus, with pain at third cartilage, *right* or left); *Pix liq.* (purulent sputum; pain at left third costal cartilage); *Myosotis* (copious sputa, emaciation, night sweat).

In pleurisy you find *Stannum* indicated by sharp, knife-like stitches, beginning in the left axilla, and extending up into the left clavicle. Sometimes they extend from the left side down into the abdomen. They are worse from bending forward, from pressure and on inspiration.

Stannum is sometimes used in functional paralysis arising from onanism or from emotions. Sometimes persons of the weak, nervous temperament I have described are so affected by emotions as to lose the power of motion. Here *Stannum* compares with *Staphisagria* and *Natrum mur.*

LECTURE LXI.

CUPRUM AND ZINCUM

Cuprum Metallicum.

Cuprum.
- Sulphur.
- Argentum nitricum, Arsenicum, Veratr. alb.
- Colocynth, Plumbum, Cholos terrapinæ.
- Stramonium, Belladonna, Hyos.

↓

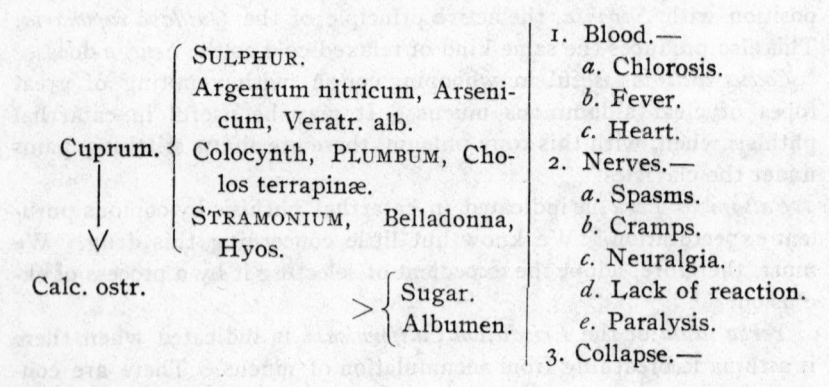

Calc. ostr.

> { Sugar. Albumen. }

1. Blood.—
   a. Chlorosis.
   b. Fever.
   c. Heart.
2. Nerves.—
   a. Spasms.
   b. Cramps.
   c. Neuralgia.
   d. Lack of reaction.
   e. Paralysis.
3. Collapse.—

Cuprum metallicum and *Cuprum aceticum* are used interchangeably by many physicians as having the same symptomatology. The original idea of those who proposed the substitution of the latter for the former was based on the supposition that the acetate of copper is soluble, while the metallic copper is not. This applies, of course, to the crude drug, but not to the potentized preparations.

Copper has for its complement *Calcarea ostrearum*. It is antidoted by sugar and albumen. *Hepar*, as a general antidote to the metals, comes into play as a dynamic antidote, as do also *Belladonna* and *Stramonium*. Copper possesses considerable interest as a prophylactic in disease. Workers in copper seldom contract Asiatic cholera. Here it resembles *Sulphur*. Unlike *Sulphur*, however, it is a remedy for the symptoms of cholera. It is indicated for the following symptoms: intense coldness of the surface of the body, blueness of the skin, cramps of the muscles, the muscles of the calves and thighs are drawn up into knots. There is considerable distress, referred by the patient to the epigastrium, and this is associated with most intense dyspnœa. So intense is the dyspnœa that the patient cannot bear his handkerchief approached to his face; it takes away his breath. Now, this picture of *Cuprum* seems to place it between *Camphor* and *Argentum nitricum*. *Camphor* has symptoms of collapse, like *Cuprum;* and *Argentum nitricum* has terrible distress in the epigastrium with dyspnœa. It differs from *Camphor* in this: *Camphor* lacks the prominence of the cramps which are ever present in the collapse of *Cuprum*.

There is another condition in which *Cuprum* may be used, and that is in the uræmia or uræmic convulsions following cholera. The character of these convulsions will appear in a few minutes when I speak of the nervous symptoms of the remedy.

We find *Cuprum* indicated in chlorosis, after the abuse of iron. The symptoms are worse in hot weather.

We also find it indicated in fever with marked tendency to frequent relapses; hence, in a sort of relapsing fever. It is not the specific relapsing fever, but rather a fever in which the relapses are the result of defective reaction.

Cuprum, when taken in large doses, produces an inflammatory colic, presenting a combination of neurotic with inflammatory symptoms; these are gastro-enteric. We find the abdomen as hard as a stone; the bowels are, at first, obstinately constipated, the constipation being succeeded at times by bloody, greenish, watery stools. The vomiting is terrific and is spasmodic in its character. It seems to be relieved by a drink of cold water. Hence it is very different from *Arsenicum*, *Veratrum* and other remedies. Now, what takes place in this group of symptoms? In the first place, *Cuprum* not only acts on the bowels, inflaming them, but it acts upon the nerves, causing constriction of fibre, particularly of the involuntary muscular fibres, as in the bloodvessels, and with this we have direct irritation producing inflammation. Now, to clearly understand the character of *Cuprum*, you must remember the other side to this picture. This condition is soon followed by collapse with great prostration, from which it is exceedingly difficult for the patient to rally. Thus, we have as a remote symptom of *Cuprum*, and one, too, which has been greatly neglected, lack of reaction. We have seen that quite a number of remedies are useful in this condition. We all know that *Sulphur* may often be used; we have learned under what circumstances *Carbo veg.* is called for; that *Laurocerasus*, *Valerian* and *Ambra grisea* are suited in some nervous temperaments; *Capsicum* in flabby, lazy individuals of lax fibre, and *Psorinum* in wellmarked psoric cases. But here we have, when *Cuprum* is the remedy, a tendency of all the symptoms to relapse. Especially is it an indication when this lack of reaction occurs in persons who are thoroughly "run down" by overtaxing both body and mind. I know of a case in which *Cuprum* prevented paralysis of both legs, and this was the indication; deciding its choice was the fact that the disease was caused by overtaxing of both brain and body.

So, too, in pneumonia, we may have to use *Cuprum* to bring about reaction before the appropriate remedy will cure. It is indicated by sudden suffocative attacks, with coldness of the surface of the body, with great prostration and dyspnœa disproportionate to the amount of solidification. The body is covered with a cold viscid sweat.

The main action of *Cuprum* and that which will call for its most frequent use in practice, is on the nervous system. We find it indicated, for instance, in spasms with affections of the brain, as in meningitis. No remedy in the materia medica excels it, and very few equal it, in this direction. We find it indicated when there has been an eruption suppressed, whether that be scarlatina, measles or erysipelas. The symptoms which call for it are these: delirium of a violent character very much like that of *Belladonna*; the patient bites the offered tumbler, loquacious delirium on awaking from sleep, or on becoming conscious he appears frightened. Here it is the exact counterpart of *Stramonium*. But it is a far deeper-acting remedy than *Stramonium*. The convulsions usually start from the brain with blueness of the face and lips, the eyeballs are rotated and there are frothing at the mouth and violent convulsive symptoms, especially of the flexor muscles. The convulsion is followed by deep sleep. Now this spasm, especially if epileptic, may be ushered in by a violent shriek or cry. There is grinding of the teeth.

Cuprum is not very frequently indicated in neuralgia, but it may sometimes be used in sudden attacks of neuralgia with active congestion affecting the nervous supply of the involuntary muscles.

Cuprum arsenicosum I have used in the third potency, on the recommendation of Dr. J. H. Marsden, for neuralgia of the abdominal viscera. I have prescribed it in cases in which no other remedy seemed to be indicated, and I believe with excellent success.

Zincum.

ZINC.
- Nervous depression.
- Undeveloped diseases from enervation.
- Brain.
  - Hemispheres.
  - Sensorium.
  - Pons medulla.
- Spine.
- Anæmia.
- Organs.
- Skin.

ZINC.
- Belladonna, Cuprum, Stramonium.
- Hyoscyamus.
- Calcarea ostrearum.   >Ign.
- Camphor.   <Nux vom.
- Plumbum.   >Hep.

Zincum metallicum is the preparation we most frequently use. You will notice the very peculiar fact that two preparations containing strychnia, *Nux vomica* and *Ignatia*, hold opposite relations to *Zinc*. *Ignatia* follows *Zinc* well, and may even act as an antidote to its effect on the nervous system. *Nux vomica* tends rather to increase the effects of *Zinc*, in fact, is inimical to it. *Hepar* also antidotes *Zinc*, as it does every other metal. It is a safe remedy to fall back on in cases of metallic poisoning when the symptoms point to no special antidote. *Zinc* often precedes *Apis* when there are sharp cutting pains all over, coming quickly, jerks of tendons in sleep, head hot, feet cold; kidneys still act.

I have had mapped out on the board some of the sphere of action of *Zinc*. I wish to impress on you all that this is not placed here as an exhaustive analysis of the remedy, nor is it intended to teach you that you are to use *Zinc* only in the diseases here named. This table is only for convenience sake, to give a sort of starting point around which you may group the symptoms of the remedy.

In poisonous doses the salts of zinc cause formication, that is, a sensation as of ants creeping over the body. This creeping or tingling is relieved by rubbing or by pressure. There is even a tremulous vibration all through the body. This is not only experienced by the patient, but is noticed, too, by the observer. Later, there appear fainting spells, with a great deal of numbness and deathly nausea. As soon as water touches the stomach, it is vomited. This is increased by acids, so, if any one should give the patient vinegar or lemon-juice, it only adds to his torment by increasing the nausea. With all this, there is vertigo. The head reels, the eyes feel as if they were being drawn together, and there is a hard heavy pressure at the root of the nose. These symptoms are followed by convulsions and stupor, and finally, if the poison cannot be antidoted, by death. I would warn you, too, if you meet with such a case of poisoning, not to give wine or other stimulants, for every symptom of *Zinc*, from head to foot, is made worse by wine.

Other remedies having aggravation from drinking wine are *Rhododendron, Glonoin, Nux vomica, Selenium, Ledum, Fluoric acid, Antimonium crudum, Pulsatilla, Arsenicum, Lycopodium, Opium* and *Silicea*.

Glonoin has congestive headache, made worse by wine.

Ledum is indicated in drawing pains in the joints, made worse by drinking wine.

Fluoric acid has aggravation from red wines.

Pulsatilla from sulphurated wines.

Antimonium crudum is suited to the bad effects of Rhenish sour wines.

Bovista, easily intoxicated. Also *Conium*.

Silicea, ebullition of blood, with aggravation from wine: *Carbo veg*. blushes up after a little wine.

Workers in zinc, after ten or twelve years' exposure, suffer from the following symptoms: pains in the back; sensitiveness of the soles of the feet; formication, numbness and coldness of the legs; sensation as of a band around the abdomen; crampy twitching of the muscles. Reflex excitability is increased so that irritation in one part of the body will produce violent jerking in another. Muscular sensibility is lessened, hence patient staggers when his eyes are closed, or when he is in the dark. There are muscular tremors which almost simulate those of shaking palsy. Still later, the gait becomes stiff, motions are spasmodic with the step on the full sole. From involvement of the sympathetic nervous system there are anæmia and progressive and general emaciation.

In studying *Zinc* as a remedy we are to remember, then, that it is a medicine which acts prominently on the nervous system. This influence which it has on the nervous tissue, is one rather of depression than stimulation. It weakens the cerebro-spinal nerves, and also those of the sympathetic, or ganglionic nerves more accurately called. It is, therefore, to be used in those diseases in which there is weakness of the nervous system. One very useful condition in which we may employ this drug comes under the second heading, undeveloped disease from enervation. By that I mean that *Zinc* is an invaluable drug when the patient is nervously too weak to develop a disease, and hence he suffers all the consequences of hidden disease, or disease spending its force on the internal organs. To give you an illustration of this in exanthematous diseases, we find *Zinc* called for in scarlatina, or in measles when the eruption remains undeveloped. As a result of the non-development of the disease, the brain suffers, as we shall see presently.

Manganese resembles *Zinc* by causing progressive wasting, staggering gait and paralysis. Like *Phosphorus* it causes acute fatty degeneration of the liver.

Now, as another evidence of this nervous condition of non-reaction, we find pains in the ovaries which are relieved during the menstrual flow. Further illustration of this action of *Zinc* will be found in the catarrhal asthma in which it is indicated. This asthma is accompanied by great constriction of the chest (*Cadmium sulph.*, *Kali chlor.* and *Cactus g.*), and is relieved as soon as the patient can expectorate, like *Sepia*, *Antimonium tart.* and *Grindelia*. So, too, in the male organs there is a local irritation which may be the result of spinal irritation, or self-abuse. This irritation is relieved by a seminal discharge.

Again, during dentition, the child gives way under the nervous strain, the teeth fail to develop; it has a slow pulse, seeming to come in long waves; it is drowsy, and lies with the back of the head pressed deeply into the pillow, with the eyes half-closed and squinting, the face pale and rather cool, or alternately red and pale. It gives forth loud cries, not exactly the *cri encephalique*, but something akin to it, with trembling all over, boring the fingers into the nose (as you find under *Cina*, *Arum triphyllum*, *Veratrum* and a few other remedies), or pulling nervously at the dry, parched lips, again reminding you of *Arum*. There will be automatic motion of different parts of the body, usually the arms and hands, and, particularly, restless, fidgety movements of the feet. This last symptom is a very strong indication for

Zincum. If still conscious enough to take water, the child drinks it hastily. In extreme cases the abdomen is hot and sunken, and the stools and urine involuntary. In milder brain symptoms the child awakes delirious, as if frightened by horrible dreams. It seems to know no one. It rolls the head from side to side. It may have convulsions, with anxious screams and springing up out of bed, gnashing the teeth and rolling the eyes. It is exceedingly cross and irritable before the attack, with hot body and great restlessness, particularly at night.

Zincum may be indicated in chorea or St. Vitus' dance, when caused by fright or suppressed eruptions, especially when the general health suffers very much. There are great depression of spirits, and irritability.

Still another form of cerebral trouble calling for *Zinc* is meningitis. Here it is indicated when, in the beginning either of a case of rheumatism, or in fact from any cause, you find these sharp, lancinating pains through the head; they are worse from wine, * or from anything that stimulates. There are, also, pressing, tearing pains in the occiput, particularly about the base of the brain; and these pains seem to shoot through the eyes, and, sympathetically, into the teeth. There is a very distressing, cramplike pain at the root of the nose, just as we found in the poisoning symptoms. Now these symptoms will suggest *Zinc* to you in quite a variety of ailments, but especially in meningitis arising from the non-development of an eruption.

So you find *Zincum* indicated in scarlatina with the brain symptoms that I have mentioned, and with the following additional symptoms: the eruption is imperfectly developed; the skin is rather livid; the child is restless and delirious, or else quiet and unconscious; even in the smooth or Sydenham scarlatina, *Zinc* may supplant *Belladonna* by reason of this enervation of the child. A still worse case than this may occur, and still *Zincum* be indicated, and that is, when the skin is bluish and cold, the body is heavy, and the pulse is almost threadlike, it is so weak and volumeless. Let us now compare *Zincum* with other remedies.

Cuprum has cerebral symptoms, convulsions with screaming out,

---

*In headache worse from wine, compare: *Rhododendron*, *Glonoin*, *Nux vomica*, *Oxalic acid* and *Selenium*.

Both *Conium* and *Zinc* have aggravation from small sips of wine; *Conium* is easily intoxicated thereby. *Zinc* has nearly all symptoms by taking small quantities.

clenching of the thumb into the palm of the hand, boring of the head into the pillow, and predominant spasm of the flexor muscles; the face is usually red, or even purple; the teeth are clenched; the child foams at the mouth; it awakens from its sleep frightened, and does not know anybody about it, just as in *Zincum* and *Stramonium*. All these symptoms in *Cuprum* are the result of a suppressed eruption. In *Zinc* they are due to an undeveloped eruption. The symptoms are more violent under *Cuprum*; and are more like those of active inflammation.

In scarlatina the case is different when *Belladonna* is indicated; it is the remedy in the smooth variety of scarlatina, in the early stages. The vomiting is violent, and the cerebral symptoms prominent. There are screaming out, wild look about the eyes and redness of the face. The throat is bright red and swollen, and the tongue covered with elevated papillæ; the patient springs up from sleep screaming, and clings to those about it. Suppose, however, this case goes on, and the rash does not come out; the child becomes pale and livid; it rolls its head in the pillow, grinds its teeth, and screams out whenever you move it, and the feet are restless; then *Belladonna*, *Cuprum* or *Lachesis* will do no good; no remedy but *Zinc* will.

If the case goes on in spite of *Zinc*, and the skin becomes livid and cold, the pulse filiform, *Camphor* may still bring about reaction, especially if there is cold sweat.

In some cases *Veratrum album* will come in.

In still others I would have you remember *Hydrocyanic acid*.

Calcarea ostrearum is often forgotten in scarlatina. It is to be placed alongside of *Zinc*, particularly in scrofulous children, when the rash is either undeveloped, or else recedes, leaving the face unnaturally pale and bloated.

Zincum is indicated in several forms of headache. One of them is a stinging, tearing headache, worse in the side of the head, greatly increased by wine; this headache is also worse after dinner. Sometimes you will find *Zinc* indicated in obstinate pain in the head, obstinate in its persistence, yet intermittent in its quality, now very severe, and now fading away, but continually returning. It is also indicated for hypochondriasis and pressure on the top of the head, increased after dinner.

You will also find *Zincum* indicated in hydrocephaloid, following cholera infantum. The child rolls its head; it awakens from sleep as if frightened, and looks around the room terrified; the occiput is apt to be hot and the forehead rather cool; there is grinding of the teeth; the eyes are sensitive to the light, and are fixed and staring; the face is sunken and pale, or alternately red and pale; the nose is dry; there is jerking of the muscles during sleep; and last, but not least, there is constant fidgety motion of the feet. In hydrocephaloid, *Zincum* is closely allied to *Calcarea phos.*

Next, I would like to speak of the action of *Zincum* on the spine. Zinc is a good remedy in disease of the spine of a functional character, especially in spinal irritation. The symptoms which call for it are these: first and foremost, dull, aching pain about the last dorsal or first lumbar vertebra, and this is worse when the patient is sitting than it is when he walks. The symptom, I can assure you, is a good indication for *Zinc.* I think that very nearly the same symptom is found under *Sepia.* It is not situated in the same locality, however, but has the same aggravation. It is also found characteristically under *Kobalt.* This backache of *Zincum* is associated with burning along the spine, which I believe to be purely subjective and not congestive in character. We also find under *Zinc*, trembling of the limbs, with a feeling as if they were about to be paralyzed; sudden spasmodic bursting sensation about the heart; the heart is beating regularly, when it suddenly seems as if it would burst through the chest; constriction of the chest, causing shortness of breath; the pulse is slow, or weak and irregular; weakness or goneness in the stomach at 11 A. M. This last symptom you will also find under *Phosphorus*, *Natrum carb.*, *Natrum phos.*, *Sulphur*, *Asafœtida*, *Hydrastis* and *Indium.* *Manganum* should be thought of in conjunction with *Zinc* when the lumbar spine is affected and there are burning pains, worse on bending backwards; legs weak; tension here and there; marked anæmia.

Zincum is also indicated in paralysis from softening of the brain, following suppressed foot-sweat, with vertigo, trembling, numbness and formication. These symptoms are relieved by friction, and greatly aggravated by wine. There may be marked ptosis with this paralysis.

In these paralytic affections, *Zincum* is similar to *Phosphorus* and *Plumbum.* It is similar to *Phosphorus*, in that both remedies suit cases of enervation and of softening of the brain with the accompanying trembling. *Phosphorus* has not the aggravation from wine or the ptosis.

Plumbum has nearly the same symptoms as *Zinc*, but there is added to these, impaired nutrition, or atrophy of the paralyzed part. There will be pains in the atrophied limbs, alternating with colic.

Now a word or two as to some local effects of *Zinc*, and we will have done with the remedy. First of all, we find it indicated in some affections of the eyes; for instance, in amblyopia, accompanied by severe headache, which is probably dependent upon some organic change in the brain or its meninges, and with severe pain at the root of the nose. The pains are particularly worse at the inner canthus of each eye. The pupils are contracted.

We may also use *Zinc* for opacities of the cornea following repeated and long-lasting attacks of inflammation of that membrane. The best preparation here is *Zincum sulphuricum.*

Pterygium may be removed by *Zinc*, particularly if there are smarting and stinging pains at the inner canthus.

Zincum is also useful for granular lids. Here again the *sulphuricum* being preferable to the *metallicum.*

It is also indicated in prosopalgia when the pains are severe and are accompanied by blueness of the eyelids.

Zincum has marked gastric and hepatic symptoms. It produces bitter taste, which is referred by the patient to the fauces. As soon as a spoonful of water reaches the stomach it is ejected. Heartburn is present, and this is increased by wine and also during pregnancy. When occuring during pregnancy it is apt to be accompanied by varicose veins of the legs. Hunger is particularly manifested towards noon. *Zincum* also affects the liver. You will find recorded in the original provings a symptom, the exact language of which I have forgotten, but which is in substance this: there is a feeling as of a hard tumor in the neighborhood of the umbilicus, and this is accompanied by griping pains. This symptom has led to the use of the drug in enlargement of the liver.

Zincum affects the abdomen something like *Plumbum*, producing griping pains about the navel, with most obstinate constipation. This is accompanied by a great deal of pressure backwards, as though the abdomen were being drawn back toward the spine. Now, in almost all cases in which *Zincum* is useful you will find that the predominant pain and pressure is on the sides of the abdomen; so it must affect principally the ascending and the descending colon. The urine often contains blood; it is sometimes turbid and loam-colored, and has a yellowish sediment. The patient cannot pass urine unless he sits cross-legged, even though the bladder be full.

The cough of *Zinc* is spasmodic, as if it would draw the chest in pieces. The sputum may be bloody. This is particularly noticed just before or during a menstrual period. It is also aggravated by eating sweet things. You will sometimes find *Zincum* helping in children, who, every time they cough, put their hands on the genital organs.

In its action on the male genital organs *Zincum* is similar to *Conium*. It is indicated in spermatorrhœa following long-lasting abuse of the genital organs, with great hypochondriasis. The face is pale and sunken, with blue rings around the eyes. There is a great local irritation. The testes are drawn firmly up against the external ring. *Conium* differs in that it lacks the excessive irritability. In this remedy, when there is urinary difficulty, the urine is apt to pass more readily while the patient is standing.

Zincum is also useful in diseases of the female organs, especially for irregularity in the menstrual function, particularly when it is associated with ulceration of the cervix uteri and boring pain in the left ovarian region. All the symptoms improve at the onset of the menstrual flow.

LECTURE LXII

FERRUM AND THE MAGNESIA SALTS.

Ferrum Metallicum.

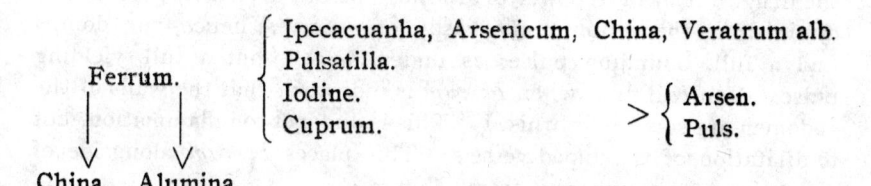

Ferrum. {Ipecacuanha, Arsenicum, China, Veratrum alb. Pulsatilla. Iodine. Cuprum.}   > {Arsen. Puls.}

∨   ∨
China. Alumina.

FERRUM has two complements, *Cinchona* or *China*, and *Alumina*. *Ferrum* and *Alumina* are complementary in chlorosis; and *Ferrum* and *Cinchona* in anæmia from loss of animal fluids.

Now the best antidote to Iron I know of is *Pulsatilla*. And, as good fortune will have it, *Pulsatilla* also antidotes *Cinchona*, which is so frequently given in combination with Iron by old-school physicians.

Ferrum acts best in young persons, male or female, who are subject to irregular distributions of blood. The cheeks are flushed a bright red, giving them an appearance of blooming health; and yet this is only a masked plethora. When they are unexcited and quiet they are apt to be pale, and the face has an earthy color. Among the evidences of this irregular distribution of blood we have the following symptoms: violent hammering headache, which is usually periodical in its return and worse after twelve o'clock at night; nose-bleed, with bright red flushing of the cheeks; the nose is filled with dark, clotted blood during an attack of catarrh; asthma, associated with an orgasm of blood to the chest, and worse after twelve o'clock at night, at which time the patient must sit up and uncover the chest. He uncovers the chest to get cool, and sits up in order to breathe, and moves slowly about for relief. *Ferrum* is also suited to hæmoptysis, especially in young boys or girls who are subject to consumption and who are just in the incipient stages of phthisis florida. Almost all these symptoms are excited by any emotion and are accompanied by great fatigue, despite the appearance of health. Even the neuralgia which *Ferrum* may cure has fulness of the bloodvessels as a concomitant condition. This neuralgia is excited by washing in cold water, especially after being overheated. The pains are of a throbbing character, and are worse at night. Almost all of these symptoms, both the congestions and the pains, are relieved by slowly walking about. Now, you may understand the action of *Ferrum* if you remember this one quality of the drug. It has the power of dilating the blood-vessels, probably by diminishing the action of the vaso-motor nerves; hence, you do not find a full, bounding pulse, as under *Aconite*, but a full, yielding pulse. You will find, when *Ferrum* is indicated, that the walls of the abdomen are sore, as if bruised. This is due, not to inflammation, but to dilatation of the blood-vessels. This places *Ferrum* alongside of *Gelsemium* and separates it from *Aconite*.

We have next to study *Ferrum* as a chlorotic remedy. We do not use *Ferrum*, or, at least, we should not, as allopathic physicians do, because, in this disease there is a defective amount of iron in the blood. That is not the homœopathic principle for giving the drug. Homœopathy aims to correct the defective supply of hæmatin which lies back of the want of iron in the blood. This deficiency is due not to want of iron in the food taken, but to want of power on the part of the system to assimilate it. Therefore, *Ferrum* is not *the* remedy in chlorosis. It may, however, be called for in that disease when the following symptoms are present: in the first place, in a general way, it is called for in erethistic chlorosis—that is, chlorosis with erethism of blood. It may be aggravated during the cold weather, less so, however, than it is during warm weather. The face is ordinarily of a pale, waxen or earthy hue, and subject, at every little emotion, to flush up red. The slightest emotion of pleasure or distress, the sudden entrance of any one into the room, the meeting of a stranger, and, in fact, anything that is calculated to disturb the mind, causes flushing up of the face. The cheeks become bright red. Now, this is not a true plethora; it is a masked case. The face is really of an earthy hue, but flushes up on any little emotion. The stomach is always out of order, the patient being subject to gastralgia and heavy pressure in the region of the stomach. With this there is a feeling as if something rolled into the throat and closed it like a valve. There is great aversion to meat, and, in fact, to anything that is really nourishing. Food has little or no taste. The patient has frequent spells of nausea which come as soon as he eats, or periodically at twelve o'clock at night. Here it reminds one of *Arsenicum*. Mucous membranes are abnormally pale. For instance, the vermilion of the lips is exchanged for a simple pale pink. In the case of a male patient the glans penis is shrivelled and white, almost as pale as the prepuce. So, too, the cavity of the mouth and the gums are almost white, showing this bloodlessness. The menses are profuse and consist of watery and lumpy blood, and are attended with labor-like pains in the abdomen. The patient is very inactive; it is with great effort that she can move about. She is relieved by exercise. She is chilly during most of the day, with bright red flushing of the cheeks in the evening. There is palpitation of the heart, well-marked bellows murmur. The blood-vessels all over the body throb violently. Sometimes the anæmia progresses so far that the patient becomes affected with œdema of the feet.

Manganese is very like Iron in its hæmatin effects but in nervous symptoms is more like *Cuprum*, *Argentum* and *Zinc*. Symptoms agreeing, it may be interpolated to favor the action of *Ferrum* in chlorosis, etc.

The *Ferrum* patient is subject to frequent congestive headaches, with pulsating pain in the head, worse usually after midnight. The face is fiery red during the attack, and the feet are cold. It is here very much like *Belladonna*, but is indicated in a very different class of cases from those calling for that remedy. Such patients always complain of vertigo or dizziness, which is worse when they rise suddenly from a lying to a sitting posture. Walking over a bridge or by some running water or riding in a car or carriage also causes this vertigo. These are the cases in which you will find *Ferrum* to succeed. An English physician has advised that *Ferrum* be administered after a meal instead of before. He thinks it acts better then. I do not know whether this is so or not.

Another use that we may make of *Ferrum*, arising from its tendency to produce ebullitions of blood, is in phthisis florida. It is indicated in young people who are subject to tuberculosis, here rivalling the well-known *Phosphorus*. It is indicated more than *Phosphorus* when there is this apparent plethora, with great oppression of the chest from any little exertion. The nostrils dilate with the efforts to breathe. There is frequent epistaxis or nose-bleed, and also hæmoptysis, the blood being bright red and coagulated. The cough is of a dry, teasing character, and is made worse after drinking anything warm. It is usually associated with bruised, sore feeling in the chest, and with dull, aching pain in the occiput. In addition to this erethistic phthisis, we may have *Ferrum* indicated later in the case when expectoration is purulent and greenish and has a very bad odor, and is mixed with blood streaks.

This reminds me of a salt of *Ferrum*, *Ferrum phosphoricum*. This is a remedy which was suggested by Schüssler in all cases of inflammation before exudation has taken place. He bases his prescription on the combined effects of *Ferrum* and *Phosphorus*. *Ferrum phos.* stands midway between *Aconite* and *Gelsemium*. In fact it develops that stage of inflammation which the pathologists describe as indicated by enlargement of the blood-vessels, paresis of the vaso-motor nerves.

Schüssler proposed *Ferrum phos.* as a substitute for *Aconite*. It has been confirmed so many times that I now offer it to you with these qualifications. The indications for *Ferrum phos.* are these: the pulse is full, round and soft; the inflammation has not yet gone on to exudation; the discharge, if it is a mucous surface that is affected, is blood-streaked. In other words, the condition calling for it is surcharged bloodvessels. If a patient with phthisis should take cold, and so become greatly prostrated, and have this blood-streaked expectoration, *Ferrum phos.* even in the two hundredth potency will quickly quiet the pulmonary congestion. So, too, in the secondary congestion following pneumonia. The right lung, for instance, is inflamed, when suddenly the left becomes congested. Here *Ferrum phos.* again acts. Or, again, on a warm summer's day, a child is exposed while perspiring, and the perspiration is checked. In consequence of this, inflammation of the bowels sets in. The stools are watery and bloody. Here, again, is a case for *Ferrum phos.* In the beginning of dysentery, *Ferrum phos.* never does any good if there is tenesmus. Then you will have to give *Mercurius* or some other remedy.

We may use the metal itself in diarrhœa. The stools contain undigested food, and come as soon as the patient attemps to eat. In summer complaint of children or cholera infantum, we find these symptoms recurring quite regularly or periodically just after midnight, when the lienteric stools may be accompanied by periodical vomiting. These symptoms of *Ferrum* place it with *Cinchona* and *Arsenic* in a little group of diarrhœa remedies, and rather in advance of *Oleander*, this last-named drug being indicated when the lienteric stools occur hours after eating. The child passes one day that which he had eaten the day before. With *Cinchona* and *Arsenic*, the stool appears more after than during eating, and with *Arsenic* more after midnight.

Argentum nitricum may also be thought of in these cases of diarrhœa. It seems as if the child had but one bowel, and that extended from mouth to anus.

In uterine hæmorrhages, *Ferrum* is useful when there is a flow of bright red blood, often mixed with coagula, and this is associated with a great deal of flushing. The face, which is ordinarily earthy and sallow, becomes bright red and flushed, breathing becomes rapid and a little labored, just as it is in *Ipecac*. The pulse itself is very much increased in frequency and in strength. *Ferrum* in hæmorrhages seems to stand between *Cinchona* and *Ipecac*. Like *Cinchona*, it is suited to very much prostrated cases in persons naturally anæmic. It is allied to *Ipecac.*, in the bright red gushing flow of blood and the difficulty of breathing.

Ipecac. suits hæmorrhage that comes with a gush. It may be associated with nausea and it may not, but there is very apt to be loud, hurried breathing.

Ferrum has sometimes been of use in prolapsus uteri; but the *Ferrum iodide* is a better preparation here. Soreness in the abdominal walls. On sitting down he feels as if something were pushed upward in the vagina.

Lastly, *Ferrum* is indicated in intermitting types of fever, particularly after the abuse of quinine. You find during the heat distension of the bloodvessels, particularly about the temples and face, throbbing headache, enlargement of the spleen, and even dropsy.

Magnesia Carbonica.

Magnesia carb. { Arsenicum, Phosphorus.
Belladonna, Camphor, Pulsatilla, Merc., Colocynth.
Ratanhia, Sepia, Cocculus.

>Pulsatilla.
>Rheum.
>Chamomilla.
>Belladonna.

Magnesia is much used in one form or another by allopaths as a purgative medicine. When thus abused several results may follow.

It may become injurious from its tendency to accumulate in the intestines as an incrustation of ammonia-magnesian phosphate, and also from its remoter effects on the nervous system. Its action on the latter is not unlike that of *Zinc,* and it may be used for similar forms of neuralgia. *Nux vomica* is the remedy for constipation resulting from large doses of the crude drug.

Rheum is also to be given for the abuse of *Magnesia* when diarrhœa, with sour, slimy stool and tenesmus, results.

Pulsatilla may be useful in some symptoms.

Colocynth is called for in case griping pains result from abuse of *Magnesia.*

Chamomilla is indicated when *Magnesia* causes neuralgia.

Almost all the symptoms of *Magnesia carb.* seem to centre around the action of the drug on the gastro-intestinal organs. All other symptoms depend upon this action more or less, or else are secondary in importance. To describe the *Magnesia carb.* patient to you, I must say that the drug acts on both adult and child. If the patient is a child, you will find it puny and sickly from defective nutrition. Milk is refused, or, if taken. causes pain in the stomach, or is passed undigested. The child is subject to frequent griping, colicky pains, which are very much like those of *Colocynth.* It draws its limbs up to relieve these abdominal pains which are also frequently relieved by motion. The stools are characteristically sour, green and slimy, are preceded by much griping and rumbling in the bowels, and have been very aptly compared in appearance to the scum on a frog pond. Sometimes, when the stool is not exactly diarrhœic, it looks as though there were lumps of tallow in it. In severe cases you will find the child poorly nourished, and its mouth full of aphthous ulcers, which are simply indications of the impoverished state of the system from defective nutrition. With these symptoms you can see how *Magnesia carb.* may be used for marasmus in children. There are several drugs which are here very similar to *Magnesia carb.,* and it will be well for us to consider them.

In the first place, *Magnesia carb.* is similar to *Colocynth*, in that it has griping, colicky pains, doubling the child up, but it is distinguished from that remedy by the green, slimy stool.

Still greater is the resemblance between *Magnesia carb.* and *Rheum.* Both have the sour, slimy stool, etc. The former is the deeper acting remedy of the two, and if you are in doubt as to which to give, *Rheum* should precede. I must say that *Rheum* is a rather treacherous remedy. With the sour, slimy, frothy stools it has griping colic and twitching of the muscles of the face and fingers during sleep.

Chamomilla resembles *Magnesia carb.* in many cases, particularly in diseases of children. In both remedies anxiety and restlessness are prominent. But in *Chamomilla* there is a yellowish-green stool, looking like chopped eggs. Both remedies have relief from moving about, and both have griping pains before stool, and both have irregularity in feeding as a cause of the illness. *Magnesia carb.* is of course the deeper acting of the two.

Magnesia carb. is also similar to *Calcarea ostrearum.* Both have sour stool, rejection of milk, and imperfect nourishment of the body. *Calcarea*, however, may readily be distinguished from the other by the sweat on the head, face and scalp, by the damp and cold feet, and by the enlargement of the abdomen.

In marasmus compare *Magnesia carb.* also with *Antimonium crudum*, *Sulphur*, *Podophyllum*, *Sepia*, and *Natrum carb.*

If the *Magnesia carb.* patient is an adult, we may have some of the following symptoms to guide us: the gastric and hepatic symptoms predominate. The patient suffers from what has been termed acid dyspepsia. Food, such as cabbage and potatoes, and starchy food generally, are indigestible in such cases. He becomes anxious and warm while eating; and at night so hot that he can't sleep; yet he dreads exposure.

Pregnant women may require *Magnesia carb.* when they suffer from toothache, and when the pains are worse at night and force the patient to get up and walk about.

There is another remedy which I shall mention in this connection, one which you would hardly think of. Some years ago, it may be twenty, a physician of this city was treating a lady in the first months of pregnancy, who suffered terribly from toothache. He gave her *Magnesia carb.* and other remedies. Still the pain continued. Dr. Lippe was called in consultation, and he thought of *Ratanhia*, which has toothache at night, compelling the patient to get up and walk about. This remedy promptly cured the case. You can remember these two remedies then, and you may place them with *Chamomilla*, which is complementary *Magnesia carb.*

The menses are usually late and scanty, and they have this peculiarity: they flow more at night or on first rising in the morning, are scanty during the day and even cease altogether in the afternoon. The flow is also more profuse between the pains. This is true, whether they be profuse or scanty. In all the *Magnesia* salts the menstrual flow is dark or black, almost like pitch.

Magnesia carb. also has some relation to rheumatism and to affections of the muscles and joints. It is suitable for rheumatism in the right shoulder. It also has rheumatic pains in the limbs, which are worse after a long walk, better from warmth, and worse in bed.

Sanguinaria is similar to *Magnesia carb.*, in that it has rheumatism affecting the right deltoid muscle. Several years ago I used *Sanguinaria* quite a number of times without any effect, and I became so disgusted with it that I announced to the class that I did not believe in it. Within a week after that I had two cases promptly cured by it.

Nux moschata is indicated in rheumatism affecting the left deltoid.

There are two cases of cataract on record as having been cured by *Magnesia carb.* In one of these the patient was predisposed to headache and boils.

MAGNESIA MURIATICA.

Magnesia mur. { Caulophyllum, Actea racemosa.
Chamomilla, Pulsatilla, Mercurius.
Sulphur, Lycopodium, Sepia.
Phosphorus, Ignatia.

>Chamomilla.

The next remedy of which I shall speak is the *Chloride of Magnesia* or *Magnesia mur.* This remedy acts particularly on women and children, especially in hysterical women and in scrofulous children.

It is indicated in women who suffer from hysterical paroxysms, with the following symptoms: after dinner the patient is seized with nausea, eructations, trembling and fainting spells. These occur after dinner because that is the principal meal, and more is eaten then than at other times. The patient is anxious and restless, and is always made worse from mental exertion. The headaches are described as congestive, with sensation as of boiling water in the cranium, or as a frontal numbness. The pains are referred to the temples, and seem to be relieved by firm pressure with the hands. They are also better from wrapping the head up warmly. The patient also complains of a

MAGNESIA MURIATICA.

sensation as of a ball rising from the stomach into the throat. This is relieved by eructation. This shows that the accumulation of gas in the stomach is the cause of this reflex symptom. She also has bearing down in the uterine region and uterine spasms. The menses are black and pitch-like, and are accompanied by pain in the back when walking, and in the thighs when sitting. She also has leucorrhœa after every stool, or following the uterine spasms. In nearly all these cases in which *Magnesia mur.* is indicated, you will find characteristic constipation, in which the stools are passed with great difficulty, being composed of hard lumps, or they are so dry that they crumble as they pass the anus. If you find that symptom present with the uterine symptoms, you may be sure that *Magnesia mur.* will help the patient.

In other cases we find the liver affected. *Magnesia mur.* is one of our best remedies for liver disease. The liver is enlarged and the abdomen bloated. There are pains in the liver, which are worse from touch or from lying on the right side. The tongue is large, coated yellow, and takes the imprint of the teeth. You will see at once how this resembles *Mercurius*, but it is differentiated from that remedy by the characteristic crumbling stool. The feet are often œdematous from interference with the portal circulation, and there are palpitation of the heart and dyspnœa, both of these last-named symptoms being reflex symptoms from the hepatic disorder.

Frequently we find *Magnesia mur.* indicated in the enlarged liver of children who are puny in their growth and rachitic. They suffer, too, from skin affections. They have what is known as tinea ciliaris, an eruption which occurs at the roots of the hairs, particularly of the eyelids. The hairs drop out. A scaly eruption appears around the hairs, the skin ulcerates, and the hairs drop out. With this tinea there are pimples on the face, and acrid ozæna, with redness and swelling and scaliness of the nose. With these symptoms there is sweat of the feet. Here we are reminded of *Silicea*, but the sweat under *Silicea* is offensive.

A general characteristic of *Magnesia mur.*, belonging to either men or women, is palpitation of the heart, which is worse when the patient is quiet, and better from moving about. The symptom has been confirmed many times. Then there is another symptom which occurs frequently in women, and that is inability to pass urine without pressing on the abdominal walls.

The analogues of *Magnesia mur.* must be studied here, or else you will not be able to separate it from similarly acting drugs. We find that in uterine spasms, *Caulophyllum* and *Actea racemosa* act like *Magnesia mur.* I must say that I believe *Caulophyllum* leads the list. I know of no other drug that produces such continued spasmodic condition of the uterus unless it be *Secale*.

Silicea ought to be mentioned as similar to *Magnesia mur.* in the treatment of scrofulous children. Both remedies have sweating of the feet, enlarged liver, rachitis, and ozæna. The difference lies in this: the *Silicea* patient has offensive-smelling sweat, both of the feet and of the head. That is one good distinction. There are many others. There is a resemblance between the headaches of the two remedies. *Silicea* and *Magnesia mur.* both have headache, relieved by wrapping the head up warmly

Mercurius is similar to *Magnesia mur.* in liver affections. It is distinguished from the latter by its diarrhœa, with tenesmus, or, more exceptionally, with gray or ashy stool.

Also similar to *Magnesia mur.* is *Ptelea*, which is useful in congestion of the liver when there is a feeling as of weight and pressure in the right hypochondrium. The liver is found to be enlarged. The patient here finds relief by lying on the right side.

I may say that the *Magnesia* salts have been placed with *Zinc* as remedies acting on the nervous system. This fact led Schüssler to *Magnesia phos.* as a nerve tonic.

LECTURE LXIII.

BARYTA CARB., STRONTIANA CARB., AND LITHIUM CARB.

BARYTA CARBONICA.

BARIUM and *Strontium* are very closely related to each other chemically. Of the elements themselves we have no provings. The carbonates of these have, however, been proved, as have also the *Muriate* and the *Sulphate of Baryta*. *Baryta* is somewhat of a poison, although there are not many cases of poisoning by it on record, because it is rarely used in domestic practice.

Baryta carb. has *Antimonium tartaricum* as its complement, particularly in the complaints of old people.

Animals poisoned with *Baryta carb.* exhibit some irritation of the abdominal organs, resembling great inflammation there, with increased peristaltic action of the bowels. The heart, too, is affected by it, the animal apparently dying from paralysis of the cardiac in systole. Its action is here very much like that of *Digitalis*. So much for the toxic action of *Baryta*.

In all its symptomatology, we find *Baryta* adapted to ailments occurring at the extremities of life, age and childhood; to old age, when there are mental symptoms and bodily weakness, and to children, when there is in addition, scrofula. The child to whom we may give *Baryta* effectively is almost an imbecile. He, very unnaturally, shows no desire to play; he sits in a corner doing nothing. He cannot remember well, and is slow in learning to talk, to read, and to understand. This slowness in learning to talk does not come from defect in the apparatus of speech—of the tongue, for instance—but it is the result of mental weakness. The child is rather emaciated, with the exception of the abdomen, which is large. The face, also, is bloated. He may have a voracious appetite, but food is not appropriated by the system, because of the diseased condition of the mesenteric glands. A case of chronic hydrocephalus in a child improved after the exhibition of *Baryta* selected by these symptoms. Adults—especially old people—have a rather peculiar aversion to strangers, and shun the approach of any unfamiliar face. They seem to have a fear of the presence of others. They imagine that they are being laughed at. They are easily angered and suffer from cowardice. You all have seen similar symptoms to these in persons of a half-imbecile state of mind from disease, whether in old age or in early life.

A peculiar mental symptom of *Baryta* which I give you on the authority of Dr. Talcott, of Middletown, N. Y., is this: the patient thinks his legs are cut off and that he is walking on his knees.

You may use *Baryta carb.* for old people when they suffer from paralysis, particularly paralysis following apoplexy. Very frequently in old people, the brain shrinks and, as the skull does not yield, there would be a vacuum formed, were it not that an effusion of serum takes place. This is followed by a more or less severe paralysis. You will find, in such cases, that the patient is childish and has loss of memory, trembling of the limbs and well-marked paralysis of the tongue. *Baryta carb.* is one of the few remedies that cause positive paralysis of the tongue. You will see these paretic symptoms also in children of this half-imbecile character of which I have spoken. The mouth is kept partly open and the saliva runs out freely. The child has a silly, vacant look, showing at once that it is *non compos mentis.*

Baryta is one of the remedies for the apoplexy of drunkards. (*Vide* lecture on *Opium.*)

Baryta also seems to induce paralysis by causing degeneration of the coats of the bloodvessels, even to the production of aneurisms.

Causticum acts similarly to *Baryta* in paralysis, but the paralysis of this remedy has more contractures or spasms.

Secale acts on the bloodvessels; but its symptoms are apt to be associated with burning and numbness; gangrene.

Colchicum and *Arsenic* have loss of sensibility of the tongue.

Both the *Muriate* and the *Carbonate of Baryta* may be used in multiple sclerosis of the brain and spinal cord. This is not an uncommon disease in infants and children in whom it may give rise to the idiotic symptoms mentioned above. These same symptoms indicate it in disseminated sclerosis occurring in old people.

For the trembling associated with this disease, *Hyoscyamus* should be thought of.

When associated with the symptoms just enumerated, you may use

Baryta for non-development of the brain in early childhood. The *Chloride of Baryta* has been used by old-school physicians for this sclerosis, and with more or less success

The remedy which most resembles *Baryta* here is *Causticum*.

The use of *Baryta* in catarrhs demands attention. It is one of the best remedies we have for the tendency to tonsillitis, particularly in scrofulous children with dry scurf on the head. *Baryta mur.* and *Baryta carb.* cause induration of connective tissue. They control proliferation of connective tissue, hence their use in tonsillitis, enlarged tonsils, indurated glands, etc., general symptoms agreeing. Every little exposure to damp or cold weather awakens anew the inflammation of the tonsils. This is not a simple sore throat, a swelling up of the mucous lining of the fauces with trouble in swallowing, but it is an actual inflammation of the tonsils with formation of pus. In these cases, you will find enlargement of the glands in the neck, under the jaw and behind the ear. *Baryta* is one of our remedies to prevent the return of this condition. It changes the constitutional tendencies of the patient. It is thus more the remedy for the effects of the trouble than for the acute symptoms. The local symptoms for the throat are principally these: the right side of the throat is worse than the left, just as you find under *Belladonna;* the throat feels worse from empty swallowing. In the treatment of tonsillitis, I frequently use the same prescription that I employ in diphtheria, namely, a gargle of alcohol and water. This seems to remove the accumulation of phlegm from the throat.

In tonsillar affections, you may compare the following remedies with *Baryta:*

Calcarea ostrearum, in fat, leuco-phlegmatic children.

Calcarea phos., in chronic cases; bones diseased.

Ignatia, large tonsils, with small, flat ulcers on them; pain between the acts of swallowing.

Hepar, large tonsils, hearing poor, sensation as of fish-bone in throat.

Lycopodium, large tonsils, studded with small indurated ulcers.

Calcarea iod. is similar to *Baryta* in some cases with enlarged glands, particularly when there are enlarged tonsils which are filled with little crypts or pockets.

Conium is suited to enlarged tonsils without any tendency to suppuration.

Baryta may also be used in children who, in addition to this tonsillitis, have post-nasal catarrh. Scabs form in the posterior nares and at the base of the uvula. The upper lip and nose are swollen just as you find in *Calcarea*, but the mental symptoms are different.

Baryta is also called for, for a chronic cough occurring in strumous or scrofulous children with swollen glands and enlarged tonsils. Every little exposure to cold or damp causes headache, backache and diarrhœa. Her *Baryta* is similar to *Dulcamara*. The ears may be involved in the catarrhal process; crackling in the ears on swallowing, reverberations in the ear on blowing the nose, sneezing, etc. The late Dr. McClatchey used *Baryta* in catarrh of the middle ear after scarlatina.

Baryta is sometimes indicated in scrofulous ophthalmia, the pains are relieved by looking downward. The general symptoms are like those of *Calcarea ostrearum*.

We find *Baryta* also indicated in old people who have what is known as suffocative catarrh, with orthopnœa. I think you can understand this when you remember the influence of *Baryta* on the voluntary and involuntary muscular fibres. It paralyzes them. In old people, the chest is very much weakened. They get a catarrh, which is not very severe, but appears suddenly in the night, with difficulty of breathing and blueness of the face, etc. *Baryta carb.* is one of the remedies that come in after the failure of *Antimonium tartaricum*. The patient complains of a sensation as of smoke or pitch in the lungs. *Baryta* should not be given in catarrhal asthma or asthma with emphysema; but when the disease is of the purely nervous variety, in the aged, when aggravation occurs in wet, warm air. You will see that its aggravations are much like those of *Aurum*.

Amblyopia, in the aged, sometimes calls for *Baryta;* the patient cannot look long at any object; sparks before the eyes when in the dark.

It is also indicated in the headaches of the aged, with aggravation after waking, after meals and near a warm stove; the patient has a stupefied feeling.

We also find *Baryta carb.* of use for the fatty tumors which occasionally appear here and there over the body. It is very easy to remove these with the knife. But it is much better to cure them by medicine, if you can do so.

In tabes mesenterica, *Baryta* is indicated, when in addition to the foregoing symptoms, the following are present: food, when swallowed, seems to pass over sore spots in the œsophagus. There is always pain in the stomach after the child eats. The stool is sometimes undigested. With this, you find the abdomen hard and swollen, and an offensive sweat on the feet, just as you find in *Silicea*.

Now, there are remedies which may be compared with *Baryta* in this form of disease. *Iodine* is similar to *Baryta* in that it is suitable in torpid cases. The complexions of the patient in the two remedies are different. The *Iodine* patient has a dark complexion, dark hair and eyes and sallow skin. There is, too, extreme hunger. If you observe the child carefully, you will find it anxious and fretful, until he eats, which relieves him for the time being; and yet he grows thin despite the quantity of food consumed. Then, there is a mental symptom which is almost always present when you find *Iodine* indicated in tabes mesenterica, and that is intolerable crossness, which is even worse than that belonging to *Antimonium crudum*.

Calcarea phosphorica is indicated in children who are weak-minded, who cannot walk, although they are old enough to do so, who are anxious and restless in their manner and who suffer from defective osseous growth. The bones are thin and brittle.

Like *Baryta*, the *Silicea* patient suffers from damp weather. He also has offensive sweat and general emaciation with the exception of the abdomen. The difference between the two remedies lies principally in the mental symptoms. The *Silicea* child is obstinate and self-willed, and, too, his head is disproportionately large.

Lactic acid has copious sweating of the feet, but is not offensive.

For the offensive foot sweat, compare *Silicea*, *Thuja*, *Nitric acid*, *Kali carb.*, *Graphites* and *Carbo veg.*

STRONTIANA CARBONICA.

Strontiana carbonica has a few symptoms that are of importance. It has more effect on the circulation than has its relative, *Baryta*. We have, as a characteristic, flushes in the face and violent pulsation of the arteries. It may be useful in case of threatening apoplexy with violent congestion of the head, and hot and red face every time the patient walks. Mere exertion increases the circulation upwards towards the head. Some erethism is shown in the chest in some patients. There is a smothering feeling about the heart; they cannot rest; there is a feeling as of a load on the chest. These are the congestive symptoms of the heart, lungs and head which suggest *Strontiana carb.*, and they may occur at the time of the climaxis when flushes of heat are so common. The peculiarity which will distinguish these symptoms from those of any other remedy is, that the head symptoms are relieved by wrapping the head up warmly, just as you find under *Silicea* and under *Magnesia mur.* These patients cannot bear the least draught of air, therefore, despite this congestive tendency, they wrap the head up warmly, though it may cause perspiration. It certainly does resemble *Silicea*, in that both remedies have congestion of the head relieved by wrapping the head up warmly. The *Silicea* congestion seems to come up the spine and go into the head. That is not characteristic of *Strontiana carb.*

Another effect that we find caused by *Strontiana carb.*, and one, too, for which it is not often used, is diarrhœa, which is worse at night, and which has this peculiar urgent character: the patient is scarcely off the vessel before he has to return. It is better towards morning at three or four o'clock.

Strontiana carb. has a marked action on the bones. It has a particular affinity for the femur, causing swelling and caries of that bone; usually in scrofulous children. This trouble is often associated with the diarrhœa just described.

Strontiana carb. causes an eruption which very much resembles that of sycosis. Hence, it has been given for a sycotic eruption on the face or other parts of the body, and which is moist, and itches and burns

Another peculiarity of the drug, and the last one I care to mention, is its effects in chronic sprains, particularly of the ankle-joint, when both *Arnica* and *Ruta* have failed. The long interference with the circulation has produced some œdema about the joint.

Lithium Carbonicum.

Lithium carb. has not a very extensive range of action nor does it greatly depress the vital forces. In its provings, debility is noticed only in connection with or as a sort of sequel of the joint affection. It is particularly useful in affections of the joints. It is efficacious in rheumatism, and, above all, in some forms of gout. Of the various organs attacked by *Lithium carb.*, the most important in the order of their importance are the heart, stomach, kidneys and bladder. The

LITHIUM CARBONICUM.

mucous membranes are also affected by the drug. At first they are unduly dry, and this dryness is followed later by thick mucous secretion. The skin does not escape. There appears an erythema, with itching of the skin, which occurs particularly about the joints, and is very annoying. It is particularly noticed along with rheumatism. Further than this, *Lithium carb.* may produce roughness of the skin and an eruption about the face resembling barbers' itch.

Studying now the symptoms of the drug with this general action before us, we find confusion of the head; headache on the vertex and in the temple, worse on awakening; the eyes pain as if sore, and it is difficult to keep the eyelids open. This vertex headache and soreness of the eyes follows suppression of the menses. The patient has pain from the left temple into the orbit of that side; relieved while eating and worse afterwards.

A very characteristic symptom of the retina, or rather of vision, is, the right half of objects vanishes.

In keeping with its effect on mucous membranes, we find the drug causing conjunctival asthenopia, just as does *Alumina*. The conjunctiva of both lids and eyeball is painfully dry and the eyes feel sore when the patient reads.

The nose is affected, too, in the *Lithium* proving, being swollen and red. Sometimes there is dryness of the nose when in the house, and mucus dropping from it when in the open air; or mucus seems to hang in strings from the posterior nares. Another symptom of *Lithium* is sensitiveness of the mucous membrane when the inspired air is unduly cold.

Lithium cures a cough which seems to come from a certain spot in the throat.

There is a form of gastralgia which *Lithium* will cure. It is accompanied by the pain in the left temple and orbit, which is better by eating.

Lithium has some effect on the bowels. Drinking chocolate or cocoa will cause diarrhœa.

Lithium irritates the neck of the bladder. This, you know, is often a symptom of rheumatic patients. The urine is turbid and flocculent. The pains extend down either ureter and into the spermatic cords or testicles, and are followed by red urine with mucous deposit.

In the female, you find *Lithium carb.* indicated when the menses are late and scanty. The provers found that all the symptoms accompanying the irregularity in menstruation were on the left side.

Now, we will consider the rheumatic symptoms of *Lithium carb.*, including under this head those of the heart also. I have succeeded, in several instances, in relieving chronic rheumatic patients by this remedy. The symptoms which indicate the drug are these: rheumatic soreness about the heart; valvular deposits will be found in many instances; mental agitation causes fluttering of the heart like *Natrum mur.*, *Sepia* and *Calc. ostr.*; very marked is the pain in the heart when the patient 'ends forward; the cardiac muscle is evidently irritated, for we find shocks or jerks about the heart; the cardiac pains are relieved when the patient urinates.

Now, the symptoms of the body, joints and limbs: tenderness, with swelling and occasional redness of the last joints of the fingers; clumsiness in walking from unwieldiness of the muscles; intense itching on the sides of the feet and hands without any apparent cause. The pains in the joints are usually worse in the knee-, ankle- and finger-joints. The whole body feels stiff and sore as if beaten. Pains go down the limbs. The whole body increases in weight and becomes puffy. I may say that this puffiness is not due to a healthy fat, but is a flabby condition which belongs to all the alkalies.

Gettysburg spring water, which contains carbonate of lithia, is very efficacious in scrofulous children when there are ulcers involving the joints, as in Pott's disease and hip-joint disease, when there are offensive pus and diarrhœa.

This character of the catarrh of *Lithium carb.* in which the inspired air feels cold is also found under *Kali bichr.*, *Æsculus*, *Cistus*, *Hydrastis* and *Corallium rubrum.*

Kali bichromicum, *Baryta carb.* *Sepia* and *Teucrium* have catarrh, with expectoration of solid chunks from the posterior nares.

In valvular deposits in the heart you may compare *Lithium carb.* with *Ledum*, *Kalmia* and *Benzoic acid*, the latter remedy being selected by the offensive character of the urine.

Zincum, *Conium* and *Aurum* have sudden jerks or shocks about the heart.

In rheumatism and gout you may compare *Kalmia* and *Calcarea ostrearum*, which resemble *Lithium* in the rheumatism of the finger-joints.

When there are nodular swellings in the joints, compare *Calcarea ostrearum*, *Natrum muriaticum*, *Benzoic acid*, *Lycopodium* and *Ammonium phos.*

LECTURE LXIV.

THE AMMONIUM PREPARATIONS.

Ammonium caust.	Blood.—
	Scorbutus.
	Uræmia.
	Carbonized blood.
Ammonium carb.	Heart.
	Mucous membranes.—
Ammonium phos.	Nose.
	Throat and larynx.
	Lungs.
Ammonium mur.	Skin.—
	Erythema.
	Scarlatina.
	Organs.

WE have on the board to-day several of the salts of ammonia, the *Carbonate of Ammonia* or *Ammonium carb.*, *Caustic Ammonia* or *Ammonium causticum*, *Muriate of Ammonia* or *Ammonium muriaticum* and *Phosphate of Ammonia* or *Ammonium phosphoricum*. The ammonium salts taken as a class, we find best suited to rather fat and bloated persons. *Ammonium carb.* is particularly indicated in fat flabby individuals of indolent disposition who lead a sedentary life. This is very different from *Nux vomica* and *Sulphur*, both of which are indicated in complaints arising from sedentary habits. But *Ammonium carb.* is especially indicated in fat lazy individuals.

Ammonium mur. is best indicated for fat sluggish individuals particularly when the adipose tissue is mostly distributed over the trunk, the legs being disproportionately thin. That is the distinction that may be made between the *Carbonate* and the *Muriate*.

The salts of ammonium exert a considerable influence over the blood. Thus if *Ammonium carb.* is taken for awhile there will be produced symptoms simulating those of scurvy. There will be hæmorrhages from the mouth, nose and bowels, showing you that there is a disintegration of the blood. The muscles become soft and flabby and there is well-marked tendency to emaciation.

We find that all the salts of ammonium act powerfully on the mucous membranes, of which tissue every one of them produces inflammation. This inflammation is of a violent character, starting with a simple feeling of burning and rawness, progressing to a complete inflammation of the mucous membrane and ending in the destruction of the epithelium, which peels off in layers and leaves a raw, burning, ulcerated surface. It is, then, not to be wondered at, that the salts of ammonia have won considerable praise in affections of the nose throat, and larynx, and somewhat of the lungs.

The ammonium salts also have an impression on the skin. When applied locally, there is produced a simple erythema followed by dermatitis and some little swelling. Soon, however, an eruption appears, and this varies with the different ammonium salts. It is at first papular, then vesicular and finally advancing to ulceration. These conditions are common to all the ammonium preparations of which we have any knowledge.

Therapeutically, the salts of ammonia are antagonized by *Veratrum viride*, *Digitalis*, *Aconite*, cold and other cardiac sedatives.

Their action is favored by heat, *Opium*, *Iodine*, *Valerian*, *Asafœtida*, *Alcohol*, etc.

AMMONIUM CARBONICUM.

Ammonium carb. { Arnica, Antimonium tart. Belladonna, Apis, Lachesis. Arsenicum, Aurum, Carbo veg., Curare. Conium, Senega, Kali bi., Calcarea ostr.

> { Camphor.
  { Arnica.
< Lachesis.

We will first study *Ammonium carb*. Let me call your attention to the fact that the *Carbonate of Ammonia* may be antidoted by *Camphor;* and some of its symptoms by *Arnica*.

Despite the apparent resemblance between *Carbonate of Ammonia* and *Lachesis*, these two drugs have been found to be inimical.

Ammonium carb. may be studied from its action on the blood. As I have already said, its prolonged use produces a scorbutic condition. The vital powers are weakened. Hæmorrhages of dark fluid blood appear. There is degeneration of blood tissue. The muscles become soft and flabby. The teeth loosen and the gums ulcerate. With these scorbutic symptoms, there is developed also a hectic form of fever.

I now take up the indications for *Ammonium carb.* in uræmia. These symptoms which I am about to give you are very important. They are not only characteristic of *Ammonium carb.* in uræmia, but also in any other disease in which this remedy may be indicated. We may find them present in scarlatina with decomposition of the blood, and also in heart disease. Now for the symptoms: you will find *Ammonium carb.* indicated for somnolence or drowsiness with rattling of large bubbles in the lungs, grasping at flocks, bluish or purplish hue of the lips from lack of oxygen in the blood, and brownish color to the tongue. You recognize in these symptoms some condition of blood-poisoning from the presence of carbonic acid. This may be in uræmia, or it may be in catarrh of the lungs, or in any other disease in which there is deficient oxygenation. The nearest analogues here are *Antimonium tartaricum*, *Carbo veg.* and *Arsenicum.*

A similar condition obtains in *Arnica* in typhoid states when the patients are drowsy and heavy, and fall asleep while answering questions.

With the symptoms just enumerated you can remember *Ammonium carb.* for œdema of the lungs or emphysema.

Ammonium carb. is also of use in poisoning by charcoal fumes. *Arnica* is sometimes of use in these cases, as is also *Bovista.*

Still another use we may make of *Ammonium carb.*, and one, too, that would hardly suggest itself to you, is in the beginning of cerebrospinal meningitis. Sometimes, in the beginning of this disease, the patient is stricken down by the violence of the poison and falls into a stupid, non-reactive state. He is cold, and the surface of the body is cyanotic. The pulse is very weak. In just such cases you should give *Ammonium carb.*, which will bring about reaction. Then you may select some more specific remedy which will cure the trouble.

I would now like to mention the action of *Ammonium carb.* on the heart. This drug is useful in dilatation of that organ. The patient suffers when ascending a height, as when going up stairs or up a hill. He also suffers intolerably in a warm room. He frequently has cough which is accompanied by bloody sputum. There is palpitation of the heart with dyspnœa and retraction of the epigastrium. You may also find cyanotic symptoms present.

Ammonium carb. is also indicated in pneumonia when there is great debility, together with symptoms pointing to the formation of heart clot.

It is also indicated in chronic bronchitis with atony of the bronchial tubes, which favors emphysema. There are copious accumulation of mucus in the lungs, dilatation of the bronchial tubes, and œdema pulmonum. The patient in these cases is weak and sluggish in his movements, coughs continually, but raises either not at all or with great difficulty. Drowsiness, or even some delirium with muttering, may be present.

Another use we may make of *Ammonium carb.* is in scarlatina. It is undoubtedly a useful remedy in the treatment of this disease, even when of a rather malignant type. We find that it produces a rash resembling that of scarlatina, but which is, however, of a miliary character. The throat is swollen internally and externally with enlargement of the glands externally, and with bluish or dark red swelling of the tonsils. The neck externally is engorged, that is, there is, in addition to the swelling of the cervical lymphatics, inflammation of the cellular tissue. The nose is often obstructed, particularly at night, causing the child to start from its sleep as if smothering. Frequently it has to lie with its mouth wide open in order to breathe. The child is drowsy, and may even go into a stupid sleep. We frequently find, too, an enlargement of the right parotid gland.

Let us now study some of the concordant remedies of *Ammonium carb.* in this disease. First of all *Belladonna*. Between this remedy and *Ammonium carb.* the resemblance is only apparent. Both remedies have right side of the throat affected, bright red rash, scarlatina and drowsiness. But the distinction between the two lies in this: there is in *Ammonium carb.* a miliary eruption on the skin, which *Belladonna* has not. The throat in *Ammonium carb.* is of a darker red than in *Belladonna*, and the drowsiness is more complete. The drowsiness of the latter remedy alternates with either wildness or starting from sleep, or restless delirium or crying out in sleep. In *Ammonium carb.* the patient is in a state of simple somnolence. The starting from sleep is not from irritation of the brain, but from stoppage of the child's breathing.

There is some resemblance between *Ammonium carb.* and *Apis*, in that both remedies have miliary rash, and both are indicated in low types of scarlatina with somnolence. *Apis* has, however, more dropsical symptoms. Whenever it is the remedy, you will find puffiness of the throat and œdema of the uvula. But you will also find inflammation or irritation of the meninges of the brain in *Apis*, as indicated by the sudden shrill crying of the child. This is a sudden shriek, and not a mere start as if frightened. There is rolling of the head in the pillow.

Lachesis, though apparently similar to *Ammonium carb.* in scarlatina, is really inimical to that remedy. It resembles *Ammonium carb.* in the blueness of the surface, in the somnolence, in the engorgement of the neck and in the dark red or bluish swelling of the throat. *Lachesis* has almost always, if not always, that extreme sensitiveness of the surface, so that the patient cannot bear to have anything touch the neck. Then, too, *Lachesis* affects more the left side and *Ammonium carb.* the right. This sensitiveness of *Lachesis* is not the same kind of soreness that you find in other remedies, as in *Apis*. This symptom is here due to a hyperæsthetic condition of the spinal nerves ramifying through the affected part. Firm pressure does not aggravate, although a light touch will.

Rhus tox. is similar to *Ammonium carb.*, in that both remedies have dark throat and both have drowsiness. It is the left parotid gland that is most likely to be affected under *Rhus;* with *Ammonium carb.*, it is the right. There is more restlessness under *Rhus*.

Next, the action of *Ammonium carb.* on the mucous membranes. This remedy is useful in nasal catarrh. The nose is stopped up at night; the patient wakens gasping for breath. He is worse at three or four o'clock A. M. The cough is dry and tickling, associated with hoarseness, and with a great deal of oppression from mucus in the chest. The nostrils are sore and raw, and sometimes, in children, there is a discharge of bluish-colored mucus. This symptom is also found under *Kali bichromicum*, *Natrum arsenicosum*, *Arundo Maurit.*, *Ammonium muriaticum* and *Ambra grisea*. At times the coryza is scalding, excoriating the upper lip, with burning in the throat and along the trachea. There is a feeling as of a lump in the throat. Dry night cough comes, which seems to threaten suffocation; copious flow of saliva, with consequent expectoration; beating like a pulse in the chest. *Ammonium carb.* is particularly suited to winter catarrhs. The sputum is slimy and contains specks of blood.

Its near relative, *Ammonium muriaticum*, will be considered presently. It is similar in these catarrhs. Differentially the *Carbonate* cures catarrhs, worse in winter, nose stopped up, worse at night, awakening the patient from sleep, gasping for breath, worse three to four A. M. Cough dry, tickling, hoarseness, chest oppressed with mucus. The *Muriate* causes stoppage of one nostril; both stopped up at night; nostrils sore and raw; discharge of bluish mucus or scalding coryza, severe burning in the throat, etc.

In the three A. M. aggravation of *Ammonium carb.*, you may compare the *Kali* salts.

In this catarrh, with stoppage of the nose, excoriating discharge and rawness down the sternum, there are a few drugs which I would have you compare. One of these is the *Ammonium causticum*, which is one of the best remedies in the whole materia medica for aphonia, with burning rawness in the throat.

Causticum and *Carbo veg* are very similar to *Ammonium carb* in this rawness and burning down the sternum.

Laurocerasus has that expectoration containing little specks of blood.

Ammonium carb. has also been used for sprains when the injured joint is hot and painful; it follows *Arnica*.

Here you may compare *Sulphuric acid* and *Ammonium mur.*

AMMONIUM MURIATICUM.

Ammonium mur. { Apis, Arnica, Natrum mur. Kali bichromicum. Sepia, Sulphur.

As I have already explained to you, *Ammonium mur.* is suited to sluggish persons, who are rather corpulent as to the body, but disproportionately thin as to the limbs. Like the *carbonate*, it produces violent inflammation of the mucous membranes. It also disturbs the circulation of the blood. The face reddens during a short, animated conversation, especially so, as you might expect, in a warm room. There are ebullitions of blood, violent throbbing in all the arteries, accompanied by anxiety and weakness, as if paralyzed. The nervous system suffers, too, from the action of *Ammonium mur.* There is a certain periodicity of symptoms, as shown in the chills and fever. The paroxysms return every seven days. There are many other symptoms of the nervous system; especially do we find this characteristic: pain in the left hip, as if the tendons were too short; this makes the patient limp when walking. While sitting there is gnawing referred to the bones.

Sciatica is very readily cured by *Ammonium mur.* when the symptoms call for it. The pains are worse while the patient is sitting, somewhat relieved while he is walking and entirely relieved when he lies down.

Ammonium mur. has also been used for the neuralgic pains which may occur in the stumps of amputated limbs. Compare *Cepa Staphisagria.*

Ammonium mur. is also useful for tearing, stitching pains from ulceration in the heels, worse at night in bed and better from rubbing.

Other remedies attacking the heels are, *Pulsatilla* (inflamed); *Causticum, Manganum,* (cannot bear the weight on them); *Antimonium crudum, Ledum, Graphites, Ignatia,* (they burn at night); *Natrum carb.*, and *Allium cepa. Sabina* is particularly suitable in plethoric women who suffer from what they call rheumatic inflammation.

Manganum is an excellent remedy in rheumatic patients when the heels are affected and the patient cannot bear any weight on the heels. In addition to this you will find that *Manganum* is indicated when the rheumatic symptoms come in dark, almost bluish, spots.

Antimonium crudum is useful in soreness of the heels, worse walking on a hard pavement.

Ledum palustre, Graphites and *Natrum carb.* cause blisters on the heels. *Sepia,* ulcers.

Allium cepa cures ulcers on the heel when developed by friction of the shoe or stocking.

Ammonium mur. has some influence on the joints. It causes a feeling of constriction in these parts. It is one of the remedies that have been used in the treatment of chronic sprains. It also affects the fibrous tissues about the joints. Thus, it is one of the remedies when there is contraction of the hamstring tendons. When the patient walks these seem to be drawn tight. This symptom is relieved on continued motion.

On the female organs, *Ammonium mur.* acts more powerfully than does *Ammonium carb.* It has a great many symptoms referred to the inguinal and hypogastric regions which would suggest the use of the drug in uterine and ovarian diseases. For instance, the patient complains of tensive pain in one or the other groin. Sometimes this symptom is described as a feeling as if she had sprained herself. There are stitches, cutting and soreness, or, what is more characteristic than all, a strained feeling in the groin, which forces the patient to walk bent. That is an indication which leads to *Ammonium mur.* in the treatment of deviations of the uterus, and also in ovarian diseases. You will find in almost all these cases the characteristic muriate stool, crumbling as it passes the anus. We have, too, a characteristic leucorrhœa attending the symptoms, a brown and lumpy or else clear and albuminous leucorrhœa, which follows every urination.

Ammonium mur., in that feeling as if sprained in the groin in women, finds its counterpart in several other remedies: in *Arnica*, which has that same strained feeling in the groin; in *Apis*, which has it all the way across the hypogastrium, with a sensation as if the skin were tight or stretched.

Next, we have to consider the action of *Ammonium mur.* on the mucous membranes. Beginning with the nose, we find that it causes coryza. The nose is "stopped-up" more at night than in the daytime. One nostril is usually stopped-up at a time; there is an excoriating, watery discharge from the nose, which makes the inside of the nostrils and upper lip sore. The throat is swollen so that the patient cannot open his mouth. The mouth and throat are filled with a viscid phlegm, which the patient expels with great difficulty. There is throbbing in the tonsils. This is characteristic of *Ammonium mur.* It is a symptom which may suggest it in tonsillitis or in scarlatina when the faucial symptoms are so severe as to produce almost complete strangling.

The chest symptoms are by no means unimportant in *Ammonium mur.* We find a cough which may accompany the foregoing symptoms or which may be separated from them. The cough is very violent, and seems to excite the salivary glands, for during it the mouth fills with saliva. Hoarseness, with burning and rawness in the larynx, necessarily belong to such an acrid remedy as *Ammonium mur.* Coldness between the shoulder-blades accompanies the chest affections, as in bronchitis and phthisis. The patient also complains of heaviness in the chest. This is also noticed in *Ammonium carb.* where it is associated with burning. Sometimes the patient will describe his sensation to you as a feeling as of a lump in the chest. Again, he will complain of certain spots in the chest which burn, throb and beat with the pulse.

Ammonium mur. may be used in chronic congestion of the liver. Depression of spirits accompanies the disease, and the stools are coated with mucus.

Ammonium Phosphoricum.

I have one or two symptoms of *Ammonium phosphoricum* to give you. It has been successfully used in the treatment of constitutional gout when there are nodes or concretions in the joints. It is not to be used for the acute symptoms, not for the twinges of pain, but when the disease has become systemic, and when concretions of urate of soda appear in the joints. The worst case of this kind I ever saw was that of a man who had been bedridden fifteen years. He showed me a box which was filled with these concretions, which he had picked out of his joints. They varied in size and looked like lumps of chalk. Some of these same concretions could be seen under the skin and along the tendons. His hands were twisted out of shape. His feet also were affected. He had a cough, which finally killed him, and he expectorated from the lungs these lumps of urate of soda. *Ammonium phos* relieved him for awhile.

LECTURE LXV.

SALTS OF LIME.—CALCAREA OSTREARUM.

Calcarea ostrearum.	Nutrition.
Calcarea caustica.	Blood. { Anæmia. / Leucocythæmia.
Calcarea fluorica.	Glands.
Calcarea phosphorica.	Bones.

There are quite a number of the salts of lime which have been more or less proven. The first one on the list is *Calcarea ostrearum* or the lime of oysters. This preparation, which was given to us by Hahnemann, was proven as *Carbonate of Lime* or *Calcarea carbonica*. It was obtained from the middle stratum of the oyster-shell, where Hahnemann supposed he could secure a perfectly pure specimen of the carbonate of lime. Chemically speaking, this is not a pure carbonate of lime, for it must contain some of the animal matter belonging to the oyster. Moreover, it always contains a trace of *Calcarea phos*. You will thus see the reason why Dr. Hering proposed to call it *Calcarea ostrearum* instead of *Calcarea carbonica*. *Calcarea caustica* is the ordinary caustic lime. *Calcarea fluorica* was proven by Dr. Bell, of Massachusetts. Of it we have a few symptoms. It is one of Schüssler's twelve tissue remedies. This combination of fluoric acid with lime gives us a very powerful drug in the treatment of diseases of the osseous system. I have already related to you a case in which *Calcarea fluorica* acted well in necrosis of the jaw. We shall also find it a useful drug in bone tumors. *Calcarea phosphorica* is also a valuable drug.

It should be your duty and your pleasure to know the distinctions between these various salts of lime, and especially between *Calcarea ostrearum* and *Calcarea phosphorica*. They are not indicated in precisely the same cases. When one is indicated, the other cannot be. They are not difficult to distinguish, so I think we will readily differentiate them.

One chapter in the history of *Calcarea phosphorica* is of some little interest. Some years ago a preparation for the cure of a certain disease was put on the market in Europe. It soon gained quite a reputation. After awhile, cures effected by it became less and less frequent. Finally, a wealthy man who failed to be cured by the preparation, sued the company for deceiving him. Analysis of the preparation became necessary. The main ingredient was found to be phosphate of lime. In the beginning the manufacturers used the phosphate of lime from bones; but later they found a cheaper way of making it in the laboratory, and without using bones at all. The company claimed that phosphate of lime is phosphate of lime, no matter how made or where found. That there is a difference between the phosphate of lime as obtained from the chemist's laboratory, and from the bones of animals, is shown by the difference in therapeutical efficacy of the two preparations, as illustrated in the above case and many others.

Calcarea sulphurica, or the *Sulphate of Lime*, is another one of Schüssler's remedies. It was proven by one of the students of the New York College. Schüssler claims that *Calcarea sulphurica* acts energetically in curing suppuration and in removing the tumefaction of boils. The proving, while not positive, rather favors this idea.

There is a use which you may make of this drug, and that is in croup; it will act like magic in a case like *Hepar*, with cough that is loose from the mucus in the larynx but which has the opposite modality as to heat and cold, namely, the child wants to be uncovered and cool.

The *Hypophosphite of Lime* given in the second decimal, has produced the following: dull heavy pain on top of the head, causing depressed feelings, fulness and oppression around the heart, fulness of head and chest; veins on hands, arms, neck and head, stand out like cords; difficult breathing, must have window open; profuse sweat all over; limbs powerless from weakness of the muscles.

All the salts of lime act prominently in the direction mentioned on the board. They all affect the nutrition of the body, hence they are of great use in infancy and childhood, when growth must be accomplished. They favor the development of bones and other tissues. You will find that some of them, the *ostrearum* and *phosphorica*, cause anæmia when pushed to the extreme. They all affect the glands and they all act on the bones.

Calcarea Ostrearum.

Calcarea ostrearum is a drug that may come into use in almost every form of disease, and is second in importance only to *Sulphur*. You will recall that it is not a perfectly pure carbonate of lime, but contains some phosphate of lime and some organic matter from the body of the oyster. Chemically it differs but slightly from the carbonate of lime made in the laboratory.

Calcarea ostrearum is suited to cases in which there is defective growth, hence it is a very necessary remedy in childhood and in infancy. It affects chiefly the vegetative system, altering materially the nutrition of the body. Under its influence secretion and absorption progress rapidly, and so it becomes a favorite remedy in cases in which the "constitution" is to be changed. The glands are readily affected by *Lime;* they swell, inflame and even become the seat of pathological deposits. This is especially true of the cervical and mesenteric lymphatics. The nervous system, is not primarily affected, but becomes eventually influenced by general nutritive failure, thus causing spasms, excitement, etc. The *Calcarea ostrearum* patient is fat and plump, rather of a bloated than of a solid, hard fat. It is especially suited for children who are scrofulous; who are fleshy, yet not well developed as to bone, brain or muscle. The face is rather pale, occasionally, however, flushing up red. Usually the color is of a watery or chalky paleness. The child is slow in its movements. It is not active, nervous, or quick, as we find in the case of the *Sulphur* child. It is peevish and self-willed, especially towards morning. Growth is irregular, so that the head is disproportionately large to the rest of the body. This defect is one of osseous growth; thus you find the fontanelles remaining open, particularly the anterior fontanelle. The abdomen is large and has been compared to an inverted saucer or basin. The features are rather large, and the lips, particularly the upper, are swollen. Dentition is slow. There is craving for boiled eggs. The scalp sweats profusely, particularly during sleep. This is not usually a warm sweat, nor is it a cold sweat; but it is cool from natural evaporation. When the child awakes, you notice the pillow damp or wet for some little space around the head. The feet are often cold and clammy. Do not, however, be deceived by this symptom, for there are some children who, by wearing too heavy a stocking, will have sweaty feet. This patient suffers from partial sweating of still other parts of the body. That is in itself an almost certain symptom of *Calcarea ostrearum*. Thus it may affect the chest or knees when all other parts of the body may be perfectly dry. Now, from this extreme picture we may have the opposite condition, one of great emaciation. The skin hangs flabby and in folds. Despite this emaciation, the abdomen remains abnormally large. Such children are scrofulous, and it is genuine scrofula, for which *Calcarea ostrearum* is indicated.

There is another form, which is tubercular in its character, and in this form we have *Phosphorus* indicated. We find the same swelling of the glands, the same indolent ulceration, and the same difficulty in learning to talk and walk, but the patient has a delicate, refined skin, and the features are sharp and rather handsome. The eyelashes are long and silky, and the hair dark and glossy. This is the kind of scrofula which will, if not neutralized, ultimately end in consumption of the lungs.

As the *Calcarea* child grows older it is slow in teething. It may even have fever or convulsions attending the tardy eruption of the teeth. In cases in which the convulsions persist, *Calcarea* is far superior to *Belladonna*. *Belladonna* may help for a while, but the deeper acting remedy must follow to complete the cure. Scrofulous inflammation of the eyes is almost always present. There are pustules on the cornea, and these threaten to destroy that membrane. The parts about the ulcer are very vascular. The child dreads artificial light in particular, although it complains bitterly of the daylight hurting its eyes on awaking in the morning. The discharges from the eyes are apt to be bland. The cornea is left more or less opaque by ulceration. *Calcarea* has often been used after the acute symptoms, to remove the corneal opacity and the chronic thickening of the eyelids. No remedy excels *Calcarea* in corneal opacities; but compare *Apis, Saccharum officinale, Cuprum, Alumen, Kali bi., Natrum sulph.*, etc.

Saccharum officinale in particular is to be remembered as similar to *Calcarea ostrearum*. This drug has been proved on several persons, and has many confirmations. It is indicated in children who are large-limbed, fat and bloated, with a tendency to dropsy. It has produced opacity of the cornea, and it ought to cure it. The mental states which lead me to the use of Cane-sugar are these: the child is dainty and capricious; he cares nothing for substantial food, but wants little "nicknacks;" he is always cross and whining, and if old enough he is indolent, and does not care to occupy himself in any way. Everything seems to be too much trouble to him.

You will find that in the eye-symptoms *Calcarea* acts better after *Sulphur* than before. It is suited to advanced cases that are sluggish and refuse to react to *Sulphur*. Hahnemann noticed that *Calcarea* particularly followed *Sulphur* when there was tendency to dilatation of the pupil .

Another remedy which holds a relation to *Calcarea ostrearum* in scrofulous and tubercular ailments is *Nitric acid*. This must be substituted for *Calcarea* if the ulcers on the cornea progress and threaten to perforate or destroy the cornea.

The *Calcarea* children are subject to eruptions on the skin, particularly eczema. This eczema is quite characteristic, too. It appears on the scalp, with a tendency to spread downwards and over the face. Frequently it appears in patches on the face or scalp, forming thick crusts, which are often white like chalk deposits. Another symptom which may suggest *Calcarea* is this: the child scratches its head on awakening from sleep. The change from sleep to activity seems to excite the itching of the existing eruption.

We find in these scrofulous children calling for *Calcarea*, inflammation of the external ear or auditory canal, and also of the middle ear or cavity of the tympanum. First, *Calcarea* produces thickening of the membrana tympani, with all the symptoms of defective hearing. There are humming, roaring and buzzing in the ears, all dependent upon the abnormal pressure on the chain of bones. The otorrhœa has a sort of pappy or fatty appearance. It is purulent, but it also has a pappy appearance, looking just like chewed-up paper. Now, on cleansing the external ear of this pus and looking at the membrana tympani, you find it perforated from previous inflammation. You will find the edge of the rupture thickened and granular, and you may even notice a tendency to the formation of polypi. The pains are of a sudden, jerking, pulsating character. In three different cases, *Calcarea* 30 produced vesicles in the auricles.

Here *Calcarea* is, according to the best authorities, to be followed by *Silicea*, if the ulceration becomes very indolent and will not heal despite the exhibition of Lime. The *Silicea* patient has a head disproportionately large to the rest of the body. The sweat appears on the whole head and face rather than on the scalp alone, and the offensive foot-sweat causes soreness of the feet. These symptoms you will recall from our lecture on *Silicea*. Besides *Silicea*, you should here compare *Calcarea* with *Hepar* and *Mercurius*.

Attending these inflammations of the eyes and ears with *Calcarea* we may have scrofulous enlargement of the lymphatic glands of the neck, axilla, etc. These are hard and firm, and yield very slowly to medicine.

We have also in these cases a coryza or chronic nasal catarrh. The wings of the nose are thickened and ulcerated. There is apt to be a moist scurfy eruption about the nostrils. There is an offensive odor, as of rotten eggs, gunpowder or manure from the nose. The nose is stopped-up, with thick yellow pus. The patient often has nose-bleed in the morning. Here you may compare *Belladonna* which follows *Calcarea* well.

Now, if the *Calcarea* children are attacked with summer complaint or a genuine cholera infantum, you will find these symptoms of the digestive organs: there will be an unusual craving for eggs. Why this is I do not know; it may be because of the sulphur in the eggs. This is a very common symptom. Milk disagrees. As soon as they take it they vomit it in sour cakes or curds. That is a strong symptom for *Calcarea*. Or the milk may pass by the bowels in white curdled lumps. There are ravenous appetite and thirst, the latter being worse toward evening. The diarrhœa, too, is worse toward evening, thus being distinguished from *Sulphur*. The stools are greenish, and may contain undigested food. They are more or less watery and sour.

In these symptoms *Calcarea ostrearum* is similar to two or three other drugs. One is *Æthusa cynapium*, or fool's parsley. This is indicated in vomiting of children, when they vomit everything they drink, particularly milk, which is ejected in white or yellowish or greenish curds. This vomiting exhausts the child, so that it at once goes to sleep.

Still another remedy is *Antimonium crudum*, which has this condition: after nursing, the child vomits its milk in little white curds, but refuses to nurse afterward; the *Æthusa* patient, on the contrary, wants to nurse again. There is also the characteristic diarrhœa of *Antimonium crudum*, which will help you to distinguish it from cases that call for *Kreosote*. If the latter remedy had no other symptom than the following it would still be invaluable, and could not be replaced: the stomach is so weak that it cannot retain or digest food, so that food is vomited either immediately or hours after eating.

Phosphorus and *Arsenicum* should also be compared in this vomiting. *Magnesium carb.*, *Ipecac* and *Sulphur* should be compared in the sour vomiting.

In diarrhœa with green stools do not forget *Calcarea phos*.

Again, we may find *Calcarea ostrearum* indicated in acute hydrocephalus in the early stages. Here, as in many other cases, it acts particularly well after *Sulphur*. It may even do good when symptoms of effusion are present. It is indicated mainly by the general constitutional symptoms present in the case.

In these cases you frequently find that it follows the previous use of *Belladonna*. You are called to attend one of these cases. You find the patient with hot head, flushed face, starting in sleep, and you give him *Belladonna*, which relieves. In a few days a relapse occurs; again you give *Belladonna*, and this time it fails. This intermittency of the disease shows that it is not a *Belladonna* case. Then you have to select another drug, which is sometimes *Sulphur* and very frequently *Calcarea*, the latter especially if the patient be the characteristic *Calcarea* child. *Belladonna* and *Calcarea* are complementary, particularly in affections of children, in brain troubles and in dentition.

Again, we may find *Calcarea ostrearum* indicated later in life, at puberty. Here it is more frequently indicated with girls than with boys. We find it called for at the time for the onset of the menses, when they are delayed. The girl is apparently plethoric, and suffers from congestions of the head and chest. She is fat and apparently robust, but if you were to examine the blood of such a patient you would find it disproportionately full of white blood-corpuscles or leucocytes. She complains of palpitation of the heart, dyspnœa and headache, worse when ascending. *Calcarea* will bring on the menstrual flow, and will relieve all these symptoms.

Again, you may find it useful at puberty for similar symptoms when tuberculosis of the lungs threatens. The patient has this dyspnœa, palpitation and rush of blood to the chest on ascending, and even hæmorrhages from the lungs. There is dry cough at night, which becomes loose in the morning. The patient has fever, which is worse in the evening, with partial sweat and soreness of the chest to touch, this soreness being worse beneath the clavicles. Digestion is greatly disturbed. The patient cannot eat any fat food without becoming sick. There is chronic tendency to diarrhœa, and with it prolapsus ani. So you see *Calcarea* is a companion to *Phosphorus*, but there is a difference between the two remedies. The difference is expressed in these few symptoms. In *Calcarea*, you find the patient scrofulous and fat, and his or her past history shows the well-marked symptoms of *Calcarea*. As children they have been slow in teething, have had slowly-closing fontanelles, and often there is yet remaining disproportionate swelling of the upper lip.

On the other hand, the *Phosphorus* patient is slender and overgrown, for his years, and narrow-chested. He has a fine grain of tissue, rather than fat and coarse as in *Calcarea*.

Calcarea is indicated late in phthisis when large cavities are forming. It acts particularly upon the right lung about its middle third. There will be pain in the middle of the right side of the chest; loud mucous râles are heard all over the chest, of course worse on the right side. Expectoration is purulent, yellowish-green and bloody. The patient has great repugnance to animal food, as meat, which passes undigested. Emaciation progresses, sweat increases, and the menses, if it is a female, become checked. These are the symptoms calling for *Calcarea* in tuberculosis.

Both *Calcarea ostrearum* and *Calcarea phosphorica* affect the middle lobes of the lungs. *Sepia* is here similar, but lacks the external sensitiveness to touch, in fact may be ameliorated thereby.

Senega is somewhat similar to *Calcarea* in fat persons, but may be distinguished, having soreness that is worse on moving the arms, especially the left arm.

Still later in life we find *Calcarea* indicated for the ailments of women, particularly for irregularities in menstruation. It is especially indicated when the menstrual flow is too frequent, coming every two or three weeks, and is profuse, amounting almost to a menorrhagia. The flow is provoked by over-exertion or by emotions. The patient complains of sweating of the head and coldness of the feet.

One of the best remedies I know of for ordinary profuse menstrual flow, coming frequently and yet without any decided constitutional character by which to judge the case, is *Trillium pendulum*, especially if the flow exhausts the patient very much. I have never given it in any potency but the sixth. That has been sufficient in all my cases.

In suppression of the menses *Calcarea* has several concordant remedies. *Belladonna* is suitable when there are hyperæmia, rush of blood to the head, subjective feeling of coldness, wakefulness, and throbbing about the temples.

Gelsemium is indicated in menstrual suppression when there is a drowsy, apathetic state.

Glonoin is an admirable remedy when there is violent throbbing about the head, and particularly if the urine is albuminous, as it may be, from congestion of the kidneys.

Aconite is indicated for suppression of menses from violent emotions, as fright

Still other drugs called for under these last-named circumstances are *Actea spicata* and *Lycopodium*.

The leucorrhœa of *Calcarea ostrearum* is rather profuse, with considerable itching and burning, and is generally milky, purulent and yellow or thick in appearance. It is especially indicated for leucorrhœa occurring before puberty, even in infants.

Another remedy that I have found very valuable in the leucorrhœa of little girls is *Caulophyllum*, when the discharge is profuse and weakens the child very much.

Sepia, *Cannabis sativa*, *Mercurius*, *Phosphorus*, *Pulsatilla* and *Cubeba* have also been sufficiently confirmed to be listed here.

Calcarea ostrearum is useful in diseases of the male sexual organs. It is one of that little group of remedies, *Nux*, *Sulphur* and *Calcarea*, first suggested by Jahr for sexual weakness arising from masturbation or other excesses in sexual indulgence. *Calcarea* is indicated when there is excessive sexual desire, but this sexual desire is more mental than physical—that is, there is more passion than the objective concomitants of passion. Erections are diminished or imperfect during coitus, emission is imperfect or premature. *Calcarea* is also indicated when, after abuse of this kind, a man settles down to a moral and quiet life. His sexual power is of a character just described, and its gratification is followed by vertigo, headache and weakness in the knees.

In milder cases, which have not been traced to so deep an origin as defective nutrition, you will find *Dioscorea* all-sufficient for the excessive loss of semen with weakness of the legs, particularly about the knees.

In old men, who, having spent their youth and early manhood in the practice of excessive venery, are just as excitable in their sexual passion at sixty as at eighteen or twenty, and yet they are physically impotent, *Agnus castus* is a good remedy. They suffer from constant dribbling of semen.

We may use *Calcarea ostrearum* from its action on the nervous system. It is indicated in nervous fevers, even in typhoid fevers, in the beginning of the disease, with these symptoms: the patient falls into a troubled sort of sleep and dreams of some perplexing subject which awakens him. He again goes to sleep and dreams of the same thing. As soon as he closes his eyes, he sees persons, objects, etc., which disappear as soon as he opens them. Later, in the course o typhoid fever, about the second week, you will find *Calcarea ostrearum* indicated when, for instance, the rash will not appear, and the patient goes into a sort of stupor. The abdomen swells and becomes more tympanitic. The patient becomes very restless and anxious and distressed, although he may be unconscious. He cries out, twitches and grasps at flocks. The body may be too hot and the limbs cold and clammy. There may be diarrhœa or constipation present. He starts up from sleep and looks about him as if frightened. A drug which is complementary to *Calcarea* here is *Lycopodium*. But diarrhœa may be present in *Calcarea*. This is never the case with *Lycopodium*.

Another use that we may make of *Calcarea ostrearum* in nervous affections is one which would not appear from a superficial study of the drug, and that is its application in insomnia. The sleeplessness that calls for this remedy does not consist simply in lying awake an hour or two, but it is that long wakefulness which is the precursor to some diseases and the accompaniment of others. For instance, during childbed a woman cannot sleep. In such cases you have this class of symptoms: she has visions on closing the eyes; she starts and twitches at every little noise, and is beside herself with anguish. The tongue is dry. She borders on the state of acute mania. *Calcarea ostrearum*, particularly in the thirtieth potency, given every three hours during the day, almost invariably produces a desire to sleep the next night. How does *Calcarea* produce it? Like opium, caffeine or chloral? No; but by bringing about a healthy sleep. Still another use of *Calcarea ostrearum* is in that unhappy affection, delirium tremens. It is indicated when there are pretty much the same symptoms as I have mentioned for the insomnia, particularly with visions of rats and mice, and of horrible objects which terrify the patient. He talks deliriously about fire and murder. He has a constant fear that he is going crazy.

Calcarea ostrearum seems to be able to cure epilepsy, not so much the paroxysms themselves, as to aid in the change of constitution by which this dreadful disease may be cured. The aura which precedes the attack in some cases begins in the solar plexus and moves upwards, and the patient is at once thrown into convulsions, a characteristic also of *Nux vomica*, *Bufo* and *Silicea*. In some cases it feels as if a mouse were running up the arm. In still others the aura may go from the epigastrium down into the uterus or into the limbs. The causes for the *Calcarea ostrearum* epilepsy are fright, suppression of some chronic eruption, and also excesses in venery. It follows *Sulphur* well in these cases. You are apt to think first of *Sulphur* for this sensation as of a mouse creeping up the arm; the symptom is just the same in *Sulphur* and *Calcarea;* the causes, also, are the same, viz., excessive venery or suppression of an eruption. *Calcarea* is particularly indicated if *Sulphur* does not cure, or if the pupils do not dilate after the use of *Sulphur*.

For the paroxysms, *Hydrocyanic acid* is a useful drug.

Artemisia vulgaris is indicated in cases which have arisen from fright, and in which the attacks are duplicated.

If indigestion starts the trouble, *Nux vomica* is the first remedy to be thought of, especially if the aura starts in the epigastrium and spreads upwards.

Calcarea ostrearum is useful in diseases of the bones and in curvatures of the spine, especially for curvatures in the dorsal region in children who are slow in learning to talk and walk, who are weak at the ankles, and turn their feet in or out according to the muscles that are affected. In weak ankles compare *Natrum carbonicum*, *Silicea*, *Carbo animalis*, *Sepia*.

There is a remedy which has been suggested for this weakness of the legs which I have never been able to confirm, and that is *Pinus sylvestris*. This is said to have cured emaciation of the lower extremities, with tardiness in learning to walk, in scrofulous children.

Calcarea ostrearum is also indicated in affections of the joints; for instance, in white swelling and in hip-joint disease. It is indicated in the second stage of these diseases, when abscesses have formed.

Now, you must learn to distinguish between *Calcarea* and *Silicea*. To the superficial observer the cases are very similar, but there are some differences which you may note. In the first place, the *Silicea* patient has sweat about the whole head, and this sweat has a sour or offensive odor; the head is unduly large, the rest of the body being rather emaciated; the sweat of the feet in *Silicea* is apt to be offensive, and produces soreness between the toes and on the soles of the feet; the face is rather of an earthy or yellowish-waxen hue. The *Silicea* child is nervous and excitable rather than sluggish, as is the case with the *Calcarea ostrearum* patient. *Silicea* has the same imperfect nutrition from defective assimilation that *Calcarea* has. There seems to be, in the *Silicea* child, a decided weakness of the cerebro-spinal nervous system; and yet, with this weakness, there is a certain amount of irritability, so that it is made worse by any external impression. Thus, if there is any tendency to epilepsy, any little emotion will tend to throw it into convulsions. There is more tendency to ulceration in *Silicea* than you find in *Calcarea*. The discharge from these ulcers is not a healthy, laudable pus, but it is rather thin and excoriating.

Calcarea ostrearum is of service in rheumatism. The symptoms indicating it are these: rheumatic affections, caused by working in water; rheumatism of the muscles of the back and shoulders after failure of *Rhus*. It is also indicated for gouty nodosities about the fingers. It may be useful in constitutional gout and in arthritis deformans.

Rhus tox. seems to be the best remedy we have for lumbago, whether the pains are better from motion or not. It seems to have a special affinity for the deep muscles of the back.

Calcarea fluorica is a good remedy to follow *Rhus* in chronic cases; for lumbago, worse on beginning to move but improving on continued motion.

Secale cornutum is indicated for sudden "catch" or "kink" in the back.

Nux vomica is called for in rheumatism of the back, when the patient is unable to turn over in bed without first sitting up.

The uses of *Calcarea* in eruptions have already been touched upon in former lectures. It is one of the best remedies in chronic urticaria. It produces herpes, one prominent locality being on the parts of the face covered by whiskers, here suggesting a comparison with *Mezereum*, which has itching in the whiskers as from vermin, scaliness; *Lithium carb.*, cheeks under the whiskers rough as a grater, itching; and *Cicuta virosa*, thick honey colored scabs in the whiskers as well as about the corners of the mouth.

LECTURE LXVI.

CALCAREA PHOSPHORICA AND HEPAR.

Calcarea Phosphorica.

Calcarea phos.
- Cinchona, Zinc, Phosphorus (hydrocephaloid).
- Dulcamara, Silicea, Sulphur.
- Rhus, Causticum.
- Sulphur, Calcarea ostr., Silicea, Phosphorus.
- Baryta c. (mental weakness).

THE complementary drugs of *Calcarea phos.* are: *Zinc*, *Ruta graveolens*, and *Sulphur*. *Zinc* you will find complementary to *Calcarea phosphorica* in hydrocephaloid; *Ruta* in affections of the joints and periosteum; and *Sulphur* pretty much as we found under *Calcarea ostrearum*.

Now there are many symptoms that are common to both *Calcarea ostrearum* and *phosphorica*. It is not a little perplexing at times, in a case which seems to call for lime, to decide which one of these preparations we should give. Perhaps I can give you distinctions enough to enable you to judge. To determine the efficacy of *Calcarea phosphorica* you must remember its ingredients, lime and phosphorus, and you will see how they are modified in their chemical combination, so that while we have some resemblances to *Calcarea* and others to *Phosphorus*, we have still other symptoms which belong to the combination, *Calcarea phosphorica*, and which are found neither in *Calcarea* nor in *Phosphorus* alone.

Calcarea phos. seems especially called for in defective nutrition, hence it is often useful in childhood as well as at puberty and in extreme old age. Beginning with the infant, we shall find it of inestimable service when the child is thin and emaciated, with sunken, rather flabby abdomen, and predisposed to grandular and osseous disease. The head is large, and both fontanelles are open. The cranial bones are unnaturally thin and brittle. The teeth develop tardily. It has curvature of the spine. The child is slow in learning to walk, and the spine is so weak that it cannot support the body. The neck is so thin and weak that it cannot support the head, which falls whichever way it happens to be inclined. The child vomits milk persistently, whether it be the breast milk or that artificially prepared from the cow. It suffers from colic after every feeding. The stools are often green, slimy and lienteric, and are accompanied by the passage of a great deal of fœtid flatus. Sometimes, the stool is very profuse, watery and hot. In cholera infantum, the stools may be of the character mentioned, or they may present a flaky appearance from the admixture of a small portion of pus. There is, in this cholera infantum, great emaciation of the whole body. The little face is pale, and the prominent parts of the body are cold. There is craving for bacon or ham. Mentally, these children are very much depressed, so that they are slow of comprehension. They seem to be stupid. Even cretinism may be developed by the continued use of *Calcarea phosphorica*. This will place it in your mind, along side of *Baryta carb.*, in mental symptoms. As the child grows in years, if not in stature, any exposure to dampness or wet causes a feeling of general aching or soreness, particularly when it is moved. The least motion is unbearable. Do not be misled by this aggravation from motion and give *Bryonia*. It is not here a symptom for *Bryonia*, for it indicates the incipient symptoms of rachitis. Every little exposure produces a feeling of heat all over the body. The periosteum and the articulations are irritated and inflamed, and cause this aggravation from motion. You will find *Calcarea phosphorica* an excellent remedy to prevent rachitis. If it fails you, you may still fall back on *Silicea*.

This sensitiveness to dampness enables us to use *Calcarea phos.* in diseases of adults. This I consider an important qualification of the drug. Thus, it is indicated in women with a feeling of weakness and distress referred to the hypogastrium with uterine displacements, and worse by passage of either stool or urine. Especially is it indicated in women whose joints ache in every change of the weather. This quality separates it from other similarly-acting drugs. The uterine symptoms are aggravated by this change in weather, a symptom that is prominent in *Calcarea phosphorica*, more so, in fact, than in either *Calcarea* or *Phosphorus*. *Phosphorus* has the gone, weak feeling in the hypogastrium, just like *Calcarea phos.*, but the modality just mentioned is absent.

So, too, we may use *Calcarea phos.* in rheumatism appearing in any change of weather. On exposure to dampness, we find stiffness of the neck, aching and soreness in the limbs and wandering pains through the limbs, particularly around the sacral region and down the legs. All these symptoms appear with every change of weather.

If the patient contracts a cold, it is associated with dryness and soreness in the throat, stitches in the chest, heat on the lower part of the chest and upper arms, and a yellow sputum.

Another use of *Calcarea phos.* arises from its action on joints. I refer to its use in the treatment of fractures. Wherever bones form a suture or joint, there *Calcarea phos.* has an action. We find it, for instance, causing pains along the sagittal suture. Again, where the sacrum unites with the iliac bones, forming the sacro-iliac symphyses, there *Calcarea phosphorica* produces pain. If during pregnancy, a woman complains of pain in this locality, *Calcarea phosphorica* ought to help her.

Now, when there is a sort of artificial suture, as there is at the point of coaptation of broken bones, there, also, *Calcarea phos.* has an action. In some cases, the fractured ends may fail to unite; you give *Calcarea phosphorica*, which stimulates the formation of callus. It is better to use a low potency of the drug in this case.

In this respect, *Calcarea phos.* compares favorably with *Symphytum*, which is also used for non-union of fracture, particularly when the trouble is of nervous origin.

Conchiolin may here be mentioned. It is useful in osteitis at the ends of the diaphyses. This "mother of pearl" causes such a disease among workmen.

We have yet another use for *Calcarea phosphorica*, and that is for school-girls, particularly when they get near the age of puberty and they are exceedingly nervous and restless. They want to go away from home, and when away, they want to come back again. They suffer from headache when at school. They develop very slowly and are often chlorotic.

We may use *Calcarea phosphorica* in children who are suffering from marasmus. They have the peculiar craving and the diarrhœa that I have already described. The face is white and pale, or else sallow. The circulation is so imperfect that the ears and nose are cold. These cases, too, have that inability of the neck to support the head, of which I have already spoken.

There is a resemblance between *Calcarea phosphorica* and *Cinchona*. The latter may prevent this extreme picture if you give it for the drowsy, exhausted condition and has cold face, that follows the frequent and protracted discharges. In these cases, the administration of *Cinchona* will bring the child up and prevent the condition calling for *Calcarea phos.*

On the other hand, you will find *Calcarea phos.* will give place to *Zinc* when you have the rolling of the head, grinding of the teeth, cold pale face, hot occiput, fidgety motion of the feet, and other symptoms of this remedy that I have already given you.

From *Baryta carb.* this drug is to be distinguished when the child under treatment is mentally stupid.

Ruta holds a complementary relationship in periosteal and articular pains. And lastly,

Silicea resembles *Calcarea phos.* especially in rachitis, but has more offensive head sweat, more constipation and a strong tendency to suppuration, boils, etc.

In aggravation from exposure to wet we may compare *Dulcamara, Sulphur, Silicea* and *Causticum.*

It is highly important to be able to distinguish between *Calcarea ostrearum* and *Calcarea phosphorica.* This you can do by comparing the descriptions I have given you to-day and yesterday, as follows: *Calcarea ostrearum* has an enlarged abdomen; *Calcarea phos.* has flabby abdomen, from the admixture of phosphorus with the lime. In cholera infantum *Calcarea ostrearum* has craving for eggs; *Calcarea phos.* for salt or smoked meats. The *Calcarea ostrearum* stools are sometimes green, but generally watery, white and mixed with curds. The *Calcarea phos.* diarrhœa has green, slimy or hot watery stools accompanied by fœtid flatus. *Calcarea ostrearum* has particularly the anterior fontanelle remaining open; *Calcarea phos.* has both anterior and posterior fontanelles open.

HEPAR SULPHURIS CALCAREA.

Hepar { Belladonna, Lachesis, Merc. Spongia, Iod., Bromine, Acon., Silicea, Sulphur.

1. Nervous system { Depresses sensorium. Irritability of all nerves.
2. Plastic exudations.
3. Suppuration.
4. Catarrhs.
5. Glands—Bones.
6. Skin.
7. Organs.
8. As an antidote to metals.

Next, we will consider *Hepar sulphuris calcarea.* This is really an impure calcium sulphide, containing traces of the sulphide of lime, organic matter possibly, and very likely, too, minute proportion of the phosphate of lime, since it is made from the middle layer of the oyster shell and flowers of sulphur. It is a valuable addition to the powers of lime and sulphur used separately. It possesses many similarities to and marked differences from its components.

Hepar has some action on the nerves. It is to be remembered as a drug that causes over-sensitiveness of the nervous system. Pain seems to be intolerable to the patient, and may even cause fainting. An inflamed part feels sore and bruised, and cannot bear the touch of the hand or even of a dressing. I mention this as a universal characteristic of the drug. I have often given *Hepar* for cold-sores in the corners of the lips when they were about to suppurate, in inflammation of the eyes and in styes and pimples, when there was present this extreme sensitiveness to touch.

Mentally, the *Hepar* patient is rather sad and low spirited, particularly in the evening. At times there is an impulse to suicide. While walking in the open air the patient feels discouraged and cross, and is annoyed by the recollection of all the past unpleasantnesses that have figured in his previous life. Memory is weakened so that he forgets words and localities. And this is most evident when he is particularly irritable. He is over-sensitive so that his speech is hasty.

Hepar is indicated in neuralgia, particularly of the right side of the face, after the abuse of mercury and after the unsuccessful exhibition of *Belladonna*, which seemed indicated, particularly after exposure to dry, cold winds. In the neuralgia and other nervous symptoms *Hepar* belongs with *Belladonna*, *Silicea* and *Sulphur*. It frequently follows *Belladonna*, as I have told you; and from *Silicea* and *Sulphur* you may distinguish it by the other symptoms. A symptom in connection with the mental irritability of the patient that I have already mentioned is hasty speech and hasty actions. We find precisely the same symptom under *Belladonna*. "Hasty speech and hasty drinking" is the way the symptom reads under the latter remedy. We find it also under *Lachesis*, *Dulcamara* and *Sulphur*. To show you that this is a genuine symptom, I will mention a case of hysterical mania cured by a physician on the other side of the ocean. He had this one symptom to guide him: the patient's speech was hasty and words rolled out in profusion. The clinching symptom was that she had taken a great deal of *Mercury*. *Hepar* cured the mental condition completely.

We next have to consider *Hepar* as a remedy in inflammation. It is suited to inflammations of a croupous form and inflammation with suppuration. In all the inflammations and congestions in which *Hepar* is the remedy, you will find that there is extreme sensitiveness of the affected part to touch. This is so characteristic that it must be present more or less prominently before *Hepar* may be the remedy. The parts feel bruised and sore, like a boil. This, as I have already said, you can carry through all the *Hepar* inflammations.

For instance, in ophthalmia, or inflammation of the eyes, or lids, you will find that the eyelids are swollen and œdematous, and sometimes, too, suppurating styes will form. With this there is a bruised sore sensation. The patient cannot bear to have the eye touched; neither can he bear the cold air. Cold air and cold applications increase the suffering, and here you have a good indication separating it from *Mercurius*. Little pimples surround the inflamed eye. Similar to *Hepar* in this particular are: *Euphrasia*, which has pimples on the cheek over which the acrid tears flow, and *Phosphorus*, which has small ulcers around the large ones.

So again in inflammation of the ear, whether of the external auditory meatus or of the middle ear, you will find the same soreness to the slightest touch.

We find *Hepar* indicated in earache when suppuration impends, after *Belladonna*, *Chamomilla* or *Pulsatilla*. It is seldom indicated in the beginning.

44

We find these same characteristics of the inflammation present in the coryza. The nose is swollen and sore to the touch, especially in the inside of the alæ or wings of the nose.

So, again, in face-ache, the bones are exquisitely sensitive to any pressure. These are all illustrations of the character of the drug. I need not multiply them, because they are found in any part of the body in which inflammation occurs.

If suppuration occurs as the result of the inflammation, we have *Hepar* indicated and exercising a double function. If you give it in a high potency when the throbbing, stabbing pains in the affected part and the general rigor show the onset of inflammation, it may abort the whole trouble. In other cases, if you see that suppuration is necessary, and wish to hasten the process, then you give *Hepar* low. In tonsillitis and in boils, particularly in the former, *Hepar* is indicated after *Belladonna* when the latter does not succeed in reducing the inflammation before suppuration commences. I will simply remind you here that I have already mentioned the distinction between *Belladonna*, *Hepar*, *Mercurius* and *Silicea* in this class of diseases.

Now, if the inflammation becomes croupous, *Hepar* may be indicated, whether it be the throat, larynx, bowels or kidneys that are involved. The characteristics indicating *Hepar* in croupous inflammation of the larynx are these: after exposure to dry, cold winds the patient becomes hoarse, with whistling breathing. Respiration is so difficult that the child throws its head far back in order to straighten the air-passages. The cough is hard, barking and ringing, and at the same time accompanied by rattling of mucus. So sensitive is the child to cold, that the least exposure, even uncovering an arm or a foot, excites a spell of coughing. Thus you see the extreme susceptibility of the patient to cold air. *Hepar* is especially indicated when the cough is worse towards morning. Occasionally *Hepar* may be given for cough which occurs before midnight, but then it must be moist and not dry.

You will see from these symptoms that *Hepar* follows rather than precedes *Aconite* and *Spongia*. *Aconite* is indicated in the beginning of croup when there are great anxiety, high fever, and distressed breathing. I would advise you to continue the *Aconite* some time after the symptoms have been relieved, because these cases are very apt to relapse.

If, however, *Aconite* fails and the cough gets worse the next night,

Spongia is usually the remedy, especially if there are dry, hard cough, sawing respiration, little or no expectoration, and starting up from sleep choking.

If towards morning, although there is increased secretion and moist sound, the croupous symptoms still continue, then the case calls for *Hepar*.

Bromine usually follows *Hepar* when the latter is unable to remove the exudate.

Hepar was used by Kafka, in Bright's disease following scarlatina. He was led to this by the power of the drug to produce fibrinous or croupous exudations. *Hepar* has succeeded in these cases many times, so that it must have some action on the kidneys. Kafka gives it after scarlatina when the urine becomes albuminous and dropsy appears.

Next we have to consider *Hepar* in ordinary catarrhs, or what is commonly called a "cold" with aching through the body. *Hepar* seldom is a remedy in the incipiency, but for the advanced stage of a "cold." If it be given at the commencement, it frequently spoils the case, whether it be one of coryza or of sore throat, because it is more suitable to what has been termed "a ripened cold" when phlegm has formed. The catarrhal process may have affected the ethmoid, with boring pain in the parts and exquisite soreness. When the patient swallows, there is a sensation as if he was swallowing a fish-bone, or as if there were something sticking in the throat. Sometimes he will describe the sensation to be as if there were a crumb of bread or toast sticking in the throat. This symptom allies *Hepar* with *Mercurius*, *Nitric acid*, *Argentum nitricum* and *Alumina*. These colds, for which *Hepar* is the remedy, are re-excited by any exposure. It is often indicated when the abuse of mercury has developed in the system a susceptibility to cold.

In affections of the lungs, we find *Hepar* indicated in two or three classes of disease. We find it called for in pneumonia, especially during the stage of resolution. It comes in late in the disease (and not in the beginning) when, during resolution, pus forms and you have present suppuration instead of the normal resolution. *Hepar* ought also to be indicated in croupous pneumonia. Here, as in all other croupous inflammations, it is called for late in the disease.

You may also give *Hepar* successfully in the treatment of that frightful disease, pulmonary tuberculosis, when, with the deposit of tubercles in one or the other apex, you have a hard, croupy cough, with production of mucus, worse in the morning. It here frequently follows *Spongia*. It may bring about absorption of the tuberculous deposit.

When a cold reaches the chest, *Hepar* does wonderfully well if the catarrh threatens to affect the capillary tubes.

A good distinction between *Hepar* and *Antimonium tartaricum* in this connection is that the latter has loose rattling mucus; the former wheezing, purring sound, as if the exudate was more tenacious. Compare also *Jaborandi*, which has increased production of bronchial mucus.

In glandular disease, *Hepar* is indicated in the stage of suppuration, when the inflammation has gone on to the formation of pus. You will find it especially useful in the treatment of bubo, whether venereal or not, especially after the abuse of mercury. Even old buboes remaining open after mercury, and discharging continually, sometimes heal under *Hepar*.

It is not uncommon to find cases of indigestion embraced under the name dyspepsia, which have resulted from a long course of mercurial treatment by physicians of the dominant school. *Hepar*, as one of the antidotes to mercury, will sometimes cure these cases. Sometimes a cure is impossible. Still, I think, relief is always obtainable from one remedy or another. We may also find *Hepar* indicated by dyspepsia, independently of this cause, by the following symptoms: there are usually a sour taste in the mouth and a longing for strong tasting substances, for alcoholic drinks, for wines, for acids, and for condiments of various kinds. These seem to relieve by stimulating the stomach; so it is the purely atonic form of dyspepsia in which *Hepar* is indicated. There is hunger, a gnawing, empty feeling in the stomach in the forenoon, a longing for something to eat. This craving for food shows the atonic condition of the stomach. At other times, although eating does him good and increases his general strength, yet it produces a fulsomeness about the stomach. He can bear no pressure about the epigastrium. Sometimes there is burning in the stomach from congestion of that organ. The bowels are usually constipated. Urging to stool is often ineffectual, although the fæces be not abnormally hard.

With *Bryonia* the stool is large, brown and dry; it is not necessarily so with *Hepar*

In *Nux vomica* the constipation is of a spasmodic, fitful urging and not ineffectual.

In these dyspeptic symptoms *Hepar* seems to be complementary to *Lachesis*, in that both have this condition: any kind of food, no matter how wholesome, provokes indigestion.

Hepar must not be forgotten in the marasmus of children. Standing as it does between *Sulphur* on one side and *Calcarea* on the other, as a combination of these two, it is here of value. The symptoms which lead you to *Hepar* in the complaints of children are these: there seems to be this same weakness of digestion; they cannot manage their food, no matter how well-selected it may be. If they are old enough, they will tell you the symptoms that I have already mentioned. If you give them any strong substance, as a preparation of beef-tea, they will show signs of enjoying it very much. Diarrhœa is present, and is usually worse during the day and after eating. The stools may be greenish or slimy, undigested, or white and sour; this last is a very important symptom. The whole child smells sour. The most prominent remedies for sour stools are *Magnesia carb.*, next to that *Calcarea ostrearum*, then *Hepar*, and lastly *Rheum*.

The symptoms for *Rheum* are as follows: sour stool; the whole child smells sour; the stools are frequent, brown and frothy, and attended with a great deal of straining and violent pain, which makes the child shriek.

If the liver is involved under *Hepar*, we find soreness and stitches in the region of that organ. The stools then become clay-colored, or even white.

The same condition is found in the bladder that we have already noticed in the rectum, viz., atony of the muscular coats. Hence when urine is voided, it passes very slowly; it drops almost perpendicularly from the meatus urinarius instead of being ejected with some force. It takes the patient some time to empty his bladder. If with this trouble of the bladder you find wetting of the bed at night, *Hepar* is the remedy. It is not often indicated in this condition, however.

In this vesical paresis you should compare *Sepia*.

The ulcers which call for *Hepar* are very sluggish and indolent, slow to heal. They are rather superficial and often serpiginous. The discharge is bloody and purulent, and has an odor like that of old cheese. They have this to characterize them, extreme sensitiveness of the border of the ulceration.

The action of *Hepar* on the skin is important. In the first place, it produces a condition of non-healing as just indicated. Every little scratch of the skin suppurates. The same is also found in *Mercurius*, *Chamomilla*, *Silicea* and *Lycopodium*. It also produces a moist eruption in the folds of the skin. There is itching, especially in the bends of the joints. When *Hepar* is called for in eczematous eruptions which have a purulent discharge, we find it indicated by these symptoms: after the abuse of salves or ointments containing zinc or mercury, and the eruption is worse in the morning and accompanied by itching. Ulcers bleed easily, are extremely sensitive and emit an odor like old cheese.

Hepar is an antidote to metallic poisoning generally, but especially to mercury and iodide of potassium. It also antidotes *Cinchona* and *Iodine*.

In symptoms of the skin *Hepar* is similar to *Carbo animalis*, *Sepia*, *Psorinum*, *Cuprum*, *Thuja*, *Zinc*, *Graphites*, *Natrum muriaticum* and *Croton tiglium*.

LECTURE LXVII.

PREPARATIONS OF SODA.

The preparations of soda are quite similar, both chemically and medicinally, to those of potash, yet this similarity is not such that they may not follow the potash salts. We will see that *Kali carb.* is complementary to *Natrum mur.* in some of its symptoms. It seems that the salts of soda are indicated particularly in complaints that arise every summer or in the spring. Hot weather, electric changes in the atmosphere, or the direct rays of the sun give rise to various ailments. For instance, we find *Natrum carb.* useful for chronic headache, traceable to exposure to the rays of the sun. Under *Natrum mur.*, we find great debility in summer; the patient feels as though he would faint away when walking in the sun.

The soda salts used in our materia medica are *Carbonate of Soda* or *Natrum carb.*, *Chloride of Sodium* or *Natrum mur.*, *Arseniate of Soda* or *Natrum arsenicosum*, *Sulphate of Soda* or *Natrum sulph.*, *Phosphate of Soda* or *Natrum phosphoricum*, *Natrum hypochlorosum* and *Borax*.

NATRUM CARBONICUM.

Natrum carbonicum is the first preparation of soda we have to consider. It is much used in the allopathic school of practice as a remedy for acidity of the stomach. It is also used by the physicians of that school in eczema; for instance, in a case in which there is chronic thickening of the skin, the affected parts are bathed in carbonate of soda. No doubt, it relieves, but it cannot cure, unless it happens to be the indicated remedy, in which case it will cure as well as palliate.

Carbonate of soda has also been introduced as a remedy for burns. In our practice the drug claims a high place, being something of a polychrest. Its most prominent action seems to be on the stomach and bowels. Many of its symptoms spread from this central point of attack.

For instance, we will find that it has mental symptoms pointing quite plainly to hypochondriasis. We find the patient *depressed and exceedingly irritable.* This is especially noticed *after a meal*, particularly after dinner, which is usually the heaviest meal. The degree of hypochondriasis seems to be measured by the stage of digestion. Just as food passes out of the stomach into the duodenum, this hypochondriacal mood lessens, and continues to do so as the food gets further down into the bowels. You will find such a patient decidedly averse to society, even to his own family. The indigestion is more marked after a vegetable diet, particularly starchy foods. The indigestion is accompanied by sour eructations, water-brash and by retching in the morning, with spasmodic contraction of both œsophagus and stomach, with little or nothing coming to the mouth and, perhaps, copious salivation. The abdomen is hard and swollen, especially so after eating. There is accumulation of flatus in the abdomen, and this, when passed, is noticed to be fœtid. There is a sort of griping colic just after a meal. The stool is difficult to expel, although not especially hard, just as we found in *Hepar* last week, and as we find still more marked in *Sepia*, which, by the way, is complementary to *Natrum carb.*

At other times, the patient suffers from diarrhœa. The stool is papescent or watery, with violent urging. This characteristic of the soda salts, you will find to be quite general. You find it also in *Natrum sulph.* It seems to be due to the purgative effect of the soda itself. Wine in such cases as this causes faintness and vertigo, not agreeing with the patient at all.

In these gastric and nervous symptoms we find the nearest analogue to *Natrum carb.* in *Sepia*, which, as I have mentioned a few moments ago, is also its complement. We find in both remedies this aversion to society and indifference to one's own family. We find, too, that both remedies have sour eructations and the formation of fœtid gas in the abdomen. I remember curing a case of dyspepsia with *Sepia*, in which there were very few gastric symptoms, nothing more than a feeling of discomfort, but the mental symptoms were prominent and always ushered in an attack of indigestion. The patient, a lady, became indifferent to her business affairs and also to her friends. She became excessively irritable. She would hardly tolerate even a civil question addressed to her. *Sepia* entirely cured this patient after she had been six or seven years under allopathic treatment. This shows you how the mental symptoms of *Sepia* come in, to enable you to decide for it as the remedy. *Natrum carb.* has almost precisely the same class of symptoms. It may not be so often indicated, but nevertheless, it comes in to supplement *Sepia* when the general symptoms are those of *Soda* rather than those of the former remedy. *Natrum carb.* has rather distension of the abdomen, with fulness and hardness, like all alkalies, while *Sepia* has more goneness and empty, sinking feeling. which food does not fill up, except, perhaps, at supper. *Natrum carb.* has one exception to the fulness of the abdomen, and that is, at ten or eleven o'clock in the morning the patient feels anxious and weak, very much as you find under *Iodine*, but eating relieves this and produces distension.

Then, again, you should remember *Natrum carb.* in connection with *Nux vomica*. Both remedies have this retching in the morning. This symptom is strongest, however, in *Nux vomica*. You are often called upon to give *Nux vomica* when it occurs in pregnant women, or after a debauch, etc. Then, too, you find *Natrum carb.* parallel with *Nux vomica* in this hypochondriasis. You must compare the two remedies carefully before you decide which you will give.

We shall see, too, that *Natrum mur.* will have to be compared with *Natrum carb.* It is necessary to distinguish between the two because they are both soda salts.

Evidence of the effect of *Natrum carb.* on the nervous system is shown by the electric changes in the atmosphere. Thus, we find it causing nervousness or anxiety, which is worse during a thunder-storm. These symptoms occur independently of the timidity which belongs to some people during thunder-storms, at which times they secrete themselves in the cellar, etc. They are due to the direct effect of the electric changes in the atmosphere on the nervous system, precisely as we find in other remedies, notably in *Phosphorus*, *Rhododendron*, *Silicea*, *Bryonia*, *Natrum muriaticum*, *Nitric acid* and *Petroleum*. So nervous and restless may the *Natrum carb.* patients become, that playing on the piano makes them worse and aggravates their complaints. It is not only the music that has this effect, but the efforts they use and the position they take. This is a common symptom in hysterical women. They get very nervous from playing on the piano or from hearing music.

Another property of *Natrum carb.* is its use in ill-effects of summer weather; this is common to all the soda salts. We find *Natrum carb.* indicated when there is a great deal of debility caused by the heat of summer, particularly when the patient is subject to chronic headaches, which are worse every time he exposes himself to the heat of the sun. *Natrum carb.* is particularly called for in the chronic effects of sunstroke. It may have been years past that the patient was overcome by the heat; and now with the return of hot weather, he suffers from headaches.

Natrum carb. also weakens the nervous system in another direction. We find it exhibiting great debility, which is marked with every exertion on the part of the patient. His walk becomes unsteady; any little obstruction on the pavement causes him to fall. His ankles turn in when he attempts to walk. I have a patient, apparently in good health, who has had five falls within one year, and, for these accidents, I can find no reason. These are the cases that require a remedy, not for the effects of the fall, but to tone up the joints or muscles. Other remedies besides *Natrum carb.* having this weakness of the ankles in children are *Sulphuric acid, Causticum, Natrum mur., Natrum hypochlorosum, Sulphur* and, perhaps, *Pinus sylvestris.* I mention this last remedy with reserve, for while it has been highly recommended in our literature for weak legs, it has failed in a number of cases.

Natrum hypochlorosum or Labarraque's liquid is not a pure salt, for it contains carbonate of soda and calx chlorinata or ordinary "chloride of lime." The indications for its use in uterine disease has already been given you in a former lecture. (See page 142.) It suits lax, flabby, indolent children who, in addition to weakness of the ankles, have curved spine with prominence of the scapulæ and eczema on the scalp and behind the ears. They are subject to purulent otonhœa, aphthæ, to scalding urine, to wetting the bed at night, and when asleep, they may have a ghastly look as if dead.

You will find that *Natrum carb.* will relieve soreness of the feet, and particularly the soles, accompanied by swelling of those parts. You may also use it for ulcers on or about the heels after a long walk. This symptom brings to mind a peculiar circumstance that I would like to mention. Certain remedies have an affinity for certain parts of the body. A soldier, who had been marching a great deal, had two ulcers, one on the heel, the other on the instep. *Natrum carb.* cured the one on the heel but not the one on the instep, which was afterwards cured by *Lycopodium. Lycopodium* acts on the instep and *Natrum carb.* on the heel. The same thing you note all over the body. There are drugs that act on the right tonsil and not at all on the left. You find some remedies which act on the great toe and not at all on the others.

On mucous membranes, too, we find *Natrum carb.*, exerting considerable influence. The crude drug has been known to produce in workmen engaged in its manufacture small ulcers on the cornea. Given internally, it has cured small corneal ulcers or phlyctenules, with great photophobia and stinging pains; particularly are these symptoms marked in scrofulous children.

The catarrhs curable by *Natrum carb.* are not commonly met with, but when they do occur, there is no drug that can take its place. The coryza is fluent, and is provoked by the least draught of air, and seems to have a periodical aggravation every other day. It is entirely relieved by sweating. Chronic cases of nasal catarrh or ozæna, even call for *Natrum carb.* when we find thick yellowish-green discharge from the nose, or hard fœtid lumps. The tip of the nose is red, the skin peels off. You find not infrequently, when *Natrum carb.* is indicated, that there will be accumulation of mucus in the posterior nares, or in the throat, in the morning, causing "hemming" and hawking until it is raised. This is a very common symptom in all the alkalies.

The cough seems to have its aggravation whenever the patient enters a warm room, and is attended with purulent green sputum of a salty taste. Among other remedies which have this cough worse in a warm room, *Bryonia* stands foremost. *Coccus cacti* has it in almost equal degree.

Natrum carb., as I have already told you, is often used in the treatment of eczema. It seems to have a particular affinity for the dorsa of the hands. The skin then becomes rough, dry and chapped. Here, again, you find *Sepia* closely related with *Natrum carb.*, being particularly indicated for this form of eruption when there are little ulcers about the joints of the hands. *Natrum carb.* also cures herpetic eruptions in yellow rings.

On the genital organs, *Natrum carb.* has some effect. Particularly do we find it indicated in diseases of females when there is pressure across the hypogastrium as if something were being pushed out. If you make an examination in these cases, you will find the os uteri indurated and misshapen. There is considerable congestion of a passive kind in the uterus, causing pulsation there during and after coitus. The extra influx of blood caused by sexual erethism brings about this pulsation. The leucorrhœa which *Natrum carb.* causes is thick and yellow, and sometimes has a putrid odor, and ceases after urinating.

There is another use you may make of *Natrum carb.*, and that is when labor pains are weak and cause a great deal of anguish, tremor and perspiration with every pain, and are relieved by gentle rubbing, which by the way is a general characteristic.

We also find *Natrum carb.* to be one of the remedies useful for expelling moles or the products of a false conception.

NATRUM SULPHURICUM.

Natrum sulphuricum would hardly have been used by members of our school had it not been alluded to by Grauvogl as the central remedy for his hydrogenoid constitution. Patients having this constitution feel every change from dry to wet; cannot tolerate sea air; nor can they eat plants that thrive near the water. They feel best on a dry day. It is this constitution in which, according to Grauvogl, the gonorrhœal poison is most pernicious. It finds here the richest soil in which it may grow rank. Therefore, he claims that if gonorrhœa occurs in such a constitution, to cure the patient not only of the local gonorrhœal discharge, but of the constitutional effects, the constitution must be altered. This he does with two remedies, *Natrum sulph.* and *Thuja*. The *Natrum sulph.* cures obstinate cases of gonorrhœa.

In the chronic effects of injury, especially to the head, *Natrum sulph.* is almost indispensable.

You will find *Natrum sulph.* especially indicated for ailments which are either aggravated or dependent upon dampness of the weather or dwelling in damp houses. You may think of *Natrum sulph.* then in the sycotic constitution of Hahnemann or the hydrogenoid of Grauvogl. It may even be necessary to give this remedy when there is no bubo or urethral discharge to be seen.

There is a kind of phthisis, not a true tuberculosis, which appears in those who have this constitution. The cough is attended with muco-purulent expectoration, loud râles are heard through the chest, and the seat of inflammation seems to be the lower lobe of the left lung. The patient complains of pain about the ninth and tenth ribs on the left side. The *Natrum sulph.* patient has a marked tendency to this catarrh of the chest. If it appears as the result of suppressing hæmorrhoids or anal fistula, *Natrum sulph.* is even more strongly indicated.

Natrum sulph. is also indicated in asthma which is excited or made worse by every spell of damp weather.

Natrum sulph. also acts on the stomach and abdomen. It produces a great deal of flatulence, belching after eating, eructations being tasteless or sour. There is a great deal of rumbling of wind in the bowels, particularly in the right side of the abdomen, probably in the ascending colon. We find, too, a subacute pain in the ileo-cæcal region, because it has some action on that portion of the intestinal tract. Associated with this there is diarrhœa, which comes on regularly in the morning after rising and returns quite regularly each day. Much wind is passed with the stools and is worse in damp weather. It is distinguished from *Sulphur* by this: with *Natrum sulph.* the diarrhœa comes on more in the forenoon after getting up, whereas, with *Sulphur* it hurries the patient out of bed.

It is distinguished from *Bryonia* which has diarrhœa on first rising in the morning by the fact that the latter has less flatus, and is aggravated by hot weather.

Natrum sulph. is also useful in affections of the left hip-joint in patients of this hydrogenoid constitution. The pains are worse at night, and arouse the patient from sleep. They cease when he turns over in bed.

Stillingia is useful for hip diseases in secondary or in inherited syphilis, with pains in and through the hip, worse at night and worse in wet weather.

LECTURE LXVIII.

NATRUM MURIATICUM

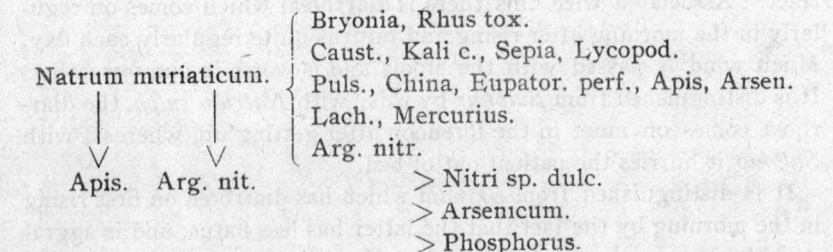

Natrum muriaticum.
{ Bryonia, Rhus tox.
Caust., Kali c., Sepia, Lycopod.
Puls., China, Eupator. perf., Apis, Arsen.
Lach., Mercurius.
Arg. nitr.

Apis.   Arg. nit.

> Nitri sp. dulc.
> Arsenicum.
> Phosphorus.

To-day we begin our study of *Natrum muriaticum* or common table-salt. This has always been held up to us as an opprobium against medicine, and as a confirmation of the fallacies of Homœopathy. A physician once said to me: "What! will you use a substance which is used in almost every food and call it a medicine, and say that you obtain good effects from it?" I can assure you, gentlemen, as I assured him, that *Natrum muriaticum* is a medicine, and I can assure you, too, that that man afterwards became a warm advocate of its medicinal virtues. When you potentize a drug you will find that you no longer have to depend upon the ordinary laws of dietetics, hygiene or chemistry, but you step into a realm which is distinct from the laws of chemistry and of physics. Medicines are then no longer subject to the grosser laws.

Natrum mur. was re-proved by a company of Austrian physicians who made heroic provings of some of our drugs. Some of these men died from the effects of their provings, so large and powerful were the doses of the medicines they took. One of the provers, whose name I have forgotten, said, when he published his provings of *Natrum mur.*, that the higher potencies of the drug produced the most symptoms, and these symptoms, moreover, were more valuable than those produced by the low. It is true of *Natrum mur.* as of most other drugs, that the high potencies act best.

You will notice on the board that I have placed *Argentum nitricum* and *Apis* as complementary to *Natrum mur. Argentum nitricum* holds a complementary relation to *Natrum mur.* It also, at times, antidotes. It acts as a chemical or as a dynamic antidote according to the quantity of the drug taken.

The relation between *Apis* and *Natrum mur.* is particularly evident in the treatment of chills and fever, and skin affections. Salt is one of the substances used to antidote the poisonous effects of bee-stings.

When salt has been abused as a condiment, sweet spirits of nitre may be used as a successful antidote. Some other effects of *Natrum mur.* are antidoted by *Arsenicum*, and still others by *Phosphorus*. I do not now recall any remedy inimical to *Natrum mur.*

Natrum muriaticum or *Chloride of Sodium* may be considered first in its physiological relations, so that we may learn something of its value as a medicine. It enters into every tissue of the body, even into the enamel of the teeth. Speaking now physiologically, it is regarded as a stimulant to the various tissues into which it enters. It exists in quite considerable quantities in the various humors of the eye, particularly in the aqueous humor and crystalline lens, and also in the vitreous humor. It has been said that its function here is to preserve the transparency of the respective tissues. Virchow, in his *Pathology*, quotes an authority who gave *Chloride of Sodium* to dogs until he produced opacity of the crystalline lens. Hence, cataract may be produced by *Natrum mur.*

Chloride of Sodium in the stomach stimulates digestion and this, too, within the bounds of physiology. It stimulates digestion in various ways. First, it improves the flavor of food. We all know how insipid certain articles of diet are unless salted. We know from physiology that if a substance has its taste enhanced, its digestibility is also increased. That which is agreeable, digests more readily than that which is unsavory. Salt also acts on the stomach itself by favoring the secretion of gastric juice. Salt acts on the glands, producing an increase in the glandular secretions. Thus we find it acting on the sudorific glands and also on the mucous glands.

Schüssler argues that salt is excreted through the mucus, which is true. Therefore, he says, that as salt has a function here, it must be the remedy for all catarrhs. That is too sweeping a conclusion for so limited a premise. It is true that if you examine healthy mucus you will find that it contains considerable salt. It is true also that *Chloride of Sodium* produces an excessive flow of normally constituted mucus. From this you may take a useful hint. Wherever you find a catarrh with a copious secretion of clear normal mucus, there *Natrum mur.* may be the remedy. We find it acting also on the sebaceous glands. These little glands are quite numerous in certain parts of the body, particularly around the wings of the nose and the cheeks. Their function is to lubricate the skin. *Natrum mur.* stimulates these, and as a result the skin becomes oily in appearance. We notice this particularly in the face, in the scalp, though it occurs, more than likely, in other parts of the body.

Salt also has a stimulating effect on the nervous system, keeping up its tone. Muscular tone is also favored by the presence of salt within the tissues of the muscles. This brings me to give you the hint that common salt may be used as an external application in weaknesses of the muscles and nerves that favor deformities of the limbs. When you first notice that a child is walking on the side of its feet, or when you meet with a case of post-diphtheritic paralysis, you may use friction with salt to great advantage. I do not mean to say that it will cure all deformities, for some arise from inflammation of the anterior gray cornua of the cord. *Chloride of Sodium* cannot cure these, for the trouble is due to organic disease.

In weak ankles study *Causticum Sulphuric acid Sulphur Natrum carb.*, etc.

Again, we may sometimes use salt in the form of the sitz-bath for obstinate amenorrhœa.

We shall frequently find *Natrum mur.* indicated when the blood is impoverished. The nutrition of the whole system, therefore, suffers. We find it indicated in anæmia, particularly in anæmia provoked by loss of fluids, hence often with women who suffer from menstrual disease and with men who suffer from loss of semen. We shall often find it indicated in scorbutic states of the system when the patient suffers more or less from scurvy. It is quite likely that the prolonged use of salt meat is a common cause of scurvy. In these cases the mouth becomes sore, ulcers form on the tongue and on the gums, and the breath has a fœtid odor. The tongue presents a mapped appearance, a symptom we also find in other remedies, as *Arsenicum*, *Rhus tox.*, *Kali bichromicum* and *Taraxacum*.

Again, as a result of this impoverishment of the blood, we find the nervous system suffering secondarily.

Natrum mur. may be given for the following symptomatic indications: the patient is emaciated, and this emaciation is very marked.

The skin is rather harsh and dry and of a yellowish hue. The patient feels greatly exhausted from any little exertion of mind or body. On account of the anæmia we have the circulation readily excited, so that every little exertion produces throbbing all over the body. The patient suffers frequently from palpitation of the heart, and this, too, is excited by every motion and every strange or sudden noise. It is often described by the patient as a sensation as though a bird's wing were fluttering in the left chest.

Mentally, we find these patients sad and tearful. You will seldom find *Natrum mur.* indicated in chronic affections unless there is this low-spirited condition of the mind. The patient seems to be made worse by any attempt at condolence. Consolation may even make her angry. This tearful condition is accompanied by palpitation of the heart and intermittent pulse. Now, this intermittent pulse does not necessarily imply organic disease of the heart, but simply a nervously weak heart.

At other times the patient is decidedly hypochondriacal, just as we have already found with *Natrum carb.* This hypochondriasis is directly associated with indigestion, as in *Natrum carb.* But there is this difference: with *Natrum mur.*, the remedy under consideration, this hypochondriasis keeps step with the degree of constipation, not alone with the indigestion, as in the other.

In addition to this melancholy mood we also have irritability developed by *Natrum mur.* The patient becomes angry at every little trifle. He stores up in his mind every little real or imaginary offence. He wakes up at night with palpitation of the heart and cannot go to sleep again, because past unpleasant events occupy his mind.

Intellectual ability is impaired. He becomes disinclined for mental work; makes mistakes, as if confused; has loss of memory; study aggravates. Frequently school girls suffer from headache, as if little hammers were pounding the head, whenever they study. Excitable, laughs immoderately at something not ludicrous; fingers move involuntarily, as in chorea; trembling of the limbs; muscular jerks; awkward; she drops things. Now add to these chronic symptoms the following, and you have a complete picture of *Natrum mur.* Excitement is always followed by melancholy, anxiety, fluttering at the heart; limbs go to sleep, with "crawling," is noted also in the lips and tongue; limbs heavy, especially in anæmic girls, whose faces are yellow, skin dry and shriveled, and menses scanty or checked. Mental emotions cause such weakness that one or more limbs are useless

Sometimes *Kali carb.* follows in menstrual difficulties. It may bring on the menses when *Natrum mur.* fails.

While on this subject of the nerves we may as well add the remaining symptoms: spinal irritation; backache relieved by lying on something hard; small of back pains, as if broken; paralyzed feeling in lumbar region, worse in the morning after rising; tongue stiff, clumsy speech; joints weak, especially the ankles, worse in the mornings This last symptom accompanied by imperfect nutrition, growing thin in spite of good appetite, has led to the successful topical and internal use of salt in children with weak ankles; the feet turn under while walking.

Now, in mental symptoms, *Natrum mur.* runs against several drugs. One of these is *Pulsatilla*, which is the most lachrymose remedy of our materia medica. But *Pulsatilla* has rather a tender, yielding disposition, that seeks consolation. The more you console her the better she likes it.

Sepia is more similar to *Natrum mur.* than is *Pulsatilla*, in that both remedies have this low-spiritedness and vehement angry disposition combined. Both have Indian-like hatred of those who have injured them. In fact, these remedies are complementary to each other. The *Sepia* patient, however, has marked indifference to her household affairs.

The patients who suffer from these mental symptoms calling for *Natrum mur.* are generally chlorotic. They suffer from leucocythæmia. The menses are often late and scanty, or else cease altogether. When the menses have not entirely ceased and are scanty they are accompanied by such marked symptoms as these: decided increase of the sadness before menses; palpitation of heart, which, too, is apt to be of this fluttering variety, and throbbing headache, which headache continues persistently after the menstrual period. The *Natrum mur.* patient frequently suffers too from uterine displacements. She has quite characteristically prolapsus uteri, which is induced particularly when she gets up in the morning. The symptom reads, "When she gets up in the morning, she must sit down to prevent prolapsus." This is a functional disease altogether. There is no organic change in the uterus, but there is great relaxation in the ligaments which support that organ. As she arises in the morning, relaxed instead of refreshed after her night's sleep, the uterus falls and she has to sit down to prevent this dragging. You will find these uterine symptoms accompanied by backache and decided spinal irritation, which is greatly relieved by lying flat on the back or by pressing a pillow firmly against the back. That I have confirmed over and over again as an excellent indication for *Natrum mur.* In addition, you will have a characteristic symptom of the bladder that is just as often present as is the prolapsus itself, and that is, cutting in the urethra after urination. That symptom, I have seen successfully applied many times. Backache and morning aggravation are symptoms which will aid you in the selection of *Natrum mur.*

Natrum mur. produces a headache, worse from any use of the mind. In the morning on awaking, there is throbbing, mostly in the forehead, as if from many little hammers beating in the head. This, too, is worse from any use of the mind. The pain is so severe at times as to make the patient almost maniacal. With this kind of headache. the tongue is dry and almost clings to the roof of the mouth, although it may look moist when put out. There is great thirst. The pulse is almost always intermittent. This helps you to distinguish it from its complement, *Sepia*, which has a similar symptom. I do not want you to forget that sharp headache of *Sepia*, in the lower part of the brain, apparently in the meninges, shooting upwards. The patient can bear neither light nor noise. The pain is usually attended with nausea and vomiting as a secondary symptom.

This headache of *Natrum mur.* resembles that of *Arsenic, Veratrum album* and *China*, none of which however have the accompanying dry tongue and intermittent pulse of the former.

Natrum mur. also produces a headache simulating that of *Bryonia;* sharp stitching about the head and sore bruised feeling about the eyeballs, especially when the eyes are moved. I may say that these headaches of *Natrum mur.* are particularly common in school children at the age of ten or eleven.

Calcarea ostrearum is also a good remedy here.

You may have occasion to use *Natrum mur.* in ciliary neuralgia, especially when the pains are periodical, returning from sunrise to sunset, being worse at mid-day.

Spigelia is a drug which also has headache or ciliary neuralgia, coming and going with the sun and worse at mid-day. The eyes feel too large.

Gelsemium and *Glonoin* have not so much neuralgia as throbbing in the head, which grows worse with the sun.

Natrum mur. also causes headache with partial blindness: here it resembles *Kali bichromicum, Iris* and *Causticum.*

Natrum mur. has a very powerful influence on the various portions of the eyes. Now all over the body, the drug produces weakness of the muscles. This is especially manifest in the muscles of the eyes. The muscles of the lids feel stiff when moving them. Letters blur and run together when looking steadily at them, as in reading. You see that there is marked asthenopia. *Natrum mur.* is especially indicated when the internal recti muscles are affected. These asthenopic symptoms depend upon a general break-down. The spine is weak and irritated, digestion is slow and imperfect, and nutrition is not as rapid or as complete as it should be.

Another form of eye disease in which *Natrum mur.* is indicated, is scrofulous ophthalmia. You will be called upon to use the drug in such cases when nitrate of silver has been abused. There are smarting and burning pains and a feeling as of sand beneath the lids. The tears are acrid and there is very marked spasmodic closure of the eyelids. You can hardly force them apart. Ulcers form on the cornea. The eyelids themselves are inflamed and agglutinated in the morning. In addition to these eye symptoms, these scrofulous children suffer from eruptions particularly marked at the border of the hair. Scabs form on the scalp and from these there oozes a corrosive matter. There are moist scabs in the angles of the lips and wings of the nose, and with these, emaciation.

In scrofulous ophthalmia you should compare with *Natrum mur., Argentum nitricum, Arsenicum* and *Graphites.*

For scabs in the corners of the mouth and wings of the nose, compare *Antimonium crudum, Graphites* and *Causticum.*

Natrum mur. also causes half-sight. Here you should compare *Aurum, Lithium carb., Lycopodium* and *Titanium.*

Natrum mur. acts on the mucous membranes. We find it indicated in catarrhs with mucous secretion abnormal in quantity rather than in quality. This hypersecretion of mucus is accompanied by paroxysms of sneezing. Fluent alternates with dry coryza. Every exposure to fresh air gives the patient cold. The wings of the nose are apt to be sore and sensitive. There is almost always in the *Natrum mur.* catarrh loss of smell, and in the acute, frequently loss of taste. *Natrum mur.* is one of the best remedies for hawking of mucus from the throat in the morning, when the symptoms call for no other remedy.

The tonsils are often very red. The uvula is elongated, probably from relaxation of its muscles. There is a constant feeling as of a plug in the throat and the patient chokes easily when swallowing. The tongue is coated in insular patches.

The cough arises from the accumulation of clear mucus in the posterior nares, pharynx and larynx. Of course, there is hoarseness. Another form of cough calling for *Natrum mur.*, is cough arising from tickling in the throat or at the pit of the stomach. This kind of cough is accompanied by bursting headache, here reminding one of *Bryonia*, and sometimes, by involuntary spurting of urine, as we find under *Scilla* and *Causticum*, and often, too, by stitches in the liver.

Natrum mur. has marked action on the male genital organs. It causes great weakness of these, giving rise to seminal emissions during sleep. These are followed by debility and great weakness. The genital organs are greatly relaxed. Wet dreams may even occur after coitus. That may seem to you an anomalous symptom, but it is not. During the act of coitus, erections are not strong and the ejaculation of semen is weak or even absent. The consequence is, there is not an entire emptying of the seminal vesicles. There is still irritation remaining there. When the man goes to sleep, this irritation, by reflex action, excites lascivious dreams. As consequences of the excessive seminal loss, we find backache, night-sweat, weakness of the legs and the melancholy which is characteristic of the remedy. *Natrum mur.* is not alone among the soda salts in this class of ailments. *Natrum phos.* was proved by gentlemen in this college. They had seminal emissions every night. At first, there seemed to be erethism with lascivious dreams, but later, emissions took place, one or two in a night, without any sensation whatever. These were followed by weakness of the back and by trembling of the knees, which felt as though they would give way.

You will find, too, that gonorrhœa is curable by *Natrum mur.*, especially when chronic. The discharge is usually clear, though it may be sometimes yellowish. There is well-marked cutting in the urethra after urination. *Natrum mur.* is especially indicated in cases that have been abused by the nitrate of silver.

Nutrition is greatly impaired under *Natrum mur.* as I have already told you. Emaciation is marked in almost every case in which it is the similimum. We may make use of this fact in children who suffer from marasmus from defective nourishment. They are thin.

particularly about the neck. They have a ravenous appetite and, despite this, they grow thin, at least they do not grow fat. Here you find it comparable with *Iodine*, but the peculiar emaciation of the neck, disproportionate to that of the body, is sufficient to distinguish it from that drug. In addition to this, you may have, at times, well-marked thirst. The child craves water all the time. This is what the laity term inward fever. There is constant heat and dryness of the mouth and throat which the water relieves. If there is constipation when *Natrum mur.* is the remedy, there is a very characteristic stool, hard, difficult to expel, fissuring the anus and, as a consequence, there is bleeding with the stool. Of course, smarting and soreness is the result of the laceration from this large stool.

Veratrum album has emaciation about the neck, especially in whooping-cough.

Lycopodium has dwindling of the upper part of the chest.

Natrum mur., like the other salts of soda, is a first-class remedy in the treatment of dyspepsia. We find it indicated when farinaceous food, particularly bread, disagrees. The symptom reads, "He is averse to bread of which he was once fond." On the other hand, there is craving for oysters, fish and salty food or for bitter things. After eating, the patient is very thirsty. There is a distressed indescribable feeling at the pit of the stomach. This is relieved by tightening the clothing, just the opposite to *Lachesis* and *Hepar;* and precisely the same as *Fluoric acid*. The constipation, which I have described, causes hypochondriasis. The patient is low-spirited and ill-humored, and this mental condition seems to keep pace with the degree of constipation. When the bowels are moved, the mind is relieved. You must use this symptom rationally. Those who have been accustomed to taking purgative medicines will almost always feel badly if their bowels remain costive longer than the usual time. They have dull headache, nasty taste in the mouth, etc., and when the bowels move, they feel better. Here, *Nux vomica* is the remedy. It is not often that undisturbed constipation produces this condition of mind, but when it does, *Natrum mur.* is the remedy.

The rectum suffers from tenesmus with slimy discharge as in chronic proctitis. Prolapsus ani with discharge of bloody mucus and water, and burning preventing sleep; dryness and smarting of rectum and anus, with tendency to erosions of the mucous membrane. Sensation of a rough substance in the rectum and yet the bowels are loose.

Constriction of the anus, fæces hard and evacuated with such exertion as to tear the anus. Chronic watery diarrhœa with dry mouth, secondary to dry stool.

In proctitis and constipation you should compare *Sepia*, which has lump in rectum: *Æsculus* and *Collinsonia*, which have sensations as of splinters or sticks in the rectum.

The extreme dryness of the rectum resembles *Alumina*, *Graphites*, *Magnesia mur.*, *Ratanhia*, *Æsculus*, etc. *Graphites* has mucus-coated stools; *Alumina* has smarting soreness; *Magnesia mur.*, crumbling stools; *Ratanhia*, feeling of splinters of glass and fissures.

We find *Natrum mur.* indicated in affections of the coarser tissues, for instance, of the skin. I have already told you how it affects the sebaceous glands. We find that it produces urticaria. The itching is very annoying. It occurs about the joints, particularly about the ankles. Wheals form on different parts of the body and these itch, smart and burn. Especially do we find *Natrum mur.* indicated when these symptoms accompany intermittent fever or occur after exposure to damp cold, especially at the seaside. Exercise makes this nettle-rash intolerably worse. Just here, we find *Natrum mur.* complementary to *Apis*.

Apis is an excellent remedy in the treatment of urticaria, but it is not so good, I have found, in the treatment of the chronic form of the disease. Here we have to use other drugs, as *Natrum mur.*, and above all, *Calcarea ostrearum*.

There is another form of eruption yet to be thought of for *Natrum mur.*, and that is herpes. Thus, we find particularly characteristic of *Natrum mur.*, what are called hydroa-labialis. They are little blisters which form on the borders of the lips and which accompany every marked case of chills and fever indicating *Natrum mur.* They are akin to what are commonly known as fever blisters. *Hepar Natrum mur.* and *Rhus tox.* are the remedies which have this symptom most marked. *Arsenicum* also has it. In the very beginning of these cold sores, the application of camphor will stop the trouble. If, however, they are well advanced, *Hepar* relieves them and prevents their return. *Camphor* is not a curative remedy, but *Hepar* is.

Herpes circinatus, a variety of ring-worm, calls for *Natrum mur.* Other remedies for this trouble are *Sepia*, *Baryta carb.* and *Tellurium*.

Another form of eruption calling for *Natrum mur.* is eczema, which appears in thick scabs, oozing pus, and matting the hair together, a crusta lactea in fact.

Lastly, I come to speak of the well-known application of *Natrum mur.* to intermittent fever. There it shares the honors long accorded to *Cinchona* and *Arsenic*. *Natrum mur.* is to be considered when the chill comes characteristically between ten and eleven A. M. The chill begins in the small of the back or in the feet. It is accompanied sometimes by thirst, and by aching pains all over the body. Sometimes urticaria complicates the case. Fever is usually violent. Thirst increases with the heat. The headache becomes more and more throbbing. So severe is this cerebral congestion at times that the patient becomes delirious. By and by, sweat breaks out quite copiously and it relieves the headache and also the other symptoms. This is the intermittent fever curable by *Natrum mur.*

When chill occurs at ten A. M., as a result of hectic fever or phthisis, *Stannum* is to be used and not *Natrum mur.*

NATRUM ARSENICATUM.

Natrum arsenicatum, or the arseniate of soda, affects markedly the mucous membranes, producing dryness and sensitiveness to dust, smoke and even to the indrawn air, and later the secretion of tough, gluey mucus, crusts, etc. This property of the drug has led to its use in catarrhs of the respiratory passages. It is indicated in a coryza which, as you will observe, resembles somewhat that of the parent arsenic. There is a copious discharge of watery fluid from the nose, and yet the nasal passages feel stuffed up. This is accompanied with dull, supra orbital headache, compressive pain at the root of the nose, dryness and smarting of the eyes, injected conjunctivæ, flushed and puffy face and dryness of the throat. There is sometimes a good deal of sneezing, which is provoked by the least draft or inhalation of cold air. All these symptoms are worse in the morning and forenoon.

This continues until the mucous secretion becomes thicker. Tough, yellow or yellowish grey mucus drops down from the post-nares into the throat, or hard, bluish mucus is blown from the nose every morning and its removal is followed by bleeding. At night and in the morning the nose is stuffed up so that the patient breathes with mouth open.

Looking at the throat, you will find it dark red, swollen, and covered with yellow gelatinous mucus which gags the patient when he attempts to hawk it out.

As the "cold" creeps downward a dry cough supervenes. There is a sensation of oppression in the chest and of stuffiness as if the lungs were full of smoke. Soreness in the supra-clavicular regions and pain over the fourth and fifth costal cartilages of the right side. The oppressed feeling in the chest has this peculiarity: it is better when the patient urinates freely, and it is aggravated by dust or smoke. You may use the remedy in bronchitis when the above symptoms are present, or even in graver forms of disease. It may be of g eat service in tuberculosis, with emaciation, dry heat of the skin, chilliness at night and thirst for small quantities of water frequently repeated.

Lastly, I have to speak of the use of *Natrum arsenicatum* in psoriasis. It should be classed here with *Arsenicum, Arsenicum iodatum* and *Sepia*. The scales are thin and whitish and when removed leave the skin slightly reddened. The eruption is apt to appear on the chest and itches when the patient warms up from exercise.

LECTURE LXIX.

BORAX VENETA.

Borax. { Staphisagria, Mercurius.
Sepia, Pulsatilla.
Bryonia.
> Chamomilla, Coffea.
Vinegar.
Wine.

BORAX is the biborate of soda. As a medicine, it won its first laurel in the nursery, where it has long been used in the treatment of sore nipples and children's sore mouth. Like all popular remedies, it has been greatly abused. Homœopathy has rescued it from the nursery and now offers it to the profession as a medicine of great value, telling when it may and when it may not be used. Underlying this sore mouth, which seems to be the keynote for the use of *Borax*, is a system or constitution which will permit of the sore mouth, that is, an illy-nourished system. Thus the infant becomes pale or of an earthy hue, its flesh grows soft and flabby; it cries a great deal when it nurses, screams out during sleep and awakens clinging to its mother as if frightened by a dream. It is excessively nervous, so much so that the slightest noise the mere rustling of paper, as well as a distant heavy noise, will arouse and frighten it. This nervous excitability qualifies the pains. For instance, in the earache, you will find that each paroxysm of pain causes the child to start nervously. The earache is accompanied by soreness, swelling and heat of the ear, just as you find in *Belladonna*, *Pulsatilla* and *Chamomilla*. There is a mucous or muco-purulent otorrhœa. *Borax* is distinguished from these remedies by this starting with the pain or from slight noises, by the paleness of the face and above all by another well-proved symptom, the dread of downward motion. Thus if the little one is sound asleep in its mother's arms and she makes the attempt to lay it down in its crib, it gives a start and awakens. If she attempts to carry it down stairs, it will cling to her as if afraid of falling. This must not be confounded with the excitability of other medicines, as *Chamomilla* and

Belladonna. It is not simply the motion that awakens the child, for the child will not awaken if it is moved without any downward motion. It must, then, be the downward motion that arouses it. The reason for this is, that the child is suffering from cerebral anæmia and this downward motion causes a feeling as though it were going to fall. This symptom may also be utilized in adults, as, for example, in the case of invalids who have been ordered to take horseback rides, but who cannot do so, because when the horse lets them down, they feel as if they were in torture. You will also find that ladies, after some exhausting disease, cannot use a rocking-chair, because when they rock backwards, they feel as if they would tumble.

The digestion in the *Borax* case is impaired, as you might infer from the defective nutrition. Colic precedes the diarrhœa in the child I am describing. The stools are usually green, or they may be soft and yellow, but they always contain mucus. Here you have another illustration of the affinity of *Borax* for mucous membranes. Aphthous inflammation of the mouth appears as a concomitant of the diarrhœa. Aphthæ form in the pouches on the inside of the cheeks, on the tongue and in the fauces. The mouth is hot, which the mother notices when the child takes hold of the nipple. The mucous membrane around these aphthæ bleeds easily. The child lets go of the nipple and cries with pain and vexation, or else refuses the breast altogether.

Similar to *Borax* are the following remedies: first, *Bryonia;* this remedy has caused and has cured infants' sore-mouth. But the characteristic symptom in *Bryonia* is this: the child refuses to nurse or makes a great fuss about it, but so soon as its mouth is moistened, it takes hold of the nipple and nurses energetically. Is not this in keeping with the character of *Bryonia?* Those of you who know anything of that drug will remember how dry the mouth is, and how devoid of secretion is the mucous tract. Hence, when the mucous membrane of the mouth is moistened the child nurses at once.

Mercurius comes in as a substitute for *Borax* when, with the sore mouth, there is profuse salivation. Water dribbles from the child's mouth. The diarrhœa is accompanied by well-marked tenesmus. These are sufficient distinctions between *Mercury* and *Borax*.

Again, you must remember a neglected remedy, and that is *Æthusa cynapium*, or the fool's parsley. This is to be preferred when the colic and crying are accompanied by the violent vomiting characteristic of this drug.

Another remedy is *Arum triphyllum*. This is readily distinguished from *Borax* by the violence of the symptoms. The inflammation of the mouth is exceedingly violent and is accompanied by soreness and scabs around the mouth and nostrils.

Another common baby symptom in the *Borax* case is that the infant screams before urinating. The urine when passed is hot and has a peculiar pungent fœtid odor. Now this is not to be confounded with gravel, which is not uncommon in little children, and which will call for *Sarsaparilla, Lycopodium, Benzoic acid*, etc.; but it is the equivalent of the inflammations of other mucous membranes, so that it compares with *Aconite, Cantharis* and another excellent baby medicine, *Petroselinum*. Do not forget this last named drug. It is not generally mentioned in our materia medicas, yet it is an excellent remedy for conditions very similar to those calling for *Borax* when there is sudden violent urging to urinate. It may be indicated even in gonorrhœa when this sudden urging is present.

Passing from child to adult, we find that although the aphthous condition is still master, we still have many of the other symptoms of *Borax*, the same difficulty in digesting food, the same weakness, and the mucous membranes still the point of attack. We find, for instance, the conjunctiva, particularly the palpebral portion, affected by *Borax*, giving you soreness especially marked along the borders of the lids. The eyelashes grow inwards instead of outwards and irritate the eyeball. You should remember it as a remedy which will sometimes help in trichiasis or "wild hairs," and here you should compare it with *Graphites*.

The nostrils ulcerate in the *Borax* case, causing a great deal of soreness, pain and swelling of the tip of the nose.

On the mucous membrane of the throat we find *Borax* having an action, being indicated, like all the soda salts, for accumulation of mucus there. But under *Borax*, the mucus is tough and difficult of detachment.

The leucorrhœa of *Borax* is clear, copious and albuminous. Like all the other secretions of *Borax*, this, too, has an unnatural warmth or heat to it.

The action of *Borax* on the lungs must not be forgotten. We find it indicated when there is cough which is accompanied by sharp sticking pain, worse through the upper part of the right chest. So sharp are these pains that they make the patient catch his breath. The expectoration has a sort of musty, mouldy odor and taste. You can often use *Borax* in lung troubles and even in phthisis when these symptoms are present.

Lastly, we have to mention a few symptoms of the skin. The skin is unhealthy; every little cut or scratch suppurates readily. There is itching of the skin, particularly on the backs of the fingers, here being something akin to the dorsal eczema of *Natrum carb*. Little ulcers form about the joints of the fingers.

The best remedy we have for these small ulcers about the joints is *Sepia*.

Lastly, *Borax* has been used in erysipelas of the face, particularly of the cheeks. The distinctive character of the drug is a feeling as though there were cobwebs on the face.

I would advise to caution your nurses, if you can do so, not to use powdered borax every time the child has a sore mouth. It may do harm if it is not indicated. I think that I have noticed after this use of the drug that the bowels suffer and the child grows paler and dwindles rapidly, which it did not do before the meddlesomeness of the nurse.

LECTURE LXX.

SALTS OF POTASH.

TOXICOLOGICALLY, potash may be of some interest to you when, by accident, caustic potash is swallowed. Its great affinity for water makes it attack the tissues with great avidity, producing very deep escharotic effects. It has more power to penetrate the tissues than have some of the other caustics nitrate of silver, for instance; hence, it has been selected as the caustic for use when it is desired to reach far into the parenchyma of a part, as in the treatment of carbuncle; when a large portion of tissue has become gangrenous and a slough must be produced, caustic potash is used. The tissues thus acted upon have a greasy appearance, which is due to the formation of a soap made from the combination of the fats with the potash. Thus it differs materially in its action from the mineral acids, which make the tissues dry and dark, almost like a mass of tinder.

When swallowed by accident, for it is seldom used for suicidal purposes, the effects of caustic potash are violent. It causes such violent contraction of the stomach that what little of it gets that far is immediately ejected by violent vomiting. If the amount of caustic taken is sufficient, it causes a brownish film over the mucous membrane, or there may be spots here and there in the mouth and throat which are denuded of their epithelium. The inflammatory process may increase to such an extent that these spots ulcerate, and as they heal they form cicatricial tissue with the subsequent unfortunate contraction and stricture of the part.

The antidotal treatment to such accidents is both chemical and mechanical; chemical, to relieve the effect of the drug, and mechanical, to relieve the trouble that remains. Vinegar. lemon-juice and large draughts of mucilaginous drinks are mostly relied upon to relieve the acute symptoms of this poisoning.

But there are many cases of slow poisoning with the potash salts, particularly when our allopathic friends use bromide of potassium so extensively. We, therefore, have the chronic effects to treat. These may require to antidote them: *Hepar*, which is an antidote to the metals in general; *Sulphur*, and other remedies may be called for according to the symptoms present.

It has been determined by experiments on mammals, that potash, particularly the carbonate, acts paralyzingly on the muscles. This accounts for the general weakness which belongs to all potash preparations. This paralyzing effect is very manifest in the case of the heart muscle, which becomes early affected in poisoning with potash, the animal eventually dying with the heart in diastole, that is, the heart is widely dilated at the moment it ceases to beat. With this hint, you would expect to find potash salts of use in great muscular weakness, in what has been termed paresis, such exhaustion as accompanies convalescence from protracted diseases as typhoid fever.

We have it on the authority of Dr. Hering, that mushrooms contain a large percentage of potash, and are therefore to be recommended as an article of diet in cases of exhaustion.

KALI BROMATUM.

The first potash preparation we will consider is *Kali bromatum* or *Bromide of Potassium*. We find that this drug is antidoted by *Hepar* mainly. It has some few analogous or concordant remedies, *Ambra grisea, Hyoscyamus, Stramonium, Tarentula* and *Mygale*.

Bromide of Potassium acts mainly upon the nervous system and acts, in two opposite directions. Primarily, it decreases reflex action; secondarily, it depresses the mind. This property of the drug to modify reflex action has led to its extravagant use in the treatment of epilepsy. It is given in progressively increasing doses until the system is affected by what is known as bromism. When the system has become saturated with the drug, then it is discontinued for awhile. The first effect of the drug seems to be to increase reflex action, particularly reflex motor action, and it is on this quality of the *Bromide of Potassium* that the allopath bases his prescription. Every little disturbance in the periphery of the nerves, every little alternation in the function of an organ, is at once reflected to the nervous centres, and produces some other disturbances, either an uncomfortable sensation, twitching of muscles, anxiety, headache or even absolute convulsions. This is the first condition of the *Bromide of Potassium*. You know that this is the starting point of almost all convulsions. Witness, for instance, a case of eclampsia, where the pressure of the child on some of the nerves in the pelvis or against an undilating os, causes spasms: or still another case, where some indigestible substance in the stomach produces convulsions. This reminds you at once of *Stramonium*, in which a bright light, by affecting the retina, reflects the irritation to the brain and causes convulsions, and of *Strychnine*, in which the slightest touch or a little draft of air, sound or odor, will renew the paroxysms.

As a result of this oversensitiveness to external impressions, we have quite a number of the characteristics of the *Bromide of Potassium*.

Many of these are symptoms of the drug calling for its exhibition in acute mania when there are sleeplessness and strange imaginations. The patient imagines that he will be poisoned ; that he is pursued by some demon that he is hated by everybody, or that his honor is at stake. Some such impression acts on the mind irresistibly, and causes him to resort to violent procedures ; thus, he will try to commit suicide in order to avoid the supposed danger. All this time, the pupils are dilated, and the face is bright red and expressive of anguish and fear. The body trembles, and the muscles twitch in various parts the body. You see how this resembles *Hyoscyamus* and they are parallel remedies in this form of disease

Kali bromatum has also acted very well in the night-terrors of children, when from over-excitement of the brain, whether it be reflex from dentition or worms, or even from affection of the brain itself, the child shrieks out in its sleep, and if old enough, will complain of seeing hob-goblins, ghosts or something of that kind. Even when that symptom occurs in impending dropsy of the brain, *Bromide of Potassium* may be the remedy.

We have another condition calling for *Kali bromatum*, and this seems to be an irritability of the nerves, not only of the brain, but of the whole body. This irritability is expressed by the following symptoms : the patient is nervous and cannot sleep, and feels better when engaged at some work. He is either busy playing with his fingers or he is walking about, or in some way occupying his mind or body in some exertion; then feels better. Simple sleeplessness will not be relieved by *Kali bromatum* unless there is this relief from activity or motion.

In this respect, I find it similar to *Tarentula*, which also has this irritation of the periphery of the nerves relieved by exercise and by rubbing. The patient plays with her dress, or with her watch-chain, as if to work off this over-irritation of the peripheral nerves. Even in the case of the headache of this remedy, the patient rubs the head against the pillow for relief.

Another remedy which is similar to *Kali bromatum* in this over-excitability, is *Ambra grisea*, which has this same sensitiveness to external impressions, the slightest influence causing excitement and difficulty in breathing. *Ambra grisea*, however, almost always has some sort of vertigo associated with its other symptoms. It is also a very quick-acting drug.

Conversely to this primary action of *Kali bromatum*, we have another, one of great depression of the cerebro-spinal nervous system. Thus we find it producing absolute loss of memory. The patient cannot remember words particularly. Associated with this symptom we find a distressing melancholy; everything looks dark and gloomy. He cares nothing for anybody nor for his occupation. This condition of things often follows excesses in venery, in which case *Kali bromatum* is an excellent remedy.

There is also a sort of ataxia developed. The patient seems to be unable to manage his legs as he should. There are numbness and tingling in the legs and in the spine; this symptom being accompanied, in the first stages, by an increase in the sexual appetite, but as the case advances it is associated with absence of erection and frequent nightly emission of semen, thus increasing the melancholy.

You will find *Bromide of Potassium* indicated for business men who have worked long and hard, who have pored over difficult problems until they have this dizziness, this staggering gait, and this benumbed feeling in the brain. It was only yesterday that I prescribed it for a business man on Third street, who has been working himself almost to death. I expect that it will relieve him promptly and effectually. He said that when he had been working at his books he would get a numbness in the back of the head, and a certain indescribable terrified feeling, as though he were going to lose his senses. Good results might also be obtained in this case by the galvanic current, the positive electrode being applied to the cervical region and the negative on the vertex. But *Kali bromatum* will give a more permanent relief.

Now, a word about *Kali bromatum* as an anti-epileptic remedy. I do not believe that it ever cured epilepsy. In almost all cases in which it has been given, it has not cured but simply suppressed the disease, and thus has produced a worse condition than the one previously existing, namely, imbecility.

Kali bromatum produces lesions of the skin. Its long-continued use gives rise to little, hard, dark red papules on the face, surrounded by little vesicles and ending in suppuration. We may, therefore, use the drug in acne, particularly that resulting from masturbation.

Another form of eruption which the *Kali bromatum* produces is a livid blotch as large as one's thumb-nail, covered with scales, and having in its centre a yellowish appearance as if it were suppurating. After a while it does suppurate and discharge, leaving a central depression, something like that of the small-pox pustule.

Still a third form of eruption, is an eczema which evidently arises from the action of *Kali bromatum* on the sebaceous or sudoriferous glands, causing an abscess in each of these and developing a scaly eruption.

Kali Hydriodicum.

The *Iodide of Potassium*, or *Kali hydriodicum*, does not, like the *Bromide of Potassium*, act on the higher tissues of the body. It seems to affect more the lowest tissues, as the fibrous, particularly the periosteum and the connective tissue wherever they may be found. It attacks the nervous tissues ultimately, probably by involving the neuroglia. The tendency of the drug is to produce infiltration, so that when it is thoroughly indicated you will almost always find an œdematous or infiltrated state of the part affected. Some of the symptoms produced by *Iodide of Potassium* are due directly to the iodine which it contains. For instance, what is known as iodine intoxication may be developed by the drug. The patient is very talkative; exhibits a great deal of anxiety about the heart; the face is flushed, the head is hot, in fact, he acts pretty much the same as one under the partial influence of liquor.

The headache which *Kali hydriodicum* causes is one of the external head, probably from the action of the drug on the aponeurosis of the occipito-frontalis muscle, because there appear sharp lumps like nodes on the scalp and these pain excessively. This may be a remote symptom of syphilis or of mercurialization, or it may appear in a patient with the rheumatic diathesis.

In affections of the eyes *Kali hydriodicum* is called for principally by the violence of the symptoms, especially in syphilitic iritis after the abuse of mecury. Now, if mercury has not been abused, I do not consider the *Iodide of Potassium* to be the best remedy. *If* there is any best remedy for iritis it is *Mercurius corrosivus*. We may also use *Kali hydriodicum* for inflammation involving both choroid and iris, the result of syphilis. More externally we find pustular keratitis, with chemosis, especially after the abuse of mercury.

Coming next to the nose, we have the following indications for the *Iodide of Potassium:* coryza or catarrh, occurring repeatedly in patients who have been mercurialized; every little cold or exposure, or every damp day causes the nose to become red and swollen; and acrid watery discharge flows from it, and the eyes smart and lachrymate, and become puffed. The patient is alternately chilly and hot, the urine is high colored (as the patient expresses it) and scanty, and there is usually some sore throat. Every exposure provokes a return of these symptoms.

Kali hydriodicum also cures this thin excoriating nasal discharge when it appears as an inheritance from syphilitic parents. The ozæna which it cures is either scrofulous, syphilitic or mercurial, or a combination of all these. The discharge may be either thin and acrid, or else thick, green and offensive, and attended with burning sensation in the nose and even perforation of the nasal bones.

Next, the action of *Iodide of Potassium* on the lungs and heart. It is not a little singular that all the preparations of *Mercurius* produce sharp, stitching pains through the lungs (through either the right or left lung, and shooting in different directions), and that the very best antidote to mercury also produces stitching pains through the lungs, particularly through the sternum to the back; worse from any motion. Now, there are two very different conditions in which *Iodide of Potassium* is indicated by these symptoms. One of these is in pneumonia, in which disease it is an excellent remedy when hepatization has commenced, when the disease localizes itself, and infiltration begins. In such cases, in the absence of other symptoms calling distinctively for *Bryonia*, *Phosphorus* or *Sulphur*, I would advise you to select either *Iodine* or *Iodide of Potassium*. It is also called for when the hepatization is so extensive that we have cerebral congestion or even an effusion into the brain as the result of this congestion. Now, the symptoms in these cases are as follows: first, they begin with very red face, the pupils are more or less dilated, and the patient is drowsy; in fact, showing a picture very much like that of *Belladonna*. If you are hasty, you may be led to give that remedy, but it does no good. The patient grows worse, the breathing becomes more heavy, and the pupils fail to react to light. You know then that you have a grave serous effusion affecting the brain, which must be speedily checked or the patient will die. Why did not *Belladonna* cure? Because *all* of the symptoms were not taken into account. The trouble did not start in the brain. The cerebral symptoms are secondary to others. What, then, is the primary trouble? You put your ear to the patient's chest and you find one or both lungs consolidated; hence the blood cannot circulate through the lungs as it should, and the different organs in the body become congested. Here then is a symptom, previously overlooked, which explains the failure of *Belladonna*. Until you have proved that *Belladonna* has produced such a condition, you cannot expect it to do any good.

Another condition in which we may use *Iodide of Potassium* is in pulmonary œdema, thus again showing the infiltration producible by the drug. This is almost always, as you know, a secondary trouble. The expectoration looks very much like soapsuds, but it is apt to be a little greenish.

We may also have *Kali hydriodicum* indicated in phthisis pulmonalis, particularly if there are present this same sort of frothy expectoration, night-sweats, and loose stools in the morning. The cough is of a violent racking, tearing character, and is worse in the morning, thus keeping up the tendency of the potash salts, to have aggravation of the chest symptoms from two to five o'clock in the morning. I may say that these symptoms of the lungs are often consecutive to Bright's disease, in which disease *Kali hydriodicum* may be the remedy.

Yerba santa is used by eclectics for phthisis of catarrhal origin. It is used empirically. There is a gentleman who has a tendency to catarrhal asthma, with thickening of the bronchial tubes and constant oppression of breathing. I treated him for a year. *Sulphur* seemed to be indicated, but was given with only partial relief. Finally, I gave him *Yerba santa* in the tincture. It so far relieved him that every morning he coughed up a quantity of sputum, and there then followed a freedom of breathing he had not had for years.

The action of *Kali hydriodicum* on the heart is also characteristic. It produces a horrible smothering feeling about the heart, awakening the patient from sleep and compelling him to get out of bed. This symptom is also found under *Lachesis*, *Kali bichromicum*, *Lactuca*, *Euphrasia*, *Graphites*, and some others.

It is also useful for repeated attacks of endocarditis or pericarditis of rheumatic origin. There are sharp, darting pains in the heart, worse from any motion, and particularly bad from walking.

In disease of the spine you will find *Kali hydriodicum* indicated by these symptoms: feeling as if the small of the back were being squeezed in a vise; bruised pain in the lumbar region and difficulty in walking; spinal meningitis with œdema or exudation, particularly when of syphilitic origin.

When gummatous tumors involve the nervous tissues *Iodide of Potassium* is your only hope.

It may also be of use when rheumatism involves the spire and paraplegia results. In these cases I think that it is the neurogl a that is attacked.

It may still further be used in rheumatism of the joints, particularly of the knee. This knee-joint is swollen and has a doughy feel; here, again, you see the tendency of the remedy to produce infiltration of tissue. There is no fluctuation to be detected. The skin above the inflamed joint is apt to be spotted, and the pains are of a gnawing, boring character, and are worse at night.

In sciatica you may give *Kali hydriodicum* when the pains are worse at night, and from lying on the affected side, and when the trouble is of mercurial or syphilitic origin.

You will find that the *Iodide of Potassium* will sometimes help you in the treatment of the so-called contracted kidney, especially when of mercurial origin.

Iodide of Potassium, like all the potash preparations, produces an eruption of a papular or of a pustular character. Especially do these appear on the scalp and down the back; when they heal they leave a cicatrix.

You may also remember *Iodide of Potassium* as a remedy for tertiary syphilis, particularly rupia.

The best antidote to *Iodide of Potassium* is *Hepar*.

LECTURE LXXI.

KALI BICHROMICUM.

TODAY I shall lecture on *Kali bichromicum*, or the *Bichromate of Potash*. You would expect in a drug having the combination of this one, to obtain not only the results of potash, which forms the base of the salt, but also the modifying influence of the chromic acid. You will find, therefore, that while there are evident general resemblances to the other *Kalis*, there are decided differences arising from the acid combined with it. *Chromic acid*, as you probably well know, is a highly irritating acid. It is a powerful escharotic, destroying animal tissue very rapidly, and penetrating quickly into the part, and so producing a deep ulcer or sore.

Kali bichromicum is a drug which acts generally, although not exclusively, on fat persons, and fat, chubby children more than on adults. We find that it possesses great virtues in inflammation of mucous surfaces, with tendency to plastic exudation and pseudo-membrane. It attacks mucous membranes, causing at first inflammation of these, violent in character and associated with a great deal of redness and swelling, and at first a production of an excessive amount of mucus, from over-action of the muciparous glands. This excessive mucous secretion is very rapidly turned into a fibrinous exudate; hence there is a tendency to the formation of false membranes.

This character of the exudation on mucous surfaces gives us the well-known characteristic of the *Bichromate of Potash*, discharges are ropy and stringy. This symptom is true of the coryza, it is true of the discharges in pharyngitis and laryngitis, and it is true of the vomited matters in gastric catarrh. It also applies to the leucorrhœa and also to the gleety discharge from urethra, which may sometimes call for *Kali bichromicum*. Illustrations, then, of this general characteristic of the drug are not wanting in any part of the body. We find this same quality of the mucous discharges even in scrofulous children, for whose diseases *Kali bichromicum* is often an excellent drug. For instance, it is indicated in inflammation of the middle ear, particularly when it affects the membrana tympani. There is ulceration not only of the membrana tympani, but also of the mucous surface of the middle ear. The distinction between *Kali bichromicum* and other remedies in these cases is that the discharge is tenacious, stringy and purulent. With this there will be earache, with pains of a sharp stitching character which shoot up into the head and down into the neck. You will find the glands of the neck swollen and also the parotid gland on the affected side. This becomes large and indurated, and pains shoot from the ear down and into the swollen parotid.

In these stringy discharges compare *Alumen, Senega, Kali carb., Asafœtida, Coccus cacti,* etc.

In diseases of the mucous membrane of the throat we find this same character to the exudation. Thus, in diphtheria, we find *Bichromate of Potash* indicated under two or three contingencies. It may be a remedy when diphtheria assumes the croupous form. The membrane is quite thick, and is dicidedly yellow-looking, like wash-leather. The tongue is coated yellow or is red, dry and glossy; pain in the throat extending to the neck or shoulder; swollen cervical glands; well defined slough in the throat. The discharges, whether coming from the nose or throat, or both, are decidedly stringy. This has been, in my mind, a sufficient distinction between *Kali bichromicum* and the *Iodides of Mercury.* When I am giving *Iodide of Mercury* in diphtheria, as soon as I find that the expectoration becomes stringy I change to *Kali bichromicum* because it suits that condition, and also because it may prevent the extension of the disease to the larynx. Although, in general, *Kali bichromicum* is suited to rather sthenic types of inflammation, yet we have indications enough to prove that it may be suited to the adynamic cases also. So far as our knowledge of this drug goes it does not produce many neurotic symptoms or blood changes, but what few are recorded belong to weariness, sleepiness and prostration, etc., and at times, especially if there is gastro-enteric inflammation, there is cold sweat, lowered temperature, pale sunken face, showing that the drug may suit actual collapse and cases of asthenic type.

The *Iodide of Mercury* is to be thought of in diphtheria when the membranous deposit is more or less profuse, involving the tonsils and posterior nares. The glands in the neck are swollen. The tongue is coated dirty yellow. There is excessive production of mucous in the throat, causing a great deal of "hawking."

Carbolic acid and *Kali permanganicum* are kindred remedies in diphtheria. Both have putridity well marked, the former associated with burning pains in the mouth to the stomach, or little or no pain, dusky red face, pale about the mouth and nose, rapid sinking of vital forces; the latter with painful throat, soreness of the muscles of the neck.

We find *Kali bichromicum* indicated in forms of inflammation of the throat other than diphtheritic. Thus, it is called for in follicular pharyngitis. The follicles of the throat become hypertrophied and look like little tubercles on the pharyngeal walls. These discharge a white cheesy-like mass, which, when crushed between the fingers, gives forth a fœtid, disagreeable odor. These are attended by a feeling of roughness and dryness in the throat, and at times by an accumulation of tenacious mucus. You will find this disease a stubborn one to treat. In addition to *Kali bichromicum*, it will be well enough to remember *Hepar*, *Kali chloricum* (especially when there is a great deal of fœtor of the breath) and *Æsculus hippocastanum*, or the horse-chestnut. *Æsculus* resembles *Kali bichromicum* very closely, but lacks the tenacious stringy mucus. There is dry, rough, burning feeling in the throat and pharynx and yet no swelling. The face is sallow and digestion is slow. There is tendency to portal congestion, as shown by deep throbbing in the hypochondrium, and constipation and hæmorrhoids.

In other cases you will have *Nux vomica* indicated by well-known symptoms, which I need not here repeat.

Still other cases call for *Secale cornutum*, which has hawking up of these little follicular exudates; *Sulphur*, *Hepar*, *Ignatia*, *Mercurius jod.*, also *Chimaphila maculata*, which produces swollen tonsils, and tensive pain in the throat on swallowing.

We have *Kali bichromicum* indicated in yet another form of throat disease which is neither scrofulous nor croupous nor diphtheritic, but syphilitic. Ulcers form on the fauces and tend to perforate. The surrounding mucous surface is of a coppery-red color.

It is also indicated in nasal catarrh. It produces, at first, dryness of the nasal mucous membrane, with tickling in the nose and sneezing, these being especially marked in the open air. The secretion from the nose is ropy and stringy, and often collects in the posterior nares. It may or may not be offensive.

In catarrh of the post-nares compare *Spigelia*, *Hydrastis*, *Natrum sulphuricum*. The latter hawks up saltish mucus every morning.

At other times, as in ozæna, there are discharges from the nostrils or posterior nares consisting of plugs, or clinkers, as they are sometimes called. Lumps of hard green mucus are hawked from the posterior nares, particularly in the morning. At other times (often in syphilitic cases) you will find ulcers which carry out the perforating character of *Chromic acid*, and tend to perforate the parts on which they are located.

Kali bichromicum is indicated in true membranous croup. It suits best, although not exclusively, light-haired, fair-complexioned children who are rather fat and chubby. The cough has a decidedly metallic sound. It has more than the mere bark of catarrnal croup. The fauces you will generally find quite red; the tonsils, perhaps, are somewhat red and a little swollen. The cough seems to descend; that is, the rattling goes down lower and lower until it apparently reaches the upper part of the epigastrium, or rather the lower third of the sternum, the irritation of the cough seeming to start from there. In this position, as well as in the throat, there seems to be a smothering, oppressive sensation; breathing becomes very labored. The child has smothering spells, arousing it from sleep, choking. The whole chest heaves with the efforts at respiration. The membrane forms quite thickly in the larynx, narrowing its lumen. The expectoration is tough and stringy, and, perhaps, mucous, and contains pieces looking like boiled macaroni. The patient is worse in the morning from three to five o'clock. Sometimes there is a tendency in these cases of croup to extend downwards and involve the trachea, and even the bronchi, giving rise to what has been termed croupous bronchitis. This is not a very common disease, but it is an exceedingly dangerous one. I remember treating a patient who, after taking *Kali bichromicum*, expectorated pieces looking like vermicelli and having numerous little branches, probably casts of the ramifications of the bronchial tubes.

One of the remedies following *Kali bichromicum* well in the throat and croupous diseases is *Lachesis*. It suits particularly when the spasmodic cough becomes so violent as to cause choking spells, and when the patient drops off to sleep, he awakens as if smothering. *Kali bichromicum* has modified the inflammation, but has not succeeded in preventing spasm of the throat. Then *Lachesis* comes in and relieves the remaining symptoms. Should the croupous symptoms increase, you may return to *Kali bichromicum*.

There is also a resemblance between *Mercurius cyanatus* and *Kali bichromicum* in diphtheritic croup.

Kaolin is very useful for membranous croup when it extends downwards, and when one of the characteristic symptoms is intense soreness along the trachea and upper part of the chest.

The mucous membrane of the stomach, too, falls under the influence of *Kali bichromicum*. The drug is so irritating that it causes gastritis. Thus it produces gastric symptoms varying in severity all the way from those of simple indigestion to those of malignant disease of the stomach. In the milder forms of dyspepsia we find it indicated when there is headache, the pain usually being supra-orbital. This may be periodical in its return, but is particularly excited by gastric irritation. Although it is neuralgic in its character, it is reflex from gastric irritation. Another form of headache which is associated with these gastric symptoms is one of a peculiar kind. The patient is affected with blindness more or less marked, objects become obscured and less distinct, the headache then begins. It is violent, and is attended by aversion to light and to noise, and the sight returns as the headache grows worse. I have met with that symptom in my practice four or five times. I have found the same symptoms precisely given under *Gelsemium*, but I have never used that drug under these circumstances, so I have not confirmed it. There are quite a number of remedies having blinding headache, but *Kali bichromicum* is the best of them. We have *Causticum* sometimes indicated for blindness with the headache, but not diminishing as the headache increases. We also find it under *Natrum mur.*, *Iris versicolor*, *Psorinum* and *Silicea*. In the latter remedy the blindness comes after the headache; in *Psorinum* before, the sight returning before the pain begins.

With this headache of *Kali bichromicum* the face is apt to be blotched and bloated, and covered with pimples or acne. It is also sallow and yellowish, as if the patient were bilious. The whites of the eyes are yellow and a little puffed. The tongue is thick and broad and scalloped on its edges, as though it had taken the imprint of the teeth.

The stomach seems to swell up immediately after a full meal, just like *Lycopodium*. The bowels are constipated, or else there is early morning diarrhœa, as you find under *Sulphur*, *Rumex*, *Bryonia* and *Natrum sulph*. The stools are watery, and are followed by tenesmus, which distinguishes this drug from *Sulphur*, *Rumex*, *Bryonia* and *Natrum sulphuricum*, all of which have morning diarrhœa. These are some of the gastric symptoms which will yield to *Kali bichromicum*. They are particularly apt to occur after excessive beer drinking. *Kali bichromicum* is one of the best remedies for the chronic effects of excessive indulgence in beer and ale.

Gnaphalium is one of the little used remedies that has diarrhœa worse in the morning. The stools are watery and offensive, with nausea and vomiting. It is sometimes useful in the beginning of cholera infantum. Urine dark, scanty. Irritability of temper, continuing even after the diarrhœa ceases.

We also find *Kali bichromicum* producing gastritis, herein very much resembling *Arsenicum*. The vomited matter is sour, and is mixed with clear mucus. You see how *Kali bichromicum* everywhere excites an over-production of mucus. The vomit may be bitter from admixture of bile. It is renewed by every attempt at eating or drinking, and is associated with a great deal of distress and burning rawness about the stomach. With this kind of vomit you may give *Kali bichromicum* in the vomiting of drunkards and in the round, perforating ulcer of the stomach.

In dysentery, *Kali bichromicum* is sometimes indicated. The disease occurs periodically in the spring or in the early part of the summer. The stools are brownish and watery, and mixed with blood and attended with great tenesmus. The distinctive symptom is the appearance of the tongue, which is dry, smooth, red and cracked.

In its action on the skin, *Kali bichromicum* causes, first of all, a rash which very much resembles that of measles. *Kali bichromicum* is particularly indicated in measles after *Pulsatilla*. The latter remedy is suited for the milder symptoms, the former for the more severe. The inflammation of the eyes grows worse with the formation of vesicles or pustules on or about the cornea. The meibomian glands or other structures of the lids ulcerate, so that the lids agglutinate, and there is more or less purulent discharge from the eyes. The ears, too, become involved, and there is a discharge from the ears of quite offensive pus. There are also violent, stitching pains which extend from the ear to the roof of the mouth and to the parotid gland on the affected side. The external auditory meatus is greatly swollen. *Kali bichromicum* is one of the best remedies we have, when measles is associated with these ear symptoms and swelling of the glands, with sharp pains shooting from the ears into the glands. There is also diarrhœa which resembles that of *Pulsatilla*, but differs from the latter in the presence of slight tenesmus. The rash is the same as we find in nearly every case of measles. In a general way, we may say that it resembles *Pulsatilla*, only it is much worse. It has the simple catarrh of *Pulsatilla*, watery or more commonly yellowish green secretions made worse and even advancing to ulceration.

We next find *Kali bichromicum*, like all the potash salts, producing papules. These papules are hard and tend to enlarge and develop into pustules. If the crude drug itself be applied to a slight abrasion in the skin its caustic action is severe enough to eat down to the bone. In extreme cases these pustules may even develop into deeply eating ulcers. Lupus, with severe burning pains, has been relieved and in some cases cured by this remedy.

We have also developed by *Kali bichromicum* symptoms resembling those of sycosis. This places the drug alongside of *Thuja*, *Pulsatilla*, and *Sarsaparilla*. We find scabs on the fingers, often about the nails, and also on the corona of the glans penis. There is a gleety discharge from the urethra, which is very often stringy, thus keeping up the general action of *Kali bichromicum* on mucous membranes. Ulcers looking like chancres, and tending to eat deeply rather than spread superficially, form about the glans penis and prepuce. In addition to these symptoms you must have the inflammation of the nose and throat of the character already described, with perforating ulcers affecting even the bones.

Kali bichromicum is also called for in inflammations of the eyes; this inflammation being rather indolent in character. There is lack of reactive power, so that ulcers form which progress slowly and show but little tendency to heal of their own accord. The same is true of the conjunctivitis, which may be of scrofulous or of sycotic origin. The lids are swollen and agglutinated, especially in the morning, with thick yellow matter, and, to keep up the indolent character of the remedy, you find very little photophobia. Sometimes we find chemosis with these cases. It is very similar to *Graphites* and *Calcarea ostr.*, in the indolent ophthalmia. *Graphites* has more cracking of the tarsi and photophobia especially in artificial light. *Calcarea* and *Kali bichrom.* meet in fat children, leukoma, etc., only *Calcarea* has the photophobia, the sweaty head and large abdomen.

You will find that iritis, whether syphilitic or not, may call for *Kali bichromicum*. It is indicated, not in the beginning but late, when there has been exudation posteriorly between the iris and crystalline lens, causing adhesions of these structures to each other. These exudations, if not too great, will be absorbed under the action of *Kali bichromicum*. Characteristic of this iritis is indolence. There is little or no photophobia and not a very decided redness attending the inflammation. This is a general hint which will guide you to *Kali bichromicum*, and will save you the memorizing of less characteristic symptoms. Do not, therefore, forget the indolence of the ulceration, the absence or deficiency of inflammatory redness and the disproportionate absence of photophobia.

We next come to the action of *Kali bichromicum* on the chest. It is indicated in bronchitis, particularly if the glands are involved. Posteriorly, on either side of the spinal column, you find dullness on percussion. The cough is of a hard, barking character, almost as in croup. It seems to start from the epigastrium. The expectoration is generally of a stringy character. Sometimes it consists of bluish lumps, and is attended with a great deal of difficulty of breathing, arising mechanically from thickening of the lining membrane of the bronchial tubes. The cough is almost always made worse after eating, and is better when warmly wrapped up in bed. There is a great deal of feeling of tightness in the epigastrium.

You must also remember *Kali bichromicum* as a remedy indicated in asthma dependent upon bronchiectasia. The bronchial tubes are filled up with this tough tenacious exudation. But we find *Kali bichromicum* indicated in another form of asthma, which is worse from three to four o'clock in the morning, and is especially liable to return in the winter weather or in summer time, when chilly. The patient is compelled to sit up in bed in order to breathe. Relief comes when the patient raises stringy mucus. This kind of asthma calls for *Kali bichromicum*, whether the patient be stout or thin. If you have this after midnight aggravation and relief from sitting up and bending forward, and from the expectoration of stringy mucus, you have a certain remedy in *Kali bichromicum*. Here is it a perfect complement to *Arsenicum*, which has nearly the same symptoms, but lacks the tenacious sputum. The low potencies have been most successful in the treatment of asthma. The high potencies have not failed, but in all of the literature that I have been able to see, the low potencies have seemed to be the most successful. Whether this is true or not, I do not know. I only give you the facts as I find them, that you may judge for yourselves.

Aralia racemosa is another remedy for asthma when the patient must sit up for relief. It seems as if he would suffocate if he did not. Dry, wheezing or loud musical whistling respiration. But the expectoration, at first scanty, later increases, is warm and of a saltish taste.

Lastly, I have to speak of the use of *Kali bichromicum* in rheumatism, particularly in rheumatism which occurs in spring or summer weather, when there are cool days or nights. The smaller joints seem to suffer. Thus we have pains about the fingers and wrists more than in any other part of the body. Pains wander about, suddenly jumping from one part of the body to another and relieved by moving the affected part. Gastric and rheumatic symptoms alternate. I have had several[1] instances in which I have been able to confirm this characteristi of the drug. It is somewhat like *Artemisia abrotanum*, in which remedy diarrhœa and piles alternate with rheumatism.

LECTURE LXXII.

CAUSTICUM.

CAUSTICUM is evidently a potash preparation, but its exact composition I do not know. Hahnemann was not able to define it, and chemists since his time have not been able to tell of what it is composed. Nevertheless it is a unique remedy, and is one that we cannot do without in practice. The drug is conveniently studied under the heads placed on the board.

Causticum.
- Carbo veg.
- Lachesis.
- Coloc.
- Rhus, Dulc., Aconite, Colch.
- Guaiacum.

- Paralysis.
- Spasms.
- Rheumatism.
- Mucous membranes.
- Skin.
- Organs.

<Phosphorus.

It has a tendency to cause paralysis and spasmodic symptoms, rheumatism, affections of the mucous membranes, and diseases of the skin and organs generally. You will recall the fact that there is an inimical relation between *Phosphorus* and *Causticum*. These remedies do not follow each other well, although indicated in the same class of diseases. This is to be remembered particularly by those who use the higher and medium potencies.

The main power of *Causticum* is the first one on the list, the paralytic weakness which the drug exhibits. This paralytic tendency is a genuine potash weakness. *Causticum* is especially suited to patients who are timid, nervous and anxious, and full of fearful fancies, particularly in the evening at twilight, when shadows grow longer and fancy more rife. The child, for instance, is afraid to go to bed in the dark. This applies not to the unfortunate child who entertains these fears by reason of faulty education, but to the child who is afraid as the result of nervous disease. As an adult, the patient is apprehensive that something is about to happen, or he feels conscience stricken, as if he had committed some crime. When closing his eyes, he sees frightful images. This is no new symptom to you, as you will recall it as belonging to several remedies. The patient, especially if a woman, is apt to be tearful and melancholy. The face is a correct picture of the mental condition, and is expressive of this low-spirited state. The face is apt to be sallow and sickly looking. The patient is either taciturn and distrustful, or is inclined to fits of anger, with scolding. This is, as you know, by no means dissimilar to *Phosphorus*, and yet you must not make the mistake of giving one, when the other is indicated. Memory fails. Any attempt at mental labor is followed by untoward symptoms, such as stitches in the temples when reading or writing, feeling of tension in the head and scalp, particularly in the forehead and about the temples. This is worse in the evening, and also on awakening from sleep. Here again it is very similar to *Phosphorus*, which also has that feeling of tension. The patient also has a rather odd sensation, and one that is not frequently met with, and that is a feeling as though there were an empty space between the brain and the cranial bones. This is relieved by warmth. As odd as this symptom may seem to you, it is not too uncommon for you to make note of. Our materia medica is not over rich in this direction, and so we ought to utilize every such symptom that we can get.

The vertigo of *Causticum* is that which belongs to an excited brain and spine, such as we find in the incipiency of paralysis, and even of locomotor ataxia. There is a tendency to fall either forward or sideways. There is with this vertigo a constant feeling of anxiety and weakness of the head. It is worse on rising and on trying to fix the mind, indicating a weakened cerebral circulation. The sight is bedimmed as though the patient were looking through a fog. Now, concomitant with these brain symptoms you have the following symptoms, one or two of which ought to be present in order to make the picture complete. The skin in these cases is apt to be dry and hot, and there is almost always constipation, which constipation is quite characteristic. It is attended with a great deal of urging, probably from defective expulsive effort in the rectal muscular fibres, with redness of the face and fulness of the bloodvessels. This symptom is very common in weak persons and in children when they are nervously debilitated.

Very characteristic of the drug is paralysis of single parts or of single nerves. Thus you may have to use it in paralysis of the facial nerve, particularly when it is the result of exposure to dry or cold winds. It may also be called for in ptosis, when the result of the same cause. *Causticum* is still further called for in paralysis of the tongue, when deglutition and speech are more or less destroyed, paralysis of the lips, and in glosso-pharyngeal paralysis. In this last-named disease, you cannot expect much improvement from any remedy. The larynx and the bladder may be attacked. These are illustrations of the local palsies which come within the range of *Causticum*. These paralyses may be caused either by deep-seated nervous disease, or, very characteristically, by exposure to cold. particularly to the intense cold of winter, when the patient is of the rheumatic diathesis.

Aconite, like *Causticum*, is useful in paralyses which are traceable to exposure to cold, especially to dry cold winds. *Aconite* suits well in the beginning, and *Causticum* more when the paralysis has become chronic and refuses to yield to the *Aconite*.

Rhus tox. and *Dulcamara* compare favorably with *Causticum* for paralysis of rheumatic origin, provoked by exposure to a damp and cold atmosphere, particularly when there have been changes from tolerably warm to cold and wet days. *Dulcamara* is suited to the beginning of such cases, and not when the trouble becomes chronic. *Rhus tox.* is suited to chronic cases.

Nux vomica and *Colchicum* are also to be thought of in paralysis from exposure.

Stammering has been cured by *Causticum* when caused by imperfect control of the tongue. In paralysis of the tongue, it may require to be fo'lowed by *Stramonium*, *Dulcamara*, *Muriatic acid* or *Baryta carbonica*.

You may also find *Causticum* indicated in paralysis which arises from apoplexy; it is not called for, for the immediate results of the stroke, not for the congestion, nor for the exudation, but for the remote symptoms, when, after absorption of the effused blood has taken place, there still remains paralysis of the opposite side of the body.

Causticum may be applied in diseases of children. It is suited to children of a scrofulous habit in whom, though emaciated generally and particularly about the feet, the abdomen is large and tumefied. They are slow in learning to talk. There is a tendency to scrofulous inflammation of the eyes, scabs form about the tarsi, the conjunctivæ become injected, and the cornea inflamed. There is a constant feeling as of sand beneath the eyelids. An eruption appears about the scalp, especially behind the ears, making this portion of the skin raw and excoriated. The discharge is slight in quantity and sticky in character. Often there is otorrhœa, purulent in its character. The child stumbles when it attempts to walk. The cause of this symptom will be found in disease of the brain or spine. These cases do not recover rapidly. There is defective nutrition in the whole nervous system. You must instruct your patients that hygienic measures must be observed in conjunction with medicinal, and that you can promise a cure if they will but be patient with you.

Other remedies which may be thought of here are, first, *Sulphuric acid* which is a good remedy for this weakness or giving way of the ankles; another is *Sulphur*, and still another, *Silicea*.

Still further, as illustrating the paralytic effect of *Causticum*, we find it causing aphonia or failure of the voice. This may or may not be catarrhal. It is associated with great weakness of the laryngeal muscles, which seem to refuse their office. This is often the case in phthisis and in laryngeal troubles, whether of a tubercular nature or not. The paralytic tendency is further illustrated in the cough. The patient is unable to expectorate. Just as under *Sepia*, *Drosera*, *Kali carb.*, *Arnica* and a few other remedies, the patient succeeds in raising the sputum so far, when it slips back into the pharynx. The remedy also has this as characteristic: the patient cannot cough deep enough for relief. In addition to these paretic symptoms in catarrhs, you may also add the following: rawness and burning down the throat and trachea, feeling as if these parts were denuded, and hoarseness with aggravation in the morning. At this time, also (consistent with the action of the potash salts generally), there is accumulation of mucus in the fauces and larynx. The sputum often tastes greasy and soapy. Drinking cold water relieves the cough. Accompanying the cough, we find pain over the hips, which is very characteristic, and, too, the cough is often associated with involuntary spurting of urine. This last symptom is very characteristic of *Causticum*. It is also found under *Natrum mur.*, *Apis*, *Phosphorus*, *Pulsatilla* and *Scilla*, which is excellent in spurting of urine in old people.

In the laryngeal symptoms, it is necessary to make a distinction between *Causticum* and *Phosphorus*. One point of difference is that *Phosphorus* often has evening aggravation of the hoarseness; *Causticum* has aggravation in the morning. Both have this nervous weakness. One symptom I have often found indicating *Phosphorus*, and that is, extreme sensitiveness of the box of the larynx. The patient dreads to cough, because it aggravates the laryngeal soreness. He dreads to talk for the same reason. Relief from cold drinks is found only under *Causticum*.

More similar to *Causticum* yet, is *Carbo veg*. Here you can make no serious mistake, because both drugs follow each other well. If you do make the mistake of giving one of these when the other is indicated, you will not injure your patient any more than from the delay caused by your imperfect selection. Both remedies have this rawness and soreness down the throat; both have hoarseness, *Carbo veg*. having aggravation in the evening and *Causticum* in the morning. The former is indicated after exposure to damp evening air; the latter, after dry, cold, severe winter weather.

Eupatorium perfoliatum is very similar to *Causticum* in that it causes hoarseness worse in the morning. Both remedies are indicated in influenza with aching all over the body, but *Eupatorium* has more soreness than burning and rawness in the chest.

In the hoarseness of singers or those who exert their voices a great deal, *Causticum* resembles *Rhus tox.*, *Graphites*, *Arum tri.* and *Selenium*.

In some cases, when *Causticum* fails in chronic hoarseness worse in the morning or evening, *Sulphur* is an all-sufficient remedy.

Still another kind of cough for which you may give *Causticum* is one which improves up to a certain point and then remains stationary, getting neither better nor worse.

Causticum is a good remedy for buzzing and roaring in the ears, or tinnitus aurium, when sounds reëcho unpleasantly in the ears. A voice which is of an ordinary tone, sounds loud and reëchoes in the ear with unpleasant confusion. When *Causticum* is the remedy, these symptoms may be concomitant with catarrh of the throat involving the Eustachian tube. They may also be symptoms of Mèniére's disease, of which affection I once cured a case with *Causticum*.

There are two drugs which you may compare here, namely, *Salicylic acid* and *Salicylate of Soda* which have caused and cured Meniere's disease.

You may also compare *Carbon bisulphide* and the well-known *Cinchona*.

When sounds reëcho in the ear, think also of *Calcarea ostr.* and *Phosphorus*.

We find *Causticum* indicated in involuntary urination or enuresis, particularly in children. It is especially called for when the accident occurs during the first sleep. The trouble is aggravated in the winter and ceases or becomes more moderate in summer. The urine is especially liable to escape involuntarily during the day in winter, as the result of any excitement.

Compare in enuresis, *Plantago major* and *Kreosote* (involuntary discharge of profuse, pale urine); *Calcarea ostr.* (fat children); *Sepia*, (little girls, worse in first sleep); *Belladonna* (nervous children); *Ferrum phos.* (during the day).

For nursing women we may use *Causticum* when over-exertion or loss of sleep threatens their supply of milk. This makes them very low-spirited, and they are apt to have this sallow, sickly complexion which is characteristic of *Causticum*.

Causticum may be used in spasmodic diseases, even in convulsions. Thus it may be used in epilepsy, particularly in *la petit mal*. When walking in the open air, the patient falls, but soon recovers. During the unconscious stage, the patient passes urine. *Causticum* may even be used when the attacks are of a convulsive nature, especially when they recur at the new moon. Now you are not to consider that the moon has anything to do with these epileptic attacks. It is only the laws which govern the relation of the planets, which regulate the tides and have to do with the periodicity of nature generally that also apply to the moon and to the disturbances within the human body; so it is that some symptoms are worse at new moon, others at full moon; some at the rise and others at the fall of the tide. It does not, therefore, follow, because the patient is worse every time at new moon, that the moon causes the aggravation. *Causticum* is, moreover, indicated in epilepsy when it is connected with menstrual irregularities, and also when it occurs at the age of puberty. In these symptoms *Causticum* is closely allied to *Calcarea ostrearum*.

Causticum is indicated in chorea when the right side of the body is affected more than the left. The muscles of the face, tongue, arm and leg are all involved in the disorderly movements. When the patient attempts to speak, words seems to be jerked out of the mouth. The patient is anxious and restless in bed at night. He must sit up and change his position. He involuntarily throws the head about, and finally he falls asleep exhausted. During sleep the legs and arms are constantly "on the go."

Lastly, we may be called upon to use *Causticum* in rheumatism, especially when the joints are stiff and the tendons shortened, drawing the limbs out of shape. It is frequently indicated in what has been termed rheumatoid arthritis. Rheumatic pains attack particularly the articulation of the jaw. They are worse from cold and are relieved by warmth.

Causticum is also useful in rheumatism of the right deltoid, here being comparable with *Phosphoric acid, Sanguinaria* and *Ferrum*.

Now, you will have to distinguish *Causticum* here from several other remedies. *Rhus tox.* also has rheumatism from exposure to cold. Some of the distinctions between it and *Causticum* I have already given you. There is yet another good one. *Rhus tox.* has restlessness and relief from motion all the time. In *Causticum* the restlessness only occurs at night. Further *Rhus* is worse in damp weather, *Causticum* in dry weather.

Guaiacum is to be preferred to *Causticum*, and follows that remedy well when, in either gout or rheumatism, there are contractions of the tendons, drawing the limbs out of shape, aggravated by any attempt at motion, particularly if there are well-developed gouty nodosities in the joints.

Colocynth is to be remembered for articular rheumatism when the joints remain stiff and unwieldy. The pains in the affected parts are of a boring character.

Causticum also acts on the skin, one of its most characteristic symptoms being warts. It is useful in the cure of these hypertrophies of the papillæ when they occur on the hands or face. I remember once giving *Causticum* to a child who had two warts on the under eyelid. At the end of the third week after taking the remedy, there was a string of warts over the inner canthus of the other eye. I believed that these resulted from the *Causticum*. Of course, I stopped the medicine. At the end of several weeks more, all the warts had disappeared, and the child has had none since. This shows you that *Causticum* really produces and cures warts.

Causticum may be called for in colic after the failure of *Colocynth*. The pains are of a griping, cutting character, and are relieved by bending double. Particularly do you find pains of this character suggesting the drug in menstrual colic. Previous to the menses, these colicky pains appear, and are associated with tearing pains in the back and limbs. The menses cease almost entirely at night, or continue for days after the normal time. All the sufferings cease entirely at night.

LECTURE LXXIII.

KALI CARBONICUM.

Kali carb.
{ Phos., Carbo veg., Arsen.
Ant. tart.
Hypophosphite of lime, Psorinum.
Caust., Senna.
Natr. m.
Lachesis.

∨
Carbo veg.

To-day I will study with you *Carbonate of potash*, known in our nomenclature as *Kali carb*. This is complementary to *Carbo veg*. and similar to it in many forms of disease, particularly in lung inflammations. Sometimes when one fails the other completes the cure; hence the origin of the complementary relation. We have quite a number of analogues to *Kali carb*., some of which have been placed on the board. We will have occasion to refer to some of these as we go on. There is also somewhat of a complementary relation between *Kali carb*. and *Phosphorus*.

Kali carb. exerts an influence over the manufacture of the blood, quantitatively as well as qualitatively. This is shown in the anæmia which the remedy causes. And is illustrated by the following symptoms: frequent chilliness; every time the patient goes out of doors, he becomes chilly if the air is in the least cool, not having the normal resistance to temperature; quite consistent with this anæmia, there is throbbing in the bloodvessels all through the body. This is not plethora, but only an appearance of plethora. It is associated with local congestions which are really anæmic in origin; the blood being normal volumetrically, but is not as rich in red corpuscles as it should be. The congestion to the head is associated with humming in the ears. The patient suffers from vertigo when he turns his head rapidly, or from riding in a carriage, or from anything that diminishes the supply of blood to the brain. He suffers from weakness of sight, especially following excessive sexual indulgence.

Again, we find *Kali carb*., by reason of this anæmia, indicated after severe or protracted diseases. It thus becomes useful for the weakness following labor or abortion when we have the following symptoms: there is a very troublesome backache, a weak, lame feeling in the small of the back, which makes walking very difficult to the patient; the patient suffers from cough and frequent sweating at night. You find persistent discharge of blood from the uterus. The urine is loaded with urates. This latter symptom, this excess of urates, shows great waste of tissue, and is evidence of the exhaustion which *Kali carb.* causes and cures.

You will recall that I mentioned *Kali carb.* as a drug which causes great exhaustion in the muscular system, and it is frequently in this kind of exhaustion that the urates are excessive in the urine.

Kali carb. acts not only on the voluntary muscles, but on the heart also. The heart becomes weakened when it is indicated. and you thus have a pulse which is irregular or intermittent, or. being rapid, is very weak. Now, this character of the pulse in *Kali carb.* will qualify every disease in which you may use the drug. It is a characteristic of the drug which lies at the very root of its symptoms; therefore, you will seldom find *Kali carb.* indicated when there is a full round pulse.

This condition of the urine, in which it is loaded with urates as evidence of exhaustion from disease, is also found under other remedies. Perhaps the best remedy in the materia medica for this symptom, other things being equal, is *Causticum.* Remember that this assertion is to be qualified. A symptom of this character has not the same value as a symptom of the mind would have. It is characteristic in its place, and yet, if symptoms more characteristic of the case indicate another drug, then you should not think of using *Causticum.* Suppose you have a patient whose other symptoms are those of *Kali carb.*, for example, a woman after confinement with backache, sweat, and other symptoms of importance, then you may give *Kali carb.* with confidence. But if you have a patient with no prominent symptoms, and with this excessive deposit of urates in the urine, *Causticum* will help you out.

Still another remedy for this symptom is *Senna,* which is one of the best remedies in the materia medica for simple exhaustion with excessive nitrogenous waste.

The particular combination of symptoms that we have under *Kali carb.*, the sweat, the backache and the weakness, are found in no other remedy. It acts as well with the high as the low potencies.

You may also remember the *Hypophosphite of Lime*, which comes near to the *Kali carb.* in the excessive sweating, weakness and pallor of the skin.

You may also remember, as akin to *Kali carb.*, *Psorinum*, which, as you have already learned, is eminently useful in convalescence from disease when there is great weakness, profuse sweat and, in addition, a mental state of abject hopelessness. The patient despairs of perfect recovery.

Next, let us look at the action of *Kali carb.* on the nervous system. Viewed mentally, the patient is excessively peevish and nervous, and is very easily startled. You often find this in women. They are startled by imaginary hallucinations; they imagine that some one is in the room or some figure comes before the mind and tantalizes them. Especially is this anxiety manifested on any noise, as the mere shutting of a door or window, particularly if the noise be unexpected. They are not only startled as many healthy persons would be under similar circumstances, but they are so frightened, that they are driven into a fit of trembling. You will sometimes find the intellect seriously impaired when *Kali carb.* is indicated. The patient does not seem to care for anything. This indifference is associated with great bodily exhaustion. When questioned, the patient, usually a female, does not seem to know exactly what to say or what she wants. The condition borders somewhat on that of *Phosphoric acid*, but still the apathy of the two remedies is not exactly the same. *Kali carb.* has not a sensorial apathy, but it has exhaustion too great to frame the answers to your questions. You will frequently find these symptoms of the mind calling for *Kali carb.* in puerperal mania and in puerperal fever.

Again, we find that spasms may occur as a symptom of the nervous system under *Kali carb.* The patient does not lose consciousness during the convulsions, hence the remedy is not indicated in true epilepsy; but it may be indicated in puerperal eclampsia, the spasms seeming to pass off with eructations of wind.

The spine suffers severely in the *Kali carb.* patient. In addition to the backache, already mentioned as the result of anæmia or of abortion, we have spinal irritation, which, by the way, is just as vague a symptom as is any other of a general character, as headache. You must always know what causes this spinal irritation. Does it come from loss of fluids, from brain troubles, from emotional causes, or what? In the *Kali carb.* patient you will find it frequently occurring with the uterine symptoms. Thus, you will have pressure in the small of the back as though there were a heavy weight pushing down there. There are also bearing down in the uterine region during the menses, burning along the spine, especially along the right side of the spine. This is not a real congestion. It is merely a subjective sensation caused by irritation of the posterior spinal nerves. The backache is worse while the patient is walking. She feels so exhausted that she must drop into a chair or support herself in some way. Sometimes you find, in the morning, a pulsation in the small of the back, quite akin to the pulsations occurring in other parts of the body. Here the drug is quite analogous to *Sepia* and the well-known *Cimicifuga*. This pulsating and drawing backache is particularly relieved when the patient lies down. This suggests a comparison between *Kali carb.* and *Natrum mur.* You will recognize at once the resemblance in the spinal symptoms, the spinal irritation, the backache and the relief from lying down. *Natrum mur.* has, particularly, relief by lying flat on the back with firm pressure. Further than this, you will find these two drugs playing into each other's hands in the treatment of amenorrhœa. Hahnemann says that *Kali carb.* will bring on the menstrual flow when *Natrum mur.*, though indicated, fails.

I once cured a singular backache with *Kali carb.* A very nervous patient came under my treatment for dyspepsia. She said to me: "There is something very strange about my case. Every time I eat a meal I suffer for half an hour or more with most intense pain in the back." This was certainly an odd symptom. I did not know where in the materia medica to find it. I hunted, and found under *Kali carb.* this symptom: pain in the spine while eating. I gave her *Kali carb.*, which cured her completely.

On the mucous membranes, *Kali carb.* acts, causing quite a series of catarrhal symptoms. We may give it in coryza with hoarseness or loss of voice. The patient catches cold at every little exposure to the fresh air. This is a very strong symptom of *Kali carb.* The *Kali carb.* patient has a tendency to obesity, and is rather weak in muscular development. With the catarrhal symptoms of this remedy there often occurs a sensation in the throat as though there were a lump there which must be swallowed. The neck is stiff and the uvula elongated. There are stinging pains in the throat when swallowing just as marked as under *Apis*.

Sometimes we have a more chronic form of catarrh in the nose: the nasal passages are obstructed, and the patient can only breathe with the mouth open. This obstruction is relieved in the open air, but returns so soon as the patient enters a warm room. There is either a discharge of fœtid green mucus or, in the morning, the nose is swollen and red, and there is a bloody discharge. There is a sticking sensation in the pharynx, as from a fish-bone lodged there, whenever the patient becomes cold. This is a good symptom for *Kali carb*. You will find it in *Allen's Encyclopædia* in large type.

Now, in addition to these symptoms, there is almost always accumulation of mucus in the pharynx. The patient "hawks and hems" in the morning. This hawking is found under every alkali, but this one peculiarity, sensation as of a fish-bone in the throat as soon as he "catches cold," *with the hawking*, is found under no other remedy. *Hepar*, *Nitric acid*. *Alumen*. *Carbo veg*. and *Argentum nitricum* all have this sensation as of a splinter or fish-bone in the throat.

In coughs, we sometimes find *Kali carb*. of use. The cough is of a paroxysmal character, and is accompanied by gagging and by vomiting of sour phlegm and of food. This suggests the use of *Kali carb*. in whooping cough, in which disease it has been very successful. Bœnninghausen has given us a characteristic symptom for *Kali carb*., namely, a little sac filled with water between the upper lids and eyebrows. You will often meet with that symptom. I would warn you not to confound it with a similar condition which is in no particular pathological at all, and that is a certain looseness of the tissues in this locality occurring in persons advanced in years.

Now for the action of *Kali carb*. on the lungs. We find it indicated in bronchitis, pneumonia and phthisis pulmonalis. I will give you the symptoms calling for it in these separate states as we go on. The most characteristic symptom of all, and one which runs through the symptomatology of the drug, is stitching pains which are prominently located in the walls of the chest. They are made worse by any motion, but unlike *Bryonia*, they come at all times independently of this aggravation. They occur characteristically in the lower third of the right lung, going through the chest to the back. They may occur all over the chest, but that above mentioned is their most frequent site. Then, too, they are erratic and wander all over the body. Here it reminds you of *Kali bichromicum*, *Pulsatilla* and *Sulphur*.

Kali carb. is indicated in infantile pneumonia or capillary bronchitis when the following symptoms are present: intense dyspnœa; although there is a great deal of mucus in the chest, it is raised with difficulty The child is so oppressed that it can neither sleep nor drink. Breathing is wheezing and whistling in character and the child has a choking cough. You should here compare *Kali carb.* carefully with *Antimonium tartaricum* and thus determine which suits the case best. One cannot be the remedy when the other is indicated.

In phthisis, *Kali carb.* is indicated when the constitution favors it. The patient has a bloated alkaline look to the face. There are also present these well-defined stitching pains through the chest and over the body, with the puffiness of the upper eyelids. Cough is difficult. The patient cannot get up the sputum. He raises it partly, when it slips backwards into the pharynx. Now, if you examine this expectoration, you will find that it is often bloody, and that there are little globules of pus scattered through it. There is an aggravation of all the symptoms from three to five o'clock in the morning. This hour of aggravation belongs to all the potash salts. There is also a very stubborn sensation, namely, chilliness at noon.

Kali carb. is indicated in cardiac inflammations, in endo- and pericarditis when these sharp stitching pains are characteristic. Do not give it too soon in the case. It is not an early remedy in cardiac disease. It is indicated rather late when there is a deposit on the cardiac valves. In such a case as this *Spigelia* is apt to precede the exhibition of *Kali carb.* The latter follows when the sharp pains persist and there is the characteristic 3 A. M. aggravation.

We find these same stitching pains under *Kali carb.* in lumbago, a very stubborn form of rheumatism. The same symptom applies in cases of impending miscarriage and during labor; sharp stitching pains in the lumbar region shooting down from the buttocks into the thighs.

The same kind of pain suggests this remedy in nephritis from cold, or from a blow over the region of the kidneys.

Lastly, in connection with the stitching pains, I want to refer you to its application in puerperal fever of the metritic form, that is, when metritis is a prominent condition. There are sharp, stabbing, cutting pains in the abdomen, the abdomen is bloated and distended, and the urine is dark and scanty, the pulse is rapid but feeble, and you have present the state of mind described in the early part of the lecture.

One more symptom and we are done with the drug, and that is its use in dyspepsia. You will find it called for in indigestion, particularly in old persons, in those who have lost a great deal of vital fluids, when there is an empty, weak feeling in the stomach before eating and bloatedness after eating, especially after soup or coffee. There are sour eructations, heart-burn, and uneasy, nervous feeling when hungry.

You see then that *Kali carb.* is a remedy indicated in a great variety of diseases. It is a drug much neglected in practice, for the same reason that many other remedies are—because the hurried and careless physician falls into routinism.

INDEX OF REMEDIES.

ABIES CANADENSIS
  prolapsus uteri, 146
ABIES NIGRA
  dyspepsia, 305, 350, 370
  mental symptoms, 305
ABROTANUM
  see Artemesia Abrotanum
ABSINTHIUM, 243
  epilepsy, 420
  delirium tremens, 243
  typhoid fever, 243
ACALYPHA INDICA
  haemoptysis, 369
  haemorrhages, 369
ACETIC ACID
  dropsy, 104
ACIDS
  remarks on the, 515
ACONITIC ACID, 315, 336
ACONITINE, 315
ACONITUM FEROX, 314
ACONITUM NAPELLUS, 314
  abortion, 325
  amenorrhoea, 674
  cerebral congestion, 320
  cholera infantum, 324
  colic 287, 324
  conjunctivitis, 321, 397
  continued fever, 316
  coryza, 294, 326
  croup, 323, 505, 684
  diarrhoea, 324
  dysmenorrhoea, 325
  dysentery, 324
  episcieritis, 321
  eyes, 321, 397
  fever, 291, 316, 318
  gastric catarrh, 324
  gastric fever, 291
  gastritis, 324
  glaucoma, 321
  haemoptysis, 324
  haemorrhages, 243
  headache, 200
  heart, 225, 322, 507, 514
  hernia, 325
  hypertrophy of the heart, 323, 508
  inflammations, 36, 99, 316
  labor, 325
  measles, 174, 326, 361
  meningitis, 294, 320, 407
  mental symptoms, 316, 321, 405
  milk fever, 325
  nephritis, 325
  nervous system, 315

ACONITUM NAPELLUS (Continued)
  neuralgia, 321, 322
  paralysis, 315, 322, 731
  pleurisy, 293, 323
  pleurodynia, 331
  pneumonia, 295, 323
  poisoning, 315
  pregnancy, 325
  puerperal fever, 321, 325
  pulse, 317
  scarlatina, 325
  serous membranes, 293
  skin, 326
  sunstroke, 320
  tetanus 180
  typhoid fever, 317
  worms, 246
ACTEA RACEMOSA, 327
  abortion, 328
  after-pains, 328
  angina pectoris, 329
  chorea, 74
  cough, 329
  dysmenorrhoea, 202, 648
  eyes, 327
  female genital organs, 143, 328, 356
  headache, 176, 328
  heart, 225
  hysteria, 76
  labor, 328
  loquacity, 39
  myalgia, 143, 327
  nervous system, 76, 143, 327
  neuralgia, 327, 356
  phthisis, 329
  pregnancy, 328
  pleurodynia, 296, 329
  puerperal mania, 328
  spinal irritation, 329, 739
  uterine diseases, 327, 356
ACTEA SPICATA
  amenorrhoea, 674
  rheumatism, 297, 327
AESCULUS HIPPOCASTANUM
  back, 606
  follicular pharyngitis, 722
  haemorrhoids, 187
AETHUSA CYNAPIUM, 450
  awkwardness, 102
  colic, 710
  dentition, 420
  vomiting, 450, 578, 671
AGARICUS MUSCARIUS
  blepharospasmus, 189
  chorea, 74, 79

INDEX OF REMEDIES.

AGARICUS MUSCARIUS (Continued)
  delirium, 423
  eyes, 203
  loquacity, 39
  spinal irritation, 329
  torticollis, 194
AGNUS CASTUS
  agalactia, 356
  sexual excesses, 674
  spermatorrhoea, 175
AILANTHUS
  diphtheria, 212, 403
  erysipelas, 417
  hay fever, 557
  scarlatina, 212, 233, 403
  typhoid fever, 403
ALCOHOL
  diphtheria, 211
ALETRIS FARINOSA
  constipation, 359
  neurasthenia, 359
  prolapsus uteri, 146
  uterine diseases, 359
ALLIUM CEPA
  see Cepa
ALLIUM SATIVA
  skin, 85
ALOE SOCOTRINA
  alimentary canal, 478
  diarrhoea, 137, 165, 166
  dysentery, 188
  female genital organs, 478
  haemorrhoids, 137, 187, 478
  headache, 137, 187
  liver, 137
  prolapsus uteri, 137
ALSTONIA SCHOLARIS, 168
  diarrhœa, 168
  intermittent fever, 168
ALUMEN
  corneal opacities, 669
  haemorrhage, 537
  typhoid fever, 537
ALUMINA, 616
  anaemia, 618
  antidotal relations, 616, 620
  aphonia, 619
  asthenopia, 619, 655
  blepharitis, 619
  blood, 618
  buboes, 620
  chlorosis, 617, 618
  complementary relations, 617
  constipation, 186, 271, 461, 617
  constitution, 617
  cough, 619
  dyspepsia, 618, 619
  eyes, 131, 619
  gastric symptoms, 619
  glands, 620
  granular lids, 619
  hypochondriasis, 618
  lead colic, 620, 621
  leucorrhoea, 618
  locomotor ataxia, 541, 618
  menses, 152, 158
  mental symptoms, 617

ALUMINA (Continued).
  mucous membranes, 618
  nasal catarrh, 617, 619
  nervous system, 195
  ozaena, 617
  ptosis, 131, 170, 618
  skin, 620
  spine, 541
  strabismus, 617, 618
  throat, 619, 685, 740
ALUMINUM MET.
  locomotor ataxia, 618
AMBRA GRISEA, 151
  asthma, 152
  constipation, 152
  cough, 151, 152, 546, 661
  epistaxis, 152
  female genital organs 151
  insomnia, 151
  leucorrhoea, 152
  lying-in, 152
  metrorrhagia, 152
  nasal catarrh, 661
  nervous system, 151, 195, 715
  reaction, defective, 121, 151, 270, 465, 629
  softening of brain and spine, 151
  varices, 152
  vertigo, 151
  whooping cough 152
AMBROSIA ARTEMESIAFOLIA
  hay fever, 332
AMMONIACUM GUMMI, 449
  asthenopia, 449
  chest symptoms, 120
  hysteria, 116, 120
AMMONIUM
  preparations of, 657
AMMONIUM BENZOICUM
  urine, 66
AMMONIUM CARB., 658
  antidotal relation, 222, 658
  asphyxia, 661
  blood, 658
  bronchitis, 660
  cerebro-spinal-meningitis, 659
  constitution, 657
  coryza, 661
  cough, 661
  emphysema, 485, 660
  heart, 601, 659
  inimical relation, 658
  menses, 65
  mucous membranes, 658
  nasal catarrh, 661
  nervous system, 79
  paralysis of the lungs, 582, 659
  pneumonia, 659
  poisoning by charcoal fumes, 659
  rhus poisoning, 222
  scarlatina, 659, 660
  sprains, 662
  scurvy, 659
  uraemia, 659
AMMONIUM CAUST.
  aphonia, 662
  coryza, 662
  diphtheria, 211

INDEX OF REMEDIES. 745

AMMONIUM CAUST. (Continued).
  skin, 85
AMMONIUM MUR., 662
  bronchitis, 664
  circulation, 662
  constitution, 657, 662
  constipation, 664
  coryza, 661, 664
  cough, 662, 664
  face, 662
  female genital organs, 663
  heels, 663
  intermittent fever, 662
  joints, 663
  leucorrhoea, 664
  liver, 187, 664
  nasal catarrh, 661
  nervous system, 662
  neuralgia, 662
  phthisis, 664
  scarlatina, 664
  sciatica, 663
  sprains, 663
  tonsillitis, 664
AMMONIUM PHOS.
  gout, 656, 665
  joints, 656
AMYGDALA AMARA
  diphtheria, 213, 414
  tonsillitis, 414
AMYGDALA PERSICA, 161
AMYL NITRITE
  See Nitrite of Amyl
ANACARDIACEAE, 217
ANACARDIUM OCCIDENTALE
  erysipelas, 221
  rhus poisoning, 221
  skin, 85, 221
ANACARDIUM ORIENTALE, 218
  antidotal relation, 222
  anus, 165
  constipation, 219
  coryza, 221
  cough, 513
  gastralgia, 497
  gastric symptoms, 219
  haemorrhoids, 220
  headache, 219
  heart, 221
  hypochondriasis, 219
  joints, 221
  mental fatigue, 219
  mental symptoms, 218, 219, 302
  pericarditis, 221
  pregnancy, 220
  profanity, 219
  rheumatism, 231
  skin, 85, 220
  spinal cord, 221
  suicidal tendency, 219
  torticollis, 231
  typhoid fever, 218
  variola, 218
  vomiting of pregnancy, 220
ANGUSTURA, 180
  caries of bones, 545
  cough, 152

ANGUSTURA (Continued).
  injuries, 180
  necrosis of lower jaw, 180
  podarthrocace, 180
  scapular pain, 282
  tetanus, 180
ANILINE SULPHATE, 479
ANISUM STELLATUM
  chest pains, 83, 306
  phthisis, 83
ANTHRACINUM
  carbuncle, 80, 232, 501
ANTIMONIUM ARSENICOSUM
  emphysema, 558
ANTIMONIUM CRUDUM, 577
  callosities, 332, 579
  complementary relations, 577
  diarrhoea, 578
  diphtheria, 580
  eczema, 579
  eyes, 580
  female genital organs, 580
  gastric catarrh, 351, 378, 578
  gout, 580
  heels, 663
  lungs, 627
  marasmus, 645
  mental symptoms, 219, 308, 577
  nails, 579
  nasal catarrh, 497
  ophthalmia, 217
  prolapsus uteri, 580
  skin, 86, 579, 702
  teeth, 340
  tongue, 578
  vomiting, 450, 578, 671
  wine, aggravation from, 632
ANTIMONIUM TART., 580
  antidotal relation, 583
  asphyxia neonatorum, 582
  capillary bronchitis, 381, 581, 686
  complementary relation, 649
  cough, 270, 582, 583
  croup, 505
  eyes, 583
  headache, 581
  intestinal symptoms, 583
  laryngismus stridulus, 504
  lungs, 627
  measles, 581, 583
  mental symptoms, 581
  ophthalmia, 300
  paralysis of the lungs, 485, 582, 650
  pneumonia, 279, 283, 295, 583
  scarlatina, 581, 583
  skin, 85, 581
  suppressed eruptions, 303, 581
  variola, 303, 581, 583
  vomiting, 265, 387
  whooping cough, 581
ANTIMONY
  remarks on preparations of, 576
APIS MELLIFICA, 98
  albuminuria, 66
  amenorrhoea, 112
  antidotal relations, 114
  aphthous sore mouth, 47

746 INDEX OF REMEDIES.

APIS MELLIFICA (Continued).
  apoplexy, 100, 269
  asthenopia, 113
  asthma, 110
  awkwardness, 102
  complementary relationships, 114
  conjunctivitis, 113, 217
  corneal opacities, 669
  cough, 111
  cystitis, 93
  diarrhoea, 114, 166
  diphtheria, 51, 95, 107, 109, 213, 413
  dropsy, 66, 67, 102
  dysuria, 245
  erysipelas, 46, 106, 232, 417
  eyes, 113, 217
  face, 44
  female genital organs, 112, 615, 664
  fever, 317
  heart, 103, 110
  hydrocephaloid, 114
  hydrocephalus, 103
  hydropericardium, 110
  hydrothorax, 103, 110
  hysteria, 100, 112
  inflammation, 99
  inimical relation, 114
  intermittent fever, 70, 107
  keratitis, 383
  kidneys, 559
  larynx, 110
  mammary abscess, 574
  meningitis, 100, 294
  mental symptoms, 99
  modalities, 114
  mode of preparation, 98
  oedema glottidis, 110
  oedema pulmonum, 110
  ovarian tumor, 64, 112
  ovaries, 64, 112
  ovaritis, 112
  panaritium, 114
  paralysis, 107
  pleurisy, 103, 472
  poisoning by, 99
  post-scarlatinal dropsy, 67
  prolapsus, 64, 113
  pulse, 317
  relationships, 114
  rheumatism, 107
  scarlatina, 100, 108, 109, 524, 660
  scrofulous ophthalmia, 113
  soreness, 36
  staphyloma, 113
  stomatitis, 95
  suppressed eruptions, 100
  synovitis, 103, 296, 353
  tubercular meningitis, 100, 103, 337, 470
  typhoid fever, 40, 100, 107, 108, 268, 523
  urine, 66
  urticaria, 106, 705
  uterus, 112
  variola, 107
  vertigo, 82
APIUM VIRUS, 98
APOCYNACEAE, 163
APOCYNUM CANNABINUM, 163

APOCYNUM CANNABINUM (Continued)
  ascites, 104
  diarrhoea, 164
  dropsy, 104, 163, 337
  fatty degeneration of heart, 164
  haemorrhoids, 165
  heart, 111, 164
  hydrocephalus, 164
  hydrothorax, 104
  joints, 164
  rheumatism, 164
  urine, 163
APOMORPHIA
  sea-sickness, 265
  vomiting, 265, 436
ARACEAE, 208
ARACHNIDA, 73
ARALIA RAC.
  asthma, 727
ARANEA DIADEMA
  bones, 81
  constitution, 80, 81
  diarrhoea, 81
  headache, 81
  intermittent fever, 80, 373
  nervous system, 81
  toothache, 81
ARCTIUM LAPPA
  crusta lactea, 168
  polyuria, 168
  rheumatism, 298
ARGEMONE MEXICANA
  skin, 274
  ape worm, 274
ARGENTUM METALLICUM, 611
  arthralgia, 509, 611
  chlorosis, 599
  debility, 611
  epilepsy, 611
  heart, 611
  joints, 611
  larynx, 611
  neuralgia, 611
  ovaries, 611, 616
  prolapsus uteri, 599, 616
ARGENTUM NITRICUM, 605
  angina pectoris, 608
  antidotal relations, 610
  asthenopia,, 609
  asthma, 608
  blepharitis, 609
  brain, 605
  cholera infantum, 610
  chorea, 629
  conjunctivitis, 347
  diarrhoea, 166, 176, 255, 610, 643
  epilepsy, 608
  eyes, 608, 619
  female genitals, 616
  gastralgia, 607
  gastro-enteric symptoms, 554
  gonorrhoea, 91
  granular conjunctivitis, 609
  headache, 605, 606
  hemicrania, 606
  kidneys, 610
  larynx, 609

INDEX OF REMEDIES. 747

ARGENTUM NITRICUM (Continued).
 locomotor ataxia, 606
 marasmus, 272. 534
 mental symptoms, 605
 mouth, 609
 nephralgia, 610
 nervous system, 606
 neurasthenia, 541
 ophthalmia, 217, 347
 ophthalmia neonatorum, 347, 608
 ovaries, 605
 paralysis, 606
 poisoning by, 600
 prosopalgia, 607
 puerperal convulsions, 608
 purulent ophthalmia, 608
 renal calculi, 610
 scrofulous ophthalmia, 702
 spinal cord, 605, 620
 throat, 609, 619, 685, 740
 urinary organs, 91
 urine, 610
 uterus, 615
 vertigo, 605
 vomiting, 607
ARNICA MONTANA, 237
 abscess, 242
 antidotal relations, 658
 apoplexy, 242, 269
 apoplexy of retina, 43
 asphyxia from charcoal, 158, 273, 659
 bed sores, 242
 bloodvessels, 238
 boils, 242
 cholera infantum, 22, 242
 conjunctivitis, 397
 cough, 152, 732
 diarrhoea, 242
 dysentery, 242
 dyspepsia, 242
 ecchymoses of the sclerotic, 190
 enteritis, 60
 female genital organs, 664
 gout, 369
 hypertrophy of heart, 225, 239, 323, 507
 hemiplegia, 242
 injuries, 239, 532
 lying-in, 242
 muscular exertion, 229, 239
 myalgia, 240
 peritonitis, 60
 pleurodynia, 296
 pyaemia, 241
 relationship, 237
 retinal apoplexy, 43
 rheumatism, 240
 skin, 242
 sprains, 229, 238, 654, 662
 soreness, 239
 testicles, 352
 typhoid fever, 40, 228, 239, 336, 402, 527, 659
 urine, 66
 vertigo, 82
 whooping cough, 242
ARNICIN, 238
ARSENICUM ALBUM, 549

ARSENICUM ALBUM (Continued)
 abdomen, 488
 albuminuria, 67, 559
 angina pectoris, 559
 antidotal relations, 372, 541
 aortitis, 486
 aphthous sore mouth, 47
 asthma, 381, 558, 727
 bladder, 271
 blood, 552
 boils, 561
 Bright's disease, 559
 burns, 97
 cancer, 552, 561
 carbuncle, 232, 552, 561
 catarrhs, 380, 557
 cholera Asiatica, 156, 553
 cholera infantum, 553
 cholera morbus, 156, 553
 chorea, 79
 collapse, 69
 complementary relations, 549
 conjunctivitis, 113, 397
 continued fever, 316, 557
 convulsions, 44
 coryza, 380, 557
 cough, 111, 152
 croup, 560
 debility, 367, 369
 delirium tremens, 269, 551
 diarrhoea, 55, 166, 370, 553, 642
 diphtheria, 110. 213, 558
 dropsy, 66, 104, 164, 337, 445, 558
 drunkards, complaints of, 55, 187
 dysentery, 488, 553
 dyspepsia, 54, 55, 185, 350, 351, 487
 eczema, 559
 endocarditis. 558
 enteritis, 553
 epilepsy, 561
 eyes, 397
 face, 44
 fatty degeneration of the heart, 572
 fever, 320, 467, 556
 fever blisters, 705
 gangrena oris, 47
 gangrene, 156, 552, 560
 gastric catarrh, 378, 379
 gastric symptoms, 54, 55, 350, 378, 487
 gastritis, 54, 185, 324, 553
 general action, 551
 haemorrhages, 482
 haemorrhoids, 487, 551
 hay fever, 332, 557
 headache, 701
 heart, 111, 164, 239, 514, 558
 hectic fever, 373
 hemicrania, 129, 561
 herpes zoster, 332
 hiccough, 203
 hydrocephaloid, 102
 hydropericardium, 111. 559
 hydrothorax, 559
 hypertrophy of the heart, 239
 hysteria, 614
 inflammation of the brain, 94
 inflammations, 96, 552

48

INDEX OF REMEDIES.

ARSENICUM ALBUM (Continued)
  intermittent fever, 69, 372, 555
  jaundice, 187
  kidneys, 67, 559
  laryngismus stridulus, 504
  lead colic, 621
  lungs, 374
  marasmus, 553
  meningitis, 102
  menorrhagia, 482
  mental symptoms, 443, 551, 612
  metrorrhagia, 65, 482
  mucous membranes, 557
  mumps, 245
  muscular exertion, 230, 521
  nervous system, 79
  neuralgia, 467, 555
  oesophagitis, 414
  ovaries, 65
  ovaritis, 552
  pericarditis, 558
  phlyctenular ophthalmia, 397
  poisoning by, 550
  prosopalgia, 614
  psoriasis, 707
  puerperal mania, 328
  retention of urine, 271
  scarlatina, 528, 558, 560
  scrofulous ophthalmia, 494, 495, 702
  skin, 559
  syncope, 37
  throat, 95, 596
  tongue, 333, 553, 698
  tuberculosis, 552
  typhoid fever, 227, 252, 430, 467, 537, 552, 555
  ulcers, 62, 63, 156, 445, 561
  uraemia, 94
  urine, 66
  urticaria, 107, 560
  vertigo, 37, 82
  vomiting, 565, 672
  wine, aggravation from, 632
ARSENICUM IODATUM
  cancer, 561
  coryza, 557
  crusta lactea, 168
  diphtheria, 558
  hay fever, 557
  psoriasis, 125, 707
  throat, 596
ARSENICUM MET.
  tongue, 454
ARTEMISIA ABROTANUM, 244
  haemorrhoids, 245
  marasmus, 245
  mumps, 245
  myelitis, 244
  rheumatism, 245
  stomach, 341
ARTEMISIA TRIDENTATA, 237
  biliousness, 244
ARTEMISIA VULGARIS, 242
  asthenopia, 243
  convulsions, 624
  emotions, 242
  epilepsy, 30, 242, 420, 676

ARTEMISIA VULGARIS (Continued).
  eyes, 243
  worms, 624
ARTICULATA, 31
ARUM MACULATUM
  skin, 85
ARUM TRIPHYLLUM, 208
  aphonia, 210, 462
  diphtheria, 233, 444, 535
  inflammation of the brain, 210
  larynx, 210
  mental symptoms, 209
  nasal catarrh, 498
  scarlatina, 208, 233, 535
  skin, 85
  sore mouth, 711
  throat, 95, 209
  uraemia, 209
ARUNDO MAUR.
  catarrh, 661
ASAFOETIDA, 449
  antidotal relations, 450, 587
  bones, 119, 450, 545
  eyes, 450
  hysteria, 119, 120, 198, 449
  iritis, 450, 602
  nervous system, 79, 119, 120, 449
  periostitis, 450
  reaction, lack of, 121
  syphilis, 602
  ulcers, 62, 119, 450, 545, 602
ASARUM EUROPAEUM
  nervous symptoms, 79, 195
ASCLEPIAS TUB.
  pleurodynia, 296
ASPARAGUS
  heart, 111
ATROPINE, 405
AURUM METALLICUM, 600
  albuminuria, 603
  antidotal relations, 586, 600
  bones, 604
  cervix uteri, 139
  cirrhosis of the liver, 36, 603
  congestions, 599
  congestion of the head, 601
  congestion of the liver, 603
  diplopia, 601
  ears, 43, 491, 602
  eyes, 601
  face, 599
  fatty degeneration of the liver, 603
  female genital organs, 603, 615
  general action, 139
  glaucoma, 601
  heart, 600, 656
  hemiopia, 601, 702
  hyperaemia, 599
  hypertrophy of the heart, 323, 601
  iritis, 450, 601
  kidneys, 559, 603
  lungs, 603
  mastoid process, caries of, 435, 491, 602
  mental symptoms, 139, 603
  nasal catarrh, 602
  orchitis, 603
  otorrhoea, 602

INDEX OF REMEDIES. 749

AURUM METALLICUM (Continued)
  ozaena, 49, 602
  pannus, 601
  prolapsus uteri, 139, 603, 613
  retinal congestion, 602
  scrofulous, 599
  scrofulous ophthalmia, 599, 601
  swelling of, 43
  syphilis, 601, 602
  testicles, 352
  throat, 602
  uterus, 139, 603, 615
AURUM MURIATICUM
  cervix uteri, 139
  heart, 601
AURUM MURIATICUM NATRONATUM
  cervix uteri, 139
  prolapsus uteri, 603

BADIAGA
  buboes, 31, 490
  enlarged lymphatics, 31
  heart 31
  syphilis, 491
BALSAM OF PERU
  bronchitis, 215
  lungs, 627
  phthisis, 627
BAPTISIA TINCTORIA, 398
  aphthae, 47
  diphtheria, 212, 403
  dysentery, 403
  enteritis, 59
  face, 44
  mental symptoms, 398, 437
  peritonitis, 59
  phthisis, 403
  relationships, 403
  scarlatina, 212
  typhoid fever, 40, 228, 239, 272, 399, 467, 523
BARYTA CARBONICA, 649
  amblyopia, 652
  aneurism, 650
  apoplexy, 268, 650
  asthma, 652
  brain, 651
  capillary bronchitis, 582
  cataract, 575
  complementary relations, 582, 649
  constitution, 649
  cough, 652
  drunkards, 268, 650
  cretinism, 679
  ears, 652
  enlarged tonsils, 651
  fatty tumors, 652
  glossoplegia, 650
  headache, 652
  herpes circinatus, 125, 705
  mental symptoms, 650, 679
  multiple sclerosis of brain and spinal cord, 650
  ophthalmia, scrofulous, 652
  paralysis, 650, 731
  paralysis of the lungs, 650
  poisoning by, 649

BARYTA CARBONICA (Continued).
  post-nasal catarrh, 652, 656
  scrofulosis, 649, 652
  senility, 649
  sweat, 653
  tabes mesenterica, 652
  throat, 651
  tonsillitis, 651
BARYTA MURIATICA
  brain, 650
  multiple sclerosis of brain and spinal cord, 650
BELLADONNA, 405
  abscess, 419, 592
  amenorrhoea, 674
  antidotal relations, 516, 600, 628
  apoplexy, 268, 269
  asthenopia, 449
  anus, 60
  biliary calculi, 192
  blepharospasm, 189
  boils, 419
  brain, 235, 320, 335, 407
  cancer, 561
  cholera infantum, 411, 419
  chorea, 77
  climaxis, 233
  colic, 419, 621
  coma, 409
  complementary relations, 406, 419, 422
  congestions, 407, 591
  conjunctivitis, 412
  convulsions, 201, 408, 420
  coryza, 326
  cough, 111, 421, 570
  delirium, 355, 429
  dentition, 249
  diarrhoea, 419
  diphtheria, 214, 413
  dysentery, 419
  enteritis, 59, 419
  enuresis, 416, 734
  epilepsy, 420
  erysipelas, 45, 106, 407, 416
  erythema, 416
  eyes, 397, 412, 449
  face, 44, 409, 411
  female genital organs, 420, 615
  fever, 292, 319, 409
  gastralgia, 414
  gastric symptoms, 350, 414
  general character, 406
  glands, 233
  haemorrhage, 368, 421
  headache, 82, 277, 408, 411
  heart, 111
  hemicrania, 128
  hydrophobia, 94
  hysteria, 77, 199
  inflammation, 99, 407, 591
  labor, 421
  laryngismus stridulus, 504
  lead colic, 621
  lungs, 627
  mammary abscess, 301, 419, 569
  measles, 174
  meningitis, 94, 101, 105, 294, 407, 409, 591

BELLADONNA (Continued)
  mental symptoms, 218, 294, 682
  menses, 421, 613
  metritis, 415
  metrorrhagia, 272, 421
  nervous system, 408
  neuralgia, 419, 613, 682
  oesophagitis, 414
  otalgia, 683, 708
  otitis media, 348, 411
  parotitis, 412
  peritonitis, 59, 415
  poisoning by, 405
  puerperal convulsions, 420
  puerperal metritis, 415
  puerperal peritonitis, 415
  pulse, 317
  pupil, 405
  quinsy, 414
  retinal congestion, 602
  rectum and anus, 60
  relationships, 419, 422
  renal colic, 191
  rheumatism, 407, 422
  scarlatina, 71, 100, 109, 233, 302, 417, 428
    443, 634, 660
  sciatica, 419
  scleritis, 412
  skin, 416
  sleep, 109, 454
  soreness, 36
  speech, 591
  sphincters, 406
  strabismus, 617
  sunstroke, 38, 320
  temperament, 406
  tetanus, 181
  throat, 95, 173, 412, 596
  tonsillitis, 414, 592
  torticollis, 194, 422
  typhlitis, 59
  typhoid fever, 292, 410
  urine, 416
  vomiting, 266, 417
BENZOIC ACID
  dysuria, 711
  enuresis, 247
  gout, 453, 656
  heart, 656
  joints, 656
  rheumatism, 453
  urine, 66, 534
BERBERIDACEAE, 451
BERBERINE, 451
BERBERIS VULGARIS, 451
  alkaloids of, 151
  backache, 361
  biliary calculi, 192, 452
  eyes, 619
  female genitals, 452
  fistula in ano, 452
  gout, 453
  joints, 453
  kidneys, 93, 451
  leucorrhoea, 452
  liver, 299, 452
  menses, 452

BERBERIS VULG. (Continued)
  metritis, 452
  peritonitis, 452
  renal colic, 93, 192
  rheumatism, 453
  stools, 452
  urinary organs, 93, 452
  urine, 452
BISMUTH
  gastralgia, 185, 415, 608
  vomiting, 565
BLATTA, 32
  dropsy, 32
BOMBUS, 98
BORAX VENETA, 708
  aphthous stomatitis, 710
  colic, 710
  constitution, 708
  cough, 710
  diarrhoea, 710
  dysuria, 711
  erysipelas, 711
  eyes, 710
  leucorrhoea, 710
  lungs, 710
  mucous membranes, 710
  nervous system, 708
  nose, 710
  otalgia, 708
  otorrhoea, 708
  phthisis, 711
  skin, 711
  throat, 710
  trichiasis, 710
  ulcers, 125, 711
BOTHROPS LANCIOLATUS
  aphasia, 33
BOVISTA, 157
  asphyxia, 158, 273, 659
  awkwardness, 102
  circulation, 157
  colic, 287
  epistaxis, 157
  headache, 158
  heart, 158
  herpes, 157
  menses, 158
  mental symptoms, 102
  metrorrhagia, 157
  oedema, 159
  speech, 425
  wine, aggravation from, 632
  urticaria, 107
BROMINE, 502
  asthma, 507
  brain, 502
  cancer, 503
  conjunctivitis, 507
  coryza, 504
  croup, 504, 684
  dentition, 504
  epistaxis, 502, 507
  glands, 503
  goitre, 503
  headache, 504
  hypertrophy of the heart, 225, 239, 507
  laryngismus stridulus, 504

BROMINE (Continued).
  mammae, 503
  mental symptoms, 502
  mucous membranes, 503
  nasal catarrh, 504
  pneumonia, 507
  scrofulous, 503
  testicles, 503
  thymus, 504
  tonsillitis, 503
  tuberculosis, 507
  ulcers, 510
  vertigo, 502
BRUCIA, 177
BRUCIA ANTIDYSENTERICA, 180
BRYONIA ALBA, 289
  alimentary canal, 298
  antidotal relations, 303, 617
  blood, 289
  bronchitis, 296, 570
  complementary relations, 303, 617
  constipation, 186, 271, 298, 461, 617, 686
  coryza, 294
  cough, 111, 296, 693, 703
  diarrhoea, 114, 299, 453, 474, 724
  dyspepsia, 298
  epistaxis, 291
  eyes, 300
  face, 246
  female genital organs, 301
  fever, 289, 317
  gastric catarrh, 378, 578
  gastric fever, 290
  gastro-enteric symptoms, 248
  glaucoma, 300
  headache, 40, 82, 289, 300, 701
  heart, 298
  hypochondriasis, 618
  intermittent fever, 229
  jaundice, 187, 299
  joints, 453
  liver, 207, 282, 298
  mammary abscess, 301
  measles, 302
  meningitis, 101, 105, 294, 407
  menses, 301
  mental symptoms, 299, 619
  milk fever, 301
  nasal cararrh, 294
  ophthalmia, 300
  peritonitis, 293
  pleurisy, 293, 295
  pleurodynia, 295, 570
  pneumonia, 295, 323
  rheumatism, 297, 353
  scarlatina, 302, 418
  serous membranes, 293
  sore mouth, 301, 710
  suppressed eruptions, 101, 294, 302
  sweat, 300
  synovitis, 103, 296, 353
  tongue, 568, 578
  toothache, 300
  torticollis, 422
  typhilitis, 59
  typhoid fever, 261, 290, 523
  whooping cough, 296

BRYONIA ALBA (Continued)
  urine, 301
BUFO
  epilepsy, 30, 547, 676
  face, 44
  peritonitis, 30
  skin, 30
  ulcers, 30, 63

CACTUS GRANDIFLORUS
  asthma, 633
  diaphragmitis, 331
  haemoptysis, 324
  heart, 225, 239
  hypertrophy of the heart, 236. 323
  neuralgia, 419, 555
  uterus, 133
CADMIUM SULPH.
  asthma, 633
  indigestion, 55
  vomiting, 554
  yellow fever, 555
CAFFEINE
  general action, 383
CALADIUM SEGUINUM
  asthma, 214
  masturbation, 247
  nymphomania, 613
  seminal emissions, 175, 215
  sexual excesses, 175, 339
  spermatorrhoea, 175, 215
  worms, 247
CAJUPUTUM, 203
CALCAREA ACETICA
  vomiting, 450
CALCAREA CAUSTICA
  skin, 85
CALCAREA FLUORICA
  bones, 519
  lumbago, 677
  osteoma, 519, 666
CALCAREA HYPOPHOSPHORICA, 667
  debility, 738
CALCAREA IOD.
  enlarged tonsils, 651
CALCAREA OSTREARUM, 668
  amenorrhoea, 673
  bones, 676
  cataract, 575
  cholera infantum, 671
  complementary relations, 672
  conjunctivitis, 235
  constitution, 493, 668, 677
  corneal opacity, 669
  corneal ulcers, 669
  convulsions, 669
  cough, 421
  delirium, 269
  delirium tremens, 269, 675
  dentition, 669
  diarrhoea, 671, 687
  eczema, 670
  enuresis, 416, 734
  epilepsy, 676, 734
  epistaxis, 671
  face, 668
  female genital organs, 145, 673
  gastric symptoms, 415

INDEX OF REMEDIES.

CALCAREA OSTREARUM (Continued)
glands, 671
gout, 453, 656, 677
headache, 701
herpes circinatus, 125
hip-joint disease, 676
hydrocephalus, 672
hysteria, 614
insomnia, 675
joints, 652, 676
leucorrhoea, 674
lumbago, 677
lungs, 627, 673
marasmus, 569, 645
meningitis, 409
menorrhagia, 673
menses, 672, 673
mental symptoms, 293, 617
nasal catarrh, 498, 671
nervous system, 195, 675
neurasthenia, 624
opacities of the cornea, 669
otitis externa, 670
otitis media, 670
otorrhoea, 670
parotitis, 443
phthisis, 536, 673
polypi, 570
post-nasal catarrh, 656
prolapsus uteri, 145
puerperal mania, 328
rheumatism, 453, 656, 677
scarlatina, 233, 418, 635
scrofulosis, 494, 495, 545, 591, 669
scrofulous ophthalmia, 494, 495, 669
seminal emissions, 175, 192
sexual excesses, 192, 339, 477, 674
sprains, 229
stomach, 132
sweat, 663
temperament, 406
throat, 498
tonsillitis, 651
tuberculosis, 470, 672
typhoid fever, 293, 442, 675
ulcers, 534
ulcers of cornea, 669
urine, 453
urticaria, 107, 667, 705
vomiting, 450, 671
CALCAREA PHOSPHORICA, 678
bones, 241, 680
chlorosis, 680
cholera infantum, 380, 679
complementary relations, 678
constitution, 678
cretinism, 679
diarrhoea, 672
female genital organs, 145, 679
fistula in ano, 452
fractures, 241, 680
hydrocephaloid, 367, 380, 636, 680
joints, 679, 680
laryngismus stridulus, 504
leucorrhoea, 145
lungs, 627, 673
marasmus, 680

CALCAREA PHOSPHORICA (Continued).
polypi, 570
prolapsus uteri, 145, 146, 625
rachitis, 679
rheumatism, 679
tabes mesenterica, 653
tonsillitis, 651
tuberculosis, 670
CALCAREA SULPHURICA
boils, 667
croup, 667
CALENDULA
injuries, 241
CALTHA
pemphigus, 87
skin, 85
CAMPHOR
antidotal relations, 116, 481, 658
cholera Asiatica, 156, 256, 484, 629
cholera morbus, 156, 380
convulsions, 45, 94
collapse, 69, 484, 629
diphtheria, 481
epistaxis, 481
erysipelas, 86
face, 44, 45
inflammation, 94
inflammation of the brain, 94
intermittent fever, 69
reaction, defective, 121
scarlatina, 635
seminal emissions, 175
skin, 85, 86
strangury, 93
sexual mania, 94
sunstroke, 38
syncope, 37, 38
tetanus, 183
urinary organs, 93
vertigo, 37
CANCHALAGUA
intermittent fever, 372
CANNABIS INDICA
backache, 361
chordee, 90
delirium tremens, 269
gonorrhoea, 90
headache, 90
kidneys, 90
mental symptoms, 89, 269
paralysis, 322
uraemia, 90
urinary organs, 90
CANNABIS SATIVA
chordee, 89
gonorrhoea, 89
leucorrhoea, 674
nephritis, 89
CANTHARIS, 84
alimentary canal, 95
antidotal relations, 93
bladder, 88
brain, 93
Bright's disease, 88
burns, 97
chordee, 96
cystitis, 88, 89, 351

INDEX OF REMEDIES.   753

CANTHARIS (Continued)
    diphtheria, 95, 435
    dysentery, 95, 253
    dysuria, 711
    eclampsia, 94
    erysipelas, 97, 106
    female genital organs, 97
    gastritis, 95
    genital organs, 96
    gonorrhoea, 96
    gravel, 89
    haematuria, 89
    hydrophobia, 94
    inflammation of the brain, 93
    labor, 97
    mucous membranes, 94
    nephritis, 88
    nymphomania, 97
    pemphigus, 87
    penis, irritation of glans, 88
    priapism, 96
    renal colic, 88, 191
    retained placenta, 97, 355
    skin, 84
    throat, 95
    uraemia, 94
    urethritis, 88
    urinary organs, 87
    urine, 306
CANTHARIS STRYGOSA
    skin, 84
CAPSICUM, 434
    asthma, 435
    bronchitis, 374, 546
    diphtheria, 435, 524
    dyspepsia, 434
    dysentery, 96, 433
    dysuria, 434
    ears, 43, 435, 491
    elongation of the uvula, 435
    general action, 434
    gonorrhoea, 91
    home sickness, 435, 528
    intermittent fever, 201, 372, 435
    mastoiditis, 43, 435, 602
    modalities, 231, 434
    neuralgia, 614
    reaction, defective, 150, 629
    skin, 85, 86, 404
    throat, 95, 435, 596
    vesicle irritability, 92
CARBO ANIMALIS, 489
    acne, 141
    ankle-joint, 676
    brain, 235
    bronchitis, 490
    buboes, 31, 489
    cancer, 490
    cervix uteri, 140
    constitution, 489
    cough, 490
    deafness, 491
    debility, 489, 490
    ears, 491
    eyes, 491
    female genital organs, 140
    gastric symptoms, 490, 496

CARBO ANIMALIS (Continued)
    glands, 489, 503
    gonorrhoea, 489
    haemorrhoids, 490
    headache, 141, 354
    heart, 134, 499
    lactation, 165, 490
    menses, 140
    otorrhoea, 491
    phthisis, 490
    pneumonia, 490
    relationships, 489
    stomach, 132, 166, 490
    syphilis, 489, 491
    uterus, 490
CARBO VEG., 481
    abscess, 483
    antidotal relationships, 481
    aortitis, 486
    aphonia, 210, 462, 484, 733
    aphthous sore mouth, 47
    asthma, 191, 485
    blood, 481
    boils, 483
    bronchorrhagia, 481
    cancer, 483
    carbuncle, 232, 483, 561
    catarrhs, 484, 662
    cholera, 156, 380, 484
    collapse, 156, 373, 484, 566
    complementary relations, 481
    constipation, 186, 486
    constitution, 481
    cough, 112, 491
    deafness, 491
    debility, 481, 491
    diphtheria, 481
    dysentery, 488
    dyspepsia, 56, 185, 486, 532
    ears, 491, 498
    emphysema, 485
    epistaxis, 157, 481
    eyes, 492
    face, 44
    female genital organs, 141
    fever, 483
    gangrene, 483
    gastric symptoms, 56, 350, 486
    gastro-enteric symptoms, 554
    glands, 484
    haemoptysis, 481
    haemorrhages, 157, 368, 481
    haemorrhoids, 57, 486
    headache, 300, 486
    hectic fever, 373, 483
    hernia, 56
    hip-joint disease, 483
    inimical relations, 481
    intermittent fever, 68, 372, 483
    leucorrhoea, 141
    menorrhagia, 482
    menses, 141
    metrorrhagia, 482
    mumps, 245
    otorrhoea, 491
    paralysis of the lungs, 485, 582
    reaction, defective, 150, 270, 465, 629

INDEX OF REMEDIES.

CARBO VEG. (Continued)
  sweat, 653
  syphilis, 491
  throat, 740
  tympanites, 253, 261, 271, 487
  typhoid fever, 228, 253, 261, 483, 566
  ulcers, 63, 482
  urine, 66
  varicose veins, 141, 441, 482
  vertebral caries, 483
  yellow fever, 483
  wine, aggravation from, 632
CARBOLIC ACID
  diphtheria, 721
  headache, 581
  skin, 85
  urine, 66
CARBON BISULPHIDE, 480
  Meniere's disease, 733
CARBONEUM OXYGENISATUM
  herpes zoster, 87
  pemphigus, 87
  skin, 87
CARBONIC OXIDE, 497, 480
CARBONS
  general characteristics of, 479
CARDUUS MARIANUS
  jaundice, 187
  liver, 187
CASCARILLA
  abdominal symptoms, 312
  constipation, 312, 497
  haemorrhage, 312
  haemorrhoids, 312
CASTOR EQUI
  sore nipples, 28
CASTOREUM, 27
  amenorrhoea, 117
  colic, 117
  convalescence, tardy, 117
  diarrhoea, 117
  menses, 121
  nervous system, 117, 195
  reaction defective, 121, 465
  typhoid fever, 27, 117
CAULOPHYLLUM
  after pains, 356
  dysmenorrhoea, 176, 648
  labor, 357
  leucorrhoea, 674
  pregnancy, 357
  prolapsus uteri, 146
  rheumatism, 297
CAUSTICUM, 729
  agalactia, 356, 734
  anger, effects of, 286
  ankle-joint, 698
  anus, 60
  aphonia, 462, 485, 732
  apoplexy, 731
  bladder, 271
  brain, 651
  catarrh, 662
  chorea, 77, 734
  colic, 735
  constitution, 729
  cough, 421, 703, 732

CAUSTICUM (Continued)
  dysmenorrhoea, 735
  ears, 733
  enuresis, 416, 734
  epilepsy, 734
  gout, 288
  headache, 702, 724
  heels, 663
  inimical relations, 481, 729
  locomotor ataxia, 730
  Meniere's disease, 733
  menses, 735
  mental symptoms, 126, 288, 729
  nature of, 729
  nervous system, 77
  paralysis, 322, 650, 729, 730
  paralysis of tongue, 731
  pemphigus, 87
  ptosis, 170, 235, 398, 731
  rectum and anus, 60
  retention of urine, 271, 735
  rheumatism, 288, 735
  scabies, 476
  scrofulosis, 731
  skin, 87, 702, 735
  tongue, 731
  torticollis, 194
  urine, 737
  vertigo, 730
  warts, 735
CEDRON
  ciliary neuralgia, 206
  intermittent fever, 80
  neuralgia, 288, 328, 374, 555
CEPA
  antidotal relations, 380
  complementary relations, 555
  coryza, 380, 398
  cough, 421
  flatulence, 445
  neuralgia after amputations, 241, 663
  ulceration of heel, 663
CHAMOMILLA, 248
  abortion, 250
  after-pains, 356
  anger, effects of, 286, 339
  antidotal relations, 616, 644
  biliousness, 249, 290
  colic, 339
  convulsions, 201
  coryza, 249
  cough, 111, 24
  dentition, 249
  diarrhoea, 243, 342, 645
  dysmenorrhoea, 202, 263
  emotions, 248
  face, 248
  gastric symptoms, 249
  insomnia, 248
  jaundice, 187, 248
  labor, 250
  lungs, 627
  menses, 263, 613
  mental symptoms, 248, 288, 344
  nervous system, 248
  neuralgia, 288, 644
  otalgia, 349, 384, 683, 708

INDEX OF REMEDIES. 755

CHAMOMILLA (Continued)
  relationships, 250
  rheumatism, 249, 353
  skin, 688
  sweat, 566
  teeth, 340, 645
  temperament, 248
CHELIDONIUM, 281
  capillary bronchitis, 283
  gastralgia, 497
  jaundice, 207
  liver, 207, 281, 299
  mental symptoms, 281
  neuralgia, 282
  relationships, 281
  pneumonia, 282, 295
  scapular pains, 281
  skin, 85
  vertigo, 82
CHENOPODIUM
  liver, 282
  scapular pains, 282
CHIMAPHILA
  bladder, 27, 92
  follicular pharyngitis, 722
  skin, 85
CHININUM ARSENICOSUM
  gastralgia, 415
CHININUM SULPH., 365
  blood, 365
  enlarged spleen, 80, 365
  infusoria, 365
  intermittent fever, 80, 371, 467
  neuralgia, 467, 555
  pemphigus, 87
  reflex action, 365
  rheumatism, 374
  skin, 85, 87, 363
  tissue waste, 365
CHLORAL
  skin, 85, 87
CHLORIDE OF GOLD AND PLATINUM
  caries and necrosis, 341
CHLORINE, 511
  antidotal relations, 511
  aphthous sore mouth, 511
  catarrh, 511
  coryza, 511
  impotence, 511
  laryngismus stridulus, 504
  nervous system, 511
  scurvy, 511
  typhoid fever, 511
CHOLOS TERRAPINAE
  cramps in muscles, 288
CHROMIC ACID
  ulcers, 723
CICUTA VIROSA
  cancer, 451
  convulsions, 44, 182, 451
  epilepsy, 182, 428, 451
  face, 44, 45
  injuries, 451
  nervous system, 79
  puerperal convulsions, 451
  skin, 451, 677
  tetanus, 178, 181, 182, 537
  worms, 451

CICUTINA, 181
CICUTOXINE, 182
CIMEX LECTULARIUS
  cough, 152
  intermittent fever, 32
CINA, 246
  asthenopia, 247
  bladder, 247
  convulsions, 246, 629
  dentition, 420
  enuresis, 247
  eyes, 247, 619
  face, 246
  intermittent fever, 247
  modalities, 247
  strabismus, 246, 617
  temperament, 247
  whooping cough, 247, 382
  worms, 246, 624
CINCHONA, 363
  abdominal symptoms, 488
  abscesses, 484
  alkaloids of, 365
  anaemia, 366
  antidotal relations, 372, 375, 551, 586
  asthenopia, 369
  biliary calculi, 192
  bowels, 370
  brain, 235
  cholera infantum, 366, 380
  colic, 272
  complementary relations, 555
  coryza, 295, 326
  debility, 367, 487
  diarrhoea, 53, 166, 370, 429, 488, 642
  dysentery, 53, 488
  dyspepsia, 53, 350, 369, 487
  enlarged spleen, 80
  face, 44
  gastric symptoms, 370, 553
  haemorrhages, 293, 367, 482, 643
  headache, 40, 369, 701
  hectic fever, 373
  hydrocephaloid, 366, 380, 680
  inimical relationships, 375, 462
  intermittent fever, 80, 229, 371
  jaundice, 374
  lungs, 374
  malarial neuralgia, 374
  marasmus, 554, 680
  Meniere's disease, 733
  mental symptoms, 293, 369
  nervous symptoms, 369
  neuralgia, 369, 374
  poisoning from, 366
  reaction, defective, 121, 150
  retained placenta, 368
  rheumatism, 374
  seminal emissions, 367, 529
  tympanites, 252, 261, 370, 487
  typhoid fever, 252, 556
  ulcers, 63
CINNABARIS
  condylomata, 311
  eyes, 594
  nasal catarrh, 595
  scarlatina, 95, 596

INDEX OF REMEDIES.

CINNABARIS (Continued)
  skin, 311
  sycosis, 311
  syphilis, 311, 595
  throat, 95, 595
CINNAMON
  haemorrhage, 369
CISTUS CANAD., 463
  nasal catarrh, 656
CITRIC ACID, 516
CITRULLUS, 285
CLEMATIS CRISPA, 86, 314
CLEMATIS ERECTA
  cancer, 561
  cystitis, 90
  gonorrhoea, 91
  orchitis, 352
  skin, 85, 86, 560
  urethra, 86, 90
CLEMATIS VIORNA
  skin, 314
COBALT
  backache, 193, 361, 636
  seminal emissions, 193
  spinal irritation, 303, 636
COCA
  muscular fatigue, 521
  reaction, defective, 121
COCCULUS INDICUS, 259
  anus, 60
  cerebro-spinal meningitis, 263
  convulsions, 262
  debility, 260, 624
  dysmenorrhoea, 202, 263
  general action, 259
  headache, 262, 354
  hernia, 189
  hysteria, 199
  menses, 262
  mental symptoms, 199
  nervous system, 195, 259
  neurasthenia, 624,
  paralysis, 315, 624
  rectum and anus, 60, 61
  sleeplessness, 361
  spinal cord, 260
  spinal irritation, 330
  stomach, 132
  tympanites, 252
  typhoid fever, 260
COCCUS CACTI
  phthisis, 627
  whooping cough, 32, 627
COCHLEARIA ARMORACEA
  skin, 85
  urinary organs, 92
CODEIN
  muscular twitchings, 265
  phthisis, 265
COFFEA ARABICUM, 383
  alkaloids of, 383
  apoplectic congestion, 384
  circulation, 385
  diarrhoea, 385
  fatigue, 385
  general action, 383
  heart, 31

COFFEA ARABICUM (Continued)
  mental symptoms, 322, 384
  skin, 384
  reaction, defective, 121
  special senses, 385
  teeth, 340
  toothache, 301, 384
COLCHICUM AUTUMNALE, 251
  abdominal symptoms, 253
  antidotal relations, 254
  Bright's disease, 254
  cholera, 59, 253
  convulsions, 59
  debility, 251
  dentition, 420
  diarrhoea, 59
  dropsy, 67, 254
  dysentery, 96, 253
  gastric symptoms, 58, 350
  gastritis, 324
  glossoplegia, 650
  gout, 253, 353
  heart, 254, 298
  hydrothorax, 254
  indigestion, 58
  paralysis, 731
  pericarditis, 254
  peritonitis, 60
  prosopalgia, 322
  rheumatism, 231, 232, 253, 298
  tympanites, 251, 261, 271, 370
  typhoid fever, 251, 271, 556
  urine, 66
COLEOPTERA, 32
COLLINSONIA
  constipation, 188
  haemorrhoids, 188
  neurasthenia, 624
  paralysis, 624
  prolapsus uteri, 188
COLOCYNTH, 285
  abdomen, 286
  antidotal relation, 288
  arthritic ophthalmia, 288, 341
  bladder, 287
  ciliary neuralgia, 288
  colic, 285, 324, 339, 419, 644
  constipation, 195
  cramps of muscles, 288
  diarrhoea, 248, 285, 644
  dysentery, 96, 286, 287
  dysmenorrhoea, 286, 287
  enteritis, 285
  glaucoma, 287
  gout, 287
  headache, 287
  hip disease, 288
  iritis, 287
  lead colic, 621
  mental symptoms, 288
  neuralgia, 285
  ovarian tumor, 285, 510
  paraphimosis, 288, 394
  rheumatism, 288, 735
  sciatica, 288
COMOCLADIA DENTATA
  erysipelas, 217

INDEX OF REMEDIES. 757

COMOCLADIA DENTATA (Continued)
  eyes, 217
  skin, 217
COMPOSITAE, 237
CONCHIOLIN
  osteitis, 680
CONIFERAE, 304
CONIINE. 181
CONIUM MACULATUM, 447
  bladder, 91
  cancer, 449, 561
  cancer of the stomach, 449
  cataract, 575
  complementary relations, 449
  constipation, 449
  cough, 361, 448
  cystitis, 450
  debility, 447
  ears, 448
  eyes, 360, 619
  glands, 448
  heart, 392, 448, 656
  hypochondriasis, 448, 638
  impotence, 564
  injuries, 449, 532
  muscular exhaustion, 336
  mental symptoms, 448
  nervous system, 447
  noma, 449
  paralysis, 318, 447
  poisoning by, 447
  post-diphtheritic paralysis, 447
  prosopalgia, 448
  rheumatism, 231
  scrofulous, 448
  seminal emissions, 175
  sexual excesses, 448, 564
  testicles, 352
  tonsils, enlargement of the, 651
  urethra, 91
  urethritis, 91
  vertigo, 448
  wine, aggravation from, 632, 634
CONVALLARIA MAJALIS
  heart, 393
  pruritus vulvae, 393
  uterus, 393
COPAIVA
  gonorrhoea, 91
  lungs, 91, 627
  pemphigus, 87
  skin, 87
  urine, 306
  urticaria, 87, 107
  vesicle irritability, 92
COPTIS ROOT, 451
CORALLIUM RUBRUM
  chancre, 311
  nasal catarrh, 656
  psora, 30
  syphilis, 30
  whooping cough, 27, 31
CORNUS FLORIDA
  intermittent fever, 371
COTURA MATURA
  skin, 85
CRABRO, 98

CROCUS
  chorea, 76, 79
  eyes, 619
  hysteria, 76, 79
  menses, 613
  muscular twitchings, 265
CROTALUS HORRIDUS
  ciliary neuralgia, 43
  cough, 111
  diphtheria, 35, 50
  ears, 43
  erysipelas, 45, 417
  haematuria, 66
  keratitis, 43
  retinal apoplexy, 43
CROTON TIGLIUM
  antidotal relations, 222
  cholera infantum, 285
  colic, 287, 312
  diarrhoea, 256, 285, 287, 312, 453
  mammary gland, 302, 503
  rhus poisoning, 222
  skin, 85, 313, 688
CUBEBS
  gonorrhoea, 91
  leucorrhoea, 674
CUCURBITA
  tape-worm, 285
CUCURBITACEAE, 284
CUPRUM ARSENICOSUM
  skin, 85
  visceral neuralgia, 630
CUPRUM METALLICUM, 628
  after-pains, 356
  antidotal relations, 628
  aortitis, 486
  asthma, 381
  chlorosis, 629
  cholera Asiatica, 628
  colic, 629
  collapse, 70, 629
  complementary relations, 628
  convulsions, 201, 629, 630, 634
  epilepsy, 630
  erysipelas, 417, 630
  face, 44
  fever, 629
  hysteria, 198
  intermittent fever, 70
  laryngismus stridulus, 504
  meningitis, 101, 630
  neuralgia, 630
  paralyisis, 537, 630
  pneumonia, 630
  reaction, defective, 464, 629
  scarlatina, 302, 443, 630, 634
  skin, 688
  sleep, 443
  suppressed eruptions, 101, 302, 424, 630, 634
  uraemia, 629
  whooping cough, 382
CURARE, 206
  catalepsy; 179
  eczema, 179

INDEX OF REMEDIES.

CURARE (Continued)
  emphysema, 207
  liver spots, 125, 179
  muscular exhaustion, 336
  nervous system, 179, 206
  paralysis, 179
  tetanus, 179
CURARINE, 179
CYANOGEN, 501
CYCLAMEN
  asthenopia, 130
  chlorosis, 359
  colic, 263, 3 0
  dysmenorrhoea, 263
  eyes, 360
  gastric symptoms, 359
  haemorrhages, 369
  headache, 130
  nasal catarrh, 348
  neurasthenia, 359
  strabismus, 617
CYPRIPEDIUM
  reaction, defective, 121
  sleep, 384

DIFFENBACHIA
  stomacace, 208
  throat, 95
DIGITALIN, 387
DIGITOXIN, 387
DIGITALIS PURPUREA, 387
  abortion, 388
  alkaloids of, 387
  balanorrhoea, 394
  brain, 393
  cerebro-spinal meningitis, 393
  chordee, 394
  collapse, 69
  cyanosis neonatorum, 389
  cystitis, 393
  dropsy, 66, 164, 396
  face, 389
  gonorrhoea, 394
  heart, 69, 111, 171, 388
  hydrocele, 390
  hydrocephalus, 337, 393
  hydropericardium, 111
  hydrothorax, 390
  jaundice, 391
  kidneys, 559
  liver, 391
  meningitis, 337, 393
  mental symptoms, 387
  paraphimosis, 394
  seminal emissions, 174, 394
  sleep, 389
  syncope, 37, 38
  urinary organs, 92
  vertigo, 37
  vesical irritation, 92
  vomiting, 388
  vomiting of pregnancy, 388
DIOSCOREA
  diarrhoea, 453, 473
  seminal emissions, 174
  sexual excesses, 339, 674
  visceral neuralgia, 285

DITAINE, 168
DOLICHOS
  dentition, 420
DORYPHORA
  gonorrhoea, 32
  urethritis, 91
DRACONTIUM
  bronchitis, 215
DROSERA
  asthma, 27
  cough, 273, 395, 732
  phthisis, 27, 273
  skin, 85
  whooping cough, 27
DULCAMARA, 433
  antidotal relations, 586
  bladder, 434
  colic, 434
  complementary relations, 434
  coryza, 434
  cystitis, 351, 434
  diarrhoea, 434, 652
  lungs, 434
  mental symptoms, 683
  myelitis, 236
  nervous system, 434
  otalgia, 434
  paralysis, 434, 731
  paralysis of the lungs, 434
  poisoning by, 433
  rheumatism, 433
  skin, 434
  spinal cord, 434
  throat, 434
  tongue, 434
  twitching of muscles, 433
  urticaria, 434

ELAPS
  diarrhoea, 58
  ears, 43
  gastro-intestinal symptoms, 58
  haemoptysis, 35
  lungs, 51
  phthisis, 51
  pneumonia, 51
  stomach, 58, 324
ELATERIUM
  cholera infantum, 284
  diarrhoea, 34, 257, 284, 395
EPIGEA
  vesical irritation, 92
EQUISETUM HYEMALE
  albuminuria, 90
  cystitis, 90, 351
  enuresis, 90
  haematuria, 90
ERGOT, 153
  convulsions, 153
ERIGERON CANADENSIS
  uterine haemorrhage, 159, 368
  vesical irritability, 92, 159
ERYODICTION CAL.
  See Yerba Santa
ESERINE, 178
EUCALYPTUS
  intermittent fever, 372

INDEX OF REMEDIES. 759

EUPATORIUM PERFOLIATUM, 244
  aphonia, 485, 733
  influenza, 244
  intermittent fever, 299, 244, 372
EUPATORIUM PURPUREUM
  intermittent fever, 244
  vesical irritation, 90, 145
EUPHORBIA COROLLATA
  cholera morbus, 312
  diarrhoea, 312
  skin, 85
  ulcers, 63
EUPHORBIA CYPARISSIAS
  skin, 86
EUPHORBIA PEPLUS
  skin, 86
EUPHORBIACEAE, 312
EUPHORBIUM
  bones, 313
  erysipelas, 46
  skin, 85, 217, 313
  ulcers, 63
EUPHRASIA, 396
  blepharitis, 396
  condylomata, 311, 398
  conjunctivitis, 397
  coryza, 380, 397
  eyes, 396, 683
  granular lids, 609
  heart, 718
  iritis, 397
  nasal catarrh, 380
  ophthalmia, 189, 683
  phlyctenular ophthalmia, 496
  ptosis, 396

FEL TAURI
  constipation, 29
FEL VULPI
  constipation, 29
FERRUM CARBONICUM
  neuralgia, 420
FERRUM IOD.
  female genital organs, 143
  prolapsus uteri, 643
FERRUM METALLICUM, 639
  anaemia, 367, 493, 640
  antidotal relations, 639
  asthma, 639
  circulation, 639
  chlorosis, 493, 640
  cholera infantum, 642
  complementary relations, 493, 639
  constitution, 639
  cough, 641
  diarrhoea, 166, 370, 642
  epistaxis, 639
  face, 640
  female genital organs, 615
  gastralgia, 640
  gastric symptoms, 496
  haemoptysis, 639, 641
  haemorrhages, 643
  headache, 639, 641
  intermittent fever, 643
  menses, 641
  neuralgia, 640

FERRUM METALLICUM (Continued)
  phthisis florida, 639, 641
  prolapsus uteri, 643
  rheumatism, 231, 249, 281, 735
  tuberculosis, 641
  uterine haemorrhage, 642
  vertigo, 641
FERRUM PHOS.
  bladder, 92
  cholera infantum, 159, 270, 642
  enuresis, 734
  diarrhoea, 159, 642
  dysentery, 642
  fever, 320
  hydroa, 159
  inflammation, 159, 642
  lungs, 159
  phthisis, 642
  pneumonia, 159, 642
  pulmonary congestion, 159, 642
  vesical irritation, 92
FLUORIC ACID, 519
  bones, 519
  caries, 519
  cicatrices, 520
  dental fistula, 519
  felons, 520
  gastric symptoms, 704
  liver, 187
  mental symptoms, 440
  muscular fatigue, 520
  naevi, 441, 521
  nails, 520
  skin, 520
  sleep, 521
  speech, 440
  syphilis, 519
  teeth, 46
  tonsillitis, 414
  varicose veins, 521
  wine, aggravation from, 632
FORMICA, 98
  albuminuria, 86
  skin, 85, 86
FORMIC ACID, 98

GAMBIER, 363
GAMBOGE
  diarrhoea, 165, 380
GAULTHERIA
  pleurodynia, 295
GELSEMINE. 169
GELSEMIUM, 169
  abortion, 176
  amenorrhoea, 674
  antidotal relations, 176
  aphonia, 170
  bilious fever, 173
  catarrh, 173
  cerebro-spinal meningitis, 172
  cervix uteri, 139, 175
  circulation, 168
  coryza, 173
  cough, 173, 174
  diarrhoea, 176, 255, 272
  diplopia, 170
  dysmenorrhoea, 176

GELSEMIUM (Continued)
dysphagia, 170, 173
emotions, 176
epididymitis, 175
face, 171
female genital organs, 175
fever, 173, 317
genital organs, 174, 175
gonorrhoea, 175
headache, 40, 171, 172, 200, 262, 300, 581, 701
heart, 170, 176
hemicrania, 128
intermittent fever, 66, 172, 229
labor, 175, 328
measles, 174, 326
muscular fatigue, 336
nervous system, 169
orchitis, 513
paralysis, 166, 170, 448, 606
passive congestion, 169
poisoning by, 168
polyuria, 171
post-diphtheritic paralysis, 171, 448, 606
prosopalgia, 174
ptosis, 170, 235, 619
puerperal convulsions, 175, 257
remittent fever, 172, 317
rheumatism, gonorrhoeal, 175
seminal emissions, 174
sexual excesses, 174, 339
skin, 174
strabismus, 171
throat, 173
tonsillitis, 173
typhoid fever, 173, 261, 401
uterus, 175, 176

GERANIUM MACULATUM
diarrhoea, 379

GETTYSBURG SPRING WATER
bones, 545
hip-joint disease, 341, 545, 656
vertebral caries, 341, 656

GLONOIN, 435
albuminuria, 437
amenorrhoea, 673
antidotal relations, 438
apoplexy, 537
apoplexy of the retina, 436
brain, 320
circulation, 278, 435
congestion of the retina, 436, 602
convulsions, 201, 437
eyes, 436
headache, 436, 701
heart, 466
inflammation of the brain, 437
injuries, 437
meningitis, 101, 320, 438
mental symptoms, 437, 500
metrorrhagia, 278
puerperal convulsions, 437, 438
retinal congestion, 436, 602
speech, 437
sun, ill effects of the, 38, 436, 437
wine, aggravation from, 632, 634

GNAPHALIUM
cholera infantum, 379

GNAPHALIUM (Continued)
diarrhoea, 379, 725
sciatica, 288, 614

GOSSYPIUM
retained placenta, 355

GRAPHITES, 492
antidotal relations, 492
aphonia, 210, 733
blepharitis, 130, 494, 619
cervix, 142
chlorosis, 493
cicatrices, 141, 496, 544
complementary relations, 492
constipation, 497
constitution, 493
cough, 498
crusta lactea, 168
deafness, 59
diarrhoea, 498
ears, 498
eczema, 234, 495
erysipelas, 97, 496
eyes, 130, 494, 580, 619, 710
female genital organs, 498
fissure in ano, 497
flatulence, 497
gastralgia, 57, 497
gastric symptoms, 57, 496
glands, 494
haemorrhoids, 497
heart, 499, 718
heels, 663
impotence, 498
indigestion, 57
leucorrhoea, 141, 493
male genital organs, 498
liver, 497
menses, 141, 493
mental symptoms, 57, 493
nasal catarrh, 497
nipples, 141
nose, 86
obesity, 493
ophthalmia, 347
ovaries, 65, 498
prolapsus uteri, 141
scrofulosis, 494
scrofulous ophthalmia, 494, 702
skin, 141, 493, 494, 495, 560, 702
styes, 404
sweat, 653
tarsal cysts, 340
throat, 498
trichiasis, 710

GRATIOLA
diarrhoea, 395

GRINDELIA ROBUSTA
heart, 171, 466
lungs, 171, 633
pneumogastric nerves, 222
skin, 222

GUAIACUM
chest pains, 306
gout, 288
growing pains, 530
phthisis, 215, 298, 329
pleurodynia, 329
rheumatism, 288, 298, 735

INDEX OF REMEDIES. 761

GUAIACUM (Continued)
  torticollis, 422

HALOGENS, 501
HAMAMELIS
  abortion, 328
  ecchymoses of the sclerotic, 190
  haematemesis, 301
  haemorrhage, 158, 369, 537
  haemorrhoids, 188
  metrorrhagia, 159, 369
  milk leg, 356
  orchitis, 352, 512
  pregnancy, 346
  retinal apoplexy, 43
  typhoid fever, 537
  varicocele, 346
  varicose veins, 366, 521
  vesical irritation, 146
  vicarious menstruation, 301
HEDEOMA
  female genitals, 146
HELLEBORUS, 334
  alkaloids of, 334
  aphthae, 48
  apoplexy, 269
  convulsions, 45
  dropsy, 66, 164, 337
  heart, 392
  hydrocephalus, 105, 337
  intermittent fever, 69
  kidneys, 559
  meningitis, 101, 336
  nephritis, 337
  scarlatina, 66, 302
  sensorium, 334
  shock, 337
  skin, 85
  tubercular meningitis, 337
  typhoid fever, 39, 335
  urine, 66
HELONIAS DIOICA
  albuminuria, 358
  debility, 135
  female genital organs, 134, 357, 616
  leucorrhoea, 358
  lying-in, 357
  mental symptoms, 134
  neurasthenia, 357
  prolapsus uteri, 146, 358
  uterine disease, 134, 615
  vaginitis, 357
HEPAR SULPHURIS CALC., 682
  abscess, 592, 684
  antidotal relations, 536, 543, 585, 600, 688, 712
  bladder, 687
  boils, 684
  Bright's disease, 685
  buboes, 686
  capillary bronchitis, 686
  catarrhs, 685
  constipation, 53, 686
  coryza, 684, 685
  cough, 234, 513, 683
  croup, 324, 506, 684
  diarrhoea, 687

HEPAR SULPH. CALC. (Continued)
  dyspepsia, 53, 686
  dysuria, 687
  ears, 43, 412, 683
  eczema, 688
  enuresis, 687
  erysipelas, 106
  eyes, 496, 683
  fever blisters, 705
  gastric symptoms, 460, 686, 704
  glands, 686
  jaundice, 187
  inflammation, 683
  liver, 687
  lungs, 627, 685
  mania, 683
  marasmus, 687
  mental symptoms, 127, 682
  mercury, abuse of, 536
  nervous system, 248, 682
  neuralgia, 682
  ophthalmia, 683
  otalgia, 683
  otitis externa, 683
  otitis media, 412, 683
  ovarian tumor, 62
  periodontitis, 46
  pneumonia, 685
  scrofulous ophthalmia, 496
  skin, 687
  styes, 496, 683
  throat, 619, 685, 740
  tonsilitis, 414, 592, 684, 685
  tonsils, 651
  tuberculosis, 513, 685
  ulcers, 62, 63, 687
HIPPOMANE MANC.
  scarlatina, 313
  skin, 86
HURA BRAS.
  skin, 85
HYDRASTIS CANADENSIS
  cancer, 510, 561
  cancer of the uterus, 510
  mucous membranes, 360
  post-nasal catarrh, 348, 656, 722
  stomach, 132
  uterus, 360
HYDRANGEA
  vesical calculus, 92
HYDROCOTYLE
  pruritus vaginae, 145
  skin, 560
  vesical irritation, 145
HYDROCYANIC ACID, 537
  asphyxia, 433
  cholera, 538
  collapse, 69, 538
  convulsions, 433, 538
  cough, 538
  dyspepsia, 517
  epilepsy, 537, 676
  face, 44, 45
  heart, 514, 538
  intermittent fever, 69
  nervous system, 537
  paralysis of brain and lungs, 336, 538

INDEX OF REMEDIES.

HYDROCYANIC ACID (Continued)
  phthisis, 538
  scarlatina, 524, 538, 635
  syncope, 37
  tetanus, 181, 537
  uraemia, 433
  vertigo, 37
HYMENOPTERA, 32, 93
HYOSCYAMUS, 426
  apoplexy, 269
  bladder, 271
  brain, 268, 427, 442
  chorea, 77, 428
  convulsions, 44, 45, 201, 428
  cough, 111, 361, 247
  delirium, 426, 429
  elongated uvula, 427
  enuresis, 416
  epilepsy, 428
  face, 44, 45
  fever, 428
  headache, 427
  hiccough, 203
  hysteria, 77, 198
  insomnia, 428
  intermittent fever, 69
  mania, 426, 430, 714
  meningitis, 427
  mental symptoms, 102, 198, 426, 427, 437, 612
  metrorrhagia, 272
  multiple sclerosis of the brain and spinal cord, 650
  nervous system, 77, 79
  nymphomania, 563
  paralysis, 426
  puerperal mania, 430
  retention of urine, 271
  scarlatina, 418, 428
  sleep, 428
  typhoid fever, 39, 228, 268
  urethritis, 91
  urine, 442
HYPERICUM
  injuries, 241
  spine, 241
  tetanus, 181

IGNATIA AMARA, 197
  antidotal relations, 204, 631
  chorea, 74, 77
  constipation, 220
  convulsions, 200
  cough, 111, 201
  deafness, 575
  emotions, 197, 200
  diphtheria, 203
  dislocation of jaw, 235
  dysmenorrhoea, 202, 263
  dyspepsia, 202
  eyes, 203
  fistula, 452
  follicular pharyngitis, 722
  gastralgia, 202
  grief, effects of, 197, 198, 528
  headache, 78, 171, 199
  hiccough, 203

IGNATIA AMARA (Continued)
  hysteria, 77, 116, 198, 200, 276
  intermittent fever, 201, 372
  joints, 235
  laryngismus stridulus, 504
  mental symptoms, 103, 197, 344, 528
  neuralgia, 203
  neurasthenia, 624
  nose, 276
  paralysis, 624
  phlyctenular ophthalmia, 203
  polyuria, 171, 200, 460
  proctalgia, 60
  prolapsus ani, 203
  rectum and anus, 60, 203
  stomach, 132
  temperament, 197
  throat, 201, 203
  tonsils, 201, 651
  toothache, 203
  worms, 203, 246
ILLICIUM ANISATUM
  lungs, 627
INDIGO
  epilepsy, 30
  worms, 203, 247
INDIUM
  gastric symptoms, 636
INULA
  female genital organs, 146
  vesical irritation, 146
IODINE, 508
  abuse of, 508
  antidotal relations, 508, 587
  aphthae, 47
  cancer, 510
  cough, 509
  croup, 506
  diarrhoea, 510
  diphtheria, 214
  glands, 509
  heart, 509
  hypertrophy of the heart, 509
  joints, 103
  laryngismus stridulus, 50
  marasmus, 703
  mental symptoms, 502, 617
  ovarian tumor, 510
  ovaries, 510
  pancreas, 510
  phthisis, 509
  pneumonia, 508
  rheumatism, 510
  scrofulosis, 509
  synovitis, 103
  tabes mesenterica, 502, 507, 653
  ulcers, 510
IPECACUANHA, 376
  abortion, 328
  alkaloids, 376
  asthma, 380, 558
  capillary bronchitis, 381, 582
  cholera infantum, 378
  colic, 378
  conjunctivitis, 383
  convulsions, 378
  coryza, 380

INDEX OF REMEDIES. 763

IPECACUANHA (Continued)
  diarrhoea, 379
  emphysema, 558
  gastric symptoms, 350, 351, 377
  general action of, 376
  haematuria, 383
  haemorrhage, 368, 482, 643
  headache, 377
  intermittent fever, 372, 382
  laryngismus stridulus, 504
  lungs, 627
  measles, 303
  mental symptoms, 377
  stomach, 132, 341
  suppressed eruption, 303
  temperament, 377, 383
  vomiting, 579, 672
  whooping-cough, 382
IPECACUANHIC ACID, 376
IPOMEA NIL
  renal colic, 92
IRIS VERSICOLOR
  cholera morbus, 256, 351, 396
  diarrhoea, 351, 371, 396
  headache, 276, 702, 784
  hemicrania, 129

JABORANDI
  asthenopia, 130
  bronchitis, 686
  eyes, 619
JACARANDA
  chancroid, 311
  condylomata, 311
JATROPHA CURCAS
  cholera Asiatica, 256, 312
JUGLANDACEAE, 207
JUGLANS CATHARTICA
  See Juglans Cinerea
JUGLANS CINEREA
  headache, 207, 262, 300
  hydrothorax, 207
  jaundice, 207, 262
  liver, 207
JUGLANS REGIA
  menses, 207

KALI BICHROMICUM, 720
  acne, 724
  anus, 60
  asthma, 727
  bronchiectasia, 727
  bronchitis, 727
  constitution, 720
  corneal opacities, 669
  corneal ulcers, 726
  cough, 662, 727
  croup, 595, 723
  diarrhoea, 724
  diphtheria, 214, 524, 595, 721
  dysentery, 61, 97, 725
  eyes, 113, 360, 726
  face, 724
  flushes of heat, 466
  follicular pharyngitis, 722
  gastric catarrh, 720
  gastric symptoms, 724

KALI BICHROMICUM (Continued)
  gastritis, 754
  gonorrhoea, 722
  headache, 702, 724
  heart, 134, 499, 718
  iritis, 726
  laryngitis, 721
  leucorrhoea, 720
  lupus, 725
  measles, 361, 725
  mucous membranes, 720
  nasal catarrh, 656, 661, 722
  otalgia, 721
  otitis media, 720
  otorrhoea, 721
  ozaena, 49, 310, 722
  pharyngitis, 721
  post-nasal catarrh, 656, 722
  rectum and anus, 60, 61
  rheumatism, 353, 728
  scrofulous ophthalmia, 113, 726
  skin, 87, 725
  sycosis, 310, 726
  syphilis, 723
  throat, 722
  tongue, 725
  ulcers, 63, 722
  whooping-cough, 32
KALI BROMATUM, 713
  acne, 716
  antidotal relations, 713
  brain-fag, 714
  cholera infantum, 380
  convulsions, 76, 713
  diarrhoea, 380
  eczema, 716
  epilepsy, 715
  locomotor ataxia, 715
  mental symptoms, 437, 606, 612, 715
  nervous system, 76, 606, 713, 715
  night terrors, 430, 714
  sexual excesses, 76, 606, 713, 715
  skin, 87, 715
  urticaria, 107
KALI CARB., 736
  abortion, 737
  aphonia, 739
  asthenopia, 130
  backache, 738, 739
  blood, 736
  capillary bronchitis, 740
  chest pains, 306
  complementary relations, 736
  coryza, 739
  cough, 732, 740
  debility, 738
  face, 44
  heart, 111, 145, 737, 741
  hydropericardium, 111
  liver, 299
  lumbago, 230, 741
  menses, 700
  mental symptoms, 443, 738
  muscular fatigue, 336
  nasal catarrh, 739
  nervous system, 195, 738
  phthisis, 536, 740, 741

INDEX OF REMEDIES.

KALI CARB. (Continued)
  pleurodynia, 296
  pneumonia, 283, 740
  puerperal convulsions, 738
  spinal irritation, 738
  stomach, 132
  sweat, 653
  throat, 739, 740
  urine, 66, 737
  vertigo, 736
KALI CHLORICUM
  antidotal relations, 586
  asthma, 633
  aphthae, 47
  follicular pharyngitis, 722
  heart, 134, 499
KALI FERROCYANICUM
  female genital organs, 144
  heart, 144
  metrorrhagia, 144
KALI HYDRIODICUM, 716
  antidotal relations, 586, 716, 719
  bones, 341
  Bright's disease, 718
  catarrh, 717
  chemosis, 717
  coryza, 717
  endocarditis, 718
  eyes, 716
  general symptoms, 716
  gummatous tumors, 719
  headache, 716
  heart, 717, 718
  iritis, 716
  joints, 103
  keratitis, 717
  kidneys, 719
  lungs, 717
  ozaena, 64, 717
  paralysis of the lungs, 582
  pericarditis, 718
  phthisis, 718
  pneumonia, 717
  pulmonary oedema, 718
  rheumatism, 719
  sciatica, 719
  skin, 87, 719
  spinal cord, 719
  synovitis, 103
  syphilis, 64, 716, 719
KALI HYDROSULPHURICUM
  skin, 85, 87
KALI NITRICUM
  heart, 499
  kidneys, 93
  skin, 87
KALI PERMANGAN.
  diphtheria, 110, 214, 524, 721
KALI SULPHURATUM
  skin, 87
KALI SULPHURICUM
  nasal catarrh, 594
KALMIA
  headache, 171, 200
  heart, 110, 214, 534, 721
  hypertrophy of the heart, 323
  neuralgia, 328, 555, 625

KALMIA (Continued)
  ptosis, 170, 235
  rheumatism, 231, 392
KAOLIN
  croup, 505, 506, 723
KOUMYSS, 28
KREOSOTUM
  acne, 196
  blepharitis, 609
  cancer, 136
  enuresis, 247, 416, 734
  female genital organs, 136, 615
  gastric symptoms, 185, 350
  leucorrhoea, 136
  menses, 136
  neuralgia, 301, 555
  skin, 560
  teeth, 48, 301, 340
  urinary symptoms, 136
  vomiting, 136, 565, 671

LAC CANINUM, 28
  constipation, 28
  diphtheria, 28, 50
  ozaena, 49
  rheumatism, 353
LAC DEFLORATUM
  diabetes, 28
  headache, 28
  prolapsus uteri, 146
LACHESIS, 36
  abscess, 592
  acne, 196
  albuminuria, 65, 66
  antidotal relations, 62, 587
  aortitis, 486
  aphthae, 47, 48
  apoplexy, 268, 269
  asthma, 51
  bladder, 416
  brain, paralysis of the, 268
  Bright's disease, 65
  bronchitis, 50
  cancer, 71
  carbuncle, 71, 80, 561
  chancre, 62
  cholera, 59
  circulation, 65
  climaxis, 37, 65, 466
  constipation, 52, 54
  coryza, 49, 294
  cough, 111, 152, 421
  croup, 723
  cystitis, 66
  delirium, 38
  delirium tremens, 269
  diarrhoea, 52
  diphtheria, 214, 444, 502
  dropsy, 65, 66
  drunkards, complaints of, 55, 58, 65, 187, 268, 477
  dysentery, 61
  dyspepsia, 561, 687
  ears, 43
  enteritis, 59
  erysipelas, 41, 45, 106, 416
  eyes, 42

INDEX OF REMEDIES. 765

LACHESIS (Continued)
 face, 43
 female genitals, 62
 flushes of heat, 466
 gastric symptoms, 52, 56, 704
 general action, 35
 haematuria, 66
 haemophilia, 575
 haemorrhoids, 52
 headache, 40, 41
 heart, 65, 111, 718
 hernia, 57
 hydropericardium, 111
 inimical relation, 659
 intermittent fever, 168, 202, 372
 jaundice, 52
 laryngismus stridulus, 504
 liver, 52, 187, 444, 477
 loquacity, 39, 423
 lungs, 374
 male genital organs, 62
 malignant pustule, 71
 meningitis, 42
 menses, 62
 mental symptoms, 36, 38, 102, 218, 437, 617
 metrorrhagia, 278
 modalities, 71
 nasal catarrh, 49, 294
 nose, 49, 51
 ovaralgia, 62
 ovarian tumors, 62
 ovaries, 62
 ovaritis, 62, 613
 ozaena, 49, 51
 paralysis of the lungs, 582
 parotitis, 443
 periproctitis, 60
 peritonitis, 59
 pneumonia, 51, 474
 post-scarlatinal dropsy, 66
 prosopalgia, 46
 puerperal mania, 328
 rectum and anus, 52
 retinal apoplexy, 43, 66
 scarlatina, 42, 70, 233, 418, 661
 scrofulous ophthalmia, 42
 sexual symptoms, 62
 skin, 86
 sleep, 36
 sore mouth, 47
 speech, 440
 stomach, 52, 58
 sunstroke, 38
 syncope, 37
 syphilis, 62
 teeth, 46
 tetanus, 44, 181
 throat, 49
 tonsillitis, 49, 592
 tuberculosis, 52
 typhlitis, 54, 59
 typhoid fever, 39, 108, 268, 402, 430
 ulcers, 62
 universal symptoms, 35
 urine, 66
 vertigo, 36, 82

LACHESIS (Continued)
 yellow fever, 55
LACHNANTHES
 intermittent fever, 69
 torticollis, 194
LACTIC ACID, 517
 diabetes mellitus, 518
 sweat, 653
LACTUCA
 heart, 718
LAC VACCINUM, 28
LAMIUM ALBUM
 haemorrhoids, 220
 headache, 220
LAPIS ALBUS
 cancer, 510
 tuberculosis, 510
LATHYRUS, 162
LAUROCERASUS
 asphyxia neonatorum, 583
 catarrhs, 662
 cough, 361, 538, 732
 liver, 477
 phthisis, 538
 reaction, defective, 464, 529
 scarlatina, 38
 syncope, 37, 38
 vertigo, 37
LEDUM
 acne, 195
 antidotal relations, 114
 drunkards' complaints, 195, 324
 ecchymoses of the sclerotic, 191
 gout, 232, 297
 haemorrhages, 369
 haemoptysis, 324
 heart, 656
 heels, 663
 injuries, 241
 lumbago, 230
 polypi, 369
 rheumatism, 232, 297, 353, 392, 548
 wine, aggravation from, 632
LEPTANDRA VIRGINICA, 395
 diarrhoea, 396, 598
 liver, 395, 598
 typhoid fever, 537
LILIUM TIGRINUM
 asthenopia, 130
 chest, 134, 346
 circulation, 127, 346
 diarrhoea, 134
 female genitals, 133, 616
 heart, 134
 leucorrhoea, 134
 mental symptoms, 17
 poisoning by, 133
 ovaries, 133
 prolapsus uteri, 133
 retroversion, 133
 subinvolution of the uterus, 133
 uterine symptoms, 133, 360
LIME
 preparations of, 666
LINARIA, 394
 enuresis, 90, 395
 fainting, 394

LITHIUM CARB., 654
  asthenopia, 655
  bladder, 655
  cough, 655
  debility, 654
  diarrhoea, 655
  eyes, 655
  gastralgia, 655
  gout, 453, 654
  headache, 55
  heart, 656
  hemiopia, 655, 702
  joints, 654, 656
  menses, 655
  mucous membranes, 655
  nasal catarrh, 655
  rheumatism, 453, 655, 656
  skin, 655, 677
  wine, 655
LOBELIA INFLATA
  asthma, 387
  hay fever, 557
  gastric symptoms, 377
  vomiting, 265
LOBELIA SYPHILITICA
  scapular pain, 282
LYCOPODIUM, 439
  abortion, 328
  amenorrhoea, 674
  aphthous sore mouth, 48
  asthma, 91
  bladder, 416
  brain, paralysis of the, 442
  blood, 441
  bronchial catarrh, 445
  capillary bronchitis, 382
  cataract, 443
  cirrhosis of the liver, 444
  colic, 722
  complementary relations, 446
  constipation, 186, 444
  constitution, 440
  convulsions, 44
  cough, 546
  diphtheria, 50, 211, 413, 443
  dropsy, 445
  dyspepsia, 131, 487
  dysuria, 443, 711
  erectile tumors, 441
  face, 44, 440
  feet, 692
  fever, 440
  flatulence, 284, 445, 497
  gastric symptoms, 444, 553, 724
  gout, 453, 656
  gravel, 443
  haemorrhoids, 441
  hectic fever, 446
  hemiopia, 702
  hernia, 189
  hydropericardium, 445
  intermittent fever, 70, 441
  joints, 656
  kidneys, 446
  labor, 328
  liver, 282, 444
  liver spots, 125

LYCOPODIUM (Continued)
  lungs, 445, 627
  mental symptoms, 37, 440
  modalities, 440
  mucous membranes, 445
  naevi, 441
  nasal catarrh, 445
  ovaries, 65
  parotitis, 442
  pneumonia, 446
  pregnancy, 441
  preparation of, 440
  pulse, 441
  renal colic, 191, 446
  retinitis, 443
  rheumatism, 231, 446, 453
  scarlatina, 211, 418, 442, 446
  scrofulosis, 545
  seminal emissions, 175, 192
  sensitiveness, 36
  sexual excesses, 192, 339
  skin, 688
  sleep, 443
  stomach, 131
  styes, 443
  temperament, 440
  tongue, 442
  tonsillitis, 414, 454, 651
  tympanites, 261, 271, 487
  typhoid fever, 430, 441, 446, 675
  ulcers, 62, 63, 445
  urine, 271, 442, 710
  varicose veins, 441
  wine, aggravation from, 632
LYTTA VITATA
  skin 84

MAGNESIA CARBONICA, 643
  abuse of, 144
  antidotal relations, 644
  cataract, 646
  colic, 644
  constitution, 644
  diarrhoea, 644, 687
  dyspepsia, 645
  marasmus, 644
  menses, 645
  neuralgia, 120, 644
  pregnancy, 645
  rheumatism, 646
  teeth, 645
  vomiting, 672
MAGNESIA MURIATICA, 646
  cataract, 575
  constipation, 647
  constitution, 646
  dysmenorrhoea, 202, 647
  dysuria, 648
  headache, 120, 646
  heart, 120, 647
  hysteria, 120, 646
  liver, 186, 647
  menses, 120, 647
  nervous system, 120, 121, 648
  ozaena, 647
  rachitis, 647
  scirrhus, 202

INDEX OF REMEDIES.

MAGNESIA MURIATICA (Continued)
  scrofulous, 648
  skin, 647
  sweat, 647
  tongue, 647
  uterus, 202, 647
MAGNESIA PHOSPHORICA
  nervous system, 648
  neuralgia, 120, 555
MAGNOLIA GRANDIFLORA
  heart, 393
MALARIA OFFICINALIS
  intermittent fever, 373
MAMMALIA, 27
MANCINELLA
  scarlatina, 86, 313
  skin, 85, 86, 313
MANGANUM
  anaemia, 641
  cough, 609
  heels, 663
  larynx, 609
  liver, 633
  marasmus, 633
  paralysis, 633
  rheumatism, 663
MEDORRHINUM
  mental symptoms, 37
MEDUSA
  urticaria, 31
MELANTHACEAE, 250
MEL CUM SALE
  metritis, 415
  uterus and ovaries, 112
MELILOTUS
  headache, 200, 277
MENISPERMACEAE, 259
MENTHA PIPERITA
  cough, 428
MENYANTHES
  headache, 354, 547
  intermittent fever, 68, 372, 483
MEPHITIS
  asthma, 27
  loquacity, 39
  nervous system, 27, 79
  sleep, 521
  whooping-cough, 27, 31
MERCURIUS ACETICUS
  vesical irritation, 92
MERCURIUS BINIOD.
  diphtheria, 214, 594
  eyes, 593
  syphilis, 491, 597
MERCURIUS CORROS.
  balanorrhoea, 394
  corneal ulcers, 593
  diphtheria, 596
  eyes, 593
  gonorrhoea, 91, 394
  iritis, 593, 602, 716
  ophthalmia neonatorum, 347
  retinitis albuminurica, 593
  syphilis, 593, 596, 602
  syphilitic nasal disease, 596
  throat, 95, 596
  typhilis, 60

MERCURIUS CORROS. (Continued)
  ulcers, 597
  urinary organs, 91
MERCURIUS CYANATUS
  croup, 723
  diphtheria, 214, 481, 524, 595
  epistaxis, 451
MERCURIUS DULCIS
  eyes, 593
  scrofulous ophthalmia, 593
MERCURIUS PROTOIOD.
  diphtheria, 595
  eyes, 593
  syphilis, 597
  ulcers of the cornea, 593
MERCURIUS SULPHURICUS
  hydrothorax, 390, 559
MERCURIUS VIVUS AND SOLUBILIS, 590
  abscess, 592
  abscess of teeth, 46
  antidotal relation, 589
  aphthous sore mouth, 47, 710
  balanorrhoea, 311
  blepharitis, 397, 593, 609
  bones, 341
  catarrhal fever, 591
  catarrh of the bowels, 591
  chancroid, 596
  congestions, 591
  conjunctivitis, 397
  constipation, 54
  corneal ulcers, 593
  coryza, 190, 594
  diarrhoea, 250, 396, 591
  diphtheria, 594
  dysentery, 54, 188, 253, 296, 324, 357
  dyspepsia, 54
  epistaxis, 591
  eyes, 397, 495, 593
  fever, 410
  felon, 592
  gastric fever, 591
  glands, 590, 596
  glans, irritation of, 88
  gonorrhoea, 91, 311, 352, 394
  haemorrhages, 591
  headache, 41, 591
  inimical relations, 543
  iritis, 311, 593
  jaundice, 187
  leucorrhoea, 674
  liver, 395, 597, 647
  male genital organs, 88
  meningitis, 591
  menorrhagia, 592
  nasal catarrh, 594
  nostalgia, 590
  orchitis, 513
  ovarian tumor, 62
  otitis media, 349
  ozaena, 49
  periodontitis, 46
  peritonitis, 592
  phimosis, 352
  pneumonia, 283, 592
  rheumatism, 51

INDEX OF REMEDIES.

MERCURIUS VIV. AND SOL. (Continued)
    scabies, 476
    scrofulosis, 590
    scrofulous ophthalmia, 496, 593
    skin, 85, 688
    sweat, 591
    syphilis, 591, 593, 596
    throat, 190, 594, 685
    tongue, 454
    tonsillitis, 414, 592, 685
    toothache, 47, 81
    typhlitis, 54, 59
    typhoid fever, 226
    ulcers, 62, 3, 534
    urinary organs, 90, 91
MERCURY
    antidotes, 189, 536, 585, 600
    poisoning by, 588
    preparations of, 584
MEZEREUM
    anus, 60
    antidotal relation, 587
    ciliary neuralgia, 205
    cough, 234
    crusta lactea, 168
    eczema, 233
    herpes zoster, 332
    neuralgia, 308, 555
    rectum and anus, 60
    skin, 85, 86, 168
    ulcers, 125, 677
MILLEFOLIUM, 243
    haematemesis, 301
    haemoptysis, 324
    haemorrhages, 243, 368
    menses, 301, 613
MINERAL KINGDOM, 455
MITCHELLA
    cervix uteri, 145
    metrorrhagia, 158
    vesical irritability, 145, 158
MOMORDICA BALSAMUM
    flatulence, 284, 445
MORPHIA
    cancer, 265
    tympanites, 265
MOSCHUS, 27, 115
    antidotal relations, 79, 116
    convulsions, 116
    headache, 116
    hysteria, 79, 116, 198, 614
    menses, 65
    mental symptoms, 79, 116
    nervous system, 115
    paralysis of the lungs, 485, 582
    pneumonia, 121
    poisoning by, 115
    reaction, defective, 121, 150
    vertigo, 37
MUREX PURPUREA
    leucorrhoea, 135
    menses, 135
    polyuria, 136
    uterus, 135
MURIATIC ACID, 521
    antidotal relations, 525
    aphthous sore mouth, 47

MURIATIC ACID (Continued)
    cirrhosis of the liver, 525
    diphtheria, 211, 524
    dropsy, 525
    gastric symptoms, 525
    general symptoms, 521
    mental symptoms, 521
    muscular exhaustion, 336, 525
    nervous system, 521
    scarlatina, 211, 524
    typhoid fever, 40, 108, 228, 403, 430, 522
    ulcers, 63
MYGALE, 73
    chordee, 75
    chorea, 75
    mental symptoms, 75
    nervous system, 73
MYLABIS CICHORII ET PHALATERII, 80
MYOSOTIS
    lungs, 627
MYRICA CERIFERA
    jaundice, 391
MYRTUS COMMUNIS
    phthisis, 83, 306

NAJA
    diphtheria, 50, 213
NAPHTHALIN
    emphysema, 558
NATRUM ARSENICOSUM (or Arsenicatum), 706
    bronchitis, 707
    catarrh, 706
    coryza, 706
    cough, 707
    diphtheria, 110, 214, 254
    face, 43
    psoriasis, 707
    scarlatina, 524
    throat, 706
    tuberculosis, 707
NATRUM CARBONICUM, 689
    ankle-joint, 676, 692
    burns, 689
    catarrhs, 693
    cervix uteri, 142, 693
    constipation, 690
    corneal ulcers, 693
    cough, 693
    debility, 692
    diarrhoea, 690
    dyspepsia, 690
    eczema, 693
    eyes, 619
    feet, 692
    female genital organs, 142, 693
    headache, 692
    heat, ill effects of, 691
    heels, 663, 692
    hypochondriasis, 689
    labor, 694
    marasmus, 645
    mental symptoms, 689
    mucous membranes, 693
    nasal catarrh, 693
    nervous system, 691

INDEX OF REMEDIES.

NATRUM CARBONICUM (Continued)
ozaena, 693
pregnancy, 691
phlyctenular ophthalmia, 693
prolapsus uteri, 142
seminal emissions, 703
skin, 689
sunstroke, 38, 691

NATRUM HYPOCHLOROSUM, 142
ankle-joint, 692
aphthous sore mouth, 48
enuresis, 692
female genitals, 143
headache, 143
otorrhoea, 692
prolapsus uteri, 143
pruritus vulvae, 143

NATRUM MURIATICUM, 696
anaemia, 698
antidotal relation, 696
anus, 60, 705
asthenopia, 130, 702
awkwardness, 102
brain-fag, 128
blepharospasm, 189
cataract, 575, 697
catarrhs, 648, 702
chlorosis, 700
chorea, 699
ciliary neuralgia, 701
conjunctivitis, 131
constipation, 704
coryza, 702
cough, 427, 703, 732
diarrhoea, 705
dyspepsia, 704
eczema, 705
elongated uvula, 427, 703
eyes, 130, 619, 702
headache, 128, 300, 699, 701, 702, 724
female genital organs, 142, 615, 700
fever blisters, 705
fright, ill effects of, 272
gonorrhoea, 703
gout, 656
grief, chronic effects of, 197, 528
headache, 128, 300, 699, 701, 702, 724
heart, 134, 499
hemiopia, 702
herpes, 705
hypochondriasis, 699, 704
intermittent fever, 108, 229, 706
leucorrhoea, 142
marasmus, 703
menses, 700
mental symptoms, 102, 126, 344, 624, 699
nervous system, 29, 606, 691
neuralgia, 625
paralysis, 170, 624, 627
prolapsus ani, 704
prolapsus uteri, 142, 146, 700
ptosis, 131
rectum and anus, 61, 705
scrofulous ophthalmia, 702
scurvy, 698
seminal emissions, 703
skin, 688, 698, 702, 705

NATRUM MURIATICUM (Continued)
spinal irritation, 329, 700, 739
sunstroke, 38
sweat, 300
throat, 702
tongue, 333, 698
urine, 66
urticaria, 705

NATRUM PHOSPHORICUM
seminal emissions, 703

NATRUM SULPHURICUM, 694
asthma, 694
constitution, 694
corneal opacities, 699
diarrhoea, 453, 474, 695, 724
eyes, 619
flatulence, 695
hip-joint disease, 695
injuries, 434, 694
jaundice, 187
phthisis, 694
sycosis, 694

NICCOLUM
stomach, 132

NICOTINUM
tetanus, 181, 182

NITRI SPIRITUS DULCIS
See Sweet Spirits of Nitre

NITRIC ACID, 533
abscess of the mastoid process, 435, 591
antidotal relations, 535, 536, 586
anus, 60, 534
aphonia, 536
aphthous sore mouth, 47, 48
balanorrhoea, 310
caries of the mastoid process, 43, 435, 491, 535, 602
catarrh, 534
chancre, 63, 535
condylomata, 310
corneal ulcers, 535, 670
cough, 536
diarrhoea, 534
diphtheria, 210, 444, 534
ears, 43, 535
fissure in ano, 497, 534
iritis, 602
leucorrhoea, 510, 534
local effects of, 533
mastoid, caries of, 43, 435, 602
mental symptoms, 219, 535
mercury, abuse of, 535
mucous membranes, 533, 534
ozaena, 49
pemphigus, 87
phthisis, 536
ptyalism, 534
rectum and anus, 60
renal colic, 610
scarlatina, 210, 534
scrofulosis, 670
skin, 85
stomacace, 534
sweat, 653
syphilis, 63, 491, 534, 535, 602
throat, 535, 609, 619, 685

49

NITRIC ACID (Continued)
  tuberculosis, 670
  typhoid fever, 522, 536
  ulcers, 63, 310, 534, 535
  urine, 534
  warts, 310, 535
NITRITE OF AMYL
  cerebral congestion, 320
  climacteric, 31, 466
  eyes, 412
  flushes of heat, 31, 466
  heart, 31
  metrorrhagia, 278
  neuralgia, 322, 419
  prosopalgia, 322
NITRO-MURIATIC ACID
  gastric symptoms, 525
NOBLE METALS, 599
NOSODES, 147
NUPHAR LUTEUM
  diarrhoea, 380
NUX JUGLANS
  crusta lactea, 168
  skin, 85
  tinea favosa, 168, 234
NUX MOSCHATA
  eyes, 619
  face, 44
  hysteria, 118, 199
  mental symptoms, 118
  nervous system, 118, 121, 248
  rheumatism, 646
NUX VOMICA, 177
  abdominal symptoms, 136
  acne, 195
  amblyopia, 189
  antidotal relations, 136, 266, 492, 562
  apoplexy, 269
  arthritic headache, 128
  asthma, 190
  atrophy of the retina, 189
  backache, 194
  bladder, 192
  blepharospasm, 189
  brain-fag, 128, 540
  brain, softening of the, 184, 564
  catarrh, 190
  colic, 186, 272, 621
  complementary relations, 183
  composition of, 177
  conjunctivitis, 189
  constipation, 184, 186, 220, 445, 686
  coryza, 190, 249, 326, 594
  cough, 111, 196
  cramps in muscles, 288
  debility, 252
  diarrhoea, 188, 287
  drunkards, complaints of, 186, 187, 189, 191, 195
  dysentery, 96, 188, 597
  dysmenorrhoea, 263
  dyspepsia, 184, 185, 350, 477, 487, 704
  dysuria, 192
  ears, 190
  ecchymoses of the sclerotic, 189
  epilepsy, 30, 547, 676

NUX VOMICA (Continued)
  epistaxis, 190
  Eustachian catarrh, 190
  eyes, 131, 189
  face, 44
  female genitals, 136, 193
  follicular tonsillitis, 722
  gastric catarrh, 378
  gastric irritability, 184
  gastric symptoms, 445
  gonorrhoea, 192
  haematuria, 192
  haemoptysis, 191
  haemorrhoids, 186, 187
  headache, 129, 183, 184, 300
  hemicrania, 129
  hernia, 189
  hypochondriasis, 618, 691
  hysteria, 276
  inimical relation, 196, 631
  intermittent fever, 196
  jaundice, 187
  labor, 193, 355
  lead colic, 621
  liver, 130, 136, 186
  liver spots, 125
  locomotor ataxia, 194
  lumbago, 194, 677
  marasmus, 554
  masturbation, 192
  menses, 193
  mental symptoms, 102, 344, 619
  metrorrhagia, 194
  modalities, 196, 440
  myelitis, 194
  nasal catarrh, 594
  nose, 276
  paralysis, 315, 731
  pregnancy, 193, 691
  prolapsus uteri, 193, 454, 625
  renal colic, 182, 191
  rheumatism, 195, 677
  scrofulous ophthalmia, 189
  seminal emissions, 175, 192
  sensitiveness, 36
  sexual excesses, 192, 339, 477
  sleep, 184, 196, 361
  spinal cord, 194, 620
  spinal irritation, 194, 330, 620
  stomacace, 190
  stomach, 59, 136
  temperament, 183
  tetanus, 537
  throat, 190
  torticollis, 194, 422
  typhoid fever, 196
  uterus, 136
  vomiting of pregnancy, 193, 220, 691
  wine, aggravation from, 632, 634

OCINUM
  renal calculi, 92
OENANTHE CROCATA
  convulsions, 428
OENOTHERA BIENNIS
  diarrhoea, 379

INDEX OF REMEDIES.

OLEANDER, 165
  abdominal organs, 165
  antidotal relations, 167
  crusta lactea, 167
  diarrhoea, 166, 371, 642
  headache, 165
  lactation, 165, 490
  mental symptoms, 165
  paralysis, 165, 166
  poisoning by, 165
  skin, 85, 166
  stomach, 132, 165
  vertigo, 165
OLEUM ANIMALE, 28
  headache, 171
  polyuria, 171
OLEUM JECORIS ASELLI
  general symptoms of, 29
  tuberculosis, 29
OLEUM RICINI COMMUNIS
  See Ricinus Communis
OPHIDIA, 33
  antidotes, 35
  general effects, 34
OPIUM, 264
  abortion, 176
  alkaloids of, 264
  antidotal relations, 266, 268, 272
  anus, 60
  apoplexy, 100, 268
  asphyxia from charcoal vapor, 273
  bladder, 271
  brain, paralysis of the, 268
  cholera infantum, 270
  colic, 272, 621
  constipation, 186, 271, 461
  convulsions, 200, 201, 270
  cough, 270
  delirium tremens, 269
  diarrhoea, 176, 255
  drunkards, complaints of, 268, 269, 270, 650
  face, 44, 420
  fever, 272
  fright, ill effects of, 270, 272
  general action of, 266
  haemoptysis, 270
  hernia, 272
  lead colic, 621
  marasmus, 271
  mental symptoms, 268
  metrorrhagia, 272
  muscular exhaustion, 336
  poisoning by, 266, 267
  puerperal fever, 272
  reaction, defective, 150, 270
  rectum and anus, 60, 61
  retention of urine, 271
  suppression of urine, 271
  suppuration of the lungs, 270
  tympanites, 267, 270
  typhlitis, 272
  typhoid fever, 39, 268, 272, 335, 336, 528
OPUNTIA VULGARIS
  diarrhoea, 379
ORTHOPTERA, 32

OSMIUM
  urine, 306
OXALIC ACID
  spinal softening, 540
  testicles, 352
OZONE, 458

PAEONIA
  fissure in ano, 497
  haemorrhoids, 497
PALLADIUM, 615
  female genital organs, 615
  headache, 615
  hysteria, 78
  mental symptoms, 64, 78, 615
  ovaritis, 64, 616
  uterus, 79, 615
PAPAVERACEAE, 264
PAREIRA BRAVA
  cystic calculus, 93
  urinary symptoms, 93, 453
PARIS QUADRIFOLIA
  eyes, 412
  headache, 547
  larynx, 610
  loquacity, 39
  mammae, 503
PASSIFLORA INCARNATA
  tetanus, 179
PAULLINIA SORBILIS
  diarrhoea, 379
  headache, 278
PENTHORUM SEDOIDES
  coryza, 348
PETROLEUM, 498
  antidotal relations, 500
  blepharitis, 499
  cough, 499
  dacryo-cystitis, 499
  diarrhoea, 499, 500
  eczema, 311, 495, 499
  eyes, 499
  dislocation of the jaw, 235
  fistula, 499
  gastralgia, 497
  gastric symptoms, 500
  headache, 172, 300
  heart, 134, 499
  lumbago, 230
  mental symptoms, 437, 500
  nervous system, 500
  ozaena, 499
  periodontitis, 46
  rheumatism, 499
  sea-sickness, 499
  skin, 31, 495, 498
  sprains, 499
  sweat, 499, 544
  sycosis, 398
  teeth, 46
  typhoid fever, 500
  vertigo, 82
  vomiting of pregnancy, 499
PETROSELINUM
  gonorrhoea, 90, 394, 450, 710
  dysuria, 710

INDEX OF REMEDIES.

PETROSELINUM (Continued)
  vesical irritation, 90
PHELLANDRIUM
  headache, 354, 450
  mammary glands, 302, 450
  phthisis, 546
PHOSPHORIC ACID, 526
  bones, 530
  cough, 530
  debility, 367, 526, 624
  diabetes, 518
  diarrhœa, 370, 530
  enuresis, 247
  epistaxis, 527
  face, 44
  fright, ill effects of, 272
  grief, ill effects of, 197, 528
  growing pains, 530
  headache, 530
  hip-joint disease, 530
  home-sickness, 528
  kidneys, 530
  masturbation, 529
  mental symptoms, 197, 471, 526, 738
  mucous membranes, 529
  neurasthenia, 367, 541, 624
  ovaries, 528
  rheumatism, 735
  seminal emissions, 529
  sensorial depression, 335, 526
  sleep, 529
  tuberculosis, 530
  typhoid fever, 228, 335, 430, 523, 527
  ulcers, 63
  uterus, 528
  vertebral caries, 530
PHOSPHORUS, 562
  alimentary tract, 567
  amblyopia, 574
  amenorrhœa, 569
  antidotal relations, 562
  aphonia, 462, 485, 570
  asthenopia, 574
  blood, 575
  bones, 545, 573
  brain fag, 540
  brain, softening of the, 184
  Bright's disease, 569
  bronchitis, 190, 570, 571
  cancer of the stomach, 568
  capillary bronchitis, 381
  cataract, 575
  chest pains, 306
  chorea, 565
  choroiditis, 574
  complementary relations, 562
  constipation, 566
  coryza, 380
  cough, 151, 421, 546, 570, 571
  croup, 570
  deafness, 574
  debility, 367
  delirium, 563
  diabetes, 568
  diarrhœa, 166, 475, 565, 568
  dyspepsia, 568

PHOSPHORUS (Continued)
  endocarditis, 572
  eyes, 574, 683
  face, 44, 45
  fatty degeneration, 540, 566, 569
  fatty degeneration of the heart, 572
  fatty degeneration of the liver, 567
  fistulae, 573
  gastric symptoms, 565, 568, 636
  grief, ill effects of, 198
  haematemesis, 301, 575
  haemophilia, 575
  haemoptysis, 301, 569
  haemorrhages, 369, 569
  headache, 563
  heart, 31, 514, 572
  hip-joint disease, 573
  hysteria, 276
  impotence, 564
  inimical relation, 729
  jaundice, 567
  kidneys, 559, 569
  laryngismus stridulus, 504
  larynx, 462, 570
  leucorrhœa, 674
  liver, 477, 565, 567
  locomotor ataxia, 564
  lungs, 627
  mammary abscess, 569
  marasmus, 469
  menses, 301, 569
  mental symptoms, 562
  myocarditis, 572
  nasal catarrh, 569
  necrosis of the lower jaw, 573
  nervous system, 562, 691
  neurasthenia, 367, 540
  nose, 276
  nymphomania, 562, 563, 569
  ozaena, 569
  pancreas, 568
  paralysis, 564, 569, 624, 636
  paralysis of the lungs, 485
  phthisis, 599, 626
  pneumonia, 279, 381, 571
  polypi, 369, 569
  retinal apoplexy, 43
  retinitis, 574
  retinitis albuminurica, 574
  rose-cold, 276
  scrofulosis, 669
  seminal emissions, 175, 540, 563
  sexual excesses, 564
  spasmodic oesophageal stricture, 568
  spinal cord, 564
  spinal irritation, 195, 563
  sweat, 566
  throat, 567
  tongue, 567
  tracheitis, 570
  tuberculosis, 470, 564, 571, 669, 673
  typhoid fever,
  ulcers, 62, 568, 574, 683
  vertebral caries, 573
  vomiting, 672
  waxy degeneration of the liver, 567

INDEX OF REMEDIES. 773

PHOSPHORUS (Continued)
  white swelling, 573
  yellow atrophy of the liver, 567

PHYSOSTIGMA
  paralysis, 178
  spinal irritation, 195, 329
  tetanus, 178, 195

PHYTOLACCA
  aphthous sore mouth, 48
  carbuncle, 561
  cicatrices, 141, 544
  convulsions, 179
  diphtheria, 213, 444
  face, 44
  heart, 225
  mammary abscess, 302
  tetanus, 179

PICRIC ACID, 538
  back, 134, 361, 539
  brain-fag, 128, 538
  brain, softening of the, 184
  general symptoms of, 538
  headache, 128, 194
  locomotor ataxia, 97
  meningitis, 97
  myelitis, 97
  neurasthenia, 539
  poisoning by, 538
  priapism, 97, 194, 539
  seminal emissions, 539
  skin, 85
  spinal irritation, 194
  vertigo, 539

PICROTOXINE, 259
  tetanus, 178

PINUS SYLVESTRIS
  joints, 676, 692

PIPER METHYSTICUM
  nervous system, 385
  vertigo, 82

PIPER NIGRUM
  skin, 58, 86

PISCES, 29

PIX LIQUIDA, 306
  bronchial catarrh, 215
  lungs, 306, 627
  phthisis, 83, 215, 306
  skin, 85, 86, 87, 306

PLANTAGO MAJOR
  enuresis, 416, 734
  otalgia, 349
  relation to tobacco, 433

PLANTAIN
  antidotal relation, 433

PLATINA, 612
  constipation, 614
  convulsions, 339, 614
  female genital organs, 65, 140, 613
  headache, 78
  hysteria, 78, 198, 613, 614
  lead colic, 614, 621
  masturbation, 339, 614
  menses, 65, 613
  mental symptoms, 127, 140, 612, 615
  neuralgia, 420, 613, 625
  nymphomania, 64, 140, 612

PLATINA (Continued)
  ovaritis, 64, 613
  prolapsus uteri, 613
  puerperal convulsions, 614
  sexual excesses, 339, 614
  uterus, 140

PLATINUM MUR.
  bones, 545, 614

PLUMBUM, 621
  abortion, 622
  antidotal relations, 621
  cerebral sclerosis, 622
  colic, 621
  constipation, 271, 461, 614, 622
  delirium, 622
  epilepsy, 622
  granular kidneys, 603, 623
  kidney, 623
  multiple cerebro-spinal sclerosis, 622
  muscles, 621
  paralysis, 621, 622, 636
  progressive muscular atrophy, 622
  rectum and anus, 60, 61
  ulcers, 63

PODOPHYLLUM PELTATUM, 453
  abdominal symptoms, 453
  biliary calculi, 454
  bilious remittent fever, 454
  cholera infantum, 59, 285
  cholera morbus, 256
  constipation, 454
  convulsions, 59
  dentition, 59, 454
  diarrhoea, 188, 250, 371, 395, 453, 474
  fever, 454
  liver, 137, 138, 453
  marasmus, 645
  prolapsus recti, 138, 454, 625
  prolapsus uteri, 138, 188, 454, 625
  skin, 85, 453
  stomach, 138
  tongue, 454
  tonsillitis, 454

POTASH SALTS
  remarks on the, 712

POTHOS FOETIDA
  asthma, 216
  hysteria, 216

PSORINUM, 148
  boils, 150
  cholera infantum, 149
  constitution, 148
  debility, 738
  diarrhoea, 149
  eczema, 234
  headache, 49, 150, 724
  herpes, 149
  night sweats, 374
  otorrhoea, 149
  pregnancy, 150
  reaction, defective, 149, 150, 270, 464
  scabies, 150
  scarlatina, 148
  sebaceous glands, 149
  skin, 149, 688
  tinea capitis, 149

INDEX OF REMEDIES.

PSORINUM (Continued)
  typhoid fever, 150
  ulcers, 149
PSEUDO-ACONITINE, 315
PTELEA
  headache, 377
  liver, 648
PULMO VULPIS
  asthma, 29
PULSATILLA NUTTALLIANA, 343
  chest-pains, 306, 361
PULSATILLA PRATENSIS, 343
    after-pains, 356
    agalactia, 356
    amenorrhoea, 355
    anaemia, 344
    antidotal relations, 343, 644
    asthenopia, 130
    backache, 361
    bronchitis, 361
    chest, 331, 345
    chlorosis, 344, 494
    circulation, 345
    complementary relations, 343
    conjunctivitis, 130, 347
    constipation, 351
    corneal ulcers, 347
    coryza, 190, 348
    cough, 234, 536, 732
    cystitis, 92, 351
    dacryo-cystitis, 347
    diarrhoea, 176, 256, 272, 351, 355
    dysmenorrhoea, 202, 263
    dyspepsia, 185, 370
    ears, 348, 708
    epistaxis, 346, 354, 355
    eyes, 130, 347
    face, 44
    female genital organs, 138, 354
    fever, 360
    fright, ill effects of, 272
    gastric catarrh, 349, 579
    gastric symptoms, 377, 496
    general character of, 343
    gonorrhoea, 310, 352
    gout, 353
    haematemesis, 301
    haemoptysis, 301, 361
    headache, 41, 353
    heart, 225, 345
    heels, 663
    hemicrania, 129
    hiccough, 203
    hydrocele, 353
    intermittent fever, 360
    jaundice, 187
    joints, 221
    labor, 193, 355
    leucorrhoea, 674
    lungs, 740
    mammary glands, 356
    measles, 174, 326, 361
    menses, 138, 301, 355
    mental symptoms, 126, 197, 343, 344, 617, 627, 700
    milk leg, 356

PULSATILLA PRATENSIS (Continued)
  mucous membranes, 347
  mumps, 245
  nasal catarrh, 348, 594
  neuralgia, 361
  ophthalmia neonatorum, 347, 608
  orchitis, 310, 352
  otalgia, 348, 683, 708
  otitis externa, 348, 354
  otitis media, 348, 349
  ozaena, 310
  pregnancy, 351, 355
  prostate gland, enlargement of the, 352
  prostatitis, 310
  purulent ophthalmia, 608
  retained placenta, 355, 356, 368
  rheumatism, 231, 310, 353
  skin, 85
  sleep, 362
  spinal irritation, 361
  sycosis, 310, 726
  synovial membranes, 353
  synovitis, 353
  temperament, 197, 344
  testicles, 352
  throat, 349
  tuberculosis, 345, 355
  urine, suppression of, 271
  urticaria, 107
  uterus, 138, 625
  varicocele, 346
  varicose veins, 346
  vesical irritation, 92
  vicarious menstruation, 301
  wine, aggravation from, 632

QUASSIA
  worms, 247
QUILLAYA SAPONARIA, 627
  coryza, 174
QUININE
  See Chinin. sulph.

RADIATA, 30
RADIX COPTIDIS, 314
RANUNCULACEAE, 314
RANUNCULUS BULBOSUS, 330
  alcoholism, 332
  diaphragmitis, 321
  eczema, 332
  epilepsy, 332
  hay fever, 332
  headache, 354
  herpes zoster, 332
  hiccough, 332
  pemphigus, 87, 332
  peritonitis, 331
  pleurisy, 331
  pleurodynia, 295, 331
  pneumonia, 331
  rheumatism, 331
  serous membranes, 331
  skin, 85, 86, 330, 332
  ulcers, 332
RANUNCULUS SCELERATUS, 333
  coryza, 333

INDEX OF REMEDIES. 775

RANUNCULUS SCEL. (Continued)
  diphtheria, 333
  headache, 354
  influenza, 87
  pemphigus, 86
  skin, 86, 87, 330, 333
  stomacace, 333
  tongue, 333
  typhoid fever, 333
  ulcers, 333

RAPHANUS
  flatulence, 271, 445

RATANHIA
  fissure in ano, 497
  toothache, 645

RHEUM
  antidotal relation, 644
  diarrhoea, 644, 687

RHODODENDRON
  nervous system, 691
  orchitis, 352
  rheumatism, 231
  wine, aggravation from, 632

RHUS GLABRA
  headache, 217

RHUS RADICANS
  headache, 222
  pleurodynia, 231, 296
  rheumatism, 231

RHUS TOXICODENDRON, 223
  antidotal relations, 223, 224
  aphonia, 733
  apoplexy, 269
  blepharospasm, 235
  brain, 235
  carbuncles, 232
  cellulitis, 232, 234
  chemosis, 113
  circulation, 223
  colic, 234
  conjunctivitis, 113, 235, 397
  coryza, 234
  cough, 234, 546
  diarrhoea, 234
  diphtheria, 213, 225, 232
  dislocation of the jaw, 235
  dropsy, 445
  dysentery, 225, 234
  eczema, 232
  enteritis, 59, 234
  erysipelas, 46, 106, 113, 221, 232
  eyes, 113, 235, 397, 609, 619
  face, 41
  fever blisters, 705
  glaucoma, 235
  granular lids, 609
  haemoptysis, 229
  heart, 223, 225, 323
  herpes zoster, 332
  hypertrophy of the heart, 223, 239, 323, 508
  influenza, 234
  inimical relation, 114
  injuries, 240
  intermittent fever, 229
  iritis, 235, 397

RHUS TOXICODENDRON (Continued)
  lumbago, 230, 677
  meningitis, 102
  mental symptoms, 226, 437
  metritis, 234
  muscular exertion, ill effects of, 229, 521
  oesophagus, 414
  otalgia, 235
  palpitation of the heart, 225
  paralysis, 236, 322, 731
  parotitis, 443
  pemphigus, 87
  periproctitis, 60
  peritonitis, 59, 225, 234
  perityphlitis, 234
  phlyctenular ophthalmia, 235
  pneumonia, 225, 227
  ptosis, 170, 235, 398
  pulse, 225
  scarlatina, 102, 109, 225, 233
  rheumatism, 230, 249, 297, 677, 735
  scrofulous ophthalmia, 235
  skin, 85, 232, 560
  sprains, 229
  sweat, 545, 566
  tongue, 226, 333, 567
  toothache, 236
  torticollis, 230
  typhlitis, 60, 234
  typhoid fever, 40, 225, 226, 292, 402, 410, 430, 523, 527, 552
  typhoid pneumonia, 227
  ulcers, 445
  urticaria, 107
  variola, 233, 234
  vertigo, 234
  vomiting, 265, 417

RHUS VENENATA, 217

RICINUS COMMUNIS
  agalactia, 313, 350
  antidote to, 313

ROBINIA
  neuralgia, 555

ROSA DAMASCENA
  hay fever, 557

RUBIACEAE, 363

RUMEX CRISPUS
  asthma, 27
  cough, 111, 421, 427, 546, 570
  diarrhoea, 474, 724
  pleurodynia, 296
  urticaria, 107

RUTA
  asthenopia, 449
  complementary relations, 681
  eyes, 449, 619
  injuries, 532, 654
  lumbago, 230
  sprains, 654

SABADILLA, 258
  influenza, 258
  intermittent fever, 229
  mental symptoms, 258
  modalities, 440
  tonsillitis, 258

SABADILLA (Continued)
  worms, 258
SABINA, 305
  abortion, 305
  condylomata, 311
  gastric symptoms, 350
  gout, 298
  menses, 613
  metrorrhagia, 305, 368
  retained placenta, 356
  rheumatism, 298, 663
SACCHARUM OFFICINALE
  corneal opacity, 669
  mental symptoms, 669
SALICYLIC ACID
  aphthae, 48
  Meniere's disease, 733
SAMBUCUS
  coryza, 249
  laryngismus stridulus, 324, 504
  laryngitis, 513
SANGUINARIA CANADENSIS, 275
  acne, 280
  aphonia, 280
  bronchitis, 374
  circulation, 276, 278
  conjunctivitis, 280
  coryza, 280
  cough, 152, 234, 278, 279, 374
  ears, 276
  general action of, 276
  haemorrhages, 278
  headache, 82, 171, 200, 276
  hemicrania, 128
  hysteria, 276
  larynx, 290
  menses, 278
  mental symptoms, 275
  metrorrhagia, 278
  nose, 276
  phthisis, 278
  pneumonia, 278
  polypi, 280, 570
  polyuria, 171
  rheumatism, 280, 646, 735
  rose-cold, 276
  skin, 275
  vertigo, 276
SANTONINE, 246
  eyes, 247, 360
SAPONIN, 627
  muscular exhaustion, 336
SARSAPARILLA
  antidotal relations, 272
  chest pains, 306
  gravel, 92, 443
  headache, 311
  marasmus, 272
  skin, 311
  stomach, 132
  sycosis, 311, 726
  tinea capitis, 311
  urine, 710
SCILLA MARITIMA
  cough, 546, 703, 732
  lungs, 627

SCOPARIUS
  dropsy, 163
SCROPHULARIACEAE, 387
SCUTELLARIA
  reaction, defective, 121
SCROPHULARIACEAE, 387
  abortion, 154
  blood, 154
  bloodvessels, 154, 650
  cataract, 575
  cholera Asiatica, 155, 554
  cholera infantum, 155
  cholera morbus, 155
  circulation, 154
  collapse, 69, 156
  constitution, 154
  convulsions, 153, 201, 437
  enuresis, 247
  epistaxis, 157
  face, 44
  female genital organs, 145
  follicular pharyngitis, 722
  gangrene, 154, 156, 560
  gastro-enteric symptoms, 155, 554
  haemorrhages, 154, 368
  intermittent fever, 69
  labor, 154
  lumbago, 677
  lungs, 374
  metrorrhagia, 145, 155, 368
  paralysis, 650
  poisoning by, 153
  prolapsus uteri, 145
  retained placenta, 154, 356
  ulcers, 63, 156
  uterus, 154
SELENIUM, 459
  aphonia, 210, 462, 733
  constipation, 460
  debility, 459
  gastric symptoms, 460
  headache, 460
  heat, ill effects of, 38, 459
  impotence, 459
  inimical relation, 462
  larynx, 461, 610
  liver, 461
  nervous system, 459
  prostatorrhoea, 459
  seminal emissions, 175, 459
  skin, 461
  sleep, 461
  sun, ill effects of, 38
  typhoid fever, 459
  urinary organs, 306
  urine, aggravation from, 462, 632
SENECIO AUREUS
  catarrh, 359
  cough, 359
  haemoptysis, 301
  menses, 301, 359
  uterus, 359
SENEGA
  aphonia, 296
  cough, 296
  phthisis, 626

INDEX OF REMEDIES.

SENEGA (Continued)
  pleurodynia, 296
  whooping cough, 32
SENNA
  debility, 737
  urine, 737
SEPIA, 122
  abortion, 146
  anaemia, 347
  ankle joint, 676
  antidotal relation, 125, 432
  arthritic headache, 128
  asthenopia, 129, 130
  backache, 361, 636
  brain fag, 128
  cataract, 130
  chlorosis, 124, 347
  chorea, 146
  circulation, 123, 124
  complementary relations, 135, 142
  circulation, 123, 124
  complexion, 123
  conjunctivitis, 130
  connective tissue, 125
  constipation, 220, 705
  constitution, 122
  cough, 732
  discovery of medicinal virtues of, 122
  dyspepsia, 131, 432
  eczema, 693
  enuresis, 734
  epistaxis, 124
  eyes, 129, 619
  female genital organs, 133, 420, 615
  gastric symptoms, 350, 490, 623
  general action of, 122
  gonorrhoea, 394
  haemorrhoids, 131
  headache, 128, 176, 701
  hemicrania, 128
  herpes, 125, 705
  herpes circinatus, 125, 705
  hypochondriasis, 690
  intermittent fever, 372
  joints, 125
  leucorrhoea, 134, 674
  liver, 131, 186
  liver spots, 125
  marasmus, 645
  menses, 133
  mental symptoms, 125, 344, 347, 617, 624, 690, 700
  neuralgia, 432
  os, induration of the, 139
  pannus, 130
  psoriasis, 125
  post-nasal catarrh, 656
  prolapsus uteri, 193, 454
  ptosis, 170, 235
  rhus poisoning, 125
  scabies, 125, 476
  seminal emissions, 175
  skin, 123, 125, 560, 688
  sphincters, 123
  spinal irritation, 136, 739
  stomach, 131

SEPIA (Continued)
  time, 124
  trachoma, 130
  ulcers, 125, 711
  urticaria, 107
  uterus, 133, 615
  venous congestion, 123
  vertigo, 82
SILICEA, 542
  abscesses, 543, 592
  ankle-joint, 676, 732
  antidotal relation, 543
  boils, 543
  bones, 519, 544
  carbuncle, 80, 543
  cataract, 575
  cellulitis, 543
  chest pains, 306
  cicatrices, 543
  complementary relation, 542
  constipation, 546
  constitution, 542, 677
  corneal ulcers, 545
  cough, 546
  diarrhoea, 546
  ears, 43, 435, 545
  enuresis, 416
  epilepsy, 547, 676
  erysipelas, 106
  fissure in ano, 497, 573
  fistula in ano, 452
  fright, ill effects of, 272
  chest pains, 306
  glands, 544
  hay fever, 332, 546, 557
  headache, 171, 200
  hemicrania, 128, 129
  hip-joint disease, 544, 573
  inimical relation, 543
  keratitis, 545
  knee-joint disease, 544
  lungs, 546
  mammary abscess, 569
  mastoid process, affections of the, 43, 545, 602
  mental symptoms, 272, 440
  mucous membranes, 545
  nasal catarrh, 546
  nervous system, 547, 691
  neuralgia, 683
  neurasthenia, 541
  otitis media, 349, 435
  otorrhoea, 43, 349, 545, 670
  ozaena, 647
  paralysis, 547
  periodontitis, 46
  phthisis, 546, 626
  polyuria, 171
  rachitis, 542, 647
  rheumatism, 548
  scrofulosis, 494, 544, 561, 648
  skin, 688
  spinal cord, 547, 548
  speech, 440
  sweat, 544, 647, 653
  tabes mesenterica, 653

SILICEA (Continued)
tetanus, 181
tonsillitis, 414, 546, 592
tuberculosis, 546
ulcers, 62, 63, 520, 544, 574
vaccination, ill effects from, 307, 542
vertebral caries, 544
vertigo, 548
wine, aggravation from, 632
wine, aggravation from, 632

SINAPIS NIGRA, 558
hay fever, 558
skin, 85

SODA
salts of, 689

SOLANACEAE, 404
SOLANINE, 162
SPIGELIA, 205
brain, 235
ciliary neuralgia, 205, 701
eyes, 205, 321, 412, 701
headache, 82, 205, 354, 392, 701
heart, 111, 206, 254, 392, 509, 741
mental symptoms, 205
neuralgia, 205, 288, 308, 321, 327, 625
post-nasal catarrh, 348, 722
prosopalgia, 322
retinitis, 205
worms, 206

SPONGIA, 512
constitution, 512
cough, 395, 506, 513
croup, 323, 506, 684
glands, 512
goitre, 512
heart, 514
hoarseness, 462
laryngeal phthisis, 513
laryngitis, 462, 513
orchitis, 512
testicles, 352, 512
tuberculosis, 513, 686

SQUILLA MARITIMA
See Scilla

STANNUM METALLICUM, 623
complementary relation, 623
debility, 624
dyspepsia, 624
epilepsy, 625
gastric symptoms, 624
hypochondriasis, 624
hysteria, 625
mental symptoms, 344, 623
mucous membranes, 626
neuralgia, 607, 625
neurasthenia, 623
paralysis, 170, 624, 627
phthisis, 623, 626, 706
pleurisy, 627
prolapsus uteri, 136, 624
stomach, 132
tongue, 624
worms, 624, 625

STAPHISAGRIA, 338
anger, ill effects of, 286, 339
antidotal relation, 340, 587

STAPHISAGRIA (Continued)
aphthous sore mouth, 47
arthritic ophthalmia, 341
bones, 340
colic, 248, 339, 341
condylomata, 311, 340
crusta lactea, 168, 340
diarrhoea, 342
eczema, 340
eyes, 340
gastric symptoms, 341, 377, 400
gout, 341
hypochondriasis, 338
injuries, 241
laparotomy, 241
lumbago, 230
mental symptoms, 248, 338, 339
mouth, 46, 340
ovaries, 339
paralysis, 170, 322, 627
pediculi, 340
prolapsus uteri, 342
sexual excesses, 193, 338
skin, 339
stomacace, 342
stomach, 132, 341, 460
styes, 340
sycosis, 340
syphilis, 340
teeth, 340
temperament, 338
testicles, 352

STICTA PULMONARIA
asthma, 27
coryza, 249
nervous system, 79

STILLINGIA
antidotal relations, 587
bones, 341
hip-joint disease, 695
ozaena, 341
syphilis, 341, 695

STRAMONIUM, 423, 628
antidotal relation, 425
asthma, 424
chorea, 74, 428
convulsions, 45, 183, 200, 423, 714
delirium, 39, 255, 423, 439
delirium tremens, 269
diarrhoea, 425
erysipelas, 425
exanthemata, 424, 425
face, 44, 45
hiccough, 203
hip-joint disease, 425
hydrophobia, 423
locomotor ataxia, 424
loquacity, 39
mania, 429
measles, 424
mental symptoms, 218, 255, 423, 424, 429
nervous system, 79
nymphomania, 425
scarlatina, 302, 418, 425, 428, 443
sleep, 443
stuttering, 425

INDEX OF REMEDIES. 779

STRAMONIUM (Continued)
  tetanus, 183
  tongue, 425, 454
  typhoid fever, 272, 431
  urine, suppression of, 271
STRONTIANA CARBONICA, 653
  apoplexy, 653
  bones, 341, 546, 654
  caries of the femur, 545
  circulation, 653
  climacteric, 654
  diarrhoea, 341, 654
  headache, 548
  neuralgia, 625
  osteitis, 341
  skin, 654
STRYCHNIA, 177
  tetanus, 177
SULPHUR, 463
  abscess, 592
  acne, 195, 468, 475
  ankle-joints, 692, 732
  antidotal relations, 272, 712
  aphonia, 473, 485, 733
  atelectasis, 382
  boils, 468
  brain-fag, 128
  brain, softening of the 184
  bronchitis, 473
  capillary bronchitis, 382
  cholera Asiatica, 478
  cholera infantum, 471, 672
  cicatrices, 544
  circulation, 135, 465
  climacteric, 654
  climaxis, 466
  congestion of the chest, 465
  congestion of the head, 465
  conjunctivitis, 321, 473
  constipation, 220, 476
  constitution, 464
  continued fever, 557
  coryza, 473
  cough, 395
  crusta lactea, 167, 468
  debility, 460, 624
  diarrhoea, 250, 453, 474, 500, 685, 695
  dropsy, 104
  dysentery, 96, 466, 474, 598
  dyspepsia, 132, 476
  eczema, 464
  enuresis, 416
  epilepsy, 676
  erysipelas, 106, 417
  eyes, 321, 473, 494, 670
  face, 44, 132, 465
  female genital organs, 134, 478
  fever, 320, 466, 557
  fistulae, 452
  flatulence, 445
  flushes of heat, 466
  gastric symptoms, 185, 455, 636
  glands, 468
  gonorrhoea, 394, 478
  haemorrhoids, 187, 465, 476
  haemoptysis, 465

SULPHUR (Continued)
  headache, 128, 581
  heart, 111, 465
  hip-joint disease, 470
  hydrocephaloid, 471
  hydrocephalus, 104, 496
  hysteria, 471
  intermittent fever, 229, 467
  keratitis, 473
  laryngitis, 473
  liver, 186, 461, 476
  lver spots, 125
  lumbago, 230
  lungs, 469, 627, 740
  marasmus, 272, 468, 554, 645
  meningitis, 101, 104, 294, 409
  mental symptoms, 37, 471, 683
  nasal catarrh, 473
  nervous system, 195, 471
  neuralgia, 467, 683
  neurasthenia, 624
  panaritium, 114
  paralysis, 236, 322, 472, 541
  peritonitis, 472
  pleurisy, 103, 472
  pneumonia, 51, 279, 466, 473
  prostatorrhoea, 459
  psora, 463
  rachitis, 468
  reaction, defective, 270, 463, 629
  retinal congestion, 602
  rheumatism, 353, 472
  scabies, 125, 475
  scarlatina, 418, 466, 524
  scrofula, 468, 494, 545, 591
  scrofulous ophthalmia, 473, 494, 495
  seminal emission, 477
  septic infection, 467
  sexual excesses, 192, 339, 477
  sleep, 361, 461
  speech, 440
  spinal congestion, 471, 541
  spinal cord, 472, 541, 620
  spinal irritation, 471
  spinal weakness, 472
  stomach, 132
  suppressed eruptions, 101, 105, 464, 470
  synovitis, 297, 472
  tabes mesenterica, 470
  throat, 498
  tongue, 293
  tonsillitis, 414, 592
  tubercular meningitis, 104, 469
  tympanites, 261
  typhoid fever, 467
  ulcers, 62
  uterine diseases, 135
  vertebral caries, 573
  vomiting, 672
  white swelling, 470
SULPHURIC ACID, 531
  alcoholism, 531
  ankle-joint, 698, 732
  aphthous sore mouth, 47, 531
  brain, 235

INDEX OF REMEDIES.

SULPHURIC ACID (Continued)
climaxis, 466
cough, 152, 531
diarrhoea, 532
diphtheria, 532
drunkards, complaints of, 58
dyspepsia, 58, 532
flushes of heat, 466
general symptoms, 531
haemorrhages, 532
haemorrhoids, 58, 531
injuries, 532, 662
marasmus, 532
mental symptoms, 531
pemphigus, 87
scarlatina, 524
skin, 85, 87
sprains, 662
typhoid fever, 531
SUMBUL
heart, 225
SWEET SPIRITS OF NITRE
sensorial depression, 335, 527
typhoid fever, 335, 336, 527
SYMPHYTUM
fractures, 241, 680
injuries, 241

TABACUM, 432
antidotal relation, 432, 433
apoplexy, 430
asphyxia, 182, 433
cholera, 432
dyspepsia, 432
gastric symptoms, 377, 432
general symptoms of, 432
heart, 432
neuralgia, 432
relation to Gelsemium, 176
renal colic, 182, 433
strangulated hernia, 433
tetanus, 182
vomiting, 387
TARAXACUM, 244
liver, 244
tongue, 229, 244, 333
typhoid fever, 228, 244
TARANTULA, 75
chorea, 74
hysteria, 75, 78
nervous system, 75, 714
poisoning by, 75
reaction, defective, 121
uterus and ovaries, 76
TARANTULA CUBENSIS, 80
carbuncle, 80
TELLURIUM
herpes circinatus, 125, 705
otitis media, 349, 412
otorrhoea, 349, 412
TEREBINTHINA, 305
albuminuria, 66
antidotal relations, 562
Bright's disease, 254, 306
bronchitis, 306
capillary bronchitis, 382

TEREBINTHINA (Continued)
cough, 306
dropsy, 66, 337
haematuria, 66, 305
hydrocephalus, 305
kidneys and bladder, 92, 305, 559
metritis, 305, 306
peritonitis, 305, 306
pneumonia, 305, 306
post-scarlatinal dropsy, 66
puerperal metritis, 415
scarlatina, 305
skin, 85, 86, 87
tympanites, 271, 370
typhoid fever, 66, 305
urticaria, 107
worms, 306
TEUCRIUM MARUM VERUM
hiccough, 203
polypi, 570
post-nasal catarrh, 656
worms, 203
THAPSIA GARGANICA
skin, 85, 86
THEA
stomach, 132, 377
THEBAINE
tetanus, 178
THERIDION, 81
antidotal relations, 81
bones, 83
headache, 82
head symptoms, 81
hemicrania, 129
hysteria, 82
neuralgia, 82
ozaena, 83
phthisis, 83
post-nasal catarrh, 348
sea-sickness, 82
spinal irritation, 82
sun, ill effects of the, 38
syncope, 37
vertigo, 37, 82
THUJA OCCIDENTALIS, 307
balanorrhoea, 309
blepharitis, 131
ciliary neuralgia, 206
circulation, 308, 309
complementary relations, 311, 543
condylomata, 309, 640
cough, 310
diarrhoea, 310
eyes, 131
female genital organs, 309, 615
gastric symptoms, 350
gonorrhoea, 91, 309
headache, 308
history of, 307
iritis, 310
marasmus, 310
mental symptoms, 258, 308, 424
nails, 310, 520
nervous system, 307
neuralgia, 308
orchitis, 310
ozaena, 310

INDEX OF REMEDIES.

THUJA OCCIDENTALIS (Continued)
  prostatitis, 309
  pseudo-cyesis, 308
  rheumatism, 309
  sclerotitis, 310
  scrofula, 310
  skin, 85, 688
  sun stroke, 38
  sweat, 653
  sycosis, 307, 309, 694, 726
  teeth, 48, 340
  tarsal tumors, 130
  urinary organs, 91
  vaccination, bad effects of, 307, 542
  variola, 308
  vertigo, 82
  warts, 309, 310
TILIA EUROPEA
  puerperal metritis, 415
TITANIUM
  hemiopia, 702
TRIFOLIUM PRATENSE
  cough, 296
  torticollis, 296
TRILLIUM PENDULUM
  epistaxis, 159
  menorrhagia, 673
  haemorrhages, 158, 159, 368

UMBELLIFERAE, 447
URTICA URENS
  agalactia, 313, 356
  urticaria, 31, 107
USTILAGO
  crusta lactea, 168
  female genital organs, 145, 157
  haemoptysis, 30
  haemorrhages, 145, 157
  menses, 301
  metrorrhagia, 157, 158
  prolapsus uteri, 145
  testes, 352
UVA URSI
  cystic calculus, 93
  cystitis, 93

VALERIANA
  hysteria, 118, 199, 256
  lumbago, 230
  nervous system, 118, 121, 248
  nose, 276
  reaction, defective, 121, 270, 465, 629
  sciatica, 230
VEGETABLE KINGDOM, 161
VERATRIA, 178
  tetanus, 178
VERATRUM ALBUM, 254
  abdominal organs, 254
  antidotal relation, 541
  cardiac debility, 257
  cholera Asiatica, 255
  cholera infantum, 156, 255, 285, 380
  cholera morbus, 255, 396, 554
  colic, 272, 287
  collapse, 69, 484, 315
  convulsions, 183, 201

VERATRUM ALBUM (Continued)
  cough, 151
  cramps, 288
  delirium, 255
  diarrhoea, 176, 255, 272, 371
  face, 44
  fright, ill effects of, 272
  headache, 200, 354, 377, 701
  heart, 257
  hemicrania, 128
  hiccough, 203
  intermittent fever, 69
  intestinal symptoms, 583
  intussusception, 255, 287
  mental symptoms, 255, 272
  nervous system, 195, 248
  neurasthenia, 624
  nymphomania, 254, 429
  poisoning by, 254
  rheumatism, 249
  scarlatina, 635
  skin, 85
  syncope, 37, 38
  tetanus, 182
  typhoid fever, 252
  vertigo, 37
  whooping cough, 704
VERATRUM VIRIDE, 257
  chorea, 257
  fever, 319
  heart, 257
  lungs, 257
  oesophagitis, 257, 414
  pneumonia, 257, 279, 319, 323
  puerperal convulsions, 257
  tetanus, 181
VERBASCUM THAPSUS
  cough, 395
  neuralgia, 395, 419
  prosopalgia, 614
VESPA, 97
  os uteri, ulceration of, 145
VIBURNUM OPULUS
  abortion, 250
  female genital organs, 146
VINCA MINOR, 167
  crusta lactea, 167
  haemorrhages, 167, 369
  menorrhagia, 167
  plica polonica, 167
VIOLA ODORATA
  rheumatism, 297
VIOLA TRICOLOR
  crusta lactea, 167
  polypi, 369
  urine, 167

WYETHIA
  hay fever, 558

XANTHOXYLUM FRAXINEUM
  after-pains, 356

YERBA SANTA
  lungs, 627
  phthisis, 215, 627, 718

INDEX OF REMEDIES.

YUCCA FILAMENTOSA
  asthma, 718
  biliousness, 299, 313
  gonorrhoea, 313
  skin, 313
  tongue, 454

ZANTHORRHIZA, 451
ZINCUM METALLICUM, 631
  amblyopia, 637
  antidotal relations, 631
  asthma, 633
  backache, 361
  brain, 367, 633
  brain, softening of the, 636
  cholera infantum, 635
  chorea, 634
  colic, 637
  complementary relations, 631
  corneal opacity, 637
  cough, 638
  dentition, 633
  dysuria, 638
  exanthemata, 424
  eyes, 637
  female genital organs, 638
  gastric symptoms, 637
  granular lids, 637
  headache, 635
  heart, 636, 656
  hydrocephaloid, 635, 680
  hypochondriasis, 638
  inimical relation, 543, 631
  liver, 637
  locomotor ataxia, 600
  measles, 425, 633
  meningitis, 102, 337, 633, **634**
  menses, 633, 638

ZINCUM METALLICUM (Continued)
  nervous symptoms, 79, 632
  neurasthenia, 541
  ovaries, 65, 633, 638
  paralysis, 636
  poisoning by, 631, 632
  prosopalgia, 637
  pterygium, 637
  rheumatism, 634
  scarlatina, 302, 633, 634
  sexual excesses, 633
  sleep, 443
  spermatorrhoea, 638
  spinal cord, 632, 636
  spinal irritation, 330, 633, 636
  suppressed eruptions, 101, 302, 367, 443, 633
  typhoidal conditions, 102
  urine, 637
  wine, aggravation from, 632, 634

ZINCUM OXIDATUM
  hypochondriasis, 448
  reaction, defective, 121
  typhoid fever, 102

ZINCUM SULPHURICUM
  corneal opacities, 637
  dysentery, 96
  granular lids, 637

ZINC, VALERIANATE OF
  hysteria, 199

ZINGIBER
  asthma, 191
  urine, 271

ZIZIA
  chorea, 74, 146
  female genital organs, 146
  mental symptoms, 146

THERAPEUTIC INDEX.

ABDOMINAL SYMPTOMS
  arsenicum, 488
  cascarilla, 312
  cinchona, 488
  colchicum, 253
  colocynth, 286
  nux vomica, 136
  oleander, 165
  podophyllum, 453
  veratrum album, 254
ABORTION
  aconite, 325
  actea racemosa, 328
  chamomilla, 250
  digitalis, 388
  gelsemium, 176
  hamamelis, 328
  ipecac, 328
  kali carb., 737
  lycopodium, 328
  opium, 484
  plumbum, 622
  sabina, 305
  secale, 154
  sepia, 146
  viburnum, 250
ABSCESSES
  belladonna, 419, 592
  carbo veg., 483
  cinchona, 484
  hepar, 592, 684
  lachesis, 492
  mercurius, 592
  silicea, 543, 592
  sulphur, 592
ABSCESS OF LUNGS
  lachesis, 51
  sulphur, 51
ABSCESS OF TEETH
  hepar, 46
  lachesis, 46
  mercurius, 46
  silicea, 46
ACNE
  carbo animalis, 141
  kali bich., 724
  kreosote, 196
  lachesis, 196
  ledum, 195
  nux vomica, 195
  sanguinaria, 280
  sulphur, 195, 468, 475
ADENOMATA
  conium, 449
AFTER-PAINS
  actea racemosa, 328

AFTER-PAINS (Continued)
  caulophyllum, 356
  chamomilla, 356
  cuprum, 356
  pulsatilla, 356
  xanthoxylum, 356
AGALACTIA
  agnus castus, 356
  causticum, 356, 734
  pulsatilla, 356
  ricinis communis, 313, 356
  urtica urens, 313, 356
ANGINA PECTORIS
  actea recemosa, 329
  argentum nitricum, 608
  arsenicum, 559
  tabacum, 432
ANKLE-JOINT
  carbo animalis, 676
  causticum, 692, 698, 732
  natrum carb., 676, 692
  natrum hypochlor., 692
  natrum mur., 692
  pinus sylvestris, 692
  sepia, 676
  silicea, 732
  sulphur, 692, 732
  sulphuric acid, 692, 698, 732
ANTIDOTAL RELATIONS, 24
  aconite, 326
  alumina, 616, 620
  ammonium carb., 658
  anacardium, 212
  antimonium tart., 583
  apis, 114
  argentum nitricum, 272, 579
  arnica, 658
  arsenicum, 541
  asafoetida, 450, 587
  aurum, 586, 600
  belladonna, 516, 600, 628
  bryonia, 303, 617
  camphor, 116, 481, 658
  cantharis, 93
  carbo veg., 481
  castor oil, 313
  cepa, 380
  chamomilla, 266, 616, 644
  chlorine, 511
  cicuta, 433
  cinchona, 372, 375, 551, 586
  colchicum, 254
  colocynth, 288
  croton tiglium, 222
  cuprum, 628
  dulcamara, 586

ANTIDOTAL RELATIONS (Continued)
ferrum, 639
gelsemium, 176
glonoin, 438
graphites, 492
hepar, 536, 543, 585, 600, 631, 688, 712
ignatia, 200, 631
iodine, 508, 587
kali brom., 713
kali chlor., 586
kali hydr., 556, 716, 719
lachesis, 62, 587
ledum, 114
magnesia carb., 644
mercury, 536, 585, 589, 600
mezereum, 587
moscnus, 116
muriatic acid, 272, 525
natrum mur., 696
nitric acid, 535, 536, 586
nux vomica, 136, 266, 492, 562
oleander, 167
ophidia, 35
opium, 266, 268, 272
petroleum, 311, 500
phosphorus, 562, 569
plantago, 433, 644
plumbum, 614, 620, 621
pulsatilla, 343, 644
rheum, 644
rhus tox., 222, 224
sarsaparilla, 272
selenium, 462
sepia, 125, 432
silicea, 543
staphisagria, 340, 586
stillingia sylvatica, 587
stramonium, 425, 628
sulphur, 272, 712
sulphuric acid, 532
tabacum, 432, 433
terebinthina, 562
theridion, 81
veratrum alb., 541
zinc, 631

ALBUMINURIA
apis, 66
arsenicum, 67, 559
aurum, 603
equisetum, 90
formica, 86
glonoin, 437
helonias, 358
lachesis, 65, 66
terebinthina, 66

ALCOHOLISM
(See also drunkards, complaints of.)
ranunculus bulbosus, 332
sulphuric acid, 531

ALIMENTARY CANAL
aloes, 478
bryonia, 298
cantharis, 95
lachesis, 51
nux vomica, 189
phosphorus, 567

ALOPECIA
selenium, 461

AMBLYOPIA
baryta carb, 652
phosphorus, 574
zincum, 637

AMENORRHOEA
aconite, 674
actea spicata, 674
apis, 112
belladonna, 674
calcarea ostr., 673
castoreum, 117
gelsemium, 674
glonoin, 673
hamamelis, 301
kali carb., 739
lycopodium, 674
natrum mur., 739
phosphorus, 569
pulsatilla, 355

ANAEMIA
(See also Chlorosis.)
alumina, 618
cinchona, 366
ferrum, 367, 483, 640
kali carb., 736
manganum, 641
natrum mur., 608
pulsatilla, 344
sepia, 347

ANALYSIS OF DRUGS, 18

ANASARCA
(See Dropsy.)

ANEURISM
baryta carb., 650

ANGER, ILL EFFECTS OF
causticum, 286
chamomilla, 286, 339
colocynth, 286, 339
staphisagria, 286, 339

ANUS
anacardium, 165
belladonna, 60
causticum, 60
cocculus, 60, 61
ignatia, 60, 203
kali bi., 60
mezereum, 60
natrum mur., 60., 705
nitric acid, 60, 534
opium, 60
plumbum, 60

AORTITIS
arsenicum, 486
carbo veg., 486
cuprum, 486
lachesis, 486

APHONIA AND HOARSENESS
bothrops lanceolatus, 33

APHONIA
ammonium caust., 662
aurum triphyl., 210, 462
carbo veg., 210., 462., 484, 733
causticum, 462, 485, 732
eupatorium perf., 485, 733

THERAPEUTIC INDEX.

APHONIA (Continued)
 gelsemium, 170
 graphites, 733
 kali carb., 739
 nitric acid, 536
 phosphorus, 462, 485., 570
 pulsatilla, 360
 rhus tox., 733
 sanguinaria, 280
 selenium, 210, 462, 733
 senega, 296
 spongia, 462
 sulphur, 473, 485, 733
APHTHOUS SORE MOUTH
 apis, 47
 arsenicum, 47
 arum triphyllum, 710
 baptisia, 47
 borax, 710
 bryonia, 301, 709
 carbo veg., 47
 chlorine, 511
 helleborus, 48
 iodine, 47
 lachesis, 47, 48
 lycopodium, 48
 mercurius, 47, 710
 muriatic acid, 47
 natrum hypochlor., 48
 nitric acid, 47, 48
 phytolacca, 48
 salicylic acid, 48
 staphisagria, 47
 sulphuric acid, 47, 532
APOPLECTIC CONGESTION
 coffea, 384
APOPLEXY
 apis, 100, 269
 arnica, 242, 269
 baryta carb., 268., 650
 belladonna, 268, 269
 causticum, 731
 glonoin, 437
 helleborus, 269
 hyoscyamus, 269
 lachesis, 268, 269
 nux vomica, 269
 opium, 100, 268
 rhus tox., 269
 strontiana carb., 653
 tabacum, 430
APOPLEXY OF THE RETINA
 arnica, 43
 crotalus, 43
 glonoin, 436
 hamamelis, 43
 lachesis, 43
 phosphorus, 43
ARTHRALGIA
 argentum met., 599, 611
ARTHRITIC HEADACHE
 nux vomica, 128
 sepia, 128
ARTHRITIS DEFORMANS
 calcarea carb., 677

ASCARIDES
 ignatia, 203
 indigo, 203
 spigelia, 206
 teucrium, 203
ASCITES
 acetic acid, 104
 apocynum cannb., 104
 lycopodium, 444
ASPHYXIA
 ammonium carb., 661
 arnica, 158, 273, 659
 bovista, 158, 273, 659
 hydrocyanic acid, 433
 tabacum, 182, 433
ASPHYXIA NEONATORUM
 antimonium tart., 582
 laurocerasus, 583
ASTHENOPIA
 alumina, 619, 655
 ammoniacum gummi, 449
 apis, 114
 argentum nitricum, 609
 artemisia vulgaris, 243
 belladonna, 449
 cina, 247
 cinchona, 369
 cyclamen, 130
 jaborandi, 130
 kali carb., 130
 lilium tigrinum, 130
 lithium carb., 130
 natrum mur., 130., 702
 phosphorus, 574
 pulsatilla, 130
 ruta, 449
 sepia, 129, 130
ASTHMA
 ambra grisea, 152
 antimonium tart., 633
 apis, 110
 aralia racemosa, 727
 argentum nitricum, 608
 arsenicum, 381, 558, 727
 baryta carb., 652
 bromine, 507
 cactus, 633
 cadmium sulph., 633
 caladium seguin, 214
 capsicum, 435
 carbo veg., 191, 485
 cuprum, 381
 drosera, 27
 ferrum met., 639
 grindelia robusta, 633
 ipecacuanha, 380, 558
 kali bich., 727
 kali chlor., 633
 lachesis, 51
 lobelia, 381
 lycopodium, 191
 mephitis, 27
 natrum sulph., 694
 nux vomica, 190
 pothos foetida, 215
 pulmo vulpis, 29

THERAPEUTIC INDEX.

ASTHMA (Continued)
  rumex crispus, 27
  sepia, 633
  stramonium, 424
  sticta, 27
  yucca, 718
  zincum, 633
  zingiber, 191
ATROPHY OF THE RETINA
  nux vomica, 189
AWKWARDNESS
  aethusa, 102
  apis melifica, 102
  ignatia, 102
  natrum mur., 102
  nux vomica., 102
BACKACHE
  aesculus hipp., 506
  agaricus, 361
  berberis, 361
  cannabis indica, 361
  chelidonium, 281
  chenopodium, 282
  cobalt, 193, 361, 632, 636
  kali carb., 738., 739
  lobelia syph., 282
  nux vomica, 194
  picric acid, 134, 361, 539
  pulsatilla, 361
  rhus tox., 361
  sepia 361, 636
  valerian, 361
  zincum, 361
BELANORRHOEA
  digitalis, 394
  mercurius corrosivus, 394
  mercurius vivus, 311
  nitric acid, 310
  thuja, 309
BILIARY CALCULI
  belladonna, 192
  berberis, 192, 452
  cinchona, 192
  podophyllum, 454
BILIOUSNESS
  artemesia tridentata, 244
  chamomilla, 249, 299
  yucca filamentosa, 299, 313
BILIOUS REMITTENT FEVER
  gelsemium, 173
  podophyllum, 453
BLADDER
  arsenicum, 271
  berberis, 451
  cantharis, 88
  cina, 247
  causticum, 271
  colocynth, 287
  conium, 91
  dulcamara, 434
  erigeron, 92
  ferrum phos, 92
  hepar, 687
  hyoscyamus, 271
  lachesis, 416

BLADDER (Continued)
  lithium carb., 655
  nux vomica, 192
  opium, 271
  pulsatilla, 92
  senecio, 359
BLADDER, STONE IN THE
  (See esical Calculus.)
BLEPHARITIS
  alumina, 619
  argentum nitr., 609
  euphrasia, 396
  graphites, 130, 494, 619
  kreosote, 609
  mercurius, 397, 593, 609
  petroleum, 499
  sepia, 130
  thuja, 131
BLEPHAROSPASMUS
  agaricus, 189
  euphrasia, 189
  natrum mur., 189.,
  rhus tox., 235
  nux vomica, 189
BLOOD
  alumina, 618
  ammonium carb., 658
  arsenicum, 552
  belladonna, 189
  bryonia, 289
  carbo veg., 481
  chininum sulph., 365
  kali carb., 736
  lycopodium 441
  phosphorus, 575
  quinine, 365
  secale, 154
  sepia, 124
BLOOD VESSELS
  arnica, 238
  secale, 154, 650
BOILS
  arnica, 242
  arsenicum, 561
  belladonna, 419
  calcarea sulph., 667
  carbo veg., 483
  hepar, 684
  psorinum 150
  silicea, 543
  sulphur, 468
BONES
  angustura, 545
  aranea diadema, 81
  asafoetida, 119, 450, 545
  aurum, 604
  calcarea flurica, 519
  calcarea ostrearum, 676
  calcarea phosphorica, 241, 680
  chloride of gold and platinum, 341
  euphorbium, 313
  fluoric acid, 519
  Gettysburg spring water, 341, 545
  kali hydriodicum, 341
  mercurius, 341
  phosphoric acid, 530

THERAPEUTIC INDEX.   787

BONES (Continued)
  posphorus, 545, 573
  platinum mur., 545, 614
  silicea, 519, 544
  staphisagria, 340
  stillingia, 341
  strontiana carb., 341, 545, 654
  symphytum 241
  theridion, 83
BOWELS, OBSTRUCTION OF
  opium, 272
BRAIN
  aconite, 320
  argentum nitricum, 605
  baryta carb., 651
  baryta mur., 650
  belladonna, 235, 320, 335, 407
  cantharis, 93
  carbo animalis, 235
  causticum, 651
  cinchona, 235
  digitalis, 393
  glonoin, 320
  hyoscyamus, 427
  natrum mur., 129
  plumbum, 622
  rhus tox., 235
  spigelis, 235
  stramonium, 425
  sulphur, 471
  sulphuric acid, 235
  zincum, 367, 633
BRAIN, CONGESTION OF THE
  amyl nitrite, 320
  belladonna, 320, 409
  glonoin, 320, 437
BRAIN-FAG
  kali bromatum, 714
  natrum mur., 128
  nux vomica, 128, 540
  phosphoric acid, 540
  phosphorus, 540
  picric acid, 128, 538
  sepia, 128
  sulphur, 128
BRAIN, INFLAMMATION OF THE
  arsenicum, 94
  arum triphyllum, 210
  belladonna, 94, 409, 437
  camphor, 94
  cantharis, 93
  glonoin, 437
  hyoscyamus, 426
BRAIN, PARALYSIS OF THE
  hydrocyanic acid, 336, 538
  hyoscyamus, 268, 442
  lachesis, 268
  lycopodium 442
  opium, 268
BRAIN, SCLEROSIS OF THE
  plumbum, 622
BRAIN, SOFTENING OF THE
  ambra grisea, 151
  nux vomica, 564
  phosphorus, 184, 564
  picric acid, 184

BRAIN, SOFTENING OF (Continued)
  piper methysticum, 385
  sulphur, 184
  zincum, 636
BRIGHT'S DISEASE
  arsenicum, 559
  cantharis, 88
  colchicum, 254
  hepar, 685
  kali hydr., 718
  lachesis, 65
  phosphorus, 569
  terebinthina, 254, 306
BRONCHIAL CATARRH AND BRONCHITIS
  ammonium carb., 660
  ammonium mur., 664
  balsam of Peru, 215
  bryonia, 296, 570
  calcarea phos, 680
  capsicum, 374, 546
  carbo animalis, 490
  carbo veg., 490
  dracontium, 215
  ipecacuanha, 381
  jaborandi, 686
  kali bichromicum, 727
  kali carbonicum, 740
  lachesis, 50
  lycopodium, 445
  natrum arsenicosum, 707
  phosphorus, 190, 570, 571
  pix liquida, 215
  pulsatilla, 361
  sanguinaria, 374
  sulphur, 473
  terebinthina, 306
  yerba santa, 215
BRONCHORRHAGIA
  carbo veg., 481
BUBOES
  alumina, 620
  badiaga, 31, 490
  belladonna, 391
  carbo animalis, 31, 489
  hepar, 686
BURNS
  arsenicum, 97
  cantharis, 97
  carbolic acid, 97
  sapo soda, 97
  soda bicarbonate, 97, 689
CALLOSITIES
  antimonium crudum, 232, 579
CANCER
  arsenicum, 552, 561
  arsenicum iod., 561
  belladonna, 561
  cantharis, 88
  bromine, 503
  carbo animalis, 490
  carbo veg., 483
  cicuta virosa, 451
  clematis, 561
  conium, 449, 561
  hydrastis, 510, 561

THERAPEUTIC INDEX.

CANCER (Continued)
  iodine, 510
  kreosote, 136
  lachesis, 71
  lapis albus, 510
  morphia, 265
  phosphorus, 568, 575
CAPILLARY BRONCHITIS
  antimonium tart., 381, 581, 686
  baryta carb., 582
  chelidonium, 283
  hepar, 686
  ipecacuanha, 381, 582
  kali carb., 740
  lycopodium, 382
  phosphorus, 381
  sulphur, 382
  terebinthina, 382
CARBUNCLE
  anthracinum, 80, 232, 561
  arsenicum, 232, 552, 561
  carbo veg., 232, 443, 501
  lachesis, 71, 80, 561
  phytolacca, 561
  rhus tox., 232
  silicea, 80, 543
  tarantula Cubensis, 80
CARDIAC DEBILITY
  veratrum album, 257
CARIES OF BONES
  angustura, 545
  aranea diadema, 81
  calcarea fluorica, 519
  fluoric acid, 519
  Gettsysburg salts, 545
  nitric acid, 535
  phosphorus, 545
  platina muriatica, 545
  silicea, 544
  strontiana carb., 545
  sulphur, 468
CATALEPSY
  curare, 179
  piper methysticum, 386
CATARACT
  baryta carbonica, 575
  calcarea ostr., 575
  conium, 575
  lycopodium, 443
  magnesia carb., 646
  magnesia mur., 646
  natrum mur., 575, 697
  phosphorus, 575
  secale, 575
  sepia, 130
  silicea, 575
CATARRHAL FEVER
  mercurius, 591
CATARRH
  (See also Mucous Membranes.)
  arsenicum, 380
  arundo maur., 661
  bryonia, 294
  carbo veg., 484, 662
  causticum, 662
  chlorine, 511

CATARRH (Continued)
  gelsemium, 173
  hepar, 685
  kali hydriodicum, 717
  laurocerasus, 662
  natrum arsenicosum, 706
  natrum carb., 693
  natrum mur., 698, 702
  nitric acid, 534
  ranunculus sceleratus, 333
  senecio, 359
CELLULITIS
  apis, 232
  rhus tox., 232, 234
  silicea, 543
CEREBRO-SPINAL MENINGITIS
  ammonium carb., 659
  cocculus, 263
  digitalis, 393
  gelsemium, 172
  oxalic acid, 540
CERVIX UTERI
  aurum metallicum, 139
  aurum muriaticum, 139
  aurum muriaticum natron., 139
  carbo animalis, 140
  gelsemium, 139, 175, 421
  graphites, 142
  kreosote, 136
  mitchella, 145
  murex, 135
  natrum carb., 693
  sepia, 139
CHANCRE
  corallium rubrum, 311
  kali hydriodicum, 64
  lachesis, 62
  lycopodium, 63
  mercurius biniod., 597
  mercurius protoiod., 597
  nitric acid, 63, 535
CHANCROID
  jacaranda, 311
  mercurius, 596
  thuja, 309
CHANGE OF LIFE
  (See Climaxis.)
CHARCOAL FUMES, ASPHYXIA FROM
  ammonium carb., 659
  arnica, 158, 273, 659
  bovista, 158, 273, 659
  opium, 273
CHEMOSIS
  rhus tox., 113
CHEST PAINS
  angustura, 282
  anisum stellatum, 83, 306
  chenopodium, 282
  fluoric acid, 306
  guaiacum, 306
  kali carb., 306
  lilium tigrinum, 134, 306, 346
  lobelia syphilitica, 282
  myrtus com., 306
  oxalic acid, 306
  phosphorus, 306

THERAPEUTIC INDEX.

CHEST PAINS (Continued)
  pix liquida, 306
  pulsatilla nut., 306, 361
  pulsatilla prat., 331, 345
  ranunculus bulbosus, 282
  sarsaparilla, 306
  silicea, 306
  sulphur, 306
  sumbul, 306
  theridion, 306

CHLOROSIS
  (See also Anaemia.)
  alumina, 617, 618
  argentum met., 599
  calcarea phosphorica, 680
  cuprum, 629
  cyclamen, 359
  ferrum, 493, 640
  graphites, 493
  manganum, 641
  natrum mur., 700
  pulsatilla, 344, 494
  sepia, 124, 347

CHOLERA ASIATICA
  arsenicum, 156, 553
  camphor, 156, 256, 484, 629
  carbo veg., 156, 380, 484
  colchicum, 59, 253
  cuprum, 628
  hydrocyanic acid, 538
  jatropha curcas, 256, 312
  lachesis, 59
  secale, 155, 554
  sulphur, 478
  tabacum, 432
  veratrum album, 255

CHOLERA INFANTUM
  aconite, 324
  argentum nitr., 610
  arnica, 22, 242
  arsenicum, 555
  belladonna, 411, 419
  calcarea ostr., 671
  calcarea phos., 300, 679
  cinchona, 366, 380
  colocynth, 287
  croton tiglium, 285
  elaterium, 284
  ferrum, 642
  ferrum phos., 159, 270, 642
  gnaphalium, 379
  helleborus, 337
  ipecacuanha, 378
  kali bromatum, 380
  opium, 270
  podophyllum, 59, 285
  psorinum, 149
  secale, 155
  sulphur, 471, 672
  veratrum alb., 156, 255, 285, 380
  zincum, 635

CHOLERA MORBUS
  argentum nitricum, 629
  arsenicum, 156
  camphor, 156, 380
  euphorbia corollata, 312

CHOLERA MORBUS (Continued)
  iris versicolor, 256, 351, 396
  podophyllum, 256
  secale, 155
  veratrum alb., 255, 296, 554

CHORDEE
  agaricus, 541
  ambra, 541
  cannabis indica, 90
  cannabis sativa, 89
  cantharis, 89, 96, 541
  capsicum, 541
  digitalis, 391
  mygale, 541
  opium, 541
  petroselinum, 541
  physostigma, 541
  platina, 541
  zincum, 541

CHOREA
  actea rac., 74
  agaricus muscarius, 74, 79
  arsenicum, 79
  belladonna, 77
  causticum, 77, 734
  crocus, 76, 79
  hyoscyamus, 77, 428
  ignatia, 74, 77
  mygale, 73
  natrum mur., 699
  phosphorus, 565
  sepia, 146
  stramonium, 74, 428
  tarentula, 74
  veratrum viride, 257, 428
  zincum, 634
  zizia, 74, 146

CHOROIDITIS
  phosphorus, **574**

CHOROIDO-RETINITIS
  nux vomica, 189

CICATRICES
  fluoric acid, **520**
  graphites, 141, 496
  phytolacca, 141, 544
  silicea, 543
  sulphur, 544

CINCHONISM, 366

CIRCULATION
  ammonium mur., 662
  amyl nitrite, 278
  bovista, 157
  coffea, 385
  ferrum, 639
  gelsemium, 168
  glonoin, 278, 435
  graphites, 493
  lachesis, 65
  lilium tigrinum, 127, 346
  pulsatilla, 345
  rhus tox., 223
  sanguinaria, 276, 278
  secale, 154
  sepia, 123, 124
  strontiana carb., 643
  sulphur, 135, 465

CIRCULATION (Continued)
  thuja, 308
CIRRHOSIS OF THE LIVER
  arum, 36, 603
  lycopodium, 444
  muriatic acid, 525
CLERGYMAN'S SORE THROAT
  arum triphyllum, 210
CLIMAXIS
  amyl nitrite, 31, 278, 466
  glonoin, 278
  lachesis, 36, 65, 278, 466
  sanguinaria, 276, 278
  strontiana carb., 654
  sulphur., 466
  sulphuric acid, 466
COLIC
  aconite, 287, 324
  aethusa cynaptum, 710
  alumina, 620, 621
  belladonna, 419, 621
  borax, 710
  bovista, 287
  castoreum, 117
  causticum, 735
  chamomilla, 339
  cinchona, 272
  colocynth, 285, 324, 339, 419, 644
  croton tiglium, 287, 312
  cuprum, 629
  cyclamen, 263, 360
  dulcamara, 434
  ipecacuanha, 378
  lycopodium, 272
  magnesia carb., 644
  nux vomica, 186, 272, 621
  opium, 272, 621
  platina, 621
  plumbum, 621
  rhus tox., 234
  staphisagria, 248, 339, 341
  veratrum album, 272, 287
  zincum, 637
COLLAPSE
  aconite, 315
  arsenicum, 69
  camphor, 69, 484, 629
  carbo veg., 156, 373, 484, 566
  cuprum, 70, 629
  digitalis, 69
  hydrocyanic acid, 69, 538
  secale, 69, 156
  veratrum album, 69, 315, 484
CONCORDANT REMEDIES, 24
CONDYLOMATA
  cinnabaris, 311
  euphrasia, 311, 398
  jacaranda, 311
  lycopodium, 63
  nitric acid, 310
  sabina, 311
  staphisagria, 311, 340
  thuja, 309, 340
CONGESTION OF THE BRAIN
  (See Brain).

CONGESTION OF THE CHEST
  ferrum phos, 159, 642
CONGESTION OF THE HEAD
  arum, 601
  sulphur, 465
CONGESTIONS
  aconite, 320
  aurum, 599, 603
  belladonna, 407, 591
  gelsemium, 169
  mercurius, 591
  sulphur, 456
CONJUCTIVITIS
  aconite, 321, 397
  apis, 113, 217
  argentum nitricum, 347
  arnica, 397
  arsenicum, 113, 397
  belladonna, 412
  bromine, 507
  calcarea ostrearum, 235
  euphrasia, 397
  ipecacuanha, 383
  mercurius cor., 347
  mercurius viv., 397
  natrum mur., 131
  nux vomica, 189
  pulsatilla, 130, 347
  rhus tox., 113, 235, 397
  sanguinaria, 280
  sepia, 130
  sulphur, 321, 473
CONNECTIVE TISSUE
  sepia, 125
CONSTIPATION
  aletris farinosa, 359
  alumina, 186, 271, 461, 617
  ambra, 152
  ammonium mur., 664
  anacardium, 219
  antimonium crud., 578
  bryonia, 186, 271, 298, 461, 617, 686
  carbo veg., 186, 486
  cascarilla, 312, 497
  collinsonia, 188
  conium, 449
  feltauri, 29
  felvulpi, 29
  graphites, 497
  hepar, 53, 686
  hydrastis, 360
  ignatia, 220
  lac caninum, 28
  lac defloratum, 28
  lachesis, 52, 54
  lycopodium, 186, 444
  natrum carb., 690
  natrum mur., 704
  nux vomica, 184, 186, 220, 445, 686
  opium, 186, 271, 461
  phosphorus, 566
  platina, 614
  plumbum, 271, 461, 614, 622
  podophyllum, 454
  pulsatilla, 351

THERAPEUTIC INDEX. 791

CONSTIPATION (Continued)
selenium, 460
sepia, 220, 705
silicea, 546
sulpnur, 220, 476
zincum, 637
CONSTITUTION
alumina, 617
ammonium carb., 657
ammonium mur., 662, 657
aranea diadema, 80
baryta carb., 649
borax, 708
calcarea ostrearum, 493, 668, 677
calcarea phos., 678
carbo animalis, 489
carbo veg., 481
causticum, 729
colocynth, 195
ferrum, 637
graphites, 493
kali bichromicum, 720
lycopodium, 440
magnesia carb., 644
magnesium mur., 646
mercurius, 54
natrum sulph., 694
nux vomica, 183
phosphorus, 562, 570
psorinum, 148
secale, 154
selenium, 460
sepia, 122
silicea, 542, 677
spongia, 512
sulphur, 464
thuja, 307
CONTINUED FEVER
(See also Fever.)
aconite, 316
arsenicum, 316, 557
sulphur, 557
CONVULSIONS
arsenicum, 44
artemisia vulg., 624
belladonna, 201, 408, 420
calcarea ostr., 669
camphor, 45, 94
chamomilla, 201
cicuta, 44, 182, 451
cina, 246, 624
cocculus, 262
colchicum, 59
cuprum, 201, 629, 630, 634
ergot, 153
glonoin, 201, 437
helleborus, 45
hydrocyanic acid, 44, 45, 433, 538
hyoscyamus, 44, 45, 201, 428
ignatia, 378
ipecacuanha, 273, 378
kali bromatum, 761, 713
lycopodium, 44
moschus, 116
oenanthe crocata, 428
opium, 200, 201, 270

CONVULSIONS (Continued)
phytolacca, 179
platina, 339, 614
podophyllum, 59
secale, 153, 201, 437
stannum, 625
stramonium, 45, 93, 200, 423, 714
strychnine, 177
veratrum album, 183, 201
CORNEA, OPACITY OF THE
alumen, 669
apis, 669
calcarea ostrearum, 669
cuprum, 669
kali bi., 669
natrum sulph., 699
saccharum offic., 669
zincum, 637
zincum sulph., 637
CORNEA, ULCERS OF THE
calcarea ostrearum, 669
kali bichromicum, 726
mercurius corrosivus, 593
mercurius protoiod., 593
mercurius vivus, 593
natrum carb., 693
nitric acid, 535, 670
podophyllum, 453
pulsatilla, 347
silicea, 545
CORYZA
(See also Nasal Catarrh.)
aconite, 294, 326
ammonium carb., 661
ammonium caust., 662
ammonium mur., 661, 664
anacardium, 221
arsenicum, 380, 557
arsenicum jod., 557
belladonna, 326
bromine, 294
bryonia, 294
cepa, 380, 398
chamomilla, 249
chlorine, 511
cinchona, 295, 326
dulcamara, 434
euphrasia, 380, 397
gelsemium, 173
hepar, 684, 685
ipecacuanha, 380
kali bichromicum, 726
kali carb., 739
kali hydriodicum, 717
lachesis, 49, 294
mercurius, 190, 594
natrum ars., 706
natrum carb., 693
natrum mur., 702
nitric acid, 534
nux vomica, 190, 249, 326, 594
penthorum sedoides, 348
phosphorus, 380
pulsatilla, 190, 348
quillaya, 174
ranunculus scel., 333

CORYZA (Continued)
rhus tox., 234
sambucus, 249
sanguinaria, 280
sticta pulmonaria, 249
sulphur, 473
verbascum, 395

COUGH
actea racemosa, 308
alumina, 619
ambra grisea, 151, 152, 546, 661
ammonium carb., 661
ammonium mur., 662, 664
anacardium, 513
angustura, 152
antimonium tart., 270, 582, 583
apis, 111
arnica, 152, 732
arsenicum, 111, 152
baryta carb., 652
belladonna, 111, 421, 570
borax, 710
bryonia, 111, 296, 693, 703
calcarea ostr., 421
capsicum, 374
carbo animalis, 490
carbo veg., 112, 491
causticum, 421, 703, 732
cepa, 422
chamomilla, 111, 249
cimex, 152
conium, 361, 448
crotalus horridus, 111
drosera, 273, 395, 732
ferrum, 641
gelsemium, 173, 174
graphites, 498
hepar, 234, 513, 683
hydrocyanic acid, 538
hyoscyamus, 111, 361, 427
ignatia, 111, 201
iodine, 509
kali bich., 662, 727
kali carb., 732, 740
lachesis, 111, 152, 421
laurocerasus, 361, 538, 732
lithium carb., 655
lycopodium, 546
manganum, 609
mentha piperita, 428
mezereum, 234
natrum ars., 707
natrum carb., 693
natrum mur., 427, 703, 732
nitric acid, 536
nux vomica, 111, 190
oleum jecoris, 29
opium, 270
petroleum, 499
phosphorus, 151, 421, 546, 570, 571
phosphoric acid, 430
pulsatilla, 234, 536, 732
rhus tox., 234, 546
rumex, 111, 421, 427, 546, 570
sanguinaria, 152, 234, 278, 279, 374
scilla, 546, 703, 732

COUGH (Continued)
senecio, 359
senega, 296
sepia, 732
silicea, 546
spongia, 395, 506, 513
sulphur, 395
sulphuric acid, 152, 531
terebinthina, 306
thuja, 310
trifolium praetense, 296
veratrum alb., 151
verbascum, 395
zinc, 638

CRAMPS
cholos terrapinae, 288
colocynth, 288
nux vomica, 288
veratrum album, 288

CRETINISM
baryta carb., 679
calcarea phos., 679

CROUP
aconite, 323, 505, 684
antimonium tart., 505
arsenicum, 560
bromine, 504, 684
calcarea sulphurica, 667
hepar, 324, 506, 684, 723
iodine, 506
kali bichromicum, 595
kaolin, 505, 506, 723
lachesis, 723
mercurius cyanatus, 723
phosphorus, 570
sanguinaria, 280
spongia, 323, 506, 684

CRUSTA LACTEA
arctium lappa, 168
arsenicum iod., 168
graphites, 168
mezereum, 168
natrum muriaticum, 705
nux juglans, 168
oleander, 167
psorinum, 149
staphisagria, 168, 340
sulphur, 167, 468
ustilago, 168
vinca minor, 167
viola tricolor, 167

CYANOSIS NEONATORUM
digitalis, 389

CYSTITIS
apis, 93
cantharis, 88, 89, 351
conium, 450
digitalis, 393
dulcamara, 351, 434
equisetum, 90, 351
lachesis, 66
pulsatilla, 92, 351

DACRYO-CYSTITIS
petroleum, 499
pulsatilla, 347

DEAFNESS
carbo animalis, 491
carbo veg., 491
graphites, 498
ignatia, 575
phosphorus, 574

DEBILITY
(see also Defective Reaction.)
argentum metallicum 611
arsenicum, 367, 369
calcarea ostrearum, 624
calcares hypophos., 738
carbo animalis, 489, 490
carbo veg., 481, 490
cinchona, 367, 487
cocculus, 260, 624
colchicum, 251
conium, 447
helonias, 135
hypophosphite of lime, 738
kali carb., 738
lithium carb., 135
muriatic acid, 522
natrum carb., 692
nux vomica, 256
phosphoric acid, 367, 526, 624
phosphorus, 367
psorinum, 738
selenium, 459
senna, 737
stannum, 624
sulphur, 460, 624
sulphuric acid, 624
veratrum album, 624

DEFECTIVE REACTION
ambra grisea, 121, 150, 270, 465, 629
asatoetida, 121
camphor, 121
capsicum, 150, 629
carbo veg., 150, 270, 465, 629
castoreum, 121, 150
coca, 121
coffea 121
cuprum, 464, 629
cypripedium, 121
laurocerasus, 150, 464, 629
moscnus, 121, 150
opium, 150
psorinum, 149, 150, 270, 464
scutellaria, 121
tarentula, 121
sulphar, 270, 462, 629
valerian, 121, 270, 465, 624
zinc oxide, 121

DELIRIUM
absinthium, 243
agaricus, 423
belladonna, 255, 429
bryonia, 290
hyoscyamus, 426, 429
lachesis, 38, 423
calcarea ostr., 269
lycopodium, 442
muriatic acid, 522
phosphorus, 563

DELIRIUM (Continued)
plumbum, 622
siramonium, 39, 255, 423, 429
veratrum alb., 255

DELIRIUM TREMENS
absinthium, 243
arsenicum, 269, 551
calcarea ostrearum, 269, 675
cannabis indica, 269
lachesis, 269
opium, 269
ranunculus bulb., 332
stramonium, 269

DENTAL FISTULA
calcarea fluorica, 519
fluoric acid, 519

DENTITION
aethusa, 420
belladonna, 249
bromine, 504
calcarea ostrearum, 669
chamomilla, 249
cina, 420
colchicum, 59, 420
dolichos, 420
kreosotum, 420
podophyllum, 59, 454
zincum, 633

DIABETES
lac defloratum, 28
lactic acid, 518
phosphoric acid, 518
phosphorus, 568

DIAPHRAGMITIS
cactus grandiflorus, 331
ranunculus bulb., 331

DIARRHOEA
aconite, 324
aloes, 137, 165, 166
astonia schol., 168
antimonium crud., 578
apis, 144, 166
apocynum, 164
aranea diadema, 81
argentum nitricum, 166, 176, 255, 610, 643
arnica, 242
arsenicum, 55, 166, 370, 553, 642
belladonna, 419
borax, 710
bryonia, 114, 299, 453, 474, 724
calcarea ostrearum, 671, 587
calcarea phosphorica, 672
castoreum, 117
chamomilla, 248, 342, 151
cinchona, 53, 166, 370, 429, 488, 642
coffea, 385
colchicum, 59
colocynth, 248, 285, 644
croton tiglium, 256, 285, 312, 453
dioscorea, 453, 475
dulcamara, 434, 652
elaps, 58
elaterium, 257, 284, 287, 395
euphorbia corollata, 312
ferrum met., 166, 370, 642
ferrum phos., 159, 642

THERAPEUTIC INDEX.

DIARRHOEA (Continued)
gamboge, 165, 180
gelsemium, 176, 255, 272
geranium, 379
gnaphalium, 374, 725
graphites, 59
gratiola, 395
hepar, 687
iodine, 510
ipecacuanha, 379
iris versicolor, 351, 371, 396
kali bichromicum, 724
kali bromatum, 380
lachesis, 52
leptandra, 396, 598
lilium tig., 134
lithium carb., 655
magnesia carb., 644, 687
mercurius, 250, 396, 591
natrum carb., 690
natrum mur., 705
natrum sulph., 453, 474, 695, 724
nitric acid, 534
nuphar luteum, 380
nux vomica, 188, 287
oenothera, 379
oleander, 166, 371, 642
opium, 176, 255
opuntia, 379
paullinia sorbilis, 379
petroleum, 499, 500
phosphoric acid, 370, 530
phosphorus, 475, 565, 568
picric acid, 540
podophyllum, 188, 250, 371, 395, 453, 474
psorinum, 149
pulsatilla, 176, 256, 272, 351
rheum, 644, 687
rhus tox., 234
rumex crispus, 474, 724
silicea, 546
staphisagria, 342
stramonium, 425
strontiana carb., 541, 654
sulphur, 250, 453, 474, 500, 695
sulphuric acid, 532
thuja, 310
veratrum album, 176, 255, 272, 371
DIPHTHERIA
ailanthus, 212, 403
alcohol, 211
ammonium caust., 211
amygdala amara, 213, 214
apis, 51, 95, 107, 109
arsenicum, 110, 213, 558
arsenicum iod., 558
arum triphyllum, 233, 444, 535
baptisia, 212, 403
belladonna, 214, 412
bromine, 214
camphor, 481
cantharis, 95, 435
capsicum, 435, 524
carbo veg., 481
carbolic acid, 721
crotalus horr., 35, 50

DIPHTHERIA (Continued)
hydrocyanic acid, 524
ignatia, 203
iodine, 214
kali bichromicum, 214, 524, 595, 721
kali permangan., 110, 214, 524, 721
lac caninum, 28, 50
lachesis, 50, 214, 444
lycopodium, 50, 211, 413, 443
mercurius biniod., 214, 594
mercurius cor., 596
mercurius cyanatus, 214, 481, 524, 595
mercurius protoiod., 595
mercurius vivus, 594
muriatic acid, 211, 524, 535
naja, 50, 213
natrum arsenicosum, 110, 214, 254
nitric acid, 210, 444, 534
phytolacca, 213, 444
ranunculus scel., 333
rhus tox., 213, 225, 232
sulphuric acid, 532
DIPHTHERIA, LARYNGEAL
lachesis, 50
DIPLOPIA
aurum, 601
gelsemium, 170
DISLOCATION OF JOINTS
ignatia, 235
petroleum, 235
rhus tox., 235
DROPSY
acetic acid, 104
apis, 66, 67, 102
apocynum can., 104, 163, 337
arsenicum, 66, 104, 164, 337, 445, 558
blatta, 32
colchicum, 67, 254
digitalis, 66, 166, 396
helleborus, 66, 164, 337
lachesis, 56, 66
lycopodium, 445
muriatic acid, 525
rhus tox., 445
scoparius, 163
sulphur, 104
terebinthina, 66, 337
DRUNKARDS, COMPLAINTS OF
arsenicum, 55, 187
ammonium mur., 187
antimonium tart., 583
baryta carb., 268, 650
carbo veg., 486
cinchona, 374
fluoric acid, 187
lachesis, 477
ledum, 195, 324
nux vomica, 186, 187, 189, 191, 195
opium, 210, 268, 269, 650
selenium, 460
staphisagria, 460
sulphur, 476
sulphuric acid, 58
DYSENTERY
aconite, 324
aloes, 188

THERAPEUTIC INDEX.

DYSENTERY (Continued)
arnica, 242
arsenicum, 488, 553
baptisia, 403
belladonna, 419
cantharis, 95, 253
capsicum, 96, 435
carbo veg., 488
cinchona, 488
colchicum, 96, 253
colocynth, 96, 286, 287
ferrum phos., 642
kali bichrom., 61, 97, 725
lachesis, 61
mercurius, 54, 188, 253, 324, 597
nux vomica, 96, 188, 597
rhus tox., 225, 234
sulphur, 96, 466, 474, 598
zincum sulph., 96

DYSMENORRHOEA
aconite, 325
actea racemosa, 202, 648
belladonna, 421
caulophyllum, 176, 648
causticum, 735
chamomilla, 209, 263
cinchona, 53
cocculus, 202, 263
colocynth, 286, 287
cyclamen, 263
gelsemium, 176
ignatia, 202, 263
magnesia mur., 202, 647
nux vomica, 263
pulsatilla, 202, 263, 355

DYSPEPSIA
abies nigra, 305, 350, 370
alumina, 618, 619
arnica, 242
arsenicum, 54, 55, 185, 487, 350, 351
bryonia, 298
cadmium sulph., 55
capsicum, 434
carbo veg., 56, 185, 486, 532
cinchona, 53, 350, 370, 487
graphites, 57
hepar, 53, 686
hydrocyanic acid, 517
ignatia, 202
ipecac, 377
kali bichromicum, 724
kali carb., 739
kreosote, 185
lachesis, 52, 687
lycopodium, 131, 487
magnesia carb., 645
mercurius, 54
natrum carb., 690
natrum mur., 704
nux vomica, 184, 350, 477, 487, 704
phosphorus, 568
pulsatilla, 186, 370
sepia, 131, 432
stannum, 624
sulphur, 132, 476
sulphuric acid, 58, 532

DYSPEPSIA (Continued)
tabacum, 432

DYSPHAGIA
gelsemium, 170, 173

DYSURIA
aconite, 710
apis, 145
arnica, 443
belladonna, 416
benzoic acid, 711
camphor, 93
cantharis, 711
capsicum, 434
colocynth, 287
digitalis, 394
hepar, 687
lycopodium, 443, 711
nitric acid, 192
nux vomica, 192
pareira brava, 453
petroselinum, 710
prunus spinosa, 443
pulsatilla, 443
sarsaparilla, 443

EARS
aurum, 43, 491, 602
baryta carb., 652
belladonna, 411, 708
borax, 708
capsicum, 43, 435, 491
carbo animalis, 491
carbo veg., 491, 498
causticum, 733
chamomilla, 708
conium, 448
crotalus, 43
dulcamara, 434
elaps, 43
graphites, 498
hepar, 43, 412, 683
lachesis, 43
nitric acid, 43, 535
nux vomica, 190
pulsatilla, 348, 708
sanguinaria, 276
silicea, 43, 435, 545
tellurium, 412

ECCHYMOSES OF THE SCLEROTIC
arnica, 190
hamamelis, 190
ledum, 191
nux vomica, 189

ECZEMA
antimonium crudum, 579
arsenicum, 559
calcarea ostrearum, 670
curare, 179
hepar, 688
hyarocotyle, 560
kali bromatum, 716
mezereum, 233
natrum carb., 693
natrum mur., 705
nux juglans, 233
petroleum, 311, 495, 499

ECZEMA (Continued)
pix liquida, 306
psorinum, 234
ranunculus bulb.,
rhus tox., 232
selenium, 461
sepia, 693
staphisagria, 340

EMOTIONS, ILL EFFECTS OF
(See Grief, Anger, etc.)

EMPHYSEMA
ammonium carb., 485, 660
antimonium arsen., 558
antimonium tart., 558
arsenicum, 558
carbo veg., 558
curare, 207
ipecac, 558
naphthalin, 558

ENDOCARDITIS
arsenicum, 558
kali carb., 741
kali hydriodicum, 718
phosphorus, 572

ENTERITIS
arnica, 60
arsenicum, 553
baptisia, 59
belladonna, 59, 419
colocynth, 285
colchicum, 60
lachesis, 59
rhus tox., 59, 234

ENURESIS
belladonna, 416, 734
benzoic acid, 247
causticum, 416, 734
calcarea ostrearum, 416, 734
cina, 247
equisetum, 90
hepar, 687
hyoscyamus, 416
kreosote, 247, 416, 734
linaria, 90, 395
natrum hydrochlor., 692
phosphoric acid, 247
plantago major, 416, 734
secale, 247
sepia, 734
silicea, 416
sulphur, 416

EPIDIDYMITIS
gelsemium, 175
pulsatilla, 352

EPILEPSY
(See also Convulsions.)
absinthium, 420
argentum metallicum, 611
argentum nitricum, 608
arsenicum, 561
artemisia vulgaris, 242, 420, 676
belladonna, 420
bufo, 30, 547, 676
calcarea ostrearum, 676, 734
causticum, 734
cicuta virosa, 182, 428, 451

EPILEPSY (Continued)
cuprum, 630
hydrocyanic acid, 537, 676
hyoscyamus, 428
indigo, 30
kali bromatum, 715
nux vomica, 30, 547, 676
oenanthe, 428
plumbum, 622
ranunculus bulb., 332
silicea, 547, 676
sulphur, 676
stannum, 625

EPISTAXIS
ambra, 152
bovista, 157
bromine, 502, 507
bryonia, 291
calcarea ostr., 671
camphor, 481
carbo veg., 157, 481
ferrum, 639
ipecac, 380
mercurius, 591
mercurius cyan., 591
nux vomica, 190
phosphorus, 569
phosphoric acid, 527
pulsatilla, 346, 354, 355
rhus tox., 527
secale, 157
sepia, 124
trillium, 159

EPITHELIOMA
arsenicum, 561
cicuta, 451
clematis, 561
hydrastis, 510, 561

ERECTILE TUMORS
lycopodium, 441

ERGOTISM, 153

ERYSIPELAS
anacardium occ., 221
apis, 46, 106, 232, 417
belladonna, 45, 106, 407, 416
borax, 711
camphor, 86
cantharis, 97, 106
comocladia, 217
crotalus, 45, 417
cuprum, 417, 630
euphorbium, 46, 86
graphites, 97, 174, 497
hepar, 106
lachesis, 41, 44, 106, 416
rhus tox., 46, 106, 113, 221, 232
silicea, 106
stramonium, 425
sulphur, 106, 417

EUSTACHIAN CATARRH
graphites, 498
nitric acid, 535
nux vomica, 190
silicea, 546

EYES
aconite, 321, 397

THERAPEUTIC INDEX. 797

EYES (Continued)
  actea racemosa, 327
  agaricus, 203
  alumina, 131, 619
  amyl nitrite, 412
  antimonium crudum, 580
  antimonium tart., 583
  apis, 113, 217
  argentum nitricum, 608, 619
  arnica, 43
  arsenicum, 113, 397, 494
  artemisia vulgaris, 243
  asafoetida, 450
  aurum, 601
  belladonna, 397, 412, 449
  berberis, 619
  borax, 710
  bryonia, 300
  calcarea ostrearum, 494, 669
  carbo animalis, 491
  carbo veg., 492
  cedron, 206
  cina, 247, 619
  cinnabaris, 594
  comocladia, 217
  conium, 360, 619
  crocus, 619
  crotalus horridus, 43
  cyclamen, 360
  euphrasia, 383, 396, 496, 609, 683
  glonoin, 436
  graphites, 130, 494, 580, 619, 710
  hepar, 496, 683
  ignatia, 203
  jaborandi, 130, 619
  kali bichromicum, 113, 360, 726
  kali carb., 130
  kali hydriodicum, 716
  kreosote, 609
  lachesis, 42
  lithium carb., 655
  mercurius, 397, 495, 593
  mercurius biniod., 593
  mercurius cor., 593
  mercurius dulcis, 593
  mercurius protoiod., 593
  mezereum, 206
  natrum carb., 619
  natrum mur., 130, 619, 702
  natrum sulph., 619
  nux moschata, 619
  nux vomica, 130, 189
  paris quadrifolia, 412
  petroleum, 499
  phellandrium, 450
  phosphorus, 574, 683
  prunus spinosa, 412
  pulsatilla, 130, 347
  rhus tox., 113, 235, 397, 609, 619
  ruta, 449, 619
  saccharum offic., 669
  santonine, 274, 360
  sepia, 129, 619
  spigelia, 205, 321, 412, 701
  staphisagria, 340
  sulphur, 321, 473, 494, 670

EYES (Continued)
  thuja, 131
  zincum, 637
  zincum sulph., 637

FACE
  aethusa, 377, 450
  ammonium mur., 662
  antimonium tart., 377
  apis, 42, 44
  arsenicum, 44
  baptisia, 44
  belladonna, 44, 409, 411
  bryonia, 246
  bufo, 44
  calcarea ostr., 668
  camphor, 44, 45
  carbo veg., 44
  cicuta, 44, 45
  cina, 246
  cinchona, 44
  cuprum, 44
  digitalis, 389
  euphorbium, 46
  ferrum, 640
  gelsemium, 171
  hydrocyanic acid, 44, 45
  hyoscyamus, 44, 45
  ipecacuanha, 246, 377
  kali bich., 724
  kali carb., 44
  lachesis, 43
  lycopodium, 44, 440
  natrum arsenicosum, 44
  nux moschata, 44
  nux vomica, 44
  opium, 44, 420
  phosphoric acid, 44
  phosphorus, 44, 45
  phytolacca, 44
  pulsatilla, 44
  rhus tox., 44
  secale, 44
  stramonium, 44, 45
  staphisagria, 338
  sulphur, 44, 465
  veratrum album, 44
FAINTING
  (See Syncope.)
FAMILY RELATION OF DRUGS, 23
FATIGUE
  coca, 521
  coffea, 385
  fluoric acid, 521
FATTY DEGENERATIONS
  apocynum, 164
  aurum, 603
  manganum, 633
  phosphorus, 540
  picric acid, 540
FATTY TUMORS
  baryta carb., 652
FEET
  lycopodium, 692
  natrum carb., 692

FELONS
  fluoric acid, 520
  mercurius, 592
FEMALE GENITAL ORGANS
  actea racemosa, 143, 328, 356
  aletris farinosa, 359
  aloes, 137, 478
  ambra grisea, 151
  ammonium mur., 663
  antimonium crud., 580
  apis mellifica, 112, 615, 664
  argentum metallicum, 616
  argentum nitricum, 616
  arnica, 664
  aurum, 139, 603, 615
  belladonna, 420, 615
  berberis, 452
  bryonia, 301
  calcarea ostrearum, 145, 673
  calcarea phos., 145, 679
  cantharis, 97
  carbo animalis, 140
  carbo veg., 141
  caulophyllum 357
  cyclamen, 359
  ferrum, 615
  ferrum jod., 143, 643
  gelsemium, 175
  graphites, 141, 498
  hedeoma, 146
  helonias, 134, 357, 616
  hydrocotyle, 145
  inula, 146
  kali ferrocyan., 144
  kreosote, 136, 615
  lachesis, 62
  lilium tigrinum, 133, 616
  mitchella, 145
  murex, 135
  natrum carb., 142, 693
  natrum hypochlorosum, 143
  natrum mur., 142, 615, 700
  nux vomica, 136, 193
  palladium, 615
  platina, 65, 140, 613
  podophyllum, 138
  pulsatilla, 138, 354
  secale, 145
  senecio, 359
  sepia, 133, 420, 615
  stannum, 138
  sulphur, 134, 478
  thuja, 309, 615
  ustilago, 145, 157
  vespa, 145
  viburnum opulus, 146, 250
  zincum, 638
  zizea, 146
FEVER
  aconite, 291, 316, 318
  apis, 317
  arsenicum, 320, 467, 552, 556
  baptisia, 467
  belladonna, 292, 319, 409
  bryonia, 289, 317
  carbo veg., 483

FEVER (Continued)
  cuprum, 629
  ferrum phos., 320
  gelsemium, 173, 317
  hyoscyamus, 428
  mercurius, 410
  lycopodium, 440
  opium, 272
  podophyllum, 454
  pulsatilla, 360
  sulphur, 320, 466, 557
  veratrum viride, 319
FEVER BLISTERS
  arsenicum, 705
  hepar, 705
  natrum mur., 705
  rhus tox., 705
FIBROUS TISSUES
  rhus tox., 235
FISTULAE
  ignatia, 542
  petroleum, 499
  phosphorus, 573
  silicea, 497, 573
  sulphur, 452
FISTULA IN ANO
  berberis, 452
  calcarea phos., 452
  graphites, 497
  lycopodium, 497
  nitric acid, 497, 534
  paeonia, 497
  petroleum, 499
  ratanhia, 497
  silicea, 542
FLATULENCE
  cepa, 445
  fel tauri, 29
  fel vulpi, 29
  graphites, 497
  lycopodium, 284, 445, 497
  momordica balsamica, 284, 445
  natrum sulph., 695
  raphanus, 271, 445
  sulphur, 445
FLUSHES OF HEAT
  amyl nitrite, 31, 466
  kali bichromicum, 466
  lachesis, 466
  sulphur, 466
  sulphuric acid, 466
FRACTURES
  calcarea phos., 680
  symphytum off., 241, 680
FRIGHT, ILL EFFECTS OF
  gelsemium, 272
  glonoin, 437
  natrum mur., 272
  opium, 270, 272
  phosphoric acid, 272
  pulsatilla, 272
  silicea, 272
  veratrum, 272

GALL-STONES
  (See Biliary Colic.)

THERAPEUTIC INDEX.

GANGRENE
  arsenicum, 47, 150, 483, 552, 560
  carbo veg., 483
  cinchona, 561
  iodine, 511
  lachesis, 560
  secale, 154, 156, 560

GASTRALGIA
  anacardium, 221
  argentum nitricum, 607
  belladonna, 414
  bismuth, 185, 415, 608
  chamomilla, 249
  chelidonium, 497
  chininum ars., 415
  ferrum, 640
  graphites, 57, 497
  ignatia, 202
  lithium carb., 655
  nux vomica, 184
  petroleum, 497
  stannum, 624

GASTRIC CATARRH
  aconite, 324
  antimonium crud., 351, 378, 578
  arsenicum, 378, 379
  bryonia, 378, 578
  ipecacuanha, 378
  kali bichromicum, 720
  nux vomica, 378
  pulsatilla, 49, 579

GASTRIC FEVER
  aconite, 291
  bryonia, 289
  mercurius, 591

GASTRIC SYMPTOMS
  (See also Gastritis, etc.)
  aconite, 324
  alumina, 619
  anacardium, 219
  antimonium crudum, 378
  antimonium tart., 583
  arsenicum, 54, 55, 350, 378, 487, 553
  belladonna, 350, 414
  bryonia, 248
  calcarea ostr., 415
  carbo animalis, 490
  carbo veg., 56, 350, 486, 554
  chamomilla, 249
  chelidonium, 481
  cinchona, 370, 553
  colchicum, 58, 350
  cyclamen, 359
  ferrum, 496
  fluoric acid, 704
  graphites, 57, 496
  hepar, 460, 686, 704
  indium, 636
  ipecacuanha, 350, 351, 377
  kali bichromicum, 724
  kreosote, 185, 350
  lachesis, 52, 56, 704
  lobelia, 377
  lycopodium, 444, 553, 724
  muriatic acid, 525
  natrum mur., 697

GASTRIC SYMPTOMS (Continued)
  nitro-muriatic acid, 525
  nux vomica, 184, 445
  petroleum, 500
  phosphorus, 565, 568, 636
  pulsatilla, 377, 496
  raphanus, 445
  sabina, 350
  selenium, 460
  sepia, 350, 490, 623
  stannum, 624
  staphisagria, 341, 377, 460
  sulphur, 195, 445, 636
  tabacum, 377, 432
  thein, 132, 377
  thuja, 350
  zincum, 637

GASTRITIS
  aconite, 324
  arsenicum, 54, 185, 324, 553
  cantharis, 95
  colchicum, 324
  kali bichromicum, 726

GASTRO-ENTERIC SYMPTOMS
  argentum nitricum, 554
  cadmium sulph., 554
  carbo veg., 554
  elaps, 58
  magnesia carb., 644
  secale cornutum, 155, 554
  veratrum album, 554

GENITAL ORGANS
  (See also Female Genital Organs.)
  apis, 112
  cantharis, 96
  croton tiglium, 86
  gelsemium, 174
  graphites, 498
  lachesis, 62
  picric acid, 97

GLANDS
  alumina, 626
  badiagia, 31
  belladonna, 233
  bromine, 503
  calcarea ostr., 671
  carbo animalis, 31, 489, 503
  carbo veg., 484
  conium, 448
  graphites, 494
  hepar, 686
  iodine, 509
  mercurius, 590, 596
  silicea, 544
  spongia, 512
  sulphur, 468

GLAUCOMA
  aconite, 321
  aurum, 601
  bryonia, 300
  colocynth, 287
  rhus tox., 235

GLOSSOPLEGIA
  baryta carb., 650
  colchicum, 650

THERAPEUTIC INDEX.

GOITRE
bromine, 503
lapis albus, 510
spongia, 512

GONORRHOEA
argentum nitricum, 91
cannabis indica, 90
cannabis sativa, 89
cantharis, 89, 96
capsicum, 91
carbo animalis, 489
chimaphila, 91
clematis, 91
copaiva, 91, 627
cubeba, 9
digitalis, 394
doryphora, 32
gelsemium, 175
kali bichromicum, 722
mercurius corrosivus, 91, 394
mercurius solubilis, 91, 311, 352, 394
natrum mur., 703
nux vomica, 192
petroselinum, 90, 394, 450, 710
pulsatilla, 310, 352
sepia, 394
sulphur, 394, 478
thuja, 91, 309
yucca, 313

GOUT
ammonium phos., 656, 665
antimonium crudum, 580
arnica, 369
benzoic acid, 453, 656
berberis vulgaris, 453
calcarea ostrearum, 453, 656, 677
causticum, 288
colchicum, 253, 353
colocynth, 288
guaiacum, 288
ledum, 232, 297
lithium carb., 453, 654
lycopodium, 453, 656
natrum mur., 656
pulsatilla, 353
sabina, 298
staphisagria, 341

GRANULAR LIDS
alumina, 619
argentum nitricum, 609
euphrasia, 609
lycopodium, 443
rhus tox., 609
zincum, 637
zincum sulph., 637

GRAVEL
cantharis, 89
lycopodium, 443
sarsaparilla, 92, 443

GRIEF, BAD EFFECTS OF
ignatia, 197, 198, 528
natrum mur., 197, 528
phosphoric acid, 197, 528

GROWING PAINS
guaiacum, 530
phosphoric acid, 530

GUMMATA
kali hydriodicum, 719

HAEMATEMESIS
hamamelis, 301
millefolium, 301
phosphorus, 575
pulsatilla, 301
ustilago, 301, 575

HAEMATURIA
cantharis, 89
crotalus, 66
equisetum, 90
ipecacuanha, 383
lachesis, 66
nux vomica, 192
terebinthina, 66, 305

HAEMAPHILLIA
bovista, 157
lachesis, 575
phosphorus, 575

HAEMOPTYSIS
acalypha indica, 369
aconite, 324
cactus, 324
carbo veg., 481
elaps, 35
ferrum, 639, 641
ledum, 324
millefolium, 324
nux vomica, 191
opium, 270
phosphorus, 301, 569
pulsatilla, 301, 361
rhus tox., 229
senecio, 301
sulphur, 465

HAEMORRHAGES
acalypha indica, 369
aconite, 243
ammonium carb., 658
aranea diadema, 80
arsenicum, 482, 487
belladonna, 368, 421
bovista, 157
carbo veg., 151, 368, 481
cascarilla, 312
cinchona, 293, 367, 482
cinnamomum, 369
cyclamen, 369
erigeron, 159, 368
ferrum, 643
ferrum phos., 159
hamamelis, 158, 369, 537
ipecacuanha, 368, 482, 643
ledum, 369
leptandra, 537
mercurius, 591
millefolium, 343, 368
mitchella, 158
phosphorus, 369, 569
sabina, 305, 368
sanguinaria, 278
secale, 154, 368
sulphuric acid, 532
trillium, 158, 159, 368

THERAPEUTIC INDEX. 801

HAEMORRHAGES (Continued)
  vinca minor, 167, 369
HAEMORRHOIDS
  abrotanum, 245
  aesculus hip., 187
  aloes, 137, 187, 478
  anacardium, 220
  apocynum, 165
  arsenicum, 55, 487
  carbo animalis, 490
  carbo veg., 57, 486
  cascarilla, 321
  collinsonia, 188
  graphites, 497
  hamamelis, 188
  lachesis, 52
  lamium album, 220
  lycopodium, 441
  nux vomica, 186, 187
  paeonia, 497
  sepia, 131
  sulphur, 187, 465, 476
  sulph. ac., 58, 531
HAY-FEVER
  ailanthus, 557
  ambrosia, 332
  arsenicum, 332, 557
  arsenicum jod., 557
  lobelia inflata, 557
  rosa damascena, 557
  ranunculus bulbosus, 332
  silicea, 332, 546, 557
  sinapis nigra, 558
  wyethia, 558
HEADACHE
  (See also Hemicrania.)
  aconite, 200
  actea racemosa, 176, 328
  aloes, 137, 187
  anacardium, 219
  antimonium tart., 581
  aranea, 81
  argentum nitricum, 605, 606
  arsenicum, 701
  baryta carb., 652
  belladonna, 82, 277, 408, 411
  bovista, 158
  bromine, 504
  bryonia, 40, 82, 289, 300, 701
  calcarea ostrearum, 701
  cannabis indica, 90
  carbo animalis, 141, 354
  carbo veg., 300, 486
  carbolic acid, 481
  castoreum, 195
  causticum, 702, 724
  chamomilla, 287
  chelidonium, 281
  cinchona, 40, 369, 701
  cocculus, 262, 354
  colocynth, 287
  cyclamen, 130
  ferrum, 639, 641
  gelsemium, 40, 171, 172, 200, 262, 300, 581, 701
  glonoin, 436, 701

HAEMORRHAGES (Continued)
  hyoscyamus, 427
  ignatia, 78, 171, 199
  ipecacuanha, 377
  iris versicolor, 277, 702, 784
  juglans cinerea, 207, 262, 300
  kali bichromicum, 702, 727
  kali hydriodicum, 716
  kalmia, 171, 200
  lac defloratum, 28
  lachesis, 40, 41
  lamium album, 220
  lithium carb., 655
  magnesia mur., 120, 656
  melilotus, 200, 277
  menyanthes, 354, 547
  mercurius, 41, 591
  moschus, 116
  natrum carb., 692
  natrum mur., 128, 300, 699, 701, 724
  nux vomica, 128, 183, 184, 300
  oleander, 165
  oleum animale, 171
  palladium, 615
  paris quadrifolia, 547
  paullinia, 278
  petroleum, 172, 300
  phellandrium, 354, 450
  phosphoric acid, 530
  phosphorus, 563
  picric acid, 128, 194
  platina, 78
  psorinum, 149, 150, 724
  ptelea, 377
  pulsatilla, 41, 353
  ranunculus bulb., 354
  ranunculus scel., 354
  rhus glabra, 217
  rhus radicans, 222
  sanguinaria, 82, 171, 200, 276
  sarsaparilla, 311
  selenium, 460
  sepia, 176, 701
  silicea, 171, 200, 547, 653, 724
  spigelia, 82, 205, 354, 392, 701
  strontiana carb., 548
  sulphur, 128, 581
  theridion, 82
  thuja, 308
  veratrum alb., 200, 354, 377, 701
  zincum, 635
HEART
  aconite, 225, 322, 507, 514
  actea racemosa, 225
  ammonium carb., 601, 659
  anacardium, 221
  apis, 103, 110
  apocynum, 111, 164
  argentum metallicum, 611
  arnica, 225, 239, 323
  arsenicum, 111, 164, 239, 314
  asparagus, 111
  aurum, 323, 600, 656
  aurum mur. natr., 601
  belladonna, 111
  benzoic acid, 656

HEART (Continued)
bovista, 158
bromine, 225, 239, 507
bryonia, 298
cactus, 225, 239
carbo animalis, 134, 499
colchicum, 254, 298
conium, 392, 448, 656
convallaria, 393
digitalis, 69, 111, 171, 388
euphrasia, 718
gelsemium, 170, 276
gloncin, 460
graphite, 499, 718.
grindelia, 171, 466
helleborus, 392
hydrocyanic acid, 514, 538
iodine, 509
kali bichromicum. 134, 499, 718
kali carb., 111, 145, 737, 741
kali chloricum, 134. 449
kali hydriodicum, 717, 718
kali nitricum, 499
kalmia, 225, 323, 392, 656
lachesis, 65, 111, 514, 718
lactuca, 718
ledum, 656
lilium tig., 134
lithium carb., 656
magnesia mur., 120, 647
natrum mur., 134, 499
petroleum, 134, 499
phosphorus, 31, 514, 572
phytolacca, 225
pulsatilla, 225
quinine, 365
rhus tox., 223, 225, 323
spigelia, 111, 206, 254, 392, 509, 741
spongia, 514
sulphur, 111, 465
sumbul, 225
tabacum, 432
veratrum alb., 257
veratrum viride, 257
zincum, 636, 656

HEART, FATTY DEGENERATION OF THE
apocynum, 164
arsenicum, 572
phosphorus, 572

HEART, HYPERTROPHY OF THE
aconite, 323, 508
arnica, 225, 239, 323, 507
arsenicum, 239
aurum, 323, 601
bromine, 225, 239, 507
cactus, 239, 323
iodine, 509
kalmia, 323
rhus tox., 223, 239, 323, 508

HEART, PALPITATION OF THE
badiaga, 31
coffea, 31
nitrite of amyl, 31
phosphorus, 31
rhus tox., 225

HEAT, ILL-EFFECTS OF
natrum carb., 691
selenium, 38, 459

HECTIC FEVER
arsenicum, 373
carbo veg., 373, 483
cinchona, 373
lycopodium, 446
stannum, 626, 706

HEELS
ammonium mur., 663
antimonium crudum, 663
causticum, 663
cepa, 663
graphites, 663.
ignatia, 663
ledum, 663
manganum, 663
natrum carb., 663, 692
pulsatilla, 663
sepia, 663

HEMICRANIA
argentum nitricum, 606
arsenicum, 129, 561
belladonna, 128
gelsemium, 128
iris versicolor, 129
nux vomica, 129
oleum animale, 171
pulsatilla, 129
sanguinaria, 128
sepia, 128
silicea, 128, 129
theridion, 129
veratrum album, 128

HEMIOPIA
aurum, 601
lithium carb., 655, 702
lycopodium, 702
natrum mur., 702
titanium, 702

HEMIPLEGIA
arnica, 242

HEPATITIS
phosphorus, 567

HERNIA
aconite, 325
carbo veg., 56
cocculus, 189
lachesis, 57
lycopodium, 189
nux vomica, 189
opium, 272
tabacum, 433

HERPES
bovista, 157
psorinum, 149
natrum mur., 705
sepia, 125, 705

HERPES CIRCINATUS
baryta carb., 125, 705
calcarea ostrearum, 125
natrum mur., 705
sepia, 125, 705
tellurium, 125, 705

THERAPEUTIC INDEX.

HERPES LABIALIS
(See Fever Blisters.)
HERPES ZOSTER
 arsenicum, 332
 carboneum oxygen., 87
 mezereum, 332
 ranunculus bulb., 332
 rhus tox., 332
HICCOUGH
 arsenicum, 203
 cajuputum, 203
 hyoscyamus, 203
 ignatia, 202
 pulsatilla, 203
 ranunculus bulb., 372
 stramonium, 203
 sulphuric acid, 203
 teucrium marum verum, 203
 veratrum album, 203
HIP-JOINT DISEASE
 calcarea ostrearum, 676
 carbo veg., 483
 colocynth, 288
 Gettysburg spring water, 341, 545, 656
 natrum sulph., 695
 phosphoric acid, 530
 phosphorus, 573
 silicea, 544, 573
 stillingia, 695
 stramonium, 425
 sulphur, 470
HOARSENESS
(See Aphonia.)
HOMESICKNESS
 capsicum, 435, 528
 mercurius, 590
 phosphoric acid, 528
HYDRARTHROSIS
 apis, 511
 iodine, 510
 sulphur, 511
HYDROCELE
 digitalis, 390
 pulsatilla, 353
HYDROCEPHALOID
 apis, 114
 arsenicum, 102
 calcarea phos., 367, 380, 636, 680
 cinchona, 366, 380, 680
 ferrum phos., 159
 oenothera bien., 379
 sulphur, 471
 zinc, 635, 680
HYDROCEPHALUS
 apis, 103
 apocynum, 164
 baryta carb., 649
 calcarea ostr., 672
 digitalis, 164, 337, 393
 helleborus, 101, 105, 337
 staphisagria, 338
 sulphur, 104, 469
 terebinth., 305
HYDROPERICARDIUM
 apis, 110
 arsenicum, 111, 559

HYDROPERICARDIUM (Continued)
 digitalis, 390
 kali carb., 111
 lachesis, 65
 lycopodium, 445
HYDROPHOBIA
 belladonna, 94
 cantharis, 94
 stramonium, 423
HYDROTHORAX
 apis, 103, 110
 apocynum cannabinum, 104
 arsenicum, 559
 colchicum, 254
 digitalis, 390
 juglans cinerea, 207
 lachesis, 65
 mercurius sulph., 390, 559
HYPEROPIA
 carbo an., 492
HYPOCHONDRIASIS
 alumina, 618
 anacardium, 219
 bryonia, 618
 conium, 448, 638
 natrum carb., 689
 natrum mur., 699, 704
 nux vomica, 618, 691
 sepia, 690
 stannum, 624
 staphisagria, 338
 zincum, 638
 zincum ox., 448
HYSTERIA
 actea racemosa, 76
 ammoniacum gummi, 116, 120
 apis, 100, 112
 arsenicum, 614
 asafoetida, 119, 120, 198, 449
 belladonna, 77, 199
 calcarea ostrearum, 614
 cocculus, 199
 crocus, 76, 79
 cuprum, 198
 hyoscyamus, 77, 198
 ignatia, 77, 116, 198, 200, 276
 magnesia mur., 120, 646
 moschus, 79, 116, 198, 614
 nux moschata, 118, 199
 nux vomica, 276
 palladium, 78
 phosphorus, 276
 platina, 78, 198, 613, 614
 sanguinaria, 276
 sepia, 124
 stannum, 625
 sulphur, 471
 tarantula, 757
 theridion, 82
 valeriana, 118, 119, 276
 valerinate of zinc, 199
ILEUS
 opium, 272
IMPETIGO
 sepia, 476

IMPOTENCE
agnus castus, 674
calcarea ostr., 674
chlorine, 511
conium, 564
graphites, 498
phosphorus, 564
selenium, 459

INFLAMMATIONS
aconite, 36, 99, 316
apis, 99
arsenicum, 94, 96, 552
belladonna, 9o, 407, 591
camphor, 04
cantharis, 94
ferrum phos., 159, 642
hepar, 687
mercurius, 591

INFLAMMATORY FEVER
arsenicum, 467

INFLUENZA
eupatorium perf., 244
ranunculus sceleratus, 333
rhus tox., 234
sabadilla, 298

INIMICAL DRUGS
ammonium carb. and lachesis, 659
apis and rhus, 114
carbo veg. and causticum, 481
cinchona and belladonna or morphia, 375
cinchona and digitalis, 393
nux and zinc, 196, 631
phos. and caust., 729
psorin. and lach., 151
ranunculus bulb. and sulph., 332
rhus tox. and apis, 114, 223
selenium and cinchona, 462
silicea and mercurius, 543, 631

INIMICAL RELATION OF DRUGS, 24

INJURIES
angustura, 180
arnica, 242, 532
calcarea phos., 241
calendula, 241
cicuta, 451
conium, 449, 532
glonoin, 437
hypericum, 241
ledum, 241
natrum sulph., 437, 694
rhus tox., 240
ruta, 532, 654
staphisagria, 241
sulphuric acid, 532
symphytum, 241

INSOMNIA
(See also Sleep.)
ambra grisea, 151
calcarea ostrearum, 675
chamomilla, 248
cocculus, 361
hyoscyamus, 428

INTERMITTENT FEVER
alstonia schol., 168
ammonium mur., 662
apis mellifica, 70, 107

INTERMITTENT FEVER (Continued)
aranea diadema, 80, 373
arsenicum, 69, 555
camphor, 69
canchalagua, 372
capsicum, 68, 201, 372, 435
carbo veg., 58, 372, 483
cedron, 80
chininum sulph., 80, 371, 467
cimex, 32
cina, 247
cinchona, 80, 229, 371
cornus florida, 371
cuprum, 70
digitalis, 69
eucalyptus, 372
eupatorium perf., 229, 244, 372
eupatorium purp., 244
ferrum, 372, 643
gelsemium, 68, 172, 229
helleborus, 69
hydrocyanic acid, 69
hyoscyamus, 69
ignatia, 201, 372
ipecacuanha, 372, 382
malaria offic., 373
lachesis, 68, 202, 372
lachnanthes, 69
lycopodium, 70, 441
menyanthes, 68, 372, 483
natrum mur., 108, 229, 706
nux vomica, 196
pulsatilla, 360
rhus tox., 229
sabadilla, 229
secale, 69
sepia, 372
sulphur, 229, 467
veratrum album, 69

IRITIS
asafoetida, 450, 602
aurum, 450, 601
colocynth, 287
euphrasia, 397
kali bichromicum, 726
kali hydriodicum, 716
mercurius, 311, 593
mercurius corros., 593, 602, 716
nitric acid, 602
rhus tox., 235, 397
thuja, 310

JAUNDICE
arsenicum, 187
bryonia, 187, 299
carduus marianus, 187
chamomilla, 187, 248
chelidonium, 207
cinchona, 374
digitalis, 391
hepar, 187
juglans cin., 207, 262
lachesis, 52
mercurius, 187, 597
myrica, 391
natrum sulph., 187

THERAPEUTIC INDEX.

JAUNDICE (Continued)
nux vomica, 187
phosphorus, 569
podophyllum, 453
pulsatilla, 187

JOINTS
ammonium mur., 663
ammonium phos., 656
anacardium, 221
apocynum, 164
argentum met., 611
benzoic acid, 453, 656
berberis, 453
bryonia, 453
calcarea ostr., 453, 656
calcarea phos., 679, 680
Gettysburg spring water, 656, 676
ignatia, 235
iodine, 103
kali hydriodicum, 103
lithium carb., 654, 656
petroleum, 235
lycopodium, 656
pinus sylvestris, 676, 692
pulsatilla, 221
rhus tox., 235, 240
sepia, 125

KERATITIS
apis, 383
crotalus, 43
kali hydriodicum, 717
silicea, 545
sulphur, 473

KIDNEYS
ammonium benz., 66
apis, 66, 559
argentum nitricum, 610
arsenicum, 67, 559
aurum, 559, 603
berberis, 93, 451
cannabis indica, 90
cantharis, 87
carbolic acid, 66
colchicum, 67
digitalis, 66, 559
helleborus, 66, 559
kali carb., 66
kali hydriodicum, 719
lachesis, 66
lycopodium, 446
natrum mur., 66
phosphoric acid, 530
phosphorus, 559, 569
plumbum, 603, 623
terebinthina, 66, 92, 305, 559

KNEE-JOINT DISEASE
silicea, 544

LABOR
aconite, 321
actea racemosa, 328
belladonna, 421
cantharis, 97
caulophyllum, 357
chamomilla, 250

LABOR (Continued)
gelsemium, 175, 328
ipecacuanha, 328
lycopodium, 328
natrum carb., 694
nux vomica, 193, 355
pulsatilla, 193, 355
secale, 154

LACTATION
(See also Agalactia.)
carbo animalis, 165, 490
oleander, 165

LAPAROTOMY
staphysagria, 241

LARYNGEAL PHTHISIS
selenium, 462
spongia, 513

LARYNGISMUS STRIDULUS
antimonium tart., 504
arsenicum, 504
belladonna, 504
bromine, 504
calcarea phos., 504
chlorine, 504
cuprum, 504
ignatia, 504
iodine, 504
ipecacuanha, 504
lachesis, 504
phosphorus, 504
sambucus, 324, 504

LARYNGITIS
apis, 110
kali bichromicum, 721
sambucus, 513
spongia, 462, 513
sulphur, 473

LARYNX
(See also Laryngeal Phthisis.)
apis, 110
argentum metallicum, 611
argentum nitricum, 609
arum triphyllum, 210
causticum, 732
eupatorium perf., 485
manganum, 609
phosphorus, 462, 570
paris quadrifolia, 610
sanguinaria,
selenium, 461, 610

LEAD-COLIC
alum, 621
alumina, 620, 621
arsenicum, 621
belladonna, 621
colocynth, 621
nux vomica, 621
opium, 621
platina, 614, 621
sulphuric acid, 621

LEUCORRHOEA
alumina, 618
ambra grisea, 152
ammonium mur., 664
berberis, 452
borax, 710

LEUCORRHOEA (Continued)
calcarea ostrearum, 674
calcarea phosphorica, 145
cannabis sat., 674
carbo veg., 141
caulophyllum, 674
cubeba, 674
graphites, 141, 493
helonias, 358
hydrastis, 360
kali bichromicum, 720
kreosote, 136
lilium tigrinum, 134
mercurius, 574
murex purpurea, 135
natrum carb., 693
natrum mur., 142
nitric acid, 310, 354
palladium, 616
phosphorus, 674
podophyllum, 454
pulsatilla, 674
rhus tox., 134
sepia, 133, 674
stannum, 625
thuja, 309

LIVER
(See also Hepatitis and Gall Stones.)
aloe, 137
ammonium mur., 187, 664
angustura, 282
aurum, 603
berberis, 299, 452
bryonia, 207, 282, 298
carduus mar., 187
chelidonium, 207, 281, 299
chenopodium, 282
digitalis, 391
fluoric acid, 187
graphites, 497
hepar, 687
juglans cin., 207
kali carb., 299
lachesis, 52, 187, 444, 477
laurocerasus, 477
leptandra, 395, 598
lobelia syph., 282
lycopodium, 282, 444
magnesia mur., 186, 647
manganum, 633
mercurius, 395, 597, 647
myrica cerifera, 391
nux vomica, 130, 136, 186
phosphorus, 477, 565, 567
podophyllum, 137, 138, 453
ptelea, 648
ranunculus bulb., 282
selenium, 461
sepia, 136, 186
sulphur, 186, 461, 476
taraxacum, 244
zincum, 637

LIVER SPOTS
curare, 125, 179
lycopodium, 125
nux vomica, 125

LIVER SPOTS (Continued)
sepia, 125
sulphur, 125

LOCOMOTOR ATAXIA
alumina, 541, 618
aluminium met., 618
argentum nitricum, 606
belladonna, 419
causticum, 730
cocculus, 261
kali bromatum, 715
nux vomica, 194
phosphorus, 564
picric acid, 97
stramonium, 424
zincum, 606

LUMBAGO
calcarea fluorica, 677
calcarea ostrearum, 677
kali carb., 230, 741
ledum, 230
nux vomica, 194, 677
petroleum, 230
rhus tox., 230, 677
ruta, 230
secale, 677
staphisagria, 230
sulphur, 230
valeriana, 230

LUNGS
ammonium carb., 659
antimonium crud., 627
antimonium tart., 627
arsenicum, 374
aurum, 603
balsam of Peru, 627
borax, 710
calcarea ostr., 627, 673
calcarea phos., 627, 673
chamomilla, 627
cinchona, 374
copaiva, 627
dulcamara, 434
elaps, 51
ferrum phos., 159, 642
grindelia, 171, 633
hepar, 627, 685
illicium anisatum, 627
ipecacuanha, 627
kali bichromicum, 740
kali carb., 740
kali hyd., 717
lachesis, 374
lycopodium, 445, 627
myosotis, 627
opium, 270
phosphorus, 627
pix liquida, 306, 327
pulsatilla, 740
scilla, 627
secale, 374
selenium, 461
senega, 673
sepia, 673
silicea, 546
spongia, 513

THERAPEUTIC INDEX.

LUNGS (Continued)
  sulphur, 469, 627, 740
  veratrum viride, 257
  yerba santa, 627
LUNGS, ABSCESS OF THE
  lachesis, 51
LUNGS, PARALYSIS OF THE
  ammonium carb., 582, 659
  ammonium mur., 664
  antimonium tart., 485, 582, 650
  baryta carb., 650
  carbo veg., 485, 582
  dulcamara, 434
  hydrocyanic acid, 336, 538
  kali hydr., 582
  lachesis, 582
  moschus, 485, 582
  phosphorus, 480
LUNGS, SPASMS OF THE
  moschus, 273
  ipecac, 273
  opium, 273
LYING-IN
  aconite, 325
  ambra grisea, 152
  arnica, 242
  arsenicum, 271
  bryonia, 301
  causticum, 250
  chamomilla, 250
  croton tiglinum, 302
  helonias, 257
  hyoscyamus, 271
  opium, 271
  phellandrium, 302
  phytolacca, 302
  pulsatilla, 355
LYMPHATIC GLANDS
  (See Glands.)
MALIGNANT PUSTULE
  lachesis, 71
MAMMARY GLAND, AFFECTIONS OF THE
  apis, 574
  belladonna, 301, 419, 569, 574
  bromine, 503
  bryonia, 301
  carbo veg., 484
  croton tiglinum, 302, 503
  paris quad., 503
  phellandrium, 302, 450
  phosphorus, 545, 569, 574
  phytolacca, 302
  pulsatilla, 356
  silicea, 569, 574
MANIA
  hepar, 683
  hyoscyamus, 246, 430, 714
  kali bromatum, 430, 714
  stramonium, 429
  sulphur, 471
MARASMUS
  abrotanum, 245
  antimonium crud., 645
  argentum nitricum, 272, 554

MARASMUS (Continued)
  arsenicum, 553
  calcarea ostrearum, 469, 645
  calcarea phosphorica, 680
  cinchona, 554, 680
  hepar, 687
  iodine, 703
  magnesia carb., 644
  manganum, 663
  natrum carb., 645
  natrum mur., 703
  nux vomica, 554
  opium, 271
  phosphorus, 469
  podophyllum, 045
  rheum, 645
  sarsaparilla, 272
  sepia, 645
  sulphur, 272, 468, 554, 645
  sulphuric acid, 532
  thuja, 310
MASTOID PROCESS, DISEASES OF
  aurum, 43, 435, 491, 602
  capsicum, 43, 435, 602
  carbo an., 491
  fluoric acid, 519
  nitric acid, 43, 435, 491, 602
  silicea, 43, 545, 602
MASTURBATION
  (See Sexual Excesses.)
MEASLES
  aconite, 174, 326, 361
  antimonium tart., 581, 583
  belladonna, 174
  bryonia, 302
  cuprum, 424
  gelsemium, 174, 326
  ipecac, 303
  kali bichromicum, 361, 725
  pulsatilla, 174, 326, 361
  stramonium, 424
  zincum, 425, 633
MENIERE'S DISEASE
  carbon bisulphide, 733
  causticum, 733
  cinchona, 733
  salicylic acid, 733
MENINGITIS
  aconite, 294, 320, 407
  apis, 100, 294
  arsenicum, 102
  arum tri., 210
  belladonna, 42, 94, 101, 105, 294, 407, 409, 591
  bryonia, 101, 105, 294, 407
  calcarea ostr., 409
  cuprum, 101, 630
  digitalis, 337, 393
  glonoin, 101
  helleborus, 101, 336.
  hyoscyamus, 427
  lachesis, 42
  mercurius, 591
  picric acid, 97
  rhus tox., 102
  sulphur, 101, 104, 294, 409

807

MENINGITIS (Continued)
zinc., 102, 337, 633, 634
MENINGITIS, TUBERCULAR
(See Meningitis.)
MENORRHAGIA
arsenicum, 482
calcarea ostrearum, 673
carbo veg., 482
cinchona, 482
ipecacuanha, 482
mercurius, 592
trillium pendulum, 673
vinca minor, 67
MENSES
ambra grisea, 152, 158
ammonium carb., 65
belladonna, 613
berberis, 452
bovista, 158
bryonia, 301
calcarea ostrearum, 672, 673
carbo an., 140
carbo veg., 141
castoreum, 121
causticum, 735
chamomilla, 263
cocculus, 262
crocus, 613
ferrum, 641
graphites, 141, 493
hamamelis, 301
juglans regia, 207
kali carb., 700
kreosote, 136
lachesis, 62
lithium carb., 655
magnesium carb., 645
magnesium mur., 120, 647
millefolium, 301, 613
moschus, 65
murex, 135
natrum mur., 700
nux vomica, 193
phosphorus, 301, 569
platina, 65, 613
pulsatilla, 138, 301, 355
sabina, 613
senecio, 301, 359
sepia, 133
ustilago, 301
zincum, 633, 638
MENTAL FATIGUE
anacardium, 219
MENTAL SYMPTOMS
abies nigra, 305
aconite, 316, 321, 409
actea racemosa, 39
agaricus, 39, 423
alumina, 617
anacardium, 218, 219, 302
antimonium crudum, 219, 308, 577
antimonium tart., 581
apis, 99
argentum nitricum, 605, 612
arsenicum, 443, 551
arum tri., 209

MENTAL SYMPTOMS (Continued)
aurum, 139, 603
baptisia, 398, 437
baryta carb., 650, 679
belladonna, 218, 294
bovista, 102
bromine, 502
bryonia, 299, 619
calcarea ostrearum, 293, 617
calcarea phosphorica, 679
cannabis indica, 89, 269
causticum, 126, 288, 729
chamomilla, 248, 288, 344
chelidonium, 281
cinchona, 293, 369
cocculus, 199
coffea, 322, 384
colocynth, 288
conium, 448
cypripedium, 384
digitalis, 389
dulcamara, 683
fluoric acid, 440
gelsemium, 232, 272
glonoin, 427, 500
graphites, 57, 493
helonias, 134
hepar, 127, 682
hyoscyamus, 102, 198, 420, 427, 437, 612
ignatia, 102, 197, 344, 528
ipecac, 377
iodine, 502, 614
kali bromatum, 437, 606, 612, 715
kali carb., 443, 748
lachesis, 36, 38, 102, 218, 437, 617, 683
lilium tigrinum, 127
lycopodium, 37, 440, 613
mercurius, 590
moschus, 79, 116
muriatic acid, 521
mygale, 75
natrum carb., 689
natrum mur., 102, 126, 142, 198, 344, 624, 699
nitric acid, 219, 535
nux moschata, 118
nux vomica, 102, 344, 618
oleander, 165
opium, 272
palladium, 64, 78, 615
paris quad., 39
petroleum, 424, 437, 500
phosphoric acid, 197, 272, 471, 526, 738
phosphorus, 562
platina, 78, 127, 612, 615
pulsatilla, 126, 197, 343, 344, 617, 623, 700
rhus tox., 226, 437
sabadilla, 258
saccharum alb., 669
sanguinaria, 275
sepia, 121, 244, 347, 617, 624, 690, 700
silicea, 272
spigelia, 205
stannum, 344, 623
staphisagria, 248, 338, 339
stramonium, 218, 255, 423, 424, 429

THERAPEUTIC INDEX.

MENTAL SYMPTOMS (Continued)
  sulphur, 37, 471, 683
  sulphuric acid, 531
  thuja, 258, 308, 424
  valerian, 118
  veratrum album, 255, 272
  zizia, 146

METRITIS
  belladonna, 414
  berberis, 452
  kali carb., 741
  mel cum sale, 112, 415
  rhus tox., 234
  terebinthina, 305, 306

METRITIS, PUERPERAL
  (See Puerperal Metritis.)

METRORRHAGIA
  ambra, 152
  arsenicum, 65, 482
  belladonna, 272, 368, 421
  bovista, 157
  cantharis, 355
  carbo an., 490
  carbo veg., 368, 482
  cinchona, 368, 482
  cinnamon, 369
  erygeron, 159, 368
  ferrum, 642
  glonoin, 278
  gossypium, 355
  hamamelis, 159, 369
  hyoscyamus, 272
  ipecacuanha, 482
  lachesis, 278
  kali ferrocyan., 144
  mercurius, 592
  millefolium, 368
  mitchella, 159
  nitrite of amyl, 278
  nux vomica, 194
  opium, 272
  pulsatilla, 355
  sabina, 305, 368
  sanguinaria, 278
  secale, 145, 155, 368
  trillium pend., 158, 368
  ustilago, 157, 158

MILK FEVER
  aconite, 325
  bryonia, 301

MILK LEG
  hamamelis, 356
  pulsatilla, 356

MISCARRIAGE
  (See Abortion.)

MORBUS BRIGHTII
  (See Bright's Disease.)

MOUTH
  apis, 47
  argentum nitricum, 609
  arsenicum, 47
  arum triphyllum, 710
  baptisia, 47
  borax, 709
  bryonia, 709
  carbo veg., 47

MOUTH (Continued)
  iodine, 47
  kali chloricum, 47
  lachesis, 46, 47
  mercurius, 709
  muriatic acid, 47
  nitric acid, 47
  staphisagria, 47, 340
  sulphuric acid, 47

MUCOUS MEMBRANES
  (See also Catarrhs.)
  alumina, 618
  ammonium carb., 658
  arsenicum, 557
  borax, 710
  bromine, 503
  cantharis, 94
  graphites, 497
  hydrastis, 360
  ipecacuanha, 376
  kali bichromicum, 720
  lithium carb., 655
  lycopodium, 445
  natrum carb., 693
  natrum mur., 142, 702
  nitric acid, 533
  petroleum, 499
  phosphoric acid, 529
  pulsatilla, 347
  senecio, 359
  silicea, 545
  stannum, 626

MULTIPLE CEREBRO-SPINAL SCLEROSIS
  baryta carb., 650
  baryta mur., 650
  hyoscyamus, 650
  plumbum, 622

MUSCULAR EXERTION, ILL-EFFECTS OF
  arnica, 229, 239
  arsenicum, 230, 521
  coca, 521
  fluoric acid, 520
  rhus tox., 229, 521

MUSCULAR EXHAUSTION
  conium, 336
  curare, 336
  gelsemium, 336
  kali carb., 336
  muriatic acid, 336, 525
  opium, 336
  saponin, 336

MYALGIA
  actea rac., 143, 327
  arnica, 240

MYELITIS
  artemisia abrotaum, 244
  dulcamara, 236
  nux vomica, 194
  picric acid, 97

MYOCARDITIS
  phosphorus, 572

NAEVI
  fluoric acid, 441, 521

810   THERAPEUTIC INDEX.

NAEVI (Continued)
  lycopodium, 441
NAILS
  antimonium crudum, 579
  fluoric acid, 520
  thuja, 310, 520
NASAL CATARRH
  alumina, 617, 619
  ambra, 661
  ammonium carb., 661
  ammonium mur., 661
  antimonium crudum, 497
  arum triphyllum, 498
  aurum, 602
  bromine, 504
  bryonia, 294
  calcarea ostrearum, 498, 671
  cinnabaris, 595
  cistus canad., 656
  corallium rubrum, 656
  cyclamen, 348
  euphrasia, 380
  graphites, 497
  hydrastis, 360
  kali bichromicum, 656, 661, 722
  kali carb., 739
  kali sulph., 594
  lachesis, 49, 294
  lithium carb., 655
  lycopodium, 445
  mercurius, 594
  natrum carb., 693
  nux vomica, 594
  phosphorus, 569
  pulsatilla, 348, 594
  sepia, 656
  silicea, 546
  sulphur, 473
  teucrium, 656
NECROSIS OF THE LOWER JAW
  angustura, 180
  calcarea fluor., 666
  phosphorus, 573
NEPHRALGIA
  argentum nitr., 613
NEPHRITIS
  aconite, 325
  cannabis sativa, 89
  cantharis, 88
  helleborus, 337
  kali carb., 741
NERVOUS SYSTEM
  actea racemosa, 76, 143, 327
  agaricus musc., 79
  alumina, 145
  ambra grisea, 151, 195, 715
  ammonium carb., 79
  ammonium mur., 662
  aranea, 81
  argentum nitricum, 606
  arnica, 369
  arsenicum, 79
  asafoetida, 79, 119, 120, 449
  asarum, 79, 195
  belladonna, 77, 408
  borax, 708

NERVOUS SYSTEM (Continued)
  bryonia, 691
  calcarea ostrearum, 195, 675
  castoreum, 117, 195
  causticum, 77
  chamomilla, 248
  cicuta, 79
  cinchona, 369
  cocculus, 195, 259
  colocynth, 287
  crocus, 71
  curare, 179, 206
  dulcamara, 434
  gelsemium, 169
  hepar, 248, 682
  hydrocyanic acid, 537
  hyoscyamus, 77, 79
  ignatia, 78
  kali bromatum, 76, 606, 713, 715
  kali carb., 195, 738
  magnesia mur., 120, 121, 648
  magnesia phos., 648
  mephitis, 27, 79
  moschus, 79, 115
  muriatic acid, 521
  mygale, 73
  natrum carb., 691
  natrum mur., 79, 606, 691
  nitric acid, 691
  nux moschata, 118, 121, 248
  opium, 267
  palladium, 78
  petroleum, 500, 691
  phosphorus, 562, 691
  piper methysticum, 82, 385
  platina, 78
  rhododendron, 691
  selenium, 459
  sepia, 123, 691
  silicea, 547, 691
  spigelia, 369
  sticta, 79
  stramonium, 79
  sulphur, 195, 471
  tarantula, 75, 714
  thuja, 307
  valeriana, 118, 121, 248
  veratrum alb., 195, 248
  zincum, 79, 632
NEURALGIA
  (See also Prosopalgia.)
  aconite, 321, 322
  actea racemosa, 327, 356
  ammonium carb., 663
  ammonium mur., 662
  amyl nitrite, 322, 419
  argentum met., 611
  arsenicum, 467, 555
  belladonna, 419, 613, 682
  cactus, 419, 555
  capsicum, 614
  cedron, 288, 328, 374, 555
  cepa, 241, 663
  chamomilla, 288, 644
  chelidonium, 282
  chininum sulph., 467, 555

THERAPEUTIC INDEX.   811

NEURALGIA (Continued)
   cinchona, 369, 374, 467
   colchicum, 322
   colocynth, 285
   cuprum, 630
   cuprum arsenicosum, 630
   dioscorea, 285
   ferrum, 640
   ferrum carb., 420
   hamamelis, 352
   hepar, 582
   ignatia, 203
   kalmia, 328, 555, 625
   kreosote, 301, 555
   magnesia carb., 120, 644
   magnesia phos., 120, 555
   mezereum, 308, 555
   natrum mur., 625
   platina, 420, 613, 625
   prunus spinosa, 288
   pulsatilla, 361
   robinia, 555
   sepia, 432
   silicea, 683
   spigelia, 205, 288, 308, 321, 327, 625
   stannum, 607, 625
   staphysagria, 663
   strontiana carb., 625
   sulphur, 467, 683
   tabacum, 432
   theridion, 82
   thuja, 308
   valerian, 555
   verbascum, 395, 419
NEURALGIA, CILIARY
   actea racemosa, 137
   cedron, 206
   colocynth, 288
   crotalus horr., 43
   mezereum, 205
   natrum mur., 701
   spigelia, 205, 701
   thuja, 206
NEURASTHENIA
   aletris farinosa, 359
   alumina, 541
   argentum nitricum, 541
   calcarea ostrearum, 624
   cocculus indicus, 624
   collinsonia, 624
   cyclamen, 359
   helonias, 357
   ignatia, 624
   natrum mur., 624
   phosphoric acid, 367, 541, 624
   phosphorus, 367, 541, 624
   picric acid, 539
   silicea, 541
   stannum, 623
   sulphur, 624
   veratrum alb., 624
   zincum, 541
NIGHT TERRORS
   kali bromatum, 413, 714
NIPPLES, SORE
   castor equi, 28

NIPPLES, CORE (Continued)
   graphites, 141
   phytolacca, 141
   sepia, 141
NOMA
   conium, 449
NOSE
   aurum, 602
   borax, 710
   graphites, 86
   ignatia, 276
   lithium carb., 655
   natrum carb., 693
   nux vomica, 276
   phosphorus, 276
   sanguinaria, 276
   valeriana, 276
NOSTALGIA
   mercurius, 590
NYMPHOMANIA
   caladium, 613
   camphor, 94
   cantharis, 97
   hyoscyamus, 563
   phosphorus, 562, 569
   platina, 64, 140, 612
   stramonium, 425
   veraturm alb., 255, 429

OBESITY
   graphites, 493
OBJECTIVE SYMPTOMS, 19
OEDEMA
   bovista, 158
OEDEMA GLOTTIDIS
   apis, 110
OEDEMA PULMONUM
   apis, 110
OESOPHAGITIS
   arsenic, 414
   belladonna, 414
   rhus tox., 414
   veratrum viride, 257, 414
OESOPHAGUS, SPASMODIC STRICTURE OF THE
   phosphorus, 568
OPHTHALMIA
   antimonium crudum, 217
   antimonium tart., 300
   argentum nitricum, 217, 234
   bryonia, 300
OPHTHALMIA, ARTHRITIS
   antimonium tart., 300
   bryonia, 300
   colocynth, 288, 341
   euphrasia, 189, 683
   staphysagria, 341
OPHTHALMIA NEONATORUM
   argentum nitricum, 347, 608
   mercurius corrosivus, 347
   pulsatilla, 347, 608
OPHTHALMIA, PURULENT
   argentum nitricum, 608
   graphites, 347
   hepar, 683
   pulsatilla, 608

OPHTHALMIA, SCROFULOUS
  apis, 113
  argentum nitricum, 702
  arsenicum, 494, 495, 702
  aurum, 601, 602
  baryta carb., 652
  calcarea ostrearum, 494, 495, 669
  conium, 448
  euphrasia, 496
  graphites, 494, 702
  hepar, 486
  kali bichromicum, 113, 725
  lachesis, 12
  mercurius, 496, 593
  mercurius, 593
  natrum mur., 702
  nux vomica, 189
  rhus tox., 235
  sulphur, 473, 494, 495

ORCHITIS
  aurum, 603
  clematis, 352
  gelsemium, 513
  hamamelis, 352, 512
  mercurius, 513
  pulsatilla, 310, 352
  rhododendron, 352
  spongia, 512
  thuja, 310

OSTEOMA
  calcarea fluorica, 519, 666

OSTEITIS
  conchiolin, 680
  stillingia, 341
  strontiana carb., 341

OTALGIA
  belladonna, 683, 708
  borax, 708
  chamomilla, 349, 384, 683, 708
  dulcamara, 434
  hepar, 683
  kali bichromicum, 721
  plantago major, 349
  pulsatilla, 348, 683, 708
  rhus tox., 235

OTITIS EXTERNA
  calcarea ostrearum, 670
  hepar, 683
  pulsatilla, 348, 354

OTITIS MEDIA
  belladonna, 348, 411
  calcarea ostrearum, 670
  hepar, 412, 683
  kali bichromicum, 720
  mercurius, 349
  pulsatilla, 348, 349
  silicea, 349, 435
  tellurium, 349, 412

OTORRHOEA
  aurum, 43, 602
  borax, 708
  calcarea ostrearum, 670
  capsicum, 43
  carbo animalis, 491
  carbo veg., 491
  elaps, 43

OTORRHOEA (Continued)
  hepar, 43, 671
  kali bichromicum, 721
  lachesis, 43
  mercurius, 671
  natrum hypochlor., 692
  nitric acid, 43
  psorinum, 149
  pulsatilla, 348
  silicea, 43, 349, 545, 670
  tellurium, 349, 412

OVARALGIA.
  colocynth, 286
  lachesis, 62

OVARIAN TUMORS
  apis, 64, 112, 510
  colocynth, 285, 510
  hepar, 62
  iodine, 510
  lachesis, 62
  mercurius, 62

OVARIES
  apis, 64, 112
  argentum metallicum, 611, 616
  argentum nitricum, 605
  arsenicum, 65
  graphites, 65, 498
  iodine, 510
  lachesis, 62
  lilium tig., 133
  lycopodium, 65
  palladium, 65
  phosphoric acid, 528
  platina, 64
  staphisagria, 339
  tarentula, 76
  zincum, 65, 633, 638

OVARITIS
  apis, 112
  arsenicum, 552
  lachesis, 62, 613
  palladium, 64, 66, 613
  platina, 64, 613

OZAENA
  alumina, 617
  aurum, 49, 602
  kali bichromicum, 49, 310, 722
  kali hyd., 64, 717
  lac caninum, 49
  lachesis, 49, 51
  magnesium mur., 647
  mercurius corr., 596
  mercurius vivus, 49
  natrum carb., 693
  nitric acid, 49
  petroleum, 499
  phosphorus, 569
  pulsatilla, 310
  silicea, 647
  stillingia, 341
  theridion, 83
  thuja, 310

PANARITIUM
  apis, 114
  sulphur, 114

THERAPEUTIC INDEX. 813

PANCREAS, AFFECTIONS OF THE
  iodine, 510
  phosphorus, 568
PANNUS
  aurum, 601
PARALYSIS
  aconite, 315, 322, 731
  antimonium tart., 537
  apis, 107
  arsenicum, 537
  baryta carb., 650, 731
  cannabis indica, 322
  causticum, 322, 650, 729, 731
  cocculus ind., 315, 624
  colchicum, 731
  collinsonia, 624
  conium, 315, 447
  cuprum, 537, 630
  curare, 179
  dulcamara, 34, 731
  gelsemium, 166, 170, 315, 448, 606
  hyoscyamus, 436
  ignatia, 624
  manganum, 663
  muriatic acid, 731
  natrum mur., 170, 624, 627
  nitric acid, 537
  nux vomica, 315, 731
  oleander, 165, 166
  phosphorus, 537, 564, 569, 624
  plumbum, 621, 622, 632
  rhus tox., 236, 322, 632
  secale, 650
  silicea, 547
  stannum, 170, 624, 672
  staphisagria, 170, 332, 627
  sulphur, 107, 236, 322, 472, 541
  zincum, 636
PARALYSIS, POST-DIPHTHERITIC
  argentum nitricum, 606
  cocculus, 448
  conium, 448
  gelsemium, 171, 448, 606
  physostigma, 178
  rhus tox., 236
  sulphur, 236
PARAPHIMOSIS
  colocynth, 288, 394
  digitalis, 394
PAROTITIS
  abrotanum, 245
  arsenicum, 245
  belladonna, 412
  calcarea ostr., 443
  carbo veg., 245
  lachesis, 443
  lycopodium, 442
  pulsatilla, 245
  rhus tox., 443
PEDICULI
  staphisagria, 340
PEMPHIGUS
  caltha, 87
  cantharis, 87
  carboneum oxygenisatum, 87
  causticum, 87

PEMPHIGUS (Continued)
  chininum sulph., 87
  copaiva, 87
  nitric acid, 87
  ranunculus bulbosus, 87, 332
  ranunculus sceleratus, 87
  rhus tox., 87
  sulphuric acid, 87
PERICARDITIS
  anacardium, 221
  arsenicum, 558
  colchicum, 254
  kali carb., 741
  kali hydr., 718
PERIODONTITIS
  hepar, 46
  lachesis, 46
  mercurius, 46
  silicea, 46
PERIOSTEUM, INURIES TO THE
  angustura, 180
  ruta, 180
PERIOSTITIS
  aranea diadema, 81
  asafoetida, 450
  stillingea, 341
PERIPROCTITIS
  lachesis, 60
  rhus tox., 60
PERITONITIS
  arnica, 60
  baptisia, 59
  belladonna, 59, 415
  berberis, 452
  bryonia, 293
  bufo, 30
  carbo veg., 57
  colchicum, 60
  lachesis, 55, 59
  lycopodium, 271
  mercurius, 592
  opium, 271
  ranunculus bulb., 331
  raphanus, 271
  rhus tox., 59, 225, 234
  sulphur, 472
  terebinth., 271, 305
PERITYPHLITIS
  rhus tox., 234
PETIT MAL
  absinthium, 420
  artemesia vulgaris, 243
  causticum, 734
PHARYNGITIS
  kali bicarbonicum, 721
  kali carbonicum, 740
  pulsatilla, 349
PHARYNGITIS FOLLICULAR
  aesculus hippocastanus, 722
  hepar, 722
  kali bichromicum 722
  kali chloricum, 722
  mercurius jodatus, 722
  nux vomica, 722
  secale, 722

THERAPEUTIC INDEX.

PHIMOSIS
  mercurius, 352
  sulphur, 478
PHLEBITIS
  lachesis, 63
PHLYCTENULAR OPHTHALMIA
  arsenicum, 397
  euphrasia, 397, 496
  graphites, 495
  ignatia, 203
  natrum carb., 693
  rhus tox., 235
PHTHISIS
  (See also Tuberculosis.)
  actea racemosa, 328
  ammonium mur., 664
  anisum stellatum, 83, 306
  balsam of Peru, 627
  baptisia, 403
  calcarea ostrearum, 536, 673
  carba animalis, 490
  carbo veg., 490
  coccus cacti, 627
  codein, 265
  conium, 448
  drosera, 27, 273
  elaps., 51
  eyrodiction, 215
  ferrum, 639, 641
  ferrum phos., 642
  guaiacum, 215, 298, 329
  hydrocyanic acid, 538
  iodine, 509
  kali carb., 536, 740
  kali hydriodicum, 718
  laurocerasus, 538
  myrtus communis, 83, 306
  natrum sulph., 694
  nitric acid, 536
  phellandrium, 546
  phosphorus, 509, 626
  pix liquida, 83, 306
  rumex, 296
  sanguinaria, 278
  senega, 626
  silicea, 546, 626
  spongia, 513
  stannum, 623, 626, 706
  sulphur, 474
  theridion, 83
  yerba santa, 215, 627, 718
PLEURISY
  aconite, 293, 323
  apis, 103, 472
  bryonia, 293, 295
  ranunculus bulbosus, 331
  stannum, 627
  sulphur, 103, 472
PLEURODYNIA
  aconite, 331
  actea racemosa, 296, 329
  arnica, 296
  asclepias tuberosa, 296
  bryonia, 295, 570
  gaultheria, 295
  guaiacum, 329

PLEURODYNIA (Continued)
  kali carb., 296
  ranunculus bulb., 295, 331
  rhus radicans, 231, 296
  rumex crispus, 296
  senega, 296
PLICA POLONICA
  vinca minor, 167
PNEUMONIA
  aconite, 295, 323
  ammonium carb., 659
  antimonium tart., 279, 283, 295, 583
  bromine, 567
  bryonia, 295, 323
  carbo animalis, 490
  carbo veg., 484, 485
  chelidonium, 282
  cuprum, 630
  elaps, 51
  ferrum phos., 159, 642
  hepar, 685
  iodine, 508
  kali carb., 283, 740
  kali hydriodicum, 717
  lachesis, 51, 474
  lycopodium, 446
  mercurius, 283, 592
  moschus, 121
  phosphorus, 279, 381, 571
  ranunculus bulb., 331
  rhus tox., 225, 227
  sanguinaria, 278
  sulphur, 51, 279, 466, 473
  terebinth., 305, 306
  veratrum viride, 257, 279, 319, 32
POLYPI
  calcarea ostrearum, 570
  calcarea phosphorica, 570
  ledum, 369
  phosphorus, 36, 570
  sanguinaria, 280
  teucrium marum verum,
  vinca minor, 369
POLYURIA
  arctium lappa, 168
  gelsemium, 460
  ignatia, 171, 460
  kalmia, 171
  lac defloratum, 460
  moschus, 136, 460
  oleum animale, 171
  phosphoric acid., 530
  sanguinaria, 171
  selenium, 460
  silicea, 171
POST-NASAL CATARRH
  baryta carb., 652, 656
  calcarea ostrearum, 656
  hydrastis, 349, 656, 722
  kali bichromicum, 656, 722
  lithium carb., 656
  natrum carb., 693
  petroleum, 499
  sepia, 656
  spigelia, 348, 722
  teucrium marum verum, 656

THERAPEUTIC INDEX. 815

POST-NASAL CATARRH (Continued)
  theridion, 348
POTT'S DISEASE
  (See Vertebral Caries.)
PREGNANCY
  actea racemosa, 328
  aconite, 325
  anacardium, 220
  apis, 112
  caulophyllum, 357
  digitalis, 388
  hamamelis, 346, 355
  lycopodium, 441
  magnesia carb., 645
  natrum carb., 691
  nux vomica, 193, 691
  psorinum, 150
  pulsatilla, 351, 355
  zincum, 637
PRIAPISM
  agaricus, 541
  ambra grisea, 541
  cantharis, 96, 541
  capsicum, 541
  mygale, 541
  opium, 541
  petroselinum, 541
  phosphorus, 541
  physostigma, 541
  picric acid, 97, 194, 539
  platina, 541
  pulsatilla, 541
PROCTALGIA
  ignatia, 60
PROCTITIS
  aesculus, 705
  collinsonia, 705
  natrum mur., 704
PROFANITY
  anacardium, 219
  nitric acid, 219
PROGRESSIVE MUSCULAR ATROPHY
  plumbum, 622
PROLAPSUS ANI
  ignatia, 203
  natrum mur., 704
  podophyllum, 138, 454, 625
PROLAPSUS UTERI
  abies canadensis, 146
  aletris farinosa, 146
  aloes, 137
  antimonium crudum, 580
  apis, 64, 113
  argentum met., 599, 616
  aurum, 139, 603, 613
  aurum muriat. natr., 603
  calcarea ostr., 145
  calcarea phos., 145, 625
  caulophyllum, 146
  collinsonia, 188
  ferrum, 643
  ferrum jod., 643
  graphites, 141
  helonias, 146, 358
  hydrastis, 360
  lac defloratum, 146

PROLAPSUS UTERI (Continued)
  lilium tigrinum, 133
  mel cum sale, 112
  melilotus, 277
  natrum hypochlorosum, 143, 146
  natrum mur., 142, 146, 700
  nux vomica, 193, 454, 625
  platina, 613
  podophyllum, 138, 188, 454, 625
  pulsatilla, 625
  secale, 145
  sepia, 193, 454
  stannum, 136, 624
  staphisagria, 342
  ustilago, 145
PROSOPALGIA
  (See also Neuralgia.)
  aconite, 321
  amyl nitrite, 322
  argentum nitricum, 607
  arsenicum, 614
  belladonna, 419
  capsicum, 614
  colchicum, 322
  conium, 449
  gelsemium, 174
  hepar, 684
  kreosote, 301
  lachesis, 46
  spigelia, 322
  stannum, 625
  verbascum 614
  zinc, 637
PROSTATE GLAND, ENLARGEMENT OF THE
  conium, 450
  pulsatilla, 352
PROSTATITIS
  pulsatilla, 310
  thuja, 309
PROSTATORRHOEA
  selenium, 459
  sulphur, 459
PRURITIS VULVAE
  caladium, 337
  convallaria, 393
  hydrocotyle, 145
  natrum hypochlor., 143
PSEUDO-CYESIS
  thuja, 308
PSORA
  corallium rubrum, 30
  psorinum, 149
  sulphur, 463
PSORIASIS
  arsenicum, 707
  arsenicum iod., 125, 707
  natrum ars., 707
  sepia, 125
PTERYGIUM
  zincum, 637
PTOSIS
  alumina, 131, 170, 618
  causticum, 170, 235, 398, 731
  euphrasia, 398
  gelsemium, 170, 235, 619

PTOSIS (Continued)
  kalmia, 170, 235
  natrum mur., 131
  rhus tox., 170, 235, 398
  sepia, 170, 235
PTYALISM
  nitric acid, 534
PUERPERAL CONVULSIONS
  argentum nitricum, 608
  belladonna, 420
  cantharis, 94
  cicuta, 451
  gelsemium, 175, 257
  glonoin, 437, 438
  kali bromatum, 713
  kali carb., 738
  platina, 614
  secale, 437
  veratrum viride, 257
PUERPERAL FEVER
  aconite, 325
  kali carb., 738, 741
  opium, 272
PUERPERAL MANIA
  actea racemosa, 328
  arsenicum 328
  calcarea ostrearum, 328
  hyoscyamus, 430
  kali carb., 738
  lachesis, 328
PUERPERAL METRITIS
  belladonna, 415
  kali carb., 741
  lachesis, 62
  mel cum sale, 415
  tilia europea, 415
  terebinthina, 305
PUERPERAL PERITONITIS
  belladonna, 415
PULSE
  aconite, 317
  apis, 317
  belladonna, 317
  lycopodium, 441
  rhus, 225
PYAEMIA
  arnica, 241

QUINSY
  belladonna, 414
  fluoric acid, 414
  hepar, 414, 592
  lachesis, 592
  mercurius, 414, 592
  silicea, 414, 592
  sulphur, 414, 592

RACHITIS
  calcarea phos., 679
  magnesia mur., 447
  phosphorus, 679
  silicea, 542, 647, 679
  sulphur, 468
REACTION, DEFECTIVE
  (See Defective Reaction.)

RECTUM
  aesculus, 705
  alumina, 705
  belladonna, 60
  causticum, 60
  cocculus, 60, 61
  graphites, 705
  ignatia, 50, 203
  kali bich., 60, 61
  lachesis, 52, 60
  magnesium mur., 705
  mezereum, 60
  natrum mur., 61, 705
  nitric acid, 60
  opium, 61
  plumbum, 60, 61
  ratanhia, 705
REMITTENT FEVER
  gelsemium, 172
  sulphur, 467
RENAL CALCULI
  argentum nitricum. 610
  belladonna, 191
  berberis, 93, 192
  cantharis, 88, 191
  ipomea nil., 92
  lycopodium, 191, 446
  nitric acid, 610
  nux vomica, 182, 191
  ocimum, 92
  tabacum, 182, 433
RETAINED PLACENTA
  cantharis, 97, 355
  cinchona, 368
  gossypium, 355
  pulsatilla, 355, 356, 368
  sabina, 356
  secale, 154, 356
  sepia, 356
RETENTION OF URINE
  (See Urine, Retention of.)
RETINA, ATROPHY OF THE
  (See Atrophy of the Retina.)
RETINAL APOPLEXY
  (See Apoplexy of the Retina.)
RETINAL CONGESTION
  aurum, 602
  belladonna, 602
  glonoin, 436, 602
  sulphur, 602
RETINAL HYPERAESTHESIA
  actea racemosa, 144
  nux vomica, 189
RETINITIS
  lycopodium, 443
  mercurius cor., 593
  phosphorus, 574
  spigelia, 205
RETINITIS ALBUMINURICA
  mercurius cor., 593
  phosphorus, 574
RETINITIS PIGMENTOSA
  lycopodium, 443
RHEUMATISM
  abrotanum, 244
  actea spicata, 297, 327

THERAPEUTIC INDEX.

RHEUMATISM (Continued)
    anacardium, 221, 231
    apis, 107
    apocynum, 164
    arctium lappa, 298
    arnica, 240
    belladonna, 407, 422
    benzoic acid, 453
    berberis, 453
    bryonia, 297, 353
    calcarea fluorica, 677
    calcarea ostrearum, 453, 656, 67.
    calcarea phos., 679
    caulophyllum, 297
    causticum, 288, 735
    chamomilla, 249, 353
    chininum sulph., 374
    cinchona, 374
    colchicum, 231, 232, 253, 298
    colocynth, 288, 735
    conium, 231
    dulcamara, 434
    ferrum, 231, 249, 281, 735
    gelsemium, 175
    guaiacum, 288, 289, 735
    iodine, 510
    kali bichromicum, 353, 728
    kali carb., 741
    kali hydriodicum, 719
    kalmia, 231, 392
    lac caninum, 353
    ledum, 232, 297, 353, 392, 548
    lithium carb., 463, 655, 656
    lycopodium, 231, 446, 453
    magnesia carb., 646
    manganum, 663
    mercurius, 311
    nux moschata, 646
    nux vomica, 195, 677
    petroleum, 499
    phosphoric acid, 735
    pulsatilla, 231, 310, 353
    ranunculus bulb., 331
    rhododendron, 231
    rhus radicans, 231
    rhus tox., 230, 249, 297, 677, 735
    sabina, 298, 663
    sanguinaria, 280, 646, 735
    secale, 677
    silicea, 548
    sulphur, 353, 472
    thuja, 309
    valerian, 230
    veratrum album, 249
    viola odorata, 297
RHUS POISONING
    ammonium carb., 222
    anacardium, 221
    croton tiglium, 222
    sepia, 125
    zincum, 634
RIGIDITY OF THE OS UTERI
    belladonna, 421
    gelsemium, 139, 175, 421
ROSE-COLD
    phosphorus, 276

ROSE-COLD (Continued)
    sanguinaria, 276
SCABIES
    causticum, 476
    mercurius, 476
    oil of lavender, 150, 476
    psorinum, 150
    sepia, 125, 476
    sulphur, 125, 475
SCARLATINA
    aconite, 325
    ailanthus, 212, 223, 403
    ammonium carb., 659, 660
    ammonium mur., 664
    anacardium, 302
    antimonium tart., 581, 583
    apis, 100, 104, 109, 524, 660
    arsenicum, 524, 558, 560
    arum triphyllum, 208, 233, 535
    baptisia, 212
    belladonna, 71, 100, 109, 233, 302, 417,
        428, 443, 634, 660
    bryonia, 302, 418
    calcarea ostrearum, 233, 418, 635
    camphor, 635
    cinnabaris, 95, 596
    cuprum, 302, 443, 630, 634
    helleborus, 66, 302
    hydrocyanic acid, 524, 538, 635
    hyoscyamus, 418, 428
    lachesis, 42, 70, 233, 418, 660
    laurocerasus, 38
    lycopodium, 211, 418, 442, 446
    mancinella, 86, 313
    muriatic acid, 211, 524
    natrum ars., 524
    nitric acid, 210, 534
    psorinum, 148
    rhus tox., 102, 109, 225, 233
    stramonium, 302, 418, 425, 428, 443
    sulphur, 418, 466, 524
    sulphuric acid, 524
    terebinthina, 66, 305
    veratrum alb., 635
    zincum, 302, 633, 634
SCIATICA
    ammonium mur., 663
    colocynth, 288
    gnaphalium, 288, 614
    kali hydriodicum, 719
    valerian, 230
SCIRRHUS
    ammonium carb., 659
    conium, 449
    lapis albus, 510
    magnesia mur., 202
SCLEROTITIS
    aconite, 321
    belladonna, 412
    thuja, 310
SCROFULOUS
    aurum, 599
    baryta carb., 649, 652
    bromine, 503
    calcarea ostrearum, 494, 497, 545, 591, 669

SCROFULOUS (Continued)
  causticum, 731
  conium, 449
  fluoric acid, 519
  graphites, 494
  iodine, 509
  lycopodium, 445
  magnesia mur., 648
  mercurius, 590
  nitric acid, 670
  oleum jecoris, 29
  phosphorus, 669
  silicea, 404, 544, 561, 648
  sulphur, 99, 494, 545, 591
  theridion, 83
  thuja, 310
SCROFULOUS OPHTHALMIA
  (See Ophthalmia, Scrofulous.)
SCURVY
  ammonium carb., 659
  chlorine, 511
  natrum mur., 698
SEA-SICKNESS
  apomorphia, 265
  petroleum, 499
  theridion, 82
SEBACEOUS GLANDS
  psorinum, 149
SEMINAL EMISSIONS
  agnus castus, 175
  caladium seg., 175, 215
  calcarea ostr., 175, 192
  camphor, 175
  cinchona, 367, 529
  cobalt, 193
  conium, 175
  digitalis, 174, 394
  dioscorea, 174
  gelsemium, 175
  lycopodium, 175, 192
  natrum carb., 703
  natrum mur., 703
  natrum phos., 703
  nux vomica, 175, 192
  phosphoric acid, 529
  phosphorus, 175, 540, 503
  picric acid, 539
  selenium, 175, 459
  sepia, 175
  sulphur, 477
SENILITY
  baryta carb., 649
SEROUS MEMBRANES
  aconite, 293
  bryonia, 293
  ranunculus bulb., 331
SEXUAL EXCESSES
  agnus castus, 674
  caladium, 175, 247, 339
  calcarea ostr., 192, 339, 477, 674
  cinchona, 367
  cobalt, 192
  conium, 448, 564
  dioscorea, 339
  gelsemium, 174, 339
  kali bromatum, 339

SEXUAL EXCESSES (Continued)
  kali carb., 736
  lycopodium, 192, 339
  nux vomica, 192, 339, 477
  phosphorus, 564
  phosphoric acid, 529
  platina, 339, 614
  stannum, 627
  staphisagria, 193, 338
  sulphur, 192, 339, 477
  zincum, 633
SHOCK
  helleborus, 337
SKIN
  aconite, 326
  alumina, 620
  ammonium caust., 85
  anacardium occid., 85, 221
  anacardium orientale, 85, 220
  antimonium crudum, 86, 579, 702
  antimonium tart., 85, 581
  argemone mex., 274
  arnica, 242
  arsenicum, 559
  arum, tri., 185
  belladonna, 416
  borax, 711
  bufo, 30
  calcarea caustica, 85
  caltha, 85
  camphor, 85, 586
  cantharis, 84
  cantharis strygosa, 84
  capsicum, 85, 86, 404
  carbolic acid, 85
  carbo animalis, 688
  carboneum oxyg., 87
  causticum, 87, 702, 735
  chamomilla, 688
  chelidoneum, 85
  chininum sulph., 87
  chloral, 87
  cicuta, 451, 677
  clematis erecta, 85, 86, 560
  clematis viorna, 314
  cochlearia, 85
  coffea, 384
  comocladia, 217
  copaiva, 87
  cotura, 85
  croton tiglium, 85, 313, 688
  cuprum ars., 85
  cuprum met., 85
  drosera, 85
  dulcamara, 434
  euphorbia cyparissias, 86
  euphorbia peplus, 86
  euphorbium off., 46, 85, 217, 313
  fluoric acid, 520
  formica, 85, 86
  gelsemium, 174
  graphites, 141, 493, 494, 495, 560, 688, 702
  grindelia robusta, 222
  hepar, 687
  hydrocotyle, 560
  hura brasiliensis, 85

THERAPEUTIC INDEX. 819

SKIN (Continued)
juglans cinerea, 207
kali bichromicum, 87, 725
kali bromatum, 87, 715
kali hydriodicum, 87, 719
kali nitricum, 87
kali sulph., 87
kreosote, 560
lachesis, 85
lithium carb., 655, 677
lycopodium, 688
lytta vitata, 84
magnesia mur., 647
mancinella, 86, 313
mercurius, 85, 688
mezereum, 85, 86, 168
natrum carb., 689
natrum mur., 688, 698, 702, 705
nitric acid, 85
nux vomica, 85, 168, 234
oleander, 166
petroleum, 311, 495, 498
picric acid, 85
piper nigrum, 85, 86
pix liquida, 85, 86, 87, 306
podophyllum, 85
psorinum, 149, 688
pulsatilla, 85
ranunculus bulb., 85, 86, 330, 332
ranunculus sceleratus, 80, 87, 330, 333
rhus tox., 85, 232, 560
sanguinaria, 276
sarsaparilla, 311
selenium, 461
sepia, 123, 125, 560, 688
silicea, 688
sinapis nigra, 85
staphisagria, 339
strontiana carb., 654
sulphur, 166, 461, 475
sulphuric acid, 85, 87
terebinthina, 85, 86, 87
thapsia garganica, 85, 86
thuja, 688
veratrum alb., 85
viola tricolor, 167
yucca filamentosa, 313
zincum, 638

SLEEP
belladonna, 109, 454
cocculus, 361
cuprum, 443
cypripedium, 384
digitalis, 389
fluoric acid, 521
hyoscyamus, 428
kali bromatum, 714
lachesis, 36
lycopodium, 443
mephitis, 521
nux vomica, 184, 196, 361
phosphoric acid, 529
pulsatilla, 362
selenium, 461
stramonium, 443
sulphur, 361, 461

SLEEP (Continued)
zincum, 443
SPEECH
bovista, 425
fluoric acid, 440
glonoin, 437
lachesis, 440
lycopodium, 440
stramonium, 425
sulphur, 440
SPERMATORRHOEA
agnus castus, 175
caladium, 175, 215
conium, 638
discorea, 174
gelsemium, 174
zincum, 638
SPINAL CONGESTION
sulphur, 471, 541
SPINAL CORD
alumina, 541
anacarium, 221
argentum nitricum, 605, 620
cocculus, 260
dulcamara, 434
hypericum, 241
kali hydriodicum, 719
nux vomica, 194, 620
phosphorus, 564
picric acid, 538
silicea, 547, 548
sulphur, 472, 541, 620
zincum, 632, 636
SPINAL CORD, SOFTENING OF THE
ambra grisea, 151
oxalic acid, 540
SPINAL IRRITATION
actea racemosa, 329, 739
agaricus, 329
cobalt, 193, 361, 636
cocculus, 330
kali carb., 738
natrum mur., 329, 700, 739
nux vomica, 194, 330, 620
phosphorus, 195, 563
physostigma, 195, 320
picric acid, 194
pulsatilla, 361
sepia, 636, 739
sulphur, 471
theridion, 82
zincum, 330, 633, 636
SPINAL WEAKNESS
sulphur, 472
SPLEEN
aranea diadema, 80
chininum sulph., 80, 365
cinchona, 80
SPOTTED FEVER
(See Cerebro-Spinal Meningitis.)
SPRAINS
ammonium carb., 662
ammonium mur., 663
arnica, 654, 662
calcarea carb., 229
petroleum, 499

THERAPEUTIC INDEX.

SPRAINS (Continued)
  rhus tox., 229
  ruta, 654
  strontiana carb., 654
  sulphuric acid, 662
STAPHYLOMA
  apis, 113
STOMACACE
  nitric acid, 534
  nux vomica, 190
  ranunculus sceleratus, 333
STOMACH
  abrotanum, 341
  actea racemosa, 132
  calcarea ostrearum, 132
  cantharis, 95
  carbo animalis, 132, 166, 490
  cocculus, 132
  colchicum, 58
  elaps, 58, 324
  hydrastis, 132
  ignatia, 132
  ipecacuanha, 132, 341
  kali carb., 132
  lachesis, 52, 58
  lycopodium, 131
  niccolum, 132
  nux vomica, 59, 132
  oleander, 132, 165
  podophyllum, 138
  sarsaparilla, 132
  sepia, 131
  stannum, 132
  staphisagria, 132, 341, 460
  sulphur, 132
  thea, 132, 377
  veratrum alb., 59
STOMACH, CANCER OF THE
  conium, 449
  phosphorus, 568, 575
STOMACH, ULCER OF THE
  phosphorus, 568
STOMATITIS
  (See also Sore Mouth.)
  apis, 95
  arum tri., 710
STRABISMUS
  alumina, 617, 618
  belladonna, 617,
  cina, 246, 617
  cyclamen, 617
  gelsemium, 171
STUTTERING
  bovista, 425
  causticum, 731
  staphysagria, 342
  stramonium, 425
STYES
  graphites, 494
  hepar, 687
  lycopodium, 443
  staphisagria, 340
SUBINVOLUTION OF THE UTERUS
  lilium tigrinum, 133
  mel cum sale, 112

SUICIDAL TENDENCY
  anacardium, 219
  antimonium crudum, 219
SUN, ILL EFFECTS OF THE
  aconite, 320
  belladonna, 320
  camphor, 38
  glonoin, 426, 437
  lachesis, 38
  natrum carb., 38, 69
  natrum mur., 38
  theridion, 38
  thuja, 38
SUPPRESSED ERUPTIONS, ILL EFFECTS OF
  antimonium tart., 303, 581
  apis, 100, 470
  bryonia, 101, 290, 302
  cuprum, 101, 302, 434, 630, 634
  helleborus, 101
  ipecacuanha, 303
  sulphur, 101, 105, 464, 470
  thuja, 308
  zinc, 101, 302, 367, 443, 633
SWEAT
  baryta carb., 653
  bryonia, 300
  calcarea carb., 668
  carbo veg., 653
  chamomilla, 566
  cinchona, 373
  graphites, 653
  kali carb., 653
  lactic acid, 653
  magnesia mur., 647
  mercurius, 591
  natrum mur., 300
  nitric acid, 653
  petroleum, 499
  phosphorus, 566
  psorinum, 374
  rhus tox., 545, 566
  silicea, 544, 647, 653
  sulphur, 374
  thuja, 653
SYCOSIS
  cinnabaris, 311
  euphrasia, 398
  kali bichromicum, 310, 726
  natrum sulph., 694
  nitric acid, 310
  petroleum, 398
  pulsatilla, 310, 726
  sabina, 311
  sarsaparilla, 311, 726
  staphisagria, 340
  thuja, 307, 309, 694, 726
SYNCOPE
  arsenicum, 37
  camphor, 37, 38
  digitalis, 37, 38
  hydrocyanic acid, 37
  lachesis, 37
  laurocerasus, 37, 38
  linaria, 394
  theridion, 37

THERAPEUTIC INDEX.

SYNCOPE (Continued)
veratrum album, 37, 38

SYNOVITIS
apis, 103, 296, 353
bryonia, 103, 296, 353
iodine, 103
kali hyd., 103
pulsatilla, 353
sulphur, 297, 472

SYPHILIS
asafoetida, 602
aurum, 601, 602
badiaga, 491
carbo animalis, 498, 491
carbo veg., 491
cinnabaris, 311, 595
corallium rubrum, 30
fluoric acid, 519
kali bichromicum, 723
kali hydriodicum, 64, 716, 719
lachesis, 62
lycopodium, 63
mercurius biniod., 491, 597
mercurius cor., 593, 596, 602
mercurius prot., 597
mercurius vivus, 591, 593, 596
nitric acid, 63, 491, 534, 535, 602
platina mur., 614
staphisagria, 340
stillingea, 341, 695

TABES MESENTERICA
baryta carb., 652
calcarea phos., 653
iodine, 502, 509, 653
silicea, 653
sulphur, 470

TAPE WORM
argemone mexicana, 274
cucurbita, 285
pumpkin seeds, 285

TARSAL CYSTS
graphites, 340
thuja, 130

TEETH
antimonium crudum, 340
chamomilla, 340, 645
coffea, 340
fluoric acid, 46
kreosote, 48, 301, 340
lachesis, 46
magnesia carb., 645
petroleum, 46
staphisagria, 340
thuja, 48, 340

TEMPERAMENT
belladonna, 406
calcarea ostrearum, 406
capsicum, 434
chamomilla, 248
cina, 247
ignatia, 197
ipecacuanha, 377, 383
lycopodium, 440
nux vomica, 183
pulsatilla, 194, 344

TEMPERAMENT (Continued)
staphisagria, 338

TESTICLES
arnica, 352
aurum, 352
bromine, 503
conium, 352
oxalic acid, 352
phosphorus, 352
pulsatilla, 352
spongia, 352, 512
staphisagria, 352
ustilago, 352

TETANUS
aconite, 180
angustura, 180
belladonna, 181
camphor, 183
cicuta, 178, 181, 182, 537
curare, 179
hydrocyanic acid, 181, 537
hypericum, 181
lachesis, 44, 81
nicotinum, 181, 182
passiflora, 179
physostigma, 178, 195
phytolacca, 179
picrotoxin, 178
pothos foetida, 216
silicea, 181
stramonium, 183
strychnia, 177
tabacum, 182
thebaine, 178
veratria, 178
veratrum album, 182
veratrum viride, 181

THROAT
(See also Tonsillitis.)
alumina, 619, 685, 740
apis, 740
argentum nitricum, 609, 619, 685, 740
arsenicum album, 95, 596
arsenicum iod., 596
arum triphyllum, 95, 209
aurum, 602
baryta carb., 651
belladonna, 95, 172, 412, 596
borax, 710
calcarea ostrearum, 498
cantharis, 95
capsicum, 95, 435, 596
carbo veg., 740
cinnabaris, 595
diffenbachia, 95
dulcamara, 434
gelsemium, 173
graphites, 498
hepar, 619, 685, 740
ignatia, 201, 203
kali bichromicum, 722
kali carb., 739, 740
lachesis, 49
mercurius, 190, 594, 685
mercurius cor., 95, 596
natrum ars., 706

THERAPEUTIC INDEX.

THROAT (Continued)
  natrum mur., 702
  nitric acid, 535. 609, 619, 685
  nux vomica, 190
  phosphorus, 567
  pulsatilla, 349
  sulphur, 498
TIC DOULOUDEUX
  aconite, 321
TINEA CAPITIS
  sarsaparilla, 311
TINEA CILIARIS
  thuja, 310
TINEA FAVOSA
  nux juglans, 168, 234
TONGUE
  antimonium crudum, 377. 578
  arsenicum album, 333, 353, 698
  arsenicum metallicum, 454
  baryta carb., 649
  bryonia, 568, 570
  causticum, 731
  colchicum, 650
  dulcamara, 434
  kali bichromicum, 725
  lycopodium, 442
  magnesia mur., 647
  mercurius, 226, 454
  natrum mur., 333, 698
  nux vomica, 377
  phosphorus, 567
  podophyllum, 454
  ranunculus sceleratus, 333
  rhus tox., 226. 333, 454, 567
  stannum, 624
  stramonium, 425, 454
  sulphur, 293
  taraxacum, 229, 244, 333
  yucca filamentosa, 454
TONSILLITIS
  ammonium mur., 664
  amygdala persica, 414
  baryta carb., 651
  belladonna, 414. 592
  bromine, 503
  calcarea ostr., 651
  calcarea phos., 651
  fluoric acid, 414
  gelsemium, 173
  hepar, 414, 592, 684, 685
  ignatia, 201, 651
  lachesis, 49, 592
  lycopodium, 414, 454, 651
  mercurius, 414, 592, 685
  nux vomica, 722
  sabadilla, 258
  silicea, 414, 546, 592
  sulphur, 414, 592
TONSILS, ENLARGEMENT OF THE
  baryta carb., 651
  bromine, 503
  calcarea iod., 651
  conium, 651
  hepar, 651
  ignatia, 651
  lycopodium, 651

TOOTHACHE
  aranea diadema, 81
  bryonia, 300
  chamomilla, 645
  coffea, 301, 384
  ignatia, 203
  magnesia carb., 645
  mercurius, 47, 81
  ratanhia, 645
  rhus tox., 236
TORTICOLLIS
  agaricus, 194
  anacardium, 231
  belladonna, 192, 422
  bryonia, 422
  causticum, 194
  guaiacum, 422
  lachnanthes, 194
  nux vomica, 194, 422
  trifolium prat., 296
TRACHEITIS
  phosphorus, 570
TRACHOMA
  sepia, 130
TRICHIASIS
  borax, 710
  graphites, 710
TUBERCULAR MENINGITIS
  apis, 100, 103, 327, 470
  helleborus, 52
  sulphur, 104, **469**
TUBERCULOSIS
  (See also Phthisis.)
  arsenicum, 558
  bromine, 507
  calcarea ostrearum, 470, 672
  calcarea phos., 670
  conium, 448
  ferrum, 641
  guaiacum, 215
  hepar, 513, 685
  lachesis, 52
  lapis albus, 510
  natrum ars., 707
  nitric acid, 670
  oleum jecoris aselli, 29
  phosphoric acid, 530
  phosphorus, 470, 564, 571, 669, 673
  pulsatilla, 345, 355
  silicea, 546
  spongia, 513, 686
  sulphur, 469, 470, 474, 572
TYMPANITES
  carbo veg., 253, 261, 271, 487
  cinchona, 252, 261, 370, 487
  cocculus, 252
  colchicum, 251, 261, 271, 370
  lycopodium, 261, 271, 487
  morphia, 265
  opium, 261, 270
  raphanus, 261
  sulphur, 261
  terebinthina, 271, 370
TYPHLITIS
  belladonna, 60
  bryonia, 60

THERAPEUTIC INDEX.

TYPHLITIS (Continued)
  lachesis, 54, 60
  mercurius, 54, 59
  mercurius cor., 60
  opium, 272
  rhus tox., 60, 234

TYPHOID FEVER AND TYPHOID CONDITIONS
  absinthium, 243
  aconite, 317
  ailanthus, 403
  alumen, 537
  anacardium, 218
  apis, 100, 107, 108, 268, 523
  arnica, 40, 228, 239, 336, 402, 527, 659
  arsenicum, 227, 252, 430, 467, 537, 552, 555
  baptisia, 40, 228, 239, 272, 399, 467, 523
  belladonna, 292, 410
  bryonia, 261, 290, 523
  calcarea ostr., 293, 442, 675
  carbo veg., 228, 253, 261, 483, 566
  castoreum, 27, 117
  chlorine, 511
  cinchona, 252, 556
  cocculus, 260
  colchicum, 251, 271, 556
  gelsemium, 173, 261, 401
  hamamelis, 537
  helleborus, 39, 335
  hydrocyanic acid, 336
  hyoscyamus, 39, 228, 268, 410, 430
  lachesis, 39, 108, 268, 402, 430
  leptandra, 537
  lycopodium, 430, 441, 446, 675
  mercurius, 226
  muriatic acid, 40, 108, 228, 403, 430, 522
  nitric acid, 522, 536
  nux vomica, 196
  opium, 39, 268, 272, 335, 336, 528
  petroleum, 500
  phosphoric acid, 228, 334, 430, 523, 527
  phosphorus, 227, 336, 527, 565, 571
  psorinum, 150
  sulphuric acid, 531
  ranunculus sceleratus, 333
  rhus tox., 40, 225, 226, 292, 402, 410, 430, 523, 527, 552
  selenium, 459
  stramonium, 272, 431
  sulphur, 467
  sweet spirits of nitre, 335, 336, 527
  taraxacum, 228, 244
  terebinthina, 66, 305
  veratrum album, 252
  zincum, 102
  zincum oxid., 102

ULCERS
  arsenicum, 62, 63, 156, 445, 561
  asafoetida, 62, 119, 450, 545, 602
  borax, 125, 711
  bromine, 510
  bufo, 30, 63
  calcarea ostrearum, 534
  carbo veg., 63, 482

ULCERS (Continued)
  chromic acid, 723
  cinchona, 63
  euphorbia corrollata, 63
  euphorbium, 63
  fluoric acid, 520
  hepar, 62, 63, 687
  iodine, 510
  kali bichromicum, 63, 722
  lachesis, 62
  lycopodium, 62, 63, 445
  mercurius, 62, 63, 534
  mercurius corr., 597
  mezereum, 125, 677
  muriatic acid, 63
  nitric acid, 63, 310, 534, 535
  phosphoric acid, 63
  phosphorus, 62, 568, 574, 683
  plumbum, 63
  psorinum, 149
  ranunculus bulb., 332
  ranunculus sceleratus, 333
  rhus tox., 445
  secale, 63, 156
  sepia, 125, 711
  silicea, 62, 63, 520, 544, 574
  sulphur, 62
  thuja, 309
  vespa, 145

URAEMIA
  ammonium carb., 659
  arsenicum, 94
  arum triphyllum, 209
  cannabis indica, 90
  cantharis, 94
  cuprum, 629
  hydrocyanic acid, 433
  plumbum, 623

URETHRA
  cantharis, 86, 90
  capsicum, 91
  clematis erecta, 90, 97
  conium, 91
  doryphora, 97

URETHRITIS
  cannabis sativa, 89
  cantharis, 88
  conium, 91
  doryphora, 91
  hyoscyamus, 91

URINARY ORGANS
  apis, 92, 93
  apocynum, 163
  argentum nitricum, 91
  berberis, 93, 452
  camphor, 93
  cannabis indica, 90
  cannabis sativa, 89
  cantharis, 87
  capsicum, 92
  chimaphila, 92
  clematis, 90
  cochlearia, 92
  conium, 91
  copaiva, 92
  cubebs, 91

URINARY ORGANS (Continued)
digitalis, 92
doryphora, 91
equisetun 90
erigeron, 92
eupatorium purp.,
ferrum phos., 92
hydrocotyle, 145
hyoscyamus, 91
kali nitricum, 93
kreosotum, 136
linaria, 90
mercurius, 90 91
mercurius aceticus, 92
mercurius cor., 91
pareira brava, 93, 453
petroselinum, 90
pulsatilla, 92, 271
selenium, 306
thuja, 91
uva ursi, 93

URINE
aconite, 710
ammonium benz., 66
apis, 66
apocynum can., 163
argentum nitricum, 610
arnica, 66
arsenicum, 66
belladonna, 416
benzoic acid, 66, 534
berberis, 452
borax, 710
bryonia, 301
calcarea ostr., 453
cantharis, 306
carbolic acid, 66
carbo veg., 66
causticum, 271, 737
colchicum, 66
copaiva, 306
digitalis, 66
helleborus, 66
hyoscyamus, 442
kali carb., 66, 737
lachesis, 66
lithium carb., 655
lycopodium, 271, 442, 710
natrum mur., 66
nitric acid., 534
opium, 66, 271
osmium, 306
pulsatilla, 271
sarsaparilla, 710
senna, 737
stramonium, 271
terebinthina, 66, 306
zincum, 637
zingiber, 271

URINE, RETENTION OF
arsenicum, 271
cantharis, 89
causticum, 271, 734
hyoscyamus, 271
opium, 271

URINE, SUPPRESSION OF THE
lycopodium, 271
pulsatilla, 271
stramonium, 271
zingiber, 271

URTICARIA
apis, 106, 705
arsenicum, 107, 560
bovista, 107
calcarea ostrearum, 107, 705
copaiva, 87, 107
dulcamara, 434
kali bromatum, 107
medusa, 31
natrum mur., 705
pulsatilla, 107
rhus tox., 107
rumex, 107
sepia, 107
terebinthina, 107
urtica urens, 107

UTERINE HAEMORRHAGE
(See Metrorrhagia.)

UTERUS
actea rac., 143, 327, 356
aletris, 359
aloe, 137
apis, 112
argentum nitr., 615
aurum, 139, 603, 615
aurum mur., 139
aurum mur. natr., 139
bovista, 157
cactus, 133
carbo an., 490
caulophyllum, 146, 356
convallaria, 393
gelsemium, 175, 176
helonias, 134, 357, 615
hydrastis, 360
kreosote, 136
lilium tigrinum, 133, 360
magnesia mur., 202, 647
mel cum sale, 112, 415
murex, 135
nux vomica, 136
palladium, 79, 615
platina, 140
podophyllum, 138
pulsatilla, 138, 625
secale, 154
senecio, 359
sepia, 133, 615
stannum, 136
sulphur, 135
tarentula, 76
ustilago, 157

UTERUS, INDURATION OF THE
magnesia mur., 202

UVULA ELONGATED
capsicum, 435
hyoscyamus, 427
mentha piperita, 428
natrum mur., 427, 703

THERAPEUTIC INDEX. 825

VACCINATION, ILL EFFECTS OF
  silicea, 307, 542
  thuja, 307, 542
VAGINITIS
  helonias, 357
VARICOCELE
  hamamelis, 346
  pulsatilla, 346
VARICOSE VEINS
  ambra, 152
  carbo veg., 141, 441, 482
  fluoric acid, 521
  hamamelis, 346, 521
  lycopodium, 441
  pulsatilla, 346
VARIOLA
  anacardium, 218
  antimonium tart., 303, 581, 583
  apis, 107
  rhus tox., 233, 234
  thuja, 308
VERTEBRAL CARIES
  carbo veg., 483
  Gettysburg water, 341, 545, 656
  phosphoric acid, 530
  phosphorus, 573
  silicea, 544
  sulphur, 573
VERTIGO
  ambra grisea, 151
  apis, 82
  argentum nitr., 608
  arsenicum, 37, 82
  bromine, 502
  camphor, 37
  causticum, 730
  chelidonium, 85
  conium, 448
  digitalis, 37
  ferrum, 641
  hydrocyanic acid, 37
  kali carb., 736
  lachesis, 36
  laurocerasus, 37
  moschus, 37
  oleander, 165
  petroleum, 82
  picric acid, 539
  piper meth., 82, 385
  rhus tox., 234
  sanguinaria, 276
  sepia, 82
  silicea, 548
  theridion, 37, 82
  thuja, 82
  veratrum alb., 37
VESICAL CALCULUS
  hydrangea, 92
  pareira brava, 93
VESICAL IRRITATION
  capsicum, 92
  capaiva, 92
  curare, 206
  digitalis, 92
  epigea, 92
  erigeron, 92, 159

VESICAL IRRITATION (Continued)
  eupatorium, purp., 90, 145
  ferrum phos., 92
  inula, 146
  mitchella repens, 145, 158
  petroselinum, 90
  pulsatilla, 92
VOMITING
  aethusa cynap., 420, 578, 671
  antimonium crud., 450, 578, 671
  antimonium tart., 265, 387
  apomorphia, 265, 436
  arsenicum, 565, 672
  belladonna, 226, 417
  bismuth, 565
  cadmium sulph., 555
  calcarea acetica, 450
  calcarea ostr., 450, 671
  colchicum, 59
  digitalis, 388
  glonoin, 266, 436
  ipecacuanha, 579, 672
  kreosote, 136, 565, 671
  lachesis, 55
  lobelia, 265, 387
  magnesia carb., 672
  nux vomica, 184
  phosphorus, 672
  rhus tox., 265, 417
  sulphur, 672
  tabacum, 387
  veratrum alb., 59
VOMITING OF PREGNANCY
  anacardium, 220
  argentum nitricum, 607
  digitalis, 388
  nux vomica, 193, 220, 691
  petroleum, 499
WARTS
  causticum, **694**
  nitric acid, 535
  thuja, 310
WAXY LIVER
  phosphorus, 567
WHITE-SWELLING
  phosphorus, 573
  sulphur, 470
WINE, AGGRAVATION FROM
  antimonium crud., 632
  bovista, 632
  carbo veg., 632
  conium, 632, 634
  fluoric acid, 632
  glonoin, 632, 634
  ledum, 632
  lycopodium, 632
  nux vomica, 632, 634
  pulsatilla, 632
  rhododendron, 632, 634
  selenium, 462, 632
  silicea, 632
  zincum, 632, 634
WHOOPING-COUGH
  ambra grisea, 152

WHOOPING-COUGH (Continued)
- antimonium tart., 581
- arnica, 242
- bryonia, 96
- cina, 247, 382
- coccus cacti, 32, 637
- corallium rubrum, 27, 31
- cuprum, 682
- drosera, 27
- ipecacuanha, 382
- kali bichromicum, 32
- kali carb., 741
- mephitis, 27, 27
- senega, 32
- veratrum album, 704

WORMS
- aconite, 246
- argemone mex., 274
- arsenicum, 632

WORMS (Continued)
- artemesia, 624
- caladium seguinum, 247
- cicuta, 451
- cina, 246, 624
- ignatia, 203, 256
- indigo, 203, 247
- quassia, 247
- sabadilla, 258
- spigelia, 206
- stannum, 624, 625
- teucrium, 203

YELLOW ATROPHY OF THE LIVER
- phosphorus, 567

YELLOW FEVER
- cadmium sulph., 555
- carbo veg., 483
- lachesis, 55

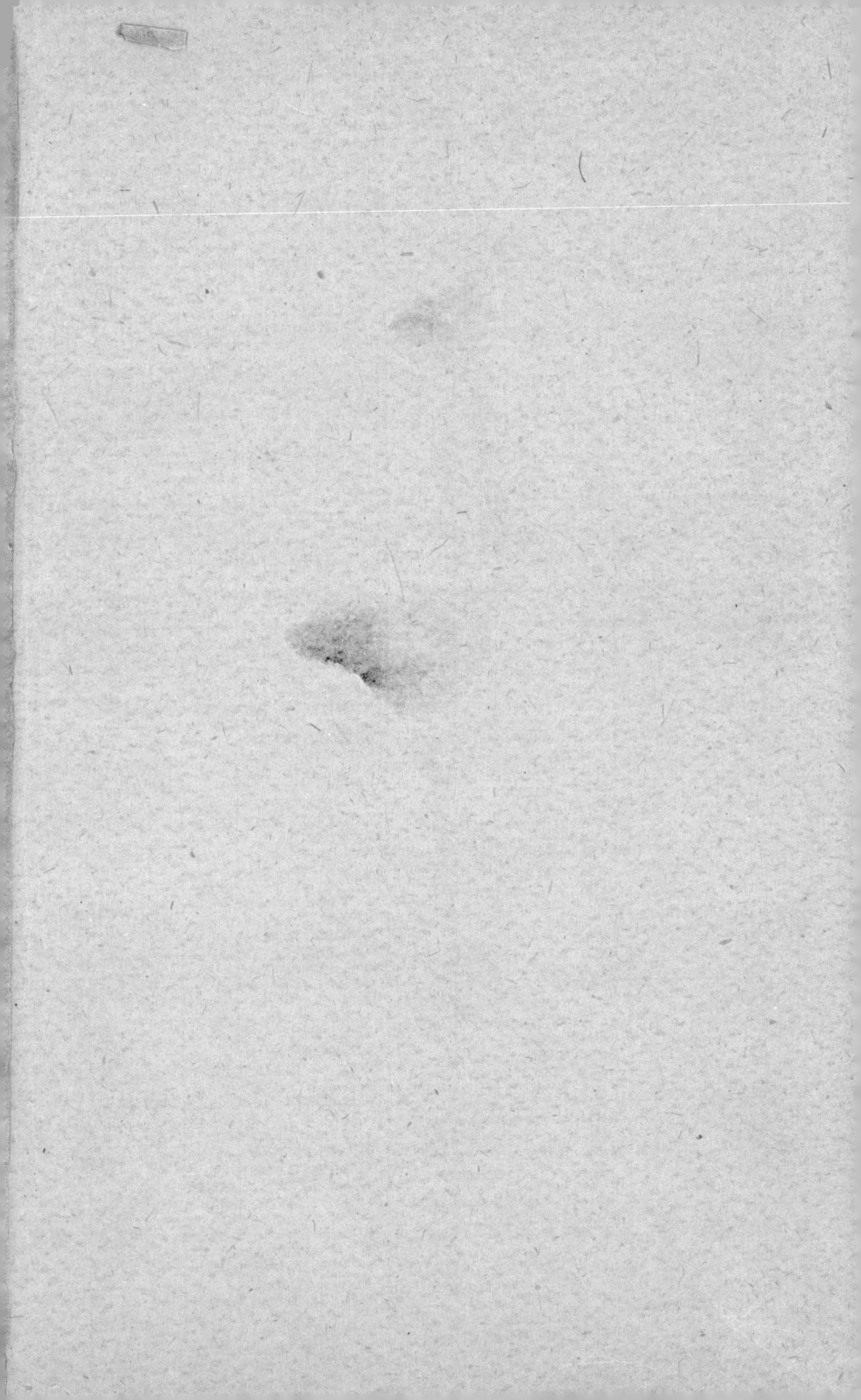

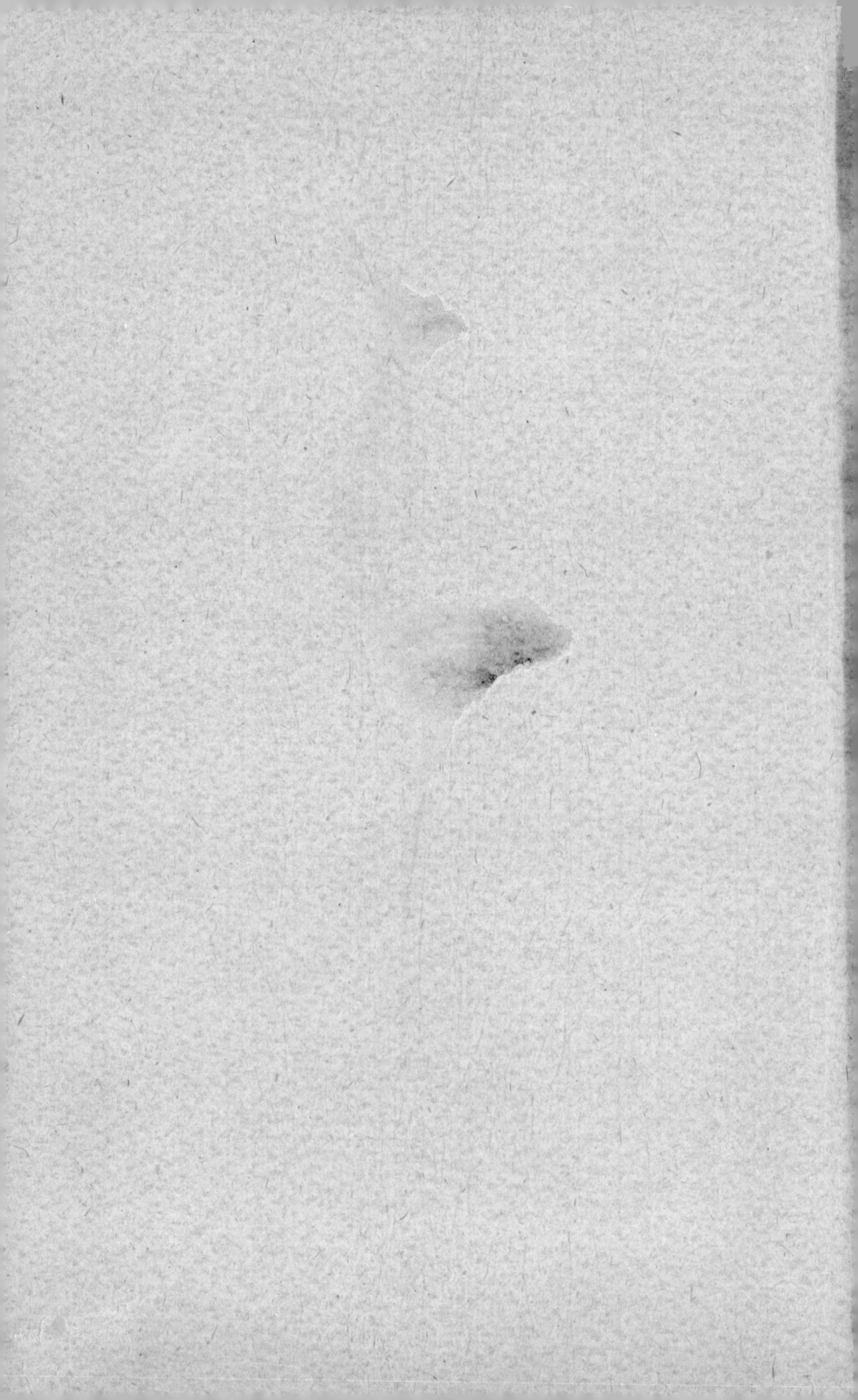